NCC B OKSTORE
832-6330
THANK YOU

SUPPLIES 1.65 1
SUPPLIES 1.65 1
NEW BOOK 23.80
NEW BOOK 47.80

you've got the book. don't stop there.

After all, why simply *read* material when you can *experience* it interactively? Why restrict yourself to classroom learning when you can have your own office, a job, and specific marketing situations to analyze and solve creatively?

Take your marketing course into the future—your future—with **MARKETING INTERACTIVE: Building Skills for Your Career**, a CD-ROM simulation developed by IRWIN and Digital Creators. **MARKETING INTERACTIVE** is a learning tool, meaning it teaches concepts from all corners of the marketing discipline, but this is no computerized trivia quiz. The material is organized by careers, not concepts, and from the moment you walk into the simulated office building, you're on your own: you decide which of five careers you want, whether it's in Personal Selling/Sales Management, Retailing, Product Management, Advertising, or Market Research. You also decide what skills and methods are best applied to that position's particular demands. When you succeed, you get promoted—just as in life.

Don't settle for a textbook—put yourself to work and gain the advantage in your class while preparing for your career. Order your copy of **MARKETING INTERACTIVE: Building Skills for Your Career**—a $26.95 value for just $13.95, a discount available *only* to our **Marketing, Fifth Edition,** customers.

Marketing Interactive
Building Skills for Your Career

William O. Bearden, *University of South Carolina*
Thomas N. Ingram, *Colorado State University*
Raymond W. LaForge, *University of Louisville*

ISBN: 0256225281
Book No. 91342300

Fill out and detach the reply card below, include a check or credit card number, and send in a stamped envelope to:
Richard D. Irwin
Attn: Colleen Suljic
Marketing Manager
1333 Burr Ridge Parkway
Burr Ridge, IL 60521-0084
csuljic@irwin.com

System Requirements: Hard drive, 486X/25 or compatible, 4 MB RAM (8 MB recommended), double-speed CD-ROM drive, 16-bit sound card (Sound Blaster compatible), SVGA 640 x 480 256-color, two-button mouse, and speakers. Compatible with Windows® 3.1, Windows® 95, and standard networks.

IRWIN

MARKETING

THE IRWIN SERIES IN MARKETING

Alreck & Settle
THE SURVEY RESEARCH HANDBOOK, 2/E

Arens
CONTEMPORARY ADVERTISING, 6/E

Belch & Belch
INTRODUCTION TO ADVERTISING AND PROMOTION: AN INTEGRATED MARKETING COMMUNICATIONS APPROACH, 3/E

Bearden, Ingram & LaForge
MARKETING: PRINCIPLES & PERSPECTIVES, 1/E

Bernhardt & Kinnear
CASES IN MARKETING MANAGEMENT, 7/E

Boyd, Walker & Larreche
MARKETING MANAGEMENT: A STRATEGIC APPROACH WITH A GLOBAL ORIENTATION, 2/E

Cateora
INTERNATIONAL MARKETING, 9/E

Churchill, Ford & Walker
SALES FORCE MANAGEMENT, 5/E

Cole & Mischler
CONSUMER AND BUSINESS CREDIT MANAGEMENT, 10/E

Cravens
STRATEGIC MARKETING, 5/E

Cravens, Lamb & Crittenden
STRATEGIC MARKETING MANAGEMENT CASES, 5/E

Crawford
NEW PRODUCTS MANAGEMENT, 5/E

Dillon, Madden & Firtle
ESSENTIALS OF MARKETING RESEARCH, 2/E

Dillon, Madden & Firtle
MARKETING RESEARCH IN A MARKETING ENVIRONMENT, 3/E

Faria, Nulsen & Roussos
COMPETE, 4/E

Futrell
ABC'S OF SELLING, 5/E

Futrell
FUNDAMENTALS OF SELLING, 5/E

Gretz, Drozdeck, & Weisenhutter
PROFESSIONAL SELLING: A CONSULTATIVE APPROACH, 1/E

Hawkins, Best & Coney
CONSUMER BEHAVIOR, 6/E

Hayes, Jenster & Aaby
BUSINESS TO BUSINESS MARKETING, 1/E

Johansson,
GLOBAL MARKETING, 1/E

Lambert & Stock
STRATEGIC LOGISTICS MANAGEMENT, 3/E

Lehmann & Winer
ANALYSIS FOR MARKETING PLANNING, 4/E

Lehmann & Winer
PRODUCT MANAGEMENT, 2/E

Levy & Weitz
RETAILING MANAGEMENT, 2/E

Levy & Weitz
ESSENTIALS OF RETAILING, 1/E

Mason, Mayer & Ezell
RETAILING, 5/E

Mason & Perreault
THE MARKETING GAME!, 2/E

Meloan & Graham
INTERNATIONAL AND GLOBAL MARKETING CONCEPTS AND CASES, 1/E

Patton
SALES FORCE: A SALES MANAGEMENT SIMULATION GAME, 1/E

Pelton, Strutton, & Lumpkin
MARKETING CHANNELS: A RELATIONSHIP MANAGEMENT APPROACH, 1/E

Perreault & McCarthy
BASIC MARKETING: A GLOBAL MANAGERIAL APPROACH, 12/E

Perreault & McCarthy
ESSENTIALS OF MARKETING: A GLOBAL MANAGERIAL APPROACH, 7/E

Peter & Donnelly
A PREFACE TO MARKETING MANAGEMENT, 7/E

Peter & Donnelly
MARKETING MANAGEMENT: KNOWLEDGE AND SKILLS, 4/E

Peter & Olson
CONSUMER BEHAVIOR AND MARKETING STRATEGY, 4/E

Peter & Olson
UNDERSTANDING CONSUMER BEHAVIOR, 1/E

Quelch
CASES IN PRODUCT MANAGEMENT, 1/E

Quelch, Dolan & Kosnik
MARKETING MANAGMENT: TEXT & CASES, 1/E

Quelch & Farris
CASES IN ADVERTISING AND PROMOTION MANAGEMENT, 4/E

Quelch, Kashani & Vandermerwe
EUROPEAN CASES IN MARKETING MANAGEMENT, 1/E

Rangan, Shapiro, & Moriarty
BUSINESS MARKETING STRATEGY: CASES, CONCEPTS & APPLICATIONS, 1/E

Rangan, Shapiro, & Moriarty
BUSINESS MARKETING STRATEGY: CONCEPTS & APPLICATIONS, 1/E

Smith & Quelch
ETHICS IN MARKETING, 1/E

Stanton, Buskirk & Spiro
MANAGEMENT OF A SALES FORCE, 9/E

Thompson & Stappenbeck
THE MARKETING STRATEGY GAME, 1/E

Walker, Boyd & Larreche
MARKETING STRATEGY: PLANNING AND IMPLEMENTATION, 2/E

Weitz, Castleberry & Tanner
SELLING: BUILDING PARTNERSHIPS, 2/E

MARKETING

FIFTH EDITION

ERIC N. BERKOWITZ
University of Massachusetts

ROGER A. KERIN
Southern Methodist University

STEVEN W. HARTLEY
University of Denver

WILLIAM RUDELIUS
University of Minnesota

IRWIN

Chicago • Bogotá • Boston • Buenos Aires • Caracas
London • Madrid • Mexico City • Sydney • Toronto

Irwin Book Team
Publisher: *Rob Zwettler*
Sponsoring editor: *Nina McGuffin*
Developmental editor: *Tricia Howland*
Marketing manager: *Colleen Suljic*
Senior project supervisor: *Rebecca Dodson*
Senior production supervisor: *Laurie Sander*
Art director: *Keith McPherson*
Assistant manager, desktop services: *Jon Christopher*
Compositor: *Carlisle Communications, Ltd.*
Typeface: *10.5/12.5 Times Roman*
Printer: *Von Hoffmann Press, Inc.*
Part/cover image: *The Stock Market © George Diebold*

Times Mirror Books

Library of Congress Cataloging-in-Publication Data

Marketing / Eric N. Berkowitz . . . [et al.]. —5th ed.
    p. cm. — (The Irwin series in marketing)
    Includes bibliographical references and indexes.
    ISBN 0-256-18968-4
    1. Marketing.   I. Berkowitz, Eric N.   II. Series.
HF5415.M29474   1997
    658.8—dc20   96–21378

Printed in the United States of America
1 2 3 4 5 6 7 8 9 0 VH 3 2 1 0 9 8 7 6

PREFACE

As the 21st century approaches, the world of marketing is entering a new and exciting era that was unimaginable only a short time ago. Electronic shopping, digizines, virtual organizations, e-cash, interactive television, and the information superhighway are just a few indications of the many new changes marketing instructors, managers, and students are likely to face in the near future. We are eager to utilize the active learning approach of *Marketing* to facilitate preparation for this extraordinary marketplace. In addition, we appreciate the opportunity to share our enthusiasm with you and we welcome you to your introduction to the field of marketing.

The Fifth Edition of *Marketing* is the result of a product development process designed to focus on customer needs, and a commitment to provide exceptional customer value. We have retained the strengths of previous editions and added new dimensions to reflect changes in the business environment and in student and instructor interests. For example, users of previous editions frequently tell us that *Marketing* provides:

- An easy-to-read, high-involvement, interactive approach to the study of marketing.
- Comprehensive and integrated coverage of traditional and contemporary marketing and business topics.
- Up-to-date and relevant examples, cases, and exercises.
- Many extended examples involving people making marketing decisions that students can easily relate to text concepts.
- A rigorous pedagogical framework and a useful decision-making orientation.
- A package of support materials to accommodate a wide range of teaching styles and formats.

These attributes remain as the foundation of our product offering, while changes in topic emphasis, the order of chapters, the number of cases, and the overall length of the book are the result of our efforts at continuous quality and coverage improvement.

We are gratified by the success of *Marketing*. The innovative pedagogical approach we developed and introduced with the first edition in 1986, and improved in subsequent editions, has helped over 350,000 students and 2,100 instructors study and teach one of the most dynamic and challenging areas of our global economic system. We have focused on creating customer value by providing exceptional knowledge, understanding, skills, decision-making tools, and support materials. This edition of *Marketing* provides you with the best revision of what we believe is the best marketing textbook available today. We hope you agree!

NEW FEATURES IN THIS EDITION

The feedback we received through our formal marketing research efforts has led to several changes in the organization of this edition:

- Global marketing topics previously covered in two chapters have been consolidated into Chapter 5, Global Marketing and World Trade, and integrated throughout the text. This change reflects a truly global view of marketing and the extensive implications of world trade on all aspects of marketing practice.

• Chapter 13, Managing Services, has been moved from the end of the text to Part IV, Satisfying Marketing Opportunities. This change is consistent with the growing recognition of services as products, and the increasing importance of service components of product offerings.

• The strategic marketing process, previously covered in three chapters, is now covered in Chapter 2 and Chapter 22. This combination of chapters allows an early introduction to a framework that integrates topics covered in-depth later in the text—while acknowledging the time constraints faced by instructors today.

• A marketing plan now appears as Appendix A following Chapter 2. In the past, many instructors have used the framework presented in Chapter 2 as a guideline for a marketing plan assignment or lecture. This appendix provides an actual, up-to-date, and relevant marketing plan as a model for students to study and use as they write marketing plans as part of their class assignments.

• Additional cases are now included at the end of the book in Appendix D. These cases allow instructors the flexibility of additional case assignments if desired. The cases address marketing topics related to products, services, and companies that students will find interesting and familiar. Some examples include: Windows 95, Starbucks, Timex, Nordstroms, Kingpin Snowboards, and the Hummer.

The content of *Marketing* has also been revised to provide complete and current coverage of emerging issues, new marketing terms, environmental trends, and changes in business practices. Examples include:

• The network organization
• Value propositions
• Total quality management
• Kaizen (continuous incremental improvement)
• Reengineering, streamlining, and restructuring
• Market orientation
• Emerging markets in South and East Asia and Eastern Europe
• Customer management teams
• Generational marketing
• Ethnic and regional marketing
• Recycling and precycling
• Intellectual property use (e.g., software piracy)
• Environmentally friendly new product development
• Global consumers and brand loyalty
• The North American Industrial Classification System (NAICS)
• Supply (channel) partnerships
• Electronic survey research
• Counterfeit brands and products
• Co-branding and co-marketing
• Emergence of "pay-for-use" services
• Cross-functional teams
• Strategic alliances
• Smart cards
• Salesforce automation
• Electronic markets (marketspace)

In addition, new sections have been added to several chapters. For example, the global marketing chapter now addresses global competition among global companies for global consumers, and the retailing chapter now includes a section on nonstore retailing which covers direct mail, telemarketing, in-home shopping, direct selling, and automatic vending. The personal selling and sales management chapter provides an up-to-date treatment of salesforce automation with a focus on information and communication technologies.

Marketplace examples have been updated to reflect the most recent activities of large and small organizations, and to provide relevant, logical illustrations of the concepts discussed in the text. Some of these include:

- Rollerblade's introduction of automatic braking technology and selection by *Business Week* as one of the best new products of the year.
- Saturn's regional marketing campaigns targeting segments of the Hispanic population.
- The "Smart Solutions" campaign used by the U.S. Postal Service as part of its aggressive new marketing strategy.
- The move by Ford, General Electric, and General Motors into consumer loans, credit cards, mortgages, commercial loans, and insurance.
- Levi Strauss's $90 million investment in new stores and computers, and its recent decision to limit investment in China as a matter of ethical policy.
- The growth of "online cafes," such as Cybersmith in Massachusetts.
- Sony's new entry into the video game market.

Several topics continue to have such an important impact on the field of marketing that they continue to receive unique coverage in separate chapters in *Marketing.* These include Ethics and Social Responsibility (Chapter 4) and Information Technology (Chapter 10). Topics which are integrated through every chapter of the text include:

- Customer value
- The impact of technology
- Ethics and social responsibility
- Global perspectives
- Cross-functional issues

Finally, the package of support materials has been expanded to provide a wide variety of value-added opportunities for students and instructors. New to the package are:

- An instructor "survival" kit which contains product samples, in-class activities, and other teaching tools that are intended to increase both student learning and participation.
- Electronic presentation slides.
- New video cases including Specialized Bicycles, Imagination Pilots, Washburn Guitars, Environsell, Sprint, and Ken Davis Products.
- Presentation CD-ROM.

In addition, we have completely revised and updated every other component of the supplement package.

HELPFUL PEDAGOGICAL FEATURES

As in previous editions, we want to involve you in the study of marketing by encouraging you to think about your personal experiences as a consumer and by asking you to take the role of a marketing decision maker. Examples of contemporary people and organizations, and their marketing decisions appear in the chapter opening vignettes, the Marketing NewsNet boxes, extended examples that are included in the text, and in the end-of-chapter cases. To help you understand potential explanations for the success or failure of marketing programs, each chapter also integrates research related to specific marketing decisions.

The book alerts the reader to special topics with corresponding icons. These include: general topics, customer value, global topics, technology, cross-functional topics, and ethics and social responsibility issues.

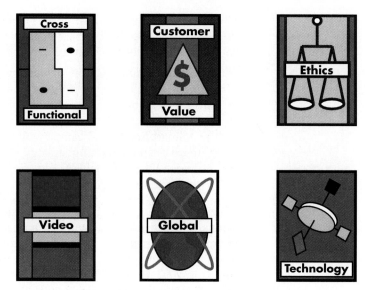

In addition, the book reinforces major concepts as they are introduced in each chapter to stimulate your understanding of them and foster your ability to apply them appropriately. At the end of every major section, Concept Checks pose two or three questions to test your recall. The Learning Objectives at the beginning of each chapter and the Summary and Key Terms and Concepts at the close provide further reinforcement.

We believe that the use of these unique learning aids lets you learn about, understand, and integrate the many marketing topics covered in our textbook, and allows you to apply them in the constantly changing marketing environment you will encounter as a consumer and a marketing manager.

THE ORGANIZATION OF *MARKETING*

The Fifth Edition of *Marketing* is divided into five parts. *Part I, Initiating the Marketing Process,* looks first at what marketing is and how it identifies and satisfies consumer needs (Chapter 1). Then Chapter 2 provides an overview of the strategic marketing process that occurs in an organization—which provides a structure for the text. Appendix A provides a sample marketing plan as a reference for students. Chapter 3 analyzes the five major environmental factors in our changing marketing environment, while Chapter 4 discusses the significance of ethics and social responsibility in marketing decisions.

Part II, Understanding Buyers and Markets, first describes, in Chapter 5, the nature and scope of world trade and the influence of cultural differences on global marketing practices. Next, Chapter 6 describes how ultimate consumers reach buying decisions. Finally, because of their important differences from ultimate consumers, industrial and organizational buyers and how they make purchase decisions are covered in Chapter 7.

In *Part III, Targeting Marketing Opportunities,* the marketing research function is discussed in Chapter 8. The process of segmenting and targeting markets and positioning products appears in Chapter 9. The increasing importance of relationship marketing, how today's marketing managers use strategic information systems, and sales forecasting are described in Chapter 10.

Part IV, Satisfying Marketing Opportunities, covers the four Ps—the marketing mix elements. Unlike most competitive textbooks, the product element is divided into the natural chronological sequence of first developing new products (Chapter 11) and then managing the existing products (Chapter 12). Services are discussed as separate product offerings and as components of product offerings (Chapter 13). Pricing is covered in terms of underlying pricing analysis (Chapter 14), followed by actual price setting (Chapter 15), and the related Appendix B, Financial Aspects of Marketing. Three chapters address the place (distribution) aspects of marketing: Marketing Channels and Wholesaling (Chapter 16), Physical Distribution and Logistics Management (Chapter 17), and Retailing (Chapter 18). Retailing is a separate chapter because of its importance and interest as a career for many of today's students. Promotion is also covered in three chapters. Chapter 19 discusses integrated marketing communications and presents an in-depth treatment of sales promotion, an activity that often exceeds advertising in the promotional budgets of many firms but receives minimal coverage in many textbooks. Chapter 19 also covers public relations. Advertising (Chapter 20) and Personal Selling and Sales Management (Chapter 21) complete the coverage of promotional activities.

Part V, Managing the Marketing Process, expands on Chapter 2 to describe specific techniques and issues related to blending the four marketing mix elements to plan, implement, and control (Chapter 22) marketing programs. The part closes with Appendix C, Career Planning in Marketing, which discusses marketing jobs themselves and how to get them, and Appendix D, Alternate Cases.

A detailed glossary, and three indexes (author; company and product; and subject) complete the book.

As we observe in Chapter 1, we genuinely hope that somewhere in *Marketing* the reader will discover not only the challenge and excitement of marketing, but possibly a career as well.

EXTENSIVE SUPPLEMENTAL RESOURCES

Providing a comprehensive and integrated package of high-quality innovative instructional supplements continues to be a priority for us. We have been involved, as authors or supervisors, in the production of all of the supplements that now accompany our text. Much attention has been given to providing elements and features in these supplements that were requested by both inexperienced and experienced instructors. As a result, each supplement contains several features not offered with any other marketing text.

Instructor's Manual The Instructor's Manual includes lecture notes, new transparency masters, discussions of the Marketing NewsNet boxes and the Ethics and Social Responsibility Alerts, and answers to the end-of-chapter Problems and Applications questions. Supplemental Lecture Notes and In-Class Activities are also provided. The Fifth Edition of the Instructor's Manual also includes teaching suggestions and detailed information about integrating the other supplements.

Transparency Acetates A set of 200 four-color overhead transparency acetates is available free to adopters. More than 50 percent of these have been developed from information outside the text. In addition, the acetates now include a greater ratio of print advertisements that demonstrate key marketing theories. Several of the ads correspond with the companies that are featured in the video cases, making it possible to teach a more integrated lecture. Each of the transparency acetates from outside of the text is accompanied by lecture notes to assist instructors in integrating the material into their lectures.

Electronic Slides New to this edition, this software includes a PowerPoint® viewer and a set of over 200 PowerPoint® slides. The slides include topics not covered in the acetate package and other key concepts covered in the text. Those instructors who have PowerPoint® can customize and add to this valuable presentation tool.

Test Bank   Our Test Bank has been developed and class tested to provide an accurate and exhaustive source of test items for a wide variety of examination styles. It contains more than 3,000 questions, categorized by topic and level of learning (definitional, conceptual, or application). The test questions for the Fifth Edition are more application oriented and include questions for each end-of-chapter video case. A Test Item Table allows instructors to select questions from any section of a chapter at any of the three levels of learning. The Test Bank includes approximately 10 essay questions, and over 100 multiple-choice questions per chapter, making it one of the most comprehensive test packages on the market. The Test Bank also includes questions for Appendices A, B, and D.

IRWIN's Computest IV   In addition to the printed format, a computerized test bank is available free to adopters. The Computest program for microcomputers allows the instructor to select from any of the questions, change if desired, or add new questions—and quickly print out a finished set customized to the instructor's course.

Video Case Studies   A unique series of 22 contemporary marketing cases is available on videotape cassettes. Each video case corresponds with chapter specific topics and an end-of-chapter case in the text. Over 60 percent of the video cases have been updated or are new. The video cases feature a variety of organizations and provide balanced coverage of services, consumer products, small businesses, Fortune 500 firms, and business-to-business examples. *Washburn Guitars, Specialized Bicycles, Imagination Pilots,* and *Ken Davis Barbecue Products* are just a few of the exciting video cases that are available with the Fifth Edition.

Study Guide   Authored by William Carner of The University of Texas, the Study Guide enables the students to learn and apply marketing principles instead of simply memorizing facts for an examination. The Study Guide includes chapter outlines for student note-taking, sample tests, critical thinking questions, and flash cards. The new format is based on the results of student focus groups.

Computer-Problem Software   This software features short cases and problems that allow students to learn about and apply marketing concepts and see the results of marketing decisions on a personal computer.

Marketing Planning Software   Revised for Windows®, the marketing plan software is designed to help students use the strategic marketing process introduced in Chapter 2 and Appendix A and discussed in detail in Chapter 22. The software provides a personal and computer-based tool for involving students in the planning process.

***Wall Street Journal* Articles**   A collection of recent *Wall Street Journal* articles with corresponding questions is provided to facilitate class discussion and add currency.

Presentation CD-ROM   IRWIN's new Instructor CD-ROM for *Marketing* will contain video clips, slides, and acetates for the text. Great for enhancing class presentations, CD-ROM enables the instructor to show video segments as they pertain to lectures or access the software or electronic slides instantly. The CD-ROM will also include the print supplements and electronic supplements so that the instructor has access to all of the supplements on one disk.

Virtual Marketing Careers CD-ROM   More than just a careers application, this innovative, interactive software puts the students in the role of several marketing professions: sales manager, brand manager, marketing research manager, advertising manager, and retail manager. The virtual reality environment gives students the opportunity to make decisions within a realistic environment and have fun while learning to apply concepts.

Instructor's "Survival Kit"   Today's students are more likely to learn and be motivated by active, participative experiences than by classic classroom lecture and discussion. While our many other supplements like video cases and transparencies enhance classroom instruction, the Instructor's "Survival Kit" contains three specific elements of special value to today's instructors:

- In-class activities. What we term "in-class activities" have appeared in our Instructor's Manual in the past, and we have received such extremely positive feedback from our customers—both instructors and students—on these that we are now putting them in a separate package so they get the attention they deserve. These may relate to a specific video case or example from the text or may be totally new. For example, some popular activities from our past editions include the "Quick Quiz" on music from Prince's Paisley Park video case, the Coke versus Pepsi taste test, and the "Ethics Quiz." These not only elicit classroom discussion, but also have a learning value in helping students understand marketing.
- "Props" to help run the in-class activities. With the time pressures on today's instructors, our goal is to make their lives simpler. So included in the survival kit are the props to run the activities, such as the labels for the Coke versus Pepsi taste test, the "quizzes" for the Paisely Park Quick Quiz (and the right answers), and the bean bags for the Total Quality Management experiment.
- Sample products. *Marketing*, in both the text and supplements, utilizes examples of offerings from both large and small firms that will interest today's students. A number of these are included in the survival kit when they may be new or unusual to students, items such as Breathe Right Nasal Strips and Hydrobands. Also, when appropriate, sample ads are included among our transparencies.

Linda Rochford of the University of Minnesota-Duluth spearheaded our efforts in developing the survival kit.

Instructor's Media Resource Guide   This all-in-one guide includes everything that the instructor needs to coordinate and utilize the media supplements. It includes recommended articles, teaching suggestions for the student software, and instructions for the CD-ROMs.

Case Teaching Notes   This supplement includes teaching notes for the video cases and supplemental cases.

Marketing Home Page   Our new home page is a source of information for student and instructors alike. The home page includes additional teaching ideas and hot links to home pages that are relevant to anyone interested more about marketing.

DEVELOPMENT OF THIS BOOK

Through each of the editions of *Marketing* we have been fortunate to utilize the extensive developmental resources of Richard D. Irwin. Building on that history, the fifth edition developmental process included several phases of evaluation and a variety of stakeholder (e.g., student, instructor, etc.) audiences. The first phase of the review process asked adopters to focus on recommendations for the organization of the text and improvements that could be made to the supplements package. The second phase encompassed a more detailed review of each chapter as the text was used by adopters in the classroom. We also surveyed students to find out what they liked about the book and what changes they would suggest. Finally, a key group of instructors who do not use the text gave us feedback on the fourth edition.

Reviewers who were vital in the changes that were made to this edition include:

Kevin W. Bittle
Johnson & Wales University

Nancy Bloom
Nassau Community College

William Carner
University of Texas at Austin

Pola B. Gupta
University of Northern Iowa

Robert C. Harris
University of Northern Colorado

James A. Henley, Jr.
University of Tennessee at Chattanooga

Donald R. Jackson
Ferris State University

Duncan G. LaBay
University of Massachusetts at Lowell

Michael R. Luthy
Drake University

Richard J. Lutz
University of Florida

H. Lee Meadow
Northern Illinois University

Janet Murray
Cleveland State University

June E. Parr
Eastern Washington University

L. William Perttula
San Francisco State University

Jean Romeo
Boston College

Craig Stacey
Northeastern University

Vincent P. Taiani
Indiana University of Pennsylvania

Tom L. Trittipo
University of Central Oklahoma

Robert S. Welsh
Central Michigan University

PRODUCT DEVELOPMENT TEAM

A special thank you is due to the following people who participated on the Product Development Team. This group of gifted instructors gave us input during every stage of development of the text and supplements package. Specifically, they critiqued the new design of the text, gave recommendations for the topic selection and editing of the video cases, and reviewed several of the supplements.

Kevin Bittle
Johnson & Wales University

Nancy Bloom
Nassau Community College

William Carner
University of Texas at Austin

Dennis Garrett
Marquette University

William George
Villanova University

Donna H. Giertz
Parkland College

Pola B. Gupta
The University of Northern Iowa

Priscilla LaBarbera
New York University

Donnie Lichtenstein
University of Colorado at Boulder

Paul Londrigan
Charles S. Mott Community College

Richard Lutz
University of Florida

Mary Ann Machanic
University of Massachusetts Boston

James Malone
University of Massachusetts

Peter McClure
University of Massachusetts Boston

Janet Murray
Cleveland State University

William Perttula
San Francisco State University

Peter Raven
Eastern Washington University

C. David Shepherd
The University of Tennessee–Chattanooga

Craig Stacey
Northeastern University

Ruth Taylor
Southwest Texas State University

Charles Vitaska
Metro State

Blaise Waguespack
Embry Riddle Aeronautical University

Rick Webb
Johnson County Community College

Robert Williams
Northern Arizona University

Janice Williams
University of Central Oklahoma

ACKNOWLEDGMENTS

The preceding section demonstrates the amount of feedback and developmental input that went into this project, and we are deeply grateful to the numerous people who have shared their ideas with us. Reviewing a book or supplement takes an incredible amount of energy and attention, and we are glad that so many of our colleagues took the time to do it. Their comments have inspired us to do our best.

Reviewers who contributed to the first four editions of this book include:

Linda Anglin
Mankato State University

William D. Ash
California State University, Long Beach

Patricia Baconride
Fort Hays State University

Siva Balasubramanian
University of Iowa

A. Diane Barlar
University of West Florida

James H. Barnes
University of Mississippi

Frederick J. Beier
University of Minnesota

Thomas M. Bertsch
James Madison University

William Brown
University of Nebraska, Omaha

William G. Browne
Oregon State University

Stephen Calcich
Norfolk State University

Gerald O. Cavallo
Fairfield University

S. Tamer Cavusgil
Michigan State University

Sang Choe
University of Southern Indiana

Clark Compton
University of Missouri, St. Louis

Ken Crocker
Bowling Green State University

Joe Cronin
University of Kentucky

James Cross
University of Nevada, Las Vegas

Lowell E. Crow
Western Michigan University

John H. Cunningham
University of Oregon

Bill Curtis
University of Nebraska, Lincoln

Dan Darrow
Ferris State University

Martin Decatur
Suffolk County Community College

Francis DeFea
El Camino College

Linda M. Delene
Western Michigan University

Paul Dion
Bryant College

William B. Dodds
Fort Lewis College

James H. Donnelly
University of Kentucky

Roger W. Egerton
Southwestern Oklahoma State University

Barbara Evans
University of Melbourne (Australia)

Charles Ford
Arkansas State University

Donald Fuller
University of Central Florida

Marc Goldberg
Portland State University

Leslie A. Goldgehn
California State, Hayward

Kenneth Goodenday
University of Toledo

James Gould
Pace University—White Plains Campus

James L. Grimm
Illinois State University

Donald V. Harper
University of Minnesota

Richard M. Hill
University of Illinois

Al Holden
St. John's University

Kristine Hovsepian
Ashland University

Jarrett Hudnal
Stephen F. Austin State University

Mike Hyman
University of North Texas

Kenneth Jameson
California State University, Dominguez Hills

James C. Johnson
St. Cloud State University

Mary Joyce
Bryant College

Herbert Katzenstein
St. John's University

Ram Kesaran
University of Detroit

Roy Klages
State University of New York at Albany

Terry Kroeten
North Dakota State University

Priscilla LaBarbera
New York University

Richard Lapidus
University of Nevada-Las Vegas

Irene Lange
California State University, Fullerton

Ed Laube
Macomb Community College

Gary Law
Cuyahoga Community College

Karen LeMasters
University of Pennsylvania

Richard C. Leventhal
Metropolital State College

Leonard Lindenmuth
State University of New York-Binghamton

Lynn Loudenback
New Mexico State University

Robert Luke
Southwest Nissouri State University

Marton L. Macchiette
Plymouth State University

Kenneth Maricle
Virginia Commonwealth University

Elena Martinez
University of Puerto Rico

James McAlexander
Iowa State University

Peter J. McClure
University of Massachusetts, Boston

Jim McHugh
St. Louis Community College at Forest Park

Gary F. McKinnon
Brigham Young University

Lee Meadow
Northern Illinois University

James Meszaros
County College of Morris

Ron Michaels
Indiana University

Stephen W. Miller
St. Louis University

Fred Morgan
University of Oklahoma

Donald F. Mulvihill
Virginia Commonwealth University

Keith Murray
Bryant University

Joseph Myslivec
Central Michigan University

Donald G. Norris
Miami University (OH)

Carl Obermiller
University of Washington

Dave Olson
North Hennepin Community College

James Olver
College of William & Mary

Philip Parron
Northwestern College

Allan Palmer
University of North Carolina, Charlotte

Dennis Pappas
Columbus Technical Institute
Richard Penn
University of Northern Iowa

John Penrose
University of Texas, Austin

William Pertula
San Francisco State University

Michael Peters
Boston College

William S. Piper
The University of Southern Mississippi-Gulf Park

Gary Poorman
Normandale Community College

Joe Puzi
Florida Atlantic University

James P. Rakowski
Memphis State University

Heikki
Brigham Young University

Robert W. Ruekert
University of Minnesota

Eberhard Seheuling
St. John's University

Starr F. Schlobohm
University of New Hampshire

Stan Scott
University of Alaska

Harold S. Sekiguchi
University of Nevada

Bob E. Smiley
Indiana State University

Allen Smith
Florida Atlantic University

Miriam B. Stamps
University of South Florida

Robert Swerdlow
Lamar University

Clint Tankeraley
Syracuse University

Andrew Thacker
California State Polytechnic University, Pomona

Fred Trawick
University of Alabama at Birmingham

Thomas L. Trittipo Central State University,
Oklahoma

Sue Umashankar
University of Arizona

Ottilia Voegtli
University of Arizona

Gerald Waddle
Clemson University

Randall E. Wade
Rogue Community College

Harlan Wallingford
Pace University

Ron Weston
Contra Costa College

Max White
Southwestern Oklahoma State University

James Wilkins
University of Southwestern Louisiana

Kaylene Williams
University of Delaware

Wilton Lelund
Southwest Texas State University

Robert Witherspoon
Triton College

Van R. Wood
Texas Tech University

William R. Wynd
Eastern Washington University

Thanks are also due to David H. Gobeli of Oregon State University who assisted in the revision of Chapter 2; Michael Blumfield of the University of Minnesota for his assistance with Appendix A; William Carner of the University of Texas-Austin who wrote the study guide; and Stuart Rogers of the University of Denver who was responsible for the testbank, assisted by Dennis N. Bristow of St. Cloud State University. Linda Rochford and Rajiv Vaidyanathan of the University of Minnesota-Duluth; Giana Eckhardt, Susan Rosen and Mark Weber of the University of Minnesota; John W. Mullins and Christina L. Grippi of the University of Denver; Krzysztof Przybylowski of the Warsaw School of Economics; and Gwen Achenreiner of Bradley University wrote or contributed significantly to the cases included in the text. Ruth Ann Smith of Virginia Polytechnic Institute and her students made valuable suggestions. Rick Armstrong, Robert Vaaler, Paul Fagan and Bruce McClean produced our videos.

The business community also provided great help in making available information that appears in the text and supplements—much of it for the first time in college materials. Thanks are due to Dwight Riskey of Frito-Lay, Inc., Bob Proscal of Honeywell, and Mary Weber of Fallon McElligott. We also acknowledge the help of L. David Ostlie of Energy Performance Systems, Alan Leeds and George Clinton of Paisley Park Records, David Dornbush and Chad Erickson of American Harvest, Barbara Jo Davis of Ken Davis Products, Randall F. Peters and Leah Peters of Paradise Kitchens, Mary Horwath of Rollerblade, Inc., James Watkins and Dr. Sarah Risch of Golden Valley Microwave Foods, and Jane Westerlund of the Caplow Co.

Staff support from the University of Massachusetts, Southern Methodist University, the University of Denver, and the University of Minnesota was essential. We gratefully acknowledge the help of Wanda Hanson, Louise Holt, Stacy Houston, Jennifer Kaczmarski, Dorothy Kleeman, and Lucy Toton for their many contributions.

Finally, we acknowledge the professional efforts of the Richard D. Irwin staff. Completion of our book and its many supplements required the attention and commitment of many editorial, production, marketing, and research personnel. Our Burr Ridge-based team included Rob Zwettler, Becky Dodson, Tricia Howland, Nina McGuffin, Keri Johnson, Charlotte Goldman, Mike Hruby, Keith McPherson, Laurie Sander, Colleen Suljic, Steve Schuetz, and many others!

Eric N. Berkowitz
Roger A. Kerin
Steven W. Hartley
William Rudelius

Contents in Brief

CONTENTS

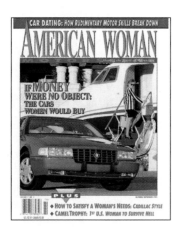

MARKETING

PART ONE

INITIATING THE MARKETING PROCESS

Satisfying consumers in local, national, and global markets. This is the essence of the marketing process described in Part I. Chapter 1 introduces the marketing process by describing the actions of Mary Horwath as she and Rollerblade, Inc., introduce in-line skates, create what *Time* magazine calls "the sport of the 90s," and plan for international growth. Chapter 2 describes how organizations such as Ben & Jerry's utilize the strategic marketing process to serve their customers. Following Chapter 2 is a sample marketing plan (Appendix A) which illustrates the outcome of the strategic marketing process and provides a reference for students to study and use. In Chapter 3 the dimensions of the business environment and how it has and will change are presented. These changes are described in terms of social, economic, technological, competitive, and regulatory forces. Finally Chapter 4 provides a framework for including ethical and social responsibility considerations in marketing decisions.

CHAPTER 1

Marketing: A Focus on the Consumer

AFTER READING THIS CHAPTER YOU SHOULD BE ABLE TO:

• Define marketing and explain the importance of (1) discovering and (2) satisfying consumer needs and wants.

• Distinguish between marketing mix elements and environmental factors.

• Describe how today's market orientation era differs from prior eras oriented to production and selling.

• Understand the meaning of ethics and social responsibility and how they relate to the individual, organizations, and society.

• Know what is required for marketing to occur and how it creates customer value and utilities for consumers.

ROLLERBLADES SKATE TO THE EXTREMES!

Did you get a ticket to the Extreme Games? Did you watch the games on TV? If not, you may not be on the cutting edge of sports! A week-long event broadcast on all-sports cable channels ESPN and ESPN2, the Extreme Games consist of 27 olympic-style competitive events including vertical ramp, street, and downhill in-line skating. Coverage of the Games was broadcast to more than 150 countries and attracted 11.1 million viewers in 8.3 million homes!

How is it possible that a sport that did not exist 10 years ago is so popular today? The answer is a marketing success story—Rollerblades![1]

In the early 1700s a Dutch inventor trying to simulate ice skating in the summer created the first roller skates by attaching spools to his shoes. His in-line arrangement was the standard design until 1863 when the first skates with rollers set as two pairs appeared. This design became the standard, and in-line skates virtually disappeared from the market.

In 1980, two Minnesota hockey-playing brothers found an old pair of in-line skates while browsing through a sporting goods store. Working in their garage, they modified the design to add polyurethane wheels, a molded boot shell, and a toe brake. They sold their product, which they dubbed "Rollerblade skates," out of the back of their truck to hockey players and skiers as a means of staying in shape during the summer. In the mid-1980s an entrepreneur bought the company from the brothers and then hired a marketing expert—Mary Horwath—to figure out how to market Rollerblade skates.[2]

On understanding the consumer "When I came here," remembers Horwath, "I knew there had to be a change." By focusing only on serious athletes who used in-line skates to train for other sports, Rollerblades had developed an image as a training product. Conversations with in-line skaters, however, convinced Horwath that using Rollerblade skates:

- Was incredible fun.
- Was a great aerobic workout and made the skater stronger and healthier.
- Was quite different from traditional roller skating, which was practiced alone, mostly inside, and by young girls.
- Would have great appeal to people other than just off-season ice skaters and skiers.

A fresh approach to the firm's marketing, advertising, and public relations was needed. Horwath explains the change:

> We decided that if we wanted to sell more skates, we had to create new reasons for people to skate. We had to create and market a new sport—the sport of in-line skating. By creating a new sport, we could stop marketing the product to only a small audience of serious athletes and begin marketing to everyone. We were the only company making in-line skates, so we knew that we would get all the publicity surrounding a new sport. If we could build a sport, Rollerblade, Inc. would grow. But our challenge was huge, because we had to build an entire sport from nothing.[3]

Horwath saw her task as changing the image in people's minds—or "repositioning"— Rollerblade skates to highlight the benefits people saw in in-line skating. "I also wanted to change the 'male-skewed' image of in-line skates," she laughs. But her task still remained: how could she gain the marketing exposure and publicity to grow an in-line skate industry on a tiny annual marketing budget of $200,000? She felt she needed what she calls "guerilla marketing"—gaining national exposure for Rollerblade skates using relatively inexpensive, creative ways to show the product to potential buyers.

Here are some of the key questions to which she and her team sought answers as they developed a marketing strategy for Rollerblade:

- What age group of potential buyers should they target?
- What benefits or points of difference should they stress to potential buyers to reposition Rollerblade skates in the minds of potential buyers?
- How should they spend their $200,000 budget to gain awareness for Rollerblade skates and get people to try them, in hopes of growing a new industry?

Looking back, it's clear that the future of the industry—and the company—hinged on finding good answers to these questions.

Rollerblade skates, marketing, and you What marketing strategy did Mary Horwath and her marketing team initiate to achieve the skyrocketing growth of in-line skating shown in Figure 1–1? By the time you reach the end of this chapter, you will know the answer to this question.

One key to how well Horwath succeeded lies in the subject of this book: marketing. In this chapter and in the rest of the book we'll introduce you to many of the people, organizations, ideas, activities, and jobs in marketing that have spawned the products and services that have been towering successes, shattering failures, or something in between.

Marketing affects all individuals, all organizations, all industries, and all countries. This text seeks not only to teach you marketing concepts, but also to demonstrate its many applications and how it affects our lives. This knowledge should make you a better consumer, help you in your career, and enable you to be a more informed citizen.

In this chapter and those that follow, you will feel the excitement of marketing. You will be introduced to the dynamic changes that will affect all of us in the future.

FIGURE 1-1

Number of in-line skaters in the United States. What led to this skyrocketing growth? For some answers, see the text.

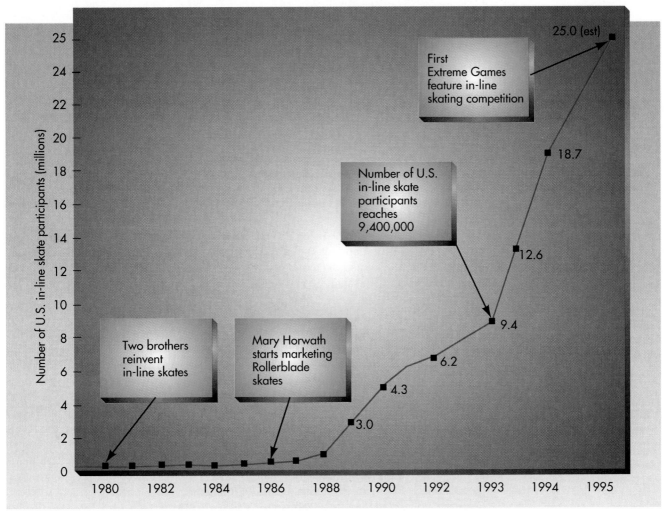

Source: "In-line skating facts," Rollerblade, Inc. report.

You will also meet many men and women—like Mary Horwath—whose marketing creativity sometimes achieved brilliant, extraordinary results. And who knows? Somewhere in these pages you may find a career.

WHAT IS MARKETING?

Being a Marketing Expert: Good News–Bad News

In many respects you are a marketing expert already. But just to test your expertise, try the "marketing expert" questions in Figure 1–2. These questions—some of them easy, others mind boggling—show the diverse problems marketing executives grapple with every day. You'll find the answers in the next few pages.

The good news: you already have marketing experience   You are somewhat of an expert because you do many marketing activities every day. You already know many marketing terms, concepts, and principles. For example, would

FIGURE 1–2

The see-if-you're-really-a-marketing-expert test

> **Answer the questions below. The correct answers are given later in the chapter.**
>
> 1. In a magazine article, a well-known actress said she often "Rollerbladed" for fun and exercise. What was Rollerblade, Inc.'s reaction? (a) delighted, (b) upset, or (c) somewhere in between. Why?
> 2. What is "Polavision"? (a) a new breathable contact lens, (b) a TV network that competes with Home Box Office, (c) special bifocal glasses, (d) instant movies, or (e) a political newspaper.
> 3. Right after World War II, International Business Machines Corporation (IBM) commissioned a study to estimate the *total* market for electronic computers. The study's results were (a) less than 10, (b) 1,000, (c) 10,000, (d) 100,000, or (e) 1 million or more.
> 4. True or false: "Customer value" is a critical marketing issue today, and the new view of it goes beyond just quality and price.
> 5. How could Mary Horwath and Rollerblade, Inc. find an inexpensive way to get prospective buyers to try their in-line skates?

you sell more Sony Walkmans at $500 or $50 each? The answer is $50, of course, so your experience in shopping for products—and maybe even selling them—already gives you great insights into the world of marketing. As a consumer, you've already been involved in thousands of marketing decisions—but mainly on the buying, not the marketing, side.

The bad news: surprises about the obvious   Unfortunately, common sense doesn't always explain some marketing decisions and actions.

An actress's saying in a national magazine that she "often Rollerbladed" (question 1, Figure 1–2) sounds like great publicity, right? But Rollerblade, Inc. was upset. Legally, Rollerblade is a registered trademark of Rollerblade, Inc. and, as a brand name, should be used only to identify its products and services. With letters to offenders and advertisements like the one below, Rollerblade, Inc. is trying to protect a precious asset: its brand identity.

Under American trademark law, if consumers generally start using a brand name as the generic term to describe the product rather than the source of the product, then the company loses its exclusive rights to the name. "Rollerblade" skates would become "rollerblade"— just another English word to describe all kinds of in-line skating. That fate has already befallen some famous American products such as

Rollerblade, Inc. ran this ad to communicate a specific message. It's also part of a "reminder" letter sent to people who *slip*. What is the message? For the answer and why it is important, see the text.

Everyday, irregardless of his homework, Jeffrey went "rollerblading" because it was to nice to lay around with his nose in a english book.

Of the seven errors in this headline, the use of "rollerblading" as a verb strikes us as the most extreme. Rollerblade® is a brand name. It is, also, technically incorrect to use "rollerblader" and "rollerblades" as nouns. Remember, the careful writer skates on in-line skates known as Rollerblade® skates.

© 1992 Rollerblade, Inc. Rollerblade and The Skate Logo are trademarks of Rollerblade, Inc.

linoleum, aspirin, cellophane, escalator, yo-yo, corn flakes, and trampoline. In fact, Random House Webster's College Dictionary says it's "almost 100 percent sure" that the word *Rollerblade* will appear in its next edition—but with a capital "R" to recognize it as a trademark.[4]

Today American firms are spending millions of dollars in both advertising and court cases to protect their important brand names. Examples are Kimberly-Clark's Kleenex tissues and towels and 3M's Scotch tape. Coca-Cola takes dozens of restaurants to court every year for serving another cola drink when the patron asks for a Coca-Cola or even a Coke. Because legal and ethical issues such as the Rollerblade skates trademark problem are so central to many marketing decisions, they are addressed throughout the book.

The point here is that although your common sense usually helps you in analyzing marketing problems, sometimes it can mislead you. This book's in-depth study of marketing augments your common sense with an understanding of marketing concepts to help you assess and make marketing decisions more effectively.

Marketing: Using Exchanges to Satisfy Needs

The American Marketing Association, representing marketing professionals in the United States and Canada, states that "**marketing** is the process of planning and executing the conception, pricing, promotion, and distribution of ideas, goods, and services to create exchanges that satisfy individual and organizational objectives."[5] Many people incorrectly believe that marketing is the same thing as advertising or personal selling; this definition shows marketing to be a far broader activity. Further, this definition stresses the importance of beneficial exchanges that satisfy the objectives of both those who buy and those who sell ideas, goods, and services—whether they be individuals or organizations.

To serve both buyers and sellers, marketing seeks (1) to discover the needs and wants of prospective customers and (2) to satisfy them. These prospective customers include both individuals buying for themselves and their households and organizations that buy for their own use (such as manufacturers) or for resale (such as wholesalers and retailers). The key to achieving these two objectives is the idea of **exchange,** which is the trade of things of value between buyer and seller so that each is better off after the trade. This vital concept of exchange in marketing is covered below in more detail.

The Diverse Factors Influencing Marketing Activities

Although an organization's marketing activity focuses on assessing and satisfying consumer needs, countless other people, groups, and forces interact to shape the nature of its activities (Figure 1–3). Foremost is the organization itself, whose mission and objectives determine what business it is in and what goals it seeks. Within the organization, management is responsible for establishing these goals. The marketing department works closely with a network of other departments and employees to help provide the customer-satisfying products required for the organization to survive and prosper.[6]

Figure 1–3 also shows the key people, groups, and forces outside the organization that influence marketing activities. The marketing department is responsible for facilitating relationships, partnerships, and alliances with the organization's customers, its shareholders (or often representatives of groups served by a nonprofit organization), its suppliers, and other organizations. Environmental forces such as social, technological, economic, competitive, and regulatory factors also shape an organization's marketing activities. Finally, an organization's marketing decisions are affected by and in turn often have an important impact on society as a whole.

FIGURE 1–3

An organization's marketing department relates to many people, groups, and forces

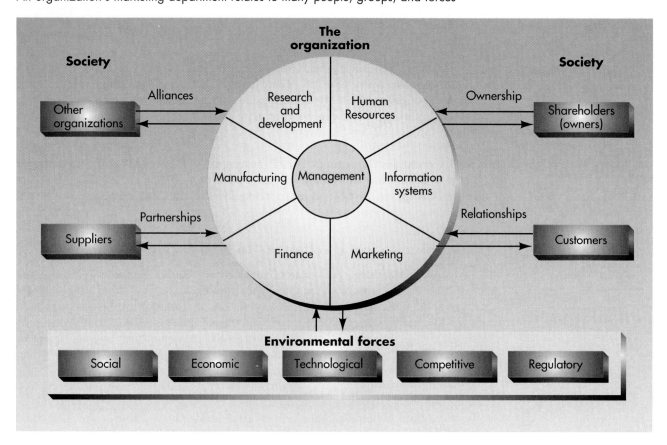

The organization must strike a continual balance among the sometimes differing interests of these individuals and groups. For example, it is not possible to simultaneously provide the lowest-priced and highest-quality products to customers and pay the highest prices to suppliers, highest wages to employees, and maximum dividends to shareholders.

Requirements for Marketing to Occur

For marketing to occur, at least four factors are required: (1) two or more parties (individuals or organizations) with unsatisfied needs, (2) a desire and ability on their part to be satisfied, (3) a way for the parties to communicate, and (4) something to exchange.

Two or more parties with unsatisfied needs   Suppose you've developed an unmet need—a desire for information about how technology is reshaping the workplace and the personal lives of consumers—but you didn't yet know that *Time Digital* magazine existed. Also unknown to you was that several copies of *Time Digital* were sitting on the magazine rack at your nearest supermarket, waiting to be purchased. This is an example of two parties with unmet needs: you, with a need for technology-related information, and your supermarket owner, needing someone to buy a copy of *Time Digital.*

Desire and ability to satisfy these needs   Both you and the supermarket owner want to satisfy these unmet needs. Furthermore, you have the money to buy the item and the time to get to the supermarket. The store's owner has not only the desire to sell *Time Digital* but also the ability to do so since it's stocked on the shelves.

A way for the parties to communicate   The marketing transaction of buying a copy of *Time Digital* will never occur unless you know the product exists and its location. Similarly, the store owner won't stock the magazine unless there's a market of potential consumers near the supermarket who are likely to buy. When you receive a free sample in the mail or see the magazine on display at the checkout lane, this communications barrier between you (the buyer) and your supermarket (the seller) is overcome.

Something to exchange   Marketing occurs when the transaction takes place and both the buyer and seller exchange something of value. In this case, you exchange your money for the supermarket's *Time Digital.* Both of you have gained something and also given up something, but you are both better off because you have each satisfied your unmet needs. You have the opportunity to read *Time Digital*, but you gave up some money; the store gave up the *Time Digital* but received money, which enables it to remain in business. This exchange process and, of course, the ethical and legal foundations of exchange are central to marketing.[7]

CONCEPT CHECK

1. What is marketing?

2. Marketing focuses on _____ and _____ consumer needs.

3. What four factors are needed for marketing to occur?

HOW MARKETING DISCOVERS AND SATISFIES CONSUMER NEEDS

The importance of discovering and satisfying consumer needs is so critical to understanding marketing that we look at each of these two steps in detail next.

New Coke was not a successful new product

Discovering Consumer Needs

The first objective in marketing is discovering the needs of prospective consumers. Sound simple? Well, it's not. In the abstract, discovering needs looks easy, but when you get down to the specifics of marketing, problems crop up.

Some product disasters   With much fanfare, a decade ago, Coca-Cola replaced its 98-year-old Coke with a better-tasting cola called New Coke. Polaroid, flushed with the success of its instant still-photography business, introduced Polavision (question 2, Figure 1–2) as the first instant home movie camera. Similarly, after investing $40 million, IBM introduced a personal computer called the PCjr.

While Coca-Cola reintroduced its original formula only 79 days after New Coke's launch, Polaroid withdrew its product, and IBM redirected its efforts to a replacement product only a short time after the products were introduced. All three firms lost millions in their failed attempts to introduce new products.

These are three of the best-known product disasters in recent U.S. history, but thousands of lesser-known products fail in the marketplace every year. One major reason is that, in each case, the firm miscalculated consumers' wants and needs for these products. In the case of New Coke, Coca-Cola provoked a nationwide uproar from old formula loyalists by failing to understand their bond with the existing product. Polaroid did not anticipate that consumers would prefer the convenience of videotape technology over Polavision. Finally, the PCjr failed because consumers did not like the keyboard, and competitors' computers were lower priced.[8]

The solution to preventing such product failures seems embarrassingly obvious. First, find out what consumers need and want. Second, produce what they do need and want and don't produce what they don't need and want. This is much more difficult than it sounds.

It's frequently very difficult to get a precise reading on what consumers want and need when they are confronted with revolutionary ideas for new products. Right after World War II, IBM asked one of the most prestigious management consulting firms in the United States to estimate the total future market for *all* electronic computers for *all* business, scientific, engineering, and government uses (question 3, Figure 1–2). The answer was less than 10! Fortunately, key IBM executives disagreed, so IBM started building electronic computers anyway. Where would IBM be today if it had assumed the market estimate was correct? Most of the firms that bought computers five years after the market study had not actually recognized they were prospective buyers because they had no understanding of what computers could do for them—they didn't recognize their own need for faster information processing.

Consumer needs and consumer wants   Should marketing try to satisfy consumer needs or consumer wants? The answer is both! Heated debates rage over this question, and a person's position in the debate usually depends on the definitions of needs and wants and the amount of freedom given to prospective customers to make their own buying decisions.

A *need* occurs when a person feels physiologically deprived of basic necessities such as food, clothing, and shelter. A *want* is a felt need that is shaped by a person's knowledge, culture, and personality. So if you feel hungry, you have developed a basic need and desire to eat something. Let's say you then want to eat an apple or a candy bar because, based on your past experience and personality, you know these will satisfy your hunger need. Effective marketing, in the form of creating an awareness of good products at convenient locations, can clearly shape a person's wants. Rollerblade in-line skates are an example.

At issue is whether marketing persuades prospective customers to buy the "wrong" things—say, a candy bar rather than an apple to satisfy hunger pangs. Certainly, marketing tries to influence what we buy. A question then arises—at what point do we want government and society to step in to protect consumers? Most consumers would say they want government to protect us from harmful drugs and unsafe cars but not from candy bars and soft drinks. The issue is not clear-cut, which is why legal and social issues are central to marketing. Because even psychologists and economists still debate the exact meanings of *need* and *want,* we shall avoid the semantic arguments and use the terms interchangeably in the rest of the book.

As shown in Figure 1–4, discovering needs involves looking carefully at prospective customers, whether they are children buying M&M's candy, college students buying Rollerblade in-line skates, or firms buying Xerox photocopying machines. A principal activity of a firm's marketing department is to carefully scrutinize its consumers to understand what they need, to study industry trends, to examine competitors' products, and to even analyze the needs of a customer's customer.

What a market is   Potential consumers make up a **market,** which is (1) people (2) with the desire and (3) with the ability to buy a specific product. All markets ultimately are people. Even when we say a firm bought a Xerox copier, we mean one or several people in the firm decided to buy it. People who are aware of their unmet needs may have the desire to buy the product, but that alone isn't sufficient. People must also have the ability to buy, such as the authority, time, and money. As we saw earlier in the definition of marketing, people may buy, or accept, more than just goods

FIGURE 1-4

Marketing's first task:
discovering consumer needs

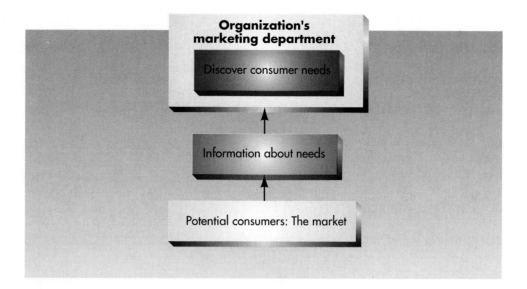

or services. For example, they may buy an idea that results in an action, such as having their blood pressure checked annually or turning down their thermostat to save energy.

Satisfying Consumer Needs

Marketing doesn't stop with the discovery of consumer needs. Since the organization obviously can't satisfy all consumer needs, it must concentrate its efforts on certain needs of a specific group of potential consumers. This is the **target market,** one or more specific groups of potential consumers toward which an organization directs its marketing program.

The four Ps: controllable marketing mix factors   Having selected the target market consumers, the firm must take steps to satisfy their needs. Someone in the organization's marketing department, often the marketing manager, must take action and develop a complete marketing program to reach consumers by using a combination of four tools, often called the *four Ps*—a useful shorthand reference to them first published by Professor E. Jerome McCarthy:[9]

- *Product.* A good, service, or idea to satisfy the consumer's needs.
- *Price.* What is exchanged for the product.
- *Promotion.* A means of communication between the seller and buyer.
- *Place.* A means of getting the product into the consumer's hands.

We'll define each of the four Ps more carefully later in the book, but for now it's important to remember that they are the elements of the marketing mix, or simply the **marketing mix.** These are the marketing manager's controllable factors, the marketing actions of product, price, promotion, and place that he or she can take to solve a marketing problem. The marketing mix elements are called *controllable factors* because they are under the control of the marketing department in an organization.

The uncontrollable, environmental factors   There are a host of factors largely beyond the control of the marketing department and its organization. These factors can be placed into five groups (as shown in Figure 1–3): social, technological, economic, competitive, and regulatory forces. Examples are what consumers themselves want and need, changing technology, the state of the economy in terms of

Dell Computer, Lands' End, and Nike provide customer value using three very different approaches. For their strategies, see the Marketing NewsNet and text.

whether it is expanding or contracting, actions that competitors take, and government restrictions. These are the **environmental factors** in a marketing decision, the uncontrollable factors involving social, economic, technological, competitive, and regulatory forces. These five forces may serve as accelerators or brakes on marketing, sometimes expanding an organization's marketing opportunities and other times restricting them. These five environmental factors are covered in Chapter 3.

Traditionally, many marketing executives have treated these environmental factors as rigid, absolute constraints that are entirely outside their influence.[10] However, recent studies and marketing successes have shown that a forward-looking, action-oriented firm can often affect some environmental factors. IBM's technical breakthroughs gave birth to the entire digital electronic computer industry, even though initial estimates of demand were low. Cable TV companies have redefined their

MARKETING NEWSNET

CUSTOMER VALUE IS WHATEVER CUSTOMERS VALUE

Until quite recently it was assumed that customer value was how prospective buyers judged a good or service on some combination of quality and price. Today, value is a much broader concept that also includes dimensions such as convenience, on-time delivery, and service. Customers now want more of the dimensions they value: if they value convenience, they want their purchase to be easy; if they value low price, they want the lowest possible price; if they value speed, they want the purchase to be extremely fast.

Curiously, to provide customer value a manufacturer, retailer, or service provider does not have to compete on all these dimensions. Research by management experts Michael Treacy and Fred Wiersema suggests that firms cannot succeed by being all things to all people. Instead they must find the unique value that they alone can deliver to a selected market. Many successful firms have chosen to deliver outstanding customer value with one of three value strategies—best price, best product, or best service.

Companies such as Wal-Mart, Southwest Airlines, Price/Costco, and Dell Computer have all been successful offering consumers the best price. Other companies such as Nike, Starbucks, Microsoft, and Johnson & Johnson claim to provide the best products on the market. Finally, companies such as Land's End and Home Depot deliver value by building long-term relationships with customers and providing exceptional service.

How should a firm choose a value proposition? By assessing its customers, competitors, and itself, say Treacy and Wiersema.

VALUE PROPOSITIONS

BEST PRICE	BEST PRODUCT	BEST SERVICE
Guaranteed low price	The best product, period.	We take care of you

competition to include telephone companies. After more than a decade of negotiations with Soviet bureaucrats, McDonald's recently opened a 700-seat restaurant in Moscow and served more than 10 million customers its first year. These technological, competitive, and regulatory factors might have forestalled productive marketing actions had they been seen as completely uncontrollable.

New standards in customer value The intensity of competition in both domestic and global markets has caused massive restructuring of many American industries and businesses, and the trend continues. American managers are seeking ways to compete more effectively in this new, more intense level of global competition. For ideas, these managers often study firms that have been successful, try to understand the reasons for their success, and then duplicate them.

One reason for the success of many firms is their focus on providing customer value. Consequently, "customer value" has become *the* critical marketing issue for both sellers and buyers (question 4, Figure 1–2). That firms gain loyal customers by providing unique value is the essence of successful marketing. What is new, however, is a more careful attempt at understanding how a firm's customers perceive value. For our purposes, **customer value** is the unique combination of benefits received by targeted buyers that includes quality, price, convenience, on-time delivery, and both before-sale and after-sale service. The Marketing NewsNet explains how companies such as Dell Computer, Lands' End, and Nike have followed very successful—but different—marketing strategies to provide value to their targeted customers.[11] We shall expand on these ideas throughout the book.

FIGURE 1-5

Marketing's second task:
satisfying consumer needs

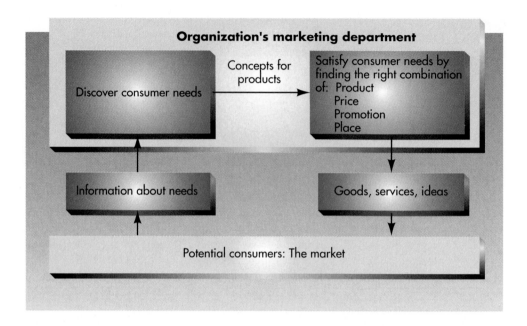

Providing customer value over a long period of time can be a challenge because firms face continually changing environmental factors. Changes in technology, competition, and regulation, in addition to issues such as globalism, diversity, ethics, and the environment, can influence consumers' perceptions of value. As a result, several important business principles are helping firms respond to changes with new or improved value offerings. *Total quality management* (TQM) programs, for example, help firms focus on the needs of the customer. Efforts at what the Japanese call *kaizen,* or continuous incremental improvement, encourage firms to do what they already do only better. Finally, *reengineering* programs involve rejecting existing assumptions, traditions, and processes and inventing new approaches to providing value. All of these approaches are likely to be part of the blueprints for success from today into the twenty-first century.[12]

The marketing program   To discover what prospective customers need, the marketing manager must translate the information from consumers into some concepts for products the firm might develop (Figure 1–5). These concepts must then be converted into a tangible **marketing program**—a plan that integrates the marketing mix to provide a good, service, or idea to prospective buyers. These prospects then react to the offering favorably (by buying) or unfavorably (by not buying), and the process is repeated. As shown in Figure 1–5, in an effective organization this process is continuous: consumer needs trigger product concepts that are translated into actual products that stimulate further discovery of consumer needs.

A marketing program for Rollerblade, Inc.   To see some specifics of an actual marketing program, let's return to the earlier example of Mary Horwath, Rollerblade, Inc., and their in-line skates.

With Rollerblade, Inc.'s small size and the limited marketing budget, Mary Horwath knew that she faced big problems in gaining awareness and consumer "trial"—actually having potential buyers put on her brand of skates and use them. Enter Guerilla Marketing 101.

Horwath started by:

• *Finding the right demographic group to target with in-line skates.* Horwath focused Rollerblade, Inc.'s marketing efforts on 18- to 35-year-old men and

Results of some of Mary Horwath's marketing efforts: attention-getting packages, Team Rollerblade, print advertisements, and demo vans.

women. They were active, health and sports conscious, and had money to spend.

- *Changing the image of—or repositioning—skating.* As Horwath observes, "We had to build a new image for in-line roller skating. People already knew about traditional roller skating, which was done inside and attracted mostly young girls. But we didn't want to be associated with that image. Our sport happened outside in the sunshine, and we built our image around freedom and excitement. This proved to be a key element of our new marketing strategy."[13]
- *Finding the right benefits—or competitive "points of difference" (discussed in Chapter 11)—to stress in marketing the Rollerblade brand of skates.* She chose three benefits and points of difference that set the tone for all subsequent marketing efforts: (1) fun, (2) fitness and health, and (3) excitement.

Now Horwath set about finding a way to use her meager budget to get exposure for Rollerblade skates and to make people aware of them and to put them on. She explains, "We knew that if people could try the skates, they would fall in love with the sport. We also knew that— although the sport was born in Minnesota—we had to make an impact in California. We wanted the sport to become part of the lifestyle in California because it was known that we would then stand a greater chance [in] the rest of the United States."[14]

So Horwath's strategy—both simple and brilliant—was to give hundreds of free skates away where they would make people most aware of the new product and also enable key "opinion leaders" to try them. Examples of recipients of the free skates and why Horwath chose them include:

- *Entertainment celebrities like Michael J. Fox, Janet Jackson, and Arnold Schwarzenegger.* These stars then turned up wearing the skates in magazine photos or on television, giving Rollerblade, Inc. lots of free publicity.

- *Cheerleaders for the Minnesota Vikings football team.* When the cheerleaders wore Rollerblade skates on the sidelines during a game, millions of TV viewers saw the skates, many for the first time.
- *Rental shops along the beaches of Southern California.* Horwath's "California strategy" involved giving hundreds of free skates to these rental shops, thereby increasing awareness of the product and enabling Californians and visitors to actually try the skates. She reasoned that major trends in the United States usually start on one of the coasts and then move inland.

These "freebies" led to tens of thousands of converts to in-line skating (see Figure 1–1), and sales of Rollerblade skates started to take off. This enabled Horwath's marketing budget to expand, and so did her ideas for promoting Rollerblade skates. She created a series of 10-kilometer in-line races across the country, involving thousands of competitors in the race—most on the Rollerblade brand. Horwath got product endorsements from the U.S. Ski Team and the Boston Bruins hockey team. She also started Team Rollerblade, a group of top men and women skaters who dance on skates and perform acrobatic stunts everywhere, from the local shopping mall to the Super Bowl and the Olympics.[15]

Because Horwath was convinced that if people tried the skates once, they would love them, she filled up "demo vans" with skates so people across the United States could try the skates for free (question 5, Figure 1–2). Action-packed skating videos that retailers could show on their VCRs, Club Rollerblade for skaters, and the how-to book *Wheel Excitement* appeared later. She even got Rollerblade skates displayed on six million Golden Grahams cereal boxes in a joint promotion with General Mills that gave away 1,000 pairs of skates. In research studies, sports medicine doctors found that in-line skating could be as healthful for people as running or bicycling. All of these activities were part of a complete marketing program for Rollerblade, Inc. that included these features:

MARKETING MIX ELEMENT	MARKETING PROGRAM ACTIVITY	RATIONALE FOR MARKETING PROGRAM ACTIVITY
Product	Continuously improved products, such as the *heel brake*, the 2-lb.-lighter Lightning skate, and the Macroblade with buckles like ski boots	Desire to make the highest-quality product necessitates continuing new product research and extensive testing to maintain and improve quality
Price	$79 to $399 a pair	Attempt to have prices that appeal to various market segments
Promotion	Free skates to key opinion leaders, 10-K races, Team Rollerblade, "demo vans," skating videos, Club Rollerblade, and book	Attempt to increase awareness of in-line skating and its benefits and to facilitate prospects' actual trial of skates
Place	Distribution and sales of Rollerblade skates at major sporting goods stores throughout the United States	Desire to make it easy for prospective buyers to buy skates

So what happened? How did Horwath and Rollerblade, Inc.'s strategy turn out? Fantastically! Rollerblade's sales doubled each year during the late 1980s. In 1990,

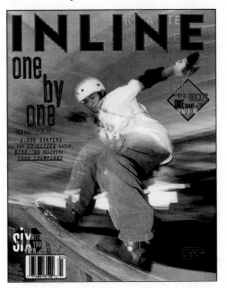

sales of in-line skates exploded and *Time* magazine called in-line skating "the sport of the 90s." In 1995, *Business Week* magazine selected Rollerblade's Bravoblades with automatic braking technology (ABT) as one of the best new products on the market.[16] Today, Rollerblade, Inc. production lines often turn out more than 20,000 pairs of skates a day.

The popularity of Rollerblades also spawned the fastest growing youth team sport—roller hockey—and the Roller Hockey International league with 19 teams in the United States and Canada. In addition, in-line skating enthusiasts can now read *Inline* magazine for reviews of new products, coverage of skating events, and information about new skating techniques.[17]

So Rollerblade, Inc. and Mary Horwath's marketing strategy had succeeded in creating a new sport and a new industry. This meant they had no problems, right? Not at all. In a free-market system, success encourages competition and imitations. Rollerblade, Inc. created the in-line skate industry, but it now must shift its efforts from marketing the sport to marketing its Rollerblade brand against new competitors. This is the marketing issue discussed in the Rollerblade case at the end of the chapter.

CONCEPT CHECK

1. An organization can't satisfy the needs of all consumers, so it must focus on one or more subgroups, which are its _____ .

2. What are the four marketing mix elements that make up the organization's marketing program?

3. What are uncontrollable variables?

HOW MARKETING BECAME SO IMPORTANT

Marketing is a driving force in the modern global economy. To understand why this is so and some related ethical aspects, let us look at (1) the evolution of the market orientation, (2) ethics and social responsibility in marketing, and (3) the breadth and depth of marketing activities.

Evolution of the Market Orientation

Many market-oriented manufacturing organizations have experienced four distinct stages in the life of their firms. We can use the Pillsbury Company as an example.

Production era   Goods were scarce in the early years of the United States, so buyers were willing to accept virtually any goods that were produced and make do with them as best they could. French economist J. B. Say described the prevailing business theory of the period: "Production creates its own demand." The central notion was that products would sell themselves, so the major concern of business firms was production, not marketing.[18]

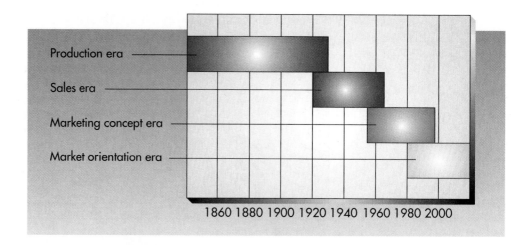

In 1869, Charles Pillsbury founded his company on the basis of high-quality wheat and the accessibility of cheap water power. Robert Keith, a Pillsbury president, described his company at this stage: "We are professional flour millers. Blessed with a supply of the finest North American wheat, plenty of water power, and excellent milling machinery, we produce flour of the highest quality. Our basic function is to mill quality flour."[19] As shown in Figure 1-6, this production era generally continued in America through the 1920s.

Sales era   About that time, many firms discovered that they could produce more goods than their regular buyers could consume. Competition became more significant, and the problems of reaching the market became more complex. The usual solution was to hire more salespeople to find new markets and consumers. Pillsbury's philosophy at this stage was summed up simply by Keith: "We must hire salespersons to sell it [the flour] just as we hire accountants to keep our books." The role of the Pillsbury salesforce, in simplified terms, was to find consumers for the goods that the firm found it could produce best, given its existing resources. This sales era continued into the 1950s for Pillsbury and into the 1960s for many other American firms (see Figure 1-6).

The marketing concept era   In the 1960s, marketing became the motivating force in Pillsbury. Since then its policy can be stated as, "We are in the business of satisfying needs and wants of consumers." This is really a brief statement of what has come to be known as the **marketing concept;** the idea is that an organization should (1) strive to satisfy the needs of consumers (2) while also trying to achieve the organization's goals.

The statement of a firm's commitment to satisfying consumer wants and needs that probably launched the marketing concept appeared in a 1952 annual report of General Electric Company:[20] "The concept introduces . . . marketing . . . at the beginning rather than the end of the production cycle and integrates marketing into each phase of the business." This statement had two important points. First, it recognized that sales is just one element of marketing—that marketing includes a much broader range of activities. Second, it changed the point at which marketing ideas are fed into the production cycle from *after* an item is produced to *before* it is designed. Clearly the marketing concept is a focus on the consumer. Unfortunately, although many companies endorsed the marketing concept and defined the purpose of their business as the creation and retention of satisfied customers, implementation of the concept proved to be very difficult.

The market orientation era   Many of the implementation issues are now being addressed by the total quality management movement. Firms such as DuPont, Marriott, and Toyota have achieved great success in the marketplace by putting huge effort into implementing the marketing concept, giving their firms what has been called a *market orientation.* An organization that has a **market orientation** focuses its efforts on (1) continuously collecting information about customers' needs and competitors' capabilities, (2) sharing this information across departments, and (3) using the information to create customer value.

A key aspect of this market orientation is that understanding consumers and competitors requires involvement of managers and employees throughout the firm. DuPont, for example, encourages employees to learn about customers' needs by participating in their "Adopt a Customer" program. Similarly, Marriott sends employees to stay in competitors' hotels and assess their facilities and services. To encourage information sharing, many firms such as Procter & Gamble, Ralston Purina, and General Mills allocate personnel and resources from many functional areas to *customer management teams.* These teams are also responsible for understanding value assessments of their suppliers and their customers' customers. Research shows that firms having a demonstrated market orientation are more profitable than those lacking it.[21]

Ethics and Social Responsibility: Balancing the Interests of Different Groups

As organizations have changed their orientation, society's expectations of marketers have also changed. Today, the standards of marketing practice have shifted from an emphasis on producers' interests to consumers' interests. In addition, organizations are increasingly encouraged to consider the social and environmental consequences of their actions. Because the interests of consumers, organizations, and society may differ, marketing managers must often find solutions acceptable to all parties. Guidelines for ethical and socially responsible behavior can help managers with the complex decisions involved in balancing consumer, organizational, and societal interests.

Ethics   Many marketing issues are not specifically addressed by existing laws and regulations. Should information about a firm's customers be sold to other organizations? Should advertising by professional service providers, such as accountants and attorneys, be restricted? Should consumers be responsible for assessing the safety of a product in "normal-use" situations? These, and many other questions, relate to **ethics,** which are the moral principles and values that govern the actions and decisions of an individual or group. Many companies, industries, and professional associations have developed codes of ethics to assist managers. Levi Strauss, for example, has developed a set of corporate statements to guide all major decisions. The company believes it "must provide clarity about our expectations and must enforce these standards throughout the corporation."[22]

Social responsibility   While many difficult ethical issues involve only the buyer and seller, others involve society as a whole. For example, suppose you buy batteries for your portable CD player, and, when their charge runs low, you throw them away. Is this just a transaction between you and the battery manufacturer? Not quite! Thrown in a trash dump, the batteries may contaminate the soil, so society will bear a portion of the cost of your battery purchase. This example illustrates the issue of **social responsibility,** the idea that organizations are part of a larger society and are accountable to society for their actions. The well-being of society at large should also

ETHICS AND SOCIAL RESPONSIBILITY ALERT

SOCIALLY RESPONSIBLE, ENVIRONMENTALLY FRIENDLY, *AND* COMPETITIVE?

Many organizations today are trying to incorporate social responsibility into their marketing activities. One reason is that socially responsible decisions are likely to have a significant positive impact on society by improving the marketplace and the environment. Another reason is that most of an organization's constituents are taking interest in the issue. Investors now evaluate environmental track records, consumers express interest in environmental issues, and employees often encourage socially responsible behavior.

Unfortunately, many environmentally friendly products have been costly to produce, and consumers have not been willing to pay a premium for them. As a result, companies often question if they can be socially responsible and competitive.

In the past, policy makers protected the environment through strict environmental regulations even if it eroded competitiveness, while companies tried to appeal to consumers with the often intangible environmental benefits of their products. More recently, some experts have suggested that the solution is innovation that either offsets the cost of improving environmental impact or increases customer value. For example, Scotchbrite Never Rust Wool Soap Pads from 3M—which are made from recycled plastic bottles—are more expensive than competitors (S.O.S. and Brillo) but superior because they don't rust or scratch.

Should companies consider social responsibility in their decision? Must environmentally friendly products be competitively priced?

---

be recognized in an organization's marketing decisions.[23] In fact, some marketing experts stress the **societal marketing concept,** the view that an organization should discover and satisfy the needs of its consumers in a way that also provides for society's well-being. The difficulty firms face as they attempt to be socially responsible and competitive is discussed in the Ethics and Social Responsibility Alert.[24]

The societal marketing concept is directly related to **macromarketing,** which looks at the aggregate flow of a nation's goods and services to benefit society.[25] Macromarketing addresses broad issues such as whether marketing costs too much, whether advertising is wasteful, and what resource scarcities and pollution side effects result from the marketing system. While macromarketing issues are addressed briefly in this book, the book's main focus is on how an individual organization directs its marketing activities and allocates its resources to benefit its customers, or **micromarketing.** An overview of this approach appears in Chapter 2. Because of the importance of ethical and social responsibility issues in marketing today, they—and related legal and regulatory actions—are discussed throughout this book. In addition, Chapter 4 focuses specifically on issues of ethics and social responsibility.

The Breadth and Depth of Marketing

Marketing today affects every person and organization. To understand this, let's analyze (1) who markets, (2) what they market, (3) who buys and uses what is marketed, (4) who benefits from these marketing activities, and (5) how they benefit.

Who markets? Every organization markets! It's obvious that business firms involved in manufacturing (Xerox, Heinz, Nike), retailing (Kmart, Toys "Я" Us, Nordstrom), and providing services (Merrill Lynch, National Broadcasting Corporation, Twentieth Century-Fox) market their offerings. Today many other types of marketing are also popular. Nonprofit organizations (San Francisco Ballet, New York Metropolitan Opera, American Museum of Natural History, your local hospital) also engage in marketing.[26] Your college or university, for example, probably has a

Marketing is used by nonprofit organizations, causes, and places.

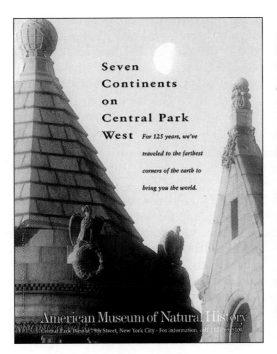

marketing program to attract students, faculty members, and donations. Places (cities, states, countries) often use marketing efforts to attract tourists, conventions, or businesses. Chile's "Make the Move" campaign is designed to attract businesses interested in a South American location. Organizations associated with special events or causes use marketing to inform and influence a target audience. These marketing activities range from announcements regarding the Olympics to government agencies discouraging smoking to private groups promoting a social cause such as literacy. Finally, individuals often use marketing to gain attention and preference. Celebrities such as Jay Leno, for example, may use marketing activities to increase the size of their "audience," while political candidates such as Bill Clinton or Bob Dole seek financial support and votes.

What is marketed?   Goods, services, and ideas are marketed. Goods are physical objects, such as toothpaste, cameras, or computers, that satisfy consumer needs. Services are intangible items such as airline trips, financial advice, or telephone calls. Ideas are intangibles such as thoughts about actions or causes. Some of these—such as lawn mowers, dry cleaning, and annual physical examinations—may be bought or accepted by individuals for their own use. Others, such as high-volume office copiers and vending machine repair services, are bought by organizations. Finally, the products marketed in today's global marketplace are increasingly likely to cross a nation's boundaries and involve exports, imports, and international marketing (covered in Chapter 5).

Who buys and uses what is marketed?   Both individuals and organizations buy and use goods and services that are marketed. **Ultimate consumers** are the people—whether 80 years or 8 months old—who use the goods and services purchased for a household. A household may consist of 1 person or 10. (The way one or more of the people in the household buys for it is the topic of consumer behavior in Chapter 6.) In contrast, **organizational buyers** are units such as manufacturers, retailers, or government agencies that buy goods and services for their own use or for resale. (Industrial and organizational buyer behavior is covered in Chapter 7.) Although the terms *consumers, buyers,* and *customers* are sometimes used for both ultimate consumers and organizations, there is no consistency on this. In this book you will be able to tell from the example whether the buyers are ultimate consumers, organizations, or both.

Who benefits?   In our free-enterprise society there are three specific groups that benefit from effective marketing: consumers who buy, organizations that sell, and society as a whole. True competition between products and services in the marketplace ensures that we consumers can find value from the best products, the lowest prices, or exceptional service. Providing choices leads to the consumer satisfaction and quality of life that we have come to expect from our economic system.

Organizations that provide need-satisfying products with effective marketing programs—for example, McDonald's, IBM, Avon, and Merrill Lynch—have blossomed, but competition creates problems for ineffective competitors. For example, Osborne Computers, DeLorean cars, and W. T. Grant retail stores were well-known names a few years ago but may now be unknown to you. Effective marketing actions result in rewards for organizations that serve consumers and in millions of marketing jobs such as those described in Appendix C.

Finally, effective marketing benefits society. It enhances competition, which, in turn, improves both the quality of products and services and lowers their prices. This makes the countries more competitive in world markets and provides jobs and a higher standard of living for their citizens.

How do consumers benefit?   Marketing creates **utility,** the benefits or customer value received by users of the product. This utility is the result of the marketing exchange process. There are four different utilities: form, place, time, and possession. The production of the good or service constitutes *form utility. Place utility* means having the offering available where consumers need it, whereas *time utility* means having it available when needed. *Possession utility* is getting the product to consumers so they can use it.

Thus, marketing provides consumers with place, time, and possession utilities by making the good or service available at the right place and right time for the right consumer. Although form utility usually arises in manufacturing activity and could be seen as outside the scope of marketing, an organization's marketing activities influence the product features and packaging. Marketing creates its utilities by bridging space (place utility) and hours (time utility) to provide products (form utility) for consumers to own and use (possession utility).

CONCEPT CHECK

1. Like Pillsbury, many firms have gone through four distinct orientations for their business: starting with the _____era and ending with today's _____era.

2. What are the two key characteristics of the marketing concept?

3. In this book the term *product* refers to what three things?

SUMMARY

1. Combining personal experience with more formal marketing knowledge will enable us to identify and solve important marketing problems.

2. Marketing is the process of planning and executing the conception, pricing, promotion, and distribution of ideas, goods, and services to create exchanges that satisfy individual and organizational objectives. This definition relates to two primary goals of marketing: *(a)* assessing the needs of consumers and *(b)* satisfying them.

3. For marketing to occur, it is necessary to have *(a)* two or more parties with unmet needs, *(b)* a desire and ability to satisfy them, *(c)* communication between the parties, and *(d)* something to exchange.

4. Because an organization doesn't have the resources to satisfy the needs of all consumers, it selects a target market of potential customers—a subset of the entire market—on which to focus its marketing program.

5. Four elements in a marketing program designed to satisfy customer needs are product, price, promotion, and place. These elements are called the *marketing mix,* the *four Ps,* or the *controllable variables* because they are under the general control of the marketing department.

6. Environmental factors, also called *uncontrollable variables,* are largely beyond the organization's control. These include social, technological, economic, competitive, and regulatory forces.

7. Customer value, perhaps *the* critical marketing issue for buyers and sellers, is the unique combination of benefits received by targeted buyers that includes quality, price, convenience, on-time delivery, and both before-sale and after-sale service.

8. In marketing terms, U.S. business history is divided into four periods: the production era, the sales era, the marketing concept era, and the current market orientation era.

9. Marketing managers must balance consumer, organizational, and societal interests. This involves issues of ethics and social responsibility.

10. Both profit-making and nonprofit organizations perform marketing activities. They market products, services, and ideas that benefit consumers, organizations, and countries. Marketing creates utilities that give benefits, or customer value, to users.

KEY TERMS AND CONCEPTS

marketing p. 9
exchange p. 9
market p. 12
target market p. 13
marketing mix p. 13
environmental factors p. 14
customer value p. 15
marketing program p. 16
marketing concept p. 20

market orientation p. 21
ethics p. 21
social responsibility p. 21
societal marketing concept p. 22
macromarketing p. 22
micromarketing p. 22
ultimate consumers p. 24
organizational buyers p. 24
utility p. 24

CHAPTER PROBLEMS AND APPLICATIONS

1. What consumer wants (or benefits) are met by the following products or services? *(a)* Carnation Instant Breakfast, *(b)* Adidas running shoes, *(c)* Hertz Rent-A-Car, and *(d)* television shopping programs.

2. Each of the four products or stores in question 1 has substitutes. Respective examples are *(a)* a ham and egg breakfast, *(b)* regular tennis shoes, *(c)* taking a bus, and *(d)* a department store. What consumer benefits might these substitutes have in each case that some consumers might value more highly than those products mentioned in question 1?

3. What are the characteristics (e.g., age, income, education) of the target market customers for the following products or services? (*a*) *National Geographic* magazine, (*b*) *Wired* magazine, (*c*) New York Giants football team, and (*d*) the U.S. Open tennis tournament.

4. A college in a metropolitan area wishes to increase its evening-school offerings of business-related courses such as marketing, accounting, finance, and management. Who are the target market customers (students) for these courses?

5. What actions involving the four marketing mix elements might be used to reach the target market in question 4?

6. What environmental factors (uncontrollable variables) must the college in question 4 consider in designing its marketing program?

7. Polaroid introduced instant still photography, which proved to be a tremendous success. Yet Polavision, its instant movie system, was a total disaster. (*a*) What benefits does each provide to users? (*b*) Which of these do you think contributed to Polavision's failure? (*c*) What research could have been undertaken that might have revealed Polavision's drawbacks?

8. Mary Horwath and Rollerblade, Inc. are now trying to grow in-line skating—and the company—globally, just as they succeeded in doing in the United States. What are the advantages and disadvantages of trying to reach new global markets?

9. Does a firm have the right to "create" wants and try to persuade consumers to buy goods and services they didn't know about earlier? What are examples of "good" and "bad" want creation? Who should decide what is good and bad?

CASE 1–1   Rollerblade, Inc.

Video

Rollerblade, Inc. is an incredible marketing success story. In just over a decade the company has created a sport that is now more popular than ameteur baseball or football. How did it happen? "Achieving success wasn't easy," reflects Mary Horwath. "It took months and years of hard work . . . and perhaps most of all, it took lots of imagination!"

THE SITUATION

But Horwath, now vice president of Marketing Services and International at Rollerblade, Inc., hears footsteps. She summarizes Rollerblade's success:

> We had introduced a product and created a sport. We had arrived. Rollerblade was rapidly becoming a part of the American way of life. But now we were faced with another challenge. It may have been a marketer's dream that people thought that in-line skating was "Rollerblading." But we knew that every skate wasn't a Rollerblade skate. And, for the first time, we had competition from other companies. We had always built brand identity during our years of building the sport. But now it was time to focus especially on marketing the Rollerblade brand. Of course we continued to build the sport because we knew that as the sport grew, so would Rollerblade, Inc.[27]

The future of the in-line skating industry looks good. In-line skating is the fastest growing sport in the United States. With more than 25 million skaters, in-line skating has now surpassed football, baseball, and soccer in total number of participants. Industry sales in 1995 were about $1 billion. Optimists see the possibility of the international in-line skate market to be even greater.

THE COMPETITION

Horwath's concern about competitors is genuine. When Rollerblade, Inc. was founded, it was the only manufacturer of in-line skates in the world. Today it has more than 30 direct competitors, most that sell lower-priced skates than Rollerblade skates through mass merchandising chains such as Wal-Mart and Target—outlets that Rollerblade, Inc. has historically avoided in favor of sporting goods stores.

MARKETS AND PRODUCTS

Horwath sees Rollerblade's primary U.S. target market as the 46 million active adults. But from skating with skaters on Rollerblade skates from Boston to San Francisco, Horwath has concluded that potential skaters are far more diverse than the 18- to 35-year-old target and that skaters use Rollerblade skates for many different reasons: for racing, for fun, for exercise, for street hockey, for complex acrobatics, and even for transportation to and from work or college.

With these diverse markets, Rollerblade, Inc. develops a variety of in-line designs targeted at different market segments. Some examples:

- *Metroblade*™. A lightweight nylon/leather walking shoe that fits into a molded skate shell designed for transportation that requires going into buildings.
- *Problade*™. Designed for serious racing for speed skaters with a low-cut leather boot and five oversize (80-mm) wheels.
- *Macroblade Equipe*™. Vented, molded plastic shell that makes a lightweight, breathable skate.
- *Mondoblade*™. Skates for starting out in in-line skating.
- *Microblade*™. Skates with wild colors, for kids.

In addition, Rollerblade offers a complete line of skating accessories that includes knee pads, wrist guards, gloves, jerseys, shorts, T-shirts, and helmets.

Designing a high-quality in-line skate is a lot more complex than it may appear. In fact, Rollerblade, Inc. holds more than 185 patents for its in-line skating products. Its industry "firsts" include polyurethane boots and wheels, metal frames, dual bearings, heel brakes, buckle closures, ventilated shells, and breathable liners. One of Rollerblade's latest innovations, Active Brake Technology (ABT), offers skaters greater speed control and stopping power. In 1995, *Business Week* magazine selected Rollerblade's Bravoblades with ABT as one of the "best new products" introduced to the market.

Because of the speeds involved in in-line skating, Rollerblade, Inc. has been an industry leader in promoting safety and the use of proper equipment. Its "Asphalt Bites^{SM}" safety awareness campaign is designed to educate consumers about the benefits of wearing full protective gear and skating safety. The campaign includes videos featuring Olympic gold-medal speed skater Bonnie Blair giving safety tips, a pocket-size in-line safety guide, and a 30-second public service announcement (for use by television stations).

GLOBAL ALLIANCES

To obtain financial strength for the future, in 1991 Rollerblade, Inc. developed an alliance with Italy's Nordica Sportsystem, a leading ski boot manufacturer. Nordica, owned by a Benetton family holding company, bought 50 percent ownership in Rollerblade, Inc. Besides capital, Nordica provides Rollerblade, Inc. with increased research, development, and manufacturing capabilities and access to global distribution networks. Today, Nordica's ski boot technology is used in many models of Rollerblade skates.

Questions

1. What trends in the environmental forces (social, economic, technological, competitive, and regulatory) identified in Figure 1–3 in the chapter (*a*) work for and (*b*) work against Rollerblade, Inc.'s growth?

2. What are the differences in marketing goals for Rollerblade, Inc., in (*a*) growing a new industry, and (*b*) marketing its Rollerblade brand of in-line skates against competition?

3. How should Mary Horwath translate the broad goals identified in question 2 into a specific marketing program—a plan that integrates product, price, promotion, and place actions?

4. Horwath believes significant opportunities exist for Rollerblade skates in global markets. To which countries or regions should she initially try to market Rollerblade skates? Why?

CHAPTER 2

Linking Marketing and Corporate Strategies

AFTER READING THIS CHAPTER YOU SHOULD BE ABLE TO:

• Describe the three organizational levels of strategy and their components.

• Describe how the three organizational levels of strategy relate to each other and how they influence the marketing function.

• Describe the strategic marketing process and its three key phases: planning, implementation, and control.

• Understand how organizations search for new marketing opportunities and select target markets.

• Explain how the marketing mix elements are blended into a cohesive marketing program.

• Describe how marketing control compares actual results with planned objectives and acts on deviations from the plan.

BEN & JERRY'S: PEACE POPS, RAINFOREST CRUNCH . . . PLUS . . . A 100-WORD ESSAY CONTEST TO FIND A NEW CEO

Have you always wanted to become president and chief executive officer (CEO) of a large ice cream company? A while back, all you had to do was send in the winning 100-word essay on "Why I Would Be a Great CEO for Ben & Jerry's."[1]

More than 22,000 aspiring ice-cream company CEOs showered Ben & Jerry's Vermont headquarters with their essays. The winner: Robert Holland, Jr. (center on the opposite page), who didn't really write an essay. He wrote a poem entitled, "Time, Value and Ice Cream."[2] Even the losers got something for their efforts. The runner-up got—you guessed it!—a lifetime supply of ice cream, and the other also-rans received a rejection letter "suitable for framing." But let's tell a bit more of the story.

Ben & Jerry's is proof that the American Dream is still alive and well. Ben Cohen and Jerry Greenfield (the Ben & Jerry's guys at left and right on the opposite page) had been high school classmates in Brooklyn. In 1978 they headed north to Vermont and started an ice cream parlor in a renovated gas station.[3] Buoyed with enthusiasm, $12,000 they had borrowed and saved, and ideas from the $5 they spent on a Penn State correspondence course in ice cream making (with perfect scores on their open-book tests!),[4] they were off and running.

By 1994 their firm, Ben & Jerry's Homemade, Inc., had more than $150 million in sales, mainly from selling its incredibly-rich ice cream. So why search for a new CEO? Ben and Jerry concluded that their firm's sales were flattening and the company's success had outgrown their ability to manage and grow it further. Also, Ben wanted to focus his energies on developing new products, and Jerry wanted to concentrate on the company's legendary social causes.

They decided they needed a new president and chief executive officer who was experienced at developing and implementing growth strategies for large firms like the one Ben & Jerry's had become. In reality, Holland's résumé entered the search in a more traditional way, one of a handful of names submitted to Ben & Jerry's by an executive-search firm.[5]

Robert Holland's experience includes working at some of the most prestigious consulting firms in the world. His challenge at Ben & Jerry's is to find strategies to foster growth—a potential problem in light of American consumers' present concerns about fat and cholesterol. At the same time, he wants to retain the founders' legendary concern for the environment and social responsibility. For example, the Peace Pops ice cream bar seeks to promote international understanding, and the Rainforest Crunch helps raise money to preserve Amazon rain forests.

Chapter 2 describes how organizations set their overall direction and link these activities to marketing strategies—the very tasks Robert Holland is facing at Ben & Jerry's. In essence, this chapter describes how organizations try to implement the marketing concept to provide genuine value to their customers.

LEVELS OF STRATEGY IN ORGANIZATIONS

This chapter first distinguishes among different kinds of organizations and the different levels within them. We then compare strategies at three different levels in an organization.

Today's Organizations: Kinds and Levels

Large organizations in existence today are often extremely complex. While this is not true for your corner deli or for some of the small businesses highlighted in our textbook cases, all of us deal in some way with huge organizations every day, so it is useful to understand both (1) the two basic kinds of organizations and (2) the levels that exist in them.

Kinds of organizations   Today's organizations can be broadly divided into business firms and nonprofit organizations. A *business firm* is a privately owned organization that serves its customers in order to earn a profit. Business firms must earn profits to survive. **Profit** is the reward to a business firm for the risk it undertakes in offering a product for sale; the money left over after a firm's total expenses are subtracted from its total revenues. In contrast to business firms, a *nonprofit organization* is a nongovernmental organization that serves its customers but does not have profit as an organizational goal. For simplicity in the rest of the book, however, the terms *firm, company, corporation,* and *organization* are used to cover both business and nonprofit operations.

Levels in organizations and how marketing links to them   Whether explicit or implicit, organizations such as Ben & Jerry's have a strategic direction. Marketing not only helps shape this direction but must also help implement it. Figure 2–1 summarizes the focus of this direction at each of the three levels in an organization.

The **corporate level** is where top management directs overall strategy for the entire organization. Multimarket, multiproduct firms such as Hewlett-Packard or Johnson & Johnson really manage a portfolio of businesses, variously termed strategic business units (SBUs), strategic business segments, and product-market units (PMUs).[6]

The term **business unit** refers to an organization that markets a set of related products to a clearly defined group of customers. The **business unit level** is the

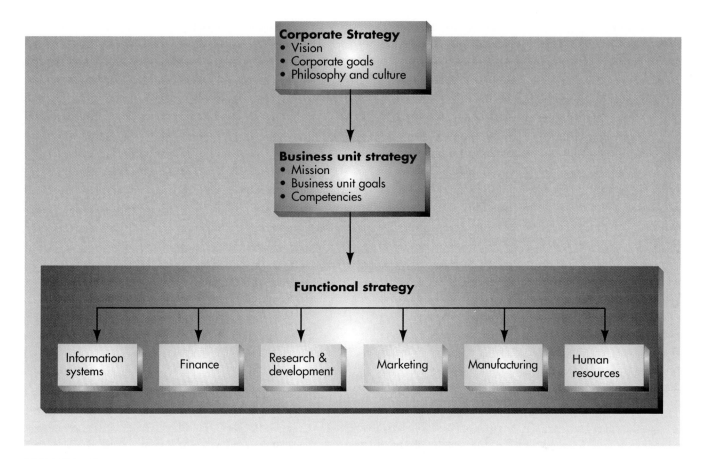

FIGURE 2–1

The three levels of strategy in organizations

level at which business unit managers set the direction for their products and markets. The strategic direction is more specific at the business level of an organization. For less complex firms with a single business focus, such as Ben & Jerry's, the corporate and business unit levels may merge.

Each business unit has marketing and other specialized activities (e.g., finance, research and development, or human resource management) at the **functional level,** which is where groups of specialists create value for the organization. The term *department* generally refers to these specialized functions, such as the marketing department or information systems department. At the functional level, the strategic direction becomes more specific and focused. So, just as there is a hierarchy of levels within organizations, there is also a hierarchy of strategic direction set by management at that level.

Marketing has a role at each of these organizational levels. In a larger corporation with multiple business units, the marketing department may be called upon to build a broad corporate image. It may also be called upon to provide comparative analyses of business unit market strengths and opportunities as part of a business portfolio analysis, which is covered later in the chapter. At the business level, the marketing department provides leadership for the other functional activities when applying the marketing concept. But it also must serve as part of a team of functional specialists that develops and implements actual programs at the functional level, which is why cross-functional teams are so vital in today's competitive world. To help develop these programs, the marketing department conducts marketing research and competitive evaluations to identify strategic marketing issues. Armed with an understanding of the marketplace, the marketing department then identifies key target markets and develops specific programs to serve them.

What is a railroad's vision for its future? How did a past nearsighted vision lead to some of today's problems? For the answer and the importance of a corporate vision, see the text.

Strategy at the Corporate Level

Complex organizations such as Coca-Cola, the railroads, and Sears, Roebuck & Co. must ask themselves not just what *business* they are in but what *portfolio of businesses* they are in. As shown in Figure 2–1, this portfolio of businesses is often coordinated with a corporate strategy consisting of a common corporate vision, common goals, and a common philosophy that unites them. We will define these terms carefully, but, in actual practice, the terms are not used rigorously and often overlap.

Developing the corporate vision   A **corporate vision** is a clear word picture of the organization's future, often with an inspirational theme. It sets the overall direction for the organization, describing what it strives to be—stretching the organization, but not beyond the imagination. Even though the terms are often used interchangeably, a vision is something to be pursued, while a mission (discussed later) is something to be accomplished. Ideally, this vision is a short sentence that can inspire employees, investors, and customers.

Coca-Cola's vision is simple but effective: "to put a Coke within arm's reach of every consumer in the world."[7] This vision clearly applies not only in the United States but worldwide. In fact, in 1996 Coca-Cola set a policy that was a "first" for a U.S. consumer products firm: It downgraded its U.S. business unit to make it just one of six international business units, thereby eliminating the very concept of "domestic" and "international" units. With only 21 percent of its revenues from U.S. sales, Coca-Cola seems to be actively pursuing its Coke-within-an-arm's-reach-of-every-consumer vision.[8]

MARKETING NEWSNET

ADDING CUSTOMER VALUE THROUGH THE QUALITY CHAIN REACTION

When W. Edwards Deming went to Japan in 1950 to help rebuild postwar Japan, he shared a very profound model with Japanese industry. This model helped launch the quality revolution that has contributed to dramatic global change in the automobile industry. For example, the market share of U.S. automobile firms in the United States has dropped from more than 99 percent in 1950 to about 40 percent today. Although many other factors contributed to this decline, the U.S. automobile industry has had to improve its product and process quality to compete effectively.

The model is shown below. It has become a mantra for the quality movement. Assuming an organization has an otherwise effective strategy and management structure in place, the model shows the additional benefits from improving the quality of products, services, and processes. The first benefit is a decrease in costs as a direct result of less waste. A consequence of less waste is greater process productivity. This allows lower prices, which combines with the improved products and services to allow the organization to compete more effectively. The ultimate payoff is that the firm stays in business and provides jobs because it provides greater value to the customers.

The amount of benefit can be quantified by looking at the cost of poor quality. Experts claim that 10 percent to 20 percent of sales revenues are needed to cover the cost of poor quality in the form of production waste and rework, complaints and warranty costs, and defective products. Motorola, after nine years of quality improvement, estimates that it has reduced the cost of poor quality to half, and it sees more room for improvement.

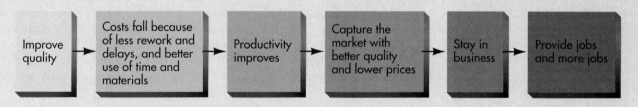

Railroads have not been so successful. They have let other forms of transportation take business away from them, possibly because their vision included only competitors and market share within the railroad business itself. The railroads have not actively sought to compete within the broader vision of transportation as a whole.[9] This narrow definition hurt railroads because they failed to design effective strategies to compete with a broad range of competitors, including airlines, trucks, bus lines, and cars. So U.S. railroads, like the U.S. auto firms described in the Marketing NewsNet box above, have had to reassess ways of delivering "quality" to their customers. Innovative Norfolk Southern Railroad has even developed a truck trailer with conventional rubber truck tires and retractable metal rail wheels that permit it to ride on either a highway or railroad at the push of a button.

Setting corporate goals   Broadly speaking, a **goal** is a targeted level of performance set in advance of work.[10] Therefore, **corporate goals** provide strategic performance targets that the entire organization must reach to pursue its vision. Several different types of goals have been identified that business firms can pursue, each of which has some strengths and limitations:

- *Profit.* Classic economic theory assumes a firm seeks to maximize long-run profit, achieving as high a financial return on its investment as possible. One difficulty with this is what is meant by *long run.* A year? Five years? Twenty years?

Ethics

ETHICS AND SOCIAL RESPONSIBILITY ALERT

THE GLOBAL DILEMMA: HOW TO ACHIEVE SUSTAINABLE DEVELOPMENT

Corporate executives and world leaders are increasingly asked to address the issue of "sustainable development," a term that involves having each country find an ideal balance between protecting its environment and providing its citizens with the additional goods and services necessary to maintain and improve their standard of living.

Eastern Europe and the nations of the former Soviet Union provide an example. Tragically, poisoned air and dead rivers are the legacies of seven decades of communist rule. With more than half of the households of many of theses nations below the poverty level, should the immediate goal be a cleaner environment or more food, clothing, housing, and consumer goods? What should the heads of these governments do? What should Western nations do to help? What should Western firms trying to enter these new, growing markets do?

Should the environment or economic growth come first? What are the societal trade-offs?

- *Sales revenue.* If profits are acceptable, a firm may elect to maintain or increase its sales level even though profitability may not be maximized. Increased sales revenue may gain promotions for key executives.
- *Market share.* A firm may choose to maintain or increase its market share, sometimes at the expense of greater profits if industry status or prestige is at stake. **Market share** is the ratio of sales revenue of the firm to the total sales revenue of all firms in the industry, including the firm itself.
- *Unit sales.* Sales revenue may be deceiving because of the effects of inflation, so a firm may choose to maintain or increase the number of units it sells, such as cars, cases of breakfast cereal, or TV sets.
- *Quality.* A firm may emphasize the need to maintain or improve the quality of its products and services, especially if quality has been poor in the past. The Marketing NewsNet box on the previous page describes W. Edwards Deming's "quality chain" that revolutionized global thinking about quality.[11]
- *Employee welfare.* A firm may recognize the critical importance of its employees by having an explicit goal stating its commitment to good employment opportunities and working conditions for them.
- *Social responsibility.* A firm may respond to advocates of corporate responsibility and seek to balance conflicting goals of consumers, employees, and stockholders to promote overall welfare of all these groups, even at the expense of profits. Ben & Jerry's is an example of such a firm.

Many private organizations that do not seek profits also exist in the United States. Examples are museums, symphony orchestras, operas, private hospitals, and research institutes. These organizations strive to provide goods or services to consumers with the greatest efficiency and the least cost. The nonprofit organization's survival depends on its meeting the needs of the consumers it serves. Although technically not falling under the definition of "nonprofit organization," government agencies also perform marketing activities in trying to achieve their goal of serving the public good. Such organizations include all levels of federal, state, and local government as well as special groups such as city schools, state universities, and public hospitals. As discussed later, marketing is an important activity for nonprofit firms and government agencies, just as it is for profit-making businesses.

Developing a corporate philosophy and culture   An organization may also have a **corporate philosophy** that establishes the values and "rules of conduct" for running it.[12] Statements such as "respecting the dignity of all employees" or "being a good citizen of the local community" are examples of corporate philosophies. The Ethics and Social Responsibility Alert describes a critical global corporate citizenship issue. An organization's **corporate culture** refers to a system of shared attitudes and behaviors held by the employees that distinguish it from other organizations. Firms around the world are frantically trying to change their corporate cultures in response to increased global competition. Hewlett-Packard, 3M, and Motorola are well-known for their corporate cultures that stimulate innovation and new product development. As described later in the chapter, George Fisher, Kodak's new chief operating officer, who came from Motorola, is working diligently to try to change Kodak's corporate philosophy and culture from one of red-tape review of every decision to one of risk taking and innovation.

CONCEPT CHECK

1. What are the three levels in today's large organizations?

2. What is the difference between corporate vision and corporate goals?

Strategy at the Business Unit Level

The strategic direction for each business unit spells out how it will help the organization accomplish its vision. This business unit strategy has three major components: mission, business unit goals, and competencies. Each component is critical and must be understood if marketing activities are to be relevant.

Defining the business unit's mission   This is probably the best-known mission statement anywhere:

> To explore strange new worlds, to seek out new life and new civilizations, to boldly go where no one has gone before.

This is the five-year mission for the Starship Enterprise, as Gene Roddenberry wrote it for the "Star Trek" adventure series. The "business unit goals" of the Starship Enterprise vary with each trip, but the competencies center on advanced technology, strong leadership, and a skilled crew. All these contribute to pursuing the vision of the Starship Enterprise's larger organization, the Federation.

The **business mission** (or **business unit mission**) is a statement that specifies the markets and product lines in which a business will compete. It communicates— ideally in one sentence—the scope of a business unit. A mission statement can dramatically affect the range of a firm's marketing activities by narrowing or broadening the competitive playing field.

The case of the Domestic Merchandising Group at Sears, Roebuck & Co. shows the tortuous path a business unit can follow as its searches for its mission in today's competitive environment. For Sears, narrower and clearer mission and business unit statements were necessary for the corporation to accomplish a very fundamental vision—to survive. In the process, Sears has become a real success story, one that required the commitment of all levels in the firm and all functional units.

In the 1980s, Sears discovered that discounters and specialty stores such as Home Depot and Toys "Я" Us were winning over more and more of Sears's traditional middle-class customers. This left Sears scrambling to find a market niche. First, it tried promoting itself as a fashion-oriented department store for higher income customers. Failing at that, Sears then experimented with budget products and finally

How does this Sears ad reflect its search for a new mission and focus? The text describes its recent success story.

"He picked up some paint supplies."

Come see the softer side of SEARS

with "everyday low prices," without success. Besides offering Allstate Insurance, in the 1980s Sears broadened its services offerings to include real estate through Coldwell Banker and financial services through Dean Witter. It also invested more than $600 million with IBM in a computerized system, Prodigy—a telephone link to Sears stores enabling consumers in their homes or offices to buy products they see advertised. It also continued its century-old catalog business.[13]

In the process of running all these different business units, Sears executives discovered that the company had lost focus—it no longer had a clear vision of what businesses it was in, who its customers really were, and how it could provide value to them. Not only was it losing sales to specialty stores, but department stores were taking other customers who wanted more ambiance and service than Sears offered. Sears's catalog was losing business to other catalog competitors and also to Wal-Mart stores, whose locations were only a few minutes' drive from most Sears catalog shoppers.

In a series of traumatic decisions in they early 1990s, Sears sold or spun off its Coldwell Banker and Dean Witter services businesses. It even completely shut down its $3-billion-a-year catalog operations—much to the delight of its Lands' End, JCPenney, Spiegel, and Fingerhut catalog competitors.

Today, the Domestic Merchandising Group at Sears believes it has rediscovered itself by redefining its mission. Its new mission, summarized in Figure 2–2, is "to sell a broad line of general merchandise and services through various types and sizes of retail facilities and direct response marketing in the United States and Puerto Rico."[14] This is further refined by focusing on middle-income women as its core customers and expanding the product offering in apparel—as reflected in "The Softer Side of Sears" marketing promotions. Even the Craftsman tools department now recognizes women as a core customer—women purchase 40 percent of the tools sold. By clearly defining the business mission, marketing activities can be more focused and effective.[15]

Specifying the business unit's goals A **business unit goal** is a performance target the business unit seeks to reach in an effort to achieve its mission. Goals measure how well the mission is being accomplished. These goals must be balanced

FIGURE 2–2

Mission and goals of
Domestic Merchandising
Group, Sears, Roebuck & Co.

BUSINESS UNIT MISSION

Domestic Merchandising sells a broad line of general merchandise and services through various types and sizes of retail facilities and direct response marketing in the United States and Puerto Rico.

BUSINESS UNIT GOALS (STRATEGIC INITIATIVES)

- Focus on the core business.
- Make Sears a more compelling place to shop.
- Improve cost and productivity.
- Focus on the market.
- Foster a winning culture.

to form a consistent, achievable pattern and should address fundamental issues such as customer satisfaction, innovation, internal processes, and, of course, financial performance.[16] In fact, the pattern of goals provides strategic direction since organizations often get what they measure.

Figure 2–2 shows that the business goals for Sears's Domestic Merchandising Group are in the form of five strategic initiatives to complement a corporate goal of increased profitability. These goals involve focusing on core businesses, making Sears a more compelling place to shop, improving cost and productivity, focusing more clearly on it customers and market, and fostering a winning culture. At the business unit level, many firms try, where possible, to construct goals that are more specific and measurable. These are often called **objectives,** which are specific, measurable performance targets and deadlines. Because there is no consistency in the use of the terms goals and objectives, the terms are used interchangeably throughout this book.

The use of quantified performance measures and targets can be illustrated by an approach developed by the Boston Consulting Group (BCG), *business portfolio analysis,* that analyzes a firm's business units (called strategic business units, or SBUs, in the BCG analysis) as though they were a collection of separate investments.[17] While used at the business unit level here, this BCG analysis has also been applied at the product line or individual product or brand level. The popularity of this kind of portfolio analysis is shown by the fact that more than 75 percent of the largest U.S. firms have used it in some form. BCG, a nationally known management consulting firm, advises its clients to locate the position of each of its SBUs on a growth-share matrix (Figure 2–3). The vertical axis is the *market growth rate,* which is the annual rate of growth of the specific market or industry in which a given SBU is competing. This axis in the figure runs from 0 to 20 percent, although in practice it might run even higher. The axis has arbitrarily been divided at 10 percent into high-growth and low-growth areas.

The horizontal axis is the *relative market share,* defined as the sales of the SBU divided by the sales of the largest firm in the industry. A relative market share of 10× (at the left end of the scale) means that the SBU has 10 times the share of its largest competitor, whereas a share 0.1× (at the right end of the scale) means it has only 10 percent of the sales of its largest competitor. The scale is logarithmic and is arbitrarily divided into high and low relative market shares at a value of 1×.

BCG has given specific names and descriptions to the four resulting quadrants in its growth-share matrix based on the amount of cash they generate for or require from the firm:

- Cash cows (lower-left quadrant) are SBUs that typically generate large amounts of cash, far more than they can invest profitably in their own product line. They

FIGURE 2-3

Boston Consulting Group
growth-share matrix for a
strong, diversified firm
showing some strategic plans

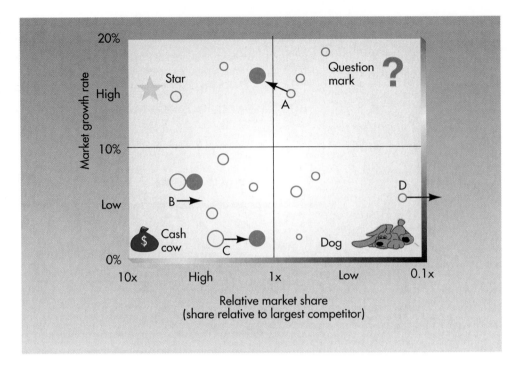

have a dominant share of a slow-growth market and provide cash to pay large amounts of company overhead and to invest in other SBUs.

- Stars (upper-left quadrant) are SBUs with a high share of high-growth markets that may not generate enough cash to support their own demanding needs for future growth. When their growth slows, they are likely to become cash cows.
- Question marks or problem children (upper-right quadrant) are SBUs with a low share of high-growth markets. They require large injections of cash just to maintain their market share, much less increase it. Their name implies management's dilemma for these SBUs: choosing the right ones to invest in and phasing out the rest.
- Dogs (lower-right quadrant) are SBUs with a low share of low-growth markets. Although they may generate enough cash to sustain themselves, they do not hold the promise of ever becoming real winners for the firm. Dropping SBUs in this quadrant from a business portfolio is generally advocated except when relationships with other SBUs, competitive considerations, or potential strategic alliances exist.[18]

The 14 circles in Figure 2–3 show the current SBUs in a strong, diversified firm. The area of each circle is proportional to the corresponding SBU's annual sales revenue.

The portfolio in Figure 2–3 is a mixed one. On the favorable side, one half of its SBUs are large and have high market shares, but, unfortunately, the other half are small with low market shares. Because most firms have limited influence on the market growth rate (the factor shown on the vertical axis), their main alternative in a growth-share matrix framework is to try to change the relative market share (the factor on the horizontal axis).

To accomplish this, management makes conscious decisions on what role each SBU should have in the future and either injects or removes cash from it. Four alternative strategies are available for each SBU. The firm can invest more in the SBU to *build* its share (SBU A in Figure 2–3). Or it can invest just enough to *hold* the SBU's share at about its current level (SBU B in the figure). Or it can *harvest* the SBU (SBU C in the figure), trying to milk its short-term cash flow even though it

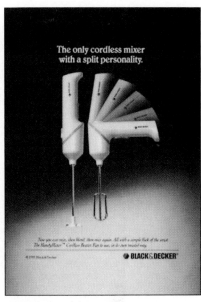

Strategies emerging from a business portfolio analysis: Intel "builds" its chip business while General Electric "divests" its small appliance business by selling it to Black & Decker.

may lose share and become a dog in the longer run. Finally, the firm can *divest* the SBU (SBU D) by phasing it out or actually selling it to gain cash to invest in the remaining SBUs.

The primary strengths of business portfolio analysis include (1) forcing a firm to assess each of its SBUs in terms of its relative market share and industry market growth rate, which, in turn, (2) requires the firm to forecast which SBUs will be cash producers and cash users in the future. Weaknesses are that (1) it is often difficult to get the information needed to locate each SBU on the growth-share matrix, (2) there are other important factors missing from the analysis such as possible synergies among the SBUs when they use the same salesforce or research and development facilities, and (3) there are problems in motivating people in an SBU that has been labeled a dog or even a cash cow and is unlikely to get new resources from the firm to grow and provide opportunities for promotion.[19] In addition, planners have had difficulty incorporating competitive information into portfolio analysis,[20] and formal experiments show the technique may not provide as effective an allocation of resources as more traditional methods of financial analysis.[21]

Specifying the business unit's competencies   Whereas the mission defines the scope of the business or business unit and the goals define its strategic performance dimensions, its **business unit competencies**—special capabilities resulting from its personnel, resources, or functional units—determine the means for achieving success.[22] These competencies should be distinctive enough to provide a **competitive advantage,** a unique strength relative to competitors, often based on quality, time, cost, or innovation.[23]

For example, if a firm such as 3M or Hewlett-Packard has a goal of generating a specific portion of its sales from new products, it must have a supporting competency in research and development. It must also have a supportive competency to manufacture and market its new products in a timely and effective way. Hewlett-Packard has a truly competitive advantage with its fast cycle time, which allows it to bring innovative products to markets in large volume rapidly.[24] In fact, in the mid-1990s Hewlett-Packard reported that more than half its orders were for products introduced the previous two years.[25] These topics are covered again in Chapters 11 and 22.

A competitive advantage from innovation and fast cycle time: Hewlett-Packard's combination color printer-copier.

Another currently popular strategy is to develop a competency in total quality management (TQM). **Quality** here means those features and characteristics of a product that influence its ability to satisfy customer needs. Firms often try to improve quality or reduce new product cycles through **benchmarking**—discovering how others do something better than your own firm so you can imitate or leapfrog competition. Benchmarking often involves studying operations in completely different businesses. When General Mills sought ideas on how to reduce the time to convert its production lines from one cereal to another, it sent a team to observe the pit crews at the Indianapolis 500 race. The result: General Mills cut its plant change-over time by more than half.

If properly done, TQM—and the resulting high quality—can often serve as a competitive advantage—because most firms have not yet adopted TQM. Also, there is evidence that the price of stocks of firms implementing a quality initiative perform slightly better than the stocks of firms that do not.[26] A note of caution, however, is that specific TQM practices of quality training, process improvement, and benchmarking may not produce a competitive advantage by themselves. Rather, more basic management competencies such as developing an open culture, empowering employees, and sustaining executive commitment must be present first. Such practices can produce an advantage, with or without a formal TQM effort, as explained in the Marketing NewsNet box.[27] Formal TQM activities can then complement these management factors to provide a further competitive advantage. This is the secret behind companies such as Ford, Motorola, and Xerox, who have gone beyond matching competitors' quality and are now using quality as a weapon themselves.

Sears appears to be developing a competitive advantage in sourcing, displaying, and selling products positioned between "mass and class." It has been wringing the costs out of its suppliers and redesigning its business processes by benchmarking with other retailers. This has allowed Sears to set prices below those of more

MARKETING NEWSNET

QUALITY AS A COMPETITIVE ADVANTAGE

Quality consultants see a quality strategy as the one solution for all organizations who want to become more competitive; some claim that quality is just as important as financial results or that it will lead to improved financial performance. A focus on quality has helped make Ford Motor Company ("Quality is Job One") more profitable and has helped propel the Ford Taurus to a best-seller. But a focus on quality has not had the same effect for General Motors' Saturn business unit. Why?

A study of 150 successful organizational turnarounds found that total quality management is not a cure-all and that typical TQM approaches have limited impact. It also noted that poor quality is only the fifth most important cause of business downturn or failure, following high costs, high debt, strategic errors, and bad investments.

Nonetheless, poor product and service quality can be competitive disadvantages, especially since customers today often demand quality on a par with competition. This is a lesson the American automobile industry has learned the hard way, and it explains why many organizations with past quality problems are inclined to pursue a quality strategy with an increased focus on their customers. However, a high cost structure or a bad strategy will not be saved by devotion to quality.

The experience with General Motors' Saturn business illustrates this. Saturn has focused on providing top value to the customers through low defects and excellent, low-pressure service. Unfortunately, Saturn has yet to make a profit after several years of operation, at least in part because of a high cost structure and a product that offers few benefits beyond the competitors' offerings. Successful organizations must emphasize quality—but not as a way to solve more fundamental strategic problems.

prestigious retail competitors. But, Sears is also using high-quality brands combined with its own private labels to find a niche slightly above mass merchandisers. Sears has invested billions of dollars to upgrade facilities, and it has relieved sales associates of administrative responsibilities to enable them to spend more time serving customers—all with an eye to pursuing the mission and goals statements in Figure 2–2.

Strategy at the Functional Level

The functional departments, such as marketing, respond to the corporate and business strategic directions by creating functional goals, which are simply extensions of the corporate and business goals. For marketing, an example of a functional goal is "to create a new image that emphasizes the soft side of merchandising," as Sears has actually done. To accomplish the functional goals requires program plans that spell out very specific marketing objectives with associated actions, responsibilities, and dates. An objective of the new Sears promotional program was to increase customer awareness about its new marketing efforts. Not only have most people heard about the "Softer Side of Sears," many are now singing the new jingles!

However, marketing does not operate by itself in an organization. When Sears launched its "Soft Side" promotional program, financial specialists had to develop a funding program, which included selling off 20 percent of the Allstate Insurance business unit and two other complete business units. This funding was used to support operations specialists, who remodeled several hundred Sears stores. Then human resource specialists had to retrain sales associates to provide better service consistent with the new market position.

Successful marketing efforts today are really cross-functional team efforts involving specialists from all the functional units to analyze, implement, and control programs to accomplish the corporate and business strategic directions. The strategic marketing process described in the next section provides the framework for making this happen.

CONCEPT CHECK

1. "Make Sears a more compelling place to shop" is an example of what kind of business unit statement?

2. What is business portfolio analysis?

3. What is a competitive advantage, and why is it important?

THE STRATEGIC MARKETING PROCESS

All approaches to planning try to find answers to these key questions:

1. Where are we now?
2. Where do we want to go?
3. How do we allocate our resources to get to where we want to go?
4. How do we convert our plans into actions?
5. How do our results compare with our plans, and do deviations require new plans and actions?

This same approach is used in the **strategic marketing process,** whereby an organization allocates its marketing mix resources to reach its target markets. This process is divided into three phases: planning, implementation, and control (Figure 2–4).

The strategic marketing process is so central to the activities of most organizations that they formalize it as a **marketing plan,** which is a road map for the marketing activities of an organization for a specified future period of time, such as one year or five years. Appendix A at the end of this chapter provides guidelines for writing a marketing plan and also presents a sample marketing plan for Paradise Kitchens,® Inc., a firm that produces and distributes a line of spicy chilies under the Howlin' Coyote® brand name. The sequence of activities that follow parallels the elements of the marketing plan that appears in Appendix A.

The following section gives an overview of the strategic marketing process that places Chapters 3 through 21 in perspective. In Chapter 22 we examine the strategic marketing process again in more depth.

Strategic Marketing Process: The Planning Phase

As shown in Figure 2–4, the planning phase of the strategic marketing process consists of the three steps shown at the top of the figure: (1) situation analysis, (2) market-product focus and goal setting, and (3) the marketing program. Let's use the recent marketing planning experiences of several companies to look at each of these steps.

Step 1: situation (SWOT) analysis   The essence of the **situation analysis** is taking stock of where the firm or product has been recently, where it is now, and where it is headed in light of the organization's plans and the external factors and trends affecting it. The situation analysis box in Figure 2–4 is the first of the three steps in the planning phase.

An effective short-hand summary of the situation analysis is a **SWOT analysis,** an acronym describing an organization's appraisal of its internal *s*trengths and *w*eaknesses and its external *o*pportunities and *t*hreats. Both the situation and SWOT analyses can be done at the level of the entire organization, the business unit, the

FIGURE 2-4

The strategic marketing process

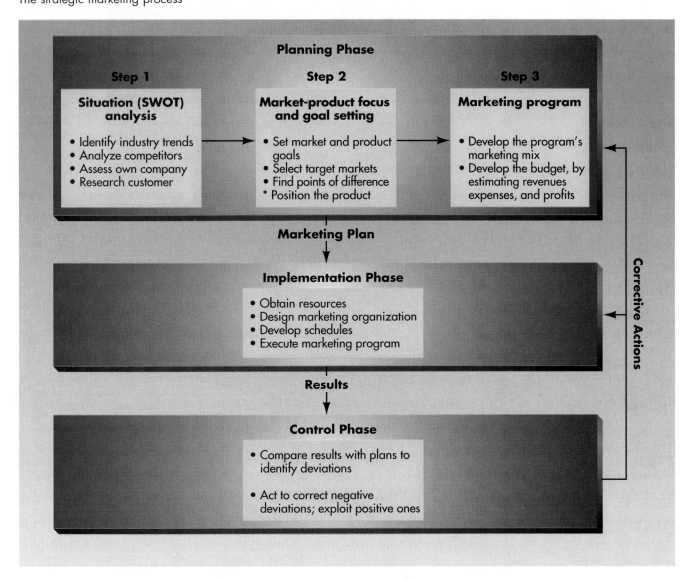

product line, or the specific product. As an analysis moves from the level of the entire organization to the specific product, it, of course, gets far more detailed. For small firms or those with basically a single product line, an analysis at the firm or product level is really the same thing. This is the case for Ben & Jerry's today—the firm for which Robert Holland, Jr., became president, as described at the start of the chapter.

Let's assume you are the consultant who provides Holland with the SWOT analysis for Ben & Jerry's shown in Figure 2–5.[28] Note that your SWOT table has four cells formed by the combination of internal versus external factors (the rows) and favorable versus unfavorable factors (the columns) that summarize Ben & Jerry's strengths, weaknesses, opportunities, and threats. A more in-depth SWOT analysis might use more detailed checklists of internal and external factors in the table. For example, internal factors might be broken down to include key elements such as the products offered and the effectiveness of the functional areas such as sales or research and development (R&D) that affect marketing activities. Similarly, external factors are often formalized in the SWOT analysis by using the external or environmental factors affecting marketing activities, such as consumer or technological trends. An

A SWOT analysis can suggest
ways for Ben & Jerry's to
leverage these well-known
products and flavors.

example of using these detailed breakdowns of internal and external factors appears
in the Paradise Kitchens SWOT in Appendix A. For simplicity, the Ben & Jerry's
SWOT does not contain this level of detail.

A SWOT analysis helps a firm identify the strategy-related factors in these four
cells that can have a major effect on the firm. However, all factors in such an analysis
are not of equal value, so the ultimate goal is to identify the *critical* factors affecting
the firm and then build on vital strengths, correct glaring weaknesses, exploit
significant opportunities, and avoid disaster-laden threats. That is a big order. This
ultimate goal is not simply to develop the SWOT analysis but to translate the results
of the analysis into specific actions to help the firm grow and succeed.

Although the SWOT analysis is a shorthand look at the situation analysis, it is
based on an exhaustive study of the four areas shown in Figure 2–4 that are the
foundation on which the firm builds its marketing program:

- Identifying trends in the firm's industry.
- Analyzing the firm's competitors.
- Assessing the firm itself.
- Researching the firm's present and prospective customers.

Examples of more in-depth analyses in these four areas appear in the marketing plan
in Appendix A and the chapters in this textbook cited in that plan.

One way for firms to utilize the SWOT results and exhaustive study of their
industry, competitors, own firm, and customers is to assess market-product strategies.
Four such strategies representing the four combinations of (1) current and new
markets and (2) current and new products appear in Figure 2–6.

As Robert Holland attempts to increase the sales revenue of Ben & Jerry's, he
must consider all four of the alternative market-product strategies shown in Figure
2–6. For example, he can try to use a strategy of *market penetration*—increasing
sales of present products in their existing markets, in this case by increasing sales of

FIGURE 2–5

Ben & Jerry's: a "SWOT" to get it growing again

LOCATION OF FACTOR	TYPE OF FACTOR	
	FAVORABLE	**UNFAVORABLE**
Internal	**STRENGTHS** • Prestigious, well-known brand name among U.S. consumers • 40% share of the U.S. super premium ice cream market • Strong position among customers built on reputation for pure ingredients and social responsibility	**WEAKNESSES** • Snags in B&J's new computerized distribution system • Need for experienced managers to help growth • Software problems in its new highly automated packing plant
External	**OPPORTUNITIES** • Growing demand for quality ice cream in overseas markets • Increasing U.S. demand for frozen yogurt and other low-fat desserts • Success of many U.S. firms in extending successful brand in one product category to others	**THREATS** • Consumer concern with fatty desserts; B&J's customers are exactly the type who read new government-ordered nutritional labels • Competes with much larger firm, whose Haagen-Dazs brand also has 40% share of this U.S. market • B&J's biggest distributor is promoting competitive products

Ben & Jerry's present ice cream products to U.S. consumers. There is no change in either the product line or the market served, but increased sales are possible through actions such as better advertising, more retail outlets, lower prices, or more effective distribution.

Market development, which for Holland means selling existing Ben & Jerry's products to new markets, is a reasonable alternative. Asian and European consumers are good candidates as possible new markets. There is good news and bad news for this strategy: increasing incomes of households in those markets present great opportunities, but the Ben & Jerry's brand is relatively unknown.

An expansion strategy using *product development* involves selling a new product to existing markets. Figure 2–6 shows that Holland could try leveraging the firm's brand, as mentioned earlier, by selling its own Ben & Jerry's brand of children's clothing in the United States. This, of course, has dangers because

FIGURE 2–6

Four market-product strategies: alternative ways to expand sales revenues for Ben & Jerry's

MARKETS	PRODUCTS	
	CURRENT	**NEW**
Current	**MARKET PENETRATION** Selling more Ben & Jerry's super premium ice cream to Americans	**PRODUCT DEVELOPMENT** Selling a new product like children's clothing under the Ben & Jerry's brand to Americans
New	**MARKET DEVELOPMENT** Selling Ben & Jerry's super premium ice cream in Asian markets for the first time	**DIVERSIFICATION** Selling a new product like children's clothing in Asian markets for the first time

Americans may not be able to see a clear connection between the company's expertise in ice cream and, say, children's clothing.

Diversification involves developing new products and selling them in new markets. This is a potentially high-risk strategy for Ben & Jerry's—and for most firms—because the company has neither previous production experience nor marketing experience on which to draw. For example, in trying to sell a Ben & Jerry's brand of children's clothing in Asia, the company has expertise neither in producing children's clothing nor in marketing to Asian consumers.

Which strategies will Ben, Jerry, and Robert Holland follow? Keep your eyes, ears, and taste buds working to discover their marketing answers in the late 1990s.

Step 2: market-product focus and goal setting Finding a focus on what product offerings will be directed toward which customers (step 2 of the planning phase in Figure 2–4) is essential for developing an effective marketing program (step 3). This focus often comes from the firm's using **market segmentation,** which involves aggregating prospective buyers into groups, or segments, that (1) have common needs and (2) will respond similarly to a marketing action. Ideally a firm can use market segmentation to identify the segments on which it will focus its efforts—its target market segments—and develop one or more marketing programs to reach them.

Goal setting here involves setting measurable marketing objectives to be achieved—possibly for a specific market, a specific product or brand, or an entire marketing program. As mentioned earlier, there is a hierarchy of goals and objectives flowing from the corporate strategy set by top management on down to the levels of the marketing managers.

We can illustrate steps 2 and 3 in the planning phase of the strategic marketing process by using the Paradise Kitchens® marketing plan from Appendix A. This firm is trying to expand its line of Howlin' Coyote® spicy chilies from 3 to 20 U.S. metropolitan markets during the last half of the 1990s. Stated simply, the five-year marketing plan for Paradise Kitchens specifies these step 2 activities:

- *Set marketing and product goals.* As mentioned later in Chapter 11, the chances of new product success are increased by specifying both market and product goals. Paradise Kitchens® will grow its present markets by expanding brands and flavors, add 17 new metropolitan markets in the next five years, enter the food-service market, and add new products.
- *Select target markets.* Howlin' Coyote® chilies will be targeted at one- to three-person households with annual incomes above $30,000 in which both adults are likely to work outside the home—adventurous consumers wanting premium-quality Southwestern/Mexican food products.
- *Find points of difference.* **Points of difference** are those characteristics of a product that make it superior to competitive substitutes. (Chapter 11 points out that this is the single most important factor in the success or failure of a new product.) For Howlin' Coyote® chilies these are unique spicy taste; quality, convenience, and a range of flavors; and premium packaging.
- *Position the product.* Howlin' Coyote® chilies will be "positioned" in consumers' minds as "very high-quality, authentic Southwestern/Mexican tasting chilies that can be prepared easily and quickly."

Details in these four elements of step 2 provide a solid foundation to use in developing the marketing program—the next step in the planning phase of the strategic marketing process.

Step 3: marketing program Activities in step 2 tell the marketing manager which customers to target and which customer needs the firm's product offerings can satisfy—the *who* and *what* aspects of the strategic marketing process. The *how*

A small business like Paradise Kitchens has a carefully developed focus for its marketing program.

aspect—step 3 in the planning phase—involves developing the program's marketing mix and its budget.

Figure 2–7 shows components of each marketing mix element that are combined to provide a cohesive marketing program. For the five-year marketing plan of Paradise Kitchens, these marketing mix activities include the following:

- *Product strategy.* Offer a current line of five Howlin' Coyote® chilies with proprietary flavoring, high-quality ingredients without preservatives, and packaging with a Southwestern motif that communicates the brand's uniqueness.
- *Price strategy.* Price Howlin' Coyote® chili at $2.89 for a 10- to 11.5-ounce package, comparable to other frozen offerings and higher than the canned and dried chili varieties.
- *Promotion strategy.* Feature in-store demonstrations to highlight the product's unique qualities, recipes using the brand to stimulate use, and various kinds of cents-off coupons to generate trial and repeat-purchase of the brand.
- *Place (distribution) strategy.* Use food distributors with current sales volumes, shifting to brokers as increased sales volumes justify them.

Putting this marketing program into effect requires that the firm commit time and money to it in the form of a budget. The budgeting process starts with a sales forecast based on estimates of units expected to be sold—probably by month, quarter, and year. Estimated expenses for the marketing mix activities comprising the marketing program are estimated and balanced against expected revenues to estimate the program's profitability. This budget is really the "sales" document presented to top management to gain approval for the budgeted resources to implement the marketing program.

FIGURE 2-7

Elements of the marketing mix
that compose a cohesive
marketing program

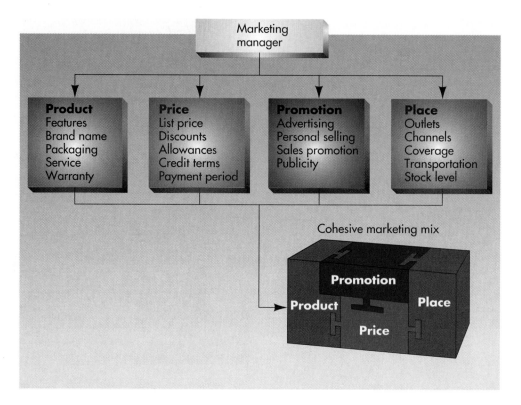

CONCEPT CHECK

1. What is the difference between a strength and an opportunity in a SWOT analysis?

2. What is market segmentation?

3. If Ben & Jerry's attempts to enter Asian markets with its super premium ice cream, which market-product strategy would it be using?

Strategic Marketing Process: The Implementation Phase

As shown in Figure 2–4, the result of the tens or hundreds of hours spent in the planning phase of the strategic marketing process is the firm's marketing plan. Implementation, the second phase of the strategic marketing process, involves carrying out the marketing plan that emerges from the planning phase. If the firm cannot put the marketing plan into effect—in the implementation phase—the planning phase was a waste of time. Figure 2–4 also shows the four components of the implementation phase: (1) obtaining resources, (2) designing the marketing organization, (3) developing schedules, and (4) actually executing the marketing program designed in the planning phase. Eastman Kodak provides a case example.

Fortune magazine provides the stage on which we can study an American firm facing both the implementation and control phases of the strategic marketing process:

> The DRAMATIC restructuring of U.S. industry won't be over, as the saying goes, until the fat lady sings. Hundreds of companies have performed massive renovations—Ford, Chrysler, Texaco, Xerox, IBM. But now the diva enters. She is the last of the great, corpulent, 20th-century American enterprises to sing the rejuvenation aria. She walks to center stage. She turns to the audience. She is Eastman Kodak.[29]

Radical change is coming to Kodak, "one of the most bureaucratic, wasteful, paternalistic, slow-moving, isolated, and beloved companies in America."[30] And the

FIGURE 2-8

Organization of a typical manufacturing firm, showing a breakdown of the marketing department

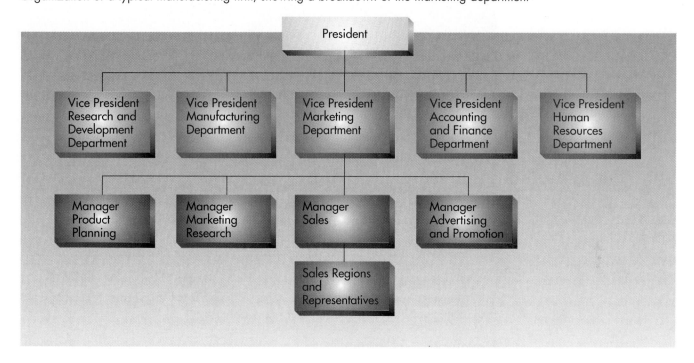

agent of change is George Fisher, its new chief executive officer, who gave up a similar job at spectacularly successful Motorola to try to move Kodak's little yellow boxes and new technologies into the twenty-first century. His early decisions are classic management and marketing lessons in implementing and controlling the activities of a corporate giant.

Obtaining resources   When George Fisher arrived at Kodak in 1994, he observed, "There are textbook types of things that are wrong with this company. Decisions are too slow. People don't take risks."[31] So he pushed some revolutionary—and—to him—obvious—decisions:

- Focus on Kodak's core business: imaging.
- Serve customer needs better, and stress quality.
- Shorten product-development cycles.
- Encourage a more dynamic, risk taking, fast-decision culture.

Fisher needed financial resources to implement these ideas, however, so he sold or spun-off Kodak's health, household-products, and chemicals businesses. The $6 billion he got for these sales provided the resources to enable Kodak to try to implement its strategy to grow its core imaging business.

Designing the marketing organization   A marketing program needs a marketing organization to implement it. This is especially true for firms such as Kodak facing constantly changing global markets. Figure 2–8 shows the organization chart of a typical manufacturing firm, giving some details of the marketing department's structure. Four managers of marketing activities are shown to report to the vice president of marketing: the managers of product planning, marketing research, sales, and advertising and promotion. Depending on the size of the organization, there may be several product planning managers—each responsible for a separate product line. Also, several regional sales managers and an international

Can't find the negative for that 20-year-old photo of the family picnic at grandma's? The solution: a do-it-yourself blowup at a very successful Kodak CopyPrint Station

sales manager may report to the manager of sales. This marketing organization is responsible for converting marketing plans to reality.

Developing schedules   One key to effective implementation is setting deadlines, which are supported by schedules of important milestones that make the deadlines achievable. "Half the people in the world have yet to take their first picture," says Fisher. So he sees huge opportunities for Kodak in global, developing markets and in digital imaging technologies that may replace film in many applications. In 1994 he set these deadlines:

- Introduce Kodak CopyPrint Stations in July 1995. Benefiting from Kodak's digital imaging technology, you can blow up your tiny 20-year-old snapshot (*not* the negative, which you've lost!) into a surprisingly clear 4×6 or 8×10 enlargement.[32]
- Introduce sleek, improved, single-use camera by spring 1995.
- Relaunch Photo CD (for compact disk) System in March 1995, this time targeting desktop computer users.
- Introduce the Advanced Photographic System (APS), a "smart" film and camera, by the end of 1996 that will store information such as shutter speed as each picture is taken, thereby improving print quality.
- Set up improved distribution networks in emerging countries such as China, Russia, India, and Brazil.

To make sure his managers meet the targets in these schedules, Fisher devised a new management compensation structure to tie salary more closely to performance.

Executing the marketing program   Marketing plans are meaningless pieces of paper without effective execution of those plans. This effective execution requires attention to detail for both marketing strategies and marketing tactics. A **marketing strategy** is the means by which a marketing goal is to be achieved, usually characterized by a specified target market and a marketing program to reach it. Although the term *strategy* is often used loosely, it implies both the end sought (target market) and the means to achieve it (marketing program).

To implement a marketing program successfully, hundreds of detailed decisions are often required, such as writing advertising copy or selecting the amount for

temporary price reductions. These decisions, called **marketing tactics,** are detailed day-to-day operational decisions essential to the overall success of marketing strategies. Compared with marketing strategies, marketing tactics generally involve actions that must be taken right away. We cannot cover many aspects of marketing tactics in detail in a book of this size, and the emphasis here is on marketing strategy—the strategic marketing process. Here are examples of both kinds of decisions Fisher made recently at Kodak:[33]

- Marketing strategy decision: develop a strategic partnership with five Japanese companies (including Fuji, Canon, and Nikon) to develop its smart film and camera—the Advanced Photographic System.
- Marketing tactics decision: assign 10 newly formed teams the responsibility of studying issues such as cycle-time improvement to squeeze excessive time and costs out of Kodak's bloated, slow-moving, new product development process.

Issues that surface at the marketing tactics level can become marketing strategy or corporate strategy issues. There are no precise lines between marketing strategies and marketing tactics because one shades into the other. Clearly, however, effective marketing program implementation requires excruciating concern for details in both marketing strategies and marketing tactics.

Strategic Marketing Process: The Control Phase

The control phase of the strategic marketing process seeks to keep the marketing program moving in the direction set for it (see Figure 2–4). Accomplishing this requires the marketing manager (1) to compare the results of the marketing program with the goals in the written plans to identify deviations and (2) to act on these deviations—correcting negative deviations and exploiting positive ones.

Comparing results with plans to identify deviations   In early 1995, shortly after George Fisher took over at Kodak, he wanted to set sales targets for the company through the end of the decade. As Fisher looked at the company's sales revenues (from continuing operations) from 1990 through 1994, he didn't like what he saw: the very flat trend, or AB in Figure 2–9. Technological innovations such as digital cameras were redefining the entire amateur photographic market. Also, Fuji was giving far greater competition in Kodak's traditional film and photographic markets than expected. These and other factors were inhibiting Kodak's growth opportunities.

Extending the 1990–1994 trend to the end of the century (BC in Figure 2–9) showed flat sales revenues, a totally unacceptable, no-growth strategy. Fisher announced that, in the five years following 1995, his goal for Kodak was to double its return on assets. Applying this same annual growth rate to sales revenue gives the target sales revenue line through the year 2000, shown as BD in Figure 2–9. This reveals a huge wedge-shaped shaded gap in the figure. Planners call this the *planning gap,* the difference between the projection of the path to reach a new goal (line BD) and the projection of the path of the results of a plan already in place (line BC).

This target goal is actually set earlier in the strategic marketing process, in the planning phase. The ultimate purpose of the firm's marketing program is to "fill in" this planning gap—in Kodak's case, to move its future sales revenue line from the essentially no-growth line BC up to the challenging high-growth target of line BD.

Having a challenging series of quantified annual sales revenue targets is not enough. Poor performance of Kodak or intense competition could result in actual sales revenues being far less than the targeted levels. This is the essence of evaluation—comparing actual results with planned objectives.

FIGURE 2-9

Evaluation and control of
Kodak's marketing program

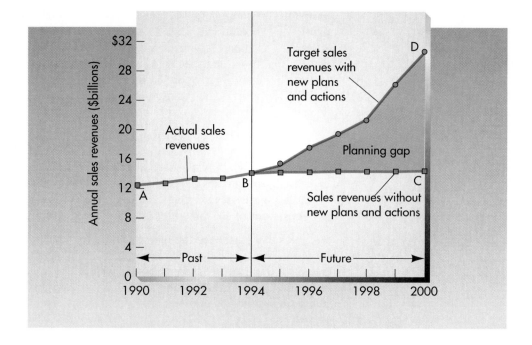

Acting on deviations   When the evaluation shows that actual performance is not up to expectations, a corrective action is usually needed to adjust and improve the program and help it achieve the planned objective. In contrast, comparing results with plans may sometimes reveal that actual performance is far better than the plan called for. In this case the marketing manager wants to uncover the reason for the good performance and act to exploit it.

After only a few months on the job, Fisher recognized the vital importance of fast action and moving new, high-quality Kodak products into the marketplace. This is the reason for the flurry of new and upgraded products released by Kodak in 1995 and 1996. Effective control at Kodak—and all organizations—requires that deviations not

Kodak is betting on its digital
imaging technologies to help
fill its planning gap.

only be identified but that positive deviations be exploited and negative ones be corrected. Two recent Kodak "mid-course corrections" to act on deviations from targets illustrate these principles:

- *Exploiting a positive deviation.* The Kodak CopyPrint Stations found spectacular consumer acceptance in enlarging small prints quickly and easily. Kodak exploited this success by not only installing several thousand of these machines around the world but by quickly designing and introducing even more sophisticated do-it-yourself machines for use by consumers in their local photo shops.[34]
- *Correcting a negative deviation.* The Photo CD System utilizing Kodak's digital imaging technologies did not gain the consumer acceptance expected, so Kodak upgraded its design and relaunched the product, this time targeting desktop computer users.[35]

The strategic marketing process is discussed in greater detail again in Chapter 22.

CONCEPT CHECK

1. What is the control phase of the strategic marketing process?

2. How do the objectives set for a marketing program in the planning phase relate to the control phase of the strategic marketing process?

SUMMARY

1. Today's large organizations, both business firms and nonprofit organizations, are often divided into three levels. These levels are, from highest to lowest, the corporate, business unit, and functional levels.

2. At the highest level, corporate strategy involves setting the strategic direction for the entire organization, using statements of corporate vision, corporate goals, and corporate philosophy and culture.

3. At the business unit level, direction comes from the business unit's mission, goals, and competencies. Concepts such as portfolio analysis, competitive advantage, total quality management, and benchmarking help the business unit achieve its mission and goals.

4. Strategy and direction at the functional level come from having the marketing department work closely with other functional units, such as manufacturing and finance, to achieve the vision, mission, and goals coming from all three organizational levels.

5. The strategic marketing process involves an organization allocating its marketing mix resources to reach its target markets. It has three phases: planning, implementation, and control.

6. The planning phase of the strategic marketing process has three steps, each with more specific elements: situation (SWOT) analysis, market-product focus and goal setting, and marketing program.

7. The implementation phase of the strategic marketing process has four key elements: obtaining resources, designing the marketing organization, developing schedules, and executing the marketing program.

8. The control phase of the strategic marketing process involves comparing results with the planned targets to identify deviations and taking actions to correct negative deviations and exploit positive ones.

KEY TERMS

profit p. 30
corporate level p. 30
business unit p. 30
business unit level pp. 30–31
functional level p. 31
corporate vision p. 32
goal p. 33
corporate goals p. 33

market share p. 34
corporate philosophy pp. 34–35
corporate culture p. 35
business (unit) mission p. 35
business unit goal p. 36
objectives p. 37
business unit competencies p. 39
competitive advantage p. 39

CHAPTER PROBLEMS AND APPLICATIONS

1. (*a*) Explain what a vision statement is. (*b*) Using Coca-Cola as an example from the chapter, explain how it gives a strategic direction to its organization. (*c*) Create a vision statement for your own career.

2. (*a*) How might top management try to change the "corporate culture" of its organization? (*b*) What has George Fisher done at Kodak to change its corporate culture?

3. Using the business unit mission statement for the Domestic Merchandising Group at Sears shown in Figure 2–2, write a comparable, plausible mission statement for its two other major groups: (*a*) the Allstate Insurance Group (selling property and liability insurance) and (*b*) the Homart Development Company (which develops and manages shopping centers and community centers).

4. Why does a product often start as a question mark and then move counterclockwise around BCG's growth-share matrix shown in Figure 2–3?

5. What organizational or business unit competencies best describe (*a*) your college or university, (*b*) your favorite restaurant, and (*c*) the company that manufactures the computer you own or use most often?

6. What is the main result of each of the three phases of the strategic marketing process? (*a*) planning, (*b*) implementation, and (*c*) control.

7. Select one strength, one weakness, one opportunity, and one threat from the SWOT analysis for Ben & Jerry's shown in Figure 2–5, and suggest a specific possible action that might result.

8. Many American liberal arts colleges have traditionally offered an undergraduate degree in liberal arts (the product) to full-time 18- to 22-year-old students (the market). How might such a college use the four market-product expansion strategies shown in Figure 2–6 to compete in the 1990s?

9. The goal-setting step in the planning phase of the strategic marketing process sets quantified objectives for use in the control phase. What actions are suggested for a marketing manager if measured results are below objectives? Above objectives?

10. Read Appendix A, "A Sample Marketing Plan." Then develop a table of contents for the Paradise Kitchens marketing plan to the level of (*a*) A-level headings and (*b*) B-level headings. (*c*) Write a 600-word executive summary for the marketing plan using the numbered headings shown in the plan.

CASE 2–1   Specialized Bicycle Components, Inc.

Video

The speaker leans forward with both intensity and pride in his voice. "We're in the business of creating a bike that delivers the customer their best possible ride," he explains. "When the customer sees our red 'S,' they say this is the company that understands the cyclist. It's a company of riders. The products they make are the rider's products." The speaker is Chris Murphy, Director of Marketing for Specialized Bicycle Components, Inc.—or just "Specialized" to serious riders.

THE COMPANY

Specialized was founded in 1974 by Mike Sinyard, a cycling enthusiast who sold his VW van for the $1,500 startup capital. Mike started out importing hard-to-find "specialized" bike components, but the company began to produce its own bike parts by 1976. Specialized introduced the first major production mountain bike in the world in 1980, revolutionizing the bike industry, and since then has maintained a reputation as the technological leader in the bike and bike accessory market. In fact, since the company's founding, its formal mission statement has remained unchanged: "To give everyone the best ride of their life!"

You probably recognize the Stumpjumper and the Rockhopper as two of the most popular mountain bikes today, both made by Specialized. The company continues to innovate, with its introduction of a European-style city bike, the Globe. It also sells road bikes and an extensive line of bike accessories, including helmets, water bottles, jerseys, and shoes. As Chris says, "The customer is buying the ride from us, not just the bike."

The first professional mountain bike racing team was created by Specialized in 1983, and Ned Overland, the

Team Specialized captain, became a six-time national champion and the first-ever world champion. Specialized also counts Ned as one of its design consultants. The company banks on the perception, and reality, that this race-proven technology trickles down to the entire line of Specialized bikes and products.

THE ENVIRONMENT

The bike market is driven by innovation and technology, and with the market becoming more crowded and competitive, the fight for the consumer is intense. Specialized divides the bike market into two categories: (1) the independent retailer, and (2) the end-user consumer. While its focus in designing the product is on the end-user consumer, it only sells directly to the retailer, and realizes a strong relationship with the dealers is a key factor for success. Steve Meineke, President of Specialized USA (the domestic unit of Specialized), refers to the on-floor salesperson as "our most important partner."

The end-user consumer is broken down into two target age-groups: the 18–25 year old college students and the 30–40 year old professional "techies." To differentiate itself from the rest of the market, Specialized positions itself as the innovator in mountain bikes—its models are what the rest of the industry imitates.

Mountain bikes account for approximately two-thirds of total industry bike sales, with road bikes accounting

for the other third. The sport of mountain biking experienced a huge surge from 1989 to 1993, but in 1994 sales began to flatten. Does Chris believe this trend will hurt Specialized? "We believe we will see growth in the next six or seven years as the entry level participants trade up—trade their lower end bikes for higher end bikes," he explains.

Specialized began cultivating what was to become an extensive global distribution network as early as 1982. It now boasts subsidiaries in twenty-five countries in Asia, North America, South America, Europe, and Australia, enabling the red "S" to become a symbol of performance-driven products around the world.

THE ISSUES

How can Specialized stay at the forefront of an industry that now includes more than twenty manufacturers? Strategic placement in the marketplace is one way. Specialized recently designed its own server, the World Ride Web, on the Internet (http://www.specialized.com/bikes/). The web site offers international mountain bike trail and road bike trail directories, e-mail access to Specialized engineers, a trail preservation network, and a dealer directory that connects users directly to dealer homepages, in addition to the standard product information. Specialized's new bike, the Globe, recently appeared on *Seinfeld* and was on display in Gap clothing stores. Specialized believes these non-traditional promotional strategies are helping to keep the Specialized name on the cutting edge and in front of the end-user consumer.

Targeting its other market segment, the dealers, Specialized launched a "Best Ride Tour." It loaded up trailers full of the new models and visited 30 cities nationwide, enabling retailers and shop employees to test ride the bikes they will be ordering for the coming year—"Ride Before You Buy."

Specialized is also eager to become involved in joint ventures to keep its technological edge. In 1989 it released the Composite wheel, which was a joint venture between Specialized and Du Pont. The wheel is so aerodynamic it actually saves a rider more than ten minutes over a 100 mile ride. Specialized also entered into a distribution relationship with GripShift in 1994, allowing the high-end gear manufacturer access to its extensive dealer network. Why is this beneficial to Specialized? It's another way to support the dealers by providing a top-notch product for its customers that Specialized can support in its marketing efforts.

Specialized sponsors races, provides racer support teams, initiates mountain biking safety programs, and is involved in trail-access advocacy groups all over the world. But, as it was in Specialized's early years, Mike sees a commitment to top quality and design as the most important factor for future success: "Even though we've been around for 20 years, this company still feels like it has something to prove. I expect it will always be that way."

Questions

These questions focus on the three steps of the planning phase of the strategic marketing process.

1. Do a SWOT analysis for Specialized. Use Figure 2–5 in Chapter 2 and Figure 1 in Appendix A as guides. In assessing internal factors (strengths and weaknesses), use the material provided in the case. In assessing external factors (opportunities and threats) augment the case material with what you see happening in the bicycle industry.

2. As part of Step 2 of the planning phase, and using your SWOT analysis, select target markets on which you might focus for present and potential bikers.

3. As part of Step 3 of the planning phase and using your answers in questions 1 and 2 above, outline Specialized's marketing programs for the target market segments you chose.

A Sample Marketing Plan

"New ideas are a dime a dozen," observes Arthur R. Kydd, "and so are new products and new technologies." Kydd should know. As chief executive officer of St. Croix Venture Partners, he and his firm have provided the seed money and venture capital to launch more than 60 startup firms in the last 25 years. Today those firms have more than 5,000 employees.

Kydd elaborates:

> I get 200 to 300 marketing and business plans a year to look at, and St. Croix provides startup financing for only two or three. What sets a potentially successful idea, product, or technology apart from all the rest is markets and marketing. If you have a real product with a distinctive point of difference that satisfies the needs of customers, you may have a winner. And you get a real feel for this in a well-written marketing or business plan.[1]

This appendix (1) describes what marketing and business plans are—including their purposes and guidelines in writing effective plans—and (2) provides a sample marketing plan.

MARKETING PLANS AND BUSINESS PLANS

After explaining the meanings, purposes, and audiences of marketing plans and business plans, this section describes some writing guidelines for them and what external funders often look for in successful plans.

Marketing and Business Plans: Meanings, Purposes, and Audiences

A *marketing plan* is a road map for the marketing activities of an organization for a specified future period of time, such as one year or five years.[2] It is important to note that no single "generic" marketing plan applies to all organizations and all situations. Rather, the specific format for a marketing plan for an organization depends on the following:

• *The target audience and purpose.* Elements included in a particular marketing plan depend heavily on (1) who the audience is and (2) what its purpose is. A marketing plan for an internal audience seeks to point the direction for future marketing activities and is sent to all individuals in the organization who must implement the plan or who will be affected by it. If the plan is directed to an external audience—such as friends, banks, venture capitalists, or potential investors—for the purpose of raising capital, it has the additional function of being an important sales document. In this case it contains elements such as the strategic plan/focus, organization, and biographies of key personnel that would rarely appear in an internal marketing plan. Also, the financial information is far more detailed when the plan is used to raise capital.

• *The kind and complexity of the organization.* A small restaurant serving a local market has a somewhat different marketing plan than Nestlé, which serves international markets. The restaurant's plan would be relatively simple and directed at serving customers in a local market. In Nestlé's case, because there is a hierarchy of marketing plans, various levels of detail would be used—such as the entire organization, the business unit, or the product/product line.

• *The industry.* Both the restaurant serving a local market and Medtronic, selling heart pacemakers globally, analyze competition. Not only are their geographic thrusts far different, but the complexities of their offerings and, hence, the time periods likely to be covered by their plans also differ. A one-year marketing plan may be adequate for the restaurant, but Medtronic may need a five-year planning horizon because product-development cycles for complex, new medical devices may be three or four years.

In contrast to a marketing plan, a *business plan* is a road map for the entire organization for a specified future period of time, such as one year or five years.[3] A key difference between a marketing plan and a business plan is that the business plan contains details on the research and development (R&D)/operations/manufacturing activities of the organization. Even for a manufacturing business, the marketing plan is probably 60 or 70 percent of the entire business plan. For businesses like a small restaurant or auto repair shop, their marketing and business plans are virtually identical.

The Most-Asked Questions by Outside Audiences

Lenders and prospective investors reading a business or marketing plan that is used to seek new capital are probably the toughest audiences to satisfy. Their most-asked questions include the following:

1. Is the business or marketing idea valid?
2. Is there something unique or distinctive about the product or service that separates it from substitutes and competitors?
3. Is there a clear market for the product or service?
4. Are the financial projections realistic and healthy?
5. Are the key management and technical personnel capable, and do they have a track record in the industry in which they must compete?
6. Does the plan clearly describe how those providing capital will get their money back and make a profit?

Rhonda M. Abrahms, author of *The Successful Business Plan,* observes that "within the first five minutes of reading your . . . plan, readers, must perceive that the answers to these questions are favorable."[4] While her comments apply to plans seeking to raise capital, the first five questions just listed apply equally well to plans for internal audiences.

Writing and Style Suggestions

There are no magic one-size-fits-all guidelines for writing successful marketing and business plans. Still, the following writing and style guidelines generally apply:[5]

- Use a direct, professional writing style. Use appropriate business terms without jargon. Present and future tenses with active voice are generally better than past tense and passive voice.
- Be positive and specific to convey potential success. At the same time, avoid superlatives ("terrific," "wonderful,"). Specifics are better than glittering generalities. Use numbers for impact, justifying projections with reasonable quantitative assumptions, where possible.
- Use bullet points for succinctness and emphasis. As with the list you are reading, bullets enable key points to be highlighted effectively and with great efficiency.
- Use "A-level" (the first level) and "B-level" (the second level) headings under the numbered section headings to help readers make easy transitions from one topic to another. This also forces the writer to organize the plan more carefully. Use these headings liberally, at least one every 200 to 300 words.
- Use visuals where appropriate. Photos, illustrations, graphs, and charts enable massive amounts of information to be presented succinctly.
- Shoot for a plan 15 to 35 pages in length, not including financial projections and appendixes. But an uncomplicated small business may require only 15 pages, while a high-technology startup may require more than 35 pages.
- Use care in layout, design, and presentation. Laser or ink-jet printers give a more professional look than do dot matrix printers or typewriters. Use 10 or 11 point type (you are now reading 10.5 point type) in the text. Use a serif type (with "feet," like that you are reading now) in the text because it is easier to read, and sans serif (without "feet") in graphs and charts. A bound report with a nice cover and clear title page adds professionalism.

These guidelines are used, where possible, in the sample marketing plan that follows.

SAMPLE FIVE-YEAR MARKETING PLAN FOR PARADISE KITCHENS,® INC.

To help interpret the marketing plan for Paradise Kitchens,® Inc. that follows, we will describe the background on the company and suggest some guidelines in interpreting the plan.

Background on Paradise Kitchens,® Inc.

With a degree in chemical engineering, Randall F. Peters spent 15 years working for General Foods and Pillsbury with a number of diverse responsibilities: plant operations, R&D, restaurant operations, and new business development. His wife Leah, with degrees in both molecular cellular biology and food science, held various Pillsbury executive positions in new category development and packaged goods and restaurants R&D. Both hobby chefs, Randy and Leah developed and perfected several spicy chili recipes in their own kitchen over a 10-year period. While driving late one night in 1989 across the Colorado prairie, they got the inspiration for their registered Howlin' Coyote® brand of chilies and decided to start their own business, Paradise Kitchens, Inc. In the company's startup years, it survived on the savings of Randy and Leah—the cofounders of Paradise Kitchens. Today Randy serves as president and CEO of Paradise Kitchens, and Leah focuses on R&D and corporate strategy. The first products entered distribution in 1990.

Interpreting the Marketing Plan

The marketing plan that follows for Paradise Kitchens, Inc. is based on an actual plan developed by the company.[6] To protect proprietary information about the company, a number of details and data have been altered, but the basic logic of the plan has been preserved. For example, to keep the plan simpler, it does not include details on a line of spicy salsas developed and marketed by Paradise Kitchens.

This sample marketing plan is intended as an *internal* road map to guide marketing activities of Paradise Kitchens for the coming five years, during which time the company plans to enter 17 new metropolitan markets.

Notes in the margins next to the Paradise Kitchens marketing plan fall into two categories:

1. *Substantive notes* are shaded blue and elaborate on the rationale or significance of an element in the marketing plan and are often keyed to chapter references in this textbook.
2. *Writing style, format, and layout notes* are shaded red and explain the editorial or visual rationale for the element.

A closing word of encouragement! Writing an effective marketing plan is hard—but challenging and satisfying—work. However, dozens of the authors' students have used effective marketing plans they wrote for class as an important part of their interviewing portfolio to show prospective employers what they could do and to help them get their first job.

The Table of Contents provides quick access to the topics in the plan, usually organized by section and subsection headings. See questions 10a and 10b at end of Chapter 2.

Seen by many experts as the single most important element in the plan, the Executive Summary, with a maximum of two pages, "sells" the document to readers through its clarity and brevity. See question 10c at the end of Chapter 2.

The Company Description highlights the recent history and recent successes of the organization.

The Strategic Focus and Plan sets the strategic direction for the entire organization, a direction with which proposed actions of the marketing plan must be consistent. This section is not included in all marketing plans. See Chapter 2.

The qualitative Mission/Vision statement focuses the activities of Paradise Kitchens for the stakeholder groups to be served. See Chapter 2.

FIVE-YEAR MARKETING PLAN
Paradise Kitchens®, Inc.

Table of Contents

1. Executive Summary

2. Company Description

Paradise Kitchens®, Inc. was started in 1989 by cofounders Randall F. Peters and Leah E. Peters to develop and market Howlin' Coyote® Chili, a unique line of single serve and microwaveable Southwestern/Mexican style frozen chili products. The Howlin' Coyote® line of chili was introduced into the Minneapolis- St. Paul market in 1990. The line was subsequently expanded to Denver in 1992 and Phoenix in 1994.

To the Company's knowledge, Howlin' Coyote® is the only premium-quality, authentic Southwestern/Mexican style, frozen chili sold in U.S. grocery stores. Its high quality has gained fast, widespread acceptance in these markets. In fact, same-store sales doubled in the last year for which data are available. The Company believes the Howlin' Coyote® brand can be extended to other categories of Southwestern/Mexican food products.

Paradise Kitchens believes its high-quality, high-price strategy has proven successful. This marketing plan outlines how the Company will extend its geographic coverage from 3 markets to 20 markets by the year 2000.

3. Strategic Focus and Plan

This section covers three aspects of corporate strategy that influence the marketing plan: (1) the mission/vision, (2) goals, and (3) core competence/ sustainable competitive advantage of Paradise Kitchens.

Mission/Vision

The mission and vision of Paradise Kitchens is to market lines of high-quality Southwestern/Mexican food products at premium prices that satisfy consumers in this fast-growing food segment while providing challenging career opportunities for employees and above-average returns to stockholders.

Box explains significance of Marketing Plan element

Box gives writing style, format, and layout guidelines

Goals

For the coming five years Paradise Kitchens seeks to achieve the following goals:

• Nonfinancial goals

1. To retain its present image as the highest-quality line of Southwestern/Mexican products in the food categories in which it competes.
2. To enter 17 new metropolitan markets.
3. To increase the production and distribution capacity to satisfy future sales while maintaining present quality.
4. To add a new product line every third year.
5. To be among the top three chili lines—regardless of packaging (frozen, canned) in one third of the metro markets in which it competes by 1998 and two thirds by 2000.

• Financial goals

1. To obtain a real (inflation adjusted) growth in earnings per share of 8 percent per year over time.
2. To obtain a return on equity of at least 20 percent.
3. To have a public stock offering by the year 2000.

In keeping with the goal of adding a new product line every third year, Paradise Kitchens is introducing a new line of salsas.

Core Competency and Sustainable Competitive Advantage

In terms of core competency, Paradise Kitchens seeks to achieve a unique ability (1) to provide distinctive, high-quality chilies and related products using Southwestern/Mexican recipes that appeal to and excite contemporary tastes for these products and (2) to deliver these products to the customer's table using effective manufacturing and distribution systems that maintain the Company's quality standards.

To translate these core competencies into a sustainable competitive advantage, the Company will work closely with key suppliers and distributors to build the relationships and alliances necessary to satisfy the high taste standards of our customers.

To improve readability, each numbered section usually starts on a new page. (This is not done in this plan to save space.)

The Situation Analysis is a snapshot to answer the question, "Where are we now?" See Chapter 2.

The SWOT Analysis identifies strengths, weaknesses, opportunities, and threats to provide a solid foundation as a springboard to identify subsequent *actions* in the marketing plan. See Chapter 2.

Each long table, graph, or photo is given a figure number and title. It then appears as soon as possible after the first reference in the text, accommodating necessary page breaks. This also avoids breaking long tables like this one in the middle. Short tables or graphs that are less than 1-1/2 inches are often inserted in the text without figure numbers because they don't cause serious problems with page breaks.

Effective tables seek to summarize a large amount of information in a short amount of space.

4. Situation Analysis

This situation analysis starts with a snapshot of the current environment in which Paradise Kitchens finds itself by providing a brief SWOT (strengths, weaknesses, opportunities, threats) analysis. After this overview, the analysis probes ever-finer levels of detail: industry, competitors, company, and consumers.

SWOT Analysis

Figure 1 shows the internal and external factors affecting the market opportunities for Paradise Kitchens. Stated briefly, this SWOT analysis highlights the great strides taken by the company in the five years since its products first appeared on grocers' shelves. In

Figure 1. SWOT Analysis for Paradise Kitchens

Internal Factors	Strengths	Weaknesses
Management	Experienced and entrepreneurial management and board	Small size can restrict options
Offerings	Unique, high-quality, high-price products	Many lower-quality, lower price competitors
Marketing	Distribution in 3 markets with excellent acceptance	No national awareness or distribution
Personnel	Good work force, though small; little turnover	Big gap if key employee leaves
Finance	Excellent growth in sales revenues	Limited resources may restrict growth opportunities when compared to giant competitors
Manufacturing	Sole supplier ensures high quality	Lack economies of scale of huge competitors
R&D	Continuing efforts to ensure quality in delivered products	

External Factors	Opportunities	Threats
Consumer/Social	Upscale market, likely to be stable; Southwestern/Mexican food category is fast-growing segment	Premium price may limit access to mass markets
Competitive	Distinctive name and packaging in its markets	Not patentable; competitors can attempt to duplicate product
Technological	Technical breakthroughs enable smaller food producers to achieve many economies available to large competitors	
Economic	Consumer income is high; convenience important to U.S. households	More households "eating out," and bringing prepared take-out into home
Legal/Regulatory	High U.S. Food & Drug Admin. standards eliminate fly-by-night competitors	

The text discussion of Figure 1 (the SWOT Analysis table) elaborates on its more important elements. This "walks" the reader through the information from the vantage of the plan's writer. (In terse plans this accompanying discussion is sometimes omitted, but is generally desirable to give the reader an understanding of what the company sees as the critical SWOT elements.)

The Industry Analysis section provides the backdrop for the subsequent, more detailed analysis of competition, the company, and the company's customers. Without an in-depth understanding of the industry, the remaining analysis may be misdirected. See Chapter 2.

Even though relatively brief, this in-depth treatment of the Spicy Southwestern/Mexican food industry in the United States demonstrates to the plan's readers the company's understanding of the industry in which it competes. It gives both external and internal readers confidence that the company thoroughly understands its own industry.

This summary of sales in the Southwestern/Mexican product category shows it is significant and provides a variety of future opportunities for Paradise Kitchens.

the Company's favor internally are its strengths of an experienced management team and board of directors, excellent acceptance of its lines in the three metropolitan markets in which it competes, and a strong manufacturing and distribution system to serve these limited markets. Favorable external factors (opportunities) include the increasing appeal of Southwestern/Mexican foods, the strength of the upscale market for the Company's products, and food-processing technological breakthroughs that make it easier for smaller food producers to compete.

These favorable factors must be balanced against unfavorable ones, the main weakness being the limited size of Paradise Kitchens relative to its competitors in terms of the depth of the management team, available financial resources, and national awareness and distribution of product lines. Threats include the potential danger that the Company's premium prices may limit access to mass markets, no legal patent protection for its foods (although it has registered its Howlin' Coyote® brand), and competition from the "eating-out" and "take-out" markets.

Industry Analysis: Trends in Spicy and Mexican Foods

In the past 10 years, hot-spice consumption has doubled in U.S. households. Currently, Mexican food and ingredients are used in 46 percent of American households. Burritos, enchiladas, and taco dinner kits, which had insignificant numbers in 1981, reached 7 percent to 16 percent of American households in 1992.

These trends reflect a generally more favorable attitude toward spicy foods on the part of Americans. Total spice consumption increased 50 percent from 1983 to 1993, according to the American Spice Trade Association. The retail grocery market for Mexican foods (excluding tortilla chips) was more than $4 billion in annual sales in 1994. The Southwestern/Mexican market includes the foods shown in Figure 2.

Figure 2.   Foods Included in the Southwestern/Mexican Product Category

Food	1994 U.S. Sales ($1,000,000)	% Change from 1993 to 1994
Dry chili mix	$121	6.0%
Canned chili	578	2.3
Salsa and sauces	1,438	10.3
Mexican frozen	602	4.5
Mexican foods canned	353	4.4
Peppers	242	2.5
Chilies	90	0.3
Mexican foods dry	1,259	5.3
Total	$4,681	6.0%

As with the Industry Analysis, the Competitors Analysis demonstrates that the company has a realistic understanding of who its major competitors are and what their marketing strategies are. Again, a realistic assessment gives confidence to both internal and external readers that subsequent marketing actions in the plan rest on a solid foundation. See Chapters 2, 3, and 8.

This page uses a "block" style and does *not* indent each paragraph, although an extra space separates each paragraph. Compare this page with page 65, which has indented paragraphs. Most readers find indented paragraphs in marketing plans and long reports are easier to follow.

Paradise Kitchens addresses the issue of the difficulty and unlikelihood of competitors jumping easily into this niche market.

The Company Analysis provides details of the company's strengths and marketing strategies that will enable it to achieve the mission, vision, and goals identified earlier. See Chapters 2, 8, and 22.

Competitors in Southwestern/Mexican Market

The chili market represents $699 million in annual sales. The products fall primarily into two groups: canned chili (81 percent of sales) and dry chili (17 percent of sales). The remaining 2 percent of sales go to frozen chili products. Besides Howlin' Coyote®, Stouffers and Marie Callender's offer frozen chilies as part of their broad line of frozen dinners and entrees. Major canned chili brands include Hormel, Wolf, Dennison, Stagg, Chili Man, and Castleberry's. Their retail prices range from $1.09 to $1.49.

Bluntly put, the major disadvantage of the segment's dominant product, canned chili, is that it does not taste very good. A taste test described in the October 1990 issue of *Consumer Reports* magazine ranked 26 canned chili products "poor" to "fair" in overall sensory quality. The study concluded, "Chili doesn't have to be hot to be good. But really good chili, hot or mild, doesn't come out of a can."

Dry mix brands include such familiar spice brands as Lawry's, McCormick, French's, and Durkee, along with smaller offerings such as Wick Fowler's and Carroll Shelby's. Their retail prices range from $1.79 to $1.99. The *Consumer Reports* study was more favorable about dry chili mixes, ranking them from "fair" to "very good." The magazine recommended, "If you want good chili, make it with fresh ingredients and one of the seasoning mixes we tested." A major drawback of dry mixes is that they require the preparers to add their own meat, beans, and tomatoes and take more preparation time than canned or frozen chilies.

The *Consumer Reports* study did not include the frozen chili entrees from Stouffer's or Marie Callender's (Howlin' Coyote® was not yet on the market at the time of the test). However, it is fair to say that these products—consisting of ground beef, chili beans, and tomato sauce—are of average quality. Furthermore, they are not singled out for special marketing or promotional programs by their manufacturers. Marie Callender's retails for $2.97, and Stouffer's retails for under $2.00.

While it is feasible for another food company to match Howlin' Coyote® and create a similar product, no known current companies are in a position to quickly match the offerings. Small companies face technical capacity issues. Large companies view the products as too much outside the mainstream of frozen-food retailing to be attracted to the market, at least initially.

Company Analysis

The husband-and-wife team that cofounded Paradise Kitchens, Inc. in 1989 has 38 years of experience between them in the food-processing business. Both have played key roles in the management of the Pillsbury Company. They are being advised by a highly seasoned group of business professionals, who have extensive understanding of the requirements for new product development.

This "introductory overview" sentence tells the reader the topics covered in the section—in this case customer characteristics and health and nutrition concerns. While this sentence may be omitted in short memos or plans, it helps readers see where the text is leading. These sentences are used throughout this plan. This textbook also generally utilizes these introductory overview sentences to aid your comprehension.

The higher-level "A heading" of Customer Analysis has a more dominant typeface and position than the lower-level "B heading" of Customer Characteristics. These headings introduce the reader to the sequence and level of topics covered. The organization of this textbook uses this kind of structure and headings.

Satisfying customers and providing genuine value to them is why organizations exist in a market economy. This section addresses the question of "Who are the customers for Paradise Kitchens's products?" See Chapters 5, 6, 7, and 8.

Currently, Howlin' Coyote® products compete in the chili and Mexican frozen entree segments of the Southwestern/Mexican food market. While the chili obviously competes as a stand-alone product, its exceptional quality means it can complement such dishes as burritos, nachos, and enchiladas and can be readily used as a smothering sauce for pasta, rice, or potatoes. This flexibility of use is relatively rare in the prepared food marketplace.

In its growth strategy, Howlin' Coyote® is retracing a path taken by such enterprising food companies as Snapple Beverages, Celestial Seasonings, and Tombstone Pizza. These companies all broke from the pack of their respective categories and established a new approach. Snapple showed that iced tea and fruit drinks can be fun and highly variable. Celestial Seasonings made tea into a "lifestyle" drink. Tombstone Pizza moved frozen pizza upscale in taste and price, creating the first alternative to "cardboard" home pizzas. Likewise, with Howlin' Coyote® Paradise Kitchens is broadening the position of frozen chili in a way that can lead to impressive market share for the new product category.

The Company now uses a single outside producer with which it works closely to maintain the consistently high quality required in its products. The greater volume has increased production efficiencies, resulting in a steady decrease in the cost of goods sold.

Customer Analysis

In terms of customer analysis, this section describes (1) the characteristics of customers expected to buy Howlin' Coyote® products and (2) health and nutrition concerns of Americans today.

Customer Characteristics. Demographically, chili products in general are purchased by consumers representing a broad range of socioeconomic backgrounds. Howlin' Coyote® chili is purchased chiefly by consumers who have achieved higher levels of education and whose income is $30,000 and higher. These consumers represent 57 percent of canned and dry mix chili users.

The five Howlin' Coyote® entrees offer a quick, tasty meal with high-quality ingredients.

This section demonstrates the company's insights into a major trend that has a potentially large impact.

The household buying Howlin' Coyote® has one to three people in it. Among married couples, Howlin' Coyote® is predominantly bought by households in which both spouses work. While women are a majority of the buyers, single men represent a significant segment. Anecdotally, Howlin' Coyote® has heard from fathers of teenaged boys who say they keep a freezer stocked with the chili because the boys devour it.

Because the chili offers a quick way to make a tasty meal, the product's biggest users tend to be those most pressed for time. Howlin' Coyote®'s premium pricing also means that its purchasers are skewed toward the higher end of the income range. Buyers range in age form 25 to 55. Because consumers in the western United States have adopted spicy foods more readily than the rest of the country, Howlin' Coyote®'s initial marketing expansion efforts will be concentrated in that region.

Health and Nutrition Concerns. Coverage of food issues in the U.S. media is often erratic and occasionally alarmist. Because Americans are concerned about their diets, studies from organizations of widely varying credibility frequently receive significant attention from the major news organizations. For instance, a study of fat levels of movie popcorn was reported in all the major media. Similarly, studies on the healthfulness of Mexican food have received prominent "play" in print and broadcast reports. The high caloric levels of much Mexican and Southwestern-style food had been widely reported and often exaggerated.

Less certain is the link between these reports and consumer buying behavior. Most indications are that while Americans are well-versed in dietary matters, they are not significantly changing their eating patterns. The experience of other food manufacturers is that Americans expect certain foods to be high in calories and are not drawn to those that claim to be low-calorie versions. Low-fat frozen pizza was a flop. Therefore, while Howlin' Coyote® is already lower in calories, fat, and sodium than its competitors, those qualities are not being stressed in its promotions. Instead, in the space and time available for promotions, Howlin' Coyote®'s taste, convenience, and flexibility are stressed.

Size of headings should give a professional look to the report and not overwhelm the reader. These two headings are too large.

5. Market-Product Focus

This section describes the five-year marketing and product objectives for Paradise Kitchens and the target markets, points of difference, and positioning of its lines of Howlin' Coyote® chilies.

Marketing and Product Objectives

Howlin' Coyote®'s marketing intent is to take full advantage of its brand potential

As noted in Chapter 11, the chances of success for a new product are significantly increased if objectives are set for the product itself and if target market segments are identified for it. This section makes these explicit for Paradise Kitchens. The objectives also serve as the planned targets against which marketing activities are measured in program implementation and control.

A heading should be spaced closer to the text that follows (and that it describes) than the preceding section to avoid confusion for the reader. This rule is *not* followed for the "Target Markets" heading, which now unfortunately appears to "float" between the preceding and following paragraphs.

This section identifies the specific niches or target markets toward which the company's products are directed. When appropriate and when space permits, this section often includes a market-product grid. See Chapter 9.

while building a base from which other revenues sources can be mined—both in and out of the retail grocery business. These are detailed in four areas below:

- Current markets. Current markets will be grown by expanding brand and flavor distribution at the retail level. In addition, same-store sales will be grown by increasing consumer awareness and repeat purchases. With this increase in same-store sales, the more desirable broker/warehouse distribution channel will become available, increasing efficiency and saving costs.

- New markets. By the end of Year 5, the chili and salsa business will be expanded to a total of 20 metropolitan areas. This will represent 55 percent of U.S. food store sales.

- Food service. Food service sales will include chili products and smothering sauces. Sales are expected to reach $580,000 by the end of Year 3 and $1.2 million by the end of Year 5.

- New products. Howlin' Coyote®'s brand presence will be expanded at the retail level through the addition of new products in the frozen-foods section. This will be accomplished through new product concept screening in Year 1 to identify new potential products. These products will be brought to market in Years 2 and 3. Additionally, the brand may be licensed in select categories.

Target Markets

The primary target market for Howlin' Coyote® products is households with one to three people, where often both adults work, with individual income typically above $30,000 per year. These households contain more experienced, adventurous consumers of Southwestern/Mexican food and want premium quality products.

To help buyers see the many different uses for Howlin' Coyote® chili, recipes are even printed on the *inside* of the packages.

An organization cannot grow by offering only "me-too products." The greatest single factor in a new product's failure is the lack of significant "points of difference" that sets it apart form competitors' substitutes. This section makes these points of difference explicit. See Chapter 11.

A positioning strategy helps communicate the company's unique points of difference of its products to prospective customers in a simple, clear way. This section describes this positioning. See Chapters 9 and 11.

Everything that has gone before in the marketing plan sets the stage for the marketing mix actions—the 4 Ps—covered in the marketing program. See Chapters 11 through 21.

This section describes in detail three key elements of the company's product strategy: the product line, its quality and how this is achieved, and its "cutting edge" packaging. See Chapters 11, 12, and 13.

Points of Difference

The "points of difference"—characteristics that make Howlin' Coyote® chilies unique relative to competitors—fall into three important areas:

- Unique taste and convenience. No known competitor offers a high-quality, "authentic" frozen chili in a range of flavors. And no existing chili has the same combination of quick preparation and home-style taste.

- Taste trends. The American palate is increasingly intrigued by hot spices, and Howlin' Coyote® brands offer more "kick" than most other prepared chilies.

- Premium packaging. Howlin' Coyote®'s high-value packaging graphics convey the unique, high-quality product contained inside and the product's nontraditional positioning.

Positioning

In the past chili products have been either convenient or tasty, but not both. Howlin' Coyote® pairs these two desirable characteristics to obtain a positioning in consumers' minds as very high-quality "authentic Southwestern/Mexican tasting" chilies that can be prepared easily and quickly.

6. Marketing Program

The four marketing mix elements of the Howlin' Coyote® chili marketing program are detailed below. Note that "chile" is the vegetable and "chili" is the dish.

Product Strategy

After first summarizing the product line, the approach to product quality and packaging are covered.

Product Line. Howlin' Coyote® chili, retailing for $2.89 for a 10- or 11.5-ounce serving, is available in five flavors. The five are:

- Green Chile Chili: braised extra-lean pork with fire-roasted green chilies, onions, tomato chunks, bold spices, and jalapeno peppers, based on a Southwestern favorite.

- Red Chile Chili: extra-lean cubed pork, deep-red acho chilies, and sweet onions; known as the "Texas Bowl of Red."

- Beef and Black Bean Chili: lean braised beef with black beans, tomato chunks, and Howlin' Coyote®'s own blend of red chilies and authentic spicing.

Using parallel structure, this bulleted list presents the product line efficiently and crisply.

- Chicken Chunk Chili: hearty chunks of tender chicken, fire-roasted green chilies, black beans, pinto beans, diced onions, and zesty spices.

- Mean Bean Chili: vegetarian, with nine distinctive bean varieties and fire-roasted green chilies, tomato chunks, onion, and a robust blend of spices and rich red chilies.

Unique Product Quality. The flavoring systems of the Howlin' Coyote® chilies are proprietary. The products' tastiness is due to extra care lavished upon the ingredients during production. The ingredients used are of unusually high quality. Meats are low-fat cuts and are fresh, not frozen, to preserve cell structure and moistness. Chilies are fire-roasted for fresher taste, not the canned variety used by more mainstream products. Tomatoes and vegetables are select quality. No preservatives or artificial flavors are used.

Packaging. Reflecting the "cutting edge" marketing strategy of its producers, Howlin' Coyote® bucks conventional wisdom in packaging. It avoids placing predictable photographs of the product on its containers. (Head to any grocer's freezer and you will be hardpressed to find a product that does not feature a heavily stylized photograph of the contents.) Instead, Howlin' Coyote®'s package shows a Southwestern motif that communicates the product's out-of-the-ordinary positioning. This approach signals the product's nontraditional qualities: "adventurous" eating with minimal fuss—a frozen meal for people who do not normally enjoy frozen meals.

A brief caption on photos and sample ads ties them to the text and highlights the reason for being included.

This Price Strategy section makes the company's price point very clear, along with its price position relative to potential substitutes. When appropriate and when space permits, this section might contain a break-even analysis. See Chapters 14 and 15.

The Southwestern motif makes Howlin' Coyote®'s packages stand out in a supermarket's freezer case.

Price Strategy

Howlin' Coyote® Chili is, at $2.89 or a 10- to 11.5-ounce package, priced comparably to the other frozen offerings and higher than the canned and dried chili varieties. However, the significant taste advantages it has over canned chilies and the convenience advantages over dried chilies justify this pricing strategy.

Elements of the Promotion Strategy are highlighted here with B-headings in terms of the three key promotional activities the company is emphasizing for its product line: in-store demonstrations, recipes featuring its Howlin' Coyote® chilies, and cents-off coupons. See Chapters 19, 20, and 21.

Photos or sample ads can illustrate key points effectively, even if they are not in color as they appear here.

<u>Promotion Strategy</u>

Key promotion programs feature in-store demonstrations, recipes, and cents-off coupons.

In-Store Demonstrations. In-store demonstrations will be conducted to give consumers a chance to try Howlin' Coyote® products and learn about their unique qualities. Demos will be conducted regularly in all markets to increase awareness and trial purchases.

Recipes. Because the products' flexibility of use is a key selling point, recipes will be offered to consumers to stimulate use. The recipes will be given at all in-store demonstrations, on the back of packages, and through a mail-in recipe book offer. In addition, recipes will be included in coupons sent by direct-mail or free-standing inserts. For new markets, recipes will be included on in-pack coupon inserts.

Cents-Off Coupons. To generate trial and repeat-purchase of Howlin' Coyote® products, coupons will be distributed in four ways:

- In Sunday newspaper inserts. Inserts are highly read and will help generate awareness. Coupled with in-store demonstrations, this has been a very successful technique so far.

Sunday newspaper inserts encourage consumer trial and provide recipes to show how Howlin' Coyote® chili can be used in summer meals.

Another bulleted list adds many details for the reader, including methods of gaining customer awareness, trial, and repeat purchases as Howlin' Coyote® enters new metropolitan areas. The lack of a space between bulleted items makes it more difficult reading for some readers compared to, say, the bulleted list on page 67.

The Place Strategy is described here in terms of both (1) the present method and (2) the new one to be used when the increased sales volume makes it feasible. See Chapters 16, 17, and 18.

All the marketing mix decisions covered in the just-described marketing program have both revenue and expense effects. These are summarized in this section of the marketing plan. See Appendix B.

Note that this section contains no introductory overview sentence. While the sentence is not essential, many readers prefer to see it to avoid the abrupt start with Past Sales Revenues.

The graph shows more clearly the dramatic growth of sales revenue than data in a table would do.

- In-pack coupons. Inside each box of Howlin' Coyote® chili will be coupons for $1 off two more packages of the chili. These coupons will be included for the first three months the product is shipped to a new market. Doing so encourages repeat purchases by new users.
- Direct-mail chili coupons. Those households that fit the Howlin' Coyote® demographics described above will be mailed coupons. This is likely to be an efficient promotion due to its greater audience selectivity.
- In-store demonstrations. Coupons will be passed out at in-store demonstrations to give an additional incentive to purchase.

Place (Distribution) Strategy

Howlin' Coyote® is distributed in its present markets through a food distributor. The distributor buys the product, warehouses it, and then resells and delivers it to grocery retailers on a store-by-store basis. This is typical for products that have moderate sales—compared with, say, staples like milk or bread. As sales grow, we will shift to a more efficient system using a broker who sells the products to retail chains and grocery wholesalers.

7. Financial Data and Projections

Past Sales Revenues

Historically, Howlin' Coyote® has had a steady increase in sales revenues since its introduction in 1990. In 1994, sales jumped spectacularly, due largely to new promotion strategies and the opportunities represented by the products' expansion to Western markets. The trend in sales revenues appears in Figure 3.

Figure 3.   Sales Revenues for Paradise Kitchens, Inc.

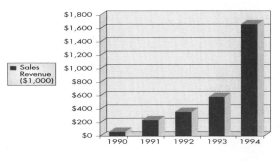

One key indicator of what future sales will be is to look at what past sales have been. Paradise Kitchens is justifiably proud of the dramatic growth in its past sales revenues and highlights this information.

Because this table is very short, it is woven into the text, rather than given a figure number and title.

Because the plan proposes to enter 17 new metropolitan markets in the coming five years (for a total of 20), it is not possible to simply extrapolate the trend in Figure 3. Instead, management's judgment must be used. Methods of making sales forecasts—including the "lost horse" technique used here—are discussed in Chapter 10.

The Five-Year Financial Projections section starts with the judgment forecast of cases sold and the resulting net sales. Gross profit and then operating profit—critical for the company's survival—are projected and show the company passes break-even and becomes profitable in Year 2. An actual plan often contains many pages of computer-generated spreadsheet projections, usually shown in an appendix to the plan.

During the five years since their introduction, Howlin' Coyote® chilies have achieved sales growth of 80 percent annually. New sales-promotion techniques have been so effective that 1994 sales have more than tripled those of 1993.

<u>Five–Year Projections</u>

Five–year financial projections for Paradise Kitchens appear below:

Financial Element	Units	Year 1 1996	Year 2 1997	Year 3 1998	Year 4 1999	Year 5 2000
Cases sold	1,000	195	353	684	889	1,249
Net sales	$1,000	2,832	5,123	9,913	12,884	18,111
Gross profit	$1,000	936	2,545	4,820	6,257	8,831
Operating profit (loss)	$1,000	(423)	339	985	2,096	2,805

These projections reflect the continuing growth in number of cases sold (with 8 packages of Howlin' Coyote® chili per case) and increasing production and distribution economies of scale as sales volume increases.

8. Organization

Paradise Kitchens's present organization appears in Figure 4. It shows the four people reporting to the President. Below this level are both the full-time and part-time employees of the Company.

At present Paradise Kitchens operates with full-time employees in only essential positions. It now augments its full-time staff with key advisors, consultants, and subcontractors. As the firm grows, people with special expertise will be added to the staff.

Figure 4.   The Paradise Kitchens Organization

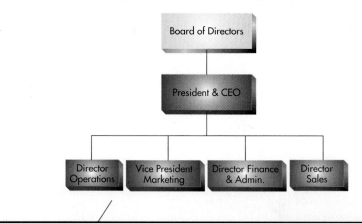

The Organization of Paradise Kitchens appears here. It reflects the bare-bones organizational structure of successful small businesses. Often a more elaborate marketing plan will show the new positions expected to be added as the firm grows. See Chapter 22.

The Implementation Plan shows how the company will turn plans into results. Gantt charts are often used to set deadlines and assign responsibilities for the many tactical marketing decisions needed to enter a new market. See Chapter 22.

The essence of Evaluation and Control is comparing actual sales with the targeted values set in the plan and taking appropriate actions. Note that the section briefly describes a contingency plan for alternative actions, depending on how successful the entry into a new market turns out to be. See Chapter 22.

Various appendixes may appear at the end of the plan, depending on the purpose and audience for them. For example, resumes of key personnel or detailed financial spreadsheets often appear in an appendix.

9. Implementation Plan

Introducing Howlin' Coyote® chilies to new metropolitan areas is a complex task and requires that creative promotional activities gain consumer awareness and initial trial among the target market households identified earlier. The anticipated rollout schedule to enter these metropolitan markets appears in Figure 5.

Figure 5.   Rollout Schedule to Enter New U.S. Markets

Year	New Markets Added	Cumulative Markets	Cumulative Percentage of U.S. Market
Today (1995)	0	3	7
Year 1 (1996)	1	4	10
Year 2 (1997)	2	6	18
Year 3 (1998)	3	9	28
Year 4 (1999)	4	13	39
Year 5 (2000)	7	20	55

10. Evaluation and Control

Monthly sales targets in cases have been set for Howlin' Coyote® chili for each metropolitan area. Actual case sales will be compared with these targets and tactical marketing programs modified to reflect the unique sets of factors in each metropolitan area. The speed of the roll-out program may increase or decrease, depending on the Paradise Kitchens's performance in the successive metropolitan markets it enters.

CHAPTER 3

The Changing Marketing Environment

AFTER READING THIS CHAPTER YOU SHOULD BE ABLE TO:

• Understand how environmental scanning provides information about social, economic, technological, competitive, and regulatory forces.

• Explain how social forces such as demographics and culture and economic forces such as macroeconomic conditions and consumer income affect marketing.

• Describe how technological changes and their ecological impacts can affect marketing.

• Understand the competitive structures that exist in a market, the role of marketing within each, and key components of competition.

• Explain the major legislation that ensures competition and regulates the elements of the marketing mix.

NEXT UP . . . GENERATION X-CELLENT

What do Michael Dell, Winona Ryder, Ethan Hawke, and 44 million 19 to 30 year olds (including you?) have in common? They are all members of the so-called Generation X—a group of consumers who spend more than $125 billion each year on computers, entertainment, economical and functional clothing, and leisure activities; who use pagers, fax machines, answering machines, and E-mail as necessities; and who may be the most educated and entrepreneurial workers in history. They are also likely to displace older generations, such as the baby boomers, as the primary influence on popular culture.

Generation X is shaping the future in many ways. They are increasingly interested in visual images rather than written words. They are closer to their parents than any previous generation, and they are delaying marriage until their education is complete and a career has been established. In addition, they readily accept racial and sexual diversity. All of these characteristics are likely to translate into a future with new lifestyles, new purchase decision approaches, and new product and service preferences.

Recognition of these changes is altering the marketplace. Because Generation X dislikes any form of hype, for example, advertisers are developing campaigns with less overstatement. Active-wear company No Fear took this idea to an extreme when it ran an ad during the Super Bowl that did not mention what the company sells. Other changes include new products and services designed for practical use rather than image or status. Small, economical automobiles such as the Geo Metro and the Chrysler Neon were some of the first offerings on the market and are already popular with Generation X.[1]

Generation X is clearly changing the marketing environment. It represents a demographic shift, an economic influence, and a force likely to increase the use of technology. Anticipating changes such as these and responding to them often means the difference between marketing success and failure. This chapter describes how the marketing environment has changed in the past and is likely to change in the future.

ENVIRONMENTAL SCANNING IN THE 1990s

Changes in the business and marketing environment are a source of opportunities and threats to be managed. The process of continually acquiring information on events occurring outside the organization in order to identify and interpret potential trends is called **environmental scanning.**

Tracking Environmental Trends

Environmental trends typically arise from five sources: social, economic, technological, competitive, and regulatory forces. As shown in Figure 3–1 and described later in this chapter, these forces affect the marketing activities of a firm in numerous ways.
To illustrate how environmental scanning is used, consider the following trend:[2]

> Coffee industry marketers have observed that the percentage of adults who drink coffee at home has declined from 83 percent in 1985 to 75 percent in 1994. Age-specific analysis indicates that coffee consumption declined among all age groups, including 18 to 24 year olds, despite the perception that young adults are leading a revival in coffee drinking.

What types of businesses are likely to be influenced by this trend? What future would you predict for coffee?
You may have concluded that this trend is likely to influence coffee manufacturers and supermarkets. If so, you are absolutely correct—manufacturers have responded by offering new flavors, and supermarkets have added coffee boutiques to try to reverse the trend. Predicting the future of coffee requires assumptions about the number of years the declining trend will continue and the rate of decline in various age groups. Did you consider these issues in your analysis? Since experts make

FIGURE 3-1

Environmental forces affecting the organization, as well as its suppliers and customers

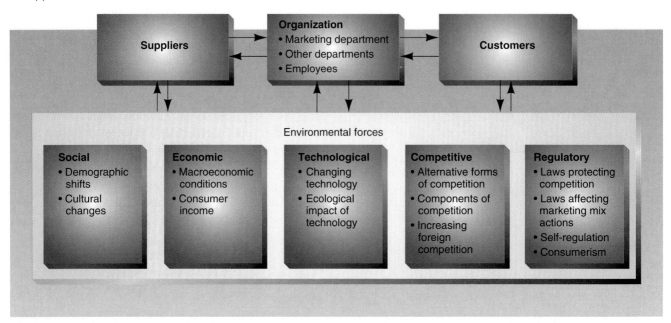

different assumptions, their forecasts range from a 30 percent decline to a 13 percent increase by 2005—a range that probably includes your forecast!

Environmental scanning also involves explaining trends. Why has coffee consumption been declining? One explanation is that consumers are switching from coffee to other beverages such as soft drinks, juices, or water. Another explanation is that preferences have shifted to better-tasting but more expensive types of coffee, and consumers have reduced their use to maintain the same level of expenditure. Identifying and interpreting trends, such as the decline in coffee consumption, and developing explanations, such as those offered in this paragraph, are essential to successful environmental scanning.

An Environmental Scan of the 1990s

What other trends might affect marketing in the 1990s? A firm conducting an environmental scan of the United States might uncover key trends such as those listed in Figure 3–2 for each of the five environmental factors. Although the list of trends is far from complete, it reveals the breadth of an environmental scan—from identifying consumers' new "do-it-yourself" attitudes and their growing desire for improved product quality and customer service to breakthroughs in information technology and competitive changes due to the restructuring of American corporations. These trends affect consumers and the businesses and nonprofit organizations that serve them. Trends such as these are covered as the five environmental forces are described in the following pages.

SOCIAL FORCES

The **social forces** of the environment include the characteristics of the population, its income, and its values. Changes in these forces can have a dramatic impact on marketing strategy.

FIGURE 3–2

An environmental scan of the United States

ENVIRONMENTAL FORCE	TREND IDENTIFIED BY AN ENVIRONMENTAL SCAN
Social	• Movement toward self-reliance and a "do-it-yourself" philosophy • Growing number and importance of older Americans • Continuing U.S. population shifts to South and West • Greater desire for product quality and customer service
Economic	• Growing concern over the U.S. budget deficit • More U.S. firms will look to foreign markets for growth • Stagnation of real per capita income of Americans • Increasing consumer debt
Technological	• Increased use of information and communication technology • Major breakthroughs in biotechnology • More problems with pollution and solid and nuclear wastes • Growing use of electronic money or "E-cash"
Competitive	• More employment in small, innovative firms • Downsizing and restructuring of many corporations • Mergers will reduce costs through economies of scale • More international competition from Europe and Asia
Regulatory	• Less regulation of U.S. firms competing in international markets • New requirements for electric cars and alternative forms of transportation • Greater concern for ethics and social responsibility in business • Renewed emphasis on self-regulation

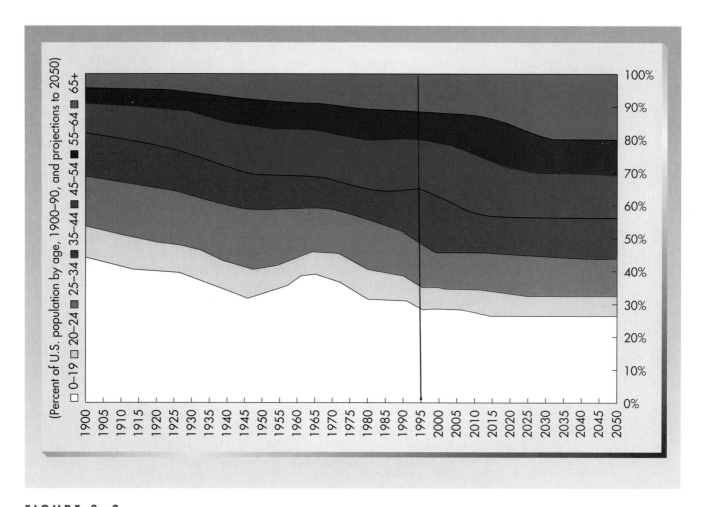

FIGURE 3-3

The changing age distribution of the U.S. population

Demographics

Describing the population according to selected characteristics such as their age, sex, ethnicity, income, and occupation is referred to as **demographics.**

The population trend   In 1995, the U.S. population was forecast to be slightly more than 262 million people. While the number of people ages 18 to 34 has declined since 1990, the number over 65 increased. These observations suggest a significant demographic trend—the graying of America. In 1960, only 9 percent of the population was over age 65; by 1995, this percentage had increased to 13 percent.[3]

The age distribution of America's population is changing (as shown in Figure 3–3) and successful companies must respond to this change. In recent years, greater marketing attention has been focused on the **mature household.** Such households are headed by people over 50 years old, who represent the fastest-growing age segment in the population. In 1990 this group represented 28 percent of the population, but this percentage will climb to 34 percent by the year 2010 and to 38 percent by 2025.[4] People over 50 control 75 percent of the net worth of U.S. households, and the over-50 category includes the period (between ages 55 and 60) when a person's income peaks.

Environmental scanning of this trend has led some companies to already begin responding to this important market. AT&T has developed products aimed at seniors, such as emergency dialing mechanisms and amplifiers. The Marriott hotel chain has

Shouldn't you live some part of your   life exactly as you please?

Club Med
Life as it should be™

Club Med promotes family vacations to aging baby boomers.

built high-rise retirement communities. General Foods uses older celebrities in its ads, such as Lena Horne for Post Bran Flakes. Beecham Products USA uses larger type on its product labels. And the demand for anti-aging products and services will grow. Johnson & Johnson, makers of Retin-A (an anti-aging lotion originally designed for treatment of pimples), found that sales of Retin-A more than tripled when consumers learned of its wrinkle reduction potential.[5]

The baby boom, Generation X and the baby boomlet   A major reason for the graying of America is that the **baby boomers**—the generation of children born between 1946 and 1965—are growing up. As the 78 million boomers have aged, their participation in the workforce and their earnings have increased, making them an important consumer market. It has been estimated that this group accounts for 56 to 58 percent of the purchases in most consumer product and service categories. In the future, their buying behavior will change to reflect greater concern for their children's future and their own retirement. Saving and financial planning will become more important concerns, and attention to quality and value will replace the focus on indulgence and luxury.[6] Companies such as Club Med and Lee jeans are refocusing their strategies to a more mature market. Club Med is trying to augment its singles image by promoting family vacations and facilities with child care in addition to vacations that cater to singles and couples, and Lee is responding to an aging baby boomer with loose-fitting jeans and advertising, "You're not a kid anymore."[7]

Generation X includes the 17 percent of the U.S. population born between 1966 and 1976. It is a generation of consumers who are not prone to extravagance and are likely to pursue lifestyles and prefer products and services that are very different from baby boomers. They are also likely to be more demanding consumers. As mentioned in the chapter opening example, marketers are now tracking this generation to identify the dominant consumption values of the 21st century.[8]

The **baby boomlet** refers to the 72 million Americans born in 1977 and later. As children, the boomlet generation already exerts influence on music, sports, computers, and video game purchases. Later in the 21st century, this group will influence markets, attitudes, and society—much like the baby boomers do now and Generation X will do soon.[9]

Because the members of each generation are distinctive in their attitudes and consumer behavior, marketers have been studying the many groups or cohorts that make up the marketplace. The Marketing NewsNet box on the next page describes seven generations that are often target markets in the United States.[10]

The American family   As the population profile has changed, so has the structure of the American family. Twenty-five years ago 40 percent of all households

MARKETING NEWSNET

TALKING ABOUT YOUR GENERATION

Businesses have discovered that they can grow bigger by targeting smaller—smaller groups of consumers that is. These groups are increasingly defined as a generation or cohort related to important life experiences. The reason is that events occurring when people first become economic adults (usually between ages 17 and 21) affect their lifelong attitudes and values. These attitudes and values are unlikely to change as a person ages. So the kind of

music that is popular during these formative years often remains the preferred type of music for life. Similarly, early lifetime experiences influence preferences in many other product and service categories.

Studies of the U.S. population have identified seven distinct groups described in the table below. Which generation are you? Your parents?

COHORT	DESCRIPTION	BORN	FAVORITE MUSIC
The Depression cohort	The G.I. generation	1912–1921	Big band
The World War II cohort	The Depression generation	1922–1927	Swing
The Postwar cohort	The silent generation	1928–1945	Frank Sinatra
The Boomers I cohort	The Woodstock generation	1946–1954	Rock and roll
The Boomers II cohort	The zoomer generation	1955–1965	Rock and roll
The Generation X cohort	The baby-buster generation	1966–1976	Grunge, rap, retro
The Boomlet cohort	The echo-boom generation	1977–	???

consisted of married couples with children. Today, that type of household is just 26 percent of the population. Nearly one fourth of all households now consist of people who live alone, while another 29 percent are married without children. The three fastest growing types of households are those with single parents, other family members, and unrelated persons.[11]

About 50 percent of all first marriages now end in divorce. The majority of divorced people eventually remarry, which has given rise to the **blended family,** one formed by the merging into a single household of two previously separated units. Today, one of every three Americans is now a stepparent, stepchild, stepsibling, or some other member of a blended family. Hallmark Cards, Inc. now has specially designed cards and verses for blended families.[12]

Population shifts A major regional shift in the U.S. population toward Western and Sunbelt states occurred in the 1980s. During the period 1990 to 1995, the states of Washington, Idaho, Utah, Colorado, Nevada, and Hawaii grew the fastest, while Massachusetts, Connecticut, Rhode Island, and North Dakota recorded losses in population. California recorded its first period of domestic out-migration, losing 1.1

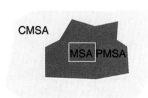

million more residents than it gained from other states, while Florida led the nation with a net gain of 640,000 in-migrants.[13]

In recent decades, people have also moved from rural areas to major cities and their suburbs. Marketers, therefore, focus on population centers, where about three fourths of the population lives. To assist marketers in gathering data on population centers, the government has a three-level classification system that reflects their degree of urbanization. From largest to smallest, these three areas are the consolidated metropolitan statistical area (CMSA), primary metropolitan statistical area (PMSA), and metropolitan statistical area (MSA), as shown in the margin and described here:

- *Consolidated metropolitan statistical area (CMSA).* The largest designation in terms of geographical area and market size. It is made up of component PMSAs, defined next, that total at least 1 million people.
- *Primary metropolitan statistical area (PMSA).* An area that is part of a larger CMSA that has a total population of 1 million or more. It must also contain counties that conform to the following standards: (1) a total population of at least 100,000, (2) a population that is at least 60 percent urban, and (3) fewer than 50 percent of the resident workers commute to jobs outside the county.
- *Metropolitan statistical area (MSA).* (1) A city having a population of at least 50,000 or (2) an urbanized area with a population in excess of 50,000, with a total metropolitan population of at least 100,000. An MSA may include counties that have close economic and social ties to the central county.

Racial and ethnic diversity   A notable trend is the changing racial and ethnic composition of the U.S population (see Figure 3–4).[14] Slightly more than one in four U.S. residents is African-American, Hispanic, Asian, or a representative of another racial or ethnic group. Diversity is further evident in the variety of peoples that make up these groups. For example, Asians consist of Chinese, Japanese, Filipinos, Koreans, Asian-Indians, people from Southeast Asia, and Pacific Islanders. Hispanics are represented by Mexicans, Puerto Ricans, Cubans, and others of Central and South American ancestry.

The racial and ethnic composition of the U.S. population is expected to change even more by 2000. From 1985 to 2000 the Hispanic and Asian populations are expected to grow by 48 percent each, the African-American population will grow by 28 percent, and the white population by only 6 percent. When one considers that 38 percent of children in the United States will be African-American, Hispanic, or Asian by 2010, the long-term consequences of their buying patterns must be understood.

FIGURE 3–4

Racial and ethnic composition and trends of the United States

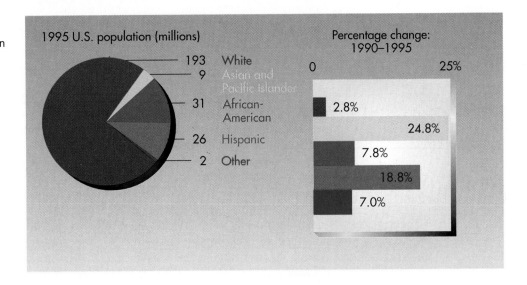

Marketers who recognize and respond to diversity in the U.S. population will be rewarded for their efforts because consumer needs will be better satisfied. The unique purchasing patterns of different racial and ethnic groups are highlighted in Chapter 6.

Regional marketing A new trend within marketing focuses not only on the shifting of consumers geographically but also on the differences in their product preferences based on where they live. This concept has been referred to as **regional marketing,** which is developing marketing plans to reflect specific area differences in taste preferences, perceived needs, or interests. For example, Procter & Gamble observed that vacuum brick-packs of coffee were relatively more popular than cans in the South. The company repackaged their Folgers brand coffee for those markets and developed a new advertising campaign. Sales of Folgers coffee increased 32 percent in the targeted markets.[15] In Chapter 9, you will learn more about this approach to the market referred to as *geographical segmentation.*

Technology has aided marketers to begin to understand the variations of regional preferences. Computerized cash registers have allowed companies to collect and analyze large amounts of sales data for geographical units as small as neighborhoods. Scott Paper found that their paper towels had a 47.7 percent share in Chicago yet only a 2.5 percent share in Los Angeles.[16] And, with advances in direct marketing approaches (described in Chapters 10 and 18), this focus on regional marketing allows a better targeting of ads and products. Ideally, Scott Paper can now create a specific campaign for their heavy users in Chicago and develop a marketing strategy to encourage new purchases in Los Angeles.

Because several ethnic groups are geographically concentrated, ethnic marketing is an increasingly important part of regional marketing. Consider, for example, that 56 percent of U.S. Asians live in California, New York, and Hawaii and that two thirds of Hispanics live in Florida, Texas, and California. Saturn combined ethnic and regional marketing by running a Spanish-language advertising campaign, using a testimonial from San Antonio, Texas, firefighter Ernest Imperial, in Texas and California. The ads were not used in Florida, where more than 55 percent of the Hispanic population is Cuban—a group for which a different Hispanic dialect was needed.[17]

Culture

A second social force, **culture,** incorporates the set of values, ideas, and attitudes of a homogeneous group of people that are transmitted from one generation to the next. Culture includes both material and abstract elements, so monitoring cultural trends in the United States is difficult but important for marketing. Cross-cultural analysis needed for global marketing is discussed in Chapter 5.

The changing roles of women and men One of the most notable changes in the United States in the past 25 years has been in the roles of women and men. These changes have had a significant impact on marketing practices.

Today some 120 million people work, nearly twice the number of 25 years ago. In 1995, more than 60 percent of married women were in the work force, and that number is expected to climb to 63 percent by 2000. And of women with children, 65 percent work outside their home, a figure that includes 50 percent of mothers with children under one year of age.[18] Not only are women working in larger numbers, but they are increasingly holding management positions—the percentage of managerial positions held by women has increased from 37 percent to more than 42 percent over 10 years. In addition, *Forbes* magazine recently reported that 11 of the largest public and private companies are now run by women.[19]

The increasing number of women in the work force has increased the number of dual-income households. To cope with the demands of managing careers and a household, men and women have learned new roles as consumers and household decision makers. For example, a recent survey indicated that 24 percent of men consider themselves the primary shopper for their household's groceries. Similarly,

Saturn combined ethnic and regional marketing by using Spanish-language promotions in some states.

women now purchase 50 percent of all new cars sold in the United States. As the roles of men and women change, marketers must adjust their marketing programs and their assumptions about how men and women shop. *Cigar Aficionado* magazine recently acknowledged a growing women's market for cigars, and *Parents* magazine has revised its coverage to reflect a growing male readership.[20]

Changing attitudes and values   Culture also includes attitudes and values. In recent years some major attitudinal changes have occurred toward work, lifestyles, and consumption. Recent study has shown a change in the work ethic. There is a growing sense that the Puritan ethic of "I live to work" may be redefined as "I work to live." Work is seen as a means to an end—recreation, leisure, and entertainment—which has contributed to a growth in sales of products such as sports equipment, vacations, and electronic stereo equipment. As attitudes toward work change, U.S. consumers are placing increased importance on quality of life.

There is greater concern for health and well-being as evidenced by the level of sports participation in the United States and increased interest in health and diet. Sears fitness products, Nike workout clothes, and Lean Cuisine dinners are but a few products developed in response to and profiting from this trend.

A change in consumption orientation is also apparent. Conspicuous consumption marked much of the past 20 years. Today, and for the foreseeable future, **value consciousness**—or the concern for obtaining the best quality, features, and performance of a product or service for a given price—will drive consumption behavior. Innovative marketers have responded to this new orientation in numerous ways. Holiday Inn Worldwide has opened Holiday Express hotels, designed to offer comfortable accommodations with room rates lower than Holiday Inns. Revlon's Charles of the Ritz, known for its upscale and expensive cosmetics, has introduced the Express Bar, a collection of modified, medium-priced cosmetics. Even American Express is adding low-fee credit cards to its line of well-known, high-priced, and exclusive green, gold, and platinum charge cards.[21]

CONCEPT CHECK

1. Explain the term *regional marketing*.

2. What are the marketing implications of blended families?

3. The work ethic of today may best be stated as "I work _____."

ECONOMIC FORCES

The third component of the environmental scan, the **economy,** pertains to the income, expenditures, and resources that affect the cost of running a business and household. We'll consider two aspects of these economic forces: a macroeconomic view of the marketplace and a microeconomic perspective of consumer income.

Macroeconomic Conditions

Of particular concern at the macroeconomic level is the inflationary or recessionary state of the economy, whether actual or perceived by consumers or businesses. In an inflationary economy, the cost to produce and buy products and services escalates as prices increase. From a marketing standpoint, if prices rise faster than consumer incomes, the number of items consumers can buy decreases. This relationship is evident in the purchase of automobiles. Today, a new car costs the equivalent of about 26 weeks' pay for an average U.S. wage earner, up from 18 weeks' pay 20 years ago.[22]

Whereas inflation is a period of price increases, recession is a time of slow economic activity. Businesses decrease production, unemployment rises, and many consumers have less money to spend. The U.S. economy experienced recessions in the early 1970s, early 1980s, and early 1990s.

Consumer expectations of an inflationary and recessionary U.S. economy is an important element of environmental scanning. Consumer spending, which accounts for two thirds of U.S. economic activity, is affected by expectations of the future. Surveys of consumer expectations are tracked over time by research organizations, who ask questions such as "Do you expect to be better or worse off financially a year from now?" Surveyors record the share of positive and negative responses to these and related questions and construct an index. The higher the index, the more favorable are consumer expectations. Figure 3–5 shows one index that charts consumer attitudes toward car purchases and car sales. As can be seen, sales are closely related to expectations. This relationship has helped Chrysler plan its automobile production and avoid overproducing cars at the onset of a recessionary economy. Levitz, the largest U.S. furniture retailer, also tracks consumer economic expectations since furniture sales reflect perceptions of the future economic environment.[23]

FIGURE 3-5

University of Michigan consumer sentiment index and automobile sales: 1970–1995

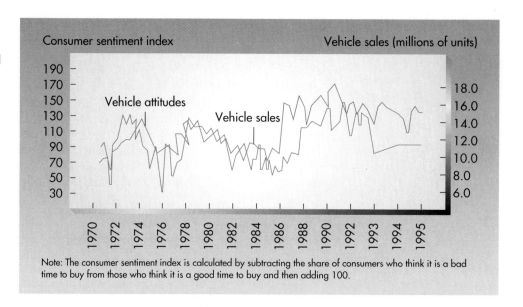

Note: The consumer sentiment index is calculated by subtracting the share of consumers who think it is a bad time to buy from those who think it is a good time to buy and then adding 100.

FIGURE 3–6

Income distribution of U.S.
households

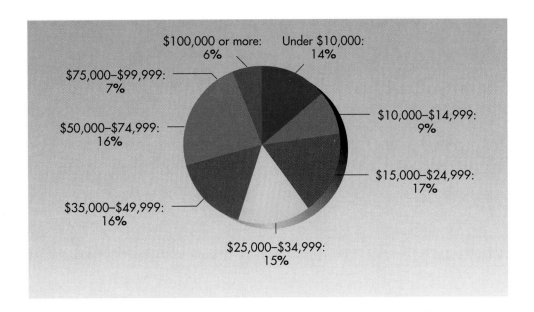

Consumer Income

The microeconomic trends in terms of consumer income are also important issues for marketers. Having a product that meets the needs of consumers may be of little value if they are unable to purchase it. A consumer's ability to buy is related to income, which consists of gross, disposable, and discretionary components.

Gross income   The total amount of money made in one year by a person, household, or family unit is referred to as **gross income.** While the typical U.S. household earned only about $10,000 of income in 1970, it earned about $37,000 in 1995. When gross income is adjusted for inflation, however, income of that typical U.S. household was relatively stable from 1970 to 1995. Figure 3–6 shows the distribution of annual income among U.S. households. More than two thirds of the households earning $100,000 or more each year are headed by college graduates.[24]

Disposable income   The second income component, **disposable income,** is the money a consumer has left after paying taxes to use for food, shelter, and clothing. Thus, if taxes rise at a faster rate than does disposable income, consumers must economize. In recent years consumers' allocation of income has shifted. For example, the proportion of disposable income devoted to eating in the home has increased, while the proportion devoted to eating out has decreased. Two environmental factors account for this: the recession of the early 1990s caused people to cut back on expenses such as eating out, and many baby boom households are in the midst of their child-raising years, causing increased spending on food at home.[25]

Discretionary income   The third component of income is **discretionary income,** the money that remains after paying for taxes and necessities. Discretionary income is used for luxury items such as vacations at a Westin resort. An obvious problem in defining discretionary versus disposable income is determining what is a luxury and what is a necessity.

The Department of Labor has calculated a budget for a household of four persons. Using these budget amounts, the Census Bureau defines a household as having discretionary income if its spendable income exceeds that of an average, similarly sized family by 30 percent or more. Based on this definition, 31 percent of U.S. households have some discretionary income, and 57 million households have none.

As consumers' discretionary income increases, so does the enjoyment of pleasure travel.

The importance of two-income couples is seen by the fact that 46 percent of these couples have discretionary income as compared with 33 percent of couples in which one spouse works and the other stays at home.

TECHNOLOGICAL FORCES

Our society is in a period of technological change. **Technology,** a major environmental force, refers to inventions or innovations from applied science or engineering research. Each new wave of technological innovation can replace existing products and companies. Do you recognize the items pictured on page 87 and what they may replace?

Technology of Tomorrow

Technological change is the result of research, so it is difficult to predict. Some of the most dramatic technological changes occurring now, however, include the following:

1. Continued improvement in the power of microprocessors.
2. The convergence of television, personal computer, and telephone technologies.
3. The emergence of the Internet or "cyberspace."
4. Greater use of electric cars and alternative forms of transportation.

These trends in technology are seen in today's marketplace. The power of microprocessors has doubled every 18 months for the past 25 years—suggesting that Intel's Pentium processor with 3.2 million transistors will be replaced by the Micro 2000 processor with more than 30 million transistors. The Internet already offers electronic magazines, shopping, and advertising, and more businesses and subscribers are becoming involved every day. Other technologies such as satellite disks, CDs and CD-ROM, and electric cars are likely to replace or substitute for existing technologies such as cable TV, records and floppy disks, and even gas-powered cars![26]

Technology's Impact on Customer Value

Advances in technology are having important effects on marketing. First, the cost of technology is plummeting—causing the customer value assessment of technology-based

Technological change leads to new products. What products might be replaced by these innovations?

products to focus on other dimensions such as quality, service, and relationships. When Computer Associates International introduced its software program Simply Money, it gave away the first million copies. Computer Associates reasoned that satisfied customers would later buy upgrades and related products. A similar approach is now used by many cellular telephone vendors, who charge little for the telephone if the purchase leads to a telephone service contract.[27]

Technology also provides value through the development of new products. Oldsmobile now offers customers an auto-navigation system that uses satellite signals to help the driver reach any destination, while Lincoln Continental's vehicles automatically adjust 24 features—including seat and steering wheel positions, temperature, choice of CDs, and suspension and steering effort settings—to the preferences of the driver. Under development are radarlike collision avoidance systems that disengage cruise control, reduce the engine speed, and even apply the brakes. Finally, research and testing are under way on auto glass that will dim—to deter theft—when the ignition is off and the car is unoccupied.[28]

Ultimately, the benefit of technology for marketers will be in allowing them to better understand and serve the consumer. A recent development has been the use of electronic maps for a host of marketing applications. Labeled *geographic information systems* (GIS), this technology records different layers of data on the same map.[29] For example, a company can now develop a map of a city with additional information, such as demographics or sales, included in the layout. The fast-food chain Arby's, Inc. uses a GIS map to select store locations. Coca-Cola uses GIS to determine the best routing for its delivery trucks. And the Census Bureau now markets its TIGER (Topologically Integrated Geographic Encoding and Reference) file, a landmark project in demography. This software will provide a minutely detailed, computerized map of the entire United States, which can be combined with a company's own database to analyze customer sales. Do you want to drive somewhere during spring break? The American Automobile Association can provide you with a GIS map. The challenge for marketers in this decade will be to keep pace with the possibilities of computer technology, as is discussed in Chapter 10.

Ecological Impact of Technology

Technology has affected society in the development of products and in the ecological balance of the world's resources. **Ecology** refers to the relationship of physical resources in the environment. There is growing recognition that decisions today on

Maps generated by geographic information systems, such as the map at right created with ESRI software, allow companies to make sophisticated marketing decisions.

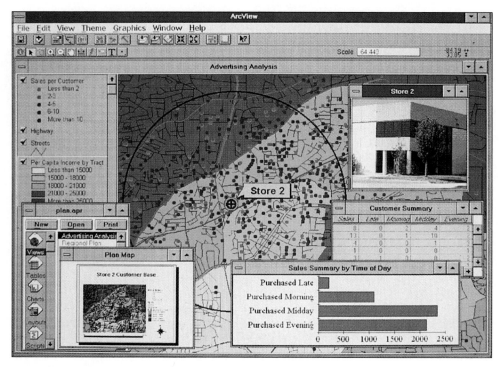

Graphic image supplied courtesy of Environmental Systems Research Institute (ESRI).

use of the earth's resources have long-term consequences to society. Such products as mercury-laden batteries, fertilizers, paints, and combustion engines have an effect on our land, air, and water, and companies are turning to technology to develop more environmentally sound alternatives. ARCO, for example, developed a reformulated gasoline, Emission Control 1, to reduce air pollution.[30]

Products that do not have obvious negative effects on the environment may also be a concern because of the growing problem of waste disposal. By 2010 total solid waste in the United States is expected to rise to 250 million tons per year from 180 million in 1988. With landfill space growing increasingly short, there is increasing pressure from consumers and regulatory groups to reduce the amount of waste associated with a product.

Many companies have responded with *recycling* programs designed to send products through the manufacturing cycle several times. The National Association for Plastic Container Recovery, for example, estimates that 50 percent of all plastic bottles are now recycled—usually to make polyester fibers that are spun into everything from sweaters to upholstery. Paper products and packaging made from recycled materials are often designated with the "chasing arrows" logo.[31] In Germany, Ford emphasizes that its cars are assembled with parts that can be recycled. The ad on page 89 showing a child's toy, exclaims "I was a car" in the headline.

Another approach is *precycling*—efforts by manufacturers to reduce waste by decreasing the amount of packaging they use. New packaging for L'eggs pantyhose is smaller but still uses the trademark egg shape, and DuPont has developed a "minisip" collapsible pouch as an alternative to milk cartons in school lunch programs. In many cases, companies respond to environmental requests made by retailers. Wal-Mart, for example, requests that its suppliers provide environmentally safe products.[32] This topic is discussed further in Chapter 4 as a matter of social responsibility. Future ecological concerns are discussed in the Marketing NewsNet box on page 90.[33]

Examples of a recycling program by Ford and a precycling program by Lever.

COMPETITIVE FORCES

The fourth component of the environmental scan, **competition,** refers to the alternative firms that could provide a product to satisfy a specific market's needs. There are various forms of competition, and each company must consider its present and potential competitors in designing its marketing strategy.

Alternative Forms of Competition

There are four basic forms of competition that form a continuum from pure competition to monopolistic competition to oligopoly to monopoly. Chapter 14 contains further discussions on pricing practices under these four forms of competition.

At one end of the continuum is *pure competition,* in which every company has a similar product. Companies that deal in commodities common to agribusiness (for example, wheat, rice, and grain) often are in a pure competition position in which distribution (in the sense of shipping products) is important but other elements of marketing have little impact.

In the second point on the continuum, *monopolistic competition,* the many sellers compete with their products on a substitutable basis. For example, if the price of coffee rises too much, consumers may switch to tea. Coupons or sales are frequently used marketing tactics.

Oligopoly, a common industry structure, occurs when a few companies control the majority of industry sales. For example, through the early 1990s a small number of large carriers controlled up to 90 percent of all sales in the airline industry. Because there are few sellers, price competition among firms is not desirable because it leads to reduced profits for all producers. This led to losses of $12 billion between 1989 and 1993. Other industries dominated by a small number of firms include the on-line service industry—America Online, CompuServe, and Prodigy—and the media industry—Viacom, Disney, and Time Warner.[34]

The final point on the continuum, *monopoly,* occurs when only one firm sells the product. It has been common for producers of goods considered essential to a

MARKETING NEWSNET

Global

USING ENVIRONMENTAL MANAGEMENT STANDARDS TO DESIGN NEW PRODUCTS

We've come a long way since the first Earth Day in 1970. Today most consumer products are designed with some consideration toward balancing environmental concerns with performance and price. The International Standards Organization recently published a guide, called ISO 14000, to provide comprehensive environmental standards for product designers around the world. What other changes are likely in the future? Consider the predictions of marketing consultant Jacquelyn Ottman:

1. *Increasing emphasis on materials use.* Although waste disposal has been a primary concern, the future may bring new policies regarding how materials are used.

2. *Longer product life.* Manufacturers will become increasingly responsible for the long-term use of their products. Landfill bans on products such as appliances will necessitate reuse and recycling and full-cost accounting, which counts the expense of getting rid of a product.

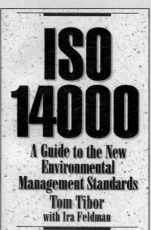

3. *Changes in consumer behavior.* Educational efforts in schools are paying off—children are more sensitive to environmental issues and more receptive to alternative product and package designs. Their influence will be particularly evident as they become adult consumers.

community: water, electricity, and telephone service. Typically, marketing plays a small role in a monopolistic setting because it is regulated by the state or federal government. Government control usually seeks to ensure price protection for the buyer. The major change in recent years has been the AT&T shift from a monopoly to a monopolistic competitor, with Sprint and MCI vying for buyers of long-distance phone service. Thus, marketing has assumed a more important role at AT&T.

Components of Competition

In developing a marketing program, companies must consider the factors that drive competition: entry, bargaining power of buyers and suppliers, existing rivalries, and substitution possibilities.[35] Scanning the environment requires a look at all of them. These factors relate to a firm's marketing mix decisions and may be used to create a barrier to entry, increase brand awareness, or intensify a fight for market share.

Entry   In considering the competition, a firm must assess the likelihood of new entrants. Additional producers increase industry capacity and tend to lower prices. A company scanning its environment must consider the possible **barriers to entry** for other firms, which are business practices or conditions that make it difficult for new firms to enter the market. Barriers to entry can be in the form of capital requirements, advertising expenditures, product identity, distribution access, or switching costs. The higher the expense of the barrier, the more likely it will deter new entrants. For example, IBM once created a switching cost barrier for companies that considered Apple Computer equipment because IBM had a different programming language for its machines.

Power of buyers and suppliers A competitive analysis must consider the power of buyers and suppliers. Powerful buyers exist when they are few in number, there are low switching costs, or the product represents a significant share of the buyer's total costs. This last factor leads the buyer to exert significant pressure for price competition. A supplier gains power when the product is critical to the buyer and when it has built up the switching costs.

Existing competitors and substitutes Competitive pressures among existing firms depend on the rate of industry growth. In slow-growth settings, competition is more heated for any possible gains in market share. High fixed costs also create competitive pressures for firms to fill production capacity. For example, hospitals are increasing their advertising in a battle to fill beds, which represent a high fixed cost.

The New Look in American Corporations

Competition has had two other important effects on corporate America: (1) the restructuring of corporations and (2) the birth and growth of many small businesses.

Restructuring corporations Although the process is known by various names—reengineering, streamlining, or **restructuring**—the result is the same: striving for more efficient corporations that can compete globally. For many firms, restructuring means reducing duplicate efforts in multiple company locations, closing or changing unprofitable plants and offices, and often laying off hundreds or thousands of employees. For example, Ford Motor Company recently merged its U.S. and European product development operations, refurbished seven plants, and reduced the number of managers by 20 percent. IBM moved 600 sales representatives from five offices to one location—a "virtual office" consisting primarily of temporary work spaces assigned by computer on the three or four days each month an employee may not be with customers. Many other companies from General Electric to much smaller firms have also restructured their organizations.

The result has been an improvement in efficiency—Ford has reduced the amount of time needed to get an engine from design to testing from 24 months to 100 days. Another result, however, has been a huge reduction in the number of middle managers in the work force. IBM alone has cut 171,000 jobs since 1986. This trend means there are fewer opportunities for those entering the work force. It also suggests that employers are shifting from a philosophy of unconditional lifetime employment to one of "lifelong employability." This view is based on the idea that employers have an obligation to provide an opportunity of self-improvement and employees have an obligation to take charge of their own careers.[36]

Another approach to restructuring has been through mergers, acquisitions, and takeovers. Consider a few of the recent examples of consolidation: Chemical Bank merged with Chase, First Union acquired First Fidelity Bancorp, Upjohn merged with Sweden's Pharmacia, Kimberly-Clark acquired Scott Paper, and Burlington Northern bought Santa Fe Pacific. What is the explanation? In general, firms are striving for market dominance by ensuring control of distribution channels, access to markets, and cost reduction through economies of scale. Businesses are also discovering that information technology will allow effective management of large and complex organizations. Experts debate whether these mergers are good for the economy. While firms that dominate a market might command higher prices, they may also be vulnerable to faster, customer-focused entrepreneurs.[37]

Regardless of the size of the organization, most firms are also changing the way employees work. Managers and employees are now empowered to make fast decisions about issues related to their job or the customers they serve. Cross-functional teams, which bring together employees from multiple functions, are used to ensure that all aspects of a product meet customer needs. Finally, continuous training is a necessity to maintain a smaller but better educated work force and to take advantage of improvements in technology and processes.

Startup and growth of small businesses   Firms that have restructured their organization often increase their reliance on **outsourcing**—contracting work that formerly was done in-house by employees in marketing research, advertising, public relations, data processing, and training departments to small, outside firms. This has been one factor triggering the major growth in new business startups and in employment in small businesses. While the 42 U.S. companies with 100,000 or more employees continue to downsize, almost two thirds of all new positions are now created by businesses with fewer than 100 employees.[38]

CONCEPT CHECK

1.   What is the difference between a consumer's disposable and discretionary income?

2.   In pure competition there are _____ number of sellers.

3.   What does restructuring a firm mean?

REGULATORY FORCES

For any organization, the marketing and broader business decisions are constrained, directed, and influenced by regulatory forces. **Regulation** consists of restrictions state and federal laws place on business with regard to the conduct of its activities. Regulation exists to protect companies as well as consumers. Much of the regulation from the federal and state levels has been passed to ensure competition and fair business practices. For consumers, the focus of legislation is to protect them from unfair trade practices and ensure their safety.

Protecting Competition

Major federal legislation has been passed to encourage competition, which is deemed desirable because it permits the consumer to determine which competitor will succeed and which will fail. The first such law was the *Sherman Antitrust Act* (1890). Lobbying by farmers in the Midwest against fixed railroad shipping prices led to the passage of this act, which forbids (1) contracts, combinations, or conspiracies in restraint of trade and (2) actual monopolies or attempts to monopolize any part of trade or commerce. Because of vague wording and government inactivity, however, there was only one successful case against a company in the nine years after the act became law, and the Sherman Act was supplemented with the *Clayton Act* (1914). This act forbids certain actions that are likely to lessen competition, although no actual harm has yet occurred.

In the 1930s the federal government had to act again to ensure fair competition. During that time, large chain stores appeared, such as the Great Atlantic & Pacific Tea Company (A&P). Small businesses were threatened, and they lobbied for the *Robinson-Patman Act* (1936). This act makes it unlawful to discriminate in prices charged to different purchasers of the same product, where the effect may substantially lessen competition or help to create a monopoly.

Product-Related Legislation

Various federal laws in existence specifically address the product component of the marketing mix. Some are aimed at protecting the company, some at protecting the consumer, and at least one at protecting both. For example, Kayser-Roth, the marketer of No Nonsense pantyhose, was recently prohibited by a federal judge from selling and advertising its Leg Looks brand of pantyhose. Why? The Leg Looks packaging too closely resembled the new packaging of L'eggs pantyhose sold by the Hanes unit of the Sara Lee Corporation. The argument made by Sara Lee Corporation attorneys was that the packaging could create confusion among consumers and harm L'eggs sales.[39]

Company protection   A company can protect its competitive position in new and novel products under the patent law, which gives inventors the right to exclude others from making, using, or selling products that infringe the patented invention. The federal copyright law is another way for a company to protect its competitive position in a product. The copyright law gives the author of a literary, dramatic, musical, or artistic work the exclusive right to print, perform, or otherwise copy that work. Copyright is secured automatically when the work is created. However, the published work should bear an appropriate copyright notice, including the copyright symbol, the first year of publication, and the name of the copyright owner, and it must be registered under the federal copyright law.

Consumer protection   There are many consumer-oriented federal laws regarding products. One of the oldest is the *Meat Inspection Act* (1906), which provides for meat products to be wholesome, unadulterated, and properly labeled. The *Food, Drug and Cosmetics Act* (1938) is one of the most important of the federal regulatory laws. This act is aimed principally at preventing the adulteration or misbranding of the three categories of products. The various federal consumer protection laws include more than 30 amendments and separate laws relating to food, drugs, and cosmetics, such as the *Poison Prevention Packaging Act* (1970), the *Infant Formula Act* (1980) and the *Nutritional Labeling and Education Act* (1990). Various other consumer protection laws have a broader scope, such as the *Fair Packaging and Labeling Act* (1966), the *Child Protection Act* (1966), and the *Consumer Product Safety Act* (1972), which established the Consumer Product Safety Commission to monitor product safety and establish uniform product safety standards. Many of these recent laws came about because of **consumerism,** a grassroots movement started in the 1960s to increase the influence, power, and rights of consumers in dealing with institutions. The *Clean Air Act* (1990), designed to curb acid rain and air pollution, and the *Telephone Consumer Protection Act* (1991), focusing on telemarketing abuses, are recent responses to consumer interests. This movement continues in the 1990s and is reflected in consumer demands for ecologically safe products and ethical and socially responsible business practices. One hotly debated issue concerns liability for environmental abuse. Read the Ethics and Social Responsibility Alert on the next page and ask yourself: Should corporate executives be personally liable for environmental offenses?[40]

Both company and consumer protection   Trademarks are intended to protect both the firm selling a trademarked product and the consumer buying it. A Senate report states that:

> The purposes underlying any trademark statute [are] twofold. One is to protect the public so that it may be confident that, in purchasing a product bearing a particular trademark which it favorably knows, it will get the product which it asks for and wants to get. Secondly, where the owner of a trademark has spent energy, time, and money in presenting to the public the product, he is protected in this investment from misappropriation in pirates and cheats.

This statement was made in connection with another product-related law, the *Lanham Act* (1946), which provides for registration of a company's trademarks. Historically, the first user of a trademark in commerce had the exclusive right to use that particular word, name, or symbol in its business. Registration under the Lanham Act provides

Ethics

ETHICS AND SOCIAL RESPONSIBILITY ALERT

SHOULD CORPORATE EXECUTIVES BE PERSONALLY LIABLE FOR ENVIRONMENTAL OFFENSES?

Public concern over air, water, and ground pollution has sparked a debate over whether corporate executives should be personally liable for their company's environmental offenses. Opinion polls indicate that 75 percent of the general public believe they should; 51 percent of large-company executives believe they should not. The U.S. Justice Department has been criticized for not aggressively pursuing executive convictions and fines. In an average year, about 100 executive convictions or guilty pleas have been made for environmental offenses, with fines ranging from several hundred thousand to millions of dollars and jail terms averaging one year. Exxon Corporation was fined $100 million for fouling Alaskan waters with oil; the president of Burlington, Massachusetts company was sentenced to two years in jail for ordering his employees to dump toxic waste down a sewer; and several judges have ordered executives to join the Sierra Club as part of their sentences.

Should corporate executives be personally liable for environmental offenses? If yes, should the penalty include both fines and prison terms? If no, who is liable?

important advantages to a trademark owner that has used the trademark in interstate or foreign commerce, but it does not confer ownership. A company can lose its trademark if it becomes generic, which means that it has primarily come to be merely a common descriptive word for the product. Coca-Cola, Whopper, and Xerox are registered trademarks, and competitors cannot use these names. Aspirin and escalator are former trademarks that are now generic terms in the United States and can be used by anyone. In 1988, the *Trademark Law Revision Act* resulted in a major change to the Lanham Act—allowing a company to secure rights to a name before actual use by declaring an intent to use the name.[41]

One of the most recent changes in trademark law is the U.S. Supreme Court's ruling that companies may obtain trademarks for colors associated with their products. The reason is that, over time, consumers may begin to associate a particular color with a specific brand. Examples of products that may benefit from the new law include NutraSweet's sugar substitute in pastel blue packages and Owens-Corning Fiberglas Corporation's pink insulation.[42]

Regulatory Controls on Pricing

The pricing component of the marketing mix is the focus of regulation from two perspectives: price fixing and price discounting. Although the Sherman Act did not outlaw price fixing, the courts view this behavior as *per se illegal* (*per se* means "through or of itself"), which means the courts see price fixing itself as illegal.

Certain forms of price discounting are allowed. Quantity discounts are acceptable; that is, buyers can be charged different prices for a product provided there are differences in manufacturing or delivery costs. Promotional allowances or services may be given to buyers on an equal basis proportionate to volume purchased. Also, a firm can meet a competitor's price "in good faith." Legal aspects of pricing are covered in more detail in Chapter 15.

Distribution and the Law

The government has four concerns with regard to distribution—earlier referred to as "place" actions in the marketing mix—and the maintenance of competition. The first, *exclusive dealing,* is an arrangement with a buyer to handle only the products of one

These products are identified by protected trademarks. Are any of these trademarks in danger of becoming generic?

manufacturer and not those of competitors. This practice is only illegal under the Clayton Act when it substantially lessens competition.

Requirement contracts require a buyer to purchase all or part of its needs for a product from one seller for a period of time. These contracts are not always illegal but depend on the court's interpretation of their impact on distribution.

Exclusive territorial distributorships are a third distribution issue often under regulatory scrutiny. In this situation, a manufacturer grants a distributor the sole rights to sell a product in a specific geographical area. The courts have found few violations with these arrangements.

The fourth distribution strategy is a *tying arrangement,* whereby a seller requires the purchaser of one product to also buy another item in the line. These contracts may be illegal when the seller has such economic power in the tying product that the seller can restrain trade in the tied product. Legal aspects of distribution are reviewed in greater detail in Chapter 16.

Advertising and Promotion Controls

Promotion and advertising are aspects of marketing closely monitored by the Federal Trade Commission (FTC), which was established by the *FTC Act of 1914.* The FTC has been concerned with deceptive or misleading advertising and unfair business practices and has the power to (1) issue cease and desist orders and (2) order corrective advertising. In issuing a *cease and desist order,* the FTC orders a company to stop practices it considers unfair. With *corrective advertising,* the FTC can require a company to spend money on advertising to correct previous misleading ads. The enforcement powers of the FTC are so significant that often just an indication of concern from the commission can cause companies to revise their promotion.

A landmark legal battle regarding deceptive advertising involved the Federal Trade Commission and Campbell Soup Co. It had been Campbell's practice to insert clear glass marbles into the bottom of soup containers used in print advertisements to bring the soup ingredients (for example, noodles or chicken) to the surface. The FTC ruled that the advertising was deceptive because it misrepresented the amount of solid ingredients in the soup, and it issued a cease and desist order. Campbell and its advertising agency agreed to discontinue the practice. Future ads used a ladle to show the ingredients.[43]

Other laws designed to regulate advertising practices include the *Federal Cigarette Labeling and Advertising Act* (1967), which requires health warnings on cigarette ads and packages, the *Public Health Cigarette Smoking Act* (1971), which prohibits advertising tobacco products on radio and television, and the *Children's Television Act* (1990), which limits the maximum amount of advertising during children's television programs to 10.5 minutes per hour on weekends and 12 minutes per hour on weekdays.

Control through Self-Regulation

The government has provided much legislation to create a competitive business climate and protect the consumer. An alternative to government control is **self-regulation,** where an industry attempts to police itself. The four major television networks have used self-regulation to set their own guidelines for TV ads for children's toys. These guidelines have generally worked well. The problem: cable TV and non-network TV have no such guidelines, and their commercials for a Barbie doll make her look almost lifelike, possibly increasing a child's desire for the doll. Critics complain that this double standard on TV commercials amounts to misleading advertising.[44] This example illustrates two problems with self-regulation: noncompliance by members and enforcement. If attempts at self-regulation are too strong, they may violate the Robinson-Patman Act. The best-known self-regulatory group is the Better Business Bureau (BBB). This agency is a voluntary alliance of companies whose goal is to help maintain fair practices. Although the BBB has no legal power, it does try to use "moral suasion" to get members to comply with its ruling.

Recently, the BBB intervened with Carnation Co. regarding their claim for Fancy Feast Gourmet Cat Food. The promotion stated that this brand was the "best-tasting gourmet canned cat food . . . cats preferred over every other brand." A competitor protested to the BBB and Carnation revised the claim. [45]

CONCEPT CHECK

1. The _____ Act was punitive toward monopolies, whereas the _____ Act was preventive.

2. Explain the Lanham Act.

3. What is a per se illegality?

Summary

1. The population of the United States is aging, and the number of typical families as seen in the 1950s is diminishing. A blended family structure is becoming more common. Baby boomers are an important target market for companies because of their proportion in the population as well as their high average disposable income.

2. Recognition of racial, ethnic, and geographical differences in product preferences has given rise to companies developing tailored marketing plans.

3. Culture represents abstract values and material possessions. Values are changing toward work, quality of life, the roles of women and men, and consumption.

4. Disposable income is the number of dollars left after taxes. Discretionary income is the money consumers have

after purchasing their necessities. The median gross income (dollars before taxes) of U.S. households has been stable since 1970 in real income terms.

5. Growing environmental concern is leading many companies to be more ecologically responsible in their development and marketing of products.

6. Competition has had two major effects on U.S. corporations: (*a*) restructuring them to improve efficiency and (*b*) stimulating the startup and growth of small businesses.

7. The Sherman Antitrust Act of 1890 made monopolies illegal, whereas the Clayton Act tried to outlaw actions believed to lead to monopolies.

8. A company's brand name or symbol can be protected under the Lanham Act, but if the name becomes generic, the company no longer has sole right to the trademark.

9. Price fixing has been viewed as illegal by the courts. However, price discounting is allowed to meet competition or to account for differences in the cost of manufacture or distribution.

10. There are four aspects of distribution reviewed by courts: exclusive dealing arrangements, requirements contracts, exclusive territorial distributorships, and tying arrangements.

11. The Federal Trade Commission monitors unfair business practices and deceptive advertising. Two methods used in enforcement are (*a*) cease and desist orders and (*b*) corrective advertising.

12. Self-regulation attempts are common to some industries and organizations, such as the Better Business Bureau. However, the effectiveness of self-regulation is coming under greater scrutiny by the courts.

KEY TERMS AND CONCEPTS

environmental scanning p. 76
social forces p. 77
demographics p. 78
mature household p. 78
baby boomers p. 79
Generation X p. 79
baby boomlet p. 79
blended family p. 80
regional marketing p. 82
culture p. 82
value consciousness p. 83
economy p. 84

gross income p. 85
disposable income p. 85
discretionary income p. 85
technology p. 86
ecology p. 87
competition p. 89
barriers to entry p. 90
restructuring p. 91
outsourcing p. 92
regulation p. 92
consumerism p. 93
self-regulation p. 96

CHAPTER PROBLEMS AND APPLICATIONS

1. For many years Gerber's has manufactured baby food in small, single-sized containers. In conducting an environmental scan, identify three trends or factors that might significantly affect this company's future business, and then propose how Gerber's might respond to these changes.

2. Describe the target market for a luxury item such as the Mercedes Benz 190 (the lowest-priced Mercedes). List four magazines in which you would advertise to appeal to this target market.

3. The growing concern with the environment was discussed in this chapter. Marketing in an ecologically sensitive manner will be more important to firms. Suggest how the following companies and products might respond to ecological concerns: (*a*) Gillette safety razor division, (*b*) KFC restaurants, and (*c*) Hallmark greeting cards.

4. In recent years in the brewing industry, a couple of large firms that have historically had most of the beer sales (Anheuser-Busch and Miller) have faced competition from many small regional brands. In terms of the continuum of competition, how would you explain this change?

5. When the airline industry became deregulated, how do you think the role of marketing changed? What elements of the marketing mix are more or less important since the deregulation?

6. The Johnson Company manufactures buttons and pins with slogans and designs. These pins are inexpensive to produce and are sold in retail outlets such as discount stores, hobby shops, and bookstores. Little equipment is needed for a new competitor to enter the market. What strategies should Johnson consider to create effective barriers to entry?

7. Why would Xerox be concerned about its name becoming generic?

CASE 3–1:   Imagination Pilots Entertainment

Video

What develops critical thinking, problem solving, and math skills, has an original musical score and sound effects, utilizes full-color graphics, and involves an adventure with the circus? The answer is one of the newest forms of edutainment—a CD-ROM game developed for children called "Where's Waldo?" The game is part of a growing number of offerings from an industry that is rapidly adapting to a wide variety of changes in the business environment. According to the *Hollywood Reporter*, which follows the new developments, "interactive start-ups face new challenges as they stake a claim in a rapidly changing market."

THE COMPANY

The developer of the "Where's Waldo?" game is a fast-growing, entrepreneurial company called Imagination Pilots Entertainment. The founder of the company, Howard Tullman, has focused on developing multimedia entertainment, educational software, and interactive "cinematic" adventures with strong game content. One of the company's first products was the interactive CD-ROM game called *Blown Away*, which was developed as part of a joint venture with MGM/United Artists and released after the movie by the same name. Imagination Pilot's *Blown Away* won the "Game of the Year" award from *Computer Life* magazine, the Gold Medal Invision Award for Best Graphic Design from *New Media* magazine, and the Innovators Software Showcase Award. Other Imagination Pilots products include *Panic in the Park* starring Erika Eleniak; *Virtual Erector Set*, which allows children to build 3-D, real-time models of vehicles; and an adventure game sequel to Arnold Schwarzenegger's movie, *Eraser*.

THE CHANGING ENVIRONMENT

Managers at Imagination Pilots are constantly monitoring social, economic, technological, competitive, and regulatory trends that may influence their business or the CD-ROM game industry. The most obvious trend, for example, is the rapid growth of the software market. Revenues for the packaged software market are expected to grow at an annual rate of 13 percent reaching $115 billion in 1997 and $153 billion by 2000. In addition, while many industries are laying off employees, the software industry is a net creator of jobs—

employing over 435,000 workers in the U.S. alone, according to the Bureau of Labor Statistics. A niche within the overall software market is the multimedia software market. Multimedia products combine video, animation, still pictures, voice, music, graphics, and text into a single system, usually on CD-ROM and very often for education or entertainment applications. Sales of CD-ROM titles have doubled each year for the past several years and now exceed $1.2 billion.

Related trends are the increasing penetration of computers into homes due to declining PC prices, and the increasing number of installed CD-ROM drives. According to Tullman, "There are only now becoming enough PC CD-ROM computers in the marketplace, in terms of total units, to permit a number of products to be successful." Although the number has been increasing at an annual rate of 25 percent, the number of worldwide CD-ROM computers was still just 21 million in 1996. The price of software is also declining while consumer expectations are increasing. Tullman observes that "the price of children's software is decreasing, and continues to decrease even while there is a greater demand for quality . . . the consumer and parents want to pay less for individual games, but they want them to be of high quality."

Increasing competition also represents a challenge for Imagination Pilots. In the children's entertainment category software developers include Electronic Arts, Acclaim Entertainment, Sierra On-Line, Broderbund, Xiphias, and a very large number of relatively small firms. In addition, as growth of computer sales slows in the corporate market, many large firms, including Microsoft, IBM, Compaq, and Apple Computer are expected to try to develop children's software as a way into the home market. Many new titles are being introduced by both past developers and new entrants—creating a very competitive market.

A final factor Imagination Pilots and other developers must consider is the possibility of regulation. Concern about the content of some games had led to a discussion about the potential need for a rating system, much like the system used for movies.

THE ISSUES

Imagination Pilots is faced with several key challenges. First, it must attempt to ensure the success of new titles planned for development. Second, it must obtain distribution for existing and future products. Although the two are related, they require attention to very different issues.

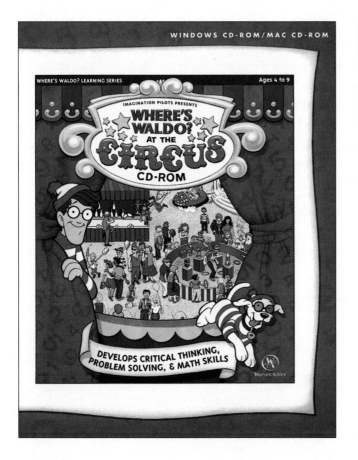

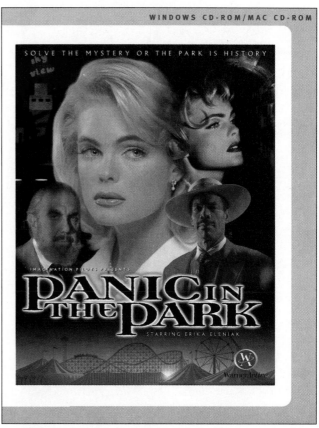

Establishing a new title in a cluttered marketplace is likely to be difficult for any software developer. Estimates suggest that from $800,000 to $1.5 million is required to develop a competitive CD-ROM product. As a result, many firms seek partnerships or alliances to spread costs and reduce risk. Recovering the investment may be difficult, however, if sales volume is low or the profit margin of each unit sold is low. Part of Imagination Pilot's strategy is to license rights to existing stories, such as "Where's Waldo?", or movies, such as *Blown Away* and *Eraser*. Tullman believes that the name recognition of licensed titles is important to ensure adequate consumer interest. Some developers of children's software have used product line extensions to extend the life of existing titles. Sierra On-line's *Quest*, for example, is now in its sixth release. New titles will need much more, though, to gain a foothold in the market.

Daniel P. Di Caro, Chief Operating Officer at Imagination Pilots, argues that "distribution is increasingly becoming the most important factor in the success of a product, assuming you have a good product to start with." In the past the traditional channel of distribution was through software specialty stores such as Egghead Software, Babbages, and Software Etc. More recently, sales have increased in computer superstores such as

CompUSA, department stores such as Sears and Wal-Mart, consumer electronic stores such as Best Buy and Circuit City, and warehouse stores such as Sam's and Office Depot. Their relationship with Warner Music Group provides Imagination Pilots with a strong distribution partner with access to many of these channels. In the future additional channels such as catalogs, interactive television channels, and kiosks may offer the company new distribution opportunities. Imagination Pilots is already testing an on-line service which makes its games available to the Internet and World Wide Web community!

Questions

1. Conduct an environmental scan for Imagination Pilots Entertainment. How are each of the five environmental forces (social, economic, technological, competitive, and regulatory) likely to influence their multimedia game business?

2. What are the key challenges facing Imagination Pilots? Describe the actions taken by Imagination Pilots to (a) ensure the success of, and (b) obtain distribution for its games.

3. What are the advantages of making Imagination Pilot's games available on-line?

We're dedicated to brewing quality beers, and to their sensible enjoyment.

The brewers of Budweiser® have been committed to brewing only the finest beer for more than one hundred years.

And we've put much of that same zeal into creating effective programs that promote, through education and awareness, responsible consumption of all alcohol beverages.

Beer is to be enjoyed…responsibly. And with your help, we can keep it that way.

Together, we can help America Know When To Say When.™

For information contact: Anheuser-Busch, Inc., Dept. of Consumer Awareness and Education, One Busch Place, St. Louis, Missouri 63118.

CHAPTER 4

Ethics and Social Responsibility in Marketing

AFTER READING THIS CHAPTER YOU SHOULD BE ABLE TO:

• Appreciate the nature and significance of ethics in marketing.

• Understand the differences between legal and ethical behavior in marketing.

• Identify factors that influence ethical and unethical marketing decisions.

• Distinguish among the different concepts of ethics and social responsibility.

• Recognize the importance of ethical and socially responsible consumer behavior.

AT ANHEUSER-BUSCH, THERE IS MORE BREWING THAN BEER

Why would a company spend more than $150 million since 1982 trying to convince people not to abuse its products and millions more to decrease litter and solid waste? Ask Anheuser-Busch, the world's largest brewer.

Anheuser-Busch has been a leader in the campaign for responsible drinking and environment-conscious disposition of its packaging. The company began promoting its "Know When to Say When" campaign for responsible drinking, first with posters in 1983 and two years later with national television commercials. In 1989, the brewery made history in the beer industry by creating a Department of Consumer Awareness and Education to encourage safe driving and responsible drinking habits. Such efforts have contributed to a sizeable decline in fatal drunk-driving accidents and a 64 percent drop in teenage drunk-driving deaths since 1982.

Anheuser-Busch continues these efforts with English- and Spanish-language versions of its "Family Talk about Drinking" program aimed at parents. With ads directed at fathers in *Sports Illustrated*, mothers in *Good Housekeeping*, and both in *Newsweek* and *Parents*, parents are invited to call a toll-free number to obtain free books to help parents address the topic of underage drinking with their children.

Responsibility at Anheuser-Busch is broader than the successful "Know When to Say When" campaign. The company is an advocate and sponsor of numerous efforts to preserve the environment. A notable example is its massive recycling effort through Anheuser-Busch Recycling Corporation (ABRC). ABRC is the world's largest recycler of aluminum cans. In 1994, ABRC recycled more than 635 million pounds of aluminum—the equivalent of more than 100 percent of the beer cans sold by Anheuser-Busch. The rationale for founding ABRC in 1978 was simple: voluntary recycling reduces litter and solid waste while conserving natural resources.

Anheuser-Busch acts on what it views as an ethical obligation to its customers with the "Know When to Say When" campaign. At the same time, the company's multifaceted efforts to protect the environment reflects its social responsibility to the general public.[1]

NATURE AND SIGNIFICANCE OF MARKETING ETHICS

Ethics are the moral principles and values that govern the actions and decisions of an individual or group.[2] They serve as guidelines on how to act rightly and justly when faced with moral dilemmas.

Ethical/Legal Framework in Marketing

A good starting point for understanding the nature and significance of ethics is the distinction between legality and ethicality of marketing decisions. Figure 4–1 helps to visualize the relationship between laws and ethics.[3] While ethics deal with personal moral principles and values, **laws** are society's values and standards that are enforceable in the courts.[4] This distinction can sometimes lead to the rationalization that if a behavior is within reasonable ethical and legal limits, then it is not really illegal or unethical. When a recent survey asked the question, "Is it OK to get around the law if you don't actually break it?" 61 percent of businesspeople who took part responded "Yes."[5] How would you answer this question?

There are numerous situations where judgment plays a large role in defining ethical and legal boundaries. Consider the following situations. After reading each, assign it to the cell in Figure 4–1 that you think best fits the situation along the ethical–legal continuum.[6]

1. More than 70 percent of the physicians in the Maricopa County (Arizona) Medical Society agreed to establish a maximum fee schedule for health services to curb rising medical costs. All physicians were required to adhere to this schedule as a condition for membership in the society. The U.S. Supreme Court ruled that this agreement to set prices violated the Sherman Act and represented price fixing, which is illegal.

2. A company in California sells a computer program to auto dealers showing that car buyers should finance their purchase rather than paying cash. The program omits the effect of income taxes and misstates the interest earned on savings over the loan period. The finance option always provides a net benefit over the cash option. Company employees agree that the program does mislead buyers, but say the company will "provide what [car dealers] want as long as it is not against the law."

3. R. J. Reynolds Tobacco Company specifically targeted African-Americans for its Uptown brand of cigarette. Public health statistics show that African-Americans have a high incidence of lung cancer and smoking-related illnesses. Also, African-American community leaders, antismoking groups, and the U.S. Secretary of Health and Human Services publicly criticized the company for this tactic. According to the company, it was within the law since cigarettes are legal products.

Did these situations fit neatly into Figure 4–1 as clearly ethical and legal or unethical and illegal? Probably not. As you read further in this chapter, you will be asked to consider other ethical dilemmas.

FIGURE 4-1

Classifying marketing
decisions according to ethical
and legal relationships

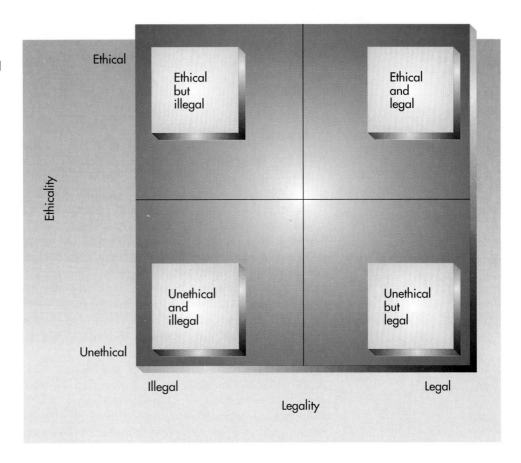

Current Perceptions of Ethical Behavior

There has been a public outcry about the ethical practices of businesspeople. Public opinion surveys show that 58 percent of U.S. adults rate the ethical standards of business executives as only "fair" or "poor"; 90 percent think white-collar crime is "very common" or "somewhat common"; 76 percent say the lack of ethics in businesspeople contributes to tumbling societal moral standards; only the U.S. government is viewed as less trustworthy than corporations among institutions in the United States; and advertising practitioners and car salespeople are thought to be among the least ethical occupations.[7] A recent survey of 1,000 senior corporate executives confirms this public perception. Two thirds of these executives think people are "occasionally" unethical in their business dealings; 15 percent believe they are "often" unethical; and 16 percent consider people "seldom" without ethics.[8]

There are at least four possible reasons the state of perceived ethical business conduct is at its present level. First, there is increased pressure on businesspeople to make decisions in a society characterized by diverse value systems.[9] Second, there is a growing tendency for business decisions to be judged publicly by groups with different values and interests. Third, the public's expectations of ethical business behavior has increased. Finally, and most disturbing, ethical business conduct may have declined.[10]

CONCEPT CHECK

1. What are ethics?

2. What are four possible reasons for the present state of ethical conduct in the United States?

UNDERSTANDING ETHICAL MARKETING BEHAVIOR

Researchers have identified numerous factors that influence ethical marketing behavior.[11] Figure 4–2 presents a framework that shows these factors and their relationships.

Societal Culture and Norms

As described in Chapter 3, *culture* refers to the set of values, ideas, and attitudes of a homogeneous group of people that are transmitted from one generation to the next. Culture also affects ethical relationships between individuals, groups, and the institutions and organizations they create. In this way, culture serves as a socializing force that dictates what is morally right and just. This means that moral standards are relative to particular societies. These standards often reflect the laws and regulations that affect social and economic behavior, including business practices, which can create moral dilemmas. For example, Levi Strauss has decided to end much of its business dealings in China because of what the company called "pervasive human rights abuses." According to its vice president for corporate marketing: "There are wonderful commercial opportunities in China. But when ethical issues collide with commercial appeal, we try to ensure ethics as the trump card. For us, ethical issues precede all others."[12]

Many of the laws affecting U.S. marketing practices were outlined in Chapter 3. Actions that restrain trade, fix prices, deceive buyers, and result in unsafe products are considered morally wrong in the United States and other countries. However, different cultures view marketing practices differently. Consider the use of another's ideas, copyright, trademark, or patent. These are viewed as intellectual property, and unauthorized use is illegal and unethical in the United States. For example, Hallmark Cards, Inc. was charged with copying the ideas of a smaller card company without its consent. The courts ruled that Hallmark must stop publishing the cards, buy back existing cards from 21,000 Hallmark stores, and pay damages to the owners of the company.[13]

Outside the United States, however, is another story.[14] U.S. companies estimate that unauthorized use of their copyrights, trademarks, and patents in countries such as China, Mexico, and Korea costs about $50 billion annually. In Korea, for instance, copying is partly rooted in its society's culture. According to a U.S. trade official, many Koreans "have the idea that the thoughts of one man should benefit all," and the Korean government rarely prosecutes infringements.

FIGURE 4–2

A framework for understanding ethical behavior

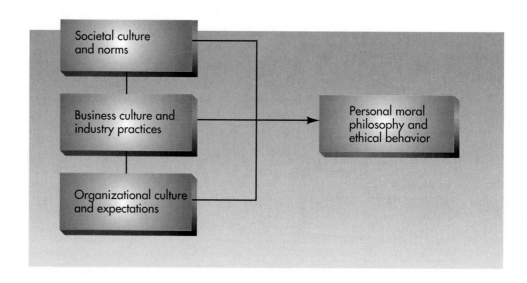

MARKETING NEWSNET

SOFTWARE PIRACY IN CYBERSPACE: THE DARK SIDE OF GLOBAL ELECTRONIC NETWORKING

Technology   The Internet links some 100 countries and an estimated 25 million computer users. The many benefits of electronic networking often overshadow its dark side: software piracy. Anyone with a computer and modem can distribute software silently, instantaneously, and illegally. Indeed, a 20-year-old U.S. college student was recently attributed with distributing an estimated $1 million worth of copyrighted programs through the Internet.

The U.S. Software Publishers Association (SPA) estimates that the unauthorized copying of computer software costs their producers the equivalent of $13 billion in worldwide sales annually. Software piracy has become pandemic in many developing countries. According to the SPA, 98 percent of the software in China is pirated, 95 percent in Russia, 92 percent in Thailand, 87 percent in India and Pakistan, 84 percent in the Czech and Slovak Republics, and 82 percent in Mexico. About 35 percent of the software used in the United States has been copied illegally.

Software programs are intellectual property, and their unauthorized use is illegal in many countries. But, for some, their reproduction and distribution is not considered unethical.

Read the accompanying Marketing NewsNet,[15] keeping in mind the ethical–legal framework in Figure 4–1. Would the unauthorized use of copyrighted computer software be considered unethical despite its prevalence?

Business Culture and Industry Practices

Societal culture provides a foundation for understanding moral behavior in business activities. *Business cultures* "comprise the effective rules of the game, the boundaries between competitive and unethical behavior, [and] the codes of conduct in business dealings."[16] Consumers have witnessed numerous instances where business cultures in the brokerage (inside trading), insurance (deceptive sales practices), and defense (bribery) industries went awry. Business culture affects ethical conduct both in the exchange relationship between sellers and buyers and in the competitive behavior among sellers.

Ethics of exchange   The exchange process is central to the marketing concept. Ethical exchanges between sellers and buyers should result in both parties being better off after a transaction.[17]

Prior to the 1960s, the legal concept of **caveat emptor**—let the buyer beware—was pervasive in the American business culture. In 1962 President John F. Kennedy outlined a **Consumer Bill of Rights** that codified the ethics of exchange between buyers and sellers. These were the right (1) to safety, (2) to be informed, (3) to choose, and (4) to be heard.

Consumers expect and often demand that these rights be protected, as have American businesses. However, exceptions exist. A. H. Robins sold the Dalkon

Supporters of animal rights advocate against using animals for product testing.

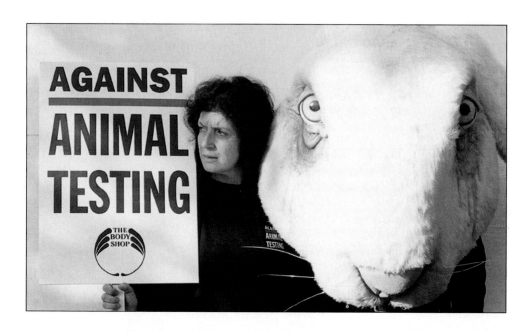

Shield, an intrauterine device, that was known to be potentially harmful to women. The company has since established a $2.5 billion fund to compensate women harmed by this device.[18]

The right to be informed means that marketers have an obligation to give consumers complete and accurate information about products and services, but this is not always the case. Dollar Rent-A-Car Systems, Inc. and Value Rent-A-Car, Inc. recently agreed to settle FTC claims that they failed to disclose mandatory extra charges such as an airport surcharge and additional charges for customers under age 25 when making price quotations through computerized reservation systems.[19]

Relating to the third right, today many supermarket chains demand "slotting allowances" from manufacturers, in the form of cash or free goods, to stock new products. This practice could limit the number of new products available to consumers and interfere with their right to choose. One critic of this practice remarked: "If we had had slotting allowances a few years ago, we might not have had granola, herbal tea, or yogurt."[20]

Finally, the right to be heard means that consumers should have access to public-policy makers regarding complaints about products and services. This right was illustrated in limitations put on telemarketing practices. Consumer complaints about late-night and repeated calls resulted in the Telephone Consumer Protection Act of 1991. Additional curbs on misrepresentation were enacted by the Federal Trade Commission in 1995 as a result of continued consumer complaints.[21] Consumer complaints against the use of animals for product testing also have led to curbs against this practice, particularly among cosmetic manufacturers.

Ethics of competition   Business culture also affects ethical behavior in competition. Two kinds of unethical behavior are most common: (1) industrial espionage and (2) bribery.

Industrial espionage is the clandestine collection of trade secrets or proprietary information about a company's competitors. About 40 percent of large U.S. and Canadian firms have uncovered espionage in some form, costing them more than $20 billion a year.[22] This practice is most prevalent in high-technology industries such as electronics, specialty chemicals, industrial equipment, aerospace, and pharmaceuticals, where technical know-how and trade secrets separate industry leaders from followers. But espionage can occur anywhere—even in the ready-to-eat cookie industry! Procter & Gamble charged that competitors photographed its plants and production lines, stole a sample of its cookie dough, and infiltrated a confidential sales presentation to learn about its technology, recipe, and marketing plan. The competitors paid Procter & Gamble $120 million in damages after a lengthy dispute.[23]

The second form of unethical competitive behavior is giving and receiving bribes and kickbacks. Bribes and kickbacks are often disguised as gifts, consultant fees, and favors. This practice is more common in business-to-business and government marketing than in consumer marketing. For example, two American Honda Motor Company executives were recently fined and sentenced to prison for extracting $15 million in kickbacks from Honda dealers and advertising agencies,[24] and a series of highly publicized trials uncovered widespread bribery in the U.S. Defense Department's awarding of $160 billion in military contracts.[25]

The prevalence of bribery in international marketing prompted legislation to curb this practice. The **Foreign Corrupt Practices Act** makes it a crime for U.S. corporations to bribe an official of a foreign government or political party to obtain or retain business in a foreign country. In the past 15 years, at least 20 individuals and corporations have been convicted or have pleaded guilty to bribery or related offenses.[26] Bribery is looked upon differently in other business cultures, however. In Denmark, bribes paid to foreign companies are a tax-deductible expense![27]

In general, ethical standards are more likely to be compromised in industries experiencing intense competition and in countries in earlier stages of economic development.[28] A survey of marketing executives in the United States, western Germany, and France revealed that western Germany was perceived as having the most ethical business culture. The United Kingdom was second, followed by the United States and France. European and U.S. marketing executives generally rate Japan and Singapore as having the most ethical business cultures in Asia. China is viewed as having the most troubling business culture.

Corporate Culture and Expectations

A third influence on ethical practices is corporate culture. *Corporate culture* reflects the shared values, beliefs, and purpose of employees that affect individual and group behavior. The culture of a company demonstrates itself in the dress ("We don't wear ties"), sayings ("The IBM Way"), and manner of work (team efforts) of employees. Culture is also apparent in the expectations for ethical behavior present in formal codes of ethics and the ethical actions of top management and co-workers.

Codes of ethics   A **code of ethics** is a formal statement of ethical principles and rules of conduct. It is estimated that 60 percent of U.S. companies and one half of European companies have some sort of ethics code, and 1 of every 10 corporate boards of directors now has a separate ethics committee to monitor company practices.[29] Ethics codes and committees typically address contributions to government officials and political parties, relations with customers and suppliers, conflicts of interest, and accurate recordkeeping. For example, General Mills provides guidelines for dealing with suppliers, competitors, and customers and recruits new employees who share these views. However, an ethics code is rarely enough to ensure ethical behavior. Johnson & Johnson has an ethics code and emphasizes that its employees be just and ethical in their behavior. But neither prohibited some of its employees from shredding papers to hinder a recent government probe into the firm's marketing of an acne cream, Retin-A.[30]

The lack of specificity is one of the major reasons for the violation of ethics codes. Employees must often judge whether a specific behavior is really unethical. The American Marketing Association has addressed this issue by providing a detailed code of ethics, which all members agree to follow. This code is shown in Figure 4–3.

Ethical behavior of management and co-workers   A second reason for violating ethics codes rests in the perceived behavior of top management and co-workers.[31] Observing peers and top management and gauging responses to unethical

CODE OF ETHICS

Members of the American Marketing Association (AMA) are committed to ethical professional conduct. They have joined together in subscribing to this Code of Ethics embracing the following topics:

Responsibilities of the Marketer

Marketers must accept responsibility for the consequence of their activities and make every effort to ensure that their decisions, recommendations, and actions function to identify, serve, and satisfy all relevant publics: customers, organizations, and society.

Marketers' professional conduct must be guided by:

1. The basic rule of professional ethics: not knowingly to do harm.
2. The adherence to all applicable laws and regulations.
3. The accurate representation of their education, training and experience.
4. The active support, practice, and promotion of this Code of Ethics.

Honesty and Fairness

Marketers shall uphold and advance the integrity, honor, and dignity of the marketing profession by:

1. Being honest in serving consumers, clients, employees, suppliers, distributors, and the public.

2. Not knowingly participating in conflict of interest without prior notice to all parties involved.
3. Establishing equitable fee schedules including the payment or receipt of usual, customary, and/or legal compensation or marketing exchanges.

Rights and Duties of Parties in the Marketing Exchange Process

Participants in the marketing exchange process should be able to expect that:

1. Products and services offered are safe and fit for their intended uses.
2. Communications about offered products and services are not deceptive.
3. All parties intend to discharge their obligations, financial and otherwise, in good faith.
4. Appropriate internal methods exist for equitable adjustment and/or redress of grievances concerning purchases.

It is understood that the above would include, *but is not limited to*, the following responsibilities of the marketer:

In the area of product development and management

- Disclosure of all substantial risks associated with product or service usage.

FIGURE 4–3

American Marketing Association Code of Ethics

behavior play an important role in individual actions. A recent study of business executives reported that 40 percent had been implicitly or explicitly rewarded for engaging in ethically troubling behavior. Moreover, 31 percent of those who refused to engage in unethical behavior were penalized, either through outright punishment or a diminished status in the company.[32] Clearly, ethical dilemmas often bring personal and professional conflict. For this reason, 35 states have laws protecting **whistle-blowers,** employees who report unethical or illegal actions of their employers. Some firms, such as General Dynamics and Dun & Bradstreet, have appointed ethics officers responsible for safeguarding these individuals from recrimination.[33]

Personal Moral Philosophy and Ethical Behavior

Ultimately, ethical choices are based on the personal moral philosophy of the decision maker. Moral philosophy is learned through the process of socialization with friends and family and by formal education. It is also influenced by the societal, business, and corporate culture in which a person finds him- or herself. Moral philosophies are of two types: (1) moral idealism and (2) utilitarianism.[34]

Moral idealism   Moral idealism is a personal moral philosophy that considers certain individual rights or duties as universal, regardless of the outcome. This philosophy exists in the Consumer Bill of Rights and is favored by moral philosophers and consumer interest groups. For example, the right to know applies to probable defects in an automobile that relate to safety.

This philosophy also applies to ethical duties. For example, Jerome LiCari, director of research for the Beech-Nut Nutrition Corporation, advised the Food and Drug Administration that Beech-Nut was selling a blend of synthetic ingredients

FIGURE 4-3—CONTINUED

- Identification of any product component substitution that might materially change the product or impact on the buyer's purchase decision.
- Identification of extra-cost added features.

In the area of promotions

- Avoidance of false and misleading advertising.
- Rejection of high-pressure manipulation, or misleading sales tactics.
- Avoidance of sales promotions that use deception or manipulation.

In the area of distribution

- Not manipulating the availability of a product for purpose of exploitation.
- Not using coercion in the marketing channel.
- Not exerting undue influence over the reseller's choice to handle the product.

In the area of pricing

- Not engaging in price fixing.
- Not practicing predatory pricing.
- Disclosing the full price associated with any purchase.

In the area of marketing research

- Prohibiting selling or fund raising under the guise of conducting research.

- Maintaining research integrity by avoiding misrepresentation and omission of pertinent research data.
- Treating outside clients and suppliers fairly.

Organizational Relationships

Marketers should be aware of how their behavior may influence or impact on the behavior of others in organizational relationships. They should not demand, encourage, or apply coercion to obtain unethical behavior in their relationships with others, such as employees, suppliers, or customers.

1. Apply confidentiality and anonymity in professional relationships with regard to privileged information.
2. Meet their obligations and responsibilities in contracts and mutual agreements in a timely manner.
3. Avoid taking the work of others, in whole or in part, and represent this work as their own or directly benefit from it without compensation or consent of the originator or owner.
4. Avoid manipulation to take advantage of situations to maximize personal welfare in a way that unfairly deprives or damages the organization or others.

Any AMA members found to be in violation of any provision of this Code of Ethics may have his or her Association membership suspended or revoked.

Source: Reprinted by permission of the American Marketing Association.

labeled as 100 percent apple juice. He did so only after his superiors ignored his internal memos. Beech-Nut was subsequently fined $2 million, the company's market share dropped 3 percent, and two executives were indicted. When asked why he acted as he did, LiCari said: "I thought apple juice should be made from apples."[35] LiCari later resigned from Beech-Nut.

Utilitarianism   An alternative perspective on moral philosophy is **utilitarianism,** which is a personal moral philosophy that focuses on "the greatest good for the greatest number," by assessing the costs and benefits of the consequences of ethical behavior. If the benefits exceed the costs, then the behavior is ethical. If not, then the behavior is unethical. This philosophy underlies the economic tenets of capitalism[36] and, not surprisingly, is embraced by many business executives and students.[37]

Some infants had allergic reactions to Nestlé's Good Start formula. Read the text to find out what the company did.

Utilitarian reasoning was apparent in Nestlé Food Corporation's marketing of Good Start infant formula, sold by Nestlé's Carnation Company. The formula, promoted as hypoallergenic, was designed to prevent or reduce colic caused by an infant's allergic reaction to cow's milk—a condition suffered by 2 percent of babies. However, some severely milk-allergic infants experienced serious side effects after using Good Start, including convulsive vomiting. Physicians and parents charged that the hypoallergenic claim was misleading, and the Food and Drug Administration investigated the matter. A Nestlé vice president defended the claim and product, saying, "I don't understand why our product should work in 100 percent of cases. If we wanted to say it was foolproof, we would have called it allergy-free. We call it hypo-, or less, allergenic."[38] Nestlé officials seemingly believed that most allergic infants would benefit from Good Start—"the greatest good for the greatest number." However, other views prevailed, and the claim was dropped from the product label.

An appreciation for the nature of ethics, coupled with a basic understanding of why unethical behavior arises, alerts a person to when and how ethical issues exist in marketing decisions. Ultimately, ethical behavior rests with the individual, but the consequences affect many.

CONCEPT CHECK

1. What rights are included in the Consumer Bill of Rights?

2. What ethical practice is addressed in the Foreign Corrupt Practices Act?

3. What is meant by moral idealism?

UNDERSTANDING SOCIAL RESPONSIBILITY IN MARKETING

As we saw in Chapter 1, the societal marketing concept stresses marketing's social responsibility by not only satisfying the needs of consumers but also providing for society's welfare. **Social responsibility** means that organizations are part of a larger society and are accountable to that society for their actions. Like ethics, agreement on the nature and scope of social responsibility is often difficult to come by, given the diversity of values present in different societal, business, and organizational cultures.

Concepts of Social Responsibility

Figure 4–4 shows three concepts of social responsibility: (1) profit responsibility, (2) stakeholder responsibility, and (3) societal responsibility.

Profit responsibility   *Profit responsibility* holds that companies have a simple duty—to maximize profits for their owners or stockholders. This view is expressed by Nobel Laureate Milton Friedman, who said, "There is one and only one social responsibility of business—to use its resources and engage in activities designed to increase its profits so long as it stays within the rules of the game, which is to say, engages in open and free competition without deception or fraud."[39] Genzyme, the maker of Ceredase, a drug that treats a genetic illness called Gaucher's disease that affects 20,000 people worldwide, has been criticized for apparently adopting this view in its pricing practices. Genzyme charges up to $200,000 for a year's worth of Ceredese. Critics claim this practice takes advantage of the federal "orphan drug" law, which grants companies a 7-year monopoly on drugs for rare diseases, and is engaged in profiteering. A Genzyme spokesperson responded by saying that Ceredase profits are below industry standards and that the company freely gives the drug to patients without insurance.[40]

Stakeholder responsibility   Frequent criticism of the profit view has led to a broader concept of social responsibility. *Stakeholder responsibility* focuses on the

Which of the three concepts of social responsibility do you think Perrier applied when it learned of quality problems with its popular water? Read the text to learn how they responded to this problem and their reasoning.

obligations an organization has to those who can affect achievement of its objectives. These constituencies include customers, employees, suppliers, and distributors. Source Perrier S.A., the supplier of Perrier bottled water, exercised this responsibility when it recalled 160 million bottles of water in 120 countries after traces of a toxic chemical were found in 13 bottles. The recall cost the company $35 million, and $40 million more was lost in sales. Even though the chemical level was not harmful to humans, Source Perrier's president believed he acted in the best interests of the firm's consumers, distributors, and employees by removing "the least doubt, as minimal as it might be, to weigh on the image of the quality and purity of our product."[41]

Societal responsibility   An even broader concept of social responsibility has emerged in recent years. *Societal responsibility* refers to obligations that organizations have to the (1) preservation of the ecological environment and (2) general public. Concerns about the environment and public welfare are represented by interest and advocacy groups such as Greenpeace, an international environmental organization.

Chapter 3 detailed the growing importance of ecological issues in marketing. Companies have responded to this concern through what is termed **green**

FIGURE 4–4

Three concepts of social responsibility

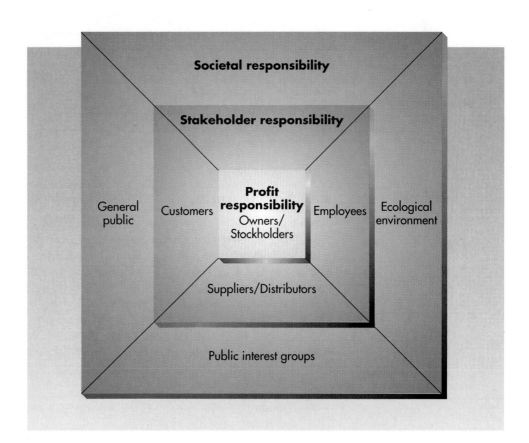

marketing—marketing efforts to produce, promote, and reclaim environmentally sensitive products. Green marketing takes many forms.[42] For example, Shell Oil Company now sells an environmentally cleaner gasoline in the nine U.S. cities with the most severe air-quality problems. H. J. Heinz (Starkist brand), Van Kamp Seafood

Procter & Gamble minimized solid waste by introducing Downy Refill, which uses 75 percent less packaging material.

(Chicken of the Sea brand), and Bumble Bee Seafoods will no longer buy tuna from fishing fleets using techniques that kill or harm dolphins. The aluminum industry recycles nearly two thirds of aluminum cans for reuse and pays consumers $1 billion annually for used cans. Procter & Gamble has introduced Downy Refill liquid fabric softener, which reduces solid waste pollution. The product's plastic bottle is reuseable, and the refill carton uses 75 percent less packaging material. Levi Strauss and Esprit have launched clothing lines using cotton that is naturally colored, thus reducing the need for dyes, a source of water pollution. These voluntary responses to environmental issues were implemented with little or no additional cost to consumers.

Socially responsible efforts on behalf of the general public are becoming more common. A formal practice is **cause-related marketing** (CRM), which occurs when the charitable contributions of a firm are tied directly to the customer revenues produced through the promotion of one of its products.[43] This definition distinguishes CRM from a firm's standard charitable contributions, which are outright donations. For example, Procter & Gamble raises funds for the Special Olympics when consumers purchase selected company products, and MasterCard International linked usage of its card with fund raising for institutions that combat cancer, heart disease, child abuse, drug abuse, and muscular dystrophy. Avon Products, Inc. focuses on different issues in different countries: breast cancer in the United States, Canada, Philippines, Mexico, Venezuela, Malaysia, and Spain; programs for women who care for senior citizens in Japan; emotional and financial support for mothers in Germany; and AIDS in Thailand. CRM programs incorporate all three concepts of social responsibility by addressing public concerns, satisfying customer needs, and enhancing corporate sales and profits.

The Social Audit

Converting socially responsible ideas into actions involves careful planning and monitoring of programs. Many companies develop, implement, and evaluate their social responsibility efforts by means of a **social audit,** which is a systematic assessment of a firm's objectives, strategies, and performance in the domain of social responsibility. Frequently, marketing and social responsibility programs are integrated, as is the case with McDonald's. The company's concern for the needs of families with children who are chronically or terminally ill was converted into some 130 Ronald McDonald Houses. These facilities, located near treatment centers, enable families to stay together during the child's care. In this case, McDonald's is contributing to the welfare of a portion of its target market.

A social audit consists of five steps:[44]

1. Recognition of a firm's social expectations and the rationale for engaging in social responsibility endeavors.

Marketing and social responsibility programs are often integrated, as is the case with McDonald's. Its concern for ill children is apparent in the opening of another Ronald McDonald House for children and their families.

2. Identification of social responsibility causes or programs consistent with the company's mission.
3. Determination of organizational objectives and priorities for programs and activities it will undertake.
4. Specification of the type and amount of resources necessary to achieve social responsibility objectives.
5. Evaluation of social responsibility programs and activities undertaken and assessment of future involvement.

Attention to the social audit on environmental matters has increased since 1989, when the Exxon *Valdez* oil tanker spilled 11 million gallons of crude oil in Alaska's Prince William Sound. This spill killed tens of thousands of birds and mammals and fouled a thousand miles of Alaskan coastline. Soon after, the Coalition for Environmentally Responsible Economics drafted guidelines designed to focus attention on environmental concerns and corporate responsibility. These guidelines, called the **Valdez Principles,** encourage companies to (1) eliminate pollutants, minimize hazardous wastes, and conserve nonrenewable resources; (2) market environmentally safe products and services; (3) prepare for accidents and restore damaged environments; (4) provide protection for employees who report environmental hazards; and (5) appoint an environmentalist to their boards of directors, name an executive for environmental affairs, and develop an environmental audit of their global operations to be made available for public inspection.[45] Numerous companies now embrace these guidelines and have environmental policy officers. Nevertheless, environmental mishaps still occur. Rockwell International was recently fined $18.5 million for illegally dumping waste in Colorado, with a cleanup expense of $200 million.[46]

Development and use of a social audit will depend on the extent to which a company's culture embraces social and environmental responsibility as part of its

MARKETING NEWSNET

AT 3M, THE CHALLENGE IS CLEAR: CREATE ENVIRONMENTALLY FRIENDLY PRODUCTS THAT PROVIDE VALUE FOR CONSUMERS

"People didn't like getting stuck by steel wool," observed Moe S. Nozari, vice president of 3M's consumer products division, after seeing the results from consumer interviews. Consumers also said they would pay a little extra for a scouring pad that didn't rust or fray. Here was an opportunity for 3M in the $300 million scouring pad market dominated by Clorox and its S.O.S. brand—provided company researchers could develop an environmentally friendly product.

At 3M, product development opportunities emanate both from consumer research and its "Pollution Prevention Pays" program. Begun in 1975, this program solicits employee suggestions on how to cut waste and recycle materials. This program has generated 4,100 ideas that have eliminated 1.3 billion pounds of pollutants from the environment and saved 3M more than $170 million.

The challenge to 3M researchers was clear: develop a scouring a pad that appealed to consumers and was environmentally friendly. The result: 3M's Scotch-Brite™ Never Rust™ Wool Soap Pad. Scotch-Brite Never Rust pad was made from recycled plastic, used a nonphosphorous soap that does not pollute rivers and streams, and was packaged in a 100 percent recycled paper box. Scotch-Brite pads were priced 12 percent

higher than competitive brands, but they still captured 16 percent of the scouring pad market and has become a tidy $20-plus million business. For good measure, the reduced waste from manufacturing cut pollution and decreased 3M's costs.

overall mission. 3M is considered an innovator in this regard. Read the accompanying Marketing NewsNet to see how 3M is responding to the need for environmentally safe products that also create customer value.[47]

Turning the Table: Consumer Ethics and Social Responsibility

Consumers also have an obligation to act ethically and responsibly in the exchange process and in the use and disposition of products. Unfortunately, consumer behavior is spotty on both counts.

Unethical practices of consumers are a serious concern to marketers.[48] These practices include filing warranty claims after the claim period, misredeeming coupons, making fraudulent returns of merchandise, providing inaccurate information on credit applications, tampering with utility meters, tapping cable TV lines, recording copyrighted music and videocassettes, and submitting phony insurance claims. The cost to marketers in lost sales revenue and prevention expenses is huge.[49] For example, consumers who redeem coupons for unpurchased products or use coupons destined for other products cost manufacturers $1 billion each year. The record industry alone loses $1 billion annually due to illegal recording, and about 12 percent of VCR owners make illegal copies of videotapes, costing producers millions of dollars in lost revenue. Electrical utilities lose between 1 and 3 percent of yearly revenues due to meter tampering.

Consumer purchase, use, and disposition of environmentally sensitive products relate to consumer social responsibility. Research indicates that consumers are sensitive to ecological issues.[50] However, research also shows that consumers (1) may be unwilling to sacrifice convenience and pay potentially higher prices to protect the environment and (2) lack the knowledge to make informed decisions dealing with the purchase, use, and disposition of products.[51]

Consumer confusion over which products are environmentally safe is also apparent, given marketers' rush to produce "green products." For example, few consumers realize that nonaerosol "pump" hairsprays are the second-largest cause of air pollution, after drying paint. In California alone, 27 tons of noxious hairspray fumes are expelled every day.[52] And "biodegradable" claims on a variety of products, including trash bags, have not proven to be accurate, thus leading to buyer confusion.[53] The FTC has recently drafted guidelines that describe the circumstances when environmental claims can be made and would not constitute misleading information. For example, an advertisement or product label touting a package as "50 percent more recycled content than before" could be misleading if the recycled content has increased from 2 percent to 3 percent.[54]

Ultimately, marketers and consumers are accountable for ethical and socially responsible behavior. The twenty-first century will prove to be a testing period for both.

CONCEPT CHECK

1. What is meant by social responsibility?

2. Marketing efforts to produce, promote, and reclaim environmentally sensitive products are called _____ .

3. What is a social audit?

Summary

1. Ethics are the moral principles and values that govern the actions and decisions of an individual or group. Laws are society's values and standards that are enforceable in the courts. Operating according to the law does not necessarily mean that a practice is ethical.

2. Ethical behavior of businesspeople has come under severe criticism by the public. There are four possible reasons for this criticism: (*a*) increased pressure on businesspeople to make decisions in a society characterized by diverse value systems, (*b*) a growing tendency to have business decisions judged publicly by groups with different values and interests, (*c*) an increase in the public's expectations for ethical behavior, and (*d*) a possible decline in business ethics.

3. Numerous external factors influence ethical behavior of businesspeople. These include the following: (*a*) societal culture and norms, (*b*) business culture and industry practices, and (*c*) organizational culture and expectations. Each factor influences the opportunity to engage in ethical or unethical behavior.

4. Ultimately, ethical choices are based on the personal moral philosophy of the decision maker. Two moral philosophies are most prominent: (*a*) moral idealism and (*b*) utilitarianism.

5. Social responsibility means that organizations are part of a larger society and are accountable to that society for their actions.

6. There are three concepts of social responsibility: (*a*) profit responsibility, (*b*) stakeholder responsibility, and (*c*) societal responsibility.

7. Growing interest in societal responsibility has resulted in systematic efforts to assess a firm's objectives, strategies, and performance in the domain of social responsibility. This practice is called a *social audit*.

8. Consumer ethics and social responsibility are as important as business ethics and social responsibility.

KEY TERMS AND CONCEPTS

ethics p. 102
laws p. 102
caveat emptor p. 105
Consumer Bill of Rights   p. 105
Foreign Corrupt Practices Act   p. 107
code of ethics p. 107
whistleblowers p. 108

moral idealism p. 108
utilitarianism p. 109
social responsibility p. 110
green marketing p. 111-112
cause-related marketing   p. 112
social audit p. 112
Valdez Principles p. 113

CHAPTER PROBLEMS AND APPLICATIONS

✓ **1.** What concepts of moral philosophy and social responsibility are applicable to the practices of Anheuser-Busch described in the introduction to this chapter? Why?

2. Five ethical situations were presented in this chapter: (*a*) a medical society's decision to set fee schedules, (*b*) the use of a computer program by auto dealers to arrange financing, (*c*) R. J. Reynolds's introduction of Uptown cigarettes, (*d*) the copying of trademarks and patents in Korea, and (*e*) the pricing of Ceredase for the treatment of a rare genetic illness. Where would each of these situations fit in Figure 4–1?

3. The American Marketing Association Code of Ethics shown in Figure 4–3 details the rights and duties of parties in

the marketing exchange process. How do these rights and duties compare with the Consumer Bill of Rights?

4. Compare and contrast moral idealism and utilitarianism as alternative personal moral philosophies.

5. How would you evaluate Milton Friedman's view of the social responsibility of a firm?

✓ **6.** The text lists several unethical practices of consumers. Can you name others? Why do you think consumers engage in unethical conduct?

7. Cause-related marketing programs have become popular. Describe two such programs that you are familiar with.

CASE 4–1   Pricing in the Pharmaceutical Industry

In 1996, U.S. consumers were projected to spend over $65 billion for prescription drugs used to treat acute and chronic ailments. Between 1985 and 1995, prescription drug prices rose 80 percent, which was twice the rate of inflation for the same period. These statistics have prompted severe criticism of pharmaceutical firms by public health officials, government agencies, and consumer advocacy groups. Pharmaceutical firm executives in the United States have responded citing the large research and development costs for drugs, extensive testing required to obtain Food and Drug Administration (FDA) approval, and marketplace uncertainties as valid reasons for high drug prices.

FAIR AND REASONABLE PRICING

A central issue in the debate concerning prescription drug pricing relates to what is a "fair and reasonable price." Critics of drug pricing spotlight instances where they believe the prices charged are excessive. For instance, Ceredase, a drug for victims of rare metabolic disorder, sells for $200,000 annually per patient. Clozapine, designed to treat schizophrenia, cost patients almost $9,000 per year. A drug to prevent an AIDS-related blindness, called Foscavir, costs $21,000 per patient annually.

Pharmaceutical firms counter critics' charges of excessive pricing using a variety of arguments. For example, the maker of Foscavir claimed the high price was necessary to recoup its financial investment in the drug. When Johnson & Johnson introduced a drug to treat colon cancer, the company cited some 1,400 studies involving 40,000 patients conducted over 25 years as the reason for the $1,250 price for a one-year supply. The price for Retrovir, an antiviral drug to treat AIDS, was justified with a variety of considerations, including its maker's "responsibility to patients and shareholders, the very real remaining uncertainties in the marketplace, and the vital need to fund our continuing research and development programs."

Debate over what is a "fair and reasonable" price for drugs typically focuses on economic versus societal factors, and the relative importance of a firm's stakeholders in setting prices. Often the final pricing decision depends on the individual judgment and moral sensitivity of the managers making the decision.

PROLIFE: PRICING ADL

Issues in the pricing of ADL, a treatment for Alzheimer's disease which affects the elderly, were recently faced by Prolife, a small pharmaceutical company. A task force of company executives was considering the pricing strategy for ADL. Two points of view were expressed: (1) pursuing a high-price strategy designed to recoup the costs of the drug quickly and getting a jump on the competition, and (2) pursuing a lower-price strategy to increase the drug's availability to victims of the disease.

Steve Vaughn, an Assistant Product Manager at Prolife, was the principal proponent of a lower-price strategy. He argued that a less aggressive price strategy made sense even though it would take slightly longer to recoup the initial investment in ADL. Having a family member afflicted with Alzheimer's disease, Mr. Vaughn felt that the ability of victims and their families to pay for the drug should be considered when setting the price for ADL. He was overruled, however, by the task force members. Believing that his views deserved attention and action, and that "bottom line" considerations did not negate his position, he lobbied other task force members and has thought about expressing his opinion to senior executives at Prolife. He was cautioned by Bill Compton, a Prolife Senior Product Manager and his mentor, to reconsider his position noting that Prolife is a business and that "rocking the boat" might not be an advantage to his career at Prolife.

Questions

1. Who are the primary stakeholders that must be considered when setting prices for prescription drugs?

2. How might the personal moral philosophies of moral idealism and utilitarianism be applied to prescription drug pricing in general and in the specific case of ADL?

3. How might the three concepts of social responsibility described in Chapter 4 be applied to prescription pricing in general and in the specific case of ADL?

4. If you were Steve Vaughn, what would you do in this situation?

PART TWO

UNDERSTANDING BUYERS AND MARKETS

Using local and global perspectives to understand people as individual consumers and as members of companies that become organizational buyers is the focus of Part II. Chapter 5 describes the nature and scope of world trade and examines the global marketing activities of such companies as McDonald's, Harley-Davidson, Campbell Soup Company, Nestlé, Caterpillar, Ford, Coca-Cola, and Procter & Gamble. Chapter 6 examines the actions buyers take in purchasing and using products, and explains how and why one product or brand is chosen over another. In Chapter 7 Bob Proscal, a marketing manager for Fiber Optics Products at Honeywell, helps explain how manufacturers, retailers, and government agencies also buy goods and services for their own use or resale. Together these chapters help marketing students understand individual, family, and organizational purchases in a variety of cultural environments.

CHAPTER 5

Global Marketing and World Trade

• Describe the nature and scope of world trade from a global perspective and its implications for the United States.

• Explain the effects of economic protectionism and the implications of economic integration for global marketing practices.

• Understand the importance of environmental factors (cultural, economic, and political) in shaping global marketing efforts.

• Describe alternative approaches firms use to enter and compete in global markets.

• Identify specific challenges marketers face when crafting worldwide marketing programs.

COMPETING IN THE GLOBAL MARKETPLACE

American marketers cannot ignore the vast potential of global markets. About 95 percent of the world's population lives outside the United States. These potential consumers possess roughly 75 percent of the world's purchasing power. Not only are global markets substantial, but many are growing faster than comparable markets in the United States—a fact not lost on both large and small global-minded companies.

Successful marketers have responded to three challenges in the global marketplace. First, they have satisfied the needs of a discriminating global consumer who increasingly purchases goods and services on the basis of value. For example, Motorola was recently chosen over three formidable Japanese competitors to produce the microprocessor for Canon's successful 35mm camera by not only meeting, but exceeding, Canon's demanding price and quality specifications. Second, these marketers have capitalized on trends favoring free trade among industrialized nations throughout the world. Recognizing the liberalization of retailing restrictions in Asian countries, Toys "Я" Us has successfully opened stores in Hong Kong, Malaysia, Taiwan, Singapore, and recently Japan—the world's second-largest toy market behind the United States. Finally, marketers have vigorously pursued opportunities in Eastern Europe and the former Soviet Union. The successful Russian-language version of *Cosmopolitan* has a print run of 430,000 copies, making it the second-largest edition of the magazine in the world, after the United States.[1]

Pursuit of global markets by American and foreign marketers ultimately results in world trade. The purpose of this chapter is to describe the nature and scope of world trade and highlight challenges involved in global marketing.

DYNAMICS OF WORLD TRADE

The dollar value of world trade has grown an average of 12 percent per year since 1970 and will approach $8 trillion in 2005. Manufactured goods and commodities account for 80 percent of world trade. Service industries, including telecommunications, transportation, insurance, education, banking, and tourism, represent the other 20 percent of world trade.

World Trade Flows

All nations and regions of the world do not participate equally in world trade. World trade flows reflect interdependencies among industries, countries, and regions and manifest themselves in country, company, industry, and regional exports and imports.

Global perspective   Figure 5–1 shows the estimated dollar value of exports and imports among North American countries, Western Europe, Asian/Pacific Rim countries, and the rest of the world, including intraregional trade flows.[2] The United States, Western Europe, Canada, and Japan together account for two thirds of world trade.[3]

Not all trade involves the exchange of money for goods or services.[4] In a world where 70 percent of all countries do not have convertible currencies or where government-owned enterprises lack sufficient cash or credit for imports, other means of payment are used. An estimated 20 percent of world trade involves **countertrade,** the practice of using barter rather than money for making global sales. As an

FIGURE 5-1

Illustrative world trade flows (billions of dollars)

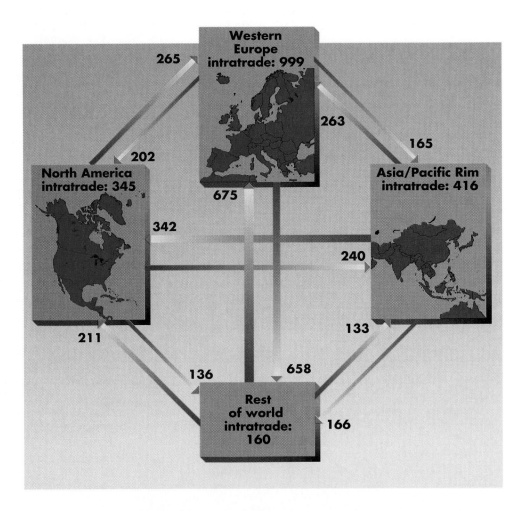

example, PepsiCo trades its soft-drink syrup concentrate in Russia in exchange for Stolichnaya vodka, which the company sells through Monsieur Henri Wines Ltd. in the United States. Initial shipments of vodka in 1973 totaled 20,000 cases; in almost 25 years, this countertrade had expanded to more than a million cases plus two oil tankers! Countertrade is popular with many Eastern European nations and developing countries.

A global perspective on world trade views exports and imports as complementary economic flows: a country's imports affect its exports and exports affect its imports.[5] Every nation's imports arise from the exports of other nations. As the exports of one country increase, its national output and income rise, which, in turn, leads to an increase in the demand for imports. This nation's greater demand for imports stimulates the exports of other countries. Increased demand for exports of other nations energizes their economic activity, resulting in higher national income, which stimulates their demand for imports. In short, imports affect exports and vice versa. This phenomenon is called the **trade feedback effect** and is one argument for free trade among nations.

Continually rising consumer income in Japan, Taiwan, India, China, South Korea, Hong Kong, and other Asian/Pacific Rim countries, fueled by their growth in exports, has prompted demand for goods and services from the United States. U.S. companies benefiting from rising consumer incomes in the Asian/Pacific Rim region include General Motors, which exports 14,000 U.S.-made cars to Taiwan annually: Johnson & Johnson, with a robust business for lotions and shampoos in South Korea; and Eastman Kodak, which dominates the $1 billion film market for professional photography in Japan.

United States perspective   The United States is the world's perennial leader in terms of **gross domestic product** (GDP), which is the monetary value of all goods and services produced in a country during one year. The United States is also among the world's leaders in exports due in large part to its global prominence in the aircraft, chemical, office equipment, pharmaceutical, telecommunications, and professional service industries. However, the U.S. percentage share of world exports has shifted downward since 1960, while its percentage share of world imports has increased. Therefore, the relative position of the United States as a supplier to the world has diminished despite an absolute growth in exports. At the same time, its relative role as a marketplace for the world has increased, particularly for automobile, textile, apparel, and consumer electronics products.[6]

The difference between the monetary value of a nation's exports and imports is called the **balance of trade.** When a country's exports exceed its imports, it incurs a surplus in its balance of trade. When imports exceed exports, a deficit has occurred. World trade trends in U.S. exports and imports are reflected in the U.S. balance of trade. Figure 5–2 shows that since 1970 two important things have happened in U.S. exports and imports. First, with a few exceptions in the 1970s, imports have significantly exceeded exports each year, indicating that the United States is running a continuing balance of trade deficit. Second, the volume of both exports and imports is about 15 to 20 times what is was in 1965—showing why almost every American is significantly affected. The effect varies from the products they buy (Samsung VCRs from Korea, Waterford crystal from Ireland, Louis Vuitton luggage from France) to those they sell (General Motors's cars to Europe, Du Pont's chemicals to the Far East) and the additional jobs and improved standard of living that result.

World trade flows to and from the United States reflect demand and supply interdependencies for goods and services among nations and industries. The three largest importers of U.S. goods and services are Canada, Japan, and Mexico. These countries purchase approximately 40 percent of U.S. exports. The three largest exporters to the United States are Japan, Canada, and Mexico.

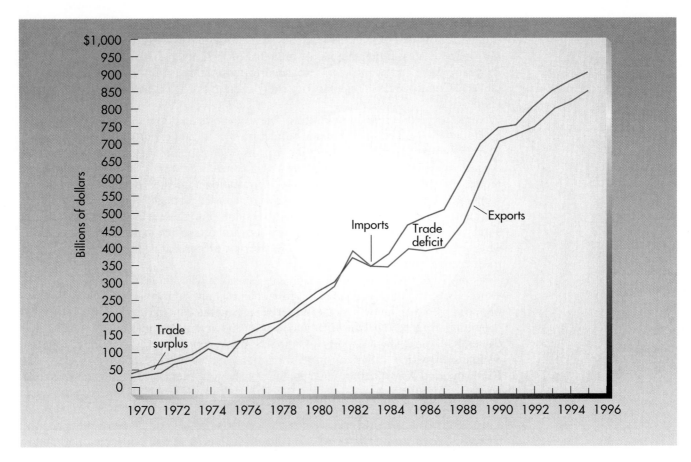

FIGURE 5–2

Trends in the U.S. balance of trade for goods and services

The United States is Asia's largest export market, buying about one third of the exports of Japan, Taiwan, South Korea, and China, a quarter of Hong Kong's exports, and 40 percent of the Philippines's exports. The trade imbalance between the United States and Asia is illustrated by the fact that Japan, China, and Taiwan combine for about four fifths of the total U.S. balance of trade deficit in the late 1990s.[7]

Competitive Advantage of Nations

As companies in many industries find themselves competing against foreign competitors at home and abroad, government policy makers around the world are increasingly asking why some companies and industries in a country succeed globally while others lose ground or fail. Harvard Business School Professor Michael Porter suggests a "diamond" to explain a nation's competitive advantage and why some industries and firms become world leaders.[8] He identified four key elements, which appear in Figure 5–3:

1. *Factor conditions.* These reflect a nation's ability to turn its natural resources, education, and infrastructure into a competitive advantage. The Dutch lead the world in the cut-flower industry because of their research in flower cultivation, packaging, and shipping—not because of their weather.
2. *Demand conditions.* These include both the number and sophistication of domestic customers for an industry's product. Japan's sophisticated consumers demand quality in their TVs and radios, thereby making Japan's producers the world leaders in the electronics industry.
3. *Related and supporting industries.* Firms and industries seeking leadership in global markets need clusters of world-class suppliers that accelerate innovation.

FIGURE 5-3

Porter's "diamond" of
national competitive
advantage

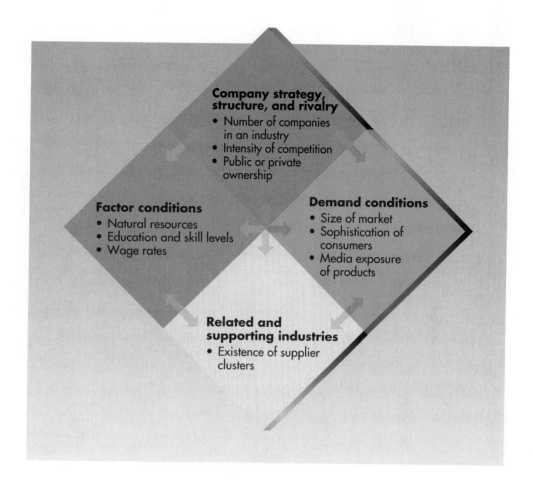

The German leadership in printing relates directly to the cluster of supporting German suppliers.

4. *Company strategy, structure, and rivalry.* These factors include the conditions governing the way a nation's businesses are organized and managed, along with the intensity of domestic competition. The Italian shoe industry has become the world leader because of intense domestic competition that enhances quality and innovation.

In Porter's study, case histories of firms in more than 100 industries were analyzed. While the strategies employed by the most successful global competitors were different in many respects, a common theme emerged—a firm that succeeds in global markets has first succeeded in intense domestic competition. Hence competitive advantage for global firms grows out of relentless, continuing improvement, innovation, and change.

It is important to note, however, that it is not essential to be a giant company to gain benefits in global markets. Numerous small firms succeed in foreign niche markets or by utilizing unique information, licenses, or technology. In fact, in one unusual respect a small regional American firm has an advantage over its huge rivals in the international arena. That is when it can trade product technology and marketing ideas with foreign firms with whom it does not compete directly. McKay Envelopes is a small firm that produces a variety of specialized packaging for photo finishers (shown in the photograph on the next page). By exchanging information with regional European printers, it is able to obtain information on new printing equipment, inks, running speeds, and printing plates that give high-quality printing—thereby gaining an advantage over its American competitors. It, in turn, provides ideas to the European printers, so the exchange benefits both parties.

For the way a small U.S. envelope firm exchanges ideas with foreign companies to be more competitive, see the text.

CONCEPT CHECK
1. What is the trade feedback effect?

2. What variables influence why some companies and industries in a country succeed globally while others lose ground or fail?

EMERGENCE OF A BORDERLESS ECONOMIC WORLD

Three trends in the late twentieth century have significantly affected world trade. One trend has been a gradual decline of economic protectionism exercised by individual countries. The second trend is apparent in the formal economic integration and free trade among nations. A third trend is evident in global competition among global companies for global consumers.

Decline of Economic Protectionism

Protectionism is the practice of shielding one or more sectors of a country's economy from foreign competition through the use of tariffs or quotas. The principal economic argument for protectionism is that it preserves jobs, protects a nation's political security, discourages economic dependency on other countries, and encourages the development of domestic industries. Read the accompanying Ethics and Social Responsibility Alert and ask yourself if protectionism has an ethical and social responsibility dimension.[9]

Tariffs and quotas discourage world trade and often result in higher domestic prices on the goods and services produced by protected industries. **Tariffs,** which are a government tax on goods or services entering a country, primarily serve to raise prices on imports. The average tariff on manufactured goods imported to the United States is 5 percent. Import tariffs on manufactured goods to Japan average 5 percent and those to Western European countries average 5.9 percent. Mexico's tariffs average 8 percent.[10]

ETHICS AND SOCIAL RESPONSIBILITY ALERT

GLOBAL ETHICS AND GLOBAL ECONOMICS: THE CASE OF PROTECTIONISM

World trade benefits from free and fair trade among nations. Nevertheless, governments of many countries continue to use tariffs and quotas to protect their various domestic industries. Why? Protectionism earns profits for domestic producers and tariff revenue for the government. There is a cost, however. For example, protectionist policies cost Japanese consumers somewhere between $75 billion and $110 billion annually. U.S. consumers pay about $70 billion each year in higher prices because of tariffs and other protective restrictions.

Sugar import quotas in the United States, automobile import quotas in many European countries, beer import tariffs in Canada, and rice import tariffs in Japan protect domestic industries but also interfere with world trade for these products. Regional trade agreements, such as those found in the provisions of the European Union and the North American Free Trade Agreement, may also pose a situation whereby member nations can obtain preferential treatment in quotas and tariffs whereas nonmember nations do not.

Protectionism, in its many forms, raises and interesting global ethical question. Is protectionism, no matter how applied, and ethical practice?

The effect of tariffs on world trade and consumer prices is substantial. Consider U.S. rice exports to Japan. The U.S. Rice Millers' Association claims that if the Japanese rice market were opened to imports by lowering tariffs, lower prices would save Japanese consumers $6 billion annually, and the United States would gain a $300 million share of the Japanese rice market.[11]

A **quota** is a restriction placed on the amount of a product allowed to enter or leave a country. Quotas can be mandatory or voluntary and may be legislated or negotiated by governments. Import quotas seek to guarantee domestic industries access to a certain percentage of their domestic market. The best-known quota concerns the mandatory or voluntary limits of foreign automobile sales in many countries. Quotas imposed by European countries make European cars 25 percent more expensive than similar models in the United States or Japan, costing European customers $40 billion per year.[12] Less visible quotas apply to the importation of mushrooms, heavy motorcycles, color TVs, and sugar. For example, U.S. sugar import quotas have existed for over 50 years and preserve about half of the U.S. sugar market for domestic producers. American consumers pay an estimated $1.6 billion annually in extra food costs because of this quota.[13]

Every country engages in some form of protectionism. However, protectionism has declined over the past 50 years due in large part to the *General Agreement on Tariffs and Trade (GATT)*. This international treaty was intended to limit trade barriers and promote world trade through the reduction of tariffs, which it did. However, GATT did not explicitly address nontariff trade barriers, such as quotas and world trade in services, which often sparked heated trade disputes between nations. As a consequence, the major industrialized nations of the world formed a permanent forum to address a broad array of world trade issues, called the **World Trade Organization** (WTO), which came into being January 1, 1995. The WTO is an institution that sets rules governing trade between its members through a panel of trade experts who (1) decide on trade disputes between members and (2) issue binding decisions. By mid-1996, 110 countries were WTO members, including the United States. These countries accounted for more than 80 percent of world trade in 1995.[14]

Rise of Economic Integration

In recent years a number of countries with similar economic goals have formed transnational trade groups or signed trade agreements for the purpose of promoting free trade among member nations and enhancing their individual economies. Three of the best-known examples are the European Union (or simply EU), the North American Free Trade Agreement, and Asian Free Trade Areas.

European Union   On January 1, 1993, 12 European countries effectively eliminated most of the barriers to the free flow of goods, services, capital, and labor across their borders. This event, after decades of negotiation, formed a single market composed of 350 million consumers with a combined gross domestic product only slightly less than that of the United States. Original members of the European Union were Great Britain, Ireland, Denmark, Belgium, the Netherlands, Luxembourg, Germany, France, Italy, Greece, Portugal, and Spain. Austria, Finland, and Sweden joined the European Union in 1995, bringing its membership to 15 countries (see Figure 5–4). The Swiss have elected not to join the European Union.[15]

Numerous marketing opportunities were made possible with creation of the European Union. Most visibly, firms no longer find it necessary to exclusively market their products and services on a nation-by-nation basis. Rather, Pan-European marketing strategies are possible due to greater uniformity in product and packaging standards, fewer regulatory differences on advertising and promotion imposed by countries, and removal of most tariffs that affect pricing practices. For example, Colgate-Palmolive Company now markets its Colgate toothpaste with one formula and package across EU countries at one price. This practice was previously impossible because of different government regulations and tariffs. Europeanwide distribution from a single location in one of the 15 EU nations also became feasible given open borders.[16] Pan-European marketing opportunities will benefit further from the adoption of a common currency called the "euro" scheduled for issuance in 2002.

FIGURE 5–4

The countries of the economic union

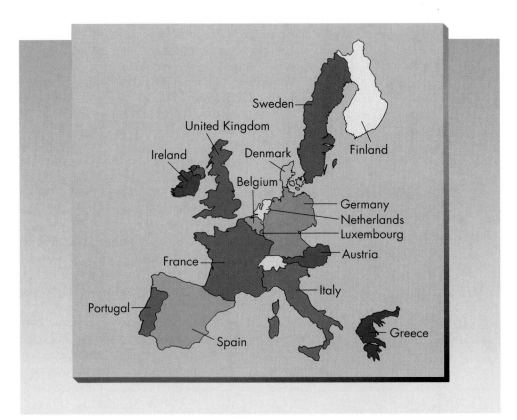

North American Free Trade Agreement   The North American Free Trade Agreement (NAFTA) became effective January 1, 1994, and lifted many trade barriers between the United States and Mexico. This agreement, when coupled with the 1988 U.S.–Canada Fair Trade Agreement, established a North American trade arrangement similar to that of the European Union. The reduction of tariffs and other provisions of NAFTA promoted relatively free trade among the United States, Canada, and Mexico and created a marketplace with about 380 million consumers. Negotiations are under way to expand NAFTA to create a Free Trade Area of the Americas by 2005. This agreement would include the United States, Canada, Mexico, and Latin American and Caribbean countries.

NAFTA has stimulated trade flows among member nations as well as cross-border manufacturing and investment. For example, Whirlpool Corporation's Canadian subsidiary stopped making washing machines in Canada and moved that operation to Ohio. Whirlpool then shifted the production of household trash compactors, kitchen ranges, and compact dryers to Canada. Ford recently invested $60 million in its Mexico City manufacturing plant to produce smaller cars and light trucks for global sales. Since the inception of NAFTA, U.S. exports of Ford vehicles from the United States to Mexico have increased more than 20-fold.[17]

Asian free trade agreements   Efforts to liberalize trade in East Asia—from Japan and the four "Little Dragons" (Hong Kong, Singapore, South Korea, and Taiwan) through Thailand, Malaysia, and Indonesia—are also growing. While the trade agreements are less formal than those underlying the European Union and NAFTA, they have reduced tariffs among countries and promoted trade.[18]

A New Reality: Global Competition among Global Companies for Global Consumers

The emergence of a largely borderless economic world has created a new reality for marketers of all shapes and sizes. Today, world trade is driven by global competition among global companies for global consumers.

Global competition   **Global competition** exists when firms originate, produce, and market their products and services worldwide. The automobile, pharmaceutical, apparel, electronics, aerospace, and telecommunications fields represent well-known industries with sellers and buyers on every continent. Other industries that are increasingly global in scope include soft drinks, cosmetics, ready-to-eat cereals, snack chips, and retailing.

Global competition broadens the competitive landscape for marketers. The familiar "Pepsi Challenge" taste comparison waged by Pepsi-Cola against Coca-Cola in the United States has been repeated around the world, most recently in India and Argentina. Procter & Gamble's Pampers and Kimberly-Clark's Huggies have taken their disposable diaper rivalry from the United States to Western Europe. Boeing, McDonnell-Douglas, and Europe's Airbus Industries can be found vying for lucrative commercial aircraft contracts on virtually every continent.[19]

Collaborative relationships also are becoming a common way to meet the demands of global competition. Global **strategic alliances** are agreements among two or more independent firms to cooperate for the purpose of achieving common goals such as a competitive advantage or customer value creation. For instance, a strategic alliance involving Duracell (United States), Toshiba (Japan), and Varta Batterie AG (Germany) has been formed to research and develop rechargeable batteries for high-power electronic products such as cellular telephones produced by Nokia (Finland) and notebook computers made by Acer (Taiwan). General Mills and Nestlé of Switzerland created Cereal Partners Worldwide for the purpose of fine-tuning Nestlé's European cereal

Avon successfully employs its direct selling approach around the world.

marketing and distributing General Mills cereals worldwide. This global alliance is expected to produce worldwide sales of $1 billion by 2000.[20]

Global companies   Three types of companies populate and compete in the global marketplace: (1) international firms, (2) multinational firms, and (3) transnational firms.[21] All three employ people in different countries, and many have administrative, marketing, and manufacturing operations (often called divisions or subsidiaries) around the world. However, a firm's orientation toward and strategy for global markets and marketing defines the type of company it is or attempts to be.

An *international firm* engages in trade and marketing in different countries as an extension of the marketing strategy in its home country. Generally speaking, these firms market their existing products and services in other countries the same way they do in their home country. Avon, for example, successfully distributes its product line through direct selling in Asia, Europe, and South America, employing virtually the same marketing strategy used in the United States.[22]

A *multinational firm* views the world as consisting of unique parts and markets to each part differently. Multinationals use a **multidomestic marketing strategy,** which means that they have as many different product variations, brand names, and advertising programs as countries in which they do business. For example, Lever Europe—a division of Unilever—markets its fabric softener known as Snuggle in the United States in 10 different European countries under seven brand names, including Kuschelweich in Germany, Coccolino in Italy, and Mimosin in France. These products have different packages, different advertising programs, and occasionally different formulas.[23]

A *transnational firm* views the world as one market and emphasizes cultural similarities across countries or universal consumer needs and wants more than differences. Transnational marketers employ a **global marketing strategy**—the practice of standardizing marketing activities when there are cultural similarities and adapting them when cultures differ. This approach benefits marketers by allowing them to realize economies of scale from their production and marketing activities.

Global marketing strategies are popular among many business-to-business marketers such as Caterpillar and Komatsu (heavy construction equipment) and Texas

A visible example of Ford's transformation from a multinational company to a transnational company is the "world car" called the Mondeo in Europe and the Ford Contour and Mercury Mystique in the United States.

Instruments, Intel, Hitachi, and Motorola (semiconductors). Consumer goods marketers such as Timex, Seiko, and Citizen (watches), Coca-Cola and Pepsi-Cola (cola soft drinks), and McDonald's (fast foods) successfully execute this strategy. Recently Ford, through its Ford 2000 initiative, embarked on a global strategy for marketing a "world car." Called the Mondeo in Europe and the Ford Contour and Mercury Mystique in the United States, this car is engineered to meet the differing needs of consumers around the world. The Ford 2000 initiative also includes significant organizational changes designed to transform Ford from a multinational company to a transnational company.[24]

Global consumers   Global competition among global companies often focuses on the identification and pursuit of global consumers. **Global consumers** consist of customer groups living in many countries or regions of the world who have similar needs or seek similar features and benefits from products or services.[25] Evidence suggests the emergence of a global middle-income class, a youth market, and an elite segment, each consuming or using a common assortment of products and services regardless of geographic location.[26] A variety of companies have capitalized on the global consumer. Whirlpool, Sony, and IKEA have benefitted from the growing global middle-income class desire for kitchen appliances, consumer electronics, and home furnishings respectively. Levi's, Nike, and Sega have tapped the global youth market as described in the Marketing NewsNet on the next page.[27] Debeers, Chanel, Gucci, and Rolls Royce successfully cater to the elite segment for luxury goods worldwide.

CONCEPT CHECK

1. What is protectionism?

2. The North American Free Trade Agreement was designed to promote free trade among which countries?

3. What is the difference between a multidomestic marketing strategy and a global marketing strategy?

MARKETING NEWSNET

THE GLOBAL TEENAGER: A MARKET OF 230 MILLION CONSUMERS

The "global teenager" market consists of 230 million 13- to 19-year-olds in Europe, North and South America, and industrialized nations of Asia who have experienced intense exposure to television (MTV broadcasts in more than 25 countries), movies, travel, and global advertising by companies such as Bennetton, Sony, Nike, and Coca-Cola. The similarities among teens in these countries are greater than their differences. For example, a global study of teenagers' rooms in 25 countries indicated it was difficult, if not impossible, to tell whether the rooms were in Los Angeles, Mexico City, Tokyo, or Paris. Why? Teens buy a common gallery of products: Nintendo and Sega video games, Levi's blue jeans, Nike athletic shoes, Procter & Gamble Cover Girl makeup, and Clearasil facial medicine. Not surprisingly, Reebok launched its Insta-Pump line of sneakers simultaneously in the United States, Germany, Japan, and 137 other countries through a global advertising campaign aimed at teens.

Teenagers around the world appreciate fashion and music and desire novelty and trendier designs and images. They also acknowledge an "Americanization" of fashion and culture based on a study of 6500 teens in 26 countries. When asked what country had the most influence on their attitudes and purchase behavior, the United States was named by 54 percent of teens from the

United States, 87 percent of those from Latin America, 80 percent of the Europeans, and 80 percent of those from the Far East. This phenomenon has not gone unnoticed by parents. As one parent in India said, "Now the youngsters dress, talk, and eat like Americans."

A GLOBAL ENVIRONMENTAL SCAN

Global companies conduct continuing environmental scans of the five sets of environmental factors described earlier in Figure 3–1 (social, economic, technological, competitive, and regulatory forces). This section focuses on three kinds of uncontrollable environmental variables—cultural, economic, and political-regulatory variables—that affect global marketing practices in strikingly different ways than those in domestic markets.

Cultural Diversity

Marketers must be sensitive to the cultural underpinnings of different societies if they are to initiate and consummate mutually beneficial exchange relationships with global consumers. A necessary step in this process is **cross-cultural analysis,** which involves the study of similarities and differences among consumers in two or more nations or societies.[28] A thorough cross-cultural analysis involves an understanding of and an appreciation for the values, customs, symbols, and language of other societies.

Values   A society's **values** represent personally or socially preferable modes of conduct or states of existence that are enduring. Understanding and working with these aspects of a society are important factors in successful global marketing. For example:[29]

- A door-to-door salesman would find selling in Italy impossible because it is improper for a man to call on a woman if she is home alone. Similarly, a popular Procter & Gamble commercial for Camay soap in Western Europe flopped when it aired in Japan. The ad, which showed a husband interrupting his wife's bath, was thought to be in poor taste since it is considered improper for a Japanese man to intrude on his wife.
- McDonald's does not sell hamburgers in its restaurants in India because the cow is considered sacred by almost 85 percent of the population.
- Germans have not been overly receptive to the use of credit cards such as Visa or MasterCard and installment debt to purchase goods and services. Indeed, the German word for debt, *schuld,* is the same as the German word for guilt.

These examples illustrate how cultural values can influence behavior in different societies. Cultural values become apparent in the personal values of individuals that affect their attitudes and beliefs and the importance assigned to specific behaviors and attributes of goods and services. These personal values affect consumption-specific values, such as the use of installment debt by Germans, and product-specific values, such as the importance assigned to credit card interest rates.

Customs **Customs** are the norms and expectations about the way people do things in a specific country. Clearly customs can vary significantly from country to country. For example, General Mills designed a cake mix especially for preparation in the rice cookers used by Japanese consumers. It failed because of a lack of understanding of Japanese consumers and customs: Japanese take pride in the purity of their rice, which they thought would be contaminated if the cooker were used to prepare another food. The 3M Company's Scotch-Brite floor-cleaning product got lukewarm sales in the Philippines. When a Filipino employee explained that consumers there often clean floors by pushing coconut shells around with their feet, 3M changed the shape of the pad to a foot and sales soared![30] Some other customs are unusual to Americans. Consider, for example, that in France, men wear more than twice the number of cosmetics than women do and that Japanese women give Japanese men chocolates on Valentine's Day.[31]

Customs also relate to nonverbal behavior of individuals in different cultural settings. The story is also told of U.S. executives negotiating a purchase agreement with their Japanese counterparts. The chief American negotiator made a proposal that was met with silence by the Japanese head negotiator. The American assumed the offer was not acceptable and raised the offer, which again was met with silence. A third offer was made, and an agreement was struck. Unknown to the American, the silence of the Japanese head negotiator meant that the offer was being considered, not rejected. The Japanese negotiator obtained several concessions from the American because of a misreading of silence! Unlike U.S. businesspeople, who tend to express opinions early in meetings and negotiations, Japanese executives prefer to wait and listen—and the higher their position, such as chief negotiator, the more they listen.[32]

Cultural symbols **Cultural symbols** are things that represent ideas and concepts. Symbols or symbolism play an important role in cross-cultural analysis because different cultures ascribe different meanings to things. So important is the role of symbols that a field of study, called **semiotics,** has emerged that examines the correspondence between symbols and their role in the assignment of meaning for people. By adroitly using cultural symbols, global marketers can tie positive symbolism to their products and services to enhance their attractiveness to consumers. However, improper use of symbols can spell disaster. A culturally sensitive global marketer will know that[33]

- North Americans are superstitious about the number 13, and Japanese feel the same way about the number 4. *Shi,* the Japanese word for four, is also the word for death. Knowing this, Tiffany & Company sells its fine glassware and china in sets of five, not four, in Japan.
- The rugged Western cowboy is a positive cultural symbol in the United States, and Philip Morris has used this symbolism in its Marlboro cigarette advertising for many years. However, in Hong Kong, the cowboy has the status of a laborer. Accordingly, the Marlboro cowboy is shown riding a white horse in Hong Kong since a white horse is a symbol of esteem in that society.

Cultural symbols evoke deep feelings. Just ask executives at Coca-Cola Company's Italian office. In a series of advertisements directed at Italian vacationers, the Eiffel

Tower, Empire State Building, and the tower of Pisa were turned into the familiar Coca-Cola bottle. However, when the white marble columns in the Parthenon that crowns Athens's Acropolis were turned into Coca-Cola bottles, the Greeks were outraged. Greeks refer to the Acropolis as the "holy rock," and a government official said the Parthenon is an "international symbol of excellence" and that "whoever insults the Parthenon insults international culture." Coca-Cola apologized for the ad.[34]

Global marketers are also sensitive to the fact that the "country of origin or manufacture" of products and services can symbolize superior or poor quality in some countries. For example, Russian consumers believe products made in Japan and Germany are superior in quality to products from the United States and the United Kingdom. Japanese consumers believe Japanese products are superior to those made in Europe and the United States.[35]

Language   Global marketers should not only know the native tongues of countries in which they market their products and services but also the nuances and idioms of a language. Even though about 100 official languages exist in the world, anthropologists estimate that at least 3,000 different languages are spoken. There are 11 official languages spoken in the European Union, and Canada has two official languages

Country of origin or manufacture of products or services can symbolize quality in some countries. For example, Italian-made shoes symbolize quality around the world.

(English and French). Fifteen major languages are spoken in India alone, although English is the official language.

English, French, and Spanish are the principal languages used in global diplomacy and commerce. However, the best language to communicate with consumers is their own, as any seasoned global marketer will attest to. Unintended meanings of brand names and messages have ranged from the absurd to the obscene:[36]

- When the advertising agency responsible for launching Procter & Gamble's successful Pert shampoo in Canada realized that the name means "lost" in French, it substituted the brand name Pret, which means "ready."
- In Italy, Cadbury Schweppes, the world's third-largest soft drink manufacturer, realized that its Schweppes Tonic Water brand had to be renamed Schweppes Tonica because "il water" turned out to be the idiom for a bathroom.
- The Vicks brand name common in the United States is German slang for sexual intimacy; therefore, Vicks is called Wicks in Germany.

Experienced global marketers use **back translation,** where a translated word or phrase is retranslated into the original language by a different interpreter to catch errors. For example, IBM's first Japanese translation of its "Solutions for a small planet" advertising message yielded "Answers that make people smaller." The error was caught and corrected.[37] Nevertheless, unintended meanings still occur in the most unlikely situations. Recently, a Japanese tire manufacturer found it necessary to publicly apologize in Brunei (a British-protected sultanate on the coast of Borneo) for the tread grooves on one of its tire brands. Some critics claimed the tread resembled a verse from the Koran, the sacred book of the Muslims written in Arabic.[38]

Cultural ethnocentricity   The tendency for people to view their own values, customs, symbols, and language favorably is well-known. However, the belief that aspects of one's culture are superior to another's is called *cultural ethnocentricity* and is a sure impediment to successful global marketing.

An outgrowth of cultural ethnocentricity exists in the purchase and use of goods and services produced outside of a country. Global marketers are acutely aware that certain groups within countries disfavor imported products, not on the basis of price, features, or performance, but purely because of their foreign origin. **Consumer ethnocentrism** is the tendency to believe that it is inappropriate, indeed immoral, to purchase foreign-made products.[39] Ethnocentric consumers believe that buying imported products is wrong because such purchases are unpatriotic, harm domestic industries, and cause domestic unemployment. The prevalence of consumer ethnocentrism in the global marketplace is unknown. However, a recent study indicated that 5 percent of consumers in the United Kingdom and France and 6 percent of consumers in Germany said that knowing a product was made in their country was the single-most important factor when considering the purchase of a product.[40] Are you an ethnocentric consumer? The Marketing NewsNet on the next page might help you answer this question.[41]

Cultural change   Cultures change slowly. Nevertheless, fewer impediments to world trade are likely to accelerate the rate of cultural change in societies around the world. A challenge facing global marketers is to anticipate how cultures are changing, particularly with respect to the purchase and use of goods and services.

An acknowledged master of anticipating cultural change and responding quickly is Nestlé, the world's largest packaged food manufacturer, coffee roaster, and chocolate maker. Nestlé derives 98 percent of its sales outside of its home country, Switzerland, because the company is always among the first to identify changing consumption patterns in diverse cultures. Consider Great Britain and Japan, with two very different cultures but a common passion—tea. Nestlé pioneered coffee marketing in both countries with its Nescafé instant coffee. The cultural preference for tea was

MARKETING NEWSNET

ARE YOU AN ETHNOCENTRIC CONSUMER?

Would you tend to agree or disagree with the following statements?

1. Buy American-made products. Keep America working.
2. It is always best to purchase American products.
3. It may cost me in the long run, but I prefer to support American products.
4. Curbs should be put on all imports.

If you tended to agree with these 4 and 13 other similar statements, you can call yourself an ethnocentric consumer.

Professors Terrence Shimp and Subhash Sharma at the University of South Carolina developed a 17-statement consumer ethnocentrism scale designed to identify the tendency of American consumers to purchase foreign- versus American-made products. Frequent agreement with statements such as those above means that a consumer would have a tendency to accentuate the positive aspects of domestic products and discount the virtues of foreign-made items.

It is important to note that consumer ethnocentrism has been observed in France, Japan, Korea, and Germany as well. In these countries, it was also found that the

more ethnocentric a consumer was, the less likely he or she was to rate the quality of foreign-made products highly. Similar conclusions have been suggested in national surveys in other parts of Europe and Asia.

The prevalence of consumer ethnocentrism in a country has important marketing implications. Specifically, consumer resistance to foreign-made products will make the task of global marketers more difficult.

changing, and Nestlé capitalized on this change. Today, Britons consume one cup of coffee for every two cups of tea. Thirty years ago, the ratio was one cup of coffee for every six cups of tea. The Japanese are now among the world's heaviest consumers of instant coffee on a per capita basis. Nestlé is a dominant coffee marketer in both countries.[42]

Economic Considerations

Global marketing also is affected by economic considerations. Therefore, a scan of the global marketplace should include (1) a comparative analysis of the economic development in different countries, (2) an assessment of the economic infrastructure in these countries, (3) measurement of consumer income in different countries, and (4) recognition of a country's currency exchange rates.

Stage of economic development   There are more than 200 countries in the world today, each of which is at a slightly different point in terms of its stage of economic development. However, they can be classified into two major groupings that will help the global marketer better understand their needs:

- *Developed* countries have somewhat mixed economies. Private enterprise dominates, although they have substantial public sectors as well. The United States, Canada, Japan, and most of Western Europe can be considered developed.

Reader's Digest learned important lessons that apply to most global firms entering foreign markets when it launched its Russian and Hungarian editions. For those lessons, see the text.

- *Developing* countries are in the process of moving from an agricultural to an industrial economy. There are two subgroups within the developing category: (1) those that have already made the move and (2) those that remain locked in a preindustrial economy. Countries such as Poland, Hungary, Australia, Israel, Venezuela, and South Africa fall into the first group. In the second group are Pakistan, Sri Lanka, Tanzania, and Chad, where living standards are low and improvement will be slow. The economies of developing countries are expected to average 5 percent annual growth compared with 2 percent annual growth for developed countries through 2000.[43]

A country's stage of economic development affects and is affected by other economic factors, as described next.

Economic infrastructure   The **economic infrastructure**—a country's communications, transportation, financial, and distribution systems—is a critical consideration in determining whether to try to market to a country's consumers and organizations. Parts of the infrastructure that North Americans or Western Europeans take for granted can be huge problems elsewhere—not only in developing nations but even in countries of Eastern Europe and the former Soviet Union where such an infrastructure is assumed to be in place. Consider, for instance, transportation and distribution systems in these countries. Two-lane roads with horse-drawn carts that limit average speeds to 35 or 40 miles per hour are commonplace—and a nightmare for firms requiring prompt truck delivery. Wholesale and retail institutions tend to be small, and 95 percent are operated by new owner-managers still learning the ways of a free market system. These conditions have prompted firms such as Danone, a French food company, to establish their own wholesale, retail, and delivery systems. Danone delivers its products to 700 shops in Russia and has set up 60 shops-in-shops, where it has its own retail sales associates and cash registers.[44]

The communication infrastructure in these countries, including telecommunications and postal systems, also differ. About one-in-ten people have a telephone. As for postal systems, *Reader's Digest* learned to send its magazine by registered mail in brown envelopes—or by private delivery services—because attractive packages tend to get "lost" frequently.[45] These problems have led to several billion dollar investments to upgrade telecommunication and postal systems in these countries.

Even the financial and legal system can cause problems. Common operating procedures among financial institutions and private properties did not exist under

FIGURE 5-5

How purchasing power differs
around the world

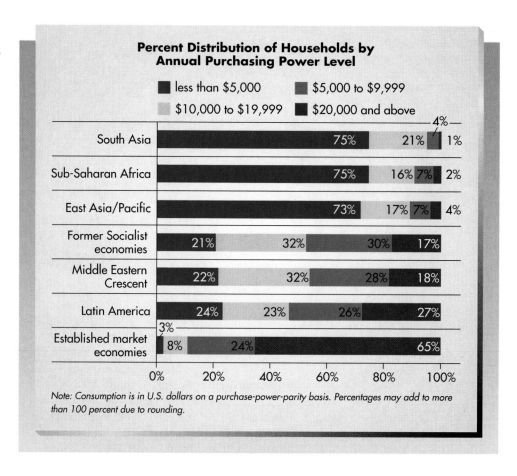

Percent Distribution of Households by Annual Purchasing Power Level

Note: Consumption is in U.S. dollars on a purchase-power-parity basis. Percentages may add to more than 100 percent due to rounding.

communism. The legal red tape involved in obtaining title to buildings and land for manufacturing, wholesaling, and retailing operations has been a huge problem. Nevertheless, Coca-Cola has invested $85 million to build two bottling and distribution facilities in Russia, and Allied Lyons has spent $30 million to build a plant to make Baskin-Robbins ice cream.[46]

Consumer income and purchasing power   A global marketer selling consumer goods must also consider what the average per capita or household income is among a country's consumers and how the income is distributed to determine a nation's purchasing power.[47] Per capita income varies greatly between nations. Average yearly per capita income in EU countries is $20,000 and is less than $200 in some developing countries such as Vietnam. A country's income distribution is important because it may give a more reliable picture of a country's purchasing power. Generally speaking, as the proportion of middle-income class households in a country increases, the greater a nation's purchasing power tends to be. Figure 5–5 shows the worldwide disparity in the percentage distribution of households by level of purchasing power. In established market economies such as those in North America and Western Europe, 65 percent of households have an annual purchasing capability of $20,000 or more. In comparison, 75 percent of households in the developing countries of South Asia have an annual purchasing power of less than $5,000.

Seasoned global marketers recognize that people in developing countries often have government subsidies for food, housing, and health care that supplement their

Currency exchange rates affect international travel and tourism.

income. Accordingly, people with seemingly low incomes are actually promising customers for a variety of products. For example, a consumer in South Asia earning the equivalent of $250 per year can afford Gillette razors. When that consumer's income rises to $1,000, a Sony television becomes affordable, and a new Volkswagen or Nissan can be bought with an annual income of $10,000. In developing countries of Eastern Europe, a $1,000 annual income makes a refrigerator affordable, and $2,000 brings an automatic washer within reach. These facts have not gone unnoticed by Whirlpool, which now aggressively markets these products in Eastern Europe.[48]

Currency exchange rates   Fluctuations in exchange rates among the world's currencies are of critical importance in global marketing. Such fluctuations affect everyone—from international tourists to global companies.

As a case in point, the strength of the U.S. dollar against foreign currencies in 1985 was a stroke of good fortune to Americans traveling abroad. Some luxury goods, such as Zeiss binoculars and Gucci handbags, were priced 30 percent to 70 percent less in Europe than in the United States. By 1995, the value of the dollar against foreign currencies had plummeted. In 1985, one U.S. dollar could be exchanged for 10.7 French francs, but in 1995 a dollar only bought 4.80 francs—less than half its value a decade earlier.

Exchange rate fluctuations have a direct impact on the prices charged and the profits made by global companies. When foreign currencies can buy more U.S. dollars, for example, U.S. products are less expensive for the foreign customer. This has been the case during the 1990s, and U.S. exports have grown accordingly.[49] Short-term fluctuations, however, can have a significant effect on the profits of global companies. Hewlett-Packard recently gained nearly a half million dollars of additional profit through exchange-rate fluctuations in one year. On the other hand, Nestlé has lost as much as a million dollars in six months due to fluctuations in the Swiss franc compared with other currencies.[50]

Political-Regulatory Climate

The political and regulatory climate for marketing in a country or region of the world lies not only in identifying the current climate but in determining how long a favorable or unfavorable climate will last. An assessment of a country or regional political-regulatory climate includes an analysis of its political stability, trade regulations, and trade incentives.

Political stability   Trade among nations or regions depends on political stability. Billions of dollars have been lost in the Middle East and the former Federal Republic of Yugoslavia as a result of internal political strife and war. Losses such as these encourage careful selection of politically stable countries and regions of the world for trade.

When instability is suspected, companies do everything they can to protect their interests. Companies may limit their trade to exporting products into the country, thereby minimizing investments in new plants in the foreign economy. Currency is converted as soon as possible. For example, some global companies are reluctant to expand operations in Hong Kong because of uncertainties about what will happen after 1997. Why? Hong Kong will become part of China in 1997 and will no longer be a British crown colony with a 150-year history of political and economic stability. Similarly, billions of dollars of investment are on hold by global companies waiting to see what kind of political stability is in store for countries in Eastern Europe, the former Soviet Union, and Latin America.

Trade regulations   Countries have a variety of rules that govern business practices within their borders. These rules can often serve as trade barriers.[51] For example, Japan has some 11,000 trade regulations. Japanese car safety rules effectively require all automobile replacement parts to be Japanese and not American or European; public health rules make it illegal to sell aspirin or cold medicine without a pharmacist present. The Malaysian government recently adopted advertising regulations warning that "advertisements must not project or promote an excessively aspirational lifestyle," and Sweden outlaws all advertisements to children.

Trade regulations also appear in free trade agreements among countries. European Union nations abide by some 10,000 rules that specify how goods are to be made and marketed. For instance, the rules for a washing machine's electrical system are detailed on more than 100 typed pages. Regulations related to contacting consumers via telephone, fax, and E-mail without their prior consent and toy advertising to children also exist. The European Union's ISO 9000 quality standards, though not a trade regulation, have the same effect on business practice. **ISO 9000** standards, developed by the International Standards Organization (ISO) in Geneva, Switzerland, refer to standards for registration and certification of a manufacturer's quality management and quality assurance system. Many European companies require suppliers to be ISO 9000 certified as a condition of doing business with them. Certified companies have undergone an on-site audit that includes an inspection of its facilities to ensure that documented quality control procedures are in place and that all employees understand and follow them. More than 100 countries have adopted ISO 9000 standards, and 40,000 certificates have been issued worldwide with about 2,000 going to U.S. firms.[52]

Trade incentives   Just as countries and regions can discourage international trade through trade barriers, they can also encourage it by offering investment incentives, helping in site location, and providing other services. Hungary is currently offering a five-year "tax holiday"—a period during which no corporate taxes will be assessed—to encourage foreign firms to develop manufacturing facilities there. The Republic of Indonesia actively promotes its modern economic infrastructure, pro-investment posture, and quality of life through a worldwide advertising and promotional campaign. In addition, a country or group of countries can establish equitable standards to enable foreign producers and products to compete fairly in their domestic markets. Free trade agreements are viewed as a trade incentive in this respect.

CONCEPT CHECK

1. Semiotics involves the study of _____.

2. When foreign currencies can buy more U.S. dollars, are U.S. products more or less expensive for a foreign consumer?

GLOBAL MARKET-ENTRY STRATEGIES

Once a company has decided to enter the global marketplace, it must select a means of market entry. Four general options exist: (1) exporting, (2) licensing, (3) joint venture, and (4) direct investment.[53] As Figure 5–6 demonstrates, the amount of financial commitment, risk, marketing control, and profit potential increases as the firm moves from exporting to direct investment.

Exporting

Exporting is producing goods in one country and selling them in another country. This entry option allows a company to make the least number of changes in terms of its product, its organization, and even its corporate goals. Host countries usually do not like this practice because it provides less local employment than under alternative means of entry.

Indirect exporting is when a firm sells its domestically produced goods in a foreign country through an intermediary. It involves the least amount of commitment and risk but will probably return the least profit. This kind of exporting is ideal for the company that has no overseas contacts but wants to market abroad. The intermediary is often a broker or agent that has the international marketing know-how and the resources necessary for the effort to succeed.

Direct exporting is when a firm sells its domestically produced goods in a foreign country without intermediaries. Most companies become involved in direct exporting

FIGURE 5–6

Alternative global market-entry strategies

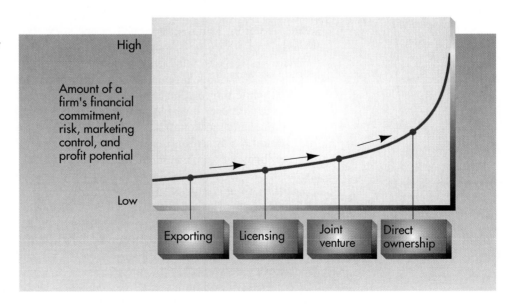

FIGURE 5-7

Exporting as a small
company, global market-entry
strategy

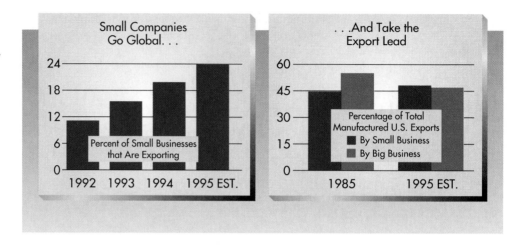

when they believe their volume of sales will be sufficiently large and easy to obtain that they do not require intermediaries. For example, the exporter may be approached by foreign buyers that are willing to contract for a large volume of purchases. Direct exporting involves more risk than indirect exporting for the company but also opens the door to increased profits.

Harley-Davidson is one company that uses an exporting strategy. It exports about one fourth of its annual production of heavyweight motorcycles. Japan, Germany, Canada, and France, in that order, represent the company's largest markets.[54] Exporting is often used by smaller U.S. businesses (those with fewer than 500 employees). As shown in Figure 5–7, one fourth of small U.S. firms engage in exporting. These firms accounted for an estimated 50.8 percent of total U.S. merchandise exports in 1995.[55]

Licensing

Under licensing, a company offers the right to a trademark, patent, trade secret, or other similarly valued items of intellectual property in return for a royalty or a fee. In international marketing the advantages to the company granting the license are low risk and a capital-free entry into a foreign country. The licensee gains information that allows it to start with a competitive advantage, and the foreign country gains employment by having the product manufactured locally. Yoplait yogurt is licensed from Sodima, a French cooperative, by General Mills for sales in the United States.

There are some serious drawbacks to this mode of entry, however. The licensor forgoes control of its product and reduces the potential profits gained from it. In addition, while the relationship lasts, the licensor may be creating its own competition. Some licensees are able to modify the product somehow and enter the market with product and marketing knowledge gained at the expense of the company that got them started. To offset this disadvantage, many companies strive to stay innovative so that the licensee remains dependent on them for improvements and successful operation. Finally, should the licensee prove to be a poor choice, the name or reputation of the company may be harmed.

Two variations of licensing, local manufacturing and local assembly, represent alternative ways to produce a product within the foreign country. With local manufacturing, a U.S. company may contract with a foreign firm to manufacture products according to stated specifications. The product is then sold in the foreign country or exported back to the United States. With local assembly, the U.S. company may contract with a foreign firm to assemble (not manufacture) parts and components that have been shipped to that country. In both cases, advantage to the foreign country

McDonald's uses franchising as a market-entry strategy and 45 percent of the company's operating income comes from non-U.S. operations.

is the employment of its people, and the U.S. firm benefits from the lower wage rates in the foreign country.

A third variation of licensing is franchising. Franchising is one of the fastest-growing market-entry strategies. By the mid-1990s, more than 30,000 franchises of U.S. firms were located in countries throughout the world. Franchises include soft-drink, motel, retailing, fast-food, and car rental operations and a variety of business services. McDonald's is a premier global franchiser: 70 percent of the company's stores are franchised, and 45 percent of the company's operating income comes from non-U.S. operations.[56]

Joint Venture

When a foreign company and a local firm invest together to create a local business, it is called a **joint venture.** These two companies share ownership, control, and profits of the new company. Investment may be made by having either of the companies buy shares in the other or by creating a third and separate entity. This was done by Caterpillar, Inc., the world's largest manufacturer of earth-moving and construction equipment. It recently created NEVAMASH with its joint venture partner, Kirovsky Zvod, a large Russian manufacturer of heavy equipment.[57]

The advantages of this option are twofold. First, one company may not have the necessary financial, physical, or managerial resources to enter a foreign market alone. The joint venture between Ericsson, a Swedish telecommunications firm, and CGCT, a French switch maker, enabled them together to beat out AT&T for a $100 million French contract. Ericsson's money and technology combined with CGCT's knowledge of the French market helped them to win the contract that neither of them could have won alone. Similarly, Ford and Volkswagen recently formed a joint venture to make four-wheel-drive vehicles in Portugal. Second, a government may require or strongly encourage a joint venture before it allows a foreign company to enter its market. This is the case in China where foreign corporations are discouraged from establishing solely owned subsidiaries. Today, more than 50,000 Chinese–foreign joint ventures operate in China.[58]

The disadvantages arise when the two companies disagree about policies or courses of action for their joint venture or when governmental bureaucracy bogs down the effort. For example, U.S. firms often prefer to reinvest earnings gained, whereas some foreign companies may want to spend those earnings. Or a U.S. firm may want to return profits earned to the United States, while the local firm or its government may oppose this—the problem now faced by many potential joint ventures in Eastern Europe, the former Soviet Union, and South Asia.

Direct Investment

The biggest commitment a company can make when entering the global market is **direct investment,** which entails a domestic firm actually investing in and owning a foreign subsidiary or division. Examples of direct investment are Honda's Marysville, Ohio, plant that produces Civics and Accords, and Nissan's Smyrna, Tennessee, plant that produces pickup trucks. Many U.S.-based global companies are also switching to this mode of entry. McDonald's chose this alternative in Great Britain and built a plant to produce 2 million buns a week when no local bakers would make them to McDonald's specifications. Reebok entered Russia in 1992 by creating a wholly owned subsidiary known as Reebok Russia.

For many firms, direct investment often follows one of the other three market-entry strategies.[59] For example, Ernst & Young, an international accounting and management consulting firm, entered Hungary first by establishing a joint venture with a local company. Ernst & Young later acquired the company, making it a subsidiary with headquarters in Budapest.[60]

The advantages to direct investment include cost savings, better understanding of local market conditions, and fewer local restrictions. Firms entering foreign markets using direct investment believe that these advantages outweigh the financial commitments and risks involved.

CONCEPT CHECK

1. What mode of entry could a company follow if it has no previous experience in global marketing?

2. How does licensing differ from a joint venture?

CRAFTING A WORLDWIDE MARKETING EFFORT

The choice of a market-entry strategy is a necessary first step for a marketer when joining the community of global companies. The next step involves the challenging task of designing, implementing, and controlling marketing programs worldwide.

Product and Promotion Strategies

Global companies have five strategies for matching products and their promotion efforts to global markets. As Figure 5–8 shows, the strategies focus on whether a

FIGURE 5–8

Five product and promotion strategies for global marketing

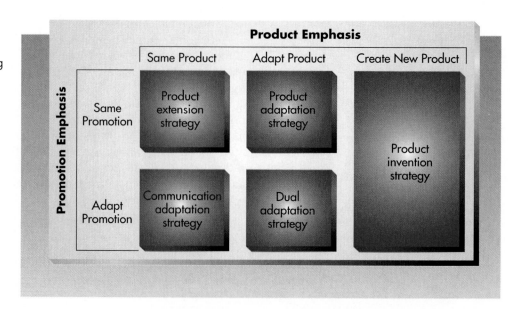

MARKETING NEWSNET

Customer

$

Value

CHEESELESS CHEETOS, DOMINO'S SQUID PIZZA, AND CAMPBELL'S DUCK-GIZZARD SOUP: AN ASIAN BUFFET OF DELECTABLE EDIBLES

Global food companies are most accommodating when it comes to adapting their products to the tastes of Asian consumers. Take Cheetos in China. The bright-orange corn puff is popular in the United States largely because of its sticky cheese covering. The Chinese, however, don't go for cheese. So executives at PepsiCo Foods International thought the unthinkable—develop cheeseless Cheetos for China! The result? The Chinese buy more than 100 million bags of Cheetos annually. What's next? Seafood-flavored Cheetos for China, of course.

Not interested in snacking? Then how about a pizza? Domino's in Japan offers a chicken teriyaki pizza, including Japanese-style grilled chicken, spinach, onion, and corn—the most common pizza topping. Domino's also offers popular squid and tuna toppings.

Campbell Soup Company has perfected the art of preparing sophisticated soups created to appeal to Asian tastes. Some Asian favorites include watercress and duck-

gizzard soup. But the company draws a line. Dog soup is out, as is shark's fin since most shark species are endangered. But snake soup is a possibility based on recent tests at the company's Hong Kong test kitchen.

company extends or adapts its product and promotion message for consumers in different countries.

A product may be sold globally in one of three ways: (1) in the same form as in its home market, (2) with some adaptations, or (3) as a totally new product.

1. *Product extension.* Selling virtually the same product in other countries is a product extension strategy. It works well for products such as Coca-Cola, Gillette razors, Wrigley's gum, and Levi's jeans. However, it didn't work for Jell-O (a more solid gelatin was preferred to the powder in England) or Duncan Hines cakes (which were seen as too moist and crumbly to eat with tea in England).

2. *Product adaptation.* Changing a product in some way to make it more appropriate for a country's climate or preferences is a product adaptation strategy. Heinz baby food offers strained lamb brains for Australians and strained brown beans in the Netherlands. Exxon sells different gasoline blends based on each country's climate. Read the accompanying Marketing NewsNet to find out how food products familiar to you are adapted to consumer preferences in Asia.[61]

3. *Product invention.* Designing a product to serve the unmet needs of a foreign nation is a product invention strategy. This is probably the strategy with the most potential since there are so many unmet needs, yet it is actually the least used. National Cash Register has followed a reverse invention strategy by introducing crank-operated cash registers in some developing nations that have unreliable or inaccessible electric power.

An identical promotion message is used for the product extension and product adaptation strategies around the world. Gillette, for example, uses the same global message for its men's toiletries: "Gillette, the Best a Man Can Get." Even though

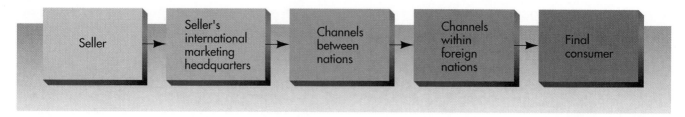

FIGURE 5–9

Channels of distribution in global marketing

Exxon adapts its gasoline for different countries, the promotion message is unchanged. "Put a Tiger in Your Tank."

Global companies may also elect to adapt their promotion message. For instance, the same product may be sold in many countries but advertised differently. As an example, L'Oreal, a French health and beauty products marketer, recently introduced its Golden Beauty brand of sun care products through its Helena Rubenstein subsidiary in Western Europe with a communication adaptation strategy.[62] Recognizing that cultural and buying motive differences related to skin care and tanning exist, Golden Beauty advertising features dark tanning for Northern Europeans, skin protection to avoid wrinkles among Latin Europeans, and beautiful skin for Europeans living along the Mediterranean Sea, even though the products are the same. Other companies use a dual adaptation strategy by modifying both their products and promotion messages. Nestlé does this with Nescafe coffee. Nescafe is marketed using different coffee blends and promotional campaigns to match consumer preferences in different countries.

Distribution Strategy

Distribution is of critical importance in global marketing. The availability and quality of retailers and wholesalers as well as transportation, communication, and warehousing facilities are often determined by a country's stage of economic development. Figure 5–9 outlines the channel through which a product manufactured in one country must travel to reach its destination in another country. The first step involves the seller; its headquarters is the starting point and is responsible for the successful distribution to the ultimate consumer.

The next step is the channel between two nations, moving the product from one country to another. Intermediaries that can handle this responsibility include resident buyers in a foreign country, independent merchant wholesalers who buy and sell the product, or agents who bring buyers and sellers together.

Once the product is in the foreign nation, that country's distribution channels take over.[63] These channels can be very long or surprisingly short, depending on the product line. In Japan fresh fish go through three intermediaries before getting to a retail outlet. Conversely, shoes only go through one intermediary. In other cases, the channel does not even involve the host country. Procter & Gamble sells its soap door to door in the Philippines because there are no other alternatives in many parts of that country. The sophistication of a country's distribution channels increases as its economic infrastructure develops. Supermarkets facilitate selling products in many nations, but they are not popular or available in many others where culture and lack of refrigeration dictate shopping on a daily rather than a weekly basis. For example, when Coke and Pepsi entered China, both had to create direct-distribution channels, investing in trucks and refrigerator units for small retailers.

Pricing Strategy

Global companies also face many challenges in determining a pricing strategy as part of their worldwide marketing effort.[64] Individual countries, even those with free trade agreements, may impose considerable competitive, political, and legal constraints on the pricing latitude of global companies. Of course, economic factors such as the costs of production, selling, and tariffs, plus transportation and storage costs, also affect global pricing decisions.

Pricing too low or too high can have dire consequences. When prices appear too low in one country, companies can be charged with dumping, a practice subject to severe penalties and fines. **Dumping** is when a firm sells a product in a foreign country below its domestic price or below its actual cost. This is often done to build a company's share of the market by pricing at a competitive level. Another reason is that the products being sold may be surplus or cannot be sold domestically and, therefore, are already a burden to the company. The firm may be glad to sell them at almost any price. The American Honey Producers' recent filing of an antidumping petition against China's bee industry is a case in point.[65] These honey producers claimed China's honey was selling for as little as $0.30 per pound in the United States when production and packaging costs were estimated to be $0.83 per pound. The result of this petition was that the International Trade Commission, an arm of the U.S. government, considered imposing a 170 percent tariff on Chinese honey as part of a recent U.S.–China trade negotiation.

When companies price their products very high in some countries but competitively in others, they face a gray market problem.[66] A **gray market,** also called parallel importing, is a situation where products are sold through unauthorized channels of distribution. A gray market comes about when individuals buy products in a lower-priced country from a manufacturer's authorized retailer, ship them to higher-priced countries, and then sell them below the manufacturer's suggested retail price through unauthorized retailers. Many well-known products have been sold through gray markets, including Olympus cameras, Seiko watches, IBM personal computers, and Mercedes-Benz cars.

CONCEPT CHECK

1. Products may be sold globally in three ways. What are they?

2. What is dumping?

SUMMARY

1. The dollar value of world trade has grown an average of 12 percent per year since 1970 and will likely approach $8 trillion in 2005. Manufactured goods and commodities account for 80 percent of world trade, while services account for 20 percent.

2. Not all world trade involves the exchange of money for goods or services. About 20 percent of world trade involves countertrade, the practice of using barter rather than money for making global sales.

3. A global perspective on world trade views exports and imports as complementary economic flows. A country's exports affect its imports and vice versa. This phenomenon is called the *trade feedback effect.*

4. The United States is the world's perennial leader in terms of gross domestic product and among the world's leaders in exports. Nevertheless, the United States has incurred a continuing balance of trade deficit since 1970.

5. The reason some companies and some industries in a country succeed globally while others do not lies in their na-

tion's competitive advantage. A nation's competitive advantage arises from specific conditions in a nation that foster success.

6. Three trends in the late twentieth century have significantly affected world trade: (1) a gradual decline of economic protectionism, (2) an increase in formal economic integration and free trade among nations, and (3) global competition among global companies for global consumers.

7. Although global and domestic marketing are based on the same marketing principles, many underlying assumptions must be reevaluated when a firm pursues global opportunities. A global environmental scan typically considers three kinds of uncontrollable environmental variables. These include cultural diversity, economic conditions, and political-regulatory climate.

8. Four global market-entry strategies are exporting, licensing, joint venture, and direct investment. The relative difficulty of global marketing, as well as the amount of financial commitment, risk, marketing control, and profit potential, increase in moving from exporting to direct investment.

9. Crafting a worldwide marketing effort involves designing, implementing, and controlling a marketing program that standardizes marketing mix elements when there are cultural similarities and adapting them when cultures differ.

KEY TERMS

countertrade p. 122
trade feedback effect p. 123
gross domestic product p. 123
balance of trade p. 123
protectionism p. 126
tariffs p. 126
quota p. 127
World Trade Organization p. 127
global competition p. 129
strategic alliances p. 129
multidomestic marketing strategy p. 130
global marketing strategy p. 130
global consumers p. 131
cross-cultural analysis p. 132

values p. 132
customs p. 133
cultural symbols p. 133
semiotics p. 133
back translation p. 135
consumer ethnocentrism p. 135
economic infrastructure p. 137
ISO 9000 p. 140
exporting p. 141
joint venture p. 143
direct investment p. 143
dumping p. 147
gray market p. 147

CHAPTER PROBLEMS AND APPLICATIONS

1. What is meant by this statement: "Quotas are a hidden tax on consumers, whereas tariffs are a more obvious one"?

2. Is the trade feedback effect described in the text a long-run or short-run view on world trade flows? Explain your answer.

3. The United States is considered to be a global leader in the development and marketing of pharmaceutical products, and Merck & Co. of New Jersey is a world leader in prescription drug sales. What explanation can you give for this situation based on the text discussion concerning the competitive advantage of nations?

4. How successful would a television commercial in Japan be if it featured a husband surprising his wife in her dressing area on Valentine's Day with a small box of chocolates containing four candies? Why?

5. As a novice in global marketing, which alternative for global market-entry strategy would you be likely to start with? Why? What other alternatives do you have for a global market entry?

6. Coca-Cola is sold worldwide. In some countries, Coca-Cola owns the bottling facilities; in others, it has signed contracts with licensees or relies on joint ventures. When selecting a licensee in each country, what factors should Coca-Cola consider?

CASE 5–1 The Coca-Cola Company: Japan

The Coca-Cola Company is the world's largest carbonated soft-drink producer. In 1994, the company sold the equivalent of 11.8 billion cases of soft drinks worldwide. Approximately 76 percent of the company's soft-drink revenues and 81 percent of soft-drink operating income arise from sales outside the United States. These statistics are not surprising since Coke and Coca-Cola are among the world's best-known trademarks.

THE COCA-COLA COMPANY: A GLOBAL ENTERPRISE

The global presence of The Coca-Cola Company is evident in numerous ways. Four of the world's top five carbonated soft drinks are sold by the company. These brands include Coca-Cola/Coca-Cola Classic, diet Coke, Coca-Cola Light, Fanta, and Sprite. The company captured 46 percent of the worldwide market for carbonated soft-drink flavor segments: cola, orange, and

EXHIBIT 1

Coca-Cola's market position in 15 countries (share of flavored, carbonated soft-drink sales)

COUNTRY	MARKET LEADER	LEADERSHIP MARGIN	SECOND PLACE
Australia	Coca-Cola	3.9–1	diet Coke
Belgium	Coca-Cola	9.0–1	Fanta
Brazil	Coca-Cola	3.7–1	Brazilian brand
Chile	Coca-Cola	4.5–1	Fanta
France	Coca-Cola	4.2–1	French brand
Germany	Coca-Cola	3.5–1	Fanta
Great Britain	Coca-Cola	1.8–1	diet Coke
Greece	Coca-Cola	3.7–1	Fanta
Italy	Coca-Cola	2.8–1	Fanta
Japan	Coca-Cola	2.2–1	Fanta
Korea	Coca-Cola	1.6–1	Korean brand
Norway	Coca-Cola	2.7–1	Coca-Cola light
South Africa	Coca-Cola	3.8–1	Sparletta
Spain	Coca-Cola	2.4–1	Spanish brand
Sweden	Coca-Cola	3.6–1	Fanta

Source: *The Coca-Cola Company 1994 Annual Report*, p. 29.

lemon-lime. Exhibit 1 illustrates the worldwide leadership position of Coca-Cola.

One of the reasons for Coca-Cola's worldwide presence is its extensive, efficient, and effective bottling network. This bottling network, which includes company-owned bottlers, joint ventures with established bottlers in various countries, and franchised bottlers, allows for Coca-Cola/Coca-Cola Classic to be distributed in more than 195 countries, Fanta and Sprite in 164 countries, and diet Coke/Coca-Cola Light in 117 countries.

Coca-Cola Marketing in Japan

The Coca-Cola Company sold its products in Japan as early as the 1920s. However, it did not establish a formal Japanese subsidiary until 1957. Since that time, the company has built a dominant position in the Japanese soft-drink market. For example, Coca-Cola is sold in 1 million stores and some 700,000 vending machines in Japan. The Coca-Cola Company captures more than 33 percent of all carbonated and noncarbonated soft drinks sold in Japan. It is estimated that the Coca-Cola brand captures 70 percent of the Japanese cola market; Coca-Cola Light captures 20 percent. Pepsi-Cola captures less than 10 percent of this market.

Industry analysts estimate that advertising spending for the Coca-Cola brand is about five times higher than the amount spent by Pepsi-Cola.

The successful entry into Japan by the Coca-Cola Company and subsequent performance provide valuable insights into global marketing in general and the need to consider cultural issues. For instance, company executives emphasize that adaptation to the local culture manifests itself in numerous ways. Its management practices focus on consensus and group-building consistent with Japanese values. Customs such as lifetime employment for Japanese employees are adopted. Efforts to localize consumer communications is also evident in the language used in advertising and the group settings featuring the consumption of the product.

Questions

1. Which of the four global market-entry strategies does Coca-Cola use most often when expanding its worldwide presence? Which strategy does it appear that Coca-Cola uses the least?

2. After watching the video tape featuring television commercials for Coca-Cola in Japan, what similarities do you see with Coca-Cola commercials in the United States?

AMERICAN WOMAN

MOTORS

Sharing the Spirit of Adventure

IF MONEY WERE NO OBJECT: THE CARS WOMEN WOULD BUY

VOLUME 7 NO. 5

10>

OCTOBER/NOVEMBER 1995

PLUS

◆ **HOW TO SATISFY A WOMAN'S NEEDS: CADILLAC STYLE**

◆ **CAMEL TROPHY: 1ST U.S. WOMAN TO SURVIVE HELL**

Consumer Behavior

• Outline the stages in the consumer decision process.

• Distinguish between three variations of the
consumer decision process: routine, limited, and
extended problem solving.

• Explain how psychological influences affect
consumer behavior, particularly purchase decision
processes.

• Identify major sociocultural influences on consumer
behavior and their effects on purchase decisions.

• Recognize how marketers can use knowledge of
consumer behavior to better understand and influence
individual and family purchases.

SAVVY AUTOMAKERS SAY: KNOW THY CUSTOM(H)ER

Who will buy 60 percent of all new cars in 2000? Who
already spends more than $65 million on new cars and
trucks for their personal use and influences 80 percent
of all new-car sales? Women—yes, women.

Until recently, automakers viewed women chiefly as
passengers not purchasers. Today most have marketing-
to-women task forces, such as Ford's Women's Marketing Committee, and have hired women design engineers
and marketing executives to help them understand this
"new" consumer. What have they learned? First,
women prefer "sporty" cars that are relatively inexpensive and fun to drive rather than "sports" cars with
bigger engines and higher price tags. Second, a car's
"feel" is important to women. Sleek exteriors and
interior designs that fit proportions of smaller drivers as
well as opening ease for doors, trunks, and hoods are
equally important. What are women's favorite models?
The Geo Storm and Toyota Paseo.

Third, women approach car buying in a deliberate
manner. Many read *American Woman Motorscene*
magazine, a bimonthly automotive lifestyle publication,
that approaches car buying, usage, and maintenance
from a woman's point of view. Fourth, while men and
women look for the same car features, their priorities
differ. Both sexes value dependability most, but more
women consider it a higher priority. Women also rank
low price and safety higher than men. Men view
appearance, horsepower, and acceleration as being more
important than women. Finally, automakers have
learned that, when shopping for cars, both sexes dislike
high-pressure tactics. Women tend to place a higher
value on how honest, sincere, polite, and helpful the
salesperson acted. Although men valued these attitudes
too, they ranked a salesperson's knowledge and willingness to negotiate higher than women.

Recognition of women as purchasers and influencers
in car buying has also altered the behavior of car
dealers. Many dealers now use a one-price policy and
have stopped negotiating a car's price. Industry research

indicates that 68 percent of new-car buyers dread the price negotiation process involved in buying a car, and women often refuse to do it at all![1]

This chapter examines **consumer behavior,** the actions a person takes in purchasing and using products and services, including the mental and social processes that precede and follow these actions. This chapter shows how the behavioral sciences help answer questions such as why people choose one product or brand over another, how they make these choices, and how companies use this knowledge to provide value to consumers.

CONSUMER PURCHASE DECISION PROCESS

Behind the visible act of making a purchase lies an important decision process that must be investigated. The stages a buyer passes through in making choices about which products and services to buy is the **purchase decision process.** This process has the five stages shown in Figure 6–1: (1) problem recognition, (2) information search, (3) alternative evaluation, (4) purchase decision, and (5) postpurchase behavior.

Problem Recognition: Perceiving a Need

Problem recognition, the initial step in the purchase decision, is perceiving a difference between a person's ideal and actual situations big enough to trigger a decision.[2] This can be as simple as finding an empty milk carton in the refrigerator; noting, as a first-year college student, that your high school clothes are not in the style that other students are wearing; or realizing that your laptop computer may not be working properly.

In marketing, advertisements or salespeople can activate a consumer's decision process by showing the shortcomings of competing (or currently owned) products. For instance, an advertisement for a compact disk (CD) player could stimulate problem recognition because it emphasizes the sound quality of CD players over that of the conventional stereo system you may now own.

Information Search: Seeking Value

After recognizing a problem, a consumer begins to search for information, the next stage in the purchase decision process. First, you may scan your memory for previous experiences with products or brands.[3] This action is called *internal search.* For frequently purchased products such as shampoo, this may be enough. Or a consumer may undertake an *external search* for information.[4] This is especially needed when past experience or knowledge is insufficient, the risk of making a wrong purchase

FIGURE 6–1

Purchase decision process

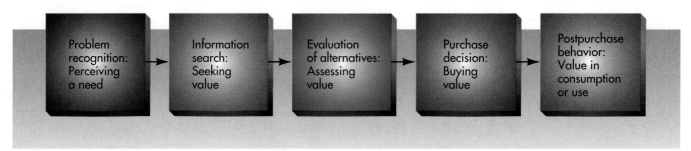

Brand	Model	Price	Disc-error correction	Track-locate speed	Bump resistance	Overall convenience	Taping ease
Onkyo	DX-C211	$270	Better	Very good	Fair	Good	Very good
Sony	CDP-C445	230	Good	Very good	Good	Better	Better
Denon	DCM-340	260	Better	Very good	Fair	Good	Very good
Technics	SL-PD1000	260	Very good	Better	Very good	Very good	Good
Philips	CDC 935	240	Very good	Very good	Better	Very good	Fair
Kenwood	DP-R6060	250	Good	Very good	Fair	Very good	Very good
Marantz	CC-45	300	Good	Very good	Better	Very good	Fair
Yamaha	CDC-645	270	Good	Very good	Fair	Very good	Very good
Teac	PD-D900	155	Good	Good	Good	Very good	Fair
Fisher	DAC-2403	265	Good	Good	Very good	Good	Very good

Rating: Better — Very good — Good — Fair — Poor

FIGURE 6–2

Consumer Reports' evaluation of carousel changer compact disk players (abridged)

Source: "CD Players," *Consumer Reports* (March 1995), p. 204

decision is high, and the cost of gathering information is low. The primary sources of external information are: (1) *personal sources,* such as relatives and friends whom the consumer trusts; (2) *public sources,* including various product-rating organizations such as *Consumer Reports,* government agencies, and TV "consumer programs"; and (3) *marketer-dominated sources,* such as information from sellers that include advertising, salespeople, and point-of-purchase displays in stores.

Suppose you consider buying an expensive or complex product, such as a CD player. You will probably tap several of these information sources: friends and relatives, CD-player advertisements, and several stores carrying CD players (for demonstrations). You might study the comparative evaluation of carousel changer CD players that appeared in *Consumer Reports,* published by a product-testing organization, a portion of which appears in Figure 6–2.

Alternative Evaluation: Assessing Value

The information search stage clarifies the problem for the consumer by (1) suggesting criteria to use for the purchase, (2) yielding brand names that might meet the criteria, and (3) developing consumer value perceptions. Based only on the information shown in Figure 6–2, what selection criteria would you use in buying a CD player? Would you use price, bump resistance, taping ease, or some combination of these and other criteria?

For some of you, the information provided may be inadequate because it does not contain all the factors you might consider when evaluating CD players. These factors are a consumer's **evaluative criteria,** which represent both the objective attributes of a brand (such as track-locate speed) and the subjective ones (such as prestige) you use to compare different products and brands.[5] Firms try to identify and capitalize on both types of criteria to create the best value for the money sought by you and other consumers.

Consumers often have several criteria for evaluating brands. (Didn't you in the preceding exercise?) Knowing this, companies seek to identify the most important evaluative criteria that consumers use when judging brands. For example, among the evaluative criteria shown in the columns of Figure 6–2, suppose that you use three in considering brands of CD players: (1) a list price under $250 (column 3), (2) overall convenience (column 7), and (3) taping ease (column 8). These criteria establish the brands in your **evoked set**—the group of brands that a consumer would consider acceptable from among all the brands in the product class of which he or she is aware.[6] Your three evaluative criteria result in only two models, Sony and Philips, in your evoked set. If these brands don't satisfy you, you can change your evaluative criteria to create a different evoked set of models.

Purchase Decision: Buying Value

Having examined the alternatives in the evoked set, you are almost ready to make a purchase decision. Two choices remain: (1) from whom to buy and (2) when to buy. For a product like a CD player, the information search process probably involved visiting retail stores, seeing different brands in catalogs, or viewing CD player promotions on a home shopping television channel. The choice of which seller to buy from will depend on such considerations as the terms of sale, your past experience buying from the seller, and the return policy. Often a purchase decision involves a simultaneous evaluation of both product attributes and seller characteristics. For example, you might choose the second-most preferred CD player brand at a store with a liberal refund and return policy versus the most preferred brand at a store with more conservative policies.

Deciding when to buy is frequently determined by a number of factors. For instance, you might buy sooner if one of your preferred brands is on sale or its manufacturer offers a rebate. Other factors such as the store atmosphere, pleasantness of the shopping experience, salesperson persuasiveness, time pressure, and financial circumstances could also affect whether a purchase decision is made or postponed.[7]

Postpurchase Behavior: Value in Consumption or Use

After buying a product, the consumer compares it with his or her expectations and is either satisfied or dissatisfied. If the consumer is dissatisfied, marketers must decide whether the product was deficient or consumer expectations too high. Product deficiency may require a design change; if expectations are too high, perhaps the company's advertising or the salesperson oversold the product's features.

Sensitivity to a customer's consumption or use experience is extremely important in a consumer's value perception. For example, research on long-distance telephone services provided by MCI, Sprint, and AT&T indicates that satisfaction or dissatisfaction affects consumer value perceptions.[8] Studies show that satisfaction or dissatisfaction affects consumer communications and repeat-purchase behavior. Satisfied buyers tell eight other people about their experience. Dissatisfied buyers complain to 22 people![9] Satisfied buyers also tend to buy from the same seller each time a purchase occasion arises. As described in the accompanying Marketing NewsNet, the financial impact of repeat-purchase behavior is significant.[10] Accordingly, firms such as General Electric (GE), Johnson & Johnson, Coca-Cola, and British Airways focus attention on postpurchase behavior to maximize customer satisfaction and retention.[11] These firms, among many others, now provide toll-free telephone numbers, offer liberalized return and refund policies, and engage in staff training to handle complaints, answer questions, and record suggestions. For

MARKETING NEWSNET

THE VALUE OF A SATISFIED CUSTOMER

Customer satisfaction is an important focus of the marketing concept. But, how much is a satisfied customer worth? This question has prompted firms to calculate the financial value of a satisfied customer over time. Frito-Lay, for example, estimates that the average loyal consumer in the southwestern United States eats 21 pounds of salty snack chips a year. At a price of $2.50 a pound, this customer spends $52.50 annually on the company's salty snacks such as Lays and Ruffles potato chips and Doritos and Tostitos tortilla chips. Exxon estimates that a loyal customer will 'spend $500 annually for its branded gasoline, not including candy, snacks, oil, or repair services purchased at its gasoline stations. Kimberly-Clark reports that a loyal customer will buy 6.7 boxes of its Kleenex tissues each year and will spend $994 on facial tissue over 60 years, in today's dollars.

These calculations have focused marketer attention on customer retention. Ford Motor Company has set a target of increasing customer retention—the percentage of Ford owners whose next car is also a Ford—from 60 percent to 80 percent. Why? Ford executives say that each additional percentage point is worth a staggering $100 million in profits!

example, GE operates a database that stores 750,000 answers about 8,500 of its models in 120 product lines to handle 3 million calls annually.[12] Research has shown that such efforts produce positive postpurchase communications among consumers and contribute to relationship building between sellers and buyers.

Often a consumer is faced with two or more highly attractive alternatives, such as a Sony or a Philips CD player. If you choose the Philips, you may think, "Should I have purchased the Sony?" This feeling of postpurchase psychological tension or anxiety is called **cognitive dissonance.** To alleviate it, consumers often attempt to applaud themselves for making the right choice. So after your purchase, you may seek information to confirm your choice by asking friends questions like, "Don't you like my CD player?" or by reading ads of the brand you chose. You might even look for negative information about the brand you didn't buy and decide that the taping ease of the Philips which was rated "fair" in Figure 6–2, was actually a serious deficiency. Firms often use ads or follow-up calls from salespeople in this postpurchase stage to try to convince buyers that they made the right decision. For many years, Buick ran an advertising campaign with the message, "Aren't you really glad you bought a Buick?"

Involvement and Problem-Solving Variations

Sometimes consumers don't engage in the five-step purchase decision process. Instead, they skip or minimize one or more steps depending on the level of **involvement,** the personal, social, and economic significance of the purchase to the consumer.[13] High-involvement purchase occasions typically have at least one of three characteristics—the item to be purchased (1) is expensive, (2) can have serious personal consequences, or (3) could reflect on one's social image. For these occasions, consumers engage in extensive information search, consider many product attributes and brands, form attitudes, and participate in word-of-mouth communication. Low-involvement purchases, such as toothpaste and soap, barely involve most of us, whereas stereo systems and automobiles are very involving. Researchers have identified three general variations in the consumer purchase process based on consumer involvement and product knowledge. Figure 6–3 summarizes some of the important differences between the three problem-solving variations.[14]

CHARACTERISTICS OF PURCHASE DECISION PROCESS	CONSUMER INVOLVEMENT HIGH ← → LOW		
	EXTENDED PROBLEM SOLVING	LIMITED PROBLEM SOLVING	ROUTINE PROBLEM SOLVING
Number of brands examined	Many	Several	One
Number of sellers considered	Many	Several	Few
Number of product attributes evaluated	Many	Moderate	One
Number of external information sources used	Many	Few	None
Time spent searching	Considerable	Little	Minimal

FIGURE 6-3

Comparison of problem-solving variations

Routine problem solving For products such as toothpaste and milk, consumers recognize a problem, make a decision, and spend little effort seeking external information and evaluating alternatives. The purchase process for such items is virtually a habit and typifies low-involvement decision making. Routine problem solving is typically the case for low-priced, frequently purchased products. It is estimated that about 50 percent of all purchase occasions are of this kind.

Limited problem solving In limited problem solving, consumers typically seek some information or rely on a friend to help them evaluate alternatives. In general, several brands might be evaluated using a moderate number of different attributes. You might use limited problem solving in choosing a toaster, a restaurant for dinner, and other purchase situations in which you have little time or effort to spend. Limited problem solving accounts for about 38 percent of purchase occasions.

Extended problem solving In extended problem solving, each of the five stages of the consumer purchase decision process is used in the purchase, including considerable time and effort on external information search and in identifying and evaluating alternatives. Several brands usually are in the evoked set, and these are evaluated on many attributes. Extended problem solving exists in high-involvement purchase situations for items such as CD players, VCRs, and investments in stocks and bonds. Firms marketing these products put significant effort into informing and educating these consumers. About 12 percent of purchase occasions fall into this category.

Situational Influences

Often the purchase situation will affect the purchase decision process. Five **situational influences** have an impact on your purchase decision process: (1) the purchase task, (2) social surroundings, (3) physical surroundings, (4) temporal effects, and (5) antecedent states.[15] The purchase task is the reason for engaging in the decision in the first place. Information searching and evaluating alternatives may differ depending on whether the purchase is a gift, which often involves the social visibility, or for the buyer's own use. Social surroundings, including the other people present when a purchase decision is made, may also affect what is purchased. Physical surroundings such as decor, music, and crowding in retail stores may alter how purchase decisions are made. Temporal effects such as time of day or the amount of time available will influence where consumers have breakfast and lunch and what is ordered. Finally, antecedent states, which include the consumer's mood or the amount of cash on hand, can influence purchase behavior and choice.

FIGURE 6-4

Influences on the consumer purchase decision process

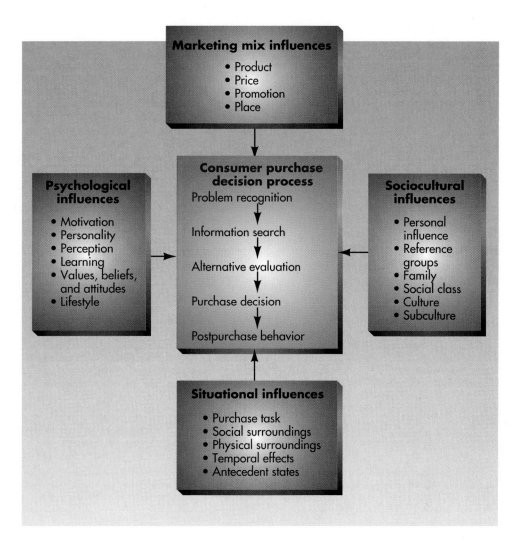

Figure 6–4 shows the many influences that affect the consumer purchase decision process. The decision to buy a product also involves important psychological and sociocultural influences, the two important topics discussed during the remainder of this chapter. Marketing mix influences are described in Chapters 11 through 21.

CONCEPT CHECK

1. What is the first step in the consumer purchase decision process?

2. The brands a consumer considers buying out of the set of brands in a product class of which the consumer is aware is called the _____ .

3. What is the term for postpurchase anxiety?

PSYCHOLOGICAL INFLUENCES ON CONSUMER BEHAVIOR

Psychology helps marketers understand why and how consumers behave as they do. In particular, concepts such as motivation and personality; perception; learning; values, beliefs, and attitudes; and lifestyle are useful for interpreting buying processes and directing marketing efforts.

FIGURE 6–5

Hierarchy of needs

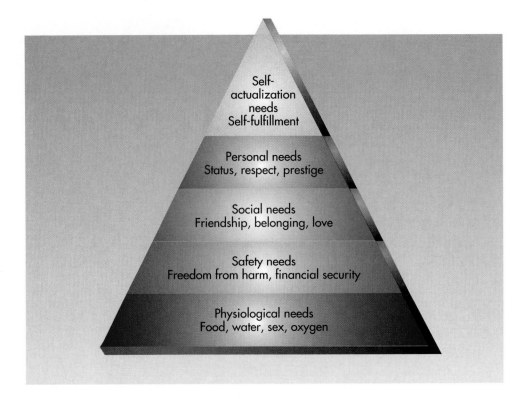

Motivation and Personality

Motivation and personality are two familiar psychological concepts that have specific meanings and marketing implications. They are both used frequently to describe why people do some things and not others.

Motivation   **Motivation** is the energizing force that causes behavior that satisfies a need. Because consumer needs are the focus of the marketing concept, marketers try to arouse these needs.

An individual's needs are boundless. People possess physiological needs for basics such as water, sex, and food. They also have learned needs, including esteem, achievement, and affection. Psychologists point out that these needs are hierarchical; that is, once physiological needs are met, people seek to satisfy their learned needs. Figure 6–5 shows one need hierarchy and classification scheme that contains five need classes.[16] *Physiological needs* are basic to survival and must be satisfied first. A Burger King advertisement featuring a juicy hamburger attempts to activate the need for food. *Safety needs* involve self-preservation and physical well-being. Smoke detector and burglar alarm manufacturers focus on these needs. *Social needs* are concerned with love and friendship. Dating services and fragrance companies try to arouse these needs. *Personal needs* are represented by the need for achievement, status, prestige, and self-respect. The American Express Gold Card and Brooks Brothers Clothiers appeal to these needs. Sometimes firms try to arouse multiple needs to stimulate problem recognition. Michelin combined security with parental love to promote tire replacement as shown in the accompanying advertisement. *Self-actualization needs* involve personal fulfillment. For example, the U.S. Army recruiting program invites you to "Be all you can be."

Personality   **Personality** refers to a person's consistent behaviors or responses to recurring situations. Although numerous personality theories exist, most identify key traits—enduring characteristics within a person or in his or her relationship with

Michelin appeals to security and parental love needs in its advertising.

A LOT OF TIRES COST LESS THAN A MICHELIN. THAT'S BECAUSE THEY SHOULD.

To everyone out there looking to save a few dollars on a set of tires, let's not mince words. You buy cheap, you get cheap.

There may be a lot of tires out there that cost less than a Michelin.

The only question is, what do you have to give up if you buy one?

Do they handle like a Michelin?

Do they last like a Michelin?

Are they as reliable as a Michelin?

Then ask yourself this: Do you really want to find out?

At Michelin, we make only one kind of tire. The very best we know how.

Because the way we see it, the last place a compromise belongs is on your car.

As a matter of fact, we're so obsessed with quality we make the steel cables that go into our steel-belted radials.

We even make many of the machines that make and test Michelin tires.

And our quality control checks are so exhaustive that they even include x-rays.

These and hundreds of other details, big and small (details that may seem inconsequential to others), make sure that when you put a set of Michelin tires on your car, you get all the mileage Michelin is famous for.

True, there may be cheaper tires. But if they don't last like a Michelin, are they really less expensive?

So the next time someone tries to save you a few dollars on a tire, tell him this: It's not how much you pay that counts. It's what you get for your money.

And then *he'll* know that *you* know that there's only one reason a tire costs less than a Michelin. It deserves to.

MICHELIN
BECAUSE SO MUCH IS RIDING ON YOUR TIRES.

others. Such traits include assertiveness, extroversion, compliance, dominance, and aggression, among others. For example, cigarette smokers have been identified as having traits such as aggression and dominance, but not compliance.[17] Research suggests that compliant people prefer known brand names and use more mouthwash and toilet soaps. In contrast, aggressive types use razors, not electric shavers, apply more cologne and after-shave lotions, and purchase signature goods such as Gucci, Yves St. Laurent, and Donna Karan as an indicator of status.

Cross-cultural analysis also suggests that residents of different countries have a **national character,** or a distinct set of personality characteristics common among people of a country or society.[18] For example, Americans and Germans are relatively more assertive than Russians and the English.

Perception

One person sees a Cadillac as a mark of achievement; another sees it as ostentatious. This is the result of **perception**—the process by which an individual selects, organizes, and interprets information to create a meaningful picture of the world.

Selective perception Because the average consumer operates in a complex environment, the human brain attempts to organize and interpret information with a process called *selective perception,* a filtering of exposure, comprehension, and retention. *Selective exposure* occurs when people pay attention to messages that are consistent with their attitudes and beliefs and ignore messages that are inconsistent. Selective exposure often occurs in the postpurchase stage of the consumer decision process, when consumers read advertisements for the brand they just bought. It also occurs when a need exists—you are more likely to "see" a McDonald's advertisement or the Golden Arches by the road when you are hungry rather than after you have eaten a pizza.

Selective comprehension involves interpreting information so that it is consistent with your attitudes and beliefs. A marketer's failure to understand this can have

ETHICS AND SOCIAL RESPONSIBILITY ALERT

THE ETHICS OF SUBLIMINAL MESSAGES

For almost 50 years, the topic of subliminal perception and the presence of subliminal messages embedded in commercial communications has sparked debate. Although there is no substantive scientific support for the concept of subliminal perception, the Federal Communications Commission denounced subliminal messages as deceptive in 1974. The Entertainment and Leisure Software Publishers Association in Great Britain is presently considering banning these messages altogether.

Subliminal messages are not illegal in the United States, however, and marketers occasionally pursue opportunities to create these messages. For example, Time Warner Interactive's Endorfun, a CD-ROM puzzle game, has a music soundtrack with more than 100 subliminal messages meant to make players feel good about themselves, even if they can't solve the puzzle. One message says, "I am a winner." Puzzle players are informed that subliminal messages exist and instructions on how to turn off the soundtrack are provided.

Do you believe that attempts to implant subliminal messages are a deceptive practice and unethical, regardless of their intent?

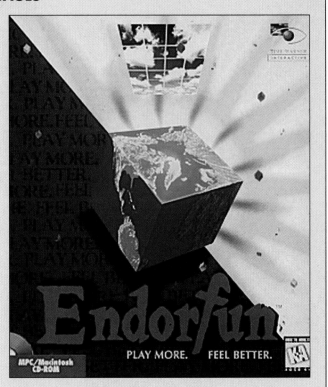

disastrous results. For example, Toro introduced a small, lightweight snowblower called the Snow Pup. Even though the product worked, sales failed to meet expectations. Why? Toro later found out that consumers perceived the name to mean that Snow Pup was a toy or too light to do any serious snow removal.[19]

Selective retention means that consumers do not remember all the information they see, read, or hear, even minutes after exposure to it. This affects the internal and external information search stage of the purchase decision process. This is why furniture and automobile retailers often give consumers product brochures to take home after they leave the showroom.

Since perception plays such an important role in consumer behavior, it is not surprising that the topic of subliminal perception is a popular item for discussion. **Subliminal perception** means that you see or hear messages without being aware of them. The presence and effect of subliminal perception on behavior is a hotly debated issue, with more popular appeal than scientific support. Indeed, evidence suggests that such messages have limited effects on behavior.[20] If these messages did influence behavior, would their use be an ethical practice? (See the accompanying Ethics and Social Responsibility Alert.[21])

Perceived risk   Perception plays a major role in the perceived risk in purchasing a product or service. **Perceived risk** represents the anxieties felt because the consumer cannot anticipate the outcomes of a purchase but believes that there may be negative consequences. Examples of possible negative consequences are the size of

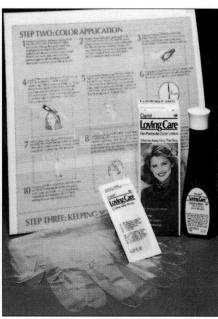

Companies use a variety of strategies to reduce consumer-perceived risk.

the financial outlay required to buy the product (Can I afford $200 for those skis?), the risk of physical harm (Is bungee jumping safe?), and the performance of the product (Will the hair coloring work?). A more abstract form is psychosocial (What will my friends say if I wear that sweater?). Perceived risk affects information search because the greater the perceived risk, the more extensive the external search phase is likely to be.

Recognizing the importance of perceived risk, companies develop strategies to reduce the consumer's risk and encourage purchases. These strategies and examples of firms using them include the following:

- Obtaining seals of approval: the Good Housekeeping seal or Underwriter's Laboratory seal.
- Securing endorsements from influential people: Elizabeth Taylor's White Diamonds fragrance.
- Providing free trials of the product: sample packages of Duncan Hines Peanut Butter Cookies mailed by P&G.
- Giving extensive usage instructions: Clairol haircoloring.
- Providing warranties and guarantees: Cadillac's four-year, 50,000-mile, Gold Key Bumper-to-Bumper warranty.

Learning

Much consumer behavior is learned. Consumers learn which information sources to use for information about products and services, which evaluative criteria to use when assessing alternatives, and, more generally, how to make purchase decisions. **Learning** refers to those behaviors that result from (1) repeated experience and (2) thinking.

Behavioral learning   *Behavioral learning* is the process of developing automatic responses to a situation built up through repeated exposure to it. Four variables are central to how consumers learn from repeated experience: drive, cue, response, and reinforcement. A *drive* is a need that moves an individual to action. Drives, such as hunger, might be represented by motives. A *cue* is a stimulus or symbol perceived by consumers. A *response* is the action taken by a consumer to satisfy the drive, and a *reinforcement* is the reward. Being hungry (drive), a consumer sees a cue (a billboard), takes action (buys a hamburger), and receives a reward (it tastes great!).

Marketers use two concepts from behavioral learning theory. *Stimulus generalization* occurs when a response elicited by one stimulus (cue) is generalized to another stimulus. Using the same brand name for different products is an application of this concept, such as Tylenol Cold & Flu and Tylenol P.M. *Stimulus discrimination* refers to a person's ability to perceive differences in stimuli. Consumers' tendency to perceive all light beers as being alike led to Budweiser Light commercials that distinguished between many types of "lights" and Bud Light.

Cognitive learning Consumers also learn through thinking, reasoning, and mental problem solving without direct experience. This type of learning, called *cognitive learning,* involves making connections between two or more ideas or simply observing the outcomes of others' behaviors and adjusting your own accordingly. Firms also influence this type of learning. Through repetition in advertising, messages such as "Advil is a headache remedy" attempt to link a brand (Advil) and an idea (headache remedy) by showing someone using the brand and finding relief.

Brand loyalty Learning is also important because it relates to habit formation—the basis of routine problem solving. Furthermore, there is a close link between habits and **brand loyalty,** which is a favorable attitude toward and consistent purchase of a single brand over time. Brand loyalty results from the positive reinforcement of previous actions. So a consumer reduces risk and saves time by consistently purchasing the same brand of shampoo and has favorable results—healthy, shining hair. There is evidence of brand loyalty in many commonly purchased products in the United States and the global marketplace. However, the incidence of brand loyalty appears to be declining in North America, Mexico, European Union nations, and Japan. Read the Marketing NewsNet on page 164 to find out which country has the lowest percentage of brand loyalists.[22]

Values, Beliefs, and Attitudes

Values, beliefs, and attitudes play a central role in consumer decision making and related marketing actions.

Attitude formation An **attitude** is a "learned predisposition to respond to an object or class of objects in a consistently favorable or unfavorable way."[23] Attitudes are shaped by our values and beliefs, which are learned. Values vary by level of specificity. We speak of American core values, including material well-being and humanitarianism. We also have personal values, such as thriftiness and ambition. Marketers are concerned with both, but focus mostly on personal values. Personal values affect attitudes by influencing the importance assigned to specific product attributes. Suppose thriftiness is one of your personal values. When you evaluate cars, fuel economy (a product attribute) becomes important. If you believe a specific car has this attribute, you are likely to have a favorable attitude toward it.

Beliefs also play a part in attitude formation. **Beliefs** are a consumer's subjective perception of *how well* a product or brand performs on different attributes. Beliefs are based on personal experience, advertising, and discussions with other people. Beliefs about product attributes are important because, along with personal values, they create the favorable or unfavorable attitude the consumer has toward certain products and services.

Attitudes toward Pepsi-Cola and Extra Strength Bayer aspirin were successfully changed by these ads. How? Read the text to find out how marketers can change consumer attitudes toward products and brands.

Attitude change   Marketers use three approaches to try to change consumer attitudes toward products and brands, as shown in the following examples.[24]

1. *Changing beliefs about the extent to which a brand has certain attributes.* To allay consumer concern that aspirin use causes an upset stomach, The Bayer Company successfully promoted the gentleness of its Extra Strength Bayer Plus aspirin.

2. *Changing the perceived importance of attributes.* Pepsi-Cola made freshness an important product attribute when it stamped freshness dates on its cans. Prior to doing so, few consumers considered cola freshness an issue. After Pepsi spent about $25 million on advertising and promotion, a consumer survey found that 61 percent of cola drinkers believed freshness dating was an important attribute![25]

3. *Adding new attributes to the product.* Chevron's Techron additive was put into its gasoline, hoping consumers would perceive this new attribute favorably, which they did.

Lifestyle

Lifestyle is a mode of living that is identified by how people spend their time and resources (activities), what they consider important in their environment (interests), and what they think of themselves and the world around them (opinions). Moreover, lifestyle reflects consumers' **self-concept,** which is the way people see themselves and the way they believe others see them.[26] Hart Schaffner & Marx, a men's clothier, focused a recent promotional campaign on this theme: "The right suit might not help you achieve success. But the wrong suit could limit your chances."

The analysis of consumer lifestyles (also called *psychographics*) has produced many insights into consumers' behavior. For example, lifestyle analysis has proven useful in segmenting and targeting consumers for new and existing products (see Chapter 9).

MARKETING NEWSNET

Global

CONSUMER BRAND LOYALTY VERSUS PRICE SEEKING IN THE GLOBAL MARKETPLACE

How widespread is brand loyalty in the global marketplace? According to a recent study of 40,000 consumers in 40 countries, 23 percent of consumers worldwide are brand loyalists. Their opposite—price seekers—account for 27 percent of consumers. Brand loyalty and price seeking appear to be related to whether a country is a developed or developing nation. Brand loyalists predominate in developing countries; price seekers predominate in developed nations. The accompanying table shows the percentage of brand loyalists and price seekers in 10 representative countries. The United States has the lowest percentage of brand loyalists. France, Germany, and Japan have the highest percentage of price seekers. This is not surprising since related research shows that the majority of consumers in these three countries believe that there is not much difference among brands of consumer products.

Brand loyalty, in general, appears to be eroding. For example, more than one half of consumers worldwide

COUNTRY	PERCENT OF CONSUMERS THAT ARE	
	BRAND LOYALISTS (%)	PRICE SEEKERS(%)
United States	11.3	35.5
Mexico	19.1	23.4
China	27.9	23.4
India	34.6	7.4
Japan	23.5	41.0
France	19.5	45.5
Germany	16.9	43.7
Spain	27.0	34.4
United Kingdom	28.7	27.2
Czech Republic	23.9	26.9

consider all brand of beer and cigarettes to be about the same, and more than 70 percent believe that all paper towels, soaps, and snack chips are alike.

Lifestyle analysis typically focuses on identifying consumer profiles. The most prominent example of this type of analysis is the Values and Lifestyles (VALS) Program developed by SRI International.[27] The VALS Program has identified eight interconnected categories of adult lifestyles based on a person's self-orientation and resources. Self-orientation describes the patterns of attitudes and activities that help people reinforce their social self-image. Three patterns have been uncovered; they are oriented toward principles, status, and action. A person's resources encompass income, education, self-confidence, health, eagerness to buy, intelligence, and energy level. This dimension is a continuum ranging from minimal to abundant. Figure 6–6 shows the eight lifestyle types and their relationships and highlights selected demographic and behavioral characteristics of each.

The VALS Program seeks to explain why and how consumers make purchase decisions. For example, *principle-oriented consumers* try to match their behavior with their views of how the world is or should be. These older consumers divide into two categories. Fulfilleds are mature, satisfied, and reflective people who value order, knowledge, and responsibility. Most are well-educated and employed in a profession. Believers, with fewer resources to draw on, are conservative, conventional people with concrete beliefs and strong attachments to family, church, and community. *Status-oriented consumers* are motivated by the actions and opinions of others. These consumers include Achievers, who are successful and career-oriented; value duty, structure, prestige and material rewards; and have abundant resources at their disposal. Strivers, with fewer resources, seek motivation, self-definition, and social approval, and define success in purely financial terms. *Action-oriented consumers* are intensely involved in social and physical activity, enjoy variety, and are risk-takers.

Most resources

ACTUALIZERS

Enjoy the "finer things."
Receptive to new products,
technologies, distribution.
Skeptical of advertising.
Frequent readers of wide
variety of publications.
Light TV viewers.

Principle   Oriented   Status   Oriented   Action   Oriented

FULFILLEDS

Little interest in image
or prestige.
Above-average consumers of
products for the home.
Like educational and public
affairs programming.
Read widely
and often.

ACHIEVERS

Attracted to premium
products.
Prime target for variety
of products.
Average TV watchers,
read business, news,
and self-help
publications.

EXPERIENCERS

Follow fashion and fads.
Spend much of disposable
income on socializing.
Buy on impulse.
Attend to advertising.
Listen to rock music.

BELIEVERS

Buy American.
Slow to change habits.
Look for bargains.
Watch TV more than average.
Read retirement, home
and garden, and
general-interest
magazines.

STRIVERS

Image conscious.
Limited discretionary incomes,
but carry credit balanes.
Spend on clothing and
personal-care products.
Prefer TV to
reading.

MAKERS

Shop for comfort,
durability, value.
Unimpressed by luxuries.
Buy the basics, listen to radio.
Read auto, home
mechanics, fishing,
outdoor
magazines.

Least resources

STRUGGLERS

Brand loyal.
Use coupons and watch
for sales.
Trust advertising.
Watch TV often.
Read tabloids and
women's
magazines.

CONSUMER TYPE	PERCENT OF POPULATION	MEDIAN AGE	MEDIAN INCOME	DISTINCTIVE PURCHASE BEHAVIORS
Actualizers	8%	43	$58,000	Possessions reflect a cultivated taste for finer things in life.
Fulfilleds	12	48	38,000	Desire product functionality, value, and durability.
Believers	17	58	21,000	Favor American products and established brands.
Achievers	10	36	50,000	Prefer products that demonstrate success to peers.
Strivers	14	34	25,000	Emulate those with impressive possessions.
Experiencers	11	26	19,000	Avid consumers of clothing, fast food, music, movies, and videos.
Makers	12	30	23,000	Unimpressed by material possessions (except those with a practical purpose).
Strugglers	16	61	9,000	Modest resources limit purchases to urgent needs.

FIGURE 6-6

VALS 2 Psychographic Segments

165

Experiencers are young, enthusiastic, impulsive, and rebellious consumers who are still formulating life values and behavior patterns. Makers too are energetic but focus their attention on practical matters related to family, work, and physical recreation. While Experiencers maintain a vicarious relationship with their surroundings, Makers experience life by working on it—building a house and raising children.

Two consumer types stand apart. Actualizers are successful, sophisticated, active, take-charge people with high self-esteem and abundant resources of all kinds. Image is important to them, not as evidence of power or status, but as an expression of taste, independence, and character. By comparison, Strugglers are poor, often uneducated, and frequently concerned about their well-being. They are the oldest of the VALS consumer types.

Each of these categories exhibits different buying behavior and media preferences. For example, Believers and Makers typically own pickup trucks and fishing gear; Actualizers are likely to own a foreign luxury car or a home computer. Actualizers, Fulfilleds, and Achievers are most likely to read business magazines such as *Fortune*. Experiencers read sports magazines, Makers read automotive magazines, and Believers are the heaviest readers of *Reader's Digest*.

CONCEPT CHECK

1. The problem with the Toro Snow Pup was an example of selective _____ .

2. What three attitude-change approaches are most common?

3. What does *lifestyle* mean?

SOCIOCULTURAL INFLUENCES ON CONSUMER BEHAVIOR

Sociocultural influences, which evolve from a consumer's formal and informal relationships with other people, also exert a significant impact on consumer behavior. These involve personal influence, reference groups, the family, social class, culture, and subculture.

Personal Influence

A consumer's purchases are often influenced by the views, opinions, or behaviors of others. Two aspects of personal influence are important to marketing: opinion leadership and word-of-mouth activity.

Opinion leadership   Individuals who exert direct or indirect social influence over others are called **opinion leaders.** Opinion leaders are more likely to be important for products that provide a form of self-expression. Automobiles, clothing, club membership, home video equipment, and PCs are products affected by opinion leaders, but appliances are not.[28] A recent study by *Popular Mechanics* magazine identified 18 million men who influence the purchases of some 85 million consumers for "do-it-yourself" products.[29]

About 10 percent of U.S. adults are opinion leaders.[30] Identifying, reaching, and influencing opinion leaders is a major challenge for companies. Some firms use sports figures or celebrities as spokespersons to represent their products, such as John Starks for Adidas and Cindy Crawford for Revlon, in the hope that they are opinion leaders. Others promote their products in media believed to reach opinion leaders. Still others use more direct approaches. For example, Chrysler Corporation recently invited influential community leaders and business executives to test drive its Dodge Intrepid, Chrysler Concorde, and Eagle Vision models. Some 6,000

Firms use sports figures or celebrities as spokespersons to represent their products, such as John Starks for Adidas and Cindy Crawford for Revlon, in the hope that they are opinion leaders.

accepted the offer, and 98 percent said they would recommend their tested car. Chrysler estimated that the number of favorable recommendations totaled 32,000.[31]

Word of mouth   People influencing each other during their face-to-face conversations is called **word of mouth.** Word of mouth is perhaps the most powerful information source for consumers because it typically involves friends viewed as trustworthy. When consumers were asked in a recent survey what most influences their buying decisions, 37 percent mentioned a friend's recommendation, and 20 percent said advertising. When a similar question was posed to Russian consumers, 72 percent said advice from friends, and 24 percent said advertising.[32]

The power of personal influence has prompted firms to promote positive and retard negative word of mouth.[33] For instance, "teaser" advertising campaigns are run in advance of new product introductions to stimulate conversations. Other techniques such as advertising slogans, music, and humor also heighten positive word of mouth. On the other hand, rumors about Kmart (snake eggs in clothing), McDonald's (worms in hamburgers), and Corona Extra beer (contaminated beer) have resulted in negative word of mouth, none of which was based on fact. Overcoming or neutralizing negative word of mouth is difficult and costly. Several food products in Indonesia, including some sold by Nestlé, were rumored to contain pork, which is prohibited to the 160 million Muslim consumers in that country. Nestlé had to spend $250,000 in advertising to counteract the rumor.[34] Firms have found that supplying factual information, providing toll-free numbers for consumers to call the company, and giving appropriate product demonstrations also have been helpful.

Reference Groups

Reference groups are people to whom an individual looks as a basis for self-appraisal or as a source of personal standards. Reference groups affect consumer purchases because they influence the information, attitudes, and aspiration levels that help set a consumer's standards.[35] For example, one of the first questions one asks others when planning to attend a social occasion is, "What are you going to wear?" Reference groups have an important influence on the purchase of luxury products but not of necessities—reference groups exert a strong influence on the brand chosen when its use or consumption is highly visible to others.[36]

Consumers have many reference groups, but three groups have clear marketing implications. A *membership group* is one to which a person actually belongs, including fraternities, social clubs, and the family. Such groups are easily identifiable and are targeted by firms selling insurance, insignia products, and charter vacations. An *aspiration group* is one that a person wishes to be a member of or wishes to be identified with, such as a professional society. Firms frequently rely on spokespeople or settings associated with their target market's aspiration group in their advertising. A *dissociative group* is one that a person wishes to maintain a distance from because of differences in values or behaviors. Believing that motorcycle ownership and usage has a "black leather-jacketed biker" stigma, Honda Motor Company has focused its promotional efforts on disassociating its motorcycles from this group.[37]

Family Influence

Family influences on consumer behavior result from three sources: consumer socialization, passage through the family life cycle, and decision making within the family.

Consumer socialization   The process by which people acquire the skills, knowledge, and attitudes necessary to function as consumers is **consumer socialization.**[38] Children learn how to purchase (1) by interacting with adults in purchase

situations and (2) through their own purchasing and product usage experiences. Research shows that children evidence brand preferences at age two, and these preferences often last a lifetime.[39] This knowledge has prompted Sony to introduce "My First Sony," a line of portable audio equipment for children; Time, Inc. to launch *Sports Illustrated for Kids;* Polaroid to develop the Cool Cam camcorder for children between ages 9 and 14; and Prodigy and America Online to create special areas where young audiences can view their children's menu—Just for Kids and Kids Only, respectively.

Family life cycle   Consumers act and purchase differently as they go through life. The **family life cycle** concept describes the distinct phases that a family progresses through from formation to retirement, each phase bringing with it identifiable purchasing behaviors.[40] Figure 6–7 illustrates the traditional progression as well as contemporary variations of the family life cycle, including the prevalence of single-person households with and without children who will account for almost one third of U.S. households in 2000.

Young singles' buying preferences are for nondurable items, including prepared foods, clothing, personal care products, and entertainment. They comprise about 9 percent of households and represent a target market for recreational travel, automobile, and consumer electronics firms. Young married couples without children are typically more affluent than young singles because usually both spouses are employed. These couples account for about 10 percent of households and exhibit preferences for furniture, housewares, and gift items for each other. Young marrieds with children represent about 17 percent of households and are driven by the needs of their children. They make up a sizeable market for life insurance, various children's products, and home furnishings. Single parents with children (8 percent of house-

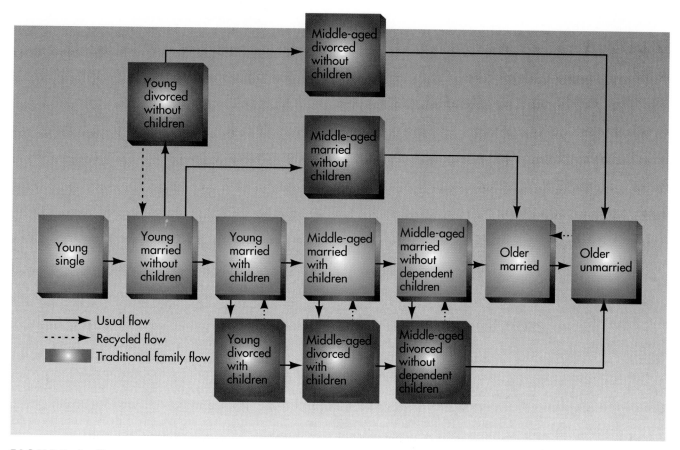

FIGURE 6-7

Modern family life cycle

holds) are the least financially secure of households with children. Their buying preferences are affected by a limited economic status and tend toward convenience foods, child care services, and personal care items.

Middle-aged married couples with children comprise about 23 percent of households and are typically better off financially than their younger counterparts. They are a significant market for leisure products and home improvement items and represent the fastest-growing family life cycle stage in the late 1990s. Middle-aged couples without children account for 20 percent of households and typically have a large amount of discretionary income. These couples buy better home furnishings, status automobiles, and financial services.

Persons in the last two phases—older married and older unmarried—make up 13 percent of households. They are a sizeable market for prescription drugs, medical services, vacation trips, and gifts for younger relatives. These consumers are expected to represent the second-fastest-growing family life cycle stage in the late 1990s.

Family decision making   A third influence in the decision-making process occurs within the family. Two decision-making styles exist: spouse-dominant and joint decision making. With a joint decision-making style, most decisions are made by both husband and wife. Spouse-dominant decisions are those for which either the husband or the wife is responsible. The types of products and services typically associated with the decision-making styles are shown in Figure 6-8.[41] However, these tendencies are changing with the rise in dual-income families. Today, 40

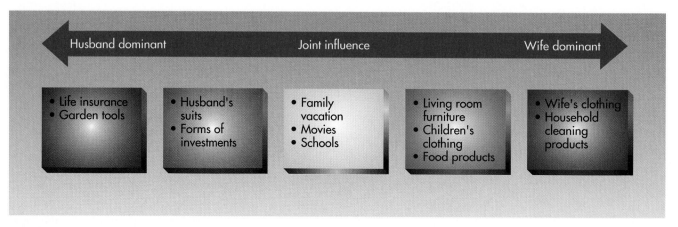

FIGURE 6-8

Influence continuum of spouse in family decision making

percent of all food-shopping dollars are spent by male customers. Women now purchase 70 percent of men's dress shirts, and Van Heusen advertises in *Vogue, Cosmopolitan,* and *Glamour* magazines.[42]

Roles of individual family members in the purchase process are another element of family decision making. Five roles exist: (1) information gatherer, (2) influencer, (3) decision maker, (4) purchaser, and (5) user. Family members assume different roles for different products and services. This knowledge is important to firms. For example, it is important for Conair marketing executives to know that 80 percent of men use hair blow dryers, but also that women are the principal decision maker and purchaser of the product.[43] Increasingly, preteens and teenagers are the information gatherers, influencers, decision makers, and purchasers of products and services items for the family, given the prevalence of working parents and single-parent households. Children under 18 currently influence more than $400 billion in annual family purchases.[44] This figure helps to explain why, for example, Nabisco, Johnson & Johnson, Apple Computer, Kellogg, and P&G often advertise between the rock videos on MTV.

Social Class

A more subtle influence on consumer behavior than direct contact with others is the social class to which people belong. **Social class** may be defined as the relatively permanent, homogeneous divisions in a society into which people sharing similar values, interests, and behavior can be grouped. A person's occupation, source of income (not level of income), and education determine his or her social class. Generally speaking, three major social class categories exist—upper, middle, and lower—with subcategories within each. This structure has been observed in the United States, Great Britain, Western Europe, and Latin America.[45]

To some degree, persons within social classes exhibit common attitudes, lifestyles, and buying behaviors. Compared with the middle classes, people in the lower classes have a more short-term time orientation, are more emotional than rational in their reasoning, think in concrete rather than abstract terms, and see fewer personal opportunities. Members of the upper classes focus on achievements and the future and think in abstract or symbolic terms.

Companies use social class as a basis for identifying and reaching particularly good prospects for their products and services. For instance, AT&T has used social class for identifying preferences for different styles of telephones, JCPenney has historically appealed to the middle classes, and *New Yorker* magazine reaches the upper classes. In general, people in the upper classes are targeted by companies for items such as financial investments, expensive cars, and evening wear. The middle classes represent a target market for home improvement centers, automobile parts stores, and personal hygiene products. The lower classes are targeted for products such as plastic figurines and scandal tabloids. Firms also recognize differences in media preferences among classes: lower and working classes prefer sports and scandal magazines, middle classes read fashion, romance, and celebrity (*People*) magazines, and upper classes tend to read literary, travel, and news magazines.

Culture and Subculture

As described in Chapter 3, culture refers to the set of values, ideas, and attitudes that are accepted by a homogeneous group of people and transmitted to the next generation. Thus we often refer to the American culture, the Latin American culture, or the Japanese culture. Cultural underpinnings of American buying patterns were described in Chapter 3; Chapter 5 explored the role of culture in global marketing.

Subgroups within the larger, or national, culture with unique values, ideas, and attitudes are referred to as **subcultures.** Various subcultures exist within the American culture. The three largest racial/ethnic subcultures in the United States are African-Americans, Hispanics, and Asians. These three groups will account for 28 percent of the U.S. population in 2000. They spend more than $700 billion annually for goods and services. Each of these groups exhibit sophisticated social and cultural behaviors that affect their buying patterns.

African-American buying patterns   African-Americans represent the largest racial/ethnic subculture in the United States in terms of population and purchasing power.

Consumer research on African-American buying patterns have focused on similarities and differences with whites.[46] When socioeconomic status differences between African-Americans and whites are removed, there are more similarities than points of difference, except for brand loyalty. African-Americans tend to exhibit higher brand loyalty than whites. However, the tendency for African-Americans to use a brand name as a dominant attribute for product evaluation declines with a rise in socioeconomic status.

Differences in buying patterns are greater within the African-American subculture, due to levels of socioeconomic status, than between African-Americans and whites of similar status. For example, Johnson Products Company, an African-American-owned firm, markets its hair care products to two segments of African-Americans—one segment seeks to achieve middle-class status, and the other does not have middle-class aspirations.[47] Furthermore, the typical African-American family is five years younger than the typical white family. This factor alone accounts for some of the observed differences in preferences for clothing, music, shelter, cars, and many other products, services, and activities.[48] Finally, it must be emphasized that, historically, African-Americans have been deprived of employment and educational opportunities in the United States. Both factors have resulted in income disparities between African-Americans and whites, which influence purchase behavior.

Recent research indicates that while African-Americans are price conscious, they are strongly motivated by quality and choice. They respond more to products such as apparel and cosmetics and advertising that appeal to their African-American pride and heritage as well as address their ethnic features and needs regardless of socioeconomic status.

Appreciation for the context in which African-Americans make purchase decisions is a necessary first step in understanding their buying patterns. Current research on African-American purchase behavior reveals that stereotypes are often misleading, as they also are for the Hispanic and Asian subcultures.

Hispanic buying patterns   About 50 percent of Hispanics in the United States are immigrants, and the majority are under the age of 25. Hispanics will surpass African-Americans as the largest ethnic/racial subculture in the United States by 2010, due in part to migration patterns.

Research on Hispanic buying practices has uncovered several consistent patterns:[49]

1. Hispanics are quality and brand conscious. They are willing to pay a premium price for premium quality and are brand loyal.
2. Hispanics prefer buying American-made products, especially those offered by firms that cater to Hispanic needs.
3. Hispanic buying preferences are strongly influenced by family and peers.
4. Hispanics consider advertising a credible product information source, and about $950 million is spent annually on advertising to them by firms in the United States.
5. Convenience of use is not an important product attribute to Hispanic homemakers with respect to food preparation or consumption, nor is low caffeine in coffee and soft drinks, low fat in dairy products, and low cholesterol in packaged foods.

Despite some consistent buying patterns, marketing to Hispanics has proven to be a challenge for two reasons. First, the Hispanic subculture is diverse and composed of Mexicans, Puerto Ricans, Cubans, and others of Central and South American ancestry. Cultural differences among these nationalities often affect product preferences. For example, Campbell Soup Company sells its Casera line of soups, beans, and sauces using different recipes to appeal to Puerto Ricans on the East Coast and

Mexicans in the Southwest. Second, a language barrier exists, and commercial messages are frequently misinterpreted when translated into Spanish. A U.S. airline painfully learned this lesson when the Spanish translation of its "We Earn Our Wings Daily" message implied that passengers often ended up dead. Campbell Soup has overcome the language issue. It provides Spanish and English labels on its soups in parts of the western and southwestern United States.

Sensitivity to the unique needs of Hispanics by firms has paid huge dividends. For example, Metropolitan Life Insurance is the largest insurer of Hispanics. Goya Foods dominates the market for ethnic food products sold to Hispanics, and Best Foods' Mazola Corn Oil captures two thirds of the Hispanic market for this product category.

Asian buying patterns   About 70 percent of Asians in the United States are immigrants, and most are under the age of 25. Recent U.S. census figures indicate

Companies often must address subcultural differences in language and custom.

that Asian-Americans are the fastest-growing racial/ethnic subculture in the United States.[50]

The Asian subculture is composed of Chinese, Japanese, Filipinos, Koreans, Asian-Indians, people from Southeast Asia, and Pacific Islanders. The diversity of the Asian subculture is so great that generalizations about buying patterns of this group are difficult to make. Consumer research on Asian-Americans suggests that individuals and families divide into two groups. "Assimilated" Asian-Americans are conversant in English, highly educated, hold professional and managerial positions, and exhibit buying patterns very much like the typical American consumer. This group buys 15 percent of the 2,500 pianos Steinway makes every year in North America. "Nonassimilated" Asian-Americans are recent immigrants and still cling to their native languages and customs. The diversity of Asian-Americans evident in language, customs, and tastes requires marketers to be sensitive to different Asian nationalities. For example, Anheuser-Busch's agricultural products division sells eight different varieties of California-grown rice, each with a different Asian label to cover a range of nationalities and tastes. The company's advertising also addresses the preferences of Chinese, Japanese, and Koreans for different kinds of rice bowls.

Studies also show that the Asian-American subculture as a whole is characterized by hard work, strong family ties, appreciation for education, and median family incomes exceeding those of white families. Moreover, this subculture is the most entrepreneurial in the United States, as evidenced by the number of Asian-owned businesses. These qualities led Metropolitan Life Insurance to identify Asians as a target for insurance following the company's success in marketing to Hispanics.

CONCEPT CHECK

1. What are the two primary forms of personal influence?

2. Marketers are concerned with which types of reference groups?

3. What two challenges must marketers overcome when marketing to Hispanics?

SUMMARY

1. When a consumer buys a product, it is not an act but a process. There are five steps in the purchase decision process: problem recognition, information search, alternative evaluation, purchase decision, and postpurchase behavior.

2. Consumers evaluate alternatives on the basis of attributes. Identifying which attributes are most important to consumers, along with understanding consumer beliefs about how a brand performs on those attributes, can make the difference between successful and unsuccessful products.

3. Consumer involvement with what is bought affects whether the purchase decision process involves routine, limited, or extended problem solving. Situational influences also affect the process.

4. Perception is important to marketers because of the selectivity of what a consumer sees or hears, comprehends, and retains.

5. Much of the behavior that consumers exhibit is learned. Consumers learn from repeated experience and reasoning. Brand loyalty is a result of learning.

6. Attitudes are learned predispositions to respond to an object or class of objects in a consistently favorable or unfavorable way. Attitudes are based on a person's values and beliefs concerning the attributes of objects.

7. Lifestyle is a mode of living reflected in a person's activities, interests, and opinions of himself or herself and the world. Lifestyle is a manifestation of a person's self-concept.

8. Personal influence takes two forms: opinion leadership and word-of-mouth activity. A specific type of personal influence exists in the form of reference groups.

9. Family influences on consumer behavior result from three sources: consumer socialization, family life cycle, and decision making within the household.

10. Within the United States there are social classes and subcultures that affect a consumer's values and behavior. Marketers must be sensitive to these sociocultural influences when developing a marketing mix.

KEY TERMS AND CONCEPTS

consumer behavior p. 152
purchase decision process p. 152
evaluative criteria p. 153
evoked set p. 154
cognitive dissonance p. 155
involvement p. 155
situational influences p. 156
motivation p. 158
personality p. 158
national character p. 159
perception p. 159
subliminal perception p. 160
perceived risk p. 160

learning p. 161
brand loyalty p. 162
attitude p. 162
beliefs p. 162
lifestyle p. 163
self-concept p. 163
opinion leaders p. 166
word of mouth p. 167
reference groups p. 167
consumer socialization p. 168
family life cycle p. 168
social class p. 170
subcultures p. 171

CHAPTER PROBLEMS AND APPLICATIONS

1. Review Figure 6–2 in the text, which shows the CD-player attributes identified by *Consumer Reports.* Which attributes are important to you? What other attributes might you consider? Which brand would you prefer?

2. Suppose research at Apple Computer reveals that prospective buyers are anxious about buying PCs for home use. What strategies might you recommend to the company to reduce consumer anxiety?

3. A Porsche salesperson was taking orders on new cars because he was unable to satisfy the demand with the limited number of cars in the showroom and lot. Several persons had backed out of the contract within two weeks of signing the order. What explanation can you give for this behavior, and what remedies would you recommend?

4. Which social class would you associate with each of the following items or actions? (*a*) tennis club membership, (*b*) an arrangement of plastic flowers in the kitchen, (*c*) *True Ro-*

mance magazine, (*d*) *Smithsonian* magazine, (*e*) formally dressing for dinner frequently, and (*f*) being a member of a bowling team.

5. Assign one or more levels of the hierarchy of needs and the motives described in Figure 6–5 to the following products: (*a*) life insurance, (*b*) cosmetics, (*c*) *The Wall Street Journal,* and (*d*) hamburgers.

6. With which stage in the family life cycle would the purchase of the following products and services be most closely identified? (*a*) bedroom furniture, (*b*) life insurance, (*c*) a Caribbean cruise, (*d*) a house mortgage, and (*e*) children's toys.

7. "The greater the perceived risk in a purchase situation, the more likely that cognitive dissonance will result." Does this statement have any basis given the discussion in the text? Why?

CASE 6–1:   Ken Davis Products, Inc.

Video

"Cooking is a lot like music," explains Barbara Jo Davis. "There are musicians who are excellent musicians and they can play any of the classical music to perfection, but they don't know how to improvise. And then there are the jazz musicians who can do both of these things."

"The same thing is true of cooks," continues Barbara. "There are the cooks who can follow a recipe . . . and will be the best cooks in the world as long as they have a recipe. But if they have to improvise, then they're lost. So what we want to do is help those who aren't the improvisers."

THE COMPANY

Barbara Jo Davis is president of Ken Davis Products, Inc., a small regional business that develops and markets barbecue sauces. The company was founded by Barbara Davis' late spouse Ken Davis. Ken owned a restaurant where he served his grandmother's recipe for barbecue sauce, and he received such positive feedback from his customers he decided to write the recipe down to ensure it would taste the same every time he made it. He called in Barbara, then a home economist for a large consumer foods corporation, to help him do it. Shortly afterwards Ken closed the restaurant, married Barbara, and began marketing his barbecue sauce full time.

Barbara Davis stayed with the consumer foods corporation, becoming a manager for the test kitchens and for the cook books, until 1988 when she left to work for Ken Davis Products full time.

While Ken Davis Products is a market leader in its region, it has not expanded nationwide. Barbara Davis explains, "What I hear consumers say again and again is the reason they buy Ken Davis barbecue sauces is because it's a local company. I think the reason we're the market leaders is because it's a personal product. People know who the person is. They can see me driving around in my car."

PRODUCTS, CUSTOMERS, AND ENVIRONMENT

In addition to the Original Ken Davis Barbecue Sauce, the company also sells Smooth and Spicy Barbecue Sauce, with jalepeno peppers added to it, and a line of marinade sauces called Jazz It Up. Through consumer testing and focus groups, Barbara Davis discovered the real problem consumers are facing when they cook is how to add flavor to the meats they are eating. Hence the Jazz It Up line of marinade sauces was born. Ken Davis Products now offers four varieties of cooking sauces—Orange Citrus, Lemon Lime, Southwestern, and Mesquite. "They're really a hybrid between marinades and cooking sauces because you can use them as an ingredient, a marinade, or even as a dipping sauce," explains Barbara Davis. This was a natural product line extension for Ken Davis Products based on its reputation in the barbecue sauce market.

The company does not target specific consumer segments because it seems the consumers are just about everybody. Barbara Davis has discovered through consumer focus groups that the barbecue sauce buying decision is still made by the female head of the household, but everybody in the family seems to participate in the decision. "Kids especially like our sauce a lot," explains Barbara Davis, "and elderly people like the Original Recipe because it's got a lot of flavor but it's not hot or spicy."

The Food and Drug Administration (FDA) recently passed legislation requiring all consumer food products to nutrition label their products in a standardized way. For small companies like Ken Davis Products, this

meant the added expense of finding an independent laboratory to analyze the products and redesigning the labels. Barbara Davis thinks this new legislation works to the advantage of Ken Davis Products, though. "New people can compare and see Ken Davis is indeed lower in sodium than most of the other barbecue sauces on the market."

THE ISSUES

Ken Davis Products prides itself on staying abreast of changing consumer tastes and trends. In addition to conducting focus groups, Barbara Davis solicits informal feedback from current and potential Ken Davis customers. She will talk to testers at an in-store sampling or even walk up to shoppers in the barbecue sauce aisle and ask them about their purchases. Barbara Davis believes, "You have to listen to your consumer because you're not in this business to please yourself. You're in business to please your consumer." In addition to discovering the latest tastes, she has learned from her customers that the primary promotional vehicle used to spread the word about Ken Davis Products is word-of-mouth.

To make the most of this strategy, Ken Davis Products participates in event marketing and in-store sampling. Ken Davis used to always say, "The best way to sell a food product is to get people to taste it, because it's ultimately the taste that will keep them as customers." Barbara Davis has found another successful strategy to get people talking about Ken Davis Products is to become involved in the community. She regularly talks to groups of young entrepreneurs or invites school children to her test kitchen to learn how to cook. "You do all of

these little things just to get people thinking Ken Davis. And they don't even know they're thinking Ken Davis half the time. But it's so ingrained that when they go to the grocery store, why would they look at those other brands?" Barbara Davis also sends out a newsletter twice a year to Ken Davis Products users with new recipe ideas and stories about the company. Today's busy family is always on the look-out for quick and easy recipes.

Ken Davis Products also uses some more traditional promotional vehicles, such as Free Standing Inserts (FSIs) in the Sunday paper and radio advertising. The FSIs include a coupon to induce new customers to try the product. The radio ads reflect the local, homegrown differentiation strategy used by Ken Davis Products. Barbara Davis does the commercials herself, which are completely unrehearsed. "That way I don't have to pay talent," she chuckles.

THE MULTIPLE ROLES OF A SMALL BUSINESSPERSON

After working for a large corporation and then becoming a small business entrepreneur, Barbara Davis is in a unique position to comment on the satisfactions and hardships of owning your own business. She stresses that you have to know everything about your business— you can't specialize like in a large corporation. You also get to make all the decisions and have the satisfaction of being a part of the process every step of the way. "But," Barbara adds, "you have to work harder than you have ever worked in your life. You have to always be working. When I was working for a corporation, I resented working all those hours because it wasn't for me. But now when I'm working all these hours I live it because I am doing if for myself. That's the reward— it's all for you."

Questions

1. In what ways have American eating habits changed over the past decade that affect a barbecue sauce manufacturer?

2. What are the two or three main (a) objective evaluative criteria and (b) subjective evaluative criteria consumers of Ken Davis barbecue sauces might use?

3. How can Ken Davis Products do marketing research on consumers to find out what they eat, to learn how they use barbecue sauces, and to get ideas for new products?

4. (a) Do you think a small, local company such as Ken Davis Products should have entered the market as a premium-priced product or a low-priced product? (b) What should its pricing strategy be today?

5. What do you see the (a) satisfactions and (b) concerns of being in business for yourself?

Source of authorship: Written by Giana Eckhardt and William Rudelius of the University of Minnesota.

CHAPTER 7

Organizational Markets and Buyer Behavior

AFTER READING THIS CHAPTER YOU SHOULD BE ABLE TO:

• Distinguish among industrial, reseller, and government markets.

• Recognize key characteristics of organizational buying that make it different from consumer buying.

• Understand how types of buying situations influence organizational purchasing.

• Recognize similarities and differences in industrial and reseller purchase behavior.

FIBER OPTICS: COMMUNICATING IN A FLASH OF LIGHT

Bob Procsal views light very differently from most people.

As marketing manager for Fiber-Optic Products at Honeywell, MICRO SWITCH Division, Procsal is responsible for fiber-optic products (like those pictured on the opposite page) that sense, modulate, and transmit infrared light for the data communications industry. Converting technology into products and bringing these products to market are part and parcel of his typical day.

Marketing fiber-optic technology and products is a challenging assignment. Buyer experience with the technology is often limited, even though potential applications are numerous in data communications, computer networks, and industrial automation. Honeywell, MICRO SWITCH Division, and other suppliers such as Hewlett-Packard, Toshiba, Mitsubishi, and ABB HAFO (Sweden) must often convey the value of fiber-optic technology and specific products through advertising, trade shows, personal selling, and demonstrations. This task often involves communicating with a diverse set of organizational buyers ranging from industrial firms to governmental agencies throughout the world and in different languages. It also requires knowing which people influence the purchasing decision; what factors they consider important when choosing suppliers and products; and when, where, and how the buying decision is made.

Procsal believes Honeywell, MICRO SWITCH Division, is poised to capture a significant share of the multibillion dollar global fiber optics market. Ultimate success will depend on continued product development that creates customer value and effective marketing to an ever-growing number of prospective buyers for fiber-optic technology in a worldwide marketplace.[1]

The challenge facing Procsal of marketing to organizations is often encountered by both small, startup corporations and large, well-established companies such as

Honeywell. Important issues in marketing to organizations are examined in this chapter, which analyzes the types of organizational buyers, key characteristics of organizational buying, and some typical buying decisions.

THE NATURE AND SIZE OF ORGANIZATIONAL MARKETS

Bob Procsal and Honeywell's MICRO SWITCH Division engage in business marketing. **Business marketing** is the marketing of goods and services to commercial enterprises, governments, and other profit and not-for-profit organizations for use in the creation of goods and services that they then produce and market to other business customers, as well as individuals and ultimate consumers.[2] Because more than half of all U.S. business school graduates take jobs in firms that engage in business marketing,[3] it is important to understand the fundamental characteristics of organizational buyers and their buying behavior.

Organizational buyers are those manufacturers, retailers, and government agencies that buy goods and services for their own use or for resale. For example, all these organizations buy computers and telephone services for their own use. However, manufacturers buy raw materials and parts that they reprocess into the finished goods they sell, whereas retailers resell the goods they buy without reprocessing them. Organizational buyers include all the buyers in a nation except the ultimate consumers. These organizational buyers purchase and lease tremendous volumes of capital equipment, raw materials, manufactured parts, supplies, and business services. In fact, because they often buy raw materials and parts, process them, and sell the upgraded product several times before it is purchased by the final organizational buyer or ultimate consumer, the aggregate purchases of organizational buyers in a year are far greater than those of ultimate consumers.

Organizational buyers are divided into three different markets: (1) industrial, (2) reseller, and (3) government markets.

Industrial Markets

There are more than 11.6 million firms in the industrial, or business, market (Figure 7–1). These **industrial firms** in some way reprocess a product or service they buy before selling it again to the next buyer. This is certainly true of a steel mill that

FIGURE 7-1

Type and number of organizational customers

TYPE OF ORGANIZATION	NUMBER	KIND OF MARKET
Manufacturers	374,000	
Mining	30,000	
Construction	1,075,000	
Farms, forestry, and fisheries	845,000	Industrial (business)
Service	6,342,000	markets—9,517,000
Finance, insurance, and real estate	577,000	
Transportation and public utilites	251,000	
Not-for-profit associations	23,000	
Wholesalers	478,000	Reseller markets—
Retailers	1,547,000	2,025,000
Government units	87,000	Government markets—87,000

Source: Based on *Statistical Abstract of the United States*, 115th ed. (Washington, D.C.: U.S. Department of Commerce, 1995).

Printed in English, the Moscow Yellow Pages lists more than 22,000 industrial, trade, joint venture, and government office telephone numbers and addresses. Read the text to find out how firms in Germany, Russia, and the United States work together to produce, promote, and distribute this directory.

converts iron ore into steel. It is also true (if you stretch your imagination) of a firm selling services, such as a bank that takes money from its depositors, reprocesses it, and "sells" it as loans to its borrowers.

The importance of services in the United States today is emphasized by the composition of the industrial markets shown in Figure 7–1. The first four types of industrial firms (manufacturers; mining; construction; and farms, forestry, and fisheries) sell physical products and represent one fourth of all the industrial firms, or about 2.3 million. The services market sells diverse services such as legal advice, auto repair, and dry cleaning. Along with finance, insurance, and real estate businesses and transportation and public utility firms, these service firms represent about 75 percent of all industrial firms, or about 7.2 million. Because of the size and importance of service firms and some 23,000 not-for-profit organizations (such as the American Red Cross), service marketing is discussed in detail in Chapter 13.

Reseller Markets

Wholesalers and retailers who buy physical products and resell them again without any reprocessing are **resellers.** In the United States there are about 1.6 million retailers and 478,000 wholesalers. In Chapters 16 through 18 we shall see how manufacturers use wholesalers and retailers in their distribution ("place") strategies as channels through which their products reach ultimate consumers. In this chapter we look at these resellers mainly as organizational buyers in terms of (1) how they make their own buying decisions and (2) which products they choose to carry.

Government Markets

Government units are the federal, state, and local agencies that buy goods and services for the constituents they serve. There are about 87,000 of these government units in the United States. Their annual purchases vary in size from the $898 million the Federal Aviation Administration intends to spend for 3,000 computerized workstations for 22 major air traffic control centers in the United States to lesser amounts spent by local school or sanitation districts.[4]

Global Organizational Markets

Industrial, reseller, and government markets also exist on a global scale. International trade statistics indicate that 9 of the 10 largest exporting industries in the United States focus on organizational customers, not ultimate consumers.

The majority of world trade involves manufacturers, resellers, and government agencies buying goods and services for their own use or for resale to others. The exchange relationships often involve numerous transactions spanning the globe as described in Chapter 5. For example, U.S.-based Rohr Industries, Inc. sells aircraft engine components to Europe's Airbus Industrie, the world's third-largest aircraft manufacturer. Airbus then sells its passenger airplanes to Japan Airlines, which flies U.S. businesspeople to the Orient. A New York City firm solicits advertising for and a publisher in Germany prints the Moscow Yellow Pages on behalf of the Moscow city government and telephone system for resale to businesses through Moscow stores, hotels, and international trade centers such as the Armand Hammer Center in Red Square. Honeywell, MICRO SWITCH Division, sells its fiber-optic technology and products to manufacturers of data communication systems worldwide through electronic component resellers in more than 20 countries and directly to national governments in Europe and elsewhere.

MEASURING DOMESTIC AND GLOBAL INDUSTRIAL, RESELLER, AND GOVERNMENT MARKETS

The measurement of industrial, reseller, and government markets is an important first step for a firm interested in gauging the size of one, two, or all three of these markets in the United States and around the world. This task has been made easier with the publication of the **North American Industry Classification System (NAICS).**[5] Effective January 1, 1997, NAICS will provide common industry definitions for Canada, Mexico, and the United States, which will help facilitate the measurement of economic activity in the three member countries of the North American Free Trade Agreement (NAFTA). NAICS replaces the Standard Industrial Classification (SIC) system, a version of which has been in place for more than 50 years in the three NAFTA member countries. The SIC neither permitted comparability across countries nor accurately measured new or emerging industries. Furthermore, NAICS will be consistent with the International Standard Industrial Classification of All Economic Activities, published by the United Nations, to facilitate measurement of global economic activity.

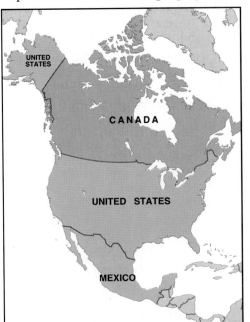

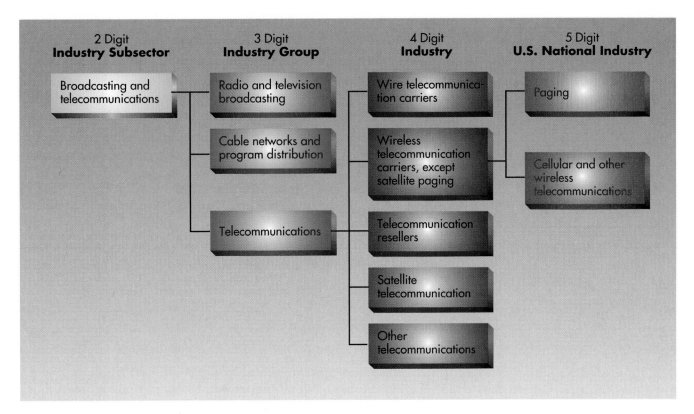

2 Digit **Industry Subsector**	3 Digit **Industry Group**	4 Digit **Industry**	5 Digit **U.S. National Industry**
Broadcasting and telecommunications	Radio and television broadcasting	Wire telecommunication carriers	Paging
	Cable networks and program distribution	Wireless telecommunication carriers, except satellite paging	Cellular and other wireless telecommunications
	Telecommunications	Telecommunication resellers	
		Satellite telecommunication	
		Other telecommunications	

FIGURE 7–2

NAICS breakdown for broadcasting and telecommunications industries (abbreviated)

The NAICS will group economic activity to permit studies of market share, demand for goods and services, import competition in domestic markets, and similar studies. Like the earlier SIC system, NAICS will designate industries with a numerical code in a defined structure. The first digit of the NAICS code will designate a sector of the economy and will be followed by a two-digit code signifying a subsector. Subsectors will be further divided into three-digit industry groups, four-digit industries, and five-digit country-specific industries. Figure 7–2 presents an abbreviated breakdown within the broadcasting and telecommunications industry to illustrate the classification scheme.

The NAICS will permit a firm to find the NAICS codes of its present customers and then obtain NAICS-coded lists for similar firms. Also, it will be possible to monitor NAICS categories to determine the growth in various sectors and industries to identify promising marketing opportunities. However, NAICS codes, like the earlier SIC codes, will have important limitations. The NAICS will assign one code to each organization based on its major economic activity, so large firms that engage in many different activities will still be given only one NAICS code. A second limitation is that five-digit National industry codes will not be available for all three countries because the respective governments will not reveal data when too few organizations exist in a category. Despite these limitations, development of NAICS represents yet another effort toward economic integration in North America and the world.

CONCEPT CHECK

1. What are the three main types of organizational buyers?

2. What is the North American Industry Classification System (NAICS)?

FIGURE 7-3

Key characteristics of organizational buying behavior

MARKET CHARACTERISTICS
- Demand for industrial products and services is derived.
- Few customers typically exist, and their purchase orders are large.

PRODUCT OR SERVICE CHARACTERISTICS
- Products or services are technical in nature and purchased on the basis of specifications.
- There is a predominance of raw and semifinished goods purchased.
- Heavy emphasis is placed on delivery time, technical assistance, postsale service, and financing assistance.

BUYING PROCESS CHARACTERISTICS
- Technically qualified and professional buyers exist and follow established purchasing policies and procedures.
- Buying objectives and criteria are typically spelled out, as are procedures for evaluating sellers and products (services).
- Multiple buying influences exist, and multiple parties participate in purchase decisions.
- Reciprocal arrangements exist, and negotiation between buyers and sellers is commonplace.

OTHER MARKETING MIX CHARACTERISTICS
- Direct selling to organizational buyers is the rule, and physical distribution is very important.
- Advertising and other forms of promotion are technical in nature.
- Price is often negotiated, evaluated as part of broader seller and product (service) qualities, typically inelastic owing to derived demand, and frequently affected by trade and quantity discounts.

CHARACTERISTICS OF ORGANIZATIONAL BUYING

Organizations are different from individuals, so buying for an organization is different from buying for yourself or your family.[6] True, in both cases the objective in making the purchase is to solve the buyer's problem—to satisfy a need or want. But unique objectives and policies of an organization put special constraints on how it makes buying decisions. Understanding the characteristics of organizational buying is essential in designing effective marketing programs to reach these buyers.

Organizational buying behavior is the decision-making process that organizations use to establish the need for products and services and identify, evaluate, and choose among alternative brands and suppliers. Some key characteristics of organizational buying behavior are listed in Figure 7-3 and discussed in the following pages.[7]

Demand Characteristics

Consumer demand for products and services is affected by their price and availability and by consumers' personal tastes and discretionary income. By comparison, industrial demand is derived. **Derived demand** means that the demand for industrial products and services is driven by, or derived from, demand for consumer products and services. For example, the demand for Weyerhaeuser's pulp and paper products is based on consumer demand for newspapers, Domino's "keep warm" pizza-to-go boxes, Federal Express packages, and disposable diapers. Derived demand is often based on expectations of future consumer demand. For instance, Whirlpool purchases parts for its washers and dryers in anticipation of consumer demand, which is affected by the replacement cycle for these products and by consumer income.

MARKETING NEWSNET

Global

THE GLOBAL INFORMATION SUPERHIGHWAY IS PAVED WITH SILICON CHIPS

The twenty-first century will witness the merging of telecommunications, information, and data networks into what has been labeled the "Information Superhighway." As new products and applications emerge for use by businesses and consumers alike, demand for microchips (the small piece of silicon that holds a complex electronic circuit) and demand for microprocessors (a miniature computer consisting of one or more microchips) will expand dramatically.

Companies that produce microchips and microprocessors will benefit from the demand derived from the sale of a multitude of products and technologies that comprise the Information Superhighway. Powerful microprocessors and multimedia graphics software will boost demand for DRAMS (dynamic random-access memory chips), a business dominated by Korean and Japanese firms. Demand for digital-signal-processing chips that speed up video and graphics will boost the fortunes of U.S.-based Texas Instruments and Europe's SGS-Thomson. Demand for multimedia chips will grow as telephone and cable TV companies begin buying video services and set-top boxes to deliver movies and interactive games to homes.

"The Information Highway will be paved with silicon," says William P. "Pat" Weber, vice chairman of Texas Instruments, and microchip demand will be driven by the telecommunication, information, and data networks that travel the highway.

As demand for the products that comprise the Information Superhighway grows, so too will the demand for the technology that makes them possible. Read the accompanying Marketing NewsNet to see how companies that produce microchips and microprocessors will benefit from the merging of telecommunications, information, and data networks on the Information Superhighway.[8]

Number of Potential Buyers

Firms selling consumer products or services often try to reach thousands or millions of individuals or households. For example, your local supermarket or bank probably serves thousands of people, and Quaker Oats tries to reach 80 million American households with its breakfast cereals and probably succeeds in selling to a third or half of these in any given year. In contrast, firms selling to organizations are often restricted to far fewer buyers. Gulfstream Aerospace Corporation can sell its business jets to fewer than 1,000 organizations throughout the world, and B. F. Goodrich sells its original equipment tires to fewer than 10 car manufacturers.

Organizational Buying Objectives

Organizations buy products and services for one main reason: to help them achieve their objectives. For business firms the buying objective is usually to increase profits

Sylvania focuses on buyers' objective of reducing costs to improve profits.

through reducing costs or increasing revenues. Southland Corporation buys automated inventory systems to increase the number of products that can be sold through its 7-Eleven outlets and to keep them fresh. Nissan Motor Company switched its advertising agency because it expects the new agency to devise a more effective ad campaign to help it sell more cars and increase revenues. To improve executive decision making, many firms buy advanced computer systems to process data. The objectives of nonprofit firms and government agencies are usually to meet the needs of the groups they serve. Thus, a hospital buys a high-technology diagnostic device to serve its patients better. Understanding buying objectives is a necessary first step in marketing to organizations. Recognizing the high costs of energy, Sylvania promotes to prospective buyers cost savings and increased profits made possible by its fluorescent lights.

Organizational Buying Criteria

In making a purchase the buying organization must weigh key buying criteria that apply to the potential supplier and what it wants to sell. **Organizational buying criteria** are the objective attributes of the supplier's products and services and the capabilities of the supplier itself. These criteria serve the same purpose as the evaluative criteria used by consumers and described in Chapter 6. Seven of the most commonly used criteria are (1) price, (2) ability to meet the quality specifications required for the item, (3) ability to meet required delivery schedules, (4) technical capability, (5) warranties and claim policies in the event of poor performance, (6) past performance on previous contracts, and (7) production facilities and capacity.[9] Suppliers that meet or exceed these criteria create customer value.

Read the text to learn how Johnson Controls, Inc., the seat supplier for Neon, played an important role in making the Neon a success.

Many organizational buyers today are transforming their buying criteria into specific requirements that are communicated to prospective suppliers. This practice, called **reverse marketing,** involves the deliberate effort by organizational buyers to build relationships that shape suppliers' products, services, and capabilities to fit a buyer's needs and those of its customers.[10] For example, consider the case of Johnson Controls, Inc., the supplier of seats for Chrysler's small car, the Plymouth Neon.[11] Johnson was able to meet Chrysler's cost target but not its safety, weight, and comfort requirements. After five 11-hour days, Johnson and Chrysler engineering and marketing staffs jointly worked out the technical details to satisfy Chrysler's performance requirements at a price acceptable to both parties. Ongoing reverse marketing efforts also exist. Harley-Davidson expects even its long-term suppliers to provide written plans of their efforts to improve quality, and it monitors the progress of these suppliers toward achieving these goals.[12]

With many U.S. manufacturers adopting a "just-in-time" (JIT) inventory system that reduces the inventory of production parts to those to be used within hours or days, on-time delivery is becoming an even more important buying criterion and, in some instances, a requirement.[13] Caterpillar trains its key suppliers at its Quality Institute in JIT inventory systems and conducts supplier seminars on how to diagnose, correct, and implement continuous quality improvement programs.[14] The just-in-time inventory system is discussed further in Chapter 17.

Size of the Order or Purchase

The size of the purchase involved in organizational buying is typically much larger than that in consumer buying. The dollar value of a single purchase made by an organization often runs into the thousands or millions of dollars. For example, Cubic Corporation was awarded a $43 million contract to install an automatic toll-collection system on the 320-mile Florida turnpike, which connects Orlando and Miami.[15] With so much money at stake, most organizations place constraints on their buyers in the

form of purchasing policies or procedures. Buyers must often get competitive bids from at least three prospective suppliers when the order is above a specific amount, such as $5,000. When the order is above an even higher amount, such as $50,000, it may require the review and approval of a vice president or even the president. Knowing how the size of the order affects buying practices is important in determining who participates in the purchase decision and makes the final decision, and also the length of time required to arrive at a purchase agreement.[16]

Buyer–Seller Relationships and Supply Partnerships

Another distinction between organizational and consumer buying behavior lies in the nature of the relationship between organizational buyers and suppliers. Specifically, organizational buying is more likely to involve complex and lengthy negotiations concerning delivery schedules, price, technical specifications, warranties, and claim policies. These negotiations can last for more than a year. This was the case when Los Alamos National Laboratory recently purchased a $35 million Cray Research T90 supercomputer that performs up to 60 million calculations per second.[17]

Reciprocal arrangements also exist in organizational buying. **Reciprocity** is an industrial buying practice in which two organizations agree to purchase each other's products and services. For example, GM purchases Borg-Warner transmissions, and Borg-Warner buys trucks and cars from GM.[18] The U.S. Justice Department frowns on reciprocal buying because it restricts the normal operation of the free market. However, the practice exists and can limit the flexibility of organizational buyers in choosing alternative suppliers. Regardless of the legality of reciprocal buying, do you believe this practice is ethical? (See the accompanying Ethics and Social Responsibility Alert.)[19]

Long-term relationships are also prevalent.[20] As an example, Scandinavian Airlines System recently announced the purchase of 35 Boeing 737–600 airliners with an option to buy another 35 in the future for a total expenditure of $2.4 billion. With aircraft deliveries beginning in late 1998 and continuing into the next century, Scandinavian Airlines cited its desire for a long-term relationship with "a professional and solid supplier" such as Boeing.[21] Dana Corporation is presently engaged in a 10-year, $2 billion contract to supply Mack Trucks with axles, clutches, and frame assemblies.

The right processor for all intelligent creatures.

Whether you're doing financial analysis or creating a multimedia presentation, choosing an Intel Pentium® processor-based PC is a smart move. That's because today's business

software requires more processing power than ever before. So when you're buying your next PC, be sure it has an Intel Pentium processor

inside. Contact Intel on the Internet at http://www.intel.com/procs/pentium/ for more information.

intel.
The Computer Inside.™

In some cases, buyer-seller relationships develop into supply partnerships.[22] A **supply partnership** exists when a buyer and its supplier adopt mutually beneficial objectives, policies, and procedures for the purpose of lowering the cost and/or increasing the value of products and services delivered to the ultimate consumer. Intel, the world's largest manufacturer of microprocessors and the "computer inside" most personal computers, is a case in point. Intel supports its suppliers by offering them quality management programs and by investing in supplier equipment that produces fewer product defects and boosts supplier productivity. Suppliers, in turn, provide Intel with consistent high-quality products at a lower cost for its customers, the makers of personal computers, and finally you, the ultimate customer. Retailers, too, are forging partnerships with their suppliers. Wal-Mart and Kmart have such a relationship with Procter & Gamble for ordering and replenishing P&G's products in their stores. By using computerized cash register scanning equipment and direct electronic linkages to P&G, these retailers can tell P&G what merchandise is needed, along with how much, when, and to which store to deliver it on a daily basis. Since supply partnerships also involve the physical distribution of goods, they are again discussed in Chapter 17.

The Buying Center: A Cross-Functional Group

For routine purchases with a small dollar value, a single buyer or purchasing manager often makes the purchase decision alone. In many instances, however, several people in the organization participate in the buying process. The individuals in this group, called a **buying center,** share common goals, risks, and knowledge important to a purchase decision. For most large multistore chain resellers, such as Sears, 7-Eleven

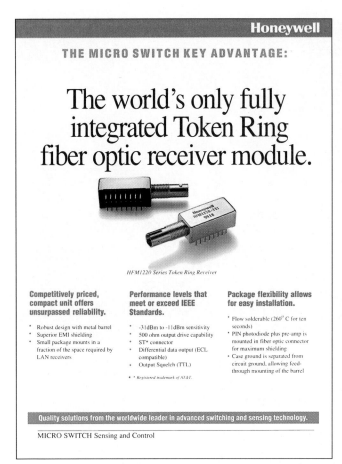

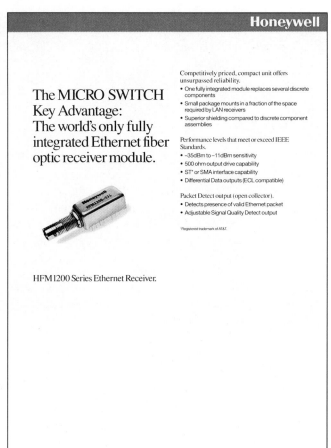

To which people in Honeywell's customer's buying center are these ads targeted: (1) engineering management or (2) design and production engineers? To understand the situation and discover the answer, see the text and the accompanying Marketing NewsNet.

convenience stores, Kmart, or Safeway, the buying center is highly formalized and is called a *buying committee*. However, most industrial firms or government units use informal groups of people or call meetings to arrive at buying decisions.

The importance of the buying center requires that a firm marketing to many industrial firms and government units understand the structure, technical and business functions represented, and behavior of these groups. One researcher has suggested four questions to provide guidance in understanding the buying center in these organizations:[23] Which individuals are in the buying center for the product or service? What is the relative influence of each member of the group? What are the buying criteria of each member? How does each member of the group perceive our firm, our products and services, and our salespeople?

Answers to these questions are difficult to come by, particularly when dealing with industrial firms, resellers, and governments outside the United States.[24] For example, U.S. firms are often frustrated by the fact that Japanese buyers "ask a thousand questions" but give few answers, sometimes rely on third-party individuals to convey views on proposals, are prone to not "talk business," and often say yes to be courteous when they mean no. U.S. firms in the global chemical industry recognize that production engineering personnel have a great deal of influence in Hungarian buying groups, while purchasing agents in the Canadian chemical industry have relatively more influence in buying decisions.

MARKETING NEWSNET

COMMUNICATING VALUE TO DIFFERENT MEMBERS OF A BUYING CENTER WITH CUSTOMIZED ADVERTISEMENTS

Different members of a buying center value different things when choosing suppliers and products. At Honeywell, MICRO SWITCH Division, the marketing staff responsible for fiber optics products develops customized advertisements for each person in a customer's buying center—design engineers, production engineers, engineering management, and purchasing agents. Design and production engineers see value in new technologies and products that are easy to design, install, and use. Engineering management is concerned with supplier capabilities, including a proven track record and service. Purchasing agents see value in low cost and reliable delivery.

Recognizing that different business and technical functions value different things, Bob Procsal, marketing manager for Fiber Optic Products, carefully chooses different messages and media to communicate to each buying center member. For instance, the ad on the left is directed toward design and production engineers and focuses on what they value. The ad on the right is designed for engineering management and deals with information they value.

Does the added effort and expense of customized advertisements pay off? Yes, it does! Inquiries about the company's line of fiber optics products increased 50 percent after this practice was implemented.

People in the buying center   The composition of the buying center in a given organization depends on the specific item being bought. Although a buyer or purchasing manager is almost always a member of the buying center, individuals from other functional areas are included depending on what is to be purchased. In buying a million-dollar machine tool, the president (because of the size of the purchase) and the production vice president or manager would probably be members. For key components to be incorporated in a final manufactured product, a cross-functional group of individuals from research and development (R&D), engineering, and quality control are likely to be added. For new word-processing equipment, experienced secretaries who will use the equipment would be members. Still, a major question in penetrating the buying center is finding and reaching the people who will initiate, influence, and actually make the buying decision.[25] The accompanying Marketing NewsNet shows how Honeywell, MICRO SWITCH Division, tailors its advertisements like those on the page to your left to reach different members of the buying centers in its customer organizations.[26]

Roles in the buying center   Researchers have identified five specific roles that an individual in a buying center can play.[27] In some purchases the same person may perform two or more of these roles.

- *Users* are the people in the organization who actually use the product or service, such as a secretary who will use a new word processor.
- *Influencers* affect the buying decision, usually by helping define the specifications for what is bought. The information systems manager would be a key influencer in the purchase of a new mainframe computer.
- *Buyers* have formal authority and responsibility to select the supplier and negotiate the terms of the contract. The purchasing manager probably would perform this role in the purchase of a mainframe computer.
- *Deciders* have the formal or informal power to select or approve the supplier that receives the contract. Whereas in routine orders the decider is usually the buyer or purchasing manager, in important technical purchases it is more likely to be someone from R&D, engineering, or quality control. The decider for a key

STAGE IN THE BUYING DECISION PROCESS	CONSUMER PURCHASE: CD PLAYER FOR A STUDENT	ORGANIZATIONAL PURCHASE: HEADPHONES FOR A CD PLAYER
Problem recognition	Student doesn't like the sound of the stereo system now owned and desires a CD player.	Marketing research and sales departments observe that competitors are including headphones on their models. The firm decides to include headphones on their own new models, which will be purchased from an outside supplier.
Information search	Student uses past experience, that of friends, ads, and *Consumer Reports* to collect information and uncover alternatives.	Design and production engineers draft specifications for headphones. The purchasing department identifies suppliers of CD player headphones.
Alternative evaluation	Alternative CD players are evaluated on the basis of important attributes desired in a CD player.	Purchasing and engineering personnel visit with suppliers and assess (1) facilities, (2) capacity, (3) quality control, and (4) financial status. They drop any suppliers not satisfactory on these factors.
Purchase decision	A specific brand of CD player is selected, the price is paid, and it is installed in the student's room.	They use (1) quality, (2) price, (3) delivery, and (4) technical capability as key buying criteria to select a supplier. Then they negotiate terms and award a contract.
Postpurchase behavior	Student reevaluates the purchase decision, may return the CD player to the store if it is unsatisfactory, and looks for supportive information to justify the purchase.	They evaluate suppliers using a formal vendor rating system and notify supplier if phones do not meet its quality standard. If problem is not corrected, they drop the firm as a future supplier.

FIGURE 7–4

Comparing the stages in consumer and organizational purchases

component being incorporated in a final manufactured product might be any of these three people.

- *Gatekeepers* control the flow of information in the buying center. Purchasing personnel, technical experts, and secretaries can all keep salespeople or information from reaching people performing the other four roles.

Stages in an Organizational Buying Decision

As shown in Figure 7–4 (and covered in Chapter 6), the five stages a student might use in buying a compact disk (CD) player also apply to organizational purchases.[28] However, comparing the two right-hand columns in Figure 7–4 reveals some key differences. For example, when a CD player manufacturer buys headphones for its units from a supplier, more individuals are involved, supplier capability becomes more important, and the postpurchase evaluation behavior is more formalized. The headphone-buying decision illustrated is typical of the steps in a purchase made by an organization.[29] Later in the chapter we will analyze more complex purchases made by industrial, reseller, and government organizations.

Types of Buying Situations

The number of people in the buying center and the length and complexity of the steps in the buying process largely depend on the specific buying situation. Researchers

BUYING CENTER DIMENSION	BUY-CLASS SITUATION	
	NEW BUY	STRAIGHT/MODIFIED REBUY
People involved	Many	Few
Decision time	Long	Short
Problem definition	Uncertain	Well-defined
Buying objective	Good solution	Low-price supplier
Suppliers considered	New/present	Present
Buying influence	Technical/operating personnel	Purchasing agent

FIGURE 7-5

How the buying situation affects buying center behavior

who have studied organizational buying identify three types of buying situations, which they have termed **buy classes.**[30] These buy classes vary from the routine reorder, or **straight rebuy,** to the completely new purchase, termed **new buy.** In between these extremes is the **modified rebuy.** Some examples will clarify the differences:

- *Straight rebuy.* Here the buyer or purchasing manager reorders an existing product or service from the list of acceptable suppliers, probably without even checking with users or influencers from the engineering, production, or quality control departments. Office supplies and maintenance services are usually obtained as straight rebuys.
- *Modified rebuy.* In this buying situation the users, influencers, or deciders in the buying center want to change the product specifications, price, delivery schedule, or supplier. Although the item purchased is largely the same as with the straight rebuy, the changes usually necessitate enlarging the buying center to include people outside the purchasing department.
- *New buy.* Here the organization is a first-time buyer of the product or service. This involves greater potential risks in the purchase, so the buying center is enlarged to include all those who have a stake in the new buy. The purchase of CD player headphones was a new buy.

Figure 7–5 summarizes how buy classes affect buying center tendencies in different ways.[31]

The marketing strategies of sellers facing each of these three buying situations can vary greatly because the importance of personnel from functional areas such as purchasing, engineering, production, and R&D often varies with (1) the type of buying situation and (2) the stage of the purchasing process.[32] If it is a new buy for the manufacturer, you should be prepared to act as a consultant to the buyer, work with technical personnel, and expect a long time for a buying decision to be reached. However, if the manufacturer has bought the component part from you before (a straight or modified rebuy), you might emphasize a competitive price and a reliable supply in meetings with the purchasing agent.

CONCEPT CHECK

1. What one department is almost always represented by a person in the buying center?

2. What are the three types of buying situations or buy classes?

The purchase of machine vision systems involves a lengthy organizational buying process.

Two Organizational New Buy Decisions

New buy purchase decisions are ones where the most purchasing expertise is needed and where both the benefits of good decisions and penalties of bad ones are likely to be greatest. This means that effective communication among people in the buying center is especially important. Tracing the stages in the buying decisions made by a manufacturer and a reseller highlights some of the similarities and differences of organizational buying. They also illustrate the challenges involved in marketing to organizations.

An Industrial Purchase: Machine Vision Systems

Machine vision is becoming widely regarded as one of the keys to the factory of the future. The chief elements of a machine vision system are its optics, light source, camera, video processor, and computer software. Vision systems are mainly used for product inspection. They are also becoming important as one of the chief elements in the information feedback loop of systems that control manufacturing processes. Vision systems, selling in the price range of $5,000, are mostly sold to original equipment manufacturers (OEMs) who incorporate them in still larger industrial automation systems, which sell for $50,000 to $100,000.

Finding productive applications for machine vision involves the constant search for technology and designs that satisfy user needs. The buying process for machine vision components and assemblies is frequently a new buy since many machine vision systems contain elements that require some custom design. Let's track five purchasing stages that a company such as the Industrial Automation Division of Siemens, a large German industrial firm, would follow when purchasing components and assemblies for the machine vision systems it produces and installs.

Problem recognition   Sales engineers constantly canvass industrial automation equipment users and manufacturers such as American National Can, Ford Motor Company, Grumman Aircraft, and many Asian and European firms for leads on upcoming industrial automation projects. They also keep these firms current on Siemens' technology, products, and services. When a firm needing a machine vision capability identifies a project that would benefit from Siemens' expertise, company engineers typically work with the firm to determine the kind of system required to meet the customer's need.

After a contract is won, project personnel must often make a **make-buy decision**—an evaluation of whether components and assemblies will be purchased from outside suppliers or built by the company itself. (Siemens' produces many components and assemblies.) When these items are to be purchased from outside suppliers, the company engages in a thorough supplier search and evaluation process.

Information search   Companies such as Siemens employ a sophisticated process for identifying outside suppliers of components and assemblies. For standard items like connectors, printed circuit boards, and components such as resistors and capacitors, the purchasing agent consults the company's purchasing databank, which contains information on hundreds of suppliers and thousands of products. All products in the databank have been prenegotiated as to price, quality, and delivery time, and many have been assessed using **value analysis**—a systematic appraisal of the design, quality, and performance of a product to reduce purchasing costs.

For one-of-a-kind components or assemblies such as new optics, cameras, and light sources, the company relies on its engineers to keep current on new developments in product technology. This information is often found in technical journals and industry magazines or at international trade shows where suppliers display their most recent innovations. In some instances, supplier representatives might be asked to make presentations to the buying center at Siemens. Such a group often consists of a project engineer; several design, system, and manufacturing engineers; and a purchasing agent.

Alternative evaluation   Three main buying criteria are used to select suppliers: price, performance, and delivery. Other important criteria include assurance that a supplier will not go out of business during the contractual period, assurance that the supplier will meet product quality and performance specifications, and service during the contractual period. Typically, two or three suppliers for each standard component and assembly are identified from a **bidders list**—a list of firms believed to be qualified to supply a given item. This list is generated from the company's purchasing databank as well as from engineering inputs. Specific items that are unique or one-of-a-kind may be obtained from a single supplier after careful evaluation by the buying center.

Firms selected from the bidders list are sent a quotation request from the purchasing agent, describing the desired quantity, delivery date(s), and specifications of the components or assemblies. Suppliers are expected to respond to bid requests within 30 days.

Purchase decision   Unlike the short purchase stage in a consumer purchase, the period from supplier selection to order placement to product delivery can take several weeks or even months. Even after bids for components and assemblies are submitted, further negotiation concerning price, performance, and delivery terms is likely. Sometimes conditions related to warranties, indemnities, and payment schedules have to be agreed on.

The purchase decision is further complicated by the fact that two or more suppliers of the same item might be awarded contracts. This practice can occur when large orders are requested. Furthermore, suppliers who are not chosen are informed why their bids were not selected.

Postpurchase behavior   As in the consumer purchase decision process, postpurchase evaluation occurs in the industrial purchase decision process, but it is formalized and often more sophisticated. All items purchased are examined in a

The American Harvest food dehydrator successfully sold by Montgomery Ward and other retailers.

formal product acceptance process. The performance of the supplier is also monitored and recorded. Performance on past contracts determines a supplier's chances of being asked to bid on future purchases, and poor performance may result in a supplier's name being dropped from the bidders list.

A Reseller Purchase: A Home Food Dehydrator

Resellers—wholesalers and retailers—resell the products they purchase without physically changing them. As a result, the stages in their buying decision process differ from those of manufacturers. As an example, let's look at Montgomery Ward's decision to stock a home food dehydrator.

Problem recognition Members of Ward's buying committee for electric appliances continually look for appealing new items to stock in its stores and sell through its catalogs. Open to new ideas, the buying committee considered a home food dehydrator, an electric device that dries fresh fruit and vegetables and competes with canning and freezing in home food preservation.

Information search Ward's committee assessed the market size to see if a genuine consumer demand exists for food dehydrators. It analyzed how the dehydrators work, their quality, and the chances that unhappy consumers would return these purchased appliances to the store for a refund.

Alternative evaluation The buying committee found no home food dehydrators of satisfactory quality that they wanted to sell. Then Montgomery Ward was approached by a new, startup firm—American Harvest—who sells its home food dehydrator under the American Harvest brand name. Initial quality-control tests showed that it met Ward's high standards for electric appliances.

A senior buyer on Ward's buying committee checked on the firm itself. He found two young entrepreneurs who had manufactured 500 such dehydrators—a number Montgomery Ward could sell in a day or two if the product "hit." These entrepreneurs were currently financed on a shoestring through bank loans obtained by using their cars as collateral. The two men had several patents on their device, and it had received the Underwriter's Laboratory approval. The Ward's buyer persuaded the two men to (1) seek better financing and (2) contract out the production of their dehydrators to a larger manufacturer that could produce them in the quantities and with the quality Montgomery Ward required.

Purchase decision   The Ward's buyer signed a contract with American Harvest for its home food dehydrator. At that time no other major chain or catalog store (for example, Sears, Target, JCPenney, or Kmart) was selling such an appliance. But although Montgomery Ward had no competition from its major rivals, there was no assurance the dehydrator would sell. On a big gamble, Montgomery Ward advertised the American Harvest dehydrator on the inside front cover of its fall catalog—an extremely valuable advertising space.

Postpurchase behavior   Ward's buyer and buying committee hit paydirt. The company sold more than 20,000 dehydrators in October and November—the peak period for using the appliance—at a retail price of $89. Montgomery Ward concluded that its decision was a good one and contracted for an expanded American Harvest line for the following fall. Today other chains such as Sears and JCPenney carry the line.

The two preceding examples of organizational purchases suggest four lessons for marketers to increase their chances of selling products and services to organizations. Firms selling to organizations must (1) understand the organization's needs, (2) get on the right bidders list, (3) find the right people in the buying center, and (4) provide value to organizational buyers.

CONCEPT CHECK

1. What is a make-buy decision?

2. What is a bidders list?

SUMMARY

1. Organizational buyers are divided into three different markets: industrial, reseller, and government. There are about 9.5 million industrial firms, 2 million resellers, and 87,000 government units.

2. Measuring industrial, reseller, and government markets is an important first step for firms interested in gauging the size of one, two, or all three markets. The newly created North American Industry Classification System (NAICS) is a convenient starting point to begin this process.

3. Many aspects of organizational buying behavior are different from consumer buying behavior. Some key differences between the two include demand characteristics, number of potential buyers, buying objectives, buying criteria, size of the order or purchase, buyer–seller relationships and partnerships, and multiple buying influences within companies.

4. The buying center concept is central to understanding organizational buying behavior. Knowing who composes the buying center and the roles they play in making purchase decisions is important in marketing to organizations. The buying center usually includes a person from the purchasing department and possibly representatives from R&D, engineering, and production, depending on what is being purchased. These people can play one or more of five roles in a purchase decision: user, influencer, buyer, decider, or gatekeeper.

5. The three types of buying situations, or buy classes, are the straight rebuy, the modified rebuy, and the new buy. These form a scale ranging from a routine reorder to a totally new purchase.

6. The stages in an organizational buying decision are the same as those for consumer buying decisions: problem recognition, information search, alternative evaluation, purchase decision, and postpurchase behavior. Examples of organizational purchases described are the purchase of machine vision technology components by an electronics manufacturer and a home food dehydrator by a reseller.

7. To market more effectively to organizations, a firm must try to understand the organization's needs, get on the right bidders list, reach the right people in the buying center, and provide value to organizational buyers.

KEY TERMS AND CONCEPTS

business marketing p. 180
organizational buyers p. 180
industrial firms p. 180
resellers p. 181
government units p. 181
North American Industry Classification System (NAICS) p. 182
organizational buying behavior p. 184
derived demand p. 184
organizational buying criteria p. 186
reverse marketing p. 187

reciprocity p. 188
supply partnership p. 189
buying center p. 189
buy classes p. 193
straight rebuy p. 193
new buy p. 193
modified rebuy p. 193
make-buy decision p. 195
value analysis p. 195
bidders list p. 195

CHAPTER PROBLEMS AND APPLICATIONS

1. Describe the major differences among industrial firms, resellers, and government units in the United States.

2. Explain how the North American Industry Classification System (NAICS) might be helpful in understanding industrial, reseller, and government markets, and discuss the limitations inherent in this system.

3. List and discuss the key characteristics of organizational buying that make it different from consumer buying.

4. What is a buying center? Describe the roles assumed by people in a buying center and what useful questions should be raised to guide any analysis of the structure and behavior of a buying center.

5. Effective marketing is of increasing importance in today's competitive environment. How can firms more effectively market to organizations?

6. A firm that is marketing multimillion-dollar wastewater treatment systems to cities has been unable to sell a new type of system. This setback has occurred even though the firm's systems are cheaper than competitive systems and meet U.S. Environmental Protection Agency (EPA) specifications. To date, the firm's marketing efforts have been directed to city purchasing departments and the various state EPAs to get on approved bidders lists. Talks with city-employed personnel have indicated that the new system is very different from current systems and therefore city sanitary and sewer department engineers, directors of these two departments, and city council members are unfamiliar with the workings of the system. Consulting engineers, hired by cities to work on the engineering and design features of these systems and paid on a percentage of system cost, are also reluctant to favor the new system. (*a*) What roles do the various individuals play in the purchase process for a wastewater treatment system? (*b*) How could the firm improve the marketing effort behind the new system?

CASE 7-1   Energy Performance Systems, Inc.

Video

"What we need," says David Ostlie matter-of-factly, "is just one electric utility to say 'yes'—to try our technology. Then the Whole-Tree Energy™ technology will speak for itself." David Ostlie is president of Energy Performance Systems, Inc. (EPS), a firm he founded in 1988 to produce environ mentally-clean, cheap electricity by growing, harvesting, transporting, drying, burning *whole* hardwood trees (trunks, branches, and all) in either (1) old retrofitted coal and oil (fossil fuel) power plants or (2) new power plants.

THE IDEA

Dave Ostlie points to three key features that make the EPS-owned and patented Whole-Tree Energy™ (WTE) technology unique:

1. Using *whole* hardwood trees. The use of whole trees saves a tremendous amount of time and energy over using wood chips—a common form for wood burned to produce electricity. "Hardwood trees" here means all broadleaf trees—mainly species such as cottonwood, aspen, birch, maple, and poplar (essentially all trees but conifers).

2. Drying the whole trees. Moisture is the culprit that leads to incomplete wood combustion and reduced energy output, resulting in emissions that lead to air pollution and acid rain. So the WTE process dries the trees to remove about 70 percent of the moisture prior to combustion, using waste heat from the combustion process itself.

3. Three-stage combustion. The whole trees burn at three levels in the furnace: (*a*) as trees in a 12-foot deep, mid-level pile, (*b*) as wood char that falls and is burned on a grate below the pile, and (*c*) as volatile gases (gasified wood) above the pile that burns cleanly like natural gas. The result is an incredibly *environmentally-clean,* efficient combustion process.

The simplicity of the technology is a big plus compared to many of the current alternative energy technologies being studied around the world.

THE COMPANY

EPS is based on the Whole-Tree Energy™ technology and owns U.S., Canadian, European, and Japanese patents. The WTE ™ technology has been scaled up in four successive tests that have demonstrated the feasibility of large-scale power production from sustained burning of whole trees. The mission of EPS: To commercialize the Whole-Tree Energy™ technology.

THE ISSUES

In assessing the Whole-Tree Energy™ technology, three critical issues soon emerge: (1) the environment and pollution, (2) jobs and economic development, and (3) buying interest of utilities.

The Environment and Pollution

Conventional coal-fired power plants, the staple for utilities, produce large volumes of SO_2, NO_x, ash, and extra CO_2 that contribute to air pollution, acid rain, and global warming. Based on test results, a WTE™ plant produces far less pollution than comparable fossil-fuel plants. Compared to a coal plant, the following levels of pollution have been demonstrated for a WTE™ plant:

- SO_2 - less than $1/400$ of that for coal (on a fuel comparison basis) because wood contains virtually no sulfur.
- NO_x - approximately $1/10$ of that for coal due to the naturally low nitrogen content of wood fuel and the multi-stage WTE™ combustion process.
- Ash - less than $1/10$ of that for coal. The ash produced can be returned to the forest or sold as a fertilizer. Coal ash is considered a hazardous waste and must be stored indefinitely in specially-designed storage ponds.
- Extra CO_2 - Coal plants release enormous amounts of CO_2 to the atmosphere by burning the remnants of prehistoric plant life—coal—in large quantities. The rapidly increasing level of atmospheric CO_2 due to the burning of fossil fuels is a significant cause of global climate change. In contrast, using biomass—including trees—as a fuel results in no net addition of CO_2 to the atmosphere because the amount of CO_2 removed over the life of the tree is equal to that released by the tree, regardless of the tree's end use.

The net effect of burning a renewable biomass—trees—instead of fossil fuels will be a reduction in air pollution, acid rain, and global warming.

Jobs and Economic Development

WTE™ plants will burn (1) hardwoods that are unsalable (not wanted by other forest product firms), (2) fast-growing energy trees raised on plantations that can be harvested as often as every five to six years and add agricultural jobs, and (3) waste wood left over by other forest product firms. Harvesting overage hardwoods actually stimulates forest regeneration and often provides better habitat for wildlife. The U.S. Forest Service reports that much of the 20 billion tons of U.S. hardwoods are overage, not wanted by the logging, paper, and pulp industries and should be harvested.

A 100 megawatt WTE™ plant—providing enough electricity for a city of 100,000 people—will provide over 600 jobs in growing, harvesting, and transporting whole trees and in the plant producing electricity. In the search for local jobs, this is a huge benefit for economic development organizations trying to increase local employment.

Buying Interest of Utilities

To avoid more electrical blackouts, U.S. utilities must add new electrical generating capacity. For EPS, this provides an opportunity, either (1) by retrofitting to use in WTE™ some of the hundreds of coal and oil-fired plants throughout the United States that are operated infrequently because of their pollution problems or (2) by building new plants to use the WTE™ technology.

In an electric utility, capacity planners project the demand for electricity by industrial, commercial, and residential users and assess the utility's ability to supply the demand. The chief executive officer makes the recommendation to add new capacity, a decision reviewed by the board of directors. The vice president of power supply probably recommends the technology to be used and the site for the new power plant.

As Ostlie talks to prospective utility customers about the WTE™ technology, six concerns emerge that are covered below.

1. Can enough heat be generated by burning wood to produce electricity? "All the skeptics said we couldn't get a high enough temperature by burning wood," says Ostlie. "But in one recent heat-release test we produced values higher than those of state-of-the-art coal plants."

2. Can whole trees be loaded, transported, and dried? Forestry experts told Ostlie he couldn't load and transport whole trees on a truck because the branches wouldn't compress. So he hired a logger and did it. The WTE™ technology calls for large-scale drying of whole trees in an air-supported dome like those used in a sports stadium.

3. Are there enough trees available at reasonable cost to support commercial-size power plants? In about 75 percent of the United States enough

Cost of producing electricity using four different fuels, cents/kilowatt-hour

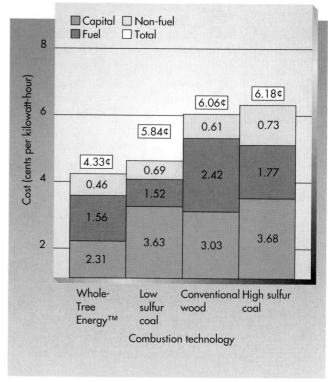

Source: Research Triangle Institute, Electric Power Research Institute and Energy Performance Systems, Inc.

biomass in the form of trees exists within a 50-mile radius to support a 100 megawatt power plant using the WTE™ technology. To support such a power plant, only about 0.1 percent of the land in a 50-mile radius of the plant would be harvested each year. Residential biomass and waste wood from pulp and timber mill operations are potential fuel sources, as are natural stands. Ultimately, much of the tree resource may come from short-rotation, hybrid tree plantations that provide farmers with an alternative cash crop.

4. What are the environmental benefits of WTE™ for utilities? Besides being increasingly sensitive to environmental concerns, a utility retrofitting a polluting electric power plant with Whole-Tree Energy™ can gain over a million dollars a year in SO_2 credits"—an incentive for a utility to offset power produced by its high-pollution plants with electricity produced by nonpolluting plants.

5. What will it cost to build a retrofitted or new WTE™ power plant? A major appeal of the WTE™ process is its simplicity relative to say, coal-fired power plants. To retrofit an existing 100 megawatt coal plant, it will cost about $25 million—thereby putting back into production an

existing plant that is of little value. To build a new 100-megawatt WTE™ plant would take about $100 million, about 25 to 30 percent less than a new fossil fuel plant.

6. What will the cost be of electricity produced by a WTE™ plant? A recent feasibility study evaluating the WTE™ technology estimated that a WTE™ power plant could produce a kilowatt-hour of electricity for 20 to 40 percent less than today's fossil fuel plants (see figure).

"It's not far away, but we've still got to make that first sale," adds Dave Ostlie.

Questions

1. In a utility's decision whether to buy and use the WTE™ technology (*a*) who comprises the buying center and (*b*) what aspects of the buying decision does each look at?

2. What are some of the key elements EPS should have in developing its strategy to market WTE™ to prospective utility buyers?

3. As a concerned citizen, (*a*) what do you see as the key benefits of the WTE™ technology and (*b*) what do you personally see as the potential "show stoppers" for WTE™—the critical things that can prevent it from being commercialized and becoming a reality.

4. A new product or technology like WTE™ requires educating a number of key groups, or "influencers", about the technology. Excluding the electric utilities themselves, (*a*) what groups, or market segments, should EPS try to reach, (*b*) what key benefits should be emphasized to each, and (*c*) what promotional methods or media should EPS use to reach each segment?

PART THREE

TARGETING MARKETING OPPORTUNITIES

CHAPTER 8
Collecting and Using Marketing Information

CHAPTER 9
Market Segmentation, Targeting, and Positioning

CHAPTER 10
Relationship Marketing, Information Technology, and Forecasting

Part Three describes how people with similar wants and needs become the target of marketing activities. The first step in this process, collecting information about prospective consumers, is discussed in Chapter 8. The information helps marketers focus their efforts on groups with common needs, or market segments. Chapter 9 describes how Reebok International develops specific products for diverse market segments such as runners, aerobic dancers, basketball players, walkers, and others. Chapter 9 also describes how automobile manufacturers have reduced the number of products offered to focus on selected consumer segments. Finally, Chapter 10 explains how new information technologies facilitate information collection and use and help marketers develop long-term cost-effective relationships with individual consumers.

CHAPTER 8

Collecting and Using Marketing Information

AFTER READING THIS CHAPTER YOU SHOULD BE ABLE TO:

• Identify five steps a person can follow in reaching a decision and the significance of each step.

• Explain the four key elements used to define a problem: the objectives, constraints, assumptions, and measures of success.

• Structure a decision into two basic components: the controllable and uncontrollable factors.

• Know three types of information collected to solve a problem: concepts, methods, and data.

• Know how questionnaires, observations, experiments, and panels are used in marketing.

• Understand how marketers identify and implement a solution and evaluate the results.

REDUCING MOVIE RISKS: LISTENING TO CONSUMERS EARLY

"Let's return Mr. Potato Head's facial features to the default position, so it's easier for the baby to bite off his nose," John Lasseter suggests to an animator. Lasseter, director and head of creative development for the movie *Toy Story,* is charged with breathing life into Mr. Potato Head, Slinky Dog, and Buzz Lightyear, using 300 Sun Microsystem's computers to produce 110,000 individual animated frames, each taking two to five hours of computer time to transfer to *Toy Story*'s final movie film. (G.I. Joe missed his curtain call. Why? The filmmakers wanted to blow his head off, and Hasbro didn't want its star treated that way.)[1]

Expensive? Very! But even *Waterworld* cost $175 million to shoot—without using animation!

So with today's typical American movie costing almost $40 million to produce and market, how can motion picture producers and directors reduce their risk of losses? One part of the answer: use marketing research to recruit people to attend sneak previews (test screenings) of a forthcoming movie and then ask them questions that might bring about improvements in the final edit of the movie.

Without turning the page, think about answers to these questions:

• Whom would you recruit for these test screenings?
• What questions would you ask them to help you in editing or modifying parts of the film?

While *Toy Story* and *Waterworld* have little else in common, they—like virtually every major U.S. movie produced today—use test screenings to modify film details to suit moviegoers' tastes. Figure 8–1 summarizes some of the key questions that are used in these test screenings—both to select the people for the screenings and to obtain the key reactions of those sitting in the screenings.

FIGURE 8-1

Marketing research questions
asked in test screenings of
movies, and how they are
used.

POINT WHEN ASKED	KEY QUESTIONS	USE OF QUESTION(S)
Before the test screening	• How old are you? • How frequently do you pay to see movies? • What movies have you seen in the last three months?	Decide if person fits profile of target audience for movie. If yes, invite to test screening. If not, don't invite.
After the test screening	• Were any characters too distasteful? Who? How? • Did any scenes offend you? Which ones? How? • How did you like the ending? If you didn't like it, how would you change it? • Would you recommend the movie to a friend?	Change aspects of some characters. Change scenes. Change or clarify ending. Overall indicator of liking and/or satisfaction with movie.

Here are some examples of changes to movies that have resulted from this kind of marketing research:

• *Adding more realism. Waterworld* scenes featuring an animated shark were reshot when preview audiences said it looked phony.[2]
• *Making the plot move faster.* Disney cut a duet by Pocahontas and John Smith in *Pocahontas* because it got in the way of the action and confused test audiences.[3]
• *Reaching a market segment more effectively.* More action footage was added for Kevin Costner when preview screening showed young males were less enthusiastic about *The Bodyguard* than young females.[4]
• *Changing an ending. Fatal Attraction* had probably the most commercially successful "ending-switch" of all time. In its sneak previews, audiences liked everything but the ending, which had Alex (Glenn Close) committing suicide and managing to frame Dan (Michael Douglas) as her murderer by leaving his fingerprints on the knife she used. The studio shot $1.3 million of new scenes for the ending that regular audiences eventually saw.[5]

Sometimes studios don't listen to customers and live to regret it. Test audiences said the length—3 hours and 11 minutes—made *Wyatt Earp* almost unbearable. Studio executives didn't listen, kept the original length, and the movie died at the box office.[6]

Besides test screenings, motion picture firms also use marketing research to do concept tests of proposed plots and to design and test the $12 million marketing campaigns that support a typical movie's launch. These examples show how marketing research is linked to marketing strategy and decisive actions, the topic of this chapter.

THE ROLE OF MARKETING RESEARCH

To place marketing research in perspective, we can describe (1) what it is, (2) some of the difficulties in conducting it, and (3) the process marketing executives can use to make effective decisions.

How can Ocean Spray introduce cranberry juice in Asian (left) and European (right) markets—when consumers there have never heard of cranberries? For Ocean Spray's decisions, see the text.

What Marketing Research Is and Does

Marketing research is the process of defining a marketing problem and opportunity, systematically collecting and analyzing information, and recommending actions to improve an organization's marketing activities.[7]

A means of reducing risk and uncertainty   Assessing the needs and wants of consumers and providing information to help design an organization's marketing program to satisfy them is the role that marketing research performs. This means that marketing research attempts to identify and define both marketing problems and opportunities and to generate and evaluate marketing actions. Although marketing research can provide few answers with complete assurance, it can reduce risk and uncertainty to increase the likelihood of the success of marketing decisions. It is a great help to the marketing managers who make the final decisions.

Anyone for horseradish in a tube?   Most marketing research is done on U.S. products developed by U.S. firms. But suppose you are asked by a marketing researcher whether you would buy horseradish-in-a-tube or a ticket on a 120 mile per hour train from New York to Washington, D.C. Can these offerings be moved successfully here from Europe (the horseradish) or Japan (its Shinkansen fast train)? Would American consumers buy them? Would Asian or European consumers buy cranberry juice—when they have never tasted cranberries? Good answers to these kinds of questions asked by marketing researchers are needed to move products successfully across international borders.

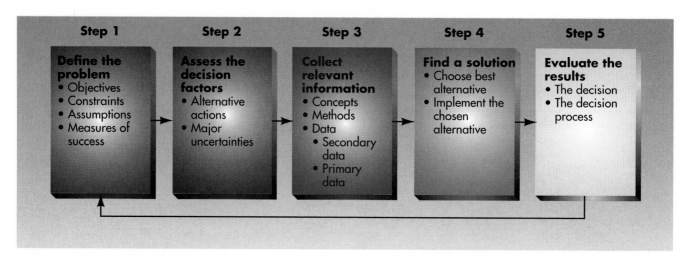

FIGURE 8–2

Five-step approach to making decisions

Why Good Marketing Research Is Difficult

The dilemmas faced by marketing researchers when trying to assess consumers' willingness to buy products or services they are not familiar with illustrate why good marketing research requires great care—especially because of the inherent difficulties in asking consumers questions. For example,

- Do consumers really know whether they are likely to buy a particular product that they probably have never thought about before? Can they really assess its advantages and disadvantages on the spur of the moment?
- Even if they know the answer, will they reveal it? When personal or status questions are involved, will people give honest answers?
- Will their actual purchase behavior be the same as their stated interest or intentions? Will they buy the same brand they say they will? To appear progressive, consumers often overstate their likelihood of buying a new product.

When people know they are being measured, the very measurement process itself can significantly affect their answers and behaviors. A task of marketing research is to overcome these difficulties to provide useful information on which marketing executives can act.

Steps in Making Effective Decisions

A **decision** is a conscious choice from among two or more alternatives. All of us make many such decisions daily. At work we choose from alternative ways to accomplish an assigned task. At college we choose from alternative courses. As consumers we choose from alternative brands. No magic formula guarantees correct decisions all the time.

Managers and researchers have tried to improve the outcomes of decisions by using more formal, systematic approaches to *decision making,* the act of consciously choosing from alternatives. People who do not use some kind of system—and many do not—may make poor decisions. The systematic approach to making decisions (or problem solving) described in this chapter uses five steps and is shown in Figure 8–2. This five-step approach provides a mental checklist for making any decision— either business or personal. For example, suppose you are the product manager for cranberry juice for Ocean Spray, the large U.S. agricultural cooperative. You have some special challenges. Because the word "cranberry" isn't a part of any foreign language, (1) you have to find a name for it and its juice, and (2) you have to design ads that will encourage foreign consumers to try the new product and acquire a liking for its bittersweet taste.[8] You might define your decision in this way:

- *Define the problem.* Select a name and a series of ads to introduce cranberry juice to Asian and European consumers. You already know that Ocean Spray's attempt to introduce a bland cranberry juice in Japan—named "Cranby"—fizzled, and the company pulled the product off the market.

- *Assess the decision factors.* Consider (1) alternative names and ads as well as (2) uncontrollable factors that might affect the success of the decision. You discover that in Taiwan Ocean Spray—*Hoshien Pei*—sounds a bit like the U.S. name and translates as "healthy refreshment," which seems like a good start. But you also learn that uncontrollable factors can affect your chances of success—after Ocean Spray tried to sell its cranberry juice to the English in bottles, belated marketing research showed that those consumers like their juices in boxes. So the marketing strategy was redesigned.

- *Collect relevant information.* Obtain information pertinent to a wise selection of a name and several ads. Test some alternative names and ads on a sample of consumers in each country to determine their local preferences.

- *Find a solution.* Select the best names and ads from among the alternatives studied, and put them into your marketing program. In French, cranberry translates as *airelle de myrtille,* which seems a bit awkward. Let's say French consumers say *le cranberry* is *okay* (literal translation: okay!) with them, despite the French uproar over the corruption of their language with English words. Also, French consumers like a sample of low-key ads you show them—sensitive to French humor. So you have a name and the ads for your French cranberry juice introduction!

- *Evaluate the results.* Assess whether the results in each country were successful or not and the reasons. Learn and apply lessons for the future.

The key point—the decision process should collect and analyze useful data that lead to effective actions.

CONCEPT CHECK

  1. What is marketing research?

  2. What are the five steps a person can use to make a decision systematically?

STEP 1: DEFINE THE PROBLEM

Toy designers at Fisher-Price Toys, the nation's top marketer of infant and preschool toys, had a problem some years back: they developed toys they thought kids would like, but how could they be certain? To research the problem, Fisher-Price gets children to play at its state-licensed nursery school in East Aurora, New York. Behind one-way mirrors Fisher-Price designers and marketing researchers watch the children use—and abuse—the toys to develop better products.

Fisher-Price's toy testing shows how to define the problem and its four key elements: objectives, constraints, assumptions, and measures of success. For example, the original model of a classic Fisher-Price toy, the chatter

Careful observation of "toy testers" in Fisher-Price's school leads to better products.

telephone, was simply a wooden phone with a dial that rang a bell. Observers noted, however, that the children kept grabbing the receiver like a handle to pull the phone along behind them, so a designer added wheels, a noisemaker, and eyes that bobbed up and down on an experimental version of the toy.

Objectives

Objectives are the goals the decision maker seeks to achieve in solving a problem. Typical marketing objectives are increasing revenues and profits, discovering what consumers are aware of and want, and finding out why a product isn't selling well. For Fisher-Price the immediate objective was to decide whether to market the old or new chatter telephone.

Constraints

The **constraints** in a decision are the restrictions placed on potential solutions by the nature and importance of the problem. Common constraints in marketing problems are limitations on the time and money available to solve the problem. Thus, Fisher-Price might set two constraints on its decision to select either the old or new version of the chatter telephone: the decision must be made in 10 weeks, and no research budget is available beyond that needed for collecting data in its nursery school.

In problem solving, there are human constraints as well that restrict the search for alternatives. Experts say that people can do a number of things to open up their minds to new solutions: (1) recast or restate the problem, (2) make the problem more explicit by writing it down or stating it aloud to a friend or co-worker (including the objectives, constraints, assumptions, and measures of success), and (3) leave it for a while to "simmer on the back burner" before attacking it afresh.

Assumptions

Assumptions are the conjectures about factors or situations that simplify the problem enough to allow it to be solved within the existing constraints. If more money or time becomes available, sometimes the assumptions themselves are investigated. For example, the product manager for the Fisher-Price chatter telephone might make these assumptions: (1) the children in the Fisher-Price nursery school are typical of all American children, and (2) an indication of their preference is the amount of time spent playing with each toy when other toys are also available.

Measures of Success

Effective decision makers specify **measures of success,** which are criteria or standards used in evaluating proposed solutions to the problem. For the Fisher-Price problem, if a measure of success were the total time children spent playing with each of the two designs, the results of observing them would lead to clear-cut actions as follows:

OUTCOME OF DATA COLLECTION	MARKETING ACTION
• Children spent more time playing with old design.	Continue with old design; don't introduce new design.
• Children spent more time playing with new design.	Introduce new design; drop old design.

One test of whether marketing research should be undertaken is if different outcomes will lead to different marketing actions. If all the research outcomes lead to the same action—such as top management sticking with the older design regardless of what the observed children liked—the research is useless and a waste of money.

In this case research results showed that kids liked the new design, so Fisher-Price introduced its noise-making pull-toy telephone, which has become a toy classic and sold millions.

Most marketing researchers would agree with philosopher John Dewey's observation that "a problem well-defined is half-solved," but they know that defining a problem is an incredibly difficult, although essential, task. For example, if the objectives are too broad, the problem may not be researchable. If they are too narrow, the value of the research results may be seriously lessened. This is why marketing researchers spend so much time in defining a marketing problem precisely and writing a formal proposal describing the research to be done.

Step 2: Assess the Decision Factors

Decision factors are the different sets of variables—the alternatives and uncertainties—that combine to give the outcome of a decision. These two sets of variables differ by the degree of control that the decision maker can exert over them. **Alternatives** are the factors over which the decision maker has control. **Uncertainties** are the uncontrollable factors that the decision maker cannot influence. In step 2 of this approach the decision maker faces the problem of

The blend of pub atmosphere with laundromat services led to the success of Duds 'n Suds.

identifying in detail (1) the principal alternatives that can be considered reasonable approaches to solving the problem and (2) the major uncertainties that can affect a particular alternative and result in its being a good or a poor solution to the problem. Taken together, the alternatives and uncertainties help define the kind of information to collect in step 3.

Alternatives: The Controllable Decision Factors

Experienced marketing managers insist on searching for more than a single alternative solution to a problem because the new alternatives may lead to better solutions. One widely used method is to start the problem statement with, "In what ways can we . . .?" For example:

- In what ways can we put our Xerox copier to new uses?
- In what ways can we put our old pipelines to new uses?
- In what ways can we put the needs of college students for socializing and washing their clothes together to start a business?

With respect to the first question, the Xerox Corporation probably exists today because although its early plain-paper photocopier was a disaster for its intended use, it did make copies that could be used in offset printing. Discovering this fact, the executives at Xerox used revenues from this application to perfect and sell the Xerox plain-paper copier. They had temporarily redefined their task to discover and produce a copier for a different application.

In one giant leap of creativity, Williams Companies moved from the petroleum business into the telecommunications business. How? By running fiber-optic telecommunications cables through 1,000 miles of unused petroleum pipeline. Today it is the fourth-largest marketer of long-distance telecommunications—in competition with AT&T, MCI, and Sprint.

To develop new alternatives, creative people often blend unusual elements into a winning combination that doesn't occur to the average person. An Iowa State University student observed that today's college students want a comfortable social atmosphere and also have to do their own laundry. The result: Duds 'N Suds, a chain of laundromat-pubs located near almost 100 college campuses across the United States.

Talking to customers, trading ideas with co-workers, holding formal brainstorming sessions, and learning from competitors are efficient ways to search for alternative ideas for improving marketing mix actions. Using these techniques to uncover new product ideas is discussed in Chapter 11.

Uncertainties: The Uncontrollable Decision Factors

Well-chosen alternatives can go haywire because of uncertainties, which can relate to factors within the firm or can involve consumers, competitors, national or international affairs, or even the weather.

Creative minds at Booz, Allen & Hamilton's research division slaved over what they were sure was a great new product idea: bubble gum a child could eat. But they could never lick two key uncertainties. First, tests with kids showed that until they got the knack of blowing bubbles, they would dribble the sticky stuff down their chins. This consumer uncertainty was also tied to a technical one: the research division found that foaming agents safe to eat made poor bubbles.

Even the weather can be a critical marketing uncertainty. Booz, Allen & Hamilton's research lab developed a temporary hair coloring the consumer applied by inserting a solid block of hair dye into a specially designed comb. It was a disaster. Researchers subsequently discovered that when people perspired on hot days, any extra dye applied to their hair ran down their foreheads and necks. One of the company's executives explained, "It just didn't occur to us to look at this under conditions where people perspire."[9]

CONCEPT CHECK

1. What are examples of constraints in solving a problem?

2. What does *measure of success* mean?

3. What is the difference between uncertainties and alternatives?

STEP 3: COLLECT RELEVANT INFORMATION

Collecting enough relevant information to make a rational, informed decision sometimes simply means using your knowledge to decide immediately. At other times it entails collecting an enormous amount of information at great expense.

Defined broadly, three kinds of information used to solve marketing problems are concepts, methods, and data. To understand the abstract topic of information, assume you are a marketing executive for Lexus and are struggling to introduce a new feature in next year's model.

Concepts

One valuable type of concept, a **hypothesis,** is a conjecture or idea about the relationship of two or more factors or what might happen in the future. Hypotheses that lead to marketing actions can come from many sources: theoretical reasoning, marketing studies, technical breakthroughs, informal conversations, educated guesses, and even suggestions from customers.

For example, as a marketing executive at Lexus, you have received a number of letters from customers suggesting improvements for the Lexus ES 300, as shown in the accompanying Marketing NewsNet box. One letter suggested that removable air-conditioner filters would be especially helpful during hay fever season. From this information you could develop a hypothesis: there is a substantial need—especially

MARKETING NEWSNET

ADDING CUSTOMER VALUE: HOW LEXUS LISTENS TO CUSTOMERS— AND INTRODUCES NEW PRODUCT FEATURES

Customers are one of the sources of new product concepts. Widely used ways of getting ideas from customers—discussed in the next few pages—are by observing past, present, and prospective customers and by asking them questions. Another important source of information is unsolicited letters that people take the time to write and mail.

Lexus gives meaning to "The Relentless Pursuit of Perfection" by listening to customers in many different ways. For example, the Lexus ES 300 luxury car may have been created by 1,400 engineers, but they utilized a number of ideas from letters sent in by Lexus owners.

Some examples of these ideas and the Lexus features that emerged to provide genuine value to customers include the following:

- Would like a signal to let you know if you've activated the remote lock. *Resulting feature*: An audible remote signal that can be volume adjusted.
- Would like suspension system for flatter cornering. *Resulting feature*: Refinements of Lexus suspension system to improve cornering.
- Removeable air conditioner filters for hay fever season. *Resulting feature*: New air filtration system to reduce pollen and dust.

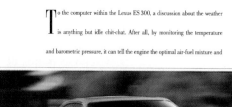

To the computer within the Lexus ES 300, a discussion about the weather is anything but idle chit-chat. After all, by monitoring the temperature and barometric pressure, it can tell the engine the optimal air-fuel mixture and

The Engine And Transmission Are Constantly Talking. As Always, Weather Is A Popular Topic.

ignition timing. To make sure this timing is as precise as possible, the computer also listens to input from the transmission. This communication translates into smooth acceleration as well as nearly imperceptible gear shifts. And, despite the constant banter, an exceedingly quiet ride. To learn more, please call 800-USA-LEXUS. We'll put you in touch with a dealer who will be more than happy to have a conversation on the subject.

LEXUS
The Relentless Pursuit Of Perfection.

© 1995 Lexus, A Division Of Toyota Motor Sales, U.S.A., Inc. Lexus reminds you to wear seatbelts and obey all speed laws. For the dealer nearest you, call 800-872-5398.

---

among people with allergies—for an improved air filtration system. A **new product concept** is a tentative description of a product or service a firm might offer for sale. A new air filtration system is a new feature—or new product concept—that Lexus wanted to consider and eventually implemented.

Methods

Methods are the approaches that can be used to solve part or all of a problem. For example, as a marketing executive at Lexus, you face a number of methodological questions, including the following:

- How do you ask prospective buyers about the value they might place on the proposed new air filtration feature?
- How do you phrase questions to try to determine which of the many new product features suggested to Lexus should be incorporated in its new model?

Millions of other people have asked exactly these same questions about millions of other products and services.

How can you find and use the methodologies that other marketing researchers have found successful? Information on useful methods is available in tradebooks, textbooks, and handbooks that relate to marketing and marketing research. Some periodicals and technical journals such as the *Journal of Marketing* and the *Journal of Marketing Research* summarize methods and techniques valuable in addressing marketing problems. Of course, a Lexus marketing executive must apply the methods that have worked for others to the particular problems that Lexus faces. Special methods vital to marketing are (1) sampling and (2) statistical inference.

Sampling   Marketing researchers often select a group of distributors, customers, or prospects, ask them questions, and treat their answers as typical of all those in whom they are interested. There are two ways of sampling, or selecting representative elements from a population: probability and nonprobability sampling. **Probability sampling** involves using precise rules to select the sample such that each element of the population has a specific known chance of being selected. For example, if a college wants to know how last year's 1,000 graduates are doing, it can put their names in a bowl and randomly select 50 names of graduates to contact. The chance of being selected—50/1,000 or 0.05—is known in advance, and all graduates have an equal chance of being contacted. This procedure helps select a sample (the 50 graduates) that is representative of the entire population (the 1,000 graduates) and allows conclusions to be drawn about the entire population.

When time and budget are limited, researchers may opt for **nonprobability sampling** and use arbitrary judgments to select the sample so that the chance of selecting a particular element may be unknown or 0. If the college decides arbitrarily to select the 50 graduates from last year's class who live closest to the college, many members of the class have been arbitrarily eliminated. This has introduced a bias that makes it dangerous to draw conclusions about the population from this geographically restricted sample.

Statistical inference   The method of **statistical inference** involves drawing conclusions about a *population* (the "universe" of all people, stores, or salespeople about which they wish to generalize) from a *sample* (some elements of the universe) taken from that population. To draw accurate inferences about the population, the sample elements should be representative of that universe. If the sample is not typical, bias can be introduced, resulting in bad marketing decisions.

Secondary Data

Figure 8–3 shows how the different kinds of marketing information fit together. **Data,** the facts and figures pertinent to the problem, are divided into two main parts: secondary data and primary data. **Secondary data** are facts and figures that have already been recorded before the project at hand, whereas **primary data** are facts and figures that are newly collected for the project.

Internal secondary data   Data that have already been collected and exist inside the business firm or other organization are internal secondary data. These include financial statements (such as the firm's balance sheet and income statement), research reports, customer letters, sales reports on customer calls, and customer lists.

External secondary data   Published data from outside the firm are external secondary data. Probably the best known are U.S. Census Bureau reports. The *U.S. Census of Population* is published every 10 years and provides detailed information on American households, such as number of people per household, their ages, their sex, household income, and education of the head of the household. These are basic

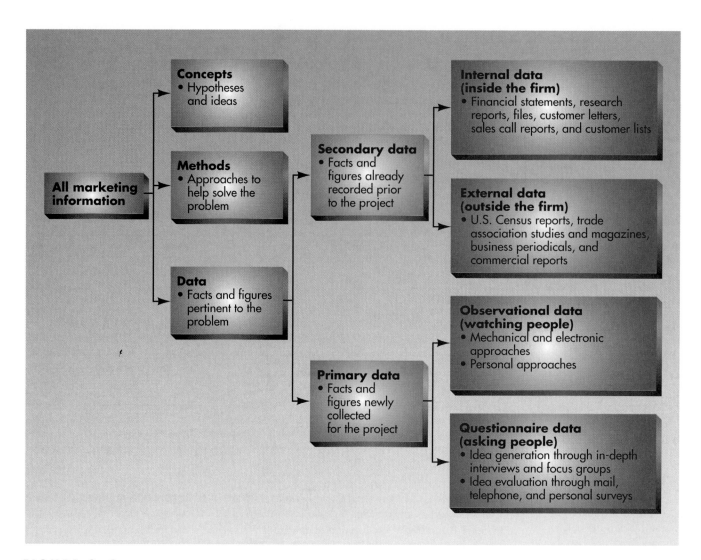

FIGURE 8–3

Types of marketing
information

sources of information used by manufacturers and retailers to identify characteristics
and trends of ultimate consumers.

Other census reports are vital to business firms selling products and services to
organizations. The *U.S. Census of Manufactures,* published about every five years,
lists the number and size of manufacturing firms by industry group (the North
American Industry Classification System described in Chapter 7). The *U.S. Census of
Retail Trade,* also published about every five years, provides comparable detailed
information on retailers.

In addition, trade associations, universities, and business periodicals provide detailed
data of value to marketing researchers. A number of different kinds of marketing research
organizations serve the needs of their clients. These fall into three categories:[10]

- *Syndicated services* provide a standard set of data on a regular basis (monthly,
  quarterly) to their clients. The best-known is the A. C. Nielsen Company's
  Nielsen television ratings, discussed later in the chapter. Both advertisers and
  advertising media follow the Nielsen ratings carefully.
- *Full-service research suppliers* contract with clients to conduct a complete
  marketing research project, including all the elements—from helping to define
  the problem and collecting and analyzing data through presenting the final
  research results in written and oral reports.

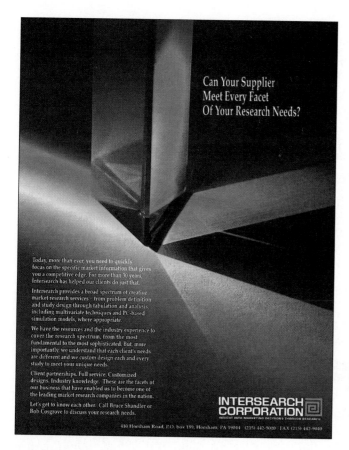

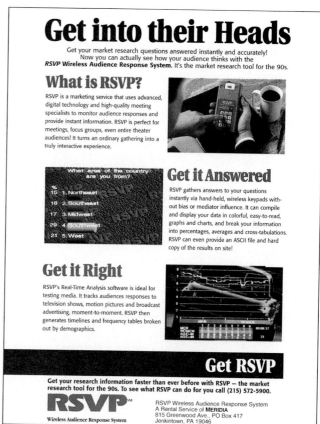

Both full-service research suppliers (left) and limited-service research suppliers (right) meet the unique needs of their clients.

- *Limited-service research suppliers* specialize in a restricted number of marketing research activities such as conducting telephone interviews or analyzing statistical data. National Research Group specializes in evaluating movies and provides motion picture companies with the kind of information discussed at the start of the chapter. Syndicated services may also be viewed as limited-service research suppliers.

While the syndicated services are generally seen as providing secondary data, in most projects the full-service and limited-service research suppliers provide primary data—the topic discussed next. CD-ROM and on-line databases, essential in today's marketing research, are discussed in Chapter 10.

Advantages and disadvantages of secondary data   A general rule among marketing people is to use secondary data first and then collect primary data. Two important advantages of secondary data are (1) the tremendous time savings if the data have already been collected and published and (2) the low cost (e.g., most census reports are available for only a few dollars each). Furthermore, a greater level of detail is often available through secondary data. Because the U.S. Census Bureau can require business establishments to report information about themselves, its industry data usually are more complete than if a private organization attempted to collect them.

However, these advantages must be weighed against some significant disadvantages. First, the secondary data may be out of date, especially if they are U.S. Census data collected only every 5 or 10 years. Second, the definitions or categories might not be quite right for your project. For example, suppose you are interested in the age group from 13 to 16, but many census data age statistics appear only from the 10 to 14 and 15 to 19 age groupings. Finally, because the data are collected for another purpose, they may not be specific enough for your needs as a marketing researcher. In such cases it may be necessary to collect primary data.

CONCEPT CHECK

1. What are methods?

2. What is the difference between secondary and primary data?

3. What are some advantages and disadvantages of *U.S. Census of Population* data?

Primary Data

There are really only two ways to collect primary data, the original data for a marketing study: (1) by observing people and (2) by asking them questions.

Observational data   Facts and figures obtained by watching, either mechanically or in person, how people actually behave is the way marketing researchers  collect **observational data.** National TV ratings, such as those of the A. C. Nielsen Company shown in Figure 8–4, are an example of mechanical observational data collected by a "people meter," which is attached to TV sets in 5,000 homes across the country. When a household member watches TV, he or she is supposed to push a button on the box and to push it again when he or she stops watching. The people meter is supposed to measure who in the household is watching what program on every TV set owned. The Nielsen TV ratings in Figure 8–4 are the percentage of people-meter households whose TV sets were tuned to the program.

 The people meter's limitations—as with all observational data collected mechanically—relate to how its measurements are taken. Critics of people meters aren't so sure the devices are measuring what they are supposed to. They are concerned that many household members, especially teenagers and the elderly, will find it annoying to hit the button every time they start or stop watching TV. A "passive people meter, in test

---

FIGURE 8–4

Nielsen ratings of the top 10 national television programs from February 5, 1996 through February 11, 1996.

RANK	PROGRAM	NETWORK	NIELSEN RATING
1	ER	NBC	25.9
2	Seinfeld	NBC	23.9
3	Friends	NBC	21.7
4	NBC Monday Night at the Movies	NBC	17.2
5	Single Guy	NBC	16.8
6	Home Improvement	ABC	16.2
7	Frasier	NBC	15.9
8	60 Minutes	CBS	15.2
9	CBS Sunday Movie	CBS	14.6
10	Walker, Texas Ranger	CBS	14.3

Focus groups enable a moderator to obtain information from 6 to 10 people at the same time.

by both Arbitron and Pretesting, can be worn on a pin or watch to measure both TV viewing and radio listening at home, at work, or in the car and is intended to address some of these problems.[11]

Nielsen ratings report the percentage of American households with TV that are watching a specific program. Precision in Nielsen ratings is critical because a change of 1 percentage point can mean gaining or losing up to $50 million during the main viewing season since advertisers pay rates based on the size of audience for a TV program. Programs that have consistently low ratings—less than 9 percent or 10 percent—often can't get advertisers and are dropped from the air.

Personal observational data, which are collected by having a person watch a marketing activity, are also a type of primary data. For example, Procter & Gamble observes how consumers bake cakes in its Duncan Hines kitchens to see if the baking instructions on the cake mix box are understood and followed correctly. Chrysler watches how drivers sit behind the wheel of a car to see if they can turn or push the radio and air conditioner knobs conveniently.

Personal observation is both useful and flexible, but it can be costly and unreliable when different observers report different conclusions in watching the same event. Also, although observation can reveal *what* people do, it cannot easily determine *why* they do it, such as why they are buying or not buying a product. This is a principal reason for using questionnaires.

Questionnaire data   **Questionnaire data** are facts and figures obtained by asking people about their attitudes, awareness, intentions, and behaviors. Because so many questions might be asked in questionnaires, it is essential that the researcher concentrate on those directly related to the marketing problem at hand. Many

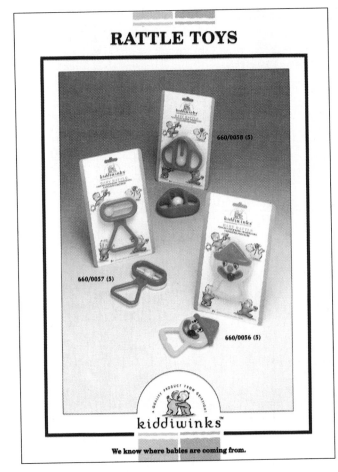

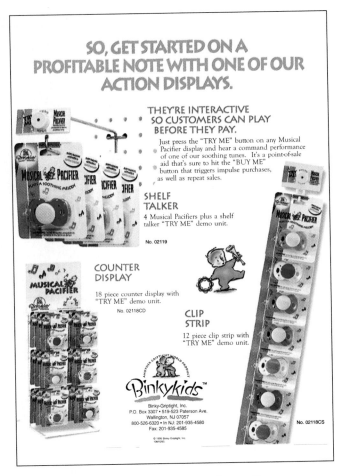

Why are the names and packages different for the British (left) and U.S. (right) markets? The answers, from talking to customers, appear in the text.

marketing researchers divide questionnaire data used for hypothesis generation from those used for hypothesis evaluation.

Marketing studies for *hypothesis generation* involve a search for ideas that can be evaluated in later research. Hamburger Helper didn't fare too well with consumers when General Mills introduced it. Initial instructions called for cooking a half pound of hamburger separately from the noodles or potatoes, which were later mixed with the hamburger. *Individual interviews* (a single researcher asking questions of one respondent) showed that consumers (1) didn't think it contained enough meat and (2) didn't want the hassle of cooking in two different pots. So the Hamburger Helper product manager changed the recipe to call for a full pound of meat and to allow users to prepare it in one dish; this converted a potential failure into a success.[12]

Focus groups are informal sessions in which 6 to 10 past, present, or prospective customers are directed by a discussion leader, or moderator, to identify what they do and don't like about the firm's products and its competitors' products, how they use the products, and special needs they have that the products don't address. Often tape recorded and conducted in special interviewing rooms with a one-way mirror, these groups enable marketing researchers and managers to hear and watch consumer reactions. The informality and peer support in an effective focus group uncover ideas that are often difficult to obtain with individual interviews.

FIGURE 8-5

Comparison of mail, telephone, and personal interview surveys

BASIS OF COMPARISON	MAIL SURVEYS	TELEPHONE SURVEYS	PERSONAL INTERVIEW SURVEYS
Cost per completed survey	Usually the least expensive, assuming adequate return rate	Moderately expensive, assuming reasonable completion rate	Most expensive, because of interviewer's time and travel expenses
Ability to probe and ask complex questions	Little, since self-administered format must be short and simple	Some, since interviewer can probe and elaborate on questions to a degree	Much, since interviewer can show visual materials, gain rapport, and probe
Opportunity for interviewer to bias results	None, since form is completed without interviewer	Some, because of voice inflection of interviewer	Significant, because of voice and facial expressions of interviewer
Anonymity given to respondent	Complete, since no signature is required	Some, because of telephone contact	Little, because of face-to-face contact

Britain's Lewis Woolf Griptight, a manufacturer of infant and toddler products, did focus group interviews about names and packaging on both U.K. and U.S. consumers before bringing a new product line to market. U.K. consumers turned thumbs down on using "Griptight" as a brand name for kids' products because they thought it sounded like "a carpet glue, a denture fixative, a kind of tire." So the firm called its product line by the name "Kiddiwinks™"—a British word for children. That name meant nothing to American parents, who thought "Binkykids™" was great because the Binky name was associated with pacifiers. As to packaging, the interviews showed that British parents were more conservative than their American couunterparts. Thus, British packaging is more serious with a stress on a rather antiseptic white, while the U.S. packaging "is more flamboyant."[13]

In *hypothesis evaluation* the marketing researcher tests ideas discovered in the hypothesis generation stage to help the marketing manager recommend marketing actions. This test usually is a mail, telephone, or personal survey of a large sample of past, present, or prospective consumers. In choosing between the three alternatives, the marketing researcher has to make important trade-offs (as shown in Figure 8–5) to balance cost against the expected quality of information obtained. The figure shows that personal interview surveys have a major advantage of enabling the interviewer to be flexible in asking probing questions or getting reactions to visual materials. In contrast, mail surveys usually have the lower cost per completed survey. Telephone surveys lie between the other two technologies in terms of flexibility and cost.

The high cost of reaching respondents in their homes using personal interviews has led to a dramatic increase in the use of *mall intercept interviews*, personal interviews of consumers while on visits to shopping centers. These face-to-face interviews reduce the cost of personal visits to consumers in their homes while providing the flexibility to show respondents visual cues such as ads or actual product samples. Technology has even made possible "virtual shopping trip" simulations by enabling a mall intercept respondent to "walk" through store aisles and "buy" products while sitting in front of a computer screen.

FIGURE 8-6

Typical problems in wording
questions

PROBLEM	SAMPLE QUESTION	EXPLANATION
Leading question	Why do you like Wendy's fresh meat hamburgers better than those of competitors made with frozen meat?	Consumer is led to make statement favoring Wendy's hamburgers.
Ambiguous question	Do you eat at fast-food restaurants regularly? ☐ Yes ☐ No	What is meant by word *regularly*—once a day, once a month, or what?
Unanswerable question	What was the occasion for your eating your first hamburger?	Who can remember the answer? Does it matter?
Two questions in one	Do you eat Wendy's hamburgers and chili? ☐ Yes ☐ No	How do you answer if you eat Wendy's hamburgers but not chili?
Nonexhaustive question	Where do you live? ☐ At home ☐ In dormitory	What do you check if you live in an apartment?
Nonmutually exclusive answers	What is your age? ☐ Under 20 ☐ 20–40 ☐ 40 and over	What answer does a 40-year-old check?

Figure 8–6 shows typical problems to guard against in wording questions to obtain meaningful answers from respondents. For example, in a question of whether you eat at fast-food restaurants regularly, the word *regularly* is ambiguous. Two people might answer "yes" to the question, but one might mean "once a day" while the other means "once or twice a year." Both answers appear as "yes" to the researcher who tabulates them, but they suggest that dramatically different marketing actions be directed to each of these two prospective consumers. Therefore, it is essential that marketing research questions be worded precisely so that all respondents interpret the same question similarly.

Suppose tonight after school you open a letter from your state legislator and see a questionnaire that includes the two questions shown here:

QUESTION	YES	NO
Environment 1 Do you think that our state should enact Gestapo-type laws that would reward citizens for spying on and reporting on other citizens for such offenses as air or water pollution?	☐	☐
University autonomy 2 Would you agree that administrators of state-supported educational institutions should be discharged for pampering revolutionaries?	☐	☐

He is looking for "no" answer to the first question and a "yes" to the second. He is "stacking the deck," using leading questions. Reporting statistical results of such biased questions would give a very distorted picture of the constituents' actual opinions. (Unfortunately these are real questions from a legislator's survey!) Hence the proper phrasing of a question is vital in uncovering useful marketing information.

Figure 8–7 shows a number of different formats for questions taken from a Wendy's survey that assessed fast-food restaurant preferences among present and

Wendy's changes continuously in response to changing customer wants.

prospective consumers. Question 1 is an example of an *open end question,* which the respondent can answer in his or her own words. In contrast, questions in which the respondent simply checks an answer are *closed-end* or *fixed alternative questions.* Question 2 is an example of the simplest fixed alternative question, a *dichotomous question* that allows only a "yes" or "no" answer.

A fixed alternative question with three or more choices uses a *scale.* Question 5 is an example of a question that uses *semantic differential scale,* a seven-point scale in which the opposite ends have one- or two-word adjectives that have opposite meanings. For example, depending on how clean the respondent feels that Wendy's is, he or she would check the left-hand space on the scale, the right-hand space, or one of the five intervening points. Question 6 uses a *Likert scale,* in which the respondent is asked to indicate the extent to which he or she agrees or disagrees with a statement.

The questionnaire in Figure 8–7 is an excerpt of a precisely worded survey that provides valuable information to the marketing researcher at Wendy's. Questions 1 to 8 inform him or her about the likes and dislikes in eating out, frequency of eating out at fast-food restaurants generally and at Wendy's specifically, and sources of information used in making decisions about fast-food restaurants. Question 9 gives details about the personal characteristics of the respondent or the respondent's household, which can be used in trying to segment the fast-food market, a topic discussed in Chapter 9.

Electronic technology has revolutionized traditional concepts of "interviews" or "surveys." Today, respondents can walk up to a kiosk in a shopping center, read questions off a screen, and key their answers into a computer on a touch screen. Even fully automated telephone interviews exist: an automated voice questions respondents over the telephone, who key their replies on a touch-tone telephone.[14]

Panels and experiments   Two special ways that observations and questionnaires are sometimes used are panels and experiments.

1 What things are most important to you when you decide to eat out and go to a restaurant?

_____

_____

_____

_____

_____

2 Have you eaten fast-food restaurant food in the past three months?
   ☐ Yes   ☐ No

3 If you answered "yes" to Question 2, how often do you eat fast food?
   ☐ Once a week or more ☐ Two or three times a month ☐ Once a month or less

4 How important is it to you that a fast-food restaurant satisfy you on the following characteristics? Check the box that describes your feelings.

CHARAC-TERISTIC	VERY IMPOR-TANT	SOME-WHAT IMPOR-TANT	IMPOR-TANT	UN-IMPOR-TANT	SOME-WHAT UNIMPOR-TANT	VERY UNIMPOR-TANT
Taste of food	☐	☐	☐	☐	☐	☐
Cleanliness	☐	☐	☐	☐	☐	☐
Price	☐	☐	☐	☐	☐	☐
Variety on menu	☐	☐	☐	☐	☐	☐

5 Check the space on the scale below that describes how you feel about Wendy's on the characteristics shown.

CHARACTERISTIC	CHECK THE SPACE DESCRIBING HOW WENDY'S IS		
Taste of food	Tasty	_ _ _ _ _ _ _ _ _	Not tasty
Cleanliness	Clean	_ _ _ _ _ _ _ _ _	Dirty
Price	Inexpensive	_ _ _ _ _ _ _ _ _	Expensive
Variety on menu	Wide	_ _ _ _ _ _ _ _ _	Narrow

Marketing researchers often want to know if consumers are changing their behavior over time, and so they take successive measurements of the same people. A **panel** is a sample of consumers or stores from which researchers take a series of measurements. For example, in this way a consumer's switching from one brand of breakfast cereal to another can be measured. Nielsen's national TV ratings are developed from its people-meter households that make up a panel and are measured repeatedly through time.

An **experiment** involves obtaining data by manipulating factors under tightly controlled conditions to test cause and effect. The interest is in whether changing one of the conditions (a cause) will change the behavior of what is studied (the effect). Both the causal conditions and the resulting behavior are variables. Two types of causal conditions can occur: (1) experimental and (2) extraneous independent variables. An **experimental independent variable** (or simply, the experimental variable) is the causal condition manipulated or controlled by the experimenter. In contrast, an **extraneous independent variable** (or simply, the extraneous variable) is the causal condition that is a result of outside factors that the experimenter cannot control. Such a variable might change the behavior of what is studied.

The change in the behavior of what is studied is called the **dependent variable.** The experimenter tries to arrange a change in the independent variable and then measure the accompanying change, or absence of it, in the dependent variable.

FIGURE 8-7

(concluded)

6 Check the box that describes your agreement with the statement.

STATEMENT	STRONGLY AGREE	AGREE	DON'T KNOW	DISAGREE	STRONGLY DISAGREE
Adults like to take their families to fast-food restaurants.	☐	☐	☐	☐	☐
Our children have a say in where the family eats.	☐	☐	☐	☐	☐

7 How important is this information about fast-food restaurants?

SOURCE OF INFORMATION	VERY IMPORTANT SOURCE	SOMEWHAT IMPORTANT SOURCE	NOT AN IMPORTANT SOURCE
Television	☐	☐	☐
Newspapers	☐	☐	☐
Billboards	☐	☐	☐
Mail	☐	☐	☐

8 In the past three months, how often have you eaten at each of these three fast-food restaurants?

RESTAURANT	ONCE A WEEK OR MORE	TWO OR THREE TIMES A MONTH	ONCE A MONTH OR LESS
Burger King	☐	☐	☐
McDonald's	☐	☐	☐
Wendy's	☐	☐	☐

9 Please answer the following questions about you and your household.
  a Are you ☐ Male ☐ Female
  b Are you ☐ Single ☐ Married ☐ Other (widowed, divorced)
  c How many children under age 18 live in your home?
    ☐ 0 ☐ 1 ☐ 2 ☐ 3 ☐ 4 ☐ 5 or more
  d What is your age?
    ☐ 24 or under ☐ 25-39 ☐ 40 or over
  e What is your approximate total annual household income?
    ☐ Less than $15,000 ☐ $15,000-$30,000 ☐ More than $30,000

In marketing experiments, the experimental independent variables are often one or more of the marketing mix variables, such as the product features, price, or advertising used. The ideal dependent variable usually is a change in purchases of an individual, household, or entire organization. If actual purchases cannot be used as a dependent variable, factors that are believed to be highly related to purchases, such as preferences in a taste test or intentions to buy, are used.

A potential difficulty with experiments is that extraneous independent variables can distort the results of an experiment and affect the dependent variable. A researcher's task is to identify the effect of the experimental variable of interest on the dependent variable when the effects of extraneous variables in an experiment might hide it. The Coke taste test experiment described in the next sections illustrates some of the potential dangers of marketing experiments.

Advantages and disadvantages of primary data   Compared with secondary data, primary data have the advantage of being more timely and specific to the problem being studied. The main disadvantages are that primary data are usually far more costly and time consuming to collect than secondary data.

ETHICS AND SOCIAL RESPONSIBILITY ALERT

Ethics

WHAT IS "TRUTH" IN REPORTING SURVEY RESULTS?

Doctors were surveyed to find out what brand of butter substitute they recommend for their patients concerned about cholesterol. The results:

- Recommend no particular brand: 80%
- Recommend Brand A: 5%
- Recommend Brand B: 4%

No other brand is recommended by more than 2 percent of the doctors. The firm owning brand A runs an ad that states: "More doctors recommend brand A than any other brand." Is this ethical? Why or why not? What kind of ethical guideline, if any, should be used to address this issue?

Ethical aspects of collecting primary data Professional marketing researchers have to make ethical decisions in collecting, using, and reporting survey data. Today's consumers feel they are bombarded by too many questionnaires and are suspicious of salespeople pretending to be marketing researchers. Using deception to collect competitive corporate intelligence is a serious problem. As described in the Ethics and Social Responsibility Alert box, another ethical issue is the incomplete reporting of data collected.[15] Using formal statements on ethical policies and instituting rewards and punishments can increase ethical behavior in marketing research.

CONCEPT CHECK

1. A mail questionnaire asks you, "Do you eat pizza?" What kind of question is this?

2. Does a mail, telephone, or personal interview survey provide the greatest flexibility for asking probing questions?

3. What is the difference between an independent and a dependent variable?

STEP 4: FIND A SOLUTION

Mark Twain once observed, "Collecting data is like collecting garbage. You've got to know what you're going to do with the stuff before you collect it." The purpose of step 4 is to analyze the collected data effectively to keep it from having the value of garbage. This requires using the data to find the alternative that best meets the measure of success the decision maker specified in defining the problem and then to put that alternative into effect. The Bair Hugger® patient warming system illustrates step 4 of the decision-making process discussed in this chapter.

Choose the Best Alternative: The Problem's Solution

The **solution** is simply the best alternative that has been identified to solve the problem. We recognize the best alternative by finding the one that best meets the measure of success established in defining the problem (step 1).

In 1985 Dr. Scott Augustine, an anesthesiologist, observed that it took a long time for patients to warm up in the recovery room after an operation. The state-of-the-art in warming patients to overcome their hypothermia at that time was either warm blankets thrown over the patient or heated water pads put under them. Dr. Augustine had a better idea—what he calls "a hair dryer blowing hot air into a double-wall

In a search for a way to warm post-operative patients—those with hypothermia—Augustine Medical's Bair Hugger® System solution revealed an entirely new market opportunity.

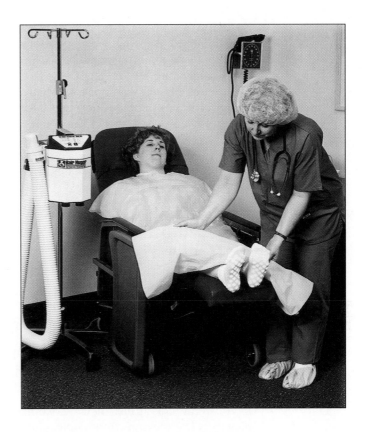

garbage bag" with holes punched on the underside so the warm air blows on the patient. He patented the idea and called it the Bair Hugger.® Bair Hugger® Total Temperature Management™ System.[16]

Dr. Augustine and his small startup company, Augustine Medical, thought they had a *solution* for the problem of warming recovery room patients around the world. But many questions still existed about the ideal design, the ideal solution. In terms of step 4—finding a solution to the problem—a team of college business students took the first prototype to 15 hospitals to get reactions from recovery room doctors and nurses. They got some very precise suggestions for improving the design, including the following:

* Reduce the size of the box containing the warming unit so it will fit under the bed, or attach to it, in a cramped recovery room.
* Lower the height of Bair Hugger® blanket lying over the patient so, the nurse can see the patient's face easily.
* Change the design so the air doesn't blow past the patient's mouth, drying out the patient's throat.

Modifying the basic design in response to this marketing research, Dr. Augustine thought he had a good solution to the patient warming problem. A tipoff: some recovery-room personnel were so excited the first time they saw the Bair Hugger® System, they tried it on a patient immediately.

Implement the Chosen Alternative

Identifying the best alternative—the potential solution—to the problem isn't enough. The difficulty is that no one may get around to putting the solution into effect. Someone must "make something happen"—see that the solution gets implemented.

In a small business, decisions can be implemented quickly—especially if the inventor and "implementer" is the company CEO. The first Bair Hugger® Warming

System was introduced in 1987. Acceptance was quick, and the Bair Hugger® has revolutionized the way recovery room patients are warmed. The advantages are striking: more comfortable patients who spend less time in the recovery room getting their temperature up to 98.6°F.

In terms of step 4, Augustine Medical introduced its Bair Hugger® to solve the patient warming problem hospitals face. Today, Augustine Medical has more than $24 million in annual sales and markets a complete line of patient warming and cooling products in 40 countries. However, as often happens with new products, things may not work out quite as well as with the Bair Hugger® System. This is the reason for evaluation, the final step in the decision process, which is discussed next.

STEP 5: EVALUATE THE RESULTS

Evaluating results is a continuing way of life for effective marketing managers. There are really two aspects of this evaluation process:

- *Evaluate the decision itself.* This involves comparing actual results with plans and the measure of success defined in step 1. If results don't achieve what is targeted, the next step is taking appropriate corrective action—the evaluation activity described in Chapter 2.
- *Evaluate the decision process used.* This involves changing the activities in one or more of the steps used in reaching a decision, such as altering the methods used to define the problem, collect the data, or implement the plan.

A careful look at the "new" Coke marketing program can reveal how marketing managers learn lessons from unpleasant results and try to move a marketing program forward.

Evaluation of the Decision Itself: The New Coke Strategy

In the early 1980s the Coca-Cola Company discovered it had a terrible dilemma: its old reliable "Formula 7X," which had been the backbone of the company for a century, was losing market share to arch-rival Pepsi-Cola. Blind taste tests (the actual brand hidden from the taster) showed that cola drinkers preferred the sweeter Pepsi to the crisper taste of the original Coke. Because of this, Coca-Cola conducted a $4 million, three-year study involving over 190,000 taste tests in search of a new formulation for Coke that consumers would prefer to the original Formula 7X and to Pepsi. So Coca-Cola marketing executives developed a new, sweeter formula for Coke, which became "new" Coke and that beat the old Coke formula 53 percent to 47 percent in blind taste tests.

For the three months following the introduction of new Coke, Coca-Cola's Atlanta headquarters was bombarded by 1,500 phone calls daily from angry Coke drinkers asking the company to return to Formula 7X. In July 1985, Coca-Cola announced the return of Formula 7X as "Coca-Cola Classic" and retained the new formulation as simply "Coke." The feedback loop in Figure 8–2 reflects this action: in the evaluation process (step 5) the company redefined its problem and went back to step 1 to initiate a new marketing program.

By offering both Coca-Cola Classic and new Coke, the company ran the danger of the two brands cannibalizing each other rather than taking market share from Pepsi—the original reason for the new formula and marketing program. So this action bought time for the Coca-Cola Company but didn't solve its most fundamental quandary: what should it do with the two brands now? As the company's marketing strategists labored over this question, one thing became evident: the original 1985 new Coke launch had inadvertently positioned new Coke against the original Coke formula in the minds of cola drinkers across the country! It had *not* done what it was intended to do—position the new Coke against Pepsi. Today, new Coke has less than 5 percent of the sales of Coke Classic.

Both the soft-drink industry and Coca-Cola executives still believe that new Coke's sweeter taste wins over Pepsi in blind taste tests. As a result, this process of continuing evaluation has given rise to the company's search for a new strategy: try to give a new life to new Coke and take great care to position it against Pepsi, not Coca-Cola Classic!

Evaluation of the Decision Process: The New Coke Strategy

Postmortems of the decision process itself help to avoid repeating the same error over and over. In the case of new Coke, the Coca-Cola Company has learned several lessons. First, marketing research lessons include the need to use a well-known brand name like Coke in taste experiments and to explain to participants that in choosing a new cola formula, the company would drop the original Coke formula.[17]

Perhaps equally important, the decision process must keep in mind the objectives of the marketing program, in this case taking market share away from Pepsi. In the original 1985 new Coke launch, the company accidentally wound up competing with itself because of the accompanying bad publicity. Future new product introductions by the company should take care that the decision process recognizes the need to avoid cannibalizing its own products.

CONCEPT CHECK

1. Why can't a marketing manager's decision making stop with selecting the best alternative to solve a problem?

2. What two factors should be evaluated after reaching a decision?

SUMMARY

1. Marketing research is the process of defining a marketing problem and opportunity, systematically collecting and analyzing information, and recommending actions to improve an organization's marketing activities. Marketing research assists in decision making. The chapter uses a five-step sequence that can lead to better decisions.

2. Defining the problem, step 1 in the sequence, involves identifying the objectives, constraints, assumptions, and measures of success related to the problem.

3. Assessing two kinds of decision factors, step 2, requires specifying both the alternatives (the controllable variables) and the uncertainties (the uncontrollable variables) that interact to lead to the outcome—good or bad—of the decision.

4. Collecting relevant information, step 3, includes considering pertinent concepts, methods, and data.

5. Secondary data have been recorded prior to the project and include those internal and external to the organization.

6. Primary data are collected specifically for the project and are obtained by either observing or questioning people. In the latter case, ideas are often generated through individual interviews and focus groups. Ideas are often evaluated using large-scale mail, telephone, or personal interview surveys. Mall intercept interviews are a form of personal interviews increasing in use because of their flexibility and lower cost.

7. Experiments manipulate a situation to measure the effect of an independent variable (cause) on the dependent variable (result or effect). With panels, repeated measurements are taken from the sample units—such as consumers or stores.

8. Finding the solution to a problem is step 4. It involves both selecting the alternative that best meets the measures of success specified in step 1 and also developing and executing a plan to put the chosen alternative into effect.

9. Step 5 in the sequence involves evaluating both the decision itself and the process used to reach it and helps the decision maker learn lessons that can be used in the future.

KEY TERMS AND CONCEPTS

marketing research p. 207
decision p. 208
objectives p. 210
constraints p. 210
assumptions p. 211
measures of success p. 211
decision factors p. 211
alternatives p. 211
uncertainties 211
hypothesis p. 213
new product concept p. 214
methods p. 214
probability sampling p. 215

nonprobability sampling p. 215
statistical inference p. 215
data p. 215
secondary data p. 215
primary data p. 215
observational data p. 218
questionnaire data p. 219
panel p. 224
experiment p. 224
experimental independent variable p. 224
extraneous independent variable p. 224
dependent variable p. 224
solution p. 226

CHAPTER PROBLEMS AND APPLICATIONS

1. Before the people meter, Nielsen obtained national TV ratings by using "audimeters" attached to TV sets in 1,170 American households. These devices measured (a) if the TV set was turned on and (b) if so, to which channel. What are the limitations of this mechanical observation method?

2. Before the people meter, Nielsen obtained ratings of local TV stations by having households fill out diary questionnaires. These gave information on (a) who was watching TV and (b) what program. What are the limitations of this questionnaire method?

3. For the two questions in the legislator's questionnaire shown in the chapter, (a) what is the factual issue for which opinions are sought, and (b) how has the legislator managed to bias the question to get the answer he wants?

4. Rework question 1 in the legislator's questionnaire to make it an unbiased question in the form of (a) an open-end question and (b) a Likert scale question.

5. Suppose Fisher-Price wants to run an experimental and control group experiment to evaluate a proposed chatter telephone design. It has two different groups of children on which to run an experiment for one week each. The control group has the old toy telephone, whereas the experimental group is exposed to the newly designed pull toy with wheels, a noisemaker, and bobbing eyes. The dependent variable is the average number of minutes during the two-hour play period that one of the children is playing with the toy, and the results are as follows:

ELEMENT IN EXPERIMENT	EXPERIMENTAL GROUP	CONTROL GROUP
Experimental variable	New design	Old design
After measurement	62 minutes	13 minutes

Should Fisher-Price introduce the new design? Why?

6. A rich aunt has decided to set you up in a business of your own choosing. To her delight, you decide on a service business—giving flying lessons in ultralight planes to your fellow college students. Some questions from the first draft of a mail questionnaire you plan to use are shown below. In terms of Figure 8–6, (a) identify the problem with each question and (b) correct it. NOTE: Some questions may have more than one problem.

a Have you ever flown in commercial airliners and in ultralight planes? ☐ Yes   ☐ No

b Why do you think ultralights are so much safer than hang gliders? _____

c At what age did you first know you like to fly?
☐ Under 10   ☐ 10 to 20   ☐ 21 to 30   ☐ Over 30

d How much did you spend on recreational activities last year?
☐ $100 or less   ☐ $401 to $800   ☐ $1,201 to $1,600
☐ $101 to $400   ☐ $801 to $1,201   ☐ $1,600 or more

e How much would you pay for ultralight flying lessons?
_____

f Would you sign up for a class that met regularly?
☐ Yes   ☐ No

7. As owner of a chain of supermarkets, you get the idea that you could sell more fresh strawberries by leaving them individually out on a tray and letting customers then fill their own pint or quart box with strawberries. (a) Describe an experiment to test this idea. (b) What are some possible measures of success?

8. Suppose on a rainy night you are driving on a two-lane highway at 50 miles per hour. As you come over the crest of the hill, you see that a car 100 yards ahead of you has plowed into a tank truck, obstructing your lane. You are afraid that too much braking will cause a bad skid, so your main choices are to steer into the left lane or into the right shoulder. Further, you can't tell if traffic is coming toward you. Apply the five steps of the decision sequence to address this problem.

CASE 8-1   Envirosell

You probably take those security cameras in stores for granted. You've assumed that you are being watched by store employees to prevent 'shrinkage,' a euphemistic expression for shoplifting. Would it surprise you to know that some of those video cameras, which you may or may not be aware of, are there conducting marketing research?

THE COMPANY

Envirosell is a New York-based consumer behavior research company that studies the relationships between consumers, products, and commercial spaces. If a company wants to know whether a point-of-purchase (P-O-P) display is effective or how the effectiveness of an in-store promotion can be improved, Envirosell can tell them through analysis of how consumers relate to the retail environment and the products within it.

Many prominent consumer products companies including General Mills, Apple Computer, Fisher-Price, Hallmark Cards, and Warner-Lambert use Envirosell to help them understand how to better reach customers. U.S. and international banking institutions such as Citibank, Banca di Roma, Credit du Nord-France, MasterCard International, food service providers like Burger King and Starbucks Coffee, retailers such as Waldenbooks/Brentano's and Blockbuster Entertainment, advertising and promotional agencies, even the U.S. Postal Service can be counted among Envirosell's customers.

THE SERVICE

Envirosell gathers data on consumer behaviors primarily through observational techniques. Trackers can be assigned to follow shoppers in stores to observe and record their behavior. Real-time video cameras and film cameras are used to record customer behavior for later analysis. A third source of information on customers is Envirosell's databases.

Paco Underhill, President of Envirosell, explains that a typical study may generate from 150 to 300 hours of video tape. What is unique about Envirosell, according to Underhill, is not how the data is collected but how it is analyzed. Envirosell takes the tape to their studios in New York where a spreadsheet is designed and from 30,000 to 50,000 data points are collected about how customers buy for a given product-service category.

This information is then presented to the client with graphs, maps, short video clips to allow the client to watch how customers shop and purchase not just the client's product/service but how customers shop and purchase in that category. For example, Fisher-Price would learn how consumers purchase toys—how easily can the child or parent see and reach the toy, how many other alternatives are examined before making a decision, are certain Fisher-Price or competitive toys examined, considered, selected or ignored more than others and how does the retail environment contribute to the way that the customer relates to the product.

Underhill feels that the Envirosell service complements other types of research that are commonly used. Attitudinal data, often collected with consumer surveys or focus groups, can provide insight into how consumers think. Scanning data utilizing the UPC (universal product code) information at point of sale tells companies what people are buying. Envirosell's observational techniques provides information on *how* customers buy. Envirosell will collect information on consumer attitudes as well but more as an addition to their observational techniques. Interviewers may intercept shoppers as they leave the store to ask them questions. This allows Envirosell to compare what customers say about what they did in the store to what they actually did based on observational data.

Underhill feels that the Envirosell service is particularly important for marketers as the retail environment grows more competitive. Increasingly, consumer decisions are made at point of sale which means understanding how consumers buy a category is critical to successful marketing programs. In addition, the increasing emphasis on relationship marketing—with a goal towards long-term, cost-effective individual relationships with customers—means that organizations needs database marketing. Database marketing or micromarketing provides the organization with continuously updated demographic and consumption information on the consumer. And that includes more than just the traditional attitudianal and sales data used in the past.

Questions

1. What are the advantages and disadvantages of Envirosell's observation techniques compared with consumer surveys?
2. Discuss how Envirosell's techniques might be combined with an in-store experiment. Give an example of a research project that could utilize such an approach.
3. What reliability issues are raised with video observational techniques? How can Envirosell attempt to control for these?

CHAPTER 9

Market Segmentation, Targeting, and Positioning

AFTER READING THIS CHAPTER YOU SHOULD BE ABLE TO:

• Explain what market segmentation is, when to use it, and the five steps involved in segmentation.

• Recognize the different factors used to segment consumer and organizational markets.

• Understand the significance of heavy, medium, and light users and nonusers in targeting markets.

• Develop a market-product grid to use in segmenting and targeting a market.

• Interpret a cross tabulation to analyze market segments.

• Understand how marketing managers position products in the marketplace.

SNEAKER WARS: BATTLING FOR KEY MARKET SEGMENTS

Putting Reeboks on Shaq's size 22 feet probably ignited the latest sneakers war between Reebok and Nike for key market segments. (If Shaq needs a last name, clearly basketball isn't your thing and you should probably talk to *any* basketball fan!) "Sneakers" here means all kinds of athletic footwear for aerobics, basketball, walking, tennis, running, and so on.

Until Reebok signed Shaq, the company's most visible market segment was women's fitness, with a product line that included a range of lower-priced casual shoes. In contrast, Nike focused largely on providing high-priced, high-quality shoes to male athletes and "wannabees." With its psychedelic "Shaqnosis" model, Reebok made a frontal attack on Nike's very loyal segment of under-18 males. Not only has Shaq become a superstar in the National Basketball Association, but his attractive, self-effacing interviews have given Reebok a powerful spokesperson to reach male athletes.[1]

Without the Shaq hype, Reebok quietly signed an endorsement contract with Rebecca Lobo of the NCAA championship University of Connecticut team. Lobo is shown at center in the photo on the opposite page with 400-meter hurdler Derrick Adkins and pro beach volleyballer Liz Masayakan as they unveiled Reebok's "Spin" line of performance sportswear and shoes for 1996 U.S. Olympians. Although getting a great deal less fanfare than Shaq, Rebecca Lobo's spokesperson role for Reebok in targeting the female segment may be even more important.[2] The reason lies in the importance of the market segments for women's sneakers. Two key factors probably underlie Reebok's signing of Lobo:

• Sales of men's sneakers are flat—not growing—and sales of high-tech basketball shoes are languishing.

• In 1994, sales of athletic footwear (sneakers) to American women 12 and older passed those of men in that age group for the first time.

233

U.S. sales in 1994 show the importance of the sneaker battle: $5.4 billion for women to $5.3 billion for men. Reebok's marketing research shows that, in 1971, 1 out of every 27 American girls was involved in sports; today this ratio is 1 in 3![3] This explains why sneaker sales to women is an important battleground, although relatively obscure to those outside the industry. Reebok has 23.4 percent of the U.S. sneaker market for women, compared with 21.7 percent for Nike, which is coming on fast in this market segment. The Marketing NewsNet box[4] shows how Nike and Reebok dominate the sneaker market, both in the United States and globally.

The Reebok strategy, making shoes designed to satisfy needs of different customers, illustrates successful market segmentation, the main topic of this chapter. It also helps explain why Reebok's sales grew by more than 100,000 percent from the early 1980s to today. We'll study Reebok's segmentation strategy more carefully in the next few pages.

After discussing why markets need to be segmented, this chapter covers the steps a firm uses in segmenting and targeting a market and then positioning its offering in the marketplace.

WHY SEGMENT MARKETS?

A business firm segments its markets so it can respond more effectively to the wants of groups of prospective buyers and thus increase its sales and profits. Nonprofit organizations also segment the clients they serve to satisfy client needs more effectively while achieving the organization's goals. Let's use the dilemma of sneaker buyers finding their ideal Reebok shoes to describe (1) what market segmentation is and (2) when it is necessary to segment markets.

What Market Segmentation Means

People have different needs and wants, even though it would be easier for marketers if they didn't. **Market segmentation** involves aggregating prospective buyers into groups that (1) have common needs and (2) will respond similarly to a marketing action. The groups that result from this process are **market segments,** a relatively homogeneous collection of prospective buyers.

The existence of different market segments has caused firms to use a marketing strategy of **product differentiation,** a strategy that has come to have two different but related meanings. In its broadest sense, product differentiation involves a firm's using different marketing mix activities, such as product features and advertising, to help consumers perceive the product as being different and better than competing products. The perceived differences may involve physical features or nonphysical ones, such as image or price.

In a narrower sense, product differentiation involves a firm's selling two or more products with different features targeted to different market segments. A firm can get into trouble when its different products blend together in consumers' minds and don't reach distinct market segments successfully. The Reebok example discussed below shows both how a manufacturer has succeeded in using a product differentiation strategy to offer different products targeted to separate market segments and also how its success is forcing new efforts to separate two groups of its shoes in consumers' minds.

Segmentation: linking needs to actions   The definition of market segmentation first stresses the importance of aggregating—or grouping—people or

MARKETING NewsNet

Global

NIKE VERSUS REEBOK: THE SNEAKER WAR OF THE WORLD

While the U.S. slugfest between Nike and Reebok provides many lessons on marketing strategy, it obscures an important point: these two companies dominate not only the U.S. market for athletic footwear but the world market as well!

The two pie charts below tell the story, using the latest data available. Together Nike and Reebok sell more than half the sneakers bought in the United States. They also sell about 43 percent of all sneakers sold in the global marketplace. Even in global sales, only Adidas—with 10 percent market share—appears to be a serious competitor in the foreseeable future.

With the U.S. sneaker war being so tough, both Reebok and Nike are looking at the $7 billion-a-year global sneaker market outside the United States. The 300 million soccer players around the world are a beckoning market segment, but in it Nike and Reebok face solidly entrenched Adidas. But learning about local consumer wants and delivering customer value isn't always easy: the English want white cricket shoes only, and the Japanese prefer ultralight running shoes. So the Nike versus Reebok war is shifting from a huge battle in the United States to global brushfire skirmishes.

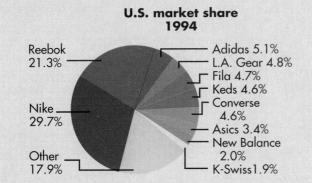

U.S. market share 1994

Reebok 21.3%
Nike 29.7%
Other 17.9%
Adidas 5.1%
L.A. Gear 4.8%
Fila 4.7%
Keds 4.6%
Converse 4.6%
Asics 3.4%
New Balance 2.0%
K-Swiss 1.9%

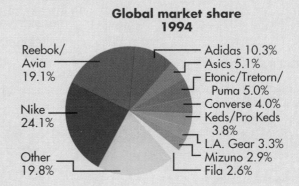

Global market share 1994

Reebok/Avia 19.1%
Nike 24.1%
Other 19.8%
Adidas 10.3%
Asics 5.1%
Etonic/Tretorn/Puma 5.0%
Converse 4.0%
Keds/Pro Keds 3.8%
L.A. Gear 3.3%
Mizuno 2.9%
Fila 2.6%

organizations in a market according to the similarity of their needs and the benefits they are looking for in making a purchase. Second, such needs and benefits must be related to specific, tangible marketing actions the firm can take. These actions may involve separate products or other aspects of the marketing mix such as price, advertising or personal selling activities, or distribution strategies—the four Ps (product, price, promotion, place).

The process of segmenting a market and selecting specific segments as targets is the link between the various buyers' needs and the organization's marketing program (Figure 9–1). Market segmentation is only a means to an end: in an economist's

FIGURE 9–1

Market segmentation links market needs to an organization's marketing program

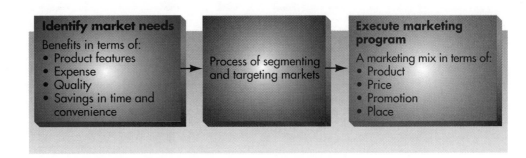

Identify market needs

Benefits in terms of:
• Product features
• Expense
• Quality
• Savings in time and convenience

Process of segmenting and targeting markets

Execute marketing program

A marketing mix in terms of:
• Product
• Price
• Promotion
• Place

terms, it relates supply (the organization's actions) to demand (customer needs). A basic test of the usefulness of the segmentation process is whether it leads to tangible marketing actions to increase sales and profitability.

How Reebok's segmentation strategy developed   In 1979 Paul Fireman, who had dropped out of college to run his family's business, wandered through an international trade fair and saw Reebok's custom track shoes. He bought the U.S. license from the British manufacturer and started producing top-of-the-line running shoes. But Fireman then saw that the running boom had peaked and he needed other outlets for his shoes. What happened next may have affected what you have on your feet this minute.

In a brilliant marketing decision, Fireman introduced the first soft-leather aerobic-dance shoe—the Reebok "Freestyle"—in 1982. The flamboyant colors of these Reebok designer sneakers captured the attention of aerobic-dance instructors and students alike. This color strategy still helps the sneakers get good display space in stores and attracts a lot of consumer attention.

Today known as Reebok International, Ltd., the firm successively introduced tennis shoes, children's shoes ("Weeboks"), and basketball shoes in 1984 and walking shoes in 1986 (see the columns in Figure 9–2). For those who don't want to buy four different pairs of shoes to run, play tennis, shoot baskets, and walk in, Reebok introduced—of course—"cross-trainers" in 1988. The Reebok Step Trainer appeared in 1991.

What segmentation strategy will Reebok use to take it into the twenty-first century? Suddenly the answer is a bit cloudy. Competitors are offering "retro" sneakers (nostalgic shoes taking you back to the 1960s and 1970s) and "street hockey" shoes (made to look like ice skates). And in 1995 arch-competitor Nike introduced "Air Swoopes,"

FIGURE 9–2

Market-product grid showing how eight different styles of Reebok shoes reach segments of customers with different needs

MARKET SEGMENT		PRODUCT (Kind of shoes)								
GENERAL	GROUP WITH NEED	RUNNING (1981)	AEROBIC (1982)	TENNIS (1984)	BASKET-BALL (1984)	CHILDREN'S (1984)	WALKING (1986)	CROSS-TRAINERS (1988)	STEP-TRAINERS (1991)	NEW PRODUCTS (1996–99)
Performance-conscious consumers (athletes)	Runners	P						P		
	Aerobic dancers		P					P		
	Tennis players			P				P		
	Basketball players				P			P		?
	Step exercisers							S	P	
Fashion-conscious consumers (nonathletes)	Comfort- and style-conscious	S	S	S	S		S	S		
	Walkers	S	S	S	S		P	P		
	Children					P				
New markets 1996–99				?						

Key: P = primary market; S = secondary market

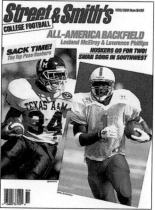

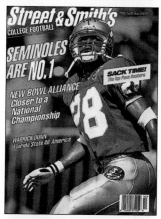

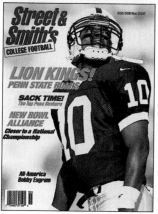

a basketball shoe targeted at women and named for Sheryl Swoopes—the Texas Tech All-American and NCAA Player of the Year. Air Swoopes is the first Nike sneaker named for a basketball player since its "Air Jordan" shoe propelled it into the No. 1 spot in sneakers.[5] Reebok's strategy includes a line of hiking and outdoor gear and a possible string of fitness clubs. But, as described earlier in the Marketing NewsNet box, the global market segment is a key focus for Reebok.

Using market-product grids   A **market-product grid** is a framework to relate the segments of a market to products offered or potential marketing actions by the firm. The grid in Figure 9–2 shows different markets of sneaker users as rows in the grid, while the columns show the different shoe products (or marketing actions) chosen by Reebok, so each cell in a market-product grid can show the estimated market size of a given product sold to a specific market segment.

The lightly shaded cells in Figure 9–2, labeled P, represent the primary market segment that Reebok targeted when it introduced each shoe. The darker shaded cells, labeled S, represent the secondary market segments that also started buying the shoe. In some cases, Reebok discovered that large numbers of people in a segment not originally targeted for a style of shoe bought it anyway. In fact, as many as 75 to 80 percent of the running shoes and aerobic-dance shoes are bought by nonathletes represented by the (1) comfort- and style-conscious and (2) walker segments shown in Figure 9–2—although walkers may object to being labeled "nonathletes." When this trend became apparent to Reebok in 1986, it introduced its walking shoes targeted directly at the walker segment.

Figure 9–2 also introduces one of the potential dangers of market segmentation for a firm: subdividing an entire market into two or more segments, thereby increasing the competition from other firms that focus their efforts on a single segment. Notice that Reebok's strategy is to reach both the performance (athletes) and fashion (nonathletes) segments. In the 1990s Reebok finds itself trying to clarify its identity among consumers who see Nike as a "performance shoe" and L.A. Gear as a "fashion shoe." In trying to compete in both markets, Reebok runs the danger of being first in neither. To be more responsive to both markets, Reebok has divided its U.S. operations into two separate units: "Technology," targeted at athletes, performance-oriented consumers, and children and "Lifestyle," targeted at style-conscious consumers.

When to Segment Markets

A business firm goes to the trouble and expense of segmenting its markets when this increases its sales revenue, profit, and ROI. When its expenses more than offset the potentially increased revenues from segmentation, it should not attempt to segment its market. The specific situations that illustrate this point are the cases of (1) one product and multiple market segments and (2) multiple products and multiple market segments.

One product and multiple market segments   When a firm produces only a single product or service and attempts to sell it to two or more market segments, it avoids the extra costs of developing and producing additional versions of the product, which often entail extremely high research, engineering, and manufacturing expenses. In this case, the incremental costs of taking the product into new product segments are typically those of a separate promotional campaign or a new channel of distribution. Although these expenses can be high, they are rarely as large as those for developing an entirely new product.

Magazines and movies are single products frequently directed to two or more distinct market segments. As shown in the margin at left, Street and Smith's official yearbook, *College Football,* uses different covers in different regions of the United States, featuring a college football star from that region. *Time* magazine now

To understand 3M's "FAB" approach to target multiple market segments with multiple products, see the text.

publishes more than 200 different U.S. editions and more than 100 international editions, each targeted at its own geographic and demographic segments and its own mix of advertisements. Movie companies often run different TV commercials featuring different aspects of a newly released film (love, or drama, or spectacular scenery) that are targeted to different market segments. Although multiple TV commercials for movies and separate covers or advertisements for magazines are expensive, they are minor compared with the costs of producing an entirely new movie or magazine for another market segment. Even Procter & Gamble is now marketing its Crest toothpaste with different advertising campaigns targeted at six different market segments, including children, Hispanics, and senior citizens.

Multiple products and multiple market segments Reebok's different styles of shoes, each targeted at a different type of user, are an example of multiple products aimed at multiple markets. Manufacturing these different styles of shoes is clearly more expensive than producing one but seems worthwhile if it serves customers' needs better, doesn't reduce quality or increase price, and adds to the sales revenues and profits.

3M uses a "FAB" acronym to develop different products for different market segments:

- F = Features of the product that are clear and that can be translated by R&D and manufacturing personnel into the specifications needed.
- A = Advantages of the product that make it clearly better than competitive products.
- B = Benefits of the product that are important to prospective buyers and can be communicated easily to them.

The four 3M Scotch™ videotapes shown in the ad are examples of using the FAB strategy to design four different videotapes, each designed to satisfy the unique needs of four slightly different market segments: (1) Scotch™ Re-Taping Tape to record favorite soaps and sport shows and then re-record, (2) Scotch™ Collections Tape that resists dust and can be used to build a home movie library, (3) Scotch™ Just for Kids Tape targeted at—what else?—kids, and (4) Scotch™ Archive Tape intended to record special family moments and to be saved permanently.

Product differentiation and market segmentation are generally effective strategies, as shown in the Reebok and 3M Scotch™ videotape examples, but they must be used with great care. The key is to assess how these strategies provide the organization with **synergy,** the increased customer value achieved through performing organizational functions more efficiently. The "increased customer value" can take many forms: more products, improved quality on existing products, lower prices, easier access to product through improved distribution, and so on. But the ultimate criterion is that customers should be better off as a result of the increased synergy.

Some car manufacturers have failed to achieve expected synergies as they offered many models and options to try to reach diverse market segments. They have concluded that the costs of developing, producing, marketing, and servicing dozens of slightly different models probably outweigh the higher prices that consumers are willing to pay for the wider array of choices.

As a result, many car manufacturers have reduced the number of options and simplified their product lines. For example, General Motors recently reduced the number of basic car platforms from 12 to 5—a "car platform" being small front-wheel drive cars or large rear-wheel drive cars. Although there are fewer choices, this provides two benefits to consumers: (1) lower prices through higher volume production of fewer models and (2) higher quality because of the ability to debug fewer basic designs.

CONCEPT CHECK

1. Market segmentation involves aggregating prospective buyers into groups that have two key characteristics. What are they?

2. What is product differentiation?

3. The process of segmenting and targeting markets is a bridge between what two marketing activities?

STEPS IN SEGMENTING AND TARGETING MARKETS

The process of segmenting a market and then selecting and reaching the target segments is divided into the five steps discussed in this section, as shown in Figure 9–3 on the next page. Segmenting a market is not a science—it requires large doses of common sense and managerial judgment.

Market segmentation and target markets can be abstract topics, so put on your entrepreneur's hat to experience the process. Suppose you own a Wendy's fast-food restaurant next to a large urban university that offers both day and evening classes. Your restaurant specializes in the Wendy's basics: hamburgers, french fries, Frosty milkshakes, and chili. Even though you are part of a chain and have some restrictions on menu and decor, you are free to set your hours of business and to undertake local advertising. How can market segmentation help?

FIGURE 9–3

The process of segmenting
and targeting markets involves
five key steps

Form Prospective Buyers into Segments

Grouping prospective buyers into meaningful segments involves meeting some specific criteria for segmentation and finding specific variables to segment the consumer or industrial market being analyzed.[6]

Criteria to use in forming the segments   A marketing manager should develop segments for a market that meet five principal criteria:

- *Potential for increased profit and ROI.* The best segmentation approach is the one that maximizes the opportunity for future profit and ROI. If this potential is maximized through no segmentation, don't segment. For nonprofit organizations, the analogous criterion is the potential for serving client users more effectively.
- *Similarity of needs of potential buyers within a segment.* Potential buyers within a segment should be similar in terms of a marketing activity, such as product features sought or advertising media used.
- *Difference of needs of buyers among segments.* If the needs of the various segments aren't appreciably different, combine them into fewer segments. A different segment usually requires a different marketing action that, in turn, means greater costs. If increased revenues don't offset extra costs, combine segments and reduce the number of marketing actions.
- *Feasibility of a marketing action to reach a segment.* Reaching a segment requires a simple but effective marketing action. If no such action exists, don't segment.
- *Simplicity and cost of assigning potential buyers to segments.* A marketing manager must be able to put a market segmentation plan into effect. This means being able to recognize the characteristics of potential buyers and then assigning them to a segment without encountering excessive costs.

The Russians' love of the dark meat on a chicken—like legs and thighs—is an example of using these five criteria in global market segmentation. Perdue's Schowell Farms in Maryland faced the dilemma of Americans preferring the white chicken meat. Discovering Russians prefer dark meat caused Perdue and other U.S. producers to increase dark-meat sales to Russia from $83 million in 1993 to $400 million in 1995.[7]

Ways to segment consumer markets   Figure 9–4 shows a number of variables that can be used to segment U.S. consumer markets. They are divided into two general categories: customer characteristics and buying situations. Some examples of how certain characteristics can be used to segment specific markets:

- *Region* (a geographical customer characteristic). Campbell's found that its canned nacho cheese sauce, which could be heated and poured directly onto

MAIN DIMENSION	SEGMENTATION VARIABLE	TYPICAL BREAKDOWNS
CUSTOMER CHARACTERISTICS		
Geographic	Region	Pacific; Mountain; West North Central; West South Central; East North Central; East South Central; South Atlantic; Middle Atlantic; New England
	City or metropolitan statistical area (MSA) size	Under 5,000; 5,000 to 19,999; 20,000 to 49,999; 50,000 to 99,999; 100,000 to 249,999; 250,000 to 499,999; 500,000 to 999,999; 1,000,000 to 3,999,999; 4,000,000 or over
	Density	Urban; suburban; rural
	Climate	Northern; Southern
Demographic	Age	Infant, under 6; 6 to 11; 12 to 17; 18 to 24; 25 to 34; 35 to 49; 50 to 64; 65 or over
	Sex	Male; female
	Family size	1 to 2; 3 to 4; 5 or over
	Stage of family life cycle	Young single; young married, no children; young married, youngest child under 6; young married, youngest child 6 or older; older married, with children; older married, no children under 18; older single; other older married, no children under 18
	Ages of children	No child under 18; youngest child 6 to 17; youngest child under 6
	Children under 18	0; 1; more than 1
	Income	Under $5,000; $5,000 to $14,999; $15,000 to $24,999; $25,000 to $34,999; $35,000 to $49,999; $50,000 or over
	Education	Grade school or less; some high school; high school graduate; some college; college graduate
	Race	Asian; African-American; Hispanic; white; other
	Home ownership	Own home; rent home
Psychographic	Personality	Gregarious; compulsive; extroverted; aggressive; ambitious
	Lifestyle	Use of one's time; values and importance; beliefs
BUYING SITUATIONS		
Benefits sought	Product features	Situation specific; general
	Needs	Quality; service; economy
Usage	Rate of use	Light user; medium user; heavy user
	User states	Nonuser; ex-user; prospect; first-time user; regular user
Awareness and intentions	Readiness to buy	Unaware; aware; informed; interested; intending to buy
		Insistence; preference; recognition; nonrecognition; rejection
	Brand familiarity	Minimum effort buying; comparison buying; special effort buying

FIGURE 9-4

Segmentation variables and breakdowns for U.S. consumer markets

nacho chips, was too hot for Americans in the East and not hot enough for those in the West and Southwest. The result: today Campbell's plants in Texas and California produce a hotter nacho cheese sauce to serve their regions than that produced in the other plants.

- *Family size* (a demographic customer characteristic). More than half of all U.S. households are made up of only one or two persons, so Campbell's packages meals with only one or two servings—from Great Starts breakfasts to L'Orient dinners.
- *Lifestyle* (a psychographic customer characteristic). Psychographic variables are consumer activities, interests, and opinions. With 70 percent of women working outside the home, millions of men are performing shopping chores their fathers

What special benefit does a MicroFridge offer and to which market segment might this appeal? The answer appears below.

didn't. Because men buy 32 percent of frozen foods and 24 percent of baby food, more firms are targeting men with their ads.[8]

- *Benefits sought* (a buying situation's characteristic). Important benefits offered to different customers are often a useful way to segment markets because they can lead directly to specific marketing actions, such as a new product, ad campaign, or distribution system. For example, what may become the hottest new appliance of the 1990s is MicroFridge, Inc.'s combination microwave/refrigerator/freezer aimed at college dorm residents. Busy, time-short consumers are making computer teleshopping for groceries a reality for 10,000 households in Chicago and San Francisco; the on-line grocery-shopping service, called

DILBERT   **by Scott Adams**

Welcome to online grocery shopping! (1) With her son looking on, Patti Landry picks out what she wants at a nearby Jewel store, where (2) one Peapod employee selects the items. Another Peapod employee delivers it, so that she and her family can eat some of these items at dinner.

"Peapod," receives the computer order and then uses its own employees to fill the orders and its own drivers to deliver them (see photos above).[9]

- **Usage rate** (quantity consumed or patronage—store visits—during a specific period; varies significantly among different customer groups). Airlines have developed frequent-flyer programs to encourage passengers to use the same airline repeatedly—a technique sometimes called "frequency marketing," which focuses on usage rate.

To obtain usage rate data, Simmons Market Research periodically surveys about 20,000 adults 18 years of age and older to discover how the products and services they buy and the media they watch relate to their demographic characteristics. Figure 9–5 shows the results of a question Simmons asks about the respondent's frequency of use (or patronage) of "fast-food and drive-in restaurants."

As shown in the right column of Figure 9–5, the importance of the segment increases as we move up the table. Among nonusers of these restaurants, pros-

FIGURE 9–5

Patronage of fast-food and drive-in restaurants by adults 18 years and older

USER OR NONUSER	SPECIFIC SEGMENT	NUMBER (1,000'S)	PERCENTAGE	ACTUAL SALES REVENUES (%)	USAGE INDEX PER PERSON*	IMPORTANCE OF SEGMENT
Users	Heavy users (14+ per month)	32,911	17.7%	43.8%	534	High
	Medium users (6–13 per month)	49,685	26.7	39.2	317	
	Light users (1–5 per month)	68,345	36.8	17.0	100	
Total Users		150,941	81.2	100.0		
Nonusers	Prospects	?	?	0	0	
	Nonprospects	?	?	0	0	
Total Nonusers		34,881	18.8	0	0	Low
Total	Users and Nonusers	185,822	100.0%	100.0%	–	

FIGURE 9-6

Comparison of various kinds
of users and nonusers for
Wendy's, Burger King, and
McDonald's restaurants

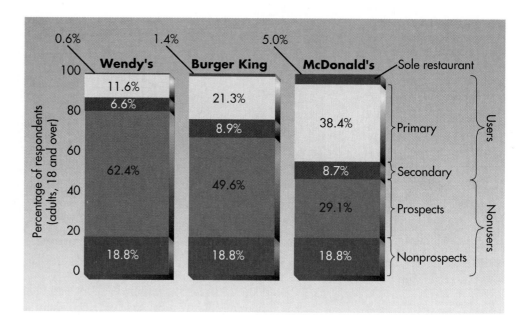

FIGURE 9-6

Comparison of various kinds
of users and nonusers for
Wendy's, Burger King, and
McDonald's restaurants

pects (who *might become* users) are more important than nonprospects (who are *never likely* to become users). Moving up the rows to the users, it seems logical that light users of these restaurants (1 to 5 times per month) are important but less so than medium users (6 to 13 times per month), who in turn are a less important segment than the critical group—the heavy users (14 or more times per month). The "Actual Sales Revenues" column in Figure 9–5 tells how much of the total monthly sales of these restaurants are accounted for by the heavy, medium, and light users.

Usage rate is sometimes referred to in terms of the **80/20 rule**, a concept that suggests 80 percent of a firm's sales are obtained from 20 percent of its customers. The percentages in the 80/20 rule are not really fixed at exactly 80 percent and 20 percent, but suggest that a small fraction of customers provide a large fraction of a firm's sales. For example, Figure 9–5 shows that the 17.7 percent of the U.S. population who are heavy users of these restaurants provide 43.8 percent of their sales revenues.

The "Usage Index per Person" column in Figure 9–5 emphasizes the importance of the heavy-user group even more. Giving the light users (1 to 5 restaurant visits per month) an index of 100, the heavy users have an index of 534. In other words, for every $1.00 spent by a light user in one of these restaurants in a month, each heavy user spends $5.34. This is the reason for the emphasis in almost all marketing strategies on effective ways to reach these heavy users. Thus, as a Wendy's restaurant owner you want to keep the heavy-user segment constantly in mind.

As part of the Simmons survey, restaurant patrons were asked if each restaurant was (1) the sole restaurant they went to, (2) the primary one, or (3) one of several secondary ones. This national information, shown in Figure 9–6, might give you, as a Wendy's owner, some ideas in developing your local strategy. The Wendy's bar in Figure 9–6 shows that your sole (0.6 percent), primary (11.6 percent), and secondary (6.6 percent) user segments are somewhat behind Burger King and far behind McDonald's, so a natural strategy is to look at these two competitors and devise a marketing program to win customers from them.

The "nonusers" part of your own bar in Figure 9–6 also provides ideas. It shows that 18.8 percent of adult Americans don't go to these restaurants in a typical month (also shown in Figure 9–5) and are really nonprospects—unlikely to ever patronize your restaurant. But the 62.4 percent of the Wendy's bar shown as prospects may be worth detailed thought. These adults use the product category (fast-food and drive-in

What variables might Panasonic use to segment the organizational markets for its Plain Paper Laser Fax? For the possible answer and related marketing actions, see the text.

restaurants) but *do not* go to Wendy's. New menu items or new promotional strategies might succeed in converting these "prospects" to "users." One key conclusion emerges about usage: in market segmentation studies, some measure of usage or revenues derived from various segments is central to the analysis.

In determining one or two variables to segment the market for your Wendy's restaurant, very broadly we find two main markets: students and nonstudents. To segment the students, we could try a variety of demographic variables, such as age, sex, year in school, or college major, or psychographic variables, such as personality characteristics, attitudes, or interests. But none of these variables really meets the five criteria listed previously—particularly the fourth criterion about leading to a feasible marketing action to reach the various segments. Four student segments that *do* meet these criteria include the following:

- Students living in dormitories (college residence halls, sororities, fraternities).
- Students living near the college in apartments.
- Day commuter students living outside the area.
- Night commuter students living outside the area.

These segmentation variables are really a combination of where the student lives and the time he or she is on campus (and near your restaurant). For nonstudents who might be customers, similar variables might be used:

- Faculty and staff members at the university.
- People who live in the area but aren't connected with the university.
- People who work in the area but aren't connected with the university.

People in each of these segments aren't quite as similar as those in the student segments, which makes them harder to reach with a marketing program or action.

Think about (1) whether the needs of all these segments are different and (2) how various advertising media can be used to reach these groups effectively.

Ways to segment organizational markets   Variables for segmenting organizational markets are shown in Figure 9–7. A product manager at Panasonic responsible for its new Plain Paper Laser Fax that doubles as a personal copier, answering machine, and autodial phone might use a number of these segmentation variables, as follows:

- *Location.* Firms located in a metropolitan statistical area (MSA) might receive a personal sales call, whereas those outside the MSA might be contacted by telephone.
- *NAICS code.* Firms categorized by the North American Industry Classification System (NAICS) code as manufacturers that deal with customers throughout the world might have different fax and answering needs than do retailers or lawyers serving local customers.
- *Number of employees.* The size of the firm is related to the volume of faxing and photocopying needs for a given industry or NAICS, so firms with a specific size range of employees might be a specific target market for Panasonic.

Form Products to Be Sold into Groups

As important as grouping customers into segments is finding a means of grouping the products you're selling into meaningful categories. If the firm has only one product or service, this isn't a problem, but when it has dozens or hundreds, these must be grouped in some way so buyers can relate to them. This is why department stores and supermarkets are organized into product groups, with the departments or aisles containing related merchandise. Likewise, manufacturers have product lines that are the groupings they use in the catalogs sent to customers.

What are the groupings for your restaurant? It could be the item purchased, such as a Frosty, chili, hamburgers, and french fries, but this is where judgment—the qualitative aspect of marketing—comes in. Students really buy an eating experience,

FIGURE 9–7

Segmentation variables and breakdowns for organizational markets

MAIN DIMENSION	SEGMENTATION VARIABLE	TYPICAL BREAKDOWNS
CUSTOMER CHARACTERISTICS		
Geographical	Region	Pacific; Mountain; West North Central; West South Central; East North Central; East South Central; South Atlantic; Middle Atlantic; New England
	Location	In MSA; not in MSA
Demographic	NAICS code	2-digit; 3-digit; 4-digit categories
	Number of employees	1 to 19; 20 to 99; 100 to 249; 250 or over
	Number of production workers	1 to 19; 20 to 99; 100 to 249; 250 or over
	Annual sales volume	Less than $1 million; $1 million to $10 million; $10 million to $100 million; over $100 million
	Number of establishments	With 1 to 19 employees; with 20 or more employees
BUYING SITUATIONS		
Nature of good	Kind	Product or service
	Where used	Installation; component of final product; supplies
	Application	Office use; limited production use; heavy production use
Buying condition	Purchase location	Centralized; decentralized
	Who buys	Individual buyer; group
	Type of buy	New buy; modified rebuy; straight rebuy

FIGURE 9–8

Selecting a target market for your fast-food restaurant next to an urban university (target market is shaded)

MARKETS	PRODUCTS: MEALS				
	BREAK-FAST	LUNCH	BETWEEN-MEAL SNACK	DINNER	AFTER-DINNER SNACK
STUDENT					
Dormitory	0	1	3	0	3
Apartment	1	3	3	1	1
Day commuter	0	3	2	1	0
Night commuter	0	0	1	3	2
NONSTUDENT					
Faculty or staff	0	3	1	1	0
Live in area	0	1	2	2	1
Work in area	1	3	0	1	0

Key: 3, Large market; 2, medium market; 1, small market; 0, no market.

or a meal that satisfies a need at a particular time of day, so the product grouping can be defined by meal or time of day as breakfast, lunch, between-meal snack, dinner, and after-dinner snack. These groupings are more closely related to the way purchases are actually made and permit you to market the entire meal, not just your french fries or Frosties.

Develop a Market-Product Grid and Estimate Size of Markets

Developing a market-product grid means labeling the markets (or horizontal rows) and products (or vertical columns), as shown in Figure 9–8. In addition, the size of the market in each cell, or the market-product combination, must be estimated. For your restaurant this involves estimating the number of, or sales revenue obtained from, each kind of meal that can reasonably be expected to be sold to each market segment. This is a form of the usage rate analysis discussed earlier in the chapter.

The market sizes in Figure 9–8 may be simple "guesstimates" if you don't have time for formal marketing research (as discussed in Chapter 8). But even such crude estimates of the size of specific markets using a market-product grid are far better than the usual estimates of the entire market.

Select Target Markets

A firm must take care to choose its target market segments carefully. If it picks too narrow a group of segments, it may fail to reach the volume of sales and profits it needs. If it selects too broad a group of segments, it may spread its marketing efforts so thin that the extra expenses more than offset the increased sales and profits.

Criteria to use in picking the target segments   There are two different kinds of criteria present in the market segmentation process: (1) those to use in dividing the market into segments (discussed earlier) and (2) those to use in actually picking the target segments. Even experienced marketing executives often confuse these two different sets of criteria. The five criteria to use in actually selecting the target segments apply to your Wendy's restaurant this way:

- *Size.* The estimated size of the market in the segment is an important factor in deciding whether it's worth going after. There is really no market for breakfasts among dormitory students (Figure 9–8), so why devote any marketing effort toward reaching a small or nonexistent market?

Wendy's can target different
market segments with different
advertising programs

- *Expected growth.* Although the size of the market in the segment may be small now, perhaps it is growing significantly or is expected to grow in the future. Night commuters may not look important now, but with the decline in traditional day students in many colleges, the evening adult education programs are expected to expand in the future. Thus, the future market among night commuters is probably more encouraging than the current picture shown in Figure 9–8.
- *Competitive position.* Is there a lot of competition in the segment now or is there likely to be in the future? The less the competition, the more attractive the segment is. For example, if the college dormitories announce a new policy of "no meals on weekends," this segment is suddenly more promising for your restaurant.
- *Cost of reaching the segment.* A segment that is inaccessible to a firm's marketing actions should not be pursued. For example, the few nonstudents who live in the area may not be economically reachable with ads in newspapers or other media. As a result, do not waste money trying to advertise to them.
- *Compatibility with the organization's objectives and resources.* If your restaurant doesn't have the cooking equipment to make breakfasts and has a policy against spending more money on restaurant equipment, then don't try to reach the breakfast segment.

As is often the case in marketing decisions, a particular segment may appear attractive according to some criteria and very unattractive according to others.

Choose the segments   Ultimately, a marketing executive has to use these criteria to choose the segments for special marketing efforts. As shown in Figure 9–8, let's assume you've written off the breakfast market for two reasons: too small market size and incompatibility with your objectives and resources. In terms of competitive position and cost of reaching the segment, you choose to focus on the four student segments and not the three nonstudent segments (although you're certainly not going to turn away business from the nonstudent segments). This combination of market-product segments—your target market—is shaded in Figure 9–8.

Take Marketing Actions to Reach Target Markets

The purpose of developing a market-product grid is to trigger marketing actions to increase revenues and profits. This means that someone must develop and execute an action plan.

Your Wendy's segmentation strategy   With your Wendy's restaurant you've already reached one significant decision: there is a limited market for breakfast, so you won't open for business until 10:30 A.M. In fact, Wendy's first attempt at a breakfast menu was a disaster and was discontinued in 1986. Wendy's evaluates possible new menu items continuously, not only to compete with McDonald's (and now its chicken fajitas and pizza) but with a complex array of supermarkets, convenience stores, and gas stations that sell reheatable packaged foods as well as new "easy-lunch" products.

Another essential decision is where and what meals to advertise to reach specific market segments. An ad in the student newspaper could reach all the student segments, but you might consider this "shotgun approach" too expensive and want a more focused "rifle approach" to reach smaller segments. If you choose three segments for special actions (Figure 9–9), advertising actions to reach them might include:

- *Day commuters* (an entire market segment). Run ads inside commuter buses and put flyers under the windshield wipers of cars in parking lots used by day commuters. These ads and flyers promote all the meals at your restaurant to a single segment of students—a horizontal cut through the market-product grid.
- *Between-meals snacks* (directed to all four student markets). To promote eating during this downtime for your restaurant, offer "Ten percent off all purchases between 2:00 and 4:30 P.M. during winter quarter." This ad promotes a single meal to all four student segments—a vertical cut through the market-product grid.
- *Dinners to night commuters.* The most focused of all three campaigns, this ad promotes a single meal to a single student segment. The campaign might consist of a windshield flyer offering a free Frosty with the coupon when the person buys a hamburger and french fries.

Depending on how your advertising actions work, you can repeat, modify, or drop them and design new campaigns for other segments you feel warrant the effort. This

FIGURE 9–9

Advertising actions to reach specific student segments

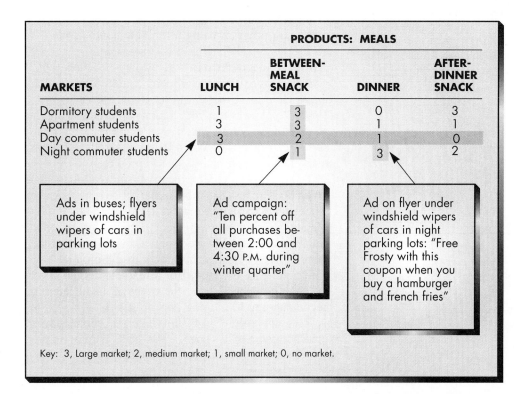

What market segments for Apple's computers are represented by these photos? The Marketing NewsNet box and text discussion provide insights into Apple's market segmentation strategy.

example of advertising your Wendy's restaurant is just a small piece of a complete marketing program using all the elements of the marketing mix.

Apple's segmentation strategy   Steven Jobs and Stephen Wozniak didn't realize they were developing today's multibillion-dollar PC industry when they invented the Apple II in a garage in 1976. Under Jobs's inspirational leadership through the early 1980s, Apple was run with a focus on products and little concern for markets. Apple's control of its brainy, creative young engineers was likened to "Boy Scouts without adult supervision."[10] When IBM entered the PC market in 1981, Apple lost significant market share, and many experts predicted it wouldn't survive.

Today Apple's chief executive officer Gilbert Amelio is seeking to formalize and give cohesiveness to Apple's market segmentation strategy and target specific Apple machines to particular market segments. The core business is built on Apple's line of Macintosh computers, which it continues to enhance. As in most segmentation situations, a single Apple product does not fit into an exclusive market niche. Rather, there is overlap among products in the product line and also among the markets to which they are directed. But a market segmentation strategy enables Apple to offer different products to meet the needs of the different market segments, as shown in the accompanying Marketing NewsNet box.

Recently Apple has introduced a more powerful line of Power Macs and incorporated Apple's speedy PowerPC chip in its products. At the same time, it faced some critical competitive problems:

MARKETING NEWSNET

APPLE'S SEGMENTATION STRATEGY: SEARCH FOR THE RIGHT NICHES

"Camp Runamok" was the nickname some computer industry wags gave to Apple Computer in the early 1980s because the entrepreneurial company had no coherent series of product lines directed at identifiable market segments.

Today, Apple has targeted its various lines of Macintosh computers at specific market segments, as shown below. Because the market-product grid shifts as a firm's strategy changes, the one shown here is based on Apple's product line in early 1996.

The market-product grid below is a simplification because each "product" is really a series of Macintosh computers in that line. Each series has computers that vary by requirements of the user, such as amount of memory needed, DOS compatibility, availability of internal CD-ROM drive, and so on. There is also an overlap of likely market segments from one product line to the other.

Nevertheless, the grid suggests a market-product strategy for Apple's product lines: Performas for home, small business, and school users; PowerBooks for travelers; and Power Macs for those needing more sophisticated applications. And coming in 1996 and 1997: a line of "info appliances" priced under $1000 targeted at home and small business users and running multimedia CD-ROMs and connecting to the Internet.

MARKETS		PRODUCTS					
		INFO APPLI-ANCES	MACINTOSH COMPUTERS			WORK-GROUP SERVERS	MONITORS & PRINTERS
SECTOR	SPECIFIC SEGMENT		PER-FORMAS	POWER-BOOKS/ DUOS	POWER MACS		
Home	Basics, games	✓	✓				✓
Small business	Administration	✓	✓				✓
School	Students/faculty		✓				✓
	Administration		✓	✓		✓	✓
College/ university	Students/faculty		✓	✓	✓	✓	✓
	Administration			✓	✓	✓	✓
Large business	Administration			✓	✓	✓	✓
	Tech./scientific				✓	✓	✓

- *Decline in market share.* Apple's market share of world sales of new personal computers fell by more than 1 percent, from 8.2 percent the last quarter of 1994 to 7.1 percent the last quarter of 1995.[11]
- *The introduction of Windows 95™.* The 1995 launch of Microsoft's Windows 95™ software system had the effect of making IBM-compatible PCs have more of the user friendliness of Apple's Macintosh line, reducing Apple's competitive advantage. Macintosh loyalists responded by noting that "Windows 95™ is Mac 89."[12]
- *Major price cuts.* Fearing a loss of market share, Apple cut the prices on some of its Macintoshes from 10 to 40 percent in late 1995 and early 1996.[13]
- *Shortage of computers for sale.* The very appealing features on its new, high-end PowerMacs and large price cuts caused demand to surge. But Apple had not forecast this huge demand, so suppliers for its unique components could not

meet Apple's production needs, causing huge 1995 shortages for those Macintoshes.[14]

During this time Apple also made some important strategic decisions such as signing up "clone makers"—a revolutionary step for Apple—that, in turn, gives potential software developers more incentive to write programs for use on Macintoshes.

To exploit Apple's strengths, CEO Gilbert Amalio in 1996 initiated an aggressive target marketing strategy:

- Stress its effectiveness in key applications such as desktop publishing, multimedia production, and education; also, design a "seamless" Internet capability into its new computers.[15]
- Continue to focus on market niches where it is strong—the home, school, business, and entertainment markets.[16] For example, a carefully crafted Macintosh Performa ad targets the home market by using the credibility of Apple's 18 years of experience in school computers to suggest readers "bring learning home with the Performa."
- Simplify the product line by focusing on its "best of class" products and introducing a new line of low-priced "info appliances" that are a TV-based, multimedia CD-ROM platform and Internet browser.[17]

Competition is fierce in all these areas. For example, almost all PC makers are now targeting the 68 million U.S. homes without a home computer, and prices are taking a nosedive. But Apple's segmentation strategy makes it optimistic.[18]

CONCEPT CHECK

1. What are some of the variables used to segment consumer markets?

2. What are some criteria used to decide which segments to choose for targets?

3. Why is usage rate important in segmentation studies?

ANALYZING MARKET SEGMENTS USING CROSS TABULATIONS

To do a more precise market segmentation analysis of your Wendy's restaurant, suppose you survey fast-food patrons throughout the metropolitan area where your restaurant is located, using the questionnaire shown in Figure 8–7. You want to use this information as best you can to study the market's segments and develop your strategy. Probably the most widely used approach today in marketing is to develop and interpret cross tabulations of data obtained by questionnaires.

Developing Cross Tabulations

A **cross tabulation,** or "cross tab," is a method of presenting and relating data having two or more variables. It is used to analyze and discover relationships in the data. Two important aspects of cross tabulations are deciding which of two variables to pair together to help understand the situation and forming the resulting cross tabulations.

Pairing the questions Marketers pair two questions to understand marketing relationships and to find effective marketing actions. The Wendy's questionnaire in Figure 8–7 gives many questions that might be paired to understand the fast-food business better and help reach a decision about marketing actions to increase revenues. For example, if you want to study your hypothesis that as the age of the

FIGURE 9–10

Two forms of a cross tabulation relating age of head of household to fast-food restaurant patronage

A. ABSOLUTE FREQUENCIES

AGE OF HEAD OF HOUSEHOLD (YEARS)	FREQUENCY			
	ONCE A WEEK OR MORE	2 OR 3 TIMES A MONTH	ONCE A MONTH OR LESS	TOTAL
24 or less	144	52	19	215
25 to 39	46	58	29	133
40 or over	82	69	87	238
Total	272	179	135	586

B. ROW PERCENTAGES: RUNNING PERCENTAGES HORIZONTALLY

AGE OF HEAD OF HOUSEHOLD (YEARS)	FREQUENCY			
	ONCE A WEEK OR MORE	2 OR 3 TIMES A MONTH	ONCE A MONTH OR LESS	TOTAL
24 or less	67.0%	24.2%	8.8%	100.0%
25 to 39	34.6	43.6	21.8	100.0
40 or over	34.4	29.0	36.6	100.0
Total	46.4%	30.6%	23.0%	100.0%

head of household increases, patronage of fast-food restaurants declines, you can cross tabulate questions 9*d* and 3.

Forming cross tabulations   Using the answers to question 3 as the column headings and the answers to question 9*d* as the row headings gives a cross tabulation, as shown in Figure 9–10, using the answers 586 respondents gave to both questions. The figure shows two forms of the cross tabulation:

- The raw data or answers to the specific questions are shown in Figure 9–10A. For example, this cross tab shows that 144 households whose head was 24 years or younger ate at fast-food restaurants once a week or more.
- Answers on a percentage basis, with the percentages running horizontally, are shown in Figure 9–10B. Of the 215 households headed by someone 24 years or younger, 67.0 percent ate at a fast-food restaurant at least once a week and only 8.8 percent ate there once a month or less.

Two other forms of cross tabulation using the raw data shown in Figure 9–10A are as described in problem 7 at the end of the chapter.

Interpreting Cross Tabulations

A careful analysis of Figure 9–10 shows that patronage of fast-food restaurants is related to the age of the head of the household. Note that as the age of the head of the household increases, fast-food restaurant patronage declines, as shown by the boxed percentages on the diagonal in Figure 9–10B. This means that if you want to reach the heavy-user segment, you should direct your marketing efforts to the segment that is 24 years old or younger.

As discussed earlier in the chapter, there are various ways to segment a consumer market besides according to age. For example, you could make subsequent cross

ETHICS AND SOCIAL RESPONSIBILITY ALERT

Ethics

CAN HEAD-TO-HEAD POSITIONING OF A NEW MEDICATION RAISE PATIENTS' COSTS WITHOUT ANY BENEFITS?

The worldwide market for thrombolytics—a medicine to break up blood clots in heart-attack victims—is $600 million a year. The pharmaceutical firm that introduced TPA (for *tissue plasminogen activator*) to compete in the thrombolytics market used high-pressure marketing and a head-to-head positioning strategy to convince doctors they should prescribe TPA rather than the traditional streptokivase. The price: $2,500 per treatment for TPA versus $220 for the older treatment.

Subsequent research showed no difference in the effectiveness of the two medicines. Researchers say U.S. doctors often accept and prescribe the latest drugs because (1) they "are enamored of new technologies," (2) they fear malpractice suits, and (3) cost is not a primary concern in the United States, in contrast to Canada and Europe.

A U.S. Senate committee is looking into what *Time* magazine calls these "overzealous marketing practices in the drug industry." What do you believe should be done?

tabulations to analyze patronage related to where students live and the meals they eat to obtain more precise information for the market-product grid in Figure 9–8.

Value of Cross Tabulations

Probably the most widely used technique for organizing and presenting marketing data, cross tabulations have some important advantages.[19] The simple format permits direct interpretation and an easy means of communicating data to management. They have great flexibility and can be used to summarize experimental, observational, and questionnaire data. Also, cross tabulations may be easily generated by today's personal computers.

Cross tabulations also have some disadvantages. For example, they can be misleading if the percentages are based on too small a number of observations. Also, cross tabulations can hide some relations because each typically only shows two or three variables. Balancing both advantages and disadvantages, more marketing decisions are probably made using cross tabulations than any other method of analyzing data.

The ultimate value of cross tabulations to a marketing manager lies in obtaining a better understanding of the wants and needs of buyers and targeting key segments. This enables a marketing manager to "position" the offering in the minds of buyers, the topic discussed next.

POSITIONING THE PRODUCT

When a company offers a product commercially, a decision critical to its long-term success is how to position it in the market on introduction. **Product positioning** refers to the place an offering occupies in consumers' minds on important attributes relative to competitive offerings. As described in the Ethics and Social Responsibility Alert, positioning strategies can also raise difficult ethical dilemmas.[20]

Two Approaches to Product Positioning

There are several approaches to positioning a new product in the market. Head-to-head positioning involves competing directly with competitors on similar product

You feel it in the seat that wraps firmly around you. You see it in the full analog gauges and ergonomic placement of the controls in front of you. You hear **Punch This.** it in the low rumble of a 215-horsepower dual overhead cam engine, straining at the bit. This is a driver's car. The Pontiac® Grand Prix® GTP Coupe. This is personal space with four-wheel independent suspension and an attitude.

This is a way to recognize your grown-up needs and, at the same time, avoid the ordinary offerings of those who simply manufacture "transportation." Get your hands on a Grand Prix. And find a great driver's road. Then do your soul a favor...PUNCH THIS.

For more information, call 1-800-2PONTIAC.

PONTIAC CARS with a 3-year/36,000-mile no-deductible bumper-to-bumper limited warranty, plus free 24-hour Roadside Assistance and Courtesy Transportation. See your dealer for details.

PONTIAC GRAND PRIX WE ARE DRIVING EXCITEMENT.

Grand Prix GTP® Coupe

USA Proud Sponsor of the 1996 U.S. Olympic Team

Riviera. Advanced technology that's designed to evoke some rather primitive emotions.

Riviera has a stronger body unit than any other luxury coupe in the world. It has a wind parting, aero-efficient shape. And a 3800 Series II Supercharged V6 engine.* All of which is designed to get your heart racing. Riviera by Buick. Express yourself. For more information, call 1-800-4-RIVIERA.

Riviera by Buick

To which market segments are these General Motors cars targeted? Do potential buyers see them as the same or different? For the company's positioning dilemma and strategy, see the text and Figure 9–11.

attributes in the same target market. Using this strategy, Dollar competes directly with Avis and Hertz, and Volvo pits its turbo-charged cars against Porsche.

Differentiation positioning involves seeking a less competitive, smaller market niche in which to locate a brand. Curtis Mathes has promoted its television sets for the quality market with the slogan, "The most expensive television sets money can buy." McDonald's, trying to appeal to the health-conscious segment, introduced its low-fat McLean Deluxe hamburger to avoid direct competition with Wendy's and Burger King. Companies also follow a differentiation positioning strategy among brands within their own product line to try to minimize cannibalization of a brand's sales or shares.

Product Positioning Using Perceptual Maps

A key to positioning a product effectively is the perceptions of consumers. In determining a brand's position and the preferences of consumers, companies obtain three types of data from consumers:

1. Evaluations of the important attributes for a product class.
2. Judgments of existing brands with the important attributes.
3. Ratings of an "ideal" brand's attributes.

From these data, it is possible to develop a **perceptual map,** a means of displaying or graphing in two dimensions the location of products or brands in the minds of

FIGURE 9–11

GM'S strategy to reposition its major car brands from 1982 to 1990 to . . . 2000(?)

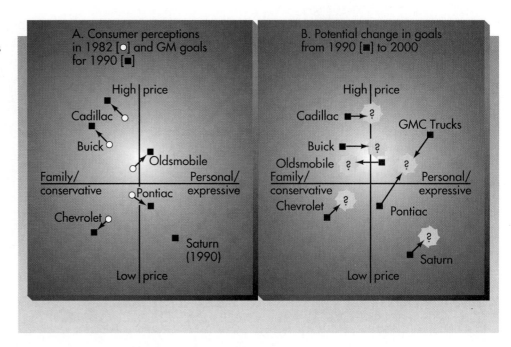

consumers. The example illustrates how a manager can use perceptual maps to see how consumers perceive competing products or brands and then take actions to try to change the product offering and the image it projects to consumers.

By the 1980s General Motors (GM) was concerned that the image of its five main models of U.S. cars—Chevrolet, Pontiac, Oldsmobile, Buick, and Cadillac—had so blurred in the minds of American consumers that they could not distinguish one brand from another. In fact, GM's Cadillac is still trying to overcome bad image problems from its 1981 decision to sell the Cimarron, an "economy" Cadillac that consumers saw as a thinly veiled Chevrolet Cavalier.

So in 1982 GM interviewed consumers and developed the perceptual map shown in Figure 9–11A. Note that the two dimensions on the perceptual map are (1) low price versus high price and (2) family/conservative versus personal/expressive appeal. Figure 9–11A shows that GM indeed had a problem. Although there was some variation in the vertical dimension (consumers' perception of price), there was little difference in the horizontal dimension (family/conservative appeal versus personal/expressive appeal). Then GM set new goals for where it wanted its models to be when its small car Saturn would be introduced (which turned out to be 1990). This involves **repositioning** the models, or changing the place an offering occupies in a consumer's mind relative to competitive offerings.

Figure 9–11A highlights the special 1980s problem GM faced in having its divisions sell nearly identical cars to nearly identical market segments: Pontiac went head-to-head with Chevrolet for younger buyers and Buick and Oldsmobile did the same for the sixtyish segment. So divisions were cannibalizing each others' sales. The figure shows that its 1990 goals included the following:

- Position Saturn as a low-priced, stylish import-fighter.
- Try to reposition Pontiac as a more personal/expressive (stylish) car and Chevrolet as a more family/conservative car.
- Try to reposition Buick as a higher priced, family/conservative car and Oldsmobile as a more stylish car.

Things didn't work out quite the way GM expected. One problem was the sudden love affair Americans had with minivans, trucks, and sports utility vehicles—trends that may be permanent or just fads. To address its positioning dilemma, GM now requires every new model to be targeted at 1 of 26 precisely defined market segments. In theory, no two models are allowed to overlap, which helps separate their positioning. While these 26 market segments have not been made public, we can look at the designs and advertising for its present lines and assess where GM wants the models to be positioned in, say, the year 2000. Figure 9–11B is just such a projection. One thing is certain: Americans of all ages want more stylish cars and are moving to the right in the positioning matrix in Figure 9–11B—especially as minivans and trucks take over more of the "family/conservative" end of the scale.[21]

Cadillac provides a case example. One question summarizes Cadillac's basic problem: how many people under 40 do you know that drive a Cadillac? The average Cadillac buyer is 63! So it's clear that Cadillac must find ways to compete with foreign rivals such as Lexus, Mercedes, and BMW. But how does Cadillac attract younger luxury-car buyers with a sleeker, smaller car without destroying its classic image and losing its present buyers?[22] One thing it didn't need was a luxury sport-utility Cadillac, which executives finally axed in 1995. Cadillac is introducing the Catera, a clone of its European-produced Opel Omega MV6, to try to attract American first-time luxury car buyers.

In 1996 GM announced an especially shocking decision: combining the Pontiac division (selling Bonneville, Grand Prix, Firebird, and Grand Am brands) and the GMC truck division (selling pickup trucks, vans, and sports utility vehicles). The new unit will target younger buyers wanting sportier cars, pickup trucks, and sports utility vehicles whose models will be positioned to emphasize "physical power and outdoor activity."[23]

Looking at GM ads and styling gives the potential repositioning of Cadillac, Pontiac, and other GM cars for the coming years. Are these projections correct? Read the ads and see for yourself. Your personal car buying decisions will affect the outcome as well.

GM's future goes far beyond the American market. With more than $16 billion in global sales in 1994, it was the largest U.S. exporter. GM also recently negotiated a joint venture with China, which represents a huge potential market for the twenty-first century.

CONCEPT CHECK

1. What is cross tabulation?

2. What are some advantages of cross tabulations?

3. Why do marketers use perceptual maps in product positioning decisions?

SUMMARY

1. Market segmentation is aggregating prospective buyers into groups that have common needs and will respond similarly to a marketing action.

2. A straightforward approach to segmenting, targeting, and reaching a market involves five steps: (*a*) form prospective buyers into segments by characteristics such as their needs, (*b*) form products to be sold into groups, (*c*) develop a market-product grid and estimate size of markets, (*d*) select target markets, and (*e*) take marketing actions to reach the target markets.

3. Marketing variables are often used to represent customer needs in the market segmentation process. For consumer markets, typical customer variables are region, metropolitan statistical area, age, income, benefits sought, and usage rate. For industrial markets, comparable variables are geographical location, size of firm, and Standard Industrial Classification (SIC) code.

4. Usage rate is an important factor in a market segmentation study. Users are often divided into heavy, medium, and light users.

5. Nonusers are often divided into prospects and non-prospects. Nonusers of a firm's brand may be important because they are prospects—users of some other brand in the product class that may be convinced to change brands.

6. Criteria used (*a*) to segment markets and (*b*) to choose target segments are related but different. The former includes potential to increase profits, similarity of needs of buyers within a segment, difference of needs among segments, and feasibility of a resulting marketing action. The latter includes market size, expected growth, the competitive position of the firm's offering in the segment, and the cost of reaching the segment.

7. A market-product grid is a useful way to display what products can be directed at which market segments, but the grid must lead to marketing actions for the segmentation process to be worthwhile.

8. Cross tabulations are widely used today in market segmentation studies to identify needs of various customer segments and the actions to reach them.

9. A company can position a product head-to-head against the competition or seek a differentiated position. A concern with positioning is often to avoid cannibalization of the existing product line. In positioning, a firm often uses consumer judgments in the form of perceptual maps to locate its product relative to competing ones.

KEY TERMS AND CONCEPTS

market segmentation p. 234
market segments p. 234
product differentiation p. 234
market-product grid p. 237
synergy p. 239
usage rate p. 243

80/20 rule p. 244
cross tabulation p. 252
product positioning p. 254
perceptual map p. 255
repositioning p. 256

CHAPTER PROBLEMS AND APPLICATIONS

1. What variables might be used to segment these consumer markets? (*a*) lawnmowers, (*b*) frozen dinners, (*c*) dry breakfast cereals, and (*d*) soft drinks.

2. What variables might be used to segment these industrial markets? (*a*) industrial sweepers, (*b*) photocopiers, (*c*) computerized production control systems, and (*d*) car rental agencies.

3. In Figure 9–9 the dormitory market segment includes students living in college-owned residence halls, sororities, and fraternities. What market needs are common to these students that justify combining them into a single segment in studying the market for your Wendy's restaurant?

4. You may disagree with the estimates of market size given for the rows in the market-product grid in Figure 9–9. Estimate the market size, and give a brief justification for these market segments: (*a*) dormitory students, (*b*) day commuters, and (*c*) people who work in the area.

5. Suppose you want to increase revenues from your fast-food restaurant shown in Figure 9–9 even further. What advertising actions might you take to increase revenues from (*a*) dormitory students, (*b*) dinners, and (*c*) after-dinner snacks from night commuters?

6. Look back at Figure 8–7. Which questions would you pair to form a cross tabulation to uncover the following relationships? (*a*) frequency of fast-food restaurant patronage and restaurant characteristics important to the customer, (*b*) age of the head of household and source of information used about fast-food restaurants, (*c*) frequency of patronage of Wendy's and source of information used about fast-food restaurants, or (*d*) how much children have to say about where the family eats and number of children in the household.

7. Look back at Figure 9–10A. (*a*) Run the percentages vertically and tell what they mean. (*b*) Express all numbers in the table as a percentage of the total number of people sampled (586) and tell what the percentages mean.

8. In Figure 9–10, (*a*) what might be other names for the three patronage levels shown in the columns? (*b*) Which is likely to be of special interest to Wendy's and why?

CASE 9–1   Paisley Park Records

Video

How do you market—and perhaps "reposition"—George Clinton, a legendary musician/songwriter? That is the marketing task facing Paisley Park Records, Prince's record label. It is also an important issue for Alan Leeds, vice president in charge of Paisley Park Records, and—of course—George Clinton, whose recording opportunities are under study.[24]

THE ARTIST

George Clinton is one of the most respected and influential musician/songwriters in the popular music industry. Since the early 1970s, he has been instrumental in the ongoing development and refinement of what is now called Urban Contemporary music. He is considered the Father of Funk, the dance-oriented rhythm and blues that has dominated African-American popular music in the last 15 years. He has also inspired musical genres from Hip Hop to Rap.

Clinton's best known work was in the late 1970s and 1980s, with the groups Parliament and Funkadelic and their amalgam P-Funk. All of the major songwriter/producers (the people who dominate Urban Contemporary music in the 1990s) claim Clinton as a mentor and an influence—this includes Prince, Jimmy Jam and Terry Lewis, Teddy Riley, L.A. and Babyface, etc.

Clinton is probably the second most sampled songwriter, behind only James Brown. "Sampling" is a term unique to the late 1980s and 1990s and is the result of the increasing use of computers in the creation of music. A "sample" is a small piece of a previously recorded song that is used in a new song or composition. Samples vary in length but generally involve a few bars of a song—sometimes only a single instrument (a guitar solo, a bass line) or all the elements (rhythm, vocals, solos). Clinton's music is sampled primarily by Rappers.

Clinton's persona is, to some extent, better known than his music. A frequent guest on David Letterman and MTV, BET, and other video-oriented programs, Clinton's long, rainbow-colored hair is a familiar trademark. His irreverent humor pokes fun at the normal image of the rock'n'roll or R&B Rhythm and Blues star. And, although he has not had a "hit" record (sales of more than half a million units) in years, he still has a large, highly loyal following.

THE COMPANY

Paisley Park Records is a small record label associated with and distributed and marketed by Warner Bros. Records. Paisley Park chooses its acts and then oversees the recording, marketing, and packaging. Warner Bros. then manufactures the records themselves, distributes them to retailers, and takes the primary responsibility for marketing the records—advertising, contacts with radio stations, television video, etc.

Make no mistake about it: Paisley Park is Prince's record label. Although run by Alan Leeds, Prince himself is the final decision maker on who the label signs and records. In that sense, Paisley Park is different from most other record companies. Most companies have large A&R (artists and repertoire) staffs; these are people who weed out the many artists seeking to be signed to the labels. At Paisley Park Records, the decisions on whom to sign are more likely to be personal than at other labels.

THE ISSUES

The marketing problem is that George Clinton has *not* had a hit record in years. In 1990, he signed a new recording contract with Prince's Paisley Park Records label. And the addition of George Clinton to that label's short roster probably was more a personal decision by

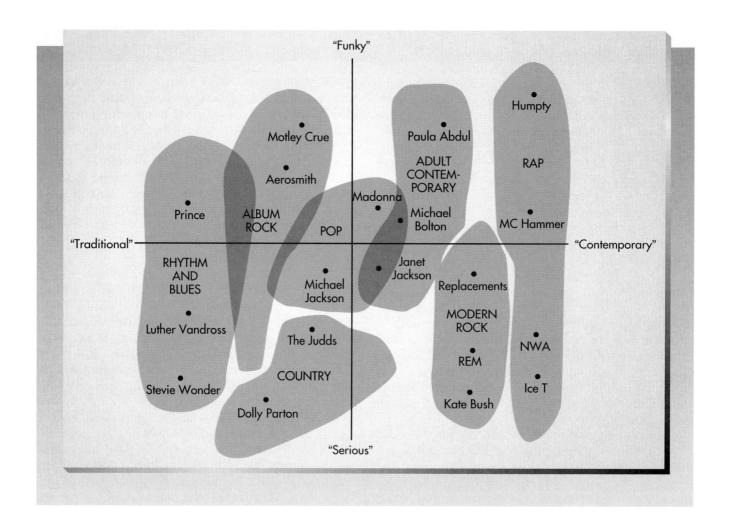

Prince—a sincere fan of Clinton—than a purely business decision. Upon signing, Prince immediately gave Clinton a small part in his moderately successful film, "Graffitti Bridge."

A significant part of Clinton's problem is that he doesn't seem to fit into any of the many market segments within the music industry—particularly the two key conduits for marketing in the industry, radio and music video television. Although he is clearly a legend in the Urban Contemporary market, Urban Contemporary program directors and DJs are not interested in his new music—they perceive Clinton as an "oldie" performer and are less likely to play his new material. Pop or CHR radio (Contemporary Hits Radio, the modern equivalent of Top 40 radio formats) see Clinton as too much an Urban Contemporary artist for their formats. And, though MTV will interview Clinton at almost any opportunity, they are very slow to play his videos. The results are that Clinton's records generally sell about 100,000 units each, based on the loyalty of his core audience.

Alan Leeds, Clinton, and his advisors want to develop a long-term strategy to reposition George Clinton.

When Clinton signed with Paisley Park, he had already completed an album, "Cinderella Theory," that was to be released on that label. The Paisley Park strategy is to use the marketing of "Cinderella Theory" to prepare the way for the release of Clinton's future albums.

As they look at Clinton's past music and marketing, several features emerge:

- Clinton's irreverent humor that viewers see on MTV and the David Letterman show is carried through on Clinton's longstanding use of "cartoon" graphics on his albums.
- Clinton's lyrics for his music have great depth and sophistication, a fact often lost on listeners and viewers.
- Traditionally George Clinton has been almost the only artist featured in his music—seldom using important backup support.

As they analyze the opportunities for repositioning George Clinton, they see two key dimensions to the music segments relative to Clinton's opportunities: (1) a traditional-to-contemporary dimension and (2) a serious-to-funky dimension. They reach two big decisions: (1) make Clinton more "contemporary" on the first dimension and (2) make Clinton more "serious" on the second dimension. Given these marketing strategy decisions, what actions should George Clinton, Alan Leeds, and Paisley Park Records take to implement these plans?

Questions

1. What are some of the key reasons an artist of the stature of George Clinton has problems getting a hit record at this stage of his career?

2. What specific market segments would you target to give new life to George Clinton's career?

3. Suppose we develop the perceptual map on the opposite page by plotting the two dimensions described in the case along the two axes. Suppose that some key *Billboard* magazine charts are positioned about as shown. (There is actually more overlap among the charts that, for simplicity, has not been shown.) What are some of the potential advantages and disadvantages of trying to reposition George Clinton to make him (*a*) more "contemporary" and (*b*) more "serious"? Locate George Clinton's (*c*) present position on the perceptual map and (*d*) the new position he is moving toward.

4. What marketing actions would you recommend to achieve the repositioning of George Clinton?

CAMP Jeep 95

CAMP HALE • COLORADO • SEPT. 8 • 9 • 10

There's Only One Jeep...

CHAPTER 10

Relationship Marketing, Information Technology, and Forecasting

AFTER READING THIS CHAPTER YOU SHOULD BE ABLE TO:

• Define and explain the use and importance of relationship marketing.

• Describe how information technology and database marketing have led to today's relationship marketing strategy.

• Describe the factors that have made relationship marketing both necessary and possible.

• Recognize structured and unstructured marketing decisions and their impact on data used in information systems.

• Recognize the top-down and buildup approaches to forecasting sales.

• Use the lost-horse and linear trend extrapolation methods to make a simple forecast.

GOOD NEWS FOR CONSUMERS: OLD-FASHIONED, PERSONALIZED RELATIONSHIPS ARE BACK!

If you own a Saturn, a Jeep, or a Harley-Davidson motorcycle you may recently have been surprised to receive a personal invitation to meet with other vehicle owners and manufacturer representatives. Saturn, for example, invited all Saturn owners to a "homecoming party" at its Spring Hill, Tennessee, assembly plant. Chrysler invited Jeep owners to a "Camp Jeep" weekend in Colorado, and Harley-Davidson regularly invites members of its Harley Owners Group (HOG) to regional, national, and international motorcycle rallies.

If you often shop from catalogs, you may have noticed that they seem to have more products that match your interests. Catalog companies can now digitally print individualized catalogs: frequent shirt buyers get extra shirt selections, book purchasers more book options, younger consumers more sporting goods, older customers more convenience items. Similarly, credit card companies such as American Express send offers in your bill that are related to recent purchases.

If you read your direct-mail offerings you have probably received personal notes such as the following:

> Thank you, Mrs. Hughes, for completing your payments on women's apparel. To show our thanks we are offering you up to 50 percent savings plus deferred payment until next January 6th.

You may have also read a magazine containing an ad with your name and a personal appeal in it.

Why are you are receiving so much attention? Firms are trying to develop long-term, personal relationships with current customers. The actions acknowledge the potential for repeat purchases and the high cost of replacing existing customers. These one-to-one marketing activities are made possible by giant databases filled with

Marketing information in today's databases can be displayed creatively to help target specific households or customers.

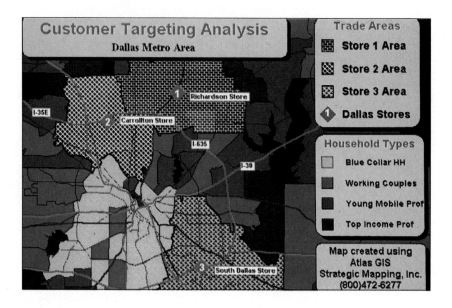

information on a household's or individual's purchase histories, sizes, anniversary and birth dates, store patronage, and television viewing behavior. They give companies the power to almost duplicate with you the kind of old-fashioned relationship small-town or neighborhood retailers had with your grandparents![1]

Welcome to the era of relationship marketing! In this context, relationship marketing has a far more specific meaning than simply good relationships with customers. Here, the term **relationship marketing** is an organization's effort to develop a long-term, cost-effective link with individual customers for mutual benefit.[2] Relationship marketing extends the concept of market segmentation described in the last chapter to marketing actions undreamed of a decade ago. For example, when using geographic market segmentation, grocery product firms and supermarket chains have found that it isn't good enough to focus on a city or even a ZIP code; they are now narrowing the target to a bull's-eye of an individual household or specific person in that household. Today's databases enable marketing strategists to identify these target customers with computer analyses and displays (like that shown above) and to reach specific households with personal, customized offers.

The result: a revolution in marketing information collection and use that will restructure the links between American and international firms and their customers into the twenty-first century. This chapter first discusses customer value in the age of information and then covers what has made relationship marketing both necessary and possible, how information technology is used in marketing, and sales forecasting.

CREATING CUSTOMER VALUE AND COMPETITIVE ADVANTAGE IN THE AGE OF INFORMATION

Advances in our ability to collect and use information have led many to refer to this period as the age of information. To understand the impact of information and information technology on consumers and businesses today let us (1) discuss the new consumer "marketspace," (2) describe the elements of information-based marketing, and (3) illustrate these concepts with the example of American Airlines' reservation system.

The New Consumer Marketspace

Consumers and businesses today face two types of markets—the traditional *marketplace,* where physical buyers and physical sellers meet, and the new information-based electronic marketplace, or *marketspace.* For example, banks offer a physical office and on-line services, airlines sell tickets at airports and through electronic reservation systems, and some newspapers are now available in print and electronic form. Other offerings, such as voice mail, may exist only in the marketspace. While the end result of transactions in the two markets may be similar, the process of creating value is very different.

When transactions occur in the marketspace, information is accessed more easily, arranged in different ways, and available in larger amounts. In addition, consumers learn about and purchase products differently than they do in the marketplace. To provide value, companies must determine how information can be useful to consumers. At Digital Equipment Corporation, for example, a World Wide Web site is available for prospective customers to contact sales representatives or search for products. Similarly, Federal Express customers can now locate a package in transit or identify the name of the person who accepts it through the FedEx World Wide Web site. Information technology such as the World Wide Web also facilitates the development of relationships between buyers and sellers in the marketspace.[3] The Marketing NewsNet box on the next page discusses some of the possible implications of continued growth of the marketspace in the future.[4]

Three Key Elements of Information-Based Marketing

Figure 10–1 shows three elements in the structure that develop continuing, one-to-one relationships between an organization and its customers: (1) information technology, (2) database marketing, and (3) relationship marketing.

Information technology   Since the advent of computers after World War II and personal computers in the 1980s, management perceptions of the value and use of information have changed significantly. Even the terms are changing: while a decade ago managers talked about *manufacturing information systems* and *marketing information systems,* the lines of separation of information among the various departments in a firm are now disappearing. So today, all generally fall under the

Individual Marketplace and Marketspace Customers

- **Relationship marketing** Goal is to have the organization develop a long-term, cost-effective individual relationship with customers.

- **Database marketing** Goal is to provide the organization with continuously updated demographic, media, and consumption information about households and individuals.

- **Information technology** Goal is to design and manage the computer and communications system of a firm to support its database marketing and relationship marketing actions.

MARKETING NEWSNET

Technology

RACING ON THE INFORMATION SUPERHIGHWAY

In his book, *The Road Ahead*, Microsoft founder Bill Gates suggests that we are witnessing a technological revolution that will change the way we buy, sell, work, learn, and communicate. Specifically, he says:

> Over the next decade, businesses worldwide will be transformed. Software will become friendlier, and companies will base the nervous systems of their organization on networks that reach every employee and beyond, into the world of suppliers, consultants, and customers.

The implications of these changes for consumers and businesses are enormous. The information superhighway will create an electronic marketplace, or "marketspace," which consists of information about products and services and electronic (rather than face-to-face) interaction in any location with a computer and a communication line. As Gates observes:

> All the goods for sale in the world will be available for you to examine, compare, and, often, customize. When you want to buy something you'll be able to tell your computer to find it for you at the best price offered by any acceptable source or ask your computer to "haggle" with the computers of various sellers.

In addition, marketing managers will be able to operate more effectively. Bill Tuszynski, manager of new-business development at Inolex Chemical Company, is an example of someone taking advantage of existing information technology. Through the Internet and other on-

line services, Bill monitors the tactics of competitors, scans chemical industry bulletin boards for product ideas, and checks "home pages" of startups that might become suppliers of materials. The Acer ad shown above emphasizes that the technology is readily available today.

Many other benefits of the information superhighway are certainly likely. Some experts suggest that company size will become less important. Others suggest that value added will become the predominant basis for product evaluations. Whatever the future holds, it is clear that the race to get there is on!

---

broader term of **information technology,** which involves designing and managing a computer and communication system to satisfy an organization's requirements for information processing and access.[5]

With the existence of today's massive databases, marketing managers are able to query and analyze data almost instantaneously. For example, a product manager at Borden, which produces Classico pasta sauce, can query a database to discover that Classico will sell well in 75 to 80 percent of West Coast stores—and which of these stores should put Classico on their shelves.[6]

Database marketing The Classico example suggests marketing strategies at the store level. Many firms have discovered this is not good enough—they need to target specific households, individuals, or organizational customers. Enter database marketing, the middle step in Figure 10–1. **Database marketing** is an organization's effort to collect demographic, media, and consumption profiles of customers in order to target them more effectively.

Relationship marketing uses personal messages to communicate with customers.

As described later in the chapter, mass media such as TV and magazines are becoming less and less cost-effective in reaching customers, so database marketing often utilizes direct marketing tools—such as catalogs—to target customers efficiently. For example, Lillian Vernon started her very successful mail-order company four decades ago at her kitchen table by putting all her merchandise in a single catalog: laundry baskets and men's slippers on one page might be followed by toys on the next. But in the last few years Lillian Vernon has shifted to a database marketing approach with the 150 million catalogs she mails annually. There are now home-oriented, children's, and Christmas-ornament catalogs targeted at customers who have purchased these kinds of merchandise from her main catalog in the past.[7]

Relationship marketing   While database marketing is a giant step beyond the traditional market segmentation strategy, it still falls short of the ideal—a near-personal or one-to-one continuing interaction between the seller and customer.[8] As shown in the top step of Figure 10–1, this leads to today's focus on relationship marketing—an organization's effort to develop a long-term, cost-effective link with individual customers for mutual benefit. Consumers benefit in several ways. First, the marketing programs directed at them should be much more efficient—exposing them only to offerings they are very likely to want or need. Second, many consumers value the personal attention and convenience of relationship marketing. Finally, the availability of detailed information about consumer preferences should eliminate unnecessary duplication of products and services.[9] Companies that are successful at relationship marketing create a competitive advantage over rivals who do not use information and information technology as an asset.

Relationship marketing applies to organizations as well as ultimate consumers.[10] For example, from its Los Angeles headquarters, Viking Office Products sends catalogs to office managers throughout the United States and in Britain and France. All its products—from office chairs to Scotch Magic Tape—come with a one-year guarantee. And if you misspelled the boss's name on a letterhead order, Viking replaces it at no cost. Because its computers have tracked every order since 1984, Viking is able to print 50 versions of its catalog, each with a different format or product mix, that are targeted at different segments. Viking's information technology and relationship marketing strategy permits, for example, a personalized offer of a 50 percent discount on binders to a bookkeeper who hasn't purchased binders in the past.[11]

SABRE: An Information Age Success Story

American Airlines uses its SABRE reservation system to obtain a competitive advantage

SABRE is a computerized travel reservation system developed by American Airlines at a cost of $1.5 billion. The system, which allows travel agents to make airline, hotel, and rental car reservations, has been so successful that it is now used by more than 29,500 travel agencies around the world and boasts an operating margin six times that of the airline business.[12] One of the reasons SABRE is so profitable is that it collects fees from:

- Other airlines for flights they book on SABRE (typically $2.25 per reservation).
- Hotels and car rental firms for reservations they receive on SABRE.
- Travel agents who lease SABRE terminals.

During one recent year, SABRE accounted for 10 percent of all hotel reservations, 20 percent of all car rentals, and 45 percent of all airline reservations made through travel agents. Along with United Airlines' Apollo computerized reservation system, the two airlines in the past decade have used their information technology capabilities to virtually preempt other channels of ticket distribution—thereby providing huge strategic marketing advantages. Such advantages for SABRE include[13]

- *Barriers to entry.* It could cost competing airlines hundreds of millions of dollars to develop and implement a system comparable to SABRE—a near-impossible task in today's deregulated airline structure.
- *Increasing switching costs.* While a travel agency might change computerized airline reservation systems, the cost of retraining agents makes such a plan very costly and likely to be error prone.
- *Competitive intelligence.* SABRE not only permits American to utilize countless sales reports by travel agency and geographic market areas, but it can react to competitors' fare reductions or scheduling changes because they must be entered *in advance* on the SABRE system.
- *Innovative marketing strategies.* To promote customer loyalty, American introduced "Advantage," the industry's first frequent-flier program, which was possible only through SABRE's capability for customer tracking.

Further, almost 100 "yield managers" working in American Airlines' Dallas headquarters use SABRE's query and analysis capability to balance fare prices, fare travel restrictions, and seat availability to try to maximize revenues.

Just as the SABRE technology gave American a competitive advantage, new technologies are now posing a threat. Ticket sales through the Internet and commercial on-line services could soon reduce the number of airline tickets sold through travel agents by 50 percent. In response, American is investing in new ways for travel agents, consumers, and corporations to purchase travel products. For example, easySABRE, a consumer version of the agent system, is now available on 12 on-line services, and Travelocity, an electronic travel service was introduced in 1996. Similarly, American is developing software for corporations to use to make travel purchases without the use of an agent.[14]

Many firms are looking for similar ways to use their information technology to achieve a competitive advantage over other firms in their industry. Examples throughout the chapter will illustrate how they are trying to achieve this.

CONCEPT CHECK

1. What is relationship marketing?

2. How do information technology and database marketing relate to relationship marketing?

3. How has SABRE provided a competitive advantage for American Airlines?

RELATIONSHIP MARKETING: THE REVOLUTION ARRIVES

As shown in Figure 10–2, relationship marketing forces today's marketing manager to be increasingly aware of many complex factors. To comprehend further how relationship marketing has revolutionized today's market segmentation and marketing mix actions, it is necessary to analyze (1) what has made relationship marketing necessary and (2) what has made relationship marketing possible.

What Makes Relationship Marketing Necessary: The Causes

Two sources of marketing problems have helped trigger the rise of relationship marketing: (1) more demanding consumers and (2) excessive business costs.

More demanding consumers   As mentioned in Chapter 3, today's consumers are constantly changing. But Box 1 in Figure 10–2 notes that one common factor remains: consumers are far more demanding than they were even five years ago. Research studies show that consumers

- *Want "personalized" offerings.* Consumers increasingly seek the combination of product and services that are tailored to their unique wants and needs. For example, 10 days after specifying their unique wants in a new car order, Japanese consumers buying a Toyota will have their built-to-order car.
- *Desire high quality and value.* Consumers are willing to pay a premium for quality, the characteristics of which Americans rank from top to bottom as:

FIGURE 10–2

Complex factors influence marketing managers as they develop relationship marketing strategies

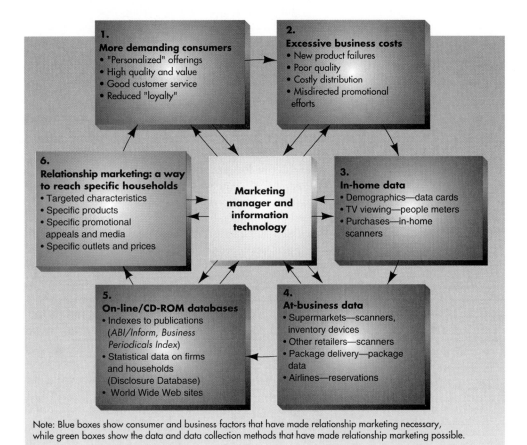

Note: Blue boxes show consumer and business factors that have made relationship marketing necessary, while green boxes show the data and data collection methods that have made relationship marketing possible.

What may lie in your future: press a touch-sensitive screen at your supermarket checkout counter to receive coupons or recipes while your bill is tallied. The text describes how checkout screens like this are replacing national TV and magazine ads.

reliability, durability, ease of maintenance, ease of use, a known or trusted brand name, and (last) low price.[15]

- *Require "caring" customer service.* Effective customer service means having the seller's representatives treat customers like they want to be treated. For IBM this means an electronic customer support system that automatically diagnoses potential trouble to alert IBM service people, who sometimes show up on a customer's doorstep *before* the glitch appears on the customer's IBM equipment.[16]
- *Have reduced loyalty to sellers.* For today's consumer, the issue is not that a product, brand, or store served their needs last year but whether it will serve their needs today. Sellers have discovered that defecting customers exact a terrible price in lost revenues, which re-emphasizes the importance of the continuing customer links of relationship marketing. Studies show that reducing customer defections by 5 percent increases the future profit stream from 30 percent to 85 percent, depending on the business. IBM estimates that if it can improve satisfaction 1 percent for worldwide customers of its world-class AS/400 minicomputers, it will increase revenues by over $200 million in the next five years.[17]

Excessive business costs   Box 2 in Figure 10–2 identifies some of the key sources of excessive business costs that have driven today's manufacturers and retailers to use relationship marketing. Poor quality can lead directly to new product failures (discussed in greater detail in Chapter 11), customer defections, and billions of dollars in lost revenues and profit. Surveys of top executives of U.S. firms show that they feel improving product and service quality is the most critical challenge facing them in the coming years.

Gaining distribution on retailers' shelves is increasingly costly and, as will be discussed in Chapter 11, may actually require manufacturers to pay for retail shelf space for new products. The cost of retail distribution has triggered relationship marketing strategies because both retailers and manufacturers now have computerized records telling them how much revenue retail shelf space should and actually does generate. Products not meeting sales targets are dropped.

In past years, large grocery product manufacturers spent hundreds of millions of dollars annually on radio, TV, and magazine advertisements. Much of this was wasted because consumers have become increasingly blasé about these messages, many of which are no longer penetrating the consumers' consciousness.[18] The result: these grocery product firms have cut back substantially on national advertising campaigns and instead use database marketing and relationship marketing strategies to select more cost-effective methods to communicate with the specific customers they want to reach. An example is the checkout-counter screen at some supermarkets (shown above) that can give customers coupons to encourage repeat purchases, buying complementary products (e.g., coupons for baby food to those buying diapers), or even switching to competing brands.

ETHICS AND SOCIAL RESPONSIBILITY ALERT

APPLYING SUNSHINE PRINCIPLES TO CONSUMER INFORMATION DATABASES

As the use of database marketing programs increases, companies are faced with increasing concerns by consumers regarding the collection and use of personal information. Legislation has addressed some of the concerns. For example, federal laws now specify that video rental stores may sell their customer lists only with customer permission and restrict cable television companies' use and release of customer information. In addition, some states now restrict the release of charity records, motor vehicle and driving records, telephone company listings, and voter registration records.

Rather than rely on regulatory restrictions, however, business professors Frank Cespedes and Jeff Smith suggest that the database marketing industry should follow a "sunshine principle." That is, database practices should be able to withstand the scrutiny of interested consumers in the light of full disclosure. Their approach includes several guidelines:

1. Data users must have the clear assent of the data subject to use personal data for database marketing purposes.
2. Companies are responsible for the accuracy of the data they use, and the data subjects should have the right to access, verify, and change information about themselves.
3. Categorizations should be based on actual behavior as well as the more traditional criteria of attitudes, lifestyles, and demographics.

What are the advantages and disadvantages of these guidelines for consumers? For companies?

As an indication of the importance of this trend, Donnelly Marketing Inc.'s annual survey of marketing practices indicates that 56 percent of manufacturers and retailers are currently building a customer database. Industry expert John Cummings estimates that more than 800 companies already operate database programs for more than 1700 brands. Most active in this group were RJR Nabisco, Ralston Purina Co., Kraft, Gerber Products, and Procter & Gamble.[19] An executive from Kraft General Foods highlighted the reason for this trend: "[When] . . . you see your heavy-user franchise, how are you going to communicate with those people through mass media?"[20]

Two potential drawbacks emerge in developing the huge databases often needed for relationship marketing. One is cost, which is estimated to be $1.74 per name for a consumer product.[21] A second drawback is the growing concern by consumers about the collection of personal information. The accompanying Ethics and Social Responsibility Alert describes guidelines that may address issues of privacy and reduce consumers' concerns.[22]

What Makes Relationship Marketing Possible: Information Technology

Marketing data have little value by themselves: they are simply facts or statistics. To translate data to information the data must be unbiased, timely, pertinent to the problem, accessible, and organized and presented in a way that helps the marketing manager make decisions that lead to marketing actions. This section covers key sources of information—including consumers' homes, businesses, single-source data services, and on-line databases—that have been revolutionized by technological break-throughs in the collection, organization, and presentation of marketing data.

In-home data   To develop relationship marketing strategies, as shown in Box 3 in Figure 10–2, marketing managers need large amounts of raw data about consumers and their households—their demographics and lifestyles, TV viewing habits, use of other promotional media (such as magazines, newspapers, and coupons), and their purchases. Historically there have been two especially severe problems in collecting these data: (1) the cost and (2) the potential bias in the data collected. Breakthroughs in technology in the past decade have addressed both issues. Recently invented "smart cards" now contain detailed data on a consumer's demographics, lifestyle, and household. In-home optical scanners used by services such as Arbitron can record purchases not captured by, say, supermarket scanners. Data on TV viewing and use of other promotional media such as coupons and direct mail are captured electronically and inexpensively with little intrusion on the consumer's activities. It is important to avoid intruding on a consumer to avoid having the measurement process alter the consumer's normal behavior. This concern is the reason Nielsen plans to replace today's people meters with "passive people meters." If these work as planned, its image-recognition computerized camera will automatically record who in the household is watching TV without the intrusion of their having to push buttons to register their TV viewing behavior.

At-business data   Business firms themselves (Box 4, Figure 10–2) collect huge volumes of detailed data for relationship marketing purposes. All of us have seen our supermarket checkout clerks use electronic optical scanners that "read" the universal product code (UPC) on our purchased items to record on our sales slip. More than 95 percent of all U.S. supermarkets with annual sales over $2 million now use scanners, whose detailed data now enable supermarkets and manufacturers to track performance weekly by store, product category, and brand level.[23] Other retailers such as department stores, mass merchandisers, and clothing stores are increasingly using scanners to track purchases.

Other businesses use electronic tracking of purchases, inventories, and reservations to facilitate their database marketing actions. The SABRE computer system used by American Airlines, described earlier in the chapter, tracks airline, hotel, and rental car reservations. UPS delivery people use hand-held computers that scan a special UPS label and double as data-input keyboards to collect real-time data that permit the location of packages to be identified throughout their trips. Kirin's sales representa-

tives use hand-held computers to track beverage inventories in the stores; then they walk to their truck to input these data into a larger computer that prints the customer's invoice and sends the data back to the company headquarters.[24] And available now at your computer store: "notepad computers" that enable you to write directly on the screen with a special stylus to create handwritten letters, numbers, and drawings while working. State Farm Insurance is developing these so that a claims adjuster for auto damages can mark the damaged auto part on an exploded-view diagram and let the notepad calculate the cost of repair, as shown at left.

A Kirin salesperson uses his hand-held computer to track beverage inventories throughout the distribution system (right), while a State Farm Insurance agent uses a notepad computer to process a claim (above).

KIND OF INFORMATION	NAME	DESCRIPTION
Indexes, abstracts, and full-text information from journals and periodicals	ABI/Research*	Covers over 800 publications on business and management topics
	Wilson Business Abstracts*†	Covers 345 journals and trade publications on business and management topics
	National Newspaper Index	Covers stories in newspapers such as the *New York Times* and *The Wall Street Journal*, plus newswire services
	Lexis Nexis	Gives full-text information from more than 650 U.S. and overseas periodicals and abstracts from more than 1,000 sources
Statistical and directory data on households, products, and companies	Compact Disclosure SEC*	Gives data on more than 11,000 publicly traded corporations required to file U.S. Security and Exchange Commission reports
	D & B Dun's Financial Records	Gives financial data on more than 750,000 public and private companies in the United States
	County and City Data Book*	Gives social/economic statistics on U.S. geographic areas from U.S. Census Bureau and 15 other federal agencies

*Also available on CD-ROM.
†Formerly called "Business Periodicals Index."

Source: Judy Wells and Nancy Herther, business reference librarians, University of Minnesota Libraries.

Single-source data: putting it all together   New marketing data services have now emerged that offer **single-source data,** information provided by a single firm on household demographics and lifestyle, purchases, TV viewing behavior, and responses to promotions such as coupons and free samples.[25] The significant advantage of single-source data is the ability of one service to collect, analyze, and interrelate all this information. BehaviorScan, offered by Information Resources, Inc., tracks about 60,000 households in 26 U.S. market areas. Campbell Soup's Swanson frozen dinners used the information from a single-source data service to shift a TV ad campaign from a serious to light theme and increase sales of Swanson dinners 14 percent.[26]

On-line and CD-ROM databases   With a personal computer, a modem, and some communications software, you can access about 5,000 on-line databases (Box 5, Figure 10–2). Hence, use of on-line databases is no longer restricted to large corporations and reference librarians. As shown in Figure 10–3, information in on-line databases divides into two general categories: (1) indexes to articles in publications, which are accessed through key word searches, and (2) statistical and directory data on households, products, and companies. When desired, this information can be transferred to the user's computer. Because of the cost of the telecommunications link to these on-line databases, many libraries obtain these databases in a CD-ROM (compact disk, read-only memory) format. Often updated monthly, one

Web sites such as Time
Warner's Pathfinder can be
useful sources of information.

CD-ROM disk can contain the same amount of information as an entire 20-volume encyclopedia. Many other sources of information can now be accessed through the Internet and the World Wide Web. Web sites often provide useful information or a means of requesting additional information.[27]

CONCEPT CHECK

1. What are the factors that have made relationship marketing (*a*) necessary and (*b*) possible?

2. How do consumer products firms use relationship marketing to reach individual households or consumers?

3. What is single-source data?

USING INFORMATION TECHNOLOGY IN MARKETING

Let's look at (1) when information technology is needed in marketing and (2) key elements in an information system.

When Information Technology Is Needed in Marketing

Not every firm needs information technology to help it make marketing decisions. The need for it is largely determined by (1) the value versus the cost of marketing information and (2) the kinds of decisions a marketing manager makes and how they relate to the information included in the information system.

Trade-offs: value versus cost of marketing data   Information and data can be valuable commodities, but they can also be very expensive. As mentioned earlier, the facts and figures that make up marketing information have no value by themselves. Their value comes from being organized and interpreted to help the decision maker reach better decisions.

In practice, a marketing manager (1) sets the priority of the data from most valuable to least valuable in solving a problem, (2) assesses the cost of collecting each kind of data, and (3) stops collecting more data on the list when the cost of collection outweighs their value in improving the decisions. Although these are very difficult guidelines to apply, they stress an important issue: the value of the data must be balanced against their cost of collection and use. Great care is needed to use information technology that is user-friendly and that assists marketing managers in reaching decisions.

Kinds of decisions a marketing manager makes   A marketing manager makes two distinctly different kinds of decisions. One type is *structured decisions,* routine and repetitive decisions for which standard solutions exist. A product manager for a grocery products manufacturer may plan dozens of sales promotions (coupons and deals) over a five-year period. For these structured decisions the manager can access the information system to determine what will be the impact on case sales of moving the promotion up two weeks or changing a coupon's price allowance.

In contrast, *unstructured decisions* are complex decisions for which there are no standard solutions. For example, a department store manager may ask for an assessment of the impact on sales of changing the department's location within the store. Researchers have found that past experience is especially important for marketing managers in making unstructured decisions such as introducing new products, but not as important for structured decisions such as scheduling consumer promotions.[28]

Marketing consultant Regis McKenna predicts that advances in information technologies will soon allow "real-time" marketing decisions. He envisions "marketing workstations" that will draw on information from a network of databases containing graphic, video, audio, and numeric information. A marketing manager will be able to simulate concepts, obtain instant feedback from others on the network, make changes, request forecasts, write production orders, design advertising, evaluate media options, and schedule the introduction and rollout! In this scenario, information technology becomes a tool for fast and intelligent marketing decisions.[29]

These and many other products are sold to the 100 million households in the *Reader's Digest* database. See the next page to learn why this database is "the best in the business."

The best information database in the consumer product industry   With a worldwide circulation of 20 million—more than that of *Time, Newsweek, U.S. News & World Report,* and *TV Guide* combined—*Reader's Digest* has the largest circulation in the world. But only 31 percent of the firm's profits come from the magazine, which has 39 foreign editions that include Russia and Hungary. The *Reader's Digest* crown jewel is its database that totals 100 million households—half outside the United States. *Fortune* magazine calls this database, simply, "the best in the business." If a household buys the book or video *A Passage to India,* it might receive another book on, perhaps, *Treasures of China,* or a video about India. The database permits relationship marketing and an inexpensive means of testing new product ideas. The firm's president says that the database tells the company the likes and dislikes of its many readers and that "our relationship with the reader is the key to the success of this company."[30]

Key Elements in an Information System

Today's marketing managers are seeking user-friendly information systems to assist them in their decisions. As shown in Figure 10–4, today's strategic information system that helps a marketing manager develop relationship marketing strategies contains five key elements:

1. *Input devices.* These means of collecting marketing data include in-store and in-home scanners, people meters, and purchase/reservation workstations.
2. *Databases.* The marketing data collected by the input devices are stored in diverse databases containing data on households, products, retailers, media, and promotions.
3. *Models.* The models provide hypotheses about the relationships among the data contained in the databases to enable the decision maker to organize, interpret,

FIGURE 10–4

Strategic information system for use in today's relationship marketing decisions

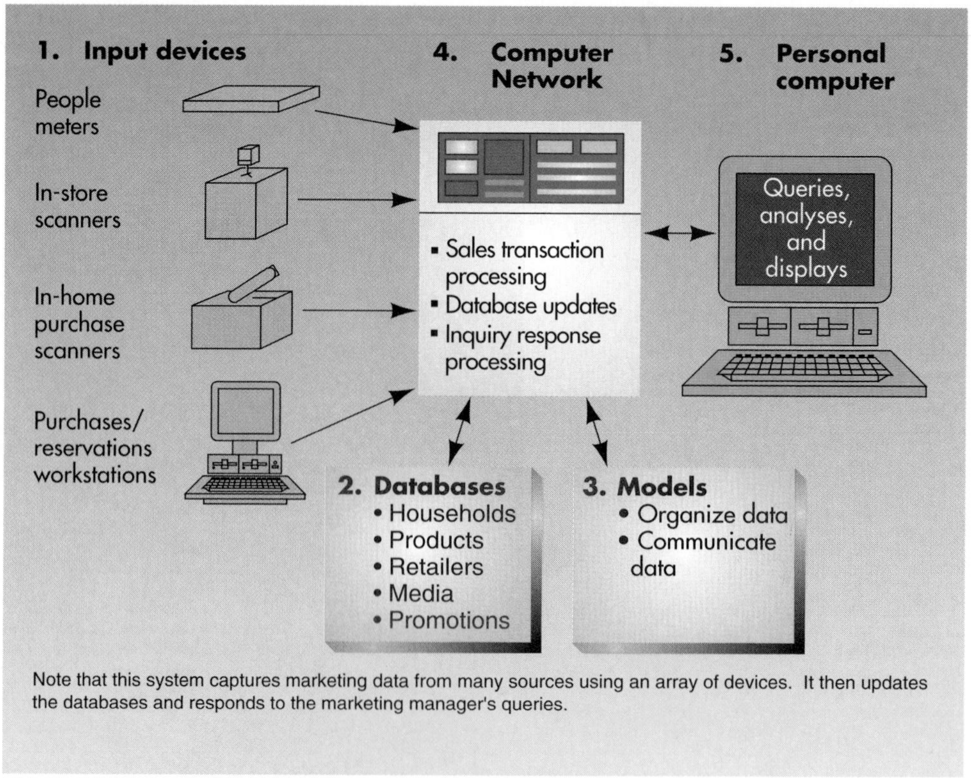

Note that this system captures marketing data from many sources using an array of devices. It then updates the databases and responds to the marketing manager's queries.

and communicate the resulting information in order to reach marketing decisions.

4. *Computer network.* This is today's main means of collecting, processing, and updating the data coming from the input devices, databases, and models.

5. *Personal computer.* The PC on the marketing manager's desk serves as an input and output device and a means of querying the system to obtain and analyze the data it contains.

An information system such as this permits a marketing manager to reach decisions using **sensitivity analysis,** asking "what if" questions to determine how changes in a factor such as price or advertising affect marketing results such as sales revenues or profits.

CONCEPT CHECK

1. What is the difference between structured and unstructured decisions for a marketing manager?

2. What are the five elements in an information system?

MARKET AND SALES FORECASTING

Forecasting or estimating the actual size of a market is critical both in relationship marketing decisions and more traditional marketing decisions. This is because overestimating the size of a market may mean wasting research and development, manufacturing, and marketing dollars on new products that fail.[31] Underestimating it may mean missing the chance to introduce successful new products. We will discuss (1) some basic forecasting terms, (2) two major approaches to forecasting, and (3) specific forecasting techniques.

Basic Forecasting Terms

Unfortunately, there are no standard definitions for some forecasting concepts, so it's necessary to take care in defining the terms used.

Market or industry potential   The term **market potential,** or **industry potential,** refers to the maximum total sales of a product by all firms to a segment under specified environmental conditions and marketing efforts of the firms. For example, the market potential for cake mix sales to U.S. consumers in 2000 might be 12 million cases—what Pillsbury, Betty Crocker, Duncan Hines, and other cake mix producers would sell to American consumers under the assumptions that (1) past patterns of dessert consumption continue and (2) the same level of promotional effort continues relative to other desserts. If one of these assumptions proves false, the estimate of market potential will be wrong. For example, if American consumers suddenly become more concerned about eating refined sugar and shift their dessert preferences from cakes to fresh fruits, the estimate of market potential will be too high.

Sales or company forecast   What one firm expects to sell under specified conditions for the uncontrollable and controllable factors that affect the forecast is the **sales forecast,** or **company forecast.** For example, Duncan Hines might develop its sales forecast of 4 million cases of cake mix for U.S. consumers in 2000, assuming past dessert preferences continue and the same relative level of advertising expenditures among it, Pillsbury, and Betty Crocker. If Betty Crocker suddenly cuts its advertising in half, Duncan Hines's old sales forecast will probably be too low.

1994 Regional State Summaries of. . .					
Region State	Population		Effective buying income		Retail sales
	1994 Total Population (Thousands)	Percentage of U.S.	1994 Total EBI ($000)	Percentage of U.S.	1994 Total Retail Sales ($000)	Percentage of U.S.
Middle Atlantic	38,175.2	14.5588	736,362,653	16.5990	307,877,940	13.7366
New Jersey	7,926.4	3.0229	181,947,935	4.1014	72,314,995	3.2265
New York	18,178.8	6.9328	347,315,780	7.8292	134,421,978	5.9975
Pennsylvania	12,070.0	4.6031	207,098,938	4.6684	101,140,967	4.5126

FIGURE 10–5

U.S. population, effective buying income, and retail sales for selected states, 1994

With both market potential estimates and sales forecasts, it is necessary to specify some significant details: the product involved (all cake mixes, only white cake mixes, or only Bundt cake mixes); the time period involved (month, quarter, or year); the segment involved (United States, Southwest region, upper-income buyer, or single-person households); controllable marketing mix factors (price and level of advertising support); uncontrollable factors (consumer tastes and actions of competitors); and the units of measurement (number of cases sold or total sales revenues).

Two Basic Approaches to Forecasting

A marketing manager rarely wants a single number for an annual forecast, such as 5,000 units or $75 million in sales revenue. Rather, the manager wants this total subdivided into elements the manager works with, such as sales by product line or sales by market segment. The two basic approaches to sales forecasting are (1) subdividing the total sales forecast (top-down forecast) or (2) building the total sales forecast by summing up the components (buildup forecast).

Top-down forecast   A **top-down forecast** involves subdividing an aggregate forecast into its principal components. A shoe manufacturer can use a top-down forecast to estimate the percentage of its total shoe sales in a state and develop state-by-state forecasts for shoe sales for the coming year. The "Survey of Buying Power" published annually by *Sales and Marketing Management* magazine is a widely used source of such top-down forecasting information.

For example, as shown in Figure 10–5, the state of New York has 6.93 percent of the U.S. population, 7.82 percent of the U.S. effective buying income, and 5.99 percent of the U.S. retail sales. If the shoe manufacturer wanted to use a single factor related to expected shoe sales, it would choose the factor that has been most closely related to shoe sales historically, in this case the percentage of U.S. retail sales. The top-down forecast would then be that 5.99 percent of the firm's sales would be made in the state of New York.

Sometimes multiple factors are considered, such as the *buying power index* (BPI) developed by *Sales and Marketing Management* magazine that gives weights of 0.2, 0.5, and 0.3, respectively, to the three previously mentioned factors, as follows:

FIGURE 10-6

Buildup approach to a
two-year sales forecast for
Martin Marietta's Aerospace
Vehicle Department

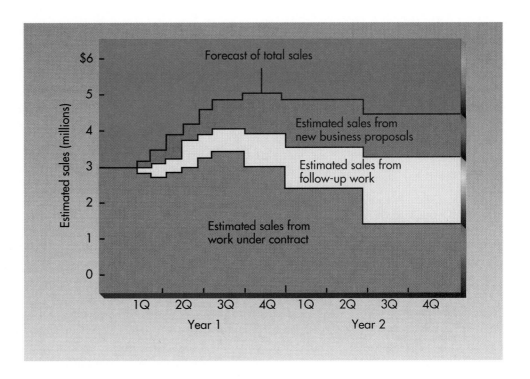

BPI = (0.2 × Percentage of population) + (0.5 × Percentage of effective
      buying income) + (0.3 × Percentage of retail sales)

= (0.2 × 6.9328) + (0.5 + 7.8292)

+ (0.3 × 5.9975)

= 1.3866 + 3.9146 + 1.7993

= 7.100 = 7.1%

Thus the BPI forecasts that 7.1 percent of the firm's shoe sales will occur in New York—significantly higher than if retail sales alone were used for the forecast. The forecast can be customized by using subclassifications of the "Survey of Buying Power" statistics. Population is reported by age group, effective buying income is reported in categories, and retail sales are reported by line of merchandise.

Buildup forecast   A **buildup forecast** involves summing the sales forecasts of each of the components to arrive at the total forecast. It is a widely used method when there are identifiable components such as products, product lines, or market segments in the forecasting problem.

Figure 10–6 shows how Martin Marietta's aerospace department uses the buildup approach to develop a sales forecast involving three broad categories of projects or products: (1) work currently under contract that can be forecast precisely, (2) follow-up work that is likely to result from current contracts, and (3) new business that results from Martin Marietta's proposals for new business, which is difficult to forecast. Each of these three forecasts is the sum of a number of individual products or projects, which for simplicity are not shown. In turn, forecasts for each of the three kinds of business can be summed to give the total sales forecast for the entire department.

Specific Sales Forecasting Techniques

Broadly speaking, three main sales forecasting techniques are available that can lead to the forecasts used in the top-down or buildup approaches. Ordered from least costly in terms of both time and money to most costly, these are (1) judgments of the decision maker, (2) surveys of knowledgeable groups, and (3) statistical methods.

Judgments of the decision maker　Probably 99.9 percent of all sales forecasts are judgments of the person who must act on the results of the forecast—the individual decision maker. An example is the forecasts of likely sales, and hence the quantity to order, for the 13,000 items stocked in a typical supermarket that must be forecast by the stock clerk or manager. A **direct forecast** involves estimating the value to be forecast without any intervening steps. Examples appear in your daily life: How many quarts of milk should I buy? How much time should I allow to drive to the game? How much money should I get out of the automated teller machine? Your mind may go through some intervening steps but so quickly you're unaware of it.

So in estimating the amount of money to get from the automated teller machine, you probably made some unconscious (or conscious) intervening estimates (such as counting the cash in your pocket or the special events you need cash for) to obtain your direct estimate. Lost-horse forecasting does this in a more structured way. A **lost-horse forecast** involves starting with the last known value of the item being forecast, listing the factors that could affect the forecast, assessing whether they have a positive or negative impact, and making the final forecast. The technique gets its name from how you'd find a lost horse: go to where it was last seen, put yourself in its shoes, consider those factors that could affect where you might go (to the pond if you're thirsty, the hayfield if you're hungry, and so on), and go there. For example, a product manager for Wilson's tennis rackets in 1996 who needed to make a sales forecast through 2000 would start with the known value of 1996 sales and list the positive factors (more tennis courts, more TV publicity) and the negative ones (competition from other sports, high prices of graphite and ceramic rackets) to arrive at the final series of annual sales forecasts.

Surveys of knowledgeable groups　If you wonder what your firm's sales will be next year, ask people who are likely to know something about future sales. Four common groups that are surveyed to develop sales forecasts are prospective buyers, the firm's salesforce, its executives, and experts.

A **survey of buyers' intentions forecast** involves asking prospective customers whether they are likely to buy the product during some future time period. For industrial products with few prospective buyers who are able and willing to predict their future buying behavior, this can be effective. For example, there are probably only a few hundred customers in the entire world for Boeing's largest airplanes, so Boeing simply surveys these prospects to develop its sales forecasts.

A **salesforce survey forecast** involves asking the firm's salespeople to estimate sales during a coming period. Because these people are in contact with customers and are likely to know what customers like and dislike, there is logic to this approach. However, salespeople can be unreliable forecasters—painting too rosy a picture if they are enthusiastic about a new product and too grim a forecast if their sales quota is based on it.

A **jury of executive opinion forecast** involves asking knowledgeable executives inside the firm—such as vice presidents of marketing, research and development, finance, and production—about likely sales during a coming period. Although this approach is fast and includes judgments from diverse functional areas, it can be biased by a dominant executive whose judgments are deferred to by the others.

A **survey of experts forecast** involves asking experts on a topic to make a judgment about some future event. A **Delphi forecast** is an example of a survey of experts and involves polling people knowledgeable about the forecast topic (often by mail) to obtain a sequence of anonymous estimates. The Delphi forecast gets its name from the ancient Greek oracle at Delphi who was supposed to see into the future. A

FIGURE 10-7

Linear trend extrapolation of sales revenues of Xerox, made at the start of 1987

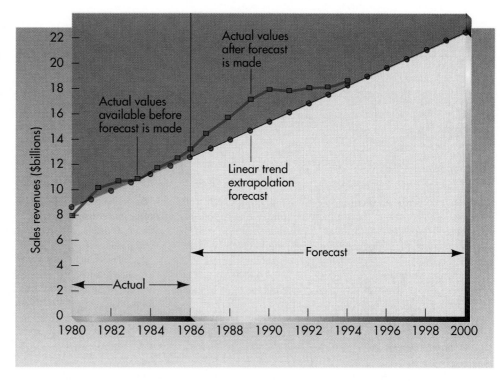

major advantage of Delphi forecasting is that the anonymous expert does not have to defend his or her views or feel obliged to agree with a supervisor's estimate.

A **technological forecast** involves estimating when scientific breakthroughs will occur. In 1963, experts used the Delphi method to estimate the year by which a limited degree of weather control would occur. Their estimate: 1990! While this technological forecast looks silly today, the technique is valuable in helping managers make new product development decisions.

Statistical methods   The best-known statistical method of forecasting is **trend extrapolation,** which involves extending a pattern observed in past data into the future. When the pattern is described with a straight line, it is *linear trend extrapolation.* Suppose that in early 1987 you were a sales forecaster for the Xerox Corporation and had actual sales revenues running from 1980 to 1986 (Figure 10–7). Using linear trend extrapolation, you draw a line to fit the past data and project it into the future to give the forecast values shown for 1987 to 2000.

If in 1995 you want to compare your forecasts with actual results, you are in for a surprise—illustrating the strength and weakness of trend extrapolation. Trend extrapolation assumes that the underlying relationships in the past will continue into the future, which is the basis of the method's key strength: simplicity. If this assumption proves correct, you have an accurate forecast. However, if this proves wrong, the forecast is likely to be wrong. In this case your forecasts from 1987 through 1993 were too low. Xerox's aggressive new product development and marketing in the late 1980s helped alter the factors underlying the linear trend extrapolation and caused the forecast to be too low. However, in 1994 the forecast and actual sales were almost identical.

In practice, marketing managers often use several of the forecasting techniques to estimate the size of markets important to them. Also, they often do three separate forecasts based on different sets of assumptions: (1) "best case" with optimistic assumptions, (2) "worst case" with pessimistic ones, and (3) "most likely case" with most reasonable assumptions.

CONCEPT CHECK

1. What is the difference between the top-down and buildup approaches to forecasting sales?

2. How do you make a lost-horse forecast?

3. What is linear trend extrapolation?

SUMMARY

1. Relationship marketing is an organization's effort to develop a long-term, cost-effective link with individual customers for mutual benefit. It represents a revolutionary extension of market segmentation and, more recently, database marketing.

2. Information and information technology are increasingly seen as a means for a firm to create customer value and to obtain a competitive advantage.

3. Relationship marketing has been made necessary by more demanding consumers and excessive business and marketing costs. More than 800 companies already operate database programs for more than 1700 brands.

4. Relationship marketing has been made possible by breakthroughs in information technology. Key sources of information include consumers' homes, businesses, single-source data services, and on-line databases.

5. Managers generally make two kinds of decisions—structured and unstructured—and must balance the value versus the cost of information.

6. Today's strategic information system used for relationship marketing has five key elements: input devices, databases, models, computer networks, and a manager's personal computer.

7. Two basic approaches to forecasting sales are the top-down and buildup methods. Three forecasting techniques are judgments of individuals, surveys of groups, and statistical methods.

8. Individual judgments are the most widely used forecasting methods. Two common examples are direct and lost-horse forecasts.

9. Asking questions of groups of people who are knowledgeable about likely future sales is another frequently used method of forecasting. Four such groups are prospective buyers, the salesforce, executives, and experts.

10. Statistical forecasting methods, such as trend extrapolation, extend a pattern observed in past data into the future.

KEY TERMS AND CONCEPTS

relationship marketing p. 264
information technology p. 266
database marketing p. 266
single-source data p. 273
sensitivity analysis p. 277
market potential p. 277
industry potential p. 277
sales forecast p. 277
company forecast p. 277
top-down forecast p. 278

buildup forecast p. 279
direct forecast p. 280
lost-horse forecast p. 280
survey of buyers' intentions forecast p. 280
salesforce survey forecast p. 280
jury of executive opinion forecast p. 280
survey of experts forecast p. 280
Delphi forecast p. 280
technological forecast p. 281
trend extrapolation p. 281

CHAPTER PROBLEMS AND APPLICATIONS

1. The chapter described two ways of electronically collecting information on a household's purchases: a scanner at the retailer's sales counter and an in-home scanner. How do these compare in terms of (*a*) quantity of a household's purchases measured and (*b*) possible bias reflected by consumers knowing they are being measured?

2. You walk up to the supermarket checkout counter with six cartons of yogurt you want to buy. (*a*) Describe circumstances under which the checkout procedure with electronic scanner (*1*) will measure all six items and (*2*) could miss the six items. (*b*) What problems do missing sales data cause for relationship marketing?

3. Compare the planned Nielsen passive people meter with the original people meter described in Chapter 8 in terms of (*a*) quality of information about TV viewing and (*b*) ability to get households to participate in the Nielsen TV panel.

4. Aim toothpaste runs an in-store experiment evaluating a coupon along with (*a*) in-store ads in half the stores and (*b*) no in-store ads in the other half of the stores.[32] The results of the Aim experiment are as follows, where a sales index of 100 indicates average store sales in the weeks before the experiment.

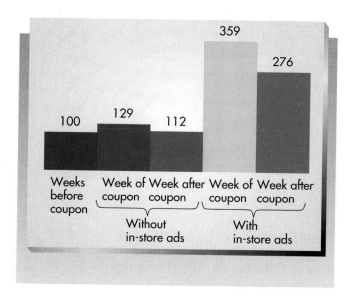

(*a*) What measures of success are appropriate? (*b*) What are your conclusions and recommendations? (*c*) How can marketers use experiments such as this?

5. Another field experiment with coupons and in-store advertising for Wisk detergent is run. The index of sales is as follows:

	WEEKS BEFORE COUPON	WEEK OF COUPON	WEEK AFTER COUPON
Without in-store ads	100	144	108
With in-store ads	100	268	203

What are your conclusions and recommendations?

6. In designing an information system, the format in which information is presented to a harried marketing manager is often vital. (*a*) If you were a marketing manager and interrogated your information system, would you rather see the results as they are shown in question 4 or question 5? (*b*) What are one or two strengths and weaknesses of each format?

7. What is the impact of information technology like that used by American Airlines (SABRE) on consumers, travel agents, corporations, and other airlines?

8. Suppose you are associate dean of your college's business school responsible for scheduling courses for the school year. (*a*) What repetitive information would you include in your information system to help schedule classes? (*b*) What special, one-time information might affect your schedule? (*c*) What standardized output reports do you have to provide? When?

9. Suppose you are to make a sales forecast using a top-down approach to estimate the percentage of a manufacturer's total U.S. sales going to each of the 50 states. You plan to use only a single factor—percentage of U.S. population, percentage of effective buying income, or percentage of retail sales. Which of the three factors would you use if your sales forecast were for each of the following manufacturers, and why? (*a*) Morton salt, (*b*) Christian Dior dresses, and (*c*) Columbia records.

10. Which of the following variables would linear trend extrapolation be more accurate for? (*a*) Annual population of the United States or (*b*) annual sales of cars produced in the United States by General Motors. Why?

CASE 10–1   UPS (A)

Reliability. Dependability. Consistency. These are the attributes that help to foster trust between buyers and sellers and provide the foundation for relationship marketing. United Parcel Service or UPS personifies this commitment to earning the customer's trust—by providing innovations that directly benefit customers in large part through the use of state-of-the-art information technology.

THE COMPANY

UPS was founded in 1907. Committed to serving the customer, UPS has grown to be the largest package and freight delivery service in the world. UPS serves every one of the companies listed in the Fortune 500, delivers to more U.S. addresses than the U.S. Postal service, reaches over 80 percent of the people on earth, and handles more than 12 million packages a day from its air hub in Louisville, Kentucky. The familiar brown trucks and vans have probably delivered packages to you or a member of your family. Today UPS is one of the largest and most profitable privately owned companies in the United States with revenues exceeding $19.5 billion and net profits of $943 million.

THE SERVICE

United Parcel Service offers a wide range of services including next-day, two-day, and three-day delivery options, Saturday delivery, 24-hour tracking and immediate confirmation of delivery, and express service to more than 200 countries and territories worldwide. In addition, UPS has recently introduced a homepage on the World Wide Web (http://www.ups.com) to allow customers to track packages, arrange same-day pickups, and access rate information for costing out shipments. UPS also makes label printers available to its largest customers so they can do their own addressing and increase efficiency.

While UPS was founded on a premise of dependable, quality service almost 90 years ago, the basis for ensuring that service has increasingly been technology based. UPS utilizes a sophisticated computer network to not only track, trace and bill for their transportation services but also to allow for customization of the service to suit the needs of the individual customer.

Information technology allows UPS to capture information electronically for almost immediate use. For example, the technology allows UPS to identify and contact the closest route driver for speedy pick-up of packages. A one-inch square UPS barcode is placed on each and every package which allows the package to be tracked through the UPS system from the sender to the intended recipient. Delivery drivers even capture the signatures from those accepting the delivery with electronic clipboards. International deliveries benefit from the UPS information system that allows for packages to clear customs before the package and plane actually arrive on the ground at their foreign destination in most cases.

UPS's commitment to relationship marketing was instrumental in their gaining a five-year, $1 billion contract with J.C. Penney for their domestic package shipments. This is not a simple agreement to carry and deliver J.C. Penney packages. Rather, it is a contract to work together to improve J.C. Penney's distribution to the mutual benefit of both parties and to create value for consumers. In the words of Ed Brockwell of UPS, "A partnership of this magnitude demands that we bring new technology and solutions to J.C. Penney which will enable them to better control costs and enhance service."

UPS, of course, benefits by obtaining what has been called "the largest distribution contract ever announced in the industry." J.C. Penney, on the other hand, benefits from UPS's expertise in the distribution business. As a result of this partnership, J.C. Penney anticipates customer service improvements and cost reductions in bar-code scanning, paperwork reduction, and increased use of electronic data interchange. So dedicated is UPS to maintaining a long-standing, mutually beneficial relationship with J.C. Penney that they assigned a full-time team, comprised of managers from Engineering, Finance, Information Services, and Customer Service to work with J.C. Penney on its distribution network.

THE COMPETITION

Federal Express is the major competitor to UPS although there are a number of other players in the delivery industry as shown in the table below. The two major rivals have each developed their own versions of computer systems designed to provide closer links between individual business customers and the package and freight delivery service provider. Federal Express pioneered the idea with PowerShip which was followed by UPS's MaxiShip. Both are database systems given to individual business customers. These systems allow shipping customers to store addresses and shipping data, print attractive mailing labels, and track packages.

Package and Freight Delivery Competitors

	Revenues (millions $)	Profits (millions $)	Number of employees
United Parcel Service	21,045	943	335,000
Federal Express	8,479	204	88,502
Pittston	2,667	27	17,829
Airborne Freight	1,071	39	17,412
Air Express Intl.	997	23	4,783

These systems also appear to encourage customer loyalty. After receiving a PowerShip system, Disney Stores increased its use of Federal Express for expedited orders from 60 to 95 percent. UPS claims that business increases at least 20 percent when a customer receives a MaxiShip system. These types of computer systems, referred to as EDI (electronic data interchange) systems

because they allow the buyer and seller to share information, help to strengthen communication and the relationship between shippers and their customers.

THE ISSUES

UPS managers face a complex set of factors which are likely to influence their relationship marketing strategies in the future. First, consumers' needs are constantly changing as they try to match specific services (e.g., next day, two day, etc.) with particular products or businesses. In addition, as businesses expand their activities into the global marketplace, the demand for delivery to a growing number of global destinations will increase. Second, UPS and its customers will continue to need new methods for reducing costs. The Web site, for example, will allow UPS to reduce the cost of human operators required for package-tracking inquiries. Similarly, customers will search for ways to manage their shipping function more efficiently. Third, improving methods of collecting customer-specific data and maintaining an up-to-date database will require continuous management of UPS's information technology. Finally, UPS managers must create personal customized services that will have value for individual customers.

Questions

1. What different types of information technologies does UPS employ? How do they increase customer satisfaction and reduce cost?

2. FedEx, and potentially other competitors, have EDI database systems to more closely link customers with the service provider. How can UPS develop a competitive advantage with their service?

3. What was the role of relationship marketing in UPS's $1 billion contract with J.C. Penney?

PART FOUR

SATISFYING MARKETING OPPORTUNITIES

Part Four covers the unique combination of products, price, place, and promotion that results in an offering for potential customers. How products are developed and managed is the focus of Chapters 11 and 12, and services are covered in Chapter 13. Pricing is covered in Chapters 14 and 15 and Appendix B. Three chapters address the place (distribution) element, which includes retailing innovations. Finally, three promotion chapters cover topics ranging from Sega's integrated marketing communication program, to advertising on ESPN's Website—Sportszone, to Julie Rasmussen's efforts to sell cosmetics in Russia, Ukraine, Kazakhstan, and the Baltics.

The innovation that produced a cast to keep an elephant's leg rigid has led to a bandage that lets a child's knee flex.

An elephant's broken leg is treated with 3M™ Vetcast™ Plus Veterinary Casting Tape, a strong, conformable tape that can bear the animal's huge weight without causing discomfort. But look beyond the physical properties of this remarkable material and you will see its essential element was the spirit of innovation that flourishes here.

The same spirit helped 3M combine multiple technologies to give active people what they've never had before in a bandage. New 3M™Active™ Strips Flexible Foam Bandages cushion and protect hard-to-bandage places like knuckles, knees and elbows, and an advanced water resistant adhesive gives extra sticking power on damp or perspiring skin.

That's the way things work at 3M. With no boundaries to imagination or barriers to cooperation, one good idea swiftly leads to another. So far there have been over 60,000 of them that make your world better, safer, more comfortable.

For a free sample of 3M Active Strips Flexible Foam Bandages, call 1-800-364-3577. That is 1-800-3M-HELPS.

Because they're flexible foam strips, 3M Active Strips Bandages stretch in every direction, conforming to the active body's twists and turns.

3M *Innovation*

CHAPTER 11

Developing New Products

AFTER READING THIS CHAPTER YOU SHOULD BE ABLE TO:

• Understand the ways in which consumer and industrial products can be classified and marketed.

• Explain the implications of alternative ways of viewing "newness" in new products.

• Analyze the factors contributing to a product's success or failure.

• Recognize and understand the purposes of each step of the new-product process.

THE AMERICAN COMPANY THAT IS A "NEW PRODUCTS MACHINE"

Consider these facts about this unique American firm:

• For years it got 25 percent of its revenues from products less than five years old. Its new boss said that wasn't good enough—it had to get 30 percent of sales from products less than four years old. So the company now does it!

• Its researchers are encouraged to spend up to 15 percent of their time on projects of their own choosing—"bootlegging time" they call it.[1] It must work. They obtain more than 500 patents a year.

• More than half its $15 billion of annual revenues from selling its 60,000 products come from outside the United States.

The company? 3M, which barely survived almost a century ago (as Minnesota Mining & Manufacturing) by selling sandpaper—when its early attempt at mining an abrasive mineral failed.

A brief look at one of 3M's important technologies—adhesives—provides us with insights into how its new products enable it to find synergies to design multiple products for multiple markets (discussed in Chapters 9 and 22). In its early years, 3M produced sandpaper by using animal glues to make the abrasive minerals adhere to the paper. While this worked, it was a flawed technology because the animal glue was water-soluble. When the sandpaper got wet, the minerals came off the paper, and the paper fell apart. This forced users to use dry sanding, with the accompanying dust. 3M's search for a better sandpaper led it into the research that makes it a world leader today in adhesives technology. Sometimes 3M wants the "sticking" to be tenacious, sometimes moderate, and sometimes just barely enough.[2]

3M's research on varnishes and glues to use on its sandpaper adhesives have led to other revolutionary new products, such as the tape for the elephant's broken leg on the opposite page. It developed an acrylate adhesive that made possible the introduction of its Scotch™ Magic™ Tape in the 1950s, a tape that can be written on. This 3M adhesives research has also led to dozens of other 3M products, including these:

- 3M™ Post-It® Notes. The adhesive enables you to stick and unstick that note to your friend over and over again.
- 3M™ Active Strips™ Flexible Foam Bandages. The adhesive allows the bandage strip to adhere to moist skin.
- 3M™ Minitran™ Transdermal Delivery System. Used for medical patches like that put behind your ear to reduce airsickness or seasickness, the system actually dissolves the drug in the adhesive in preparation for delivery to the user.
- 3M™ Bow Magic™ Pull Bows. The adhesive bonds four flat pieces of ribbon together that becomes a beautiful bow with just a tug. The latest addition to this line: 3M™ Easy Stick™ Pull Bows with self-stick adhesive on the banding ribbon.[3]
- 3M high-strength structural adhesives. These adhesives make a continuous bond, for example, in cars and airplanes, that's tighter and stronger than spot welds and reduces rattles and weight.

Yes, interested reader, key components of the car you're driving and the airplane you took that last trip in are probably held together by a high-tech 3M glue—oops—adhesive!

The essence of marketing is in developing products such as a new, technologically advanced adhesives to meet buyer needs. A **product** is a good, service, or idea consisting of a bundle of tangible and intangible attributes that satisfies consumers and is received in exchange for money or some other unit of value. Tangible attributes include physical characteristics such as color or sweetness, and intangible attributes include becoming healthier or wealthier. Hence, a product includes the breakfast cereal you eat, the accountant who fills out your tax return, or the American Red Cross, which provides you self-satisfaction when you donate your blood. In many instances we exchange money to obtain the product, whereas in other instances we exchange our time and other valuables, such as our blood.

The life of a company often depends on how it conceives, produces, and markets new products. This is the exact reason that 3M Chief Executive L. D. (Desi) DeSimone has set a company target of 30 percent of sales revenue each year from products that didn't exist four years earlier. In this chapter we discuss the decisions involved in developing and marketing a new product. Chapter 12 covers the process of managing existing products.

THE VARIATIONS OF PRODUCTS

A product varies in terms of whether it is a consumer or industrial good. For most organizations the product decision is not made in isolation because companies often offer a range of products. To better appreciate the product decision, let's first define some terms pertaining to products.

Product Line and Product Mix

A **product line** is a group of products that are closely related because they satisfy a class of needs, are used together, are sold to the same customer group, are distributed through the same type of outlets, or fall within a given price range.[4] Polaroid has two major product lines consisting of cameras and film; Adidas's product lines are shoes and clothing; the Mayo Clinic's product lines consist of inpatient hospital care, outpatient physician services, and medical research. Each product line has its own marketing strategy.

Within each product line is the *product item,* a specific product as noted by a unique brand, size, or price. For example, Downy softener for clothes comes in

Nike's striking ads gain attention for its lines of shoes and clothing.

12-ounce and 22-ounce sizes; each size is considered a separate item and assigned a distinct ordering code, or *stock keeping unit (SKU)*.

The third way to look at products is by the **product mix,** or the number of product lines offered by a company. Cray Research has a single product line consisting of supercomputers, which are sold mostly to governments and large businesses. American Brands, Inc., however, has many product lines consisting of cigarettes (Pall Mall), sporting equipment (Titleist golf balls), distilled beverages (Jim Beam liquors), and even services (Pinkerton security).

Classifying Products

Both the federal government and companies classify products, but for different purposes. The government's classification method helps it collect information on industrial activity. Companies classify products to help develop similar marketing strategies for the wide range of products offered. Two major ways to classify products are by degree of product tangibility and type of user.

Degree of tangibility   Classification by degree of tangibility divides products into one of three categories. First is a *nondurable good,* an item consumed in one or a few uses, such as food products and fuel. A *durable good* is one that usually lasts over an extended number of uses, such as appliances, automobiles, and stereo equipment. *Services* are defined as activities, benefits, or satisfactions offered for sale, such as marketing research, health care, and education. According to this classification, government data indicate that the United States is becoming a service economy, the reason for a separate chapter (Chapter 13) on the topic.

This classification method also provides direction for marketing actions. Nondurable products such as Wrigley's gum are purchased frequently and at relatively low cost. Advertising is important to remind consumers of the item's existence, and wide distribution in retail outlets is essential. A consumer wanting Wrigley's Spearmint Gum would most likely purchase another brand of spearmint gum if Wrigley's were not available. Durable products, however, generally cost more than nondurable goods and last longer, so consumers usually deliberate longer before purchasing them. Therefore, personal selling is an important component in durable-product marketing because it assists in answering consumer questions and concerns.

Marketing is increasingly being used with services. Services are intangibles, so a major goal in marketing is to make the benefits of purchasing the product real to consumers. Thus, Northwest Airlines shows the fun of a Florida vacation or the joy of seeing grandparents. People who provide the service are often the key to its success in the market because consumers often evaluate the product by the service provider they meet—the Hertz reservation clerk, the receptionist at the university admissions office, or the nurse in the doctor's office.

Type of user   The second major type of product classification is according to the user. **Consumer goods** are products purchased by the ultimate consumer, whereas **industrial goods** are products used in the production of other products for ultimate consumers. In many instances the differences are distinct: Oil of Olay face moisturizer and Bass shoes are clearly consumer products, whereas DEC computers and high-tension steel springs are industrial goods used in producing other products or services.

There are difficulties, however, with this classification because some products can be considered both consumer and industrial items. A Macintosh computer can be sold to consumers as a final product or to industrial firms for office use. Each classification results in different marketing actions. Viewed as a consumer product, the Macintosh would be sold through computer stores. As an industrial product, the Macintosh might be sold by a salesperson offering discounts for multiple purchases. Classifying by the type of user focuses on the market and the user's purchase behavior, which determine the marketing mix strategy.

The Tiffany brand of silver is an example of a specialty good.

BASIS OF COMPARISON	TYPE OF CONSUMER GOOD			
	CONVENIENCE	**SHOPPING**	**SPECIALTY**	**UNSOUGHT**
Product	Toothpaste, cake mix, hand soap, laundry detergent	Cameras, TVs, briefcases, clothing	Rolls Royce cars, Rolex watches	Burial insurance, thesaurus
Price	Relatively inexpensive	Fairly expensive	Usually very expensive	Varies
Place (distribution)	Widespread; many outlets	Large number of selective outlets	Very limited	Often limited
Promotion	Price, availability, and awareness stressed	Differentiation from competitors stressed	Uniqueness of brand and status stressed	Awareness is essential
Brand loyalty of consumers	Aware of brand, but will accept substitutes	Prefer specific brands, but will accept substitutes	Very brand loyal; will not accept substitutes	Will accept substitutes
Purchase behavior of consumers	Frequent purchases; little time and effort spent shopping; routine decision	Infrequent purchases; comparison shopping; uses decision time	Infrequent purchases; extensive time spent to decide and get the item	Very infrequent purchases, some comparison shopping

FIGURE 11–1   Classification of consumer goods

CLASSIFYING CONSUMER AND INDUSTRIAL GOODS

Because the buyer is the key to marketing, consumer and industrial product classifications are discussed in greater detail.

Classification of Consumer Goods

Convenience, shopping, specialty, and unsought products are the four types of consumer goods. They differ in terms of (1) effort the consumer spends on the decision, (2) attributes used in purchase, and (3) frequency of purchase.

Convenience goods are items that the consumer purchases frequently, conveniently, and with a minimum of shopping effort. **Shopping goods** are items for which the consumer compares several alternatives on criteria, such as price, quality, or style. **Specialty goods** are items, such as Tiffany sterling silver, that a consumer makes a special effort to search out and buy. **Unsought goods** are items that the consumer either does not know about or knows about but does not initially want. Figure 11–1 shows how the classification of a consumer product into one of these four types results in different aspects of the marketing mix being stressed. Different degrees of brand loyalty and amounts of shopping effort are displayed by the consumer for a product in each of the four classes.

The manner in which a consumer good is classified depends on the individual. One person may view a camera as a shopping good and visit several stores before deciding on a brand, whereas a friend may view cameras as a specialty good and will only buy a Nikon.

The product classification of a consumer good can change the longer a product is on the market. When first introduced, the Litton microwave oven was unique, a specialty good. Now there are competing brands on the market, and microwaves are a shopping good for many consumers.

Classification of Industrial Goods

A major characteristic of industrial goods is that their sales are often the result of *derived demand;* that is, sales of industrial products frequently result (or are derived) from the sale of consumer goods. For example, if consumer demand for Fords (a consumer product) increases, the company may increase its demand for paint spraying equipment (an industrial product). Industrial goods are classified not only on the attributes the consumer uses but also on how the item is to be used. Thus, industrial products may be classified as production or support goods.

Production goods   Items used in the manufacturing process that become part of the final product are **production goods.** These include raw materials such as grain or lumber, as well as component parts. For example, a company that manufactures door hinges used by GM in its car doors is producing a component part. As noted in Chapter 7, the marketing of production goods is based on factors such as price, quality, delivery, and service. Marketers of these products tend to sell directly to industrial users.

Support goods   The second class of industrial goods is **support goods,** which are items used to assist in producing other goods and services. Support goods include installations, accessory equipment, supplies, and services.

- *Installations* consist of buildings and fixed equipment. Because a significant amount of capital is required to purchase installations, the industrial buyer deals directly with construction companies and manufacturers through sales representatives. The pricing of installations is often by competitive bidding.
- *Accessory equipment* includes tools and office equipment and is usually purchased in small-order sizes by buyers. As a result, instead of dealing directly with buyers, sellers of industrial accessories use distributors to contact a large number of buyers.
- *Supplies* are similar to consumer convenience goods and consist of products such as stationery, paper clips, and brooms. These are purchased with little effort, using the straight rebuy decision sequence discussed in Chapter 7. Price and delivery are key factors considered by the buyers of supplies.
- *Services* are intangible activities to assist the industrial buyer. This category can include maintenance and repair services and advisory services such as tax or legal counsel. The reputation of the seller of services is a major factor in marketing these industrial goods.

CONCEPT CHECK

1. Explain the difference between product mix and product line.

2. What are the four main types of consumer goods?

3. To which type of good (industrial or consumer) does the term *derived demand* generally apply?

New Products and Why They Fail

New products are the lifeblood of a company and keep it growing, but the financial risks are large. Before discussing how new products reach the stage of commercialization when they are available to the consumer, we'll begin by looking at *what* a new product is.

Sony's Data Discman: a revolutionary new product that may replace some books.

What Is a New Product?

The term *new* is difficult to define. Does changing the color of a laundry detergent mean it is a new product, as a new hot-air appliance that cooks like a regular oven but with the speed of a microwave would be considered new? There are several ways to view the newness of a product.

Newness compared with existing products   If a product is functionally different from existing offerings, it can be defined as new. The microwave oven and automobile were once functionally new, but for most products the innovation is more a modification of an old product than a dramatic functional change.

Newness in legal terms   The Federal Trade Commission (FTC) advised that the term *new* be limited to use with a product up to six months after it enters regular distribution. The difficulty with this suggestion is in the interpretation of the term *regular distribution.*

Breathe Right® strips: what kind of innovation are they and what does this mean for marketing strategy? For the answers see the text and Figure 11-2.

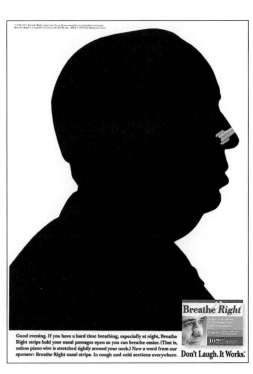

FIGURE 11-2   Consumption effects define newness

	LOW DEGREE OF CHANGE BEHAVIOR AND LEARNING NEEDED BY CONSUMER HIGH		
BASIS OF COMPARISON	**CONTINUOUS INNOVATION**	**DYNAMICALLY CONTINUOUS INNOVATION**	**DISCONTINUOUS INNOVATION**
Definition	Requires no new learning by consumers	Disrupts consumer's normal routine but does not require totally new learning	Establishes new consumption patterns among consumers
Examples	Sensor and New Improved Tide	Electric toothbrush, compact disk player, and automatic flash unit for cameras	VCR, Jet Stream Oven, and home computer
Marketing emphasis	Generate awareness among consumers and obtain widespread distribution	Advertise benefits to consumers, stressing point of differentiation and consumer advantage	Educate consumers through product trial and personal selling

Newness from the company's perspective   Successful companies are starting to view newness and innovation in their products at three levels. At the lowest level, which usually involves the least risk, is a product line extension. This is an incremental improvement of an exciting or important product for the company, such as Frosted Cheerios or Diet Cherry Coke or Sensor for Women—extensions of the basic Cheerios or Diet Coke or men's Sensor product lines, respectively. At the next level is a significant jump in the innovation or technology, such as Sony's leap from the micro tape recorder to the Walkman. The third level is true innovation, a truly revolutionary new product, like the first Apple computer in 1976. Some people wonder whether Sony's Data Discman—a portable electronic book using a removable disk, which may lead to novels, textbooks, and encyclopedias on disks—could be such an innovation.[5] Effective new product programs in large firms deal at all three levels.

Newness from the consumer's perspective   A fourth way to define new products is in terms of their effects on consumption. This approach classifies new products according to the degree of learning required by the consumer, as shown in Figure 11-2.

With *continuous innovation,* no new behaviors must be learned. Breathe Right® nasal strips are an example. In the 1994 Super Bowl San Francisco wide receiver Jerry Rice had what looked like a piece of adhesive tape across his nose. In fact, it was actually a Breathe Right® strip that helped hold his nasal passages open and let him breathe. Partly as a result of the free Super Bowl publicity, sales of Breathe Right® strips skyrocketed—and not just for athletes. The main target market: everyday people who snore. In November, 1995, the U.S. Food and Drug Administration allowed the manufacturer to market the device as a snoring cure when tests showed that 75 percent of people snored less often and less loudly when using the strip than when they didn't. The beauty of this innovation is that neither Jerry Rice nor typical people have to change their behaviors to adopt the product. With consumer products requiring minimal consumer education, such as Breathe Right® strips, effective marketing depends on generating awareness and having strong distribution in appropriate outlets.

With *dynamically continuous innovation,* only minor changes in behavior are required for use. An example is built-in, fold-down child seats such as those available in Chrysler minivans. Built-in car seats for children require only minor bits of

The Jet-Stream Oven: a discontinuous innovation requiring consumer education and learning.

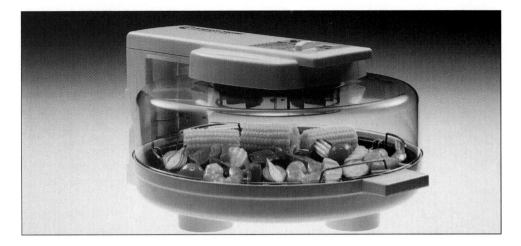

education and changes in behavior, so the marketing strategy is to educate prospective buyers on their benefits, advantages, and proper use.

A *discontinuous innovation* involves making the consumer learn entirely new consumption patterns in order to use the product. In the 1990s American Harvest, a small Midwestern firm, introduced its Jet-Stream Oven—a revolutionary cooking idea that involves moving hot air at high speeds to do the cooking. (See the American Harvest video case at the end of the chapter.) In achieving its claim of "Finally! . . . oven quality, microwave fast," the Jet-Stream Oven requires consumers to learn how to use it properly. Hence, marketing efforts involve not only gaining consumer awareness but also educating consumers on both the benefits and proper use of the innovative product. Personal selling and creative advertising are often needed to achieve this consumer education—activities that can cost millions of dollars for some discontinuous innovations.

Why Products Fail

The thousands of product failures that occur every year cost American businesses billions of dollars. Some estimates place new-product failure rates as high as 80 percent. To learn marketing lessons and convert those potential failures to successes, we can analyze why new products fail and then study several failures in detail. As we

New product success or failure? For the special problems these products face, see the text.

go through the new-product process later in the chapter, we can identify ways such failures might have been avoided—admitting that hindsight is clearer than foresight.

Marketing reasons for new-product failures   Both marketing and nonmarketing factors contribute to new-product failures, as shown in the accompanying Marketing NewsNet box.[6] Using the research results from several studies[7] on new-product success and failure and also those described in the Marketing Newsnet box, we can identify seven critical marketing factors—sometimes overlapping—that often separate new product winners and losers:

1. *Insignificant "point of difference."* Shown as the most important factor in the Marketing NewsNet box, a distinctive "point of difference" is essential for a new product to defeat competitive ones—through having superior characteristics that deliver unique benefits to the user. In the mid-1990s General Mills introduced "Fingos," a sweetened cereal flake about the size of a corn chip. Consumers were supposed to snack on them dry, but they didn't.[8] The point of difference was not important enough to get consumers to give up competing snacks such as popcorn, potato chips, or Cheerios from the box late at night.

2. *Incomplete market and product definition before product development starts.* Ideally, a new product needs a precise *protocol,* a statement that, before product development begins, identifies (1) a well-defined target market; (2) specific customers' needs, wants, and preferences; and (3) what the product will be and do. Without this precision, loads of money disappear as R&D tries to design a vague product for a phantom market. This combines factors 2 and 5 in the Marketing NewsNet box. Prodigy Service, an on-line service that is a joint venture of IBM and Sears Roebuck, has struggled for years to make money because dynamic changes in the marketplace make it difficult to know what services to sell to whom.[9]

3. *Too little market attractiveness.* Shown as Factor 8 in the Marketing NewsNet, market attractiveness refers to the ideal situation every new product manager looks for: a large target market with high growth and real buyer need. But often, when looking for ideal market niches, the target market is too small and competitive to warrant the R&D, production, and marketing expenses necessary to reach it. In the early 1990s Kodak discontinued its Ultralife lithium battery. Seen as a major breakthrough because of its 10-year shelf life, the battery was touted as lasting twice as long as an alkaline battery. Yet the product was only available in the 9-volt size, which accounts for less than 10 percent of the batteries sold in the United States.

4. *Poor execution of the marketing mix.* Coca-Cola thought its Minute Maid Squeeze-Fresh frozen orange juice concentrate in a squeeze bottle was a hit. The idea was that consumers could make one glass of juice at a time, and the concentrate stayed fresh in the refrigerator for over a month. After two test markets, the product was finished. Consumers loved the idea, but the product was messy to use, and the advertising and packaging didn't educate them effectively on how much concentrate to mix.

5. *Poor product quality on critical factors.* Overlapping somewhat with point 1, this factor stresses that poor quality on one or two critical factors can kill the product, even though the general quality is high. For example, the Japanese, like the British, drive on the left side of the road. Until 1996 U.S. carmakers sent Japan few right-drive cars—unlike German carmakers who exported right-drive models in a number of their brands.[10]

6. *Bad timing.* The product is introduced too soon, too late, or at a time when consumer tastes are shifting dramatically. Good timing is a special problem with fad or fashion products (discussed in Chapter 12). Exploding sales to consumers of T-shirts and sweatshirts with names of professional sports teams turned to huge piles of unbought merchandise in 1995, following the baseball

MARKETING NEWSNET

WHAT SEPARATES NEW-PRODUCT WINNERS AND LOSERS

What makes some products winners and others losers? Knowing this answer is a key to a new-product strategy. R. G. Cooper and E. J. Kleinschmidt, studied 203 new industrial products to find the answers shown below.

The researchers defined the "product success rate" of new products as the percentage of products that reached the company's own profitability criteria. Product "winners" are the best 20 percent of performers and "losers" are the worst 20 percent.

Factor Affecting Product Success Rate	Comparison	Winners–Losers
1. Point of difference, or uniquely superior product	18% Bottom 20% / 98% Top 20%	80%
2. Well-defined product before actual development starts	26% / 85%	59%
3. Synergy, or fit, with firm's R&D, engineering, and manufacturing capabilities	29% / 80%	51%
4. Quality of execution of technological activities	30% / 76%	46%
5. Quality of execution of activities before actual development starts	31% / 75%	44%
6. Synergy, or fit, with marketing mix activities	31% / 71%	40%
7. Quality of execution of marketing mix activities	32% / 71%	39%
8. Market attractiveness, ones with large markets, high growth, significant buyer need	43% / 74%	31%

0 20 40 60 80 100
% of Products in Each Group

strike and hockey lockout that alienated many fans. Also, the sports fashions changed. Now hot among kids are sports-related clothes featuring in-your-face slogans like "Life is a contact sport" and "You let up, you lose."[11]

7. *No economical access to buyers.* Grocery products provide an example. Today's mega-supermarkets carry 30,000 different products (meaning they carry 30,000 different SKUs). With more than 15,000 new food products introduced each year, the fight for shelf space is tremendous in terms of costs for advertising, distribution, and shelf space.[12] Because shelf space is judged in terms of sales per square foot, Thirsty Dog! (a zesty beef-flavored, vitamin enriched, mineral loaded, lightly-carbonated bottled water for your dog) must displace an existing product on the supermarket shelves. Many small manufacturers simply do not have the money to gain effective exposure for their products.

FIGURE 11-3

Why did these new products fail?

As explained in detail in the text, new products often fail because of one or a combination of seven reasons. Look at the two products described below, and try to identify which reason explains why they failed in the marketplace:

- Del Monte's Barbecue Ketchup that contained finely chopped onions and was aimed at the heavy ketchup-eating segment.
- Mennen's Real deodorant, a cream-like antiperspirant developed for women, that was applied like a roll-on.

Compare your insights with those in the text.

A look at some failures Before reading further, study the product failures described in Figure 11–3, and try to identify which of the seven reasons is the most likely explanation for their failure. The two examples are discussed in greater detail below.

Del Monte aimed its Barbecue Ketchup to the heavy ketchup-using segment—children and teenagers. The problem is that most consumers in this segment hate onions, so the product's difference—onions mixed with regular ketchup—worked against it. As a result, the target market was too small. The product was subsequently reintroduced as a gourmet sauce for meat cooked on outdoor grills.

Poor execution of the marketing mix hurt Real, Mennen's deodorant. The product was introduced with a $14 million advertising campaign. One problem, though, was that customers found that if they twisted the dispenser too hard, too much cream came out, creating an instant mess. Also, the name Real gave little indication of the product or its benefits.

Developing successful new products may sometimes involve luck, but more often it involves having a product that really meets a need and has significant points of difference over competitive products. The likelihood of success is improved by paying attention to the early steps of the new-product process described in the next section of the text.

CONCEPT CHECK

1. From a consumer's viewpoint, what kind of innovation would an improved electric toothbrush be?

2. What does "insignificant point of difference" mean as a reason for new-product failure?

THE NEW-PRODUCT PROCESS

Companies such as General Electric, Sony, or Procter & Gamble take a sequence of steps before their products are ready for market. Figure 11–4 shows the seven stages of the **new-product process,** the sequence of activities a firm uses to

FIGURE 11-4

Stages in the new-product process

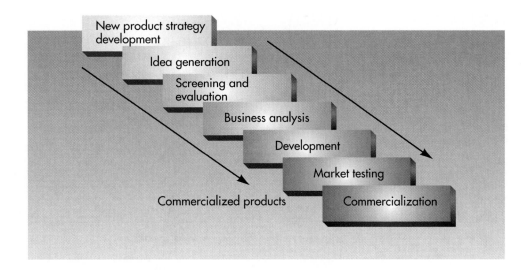

identify business opportunities and convert them to a saleable good or service. This sequence begins with new-product strategy development and ends with commercialization.

New-Product Strategy Development

For companies, **new-product strategy development** involves defining the role for a new product in terms of the firm's overall corporate objectives. This step in the new-product process has been added by many companies recently to provide a needed focus for ideas and concepts developed in later stages.

Objectives of the stage: identify markets and strategic roles   During this new-product strategy development stage the company uses the environmental scanning process described in Chapter 3 to identify trends that pose either opportunities or threats. Relevant company strengths and weaknesses are also identified. The outcome of new-product strategy development is not new-product ideas but identifying markets for which new products will be developed and strategic roles new products might serve—the vital protocol activity explained earlier in the discussion of the Marketing NewsNet on new-product winners and losers.

Booz, Allen & Hamilton, Inc., a national consulting firm, asked firms what strategic role was served by their most successful recent product. These roles, shown in Figure 11–5, help define the direction of new-product development and divide into externally and internally driven factors.

Henry C. Yuen is an example of using an externally driven action to preempt a market segment (Figure 11–5). Not your typical TV couch potato, Yuen tried to tape a baseball game and got only snow. Unlike the rest of us who might just have mumbled, Yuen took his PhD degree in mathematics and co-invented "VCR Plus"—the device millions of TV fans use to set their VCRs by punching in numbers from newspaper listings. To maintain his firm's role as a market innovator (an internally driven strategic role in Figure 11–5), in 1996 he launched "Guide Plus)," which allows viewers to use their VCR to select from the blizzard of today's programs by simply clicking one remote control button.[13]

Cross-functional teams   Another key to 3M's success in new-product development is its use of *cross-functional teams,* a small number of people from different departments in an organization who are mutually accountable to a common set of performance goals. Teams are especially important in new-product development so

FIGURE 11 – 5

Strategic roles of most
successful new products

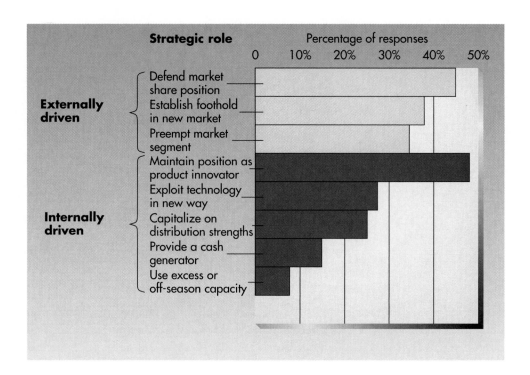

that individuals from R&D, marketing, manufacturing, finance, and so forth can simultaneously search together in a constructive environment for new product and market opportunities. In the past 3M and other firms often utilized these department people in sequence—possibly resulting in R&D designing new products that the manufacturing department couldn't produce economically and that the marketing department couldn't sell. A 3M cross-functional team developed a more environmentally responsible method for manufacturing an emulsifier, without compromising product quality.

Bringing people together from different departments can also lead to great synergies. At 3M the lighting technology that led to its overhead projectors 30 years ago has resulted in $800 million a year sales in lighting-related products that range from highway reflective signs to crystalline structures used on high-tech sandpapers. Marketing synergies also occur, as when a 3M cross-functional team came up with a new venue—the Home Shopping Network—to promote an extended line of 3M™ Bow Magic™ Pull Bows.[14]

3M's experiences suggest some conclusions about today's style of teamwork:

- Teams are ongoing, not just a one-shot effort.
- Teamwork takes time because the members have to learn about each other and find a comfort level.
- Team members can—and do—disagree, and that's okay.
- Teams can be informal or formal, depending on the task that needs doing.
- Teams need "champions," individuals willing and able to carry messages and requests to management and to move the project forward.

Because program and product champions are so important in marketing, they are discussed again in Chapter 22.

Idea Generation

Developing a pool of concepts as candidates for new products, or **idea generation,** must build on the previous stage's results. New-product ideas are generated by consumers, employees, basic R&D, and competitors.

Ultra Pampers: Understanding the needs of Japanese consumers led to a new-product success.

Customer suggestions   Procter & Gamble surveyed Japanese parents and found that they changed their babies' diapers far more frequently than American parents. In response to this market difference, P&G developed Ultra Pampers, a more absorbent diaper that makes frequent changing less necessary. Today, Ultra Pampers is the market leader in Japan.

Companies often analyze consumer complaints or problems to discover new-product opportunities. They also pose complaints to a sample of consumers, who are asked to suggest products with such deficiencies in order to identify new product opportunities. Listening to growing concerns about cholesterol and fat in its food, McDonald's reformulated its shakes with a low-fat mixture and introduced a low-fat hamburger.

Employee and co-worker suggestions   Employees may be encouraged to suggest new product ideas through suggestion boxes or contests. The idea for General Mills's $350 million-a-year Nature Valley Granola Bars came when one of its marketing managers observed co-workers bringing granola to work in plastic bags.

Research and development breakthroughs   Another source of new products is a firm's basic research, but the costs can be huge. Sony is the acknowledged world leader in new-product development in electronics. Its scientists and engineers produce an average of four new products each business day. Sony's research and development breakthroughs have led to innovative products, and its ability to manufacture and market those products has made it a legend in the electronics industry, popularizing VCRs, the Walkman, and—coming into your future?—the Data Discman. Consultants studying the new-product and innovation process say firms need a dual approach to get the most from their R&D: (1) create cultures where new ideas can thrive and (2) have systems that will sift those ideas through the development process and get them to market with lightning speed. Sony seems to have done this for four decades.

R&D's search for new-product ideas can take it to some pretty strange places. Shaman Pharmaceuticals has spent tens of millions of dollars going into the rain forests of South American jungles to observe native healers' (called "shamans") knowledge of medicinal plants to find curative compounds that could then lead to mass-produced drugs. So far it has found two chemicals that may be on your drug store shelves in a few years. Pharmaceutical giants Merck and Eli Lilly are doing much the same thing. University research scientists can use a similar approach. University of Wisconsin Professor Goran Hellekant has patented Brazzein, a protein with 1000 times the sweetness of sugar, that has been consumed for generations by West Africans.[15]

Professional R&D laboratories also provide new-product ideas. Labs at Arthur D. Little helped put the crunch in Cap'n Crunch cereal and the flavor in Carnation Instant Breakfast. Because broccoli is increasingly felt to contain cancer-fighting properties, Little's labs are trying to find ways to make the vegetable more appealing to today's consumers. Some ideas now in test: sweetened broccoli-based vegetable juices and a chocolate-flavored powdered broccoli-juice drink mix. An idea sent back to the drawing boards: broccoli cereal.[16]

Competitive products   New-product ideas can also be found by analyzing the competition. A six-person intelligence team from the Marriott Corporation spent six months traveling around the country staying at economy hotels. The team assessed the competition's strengths and weaknesses on everything from the soundproof qualities of the rooms to the softness of the towels. Marriott then budgeted $500 million for a new economy hotel chain, Fairfield Inns.

Screening and Evaluation

The third stage of the new product process is **screening and evaluation,** which involves internal and external evaluations of the new-product ideas to eliminate those that warrant no further effort.

Internal approach   Internally, the firm evaluates the technical feasibility of the proposal and whether the idea meets the new-product strategy objectives defined in step 1. In 1957 Earl Bakken, founder of Medtronic, built the first external portable heart pacemaker. Working with a team of scientists, Medtronic later built the first implantable pacemaker—a device enabling bedridden people suffering from heart problems to regain their normal, productive lives.

In the mid-1980s Medtronic concluded it had to broaden its products beyond its heart pacemaker line and embarked on a systematic search for new products. In the process it developed an astute new-product development process that reduces the likelihood of failure. Continuing internal evaluation is one key. After investing $10 million in an angioplasty catheter project, Medtronic's evaluation concluded the device was two years behind the competition and shut the project down. But Medtronic redeployed people working on that project that helped lead to four generations of implantable heart defibrillators (devices that regulate an erratic heart beat) introduced in a two-year period—keeping it well ahead of competitors.[17]

External approach   Concept tests are external evaluations that consist of preliminary testing of the new-product idea (rather than the actual product) with consumers. Concept tests usually rely on written descriptions of the product but may be augmented with sketches, mockups, or promotional literature. Several key questions are asked during concept testing: How does the customer perceive the product? Who would use it? How would it be used?

For external evaluations, Medtronic often uses external panels of doctors who initially see and evaluate concepts rather than physical devices. Only after the device

A year's worth of consumer interviews went into the development of Sun Chips.

makes sense to the panel does Medtronic actually design and build it, which is the most expensive and risky stage of the new-product development process.

Frito-Lay spent a year interviewing 10,000 consumers about the concept of a multigrain snack chip. The company experimented with 50 different shapes before settling on a thin, rectangular chip with ridges and a slightly salty, nutty flavor. The product, Sun Chips, is highly successful.

CONCEPT CHECK

1. What step in the new-product process has been added in recent years?

2. What are four sources of new-product ideas?

3. What is the difference between internal and external screening and evaluation approaches used by a firm in the new-product process?

Business Analysis

Business analysis involves specifying the features of the product and the marketing strategy needed to commercialize it and making necessary financial projections. This is the last checkpoint before significant capital is invested in creating a prototype of the product. Economic analysis, marketing strategy review, and legal examination of the proposed product are conducted at this stage. It is at this point that the product is analyzed relative to the firm's marketing and technological synergies, two criteria noted in the Marketing NewsNet shown earlier in the chapter.

The marketing strategy review studies the new-product idea in relation to the marketing program to support it. The proposed product is assessed to determine whether it will help or hurt sales of existing products. Likewise, the product is examined to assess whether it can be sold through existing channels or if new outlets will be needed.

After the product's important features are defined, economic considerations focus on several issues, starting with costs of R&D, production, and marketing. For financial projections, the firm must also forecast the possible revenues from future product sales and forecast market shares. In this stage the firm also estimates how many units of the product must be sold to cover the costs of production and projects a return on investment to determine the profitability.

Microsoft's Windows 95, called "one of the most strategic products ever to hit the personal-computer market" by *The Wall Street Journal,* provides an example. The initial target market for Windows 95 was the existing Microsoft operating systems, MS DOS and Windows 3.1, which run about 100 million computers around the globe and together have an 80 percent market share. Sales projections include 30 million units sold in the four months after release and possibly 100 million units a year starting in 1998. The business analysis underlying this new-product decision involved recognizing that Windows 95 required 15,000,000 lines of computer code and total R&D and marketing costs of $400 million. One reason for this complexity and cost: Microsoft imposed a huge design burden on itself by promising

Customers examine the Japanese language version of Windows 95™, moments past midnight, November 23, 1995 when it was first released in Japan.

compatibility with past software. Hundreds of customer users in the field tried for months to get the bugs out.[18]

As an important aspect of the business analysis, the proposed new product is studied to determine whether it can be protected with a patent or copyright. An attractive new-product proposal is one in which the technology, product, or brand cannot easily be copied. This includes counterfeiting concerns, such as those discussed in the Ethics and Social Responsibility Alert.[19]

Development

Product ideas that survive the business analysis proceed to actual **development,** turning the idea on paper into a prototype. This results in a demonstrable, producible product in hand. Outsiders seldom understand the technical complexities of the development stage, which involves not only manufacturing the product but also performing laboratory and consumer tests to ensure that it meets the standards set. Design of the product becomes an important element.

Liquid Tide, introduced by P&G, looks like a simple modification of its original Tide detergent. However, P&G sees this product as a technological breakthrough: the first detergent without phosphates that cleans as well as existing phosphate detergents.

To achieve this breakthrough, P&G spent 400,000 hours and combined technologies from its laboratories in three countries. The new ingredient in Liquid Tide that helps suspend the dirt in wash water came out of the P&G research lab in Cincinnati. The cleaning agents in the product came from P&G scientists in Japan. Cleaning agent technology is especially advanced in Japan because consumers there wash clothes in colder water (about 70°F) than consumers in the United States (95°F) and Europe (160°F). P&G scientists thought that Liquid Tide also needed water-softening ingredients to make the cleaning agents work better. For this technology it turned to P&G's lab in Belgium, whose experience was based on European water, which has more than twice the mineral content of U.S. wash water.

ETHICS AND SOCIAL RESPONSIBILITY ALERT

Ethics

COUNTERFEIT BRANDS AND PRODUCTS: WHAT COSTS IN LOST SALES, LOST JOBS . . . AND LOST LIVES?

Los Angeles and New York City vie to be #1 in a very dubious category: producer of more merchandise with counterfeit brands and labels than any other American city!

Want a Microsoft CD-ROM encyclopedia? A Disney T-shirt? An "official" National Football League jersey? A Louis Vuitton purse? Or better yet, a $15,000 Cartier watch for $20? LA and the Big Apple are the places to be—but these kinds of goods are increasingly available across the United States.

It's no longer just branded items that are counterfeit. Regular products with no special brand are moving into U.S. markets—many with potentially dire consequences.

Fake birth control pills have caused internal bleeding, phony brake pads have led to car crashes, and bogus bolts have damaged aircraft engines! A lot of this counterfeiting is done offshore and the items smuggled into the United States, so Los Angeles and New York have no monopoly.

No one knows the exact costs, but they are enormous. Brand and trademark forgeries alone are estimated to cost U.S. Industries about $200 billion a year. Foreign counterfeiting of U.S. products is estimated to cost about 750,000 U.S. jobs.

So what's the big deal? Who really loses? What should be done? Who should do it? And pay for it?

The prototype product is tested in the laboratory to see if it achieves the physical standards set for it. Mattel submits its dolls and toys to rigorous tests: it clamps Barbie's foot in steel jaws, then pulls on her head with a wire to make sure her skin or head can't crack, cut, or choke future owners. Prototypes of disposable consumer goods are also subjected to consumer tests, often in-home placements of the product to see if consumers actually perceive it as a better product after they use it. In a blind test consumers preferred Liquid Tide nine to one over the detergent of their own choice tested in their washers.

Industrial products often have special, exacting test requirements. For example, jet engines for commercial aircraft have to pass a "bird strike test" and have minimal

Mattel's laboratory testing subjects its toys and dolls, like Barbie here, to extreme tests to assure quality and protect children.

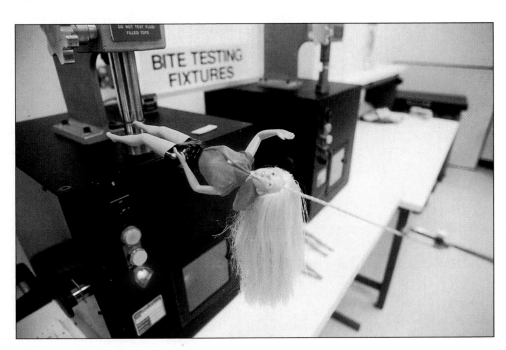

Why do you want General
Electric to pass the "bird strike
test" on its new GE90 jet
engine? For the answer, see
the text.

engine damage when a carasses of ducks or gulls are fired into the whirling jet
engine operating on a test stand. Why this weird field test? To simulate the conditions
that might occur when your plane ingests an unfortunate seagull or duck standing
around on the runway at takeoff. General Electric's huge new GE90 will be used to
power many future Boeing 777 commercial jets. As a result of tests like these GE
engineers redesigned the GE 90's jet engine blades, and it passed its next bird strike
test with flying colors.[20]

Market Testing

The **market testing** stage of the new-product process involves exposing actual
products to prospective consumers under realistic purchase conditions to see if they
will buy. Often a product is developed, tested, refined, and then tested again to get
consumer reactions through either test marketing or purchase laboratories.

Test marketing   Test marketing involves offering a product for sale on a limited
basis in a defined area. This test is done to determine whether consumers will actually
buy the product and to try different ways of marketing it. Only about a third of the
products test marketed do well enough to go on to the next phase. These market tests
are usually conducted in cities that are viewed as being representative of U.S.
consumers. Figure 11–6 shows the cities commonly used for market tests.

In examining the commercial viability of the new product, companies measure
sales in the test area, often with *store audits* that measure the sales in grocery stores
and the number of cases ordered by a store from the wholesaler. This gives the
company an indication of potential sales volume and market share in the test area.

Market tests are also used to check other elements of the marketing mix besides
the product itself such as price, level of advertising support, and distribution. In test
marketing its new compact drink dispenser for small and medium offices, Coca-Cola
analyzed both the distribution channel and the advertising. During the market test,
Coca-Cola discovered that office managers are the people who decide whether

FIGURE 11-6

The most popular test markets

machines are installed in break rooms. Targeting office managers, Coca-Cola introduced its successful dispenser, called BreakMate, in the early 1990s.

There are difficulties with test marketing, a primary one being how well the results can be projected. Representativeness of the test market to the target market for the product is very important. Market tests also are time consuming and expensive because production lines as well as promotion and sales programs must be set up. Costs can run over a million dollars, the exact amount depending on the size of the city and the cost of buying media time or space to advertise the product. Market tests also reveal plans to competitors, sometimes enabling them to get a product into national distribution first or to take actions to disrupt the test markets. When a product can be easily copied by a competitor, test marketing may not be used. Although Hunt-Wesson got its Prima Salsa Tomato Sauce into the test market first, Chesebrough-Pond's Ragu Extra Thick & Zesty beat it into national introduction. Competitors can also try to sabotage test markets. Pepsi ran Mountain Dew Sport Drink in a test market and Gatorade counterattacked furiously with ads and coupons. Pepsi pulled the product off the market. With such problems, some firms skip test markets completely or use simulated test markets.

Simulated test markets   Because of the time, cost, and confidentiality problems of test markets, manufacturers often turn to *simulated* (or *laboratory*) *test markets* (*STM*), a technique that simulates a full-scale test market but in a limited fashion. STMs are often run in shopping malls, where consumers are questioned to identify who uses the product class being tested. Willing participants are questioned on usage, reasons for purchase, and important product attributes. Qualified persons are then shown TV commercials or print ads for the test product along with competitors' advertising and are given money to make a decision to buy or not buy a package of the product (or the competitors') from a real or simulated store environment. If the test product is not purchased, the consumer may receive it as a free sample. Participants are interviewed later for their reactions and the likelihood of repurchase. Based on these reactions, the company may decide to proceed to the last stage of the new product process.

Market testing is a valuable step in the new-product process, but not all products can use it. Testing a service beyond the concept level is very difficult because the service is intangible and consumers can't see what they are buying. Similarly, market testing of expensive consumer products such as cars or VCRs or costly industrial products like jet engines or computers is impractical.

Test markets in supermarkets can be valuable, but they also alert competitors.

Commercialization

Finally, the product is brought to the point of **commercialization**—positioning and launching it in full-scale production and sales. Companies proceed very carefully at the commercialization stage because this is the most expensive stage for most new products, especially consumer products.

Increasing the success rate of new products   In recent years, companies have begun to recognize that speed is important in bringing a new product to market. Recent studies have shown that high-tech products coming to market on time are far more profitable than those arriving late. As a result, some companies—such as Sony, NEC, Honda, AT&T, and Hewlett-Packard—have overlapped the sequence of stages described in this chapter. With this approach, termed *parallel development* (the simultaneous development by cross-functional teams of both the product and the production process), marketing, manufacturing, and R&D personnel stay with the product from conception to production. The results are a significant reduction in new-product development times. Honda has cut car development from five years to three, while Hewlett-Packard has reduced the development time for computer printers from 54 months to 22.

The risks and uncertainties of the commercialization stage   The job is far from over when the new product gets to the commercialization stage. In fact, disasters still often occur. Some examples include the following:

- The high quality of the 5 or 50 prototypes that were handcrafted in the R&D lab with lots of tender loving care can't be replicated on the mass-production lines.
- Costs have gotten so far beyond original budgets that customers won't buy the product at the new price point that must be set to make a profit.
- Buyers can't understand the benefits of the new product without extensive, costly education activities—necessitating new training of the sales force and distributors, along with new videos and infomercials.

Effective cross-functional teams at Hewlett-Packard have reduced new-product development times significantly.

- Competitors introduce their new product a few weeks before the firm's own product hits the market, making the product obsolete before potential customers ever see it.

The last point in the list—bad timing—gives new product managers nightmares. IBM, for example, killed several laptop computer prototypes because competitors introduced better, more advanced machines to the market before IBM. Even well-accepted brands and products that reach the market late can represent significant lost sales. In the mid-1990s General Motors lost at least 100,000 Chevrolet Cavalier and Pontiac Sunfire sales when it couldn't simultaneously retool a factory and introduce new models. It probably lost sales, too, when it announced in 1995 that many new model launches were going to be delayed by six months to two years, extending some introductions to 1998 and 1999.[21]

Grocery products have special problems at the commercialization stage. Because space is so limited on supermarket shelves, many require manufactures to pay a **slotting fee,** a payment a manufacturer make to place a new item on a retailer's shelf. This can run to several million dollars for a single product. But there's even another potential expense. If a new grocery product does not achieve a predetermined sales target, some retailers require a **failure fee,** a penalty payment by a manufacturer to compensate the retailer for sales its valuable shelf space never made. To minimze the financial risk of a new product failure, many grocery product manufacturers use *regional rollouts,* introducing the product sequentially into geographical areas of the United States to allow production levels and marketing activities to build up gradually.

Figure 11–7 identifies the purpose of each stage of the new-product process and the kinds of marketing information and methods used. The figure also suggests information that might help avoid some new product failures. Although using the new-product process does not guarantee successful products, it does increase a firm's success rate.

STAGE OF PROCESS	PURPOSE OF STAGE	MARKETING INFORMATION AND METHODS USED
New product strategy development	Identify new product niches to reach in light of company objectives	Company objectives; assessment of firm's current strengths and weaknesses in terms of market and product
Idea generation	Develop concepts for possible products	Ideas from employees and co-workers, consumers, R&D, and competitors; methods of brainstorming and focus groups
Screening and evaluation	Separate good product ideas from bad ones inexpensively	Screening criteria, concept tests, and weighted point systems
Business analysis	Identify the product's features and its marketing strategy, and make financial projections	Product's key features, anticipated marketing mix strategy; economic, marketing, production, legal, and profitability analyses
Development	Create the prototype product, and test it in the laboratory and on consumers	Laboratory and consumer tests on product prototypes
Market testing	Test product and marketing strategy in the marketplace on a limited scale	Test markets, simulated test markets (STMs)
Commercialization	Position and offer product in the marketplace	Perceptual maps, product positioning, regional rollouts

FIGURE 11–7   Marketing information and methods used in the new-product process

---

CONCEPT CHECK

1. How does the development stage of the new-product process involve testing the product inside and outside the firm?

2. What is a test market?

3. What is commercialization of a new product?

SUMMARY

1. A product is a good, service, or idea consisting of a bundle of tangible and intangible attributes that satisfies consumers and is received in exchange for money or some other unit of value. A company's product decisions involve the product item, product line, and range of its product mix.

2. Products can be classified by tangibility and by user. By degree of tangibility, products divide into nondurable goods, durable goods, and services. By user, the major distinctions are consumer or industrial goods. Consumer goods consist of convenience, shopping, and specialty products. Industrial goods are for either production or support.

3. There are several ways to define a new product, such as the degree of distinction from existing products, a time base

specified by the FTC, a company perspective, or effect on a consumer's usage pattern.

4. In terms of its effect on a consumer's use of a product, a discontinuous innovation represents the greatest change and a continuous innovation the least. A dynamically continuous innovation is disruptive but not totally new.

5. The failure of a new product is usually attributable to one of seven marketing reasons: insignificant point of difference, incomplete market and product definition before product development begins, too little market attractiveness, poor execution of the marketing mix, poor product quality on critical factors, bad timing, and no economical access to buyers.

6. The new-product process consists of seven stages. Objectives for new products are determined in the first stage, new-product strategy development; this is followed by idea generation, screening and evaluation, business analysis, development, market testing, and commercialization.

7. Ideas for new products come from several sources, including consumers, employees, R&D laboratories, and competitors.

8. Screening and evaluation can be done internally or externally.

9. Business analysis involves defining the features of the new product, a marketing strategy to introduce it, and a financial forecast.

10. Development involves not only producing a prototype product but also testing it in the lab and on consumers to see that it meets the standards set for it.

11. In market testing new products, companies often rely on market tests to see that consumers will actually buy the product when it's offered for sale and that other marketing mix factors are working. Products surviving this stage are commercialized—taken to market.

Key Terms and Concepts

product p. 290
product line p. 290
product mix p. 291
consumer goods p. 292
industrial goods p. 292
convenience goods p. 293
shopping goods p. 293
specialty goods p. 293
unsought goods p. 293
production goods p. 294
support goods p. 294

new-product process p. 300
new-product strategy development p. 301
idea generation p. 302
screening and evaluation p. 304
business analysis p. 305
development p. 306
market testing p. 308
commercialization p. 310
slotting fee p. 311
failure fee p. 311

Chapter Problems and Applications

1. Products can be classified as either consumer or industrial goods. How would you classify the following products? (*a*) Johnson's baby shampoo, (*b*) a Black & Decker two-speed drill, and (*c*) an arc welder.

2. Are products such as Nature Valley Granola bars and Eddie Bauer hiking boots convenience, shopping, specialty, or unsought goods?

3. Based on your answer to problem 2, how would the marketing actions differ for each product and the classification to which you assigned it?

4. In terms of the behavioral effect on consumers, how would a PC, such as a Macintosh PowerBook or an IBM ThinkPad, be classified? In light of this classification, what actions would you suggest to the manufacturers of these products to increase their sales in the market?

5. Several alternative definitions were presented for a new product. How would a company's marketing strategy be affected if it used (*a*) the legal definition or (*b*) a behavioral definition?

6. What methods would you suggest to assess the potential commercial sucess for the following new products? (*a*) A new, improved ketchup, (*b*) a three-dimensional television system that took the company 10 years to develop, and (*c*) a new children's toy on which the company holds a patent.

7. Look back at Figure 11–5, which outlines the roles for new products. If a company followed the role of defending market share position, what type of positioning strategy might be implemented?

8. Concept testing is an important step in the new-product process. Outline the concept tests for (*a*) an electrically powered car and (*b*) a new loan payment system for automobiles that is based on a variable rate interest. What are the differences in developing concept tests for products as opposed to services?

CASE 11–1   American Harvest

Video

"Veiled market potential" was what their ideal product was supposed to have. David Dornbush and Chad Erickson were college friends who had decided to try to find a product to market that could form the basis of a new business they could start.

THE IDEA

Watching a television talk show one day when he was supposed to be studying, Dave Dornbush found *the* product—a home food dehydrator. He sold Chad on the notion that a home food dehydrator had "veiled market potential," and they were in business. The "veiled" part was important because they didn't want to spend time and money developing a product only to have General Electric or Sunbeam jump in and take their market away, but it couldn't be so veiled that consumers couldn't understand the product and want to buy it. This also meant it should be patentable, involve relatively low technology, and have a practical appeal to consumers. "We weren't interested in being the first of 16 companies to make a new kind of popcorn popper—or a gift hot dogger that would be used only twice a year," Dornbush explains.

THE COMPANY

So Dornbush and Erickson formed Alternative Pioneering Systems, Inc., and went into business. However, it was a long way from seeing a crude home food dehydrator on TV to manufacturing and marketing a better one. As Erickson puts it, "We went through our own Industrial Revolution."

Their first model, developed in two weeks, dried food successfully. They glued a few models together in their college's carpentry shop, took them around in the back of their cars to some trade shows, and knew success was just around the corner. But that "corner" was still several years away. The product was overengineered, cost too much, and the subcontractor that manufactured and assembled the product was producing 25 percent defective dehydrators, making for some very unhappy customers. When Dave and Chad discovered the problems, they redesigned the dehydrator, moved the assembly in-house, and beefed up quality control and inspection activities. To get money for a bank loan

to do this, they put their cars up for collateral. Success with the Harvest Maid dehydrator came when they sold Montgomery Ward on carrying the product.

THE ISSUES

But Dornbush and Erickson concluded they shouldn't be a one-product company and searched for a second product. They studied different ways of cooking food—even to suspending a frozen french fry on a thread and cooking it with hot air. Their search narrowed to a potential product that would have the key benefits of two existing cooking appliances—the cooking quality of a regular oven with the speed of a microwave oven. After five years of research, development, trial, and error, they introduced their patented Jet Stream Oven, a product that provides "oven quality food, microwave fast". In fact, promotions for the Jet Stream Oven stress that it can do *nine* different cooking functions, such as grilling, broiling, and baking. Its suggested retail price is $250, and it is distributed nationally.

A key design feature of the Jet Stream Oven is that it moves hot air in a "cyclonic" movement in the device at 2,200 feet per minute, a complex technical feat that took several years to develop. This cooking action enables the Jet Stream Oven to sear the surface of the item being cooked—whether it's a dinner roll or roast turkey—thereby increasing the moisture in the food being cooked. The result is more tasty, nutritious food that is finished in about one-third of the time of the regular oven. Consumer response to the Jet Stream Oven is overwhelmingly favorable.

With the advent of the new line of Jet Stream Ovens, Dornbush and Erickson repositioned the brand name for all their products marketed in the United States to "American Harvest." Dornbush and Erickson believe that this brand name has broader consumer appeal and has better application to a broader range of future products. Dornbush and Erickson also concluded that the Jet Stream Oven was too complex a product to try to sell with simple print ads or 30-second TV ads. The result: They chose to use a series of spectacularly successful 30-minute TV "infomercials" that could tell a more complete story about their product.

The "newness" of the Jet Stream Oven is a two-edged sword for Dornbush and Erickson. On the plus side, it permits them to stress the unique points of difference of the product. On the minus side, it raises questions about just how to "position" a product that is defining a whole new product category in consumers' eyes: at a price of over $200, what cooking appliances should it be positioned against?

The new-product process also poses challenges for Dornbush and Erickson. Some of the questions include getting feedback from the market on product improvements and making critical decisions about patents and packaging. Being a small business, these new product activities must be done efficiently without excessive expenses.

Questions

1. (*a*) How should American Harvest "position" its Jet Stream Oven, which is really a totally new product category? (*b*) What are the advantages and disadvantages of such "newness" in this revolutionary product?

2. (*a*) What "points of difference" should American Harvest stress in marketing the Jet Stream Oven? (*b*) What are the demographic characteristics of the target market households for the Jet Stream Oven?

3. In looking at American Harvest's new product development process, what activities should it use in idea generation, evaluation, and testing of product improvements, and getting market feedback on the Jet Stream Oven?

4. Evaluate the Jet Stream Oven on the following five factors that are common reasons for new product failure: (*a*) size of market, (*b*) significant points of difference, (*c*) product quality, (*d*) access to consumers, and (*e*) timing.

CHAPTER 12

Managing the Product

- Explain the product life-cycle concept and relate a marketing strategy to each stage.

- Recognize the differences in product life cycles for various products and their implications for marketing decisions.

- Understand alternative approaches to managing a product's life cycle.

- Identify the attributes of a successful brand name.

- Explain the rationale for alternative brand name strategies employed by companies.

- Understand the benefits of packaging and warranties in the marketing of a product.

FOR GATORADE, SUCCESS IS FOUND IN THE SWEET SMELL OF SWEAT

Bill Smithburg is a Gatorade kind of person. He runs, bikes, helicopter-skis down Canadian mountains, and enjoys skating with his Rollerblades along Lake Michigan, near his Chicago home. "Competition is a way of life," insists Smithburg, the chief executive officer of Quaker Oats and the maker of Gatorade. "If you don't have a really tough competitor you ought to invent one."

Gatorade captures 81 percent of the $1 billion U.S. sports drink market and thrives on both athletic and marketing competition. Like Kleenex in the tissue market and Jello among gelatin desserts, Gatorade has become synonymous with sports drinks. Concocted in 1965 at the University of Florida as a rehydration beverage for the school's football team, the drink was called "Gatorade" by an opposing team's coach after watching his team lose to the Florida Gators in the Orange Bowl. The name stuck, and a new beverage product class was born. Today, Gatorade is the official sports drink of Major League Baseball, the National Football League, the National Basketball Association, and the National Hockey League.

The Stokely-Van Camp Co. bought the Gatorade formula in 1967 and commercialized the product. The original Gatorade was a liquid with a lemon-lime flavor. An orange flavor was added in 1971 and a fruit-punch flavor in 1983. Instant Gatorade was introduced in 1979. Quaker Oats purchased Stokely-Van Camp in 1983, at which time Gatorade sales were $97 million. Quaker Oats executives immediately began to build sales through a variety of means. Gatorade Light was introduced, and more flavors were added, bringing the number to nine by 1997. Multiple package sizes were offered using different containers—glass and plastic bottles and aluminum cans. Distribution expanded first to include convenience stores and supermarkets followed by vending machines and fountain service in 1996. Advertising and promotion effectively conveys the product's benefits and links to athletic competition using popular athletes such as Michael Jordan to communicate its message: "Life is a sport, so drink it up." International opportunities are vigorously pursued, and Gatorade is now sold in 27 countries. Quaker Oats expects Gatorade sales in Europe, Latin America, and Asia to increase to $1 billion by the year 2000.

Gatorade has deflected the marketing efforts of 50 to 60 competing sports drink brands since 1967. In 1994, Gatorade faced its most serious challengers with the introduction of Coca-Cola's PowerAde and Pepsico's All Sport. A Coca-Cola spokesperson said, "The sports drink market is a ripe apple to be plucked." A Gatorade executive replied, "We've stepped up spending in the past to counter new competition, and it's likely we'll do it again." Advertising spending for Gatorade now exceeds the total expenditure for PowerAde and All Sport combined. But, Gatorade has been double-teamed with (1) All Sport adding basketball hoopster Shaquille O'Neal to its roster of product endorsers and (2) PowerAde being named as the official sponsor of the 1996 Olympics. Ever confident, Bill Smithburg says, "Sports beverages is our arena. We don't feel we're at a disadvantage."[1]

The marketing of Gatorade for 30 years illustrates the effective management of a product in the marketplace. This chapter shows how the actions taken by Gatorade executives are typical of those made by successful marketers in managing products and brands.

PRODUCT LIFE CYCLE

Products, like people, have been viewed as having a life cycle. The concept of the **product life cycle** describes the stages a new product goes through in the marketplace: introduction, growth, maturity, and decline (Figure 12–1).[2] There are two curves shown in this figure, total industry sales revenue and total industry profit, which represent the sum of sales revenue and profit of all firms producing the product. The reasons for the changes in each curve and the marketing decisions involved are discussed in the following pages.

Introduction Stage

The introduction stage of the product life cycle occurs when a product is first introduced to its intended target market. During this period, sales grow slowly, and profit is minimal. The lack of profit is often the result of large investment costs in product development, such as the $200 million spent by Gillette to develop the Sensor razor shaving system. The marketing objective for the company at this stage is to create consumer awareness and stimulate trial—the initial purchase of a product by a consumer.

Companies often spend heavily on advertising and other promotion tools to build awareness among consumers in the introduction stage. For example, Frito-Lay spent $30 million to promote its SunChips multigrain snacks to consumers and retailers, and Gillette spent $35 million in advertising alone to introduce the Sensor razor to consumers.[3] These expenditures are often made to stimulate *primary demand,* or desire for the product class (such as multigrain snack chips), rather than for a specific brand since there are no competitors with the same product. As competitors introduce their own products and the product progresses along its life cycle, company attention is focused on creating *selective demand,* or demand for a specific brand.

Other marketing mix variables also are important at this stage. Gaining distribution is often a challenge because channel intermediaries may be hesitant to carry a new product. Moreover, in this stage a company often restricts the number of variations of the product to ensure control of product quality. For example, SunChips originally came in only two flavors and Gatorade in only one. Gillette originally offered only a single version of the Sensor razor.

FIGURE 12-1

How stages of the product life cycle relate to a firm's marketing objectives and marketing mix actions

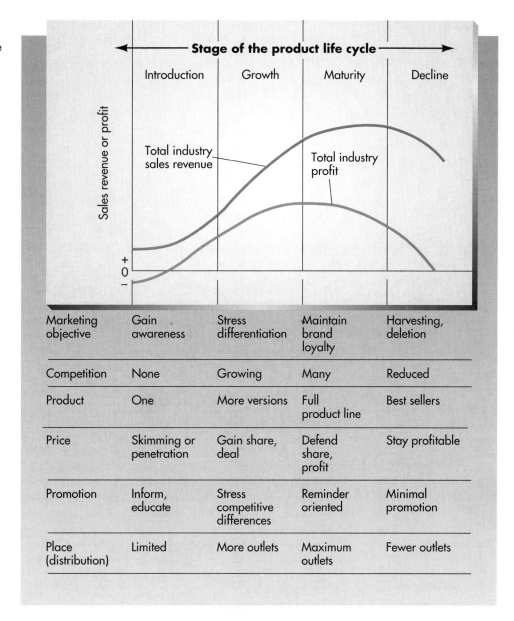

	Introduction	Growth	Maturity	Decline
Marketing objective	Gain awareness	Stress differentiation	Maintain brand loyalty	Harvesting, deletion
Competition	None	Growing	Many	Reduced
Product	One	More versions	Full product line	Best sellers
Price	Skimming or penetration	Gain share, deal	Defend share, profit	Stay profitable
Promotion	Inform, educate	Stress competitive differences	Reminder oriented	Minimal promotion
Place (distribution)	Limited	More outlets	Maximum outlets	Fewer outlets

During introduction, pricing can be either high or low. A high initial price may be used as part of a *skimming* strategy to help the company recover the costs of development as well as capitalize on the price insensitivity of early buyers. 3M is a master of this strategy. According to a 3M manager, "We hit fast, price high, and get the heck out when the me-too products pour in."[4] High prices also tend to attract competitors more eager to enter the market because they see the opportunity for profit. To discourage competitive entry, a company can price low, referred to as *penetration pricing*. This pricing strategy also helps build unit volume, but a company must closely monitor costs. These and other pricing techniques are covered in depth in Chapter 15.

Figure 12-2 charts the stand-alone fax machine product life cycle for business use in the United States from the early 1970s through 1996.[5] As shown, sales grew slowly in the 1970s and early 1980s after Xerox pioneered the first lightweight portable fax machine that sent and received documents. Fax machines were originally sold direct to businesses through company salespeople and were premium priced. The average price for a fax machine in 1980 was $12,700. By today's standards, those fax machines were primitive. They contained mechanical parts, not electronic circuitry, and offered few of the features seen in today's models.

FIGURE 12-2

Product life cycle for the
stand-alone fax machine for
business use: 1970–1996

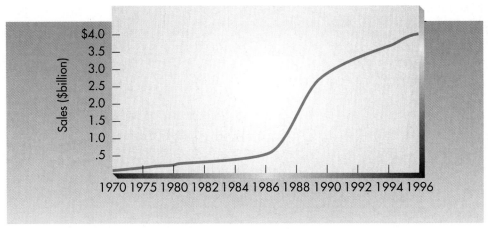

Source: Chart drawn from Dataquest, Inc., statistics. Used with permission.

Several product classes are poised to enter the introductory stage of the product life cycle or have been only recently commercialized. These include high-definition television (HDTV) and electronic imaging cameras. Electric vehicles have been in the introductory stage and are about to enter a period of rapid growth worldwide. Read the accompanying Marketing NewsNet to find out when, why, and how this will happen.[6]

Growth Stage

The second stage of the product life cycle, growth, is characterized by rapid increases in sales. It is in this stage that competitors appear. For example, Figure 12–2 shows the dramatic increase in sales of fax machines from 1986 to 1990. The number of companies selling fax machines was also increasing, from one in the early 1970s to four in the late 1970s to seven manufacturers in 1983, which sold nine brands. By 1990 there were some 25 manufacturers and 60 possible brands from which to choose.

The result of more competitors and more aggressive pricing is that profit usually peaks during the growth stage. For instance, the average price for a fax machine declined from $3,300 in 1985 to $1,500 in 1990. At this point the emphasis of advertising shifts to stimulating selective demand, in which product benefits are compared with those of competitors' offerings.

Product sales in the growth stage grow at an increasing rate because of new people trying or using the product and a growing proportion of *repeat purchasers*—people who tried the product, were satisfied, and bought again. As a product moves through the life cycle, the ratio of repeat to trial purchasers grows. Failure to achieve substantial repeat purchasers usually means an early death for a product. Alberto-Culver introduced Mr. Culver's Sparklers, which were solid air fresheners that looked like stained glass. The product moved quickly from the introduction to the growth stage, but then sales plummeted. The problem was there were almost no repeat purchasers because buyers treated the product like cheap window decorations, left them there, and didn't buy new ones. Durable fax machines meant that replacement purchases were rare; however, it was common for more than one machine to populate a business as their use became more widespread. In 1994, there was one fax machine for every eight people in a business in the United States.

Changes start to appear in the product during the growth stage. To help differentiate a company's brand from those of its competitors, an improved version or new features are added to the original design, and product proliferation occurs. Changes in fax machines included (1) models with built-in telephones; (2) models that used plain, rather than thermal, paper for copies; (3) models that integrated telex for electronic mail purposes; and (4) models that allowed for secure (confidential)

MARKETING NEWSNET

PLUGGING INTO THE WORLDWIDE POWER SURGE FOR ELECTRIC VEHICLE SALES

Technology

Automobile industry analysts have been enamored with electric vehicles (EVs) since the 1950s when the first prototypes were developed. General Motors and France's PSA/Peugeot-Citroen Group have gone beyond talk and invested $300 million and $100 million, respectively, to produce commercially viable EVs, believing their time has come. Japanese automakers have formed the Japan Electric Vehicle Association to research, develop, and popularize EVs in Japan.

Automakers worldwide believe the product life cycle for EVs will evidence an introductory stage starting in 1995 followed by rapid growth in sales beginning in the year 2000. Why then? Strict regulations on gasoline emissions and pollution in the United States, Western Europe, and Japan will go into effect at that time. The majority of EVs sold will be small service vehicles operated by national, state, and local government agencies. However, assuming advances in automobile battery technology occur, two- and four-seat cars will become viable.

Are you interested in buying an EV? You can purchase a Peugeot 106/Citroen AX subcompact in France today

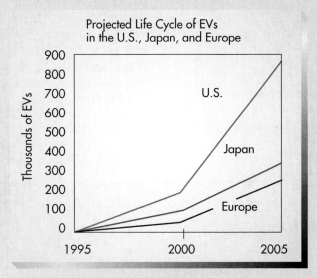

Projected Life Cycle of EVs in the U.S., Japan, and Europe

for about $10,700. You will have to wait until 1998 to buy General Motors' Impact sports car for about $40,000 at your local Saturn dealer.

transmissions. For SunChips and Gatorade, new flavors and package sizes were added during the growth stage. Gillette introduced an advanced design of its Sensor razor, Sensor Excel, and produced a Sensor razor for women.

In the growth stage it is important to gain as much distribution for the product as possible. In the retail store, for example, this often means that competing companies fight for display and shelf space. Expanded distribution in the fax industry is an example. In 1986, early in the growth stage, only 11 percent of office machine dealers carried this equipment. By the mid-1990s, more than 70 percent of these dealers carried fax equipment, distribution was expanded to other stores selling electronic equipment, and the fight continues for which brands will be displayed.

Numerous product classes or industries are in the growth stage of the product life cycle. Examples include disposable 35-mm cameras, cellular telephones, nonalcoholic beer, and laptop computers.

Maturity Stage

The third stage, maturity, is characterized by a gradual leveling off of total industry sales or product class revenue. Also, marginal competitors begin to leave the market. Most consumers who would buy the product are either repeat purchasers of the item or have tried and abandoned it. Sales increase at a decreasing rate in the maturity stage as few new buyers enter the market. Profit declines because there is fierce price competition among many sellers and the cost of gaining each new buyer at this stage is greater than the resulting revenue.

Marketing expenses in the maturity stage are often directed toward holding market share through further product differentiation, and price competition continues through rebates and price discounting. Companies also focus on retaining distribution outlets. A major factor in a company's strategy is to reduce overall marketing costs by improving its promotional and distribution efficiency.

Stand-alone fax machines for business use entered the maturity stage in early 1991. Sixty-five percent of industry sales were captured by five producers at this time (Sharp, Muratec, Canon, Panasonic, and Ricoh), reflecting the departure of many marginal competitors. Industry sales growth had slowed in the mid-1990s compared with triple-digit average annual dollar sales increases in the late 1980s. By early 1996, there were an estimated 25 million stand-alone fax machines for business use installed throughout the world.

Numerous product classes and industries are in the maturity stage of their product life cycle. These include carbonated soft drinks, automobiles, and TVs.

Decline Stage

The decline stage occurs when sales and profits begin to drop. Frequently, a product enters this stage not because of any wrong strategy on the part of the company but because of environmental changes. New technology led to video cameras, which pushed 8-mm movie cameras into decline. Similarly, the merging of personal computer and facsimile technology began to replace the stand-alone fax machine in 1994. The decline stage for stand-alone fax machines for business use is projected for the year 2000 with the growth of E-mail. Advertising and promotional support for a product in this stage diminish as does investment in major product development. Products in the decline stage tend to consume a disproportionate share of management time and financial resources relative to their potential future worth. To handle a declining product, a company follows one of two strategies: deletion or harvesting.

Deletion   Product *deletion*, or dropping the product from the company's product line, is the most drastic strategy. Since a residual core of consumers still consume or use a product even in the decline stage, product elimination decisions are not taken lightly. When Coca-Cola decided to drop what is now known as Classic Coke, consumer objection was so intense that the company brought the product back.

Harvesting   A second strategy, *harvesting*, is when a company retains the product but reduces marketing support costs.[7] The product continues to be offered, but salespeople do not allocate time in selling nor are advertising dollars spent. The purpose of harvesting is to maintain the ability to meet customer requests. For example, Gillette continues to sell its Liquid Paper correction fluid for use with typewriters in the era of word-processing equipment.

Some Dimensions of the Product Life Cycle

Some important aspects of product life cycles are (1) their length, (2) the shape of their curves, and (3) how they vary with different levels of the products.

Length of the product life cycle   There is no exact time that a product takes to move through its life cycle. As a rule, consumer products have shorter life cycles than industrial products. For example, many new consumer food products such as SunChips move from the introduction stage to maturity in 18 months. The availability of mass communication vehicles informs consumers faster and shortens life cycles. Also, the rate of technological change tends to shorten product life cycles as new product innovation replaces existing products. This is happening with stand-alone fax machines.

FIGURE 12-3

Alternative product life cycles

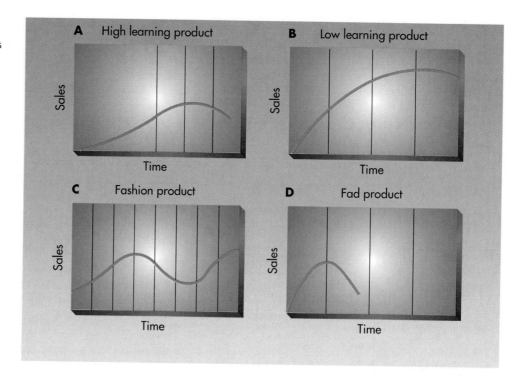

The shape of the product life cycle The product life-cycle curve shown in Figure 12–1 might be referred to as a *generalized life cycle,* but not all products have the same shape to their curve. In fact, there are several different life-cycle curves, each type suggesting different marketing strategies. Figure 12–3 shows the shape of life-cycle curves for four different types of products: high learning, low learning, fashion, and fad products.

A *high learning product* is one for which significant education of the customer is required and there is an extended introductory period (Figure 12–3A). Products such as home computers had this type of life-cycle curve because consumers have to understand the benefits of purchasing the product or be educated in a new way of performing a familiar task. Convection ovens, for example, necessitate that the consumer learn a new way of cooking and alter familiar recipes.

In contrast, for a *low learning product* sales begin immediately because little learning is required by the consumer, and the benefits of purchase are readily understood (Figure 12–3B). This product often can be easily imitated by competitors, so the marketing strategy is to broaden distribution quickly. In this way, as competitors rapidly enter, most retail outlets already have the innovator's product. It is also important to have the manufacturing capacity to meet demand. A recent example of a successful low learning product is Frito-Lay's SunChips, discussed earlier. SunChips achieved $100 million in sales the first year it was introduced.

A *fashion product* (Figure 12–3C), such as hemline lengths on skirts or lapel widths on sports jackets, is introduced, declines, and then seems to return. Life cycles for fashion products most often appear in women's and men's clothing styles. The length of the cycles may be years or decades.

A *fad,* such as wall walkers or toe socks, experiences rapid sales on introduction and then an equally rapid decline (Figure 12–3D). These products are typically novelties. They include car tatoos sold in southern California and described as the first removable and reusable graphics for automobiles and vinyl dresses, fleece bikinis, and an AstroTurf miniskirt made by Thump, Inc., a Minnesota clothing company.[8]

The product level: class, form, and brand The product life shown in Figure 12–1 is a total industry or product class curve. Yet, in managing a product it

FIGURE 12-4

Video game life cycle by
product class, product form,
and brand

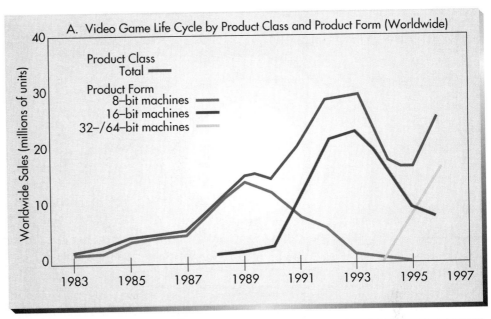

A. Video Game Life Cycle by Product Class and Product Form (Worldwide)

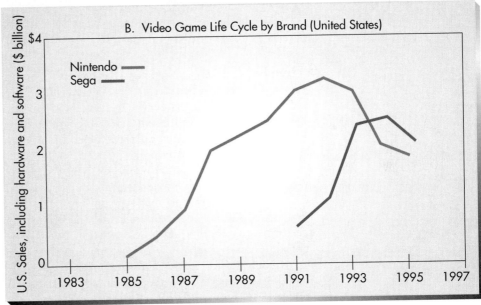

B. Video Game Life Cycle by Brand (United States)

is important to often distinguish among the multiple life cycles (class, form, and brand) that may exist. **Product class** refers to the entire product category or industry, such as video games shown in Figure 12–4A.[9] **Product form** pertains to variations within the class. For video games, product form exists in the computing capability of game players such as 8-, 16- and 32/64-bit machines. Game players have a life cycle of their own and typically move from the introduction stage to maturity in six years. A final type of life-cycle curve can represent a video game brand, apparent in the U.S. sales of Nintendo and Sega charted in Figure 12–4B. Sales of these brands are driven by the purchase of their game players and the number and quality of their games. A new product form and brand cycle began in 1995 with the introduction of 32/64-bit machines and a new competitor, Sony's PlayStation game player. Sony will compete with Sega's Saturn and Nintendo's Ultra 64 game players and games.

The life cycle and consumers   The life cycle of a product depends on sales to consumers. Not all consumers rush to buy a product in the introductory stage, and the shapes of the life-cycle curves indicate that most sales occur after the product has

FIGURE 12–5

Five categories and profiles of product adopters

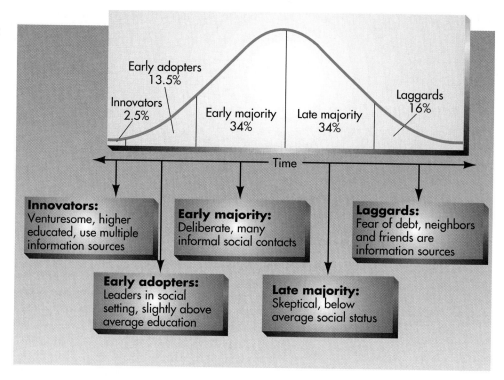

been on the market for some time. In essence, a product diffuses, or spreads, through the population, a concept called the *diffusion of innovation.*[10]

Some people are attracted to a product early, while others buy it only after they see their friends with the item. Figure 12–5 shows the consumer population divided into five categories of product adopters based on when they adopt a new product. Brief profiles accompany each category. For any product to be successful, it must be purchased by innovators and early adopters. This is why manufacturers of new pharmaceuticals try to gain adoption by leading hospitals, clinics, and physicians that are widely respected in the medical field. Once accepted by innovators and early adopters, the adoption of new products moves on to the early majority, late majority, and laggard categories.

Several factors affect whether a consumer will adopt a new product or not. Common reasons for resisting a product in the introduction stage are usage barriers (the product is not compatible with existing habits), value barriers (the product provides no incentive to change), risk barriers (physical, economic, or social), and psychological barriers (cultural differences or image).[11]

Companies attempt to overcome these barriers in numerous ways. For example, Golden Valley Microwave Foods initially distributed its shelf-stable Act II microwave popcorn through vending machines—not through the more traditional supermarket chains—to introduce the product to consumers (see the case at the end of the chapter). The result? A very successful introduction that gained consumer trials and eventual acceptance of the product targeted at microwave oven owners. When Lever Brothers introduced its Lever 2000 triple-threat skin soap bar that moisturizes, deodorizes, and kills bacteria, it had to give consumers an incentive to change from their current soap. How? The company sent samples of the new product to half of all U.S households and recorded sales of $27.6 million.[12]

1. Advertising plays a major role in the _____ stage of the product life cycle, and _____ plays a major role in maturity.

2. How do high learning and low learning products differ?

3. What does the life cycle for a fashion product look like?

MANAGING THE PRODUCT LIFE CYCLE

An important task for a firm is to manage its products through the successive stages of their life cycles. This section discusses the role of the product manager, who is usually responsible for this, and analyzes three ways to manage a product through its life cycle: modifying the product, modifying the market, and repositioning the product.

Role of a Product Manager

The product manager (sometimes called *brand manager*) manages the marketing efforts for a close-knit family of products or brands.[13] Introduced by P&G in 1928, the product manager style of marketing organization is used by consumer goods firms such as General Foods and Frito-Lay and by industrial firms such as Intel and Hewlett-Packard. The U.S. Postal Service and General Motors recently began using product managers as well. All product managers are responsible for managing existing products through the stages of the life cycle, and some are also responsible for developing new products. Product managers' marketing responsibilities include developing and executing a marketing program for the product line described in an annual marketing plan and approving ad copy, media selection, and package design. The role of product managers in planning, implementing, and controlling marketing strategy is covered in depth in Chapter 22.

Modifying the Product

Product modification involves altering a product's characteristic, such as its quality, performance, or appearance, to try to increase and extend the product's sales. Wrinkle-free cotton slacks sold by Levi Strauss, Haggar, and Farah revitalized sales of men's casual pants and now account for 60 percent of the men's cotton pants product class sales. A modest modification of Black & Decker's Phillips screwdriver, which prevents the tip from slipping out of the screw, expanded sales substantially.[14]

New features, packages, or scents can be used to change a product's characteristics and give the sense of a revised product. Procter & Gamble revamped Pantene shampoo and conditioner with a new vitamin formula and relaunched the brand with a multimillion dollar advertising and promotion campaign. The result? Pantene, a brand first introduced in the 1940s, became the top-selling shampoo and conditioner in the United States in an industry with more than 1,000 competitors.[15]

Modifying the Market

With **market modification** strategies, a company tries to increase a product's use among existing customers, create new use situations, or find new customers.

Increasing use   Promoting more frequent usage has been a strategy of Campbell Soup Company. Since soup consumption rises in the winter and declines during the summer, the company now advertises more heavily in warm months to encourage consumers to think of soup as more than a cold-weather food. Similarly, The Florida Orange Growers Association advocates drinking orange juice throughout the day rather than for breakfast only.

Mars, Inc. successfully extends the life cycle of its M&M's candy by finding new use situations.

Secretly, all chocolate chips harbor a desire to splash around in a colorful candy shower.

M&M's'® Mini Chocolate Baking Bits. Perhaps it was cruel to put them so close to other chocolate chips in the baking aisle. But these special Mini "M&M's" are for baking. Smaller and available in either semi-sweet or milk chocolate. Use them in any recipe that calls for chocolate chips. Or if the colors really inspire you, call 1-800-627-7852 for more recipes.

But no matter what you bake, don't put the results next to anything made with chocolate chips.

Ordinary chips start to feel naked.

"M&M's" Mini Baking Bits are ¹/₅ the size of regular "M&M's."

© Mars, Incorporated 1995   Contact us on the Internet http://www.baking.M-Ms.com

Creating new use situation   Finding new uses for an existing product has been the strategy behind Woolite, a laundry soap. Originally intended for the hand washing of woolen material, Woolite now promotes itself for use with all fine clothing items. Mars, Inc. suggests a new-use situation when it markets its M&M's candy as a replacement for chocolate chips in baked goods.

Finding new users   To prevent sales declines in wall-to-wall carpeting, carpet manufacturers found new user groups such as schools and hospitals. To expand company sales, Nautilus, a manufacturer of fitness equipment for gyms, entered the home market. Commercial accounts represented 95 percent of the company's sales, but the home market has a $1 to $5 billion sales potential. Pharmacia & Upjohn, Inc. first targeted men for its Rogaine Topical Solution, a drug to restore hair growth, but later marketed this product to women.

Repositioning the Product

Often a company decides to reposition its product or product line in an attempt to prevent sales decline. *Product repositioning* is changing the place a product occupies in a consumer's mind relative to competitive products. A firm can reposition a product by changing one or more of the four marketing mix elements. Four factors that trigger a repositioning action are discussed next.

Reacting to a competitor's position   One reason to reposition a product is because a competitor's entrenched position is adversely affecting sales and market share. Procter & Gamble recently repositioned its venerable Ivory soap bar in response to the success of Lever 2000, sold by Lever Brothers. Lever 2000, a bar soap that moisturizes, deodorizes, and kills bacteria, eroded P&G's dominance of the bar soap market. P&G responded with its own triple-threat soap called New Ivory Ultra Safe Skin Care Soap. The problem? The new Ivory doesn't float![16]

Reaching a new market   Dannon Yogurt introduced Yop, a liquid yogurt, in France. The product flopped because the French were not interested in another dairy product. When Dannon repositioned Yop as a soft drink for the health-conscious French consumer, sales soared.[17]

Oscar Mayer capitalizes on the popularity of the "better-for-you" trend in the food industry with its new Low Fat LUNCHABLES® product line.

Repositioning can involve more than changing advertising copy. The New Balance Company changed its product's position as a running shoe for the serious runner to a shoe for the mass market. The distribution strategy was altered from selling only through specialty running stores to selling through discount and department stores as well.

Catching a rising trend   Changing consumer trends can also lead to repositioning. The recent popularity of low-fat or fat-free foods is an example.[18] Today, about two thirds of U.S. consumers say that a food's fat content is a concern to them. Nabisco's SnackWell line of cookies and crackers and Oscar Mayer Low-Fat Lunchables were among the first to capitalize on this "better-for-you" trend in the food industry. At Kraft Foods, fat-free and reduced-fat versions of its existing products total about $3 billion in sales annually.

Changing the value offered   In repositioning a product, a company can decide to change the value it offers buyers and trade up or down. **Trading up** involves adding value to the product (or line) through additional features or higher quality materials. Japanese automakers built their reputations with reliable and affordable cars. Many have since traded up, as evidenced by Honda's Acura, Toyota's Lexus, and Nissan's Infiniti, to compete in the luxury sedan market historically occupied by Mercedes-Benz and Cadillac. Dog food manufacturers also have traded up by offering super premium foods based on "life-stage nutrition." Mass merchandisers can trade up by adding a designer clothes section to their store, as shown by recent actions by Sears and JCPenney.

Trading down involves reducing the number of features, quality, or price. For example, airlines have added more seats, thus reducing leg room, and eliminated extras, such as snack service and food portions. Trading down often exists when companies engage in **downsizing**—reducing the content of packages without changing package size and maintaining or increasing the package price. For instance, Fabergé's Brut antiperspirant deodorant spray comes in its regular-size can at the same price, but the content has been reduced from five ounces to four.[19] Firms have been criticized for this practice, as described in the accompanying Ethics and Social Responsibility Alert.[20]

ETHICS AND SOCIAL RESPONSIBILITY ALERT

Ethics

CONSUMERS ARE PAYING MORE FOR LESS IN DOWNSIZED PACKAGES

For more than 30 years, Starkist put 6.5 ounces of tuna into its regular-sized can. Today, Starkist puts 6.125 ounces of tuna into its can but charges the same price. Colgate-Palmolive's Ajax king-size laundry detergent package has remained the same size, but the contents have been cut from 61 ounces to 55 ounces and the package price increased from $2.59 to $2.79. Procter & Gamble cut the number of Pampers disposable diapers in its packages while leaving the price the same. The price of Mennen Speed Stick deodorant has not changed, but it now comes in a larger package with 2.25 ounces of deodorant versus 2.5 ounces in the previous, smaller package.

Consumer advocates charge that "downsizing" packages while maintaining or increasing prices is a subtle and unannounced way of taking advantage of consumer's buying habits. Manufacturers argue that this practice is a way of keeping prices from rising beyond psychological barriers for their products.

Is downsizing an unethical practice if manufacturers do not inform consumers that the package contents are less than they were previously?

CONCEPT CHECK

1. How does a product manager help manage a product's life cycle?

2. What does "creating new use situations" mean in managing a product's life cycle?

3. Explain the difference between trading up and trading down in repositioning.

BRANDING

A basic decision in marketing products is **branding,** in which an organization uses a name, phrase, design, symbols, or combination of these to identify its products and distinguish them from those of competitors. A **brand name** is any word, "device" (design, sound, shape, or color), or combination of these used to distinguish a seller's goods or services. Some brand names can be spoken, such as a Gatorade. Other brand names cannot be spoken, such as the rainbow-colored apple (the *logotype* or *logo*) that Apple Computer puts on its machines and in its ads. A **trade name** is a commercial, legal name under which a company does business. The Campbell Soup Company is the trade name of that firm.

A **trademark** identifies that a firm has legally registered its brand name or trade name so the firm has its exclusive use, thereby preventing others from using it. In the United States, almost 700,000 trademarks are registered with the U.S. Patent and Trademark Office, and these trademarks are protected under the Lanham Act. A well-known trademark can help a company advertise its offerings to customers and develop their brand loyalty. Figure 12–6 shows examples of well-known trademarks.

Because a good trademark can help sell a product, *product counterfeiting,* which involves low-cost copies of popular brands not manufactured by the original producer, has been a growing problem. Counterfeit products can steal sales from the original manufacturer or hurt the company's reputation. Counterfeiting losses to U.S. companies exceed $50 billion in every year. To protect against counterfeiting, the U.S. government passed the Trademark Counterfeiting Act, which makes

FIGURE 12-6

Examples of well-known
trademarks, brand names,
and trade names.

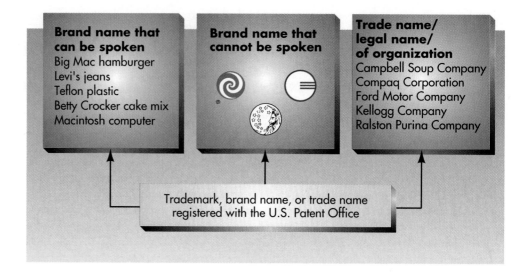

FIGURE 12-6

Examples of well-known trademarks, brand names, and trade names.

counterfeiting a federal offense with offenders subject to prison sentences, damage payments, and seizure of counterfeit merchandise.

Trademark protection is a significant issue in global marketing. For instance, the transformation of the Soviet Union into individual countries has meant that many U.S. firms, such as Xerox, have had to reregister trademarks in each of the republics to prohibit misuse and generic use ("xeroxing") of their trademarks by competitors and consumers. Is trademark registration a routine process in these republics? For some, yes, but not when Smirnoff vodka squared off with Smirnov vodka in Russia as detailed in the accompanying Marketing NewsNet.[21]

The Value of Brands

Branding policy is important not only for manufacturers but also for retailers and consumers. Retailers value branding because consumers shop at stores that carry their desired brands. Some retailers have created their own store brands to further enhance loyalty from their customers. Sears exclusively offers the Kenmore brand for its appliance line and Craftsman as the brand for tools.

A good brand name is of such importance to a company that it has led to a concept called **brand equity,** the added value a given brand name gives to a product beyond the functional benefits provided.[22] This value has two distinct advantages. First, brand equity provides a competitive advantage, such as the Sunkist label that implies quality fruit and the Gatorade name that defines sport drinks. A second advantage is that consumers are often willing to pay a higher price for a product with brand equity. Brand equity, in this instance, is represented by the premium a consumer will pay for one brand over another when the functional benefits provided are identical. Intel microchips, Kodak film, Duracell batteries, Microsoft computer software, and Louis Vuitton luggage all enjoy a price premium arising from brand equity.

Consumers, however, may benefit most from branding. Recognizing competing products by distinct trademarks allows them to be more efficient shoppers. Consumers can recognize and avoid products with which they are dissatisfied, while becoming loyal to other, more satisfying brands. As discussed in Chapter 6, brand loyalty often eases consumers' decision making by eliminating the need for an external search. Also, the expense of establishing a brand on the marketplace means that some brands are reintroduced years after they apparently died. For example, Buick recently resurrected its Roadmaster brand after the name had been discontinued for about 20 years.

MARKETING NEWSNET

Global

SMIRNOFF VERSUS SMIRNOV: A TANGLED TRADEMARK IN RUSSIA

Smirnoff is the largest selling vodka brand in the world with roots in Russia, one of the world's largest vodka-drinking markets. Smirnoff's formula came from Pyotr Smirnov, a nineteenth century Russian vodka baron and friend of the Czar of Russia. Heublein, Inc. bought the Smirnoff recipe for $14,000 in 1939 from Rudolf Kunett, who obtained it from Pyotr Smirnov's son, Vladimir. Vladimir had fled to Paris after the Russian Revolution in 1917 and opened a vodka distillery under the Smirnoff name.

Smirnoff's Russian heritage made the brand's entry into the Soviet Union in 1988 akin to a homecoming. The brand quickly became the Number 1 imported vodka. When the Soviet Union dissolved into individual countries, Heublein began registering the Smirnoff trademark in each country, including Russia. To its surprise, in July 1991, Boris Smirnov (shown in the photo), Pyotr Smirnov's great-great grandson had already registered the Smirnov trademark in Russia. His company, Pyotr A. Smirnov & Descendants, was created to produce vodka and wines.

So what is the problem? Smirnoff and Smirnov are two Anglicized versions of one Russian name. When translated into Russian, both names are spelled the same. In 1993, the Court of Appeals of the Russian Committee on Patents & Trademarks ruled that Heublein had exclusive rights to the Smirnoff name, and the Smirnov name was not protected. But the court did not say

whether Pyotr A. Smirnov & Descendants could sell vodka with the name "Genuine Smirnov." In 1995, two Russian court decisions sided with Pyotr A. Smirnov & Descendants.

The legal battle continues as both sides claim lineage to Pyotr Smirnov and the Smirnoff (Smirnov) name. Boris Smirnov says that Vladimir gave up his share of the original family-owned company and therefore had no legal right to sell the recipe. Heublein disagrees, arguing it is the "successor to Vladimir Smirnov." The outcome has immense financial implications. Russians consume more than 500 million gallons of vodka annually.

Licensing

The value of brand equity is evident in the strategy of licensing. **Licensing** is a contractual agreement whereby a company allows another firm to use its brand name, patent, trade secret, or other property for a royalty or a fee. Licensing can be very profitable to a licensor, and a licensee as annual worldwide retail sales of licensed products exceed $100 billion.[23] Playboy has earned more than $260 million licensing its name for merchandise ranging from shoes in the United States to wallpaper in Europe and cooking classes in Brazil. Murjani has sold more than $500 million of clothing worldwide bearing the Coca-Cola logo. The U.S. Postal Service expects to earn more than $1 million in royalty revenue from licensing the likeness of its popular Elvis Presley stamp.

Licensing also assists companies in entering global markets with minimal risk. PepsiCo Foods International licensed Elite Foods in Israel to produce and market Frito-Lay's Ruffles potato chips and Chee-tos cheese-flavored corn puffs. These brands capture 15 percent of the salty snack market in Israel.[24]

Ruffles and Chee-tos are in Israel now, and more PepsiCo Foods International snack items may follow. Entry into Israel was made possible through a licensing agreement with Elite Foods in Israel.

Picking a Good Brand Name

We take brand names such as Dial, Sanyo, Porsche, and Danskin for granted, but it is often a difficult and expensive process to pick a good name. Five criteria are mentioned most often in selecting a good brand name. [25]

The name should suggest the product benefits. For example, Accutron (watches), Easy Off (oven cleaner), Glass Plus (glass cleaner), Cling-Free (antistatic cloth for drying clothes), and Tidy Bowl (toilet bowl cleaner) all clearly describe the benefits of purchasing the product.

The name should be memorable, distinctive, and positive. In the auto industry, when a competitor has a memorable name, others quickly imitate. When Ford named a car the Mustang, Pintos, Colts, Mavericks, and Broncos soon followed. The Thunderbird name led to the Phoenix, Eagle, Sunbird, and Firebird.

The name should fit the company or product image. Sharp is a name that can apply to audio and video equipment. Excedrin, Anacin, and Nuprin are scientific-sounding names, good for an analgesic. However, naming a personal computer PCjr, as IBM did with its first computer for home use, neither fit the company nor the product. PCjr, sounded too much like a toy and stalled IBM's initial entry into the home-use market.

The name should have no legal or regulatory restrictions. Legal restrictions produce trademark infringement suits, and regulatory restrictions arise through improper use of words. For example, the U.S. Food and Drug Administration discourages the use of the word *heart* in food brand names. This restriction led to changing the name of Kellogg's Heartwise cereal to Fiberwise, and Clorox's Hidden Valley Ranch Take Heart Salad Dressing had to be modified to Hidden Valley Ranch Low-Fat Salad Dressing.[26]

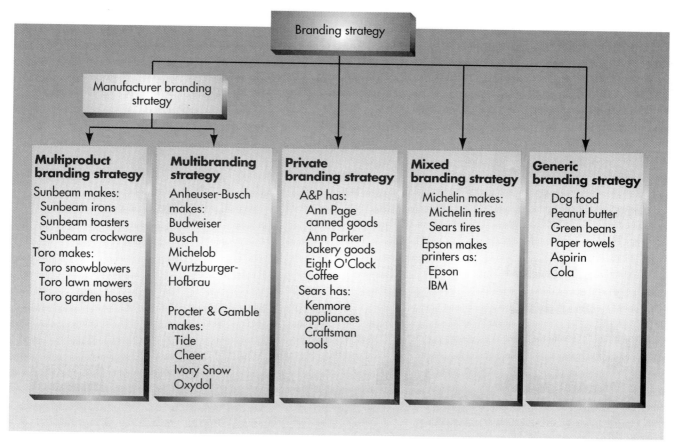

FIGURE 12–7

Alternative branding strategies

Finally, the name should be simple (such as Bold laundry detergent, Sure deodorant, and Bic pens) and should be emotional (such as Joy and My Sin perfumes). In the development of names for international use, having a nonmeaningful brand name has been considered a benefit. A name such as Exxon does not have any prior impressions or undesirable images among a diverse world population of different languages and cultures. The 7Up name is another matter. In Shanghai, China, the phrase means "death through drinking" in the local dialect, and sales have suffered as a result.[27]

Branding Strategies

In deciding to brand a product, companies have several possible strategies, including manufacturer branding, reseller branding, or mixed branding approaches.

Manufacturer branding   With **manufacturer branding,** the producer dictates the brand name using either a multiproduct or multibrand approach. **Multiproduct branding** is when a company uses one name for all its products. This approach is often referred to as a *blanket* or *family* branding strategy (Figure 12–7).

There are several advantages to multiproduct branding. Capitalizing again on brand equity, consumers who have a good experience with the product will transfer this favorable attitude to other items in the product class with the same name. Therefore, this brand strategy makes possible *line extensions,* the practice of using a current brand name to enter a new market segment in its product class. Campbell Soup Company effectively employs a multiproduct branding strategy with soup line extensions. It offers regular Campbell soup, home-cooking style, chunky, and "healthy request" varieties and more than 100 soup flavors. This strategy can also

Black & Decker uses a multibranding strategy to reach different market segments. Black & Decker markets its line of tools for the do-it-yourselfer market with the Black & Decker name, but uses the DeWalt name for its professional tool line.

result in lower advertising and promotion costs because the same name is used on all products, thus raising the level of brand awareness.

A strong brand equity also allows for *brand extension,* the practice of using a current brand name to enter a completely different product class.[28] For instance, the equity in the Tylenol name as a trusted pain reliever allowed Johnson & Johnson to successfully extend this name to Tylenol Cold & Flu and Tylenol PM, a sleep aid. Fisher-Price, an established name in children's toys, was able to extend this name to children's shampoo and conditioners and baby bath and lotion products.

However, there is a risk with brand extensions. Too many uses for one brand name can dilute the meaning of a brand for consumers. Marketing experts claim this has happened to the Arm & Hammer brand given its use for toothpaste, laundry detergent, cat litter, air freshener, carpet deodorizer, and anti-perspirant.[29]

A recent variation on brand extensions is the practice of **co-branding,** the pairing of two brand names of two manufacturers on a single product.[30] For example, Hershey Foods has teamed with General Mills to offer a co-branded breakfast cereal called Reese's Peanut Butter Puffs and with Nabisco to provide Chips Ahoy cookies using Hershey's chocolate morsels. Citibank co-brands MasterCard and Visa with American Airlines and Ford. Co-branding benefits firms by allowing them to enter new product classes and capitalize on an already established brand name in that product class.

An alternative manufacturer's branding strategy, **multibranding,** involves giving each product a distinct name. Multibranding is a useful strategy when each brand is intended for a different market segment. P&G makes Camay soap for those concerned with soft skin and Safeguard for those who want deodorant protection. Black & Decker markets its line of tools for the household do-it-yourselfer segment with the Black & Decker name, but uses the DeWalt name for its professional tool line. Disney uses the Touchstone Pictures name for films directed at adults and its Disney name for children's films.

Kodak, in a recent departure from its multiproduct branding strategy in Japan, now uses a mixed branding strategy in that country. Read the text to find out why Kodak has modified its branding strategy in Japan.

Multibranding strategies become more complex in the gobal marketplace. As an example, P&G uses multiple brand names for the same product when competing internationally. For instance, PertPlus shampoo is sold as Rejoice in Hong Kong, PertPlus in the Middle East, and Vidal Sassoon in the United Kingdom. However, international branding strategies do differ. In Japan, where corporate names are important, P&G markets the company's name prominently with the brand name of the product.

Compared with the multiproduct approach, promotional costs tend to be higher with multibranding. The company must generate awareness among consumers and retailers for each new brand name without the benefit of any previous impressions. The advantages of this approach are that each brand is unique to each market segment and there is no risk that a product failure will affect other products in the line.

The multibranding approach in Europe is slowly being replaced by **euro-branding,** the strategy of using the same brand name for the same product across all countries in the 15-nation European Union. This strategy has many of the benefits linked with multiproduct branding in addition to making Pan-European advertising and promotion programs possible.

Private branding   A company uses **private branding,** often called *private labeling* or *reseller branding,* when it manufactures products but sells them under the brand name of a wholesaler or retailer. Radio Shack, Sears, and Kmart are large retailers that have their own brand names. Food products are often private labeled for supermarkets. Private brands account for 14 percent of U.S. food sales, 36 percent of British food sales, and about 18 percent of food sales in France and Germany.[31]

Matsushita of Japan manufactures VCRs for Magnavox, GE, Sylvania, JCPenney, and Curtis Mathes. The advantage to the manufacturer is that promotional costs are shifted to the retailer or other company, and the manufacturer can often sell more units through others than by itself. There is a risk, though, because the manufacturer's sales depend heavily on the efforts of others.

Mixed branding   A compromise between manufacturer and private branding is **mixed branding,** where a firm markets products under its own name and that of a reseller because the segment attracted to the reseller is different from their own market. Sanyo and Toshiba manufacture television sets for Sears as well as for themselves. This process is similar to Michelin's, which manufactures tires for Sears as well as under

MARKETING NEWSNET

CREATING CUSTOMER VALUE THROUGH PACKAGING: PEZ HEADS DISPENSE MORE THAN CANDY

Customer value can assume numerous forms. For Pez Candy, Inc., customer value manifests itself in some 250 Pez character candy dispensers. Each 99 cent refillable dispenser ejects tasty candy tablets in a variety of flavors that delight preteen and teens alike.

Pez was formulated in 1927 by Austrian food mogul Edward Haas III and successfully sold in Europe as an adult breath mint. Pez, which comes from the German word for peppermint, *pfefferminz*, was originally packaged in a hygienic, headless plastic dispenser. Pez first appeared in the United States in 1953 with a headless dispenser, marketed to adults. After conducting extensive marketing research, Pez was repositioned with fruit flavors, repackaged with licensed character heads on top of the dispenser, and remarketed as a children's product in the mid-1950s. Since then, most top-level licensed characters and hundreds of other characters have become Pez heads. Consumers eat more than 1 billion Pez tablets annually, and company sales growth exceeds that of the candy industry as a whole.

The unique Pez package dispenses a "use experience" for its customers beyond the candy itself, namely, fun. An fun translates into a 98 percent awareness level for Pez among teenagers and 89 percent among mothers with children. Pez has not advertised its product for years. With that kind of awareness, who needs advertising?

its own name. Kodak recently adopted a mixed branding approach in Japan to increase its sales of 35-mm film. In addition to selling its Kodak brand, the company now makes "COOP" private label film for the Japanese Consumer Cooperative Union, which is a group of 2,500 stores. Priced 38 percent below its Kodak brand, the private label seeks to attract the price-sensitive Japanese consumer.[32]

Generic branding An alternative branding approach is the **generic brand,** which is a no-brand product such as dog food, peanut butter, or green beans. There is no identification other than a description of the contents. The major appeal is that the price is up to one third less than that of branded items. Generic brands account for less than 1 percent of total grocery sales.[33] The limited appeal of generics has been attributed to the popularity of private brands and greater promotional efforts for manufacturer brand-name items. Consumers who use generics see these products as being as good as brand-name items, and, in light of what they expect, users of these products are relatively pleased with their purchases.

PACKAGING

The **packaging** component of a product refers to any container in which it is offered for sale and on which information is communicated. To a great extent, the customer's first exposure to a product is the package, and it is an expensive and important part of the marketing strategy. For Pez Candy, Inc., the character head-on-a-stick plastic container that dispenses a miniature brick candy is the central element of its marketing strategy as described in the accompanying Marketing NewsNet.[34]

New packaging for well-known products creates customer value.

Creating Customer Value through Packaging

Today's packaging costs exceed $50 billion, and an estimated 10 cents of every dollar spent by a consumer goes to packaging. Despite the cost, packaging is essential because packages provide important benefits for the manufacturer, retailer, and ultimate consumer.

Communication benefits   A major benefit of packaging is the information on it conveyed to the consumer, such as directions on how to use the product and the composition of the product, which is needed to satisfy legal requirements of product disclosure. For example, a new labeling system for packaged and processed foods, which created a uniform format for nutritional and dietary information, became effective in 1994 at a cost of $2 billion to food companies. Other information consists of seals and symbols, either government required or commercial seals of approval (such as the Good Housekeeping seal).

Functional benefits   Packaging often plays an important functional role, such as convenience, protection, or storage. Quaker State has changed its oil containers to eliminate the need for a separate spout, and Borden has changed the shape of its Elmer's Wonder Bond adhesive to prevent clogging of the spout.

The convenience dimension of packaging is becoming increasingly important. A Richard Simmons salad dressing is sold in a pump-top bottle, microwave popcorn has been a major market success, and Folgers coffee is now packaged in single-serving portions.

Consumer protection has become an important function of packaging, including the development of tamper-resistant containers. Today, companies commonly use safety seals or pop-tops that reveal previous opening. Nevertheless, no package is truly tamper resistant. U.S. law now provides for maximum penalties of life imprisonment and $250,000 fines for package tampering.[35]

Can you name this soft drink brand?

Another functional value of packaging is in extending storage and *shelf life* (the time a product can be stored before it spoils). New technology allows products requiring refrigeration to be packaged in paper-sealed containers, which dramatically increases their shelf life.

Perceptual benefits A third component of packaging is the perception created in the consumer's mind. Just Born Inc., a candy manufacturer of such brands as Jolly Joes and Mike and Ike Treats, discovered the importance of this component of packaging. For many years the brands were sold in old-fashioned black and white packages, but when the packaging was changed to four color, with animated grape and cherry characters, sales increased 25 percent. Procter & Gamble changes the packaging for Clearasil every year to give the appearance of a new cream, which is important to the target market of teenagers who purchase the product. Coca-Cola has brought back its famous pale-green, contoured 8-ounce bottle to attract consumers who remember drinking soft drinks from glass bottles, not from aluminum cans and large plastic bottles. A worldwide sales increase of 8 percent was linked to the new-old bottle. In Japan and Spain, sales increases were 23 percent and 30 percent, respectively.[36] The popularity of the contoured bottle has led Coca-Cola to experiment with a contoured aluminum can in Europe. If successful, expect to see this can in the United States in 1999 or sooner.

A package can connote status, economy, or even product quality. Equally fresh potato chips were wrapped in two different types of bags: wax paper and polyvinyl. Consumers rated the chips in the polyvinyl as crisper and even tastier, even though the chips were identical.[37]

In the past, the color of packages was selected subjectively. For example, the famous Campbell's soup can was the inspiration of a company executive who liked Cornell University's red and white football uniforms. Today, there is greater

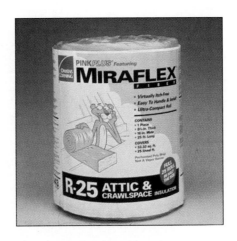

recognition that color affects consumers' perceptions. When the color of the can of Barrelhead Sugar-Free Root Beer changed to beige from blue, consumers said it tasted more like old-fashioned root beer.[38] And Owens-Corning judged the pink color of its fiber insulation to be so important that the color was given trademark status by the courts.[39]

Global Trends in Packaging

Two global trends in packaging originating in the mid-1990s will continue into the twenty-first century. One trend involves the environmental effects of packaging, the other focuses on packaging health and safety concerns.

Environmental sensitivity   Because of widespread worldwide concern about the growth of solid waste and the shortage of viable landfill sites, the amount, composition, and disposal of packaging material continues to receive much attention.[40] Recycling packaging material is a major thrust. Procter & Gamble now uses recycled cardboard in 70 percent of its paper packaging and is packaging Tide, Cheer, Era, and Dash detergents in jugs that contain 25 percent recycled plastic. Spic and Span liquid cleaner is packaged in 100 percent recycled material. Other firms, such as the large U.K. retailer Gainsbury, emphasize the use of less packaging material. Gainsbury examines every product it sells to ensure that each uses only the minimum material necessary for shipping and display. Not surprisingly, when ARCO, one of the world's largest petrochemical firms, recently announced that its new packaging material would reduce packaging volume by 40 percent compared with corrugated paper shipping containers, the news was favorably received by manufacturers and retailers alike.

European countries have been trendsetters concerning packaging guidelines and environmental sensitivity. Many of these guidelines now exist in provisions governing trade to and within the European Union. In Germany, for instance, 80 percent of packaging material must be collected, and 80 percent of this amount must be recycled or reused to reduce solid waste in landfills. U.S. firms marketing in Europe have responded to these guidelines, and ultimately benefitted U.S. consumers. The history of Procter & Gamble's Downy Refill liquid fabric softener is an example. The product's plastic bottle is reusable, and the refill carton uses 75 percent less packaging material. First introduced in Germany in 1987, the product moved to Canada in 1989, and then to the United States in late 1990. Downy Refill now accounts for more than 40 percent of Downy's U.S. sales.[41]

Increasingly, firms are using life-cycle analysis (LCA) to examine the environmental effect of their packaging at every stage from raw material sources and production through distribution and disposal. A classic use of LCA was the decision by McDonald's to abandon the polystyrene clam-shells it used to package its

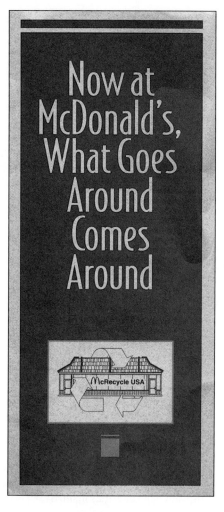

hamburger. LCA indicated that the environment would be better served if the amount of solid waste packaging was reduced than if the polystyrene shells were recycled. McDonald's elected to package its hamburgers in a light wrap made of paper and polyethylene and eliminate the polystyrene package altogether.

Health and safety concerns   A second trend involves the growing health and safety concerns of packaging materials. Today, a majority of U.S. and European consumers believe companies should make sure products and their packages are safe, regardless of the cost, and companies are responding to this view in numerous ways.[42] For instance, studies by the U.S. Food and Drug Administration suggest that microwave heating of some packages can lead to potentially cancer-causing agents seeping into food products. The major concern relates to packaging that contains heat susceptors—thin, metalicized plastic film strips that help brown microwaveable food. Du Pont, 3M, and Raytheon, among other firms, are working to develop alternatives in anticipation of regulatory changes regarding packaging.[43] Most butane lighters sold today, such as those made by BIC, contain a child-resistant safety latch to prevent misuse and accidental fire.

PRODUCT WARRANTY

A final component for product consideration is the **warranty,** which is a statement indicating the liability of the manufacturer for product deficiencies. There are various degrees of product warranties with different implications for manufacturers and customers.

The Variations of a Warranty

Some companies offer *express warranties,* which are written statements of liabilities. In recent years the government has required greater disclosure on express warranties to indicate whether the warranty is a limited-coverage or full-coverage alternative. A *limited-coverage warranty* specifically states the bounds of coverage and, more important, areas of noncoverage, whereas a *full warranty* has no limits of noncoverage. Cadillac is a company that boldly touts its warranty coverage. The Magnuson-Moss Warranty/FTC Improvement Act (1975) regulates the content of consumer warranties and so has strengthened consumer rights with regard to warranties.

With greater frequency, manufacturers are being held to *implied warranties,* which assign responsibility for product deficiencies to the manufacturer. Studies show that warranties are important and affect a consumer's product evaluation. Brands that have limited warranties tend to receive less positive evaluations compared with full-warranty items.

The Growing Importance of Warranties

Warranties are important in light of increasing product liability claims. In the early part of this century the courts protected companies, but the trend now is toward "strict liability" rulings, where a manufacturer is liable for any product defect, whether it followed reasonable research standards or not. This issue is hotly contested by companies and consumer advocates.

Warranties represent much more to the buyer than just protection from negative consequences—they can hold a significant marketing advantage for the producer. Sears has built a strong reputation for its Craftsman tool line with a simple warranty: if you break a tool, it's replaced with no questions asked. Zippo has an equally simple guarantee: "If it ever fails, we'll fix it free."

CONCEPT CHECK

1. How does a generic brand differ from a private brand?

2. Explain the role of packaging in terms of perception.

3. What is the difference between an expressed and an implied warranty?

SUMMARY

1. Products have a finite life cycle consisting of four stages: introduction, growth, maturity, and decline. The marketing objectives for each stage differ.

2. In the introductory stage the need is to establish primary demand, whereas the growth stage requires selective demand strategies. In the maturity stage the need is to maintain market share; the decline stage necessitates a deletion or harvesting strategy.

3. There are various shapes to the product life cycle. High learning products have a long introductory period, and low learning products rapidly enter the growth stage. There are also different curves for fashions and fads. Different product life-cycle curves can exist for the product class, product form, and brand.

4. In managing a product's life cycle, changes can be made in the product itself or in the target market. Product modification approaches include changes in the quality, performance, or appearance. Market modification approaches entail increasing a product's use among existing customers, creating new use situations, or finding new users.

5. Product repositioning can come about by reacting to a competitor's position, reaching a new market, capitalizing on a rising trend, or changing the value offered in a product.

6. Branding enables a firm to distinguish its product in the marketplace from those of its competitors. A good brand name should suggest the product benefits, be memorable, fit the company or product image, be free of legal restrictions, and be simple and emotional. A good brand name is of such importance that is has led to a concept of brand equity, the added value a given brand name gives to a product beyond the functional benefits provided.

7. Licensing of a brand name is being used by many companies. The company allows the name to be used without having to manufacture the product.

8. Manufacturers can follow one of three branding strategies: a manufacturer's brand, a reseller brand, or a mixed brand approach. With a manufacturer's branding approach, the company can use the same brand name for all products in the line (multiproduct, or family, branding) or can give products different brands (multibranding).

9. A reseller, or private, brand is used when a firm manufactures a product but sells it under the brand name of a wholesaler or retailer. A generic brand is a product with no identification of manufacturer or reseller that is offered on the basis of price appeal.

10. Packaging provides communication, functional, and perceptual benefits. The two global emerging trends in packaging are greater concerns regarding the environmental impact and the health and safety of packaging materials.

11. The warranty, a statement of a manufacturer's liability for product deficiencies, is an important aspect of a manufacturer's product strategy.

KEY TERMS

product life cycle p. 318
product class p. 324
product form p. 324
product modification p. 326

market modification p. 326
trading up p. 328
trading down p. 328
downsizing p. 328

CHAPTER PROBLEMS AND APPLICATIONS

1. Listed here are three different products in various stages of the product life cycle. What marketing strategies would you suggest to these companies? (*a*) GTE cellular telephone company—growth stage, (*b*) Mountain Stream tap-water purifying systems—introductory stage, and (*c*) hand-held manual can openers—decline stage.

2. It has often been suggested that products are intentionally made to break down or wear out. Is this strategy a planned product modification approach?

3. The product manager of GE is reviewing the penetration of trash compactors in American homes. After more than a decade in existence, this product is in relatively few homes. What problems can account for this poor acceptance? What is the shape of the trash compactor life cycle?

4. For several years Ferrari has been known as the manufacturer of expensive luxury automobiles. The company plans to attract the major segment of the car-buying market who purchase medium-priced automobiles. As Ferrari considers this trading-down strategy, what branding strategy would you recommend? What are the trade-offs to consider with your strategy?

5. The nature of product warranties has changed as the federal court system reassesses the meaning of warranties. How does the regulatory trend toward warranties affect product development?

CASE 12–1   Golden Valley Microwave Foods, Inc.

"Do you know how to identify the pioneers?" asks Jim Watkins. "They're the ones face down in the mud with arrows in their backs," he answers very descriptively. Watkins should know. As one of the food industry's foremost entrepreneurs, he has been responsible for improving microwave popcorn, developing nutritious microwave breakfasts, and introducing the first brown-and-crisp microwave french fries.

THE IDEA

After working at Pillsbury from 1971 to 1978 on a research team developing microwave foods, Jim Watkins hit a roadblock. Pillsbury executives were not enthusiastic about the team's new product ideas because less than 15 percent of U.S. households had microwave ovens and they felt consumers preferred conventional ovens.

So Watkins started his own firm—Golden Valley Microwave Foods, Inc. (GVMF). Watkins believed that the convenience of microwave cooking would appeal to consumers. He also knew, however, that a small, start-up company would have difficulty competing in an industry dominated by large, well-established corporations. Wat-

kins's solution was to focus on high-quality microwave-only foods that required significant technological input. He says: "We had the conviction that by combining low-cost production and aggressive marketing skills with high-quality products developed expressly for the microwave oven, our company could not only survive but prevail."

THE COMPANY

Golden Valley initially focused its efforts on microwave popcorn—a product that has grown from a junk food to a health food (low calorie, high fiber). After years of testing, GVMF researchers developed an innovative packaging technology for popcorn. It used a laminated paper that focused microwave energy and allowed more complete popping of the corn. This was important because consumers had expressed concern about unpopped kernels in competitive products, and it gave the Golden Valley product an important advantage over competing popcorns—or a "point of difference." In addition, the new technology allowed the use of low-power microwave ovens (about 50 percent of all microwaves) and, therefore, increased the size of the potential market.

Distribution was critical for a product such as popcorn. Unfortunately, GVMF had no other products to

offer supermarkets, which preferred dealing with large manufacturers. GVMF distributed the popcorn through vending machines and discount stores and had 50 percent of the non-grocery popcorn market. Today nearly 90 percent of American homes have microwave ovens. This means interest in microwave foods has increased but so has competition from firms like Orville Redenbacher and Pillsbury.

To continue its growth GVMF needed additional products. Golden Valley introduced microwave pancakes as its second product and began development of microwave french fries. Again Watkins was determined to address consumers' needs, and, if possible, exceed their expectations. He hired Dr. Sara Risch as Director of Advanced Technologies to help design the product. According to Dr. Risch the "target in developing the microwave french fry was to try to get what consumers consider the gold standard for french fries, and that is something that comes out of a deep-fat fryer—a shoestring potato that is crisp and lightly brown." The result is a unique package that will crisp and brown each french fry individually, and that, Watkins believes, can unlock a much larger market by offering a restaurant-quality product.

In the microwaveable french fries market, Golden Valley faces two sizeable competitors: J. R. Simplot, a privately-held Idaho potato processor, and the Ore-Ida division of Heinz. To have the financial resources to compete in this market, Golden Valley forms a joint venture with ConAgra, a large U.S. food company.

THE ISSUES

Watkins knows that if Golden Valley is to build a reputation as a leader in microwave foods, it must continue to develop new products, market them effectively, and increase its distribution. Because GVMF's popcorn and french fries are at different stages of their product life cycles, somewhat different marketing strategies are needed.

Finally, with sales in 30 countries, GVMF has begun to follow the penetration of microwave ovens around the world. Microwave ovens are currently found in approximately 40 percent of Japanese homes and 30 percent of home kitchens in the United Kingdom. Throughout Western Europe the increasing demand for microwave ovens makes them the single fastest-growing home appliance. Some countries, however, present special problems. The United Kingdom, for example, thinks of popcorn as a candy or child's food rather than the salty snack it is in the United States. Germans and French consumers sprinkle sugar on their popcorn, and Swedes like theirs very buttery. Many Mexicans like jalapeno-flavored popcorn.

Questions

1. What points of difference should GVMF offer its customers with (a) popcorn and (b) french fries?

2. What criteria should GVMF use to select new products?

3. Looking at GVMF's product line in the accompanying photo, (a) what kind of branding strategy does it use, and (b) what benefits and dangers does the strategy pose?

4. What functions does GVMF's packaging perform for its popcorn and french fries?

5. (a) At what stage of their product life cycles are GVMF's popcorn and french fries? (b) What marketing strategies seem appropriate for each?

6. What unique marketing issues does GVMF face as it pursues growth in international markets?

Managing Services

• Describe four unique elements of services.

• Recognize how services differ and how they can be classified.

• Understand the way in which consumers purchase and evaluate services.

• Develop a customer contact audit to identify service advantages.

• Understand the important role of internal marketing in service organizations.

• Explain the role of the four Ps in the services marketing mix.

SKI RESORTS' NEW TARGET MARKET: HOT DOGS!

When growth in the $3 billion U.S. ski industry slowed several years ago, ski resorts began looking for new ways to increase sales. Like many businesses, the resorts investigated marketing actions ranging from pursuing new products (in this case new services) and new markets to changing their pricing and promotion practices. The changes have excited many consumers. Carol Brownson, an avid skier, says, "If this is as close to heaven as I can get, that's O.K. It's pretty close."

The range of new services offered by ski resorts has increased dramatically. Aspen's Ski School now offers day-long back-country expeditions. Sugarbush in Vermont recently introduced guided tours that they call "woods skiing." Colorado's Purgatory Resort created four-day lift tickets that let skiers trade one or more days for a visit to a national park, a gambling excursion, or a train trip. Many resorts have also opened new terrain left in its natural state and have added snowshoeing, dogsledding, and snowboarding to their offerings.

Slow growth in the number of new skiers means that ski resorts must select specific target markets. At Kirkwood, California, Bridger Bowl, Montana, Stowe, Vermont, and Telluride, Colorado, steep slopes are used to attract "extreme" skiers and "hot dogs" who are bored with the gentler runs. Other niches include children, the over 50 age group, Europeans, and snowboarders. Research has revealed that 80 percent of the world's skiers live outside the United States, and snowboarders now account for 11 percent of all resort visits.

Ski resorts—and all service organizations—face another special challenge: matching demand and capacity. Historically, ski areas could attract consumers only during the winter months, leaving their resorts idle the rest of the year. Ski areas across the United States, however, are now learning how to attract enthusiasts of another sport—mountain biking. The International Mountain Bicycling Association estimates that the number of ski resorts open to bikes has grown from 20 to 200 in the past four years. Mammoth Mountain in

California, for example, reported that 50,000 visitors paid to ride on its 60 miles of trails last summer.[1]

As the actions of the U.S. ski industry illustrate, the marketing of services is unique and challenging. In this chapter we discuss how services differ from traditional products (goods), how service consumers make purchase decisions, and the ways in which the marketing mix is used.

THE UNIQUENESS OF SERVICES

As noted in Chapter 1, **services** are intangible items such as airline trips, financial advice, or automobile repair that an organization provides to consumers. To obtain these services, consumers exchange money or something else of value, such as their own time.

Services have quickly become one of the most important components of the U.S. economy. About 90 percent of the 2.7 million new jobs created each year are in the services sector. In addition, more than half of the gross domestic product now comes from services. As shown in Figure 13–1, services accounted for $3.777 trillion in 1995, which was an increase of more than 200 percent since 1980. Services also represent a large export business—the $200 billion of services exports in 1995 is one of the few areas in which the United States has a trade surplus.[2]

The growth in this sector is the result of increased demand for services that have been available in the past and the increasing interest in new services. Capital Concierge in Washington, D.C., for example, provides personal and business services to 50,000 people in 85 buildings. If a customer has a wish, from picking up dry cleaning to finding hard-to-get concert tickets, founder Mary Naylor and her 85 employees make it come true. Other new services include mobile banks, such as the one operated by Huntington National Bank in Cincinnati, to serve low- to middle-income neighborhoods; International Video Yearbooks, a video service available to high schools; and On-Call, a 24-hour interactive movie and video review service, featuring film critic Leonard Maltin. In California, Oasis Laundries, Inc. offers laundromats with big-screen TVs, video games, snack bars, and attendants. These firms and many others like them are examples of the groundbreaking and imaginative services that will play a role in our economy in the future.[3]

FIGURE 13–1

Importance of services in the U.S. Gross Domestic Product (GDP)

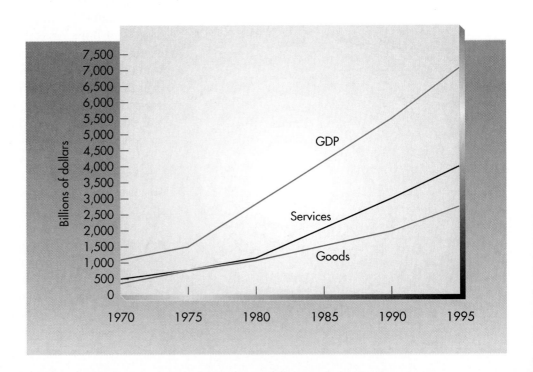

Why do many services emphasize their tangible benefits? The answer appears in the text.

The Four I's of Services

There are four unique elements to services: intangibility, inconsistency, inseparability, and inventory. These four elements are referred to as the **four I's of services.**

Intangibility   Services are intangible; that is, they can't be held, touched, or seen

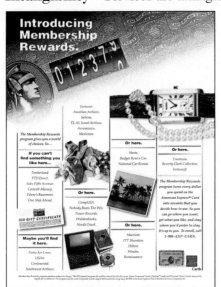

before the purchase decision. In contrast, before purchasing a traditional product, a consumer can touch a box of laundry detergent, kick the tire of an automobile, or sample a new breakfast cereal. A major marketing need for services is to make them tangible or show the benefits of using the service. A Continental Airlines advertisement shows a traveler enjoying legroom, an entertainment system, and other benefits of a business class fare; American Express emphasizes the gifts available to cardholders through its Membership Rewards program; and a leading insurance company says, "You're in Good Hands with Allstate."

Inconsistency   Developing, pricing, promoting, and delivering services is challenging because the quality of a service is often inconsistent. Since services depend on the people who provide them, their quality varies with each person's capabilities and day-to-day job performance. Inconsistency is much more of a problem in services than it is with tangible goods. Tangible products can be good or bad in terms of quality, but with modern production lines the quality will at least be consistent. On the other hand, one day the Philadelphia Phillies baseball team may have great hitting and pitching and look like a pennant winner and the next day lose by 10 runs. Or a soprano at New York's Metropolitan Opera may have a bad cold and give a less-than-perfect performance. Whether the service involves tax assistance at Arthur Andersen or guest relations at the Hyatt Regency, organizations attempt to reduce inconsistency through standardization and training.[4]

People play an important role in the delivery of many services.

Inseparability   A third difference between services and goods, and related to problems of consistency, is inseparability. In most cases, the consumer cannot (and does not) separate the deliverer of the service from the service itself. For example, to receive an education, a person may attend a university. The quality of the education may be high, but if the student has difficulty interacting with instructors, finds counseling services poor, or does not receive adequate library or computer assistance, he or she may not be satisfied with the educational experience. Students' evaluations of their education will be influenced primarily by their perceptions of instructors, counselors, librarians, and other people at the university.

Inventory   Inventory of services is different from that of goods. Inventory problems exist with goods because many items are perishable and because there are costs associated with handling inventory. With services, inventory carrying costs are more subjective and are related to **idle production capacity,** which is when the service provider is available but there is no demand. The inventory cost of a service is the cost of paying the person used to provide the service along with any needed equipment. If a physician is paid to see patients but no one schedules an appointment, the fixed cost of the idle physician's salary is a high inventory carrying cost. In some service businesses, however, the provider of the service is on commission (the Merrill Lynch stockbroker) or is a part-time employee (a counterperson at McDonald's).

FIGURE 13–2

Inventory carrying costs of services

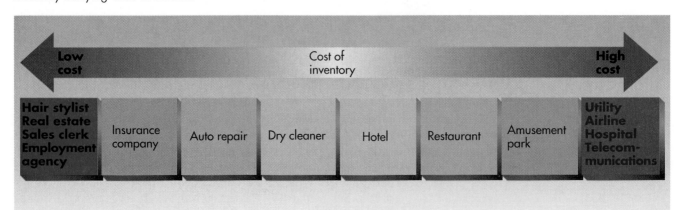

FIGURE 13-3

Service continuum

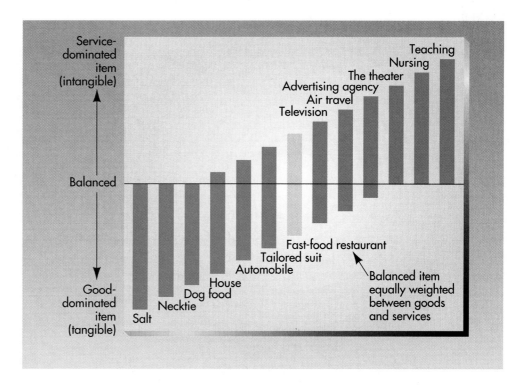

In these businesses, inventory carrying costs can be significantly lower or nonexistent because the idle production capacity can be cut back by reducing hours or having no salary to pay because of the commission compensation system. Figure 13–2 shows a scale of inventory carrying costs represented on the high side by airlines and hospitals and on the low end by real estate agents and hair stylists. The inventory carrying costs of airlines is high because of high-salaried pilots and very expensive equipment. In contrast, real estate agents and hair stylists work on commission and need little expensive equipment to conduct business.

The Service Continuum

The four I's differentiate services from goods in most cases, but many companies are not clearly service-based or good-based organizations. Is IBM a computer company or service business? Does Dow Jones provide only goods in the sense of publishing *The Wall Street Journal,* or does it consider itself a service in terms of up-to-date business information? As companies look at what they bring to the market, there is a range from the tangible to the intangible or good-dominant to service-dominant offerings referred to as the **service continuum** (Figure 13–3).

Teaching, nursing, and the theater are intangible, service-dominant activities, and intangibility, inconsistency, inseparability, and inventory are major concerns in their marketing. Salt, neckties, and dog food are tangible goods, and the problems represented by the four I's are not relevant in their marketing. However, some businesses are a mix of intangible service and tangible good factors. A clothing tailor provides a service but also a good, the finished suit. How pleasant, courteous, and attentive the tailor is to the customer is an important component of the service, and how well the clothes fit is an important part of the product. As shown in Figure 13–3, a fast-food restaurant is about half tangible goods (the food) and half intangible services (courtesy, cleanliness, speed, convenience).

Classifying Services

Throughout this book, marketing organizations, techniques, and concepts are classified to show the differences and similarities in an organized framework. Services can

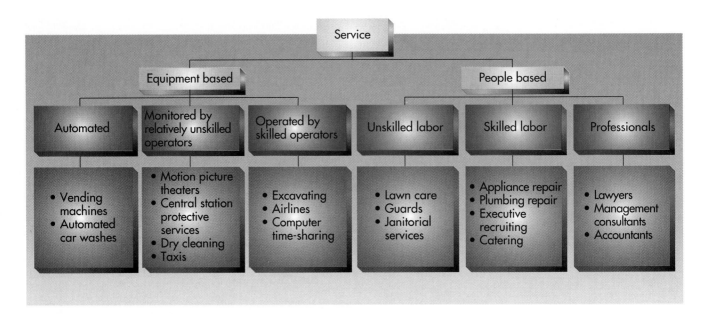

FIGURE 13-4   Service classifications

also be classified in several ways, according to (1) whether they are delivered by people or equipment, (2) whether they are profit or nonprofit, or (3) whether or not they are government sponsored.

Delivery by people or equipment   As seen in Figure 13–4, companies offering services provided by professionals include management consulting firms such as Booz, Allen & Hamilton. Skilled labor is required to offer services such as Sears appliance repair or Sheraton catering service. Unskilled labor such as that used by Brinks store-security forces is also a service provided by people.

Equipment-based services do not have the marketing concerns of inconsistency because people are removed from provision of the service. Electric utilities, for example, can provide service without frequent personal contact with customers. To keep in touch with their customers, many utilities such as the Public Service Company of New Mexico now conduct frequent marketing research efforts.[5]

Profit or nonprofit organizations   Many organizations involved in services also distinguish themselves by their tax status as profit or nonprofit organizations. In contrast to *profit organizations, nonprofit organizations'* excesses in revenue over expenses are not taxed or distributed to shareholders. When excess revenue exists, the money goes back into the organization's treasury to allow continuation of the service. Based on the corporate structure of the nonprofit organization, it may pay tax on revenue-generating holdings not directly related to its core mission. The 600,000 nonprofit organizations in the United States now generate 10 percent of the gross domestic product.[6]

The American Red Cross, United Way, Greenpeace, St. Mary's Health Center in St. Louis, and the University of Florida are nonprofit organizations. Such organizations historically have not used marketing practices in the belief that they were inappropriate. In recent years, however, nonprofit organizations such as hospitals, universities, and museums have turned to marketing to increase their revenues. The accompanying Marketing NewsNet box describes some of the changes nonprofit organizations have undertaken.[7]

Nonprofit and government services often advertise.

YOUR GREAT GREAT GREAT GREAT GREAT GREAT GREAT GREAT GREAT GREAT GREAT
GREAT GREAT GREAT GREAT GREAT GREAT GREAT GREAT GREAT GREAT GREAT GREAT
GREAT GREAT GREAT GREAT GREAT GREAT GREAT GREAT GREAT GREAT GREAT GREAT
GREAT GREAT GREAT GREAT GREAT GREAT GREAT GREAT GREAT GREAT GREAT GREAT
GREAT GREAT GREAT GREAT GREAT GREAT GREAT GREAT GREAT GREAT GREAT GREAT
GREAT GREAT GREAT GREAT GREAT GREAT GREAT GREAT GREAT GREAT GREAT GREAT
GREAT GREAT GREAT GREAT GREAT GREAT GREAT GREAT GREAT GREAT GREAT GREAT
GREAT GREAT GREAT GREAT GREAT GREAT GREAT GREAT GREAT GREAT GREAT GREAT
GREAT GREAT GREAT GREAT GREAT GREAT GREAT GREAT GREAT GREAT GREAT GREAT
GREAT GREAT GREAT GREAT GREAT GREAT GREAT GREAT GREAT GREAT GREAT GREAT
GREAT GREAT GREAT GREAT GREAT GREAT GREAT GREAT GREAT GREAT GREAT GREAT
GREAT GREAT GREAT GREAT GREAT GREAT GREAT GREAT GREAT GREAT GREAT GREAT
GREAT GREAT GREAT GREAT GREAT GREAT GREAT GREAT GREAT GREAT GREAT GREAT
GREAT GREAT GREAT GREAT GREAT GREAT GREAT GREAT GREAT GREAT GREAT GREAT
GREAT GREAT GREAT GREAT GREAT GREAT GREAT GREAT GREAT GREAT GREAT GREAT
GREAT GREAT GREAT GREAT GREAT GREAT GREAT GREAT GREAT GREAT GREAT GREAT
GREAT GREAT GREAT GREAT GREAT GREAT GREAT GREAT GREAT GREAT GREAT GREAT
GREAT GREAT GREAT GREAT GREAT GREAT GREAT GREAT GREAT GREAT GREAT GREAT
GREAT GREAT GREAT GREAT GREAT GREAT GREAT GREAT GREAT GREAT GREAT GREAT
GREAT GREAT **GRANDCHILDREN WILL DIE**   **BEFORE THIS DOES.**

Stop the nuclear industry from churning ———— out more radioactive waste.
Write to Greenpeace, Suite #201 A, 1436 "U" Street, NW, Washington, DC 20009.

MARKETING NEWSNET

THE GIRL SCOUTS TAKE A MARKETING COURSE

For many years, nonprofit agencies avoided the word *marketing.* They were concerned that marketing activities were inappropriate for organizations not motivated by profit. Today, that attitude is changing. As John Garrison, president of the National Easter Seal Society, explains, "Almost everyone now realizes that commitment isn't enough anymore. You also have to have professionalism or you're going to go out of business."

The Girl Scouts of the U.S.A. is a good example. Faced with eight straight years of falling membership, CEO Frances Hesselbein began asking questions such as "What is our business?", "Who is the customer?", and "What does the customer value?" Market studies showed that girls had changed—they were now more interested in areas such as science, the environment, and business—but the Girl Scouts had not. By focusing on contemporary issues, encouraging equal access to all types of girls, and becoming customer-oriented, the Girl Scouts reversed its membership trend and now serves more than 2 million young girls.

Other nonprofit organizations are also utilizing marketing techniques:

- The United Way used focus groups to discover that people didn't know how United Way worked. In response, United Way launched a national TV ad campaign describing how individuals received assistance.
- The American Red Cross raised $300,000 using cause-related marketing techniques in conjunction with MasterCard International.
- The YMCA reorganized to include three new divisions: corporate communications, public relations, and marketing.

As the number of nonprofit organizations with interest in marketing grows, so does the need for marketing education. Planned Parenthood's headquarters has developed a marketing training program available to members of the 178 affiliate chapters. J. Carter Brown, director of the National Gallery of Art, got an MBA degree. Many other organizations send their managers to marketing seminars and executive training programs. Because so many nonprofit organizations rely on volunteers, management expert Peter Drucker has observed that the training of volunteers to create unpaid professionals "may be the most important development in American society today."

Government sponsored or not   A third way to classify services is based on whether they are government sponsored. Although there is no direct ownership and

they are nonprofit organizations, governments at the federal, state, and local levels provide a broad range of services. The United States Postal Service, for example, has adopted many marketing activities. Their "We Deliver for You" campaign is designed to change its image of a huge bureaucracy and to focus the organization's efforts on customer satisfaction. Another marketing program, designing and promoting collector stamps such as the all-time best-selling Elvis Presley stamp, is expected to generate $1 billion in revenue by the year 2000. Government sponsorship does not limit competition, however. Britain's Royal Mail recently opened an office in Manhattan to compete with the U.S. Postal Service for international direct mail business.[8]

CONCEPT CHECK

1. What are the four I's of services?

2. Would inventory carrying costs for an accounting firm with certified public accountants be (*a*) high, (*b*) low, or (*c*) nonexistent?

3. To eliminate service inconsistencies, companies rely on _____ and _____.

HOW CONSUMERS PURCHASE SERVICES

Colleges, hospitals, hotels, and even charities are facing an increasingly competitive environment. Successful service organizations, like successful product-oriented firms, must understand how the consumer makes a service purchase decision and quality evaluation and in what ways a company can present a differential advantage relative to competing offerings.

The Purchase Process

The intangible and inseparable aspects of services affect the consumer's evaluation of the purchase. Because services cannot be displayed, demonstrated, or illustrated, consumers cannot make a prepurchase evaluation of all the characteristics of services.[9] Similarly, because services are produced and consumed simultaneously, the buyer must participate in producing the service and that participation can affect the evaluation of the service. Figure 13–5 portrays how different types of goods and services are evaluated by consumers. Tangible goods such as clothing, jewelry, and furniture have *search* properties, such as color, size, and style, which can be determined before purchase. Services such as restaurants and child care have *experience* properties, which can only be discerned after purchase or during consumption. Finally, services provided by specialized professionals such as medical diagnoses and legal services have *credence* properties, or characteristics that the

FIGURE 13-5

How consumers evaluate
goods and services

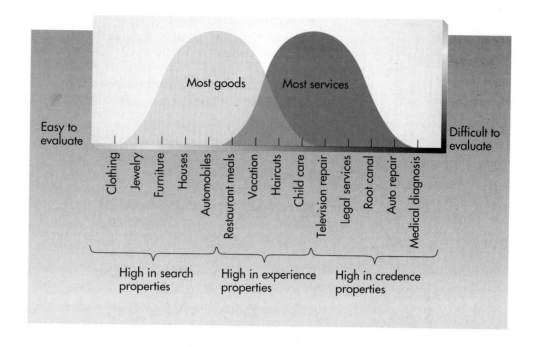

consumer may find impossible to evaluate even after purchase and consumption.[10] To reduce the uncertainty created by these properties, service consumers turn to personal sources of information such as early adopters, opinion leaders, and reference group members during the purchase decision process.[11]

Assessing Service Quality

Once a consumer tries a service, how is it evaluated? Primarily by comparing expectations about a service offering to the actual experience a consumer has with the service.[12] Differences between the consumer's expectations and experience are identified through **gap analysis.** This type of analysis asks consumers to assess their expectations and experiences on dimensions of service quality such as those described in Figure 13–6.[13] Expectations are influenced by word-of-mouth communications, personal needs, past experiences, and promotional activities, while actual

FIGURE 13-6

Dimensions of service quality

DIMENSION AND DEFINITION	EXAMPLES OF QUESTIONS STOCK BROKERAGE CUSTOMERS MIGHT ASK
Reliability: Ability to perform the promised service dependably and accurately	Does my stockbroker follow exact instructions to buy or sell?
Tangibles: Appearance of physical facilities, equipment, personnel, and communication materials	Is the monthly report easy to read and understand?
Responsiveness: Willingness to help customers and provide prompt service	Is my stockbroker willing to answer my questions?
Assurance: Knowledge and courtesy of employees and their ability to convey trust and confidence	Does my broker refrain from acting busy or being rude when I ask questions?
Empathy: Caring, individualized attention provided customers	Does my broker try to determine what my specific financial objectives are?

experiences are determined by the way an organization delivers its service.[14] The relative importance of the various dimensions of service quality varies by the type of service.[15] In the fast-food industry, Burger King is an example of a firm trying to implement gap analysis. According to Barry Gibbons, Burger King's CEO, the company is "measuring our performance against their [customer's] expectations" by using a 24-hour hot line to receive 4,000 customer calls per day.[16]

Customer Contact Audit

Consumers judge services on the entire sequence of steps that make up the service process. To focus on these steps or "service encounters," a firm can develop a **customer contact audit**—a flowchart of the points of interaction between consumer and service provider.[17] This is particularly important in high-contact services such as hotels, educational institutions, and automobile rental agencies.[18] Figure 13–7 is a consumer contact audit for renting a car from Hertz. Look carefully at the sequence.

A customer's car rental activities   A customer decides to rent a car and (1) makes a telephone reservation (see Figure 13–7). An operator answers and receives the information (2) and checks the availability of the car at the desired location (3). When the customer arrives at the rental site (4), the reservation system is again accessed, and the customer provides information regarding payment, address, and driver's license (5). A car is assigned to the customer (6), who proceeds by bus to the car pickup (7). On return to the rental location (8), the car is parked and the customer checks in, providing information on mileage, gas consumption, and damages (9). A bill is subsequently prepared (10).

Each of the steps numbered 1 to 10 is a customer contact point where the tangible aspects of Hertz service are seen by the customer. Figure 13–7, however, also shows a series of steps lettered A to E that involve two levels of inspections on the automobile. These steps are essential in providing a car that runs, but they are not points of customer interaction. To create a service advantage, Hertz must create a competitive advantage in the sequence of interactions with the customer.

CONCEPT CHECK

1. What are the differences between search, experience, and credence properties?

2. Hertz created its differential advantage at the points of _____ in their customer contact audit.

MANAGING THE MARKETING OF SERVICES

Just as the unique aspects of services necessitate changes in the consumer's purchase process, the marketing management process requires special adaptation.[19] As emphasized earlier in the chapter, in services marketing the employee plays a central role in attracting, building, and maintaining relationships with customers.[20] This aspect of services marketing has led to a concept called internal marketing.[21]

Internal marketing is based on the notion that a service organization must focus on its employees, or internal market, before successful programs can be directed at customers.[22] The internal marketing concept holds that an organization's employees

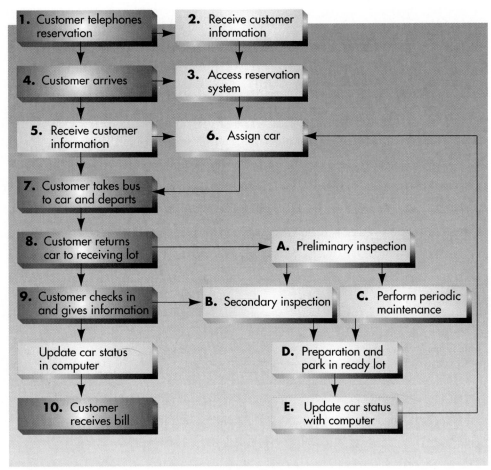

Source: Adapted from W. Earl Sasser, R. Paul Olsen, and D, Daryl Wyckoff, *Management of Service Operations: Text, Cases, and Readings* (Boston: Allyn & Bacon, 1978).

(its "internal market") will be influenced to develop a market orientation if marketing-like activities are directed at them. This idea suggests that employees and employee development through recruitment, training, communication, and administration are critical to the success of service organizations.[23] See the Marketing NewsNet box on the next page for an example of the importance of employees in guaranteeing customer satisfaction.[24]

Let's use the four Ps framework of the text for discussing the marketing mix for services.

Product (Service)

To a large extent, the concepts of the product component of the marketing mix discussed in Chapters 11 and 12 apply equally well to Cheerios (a good) and to American Express (a service). Yet there are three aspects of the product/service element of the mix that warrant special attention: exclusivity, brand name, and capacity management.

Exclusivity   Chapter 11 pointed out that one favorable dimension in a new product is its ability to be patented. Remember that a patent gives the manufacturer

MARKETING NEWSNET

Customer

$

Value

TO INCREASE CUSTOMER VALUE, LET EMPLOYEES GUARANTEE THE SERVICE

How can service organizations increase the value of their offering? For a growing number of firms the answer is a guarantee of satisfaction. At Delta Dental Plan of Massachusetts, for example, customers receive refunds for "service failures." Similarly, a California hospital reduces its bill by 25 percent if a patient has to wait more than five minutes for emergency room care, Domino's Pizza reduces the price of a pizza by $3 if it is not delivered in 30 minutes, and UPS refunds shipping charges if its guaranteed delivery service is late.

Although a guarantee can provide service firms with a means to differentiate themselves from competitors, the inconsistency of services suggests that the potential for payout could be substantial. The key to justifying this expense is to use the payout feedback in an employee development and service improvement process. Thus, implementing a guarantee program requires several steps:

1. Understand client needs.
2. Clearly specify guarantees and payouts.
3. Empower employees to honor the guarantees.
4. Use the service failures to identify problems and improve the service delivery process.

By empowering employees to act, an organization ensures customers that the guarantee is valid and encourages employees to be involved in continuous improvement efforts.

At Ritz-Carlton Hotels, front-desk clerks are now authorized to take off up to $2,000 from a guest's bill if they are not satisfied. The benefits include increased

customer loyalty, an organization focused on customer satisfaction, and reduced managerial costs due to the reduced need for supervisors.

So the next time you're evaluating the services provided by a bank, hotel, advertising agency, accounting firm, doctor, lawyer, dentist, or any service provider, don't be surprised if you're offered a guarantee!

---

of a product exclusive rights to its production for 17 years. A major difference between products and services is that services cannot be patented. Hence the creator of a successful fast-food hamburger chain could quickly discover the concept being copied by others. Domino's Pizza, for example, has seen competitors copy the quick delivery advantage that propelled the company to success.

Branding   An important aspect in marketing goods is the branding strategy used. However, because services are intangible and, therefore, more difficult to describe, the brand name or identifying logo of the service organization is particularly important in consumer decisions.[25] The financial services industry, for example, has failed to use branding to distinguish what consumers perceive to be similar offerings by banks, mutual fund companies, brokerage firms, and insurance companies. Federal Express, however, is a strong service brand name because it suggests the possibility that it is government sanctioned, and it describes the nature and benefit (speed) of the

Logos create service identities.

service.[26] Take a look at the figures at the top of this page to determine how successful some companies have been in branding their service by name, logo, or symbol.

Capacity management   Most services have a limited capacity due to the inseparability of the service from the service provider and the perishable nature of the service. For example, a patient must be in the hospital at the same time as the surgeon to "buy" an appendectomy, and only one patient can be helped at that time. Similarly, no additional surgery can be conducted tomorrow because of an unused operating room or an available surgeon today—the service capacity is lost if it is not used. So the service component of the mix must be integrated with efforts to influence consumer demand.[27] This is referred to as **capacity management.**

Service organizations must manage the availability of the offering so that (1) demand matches capacity over the duration of the demand cycle (for example, one day, week, month, year), and (2) the organization's assets are used in ways that will maximize the return on investment (ROI).[28] Figure 13–8 shows how a hotel tries to

FIGURE 13-8

Managing capacity in a hotel

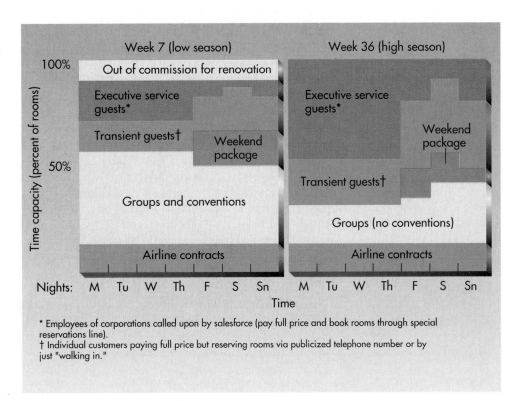

* Employees of corporations called upon by salesforce (pay full price and book rooms through special reservations line).
† Individual customers paying full price but reserving rooms via publicized telephone number or by just "walking in."

Price influences perceptions of services.

manage its capacity during the high and low seasons. Differing price structures are assigned to each segment of consumers to help moderate or adjust demand for the service. Airline contracts fill a fixed number of rooms throughout the year. In the slow season, when more rooms are available, tour packages at appealing prices are used to attract groups or conventions, such as an offer for seven nights in Orlando at a reduced price. Weekend packages are also offered to buyers. In the high-demand season, groups are less desirable because guests who will pay high prices travel to Florida on their own.

Pricing

In the service industries, *price* is often referred to in various ways. Hospitals refer to charges; consultants, lawyers, physicians, and accountants to fees; airlines to fares; and hotels to rates.

Role of pricing   Pricing services plays two essential roles: (1) to affect consumer perceptions and (2) to be used in capacity management. Because of the intangible nature of services, price can indicate the quality of the service. Would you wonder about the quality of a $100 surgery? Studies have shown that when there are few well-known cues by which to judge a product, consumers use price.[29] Look at the accompanying ad for dental services. Would you have concerns about the offer or think it's a good value for the money?

The capacity management role of price is also important to movie theaters, airlines, restaurants, and hotels. Many service businesses use **off-peak pricing,** which consists of charging different prices during different times of the day or days of the week to reflect variations in demand for the service. Airlines offer discounts for weekend travel, and movie theaters offer matinee prices. Sunrise Hospital in Las Vegas offered a 5 1/4 percent rebate on the total hospital bill to patients admitted on a Friday or Saturday so it could level out the demand for surgical suites.[30]

Place (Distribution)

Place or distribution is a major factor in developing a service marketing strategy because of the inseparability of services from the producer. Rarely are intermediaries involved in the distribution of a service; the distribution site and service deliverer are the tangible components of the service.

Historically in professional services marketing, little attention has been paid to distribution. But as competition grows, the value of convenient distribution is being

Services need promotional
programs.

recognized. Hairstyling chains such as Fantastic Sam's Family Haircutters, legal
firms such as the Hyatt chain, and accounting firms such as Deloitte and Touche all
use multiple locations for the distribution of services. In the banking industry,
customers of participating banks using the Cirrus system can access any one of
thousands of automatic teller systems throughout the United States.

Promotion

The value of promotion, specifically advertising, for many services is to show the
benefits of purchasing the service, such as the outcome of using United Airlines. It is
valuable to stress availability, location, consistent quality, and efficient, courteous
service.[31] In addition, services must be concerned with their image. Promotional
efforts, such as Singapore Airline's "Experience an Original" campaign or Merrill
Lynch's use of the bull in its ads, contribute to image and positioning strategies.[32] In
most cases promotional concerns of services are similar to those of products.

In the past, advertising has been viewed negatively by many nonprofit and
professional service organizations. In fact, professional groups such as law, dentistry,
and medicine had previously barred their members from advertising by their
respective professional codes of conduct. A Supreme Court case in 1976, however,
struck down this constraint on professional services advertising.[33] Although opposi-
tion to advertising remains strong in some professional groups, the barriers to promotion are being broken down. In recent years, advertising has been used by religious
groups; legal, medical, and dental services; educational institutions; and many other
service organizations. Attorney Rosalie Osias of Long Island, New York, more than
doubled the number of cases at her real estate and banking law practice by running ads
in two trade newspapers covering the mortgage banking industry in New York.[34]

Another form of promotion, publicity, has played a major role in the promotional
strategy of nonprofit services and some professional organizations. Nonprofit organizations such as public school districts, the Chicago Symphony Orchestra, religious
organizations, and hospitals have used publicity to disseminate their messages.
Because of the heavy reliance on publicity, many services use public service

announcements (PSAs), and because PSAs are free, nonprofit groups have tended to rely on them as the foundation of their media plan.[35] However, as discussed in Chapter 19 on promotion, the timing and location of a PSA are under the control of the medium, not the organization. So the nonprofit service group cannot control who sees the message or when the message is given.

SERVICES IN THE FUTURE

What can we expect from the services industry in the future? New and better services, of course, and an unprecedented variety of suppliers. The changes will be driven by three factors—deregulation, technological development, and consumer interests.

One by one, transportation, telecommunications, financial services, professional services, and other services have gone through some kind of regulatory changes. The changes have generally led to a greater variety of services and, most recently, to a convergence of many of the suppliers of services. Banks, brokerages, and insurance companies, for example, all want to offer one-stop shopping for financial services. Other businesses we traditionally think of as manufacturers are adding services. Ford, General Electric, and General Motors, for example, now offer consumer loans, credit cards, mortgages, commercial loans, and insurance. In recognition of the growing importance of services to most businesses, *Fortune* magazine's ranking of the 500 largest companies in the United States now includes industrial and service firms.

Technological changes are also likely to change the service industry. Perhaps the most dramatic is the trend toward "pay-for-use" services. The information superhighway will soon make it possible to obtain movies, software programs, video games, photographs, and virtually all digital information electronically for a fee. Electronic banking, E-mail, and on-line services are already taking advantage of the changes. Technology is also changing the way some services operate. United Airlines, for example, is replacing traditional paper tickets with electronic versions called e-tickets, and many stock brokerages such as Schwab now encourage customers to use their computers to buy and sell stock. Future readers of this book may simply use their computer and a cable or telephone connection to read assigned pages or to download a copy of the book to a compact disk![36]

Technological changes have expanded the variety of services available and changed the way some services operate.

So easy to forget.

With E-Ticket, there's no paper ticket to remember.

UNITED AIRLINES

Announcing the future of trading

e.Schwab

from one of the biggest names in trading.

Other changes in services are being driven by changes in consumer interests. According to Barbara Feigin of Grey Advertising's Strategic Services, "time will be the currency" of the future. Consumers will search for new services that reduce the time needed to go to the post office, bank, or supermarket or to prepare food, clean clothes, or maintain their homes. In addition, experts say that consumers will become sensitive to environmental issues, and services such as the low-environmental-impact travel service offered by the Audubon Society will be in increasing demand.[37] See the accompanying Ethics and Social Responsibility Alert on page 360 for a discussion of some of the difficult questions facing these new services.[38]

CONCEPT CHECK

1. Matching demand with capacity is the focus of _____ management.

2. How does a movie theater use off-peak pricing?

3. What factors will influence future changes in services?

SUMMARY

1. Services have four unique elements: intangibility, inconsistency, inseparability, and inventory.

2. Intangible refers to the difficulty of communicating the service benefits. Inconsistency refers to the difficulty of providing the same level of quality each time a service is purchased. Inseparable means that service deliverers represent the service quality. Inventory costs for services are related to the cost of maintaining production capacity.

3. Services can be classified in several ways. The primary distinction is whether they are provided by people or equipment. Other distinctions of services are in terms of tax status (profit versus nonprofit) or whether the service is provided by a government agency.

4. Consumers can evaluate three aspects of goods or services: search properties, experience properties, and credence properties.

5. A gap analysis determines if consumers' expectations are different from their actual experiences.

6. A customer contact audit is a flowchart of the points of interaction between a service provider and its customers, where competitive differential advantages should be created.

7. Internal marketing, which focuses on an organization's employees, is critical to the success of a service organization.

8. Because services cannot be patented, unique offerings are difficult to protect. In addition, because services are intangible, brands and logos (which can be protected) are particularly important to help distinguish among competing service providers.

9. The inseparability of production and consumption of services means that capacity management is important in the service element of the mix. This process involves smoothing demand to meet capacity.

10. The intangible nature of services makes price an important cue to indicate service quality to the consumer.

11. Inseparability of production and consumption in services eliminates intermediaries in most service marketing. Distribution is important as a tangible component of a service offering.

12. Historically, promotion has not been viewed favorably by many nonprofit and professional service organizations. In recent years this attitude has changed, and service organizations have increased their promotional activities.

KEY TERMS AND CONCEPTS

services p. 346
four I's of services p. 347
idle production capacity p. 348
service continuum p. 349
gap analysis p. 353

customer contact audit p. 354
internal marketing p. 354
capacity management p. 357
off-peak pricing p. 358

CHAPTER PROBLEMS AND APPLICATIONS

1. Explain how the four I's of services would apply to a Marriott Hotel.

2. Idle production capacity may be related to inventory or capacity management. How would the pricing component of the marketing mix reduce idle production capacity for (*a*) a car wash, (*b*) a stage theater group, and (*c*) a university?

3. What are the search, experience, and credence properties of an airline for the business traveler and pleasure traveler? What properties are most important to each group?

4. Outline the customer contact audit for the typical deposit you make at your neighborhood bank.

5. The text suggests that internal marketing is necessary before a successful marketing program can be directed at consumers. Why is this particularly true for service organizations?

6. Outline the capacity management strategies that an airline must consider.

7. Draw the channel of distribution for the following services: (*a*) a restaurant, (*b*) a hospital, and (*c*) a hotel.

8. How does off-peak pricing influence demand for services?

9. In recent years, many service businesses have begun to provide their employees with uniforms. Explain the rationale behind this strategy in terms of the concepts discussed in this chapter.

10. Look back at the service continuum in Figure 13–3. Explain how the following points in the continuum differ in terms of consistency: (*a*) salt, (*b*) automobile, (*c*) advertising agency, and (*d*) teaching.

CASE 13–1 The Philadelphia Phillies, Inc.

Video

Marketing is always full of surprises! In professional baseball it even involves settling disputes between the "Phillie Phanatic"—the green furry mascot of the Philadelphia Phillies—and Tommy Lasorda, manager of the Los Angeles Dodgers.

This is one reason David Montgomery never gets bored. "When I finished business school, I had to choose between a marketing research job at a large paper products company or marketing the Philadelphia Phillies," explains Montgomery, the executive vice president of the Philadelphia Phillies. "And it was no real decision because there never has been one day on this job that wasn't different and exciting," he says.

THE ORGANIZATION

Like other teams in professional sports, over the years the Phillies team has had its ups and downs. But the team has provided some great baseball for loyal Phillies' fans: National League East divisional titles in 1976, 1977, 1978, 1980, 1983, and 1993; National League pennants

in 1980, 1983, and 1993; and a World Series title in 1980. The team moved into newly built Veterans Stadium in 1971, which the Philadelphia Eagles football team also uses.

"We're a private business that serves the public," continues David Montgomery, "and we've got to make sure our revenues more than cover our expenses." He identifies these key sources of revenues and gives the approximate annual percentages of each (see accompanying table).

SERVICE	PERCENTAGE OF VISITS	AVERAGE CHARGE
Personal illness	39%	$25
Physical examinations	14	25
Workers' compensation	25	39
Employment or insurance examinations	19	47
Emergency	3	67

Balanced against these revenues are some major expenses that include players' salaries (some exceeding several million dollars annually) and salaries of more than 70 full-time employees. Other expenses are those for scouting and drafting 40 to 60 new players per year, operating six minor-league farm clubs, and renting and operating (with a labor force of 400 persons per game) Veterans Stadium for the Phillies' 81 home games.

THE ISSUES

Many of these revenues depend on fan attendance, which typically exceeds more than 2 million annually at Phillies' home games. But marketing appeals and promotions that work with more traditional, stable products don't always apply here. "In sports marketing, you're not so sure exactly what you can say," comments Montgomery. "It's difficult to promise a pennant-winning club when reality may be entirely different."

Promotions of special events generate fan attendance—and even first-time visits by people who have never seen a major league baseball game. "Our special promotions fall into two categories—promotional or premium gift days and event days," explains Jo-Anne Levy, the Phillies' assistant director of marketing. Gift days involve free gifts like hats, jackets, and sunglasses, whereas event days are things like camera night, fireworks, and the old-timers' game. Local and national businesses often pay the Phillies to "cosponsor" the gift days, which often means putting their name on the product.

Some special event days have been more "special" than even Levy had hoped. One was the ostrich race in which a frightened Phillies' broadcaster wound up in the first row of the stands when the ostrich pulling him and his cart panicked in front of the crowd.

Planning the special events promotions and advertising starts the July or August of the preceding season. This often involves personal appearances by Phillies players, advertising, and publicity to try to sell tickets in February, March, and April—*before* the regular season starts. Reflecting the loyalty of the fanatical Philadelphia fans, in 1978 Phillies marketing personnel dreamed up a mascot for the team—the Phillie Phanatic. This friendly green, furry animal is present at all home Phillies games and makes many public relations appearances throughout the year.

A major league sports team has a special dimension for its community. Comments Dennis Mannion, the Phillies director of marketing: "The bottom line is the impact you have on the community itself. What you do for your community and what you can give to it often translates into what you will get back."

Questions

1. What is the "product" that the Phillies should market? What appeals should the Phillies use?

2. How does "marketing the Philadelphia Phillies" differ from marketing a consumer product such as a breakfast cereal or cake mix?

3. Considering all four elements of the promotional mix (advertising, personal selling, sales promotion, and publicity), what specific promotional activities should the Phillies use? Which should be used off-season? On-season?

4. What kind of special promotions and special events can the Phillies use to increase attendance by targeting segments based on (*a*) age (14 and under versus 15 and over), (*b*) sex (females versus males), and (*c*) fans versus people who have never been to a baseball game?

CHAPTER 14

Pricing: Relating Objectives to Revenues and Costs

AFTER READING THIS CHAPTER YOU SHOULD BE ABLE TO:

• Identify the elements that make up a price.

• Recognize the constraints on a firm's pricing latitude and the objectives a firm has in setting prices.

• Explain what a demand curve is and how it affects a firm's total and marginal revenue.

• Recognize what price elasticity of demand means to a manager facing a pricing decision.

• Explain the role of costs in pricing decisions.

• Calculate a break-even point for various combinations of price, fixed cost, and unit variable cost.

THE CASE OF THE $660 MILLION PRICE CUT

By all conventional measures Boeing is the world leader in the design, manufacture, and marketing of commercial jet aircraft: after ushering in jet-age air travel with the Boeing 707 three decades ago, it has built almost 8,000 jetliners—more than all other manufacturers in the world combined.[1]

Still, when it comes to setting price, Boeing sweats the details like small and large organizations the world over. Consider some of the problems it faces today in the 1990s:

• U.S. deregulation of airlines. This has led to intense competition and cost controls among U.S. airlines, reflected in everything from the bankruptcies of some to intense fare wars among others to that bagel or croissant "lunch" you had on your last flight.

• High operating costs on many international airlines. The costs of operating a jetliner plus the recessions in Japan and Europe have made airline executives frantic in these countries. Because the recession and the strong yen have grounded many of its core first-class customers, Japan Airlines (JAL) has sought ways to drastically cut costs. For instance, on a recent JAL flight to Hawaii, foreign crew members were substituted for the Japanese crew. The newly hired Thai flight attendants earn about five percent of the annual salary of their Japanese counterparts, and the Irish pilot and Canadian copilot earn about half as much.[2]

• Competition from the Airbus Industrie consortium. Composed of key aerospace partners from France, Great Britain, Germany, and Spain, Airbus Industrie is a formidable international competitor that bids on jetliner purchases around the world.

The effect of all of this on Boeing? Annual revenues fell from a peak of $30 billion in 1992 to $22 billion in 1994 as sales of jetliners plummeted.

365

So what's a company to do? Boeing's answer: cut price . . . big time! Working with General Electric (GE), its jet-engine supplier, Boeing faced intense competition with McDonnell Douglas and Airbus Industrie for a 55-plane order from Scandinavian Airline System (SAS). Boeing won the order by agreeing to sell its 100-passenger 737-600 jetliners to SAS for $20 million each, a $12 million (38 percent) reduction from its regular price. And for 55 jetliners that adds up to a $660 million price cut![3]

Cutting price isn't always the solution. As we'll see in this chapter, a firm can go bankrupt if, in the long run, the prices customers pay don't cover its production and marketing expenses and also provide some profit. In fact, cutting price didn't succeed when Boeing sought an order for 40 new upgraded 737s from Northwest Airlines for a $50 million "list" price each. Instead, Northwest decided to refurbish 40 of its old DC-9s for $5 million apiece and operate them for another 15 years.[4]

Innovative companies now recognize that value for their customers is more than simply a low price. As shown in the Marketing NewsNet below,[5] Boeing has utilized cross-functional teams to improve jetliner designs as well as to speed up jetliner and spare parts delivery to customers. But as the box shows, sometimes what is seen as

---

MARKETING NEWSNET

JETLINER CROSS-FUNCTIONAL TEAMS AND CUSTOMER VALUE: NO LONGER SLEEPY IN SEATTLE

The new economics of jetliner production and use has awakened Boeing, the Seattle giant that is the area's largest employer. In recent years Boeing utilized a variety of cross-functional teams to add genuine value for its customers—both the airlines that buy Boeing jetliners and the passengers that ride in them.

Boeing's cross-functional teams blend not only employees from different functional areas within the firm but also its suppliers and customers as well. Here are some actions triggered by these teams:

- Introduction of a new 737-800 model. This upgrade of the 737 series—the best selling jetliner in aviation history—offers the airline customers more range, more speed, and better operating economics.
- Next-day shipment on routine spare parts. This was a drastic improvement over the previous 10-day Boeing standard, which, in turn, was three times better than the industry standard.
- Reduction of order cycle time by 45 percent. This means that the time from receiving a jetliner order until delivery has been reduced from 18 months to 10—with a new target of 8 months.

Further, in 1995 Boeing's flagship customer, United Airlines, put the Boeing 777 into service. Listening to passengers like you, the Boeing Triple-7 provides some great customer-value innovations: 6'4" of center aisle

headroom, a 5.7-inch TV screen in the seatback in front of each passenger, and most seats that are 18.5 inches wide—1.5 inches wider than most economy jetliner seats.

But the airlines wanted customer value, too, in the form of the flexibility to reconfigure seats to handle different uses for the plane, which generates a conflict between the customer value of the airlines and that of passengers. Until things change, you might avoid seats in rows 16, 31, 40, and 43. They're still only 17 inches wide! So delivering customer value for all of a firm's customers often requires some difficult trade-offs.

greater customer value for one group (reconfiguration flexibility for airlines) can conflict with that for another (wider seats for all the passengers).[6]

Welcome to the fascinating—and intense—world of pricing, where myriad forces come together in the specific price prospective buyers are asked to pay. This chapter and Chapter 15 cover important factors used in setting prices.

NATURE AND IMPORTANCE OF PRICE

The price paid for goods and services goes by many names . You pay *tuition* for your education, *rent* for an apartment, *interest* on a bank credit card, and a *premium* for car insurance. Your dentist or physician charges you a *fee,* a professional or social organization charges *dues,* and airlines flying their Boeing—or other—jetliners charge a *fare.* In business, a consultant may require a *retainer* for services rendered, an executive is given a *salary,* a salesperson receives a *commission,* and a worker is paid a *wage.* Of course, what you pay for clothes or a haircut is termed a *price.*

What Is a Price?

These examples highlight the many varied ways that price plays a part in our daily lives. From a marketing viewpoint, **price** is the money or other considerations (including other goods and services) exchanged for the ownership or use of a good or service. For example, Shell Oil recently exchanged 1 million pest control devices for sugar from a Caribbean country, and Wilkinson Sword exchanged some of its knives for advertising used to promote its razor blades. This practice of exchanging goods and services for other goods and services rather than for money is called **barter.** These transactions account for billions of dollars annually in domestic and international trade.

For most products and services, money is exchanged, although the amount is not always the same as the list or quoted price, because of the discounts, allowances, and extra fees shown in Figure 14–1. Suppose you decide to buy two identical

ITEM PURCHASED	PRICE	=	LIST PRICE	−	DISCOUNTS AND ALLOWANCES	+	EXTRA FEES
New car bought by an individual	Final price	=	List price	−	Quantity discount Cash discount Trade-ins	+	Financing charges Special accessories
Term in college bought by a student	Tuition	=	Published tuition	−	Scholarship Other financial aid Discounts for number of credits taken	+	Special activity fees
Bank loan obtained by a small business	Principal and interest	=	Amount of loan sought	−	Allowance for collateral	+	Premium for uncertain creditworthiness
Merchandise bought from a wholesaler by a retailer	Invoice price	=	List price	−	Quantity discount Cash discount Seasonal discount Functional or trade discount	+	Penalty for late payment

PRICE EQUATION

FIGURE 14–1   The price of four different purchases

How do consumers relate *value* to *price,* as in the new Kohler walk-in bathtub that is safe for children and elderly alike? For a discussion of this important issue, see the text.

Lamborghini Diable VTs because their 492-horsepower engines can move you from 0 to 60 mph in 4.1 seconds.[7] (You need *two,* in case one is in the shop.) The list price is $255,000 each. As a quantity discount for buying two, you get $28,000 off the list price for each. You agree to pay half down and the other half when the cars are delivered, which results in a financing fee of $15,000 per car. You are allowed $1,000 for your only trade—your 1985 Honda—amounting to $500 off the price of each Diablo VT.

Applying the "price equation" (as shown in Figure 14–1) to your purchase, your price per car is:

Price = List price − Discounts and allowances + Extra fees

   = $255,000 − ($20,000 + $500) + $15,000

   = $249,500

Are you still interested? Perhaps you might look at the Dodge Viper or Aston Martin to compare prices. Figure 14–1 also illustrates how the price equation applies to a variety of different products and services.

Price as an Indicator of Value

From a consumer's standpoint, price is often used to indicate value when it is paired with the perceived benefits of a product or service. Specifically, **value** can be defined as the ratio of perceived benefits to price, or:[8]

$$\text{Value} = \frac{\text{Perceived benefits}}{\text{Price}}$$

This relationship shows that for a given price, as perceived benefits increase, value increases. Also, for a given price, value decreases when perceived benefits decrease. Creative marketers engage in **value-pricing**, the practice of simultaneously increasing product and service benefits and maintaining or decreasing price.

For some products, price influences the perception of overall quality, and ultimately value, to consumers.[9] For example, in a survey of home furnishing buyers, 84 percent agreed with the following statement: "The higher the price, the higher the quality." For computer software it has been shown that consumers believe a low price implies poor quality.[10]

Consumer value assessments are often comparative. Here value involves the judgment by a consumer of the worth and desirability of a product or service relative to substitutes that satisfy the same need. In this instance a "reference value" emerges, which involves comparing the costs and benefits of substitute items. For example, Kohler recently introduced a walk-in bathtub that is safe for children and the elderly. Although priced higher than conventional step-in bathtubs, it has proven very successful because buyers place great "value" on the extra safety.

Price in the Marketing Mix

Pricing is also a critical decision made by a marketing executive because price has a direct effect on a firm's profits. This is apparent from a firm's **profit equation**:

Profit = Total revenue − Total cost

or

Profit = (Unit price × Quantity sold) − Total cost

What makes this relationship even more important is that price affects the quantity sold, as illustrated with demand curves later in this chapter. Furthermore, since the quantity sold sometimes affects a firm's costs because of efficiency of production, price also indirectly affects costs. So pricing decisions influence both total revenue and total cost, which makes pricing one of the most important decisions marketing executives face.

The importance of price in the marketing mix necessitates an understanding of six major steps involved in the process organizations go through in setting prices (Figure 14–2):

- Identify pricing constraints and objectives.
- Estimate demand and revenue.
- Determine cost, volume, and profit relationships.
- Select an approximate price level.

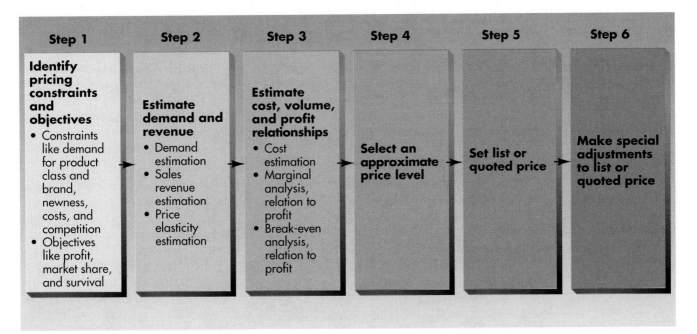

FIGURE 14-2   Steps in setting price

- Set list or quoted price.
- Make special adjustments to list or quoted price.

The first three steps are covered in this chapter and the last three in Chapter 15.

STEP 1: IDENTIFYING PRICING CONSTRAINTS AND OBJECTIVES

To define a problem, Chapter 8 showed that it is important to consider both the objectives and constraints that narrow the range of alternatives available to solve it. These same principles apply in solving a pricing problem. Let's first review the pricing constraints so that we can better understand the nature of pricing alternatives.

Identifying Pricing Constraints

Factors that limit the latitude of prices a firm may set are **pricing constraints**. Consumer demand for the product clearly affects the price that can be charged. Other constraints on price are set by factors within the organization: newness of the product, whether it is part of a product line, and cost of and flexibility in changing a price. Competitive factors such as the nature of competition and price set by competitors also restrict the latitude of an organization's ability to set price. Legal and regulatory constraints on pricing are discussed in Chapter 15.

Demand for the product class, product, and brand   The number of potential buyers for the product class (such as cars), product (sports cars), and brand (Lamborghini) clearly affects the price a seller can charge. So does whether the item is a luxury—like a Lamborghini—or a necessity—like bread and a roof over your head. In fact, as shown in the Ethics and Social Responsibility Alert, the name "Kona" is so prized among coffee drinkers that putting this name on nonKona coffee can command a premium price.[11] The nature of demand is discussed later in the chapter.

Newness of the product: stage in the product life cycle   The newer a product and the earlier it is in its life cycle, the higher is the price that can usually be charged. When NutraSweet was introduced in 1983, it was the only nonartificial sugar substitute that was safe to use, contained few calories, and was sweeter than sugar. The newness of the product coupled with patent protection meant that a premium price of $92 per pound could be charged. However, once its patent expired in 1992, rivals emerged (such as Johnson & Johnson's sweetener Sucralose), which affected the pricing latitude for NutraSweet. NutraSweet's price per pound has fallen by about half.

Single product versus a product line   When Sony introduced its CD player, not only was it unique and in the introductory stage of its product life cycle but also it was the *only* CD player Sony sold, so the firm had great latitude in setting a price. Now, with a line of CD player products, the price of individual models has to be consistent with the others based on features provided and meaningful price differentials that communicate value to consumers.

ETHICS AND SOCIAL RESPONSIBILITY ALERT

Ethics

GETTING AN UNFAIR PRICE PREMIUM FROM THAT MAGIC "KONA" NAME

Javaheads of America, arise! That may not be real Kona coffee you're scarfing by the "grande" from your local coffee shop!

Many coffee aficionados put Kona coffee in a class by itself because of its distinctive taste, which is strong but not bitter. However, true Kona coffee is raised in a tiny area on the western slopes of Hawaii, the Big Island, where the right combination of sun and cloud cover provide ideal growing conditions.

The problem? The tiny growing area and the wages of Hawaiian coffee pickers that are often 15 to 20 times their Central and South American counterparts makes pure Kona coffee very expensive—about $20 a pound.

(The Starbucks gourmet coffee chain was recently selling 100 percent Kona coffee for $18.95 a pound.) The result is that many "Kona coffees" sold in the U.S. may contain only 10 percent Kona coffee. . . or even as little as "at least one bean," according to a coffee expert quoted by *The Wall Street Journal*. The remainder is made up of blends of cheaper Central and South American coffees.

This is a big concern to many coffee growers in Kona. They believe that some coffee packers are using the prestigious "Kona" name in labeling their coffees to get a premium price from unsophisticated coffee consumers who don't really know what they are buying.

Is this use of the Kona name unfair? Unethical? Illegal? What should be done? Who should do it?

Cost of producing and marketing the product   In the long run, a firm's price must cover all the costs of producing and marketing a product. If the price doesn't cover the cost, the firm will fail, so in the long run a firm's costs set a floor under its price. Regent Air and McClain Airlines painfully learned this lesson. Both airlines provided luxury transcontinental air service for one-way airfares as high as $1,000. Unfortunately, the total cost of providing this red-carpet service exceeded the total revenue and both companies failed.

Cost of changing prices and time period they apply   If Scandinavian Airlines asks General Electric (GE) to provide spare jet engines to power the new Boeing 737 it just bought, GE can easily set a new price for the engines to reflect its latest information since only one buyer has to be informed. But if J. Crew or L. L. Bean decides that sweater prices are too low in its winter catalogs after thousands of catalogs have been mailed to customers, it has a big problem. It can't easily inform thousands of potential buyers that the price has changed, so J. Crew or L. L. Bean must consider the cost of changing prices and the time period for which they apply in developing the price list for its catalog items. In actual practice, research indicates that most firms change the price for their major products once a year.[12]

Type of competitive markets   The seller's price is constrained by the type of market in which it competes. Economists generally delineate four types of competitive markets: pure monopoly, oligopoly, monopolistic competition, and pure competition. Figure 14–3 shows that the type of competition dramatically influences the latitude of price competition and, in turn, the nature of product differentiation and extent of advertising. A firm must recognize the general type of competitive market it is in to understand the latitude of both its price and nonprice strategies. For example,

- *Pure monopoly.* Pacific Power & Light, an electric power company, receives approval from the state utility commission for the rates it can charge California

	TYPE OF COMPETITIVE MARKET			
STRATEGIES AVAILABLE	**PURE MONOPOLY** (One seller who sets the price for a unique product)	**OLIGOPOLY** (Few sellers who are sensitive to each other's prices)	**MONOPOLISTIC COMPETITION** (Many sellers who compete on nonprice factors)	**PURE COMPETITION** (Many sellers who follow the market price for identical, commodity products)
Price competition	None: sole seller sets price	Some: price leader or follower of competitors	Some: compete over range of prices	Almost none: market sets price
Product differentiation	None: no other producers	Various: depends on industry	Some: differentiate products from competitors'	None: products are identical
Extent of advertising	Little: purpose is to increase demand for product class	Some: purpose is to inform but avoid price competition	Much: purpose is to differentiate firm's products from competitors'	Little: purpose is to inform prospects that seller's products are available

FIGURE 14–3   Pricing, product, and advertising strategies available to firms in four types of competitive markets

consumers. In most areas of the state it is the only source of electricity for consumers and runs public-service ads to show them how to conserve electricity.

- *Oligopoly.* The few sellers of aluminum (Reynolds, Alcoa) or American-built, mainframe computers try to avoid price competition because it can lead to disastrous price wars in which all lose money. Yet firms in such industries stay aware of a competitor's price cuts or increases and may follow suit. The products can be undifferentiated (aluminum) or differentiated (mainframe computers), and informative advertising that avoids head-to-head price competition is used.

- *Monopolistic competition.* Dozens of regional, private brands of peanut butter compete with national brands like Skippy and Jif. Both price competition (regional, private brands being lower than national brands) and nonprice competition (product features and advertising) exist.

- *Pure competition.* Hundreds of local grain elevators sell corn whose price per bushel is set by the marketplace. Within strains, the corn is identical, so advertising only informs buyers that the seller's corn is available.

Competitors' prices   A firm must know or anticipate what specific price its present and potential competitors are charging now or will charge. When the NutraSweet Company planned the market introduction of Simplesse® all natural fat substitute, it had to consider the price of fat replacements already available as well as potential competitors including Procter & Gamble's Olestra, Pfizer Inc.'s VeriLo, and the Stellar brand made by A. E. Staley Company.

Identifying Pricing Objectives

Expectations that specify the role of price in an organization's marketing and strategic plans are **pricing objectives**. To the extent possible, these organizational

pricing objectives are also carried to lower levels in the organization, such as in setting objectives for marketing managers responsible for an individual brand. H. J. Heinz, for example, has specific pricing objectives for its Heinz ketchup brand that vary by country. Chapter 2 discussed six broad objectives that an organization may pursue, which tie in directly to the organization's pricing policies.

Profit   Three different objectives relate to a firm's profit, usually measured in terms of return on investment (ROI) or return on assets. One objective is *managing for long-run profits,* which is followed by many Japanese firms that are willing to forgo immediate profit in cars, TV sets, or computers to develop quality products that can penetrate competitive markets in the future. A *maximizing current profit* objective, such as during this quarter or year, is common in many firms because the targets can be set and performance measured quickly. American firms are sometimes criticized for this short-run orientation. A *target return* objective involves a firm such as Du Pont or Exxon setting a goal (such as 20 percent) for pretax ROI. These three profit objectives have different implications for a firm's pricing objectives.

Sales   Given that a firm's profit is high enough for it to remain in business, its objectives may be to increase sales revenue. The hope is that the increase in sales revenue will in turn lead to increases in market share and profit. Cutting price on one product in a firm's line may increase its sales revenue but reduce those of related products. Objectives related to sales revenue or unit sales have the advantage of being translated easily into meaningful targets for marketing managers responsible for a product line or brand—far more easily than with an ROI target, for example.

Market share   Market share is the ratio of the firm's sales revenues or unit sales to those of the industry (competitors plus the firm itself). Companies often pursue a market share objective when industry sales are flat or declining and they want to get a larger share. Anheuser-Busch has adopted this objective in the brewing industry. According to August A. Busch III, the company's chief executive officer, "We want 50 percent of the [beer] market in the mid-1990s."[13] Although increased market share is a primary goal of some firms, others see it as a means to other ends: increasing sales and profits.

Unit volume Many firms use unit volume, the quantity produced or sold, as a pricing objective. These firms often sell multiple products at very different prices and are sensitive to matching production capacity with unit volume. Using unit volume as an objective, however, can sometimes be misleading from a profit standpoint. Volume can be increased by employing sales incentives (such as lowering prices, giving rebates, or offering lower interest rates). By doing this the company chooses to lower profits in the short run to quickly sell its product. This happened recently when Fiat offered $1,600 rebates and zero-interest financing in Italy on its $10,000 Uno compact car.[14]

Survival In some instances, profits, sales, and market share are less important objectives of the firm than mere survival. Continental Airlines has struggled to attract passengers with low fares, no-penalty advance-booking policies, and aggressive promotions to improve the firm's cash flow. This pricing objective has helped Continental to stay alive in the competitive airline industry.

Social responsibility A firm may forgo higher profit on sales and follow a pricing objective that recognizes its obligations to customers and society in general. Medtronics followed this pricing policy when it introduced the world's first heart pacemaker. Gerber supplies a specially formulated product free of charge to children who cannot tolerate foods based on cow's milk. Government agencies, which set many prices for services they offer, use social responsibility as a primary pricing objective. As a result, in the arid South and Southwest the federal government sells water to users at a price that is only about one fifth of the total cost of providing it.

CONCEPT CHECK

1. What do you have to do to the list price to determine the final price?

2. How does the type of competitive market a firm is in affect its latitude in setting price?

STEP 2: ESTIMATING DEMAND AND REVENUE

Basic to setting a product's price is the extent of customer demand for it. Marketing executives must also translate this estimate of customer demand into estimates of revenues the firm expects to receive.

Fundamentals of Estimating Demand

Newsweek decided to conduct a pricing experiment at newsstands in 11 cities throughout the United States.[15] At that time, Houston newsstand buyers paid $2.25.

In Fort Worth, New York, Los Angeles, San Francisco, and Atlanta, newsstand buyers paid the regular $2.00 price. In San Diego, the price was $1.50. The price in Minneapolis–St. Paul, New Orleans, and Detroit was only $1.00. By comparison, the regular newsstand price for *Time* and *U.S. News & World Report, Newsweek's* competitors, was $1.95. Why did *Newsweek* conduct the experiment? According to a *Newsweek* executive, at that time, "We want to figure out what the demand curve for our magazine at the newsstand is." And you thought that demand curves only existed to confuse you on a test in basic economics!

The demand curve   A **demand curve** shows a maximum number of products consumers will buy at a given price. Demand curve D_1 in Figure 14–4 shows the newsstand demand for *Newsweek* under present conditions. Note that as price falls, people buy more. But price is not the complete story in estimating demand. Economists stress three other key factors:

1. *Consumer tastes.* As we saw in Chapter 3, these depend on many factors such as demographics, culture, and technology. Because consumer tastes can change quickly, up-to-date marketing research is essential.
2. *Price and availability of other products.* As the price of close substitute products falls (the price of *Time*) and their availability increases, the demand for a product declines (the demand for *Newsweek*).
3. *Consumer income.* In general, as real consumer income (allowing for inflation) increases, demand for a product also increases.

The first of these two factors influences what consumers *want* to buy, and the third affects what they *can* buy. Along with price, these are often called **demand factors**, or factors that determine consumers' willingness and ability to pay for goods and services.

Movement along versus shift of a demand curve   Demand curve D_1 in Figure 14–4 shows that as the price is lowered from $2 to $1.50, the quantity demanded increases from 3 million (Q_1) to 4.5 million (Q_2) units per year. This is an example of a movement along a demand curve and assumes that other factors (consumer tastes, price and availability of substitutes, and consumer income) remain unchanged.

What if some of these factors change? For example, if advertising causes more people to want *Newsweek,* newsstand distribution is increased, and consumer incomes double, then the demand increases. This is shown in Figure 14–4 as a shift of the demand curve to the right, from D_1 to D_2. This increased demand means that more *Newsweek* magazines are wanted for a given price: at a price of $2, the demand is 6 million units per year (Q_3) on D_2 rather than 3 million units per year (Q_1) on D_1.

For any downward-sloping, straight-line demand curve, the marginal revenue curve always falls at a rate twice as fast as the demand curve. As shown in Figure 14–6A, the marginal revenue becomes $0 per unit at a quantity sold of 4.5 million units—the very point at which total revenue is maximum (see Figure 14–6B). Because a rational marketing manager would never operate in the region of the demand curve in which marginal revenue is negative, only the positive portion is shown in typical graphs of demand curves, as is done in Figure 14–6A.

What price did *Newsweek* select after conducting its experiment? It kept the price at $2.00. However, through expanded newsstand distribution and more aggressive advertising, *Newsweek* was later able to shift its demand curve to the right and charge a price of $2.50 without affecting its newsstand volume.

Price elasticity of demand   With a downward-sloping demand curve, we have been concerned with the responsiveness of demand to price changes. This can be conveniently measured by **price elasticity of demand**, or the percentage change in quantity demanded relative to a percentage change in price. Price elasticity of demand (E) is expressed as follows:

$$E = \frac{\text{Percentage change in quantity demanded}}{\text{Percentage change in price}}$$

Because quantity demanded usually decreases as price increases, price elasticity of demand is usually a negative number. However, for the sake of simplicity and by convention, elasticity figures are shown as positive numbers.

Price elasticity of demand assumes three forms: elastic demand, inelastic demand, and unitary demand elasticity. *Elastic demand* exists when a small percentage decrease in price produces a larger percentage increase in quantity demanded. Price elasticity is greater than 1 with elastic demand. *Inelastic demand* exists when a small percentage decrease in price produces a smaller percentage increase in quantity demanded. With inelastic demand, price elasticity is less than 1. *Unitary demand* exists when the percentage change in price is identical to the percentage change in quantity demanded. In this instance, price elasticity is equal to 1.

Price elasticity of demand is determined by a number of factors. First, the more substitutes a product or service has, the more likely it is to be price elastic. For example, butter has many possible substitutes in a meal and is price elastic, but gasoline has almost no substitutes and is price inelastic. Second, products and services considered to be necessities are price inelastic. For example, open-heart surgery is price inelastic, whereas airline tickets for a vacation are price elastic. Third, items that require a large cash outlay compared with a person's disposable income are price elastic. Accordingly, cars and yachts are price elastic; books and movie tickets tend to be price inelastic.

Price elasticity is important to marketing managers because of its relationship to total revenue. For example, with elastic demand, total revenue increases when price decreases, but decreases when price increases. With inelastic demand, total revenue increases when price increases and decreases when price decreases. Finally, with unitary demand total revenue is unaffected by a slight price change.

Because of this relationship between price elasticity and a firm's total revenue, it is important that marketing managers recognize that price elasticity of demand is not the same over all possible prices of a product. Figure 14–6B illustrates this point using the *Newsweek* demand curve shown in Figure 14–6A. As the price decreases from $2.50 to $2, total revenue increases, indicating an elastic demand. However, when the price decreases from $1 to 50 cents, total revenue declines, indicating an inelastic demand. Unitary demand elasticity exists at a price of $1.50.

Price elasticities for brands and product classes   Marketing executives also recognize that the price elasticity of demand is not always the same for product

What are the marketing secrets of the entrepreneur who entered the frozen-entree fray, against the advice of experts? For the answer, see the text and the Marketing NewsNet box.

classes (such as stereo receivers) and brands within a product class (such as Sony and Marantz). For example, marketing experiments on brands of cola, coffee, and snack and specialty foods generally show elasticities of 1.5 to 2.5, indicating they are price elastic. By comparison, entire product classes of fruits and vegetables have elasticities of about 0.8—they are price inelastic.[16]

Recently, the price elasticity of demand for cigarettes has become a hotly debated public health issue and a matter of corporate ethics and social responsibility. Research generally shows that cigarettes are price inelastic.[17] However, price elasticity differs by the age of the smoker. Because 12 to 17 year olds often have limited "spending money," this group is very price elastic in its demand for cigarettes. As a result, many legislators recommend far higher excise taxes on cigarettes to increase their prices significantly with the goal of reducing teen-age smoking. So price elasticity is not only a relevant concept for marketing managers, it is also important for public policy affecting pricing practices.[18]

CONCEPT CHECK

1. What is the difference between a movement along and a shift of a demand curve?

2. What does it mean if a product has a price elasticity of demand that is greater than 1?

STEP 3: ESTIMATING COST, VOLUME, AND PROFIT RELATIONSHIPS

While revenues are the moneys received by the firm from selling its products or services to customers, costs or expenses are the moneys the firm pays out to its employees and suppliers. Marketing managers often use marginal analysis and break-even analysis to relate revenues and costs at various levels of units sold, topics covered in this section.

MARKETING NEWSNET

THE SECRETS OF A FOOD ENTREPRENEUR: PAY ATTENTION TO DETAIL AND CONTROL COSTS

"I think I'm well liked by my employees," he says, "but I'm a [soft expletive] on quality. If the pasta is a little mushy, I get a lot of upset." The speaker is Jeno Paulucci, chief executive officer of Luigino's foods and called the "nation's most accomplished food entrepreneur in recent times" by *Fortune* magazine. Across five decades and through three huge new-food businesses, Paulucci's secrets have remained consistent: (1) a passion for detail and (2) low, low overhead to control costs. The effect has been to provide genuine value to customers that, in turn, has resulted in huge success for his three separate businesses, described here.

Chun King Foods. In 1945 Paulucci became a local legend—the son of Italian immigrant parents selling Chinese food to mostly Scandinavian customers on Minnesota's Iron Range. But Chun King took off when GIs returning from World War II sought the convenience—and customer value—of easy-to-prepare dinners. In 1966 Paulucci sold Chun King to what was then R.J. Reynolds for $63 million.

Jenos. He took the cash and started producing pizzas and pizza rolls. How did Paulucci get the idea for pizza rolls? His response: "I had to do something with my egg roll machines"—a low cost way of utilizing his leftover Chun King equipment. By 1972 Jeno's was the U.S. leader in frozen pizza and frozen hot snacks. But Paulucci got bored with the business and sold it to Pillsbury for $150 million in 1985. Paulucci's quality concern: "The pies got smaller, with more artificial ingredients. I didn't like making food that way."

Luiginos. In 1990, against the judgment of experts, Paulucci entered the overcrowded frozen-entree fray, competing with giant brands such as Stouffer, Healthy Choice, and Weight Watchers. Paulucci was unfazed and observes, "All those big companies with all their overhead—I knew if we paid attention to the little things our plan would work." Two examples: (1) Paulucci packs the pasta in his Michelina's Italian dinners separately from the sauce to improve flavor, and (2) he sells his Italian dinners for about half the price of competitors—by controlling his costs.

His credo: "Gold is in the details"—which applies to customer value, costs, and prices.

The Importance of Controlling Costs

The profit equation described at the beginning of the chapter showed that Profit = Total revenue − Total cost. Therefore, understanding the role and behavior of costs is critical for all marketing decisions, particularly pricing decisions. Four cost concepts are important in pricing decisions: **total cost, fixed cost, variable cost**, and **marginal cost** (Figure 14–7).

Many firms go bankrupt because their costs get out of control, causing their total costs to exceed their total revenues over an extended period of time. This is why sophisticated marketing managers make pricing decisions that balance both their revenues and costs. An example, described in the Marketing NewsNet box, is that of an entrepreneur who has achieved spectacular success in three different food businesses by controlling costs and attending to critical details that ensure that his products provide genuine value to customers. Controlling costs carefully has enabled him to sell his Michelina's Italian dinners at prices well below those of his competitors.[19]

Marginal Analysis and Profit Maximization

A basic idea in business, economics, and indeed everyday life is marginal analysis. In personal terms, marginal analysis means that people will continue to do something as long as the incremental return exceeds the incremental cost. This same idea holds true

FIGURE 14-7

Fundamental cost concepts

> *Total cost (TC)* is the total expense incurred by a firm in producing and marketing the product. Total cost is the sum of fixed cost and variable cost.
>
> *Fixed cost (FC)* is the sum of the expenses of the firm that are stable and do not change with the quantity of product that is produced and sold. Examples of fixed costs are rent on the building, executive salaries, and insurance.
>
> *Variable cost (VC)* is the sum of the expenses of the firm that vary directly with the quantity of product that is produced and sold. For example, as the quantity sold doubles, the variable cost doubles. Examples are the direct labor and direct materials used in producing the product and the sales commissions that are tied directly to the quantity sold. As mentioned above:
>
> $$TC = FC + VC$$
>
> Variable cost expressed on a per unit basis is called *unit variable cost (UVC)*.
>
> *Marginal cost (MC)* is the change in total cost that results from producing and marketing one additional unit:
>
> $$MC = \frac{\text{Change in TC}}{1 \text{ unit increase in Q}} = \frac{\Delta TC}{\Delta Q} = \text{slope of TC curve}$$

in marketing and pricing decisions. In this setting, **marginal analysis** means that as long as revenue received from the sale of an additional product (marginal revenue) is greater than the additional cost of production and selling it (marginal cost), a firm will expand its output of that product.[20]

Marginal analysis is central to the concept of maximizing profits. In Figure 14–8A, marginal revenue and marginal cost are graphed. Marginal cost starts out high at lower quantity levels, decreases to a minimum through production and marketing efficiencies, and then rises again due to the inefficiencies of overworked labor and equipment. Marginal revenue follows a downward slope. In Figure 14–8B, total cost and total revenue curves corresponding to the marginal cost and marginal revenue curves are

FIGURE 14-8

Profit maximization pricing

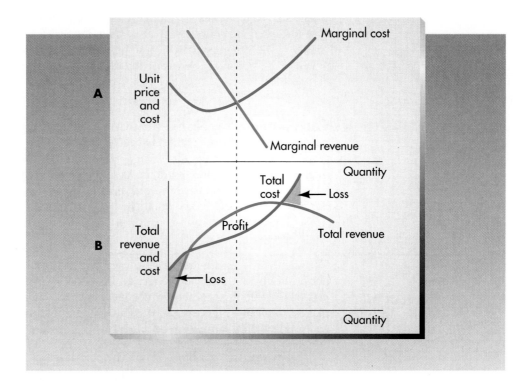

QUANTITY SOLD (Q)	PRICE PER BUSHEL (P)	TOTAL REVENUE (TR) (P × Q)	UNIT VARIABLE COST (UVC)	TOTAL VARIABLE COSTS (TVC) (UVC × Q)	FIXED COST (FC)	TOTAL COST (TC) (FC + VC)	PROFIT (TR − TC)
0	$2	$ 0	$1	$ 0	$2,000	$2,000	−$2,000
1,000	2	2,000	1	1,000	2,000	3,000	−1,000
2,000	2	4,000	1	2,000	2,000	4,000	0
3,000	2	6,000	1	3,000	2,000	5,000	1,000
4,000	2	8,000	1	4,000	2,000	6,000	2,000
5,000	2	10,000	1	5,000	2,000	7,000	3,000
6,000	2	12,000	1	6,000	2,000	8,000	4,000

FIGURE 14–9

Calculating a break-even point

graphed. Total cost initially rises as quantity increases but increases at the slowest rate at the quantity where marginal cost is lowest. The total revenue curve increases to a maximum and then starts to decline, as shown in Figure 14–6B.

The message of marginal analysis, then, is to operate up to the quantity and price level where marginal revenue equals marginal cost (MR = MC). Up to the output quantity at which MR = MC, each increase in total revenue resulting from selling one additional unit exceeds the increase in the total cost of producing and marketing that unit. Beyond the point at which MR = MC, however, the increase in total revenue from selling one more unit is less than the cost of producing and marketing that unit. At the quantity at which MR = MC, the total revenue curve lies farthest above the total cost curve, they are parallel, and profit is a maximum.

Break-Even Analysis

Marketing managers often employ a simpler approach for looking at cost, volume, and profit relationships, which is also based on the profit equation.[21] **Break-even analysis** is a technique that analyzes the relationship between total revenue and total cost to determine profitability at various levels of output. The **break-even point** (BEP) is the quantity at which total revenue and total cost are equal and beyond which profit occurs. In terms of the definitions in Figure 14–7:

$$\text{BEP}_{\text{Quantity}} = \frac{\text{Fixed cost}}{\text{Unit price} - \text{Unit variable cost}}$$

Calculating a break-even point   Consider, for example, a corn farmer who wishes to identify how many bushels of corn he must sell to cover his fixed cost at a given price. Suppose the farmer had a fixed cost (FC) of $2,000 (for real estate taxes, interest on a bank loan, and other fixed expenses) and a unit variable cost (UVC) of $1 per bushel (for labor, corn seed, herbicides, and pesticides). If the price (P) is $2 per bushel, his break-even quantity is 2,000 bushels:

$$\text{BEP}_{\text{Quantity}} = \frac{\text{FC}}{\text{P} - \text{UVC}} = \frac{\$2,000}{\$2 - \$1} = 2,000 \text{ bushels}$$

The shaded row in Figure 14–9 shows that the break-even quantity at a price of $2 per bushel is 2,000 bushels since, at this quantity, total revenue equals total cost. At less than 2,000 bushels the farmer incurs a loss, and at more than 2,000 bushels he makes a profit. Figure 14–10 shows a graphic presentation of the break-even analysis, called a **break-even chart**.

Applications of break-even analysis   Because of its simplicity, break-even analysis is used extensively in marketing, most frequently to study the impact on

FIGURE 14–10

Break-even analysis chart

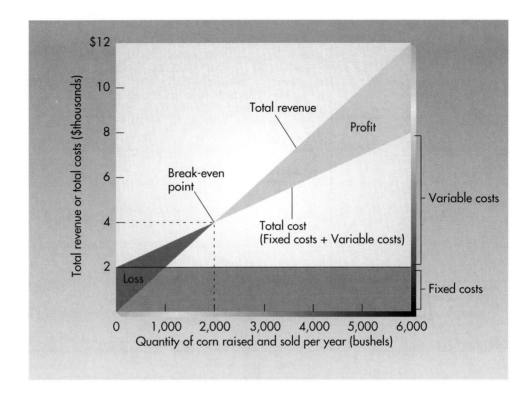

profit of changes in price, fixed cost, and variable cost. The mechanics of break-even analysis are the basis of the widely used electronic spreadsheets offered by computer programs such as Microsoft Excel or Lotus 1-2-3 that permit managers to answer hypothetical "what if . . ." questions about the effect of changes in price and cost on their profit.

An example will show the power of break-even analysis. As described in Figure 14–11, if an electronic calculator manufacturer automates its production, thereby increasing fixed cost and reducing variable cost by substituting machines for workers, this increases the break-even point from 333,333 to 500,000 units per year.

But what about the impact of the higher level of fixed cost on profit? Remember, profit at any output quantity is given by:

Profit = Total revenue − Total cost

$$= (P \times Q) - [FC + (UVC \times Q)]$$

So profit at 1 million units of sales before automation is:

Profit $= (P \times Q) - [FC + (UVC \times Q)]$

$$= (\$10 \times 1,000,000) - [\$1,000,000 + (\$7 \times 1,000,000)]$$

$$= \$10,000,000 - \$8,000,000$$

$$= \$2,000,000$$

After automation, profit is:

Profit $= (P \times Q) - [FC + (UVC \times Q)]$

$$= (\$10 \times 1,000,000) - [\$4,000,000 + (\$2 \times 1,000,000)]$$

$$= \$10,000,000 - \$6,000,000$$

$$= \$4,000,000$$

Automation, by adding to fixed cost, increases profit by $2 million at 1 million units of sales. Thus, as the quantity sold increases for the automated plant, the

FIGURE 14–11

The cost trade-off: fixed versus variable costs

Executives in virtually every mass-production industry—from locomotives and cars to electronic calculators and breakfast cereals—are searching for ways to increase quality and reduce production costs to remain competitive in world markets. Increasingly they are substituting robots, automation, and computer-controlled manufacturing systems for blue- and white-collar workers.

To understand the implications of this on the break-even point and profit, consider this example of an electronic calculator manufacturer:

BEFORE AUTOMATION			**AFTER AUTOMATION**		
P	=	$10 per unit	P	=	$10 per unit
FC	=	$1,000,000	FC	=	$4,000,000
UVC	=	$7 per unit	UVC	=	$2 per unit
BEP$_{Quantity}$	=	$\dfrac{FC}{P - UVC}$	BEP$_{Quantity}$	=	$\dfrac{FC}{P - UVC}$
	=	$\dfrac{\$1,000,000}{\$10 - \$7}$		=	$\dfrac{\$4,000,000}{\$10 - \$2}$
	=	333,333 units		=	500,000 units

The automation increases the fixed cost and increases the break-even quantity from 333,333 to 500,000 units per year. So if annual sales fall within this range, the calculator manufacturer will incur a loss with the automated plant, whereas it would have made a profit it if had not automated.

But what about its potential profit if it sells 1 million units a year? Look carefully at the two break-even charts below, and see the text to check your conclusions:

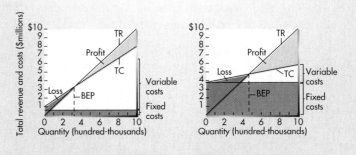

potential increase or leverage on profit is tremendous. This is why with large production and sales volumes, automated plants for GM cars or Texas Instruments calculators produce large profits. Also, firms in other industries, such as airline, railroad, and hotel and motel industries, that require a high fixed cost can reap large profits when they go even slightly beyond the break-even point.

CONCEPT CHECK

1. What is the difference between fixed cost and variable cost?

2. What is a break-even point?

SUMMARY

1. Price is the money or other considerations exchanged for the ownership or use of a product or service. Although price typically involves money, the amount exchanged is often different from the list or quoted price because of allowances and extra fees.

2. Consumers use price as an indicator of value when it is paired with the perceived benefits of a good or service. Sometimes price influences consumer perceptions of quality itself and at other times consumers make value assessments by comparing the costs and benefits of substitute items.

3. Pricing constraints such as demand, product newness, costs, competitors, other products sold by the firm, and the type of competitive market restrict a firm's pricing latitude.

4. Pricing objectives, which specify the role of price in a firm's marketing strategy, may include pricing for profit, sales revenue, market share, unit sales, survival, or some socially responsible price level.

5. A demand curve shows the maximum number of products consumers will buy at a given price and for a given set of

(*a*) consumer tastes, (*b*) price and availability of other products, and (*c*) consumer income. When any of these change, there is a shift of the demand curve.

6. Important revenue concepts include total revenue, average revenue, and marginal revenue.

7. Price elasticity of demand measures the sensitivity of units sold to a change in price. When demand is elastic, a reduction in price is more than offset by an increase in units sold, so that total revenue increases.

8. It is necessary to consider cost behavior when making pricing decisions. Important cost concepts include total cost, variable cost, fixed cost, and marginal cost.

9. Break-even analysis shows the relationship between total revenue and total cost at various quantities of output for given conditions of price, fixed cost, and variable cost. The break-even point is where total revenue and total cost are equal.

KEY TERMS AND CONCEPTS

price p. 367
barter p. 367
value p. 368
value-pricing p. 368
profit equation p. 369
pricing constraints p. 370
pricing objectives p. 373
demand curve p. 375
demand factors p. 375
total revenue p. 376
average revenue p. 376

marginal revenue p. 376
price elasticity of demand p. 378
total cost p. 380
fixed cost p. 380
variable cost p. 380
marginal cost p. 380
marginal analysis p. 381
break-even analysis p. 382
break-even point p. 382
break-even chart p. 382

CHAPTER PROBLEMS AND APPLICATIONS

1. How would the price equation apply to the purchase price of (*a*) gasoline, (*b*) an airline ticket, and (*c*) a checking account?

2. What would be your response to the statement, "Profit maximization is the only legitimate pricing objective for the firm"?

3. How is a downward-sloping demand curve related to total revenue and marginal revenue?

4. A marketing executive once said, "If the price elasticity of demand for your product is inelastic, then your price is probably too low." What is this executive saying in terms of the economic principles discussed in this chapter?

5. A marketing manager reduced the price on a brand of cereal by 10 percent and observed a 25 percent increase in quantity sold. The manager then thought that if the price were reduced by another 20 percent, a 50 percent increase in quantity sold would occur. What would be your response to the marketing manager's reasoning?

6. A student theater group at a university has developed a demand schedule that shows the relationship between ticket prices and demand based on a student survey, as follows:

TICKET PRICE	NUMBER OF STUDENTS WHO WOULD BUY
$1	300
2	250
3	200
4	150
5	100

a. Graph the demand curve and the total revenue curve based on these data. What ticket price might be set based on this analysis?

b. What other factors should be considered before the final price is set?

7. Touché Toiletries, Inc. has developed an addition to its Lizardman Cologne line tentatively branded Ode d'Toade Cologne. Unit variable costs are 45 cents for a 3-ounce bottle, and heavy advertising expenditures in the first year would result in total fixed costs of $900,000. Ode d'Toade Cologne is priced at $7.50 for a 3-ounce bottle. How many bottles of Ode d'Toade must be sold to break even?

8. Suppose that marketing executives for Touché Toiletries reduced the price to $6.50 for a 3-ounce bottle of Ode d'Toade and the fixed costs were $1,100,000. Suppose further that the unit variable cost remained at 45 cents for a 3-ounce bottle. (*a*) How many bottles must be sold to break even? (*b*) What dollar profit level would Ode d'Toade achieve if 200,000 bottles were sold?

9. Executives of Random Recordings, Inc. produced an album entitled *Sunshine/Moonshine* by the Starshine Sisters Band. The cost and price information was as follows:

Album cover	$ 1.00	per album
Songwriter's royalties	0.30	per album
Recording artists' royalties	0.70	per album
Direct material and labor costs to produce the album	1.00	per album
Fixed cost of producing an album (advertising, studio fee, etc.)	100,000.00	
Selling price	7.00	per album

a. Prepare a chart like that in Figure 14–10 showing total cost, fixed cost, and total revenue for album quantity sold levels starting at 10,000 albums through 100,000 albums at 10,000 album intervals, that is, 10,000, 20,000, 30,000, and so on.
b. What is the break-even point for the album?

CASE 14–1   Washburn International, Inc.

Video

"The relationship between musicians and their guitars is something really extraordinary—and is a fairly strange one," says Brady Breen in a carefully-understated tone of voice. Breen has the experience to know. He's production manager of Washburn International, one of the most prestigious guitar manufacturers in the world. Washburn's instruments range from one-of-a-kind, custom-made acoustic and electric guitars and basses to less-expensive, mass-produced ones.

THE COMPANY AND ITS HISTORY

The modern Washburn International started in 1977 when a small Chicago firm bought the century-old Washburn brand name and a small inventory of guitars, parts, and promotional supplies. At that time annual revenues of the company were $300,000 for the sale of about 2,500 guitars. Washburn's first catalog, appearing in 1978, told a frightening truth:

> Our designs are translated by Japan's most experienced craftsmen, assuring the consistent quality and craftmanship for which they are known.

At that time the American guitar-making craft was at an all-time low. Guitars made by Japanese firm's such as Ibane and Yamaha were in use by an increasing number of professionals.

Times have changed for Washburn. Today the company sells about 250,000 guitars a year. Annual sales

exceed $50 million. All this resulted from Washburn's aggressive marketing strategies to develop product lines with different price points targeted at musicians in distinctly different market segments.

THE PRODUCTS AND MARKET SEGMENTS

Arguably the most trendsetting guitar developed by the modern Washburn company appeared in 1980. This was the Festival Series of cutaway, thin-bodied flattops, with built-in bridge pickups and controls, which went on to become the virtual standard for live performances. John Lodge of the Moody Blues endorsed the 12-string version—his gleaming white guitar appearing in both concerts and ads for years. In the time since the Festival Series appeared, countless rock and country stars have used these instruments including Bob Dylan, Dolly Parton, Greg Allman, John Jorgenson, and George Harrison.

Until 1991 all Washburn guitars were manufactured in Asia. That year Washburn started building its high-end guitars in the United States. Today Washburn marketing executives divide its product line into four levels. From high-end to low-end these are:

- One-of-a-kind, custom units
- Batch-custom units
- Mass-customized units
- Mass-produced units

The one-of-a-kind custom units are for the many stars that use Washburn instruments. The mass-produced units targeted at first-time buyers are still manufactured in Asian factories.

PRICING ISSUES

Setting prices for its various lines presents a continuing challenge for Washburn. Not only do the prices have to reflect the changing tastes of its various segments of musicians, but the prices must also be competitive with the prices set for guitars manufactured and marketed globally. In fact, Washburn and other well-known guitar manufacturers have a prestige-niche strategy. For Washburn this involves endorsements by internationally-known musicians who play its instruments and lend their names to lines of Washburn signature guitars. This has the effect of reducing the price elasticity or price sensitivity for these guitars. Stars playing Washburn guitars like Nuno Bettencourt, David Gilmour of Pink Floyd, Joe Perry of Aerosmith, and Darryl Jones of the Rolling Stones have their own lines of signature guitars—the "batch-custom" units mentioned above.

Joe Baksha, Washburn's executive vice president, is responsible for reviewing and approving prices for the company's lines of guitars. Setting a sales target of 2,000 units for a new line of guitars, he is considering a suggested retail price of $329 per unit for customers at one of the hundreds of retail outlets carrying the Washburn line. For planning purposes, Baksha estimates half of the final retail price will be the price Washburn nets when it sells its guitar to the wholesalers and dealers in its channel of distribution.

Looking at Washburn's financial data for its present Chicago plant, Baksha estimates that this line of guitars must bear these fixed costs:

Rent and taxes	= $12,000
Depreciation of equipment	= $ 4,000
Management and quality control program	= $20,000

In addition, he estimates the variable costs for each unit to be:

Direct materials	= $25/unit
Direct labor	= 8 hours/unit @ $14/hour

Carefully-kept production records at Washburn's Chicago plant make Baksha believe that these are reasonable estimates. He explains, "Before we begin a production run, we have a good feel for what our costs will be. The U.S.-built N-4, for example, simply costs more than one of our foreign-produced Mercury or Wing series electrics."

Caught in the global competition for guitar sales, Washburn searches for ways to reduce and control costs. After much agonizing, the company decides to move to Nashville, Tennessee. In this home of country music, Washburn expects to lower its manufacturing costs because there are many skilled workers in the region, and its fixed costs will be reduced by avoiding some of the expenses of having a big city, Chicago, location. Specifically, Washburn projects that it will reduce its rent and taxes expense by 40 percent and the wage rate it pays by 15 percent in relocating from Chicago to Nashville.

Questions

1. What factors are most likely to affect the demand for the lines of Washburn guitars (*a*) bought by a first-time guitar buyer and (*b*) bought by a sophisticated musician who wants a signature model signed by David Gilmour or Joe Perry?

2. For Washburn what are examples of (*a*) shifting the demand curve to the right to get a higher price for a guitar line (movement *of* the demand curve) and (*b*) pricing decisions involving moving *along* a demand curve?

3. In Washburn's Chicago plant what is the break-even point for the new line of guitars if the retail price is (*a*) $329, (*b*) $359, and (*c*) $299? Also, (*d*) if Washburn achieves the sales target of 2,000 units at the $329 retail price, what will its profit be?

4. Assume that Washburn moves its production to Nashville and that the costs are reduced as projected in the case. Then, what will be the (*a*) new break-even point at a $329 retail price for this line of guitars and (*b*) the new profit if it sells 2,000 units?

5. If for competitive reasons, Washburn eventually has to move all its production back to Asia, (*a*) which specific costs might be lowered and (*b*) what additional costs might it expect to incur?

CHAPTER 15

Pricing: Arriving at the Final Price

AFTER READING THIS CHAPTER YOU SHOULD BE ABLE TO:

• Understand how to establish the initial "approximate price level" using demand-oriented, cost-oriented, profit-oriented, and competition-oriented approaches.

• Identify the major factors considered in deriving a final list or quoted price from the approximate price level.

• Describe adjustments made to the approximate price level based on geography, discounts, and allowances.

• Prepare basic financial analyses useful in evaluating alternative prices and arriving at the final sales price.

• Describe the principal laws and regulations affecting pricing practices.

VIDEOPHONE 2500: A PICTURE IS WORTH . . ?

How much would you pay to see the person you are talking to on the telephone? Executives responsible for VideoPhone 2500 are seeking the answer to this question. VideoPhone 2500 is the latest incarnation of a technology dating back to the 1960s when AT&T launched its Picturephone. AT&T reportedly spent $500 million on Picturephone, expecting that it would become a $1 billion business by 1980. These expectations were not met, and the product was discontinued in 1978. Picturephone was resurrected in 1992 as VideoPhone 2500. This time a senior company executive predicted that there would be "millions" of these phones in use by 1994. However, by mid-1994, only about 30,000 units had been sold worldwide, half of which were installed in the United States. Almost 40,000 were in use by early 1996.

Why haven't VideoPhone 2500 sales skyrocketed? The problem appears to reside in its perceived value marked by (1) the quality of the picture and (2) the price of the product. Engineers are working on picture quality. Adopting recent breakthroughs in what are called compression technologies, engineers believe they can deliver a still clearer video picture over conventional telephone lines. As for price, a senior company executive believes the right retail price for the VideoPhone 2500 is under $500, or about half of the present suggested retail price of $999.99 and one third the $1,499 price when it was introduced in 1992.[1]

The challenge facing VideoPhone 2500 involves the imaginative application of technology at a price point that creates value for the consumer. Consumer demand, cost, competition, and profit considerations will all play a part in the pricing decision.

This chapter describes how companies select an approximate price level, highlights important considerations

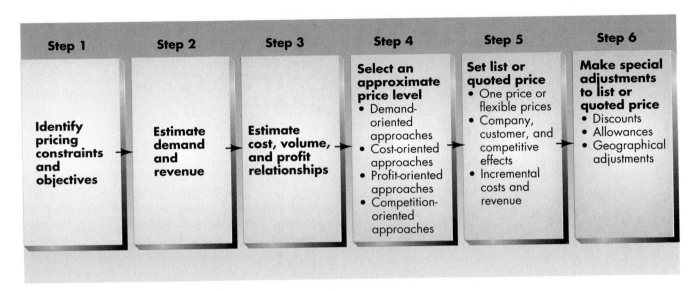

FIGURE 15-1   Steps in setting price

in setting a list or quoted price, and identifies various price adjustments that can be made to prices set by the firm—the last three steps an organization uses in setting price (Figure 15-1). In addition, an overview of legal and regulatory aspects of pricing is provided.

STEP 4: SELECT AN APPROXIMATE PRICE LEVEL

A key to a marketing manager's setting a final price for a product is to find an "approximate price level" to use as a reasonable starting point. Four common approaches to helping find this approximate price level are (1) demand-oriented, (2) cost-oriented, (3) profit-oriented, and (4) competition-oriented approaches (Figure 15-2). Although these approaches are discussed separately below, some of them overlap, and an effective marketing manager will consider several in searching for an approximate price level.

Demand-Oriented Approaches

Demand-oriented approaches weigh factors underlying expected customer tastes and preferences more heavily than such factors as cost, profit, and competition when selecting a price level.

Skimming pricing   A firm introducing a new or innovative product can use **skimming pricing,** setting the highest initial price that customers really desiring the product are willing to pay. These customers are not very price sensitive because they weigh the new product's price, quality, and ability to satisfy their needs against the same characteristics of substitutes. As the demand of these customers is satisfied, the firm lowers the price to attract another, more price-sensitive segment. Thus, skimming pricing gets its name from skimming successive layers of "cream," or customer segments, as prices are lowered in a series of steps.

Skimming pricing is an effective strategy when (1) enough prospective customers are willing to buy the product immediately at the high initial price to make these sales profitable, (2) the high initial price will not attract competitors, (3) lowering price has

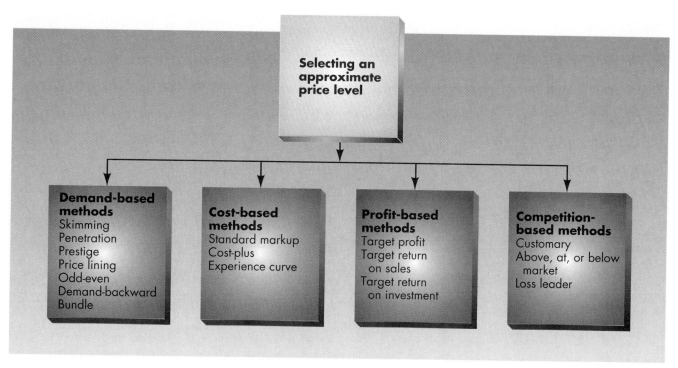

FIGURE 15-2   Four approaches for selecting an approximate price level

only a minor effect on increasing the sales volume and reducing the unit costs, and (4) customers interpret the high price as signifying high quality. These four conditions are most likely to exist when the new product is protected by patents or copyrights or its uniqueness is understood and valued by customers. StarSignal, a small California firm, has adopted a skimming strategy for its $26,000 fax machine, which prints color documents.[2] Nintendo and Sega used this strategy for their CD-ROM video-game systems when they were introduced in the early 1990s.[3]

Penetration pricing   Setting a low initial price on a new product to appeal immediately to the mass market is **penetration pricing,** the exact opposite of skimming pricing. Sony Corporation consciously chose a penetration strategy when it introduced its PlayStation video-game player first in Japan and later in the United States. Read the Marketing NewsNet on the next page that describes how Sony's penetration strategy made it a front-runner in the latest generation of video games.[4]

The conditions favoring penetration pricing are the reverse of those supporting skimming pricing: (1) many segments of the market are price sensitive, (2) a low initial price discourages competitors from entering the market, and (3) unit production and marketing costs fall dramatically as production volumes increase. A firm using penetration pricing may (1) maintain the initial price for a time to gain profit loss from its low introductory level or (2) lower the price further, counting on the new volume to generate the necessary profit.

In some situations penetration pricing may follow skimming pricing. A company might initially price a product high to attract price-insensitive consumers and recoup initial research and development costs and introductory promotional expenditures. Once this is done, penetration pricing is used to appeal to a broader segment of the population and increase market share.[5] Apple Computer and Digital Equipment did this in Japan recently when each cut their personal computer prices to increase their respective market shares.[6]

MARKETING NEWSNET

Global

SONY'S PLAYSTATION IS STIMULATING AND ITS PRICE IS PENETRATING

How did a new entrant break into the $6 billion global video-game market dominated by a few entrenched competitors such as Japan's Sega Enterprises, Ltd. and Nintendo and the Dutch firm, Philips Electronics NV? Ask Sony Corporation executive Olaf Olafsson. He would say, "We had the right price, the right technology, and the right software" in the introduction of its PlayStation video game first in Japan and then in the United States, the world's two largest video-game markets.

PlayStation made Sony a front-runner in the race to offer greater computing power for game users, improved color, and better animation to heighten game play. First introduced in Japan in December 1994, PlayStation sold 1 million units during its first six months. In September 1995, PlayStation was launched in the United States with an introductory price of $299—$100 less than the list price for the advanced Saturn game player by Sega Enterprises, Ltd., which debuted four months earlier. PlayStation unit sales in its first six months of commercialization were estimated to be more than five times higher than Saturn unit sales for a comparable period.

Sony's pricing strategy for a new game player broke the competitive rules. Previous introductions of technologically advanced video-game systems by Sega and Nintendo had employed skimming pricing strategies. Sony's penetration strategy was designed to quickly gain market share, attract price-sensitive consumers, discourage competitors from entering the market, and, according to Olaf Olafsson, "achieve a massive mass market." The strategy accomplished its objective.

Prestige pricing   As noted in Chapter 14, consumers may use price as a measure of the quality or prestige of an item so that as price is lowered beyond some point, demand for the item actually falls. **Prestige pricing** involves setting a high price so that status-conscious consumers will be attracted to the product and buy it (Figure 15–3A). The demand curve slopes downward and to the right between points A and B but turns back to the left between points B and C since demand is actually reduced between points B and C. From A to B buyers see the lowering of price as a bargain and buy more; from B to C they become dubious about the quality and prestige and buy less. A marketing manager's pricing strategy here is to stay above price P_0 (the initial price). Heublein, Inc. successfully repositioned its Popov brand of vodka to make it a prestige brand. It increased price by 8 percent, which led to a 1 percent decline in market share but a whopping 30 percent increase in profit.[7]

Rolls-Royce cars, diamonds, perfumes, fine china, Swiss watches, and crystal have an element of prestige pricing appeal in them and may sell worse at lower prices than at higher ones. The recent success of Swiss watchmaker TAG Heuer is an example. The company raised the average price of its watches from $250 to $1,000, and its sales volume increased sevenfold![8]

Price lining   Often a firm that is selling not just a single product but a line of products may price them at a number of different specific pricing points, which is called **price lining.** For example, a discount department store manager may price a

FIGURE 15-3

Demand curves for two types of demand-oriented approaches

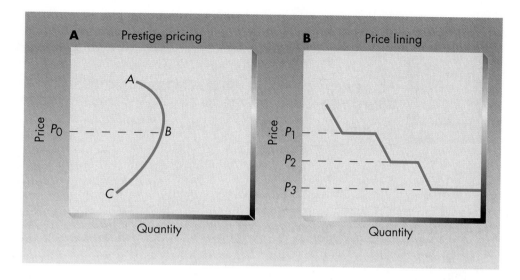

line of women's dresses at $59, $79, and $99. As shown in Figure 15-3B, this assumes that demand is elastic at each of these price points but inelastic between these price points. In some instances all the items might be purchased for the same cost and then marked up at different percentages to achieve these price points based on color, style, and expected demand. In other instances manufacturers design products for different price points, and retailers apply approximately the same markup percentages to achieve the three or four different price points offered to consumers. Sellers often feel that a limited number (such as three or four) of price points is preferable to 8 or 10 different ones, which may only confuse prospective buyers.[9]

Odd-even pricing   Sears offers a Craftsman radial saw for $499.99, the suggested retail price for VideoPhone 2500 is $999.99, and Kmart sells Windex glass cleaner on sale for 99 cents. Why not simply price these items at $500, $1,000, and $1, respectively? These firms are using **odd-even pricing,** which involves setting prices a few dollars or cents under an even number. The presumption is that consumers see the Sears radial saw as priced at "something over $400" rather than "about $500." In theory, demand increases if the price drops from $500 to $499.99. There is some evidence to suggest this does happen. However, consumers may interpret these odd-ending prices as meaning lower quality.[10]

Demand-backward pricing   Manufacturers sometimes estimate the price that consumers would be willing to pay for a relatively expensive item, such as a shopping good. They then work backward through the markups taken by retailers and wholesalers to determine what price they can charge wholesalers for the product. This practice, called **demand-backward pricing,** results in the manufacturer deliberately adjusting the composition and quality of the component parts in the product to achieve the target price. This pricing practice is used with great success by Compaq Computer Corporation as illustrated in the Marketing NewsNet on the next page.[11]

Bundle pricing   A frequently used demand-oriented pricing practice is **bundle pricing**—the marketing of two or more products in a single "package" price. For example, American Airlines offers vacation packages that include airfare, car rental, and lodging. Bundle pricing is based on the idea that consumers value the package more than the individual items. This is due to benefits received from not having to make separate purchases and enhanced satisfaction from one item given the presence of another. Moreover, bundle pricing often provides a lower total cost to buyers and

Marketing NewsNet

Cross **Functional**

ACHIEVING A TARGET PRICE: CROSS-FUNCTIONAL PLANNING PAYS A CUSTOMER VALUE DIVIDEND TO COMPAQ COMPUTER

Personal computer buyers in the 1990s demand better hardware and more software and expect to pay less for computing power and reliability. It is therefore understandable that creating and sustaining customer value in the PC industry is a constant challenge. Compaq Computer Corporation has met the customer value challenge and sells more personal computers than any other firm in the United States. One reason for Compaq's success has been its focus on target pricing.

Target pricing at Compaq involves cross-functional planning and integration. It begins by first determining what the final retail list price to the buyer should be, followed by the subtraction of retailer markup (about 15 percent) and the company's desired profit margin. Managers of the materials, engineering, manufacturing, and marketing functions resolve among themselves how to allocate the remaining costs to make a product that provides the desired features at the desired retail price point.

Target pricing at Compaq demands discipline, teamwork, originality, and a collective commitment to develop products at prices that PC buyers are willing to pay. Does it work? With target pricing, Compaq built a $3 billion business in home computers from scratch in two years.

lower marketing costs to sellers.[12] For example, Microsoft Corporation sells a "bundle" of spreadsheet and word-processing software in its Office package for $750. Priced separately, items in the bundle could cost a buyer $2,190.[13]

CONCEPT CHECK

1. What are the circumstances in pricing a new product that might support skimming or penetration pricing?

2. What is odd-even pricing?

Cost-Oriented Approaches

With cost-oriented approaches the price setter stresses the supply or cost side of the pricing problem, not the demand side. Price is set by looking at the production and marketing costs and then adding enough to cover direct expenses, overhead, and profit.

Standard markup pricing Managers of supermarkets and other retail stores have such a large number of products that estimating the demand for each product as

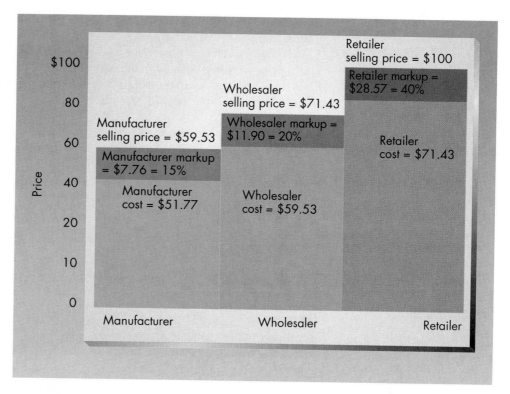

a means of setting price is impossible. Therefore, they use **standard markup pricing,** which entails adding a fixed percentage to the cost of all items in a specific product class. This percentage markup varies depending on the type of retail store (such as furniture, clothing, or grocery) and on the product involved. High-volume products usually have smaller markups than do low-volume products. Supermarkets such as Kroger, Safeway, and Jewel have different markups for staple items and discretionary items. The markup on staple items like sugar, flour, and dairy products varies from 10 percent to 23 percent, whereas markups on discretionary items like snack foods and candy ranges from 27 percent to 47 percent. These markups must cover all expenses of the store, pay for overhead costs, and contribute something to profits. For supermarkets these markups, which may appear very large, result in only a 1 percent profit on sales revenue if the store is operating efficiently. By comparison, consider the markups on snacks and beverages purchased at your local movie theater. The markup on soft drinks is 87 percent, 65 percent on candy bars, and a whopping 90 percent on popcorn! An explanation of how to compute a markup, along with operating statement data and other ratios, is given in Appendix B to this chapter.

Figure 15-4 shows the way standard markups combine to establish the selling price of the manufacturer to the wholesaler, the wholesaler to the retailer, and the retailer to the ultimate consumer. For example, the markups on a home appliance (for simplicity, sold to consumers for exactly $100) can increase as the product gets closer to the ultimate consumers; that is, the manufacturer has a 15 percent markup on its cost, the wholesaler 20 percent, and the retailer 40 percent.

These larger markups later in the channel reflect the fact that as the product gets closer to the ultimate consumer, the seller has a smaller volume of the product and must provide a greater number of services or amount of individual attention to the buyer. The manufacturer gets $59.53 for selling the appliance to the wholesaler, who gets $71.43 from the retailer, who gets $100 from the ultimate consumer. As noted in the discussion of demand-backward pricing, if the manufacturer targets the price to the ultimate consumer at \$100, it must verify that this includes adequate markups for the retailer, wholesaler, and itself.

Cost-plus pricing   Many manufacturing, professional services, and construction firms use a variation of standard markup pricing. **Cost-plus pricing** involves summing the total unit cost of providing a product or service and adding a specific amount to the cost to arrive at a price. Cost-plus pricing generally assumes two forms. With *cost-plus percentage-of-cost pricing,* a fixed percentage is added to the total unit cost. This is often

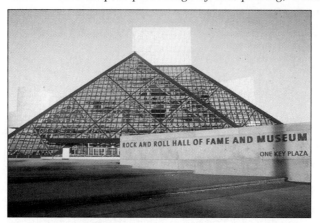

used to price one- or few-of-a-kind items, as when an architectural firm charges a percentage of the construction costs of, say, the \$92 million Rock and Roll Hall of Fame and Museum in Cleveland, Ohio. In buying highly technical, few-of-a-kind products such as hydro-electric power plants or space satellites, country governments have found that general contractors are reluctant to specify a formal, fixed price for the procurement. Therefore, they use *cost-plus fixed-fee pricing,* which means that a supplier is reimbursed for all costs, regardless of what they turn out to be, but is allowed only a fixed fee as profit that is independent of the final cost of the project. For example, suppose that the National Aeronautics and Space Administration agreed to pay McDonnell Douglas \$1.2 billion as the cost of a space shuttle and agreed to a \$100 million fee for providing that space shuttle. Even if McDonnell Douglas's cost increased to \$2 billion for the space shuttle, its fee would remain \$100 million.

The rising cost of legal fees has prompted some law firms to adopt a cost-plus pricing approach. Rather than billing clients on an hourly basis, lawyers and their clients agree on a fixed fee based on expected costs plus a profit for the law firm.[14] Many advertising agencies also use this approach. Here, the client agrees to pay the agency a fee based on the cost of its work plus some agreed-on profit, which is often a percentage of total cost.[15]

Experience curve pricing   The method of **experience curve pricing** is based on the learning effect, which holds that the unit cost of many products and services declines by 10 percent to 30 percent each time a firm's experience at producing and selling them doubles.[16] This reduction is regular or predictable enough that the average cost per unit can be mathematically estimated. For example, if the firm estimates that costs will fall by 15 percent each time volume doubles, then the cost of the 100th unit produced and sold will be about 85 percent of the cost of the 50th unit, and the 200th unit will be 85 percent of the 100th unit. Therefore, if the cost of the 50th unit is \$100, the 100th unit would cost \$85, the 200th unit would be \$72.25, and so on. Since prices often follow costs with experience curve pricing, a rapid decline in price is possible. Japanese and U.S firms in the electronics industry often adopt this pricing approach. This cost-based pricing approach complements the demand-based pricing strategy of skimming followed by penetration pricing. For example, CD player prices have decreased from \$900 to less than \$200, fax machine prices have declined from \$1,000 to under \$300, and cellular telephones that sold for \$4,000 are now priced below \$99. Figure 15–5 displays the relationship between volume increases in cellular phone sales and the average cost of the least expensive model.[17]

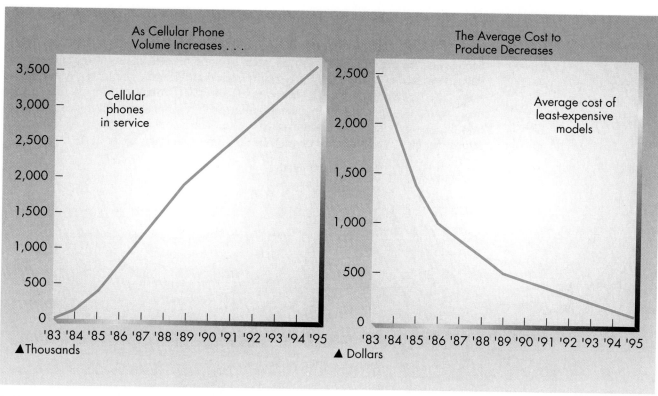

FIGURE 15-5   Cellular phone unit sales and average cost

Profit-Oriented Approaches

A price setter may choose to balance both revenues and costs to set price using profit-oriented approaches. These might either involve a target of a specific dollar volume of profit or express this target profit as a percentage of sales or investment.

Target profit pricing   A firm may set an annual target of a specific dollar volume of profit, which is called **target profit pricing.** Suppose a picture framing store owner wishes to use target profit pricing to establish a price for a typical framed picture and assumes the following:

- Variable cost is a constant $22 per unit.
- Fixed cost is a constant $26,000.
- Demand is insensitive to price up to $60 per unit.
- A target profit of $7,000 is sought at an annual volume of 1,000 units (framed pictures).

The price can be calculated as follows:

Profit = Total revenue − Total cost

Profit = (P × Q) − [FC + (UVC × Q)]

$7,000 = (P × 1,000) − [$26,000 + ($22 × 1,000)]

$7,000 = 1,000P − ($26,000 + $22,000)

1,000P = $7,000 + $48,000

P = $55

Note that a critical assumption is that this higher average price of a framed picture will not cause the demand to fall.

Target return-on-sales pricing   A difficulty with target profit pricing is that although it is simple and the target involves only a specific dollar volume, there is no benchmark of sales or investment used to show how much of the firm's effort is needed to achieve the target. Firms such as supermarket chains often use **target return-on-sales pricing** to set typical prices that will give the firm a profit that is a specified percentage, say, 1 percent, of the sales volume. Suppose the owner decides to use target return-on-sales pricing for the frame shop and makes the same first three assumptions shown previously. The owner now sets a target of 20 percent return on sales at an annual volume of 1,250 units. This gives

$$\text{Target return on sales} = \frac{\text{Target profit}}{\text{Total revenue}}$$

$$20\% = \frac{\text{TR} - \text{TC}}{\text{TR}}$$

$$0.20 = \frac{\text{P} \times \text{Q} - [\text{FC} + (\text{UVC} \times \text{Q})]}{\text{TR}}$$

$$0.20 = \frac{\text{P} \times 1{,}250 - [\$26{,}000 + (\$22 \times 1{,}250)]}{\text{P} \times 1{,}250}$$

$$\text{P} = \$53.50$$

So at a price of $53.50 per unit and an annual quantity of 1,250 frames,

TR = P × Q = \$53.50 × 1,250 = \$66,875

TC = FC + (UVC × Q) = 26,000 + (22 × 1,250) = \$53,500

Profit = TR − TC = \$66,875 − \$53,500 = \$13,375

As a check,

$$\text{Target return on sales} = \frac{\text{Target profit}}{\text{Total revenue}} = \frac{\$13{,}375}{\$66{,}875} = 20\%$$

Target return-on-investment pricing   Firms such as GM and many public utilities set annual return-on-investment (ROI) targets such as ROI of 20 percent. **Target return-on-investment pricing** is a method of setting prices to achieve this target.

Suppose the store owner sets a target ROI of 10 percent, which is twice that achieved the previous year. She considers raising the average price of a framed picture to $54 or $58—up from last year's average of $50. To do this, she might improve product quality by offering better frames and higher quality matting, which will increase the cost but will probably offset the decreased revenue from the lower number of units that can be sold next year.

To handle this wide variety of assumptions, today's managers use computerized spreadsheets to project operating statements based on a diverse set of assumptions. Figure 15–6 shows the results of computerized spreadsheet simulation, with assumptions shown at the top and the projected results at the bottom. A previous year's operating statement results are shown in the column headed "Last Year," and the assumptions and spreadsheet results for four different sets of assumptions are shown in columns A, B, C, and D.

In choosing a price or another action using spreadsheet results, the decision maker must (1) study the results of the computer simulation projections and (2) assess the realism of the assumptions underlying each set of projections. For example, the store owner sees from the bottom row of Figure 15–6 that all four spreadsheet simulations exceed the after-tax target ROI of 10 percent. But, after more thought, she judges it to be more realistic to set an average price of $58 per unit, allow the unit variable cost to increase by 20 percent to account for more expensive framing and matting, and

ASSUMPTIONS OR RESULTS	FINANCIAL ELEMENT	LAST YEAR	SIMULATION			
			A	B	C	D
Assumptions	Price per unit (P)	$ 50	$ 54	$ 54	$ 58	$ 58
	Units sold (Q)	1,000	1,200	1,100	1,100	1,000
	Change in unit variable cost (UVC)	0%	+10%	+10%	+20%	+20%
	Unit variable cost	$ 22.00	$ 24.20	$ 24.20	$ 26.40	$ 26.40
	Total expenses	$ 8,000	Same	Same	Same	Same
	Owner's salary	$18,000	Same	Same	Same	Same
	Investment	$20,000	Same	Same	Same	Same
	State and federal taxes	50%	Same	Same	Same	Same
Spreadsheet simulation results	Net sales (P ×Q)	$50,000	$64,800	$59,400	$63,800	$58,000
	Less: COGS (Q × UVC)	22,000	29,040	26,620	29,040	26,400
	Gross margin	$28,000	$35,760	$32,780	$34,760	$31,600
	Less: total expenses	8,000	8,000	8,000	8,000	8,000
	Less: owner's salary	18,000	18,000	18,000	18,000	18,000
	Net profit before taxes	$ 2,000	$ 9,760	$ 6,780	8,760	$ 5,600
	Less: taxes	1,000	4,880	3,390	4,380	2,800
	Net profit after taxes	$ 1,000	$ 4,880	$ 3,390	$ 4,380	$ 2,800
	Investment	$20,000	$20,000	$20,000	$20,000	$20,000
	Return on investment	5.0%	24.4%	17.0%	21.9%	14.0%

FIGURE 15-6

Results of computer spreadsheet simulation to select price to achieve a target return on investment

settle for the same unit sales as the 1,000 units sold last year. She selects simulation D in this computerized spreadsheet approach to target ROI pricing and has a goal of 14 percent after-tax ROI. Of course, these same calculations can be done by hand, but this is far more time consuming.

Competition-Oriented Approaches

Rather than emphasize demand, cost, or profit factors, a price setter can stress what competitors or "the market" is doing.

Customary pricing   For some products where tradition, a standardized channel of distribution, or other competitive factors dictate the price, **customary pricing** is used. Tradition prevails in the pricing of Swatch watches. The $40 customary price for the basic model has not changed in 10 years.[18] Candy bars offered through standard vending machines have a customary price of 50 cents, and a significant departure from this price may result in a loss of sales for the manufacturer. Hershey typically has changed the amount of chocolate in its candy bars depending on the price of raw chocolate rather than vary its customary retail price so that it can continue selling through vending machines.

Above-, at-, or below-market pricing   For most products it is difficult to identify a specific market price for a product or product class. Still, marketing managers often have a subjective feel for the competitors' price or market price. Using this benchmark, they then may deliberately choose a strategy of **above-, at-, or below-market pricing.**

Among watch manufacturers, Rolex takes pride in emphasizing that it makes one of the most expensive watches you can buy—a clear example of above-market pricing. Manufacturers of national brands of clothing such as Hart Schaffner & Marx and Christian Dior and retailers such as Neiman-Marcus deliberately set premium prices for their products.

ETHICS AND SOCIAL RESPONSIBILITY ALERT

Ethics

FLEXIBLE PRICING: IS THERE RACE AND GENDER DISCRIMINATION IN BARGAINING FOR A NEW CAR?

What do 60 percent of perspective buyers dread when looking for a new car? That's right! They dread negotiating the price. Price bargaining, however, has a more serious side and demonstrates shortcomings of flexible pricing when purchasing a new car: the potential for price discrimination by race and gender. Recent research among 153 car dealers in a large Midwestern city suggests that car dealers offer male and female African-Americans and white females higher prices than white males even though all buyers used identical bargaining strategies when negotiating the price of a new car.

African-American males were typically offered the highest price, followed by African-American females, white females, and white males.

New car price bargaining has been eliminated by an increasing number of car dealers, most notably Saturn dealers. Saturn's no haggle, one-price policy for new cars has been recently expanded to pre-owned or used Saturns. According to a Saturn executive, "People don't want to dicker on price, period, whether it's a house, suit of clothes, or a car. When you have to dicker, you feel uncomfortable because you always feel you paid too much." In certain instances, some consumers do.

Large mass-merchandise chains such as Sears and Montgomery Ward generally use at-market pricing. These chains often establish the going market price in the minds of their competitors. Similarly, Revlon and Cluett Peabody & Company (the maker of Arrow shirts) generally price their products "at market." They also provide a reference price for competitors that use above- and below-market pricing.

In contrast, a number of firms use a strategy of below-market pricing. Manufacturers of all generic products and retailers who offer their own private brands of products ranging from peanut butter to shampoo deliberately set prices for these products about 8 percent to 10 percent below the prices of nationally branded competitive products such as Skippy peanut butter, Vidal Sassoon shampoo, or Crest toothpaste. Below-market pricing also exists in business-to-business marketing. Hewlett-Packard, for instance, consciously prices its line of office personal computers below Compaq and IBM to promote a value image among corporate buyers.[19]

Loss-leader pricing   For a special promotion many retail stores deliberately sell a product below its customary price to attract attention to it. For example, Pechin's, a legendary supermarket 50 miles south of Pittsburgh, prices rib steaks at $2.29 a pound, which is below its cost. The purpose of this **loss-leader pricing** is not to increase sales of the rib steaks but to attract customers in hopes they will buy other products as well, particularly the discretionary items carrying large markups. This tactic works for Pechin's, which has five times the sales of a typical supermarket.[20] Likewise, mass merchandisers such as Target have sold home videos at half their customary price to attract customers to their stores. According to an industry observer, "Video is one of the mass merchandisers' favorite traffic-building devices."[21]

CONCEPT CHECK

1. What is standard markup pricing?

2. What profit-based pricing approach should a manager use if he or she wants to reflect the percentage of the firm's resources used in obtaining the profit?

3. What is the purpose of loss-leader pricing when used by a retail firm?

Step 5: Set the List or Quoted Price

The first four steps in setting price covered in Chapter 14 and this chapter result in an approximate price level for the product that appears reasonable. But it still remains for the manager to set a specific list or quoted price in light of all relevant factors.

One-Price versus Flexible-Price Policy

A seller must decide whether to follow a one-price or flexible-price policy. A **one-price policy** is setting the same price for similar customers who buy the same

Many one-price retailers use below-market pricing.

product and quantities under the same conditions. Saturn Corporation uses this approach in its "no haggle, one-price" price for both new and used Saturn cars. Some retailers such as Dollar Bill$, Your $10 Store, and Fashions $9.99 have married this policy with a below-market approach to include all merchandise in their stores. At One Price Clothing Stores, Inc. all of women's sportswear, blouses, and skirts are priced at $7![22] In contrast, a **flexible-price policy** is offering the same product and quantities to similar customers but at different prices. As noted at the end of this chapter, there are legal constraints under the Robinson-Patman Act to prevent carrying a flexible-price policy to the extreme of price discrimination.

Prices paid by an ultimate consumer illustrate the differences in these two policies, although the same principles apply to manufacturers and wholesalers as well. When you buy a Wilson Sting tennis racket from a discount store, you are offered the product at a single price. You can buy it or not, but there is no variation in the price under the seller's one-price policy. But with a house, the seller generally uses a flexible-price policy, and you might negotiate a purchase at a price that lies within a range of prices. Flexible prices give sellers greater discretion in setting the final price in light of demand, cost, and competitive factors.

Car dealers have traditionally used flexible pricing based on buyer–seller negotiations to agree on a final sale price. However, as detailed in the Ethics and Social Responsibility Alert on the previous page, flexible pricing may result in race and gender discrimination.[23]

Company, Customer, and Competitive Effects

As the final list or quoted price is set, the effects on the company, customers, and competitors must be assessed.

Company effects   For a firm with more than one product, a decision on the price of a single product must consider the price of other items in its product line or related product lines in its product mix. Within a product line or mix there are usually some products that are substitutes for one another and some that complement each other. Frito-Lay recognizes that its tortilla chip product line consisting of Baked Tostitos, Tostitos, and Doritos brands are partial substitutes for one another and its bean and cheese chip dip line and salsa sauces complement the tortilla chip line.

Frito-Lay recognizes that its tortilla chip products are partial substitutes for one another and its bean and cheese dips and salsa sauces complement tortilla chips. This knowledge is used for Frito-Lay product-line pricing.

A manager's challenge when marketing multiple products is **product-line pricing,** the setting of prices for all items in a product line. When setting prices, the manager seeks to cover the total cost and produce a profit for the complete line, not necessarily for each item. For example, the $299 penetration price for Sony's PlayStation video-game player was likely below its cost, but the price of its video games (complementary products) was set high enough to cover the loss and deliver a handsome profit for the PlayStation product line.[24]

Product-line pricing involves determining (1) the lowest priced product and price, (2) the highest priced product and price, and (3) price differentials for all other products in the line.[25] The lowest and highest priced items in the product line play important roles. The highest priced item is typically positioned as the premium item in quality and features. The lowest priced item is the traffic builder designed to capture the attention of the hesitant or first-time buyer. Price differentials between items in the line should make sense to customers and reflect differences in their perceived value of the products offered. Behavioral research also suggests that the price differentials should get larger as one moves up the product line.

Customer effects   In setting price, retailers weigh factors heavily that satisfy the perceptions or expectations of ultimate consumers, such as the customary prices for a variety of consumer products. Retailers have found that they should not price their store brands 20 to 25 percent below manufacturers' brands. When they do, consumers often view the lower price as signaling lower quality and don't buy.[26] Manufacturers and wholesalers must choose prices that result in profit for resellers in the channel to gain their cooperation and support. Toro failed to do this on its lines of lawn mowers and snow throwers. It decided to augment its traditional hardware outlet distribution by also selling through big discounters such as Kmart and Target. To do so, it set prices for the discounters substantially below those for its traditional hardware outlets. Many unhappy hardware stores abandoned Toro products in favor of mowers and snow throwers from other manufacturers.

FIGURE 15-7

The power of marginal analysis in real-world decisions

Suppose the owner of a picture framing store is considering buying a series of magazine ads to reach her up-scale target market. The cost of the ads is $1,000, the average price of a framed picture is $50, and the unit variable cost (materials plus labor) is $30.

This is a direct application of marginal analysis that an astute manager uses to estimate the incremental revenue or incremental number of units that must be obtained to at least cover the incremental cost. In this example, the number of extra picture frames that must be sold is obtained as follows:

$$\text{Incremental number of frames} = \frac{\text{Extra fixed cost}}{\text{Price} - \text{Unit variable cost}}$$

$$= \frac{\$1,000 \text{ of advertising}}{\$50 - \$30}$$

$$= 50 \text{ frames}$$

So unless there are some other benefits of the ads, such as long-term goodwill, she should only buy the ads if she expects they will increase picture frame sales by at least 50 units.

Competitive effects   A manager's pricing decision is immediately apparent to most competitors, who may retaliate with price changes of their own. Therefore, a manager who sets a final list or quoted price must anticipate potential price responses from competitors. Regardless of whether a firm is a price leader or follower, it wants to avoid cutthroat price wars in which no firm in the industry makes a satisfactory profit. As an example, price wars in the U.S. airline industry in the early 1990s resulted in carrier losses exceeding $12 billion, the collapse of three airlines (Eastern, Pan Am, and Midway), and the bankruptcy of three others.[27] Price reductions as little as 1 cent can have a significant effect in a highly competitive environment. This is the case in the residential long-distance telephone industry, where AT&T, MCI, Sprint, and ITT compete head-to-head for customers. Each time a competitor lowers its per-minute charge by a penny and AT&T matches the price, it gives up $1 billion in revenues.[28]

Balancing Incremental Costs and Revenues

When a price is changed or new advertising or selling programs are planned, their effect on the quantity sold must be considered. This assessment, called *marginal analysis* (Chapter 14), involves a continuing, concise trade-off of incremental costs against incremental revenues.

Do marketing and business managers really use marginal analysis? Yes, they do, but they often don't use phrases like *marginal revenue, marginal cost,* and *elasticity of demand.*

Think about these managerial questions:

- How many extra units do we have to sell to pay for that $1,000 advertisement?
- How much savings on unit variable cost do we have to get to keep the break-even point the same if we invest in a $10,000 labor-saving machine?
- Should we hire three more salespeople or not?

All these questions are a form of managerial or incremental analysis, even though these exact words are not used.

Figure 15-7 shows the power—and some limitations—of marginal analysis applied to a marketing decision. Note that the frame store owner must either conclude that a simple advertising campaign will more than pay for itself in additional sales or not undertake the campaign. The decision could also have been made to increase the

FIGURE 15-8

Three special adjustments to
list or quoted price

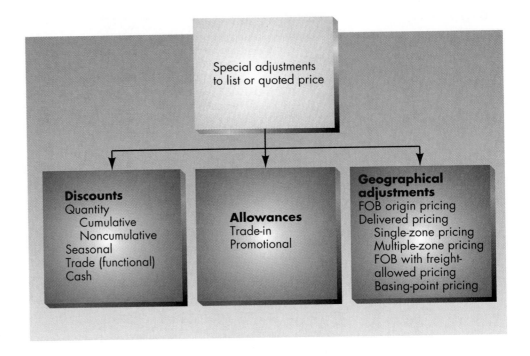

average price of a framed picture to cover the cost of the campaign, but the principle
still applies: expected incremental revenues from pricing and other marketing actions
must more than offset incremental costs.

The example in Figure 15–7 shows both the main advantage and difficulty of
marginal analysis. The advantage is its common-sense usefulness, and the difficulty
is obtaining the necessary data to make decisions. The owner can measure the cost
quite easily, but the incremental revenue generated by the ads is difficult to measure.
She could partly solve this problem by offering $2 off the purchase price with use of
a coupon printed in the ad to see which sales resulted from the ad.

STEP 6: MAKE SPECIAL ADJUSTMENTS TO THE LIST OR QUOTED PRICE

When you pay 50 cents for a bag of M&Ms in a vending machine or receive a quoted
price of $5,000 from a contractor to build a new kitchen, the pricing sequence ends
with the last step just described: setting the list or quoted price. But when you are a
manufacturer of M&M candies or gas grills and sell your product to dozens or
hundreds of wholesalers and retailers in your channel of distribution, you may need
to make a variety of special adjustments to the list or quoted price. Wholesalers also
must adjust list or quoted prices they set for retailers. Three special adjustments to the
list or quoted price are (1) discounts, (2) allowances, and (3) geographical adjustments (Figure 15–8).

Discounts

Discounts are reductions from list price that a seller gives a buyer as a reward for
some activity of the buyer that is favorable to the seller. Four kinds of discounts are
especially important in marketing strategy: (1) quantity, (2) seasonal, (3) trade
(functional), and (4) cash discounts.

Quantity discounts   To encourage customers to buy larger quantities of a
product, firms at all levels in the channel of distribution offer **quantity discounts,**
which are reductions in unit costs for a larger order.[29] For example, an instant

Toro uses seasonal discounts to stimulate consumer demand.

photocopying service might set a price of 10 cents a copy for 1 to 25 copies, 9 cents a copy for 26 to 100, and 8 cents a copy for 101 or more. Because the photocopying service gets more of the buyer's business and has longer production runs that reduce its order-handling costs, it is willing to pass on some of the cost savings in the form of quantity discounts to the buyer.

Quantity discounts are of two general kinds: noncumulative and cumulative. *Noncumulative quantity discounts* are based on the size of an individual purchase order. They encourage large individual purchase orders, not a series of orders. This discount is used by Federal Express to encourage companies to ship a large number of packages at one time. *Cumulative quantity discounts* apply to the accumulation of purchases of a product over a given time period, typically a year. Cumulative quantity discounts encourage repeat buying by a single customer to a far greater degree than do noncumulative quantity discounts. A recent decision by Burger King to replace Pepsi-Cola with Coca-Cola in its outlets was based on the cumulative quantity discounts offered by Coca-Cola on its syrup.[30]

Seasonal discounts   To encourage buyers to stock inventory earlier than their normal demand would require, manufacturers often use seasonal discounts. A firm such as Toro that manufactures lawn mowers and snow throwers offers seasonal discounts to encourage wholesalers and retailers to stock up on lawn mowers in January and February and on snow throwers in July and August—five or six months before the seasonal demand by ultimate consumers. This enables Toro to smooth out seasonal manufacturing peaks and troughs, thereby contributing to more efficient production. It also rewards wholesalers and retailers for the risk they accept in assuming increased inventory carrying costs and having supplies in stock at the time they are wanted by customers.

Trade (functional) discounts   To reward wholesalers and retailers for market-ing functions they will perform in the future, a manufacturer often gives trade, or functional, discounts. These reductions off the list or base price are offered to

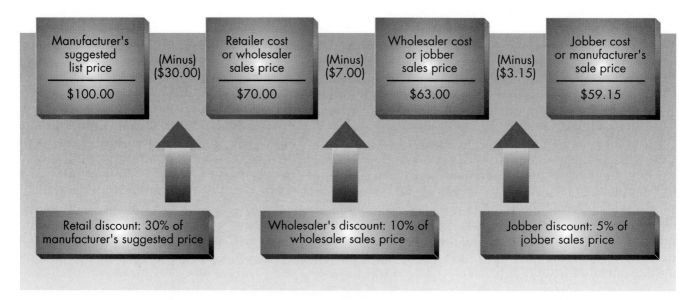

FIGURE 15–9

The structure of trade discounts

resellers in the channel of distribution on the basis of (1) where they are in the channel and (2) the marketing activities they are expected to perform in the future.

Suppose a manufacturer quotes price in the following form: list price—$100 less 30/10/5. The first number in the percentage sequence always refers to the retail end of the channel, and the last number always refers to the wholesaler or jobber closest to the manufacturer in the channel. The trade discounts are simply subtracted one at a time. This price quote shows $100 is the manufacturer's suggested retail price; 30 percent of the suggested retail price is available to the retailer to cover costs and provide a profit of $30 ($100 × 0.3 = $30); wholesalers closest to the retailer in the channel get 10 percent of their selling price ($70 × 0.1 = $7); and the final group of wholesalers in the channel (probably jobbers) that are closest to the manufacturer get 5 percent of their selling price ($63 × 0.05 = $3.15). Thus, starting with the manufacturer's retail price and subtracting the three trade discounts shows that the manufacturer's selling price to the wholesaler or jobber closest to it is $59.85 (Figure 15–9).

Traditional trade discounts have been established in various product lines such as hardware, food, and pharmaceutical items. Although the manufacturer may suggest the trade discounts shown in the example just cited, the sellers are free to alter the discount schedule depending on their competitive situation.

Cash discounts   To encourage retailers to pay their bills quickly, manufacturers offer them cash discounts. Suppose a retailer receives a bill quoted at $1,000, 2/10 net 30. This means that the bill for the product is $1,000, but the retailer can take a 2 percent discount ($1,000 × 0.02 = $20) if payment is made within 10 days and send a check for $980. If the payment cannot be made within 10 days, the total amount of $1,000 is due within 30 days. It is usually understood by the buyer that an interest charge will be added after the first 30 days of free credit.

Naive buyers may think that the 2 percent discount offered is not substantial. What this means is that the buyer pays 2 percent on the total amount to be able to use that amount an extra 20 days—from day 11 to day 30. In a 360-day business year, this is an effective annual interest rate of 36 percent (2% × 360/20 = 36%). Because the effective interest rate is so high, firms that cannot take advantage of a 2/10 net 30 cash discount often try to borrow money from their local banks at rates far lower than the 36 percent they must pay by not taking advantage of the cash discount.

Retailers provide cash discounts to consumers as well to eliminate the cost of credit granted to consumers. These discounts take the form of discount-for-cash policies.

Allowances

Allowances—like discounts—are reductions from list or quoted prices to buyers for performing some activity.

Trade-in allowances   A new car dealer can offer a substantial reduction in the list price of that new Ford Taurus by offering you a trade-in allowance of $500 for your 1985 Chevrolet. A trade-in allowance is a price reduction given when a used product is part of the payment on a new product. Trade-ins are an effective way to lower the price a buyer has to pay without formally reducing the list price.

Promotional allowances   Sellers in the channel of distribution can qualify for **promotional allowances** for undertaking certain advertising or selling activities to promote a product. Various types of allowances include an actual cash payment or an extra amount of "free goods" (as with a free case of pizzas to a retailer for every dozen cases purchased). Frequently, a portion of these savings is passed on to the consumer by retailers.

Some companies, such as Procter & Gamble, have chosen to reduce promotional allowances for retailers by using everyday low pricing. **Everyday low pricing** (EDLP) is the practice of replacing promotional allowances with lower manufacturer list prices. EDLP promises to reduce the average price to consumers while minimizing promotional allowances that cost manufacturers billions of dollars every year. However, EDLP does not necessarily benefit supermarkets as described in the Marketing NewsNet on the next page.[31]

Geographical Adjustments

Geographical adjustments are made by manufacturers or even wholesalers to list or quoted prices to reflect the cost of transportation of the products from seller to buyer. The two general methods for quoting prices related to transportation costs are (1) FOB origin pricing and (2) uniform delivered pricing.

FOB origin pricing   FOB means "free on board" some vehicle at some location, which means the seller pays the cost of loading the product onto the vehicle that is used (such as a barge, railroad car, or truck). **FOB origin pricing** usually involves the seller's naming the location of this loading as the seller's factory or warehouse (such as "FOB Detroit" or "FOB factory"). The title to the goods passes to the buyer at the point of loading, so the buyer becomes responsible for picking the specific mode of transportation, for all the transportation costs, and for subsequent handling of the product. Buyers farthest from the seller face the big disadvantage of paying the higher transportation costs.

Uniform delivered pricing   When a **uniform delivered pricing** method is used, the price the seller quotes includes all transportation costs. It is quoted in a contract as "FOB buyer's location," and the seller selects the mode of transportation, pays the freight charges, and is responsible for any damage that may occur since the seller retains title to the goods until delivered to the buyer. Although they go by various names, four kinds of delivered pricing methods are (1) single-zone pricing, (2) multiple-zone pricing, (3) FOB with freight-allowed pricing, and (4) basing-point pricing.

In *single-zone pricing* all buyers pay the same delivered price for the products, regardless of their distance from the seller. This method is also called *postage stamp pricing* because it is the way that U.S. postal rates are set for first-class mail. So although a store offering free delivery in a metropolitan area has lower transportation costs for goods shipped to customers nearer the store than for those shipped to distant ones, customers pay the same delivered price.

MARKETING NEWSNET

Customer $ Value

EVERYDAY LOW PRICES AT THE SUPERMARKET = EVERYDAY LOW PROFITS: CREATING CUSTOMER VALUE AT A COST

Who wouldn't welcome low retail prices everyday? The answer is supermarket chains. That's why 76 percent of U.S. grocery stores haven't adopted this practice. Supermarkets prefer Hi-Lo pricing based on frequent specials where prices are temporarily lowered then raised again. Hi-Lo pricing reflects allowances that manufacturers give supermarkets to push their product. Consider a New York City supermarket whose advertisement is shown here. It regularly pays $1.15 for a can of Bumble Bee white tuna ($55.43 ÷ 48 = $1.15), but the allowances reduces the cost to 96 cents. A price special of 99 cents still provides a 3 cent retail markup ($0.99 retail price in ad − $0.96 cost). When the price on tuna returns to its regular level, the store's gross margin on tuna increases substantially on those cans that were bought with the allowance but not sold during the price special promotion.

Everyday low pricing (EDLP) eliminates manufacturer allowances and can reduce average retail prices by up to 10 percent. While EDLP provides lower average prices than Hi-Lo pricing, EDLP does not allow for deeply discounted price specials. EDLP can create everyday customer value and modestly increase supermarket sales—but at a cost. Already slim supermarket chain

profits can slip by 18 percent with EDLP without the benefit of allowances as described earlier. Also, some argue that EDLP without price specials is boring for many grocery shoppers who welcome price specials. EDLP has been hailed as "value pricing" by manufacturers, but supermarkets view it differently. For them, EDLP means "Everyday Low Profits!"

In *multiple-zone pricing* a firm divides its selling territory into geographic areas or zones. The delivered price to all buyers within any one zone is the same, but prices across zones vary depending on the transportation cost to the zone and the level of competition and demand within the zone. The U.S postal system uses multiple-zone pricing for mailing packages. This system is also used in setting prices on long distance phone calls.

With *FOB with freight-allowed pricing,* also called *freight absorption pricing,* the price is quoted by the seller as "FOB plant—freight allowed." The buyer is allowed to deduct freight expenses from the list price of the goods, so the seller agrees to pay, or "absorbs," the transportation costs.

Basing-point pricing involves selecting one or more geographical locations (basing point) from which the list price for products plus freight expenses are charged to the buyer. For example, a company might designate St. Louis as the basing point and charge all buyers a list price of $100 plus freight from St. Louis to their location. Basing-point pricing methods have been used in the steel, cement, and lumber industries where freight expenses are a significant part of the total cost to the buyer and products are largely undifferentiated.

Legal and Regulatory Aspects of Pricing

Arriving at a final price is clearly a complex process. The task is further complicated by legal and regulatory restrictions. Chapter 3 described the regulatory environment

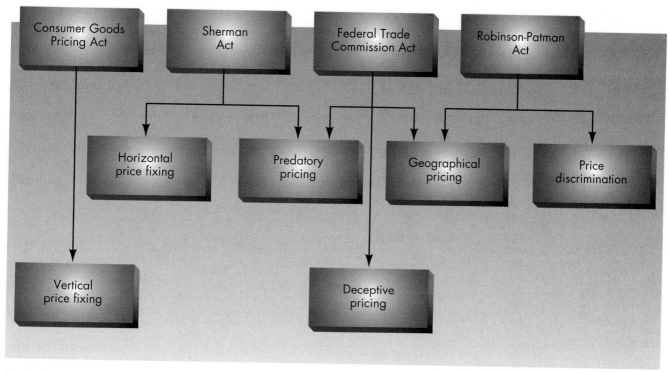

FIGURE 15–10

Pricing practices affected by legal restrictions

of companies. Here we elaborate on the specific laws and regulations affecting pricing decisions. Five pricing practices have received the most scrutiny: (1) price fixing, (2) price discrimination, (3) deceptive pricing, (4) geographical pricing, and (5) predatory pricing[32] (Figure 15–10).

Price fixing   A conspiracy among firms to set prices for a product is termed **price fixing.** Price fixing is illegal per se under the Sherman Act (*per se* means in and of itself). When two or more competitors explicitly or implicitly set prices, this practice is called *horizontal price fixing.* For example, several U.S. airlines recently agreed to pay a total of $44 million in costs and $368.5 million in discount fare coupons to settle charges of illegally setting ticket prices.[33]

Vertical price fixing involves controlling agreements between independent buyers and sellers (a manufacturer and a retailer) whereby sellers are required to not sell products below a minimum retail price. This practice, called *resale price maintenance,* was declared illegal per se in 1975 under provisions of the Consumer Goods Pricing Act. Nevertheless, in 1995, Reebok International and its Rockport Company subsidiary agreed to settle government charges that they tried to fix the prices of their footwear with retailers. The companies agreed to pay $9.5 million in the settlement.[34]

It is important to recognize that a manufacturer's "suggested retail price" is not illegal per se. The issue of legality only arises when manufacturers enforce such a practice by coercion. Furthermore, there appears to be a movement toward a "rule of reason" in pricing cases. This rule holds that circumstances surrounding a practice must be considered before making a judgment about its legality. The rule of reason perspective is the direct opposite of the per se rule, which holds that a practice is illegal in and of itself.

Price discrimination   The Clayton Act as amended by the Robinson-Patman Act prohibits **price discrimination**—the practice of charging different prices to different buyers for goods of like grade and quality. However, not all price differences are illegal; only those that substantially lessen competition or create a

FIGURE 15-11

Five most common deceptive
pricing practices

- *Bait and switch.* A deceptive practice exists when a firm offers a very low price on a product (the bait) to attract customers to a store. Once in the store, the customer is persuaded to purchase a higher-priced item (the switch) using a variety of tricks, including (1) downgrading the promoted item and (2) not having the item in stock or refusing to take orders for the item.
- *Bargains conditional on other purchases.* This practice may exist when a buyer is offered "1-Cent Sales," "Buy 1, Get 1 Free," and "Get 2 for the Price of 1." Such pricing is legal only if the first items are sold at the regular price, not a price inflated for the offer. Substituting lower-quality items on either the first or second purchase is also considered deceptive.
- *Comparable value comparisons.* Advertising such as "Retail Value $100.00, Our Price $85.00," is deceptive if a verified and substantial number of stores in the market area did not price the item at $100.
- *Comparisons with suggested prices.* A claim that a price is below a manufacturer's suggested or list price may be deceptive if few or no sales occur at that price in a retailer's market area.
- *Former price comparisons.* When a seller represents a price as reduced, the item must have been offered in good faith at a higher price for a substantial previous period. Setting a high price for the purpose of establishing a reference for a price reduction is deceptive.

monopoly are deemed unlawful. Moreover, "goods" is narrowly defined and does not include discrimination in services.

A unique feature of the Robinson-Patman Act is that it allows for price differentials to different customers under the following conditions:

1. When price differences charged to different customers do not exceed the differences in the cost of manufacture, sale, or delivery resulting from differing methods or quantities in which such goods are sold or delivered to buyers. This condition is called the *cost justification defense.*
2. Price differences resulting from meeting changing market conditions, avoiding obsolescence of seasonal merchandise including perishables or closing out sales.
3. When price differences are quoted to selected buyers in good faith to meet competitors' prices and are not intended to injure competition. This condition is called the *meet the competition defense.*

The Robinson-Patman Act also covers promotional allowances. To legally offer promotional allowances to buyers, the seller must do so on a proportionally equal basis to all buyers distributing the seller's products. In general, the rule of reason applies frequently in price discrimination cases and is often applied to cases involving flexible pricing practices of firms.

Deceptive pricing　Price deals that mislead consumers fall into the category of deceptive pricing. Deceptive pricing is outlawed by the Federal Trade Commission Act. The FTC monitors such practices and has published a regulation titled "Guides against Deceptive Pricing" designed to help businesspeople avoid a charge of deception. The five most common deceptive pricing practices are described in Figure 15–11. As you read about these practices it should be clear that laws cannot be passed and enforced to protect consumers and competitors against all of these practices, so it is essential to rely on the ethical standards of those making and publicizing pricing decisions.

Geographical pricing　FOB origin pricing is legal, as are FOB freight-allowed pricing practices, providing no conspiracy to set prices exists. Basing-point pricing can be viewed as illegal under the Robinson-Patman Act and the Federal Trade

Commission Act if there is clear-cut evidence of a conspiracy to set prices. In general, geographical pricing practices have been immune from legal and regulatory restrictions, except in those instances in which a conspiracy to lessen competition exists under the Sherman Act or price discrimination exists under the Robinson-Patman Act.

Predatory pricing   **Predatory pricing** is the practice of charging a very low price for a product with the intent of driving competitors out of business. Once competitors have been driven out, the firm raises its prices. This practice is illegal under the Sherman Act and the Federal Trade Commission Act. Proving the presence of this practice has been difficult and expensive because it must be shown that the predator explicitly attempted to destroy a competitor and the predatory price was below the defendant's average cost.

CONCEPT CHECK

1. Why would a seller choose a flexible-price policy over a one-price policy?

2. If a firm wished to encourage repeat purchases by a buyer throughout a year, would a cumulative or noncumulative quantity discount be a better strategy?

3. Which pricing practices are covered by the Sherman Act?

SUMMARY

1. Four general methods of finding an approximate price level for a product or service are demand-oriented, cost-oriented, profit-oriented, and competition-oriented pricing approaches.

2. Demand-oriented pricing approaches stress consumer demand and revenue implications of pricing and include seven types: skimming, penetration, prestige, price lining, odd-even, demand-backward, and bundle pricing.

3. Cost-oriented pricing approaches emphasize the cost aspects of pricing and include three types: standard markup, cost-plus, and experience curve pricing.

4. Profit-oriented pricing approaches focus on a balance between revenues and costs to set a price and include three types: target profit, target return-on-sales, and target return-on-investment pricing.

5. Competition-oriented pricing approaches stress what competitors or the marketplace are doing and include three types: customary; above-, at-, or below-market; and loss-leader pricing.

6. Given an approximate price level for a product, a manager must set a list or quoted price by considering factors such as one-price versus a flexible-price policy; the effects of the proposed price on the company, customer, and competitors; and balancing incremental costs and revenues.

7. List or quoted price is often modified through discounts, allowances, and geographical adjustments.

8. Legal and regulatory issues in pricing focus on price fixing, price discrimination, deceptive pricing, geographical pricing, and predatory pricing.

KEY TERMS AND CONCEPTS

skimming pricing p. 390
penetration pricing p. 391
prestige pricing p. 392
price lining p. 392
odd-even pricing p. 393
demand-backward pricing p. 393
bundle pricing p. 393
standard markup pricing p. 395
cost-plus pricing p. 396
experience curve pricing p. 396

target profit pricing p. 397
target return-on-sales pricing p. 398
target return-on-investment pricing p. 398
customary pricing p. 399
above-, at-, or below-market pricing p. 399
loss-leader pricing p. 400
one-price policy p. 401
flexible-price policy p. 401
product-line pricing p. 402
quantity discounts p. 404

Chapter Problems and Applications

1. Under what conditions would a camera manufacturer adopt a skimming price approach for a new product? A penetration approach?

2. What are some similarities and differences between skimming pricing, prestige pricing, and above-market pricing?

3. A producer of microwave ovens has adopted an experience curve pricing approach for its new model. The firm believes it can reduce the cost of producing the model by 20 percent each time volume doubles. The cost to produce the first unit was $1,000. What would be the approximate cost of the 4,096th unit?

4. The Hesper Corporation is a leading manufacturer of high-quality upholstered sofas. Current plans call for an increase of $600,000 in the advertising budget. If the firm sells its sofas for an average price of $850 and the unit variable costs are $550, then what dollar sales increase will be necessary to cover the additional advertising?

5. Suppose executives estimate that the unit variable cost for their VCR is $100, the fixed cost related to the product is $10 million annually, and the target volume for next year is 100,000 recorders. What sales price will be necessary to achieve a target profit of $1 million?

6. A manufacturer of motor oil has a trade discount policy whereby the manufacturer's suggested retail price is $30 per case with the terms of 40/20/10. The manufacturer sells its products through jobbers, who sell to wholesalers, who sell to gasoline stations. What will the manufacturer's sale price be?

7. What are the effective annual interest rates for the following cash discount terms? (*a*) 1/10 net 30, (*b*) 2/10 net 30, and (*c*) 2/10 net 60.

8. Suppose a manufacturer of exercise equipment sets a suggested price to the consumer of $395 for a particular piece of equipment to be competitive with similar equipment. The manufacturer sells its equipment to a sporting goods wholesaler who receives a 25 percent markup and a retailer who receives a 50 percent markup. What demand-oriented pricing approach is being used, and at what price will the manufacturer sell the equipment to the wholesaler?

9. Is there any truth in the statement, "Geographical pricing schemes will always be unfair to some buyers?" Why or why not?

Case 15–1   My Own Meals

Video

"The kids generally like the fast-food meals. I tend to not like them because I try to stay away from the high fat," says Angela Harmon, mother of three young girls. "I have to have something that is nutritious and fast," remarks Mary Champlain, mother of two. Comments like these and her own experiences led Mary Anne Jackson to conclude that there was an opportunity to provide parents with better children's food options. As Mary explains, "being a busy working mother, I knew that there was a need for this type of product in the marketplace."

The Idea

Mary's insight about the marketplace was supported by several socioeconomic trends. For example:

- More than 65 percent of working mothers now have school-age children, the highest percentage ever.

- About 90 percent of children under the age of 7 eat at McDonald's at least 4 times per month.
- More than 90 percent of homes in the United States now have microwave ovens.
- Women already represent almost half of the total workforce. By the year 2000, two out of three new entrants into the labor force will be women.

With this evidence, some food industry experience and business education, and a lot of entrepreneurial spirit, Mary Anne Jackson set out to satisfy the need for nutritious, convenient children's meals. Her idea: develop a line of healthy, microwaveable meals for children 2 to 10 years old.

The Company

Ms. Jackson started by founding a company, My Own Meals, Inc., with a line of five healthy microwaveable meals. The meals were offered in shelf-stable "retort" packages, which are like flexible cans. This created a whole new category of prepared foods, and raised more than a few eyebrows among the major food companies. Mary observed that "The need for children's meals was not being addressed in the past, and I think this was because most major food companies are run by men." Eventually, however, the big companies challenged My Own Meals with their own entries into the new category. Tyson, Banquet (Con Agra), and Hormel each introduced new children's meals, although Tyson and Banquet launched frozen meals. The competition reinforced Mary's efforts, "Having competitors come into the marketplace justified the existence of the category," she explains.

The product line was developed using a lot of marketing research—hundreds of busy mothers provided input about product quality, usage rates, and price. The results indicated that customers would serve their children high-quality meals between 3 and 4 times each month and that they would be willing to pay approximately $2.30 for each meal. Based on this information Mary estimated that the potential retail market was $500 million!

THE ISSUE: SETTING RETAIL PRICES

"We were trying to decide if we were priced appropriately and competitively for the marketplace, and we decided that we would look at the price elasticity for our product line," observes Mary Anne Jackson. "We found that the closer we came to $3.00 a unit, the lower the volume was, and overall we were losing revenues and profits," said Jackson.

To arrive at final retail prices for her company's products Mary Anne Jackson considered factors related to demand, cost, profit, and competition. For example, because lower-quality brands had entered the market, My Own Meals needed a retail price that reflected the superior quality of its products. "We're premium priced because we're a higher quality product than any of our competitors. If we weren't, our quality image would be lowered to the image that they have," explains Jackson.

At some stores, however, prices approached $3.00 and consumer demand decreased.

To estimate the prices consumers would see on their shelves, Jackson needed to estimate the cost of producing the meals and add My Own Meal's markup. Then she determined the markup of each of the distribution channels—retail grocery stores, mass merchants, day care centers, and military commissaries—would add to reach the retail price. The grocery stores were very concerned about profitability and used a concept called direct product profitability (DPP) to determine prices and shelf space. "They want to know how much money they make on each square foot of the shelf dedicated to each product line. I had to do a DPP analysis to show them why they were making more on our products for our space than the competition," remarks Mary Anne Jackson. Finally, Mary considered competitors' prices which were:

- Looney Toons (Tyson) $2.49
- Kid Cuisine (Banquet) $1.89
- Kid's Kitchen (Hormel) $1.19

Mary knew that it was important to consider all of these factors in her pricing decisions. The price would influence the interest of consumers and retailers, the reactions of competitors, and ultimately the success of My Own Meals!

Questions

1. In what ways are the demand factors of (*a*) consumer tastes, (*b*) price and availability of substitute products, and (*c*) consumer income important in influencing consumer demand for My Own Meals products?
2. How can (*a*) demand-based, (*b*) cost-based, (*c*) profit-based, and (*d*) competition-based approaches be used to help My Own Meals arrive at an approximate price level?
3. Why might the retail price of My Own Meal's products be different in grocery stores, mass merchants, day care centers, and military commissaries?

Financial Aspects of Marketing

Basic concepts from accounting and finance provide valuable tools for marketing executives. This appendix describes an actual company's use of accounting and financial concepts and illustrates how they assist the owner in making marketing decisions.

THE CAPLOW COMPANY

An accomplished artist and calligrapher, Jane Westerlund, decided to apply some of her experience to the picture framing business in Minneapolis. She bought an existing retail frame store, The Caplow Company, from a friend who owned the business and wanted to retire. She avoided the do-it-yourself end of the framing business and chose three kinds of business activities: (1) cutting the frame, mats, and glass for customers who brought in their own pictures or prints to be framed, (2) selling prints and posters that she had purchased from wholesalers, and (3) restoring high-quality frames and paintings.

To understand how accounting, finance, and marketing relate to each other, let's analyze (1) the operating statement for her frame shop, (2) some general ratios of interest that are derived from the operating statement, and (3) some ratios that pertain specifically to her pricing decisions.

The Operating Statement

The operating statement (also called an *income statement* or *profit-and-loss statement*) summarizes the profitability of a business firm for a specific time period, usually a month, quarter, or year. The title of the operating statement for The Caplow Company shows it is for a one-year period (Figure B–1). The purpose of an operating statement is to show the profit of the firm and the revenues and expenses that led to that profit. This information tells the owner or manager what has happened in the past and suggests actions to improve future profitability.

The left side of Figure B–1 shows that there are three key elements to all operating statements: (1) sales of the firm's goods and services, (2) costs incurred in making and selling the goods and services, and (3) profit or loss, which is the difference between sales and costs.

Sales elements The sales element of Figure B–1 has four terms that need explanation:

- *Gross sales* are the total amount billed to customers. Dissatisfied customers or errors may reduce the gross sales through returns or allowances.
- *Returns* occur when a customer gives the item purchased back to the seller, who either refunds the purchase price or allows the customer a credit on subsequent purchases. In any event, the seller now owns the item again.

- *Allowances* are given when a customer is dissatisfied with the item purchased and the seller reduces the original purchase price. Unlike returns, in the case of allowances the buyer owns the item.
- *Net sales* are simply gross sales minus returns and allowances.

The operating statement for The Caplow Company shows that

Gross sales	$80,500
Less: Returns and allowances	500
Net sales	$80,000

The low level of returns and allowances shows the shop generally has done a good job in satisfying customers, which is essential in building the repeat business necessary for success.

FIGURE B-1

Examples of an operating statement

THE CAPLOW COMPANY
Operating Statement
For the Year Ending December 31, 1996

Sales	Gross sales			$80,500
	Less: Returns and allowances			500
	Net sales			$80,000
Costs	Cost of goods sold:			
	Beginning inventory at cost		$ 6,000	
	Purchases at billed cost	$21,000		
	Less: Purchase discounts	300		
	Purchases at net cost	20,700		
	Plus freight-in	100		
	Net cost of delivered purchases		20,800	
	Direct labor (framing)		14,200	
	Cost of goods available for sale		41,000	
	Less: Ending inventory at cost		5,000	
	Cost of goods sold			36,000
	Gross margin (gross profit)			$44,000
	Expenses:			
	Selling expenses:			
	Sales salaries	2,000		
	Advertising expense	3,000		
	Total selling expense		5,000	
	Administrative expenses:			
	Owner's salary	18,000		
	Bookkeeper's salary	1,200		
	Office supplies	300		
	Total administrative expense		19,500	
	General expenses:			
	Depreciation expense	1,000		
	Interest expense	500		
	Rent expense	2,100		
	Utiltiy expenses (heat, electricity)	3,000		
	Repairs and maintenance	2,300		
	Insurance	2,000		
	Social security taxes	2,200		
	Total general expense		13,100	
	Total expenses			37,600
Profit or loss	Profit before taxes			$ 6,400

Cost elements   The *cost of goods sold* is the total cost of the products sold during the period. This item varies according to the kind of business. A retail store purchases finished goods and resells them to customers without reworking them in any way. In contrast, a manufacturing firm combines raw and semifinished materials and parts, uses labor and overhead to rework these into finished goods, and then sells them to customers. All these activities are reflected in the cost of goods sold item on a manufacturer's operating statement. Note that the frame shop has some features of a pure retailer (prints and posters it buys that are resold without alteration) and a pure manufacturer (assembling the raw materials of molding, matting, and glass to form a completed frame).

Some terms that relate to cost of goods sold need clarification:

- *Inventory* is the physical material that is purchased from suppliers, may or may not be reworked, and is available for sale to customers. In the frame shop inventory includes molding, matting, glass, prints, and posters.
- *Purchase discounts* are reductions in the original billed price for reasons such as prompt payment of the bill or the quantity bought.
- *Direct labor* is the cost of the labor used in producing the finished product. For the frame shop this is the cost of producing the completed frames from the molding, matting, and glass.
- *Gross margin (gross profit)* is the money remaining to manage the business, sell the products or services, and give some profit. Gross margin is net sales minus cost of goods sold.

The two right-hand columns in Figure B–1 between "Net sales" and "Gross margin" calculate the cost of goods sold:

Net sales		$80,000
Cost of goods sold		
Beginning inventory at cost	$ 6,000	
Net cost of delivered purchases	20,800	
Direct labor (framing)	14,200	
Cost of goods available for sale	41,000	
Less: ending inventory at cost	5,000	
Cost of goods sold		36,000
Gross margin (gross profit)		$44,000

This section considers the beginning and ending inventories, the net cost of purchases delivered during the year, and the cost of the direct labor going into making the frames. Subtracting the $36,000 cost of goods sold from the $80,000 net sales gives the $44,000 gross margin.

Three major categories of expenses are shown in Figure B–1 below the gross margin:

- *Selling expenses* are the costs of selling the product or service produced by the firm. For The Caplow Company there are two such selling expenses: sales salaries of part-time employees waiting on customers and the advertising expense of simple newspaper ads and direct-mail ads sent to customers.
- *Administrative expenses* are the costs of managing the business, and, for The Caplow Company, include three expenses: the owner's salary, a part-time bookkeeper's salary, and office supplies expense.
- *General expenses* are miscellaneous costs not covered elsewhere; for the frame shop these include seven items: depreciation expense (on her equipment), interest expense, rent expense, utility expenses, repairs and maintenance expense, insurance expense, and social security taxes.

As shown in Figure B–1, selling, administrative, and general expenses total $37,600 for The Caplow Company.

Jane Westerlund (left) and an assistant assess the restoration of a gold frame for regilding.

Profit element   What the company has earned, the *profit before taxes,* is found by subtracting cost of goods sold and expenses from net sales. For The Caplow Company, Figure B–1 shows that profit before taxes is $6,400.

General Operating Ratios to Analyze Operations

Looking only at the elements of Caplow's operating statement that extend to the right-hand column highlights the firm's performance on some important dimensions. Using operating ratios such as *expense-to-sales-ratios* for expressing basic expense or profit elements as a percentage of net sales gives further insights:

ELEMENT IN OPERATING STATEMENT	DOLLAR VALUE	PERCENTAGE OF NET SALES
Gross sales	$80,500	
Less: Returns and allowances	500	
Net sales	80,000	100%
Less: Cost of goods sold	36,000	45
Gross margin	44,000	55
Less: Total expenses	37,600	47
Profit (or loss) before taxes	$ 6,400	8%

Westerlund can use this information to compare her firm's performance from one time period to the next. To do so, it is especially important that she keep the same definitions for each element of her operating statement, also a significant factor in using the electronic spreadsheets discussed in Chapter 15. Performance comparisons between periods are more difficult if she changes definitions for the accounting elements in the operating statement.

   She can use either the dollar values or the operating ratios (the value of the element of the operating statement divided by net sales) to analyze the firm's

NAME OF FINANCIAL ELEMENT OR RATIO	WHAT IT MEASURES	EQUATION
Selling price ($)	Price customer sees	Cost of goods sold (COGS) + Markup
Markup ($)	Dollars added to COGS to arrive at selling price	Selling price − COGS
Markup on selling price (%)	Relates markup to selling price	$\dfrac{\text{Markup}}{\text{Selling price}} \times 100 = \dfrac{\text{Selling price} - \text{COGS}}{\text{Selling Price}} \times 100$
Markup on cost (%)	Relates markup to cost	$\dfrac{\text{Markup}}{\text{COGS}} \times 100 = \dfrac{\text{Selling price} - \text{COGS}}{\text{COGS}} \times 100$
Markdown (%)	Ability of firm to sell its products at initial selling price	$\dfrac{\text{Markdowns}}{\text{Net sales}} \times 100$
Stockturn rate	Ability of firm to move its inventory quickly	$\dfrac{\text{COGS}}{\text{Average inventory at cost}}$ or $\dfrac{\text{Net sales}}{\text{Average inventory at selling price}}$
Return on investment (%)	Profit performance of firm compared with money invested in it	$\dfrac{\text{Net profit after taxes}}{\text{Investment}} \times 100$

FIGURE B−2 How to calculate selling price, markup, markdown, stockturn, and return on investment

performance. However, the operating ratios are more valuable than the dollar values for two reasons: (1) the simplicity of working with percentages rather than dollars and (2) the availability of operating ratios of typical firms in the same industry, which are published by Dun & Bradstreet and trade associations. Thus, Westerlund can compare her firm's performance not only with that of *other* frame shops but also with that of *small* frame shops that have annual net sales, for example, of under $100,000. In this way she can identify where her operations are better or worse than other similar firms. For example, if trade association data showed a typical frame shop of her size had a ratio of cost of goods sold to net sales of 37 percent, compared with her 45 percent, she might consider steps to reduce this cost through purchase discounts, reducing inbound freight charges, finding lower cost suppliers, and so on.

Ratios to Use in Setting and Evaluating Price

Using The Caplow Company as an example, we can study four ratios that relate closely to setting a price: (1) markup, (2) markdown, (3) stockturns, and (4) return on investment. These terms are defined in Figure B−2 and explained below.

Markup Both markup and gross margin refer to the amount added to the cost of goods sold to arrive at the selling price, and they may be expressed either in dollar or percentage terms. However, the term *markup* is more commonly used in setting retail prices. Suppose the average price Westerlund charges for a framed picture is $80. Then in terms of the first two definitions in Figure B−2 and the earlier information from the operating statement,

ELEMENT OF PRICE	DOLLAR VALUE
Cost of goods sold	$36
Markup (or gross margin)	44
Selling price	$80

The third definition in Figure B–2 gives the percentage markup on selling price:

$$\text{Markup on selling price (\%)} = \frac{\text{Markup}}{\text{Selling price}} \times 100$$

$$= \frac{44}{80} \times 100 = 55\%$$

And the percentage markup on cost is obtained as follows:

$$\text{Markup on cost (\%)} = \frac{\text{Markup}}{\text{Cost of goods sold}} \times 100$$

$$= \frac{44}{36} \times 10 = 122.2\%$$

Inexperienced retail clerks sometimes fail to distinguish between the two definitions of markup, which (as the preceding calculations show) can represent a tremendous difference, so it is essential to know whether the base is cost or selling price. Marketers generally use selling price as the base for talking about "markups" unless they specifically state that they are using cost as a base.

Retailers and wholesalers that rely heavily on markup pricing (discussed in Chapter 15) often use standardized tables that convert markup on selling price to markup on cost, and vice versa. The two equations below show how to convert one to the other:

$$\text{Markup on selling price (\%)} = \frac{\text{Markup on cost (\%)}}{100\% + \text{Markup on cost (\%)}} \times 100$$

$$\text{Markup on cost (\%)} = \frac{\text{Markup on selling price (\%)}}{100\% - \text{Markup on selling price (\%)}} \times 100$$

Using the data from The Caplow Company gives

$$\text{Markup on selling price (\%)} = \frac{\text{Markup on cost (\%)}}{100\% + \text{Markup on cost (\%)}} \times 100$$

$$= \frac{122.2}{100 + 122.2} \times 100 = 55\%$$

$$\text{Markup on cost (\%)} = \frac{\text{Markup on selling price (\%)}}{100\% - \text{Markup on selling price (\%)}} \times 100$$

$$= \frac{55}{100 - 55} \times 100 = 122.2\%$$

The use of an incorrect markup base is shown in Westerlund's business. A markup of 122.2 percent on her cost of goods sold for a typical frame she sells gives 122.2% × $36 = $44 of markup. Added to the $36 cost of goods sold, this gives her selling price of $80 for the framed picture. However, a new clerk working for her who erroneously priced the framed picture at 55 percent of cost of goods sold set the final price at $55.80 ($36 of cost of goods sold plus 55% × $36 = $19.80). The error, if repeated, can be disastrous: frames would be accidentally sold at $55.80, or $24.20 below the intended selling price of $80.

Markdown   A markdown is a reduction in a retail price that is necessary if the item will not sell at the full selling price to which it has been marked up. The item might not sell for a variety of reasons: the selling price was set too high or the item is out of style or has become soiled or damaged. The seller "takes a markdown" by lowering the price to sell it, thereby converting it to cash to buy future inventory that will sell faster.

The markdown percentage cannot be calculated directly from the operating statement. As shown in the fifth item of Figure B–2, the numerator of the markdown percentage is the total dollar markdowns. Markdowns are reductions in the prices of goods that are purchased by customers. The denominator is net sales.

A customer discusses choices of framing and matting for her print with Jane Westerlund.

Suppose The Caplow Company had a total of $700 in markdowns on the prints and posters that are stocked and available for sale. Since the frames are custom made for individual customers, there is little reason for a markdown there. Caplow's markdown percent is then

$$\text{Markdown}(\%) = \frac{\text{Markdowns}}{\text{Net sales}} \times 100$$

$$= \frac{\$700}{\$80,000} \times 100$$

$$= 0.875\%$$

Other kinds of retailers often have markdown ratios several times this amount. For example, women's dress stores have markdowns of about 25 percent, and menswear stores have markdowns of about 2 percent.

Stockturn rate   A business firm is anxious to have its inventory move quickly, or "turn over." Stockturn rate, or simply stockturns, measures this inventory movement. For a retailer a slow stockturn rate may show it is buying merchandise customers don't want, so this is a critical measure of performance. When a firm sells only a single product, one convenient way to measure stockturn rate is simply to divide its cost of goods sold by average inventory at cost. The sixth item in Figure B–2 shows how to calculate stockturn rate using information in the following operating statement:

$$\text{Stockturn rate} = \frac{\text{Cost of goods sold}}{\text{Average inventory at cost}}$$

The dollar amount of average inventory at cost is calculated by adding the beginning and ending inventories for the year and dividing by 2 to get the average. From Caplow's operating statement, we have

$$\text{Stockturn rate} = \frac{\text{Cost of goods sold}}{\text{Average inventory at cost}}$$

$$= \frac{\text{Cost of goods sold}}{\dfrac{\text{Beginning inventory} + \text{Ending inventory}}{2}}$$

$$= \frac{\$36,000}{\dfrac{\$6,000 + \$5,000}{2}}$$

$$= \frac{\$36,000}{\$5,500}$$

$$= 6.5 \text{ stockturns per year}$$

What is considered a "good stockturn" varies by the kind of industry. For example, supermarkets have limited shelf space for thousands of new products from manufacturers each year, so they watch stockturn carefully by product line. The stockturn rate in supermarkets for breakfast foods is about 17 times per year, for pet food about 22 times, and for paper products about 25 times per year.

Return on investment   A better measure of the performance of a firm than the amount of profit it makes in a year is its ROI, which is the ratio of net income to the investment used to earn that net income. To calculate ROI, it is necessary to subtract income taxes from profit before taxes to obtain net income, then divide this figure by the investment that can be found on a firm's balance sheet (another accounting statement that shows the firm's assets, liabilities, and net worth). While financial and accounting experts have many definitions for "investment," an often-used definition is "total assets."

For our purposes, let's assume that Westerlund has total assets (investment) of $20,000 in The Caplow Company, which covers inventory, store fixtures, and framing equipment. If she pays $1,000 in income taxes, her store's net income is $5,400, so her ROI is given by the seventh item in Figure B–2:

$$\text{Return on investment} = \text{Net income/investment} \times 100$$

$$= \$5,400/\$20,000 \times 100$$

$$= 27\%$$

If Westerlund wants to improve her ROI next year, the strategies she might take are found in this alternative equation for ROI:

$$\text{ROI} = \text{Net sales/investment} \times \text{Net income/net sales}$$

$$= \text{Investment turnover} \times \text{Profit margin}$$

This equation suggests that The Caplow Company's ROI can be improved by raising turnover or increasing profit margin. Increasing stockturns will accomplish the former, whereas lowering cost of goods sold to net sales will cause the latter.

CHAPTER 16

Marketing Channels and Wholesaling

AFTER READING THIS CHAPTER YOU SHOULD BE ABLE TO:

• Explain what is meant by a marketing channel of distribution and why intermediaries are needed.

• Recognize differences between marketing channels for consumer and industrial products and services.

• Describe the types and functions of firms that perform wholesaling activities.

• Distinguish among traditional marketing channels and different types of vertical marketing systems.

• Describe factors considered by marketing executives when selecting and managing a marketing channel.

REIGNING CATS AND DOGS WAG PET INDUSTRY MARKETING CHANNELS

Fido's bark and Fifi's purr are a nurturing pet owner's sound of music. Pet pampering has the sound of money for companies that market pet foods, toys, clothing, accessories, and furniture.

More than one half of all U.S. households care for 54 million dogs, 62 million cats, and countless fish, birds, and hamsters, all of whom get hungry. Annual pet food sales top $9 billion, and another $9 billion-plus is spent for pet supplies and health care. Surprised? Don't be. A recent survey revealed that one half of U.S. pet owners consider themselves "Mom and Dad" to their animal companions.

A decade ago, supermarkets sold 95 percent of pet products; small pet stores sold the rest. But the 1990s witnessed a distribution revolution that took a huge bite out of supermarket sales. Superpremium pet brands, such as Hill's Science Diet, Iams, and Nutro Pet Food, posed the first challenge to supermarkets. These and similar brands, which now capture 20 percent of the pet food market, were initially sold only at veterinarians' offices and pet stores. The next assault came from nongrocery outlets such as Wal-Mart. The latest bite has come from pet superstores—PetsMart, Petco, Petstuff, and Pet Food Warehouse—which now capture more than 40 percent of pet product sales.

Pet superstores cater to pets and their adoptive parents. Animals and their companions prowl aisles filled with everything a discriminating shopper could want—doggy dental floss, bones, purple aquarium gravel, hamster starter kits, and bins of toys, balls, stuffed playthings, and treats—many at a pet's eye level to stimulate impulse purchases. Pet food and supplements are plentiful as are sweaters, hats, and colorful collars and leashes. Some stores offer pet grooming and in-house veterinary services.

The distribution revolution in the pet products industry is illustrative of changes in marketing channels occurring in other industries, including home-improvement supplies (Home Depot), office equipment (Office Max), children's toys (Toys "Я" Us), where the superstore concept has emerged. In each instance, product manufacturers and intermediaries that supply these stores have had to adjust their marketing practices in ways described later in this chapter.[1]

This chapter focuses on marketing channels of distribution and why they are an important component in the marketing mix. It then shows how such channels benefit consumers and the sequence of firms that make up a marketing channel. Finally, it describes factors that influence the choice and management of marketing channels, including channel conflict and legal restrictions.

NATURE AND IMPORTANCE OF MARKETING CHANNELS

Reaching prospective buyers, either directly or indirectly, is a prerequisite for successful marketing. At the same time, buyers benefit from distribution systems used by firms.

Defining Marketing Channels of Distribution

You see the results of distribution every day. You may have purchased Lay's Potato Chips at the 7-Eleven store, your lunch at McDonald's, and Levi's jeans at Sears. Each of these items was brought to you by a marketing channel of distribution, or simply a **marketing channel,** which consists of individuals and firms involved in the process of making a product or service available for use or consumption by consumers or industrial users.

Marketing channels can be compared with a pipeline through which water flows from a source to terminus. Marketing channels make possible the flow of goods from a producer, through intermediaries, to a buyer. Intermediaries go by various names (Figure 16–1) and perform various functions.[2] Some intermediaries actually purchase items from the seller, store them, and resell them to buyers. For example, Sunshine Biscuits produces cookies and sells them to food wholesalers. The wholesalers then sell the cookies to supermarkets and grocery stores, which, in turn, sell them to consumers. Other intermediaries such as brokers and agents represent sellers but do not actually take title to products—their role is to bring a seller and

FIGURE 16–1

Terms used for marketing intermediaries

TERM	DESCRIPTION
Middleman	Any intermediary between manufacturer and end-user markets
Agent or broker	Any intermediary with legal authority to act on behalf of the manufacturer
Wholesaler	An intermediary who sells to other intermediaries, usually to retailers; usually applies to consumer markets
Retailer	An intermediary who sells to consumers
Distributor	An imprecise term, usually used to describe intermediaries who perform a variety of distribution functions, including selling, maintaining inventories, extending credit, and so on; a more common term in industrial markets but may also be used to refer to wholesalers
Dealer	An even more imprecise term that can mean the same as distributor, retailer, wholesaler, and so forth

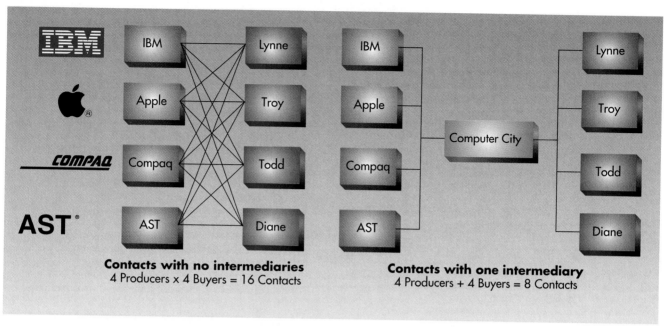

Contacts with no intermediaries
4 Producers x 4 Buyers = 16 Contacts

Contacts with one intermediary
4 Producers + 4 Buyers = 8 Contacts

FIGURE 16-2

How intermediaries minimize transactions

buyer together. Century 21 real estate agents are examples of this type of intermediary. The importance of intermediaries is made even clearer when we consider the functions they perform and the value they create for buyers.

Value Created by Intermediaries

Few consumers appreciate the value created by intermediaries; however, producers recognize that intermediaries make selling goods and services more efficient because they minimize the number of sales contacts necessary to reach a target market. Figure 16–2 shows a simple example of how this comes about in the personal computer industry. Without a retail intermediary (such as Computer City), IBM, Apple, Compaq, and AST would each have to make four contacts to reach the four buyers shown who are in the target market. However, each producer has to make only one contact when Computer City acts as an intermediary. Equally important from a macromarketing perspective, the total number of industry transactions is reduced from 16 to 8, which reduces producer cost and hence benefits the consumer. This simple example also illustrates why computer manufacturers constantly compete with each other to gain access to computer retailers such as Computer City and Circuit City.

Functions performed by intermediaries   Intermediaries make possible the flow of products from producers to buyers by performing three basic functions (Figure 16–3).[3] Most prominently, intermediaries perform a transactional function that involves buying, selling, and risk taking because they stock merchandise in anticipation of sales. Intermediaries perform a logistical function evident in the gathering, storing, and dispersing of products (see Chapter 17 on physical distribution). Finally, intermediaries perform facilitating functions, which assist producers in making goods and services more attractive to buyers.

All three groups of functions must be performed in a marketing channel, even though each channel member may not participate in all three. Channel members often negotiate about which specific functions they will perform. Sometimes conflict results, and a breakdown in relationships among channel members occurs. This happened recently when PepsiCo, Inc. terminated its marketing and distribution arrangement with its bottler in France, citing poor performance. However, because all

FIGURE 16-3

Marketing channel functions
performed by intermediaries

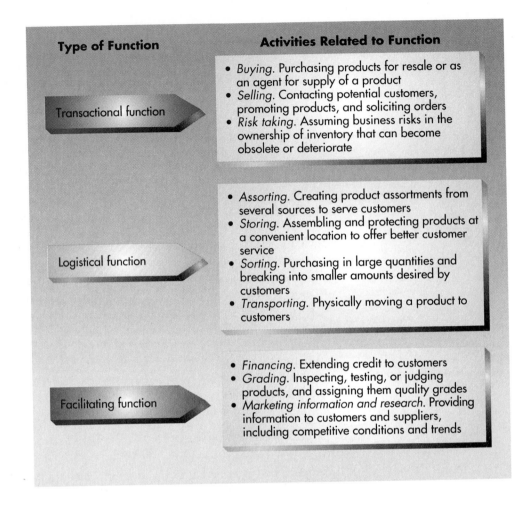

channel functions had to be performed, PepsiCo could eliminate this intermediary but not the functions it performed. So PepsiCo either had to find another bottler (which it did) or set up its own bottling operation to perform the channel functions.[4]

Consumer benefits from intermediaries Consumers also benefit from intermediaries. Having the goods and services you want, when you want them, where you want them, and in the form you want them is the ideal result of marketing channels. In more specific terms, marketing channels help create value for consumers through the four utilities described in Chapter 1: time, place, form, and possession. Time utility refers to having a product or service when you want it. For example, Federal Express provides next-morning delivery. Place utility means having a product or service available where consumers want it, such as having a Gulf gas station located on a long stretch of lonely highway. Form utility involves enhancing a product or service to make it more appealing to buyers, for example, tailoring services provided by the men's shop in Foley's Department Store in Houston. Possession utility entails efforts by intermediaries to help buyers take possession of a product or service, such as having airline tickets delivered by a travel agency.

CONCEPT CHECK

1. What is meant by a marketing channel?

2. What are the three basic functions performed by intermediaries?

CHANNEL STRUCTURE AND ORGANIZATION

A product can take many routes on its journey from a producer to buyers, and marketers search for the most efficient route from the many alternatives available.

Marketing Channels for Consumer Goods and Services

Figure 16–4 shows the four most common marketing channels for consumer goods and services. It also shows the number of levels in each marketing channel, as evidenced by the number of intermediaries between a producer and ultimate buyers. As the number of intermediaries between a producer and buyer increases, the channel is viewed as increasing in length. Thus the producer → wholesaler → retailer → consumer channel is longer than the producer → consumer channel.

Channel A represents a **direct channel** because a producer and ultimate consumers deal directly with each other. Many products and services are distributed this way. A number of insurance companies sell their financial services using a direct channel and branch sales offices, and World Book Educational Products sells its encyclopedias door-to-door. Schwan's Sales Enterprises of Marshall, Minnesota, markets a full line of frozen foods in 49 states and parts of Canada using door-to-door salespeople who sell from refrigerated trucks. Because there are no intermediaries with a direct channel, the producer must perform all channel functions.

The remaining three channel forms are **indirect channels** because intermediaries are inserted between the producer and consumers and perform numerous channel functions.

Channel B, with a retailer added, is most common when a retailer is large and can buy in large quantities from a producer or when the cost of inventory makes it too expensive to use a wholesaler. Manufacturers such as GM, Ford, and Chrysler use this channel, and a local car dealer acts as a retailer. Why is there no wholesaler? So

FIGURE 16–4

Common marketing channels for consumer goods and services

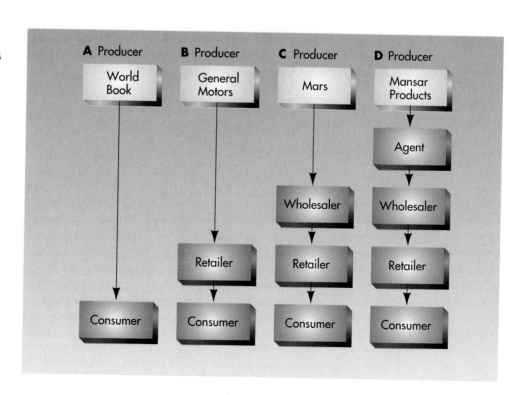

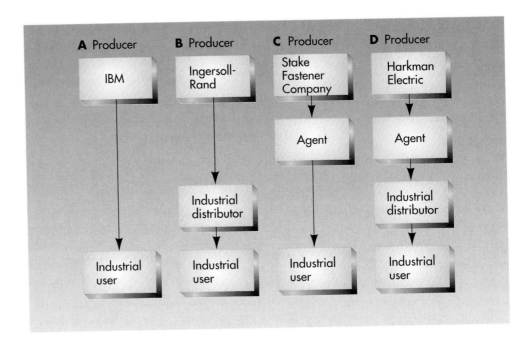

many variations exist in the product that it would be impossible for a wholesaler to stock all the models required to satisfy buyers; in addition, the cost of maintaining an inventory would be too high. However, large retailers such as Sears, 7-Eleven, Safeway, and JCPenney buy in sufficient quantities to make it cost effective for a producer to deal with only a retail intermediary.

Adding a wholesaler in Channel C is most common for low-cost, low-unit value items that are frequently purchased by consumers, such as candy, confectionary items, and magazines. For example, Mars sells its line of candies to wholesalers in case quantities; then they can break down (sort) the cases so that individual retailers can order in boxes or much smaller quantities.

Channel D, the most indirect channel, is employed when there are many small manufacturers and many small retailers and an agent is used to help coordinate a large supply of the product. Mansar Products, Ltd. is a Belgian producer of specialty jewelry that uses agents to sell to wholesalers in the United States, which then sell to many small retailers.

Marketing Channels for Industrial Goods and Services

The four most common channels for industrial goods and services are shown in Figure 16–5. In contrast with channels for consumer products, industrial channels typically are shorter and rely on one intermediary or none at all because industrial users are fewer in number, tend to be more concentrated geographically, and buy in larger quantities (see Chapter 7).

Channel A, represented by IBM's large, mainframe computer business, is a direct channel. Firms using this channel maintain their own salesforce and are responsible for all channel functions. This channel arrangement is employed when buyers are large and well defined, the sales effort requires extensive negotiations, and the products are of high unit value and require hands-on expertise in terms of installation or use.

Channels B, C, and D are indirect channels with one or more intermediaries to reach industrial users. In Channel B an **industrial distributor** performs a variety of marketing channel functions, including selling, stocking, and delivering a full product assortment and financing. In many ways, industrial distributors are like wholesalers in consumer channels. Ingersoll-Rand, for example, uses industrial distributors to sell its line of pneumatic tools.

Channel C introduces a second intermediary, an *agent,* who serves primarily as the independent selling arm of producers and represents a producer to industrial users. For example, Stake Fastener Company, a California-based producer of industrial fasteners, has an agent call on industrial users rather than employing its own salesforce.

Channel D is the longest channel and includes both agents and distributors. For instance, Harkman Electric, a small Texas-based producer of electric products, uses agents to call on distributors who sell to industrial users.

Multiple Channels and Strategic Alliances

In some situations producers use **dual distribution,** an arrangement whereby a firm reaches different buyers by employing two or more different types of channels for the same basic product.[5] For example, GE sells its large appliances directly to home and apartment builders but uses retail stores to sell to consumers. In some instances, firms use multiple channels when a multibrand strategy is employed (see Chapter 12). Hallmark sells its Hallmark greeting cards through Hallmark stores and select department stores, and its Ambassador brand of cards through discount and drugstore chains. In other instances, a firm will distribute modified products through different channels. Zoecon Corporation sells its insect control chemicals to professional pest-control operators such as Orkin and Terminex. A modified compound is sold to the Boyle-Midway Division of American Home Products for use in its Black-Flag Roach Ender brand.

A recent innovation in marketing channels is the use of **strategic channel alliances,** whereby one firm's marketing channel is used to sell another firm's products.[6] An alliance between Pepsi-Cola and Thomas J. Lipton Company is a case in point. Lipton relies on Pepsi-Cola's extensive bottling network to distribute Lipton Original, a ready-to-drink iced tea sold only in bottles. Strategic alliances are very popular in global marketing, where the creation of marketing channel relationships is expensive and time-consuming. For example, General Motors distributes the Swedish Saab through its dealers in Canada. And Kraft Foods uses the distribution system of Ajinomoto, a major Japanese food company, to market its Maxwell House coffee in Japan.

These examples illustrate the creative routes to the marketplace available through dual distribution and strategic channel alliances. They also show how innovative firms can reach more buyers and increase sales volume. Read the Marketing NewsNet on the next page so you won't be surprised when you are served Nestlé (not General Mills) Cheerios in Europe, Mexico, and parts of Asia.[7]

Direct Marketing Channels

Increasingly, many firms are using direct marketing to reach buyers. **Direct marketing** allows consumers to buy products by interacting with various advertising media without a face-to-face meeting with a salesperson.[8] Direct marketing includes mail-order selling, direct-mail sales, catalog sales, telemarketing, video-text such as Prodigy, and televised home shopping (for example, the Home Shopping Network). One of every $15 in U.S. sales is related to direct marketing.[9]

Some firms sell products almost entirely through direct marketing. These firms include L. L. Bean (apparel), Sharper Image (expensive gifts and novelties), and Gateway 2000 (personal computers). Manufacturers such as Nestlé and Sunkist, in addition to using traditional channels composed of wholesalers and retailers, employ

MARKETING NEWSNET

NESTLÉ AND GENERAL MILLS: CEREAL PARTNERS WORLDWIDE

Can you say Nestlé Cheerios *miel amandes?* Millions of French start their day with this European equivalent of General Mills's Honey Nut Cheerios, made possible by Cereal Partners Worldwide (CPW). CPW is the food industry's first strategic alliance designed to be a global business; it joined the cereal manufacturing and marketing capability of U.S.-based General Mills with the worldwide distribution clout of Swiss-based Nestlé.

From its headquarters near Lake Geneva, Switzerland, CPW first launched General Mills cereals under the Nestlé label in France, the United Kingdom, Spain, Portugal, and Italy in 1991, and recorded sales of $250 million. In 1992, distribution moved to include Mexico, Italy, and Germany. Asia—particularly the Philippines and Thailand—was targeted in 1993 and 1994. CPW expects to achieve its goal of $1 billion in sales by 2000. The General Mills–Nestlé strategic alliance is also likely to increase the ready-to-eat worldwide market share

of these companies, which are already rated as the two best-managed firms in the world.

---

direct marketing through catalogs and telemarketing to reach more buyers. At the same time, retailers such as JCPenney use direct marketing techniques to augment conventional store merchandising activities. Some experts believe that direct marketing will account for 20 percent of all retail transactions in the United States and 10 percent of retail transactions in Europe in the late 1990s. Direct marketing is covered in greater depth in Chapter 18.

A Closer Look at Channel Intermediaries

Channel structures for consumer and industrial products assume various forms based on the number and type of intermediaries. Knowledge of the roles played by these intermediaries is important for understanding how channels operate in practice.

The terms *wholesaler, agent,* and *retailer* have been used in a general fashion consistent with the meanings given in Figure 16–1. However, on closer inspection, a variety of specific types of intermediaries emerges. Figure 16–6 shows a common classification of intermediaries that engage in wholesaling activities—those activities involved in selling products and services to those who are buying for the purposes of resale or business use. Intermediaries engaged in retailing activities are discussed in detail in Chapter 18. Figure 16–7 describes the functions performed by major types of independent wholesalers.[10]

Merchant wholesalers   Merchant wholesalers are independently owned firms that take title to the merchandise they handle. They go by various names, including industrial distributor (described earlier). About 83 percent of the firms engaged in wholesaling activities are merchant wholesalers.

Merchant wholesalers are classified as either full-service or limited-service wholesalers, depending on the number of functions performed. Two major types of

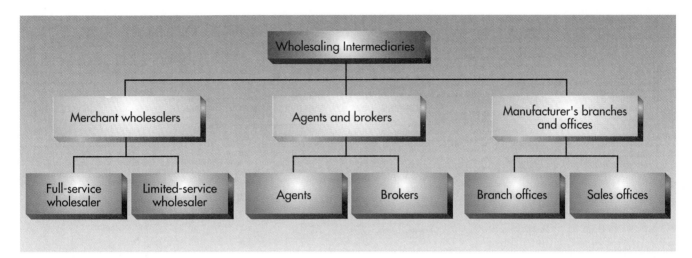

FIGURE 16-6

Types of wholesaling intermediaries

full-service wholesalers exist. **General merchandise** (or *full-line*) **wholesalers** carry a broad assortment of merchandise and perform all channel functions. This type of wholesaler is most prevalent in the hardware, drug, and clothing industries. However, these wholesalers do not maintain much depth of assortment within specific product lines. **Specialty merchandise** (or *limited-line*) **wholesalers** offer a relatively narrow range of products but have an extensive assortment within the product lines carried. They perform all channel functions and are found in the health foods, automotive parts, and seafood industries.

Four major types of limited-service wholesalers exist. **Rack jobbers** furnish the racks or shelves that display merchandise in retail stores, perform all channel functions, and sell on consignment to retailers, which means they retain the title to the products displayed and bill retailers only for the merchandise sold. Familiar products such as hosiery, toys, housewares, and health and beauty aids are sold by rack jobbers. **Cash and carry wholesalers** take title to merchandise but sell only to buyers who call on them, pay cash for merchandise, and furnish their own transportation for merchandise. They carry a limited product assortment and do not make deliveries, extend credit, or supply market information. This wholesaler is common in electric supplies, office supplies, hardware products, and groceries. **Drop shippers,** or *desk jobbers,* are wholesalers who own the merchandise they sell but do not physically handle, stock, or deliver it. They simply solicit orders from retailers and other wholesalers and have the merchandise shipped directly from a producer to a buyer. Drop shippers are used for bulky products such as coal, lumber, and chemicals, which are sold in extremely large quantities. **Truck jobbers** are small wholesalers who have a small warehouse from which they stock their trucks for distribution to retailers. They usually handle limited assortments of fast-moving or perishable items that are sold for cash directly from trucks in their original packages. Truck jobbers handle products such as bakery items, dairy products, meat, and tobacco.

Agents and brokers   Unlike merchant wholesalers, agents and brokers do not take title to merchandise and typically provide fewer channel functions. They make their profit from commissions or fees paid for their services, whereas merchant wholesalers make their profit from the sale of the merchandise they own.

Manufacturer's agents and selling agents are the two major types of agents used by producers. **Manufacturer's agents,** or *manufacturer's representatives,* work for several producers and carry noncompetitive, complementary merchandise in an exclusive territory. Manufacturer's agents act as a producer's sales arm in a territory

FUNCTIONS PERFORMED	MERCHANT WHOLESALERS						AGENTS AND BROKERS		
	FULL SERVICE		LIMITED SERVICE						
	GENERAL MERCHANDISE	SPECIALTY MERCHANDISE	RACK JOBBERS	CASH AND CARRY	DROP SHIPPERS	TRUCK JOBBERS	MANUFACTURER'S AGENTS	SELLING AGENTS	BROKERS
TRANSACTIONAL FUNCTIONS									
Buying	Yes ★	Yes	Yes	Yes	Yes	Yes	No	No	No
Sales calls on customers	Yes	Yes	Yes	sometimes	Yes	Yes	Yes	Yes	Yes
Risk taking (taking title to products)	Yes	Yes	Yes	Yes	Yes	Yes	No	No	No
LOGISTICAL FUNCTIONS									
Creates product assortments	Yes	Yes	Yes	Yes	No	Yes	sometimes	sometimes	Yes
Stores products (maintains inventory)	Yes	Yes	Yes	Yes	sometimes	Yes	sometimes	sometimes	sometimes
Sorts products	Yes	Yes	Yes	Yes	Yes	Yes	sometimes	sometimes	sometimes
Transports products	Yes	Yes	Yes	no	no	Yes	sometimes	sometimes	sometimes
FACILITATING FUNCTIONS									
Provides financing (credit)	Yes	Yes	Yes	no	Yes	no	no	sometimes	no
Provides market information and research	Yes	Yes	sometimes	no	sometimes	sometimes	Yes	Yes	Yes
Grading	Yes	Yes	sometimes	no	sometimes	sometimes	sometimes	Yes	Yes

★ Key: ●, Yes; ●, sometimes; ●, no.

FIGURE 16-7

Functions performed by independent wholesaler types

and are principally responsible for the transactional channel functions, primarily selling. They are used extensively in the automotive supply, footwear, and fabricated steel industries. However, Swank Jewelry, Japanese computer firms, and Apple have used manufacturer's agents as well. By comparison, **selling agents** represent a single producer and are responsible for the entire marketing function of that producer. They design promotional plans, set prices, determine distribution policies, and make recommendations on product strategy. Selling agents are used by small producers in the textile, apparel, food, and home furnishing industries.

    Brokers are independent firms or individuals whose principal function is to bring buyers and sellers together to make sales. Brokers, unlike agents, usually have no continuous relationship with the buyer or seller but negotiate a contract between two parties and then move on to another task. Brokers are used extensively by producers of seasonal products (such as fruits and vegetables) and in the real estate industry.

MARKETING NEWSNET

MR. COFFEE + AGENTS + BROKERS = CUSTOMER VALUE

Vincent Marotta hated the way coffee tasted, but he was convinced that its poor taste was caused not by bad coffee but by the machines that brewed it. In 1972, he developed the prototype for what is now known as Mr. Coffee, the first electric-drip coffee maker. By 1996 more than 50 million Mr. Coffees had been sold, as well as billions of coffee filters. Was Mr. Coffee's success only a result of a high-quality product that satisfied a need? Not quite. Distribution played an integral role in creating value for customers.

Mr. Coffee and its filters were sold by manufacturer's agents who called on appliance and mass merchandise stores. In time, however, it became apparent that Mr. Coffee users found it inconvenient to visit appliance and mass merchandise stores to buy replacement filters. These customers would benefit by having filters in the stores where they bought their coffee, namely, in the 170,000 retail food outlets throughout the United States. Therefore, a national network of food brokers was hired to sell Mr. Coffee filters to supermarkets and grocery stores. The

result? It is estimated that about 75 percent of Mr. Coffee's filter sales come from retail food outlets.

When the company introduced the Ice Tea Pot by Mr. Coffee, it used its network of manufacturer's agents to call on appliance and mass merchandise stores. Filters were sold by food brokers to retail food outlets, and another success was brewed.

A unique broker that acts in many ways like a manufacturer's agent is a food broker, representing buyers and sellers in the grocery industry. Food brokers differ from conventional brokers because they act on behalf of producers on a permanent basis and receive a commission for their services. For example, Nabisco uses food brokers to sell its candies, margarine, and Planters peanuts, but it sells its line of cookies and crackers directly to retail stores. Do agents and brokers create value for customers? The accompanying Marketing NewsNet describes how Mr. Coffee used both manufacturer's agents and brokers to become a leader in the electric-drip coffee maker market.[11]

Manufacturer's branches and offices   Unlike merchant wholesalers, agents, and brokers, manufacturer's branches and offices are wholly owned extensions of the producer that perform wholesaling activities. Producers will assume wholesaling functions when there are no intermediaries to perform these activities, customers are few in number and geographically concentrated, or orders are large or require significant attention. Wholesaling activities performed by producers are conducted by means of a branch office or sales office. A *manufacturer's branch office* carries a producer's inventory, performs the functions of a full-service wholesaler, and is an alternative to a merchant wholesaler. A *manufacturer's sales office* does not carry inventory, typically performs only a sales function, and serves as an alternative to agents and brokers.

Vertical Marketing Systems and Channel Partnerships

The traditional marketing channels described so far represent a loosely knit network of independent producers and intermediaries brought together to distribute goods and

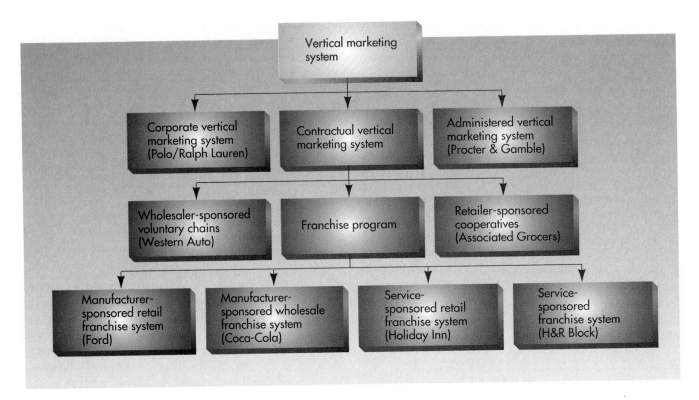

FIGURE 16-8

Types of vertical marketing systems

services. However, new channel arrangements have emerged for the purpose of improving efficiency in performing channel functions and achieving greater marketing effectiveness. These new arrangements are called vertical marketing systems and channel partnerships. **Vertical marketing systems** are professionally managed and centrally coordinated marketing channels designed to achieve channel economies and maximum marketing impact.[12] Figure 16–8 depicts the major types of vertical marketing systems: corporate, contractual, and administered.

Corporate systems   The combination of successive stages of production and distribution under a single ownership is a *corporate vertical marketing system.* For example, a producer might own the intermediary at the next level down in the channel. This practice, called *forward integration,* is exemplified by Polo/Ralph Lauren, which manufactures clothing and also owns apparel shops. Other examples of forward integration include Goodyear, Singer, Sherwin Williams, and the building materials division of Boise Cascade. Alternatively, a retailer might own a manufacturing operation, a practice called *backward integration.* For example, Kroger supermarkets operate manufacturing facilities that produce everything from aspirin to cottage cheese, for sale under the Kroger label.

Contractual systems   Under a *contractual vertical marketing system,* independent production and distribution firms integrate their efforts on a contractual basis to obtain greater functional economies and marketing impact than they could achieve alone. Contractual systems are the most popular among the three types of vertical marketing systems and are estimated to account for about 40 percent of all retail sales.

   Three variations of contractual systems exist. *Wholesaler-sponsored voluntary chains* involve a wholesaler that develops a contractual relationship with small, independent retailers to standardize and coordinate buying practices, merchandising programs, and inventory management efforts. With the organization of a large number of independent retailers, economies of scale and volume discounts can be achieved to compete with chain stores. Western Auto, IGA, and Ben Franklin stores

FIGURE 16-9

Franchise sales and
establishment growth

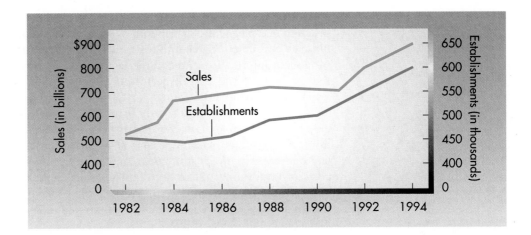

represent wholesaler-sponsored voluntary chains. *Retailer-sponsored cooperatives* exist when small, independent retailers form an organization that operates a wholesale facility cooperatively. Member retailers then concentrate their buying power through the wholesaler and plan collaborative promotional and pricing activities. Examples of retailer-sponsored cooperatives include Associated Grocers and Certified Grocers.

The most visible variation of contractual systems is **franchising,** a contractual arrangement between a parent company (a franchisor) and an individual or firm (a franchisee) that allows the franchise to operate a certain type of business under an established name and according to specific rules. As shown in Figure 16–9, franchises generate more than $900 billion in sales through about 600,000 outlets annually in the United States. Franchise sales will exceed $2 trillion by 2000 and will account for more than 40 percent of U.S. retail sales.[13] Four types of franchise arrangements are most popular. Manufacturer-sponsored retail franchise systems are most prominent in the automobile industry, where a manufacturer such as Ford licenses dealers to sell its cars subject to various sales and service conditions. Manufacturer-sponsored wholesale systems are evident in the soft-drink industry, where Pepsi-Cola licenses wholesalers (bottlers) who purchase concentrate from Pepsi-Cola and then carbonate, bottle, promote, and distribute its products to supermarkets and restaurants. Service-sponsored retail franchise systems are provided by firms that have designed a unique approach for performing a service and wish to profit by selling the franchise to others. Holiday Inn, Avis, and McDonald's represent this franchising approach. Service-sponsored franchise systems exist when franchisors license individuals or firms to dispense a service under a trade name and specific guidelines. Examples include Snelling and Snelling, Inc. employment services, and H&R Block tax services. Service-sponsored franchise arrangements are the fastest-growing type of franchise in the 1990s. Franchising is discussed further in Chapter 18.

Administered systems   In comparison, *administered vertical marketing systems* achieve coordination at successive stages of production and distribution by the size and influence of one channel member rather than through ownership. P&G, given its broad product assortment ranging from disposable diapers to detergents, is able to obtain cooperation from supermarkets in displaying, promoting, and pricing its products. Wal-Mart can obtain cooperation from manufacturers in terms of product specifications, price levels, and promotional support, given its position as the world's largest retailer.

Channel partnerships   Increasingly, channel members are forging channel partnerships akin to supply partnerships described in Chapter 7. A **channel**

partnership consists of agreements and procedures among channel members for ordering and physically distributing a producer's products through the channel to the ultimate consumer.[14] A central feature of channel partnerships is the collaborative use of modern information and communication technology to better serve customers and reduce the time and cost of performing channel functions.

The partnership Levi Strauss & Company has with Modell's Sporting Goods in New York is a case in point.[15] By using point-of-sale scanning equipment and direct electronic linkage to Levi Strauss in San Francisco, Modell's can instantaneously inform Levi Strauss what styles and sizes of jeans are needed, create purchase orders, and convey shipping instructions without any human involvement. The result? The costs of performing transaction, logistic, and facilitating functions are substantially reduced, and the customer is virtually assured of having his or her preferred 501 Levi jeans in stock. The role of information and communication technology in the management of physical distribution and logistics is discussed further in Chapter 17.

CONCEPT CHECK	**1.**	What is the difference between a direct and an indirect channel?
	2.	Why are channels for industrial products typically shorter than channels for consumer products?
	3.	What is the principal distinction between a corporate vertical marketing system and an administered vertical marketing system?

CHANNEL CHOICE AND MANAGEMENT

Marketing channels not only link a producer to its buyers but also provide the means through which a firm implements various elements of its marketing strategy. Therefore, choosing a marketing channel is a critical decision.

Factors Affecting Channel Choice and Management

The final choice of a marketing channel by a producer depends on a number of factors that often interact with each other.

Environmental factors   The changing environment described in Chapter 3 has an important effect on the choice and management of a marketing channel. For example, the Fuller Brush Company, which is a name synonymous with door-to-door selling, now uses catalogs and has opened retail stores in some cities. Rising employment among women, resulting in fewer being at home during working hours, prompted this action. Advances in the technology of growing, transporting, and storing perishable cut flowers has allowed Kroger to eliminate flower wholesalers and buy direct from flower growers around the world. Today, Kroger's annual cut-flower sales exceed $100 million, making it one of the largest flower retailers in the United States.[16]

Consumer factors   Consumer characteristics have a direct bearing on the choice and management of a marketing channel. Determining which channel is most appropriate is based on answers to fundamental questions such as: Who are potential customers? Where do they buy? When do they buy? How do they buy? What do they buy? These answers also indicate the type of intermediary best suited to reaching target buyers. For example, Ricoh Company, Ltd. studied the serious (as opposed to recreational) camera user and concluded that a change in marketing channels was

Technology helped Kroger become one of the nation's largest flower retailers.

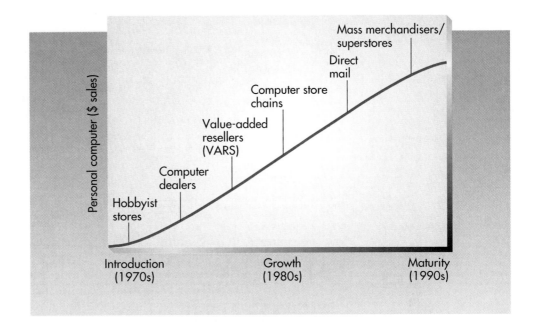

necessary. The company terminated its contract with a wholesaler who sold to mass merchandise stores and began using manufacturer's agents who sold to photo specialty stores. These stores agreed to stock and display Ricoh's full line and promote it prominently, and sales volume tripled within 18 months.[17]

Product factors   In general, highly sophisticated products such as large, scientific computers, unstandardized products such as custom-built machinery, and products of high unit value are distributed directly to buyers. Unsophisticated, standardized products with low unit value, such as table salt, are typically distributed through indirect channels. A product's stage in the life cycle also affects marketing channels. Figure 16–10 shows the dominant retail marketing channel for personal computers since their introduction in the 1970s.[18]

Company factors   A firm's financial, human, or technological capabilities affect channel choice. For example, firms that are unable to employ a salesforce might use manufacturer's agents or selling agents to reach wholesalers or buyers. If a firm has multiple products for a particular target market, it might use a direct channel, whereas firms with a limited product line might use intermediaries of various types to reach buyers.

Company factors also apply to intermediaries. For example, personal computer hardware and software producers wishing to reach business users might look to value-added resellers such as Micro Age, which has its own salesforce and service staff that calls on businesses.

Channel Design Considerations

Recognizing that numerous routes to buyers exist and also recognizing the factors just described, marketing executives typically consider three questions when choosing a marketing channel and intermediaries:

1. Which channel and intermediaries will provide the best coverage of the target market?
2. Which channel and intermediaries will best satisfy the buying requirements of the target market?
3. Which channel and intermediaries will be the most profitable?

Target market coverage   Achieving the best coverage of the target market requires attention to the density and type of intermediaries to be used at the retail level of distribution. Three degrees of distribution density exist: intensive, exclusive, and selective. **Intensive distribution** means that a firm tries to place its products and services in as many outlets as possible. Intensive distribution is usually chosen for convenience products or services; for example, chewing gum, automatic teller machines, and soft drinks. Increasingly, medical services are distributed in this fashion.

Exclusive distribution is the extreme opposite of intensive distribution because only one retail outlet in a specified geographical area carries the firm's product. Exclusive distribution is typically chosen for specialty products or services; for example, automobiles, some women's fragrances, men's suits, and yachts. Sometimes manufacturers sign exclusive distribution agreements with retail chain stores. Hewlett-Packard originally sold its personal computers for home use only through Circuit City, but it has since broadened its distribution.

Selective distribution lies between these two extremes and means that a firm selects a few retail outlets in a specific area to carry its products. This is the most common form of distribution intensity and is usually associated with shopping goods or services such as Rolex watches, Ben Hogan golf clubs, and Henredon furniture.

The type or availability of a retail outlet will also influence whether a target market is reached. For example, the L'eggs division of the Hanes Corporation distributes fashionable white pantyhose to nurses through catalogs because supermarkets and department stores do not typically carry these items.

Satisfying buyer requirements   A second consideration in channel design is gaining access to channels and intermediaries that satisfy at least some of the interests buyers might want fulfilled when they purchase a firm's products or services. These interests fall into four categories: (1) information, (2) convenience, (3) variety, and (4) attendant services.

Information is an important requirement when buyers have limited knowledge or desire specific data about a product or service. Properly chosen intermediaries communicate with buyers through in-store displays, demonstrations, and personal selling. Computer stores originally grew in popularity as a source for small computers because they provided such information. Similarly, direct sales firms such as Amway, Avon, and Tupperware have been able to identify the unique information needs of Japanese women and successfully communicate the benefits of their products and method of selling. Amway is one of the fastest-growing firms in Japan, and Avon records more than \$350 million in Japanese sales each year through direct selling.[19]

Convenience has multiple meanings for buyers, such as proximity or driving time to a retail outlet. For example, 7-Eleven stores with more than 6,000 outlets nationwide satisfy this interest for buyers, and candy and snack food firms benefit by

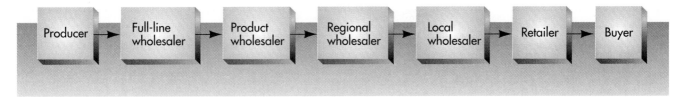

FIGURE 16-11   Marketing channel for soap in Japan

gaining display space in these stores. For other consumers, convenience means a minimum of time and hassle. The rapid growth of Jiffy Lube and Minit-Lube, which promise to change engine oil and filters in less than 10 minutes, appeal to this aspect of convenience.

Variety reflects buyers' interest in having numerous competing and complementary items from which to choose. Variety is evident in both the breadth and depth of products and brands carried by intermediaries, which enhances their attraction to buyers. Thus, manufacturers of pet food and supplies seek distribution through pet superstores such as Petco and PetsMart, which offer a wide array of pet products.

Attendant services provided by intermediaries are an important buying requirement for products such as appliances that require delivery, installation, and credit. Therefore, Whirlpool seeks dealers that provide such services.

Profitability   The third consideration in designing a channel is profitability, which is determined by the margins earned (revenues minus cost) for each channel member and for the channel as a whole. Channel cost is the critical dimension of profitability. These costs include distribution, advertising, and selling expenses associated with different types of marketing channels. The extent to which channel members share these costs determines the margins received by each member and by the channel as a whole.

Global Dimensions of Marketing Channels

Marketing channels around the world reflect traditions, customs, geography, and the economic history of individual countries and societies. Even so, the basic marketing channel functions must be performed. But differences do exist, and are illustrated by highlighting marketing channels in Japan—the world's second-largest economy and the second-largest U.S.–world trade partner.

For the answer to how Schick became the razor and blade market share leader in Japan read the text.

Intermediaries outside Western Europe and North America tend to be small, numerous, and often owner operated. Japan, for example, has less than one half of the population and a land mass less than 5 percent of the United States. However, Japan and the United States have about the same number of wholesalers and retailers. Why? Japanese marketing channels tend to include many intermediaries based on tradition and lack of storage space. As many as five intermediaries are involved in the distribution of soap in Japan compared with one or two in the United States (see Figure 16–11).[20]

Understanding marketing channels in global markets is often a prerequisite to successful marketing. For example, Gillette attempted to sell its razors and blades through company salespeople in Japan as it does in the United States, thus eliminating wholesalers traditionally involved in marketing toiletries. Warner-Lambert Company sold its Schick razors and blades through the traditional Japanese channel involving wholesalers. The result? Gillette holds 10 percent of the Japanese razor and blade market, and Schick holds 62 percent.[21]

Channel relationships also must be considered. In Japan, the distribution *keiretsu* (translated as "alignments") bonds producers and intermediaries together.[22] The bond, through vertical integration and social and economic ties, ensures that each

MARKETING NEWSNET

Global

CREATIVE COSMETICS AND CREATIVE MARKETING IN JAPAN

How does a small U.S. cosmetics firm sell 1.5 million tubes of its lipstick in Japan annually? Fran Wilson Creative Cosmetics executives attribute their success to a top-quality product, an effective advertising program, and distribution. The firm's Moodmatcher lip coloring comes in green, orange, silver, black, and six other funky hues that change to a shade of pink, coral, or red, depending on a woman's chemistry when it's applied.

The company does not sell to department stores. According to a company spokesperson, "Shiseido and Kanebo keep all the other Japanese or import brands out of the major department stores." Rather, the company sells its Moodmatcher lipstick through a Japanese distributor and marketing channel that reaches Japan's 40,000 beauty salons. The result? The company captures 20 percent of the $4.3 million of lipsticks exported annually to Japan by U.S. companies.

channel member benefits from the distribution alignment. The dominant member of the distribution *keiretsu,* which is typically a producer, has considerable influence over channel member behavior, including which competing products are sold by other channel members. Well-known Japanese companies such as Matsushita (electronics), Nissan and Toyota (automotive products), Nippon Gakki (musical instruments), and Kirin (and other brewers and distillers) employ the distribution *keiretsu* extensively. Shiseido and Kanebo, for instance, influence the distribution of cosmetics through Japanese department stores. Nevertheless, Fran Wilson Creative Cosmetics of New York City has been able to capture 20 percent of the lipsticks exported to Japan by U.S. companies. Read the accompanying Marketing NewsNet to find out how this creative marketer did it.[23]

Channel Relationships: Conflict, Cooperation, and Law

Unfortunately, because channels consist of independent individuals and firms, there is always potential for disagreements concerning who performs which channel functions, how profits are allocated, which products and services will be provided by whom, and who makes critical channel-related decisions. These channel conflicts necessitate measures for dealing with them. Sometimes they result in legal action.

Conflict in marketing channels   Channel conflict arises when one channel member believes another channel member is engaged in behavior that prevents it from achieving its goals. Two types of conflict occur in marketing channels: vertical conflict and horizontal conflict.

Vertical conflict occurs between different levels in a marketing channel; for example, between a manufacturer and a wholesaler or retailer or between a wholesaler and a retailer. Three sources of vertical conflict are most common. First,

conflict arises when a channel member bypasses another member and sells or buys products direct. This conflict emerged when Jenn-Air, a producer of kitchen appliances, decided to terminate its distributors and sell direct to retailers. Conflict also arose when Wal-Mart elected to purchase products direct from manufacturers rather than through manufacturer's agents.[24] Second, disagreements over how profit margins are distributed among channel members produce conflict. This happened when Businessland and Compaq Computer Corporation disagreed over how price discounts were applied in the sale of Compaq's products. Compaq Computer stopped selling to Businessland for 13 months until the issue was resolved.[25] A third conflict situation arises when manufacturers believe wholesalers or retailers are not giving their products adequate attention. For example, H. J. Heinz Company found itself in a conflict situation with its supermarkets in Great Britain when the supermarkets promoted and displayed private brands at the expense of Heinz brands.[26]

Horizontal conflict occurs between intermediaries at the same level in a marketing channel, such as between two or more retailers (Target and Kmart) or two or more wholesalers that handle the same manufacturer's brands. Two sources of horizontal conflict are most common. First, horizontal conflict arises when a manufacturer increases its distribution coverage in a geographical area. For example, a franchised Cadillac dealer in Chicago might complain to GM that another franchised Cadillac dealer has located too close to its dealership. Second, dual distribution causes conflict when different types of retailers carry the same brands. For instance, the launch of Elizabeth Taylor's Black Pearls fragrance by Elizabeth Arden was put on hold when department store chains such as May and Dillard refused to stock the item once they learned that mass merchants Sears and JCPenney would also carry the brand. Elizabeth Arden subsequently introduced the brand only through department stores in 1996.[27]

Cooperation in marketing channels   Conflict can have destructive effects on the workings of a marketing channel, so it is necessary to secure cooperation among channel members. One means is through a **channel captain,** a channel member that coordinates, directs, and supports other channel members. Channel captains can be producers, wholesalers, or retailers. P&G assumes this role because it has a strong consumer following in brands such as Crest, Tide, and Pampers. Therefore, it can set policies or terms that supermarkets will follow. McKesson-Robbins, a drug wholesaler, is a channel captain because it coordinates and supports the product flow from numerous small drug manufacturers to more than 20,000 drugstores and nearly 6,000 hospitals nationwide. Wal-Mart and Home Depot are retail channel captains because of their strong consumer image, number of outlets, and purchasing volume.

FIGURE 16-12

Channel strategies and practices affected by legal restrictions

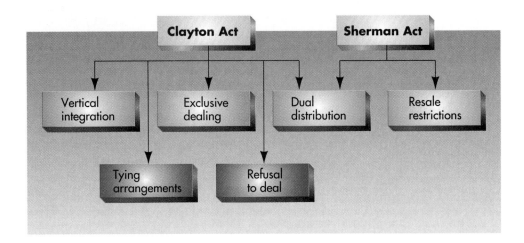

A firm becomes a channel captain because it is typically the channel member with the ability to influence the behavior of other members.[28] Influence can take four forms. First, economic influence arises from the ability of a firm to reward other members given its strong financial position or customer franchise. Microsoft Corporation and Toys "Я" Us have such influence. Expertise is a second source of influence over other channel members. For example, American Hospital Supply helps its customers (hospitals) manage inventory and streamline order processing for hundreds of medical supplies. Third, identification with a particular channel member may also create influence for that channel member. For instance, retailers may compete to carry the Ralph Lauren line, or clothing manufacturers may compete to be carried by Neiman-Marcus, Nordstrom's, or Bloomingdale's. In both instances the desire to be associated with a channel member gives that firm influence over others. Finally, influence can arise from the legitimate right of one channel member to dictate the behavior of other members. This situation would occur under contractual vertical marketing systems where a franchisor could legitimately direct how a franchisee behaves. Other means for securing cooperation in marketing channels rest in the different variations of vertical marketing systems.

Channel influence can be used to gain concessions from other channel members. For instance, some large supermarket chains expect manufacturers to pay allowances, in the form of cash or free goods, to stock and display their products. Some manufacturers call these allowances "extortion" as described in the Ethics and Social Responsibility Alert.[29]

Legal considerations Conflict in marketing channels is typically resolved through negotiation or the exercise of influence by channel members. Sometimes conflict produces legal action. Therefore, knowledge of legal restrictions affecting channel strategies and practices is important. Some restrictions were described in Chapter 15, namely vertical price-fixing and price discrimination. However, other legal considerations unique to marketing channels warrant attention.[30]

In general, suppliers can select whomever they want as channel intermediaries and may refuse to deal with whomever they choose. This right was established in the case of the *United States* v. *Colgate and Company* in 1919. However, the Federal Trade Commission and the Justice Department monitor channel practices that restrain competition, create monopolies, or otherwise represent unfair methods of competition under the Sherman Act (1890) and the Clayton Act (1914). Six practices have received the most attention (Figure 16–12).

Dual distribution, although not illegal, can be viewed as anticompetitive in some situations. The most common situation arises when a manufacturer distributes through its own vertically integrated channel in competition with independent wholesalers and retailers that also sell its products. If the manufacturer's behavior is viewed as an attempt to lessen competition by eliminating wholesalers or retailers, then such action would violate both the Sherman and Clayton Acts.

Vertical integration is viewed in a similar light. Although not illegal, this practice is sometimes subject to legal action under the Clayton Act if it has the potential to lessen competition or foster monopoly.

The Clayton Act specifically prohibits exclusive dealing and tying arrangements when they lessen competition or create monopolies. *Exclusive dealing* exists when a supplier requires channel members to sell only its products or restricts distributors from selling directly competitive products. *Tying arrangements* occur when a supplier requires a distributor purchasing some products to buy others from the supplier. These arrangements often arise in franchising. They are illegal if the tied products could be purchased at fair market values from other suppliers at desired quality standards of the franchiser. Full-line forcing is a special kind of tying arrangement. This practice involves a supplier requiring that a channel member carry its full line of products in order to sell a specific item in the supplier's line.

Even though a supplier has a legal right to choose intermediaries to carry and represent its products, a *refusal to deal* with existing channel members may be illegal under the Clayton Act. For example, Eastman Kodak Company has been charged with refusing to sell replacement parts for its photocopiers and other equipment to independent dealers.[31]

Resale restrictions refer to a supplier's attempt to stipulate to whom distributors may resell the supplier's products and in what specific geographical areas or territories they may be sold. These practices have been prosecuted under the Sherman Act. Today, however, the courts apply the "rule of reason" in such cases and consider whether such restrictions have a "demonstrable economic effect."

CONCEPT CHECK

1. What are the three degrees of distribution density?

2. What are the three questions marketing executives consider when choosing a marketing channel and intermediaries?

3. What is meant by "exclusive dealing?"

SUMMARY

1. A marketing channel consists of individuals and firms involved in the process of making a product or service available for use by consumers or industrial users.

2. Intermediaries make possible the flow of products and services from producers to buyers by performing transactional, logistical, and facilitating functions. At the same time, intermediaries create time, place, form, and possession utility.

3. Channel structure describes the route taken by products and services from producers to buyers. Direct channels represent the shortest route because producers interact directly with buyers. Indirect channels include intermediaries between producers and buyers.

4. In general, marketing channels for consumer products and services contain more intermediaries than do channels for industrial products and services. In some situations, producers use multiple channels and strategic channel alliances.

5. Numerous types of wholesalers can exist within a marketing channel. The principal distinction between the various types of wholesalers lies in whether they take title to the items they sell and the channel functions they perform.

6. Vertical marketing systems are channels designed to achieve channel function economies and marketing impact. A vertical marketing system may be one of three types: corporate, administered, or contractual.

7. Marketing managers consider environmental, consumer, product, and company factors when choosing and managing marketing channels.

8. Channel design considerations are based on the target market coverage sought by producers, the buyer requirements to be satisfied, and the profitability of the channel. Target market coverage comes about through one of three levels of distribution density: intensive, exclusive, and selective distribution. Buyer requirements are evident in the amount of information, convenience, variety, and service sought by consumers. Profitability relates to the margins obtained by each channel member and the channel as a whole.

9. Marketing channels in the global marketplace reflect traditions, customs, geography, and the economic history of individual countries and societies. These factors influence channel structure and relationships among channel members.
10. Conflicts in marketing channels are inevitable. Vertical conflict occurs between different levels in a channel. Horizon-

tal conflict occurs between intermediaries at the same level in the channel.
11. Legal issues in the management of marketing channels typically arise from six practices: dual distribution, vertical integration, exclusive dealing, tying arrangements, refusal to deal, and resale restrictions.

KEY TERMS AND CONCEPTS

marketing channel p. 424
direct channel p. 427
indirect channels p. 427
industrial distributor p. 428
dual distribution p. 429
strategic channel alliances p. 429
direct marketing p. 429
general merchandise wholesalers p. 431
specialty merchandise wholesalers p. 431
rack jobbers p. 431
cash and carry wholesalers p. 431
drop shippers p. 431

truck jobbers p. 431
manufacturer's agents p. 431
selling agents p. 432
brokers p. 432
vertical marketing systems p. 434
franchising p. 435
channel partnership p. 435–36
intensive distribution p. 438
exclusive distribution p. 438
selective distribution p. 438
channel captain p. 441

CHAPTER PROBLEMS AND APPLICATIONS

1. A distributor for Celanese Chemical Company stores large quantities of chemicals, blends these chemicals to satisfy requests of customers, and delivers the blends to a customer's warehouse within 24 hours of receiving an order. What utilities does this distributor provide?
2. Suppose the president of a carpet manufacturing firm has asked you to look into the possibility of bypassing the firm's wholesalers (who sell to carpet, department, and furniture stores) and selling direct to these stores. What caution would you voice on this matter, and what type of information would you gather before making this decision?
3. What type of channel conflict is likely to be caused by dual distribution, and what type of conflict can be reduced by direct distribution? Why?

4. How does the channel captain idea differ among corporate, administered, and contractual vertical marketing systems with particular reference to the use of the different forms of influence available to firms?
5. Comment on this statement: "The only distinction among merchant wholesalers and agents and brokers is that merchant wholesalers take title to the products they sell."
6. How do specialty, shopping, and convenience goods generally relate to intensive, selective, and exclusive distribution? Give a brand name that is an example of each goods-distribution matchup.

CASE 16–1   Creston Vineyards

Video

Larry Rosenbloom's customers include individuals, retail stores, restaurants, hotels, and even the White House! Because of the many types and large numbers of customers, distribution is as important as production at Creston Vineyards. As Larry explains, "We need distributors in our business . . . as most other [businesses] do, to get the product to the end user, to the consumer."

THE COMPANY

In 1772 Franciscan Padres introduced wine to the La Panza Mountains of California when they founded Mission San Luis Obispo south of what is now San Francisco. The potential of the region for growing grapes remained a secret, however, until 1980 when Stephanie and Larry Rosenbloom purchased an abandoned ranch and started Creston Vineyards. Because it takes several years for vines to grow and produce grapes, Creston did not sell its first wine until 1982. Today, the 569 acre ranch has 155 acres of planted vineyards and produces over 55,000 cases of eight varieties of wines. The production facilities include a 15,000 square foot winery and 2,000 square feet of laboratory and office space.

Since 1982 Creston wines have won over 500 awards in wine tasting events and competitions. In addition, the Rosenblooms are particularly proud of the fact that their wine was served at the inaugurations of Presidents Reagan, Bush, and Clinton. It was at the inaugurations that Creston conceived the concept of an "Artist Collection" of labels—painted by James Paul Brown, who also painted the presidents' portraits. The artistic labels added another dimension of distinctiveness to the Creston products. In fact, Creston's success has attracted the attention of Mondavi, Beringer, Kendall-Jackson, J. Lohr, and several other large Northern California wineries which have recently purchased land and started vineyards near the Creston location.

THE INDUSTRY AND DISTRIBUTION CHANNELS

The wine industry is undergoing several very interesting changes. First, sales have increased in recent years after a general decline since 1984. The decline was attributed to changing consumer demographics, shifting buying habits, and concerns about the economy. At least some of the recent interest in wine is related to the press reports suggesting the possible health benefits of red wine. A second change is the significant increase in the price of wine due to a low supply of good international wines and changing exchange rates, and an infestation of vine-eating insects (phylloxera) on over 20 percent of California's vineyards. Finally, many wine producers are trying to change the image of wine from a beverage only for special occasions and gourmet foods to a beverage for any occasion.

The industry also faces several distribution challenges. The large number of wine producers and the variety of consumers requires a sophisticated system of distribution channels. By combining different types of intermediaries the industry is able to meet the requirements of many customers. In addition, because the sale of wine is regulated, the use of multiple distribution channels facilitates the sale of wine in many locations.

One of the most common channels of distribution involves a distributor buying wine directly from the vineyard and reselling it to retail stores and restaurants within a geographic area. Some distributors, however, may not need quantities large enough to warrant purchasing directly from the vineyard. They usually purchase several brands at the same time from a warehouse. A broker may facilitate sales by providing information to distributors, training the distributor's salesforce, and even assisting in sales calls to retailers. John Drady, one of twelve brokers for Creston Vineyards explains: "It's very important that we translate our knowledge and our selling skills to the distributor's salespeople so they can, in turn, go out and [sell] more readily on their own."

Other channels are also used by Creston. In California, for example, Creston can sell directly to any customer. The vineyard also sells directly to some large retailers, such as Trader Joe's. Another channel of distribution is through wine clubs which provide club members with information about wines and an average of six wines per year. The popularity of wine clubs has been increasing and they now account for 15 percent of Creston's sales. The newest type of distribution channel is through on-line services. Creston now has a page on the World Wide Web that provides information about its wines and allows orders to be shipped directly to consumers in 12 states where direct sales are legal.

THE ISSUES

In an industry with thousands of products and hundreds of producers, Creston is relatively new and small. Selecting and managing its distribution channels to best meet the needs of many constituents is a key task. Providing marketing assistance, product information, and appropriate assortment, transportation, storage, and credit are just a few of the functions the warehouse, brokers, distributors, and retailers may provide as the product moves from the vineyard to the end user.

Creston also faces a situation where new, and possibly more efficient, channels are becoming available. Direct sales, wine clubs, and on-line services have generated substantial sales for Creston. Other channels, or new variations of existing channels, may also be available in the future. Overall, Creston must continue to utilize distribution channels to provide value to customers ranging from large retailers, to hotels and restaurants, to individuals, to the White House!

Questions

1. What functions must be performed by intermediaries in the wine industry?

2. What intermediaries and distribution channels are currently used by Creston vineyards?

3. How do different channels of distribution reach different segments? Are there any segments Creston does not reach with its current segments?

CHAPTER 17

Physical Distribution and Logistics Management

AFTER READING THIS CHAPTER YOU SHOULD BE ABLE TO:

• Explain what physical distribution and logistics management are and how they relate to the marketing mix.

• Understand the nature of logistics trade-offs among transportation, inventory, and other logistics elements.

• Understand how managers trade off different "logistics costs" relative to customer service in order to reach a logistics decision.

• Recognize how customer service in logistics decisions contributes to customer value and successful marketing programs.

• Describe the major logistics functions of transportation, warehousing and materials handling, order processing, and inventory management.

$500 MILLION TO $1 BILLION LOST SALES . . . AND NO. 1, TOO!

The year 1994 was a red-letter year for Compaq Computer. It became the world's No. 1 producer of PCs, but the company estimates it lost $500 million to $1 billion during the year because its hot-selling laptops and desktops weren't available when and where its customers—31,000 distributors, wholesalers, and retailers around the world—wanted them! Compaq's chief financial officer, Daryl White, told *Fortune* magazine:

> We've done most of what we need to do to be more competitive. We've changed the way we develop products, manufacture, market, and advertise. The one piece of the puzzle we haven't addressed is logistics. It's the next source of competitive advantage. The possibilities are just astounding.[1]

We can excuse Mr. White, however, for being just a little too modest about Compaq's logistics actions over the past three years. Consider, in fact, that Compaq

• *Quintupled* production from 1991 to 1994 *without* expanding factory space, partly due to cooperation with suppliers to reduce inventories of unassembled components.
• Took an idea from Wal-Mart and moved the component inventories off its factory floor in Houston to a warehouse 12 miles away and leased by 35 of its suppliers.
• Cut the average time a computer spends on the floor of its distribution center in Houston from four weeks to two weeks.

Still, Compaq isn't out of the woods, logistically speaking. Like most computer companies, observes *Fortune* magazine, Compaq's 40 percent on-time delivery record to its customers could put it into bankruptcy court if it were an airline.[2]

To address this problem Compaq initiated a program to avoid building computers for inventory. By the time you read this, Compaq expects that its production facilities will be linked to its distributors so that *every* computer it produces will be built to the specifications of an ultimate buyer or user.

Welcome to the very unglamorous—but increasingly critical—world of physical supply, physical distribution, and logistics management. The essence of the problem is simple: it makes no sense to have brilliant marketing programs to sell world-class products if the products aren't available at the right time, at the right place, and in the right form and condition that customers want them. It's finding the continuing solutions through time that's always the problem. This chapter examines the physical distribution process, which moves products from producer to consumer, and how a firm balances distribution costs against the need for effective customer service.

SIGNIFICANCE OF PHYSICAL DISTRIBUTION AND LOGISTICS MANAGEMENT

We often hear the term *physical distribution,* but may rarely hear the term *logistics.* In this section we shall contrast the two concepts, describe the increasing importance of logistics and how these activities vary among firms, and relate logistics to marketing strategy decisions.

Relating Physical Supply, Physical Distribution, and Logistics

Generally, marketing managers use **physical distribution management** to mean organizing the movement and storage of a finished product to the customer. Logistics implies a broader view and attempts to coordinate both the inbound flow of raw materials *and* the outbound flow of finished product. Because these two flows are not simply mirror images of each other, we prefer to discuss the broader term of logistics, or *logistics management,* in this chapter. **Logistics management** is organizing the cost-effective *flow* of raw materials, in-process inventory, finished goods, and related information from point-of-origin to point-of-consumption to satisfy *customer requirements.*[3]

Three elements of this definition deserve emphasis. First, logistics deals with decisions needed to move a product from the source of raw materials to consumption, or the *flow* of the product. Second, those decisions have to be made in a *cost-effective* manner. While it is important to drive down the costs of a firm's logistics system, there is a limit—the third point of emphasis. A firm needs to drive down logistics costs as long as it can deliver expected *customer service,* which means satisfying customer requirements. In other words, customer needs determine the outputs of the logistics system, and hence the role of management is to see that those needs are satisfied in the most cost-effective manner.

Figure 17–1 demonstrates the relation of physical supply, physical distribution, and logistics to the operations of a manufacturing firm. This chart shows how the firm receives its physical supply in the form of raw materials and parts from its suppliers, converts these to finished products, and then engages in the distribution of these products to its customers. Note that these concepts also apply to nonmanufacturing firms, such as retailers and wholesalers, for which the inbound activities include the finished goods that are resold to customers without physical modification.

Increasing Importance of Logistics Systems

Several factors account for the trend of increased emphasis on logistics systems. There has been a large growth in the differentiation of products in order to respond to consumer demands. The effect of this increased product differentiation is that inventory control has become more complex, and thus there are many more things to

FIGURE 17-1

Relation of physical supply, physical distribution, and logistics to a manufacturing firm's operations

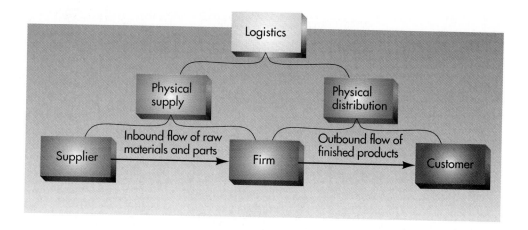

keep track of. Consider, for example, that L.L. Bean must track more than 50,000 separate items when each product is divided by size, color, and other distinguishing features.[4] In today's environment, the increasing costs of carrying inventory make it clear that inventories cannot grow unchecked. Thus, while firms are under pressure to provide high levels of customer service by having many items available, they need to control the cost of such service.

Such dramatic savings in inventory are possible when efficient transportation systems and information technology can be substituted for inventory. A significant development that allowed this substitution to take place was the federal deregulation of the transportation industries, effectively accomplished by 1980. This permitted manufacturers, wholesalers, and retailers to benefit from increased flexibility, particularly when dealing with railroads and truck lines. Also, continuously upgraded computer and information technology has permitted efficient tracking of the thousands of items manufacturers produce.

In the 1990s, industries outside the manufacturing sector have discovered the importance of powerful distribution networks—sectors as diverse as banking and entertainment. In fact, strategists are concluding that control of the distribution networks is often more important than producing the original good or service. Some examples of powerful distribution networks and some guiding principles of today's competitive environment seeking creative ways to add customer value appear in the Marketing NewsNet box on the next page.[5]

How Movement and Storage Activities Vary among Firms

For firms that don't physically move or store many items, logistics costs will be minor. For example, insurance companies and banks distribute mainly paperwork, and most of their inbound materials are supplies. At the other end of the spectrum are firms that produce many products from diverse raw materials at widely separated plants, and which, in turn, distribute products to widely dispersed markets. For large consumer product companies that compete both nationally and internationally, such as Procter & Gamble, the range of logistics problems can be enormous. For example, P&G produces approximately 80 different brands, all of which require a different mix of raw materials. The logistics system has to move all the raw materials to the appropriate manufacturing plant, and then distribute the finished products (brands) to the marketplace. This involves moving products to thousands of wholesalers and retailers around the world. In addition, P&G's logistics managers must also control a number of information flows, including how much inventory is where, the order processing system for customers, the reordering process from the factories, and the level of customer service that the logistics system is delivering. Because of the scope

MARKETING NEWSNET

DESIGNING DISTRIBUTION NETWORKS TO ENSURE ACCESS TO CUSTOMERS: EASIER SAID THAN DONE!

Technology

In many industries the "small is beautiful" era of the 1970s and 1980s is gone. Its replacement: a drive to control strong distribution networks to ensure continuing access to important target market customers for producers of goods and services. Although the industries may differ, some common threads emerge. Let's look at (1) some industry examples and (2) some guiding principles.

Industry Examples

"Distribution networks" here can mean either the physical transportation of goods or electronic transmission of services, such as

- *Mass merchandise chains.* CostCo, Home Depot, and Wal-Mart gain access to customers by moving both products and inventory information very efficiently.
- *Banks and financial institutions.* Putting your card into an automated teller machine (ATM) a few years ago may have been a problem: The ATM may not have talked to your bank. Now they connect—often globally—so large banks and other financial institutions have been acquiring smaller ones.
- *Movie producers and TV/cable/telephone systems.* The Walt Disney acquisition of Capital Cities/ABC is but the first of a complex series of corporate combinations directed at linking Hollywood's

entertainment to an electronic delivery system—from TV and cable companies to telephone companies.

Guiding Principles

Some principles seem to emerge from the 1990s experiences. Specifically, huge distribution networks

- *Demand centralized control.* In this age of decentralization, delegation, and empowerment, the opposite is true for distribution networks: a centralized system is essential to achieve the synergies needed.
- *Require efficient electronic links, such as software and telecommunications systems.* This applies whether the distribution network is in retailing, banking, or entertainment.
- *Transcend departmental, corporate, and often national boundaries.* This means many different groups, with different orientations, need "buy-in" for success. Technology (the preceding bullet) is the easy part. Changing people's ingrained behavior is much harder.

Across dozens of industries, the close of the 1990s will see these guiding principles take on new meanings in very diverse forms. But the goal is clear: organizations are increasingly seeking ways to provide genuine values to customers in order to gain their loyalty.

---

of P&G's logistics problems, it has learned to simplify matters by working closely with its major distributors or customers, such as Wal-Mart where it has located a dozen P&G employees.

The relative importance of logistics to a firm can be evaluated on a number of key factors:

- Number, weight, volume, and perishability of raw materials and final products.
- Number of material supply points.
- Number of material processing points.
- Number of product consumption points.

As the number of any of these factors increases, the complexity and cost of the logistics system increase as well. On a national basis, the total logistics costs for U.S. firms in 1993 to wrap, bundle, load, store, unload, sort, reload, and transport goods was $670 billion, about 10.5 percent of gross-domestic product.[6]

For all U.S. firms (including manufacturers, wholesalers, and retailers), for every dollar of sales about 8 cents is spent on distribution costs.

Hand-held computers and bar coding have reduced delay and lost shipments and improved customer service significantly.

Relation of Logistics to Marketing Strategy

Recalling your own shopping experiences can show the critical relationship between marketing and logistics. Consider your disappointment after traveling to a store—in response to an advertised sale—only to find that the items were out of stock or had been lost or damaged in transit. Imagine how a manufacturer such as Compaq (described at the start of the chapter) reacts upon learning that the product was not on the shelf, after spending huge sums on its extensive promotional campaign. The bottom line is that poorly executed logistics can do serious damage to an otherwise excellent marketing strategy. To demonstrate the importance of logistics' relationship to marketing, consider how logistics impacts the 4 Ps—product factors, pricing factors, promotional factors, and place factors.

A logistics manager's nightmare: how to get this dual-pack on a retailer's shelf while balancing logistics and marketing benefits and costs.

Product factors The physical characteristics of the product, as well as its raw materials, will often dictate what kinds of transportation can be used, the length of time inventory can be accumulated, and whether markets can be served from one or many locations. One physical characteristic that has important logistics implications is the perishability of the product, or its *shelf-life*. For example, the distribution of fresh foods requires timely transportation and low inventories to minimize spoilage. Time-dated food materials must be kept fresh on the store shelves and not allowed to spoil in the warehouse. These products may require specialized transport and storage facilities, such

ETHICS AND SOCIAL RESPONSIBILITY ALERT

Ethics

WHAT ARE THE SOCIAL COSTS OF PACKAGING?

Some experts believe that the logistic systems of many firms depend too heavily on packaging. While efficient packaging materials allow a firm to use cheaper modes of transportation or less specialized warehouse services, these benefits are offset by costs imposed on society in general. Specifically, what should society do with the excessive packaging that comes with the product? In many cases, the packaging material is difficult to dispose of or is quickly filling landfills. Further, the focus on recycled products is a complicated issue and has its own costs and benefits. For example, Procter & Gamble has just introduced a plastic bottle for its Ultra Downy fabric softener that is made of 100 percent recycled plastic. However, because P&G will color the bottle as part of its marketing program, the bottle will be difficult to recycle once it is used.

What are the benefits and costs to society of such packaging trends? What should communities do to counter the trend of overpackaging? What are the responsibilities of global citizens to counteract the trend of overpackaging?

as refrigerated vehicles. Other products have a very short time frame in which to retain their freshness, such as fresh cut flowers, fresh seafoods, or out-of-town newspapers. These require premium transportation, such as air freight, and, in some cases, they can only be distributed to a regional market. For example, newspapers such as *The New York Times* are printed in a number of cities around the country for regional distribution the same day.

One of the most important links between a product's physical characteristics and logistics is the product package. On the one hand, the marketer views the package as an important point-of-purchase promotional device. On the other hand, there are many logistical implications associated with the packaging decision. Does the protective packaging reduce the density of the products so that less product can be loaded into the transport vehicle or warehouse? If so, logistics costs will increase. Does the product's package require it to be placed in an exterior package or carton? In this case, additional handling will be required at the retail level to prepare the product for sale. As described in the accompanying Ethics and Social Responsibility Alert, package features can make handling, stacking, filling, or disposing of the package more difficult, and once again logistics costs will increase.[7]

When the computerized inventory monitoring network in a logistics system breaks down, major problems can occur. For example, Rubbermaid, which makes dozens of products, such as containers and toys, recently got in hot water with Wal-Mart—its most important distributor. Rubbermaid offered an end-of-quarter deep discount price cut to some customers, but not Wal-Mart. Needless to say, Wal-Mart was furious when it found out and proceeded to feature promotional materials for Sterilite, one of Rubbermaid's rising competitors.[8]

Pricing factors   Pricing interacts with logistics in several ways. As mentioned in the discussion of geographical pricing adjustments in Chapter 15, price quotations such as FOB origin assign responsibility for arranging and paying for transportation services to the buyer. Logistics costs are also important for determining quantity discounts. According to the Robinson-Patman Act, the "cost justification" defense for discriminatory prices limits discounts to differences in the cost of manufacture, sale, or delivery of various quantities. Although in practice it may be difficult to adequately document differences in selling or manufacturing costs, transportation rate structures make quantity discounts provided by the carrier easy to document for regulators.

Promotional factors   Promotion interacts with logistics in the areas of advertising, sales promotion, and personal selling. Advertising and promotional campaigns must be planned and coordinated with the logistics system to ensure product availability at the appropriate time. For example, General Motors learned that an eight-week wait was a big turn-off for Floridians thinking about buying a Cadillac, 11 percent of whom then bought a car from a competitor rather than wait for delivery. Cadillac is testing the feasibility of customer responsiveness as a competitive differentiator with the objective of delivering popularly configured Cadillacs to customers immediately from dealers' lots, with overnight delivery if the vehicle isn't available on site. For those customers who desire a more custom configuration, Cadillac is taking their orders, assembling and delivering their exact Cadillacs within three weeks under the "Cadillac Custom Rapid Delivery" process.[9] So distribution can and must be synchronized to ensure timely and efficient handling of orders.

Place factors   It is the responsibility of logistics to get the product to the right place at the right time in usable conditions. Logistics also plays an important part in determining where a firm locates its plants and distribution centers relative to markets. Such decisions must consider transportation costs as well as the ability of the product to be transported long distances and be stored for long periods of time.

Effective logistics can also help gain access to key distribution outlets. In the Nike-Reebok "sneaker war," two critical market segments are teens and Generation X buyers, who are often willing to pay $80, $90, or more for a pair of shoes. These segments are core customers of the Foor Locker chain. Recently, Nike has been winning in Foot Locker sales because—among other things—Reebok needs to overhaul its information-tracking system and fix its distribution snags, which have resulted in limited customer exposure to its lines in Foot Locker outlets. If Reebok fixes these problems—and with "Shaq" in its ads—it will remain a formidable competitor for Nike.[10]

CONCEPT CHECK

1. What are the three important characteristics of the logistics concept?

2. Why are distribution networks in industries as diverse as retailing and banking increasingly important in the 1990s?

3. How does logistics interact with the product element of the marketing mix?

OBJECTIVES OF THE LOGISTICS SYSTEM

The objective of a logistics system is to minimize relevant logistics costs while delivering maximum customer service. Recently, firms have begun to realize that logistics costs are also dependent on their relationship with suppliers, carriers, and customers. This has led to the practice of forming "strategic alliances" among buyers, sellers, and the transportation system that connects them. For example, to handle its more than 3 billion packages and documents a year, in 1995, JC Penney signed a $1 billion, five-year contract with United Parcel Service (UPS). A full-time UPS manager now works on-site at Penney's to improve the tasks of tracking inventory, billing customers, and managing warehouses. Similarly, Roadway Logistics Services took over the responsibility of all inbound and outbound shipments of Dell computers.[11]

Such strategic alliances are often supported by sophisticated information systems that involve shared databases of customer information and **electronic data interchange (EDI),** computers linked in two different firms to transmit documents such as

FIGURE 17-2

How total logistics cost varies
with number of warehouses
used

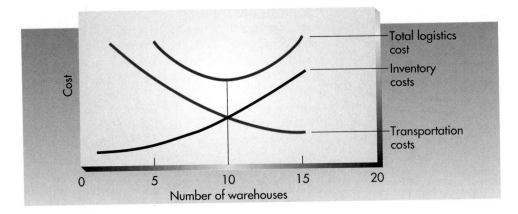

purchase orders, bills of lading, and invoices. For example, Schneider National, a logistics firm in Green Bay, Wisconsin, equips its trucks with on-board computers that can communicate by satellite. The system allows hundreds of Schneider customer-service representatives located in Green Bay to use its EDI techology to tell its clients precisely when trucks will arrive and what is on them.[12] This provides Schneider's customers much more meaningful information than the traditional "it will be there sometime in the morning or afternoon."

Total Logistics Cost Concept

For our purposes **total logistics cost** includes expenses associated with transportation, materials handling and warehousing, inventory, stockouts (being out of inventory), and order processing. A more complete list of decisions that are associated with the flow of product and make up total logistics cost includes the following:

- Traffic and transportation.
- Warehousing and storage.
- Packaging.
- Materials handling.
- Inventory control.
- Order processing.
- Customer service level.
- Plant and warehouse site location.
- Return goods handling.

Note that many of these costs are interrelated so that changes in one will impact the others. For example, as the firm attempts to minimize its transportation costs by shipping in larger quantities, it will also experience an increase in inventory levels. Larger inventory levels will not only increase inventory costs but should also reduce stockouts. It is important, therefore, to study the impact on all of the logistics decision areas when considering a change.

Figure 17–2 provides a graphic example. An oft-used logistics strategy is for a firm to have a number of warehouses, which receive shipments in large quantities and then redistribute smaller shipments to local customers. As the number of warehouses increases, inventory costs rise and transportation costs fall. That is, more inventory is warehoused, but it is transported in volume closer to customers. The net effect is to minimize the total costs of the logistics system shown in Figure 17–2 by having 10 warehouses. This means the total cost curve is minimized at a point where neither of the two individual cost elements is at a minimum but the overall system is.

Studying its total logistics cost has had revolutionary consequences for National Semiconductor, which produces computer chips. In two years it cut its standard delivery time 47 percent, reduced distribution costs 2.5 percent, and increased sales

FIGURE 17-3

Logistics managers balance
total logistics cost factors
against customer service
factors

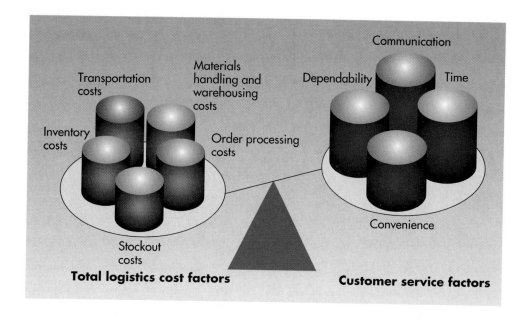

FIGURE 17-3

Logistics managers balance total logistics cost factors against customer service factors

34 percent by shutting down six warehouses around the world and air-freighting its microchips from its huge distribution center in Singapore. It does this even though it has six factories in Israel, Britain, and the United States. National also discovered that a lot of its chips were actually profit-losers, and it cut the number of products it sells by 45 percent, thereby simplifying logistics and increasing profits.[13]

Customer Service Concept

If logistics is a *flow*, the end of it—or *output*—is the service delivered to customers. However, service can be expensive. One firm found that to increase on-time delivery from a 95 percent rate to a 100 percent rate tripled total logistics costs. Higher levels of service require tactics such as more inventory to reduce stockouts, more expensive transportation to improve speed and lessen damage, and double or triple checking of orders to ensure correctness. A firm's goal should be to provide adequate customer service while controlling logistics costs. Customer service is now seen not merely as an expense but as a strategic tool for increasing customer satisfaction and sales. For example, a 3M survey about customer service among 18,000 European customers in 16 countries revealed surprising agreement in all countries about the importance of customer service. Respondents stressed factors such as condition of product delivered, on-time delivery, quick delivery after order placement, and effective handling of problems.[14]

Within the context of logistics, **customer service** is the ability of a logistics system to satisfy users in terms of time, dependability, communication, and convenience.[15] As suggested by Figure 17–3, a logistics manager's key task is to balance these four customer service factors against total logistics cost factors.

Time   In a logistics setting, time refers to **lead time** for an item, which means the lag from ordering an item until it is received and ready for use. This is also referred to as **order cycle time** or **replenishment time** and may be more important to retailers or wholesalers than consumers. The various elements that make up the typical order cycle include recognition of the need to order, order transmittal, order processing, documentation, and transportation. A current emphasis on logistics is to reduce lead time so that the inventory levels of customers may be minimized. Another emphasis is to make the process of reordering and receiving products as simple as possible, often through electronic data interchange and other computer-

Stacking containers two high doubles a train's capacity and leads to significant logistics efficiencies and better customer service.

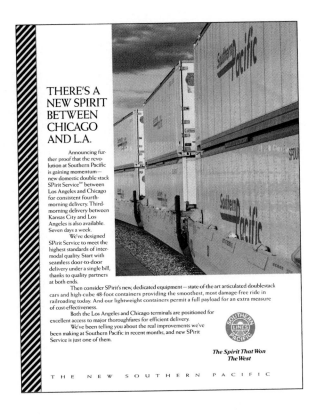

based ordering and inventory systems. The order processing portion of lead time will be discussed later in this chapter.

Dependability   Dependability is the consistency of replenishment. This is important to both intermediaries and consumers. It can be broken into three elements: consistent lead time, safe delivery, and complete delivery. Consistent service allows planning (such as appropriate inventory levels), whereas inconsistencies create surprises. Intermediaries may be willing to accept longer lead times if they know about them in advance and can thus make plans. While surprise delays may shut down a production line, early deliveries will be almost as troublesome because of the problems of storing the extra inventory. Dependability is essential for the just-in-time strategies discussed at the end of the chapter.

Communication   Communication is a two-way link between buyer and seller that helps in monitoring service and anticipating future needs. Status reports on orders are a typical example of improved communication between buyer and seller. The increased communication capability of transportation carriers (such as Schneider National, noted earlier) has enhanced the accuracy of such tracing information and improved the ability of buyers to schedule shipments. Note, however, that such information is still reactive and is not a substitute for consistent on-time deliveries. Therefore, some firms have established strategic alliances in an effort to institutionalize a more proactive flow of useful information that, in turn, improves on-time deliveries. Hewlett-Packard (HP), a high-tech computer printer manufacturer, recently turned its inbound raw materials over to a logistics firm, Roadway Logistics. HP lets Roadway manage the warehousing and coordinate parts delivery so that HP can focus on its printer business. In the process, HP estimates it has cut its warehouse operating costs by about 10 percent.[16]

Convenience   The concept of convenience for a logistics manager means that there should be a minimum of effort on the part of the buyer in doing business with

FIGURE 17-4

Examples of customer service
standards

TYPE OF FIRM	CUSTOMER SERVICE STANDARD
Wholesaler	At least 98% of orders filled accurately
Manufacturer	Order cycle time of no more than 5 days
Retailer	Returns accepted within 30 days
Airline	At least 90% of arrivals on time
Trucker	A maximum of 5% loss and damage per year
Restaurant	Lunch served within 5 minutes of order

the seller. Is it easy for the customer to order? Are the products available from many outlets? Does the buyer have to buy huge quantities of the product? Will the seller arrange all necessary details, such as transportation? The seller must concentrate on removing unnecessary barriers to customer convenience.

Customer Service Standards

Firms that operate effective logistics systems usually develop a set of written customer service standards. These serve as objectives and provide a benchmark against which results can be measured for control purposes. In developing these standards, information is collected on customers' needs. It is also necessary to know what competitors offer as well as the willingness of customers to pay a bit more for better service. After these and similar questions are answered, realistic standards are set and an ongoing monitoring program is established. Note that the examples in Figure 17–4 suggest that customer service standards will differ by type of firm.

CONCEPT CHECK

1. What is a current strategy adopted by firms attempting to squeeze costs from their logistics system while delivering customer service?

2. In what ways do key customer service factors differ between a manufacturer and a retailer?

3. What is the relationship between transportation costs and volume shipped? What impact does it have on the pricing of the firm?

MAJOR LOGISTICS FUNCTIONS

Four key elements in a logistics system include (1) transportation, (2) warehousing and materials handling, (3) order processing, and (4) inventory management. These are described in more detail in the following sections.

Transportation

Transportation provides the movement of goods necessary in a logistics system. There are five basic modes of transportation: railroads, motor carriers, air carriers, pipelines, and water carriers, and modal combinations involving two or more modes, such as highway trailers on a rail flatcar.

Prior to 1980 all modes of transportation were regulated to various degrees by the federal and state governments. This severely restricted the ability of carriers to market their services to different-sized customers or market niches. By 1980 the federal government had relaxed much of the economic regulation for railroads, trucks, and air carriers. This has resulted in an increased ability of carriers to

FIGURE 17-5

Advantages and
disadvantages of five modes
of transportation

MODE	RELATIVE ADVANTAGES	RELATIVE DISADVANTAGES
Rail	Full capability Extensive routes Low cost	Some reliability, damage problems Not always complete pickup and delivery Sometimes slow
Truck	Complete pickup and delivery Extensive routes Fairly fast	Size and weight restrictions Higher cost More weather sensitive
Air	Fast Low damage Frequent departures	High cost Limited capabilities
Pipeline	Low cost Very reliable	Limited routes (accessibility) Slow
Water	Low cost Huge capacities	Slow Limited routes and schedules More weather-sensitive

customize their services and market them toward target customer groups, just like any other industry in the economy.

All modes can be evaluated on six basic service criteria:

- *Cost.* Charges for transportation.
- *Time.* Speed of transit.
- *Capability.* What can be realistically carried with this mode.
- *Dependability.* Reliability of service regarding time, loss, and damage.
- *Accessibility.* Convenience of the mode's routes (such as pipeline availability).
- *Frequency.* Scheduling.

Figure 17–5 summarizes service advantages and disadvantages of five of the modes of transportation available.

Railroads Railroads carry heavy, bulky items over long distances. Of the commodities tracked by the rail industry, coal, farm products, chemicals, and nonmetallic minerals represent nearly 70 percent of the total tonnage. (Coal represents 40 percent of the total.)[17] Railroads have the ability to carry larger shipments than trucks (in terms of total weight per vehicle), but their routes are less extensive. Service innovations include unit trains and intermodal service. A *unit train* is dedicated to one commodity (often coal), using permanently coupled cars that run a continuous loop from a single origin to a single destination and back. Even though the train returns empty, the process captures enough operating efficiencies to make it one of the lowest cost transportation alternatives available. Unit trains are held to a specific schedule so that the customers can plan on reliable delivery and usually carry products that can be loaded and unloaded quickly and automatically.

Railroads have been able to apply the unit train concept to **intermodal transportation,** which involves combining different transportation modes to get the best features of each. The result is a service that attracts high-valued freight, which would normally go by truck. The most popular combination is truck-rail, also referred to as *piggyback* or *trailer on flatcar (TOFC).* The other popular use of an intermodal combination is associated with export/import traffic and uses containers in place of trailers. These containers can be loaded on ships, trains, and truck trailers, so in terms of the on-land segment of international shipments, a container is handled the same way as a trailer. Containers are used in international trade because they take up less

Export/import shippers use containers to move a wide variety of products, including perishable ones.

space on ocean-going vessels. In the mid-1990s, railroads handled about 7 million carloads of intermodal shipments, which included both domestic and international traffic, about double the amount of a decade earlier.

Motor carriers   In contrast to the railroad industry, the for-hire motor carrier industry is composed of many small firms, including as many as 500,000 independent truckers and firms that own their own trucks for transporting their own products.

The greatest advantage of motor carriers is the complete door-to-door service. Trucks can go almost anywhere there is a road, and with the design of specialized equipment they can carry most commodities. Their physical limitations are size and weight restrictions enforced by the states. Trucks have the reputation for maintaining a better record than rail for loss and damage and providing faster, more reliable service, especially for shorter distances. As a result, trucks carry higher-valued goods that are time-sensitive and expensive to carry in inventory. The trade-off is that truck rates are substantially higher than rail rates.

Air carriers and express companies   Air freight is costly, but its speed may create savings in lower inventory. The items that can be carried are limited by space constraints and are usually valuable, time-sensitive, and lightweight, such as perishable flowers, clothing, and electronic parts. Products moved in containers are especially amenable to this mode of shipment. Specialized firms provide ground support in terms of collecting shipments and delivering them to the air terminal. When air freight is handled by the major airlines—such as American, United, Delta, or Northwest—it is often carried as cargo in the luggage space of scheduled passenger flights. This strategy allows the airline to utilize excess capacity that would otherwise be lost.

Freight forwarders   **Freight forwarders,** already mentioned a number of times, are firms that accumulate small shipments into larger lots and then hire a carrier to move them, usually at reduced rates. Recall that transportation companies provide rate incentives for larger quantities. Forwarders collect many small shipments

United Airlines Cargo
provides fast, global
delivery—often utilizing
containers.

consigned to a common destination and pay the carrier the lower rate based on larger volume, so they often convert shipments that are less-than-truckload (LTL) into full truckloads, thereby receiving better shipping rates. The rates charged by the forwarder to the individual shippers, in turn, are somewhat less than the small quantity rate, and the difference is the forwarder's margin. In general, the shipment receives improved service at lower cost. While forwarders may specialize in a particular mode—such as air freight—they are available for all modes of transportation. International freight forwarders play an equally important role in the export/import trades.

Air freight forwarders are an example of specialization in one transportation mode. In some cases, airlines will subcontract excess space to *air freight forwarders* or *express companies,* which are firms that market air express services to the general public. Where markets are large enough, major airlines have responded with pure air freight service between specific airports—often involving international destinations.

CONCEPT CHECK

1. What are some new kinds of train service offered by railroads to compete more effectively with other modes of transportation?

2. What is intermodal transportation?

3. What are the inherent advantages of truck transportation?

Warehousing and Materials Handling

Warehouses may be classified in one of two ways: (1) storage warehouses and (2) distribution centers. In *storage warehouses* the goods are intended to come to rest for some period of time, as in the aging of products or in storing household goods.

MARKETING NEWSNET

Technology

MARKETING STRATEGY WHODUNIT: AND WHERE ARE THEY TODAY?

By the last page of a whodunit, it's pretty clear who the killer was.

But when you're actually involved in a real-life drama, it's often anything but obvious who will emerge the winner. Marketing strategy is an example,

which is why marketing is such a challenge for many people. Study the snapshot history of the two retail chains here called Chain A and Chain B. Then try to tell (1) the names of each chain, (2) where it is today, and (3) how and why it got to this point. See the text for answers.

BASIS OF COMPARISON	CHAIN A	CHAIN B
How it looked in 1962	• 2,223 stores • $26 billion in sales	• 1,198 stores • $16 billion in sales
Initial mission	Offer customer value to typical Americans	Offer customer value to typical Americans
Location of stores	U.S. cities and suburbs	Southern U.S. small towns
Marketing mix strategies from 1962–1995: Product offerings and branding strategy	Wide selection; private brands like Jaclyn Smith's	Wide selection; stress national brands
Pricing strategy	Low discount prices	Lowest discount prices possible
Promotion strategy	Heavy national marketing and advertising campaigns	Virtually no national advertising
Place strategy	Add outlets across the U.S.	Move outside southern U.S. and into major metro areas
Diversification strategy	Add specialty stores offering books, office supplies, sporting goods, "warehouse clubs"	Add "supercenters" that are combination discount store and supermarket
Logistics strategy	Limited activities	Invest in regional distribution centers, computerized inventory systems

Distribution centers, on the other hand, are designed to facilitate the timely movement of goods and represent a very important part of the logistics system. Distribution centers are the focus of the following discussion and represent the second most significant cost for logistics systems.

Distribution centers not only allow firms to hold their stock in decentralized locations but are also used to facilitate sorting and consolidating products from different plants or different suppliers. Some physical transformation can also take place in distribution centers such as mixing or blending different ingredients, labeling, and repackaging. They may also serve as sales offices and order processing centers.

The "whodunit" in the Marketing NewsNet box is a classic case study on the effectiveness of well-placed distribution centers coupled with sophisticated computerized information systems to control inventory and reduce stockout. Chain A is Kmart, and Chain B is Wal-Mart. Note that Wal-Mart has used its distribution centers and information systems to lower retail prices, thereby increasing customer value. Kmart's specialty stores and private brands have come in a distant second to Wal-Mart's strategy. And today, Wal-Mart's sales are nearly $50 billion a year more than Kmart's.[18]

MARKETING NEWSNET

FLY-BY-NIGHT IDEA + CUSTOMER SERVICE + KISS = FEDERAL EXPRESS

Armed with one of his college term papers, which got a C− grade, Frederick W. Smith didn't build a better mousetrap and wait for the world to beat a path to his door. Instead, he set out to show the world that with his simple new innovation *he* could beat a path to everybody else's door.

He gave the name *Federal Express* to his door-to-door parcel service that uses orange, white, and purple jets. And he advertised "absolutely, positively overnight" delivery for his small-parcel service—limited to 70 pounds, the weight one person can carry. "I figured we had to be enormously reliable," says Smith, "since our service is frequently used for expensive spare parts, live organs, or other emergency shipments."

But Federal Express (FedEx) isn't your typical "fly-by-night" outfit. After all, Smith *did* write his term paper at Yale, and he *did* use a family trust of $4 million to get started—and Federal Express *did* lose $27 million in its first 26 months of operation.

What Smith had was a good idea, a good understanding of customer service, and the tenacity and resources to stick with it. First, Smith reasoned, he had to own his own jet aircraft so *all* parcels could be picked up early in the evening, flown to a single sorting center (Memphis), and rerouted to their final destination before dawn. The KISS (keep it simple, stupid) concept worked to

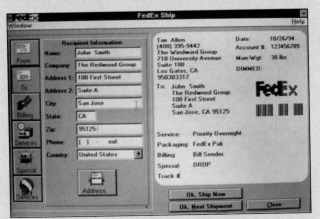

the company's advantage in the early years. Always looking for a better idea, FedEx recently introduced "FedEx Ship"—a shipping software solution in both Mac and Windows™ versions that lets any customer order pickups, print their shipping labels, and track their express deliveries without touching a telephone. Of course, FedEx benefits, too, by cutting telephone traffic and package pickup costs, and also eliminating paperwork errors that might impact sorting. This is essential in the competitive domestic marketplace where U.S. domestic operating margins have fallen from 12 percent to 7 percent in five years.

And in its international segment, FedEx is turning a profit after losing $1 billion over an eight-year period.

Materials handling, which involves moving goods over short distances into, within, and out of warehouses and manufacturing plants, is a key part of warehouse operations. The two major problems with this activity are high labor costs and high rates of loss and damage. Every time an item is handled, there is a chance for loss or damage. Common materials handling equipment includes forklifts, cranes, and conveyors. Recently, materials handling in warehouses has been automated by using computers and robots to reduce the cost of holding, moving, and recording the inventories of stores.

Order Processing

There are several stages in the processing of an order, and a failure at any one of them can cause a problem with the customer. The process starts with transmitting the order by a variety of means such as computer or electronic data interchange (EDI). This is followed by entering the order in the appropriate databases and sending the information to those needing it. For example, a regional warehouse is notified to prepare an order. After checking inventory, a new quantity may need to be reordered from the production line, or purchasing may be requested to reorder from a vendor.

Storage warehouses often stock a large, stable volume of goods.

If the item is currently out of stock, a "backorder" is created, and the whole process of keeping track of a small part of the original order must be managed. In addition, credit may have to be checked for some customers, all paperwork associated with the order must be prepared, transportation must be arranged, and a confirmation of the order must be sent. Order processing systems are generally evaluated in terms of speed and accuracy.

Inventory Management

Inventory management is one of the primary responsibilities of the logistics manager. The major problem is maintaining the delicate balance between too little and too much. Too little inventory may result in poor service, stockouts, brand switching, and loss of market share; too much leads to higher costs because of the money tied up in inventory and the chance that it may become obsolete.

Creative inventory management practices can make possible cost savings elsewhere in the logistics system. For example, IBM has begun closing many of its parts warehouses because Federal Express's reliable overnight delivery (see the Marketing NewsNet box) enables FedEx to inventory high-priced IBM parts at its sorting hubs and deliver them quickly to IBM customers.[19]

Reasons for inventory   Traditionally, carrying inventory has been justified on several grounds: (1) to offer a buffer against variations in supply and demand, often caused by uncertainty in forecasting demand; (2) to provide better service for those customers who wish to be served on demand; (3) to promote production efficiencies; (4) to provide a hedge against price increases by suppliers; (5) to promote purchasing and transportation discounts; and (6) to protect the firm from contingencies such as strikes and shortages.

Inventory costs   Specific inventory costs are often hard to detect because they are difficult to measure and occur in many different parts of the firm. A classification of inventory costs includes the following:

Materials handling through automation.

- *Capital costs.* The opportunity costs resulting from tying up funds in inventory instead of using them in other, more profitable investments; these are related to interest rates.
- *Inventory service costs.* Items such as insurance and taxes that are present in many states.
- *Storage costs.* Warehousing space and materials handling.
- *Risk costs.* Possible loss, damage, pilferage, perishability, and obsolescence.

Storage costs, risk costs, and some service costs vary according to the characteristics of the item inventoried. For example, perishable products or highly seasonal items have higher risk costs than a commodity type product such as lumber. Capital costs are always present and are proportional to the *values* of the item and prevailing interest rates. The costs of carrying inventory vary with the particular circumstances but quite easily could range from 10 to 35 percent for different firms.

Newer inventory strategies Conventional wisdom during the 1970s and 1980s was that a firm should protect itself against uncertainty by maintaining a reserve inventory at each of its production and stocking points. This has been described as a "just-in-case" philosophy of inventory management and led to unnecessary high levels of inventory. In contrast is the **just-in-time (JIT) concept,** which is an inventory supply system that operates with very low inventories and requires fast, on-time delivery. When parts are needed for production, they arrive from suppliers "just in time," which means neither before nor after they are needed. Note that JIT is used in situations where demand forecasting is reliable, such as when supplying a production line, and is not suitable for inventories that are to be stored over significant periods of time.

Saturn's manufacturing operation in Spring Hill, Tennessee, uses a sophisticated JIT system. A central computerized system directs trucks to deliver pre-inspected parts at specific times 21 hours a day, six days a week to one of the plant's 56 receiving docks. Incredibly, the JIT system must coordinate Saturn's 339 suppliers located in 39 states, each supplier being an average of 550 miles away from the Spring Hill facility. Does the JIT system work for Saturn? The answer is a resounding yes. In four years of operation, the Saturn production line has been shut down only

The key to Saturn's JIT System: a Ryder truck driver downloads a key-shaped floppy disk from an on-board computer to get delivery instructions.

once—for 18 minutes!—because the right part was not delivered at the right place and time. The on-site inventory is so low that Saturn's inventory turns over 300 times a year.

Ryder System, the largest logistics management firm in the United States, is charged with making Saturn's JIT system work smoothly. Ryder long-haul trucks and their drivers are the most expensive part of the system. The key—very literally—to this JIT system is a computer disk in the form of a plastic key that drivers plug into an on-truck computer. The computer screen then tells the driver where to go, the route to use, and how much time to spend getting there.[20]

Proponents cite several advantages to JIT. First, there are the financial advantages that come from lower inventory levels and faster turnover. Second, the Japanese experience suggests that JIT yields better reliability in production scheduling and product quality. However, for JIT to work properly, suppliers must be able to provide fast, reliable deliveries or there will be failures relative to customer service. Consequently, with JIT the supplier assumes more responsibility and risk for inventory, quality products, and on-time delivery than formerly.

CONCEPT CHECK

1. What are the basic trade-offs between the modes of transportation?

2. What types of inventory should use storage warehouses and which type should use distribution centers?

3. What are the strengths and weaknesses of a just-in-time system?

SUMMARY

1. Logistics management includes the coordination of the flows of both inbound and outbound goods, an emphasis on making these flows cost-effective, and customer service.

2. The importance of logistical activities varies among firms. The complexity of the system increases with the width of the product line, number of supply points, and number of geographic markets served.

3. Although some marketers may pay little attention to logistics, they do so at their own peril. Logistics directly affects the success of the marketing program and all areas of the marketing mix. In the 1990s powerful distribution networks to control access to customers through efficient logistics systems are gaining strategic importance.

4. The total logistics cost concept suggests that a system of interrelated costs is present such as transportation, materials handling and warehousing, inventory, and stockout costs.

5. Minimizing total logistics cost is irrelevant without specifying an acceptable customer service level that must be maintained. The importance of customer service varies among industries.

6. Although key customer service factors depend on the situation, important elements of the customer service program are likely to be time-related dependability, communications, and convenience.

7. The modes of transportation (e.g., railroads, motor carriers, air carriers, and trucks) offer shippers different service benefits. Better service often costs more, although it should result in savings in other areas of the logistics system.

8. The function of warehousing in a logistics system is to facilitate storage and movement of goods. Distribution centers provide flexibility and facilitate sorting and consolidating products from different plants or different suppliers.

9. Inventory management is critical since too much inventory greatly increases costs and too little may result in stockouts. Various methods are available to manage inventory. A currently popular approach is the just-in-time concept, which attempts to minimize inventory in the system.

10. Some buyers and sellers have developed strategic alliances designed to make the logistics transaction as efficient as possible.

KEY TERMS AND CONCEPTS

physical distribution management p. 448
logistics management p. 448
electronic data interchange (EDI) p. 453
total logistics cost p. 454
customer service p. 455
lead time p. 455

order cycle time p. 455
replenishment time p. 455
intermodal transportation p. 458
freight forwarders p. 459
materials handling p. 462
just-in-time (JIT) concept p. 464

CHAPTER PROBLEMS AND APPLICATIONS

1. List several companies to which logistical activities are unimportant. Also list several whose focus is only on the inbound or outbound side.

2. Give an example of how logistical activities might affect trade promotion strategies.

3. What are some types of businesses in which order processing may be among the paramount success factors?

4. What behavioral problems might arise to negate the logistics concept within the firm?

5. List the customer service factors that would be vital to buyers in the following types of companies: (*a*) manufacturing, (*b*) retailing, (*c*) hospitals, and (*d*) construction.

6. Name some cases when extremely high service levels (e.g., 99 percent) would be warranted.

7. Name the mode of transportation that would be the best for the following products: (*a*) farm machinery, (*b*) cut flowers, (*c*) frozen meat, and (*d*) coal.

8. The auto industry is a heavy user of the just-in-time concept. Why? What other industries would be good candidates for its application? What do they have in common?

9. Look again at Figure 17–2. Explain why as the number of warehouses increases, (*a*) inventory costs rise and (*b*) transportation costs fall.

10. How has Wal-Mart's investment in (*a*) regional distribution centers and (*b*) computerized inventory systems contributed to its low retail prices?

CASE 17–1   Navistar International (B)

How important is logistics management in today's business environment? Just ask managers at the Navistar International Corporation, which produces up to 400 customized trucks each day!

THE COMPANY

Navistar International is one of the largest manufacturers of medium and heavy trucks in the world. Much of its success can be attributed to the sophisticated use of micromarketing actions (described in Chapter 10) that deliver a customized truck equipped with features designed to improve the productivity of each specific customer. This strategy, however, created a problem—a huge inventory of parts. Tailoring a truck to the unique needs of each buyer requires that Navistar keep 80,000 parts, some of which are needed by only one or just a few customers.

Navistar's success is also the result of superior product quality. The manufacturing department focuses much of its effort on ensuring that there are few defects in Navistar trucks. This attention to quality, however, slowed the manufacturing process so that Navistar's order cycle time reached 100 days. In fact, one measure of manufacturing efficiency, the percentage of trucks delivered to the customer on time, indicated that 40 percent of Navistar's deliveries were late.

Managers at Navistar realized that to satisfy customer requirements they needed to reduce order cycle time and inventory costs while maintaining high-quality customized products. Logistics management approaches, which balance the needs of the sales, engineering, and manufacturing departments, were an obvious potential solution.

LOGISTICS MANAGEMENT AT NAVISTAR

In response to these issues, Navistar developed an elaborate material requirement planning (MRP) system to manage the purchase of parts and components from its many suppliers. Navistar also developed an electronic data interchange (EDI) with its major suppliers that allowed specifications, quotes, purchase orders, invoices, and even payments to be made electronically. The system was responsible for the elimination of millions of pieces of paper and the errors and inefficiencies caused by the manual processing of thousands of orders. Finally, a just-in-time system (JIT) was added to match deliveries of supplies with its manufacturing requirements.

These systems have helped Navistar begin to integrate the many complex tasks of producing custom-built trucks. In addition, the systems have helped dealers to improve their customer service. Dealers can now submit their orders electronically and receive information about the lead time of the specified components and the probable delivery date of the completed truck. In the future, as Navistar continues to improve its systems, current status of orders, delivery schedule adjustments, and other important information should be available to dealers.

Navistar has set challenging goals for its logistics management systems. First, it hopes to achieve 100 percent on-time delivery ("slot credibility"). Second, managers hope that Navistar can reduce its order cycle time to 30–45 days. Finally, the company is determined to minimize inventory. Overall, Navistar believes these changes will represent increased value for its customers and allow Navistar to maintain its dominant position in the truck market.

Questions

1. What factors helped Navistar managers realize that logistics management approaches might help them better satisfy customer requirements?

2. What systems did Navistar develop to improve its production process? How can Navistar measure their impact?

3. Explain how the new systems have improved Navistar's customer service.

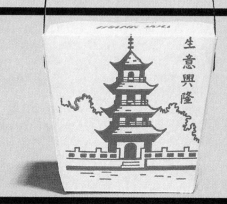

CHAPTER 18

Retailing

AFTER READING THIS CHAPTER YOU SHOULD BE ABLE TO:

• Identify retailers in terms of the utilities they provide.

• Explain the alternative ways to classify retail outlets.

• Understand the many methods of nonstore retailing.

• Classify retailers in terms of the retail positioning matrix.

• Develop retailing mix strategies over the life cycle of a retail store.

VIRTUAL RETAILING MAY SOON LET YOU SHOP WHILE YOU FLOP!

Imagine that you are watching "Seinfeld" on TV and you like the shirt Jerry or Elaine is wearing. You click on it with your remote control, and a windows-style menu asks if you want to buy it. You click on "yes," and another menu asks for your color preference—you choose blue. Additional menus list your credit cards and your campus, home, and work addresses—you indicate how to pay for and where to send your purchase. Because your computer knows your size information, it sends the data electronically to the factory where a shirt is custom-made for you. An overnight service delivers the shirt to your door the next morning—possibly before you are awake!![1]

Sound unlikely? Only if you haven't been watching the extraordinary boom in electronic shopping. Popular TV shopping channels such QVC and Home Shopping Network are being joined by a wide variety of on-line shopping services. CUC International shopping service, for example, has 34 million members who can use their computers or telephones to order directly from more than 600 manufacturers. Similarly, Peapod, an on-line "virtual supermarket" in Chicago and San Francisco, lets shoppers review product information, place orders, and select next-day delivery times with a few computer keystrokes. Other forms of interactive merchandising such as video-on-demand and on-line services such as Prodigy, CompuServe, and America Online are increasing the likelihood that we may soon just "click" to buy.[2]

The dramatic growth of electronic shopping is just one example of the dynamic and exciting nature of retailing today. This chapter examines the critical role retailing plays as a component of many distribution channels and the challenging decisions retailers face as they strive to create value for their customers.

What types of products will consumers buy directly through catalogs, the mail, computers, or telephone? In what type of store will consumers look for products they don't buy directly? How important is the location of the store? Will customers expect services such as alterations, delivery, installation, or repair? What price should be charged for each product? These are difficult and important questions that are an integral part of retailing. In the channel of distribution, retailing is where the customer meets the product. It is through retailing that exchange (a central aspect of marketing) occurs. **Retailing** includes all activities involved in selling, renting, and providing goods and services to ultimate customers for personal, family, or household use.

THE VALUE OF RETAILING

Retailing is an important marketing activity. Not only do producers and consumers meet through retailing actions, but retailing also creates customer value and has a significant impact on the economy. To consumers, the value of retailing is in the form of utilities provided. Retailing's economic value is represented by the people employed in retailing as well as by the total amount of money exchanged in retail sales.

Consumer Utilities Offered by Retailing

The utilities provided by retailers create value for consumers. Time, place, possession, and form utilities are offered by most retailers in varying degrees, but one utility is often emphasized more than others. Look at Figure 18–1 to see how well you can match the retailer with the utility being emphasized in the description.

Providing minibanks in supermarkets, as Wells Fargo does, puts the bank's products and services close to the consumer, providing place utility. By providing financing or leasing and taking used cars as trade-ins, Saturn makes the purchase easier and provides possession utility. Form utility—production or alteration of a product—is offered by Levi Strauss & Co. as it creates "Personal Pair" Jeans for Women to meet each customer's specifications. Finding toy shelves stocked in May is the time utility dreamed about by every child (and many parents) who enters Toys "Я" Us. Many retailers offer a combination of the four basic utilities. Some

FIGURE 18–1

Which company best represents which utilities?

Wells Fargo	One of the best-run banks in the United States, Wells Fargo is intensifying its drive to reach retail customers by opening minibanks in supermarkets. This new form of banking is designed to complement ATMs, which already dispense 75% of the bank's cash.
Saturn	Saturn dealers have adopted a one-price strategy that eliminates the need for negotiating. Instead, all customers are offered the same price. Test drives, financing, trade-ins, leasing are all offered to encourage customers to purchase a Saturn.
Levi Strauss	In the next five years, Levi Strauss & Co. will open 100 Original Levi's Stores where in-store computers are used to create personal-fit jeans. An order for Levi's "Personal Pair" Jeans for Women specifies the customer's measurements, style, and color preferences and can be delivered in approximately three weeks.
Toys "Я" Us	A distinctive toy store with a backwards R, this company is what every kid dreams about. Walking into a Toys "Я" Us store is like living under a Christmas tree. Unlike most stores, which reduce their space allotted to toys after the holiday season, a huge selection of toys is always available at Toys "Я" Us.

Can You Match Them?

Time	Place	Possession	Form
____	____	____	____

supermarkets, for example, offer convenient locations (place utility) and are open 24 hours (time utility). In addition, consumers may seek additional utilities such as entertainment, recreation, or information.[3]

The Global Economic Impact of Retailing

Retailing is also important to the U.S. and global economies. Three of the 20 largest businesses in the United States are retailers (Wal-Mart, Sears, and Kmart).[4] Wal-

Mart's $93 billion of sales in 1995 surpassed the gross domestic product of Finland for that same year. Sears, Wal-Mart, and Kmart together have more than 1.2 million employees—more people than live in Austin, Texas, and Spokane, Washington, combined! Many other retailers, including food stores, automobile dealers, and general merchandise outlets, are also significant contributors to the U.S. economy (Figure 18–2).[5]

Outside of the United States, large retailers include Karstadt in Germany, Nichii in Japan, Coles Meyer in Australia, Marks & Spencer in Britain, and Carrefour in France. In emerging economies such as China and Mexico, a combination of local and global retailers are evolving. Wal-Mart, for example, has 277 stores outside the United States, many through joint ventures. The Marketing NewsNet on the following page describes the incredible expansion currently under way![6] In the Arabian Gulf Dubai is promoting itself as a gateway to the Middle East with the

FIGURE 18–2   Retail sales, by type of business

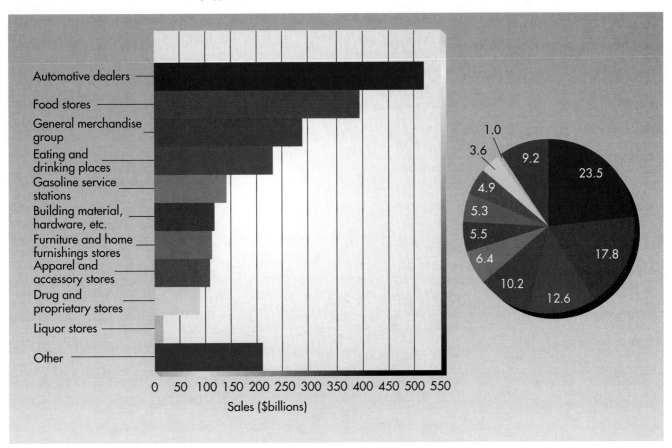

MARKETING NEWSNET

Global

MEGA-MERCHANTS ARE BUSTING BORDERS!

Around the world, customer wants and needs are converging, and retailers are responding with frenzied global expansion. Experts estimate that retailers will spend $5 billion during the next two years opening new stores in foreign countries. Wal-Mart, for example, has plans to open stores in Brazil, Argentina, Hong Kong, and China. Home Depot will open 50 stores in Canada, while Office Depot, Saks Fifth Avenue, and JCPenney are expanding into Mexico. Italy's Bennetton already has stores in 120 countries, and Britain's Marks & Spencer has grown to 150 stores around the world.

Why are retailers expanding so rapidly? One reason is that the U.S. and European markets are saturated with retailers. Therefore, large merchants are looking for new places to invest. A second reason, however, is that retailers would like to transform their store names into global brands—a move that will allow them to sell higher

margin private-label goods, avoid price wars, and better negotiate with suppliers. Keith Oates of Marks & Spencer says, "we'll be a global brand in time, like Coca-Cola."

"Dubai Shopping Festival." More than 3000 retail outlets participate by offering sales, discounts, special offers and other promotions. Each day the festival also holds a free drawing for a $16,000 bar of gold and a raffle for two Lexus automobiles. Because the event attracts more than 2 million shoppers retailers are eager to expand their global participation in Dubai and other growing markets.

CONCEPT CHECK

1. When Levi Strauss makes jeans cut to a customer's exact measurements, what utility is provided?

2. Two measures of the importance of retailing in the global economy are _____ and _____ .

CLASSIFYING RETAIL OUTLETS

For manufacturers, consumers, and the economy, retailing is an important component of marketing that has several variations. Because of the large number of alternative forms of retailing, it is easier to understand the differences among retail institutions by recognizing that outlets can be classified in several ways:

- **Form of ownership.** Who owns the outlet.
- **Level of service.** The degree of service provided to the customer.
- **Merchandise line.** How many different types of products a store carries and in what assortment.

Within each method of classification there are several alternative types of outlets, as shown in Figure 18–3 and explained in the following pages.

FIGURE 18-3

Classifying retail outlets

METHOD OF CLASSIFICATION	DESCRIPTION OF RETAIL OUTLET
Form of ownership	Independent retailer Corporate chain Contractual system • Retailer-sponsored cooperative • Wholesaler-sponsored voluntary chain • Franchise
Level of service	Self-service Limited-service Full-service
Merchandise line	Depth • Single line • Limited line Breadth • General merchandise • Scrambled merchandising

Form of Ownership

Independent retailer   One of the most common forms of retail ownership is the independent business, owned by an individual. The number of small retailers has grown at a rate of 15 percent to 775,000 companies that dominate employment in hardware, sporting goods, jewelry, and gift stores. They are also popular retailers of auto supplies, books, paint, cameras, and women's accessories. The advantage of this form of ownership for the owner is that he or she can be his or her own boss. For customers, the independent store can offer convenience, quality, personal service, and lifestyle compatibility.[7]

Corporate chain   A second form of ownership, the corporate chain, involves multiple outlets under common ownership. If you've ever shopped at Dayton's, Hudson's, Marshall Field's, Mervyn's, or Target, you've shopped at a chain outlet owned by the Dayton Hudson Corporation.

In a chain operation, centralization in decision making and purchasing is common. Chain stores have advantages in dealing with manufacturers, particularly as the size of the chain grows. A large chain can bargain with a manufacturer to obtain good service or volume discounts on orders. Kmart's large volume makes it a strong negotiator with manufacturers of most products. The power of chains is seen in the retailing of computers: small independents buy at 75 percent of list price, but large chains such as Comp USA, Circuit City, and Best Buy may pay only 60 to 65 percent of list price.[8] Consumers also benefit in dealing with chains because there are multiple outlets with similar merchandise and consistent management policies.

Retailing has become a high-tech business for many large chains. Wal-Mart, for example, has developed a sophisticated inventory management and cost control system that allows rapid price changes for each product in every store. Although the technology requires a substantial investment, it is a necessary competitive tool today—a lesson illustrated by Mexico's largest drugstore chain. When Wal-Mart, Price Club, and other discounters opened stores in Mexico, Formacias Benavides used its state-of-the-art computer system to match prices on popular pharmaceutical products that were also available in the new competitors' stores.[9]

Contractual system   Contractual systems involve independently owned stores that band together to act like a chain. The three kinds described in Chapter 16 are retailer-sponsored cooperatives, wholesaler-sponsored voluntary chains, and fran-

FRANCHISE	TYPE OF BUSINESS	TOTAL START-UP COST	NUMBER OF FRANCHISES
McDonald's	Fast-food restaurant	$385,000–$520,000	10,339
7-Eleven Stores	Convenience store	$12,500–$162,000	3,031
The Maids	Cleaning service	$27,500–$32,500	244
Discovery Zone	Children's fitness center	$355,000–$540,000	30
Jiffy Lube	Automobile fluid service	$158,000–$164,000	875
Mail Boxes Etc.	Postal services	$93,500–$137,400	2500
Duds 'N Suds	Laundry and snack bar	$220,000	85

chises. One retailer-sponsored cooperative is the Associated Grocers, which consists of neighborhood grocers that all agree with several other independent grocers to buy their meat from the same wholesaler. In this way, members can take advantage of volume discounts commonly available to chains and also give the impression of being a large chain, which may be viewed more favorably by some consumers. Wholesaler-sponsored voluntary chains such as Ace Hardware and Independent Grocers' Alliance (IGA) try to achieve similar benefits.

As noted in Chapter 16, in a franchise system an individual or firm (the franchisee) contracts with a parent company (the franchisor) to set up a business or retail outlet.

McDonald's, Holiday Inn, Midas, and H&R Block all involve some level of franchising. The franchisor usually assists in selecting the store location, setting up the store, advertising, and training personnel. The franchisee pays a one-time franchise fee and an annual royalty, usually tied to the store's sales. Although this might be seen as a relatively new phenomenon, this ownership approach has been used with gas stations since the early 1900s.[10] Franchising is attractive because of the opportunity for people to enter a well-known, established business where managerial advice is provided. Also, the franchise fee may be less than the cost of setting up an independent business. The International Franchise Association recently reported that franchising is one of the strongest segments of the economy, generating close to $800 billion in sales and more than 160,000 new jobs each year.[11]

Franchise fees paid to the franchisor can range from as little as $10,000 for a Dominos Pizza franchise to $50,000 for a TGI Friday restaurant franchise.[12] When the fees are combined with other costs such as real estate and equipment, however, the total investment can be substantial. Figure 18–4 shows some businesses that can be entered through franchise, along with the total costs of becoming a franchisee. By selling franchises, an organization reduces the cost of expansion but loses some control. A good franchisor, however, will maintain strong control of the outlets in terms of delivery and presentation of merchandise.

Level of Service

Even though most customers perceive little variation in retail outlets by form of ownership, differences among retailers are more obvious in terms of level of service. In some department stores, such as Loehman's, very few services are provided. Some grocery stores, such as the Cub chain, have customers bag the food themselves. Other outlets, such as Neiman Marcus, provide a wide range of customer services from gift wrapping to wardrobe consultation.

Self-service   Self-service is at the extreme end of the level of service continuum because the customer performs many functions and little is provided by the outlet. Home building supply outlets, discount stores, and gas stations are often self-service. Warehouse stores, usually in buildings several times larger than a conventional store, are self-service with all nonessential customer services eliminated. Several new forms of self-service include Federal Express's placement of hundreds of self-service package shipping stations in retail stores such as Target and Sam's Club and a self-service scanning system called the Portable Personal Shopper now used by some grocery stores in The Netherlands and being considered for testing by Kroger stores in the United States.[13]

Limited service   Limited-service outlets provide some services, such as credit, merchandise return and telephone ordering, but not others, such as custom-made clothes. Department stores typically are considered limited-service outlets.

Full-service   Full-service retailers, which include most specialty stores and some department stores, provide many services to their customers. Nordstrom, a Seattle-based retail chain, for example, is legendary for its customer service. The store typically has 50 percent more salespeople on the floor than similar-sized stores. Salespeople often write customers thank-you notes, or deliver purchases to customers' homes. In most stores, customers are serenaded by the sounds of a grand piano. These activities are reflected in a biannual industry customer satisfaction survey—the Retail Satisfaction Index—which ranks Nordstrom highest in terms of personalized attention and professional salespeople.[14]

Merchandise Line

Retail outlets also vary by their merchandise lines, the key distinction being the breadth and depth of the items offered to customers (Figure 18–5). **Depth of**

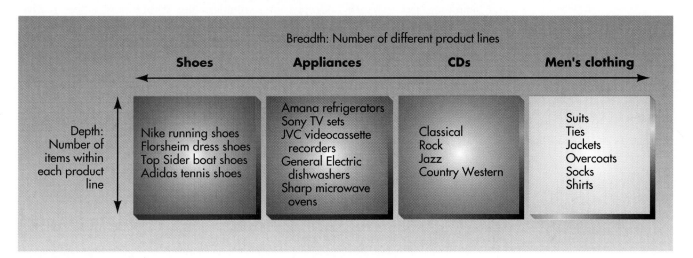

FIGURE 18-5   Breadth versus depth of merchandise lines

product line means that the store carries a large assortment of each item, such as a shoe store that offers running shoes, dress shoes, and children's shoes. **Breadth of product line** refers to the variety of different items a store carries.

Depth of line   Stores that carry a considerable assortment (depth) of a related line of items are limited-line stores. Herman's sporting goods stores carry considerable depth in sports equipment ranging from weight-lifting accessories to running shoes. Stores that carry tremendous depth in one primary line of merchandise are single-line stores. Victoria's Secret, a nationwide chain, carries great depth in women's lingerie. Both limited- and single-line stores are often referred to as *specialty outlets.*

Specialty discount outlets focus on one type of product, such as electronics (Circuit City), business supplies (Staples), or books (Barnes and Noble) at very competitive prices. These outlets are referred to in the trade as *category killers* because they often dominate the market. Toys "Я" Us, for example, controls 22 percent of the toy market.[15]

Breadth of line   Stores that carry a broad product line, with limited depth, are referred to as *general merchandise stores.* For example, a large department store carries a wide range of different types of products but not unusual sizes. The breadth and depth of merchandise lines are important decisions for a retailer. Traditionally, outlets carried related lines of goods. Today, however, **scrambled merchandising**, offering several unrelated product lines in a single store, is common. The modern drugstore carries food, camera equipment, magazines, paper products, toys, small hardware items, and pharmaceuticals. Supermarkets rent video tapes, develop film, and sell flowers.

A form of scrambled merchandising, the **hypermarket**, has been successful in Europe since the late 1960s. These hypermarkets are large stores (more than 200,000 square feet) offering a mix of 40 percent food products and 60 percent general merchandise. Prices are typically 5 to 20 percent below discount stores. The general concept behind the stores is simple: offer consumers everything in a single outlet, eliminating the need to stop at more than one location.

Despite their success in Europe, hypermarkets have not been popular in the United States. When Wal-Mart opened four Hypermart USA stores and Kmart opened three American Fare stores, they discovered that U.S. shoppers were uncomfortable with the huge size of the stores. In addition, the competitive environment was tough: warehouse stores beat hypermarkets on price, category killers beat them on selection, and discounters beat them on location.

Searching for a better concept, some retailers are trying new stores, called *supercenters,* which combine a typical merchandise store with full-size grocery. Wal-Mart already operates more than 100 supercenters and has plans to open 100 more, while rival Kmart has close to 100 Super Kmart Centers.[16] Figure 18–6 shows the differences between discount stores, supercenters, and hypermarkets.[17]

FIGURE 18-6

Differences in store concepts

	DISCOUNT STORE	**SUPERCENTER**	**HYPERMARKET**
Average size (in square feet)	70,000	150,000	230,000
Number of employees	200–300	300–350	400-600
Annual sales ($ millions per store)	$10–$20	$20–$50	$75–$100
Gross margin	18%–19%	15%–16%	7%–8%
Number of items stocked	60,000–80,000	100,000	60,000–70,000

Scrambled merchandising is convenient for consumers because it eliminates the number of stops required in a shopping trip. However, for the retailer this merchandising policy means there is competition between very dissimilar types of retail outlets, or **intertype competition**. A local bakery may compete with a department store, discount outlet, or even a local gas station. Scrambled merchandising and intertype competition make it more difficult to be a retailer.

CONCEPT CHECK

1. Centralized decision making and purchasing are an advantage of _____ _____ ownership.

2. What are some examples of new forms of self-service retailers?

3. Would a shop for big men's clothes carrying pants in sizes 40 to 60 have a broad or deep product line?

Nonstore Retailing

Most of the retailing examples discussed earlier in the chapter, such as corporate chains, department stores, and limited- and single-line specialty stores, involve store retailing. Many retailing activities today, however, are not limited to sales in a store. Nonstore retailing occurs outside a retail outlet such as through direct marketing (described in Chapter 16), direct selling, and automatic vending.[18]

Direct Marketing

Few areas of retailing have grown as rapidly as direct marketing. What was once a specialized activity is now a set of fashionable tools used by virtually every type of business. Direct marketing includes direct mail, telemarketing, and in-home shopping.

Direct mail Of the $300 billion in annual U.S. sales generated by direct marketing activities, approximately 50 percent are the result of direct mail programs, including catalogs. Direct mail retailing is attractive because it eliminates the cost of a store and clerks. In addition, it improves marketing efficiency through segmentation and targeting and creates customer value by providing a fast and convenient means of making a purchase. Direct marketers, for example, offer rural Japanese farmers outdoor gear at discount prices through direct mail campaigns—and deliver within 72 hours![19]

As consumers' direct mail purchases have increased, the number of catalogs and the number of products sold through catalogs has skyrocketed. A typical household now receives more than 50 of the 12 billion catalogs mailed each year. The competition combined with higher paper and postal costs, however, have hurt large catalog merchants such as Sears—which closed its 100-year-old general catalog business in 1993—and Spiegel—which is substantially reducing the size of its "Big Book." A successful approach now used by many catalog retailers is to send specialty catalogs to market niches identified in their databases. L. L. Bean, a longstanding catalog retailer, has developed an individual catalog for fly fishing enthusiasts. Similarly, Lillian Vernon Corporation sends a specialty catalog called "Lilly's Kids" to customers with children or grandchildren and a "Welcome" catalog of household items to customers who change their address.[20]

Creative forms of catalog retailing are also being developed. Boston's Bay Banks, Inc., for example, offers 160 financial products, ranging from checking accounts to student loans, in a colorful 53-page catalog. Victoria's Secret mails as many as 45 catalogs a year to its customers to generate mail-order and 800 number business and to increase traffic in its 600 stores. Interactive Catalog Corporation offers multiple catalogs on disks to owners of home computers with CD-ROM capabilities.[21]

Telemarketing   Another form of direct marketing, called **telemarketing**, involves using the telephone to interact with and sell directly to consumers. Compared with direct mail, telemarketing is often viewed as a more efficient means of targeting consumers, although the two techniques are often used together. Information Management Network, a Dallas-based company, for example, sends direct mail to 30 million names each year to generate 650,000 responses from people who are then contacted by telemarketers. At Ryder Consumer Truck Rental, well-trained agents talk to 15 prospective customers each hour, while the staff of 24 at Lens Express makes 100,000 calls each month. Telemarketing has grown in popularity as companies search for ways to cut costs but still provide convenient access to their customers. According to the American Telemarketing Association, telemarketing sales reached $500 billion in 1994.[22]

As the use of telemarketing grows, consumer privacy has become a topic of discussion among consumers, Congress, the Federal Trade Commission, and businesses. Issues such as industry standards, ethical guidelines, and new privacy laws are evolving to provide a balance between the varying perspectives. The accompanying Ethics and Social Responsibility Alert offers some of the details of the debate.[23]

In-home shopping   In-home shopping includes several relatively new forms of nonstore retailing—television-assisted retailing and computer-assisted retailing. TV shopping is possible when consumers watch a shopping channel on which products are displayed; orders are then placed over the telephone. Two popular programs, Home Shopping Network and QVC, reach 60 million households and recently accounted for combined sales of more than $2 billion. Because these programs have traditionally attracted 40- to 50-year-old women, other programs such as MTV Network's "The Goods" and "House of Style," with spokesperson Cindy Crawford, and QVC's "Q2" are designed to attract younger audiences. A limitation of TV shopping has been the lack of buyer-seller interaction and the inability of consumers to control the items they see. But two new technologies—fiber optics and digital compression—will soon allow consumers to choose from as many as 500 channels and interact with the program source.[24]

CompuServe and Cybersmith Online Cafes are just two of many ways consumers can gain access to products and services online.

ETHICS AND SOCIAL RESPONSIBILITY ALERT

Ethics

IS PERSONAL PRIVACY FOR SALE?

MasterCard International recently asked 507 people for their views about direct marketing and discovered that 75 percent agreed, "We need to find ways to stop business and government from collecting information about the average person." The Federal Trade Commission has adopted new rules for telemarketers, and more than half of the state legislatures have introduced or enacted legislation likely to affect nonstore retailers. Some of the key issues and questions include the following:

- *Disclosure.* Should companies be required to disclose to consumers that information about them is being collected?
- *Knowledge.* Should businesses be limited in the types and amount of information collected about individuals?

- *Suppression.* Should consumers be able to remove themselves from databases?

Some experts argue that the First Amendment specifies there should be no restrictions on the collection and use of data. Many businesses advocating self-regulation have adopted privacy principles to guide their marketing practices. The Direct Marketing Association developed the Mail Preference Service as a means for consumers to remove their names from mailing lists. Finally, consumers in the MasterCard survey indicated that they would be more willing to disclose personal information in exchange for an incentive. What were the incentives most preferred by respondents? Better protection against fraud and lower finance charges.

What is your opinion about these privacy issues?

Computer-assisted retailing (sometimes called videotex) allows customers to view product information on their computer and then order the desired item electronically. Several companies have entered this form of retailing in recent years. The largest are America Online, CompuServe, and Prodigy. Other online services include General Electric's Genie, Apple Computer Inc.'s e·world and Microsoft's Microsoft Network. For a monthly connect-time fee (such as Prodigy's $9.95 per month), these companies provide customers with access to a databank of products. Prodigy, for example, has merchandise from stores such as Sears, catalogs such as Speigel, and manufacturers such as Xerox and Sony. Travel reservations, stock transactions, and encyclopedia searches can also be made via this system. Prodigy charges retailers up to $25,000 to sign up on the service, and there is an ongoing fee of approximately one third of the retailer's gross margin.[25] Prodigy currently has 1.2 million subscribers and more than 160 advertising accounts.[26]

Many other electronic markets are being developed on the Internet and its World Wide Web, a global network of networks that enables computers to communicate directly. Chrysler and Coca-Cola, for example, have developed "Web sites" that provide company and product information to on-line computer users. The on-line audience is already global—while there are 6 million U.S. on-line subscribers, there are 25 million Internet users. Future growth will likely follow the penetration of computers into homes, currently ranging from 37 percent in the United States to 15 percent in France. Owning a computer isn't a necessity, however, as many "on-line cafes" now provide guests with access to computer stations linked to the Internet. In Massachusetts, a new retail outlet called Cybersmith offers 52 computer stations to customers at a rate of 17.5 cents a minute.[27]

Direct Selling

Direct selling, sometimes called door-to-door retailing, involves direct sales of goods and services to consumers through personal interactions and demonstrations in their

Vending machines serve customers when and where stores cannot.

home or office. A variety of companies, including familiar names such as Fuller Brush, Avon, World Book, and Mary Kay Cosmetics, have created an industry with more than $16 billion in sales by providing consumers with personalized service and convenience. In the United States, however, sales have been declining as retail chains such as Wal-Mart begin to carry similar products at discount prices and as the increasing number of dual-career households reduces the number of potential buyers at home.

In response to the changes in the United States, many direct selling retailers are expanding into other markets. Avon, for example, already has 1.3 million sales representatives in 26 countries including Mexico, Poland, Argentina, and China. Similarly, other retailers such as Amway, Herbalife, and Electrolux are rapidly expanding in Europe. Stanhome, Inc. tested international direct selling of home cleaning products in Italy and France and has already reached $200 million in sales! Direct selling is likely to continue to grow in markets where the lack of effective distribution channels increases the importance of door-to-door convenience and where the lack of consumer knowledge about products and brands will increase the need for a person-to-person approach.[28]

Automatic Vending

Direct marketing also encompasses vending machines, which make it possible to serve customers when and where stores cannot. Maintenance and operating costs are high, so product prices in vending machines tend to be higher than those in stores. Typically, small convenience products are available in vending machines. Of the 3 million vending machines currently in use, more than 1.8 million are soft drink machines. Improved technology, however, may soon allow vending machines to accept credit cards—a change that will permit more expensive items to be sold through this form of retailing. Some airports, for example, now have vending machines that sell software to commuters with laptop computers. Another improvement in vending machines—the use of modems to notify retailers when their machines are empty—is expected to increase the current $29 billion in sales by 10 percent.[29]

CONCEPT CHECK

1. Successful catalog retailers often send _____ catalogs to _____ markets identified in their databases.

2. How are on-line shopping services and the Internet changing retailing?

3. Where are direct selling retail sales growing? Why?

Retailing Strategy

This section identifies how a retail store positions itself and describes specific actions it can take to develop a retailing strategy.

Positioning a Retail Store

The classification alternatives presented in the previous sections help determine one store's position relative to its competitors.

Retail positioning matrix   The **retail positioning matrix** is a matrix developed by the MAC Group, Inc., a management consulting firm.[30] This matrix positions retail outlets on two dimensions: breadth of product line and value added. As defined previously, breadth of product line is the range of products sold through each outlet. The second dimension, *value added*, includes elements such as location (as with 7-Eleven stores), product reliability (as with Holiday Inn or McDonald's), or prestige (as with Saks Fifth Avenue or Brooks Brothers).

The retail positioning matrix in Figure 18–7 shows four possible positions. An organization can be successful in any position, but unique strategies are required within each quadrant. Consider the four stores shown in the matrix:

1. Bloomingdale's has high value added and a broad product line. Retailers in this quadrant pay great attention to store design and product lines. Merchandise often has a high margin of profit and is of high quality. The stores in this position typically provide high levels of service.
2. Kmart has low value added and a broad line. Kmart and similar firms typically trade a lower price for increased volume in sales. Retailers in this position focus on price with low service levels and an image of being a place for good buys.
3. Tiffany's has high value added and a narrow line. Retailers of this type typically sell a very restricted range of products that are of high status quality. Customers are also provided with high levels of service.
4. Kinney has low value added and a narrow line. Such retailers are specialty mass merchandisers. Kinney, for example, carries attractively priced shoes for the entire family. These outlets appeal to value-conscious consumers. Economies of scale are achieved through centralized advertising, merchandising, buying, and distribution. Stores are usually the same in design, layout, and merchandise; hence they are often referred to as "cookie-cutter" stores.

Keys to positioning   To successfully position a store, it must have an identity that has some advantages over the competitors yet is recognized by consumers. A company can have outlets in several positions on the matrix, but this approach is usually done with different store names. Dayton-Hudson, for example, owns Dayton's and Hudson's department stores (with high value added and a broad line) and Target discount stores (low value added and a broad line). Shifting from one box

FIGURE 18-7

Retail positioning matrix

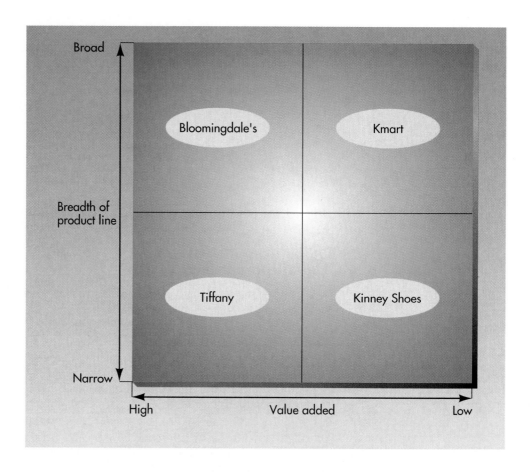

in the retail positioning matrix to another is also possible, but all elements of retailing strategy must be reexamined. For example, JCPenney has modified the visual presentation of its stores and changed the assortment of its merchandise to reposition itself from a mass merchandiser competing with Sears to a contemporary department store competing with stores such as Macys.[31]

Retailing Mix

In developing retailing strategy, managers work with the **retailing mix**, which includes the (1) goods and services, (2) physical distribution, and (3) communications tactics chosen by a store (Figure 18–8).[32] Decisions relating to the mix focus on the consumer. Each of the areas shown is important, but we will cover only three basic areas: (1) pricing, (2) store location, and (3) image and atmosphere. The communications and promotion components are discussed in Chapter 20 on advertising and Chapter 21 on personal selling.

Retail pricing   In setting prices for merchandise, retailers must decide on the markup, markdown, and timing for markdowns. As mentioned in the appendix to Chapter 15, the *markup* refers to how much should be added to the cost the retailer paid for a product to reach the final selling price. Retailers decide on the *original markup*, but by the time the product is sold, they end up with a *maintained markup*. The original markup is the difference between retailer cost and initial selling price. When products do not sell as quickly as anticipated, their price is reduced. The difference between the final selling price and retailer cost is the maintained markup, which is also called the *gross margin.*

   Discounting a product, or taking a *markdown,* occurs when the product does not sell at the original price and an adjustment is necessary. Often new models or styles

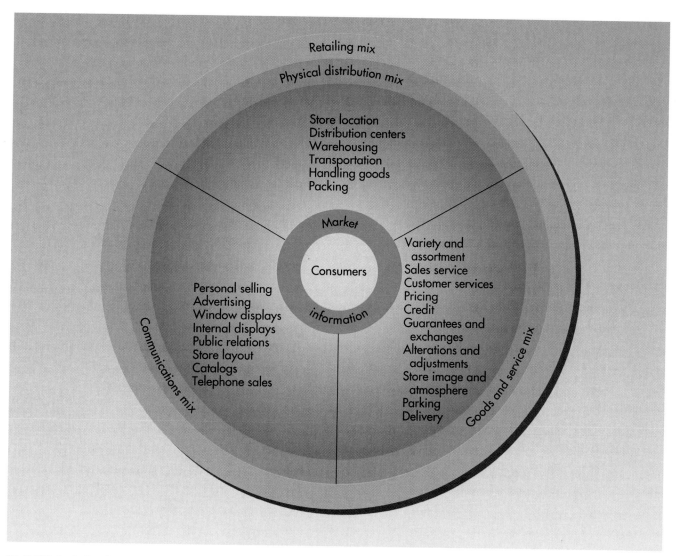

Store location
Distribution centers
Warehousing
Transportation
Handling goods
Packing

Retailing mix

Physical distribution mix

Market

Consumers

information

Variety and
  assortment
Sales service
Customer services
Pricing
Credit
Guarantees and
  exchanges
Alterations and
  adjustments
Store image and
  atmosphere
Parking
Delivery

Personal selling
Advertising
Window displays
Internal displays
Public relations
Store layout
Catalogs
Telephone sales

Communications mix

Goods and service mix

FIGURE 18-8

The retailing mix

force the price of existing models to be marked down. Discounts may also be used to increase demand for complementary products.[33] For example, retailers might take a markdown on stereos to increase sales of CDs or reduce the price of cake mix to generate frosting purchases.

Although most retailers plan markdowns, many retailers use price discounts as part of their regular merchandising policy. In March 1989, Sears closed its 824 U.S. stores for 48 hours to lower its shelf prices on 50,000 items and begin an *everyday low pricing* strategy. Although Sears was not successful with its switch, emphasizing consistently low prices and eliminating most markdowns or sales has become a successful strategy for retailers like Wal-Mart and Home Depot.[34] Because consumers often use price as an indicator of product quality, however, the brand name of the product and the image of the store become important decision factors in these situations.[35]

A final issue, *timing,* involves deciding when to discount the merchandise. Many retailers take a markdown as soon as sales fall off to free up valuable selling space and cash. However, other stores delay markdowns to discourage bargain hunters and maintain an image of quality. There is no clear answer, but retailers must consider how the timing might affect future sales.

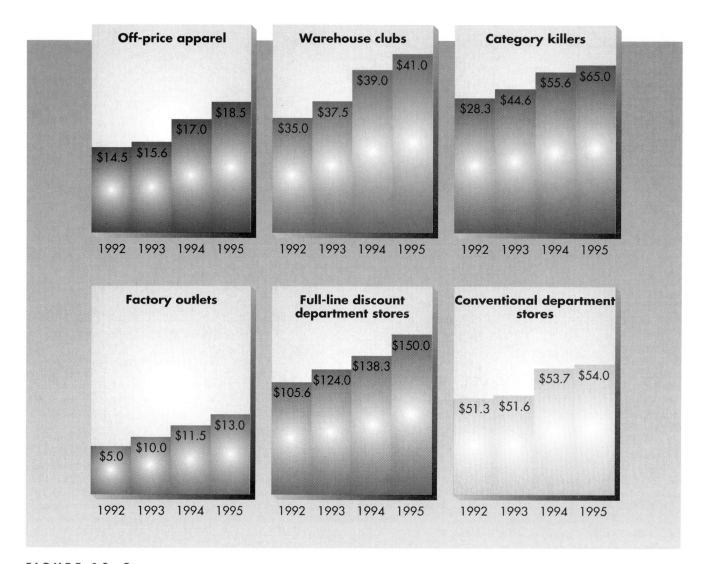

FIGURE 18–9

Retail sales trends ($ billions)

Off-price retailing is a retail pricing practice that is most commonly found in clothing sales. **Off-price retailing** involves selling brand-name merchandise at lower than regular prices. In 1995, off-price apparel retailer sales grew to $18.5 billion.[36] Figure 18–9 shows the growth of off-price clothing retailers compared with other types of retail outlets. The difference between the off-price retailer and a discount store is that off-price merchandise is bought by the retailer from manufacturers with excess inventory at prices below wholesale prices, while the discounter buys at full wholesale price (but takes less of a markup than do traditional department stores). Because of this difference in the way merchandise is purchased by the retailer, selection at an off-price retailer is unpredictable, and searching for bargains has become a popular activity for many consumers. "It's more like a sport than it is like ordinary shopping," says Christopher Boring of Columbus, Ohio's Retail Planning Associates.[37] Savings to the consumer at off-price retailers are reported as high as 70 percent off the prices of a traditional department store.

There are two variations of off-price retailing. One is the warehouse club. These large stores (more than 100,000 square feet) began as rather stark outlets with no elaborate displays, customer service, or home delivery. They require an annual membership fee (usually $25) for the privilege of shopping there. While a typical

Kmart stocks 100,000 items, warehouse clubs carry about 3,500 items and usually stock just one brand name of appliance or food product. Service is minimal, and customers usually pay by cash or check. However, the extremely competitive pricing of merchandise makes warehouse clubs attractive.[38] The major warehouse clubs in the United States, which account for 90 percent of the sales, include Wal-Mart's Sam's Clubs, Price Company's Price Club, and Costco Warehouse Club. Sales of these off-price retailers have grown dramatically, as shown in Figure 18–9, reaching $41 billion in 1995 (compared with $4 billion in 1985).[39] One of the leading warehouse clubs, Sam's, has added more services to encourage more warehouse shoppers to visit the store.

A second variation is the factory outlet store. These outlets, such as Van Heusen Factory Store, Bass Shoe Outlet, and Oneida Factory Store, offer products for 25 to 30 percent off the suggested retail price. Manufacturers use the stores to clear excess merchandise and to reach consumers who focus on value shopping. The number of factory outlet centers has increased from 183 in 1990 to 338, with sales of $13 billion, in 1995. Some experts expect the next trend to combine outlet stores, off-price retailers, and department store clearance centers in "value-retail centers."[40]

Store location   A second aspect of the retailing mix involves deciding where to locate the store and how many stores to have. Department stores, which started downtown in most cities, have followed customers to the suburbs, and in recent years more stores have been opened in large regional malls. Most stores today are near several others in one of five settings: the central business district, the regional center, the community shopping center, the strip, or the power center.

The **central business district** is the oldest retail setting, the community's downtown area. Until the regional outflow to suburbs, it was the major shopping area, but the suburban population has grown at the expense of the downtown shopping area. Detroit, experiencing a decade of population decline, lost its last major department store in 1982 when Hudson's left the central city.

Regional shopping centers are the suburban malls of today, containing up to 100 stores. The typical drawing distance of a regional center is 5 to 10 miles from the mall. These large shopping areas often contain two or three *anchor stores,* which are well-known national or regional stores such as Sears, Saks Fifth Avenue, and Bloomingdale's. The largest variation of a regional center is the West Edmonton Mall in Alberta, Canada. The shopping center is a conglomerate of 600 stores, six amusement centers, 110 restaurants, and a 355-room Fantasyland hotel.[41] The Marketing NewsNet on the following page discusses the changes many malls are making to attract customers.[42]

A more limited approach to retail location is the **community shopping center**, which typically has one primary store (usually a department store branch) and often about 20 to 40 smaller outlets. Generally, these centers serve a population base of about 100,000.

Not every suburban store is located in a shopping mall. Many neighborhoods have clusters of stores, referred to as a **strip location**, to serve people who are within a 5- to 10-minute drive and live in a population base of under 30,000. Gas station, hardware, laundry, and grocery outlets are commonly found in a strip location. Unlike the larger shopping centers, the composition of these stores is usually unplanned. A variation of the strip shopping location is called the **power center**, which is a huge shopping strip with multiple anchor (or national) stores. Power centers are seen as having the convenient location found in many strip centers and the additional power of national stores. These large strips often have two to five anchor stores and often contain a supermarket, which brings the shopper to the power center on a weekly basis.[43]

Several new types of retail locations include carts, kiosks, and wall units. These forms of retailing have been popular in airports and mall common areas because they

MARKETING NewsNet

Customer

$

Value

THERE IS MAGIC IN THE MALLS!

Have you noticed anything different about your favorite mall lately? Chances are you've seen a variety of changes from new stores to new store designs to entertainment. Why? Because malls are struggling to reinvent themselves and once again become primary shopping destinations for consumers. Some retailing experts believe that if malls don't make significant changes soon, as many as 300 of the 1800 regional shopping centers in the United States may soon be forced to close.

Two trends are responsible for the concern. First, consumers have become value shoppers and, therefore, are less likely to shop at what they perceive to be full-price retailers. Second, an increasingly important segment, Generation X is easily bored by traditional merchandise approaches—making long shopping trips unlikely. Department stores and chains such as the Limited and the Gap have been the first to feel the impact of these trends. Others are watching closely to see if a comeback is possible.

One approach being used to lure customers back is to change the mix of specialty stores in the mall to be more consistent with the needs of regional markets. Another approach is to create a store design that allows interactive merchandising. Oshman's sporting goods stores contain a skating rink, basketball court, and an in-line skating track so customers can try equipment prior to purchase. Similarly, large consumer electronics stores often include a listening bar and testing area.

The most widely used approach, however, is entertainment. Malls are trying to add value to the shopping experience with movies, video arcades, restaurants, bars, and even amusement parks. The most

elaborate example, The Forum Shops mall next to Caesars Palace in Las Vegas, offers a gallery of statues, upscale restaurants, fountains with robotic shows, and Roman processions. The success of malls that have already made some of these changes suggests that many consumers like the magic of the transformations. What about you?

provide consumers with easy access and rental income for the property owner. Retailers benefit from the relatively low cost compared with a regular store.

Retail image and atmosphere   Deciding on the image of a retail outlet is an important retailing mix factor that has been widely recognized and studied since the late 1950s. Pierre Martineau described image as "the way in which the store is defined in the shopper's mind," partly by its functional qualities and partly by an aura of psychological attributes.[44] In this definition, *functional* refers to mix elements such as price ranges, store layouts, and breadth and depth of merchandise lines. The psychological attributes are the intangibles such as a sense of belonging, excitement, style, or warmth. Image has been found to include impressions of the corporation that operates the store, the category or type of store, the product categories in the store, the brands in each category, merchandise and service quality, and the marketing activities of the store.[45]

Closely related to the concept of image is the store's atmosphere or ambiance. Many retailers believe that sales are affected by layout, color, lighting, and music in the store as well as by how crowded it is. In addition, the physical surroundings that influence customers may affect the store's employees.[46]

In creating the right image and atmosphere, a retail store tries to identify its target audience and what the target audience seeks from the buying experience so the store will fortify the beliefs and the emotional reactions buyers are seeking.[47] Sears, for example, is attempting to shift from its appliance and tool image by targeting middle-income women with its "Softer Side of Sears" campaign.[48]

CONCEPT CHECK

1. What are the two dimensions of the retail positioning matrix?

2. How does original markup differ from maintained markup?

3. A huge shopping strip with multiple anchor stores is a _____ center.

THE CHANGING NATURE OF RETAILING

Retailing is the most dynamic aspect of a channel of distribution. Stores such as factory outlets show that new retailers are always entering the market, searching for a new position that will attract customers. The reason for this continual change is explained by two concepts: the wheel of retailing and the retail life cycle.

The Wheel of Retailing

The **wheel of retailing** describes how new forms of retail outlets enter the market.[49] Usually they enter as low-status, low-margin stores such as a drive-in hamburger stand with no indoor seating and a limited menu (Figure 18–10, box 1). Gradually these outlets add fixtures and more embellishments to their stores (in-store seating, plants, and chicken sandwiches as well as hamburgers) to increase the attractiveness for customers. With these additions, prices and status rise (box 2). As time passes, these outlets add still more services and their prices and status increase even further (box 3). These retail outlets now face some new form of retail outlet that again appears as low-status, low-margin operator (box 4), and the wheel of retailing turns as the cycle starts to repeat itself.

In the 1950s, McDonald's and Burger King had very limited menus of hamburgers and french fries. Most stores had no inside seating for customers. Over time, the wheel of retailing for fast-food restaurants has turned. These chains have changed by altering their stores and expanding their menus. Today, McDonald's is testing new products such as pizza and pasta, new formats such as the McDonald's Cafe introduced in Maine, and new decor options such as the 50s-style store opened in Chicago. The changes are leaving room for new forms of outlets such as Checkers Drive-In Restaurants. The chain opened fast-food stores that offered only the basics—burgers, fries, and cola, a drive-through window, and no inside seating—and now has over 400 stores.[50] The wheel is turning for other outlets too—Boston Chicken has now become Boston Market as turkey, meat loaf, and ham have been added to the menu. For still others, the wheel has come full circle. Taco Bell is now

FIGURE 18–10

The wheel of retailing

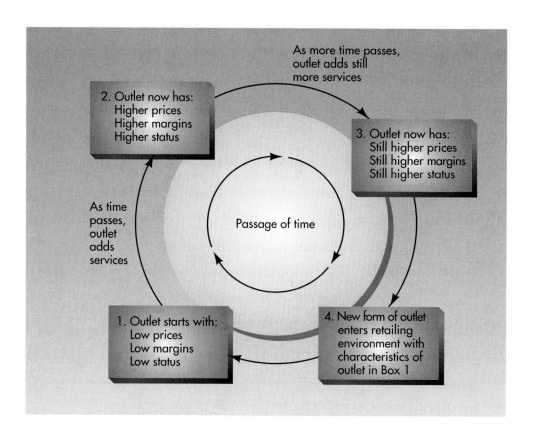

opening small, limited-offering outlets in gas stations, discount stores, or "wherever a burrito and a mouth might possibly intersect."[51]

Discount stores were a major new retailing form in the 1960s and priced their products below those of department stores. As prices in discount stores rose, in the 1980s they found themselves over-priced compared with a new form of retail outlet—the warehouse retailer. Today, off-price retailers and factory outlets are offering prices even lower than warehouses!

The Retail Life Cycle

The process of growth and decline that retail outlets, like products, experience is described by the **retail life cycle**.[52] Figure 18–11 shows the retail life cycle and the position of various current forms of retail outlets on it. Early growth is the stage of emergence of a retail outlet, with a sharp departure from existing competition. Market share rises gradually, although profits may be low because of startup costs. In the next stage, accelerated development, both market share and profit achieve their greatest growth rates. Usually multiple outlets are established as companies focus on the distribution element of the retailing mix. In this stage some later competitors may

FIGURE 18–11

The retail life cycle

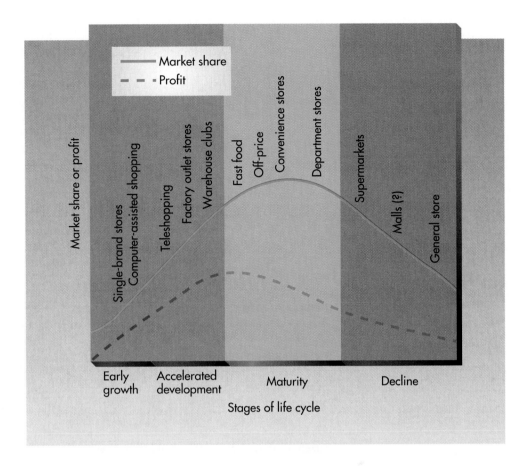

The retail life cycle diagram shows Market share (solid line) and Profit (dashed line) plotted against Stages of life cycle. The vertical axis is labeled "Market share or profit." The horizontal axis stages are: Early growth, Accelerated development, Maturity, and Decline.

Retail forms positioned along the curve: Single-brand stores, Computer-assisted shopping, Teleshopping, Factory outlet stores, Warehouse clubs, Fast food, Off-price, Convenience stores, Department stores, Supermarkets, Malls (?), General store.

enter. Wendy's, for example, appeared on the hamburger chain scene almost 20 years after McDonald's had begun operation. The key goal for the retailer in this stage is to establish a dominant position in the fight for market share.

The battle for market share is usually fought before the maturity phase, and some competitors drop out of the market. In the wars among hamburger chains, Jack In The Box, Gino Marchetti's, and Burger Chef used to be more dominant outlets. New retail forms enter in the maturity phase, stores try to maintain their market share, and price discounting occurs. In the early 1990s, major fast-food chains such as Wendy's and McDonald's began to aggressively discount their prices. McDonald's introduced its Extra Value Meal, a discounted package of burger, fries, and drink, while Wendy's followed with a kid's Value Menu.

The challenge facing retailers is to delay entering the decline stage in which market share and profit fall rapidly. Specialty apparel retailers, such as the Gap, Limited, Benetton, and Ann Taylor have noticed a decline in market share after a decade of growth. To prevent further decline, these retailers will need to find ways of discouraging their customers from moving to low-margin, mass-volume outlets or high-price, high-service boutiques.[53]

FUTURE CHANGES IN RETAILING

Three exciting trends in retailing—the increasing impact of technology, the dramatic changes in the way we shop, and the growing importance of brands—are likely to lead to many changes for retailers and consumers in the future.

The Impact of Technology

One of the most significant changes retailers may face in the future is the way consumers pay for purchases. It is already possible to travel through coinless tollbooths in California, ride on tokenless subways in New York City, Washington, D.C., and San Francisco, and pay mortgages with an electronic transfer of funds. In anticipation of a cashless society some retailers such as Safeway, Burger King, the *Philadelphia Inquirer*, and even some taxis in Manhattan are now accepting credit cards. While credit card transactions are currently only 9 percent of all purchases, they are expected to reach 15 percent by 2001.

Credit cards, however, are likely to be replaced by smart cards, which look the same as credit cards but store information on computer chips instead of magnetic strips. They will hold information about bank accounts and amounts of available funds, and they will contain customer purchase information such as airline seat preferences and clothing sizes. The idea is already popular in Europe and Asia where over 33 million smart cards are in use. Benefits for consumers include faster service—a smart card transaction is much faster than having a check or credit card approved—and they are a convenient method of paying for small dollar-amount transactions. Merchants will also benefit because they will save the 5 to 7 percent usually paid to credit card companies or lost in handling. Currently the absence of processing equipment is slowing the use of smart cards in the U.S. Recent investments by several companies are likely to help, however. Visa U.S.A., Inc., for example, launched a smart card at the Olympics and placed 5,000 terminals for their use throughout Atlanta. Similarly, U.S. West has equipped 16,000 pay phones in five cities for smart card use![54]

Changing Shopping Behavior

In recent years consumers have become precision shoppers. The number of stores consumers visit and the number of times they visit those stores each month is declining. Shoppers are demanding convenient hours and locations, outstanding service, and reasonable prices from retailers. As a result, familiar forms of retailers such as supermarkets, travel agencies, and car dealerships are likely to change or be replaced by new types of retailers. Byerly's, a supermarket chain expanding from Minneapolis to Chicago, offers rushed shoppers a wide variety of premium ready-to-eat entrees, in a carpeted store. TravelFest Superstores in Austin, Texas, offer one-stop shopping for travelers. Visa applications, traveler's checks, luggage, newspapers from around the world, and traditional tickets and reservations are available in the stores from 9 A.M. to 11 P.M. Even car dealers are changing. CarMax offers no-haggle pricing, an inventory of 500 to 1,000 cars, written offers on trade-in vehicles, guarantees and extended warranties, financing, and 1-hour transactions if a car is purchased.

Another response to the changes in consumers' preferences is a form of co-branding where two retailers share a location. For example, McDonald's has developed partnerships with Wal-Mart, Home Depot, Amoco, and Chevron that will lead to thousands of satellite outlets in the retail stores and gas stations. Starbucks Coffee Co. has opened cafes in over 100 Barnes & Noble bookstores. And KFC, which attracts a strong dinner crowd, will partner with Taco Bell, which is stronger in the lunch market, at 800 of its stores. Retailers hope that consumers will appreciate the convenience of the new locations.[55]

The Importance of Brands

The use of brands is also changing dramatically. Many retailers have developed their own private-label brands to increase customer loyalty. As a result, many manufacturers have opened their own stores. Single-brand, or company, stores such as the 68,000 square-foot Nike Town in Chicago allow manufacturers to display their entire

product line in a controlled "showcase." Other company stores include Speed Authentic Fitness Stores, Original Levi's Stores, OshKosh B'Gosh Stores, and Reebok Concept Stores. Many other manufacturers are showing interest in the concept.

Two of the most successful variations of the company store trend are the Disney and Warner studio stores. The 268 Disney stores and the 67 Warner stores market characters such as Mickey Mouse, Peter Pan, Bugs Bunny, and the Tasmanian Devil directly to the public. While both companies are fortunate to have several characters to promote, they have discovered that preferences vary throughout the world. In British stores, for example, Winnie the Pooh is the top seller, while Bambie and Thumper are preferred in France, and Mickey and Minnie are the first choices in Japan![56]

Most consumers associate strong brand names with specific products such as Coke or Tide, or particular companies such as Microsoft or Motorola. In the future, however, many large merchants will be trying to turn their store names into world brands. The changing role of products, stores, and manufacturers as popular, well-known brands is likely to generate many more changes in the dynamic practice of retailing!

CONCEPT CHECK

1. According to the wheel of retailing, when a new retail form appears, how would you characterize its image?

2. Market share is usually fought out before the _____ stage of the retail life cycle.

3. What is a smart card?

SUMMARY

1. Retailing provides a number of values to the consumer in the form of various utilities: time, place, possession, and form. Economically, retailing is important in terms of the people employed and money exchanged in retail sales.

2. Retailing outlets can be classified along several dimensions: the form of ownership, level of service, or merchandise line.

3. There are several forms of ownership: independent, chain, retailer-sponsored cooperative, wholesaler-sponsored chain or franchise.

4. Stores vary in the level of service, being self-service, limited service, or full service.

5. Retail outlets vary in terms of the breadth and depth of their merchandise lines. Breadth refers to the number of different items carried, and depth refers to the assortment of each item offered.

6. Nonstore retailing includes direct marketing, direct selling, and automatic vending. Direct marketing includes direct mail, telemarketing, and in-home shopping.

7. A retail store positions itself on two dimensions: breadth of product line and value added, which includes elements such as location, product reliability, and prestige.

8. Retailing strategy is based on the retailing mix, consisting of goods and services, physical distribution, and communication tactics.

9. In retail pricing, retailers must decide on the markup, markdown, and timing for the markdown. Off-price retailers offer brand-name merchandise at lower than regular prices. This retailing form is most common in the clothing industry.

10. Retail store location is an important retail mix decision. The common alternatives are the central business district, a regional shopping center, a community shopping center, or a strip location. A variation of the strip location is the power center, which is a strip location with multiple national anchor stores and a supermarket.

11. Retail image and atmosphere help retailers create the appropriate buying experience for their target market.

12. New retailing forms are explained by the wheel of retailing. Stores enter as low-status, low-margin outlets. Over time, they add services and raise margins, which allows a new form of low-status, low-margin retailing outlet to enter.

13. Like products, retail outlets have a life cycle consisting of four stages: early growth, accelerated development, maturity, and decline.

14. Technology will change the way consumers pay for purchases in the future. Smart cards may lead to a cashless society.

KEY TERMS AND CONCEPTS

retailing p. 470
form of ownership p. 472
level of service p. 472
merchandise line p. 472
depth of product line p. 475
breadth of product line p. 476
scrambled merchandising p. 476
hypermarket p. 476
intertype competition p. 477
telemarketing p. 478

retail positioning matrix p. 481
retailing mix p. 482
off-price retailing p. 484
central business district p. 485
regional shopping centers p. 485
community shopping center p. 485
strip location p. 485
power center p. 485
wheel of retailing p. 487
retail life cycle p. 488

CHAPTER PROBLEMS AND APPLICATIONS

1. Discuss the impact of the growing number of dual-income households on (*a*) nonstore retailing and (*b*) the retail mix.

2. How does value added affect a store's competitive position?

3. In retail pricing, retailers often have a maintained markup. Explain how this maintained markup differs from original markup and why it is so important.

4. What are the similarities and differences between the product and retail life cycles?

5. How would you classify Kmart in terms of its position on the wheel of retailing versus that of an off-price retailer?

6. Develop a chart to highlight the role of each of the three main elements of the retailing mix across the four stages of the retail life cycle.

7. In Figure 18–7 Kinney Shoes was placed on the retail positioning matrix. What strategies should Kinney follow to move itself into the same position as Tiffany?

8. Breadth and depth are two important components in distinguishing among types of retailers. Discuss the breadth and depth implications of the following retailers discussed in this chapter: (*a*) Levi Strauss, (*b*) Wal-Mart, (*c*) L. L Bean, and (*d*) Circuit City.

9. According to the wheel of retailing and the retail life cycle, what will happen to factory outlet stores?

10. The text discusses the development of television-assisted retailing and computer-assisted retailing in the United States. How does the development of each of these retailing forms agree with the implications of the retail life cycle?

CASE 18–1 Mall of America

Video

"Surely the most mighty and colossal and stupendous shopping and entertainment experience there ever was." In a different era these words might have been attributed to P. T. Barnum; today, however, they describe the Mall of America. The mall is the largest, fully enclosed combination retail and family entertainment complex in the United States—a one-stop destination designed to offer extensive guest services, convenience, family entertainment, and fun!

THE IDEA

The idea began with Canada's Ghermezian brothers who had built a similar mall in Edmonton, Alberta. They teamed up with Indianapolis-based Melvin and Herbert Simon who had built 202 shopping centers in the United States. Together they planned to design and build a mall that would attract people who wanted to shop and to be entertained. In fact, the Simons and Ghermezians hoped they could create a mall that would attract entire families for vacations!

THE MALL

Seven years later the Mall of America opened in Minneapolis, Minnesota, to more than 1 million eager visitors in its first week of operation. The size of the mall—4.2 million square feet—has been difficult for anyone to anticipate. Visitors find anchor stores Bloomingdale's, Macy's, Nordstrom, and Sears and hundreds of specialty stores surrounding a seven-acre entertainment theme park with more than 50 rides.

Other unique aspects of the mall include the following:

* The LEGO Imagination Center—a 6,000-square-foot showplace of LEGO models ranging from clowns to castles to dinosaurs.
* Recycle Now—an in-house recycling plant with displays explaining how recycling can impact the environment.
* Wilderness Theater—a "ranger station" that lets kids and adults learn about birds, mammals, insects, and reptiles through up-close experiences.
* Golf Mountain—a two-level, 18-hole miniature golf course lushly landscaped with seven waterfalls, two streams, trees, and plants.

In addition, the Mall of America has things you would find in other malls—but in larger quantities. For example, the Mall has 12,750 free parking spaces, 17 elevators, 44 escalators, a shuttle bus that runs to the airport every half hour, and 10,000 employees!

THE ISSUES

To ensure that the Mall of America would be a success, managers faced two huge challenges—to find hundreds of retailers to open stores in the mall and to attract more than 40 million visitors each year. Because many retailers were concerned about the uncertainties associated with the new mall, special rent incentives were offered to attract key stores. In addition, small outlets were offered assistance with store layout, lighting, and displays to reduce initial costs for new merchants and ensure that the general decor of the mall would be consistent.

The market for potential visitors was defined in terms of two groups—shoppers and tourists. Shoppers may include the 2.5 million residents of Minneapolis and St. Paul, Minnesota, the 4.8 million people who live within a 150-mile radius, and the 27 million people who live within 400 miles (a day's drive). Tourists were expected from the neighboring 11 states and 2 Canadian provinces. In addition, more than 2,500 bus tours from across the United States and 90 tour groups from Japan have visited the mall.

Mall of America managers are determined to continue its success by keeping current retailers happy, finding new retailers to open stores in the mall, and by maintaining the steady stream of shoppers and tourists. After all what could be more "mighty and colossal and stupendous" than the Mall of America!

Questions

1. What environmental factors suggest that the concept of a mall the size of the Mall of America would be successful? Unsuccessful?

2. What were the primary challenges facing managers as they designed and built the Mall of America?

3. Design a marketing campaign to obtain 40 million visitors to the Mall of America each year.

CHAPTER 19

Integrated Marketing Communications, Sales Promotion, and Public Relations

AFTER READING THIS CHAPTER YOU SHOULD BE ABLE TO:

• Explain the communication process and its elements.

• Understand the promotional mix and the uniqueness of each component.

• Select the promotional approach appropriate to a product's life-cycle stage and characteristics.

• Differentiate between the advantages of push and pull strategies.

• Understand the alternative strengths and weaknesses of consumer-oriented and trade-oriented sales promotions.

• Appreciate the value of an integrated marketing communications approach.

WHY IS JAMES BOND DRIVING A BMW?

Since 1963, in a series of 16 movies including box-office hits *Dr. No, You Only Live Twice, Diamonds Are Forever,* and *License to Kill,* James Bond, British secret agent 007, has driven his signature automobile—the sporty Aston-Martin. In the most recent Bond thriller, *Goldeneye,* however, Bond drives the new BMW Z3 roadster.

Why the switch after more than 30 years? Primarily because of a promotional agreement between movie studio Metro-Goldwyn-Mayer and automaker BMW. In exchange for the on-screen exposure, BMW promoted the film on TV, in car showrooms, and on airplanes. The agreement provided benefits for both partners: the marketing efforts reached new audiences and almost guaranteed the success of the movie, and BMW received more than 6,000 orders for the new automobile.

Other movies have also used brand-name products. It was Steven Speilberg's placement of Hershey's Reese's Pieces in *E.T.* that brought a lot of interest to the concept. Similarly, when Tom Cruise wore Bausch and Lomb's Ray-ban sunglasses in *Risky Business* and its Aviator sunglasses in *Top Gun*—and sales skyrocketed from 100,000 to 7,000,000 pairs in five years—the potential impact of "product placement" was recognized. You might remember that Tom Hanks received a pair of Nike running shoes in *Forrest Gump,* Clint Eastwood and Rene Russo ate Breyer's Ice Cream in *In the Line of Fire,* and Nicholas Cage and Bridget Fonda wore Rollerblade in-line skates in *It Could Happen to You.* In *Ace Ventura: When Nature Calls,* Jim Carey passes a Subway billboard while driving through Africa.

It's not just movies, though. Other outlets include music videos, televisions shows, game shows, and even other companies' commercials. NBC's top-rated "Seinfeld" has included Junior Mints, Snapple, Colombo frozen yogurt, Rold Gold pretzels, and diet Coke in its episodes. "Baywatch" receives Adidas shoes and Speedo swimsuits that are often used on the program. "Home Improvement" actors have modeled Logo Athletic jackets, and "ER" actors use Compaq computers. Mazda recently placed a Miata in a Chevron ad.[1]

Placement of products in the many media alternatives available today is becoming an important part of marketing and promotion. Applications of the technique demonstrate the importance of creativity in communicating with potential customers. In addition, to ensure that a consistent message is delivered through product placement and all promotional activities, a process that integrates marketing communications is a necessity.

Promotion represents the fourth element in the marketing mix. The promotional element comprises a mix of tools available for the marketer called the *promotional mix,* which consists of advertising, personal selling, sales promotion, and public relations. All of these elements can be used to (1) inform prospective buyers about the benefits of the product, (2) persuade them to try it, and (3) remind them later about the benefits they enjoyed by using the product. This chapter first gives an overview of the communication process and the promotional elements used in marketing and then discusses sales promotion and public relations. Chapter 20 covers advertising, and Chapter 21 discusses personal selling.

THE COMMUNICATION PROCESS

Communication is the process of conveying a message to others and requires six elements: a source, a message, a channel of communication, a receiver, and the processes of encoding and decoding[2] (Figure 19–1). The **source** may be a company or person who has information to convey. The information sent by a source, such as a description of a new weight reduction drink, forms the **message.** The message is conveyed by means of a **channel of communication** such as a salesperson, advertising media, or public relations tools. Consumers who read, hear, or see the message are the **receivers.**

FIGURE 19–1

The communication process

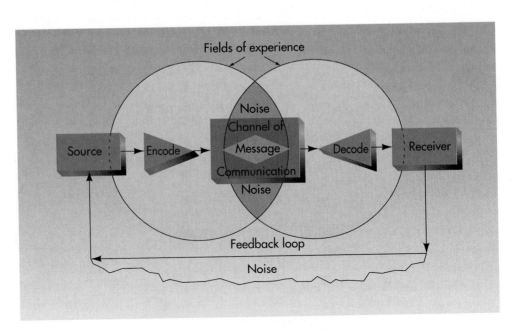

Encoding and Decoding

Encoding and decoding are essential to communication. **Encoding** is the process of having the sender transform an abstract idea into a set of symbols. **Decoding** is the reverse, or the process of having the receiver take a set of symbols, the message, and transform them back to an abstract idea. Look at the accompanying automobile advertisement: who is the source, and what is the message?

Decoding is performed by the receivers according to their own frame of reference: their attitudes, values, and beliefs.[3] In the ad, Lexus is the source and the message is this advertisement, which appeared in *Forbes* magazine (the channel). How would you interpret (decode) this advertisement? The picture and text in the advertisement show that the source's intention is to introduce a unique product and to position Lexus as a company in "the relentless pursuit of perfection"—a position the source believes will appeal to the upper-income readers of the magazine.

The process of communication is not always a successful one. Errors in communication can happen in several ways. The source may not adequately transform the abstract idea into an effective set of symbols, a properly encoded message may be sent through the wrong channel and never make it to the receiver, the receiver may not properly transform the set of symbols into the correct abstract idea, or finally, feedback may be so delayed or distorted that it is of no use to the sender. Although communication appears easy to perform, truly effective communication can be very difficult.

For the message to be communicated effectively, the sender and receiver must have a mutually shared **field of experience**—similar understanding and knowledge. Figure 19–1 shows two circles representing the fields of experience of the

A source and a message.

sender and receiver, which overlap in the message. Some of the better-known communication problems have occurred when U.S. companies have taken their messages to cultures with different fields of experience. Many misinterpretations are merely the result of bad translations. For example, General Motors made a mistake when its "Body by Fisher" claim was translated into Flemish as "Corpse by Fisher."[4]

Feedback

Figure 19–1 shows a line labeled *feedback loop*. **Feedback** is the communication flow from receiver back to sender and indicates whether the message was decoded and understood as intended. Chapter 20 reviews approaches called *pretesting* that ensure that advertisements are decoded properly.

Noise

Noise includes extraneous factors that can work against effective communication by distorting a message or the feedback received (Figure 19–1). Noise can be a simple error, such as a printing mistake that affects the meaning of a newspaper advertisement, or using words or pictures that fail to communicate the message clearly. Noise can also occur when a salesperson's message is misunderstood by a prospective buyer, such as when a salesperson's accent, use of slang terms, or communication style make hearing and understanding the message difficult.

CONCEPT CHECK

1. What are the six elements required for communication to occur?

2. A difficulty for U.S. companies advertising in international markets is that the audience does not share the same _____ .

3. A misprint in a newspaper ad is an example of _____ .

THE PROMOTIONAL ELEMENTS

To communicate with consumers, a company can use one or more of four promotional alternatives: advertising, personal selling, sales promotion, and public relations. Figure 19–2 summarizes the distinctions among these four elements. Three of these elements—advertising, sales promotion, and public relations—are often said to use *mass selling* because they are used with groups of prospective buyers. In contrast, personal selling uses *person-to-person interaction* between a seller and a prospective buyer. Personal selling activities include face-to-face, telephone, and interactive electronic communication.

Advertising

Advertising is any paid form of nonpersonal communication about an organization, good, service, or idea by an identified sponsor. The *paid* aspect of this definition is important because the space for the advertising message normally must be bought. An occasional exception is the public service announcement, where the advertising time or space is donated. A full-page, four-color ad in *Time* magazine, for example, costs $156,000. The *nonpersonal* component of advertising is also important. Advertising involves mass media (such as TV, radio, and magazines), which are

FIGURE 19-2

The promotional mix

PROMOTIONAL ELEMENT	MASS VERSUS PERSON-TO-PERSON	PAYMENT	STRENGTHS	WEAKNESSES
Advertising	Mass	Fees paid for space or time	• Efficient means for reaching large numbers of people	• High absolute costs • Difficult to receive good feedback
Personal selling	Person-to-person	Fees paid to salespeople as either salaries or commissions	• Immediate feedback • Very persuasive • Can select audience • Can give complex information	• Extremely expensive per exposure • Messages may differ between salespeople
Public relations	Mass	No direct payment to media	• Often most credible source in the consumer's mind	• Difficult to get media cooperation
Sales promotion	Mass	Wide range of fees paid, depending on promotion selected	• Effective at changing behavior in short run • Very flexible	• Easily abused • Can lead to promotion wars • Easily duplicated

nonpersonal and do not have an immediate feedback loop as does personal selling. So before the message is sent, marketing research plays a valuable role; for example, it determines that the message is understood by the target market and that the target market will actually see the medium chosen.

An attention-getting advertisement.

There are several advantages to a firm using advertising in its promotional mix. It can be attention-getting—as with this Eastpak ad—and also communicate specific product benefits to prospective buyers. By paying for the advertising space, a company can control *what* it wants to say and, to some extent, to *whom* the message is sent. If a stereo company wants college students to receive its message about CD players, advertising space is purchased in a college campus newspaper. Advertising also allows the company to decide *when* to send its message (which includes how often). The nonpersonal aspect of advertising also has its advantages. Once the message is created, the same message is sent to all receivers in a market segment. If the message is properly pretested, the company can trust that the same message will be decoded by all receivers in the market segment.

Advertising has some disadvantages. As shown in Figure 19–2 and discussed in depth in Chapter 20, the costs to produce and place a message are significant, and the lack of direct feedback makes it difficult to know how well the message was received.

Personal Selling

The second major promotional alternative is **personal selling,** defined as the two-way flow of communication between a buyer and seller, designed to influence a person's or group's purchase decision. Unlike advertising, personal selling is usually face-to-face communication between the sender and receiver (although telephone and electronic sales are growing). Why do companies use personal selling?

There are important advantages to personal selling, as summarized in Figure 19–2. A salesperson can control to *whom* the presentation is made. Although some control is available in advertising by choosing the medium, some people may read the college newspaper, for example, who are not in the target audience for CD players. For the CD-player manufacturer, those readers outside the target audience are *wasted coverage.* Wasted coverage can be reduced with personal selling. The personal component of selling has another advantage over advertising in that the seller can see or hear the potential buyer's reaction to the message. If the feedback is unfavorable, the salesperson can modify the message.

The flexibility of personal selling can also be a disadvantage. Different salespeople can change the message so that no consistent communication is given to all customers. The high cost of personal selling is probably its major disadvantage. On a cost-per-contact basis, it is generally the most expensive of the four promotional elements.

Public Relations

Public relations is a form of communication management that seeks to influence the feelings, opinions, or beliefs held by customers, prospective customers, stockholders, suppliers, employees, and other publics about a company and its products or services.[5] Many tools such as special events, lobbying efforts, annual reports, and image management may be used by a public relations department, although publicity often plays the most important role. **Publicity** is a nonpersonal, indirectly paid presentation of an organization, good, or service. It can take the form of a news story, editorial, or product announcement. A difference between publicity and both advertising and personal selling is the "indirectly paid" dimension. With publicity a company does not pay for space in a mass medium (such as television or radio) but attempts to get the medium to run a favorable story on the company. In this sense there is an indirect payment for publicity in that a company must support a public relations staff.

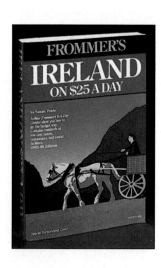

An advantage of publicity is credibility. When you read a favorable story about a company's product (such as a glowing restaurant review), there is a tendency to believe it. Travelers throughout the world have relied on Arthur Frommer's guides such as *Ireland on $25 a Day.* These books outline out-of-the-way, inexpensive restaurants, hotels, inns, and bed-and-breakfast rooms, giving invaluable publicity to these establishments. Such businesses do not (nor can they) buy a mention in the guide, which in recent years has sold millions of copies.

The disadvantages of publicity relate to the lack of the user's control over it. A company can invite a news team to preview its innovative exercise equipment and hope for a favorable mention on the 6 P.M. newscasts. But without buying advertising time, there is no guarantee of any mention of the new equipment or that it will be aired when the target audience is watching. The company representative who calls the station and asks for a replay of the story may be told, "Sorry, it's only news once." With publicity there is little control over what is said, to whom, or when. As a result, publicity is rarely the main component of a promotional campaign.

Sales Promotion

A fourth promotional element is **sales promotion,** a short-term inducement of value offered to arouse interest in buying a good or service. Used in conjunction with advertising or personal selling, sales promotions are offered to intermediaries as well as to ultimate consumers. Coupons, rebates, samples, and sweepstakes are just a few examples of sales promotions discussed later in this chapter.

The advantage of sales promotion is that the short-term nature of these programs (such as a coupon or sweepstakes with an expiration date) often stimulates sales for their duration. Offering value to the consumer in terms of a cents-off coupon or rebate provides an incentive to buy.

Sales promotions cannot be the sole basis for a campaign because gains are often temporary and sales drop off when the deal ends.[6] Advertising support is needed to convert the customer who tried the product because of a sales promotion into a long-term buyer.[7] If sales promotions are conducted continuously, they lose their effectiveness. Customers begin to delay purchase until a coupon is offered, or they question the product's value. Some aspects of sales promotions also are regulated by the federal government. These issues are reviewed in detail later in this chapter.

CONCEPT CHECK

1. Explain the difference between advertising and publicity when both appear on television.

2. Which promotional element should be offered only on a short-term basis?

3. Cost per contact is high with the _____ element of the promotional mix.

INTEGRATED MARKETING COMMUNICATIONS—DEVELOPING THE PROMOTIONAL MIX

A firm's **promotional mix** is the combination of one or more of the promotional elements it chooses to use. In putting together the promotional mix, a marketer must consider several issues. First, the balance of the elements must be determined. Should advertising be emphasized more than personal selling? Should a promotional rebate be offered? Would public relations activities be effective? Several factors affect such decisions: the target audience for the promotion,[8] the stage of the product's life cycle, characteristics of the product, decision stage of the buyer, and even the channel of distribution. Second, because the various promotional elements are often the responsibility of different departments, coordinating a consistent promotional effort is necessary. A promotional planning process designed to ensure integrated marketing communications can facilitate this goal.

The Target Audience

Promotional programs are directed to the ultimate consumer, to an intermediary (retailer, wholesaler, or industrial distributor), or to both. Promotional programs directed to buyers of consumer products use mass media. Geographical dispersion and the number of potential buyers are the primary reasons for a mass approach. Personal selling is used at the place of purchase, generally the retail store.

Advertising directed to industrial buyers is used selectively in trade publications, such as *Fence* magazine for buyers of fencing material. Because industrial buyers often have specialized needs or technical questions, personal selling is particularly important. The salesperson can provide information and the necessary support after sales.

Intermediaries are often the focus of promotional efforts. As with industrial buyers, personal selling is the major promotional ingredient. The salespeople inform retailers about future advertising campaigns directed at ultimate users, for example, and they assist retailers in making a profit. Intermediaries' questions often pertain to the allowed markup, merchandising support, and return policies, which are best handled by a salesperson.

The Product Life Cycle

Purina Puppy Chow: a product in the maturity stage of its life cycle.

All products have a product life cycle (see Chapter 12), and the composition of the promotional mix changes over the four life-cycle stages, as shown for Purina Puppy Chow in Figure 19–3.

Introduction stage   Informing consumers in an effort to increase their level of awareness is the primary promotional objective in the introduction stage of the product life cycle. In general, all the promotional mix elements are used at this time, although the use of specific mix elements during any stage depends on the product and situation. Stories on Purina's new nutritional food are placed in *Dog World* magazine, trial samples are sent to registered dog owners in 10 major cities, advertisements are placed during reruns of the TV show "Lassie," and the salesforce begins to approach supermarkets to get orders. Advertising is particularly important as a means of reaching as many people as possible to build up awareness and interest. Publicity may even begin slightly before the product is commercially available.

Growth stage   The primary promotional objective of the growth stage is to persuade the consumer to buy the product—Purina Puppy Chow—rather than substitutes, so the marketing manager seeks to gain brand preference and solidify distribution. Sales promotion assumes less importance in this stage, and publicity is not a factor because it depends on novelty of the product. The primary promotional element is advertising, which stresses brand differences. Personal selling is used to

FIGURE 19–3

Promotional tools used over the product life cycle of Purina Puppy Chow

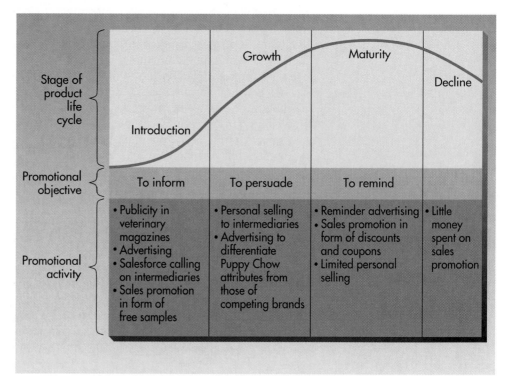

solidify the channel of distribution. For consumer products such as dog food, the salesforce calls on the wholesalers and retailers in hopes of increasing inventory levels and gaining shelf space. For industrial products, the salesforce often tries to get contractual arrangements to be the sole source of supply for the buyer.

Maturity stage   In the maturity stage the need is to maintain existing buyers, and advertising's role is to remind buyers of the product's existence. Sales promotion, in the form of discounts and coupons offered to both ultimate consumers and intermediaries, is important in maintaining loyal buyers. In a test of one mature consumer product, it was found that 80 percent of the product's sales at this stage resulted from sales promotions.[9] Price cuts and discounts can also significantly increase a mature brand's sales. The salesforce at this stage seeks to satisfy intermediaries. An unsatisfied customer who switches brands is hard to replace.

Decline stage   The decline stage of the product life cycle is usually a period of phaseout for the product, and little money is spent in the promotional mix—especially in sales promotions.

Product Characteristics

The proper blend of elements in the promotional mix also depends on the type of product. Three specific characteristics should be considered: complexity, risk, and ancillary services. *Complexity* refers to the technical sophistication of the product and hence the amount of understanding required to use it. It's hard to provide much

IBM must consider product characteristics such as complexity, risk, and ancillary services when designing its promotional mix.

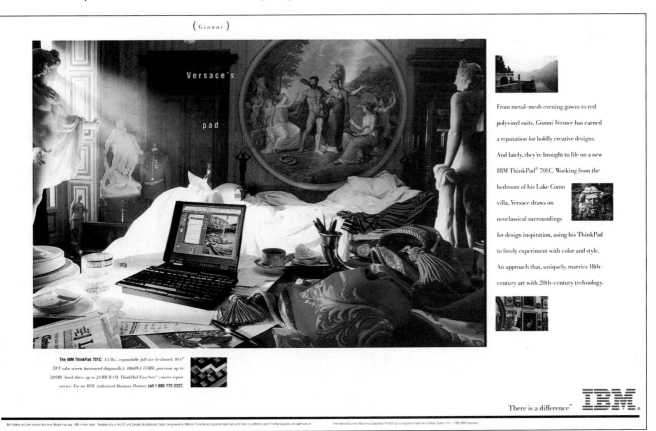

information in a one-page magazine ad or 30-second television ad, so the more complex the product, the greater the emphasis on personal selling.

A second element is the degree of *risk* represented by the product's purchase. Risk for the buyer can be assessed in terms of financial risk, social risk, and physical risk. A hair transplant procedure, for example, might represent all three risks—it may be expensive, people can see and evaluate the purchase, and there may be a chance of physical harm. Although advertising helps, the greater the risk, the greater the need for personal selling.

The level of *ancillary services* required by a product also affects the promotional strategy. Ancillary services pertain to the degree of service or support required after the sale. This characteristic is common to many industrial products and consumer purchases. Who will repair your automobile or VCR? Advertising's role is to establish the seller's reputation. However, personal selling is essential to build buyer confidence and provide evidence of customer service.

Stages of the Buying Decision

Knowing the customer's stage of decision making can also affect the promotional mix. Figure 19–4 shows how the importance of the three directly paid promotional elements varies with the three stages in a consumer's purchase decision.

Prepurchase stage In the prepurchase stage advertising is more helpful than personal selling because advertising informs the potential customer of the existence of the product and the seller. Sales promotion in the form of free samples also can play an important role to gain low-risk trial. When the salesperson calls on the customer after heavy advertising, there is some recognition of what the salesperson represents. This is particularly important in industrial settings in which sampling of the product is usually not possible.

Purchase stage At the purchase stage the importance of personal selling is highest, whereas the impact of advertising is lowest. Sales promotion in the form of coupons, deals, point-of-purchase displays, and rebates can be very helpful in

FIGURE 19–4

How the importance of three promotional elements varies during the consumer's purchase decision

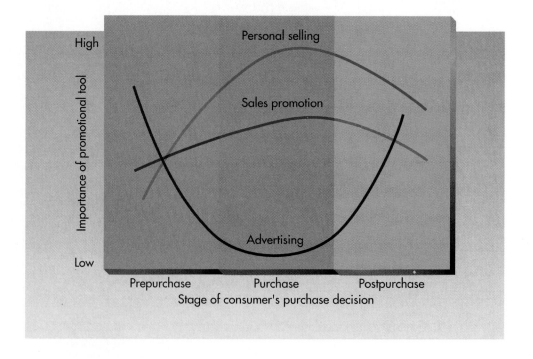

encouraging demand. In this stage, although advertising is not an active influence on the purchase, it is the means of delivering the coupons, deals, and rebates that are often important.

Postpurchase stage   In the postpurchase stage the salesperson is still important. In fact, the more personal contact after the sale, the more the buyer is satisfied. Advertising is also important to assure the buyer that the right purchase was made. Advertising and personal selling help reduce the buyer's postpurchase anxiety.[10] Sales promotion in the form of coupons can help encourage repeat purchases from satisfied first-time triers.

Channel Strategies

Chapter 16 discussed the channel flow from producer to intermediaries to consumer. Achieving control of the channel is often difficult for the manufacturer, and promotional strategies can assist in moving a product through the channel of distribution. This is where a manufacturer has to make an important decision about whether to use a push strategy, pull strategy, or both in its channel of distribution.[11]

Push strategy   Figure 19–5A shows how a manufacturer uses a **push strategy,** directing the promotional mix to channel members to gain their cooperation in ordering and stocking the product. In this approach, personal selling and sales promotions play major roles. Salespeople call on wholesalers to encourage orders and provide sales assistance. Sales promotions, such as case discount allowances (20 percent off the regular case price), are offered to stimulate demand. By pushing the product through the channel, the goal is to get channel members to push it to their customers.

Anheuser-Busch, for example, spends a significant amount of its marketing resources on maintaining its relationship with its distributors, and through them, with retailers. At a recent meeting of its wholesalers and salespeople, Anheuser-Busch

FIGURE 19–5

A comparison of push and pull promotional strategies

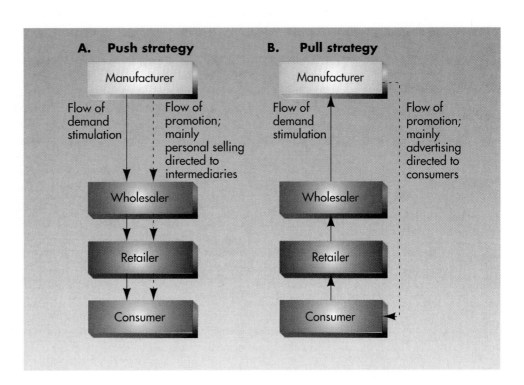

announced that it would provide $250 million of marketing support for its Budweiser brand—an action designed to maintain channel dominance. The company also arranges group discounts on purchase of trucks, insurance, and the computers that wholesalers use to order beer. Even specialized computer software is provided to help retailers maximize the shelf space of Anheuser-Busch products.[12]

"It's a patch. Ask your doctor about it."

NICODERM
(nicotine transdermal system)

Pull strategy In some instances manufacturers face resistance from channel members who do not want to order a new product or increase inventory levels of an existing brand. As shown in Figure 19–5B, a manufacturer may then elect to implement a **pull strategy** by directing its promotional mix at ultimate consumers to encourage them to ask the retailer for the product. Seeing demand from ultimate consumers, retailers order the product from wholesalers and thus the item is pulled through the intermediaries. Pharmaceutical companies, for example, historically marketed only to doctors. This year they spent more than $200 million to advertise prescription drugs directly to consumers. The strategy is designed to encourage consumers to ask their physicians for a specific drug by name—pulling it through the channel. Successful advertising strategies, such as Nicoderm's "Ask your doctor . . ." campaign, can have dramatic effects on the sales of a product.[13]

Integrated Marketing Communications

In the past the promotional elements were regarded as separate functions handled by experts in separate departments. The salesforce designed and managed its activities independently of the advertising department, and sales promotion and public relations were often the responsibility of outside agencies or specialists. The result was often an overall communication effort that was uncoordinated and, in some cases, inconsistent. Dairy Queen, for example, was left with unused inventory of a summertime premium when the movie *Radio Flyer,* which contained a product placement of the premium, was released late and other promotion elements did not support the giveaway.[14] Today the concept of designing marketing communications programs that coordinate all promotional activities—advertising, personal selling, sales promotion, and public relations—to provide a consistent message across all audiences is referred to as **integrated marketing communications** (IMC).

The key to developing successful IMC programs is to create a process that facilitates their design and use. A tool used to evaluate a company's current process is the IMC audit. The audit analyzes the internal communication network of the company, identifies key audiences, evaluates customer databases, assesses messages in recent ads, public relations releases, packaging, video news releases, signage, sales promotion pieces, and direct mail and determines managers' knowledge of IMC.[15] While many organizations are interested in improving their IMC process, a recent survey suggests that fewer than one third have been successful at implementing IMC. The reasons include lack of expertise, lack of budget, and lack of management approval.[16]

Once the IMC process is implemented, most organizations want to assess its benefits. The tendency is to try to determine which element of promotion "works" better. In an integrated program, however, media advertising might be used to build awareness, sales promotion to generate an inquiry, direct mail to provide additional information to individual prospects, and a personal sales call to complete the transaction. The tools are used for different reasons, and their combined use creates a synergy that should be the focus of the assessment.[17] The accompanying Marketing NewsNet box describes some of the many promotional activities Sega integrated to pass Nintendo as the leading maker of videogames.[18]

MARKETING NEWSNET

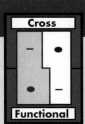

IMC HAS SEGA SCREAMING

In recent years Sega has overtaken rival Nintendo as the top selling brand in the $6 billion videogame industry. Much of the company's success is due to its extraordinary integrated marketing communications program—an effort that earned Sega *Advertising Age*'s Promotional Marketer of the Year Award. The campaign began with a TV commercial featuring a loud voiceover of the word "Sega," which soon had children and adults nationwide doing "the Sega scream." Sega followed the advertising with a variety of integrated promotions, including the following:

- An on-line contest allowing users to download Sega President Tom Kalinski's scream and to upload to Sega their best version of the scream.
- A 50-campus merchandise sampling and testing event organized by students.
- Sponsorship of Sports Byline USA.
- Introduction of the Sega Channel on cable television.
- An exclusive agreement with CompuServe on-line service.
- Establishment of an Internet site.
- A national contest involving hundreds of thousands of videogame players. Finalists were flown to San

Francisco's Alcatraz Prison for a face-off television by MTV!

Sega even arranged for special limited-time Lifesavers flavors to promote its Sega Genesis and Sonic 3 products. Tom Abramson, vice president of marketing at Sega, describes their approach: "Advertising sets the stage for our attitude and gets us into the heads of our consumers, but we use promotions and events to get Sega into the hands of consumers every day."

CONCEPT CHECK

1. For consumer products, why is advertising emphasized more than personal selling?

2. Explain the differences between a push strategy and a pull strategy.

3. Integrated marketing communications programs provide a _____ message across all audiences.

SALES PROMOTION

The Importance of Sales Promotion

Sales promotion is a supplemental ingredient of the promotional mix and is not as visible as advertising, but more than $200 billion is spent annually on it. As shown in Figure 19–6, during the 1980s there was a major shift of dollars from media advertising to trade and consumer promotion. By 1993 about 75 percent of these expenditures were for trade and consumer promotion.[19] More recently, however, promotion expenditures shifted as an increasing share of promotion budgets was allocated to

FIGURE 19-6

Trends in expenditures for media advertising, trade promotion, and consumer promotion

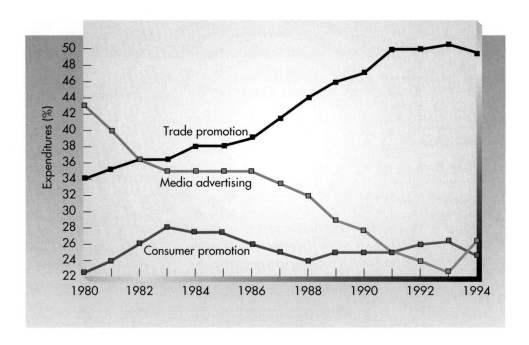

media advertising. The shift indicates a trend toward integrated, consumer-oriented advertising and promotion programs and away from traditional trade promotion. Selection and integration of the many promotion techniques requires a good understanding of the advantages and disadvantages of each kind of promotion.[20]

Consumer-Oriented Sales Promotions

Directed to ultimate consumers, **consumer-oriented sales promotions,** or simply consumer promotions, are sales tools used to support a company's advertising and personal selling. The alternative consumer-oriented sales promotion tools include coupons, deals, premiums, contests, sweepstakes, samples, continuity programs, point-of-purchase displays, rebates, and product placement (see Figure 19-7).

Coupons   Coupons are sales promotions that usually offer a discounted price to the consumer, which encourages trial. Approximately 320 billion coupons are distributed in the United States each year. In 1994, the face value of distributed coupons was about $211 billion, and the total value of redeemed coupons was $4.3 billion.[21]

Do coupons help increase sales? Studies suggest that market share does increase during the period immediately after coupons are distributed.[22] There are also indications, however, that couponing can reduce gross revenues by lowering the price paid by already-loyal consumers.[23] Therefore, the 9,000 manufacturers who currently use coupons are particularly interested in coupon programs directed at potential first-time buyers. One means of focusing on these potential buyers is through electronic in-store coupon machines that match coupons to your most recent purchases.[24]

Coupons are often far more expensive than the face value of the coupon; a 25¢ coupon can cost three times that after paying for the advertisement to deliver it, dealer handling, clearinghouse costs, and redemption. In addition, misredemption, or paying the face value of the coupon even though product was not purchased, should be added to the cost of the coupon. See the accompanying Ethics and Social Responsibility Alert for additional information about misredemption.[25]

Deals   Deals are short-term price reductions, commonly used to increase trial among potential customers or to retaliate against a competitor's actions. For example,

ETHICS AND SOCIAL RESPONSIBILITY ALERT

COUPON SCAMS COST MANUFACTURERS $800 MILLION EACH YEAR

Coupon fraud has become a serious concern for consumer goods manufacturers. How serious? The Coupon Information Center estimates that companies pay out coupon refunds of more than $800 million a year to retailers and individuals who don't deserve them. That adds a huge cost to promotions designed to help consumers.

The methods used by the cheaters are becoming very sophisticated. For example:

- Some scam artists set up a fake store and send coupons to manufacturers for payment.
- Coupon collectors often sell coupons by the pound to retailers who are paid full face value by manufacturers, even though the products were not sold.

- Retailers increase their refunds by adding extra coupons to those handed in by shoppers.
- Counterfeiters print rebate forms and proofs of purchase to collect big cash rebates without buying the products.

Other methods range from the use of high-tech color copying machines to simply running coupons through the washing machine to give them a handled look.

Some of the steps being taken to reduce coupon and rebate fraud include requiring handwritten redemption requests, printing coupons and forms in at least two colors, keeping expiration dates short, and requiring proof of purchase.

What are your reactions to misredemption? Should actions be taken against coupon fraud?

---

if a rival manufacturer introduces a new cake mix, the company responds with a "two packages for the price of one" deal. This short-term price reduction builds up the stock on the kitchen shelves of cake mix buyers and makes the competitor's introduction more difficult.

Premiums A promotional tool often used with consumers is the premium, which consists of merchandise offered free or at a significant savings over retail. This latter type of premium is called *self-liquidating* because the cost charged to the consumer covers the cost of the item. Burger King, for example, gave away more than 50

Friday's and Hertz attract prospective customers with coupons.

KIND OF SALES PROMOTION	OBJECTIVES	ADVANTAGES	DISADVANTAGES
Coupons	Stimulate demand	Encourage retailer support	Consumers delay purchases
Deals	Increase trial; retaliate against competitor's actions	Reduce consumer risk	Consumers delay purchases; reduce perceived product value
Premiums	Build goodwill	Consumers like free or reduced-price merchandise	Consumers buy for premium, not product
Contests	Increase consumer purchases; build business inventory	Encourage consumer involvement with product	Require creative or analytical thinking
Sweepstakes	Encourage present customers to buy more; minimize brand switching	Get customer to use product and store more often	Sales drop after sweepstakes
Samples	Encourage new product trial	Low risk for consumer	High cost for company
Continuity programs	Encourage repeat purchases	Help create loyalty	High cost for company
Point-of-purchase displays	Increase product trial; provide in-store support for other promotions	Provide good product visibility	Hard to get retailer to allocate high-traffic space
Rebates	Encourage customers to purchase; stop sales decline	Effective at stimulating demand	Easily copied; steal sales from future; reduce perceived product value
Product placement	Introduce new products; demonstrate product use	Positive message in a noncommercial setting	Little control over presentation of product

FIGURE 19–7

Sales promotion alternatives

million collectible toys resembling characters in Disney's movie *The Lion King*. Procter & Gamble proved that premiums do not have to be inexpensive when it offered an O-gauge model train set for $79.95 and three proofs of purchase from any of six P&G brands.[26] By offering a premium, companies encourage customers to return frequently or to use more of the product.

Contests   A fourth sales promotion in Figure 19–7, the contest, is where consumers apply their analytical or creative thinking to try to win a prize. For example, McDonald's and the United States Postal Service cosponsored a contest that asked children to design stamps that reflected environmental awareness. Despite a complex set of rules, 150,000 kids ages 8 to 13 submitted entries. Today the designs of four winners are available on actual postage stamps.[27]

Sweepstakes   *Reader's Digest* and Publisher's Clearing House are two of the better-promoted sweepstakes. These sales promotions require participants to submit some kind of entry form but are purely games of chance requiring no analytical or creative effort by the consumer. In October 1969 the Federal Trade Commission issued trade rules covering sweepstakes, contests, and games to regulate their fairness, ensure that the chance for winning is represented honestly, and guarantee that the prizes are actually awarded.[28]

Samples   Another common consumer sales promotion is sampling, which is offering the product free or at a greatly reduced price. Often used for new products, sampling puts the product in the consumer's hands. A trial size is generally offered that is smaller than the regular package size. If consumers like the sample, it is hoped they will remember and buy the product. Taco Bell, for example, recently introduced its new low-fat Border Lights fare by giving away 8 million free tacos and burritos in one day. While the samples cost between $8 million and $12 million, Taco Bell reports that consumers returned to purchase more than $800 million worth of Border Lights in the six months following the promotion. Overall, companies invest more than $700 million in sampling programs each year.[29]

Continuity programs   Continuity programs are a sales promotion tool used to encourage and reward repeat purchases by acknowledging each purchase made by a consumer and offering a premium as purchases accumulate. Trading stamps, which were first used by supermarkets and gas stations in the 1960s and 1970s, are an example. More recently airlines and hotels have used frequent-flyer and frequent-traveler programs to reward loyal customers. Chart House Enterprises, a 34-year-old chain of 65 restaurants, recently launched a frequent-diner program that allows members to earn "points" toward dining certificates for every dollar they spend. In addition, members who dine at all 65 Chart House restaurants earn a pair of round-the-world airline tickets.[30] Even GM has a continuity program—a credit card that allows consumers to accumulate up to $3,500 in "points" toward the purchase of a new Chevrolet, Pontiac, Oldsmobile, Buick, or Cadillac.[31]

Point-of-purchase displays   In a store aisle, you often encounter a sales promotion called a *point-of-purchase display*. These product displays take the form of advertising signs, which sometimes actually hold or display the product, and are

Taco Bell used free samples to introduce its new low-fat products.

A gravity-feed bin that doubles as a point-of-purchase display.

often located in high-traffic areas near the cash register or the end of an aisle. The accompanying picture shows gravity-feed bins that Nabisco uses for its animal crackers; it helps ensure product freshness, provides storage, and captures the consumer's attention as an end-aisle, point-of-purchase display.[32] A recent survey of retailers found that 87 percent plan to use more point-of-purchase materials in the future, particularly for products that can be purchased on impulse.[33]

Some studies estimate that two thirds of a consumer's buying decisions are made in the store. This means that grocery product manufacturers want to get their message to you at the instant you are next to their brand in your supermarket aisle—perhaps through a point-of-purchase display. At many supermarkets this may be done through Actmedia's in-store marketing network. Supermarket shopping cart displays, video screens in the aisles, and audio messages remind shoppers about products they might consider buying. The advantage of these methods of promotion is that they do not rely on the consumers' ability to remember the message for long periods of time. Other in-store promotions such as interactive kiosks are also becoming popular.[34]

Rebates   Another consumer sales promotion in Figure 19–7, the cash rebate, offers the return of money based on proof of purchase. This tool has been used heavily by car manufacturers facing increased competition. Turner Home Entertainment offered purchasers of its home video *The Swan Princess,* a $5 rebate through a collaborative agreement, or *tie-in,* with Pillsbury, which printed the offer on 20 million packages.[35] When the rebate is offered on lower-priced items, the time and trouble of mailing in a proof-of-purchase to get the rebate check means that many buyers—attracted by the rebate offer—never take advantage of it. However, this "slippage" is less likely to occur with frequent users of rebate promotions.[36] In fact, a firm now offers a 900 number for consumers to call for information about rebates and for personalized rebate certificates.[37]

Product placement   A final consumer promotion, **product placement,** involves the use of a brand-name product in a movie, television show, video, or a commercial for another product. Companies are usually eager to gain exposure for their products, and the studios believe that product placements add authenticity to the film or program. The studios also receive fees—usually $40,000—although merchandise may be offered instead of cash. Ford Explorers appeared in *Jurassic Park* because Ford agreed to supply 10 of the vehicles and sell them at wholesale to the production company members after the filming was completed. How are product placements arranged? Many companies simply send brochures and catalogs to the studio resource departments; others are approached by agents who review scripts to find promising scenes where a product might be used.[38]

Trade-Oriented Sales Promotions

Trade-oriented sales promotions, or simply trade promotions, are sales tools used to support a company's advertising and personal selling directed to wholesalers, retailers, or distributors. Some of the sales promotions just reviewed are used for this

Point-of-purchase displays reach consumers while they are making many purchase decisions.

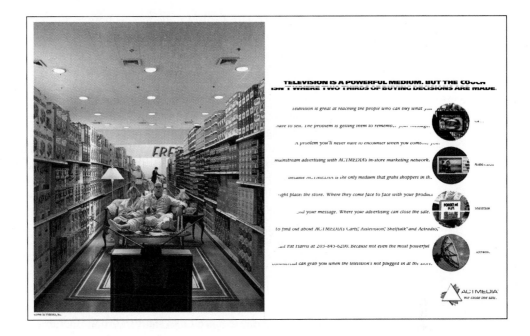

purpose, but there are three other common approaches targeted uniquely to these intermediaries: (1) allowances and discounts, (2) cooperative advertising, and (3) training of distributors' salesforces.

Allowances and discounts   Trade promotions often focus on maintaining or increasing inventory levels in the channel of distribution. An effective method for encouraging such increased purchases by intermediaries is the use of allowances and discounts. However, overuse of these "price reductions" can lead to retailers changing their ordering patterns in the expectation of such offerings. Although there are many variations that manufacturers can use with discounts and allowances, three common approaches include the merchandise allowance, the case allowance, and the finance allowance.[39]

Reimbursing a retailer for extra in-store support or special featuring of the brand is a *merchandise allowance.* Performance contracts between the manufacturer and trade member usually specify the activity to be performed, such as a picture of the product in a newspaper with a coupon good at only one store. The merchandise allowance then consists of a percentage deduction from the list case price ordered during the promotional period. Allowances are not paid by the manufacturer until it sees proof of performance (such as a copy of the ad placed by the retailer in the local newspaper).

A second common trade promotion, a *case allowance,* is a discount on each case ordered during a specific time period. These allowances are usually deducted from the invoice. A variation of the case allowance is the "free goods" approach, whereby retailers receive some amount of the product free based on the amount ordered, such as 1 case free for every 10 cases ordered.[40]

A final trade promotion, the *finance allowance,* involves paying retailers for financing costs or financial losses associated with consumer sales promotions. This trade promotion is regularly used and has several variations. One type is the floor stock protection program—manufacturers give retailers a case allowance price for products in their warehouse, which prevents shelf stock from running down during the promotional period. Also common are freight allowances, which compensate retailers that transport orders from the manufacturer's warehouse.

Cooperative advertising   Resellers often perform the important function of promoting the manufacturer's products at the local level. One common sales promotional activity is to encourage both better quality and greater quantity in the local advertising efforts of resellers through **cooperative advertising.** These are programs by which a manufacturer pays a percentage of the retailer's local advertising expense for advertising the manufacturer's products.

Usually the manufacturer pays a percentage, often 50 percent, of the cost of advertising up to a certain dollar limit, which is based on the amount of the purchases the retailer makes of the manufacturer's products. In addition to paying for the advertising, the manufacturer often furnishes the retailer with a selection of different ad executions, sometimes suited for several different media. A manufacturer may provide, for example, several different print layouts as well as a few broadcast ads for the retailer to adapt and use.[41]

Training of distributors' salesforces One of the many functions the intermediaries perform is customer contact and selling for the producers they represent. Both retailers and wholesalers employ and manage their own sales personnel. A manufacturer's success often rests on the ability of the reseller's salesforce to represent its products.

Thus, it is in the best interest of the manufacturer to help train the reseller's salesforce. Because the reseller's salesforce is often less sophisticated and knowledgeable about the products than the manufacturer might like, training can increase their sales performance. Training activities include producing manuals and brochures to educate the reseller's salesforce. The salesforce then uses these aids in selling situations. Other activities include national sales meetings sponsored by the manufacturer and field visits to the reseller's location to inform and motivate the salesperson to sell the products. Manufacturers also develop incentive and recognition programs to motivate reseller's salespeople to sell their products.

CONCEPT CHECK

1. Which sales promotional tool is most common for new products?

2. What's the difference between a coupon and a deal?

3. Which trade promotion is used on an ongoing basis?

PUBLIC RELATIONS

As noted previously, public relations is a form of communication management that seeks to influence the image of an organization and its products and services. Public relations efforts may utilize a variety of tools and may be directed at many distinct audiences. While public relations personnel usually focus on communicating positive aspects of the business, they may also be called on to minimize the negative impact of a problem or crisis. Intel, for example, had already shipped millions of its Pentium microprocessor chips when it was revealed that the chip had a flaw that caused mathematical errors.[42] Unfortunately, the company initially denied the seriousness of the problem, creating a more difficult situation for the public relations department. The most frequently used public relations tool is publicity.

Publicity Tools

In developing a public relations campaign, several methods of obtaining nonpersonal presentation of an organization, good, or service without direct cost—**publicity tools**—are available to the public relations director. Many companies frequently use the *news release,* consisting of an announcement regarding changes in the company

Uma Thurman uses publicity to promote her movies.

or the product line. The objective of a news release is to inform a newspaper, radio station, or other medium of an idea for a story. A recent study found that more than 40 percent of all free mentions of a brand name occur during news programs.[43]

A second common publicity tool is the *news conference.* Representatives of the media are all invited to an informational meeting, and advance materials regarding the content are sent. This tool is often used when negative publicity—as in the cases of the Ford Pinto fires, the Tylenol poisonings, the Audi 5000 acceleration problem, and the Exxon Valdez oil spill—requires a company response.[44]

Nonprofit organizations rely heavily on *PSAs (public service announcements),* which are free space or time donated by the media. For example, the charter of the American Red Cross prohibits any local chapter from advertising, so to solicit blood donations local chapters often depend on PSAs on radio or television to announce their needs.

Finally, today many high-visibility individuals are used as publicity tools to create visibility for their companies, their products, and themselves. Michael Eisner uses visibility to promote Disney, Uma Thurman uses it to promote her movies, and Bob Dole uses it to promote himself as a political candidate. These publicity efforts are coordinated with news releases, conferences, advertising, donations to charities, volunteer activities, endorsements, and any other activities that may have an impact on public perceptions.[45]

INCREASING THE VALUE OF PROMOTION

Today's customers seek value from companies that provide leading-edge products, hassle-free transactions at competitive prices, and customer intimacy.[46] Promotion practices have changed dramatically to improve transactions and increase customer intimacy by (1) emphasizing long-term relationships, and (2) increasing self-regulation.

Building Long-Term Relationships with Promotion

In 1970, manufacturers offered retailers promotional discounts of approximately 4 percent to encourage special purchases of a product; more recently, as managers have been pressured to produce short-term sales increases, the discounts have averaged about 15 percent. Although this sounds like good news, consumers didn't always receive the discount. The reason: in a practice called *forward buying* supermarkets often purchased more merchandise than they planned to sell during the promotion, only to sell the remaining stock at a regular price later, or the retailer would often "divert" part of the shipment by selling it to a supermarket that had not been offered the manufacturer's discount. In either case, only 30 percent of the discount actually reached the consumer. Over time, retailers began to focus on products offered with discounts, and consumers learned to shop for what was on sale.

In an effort to increase the customer value of trade promotions, consumer goods manufacturers such as P&G are trying to put an end to the discount war. Their first action was to reduce the number of discounts that they offer stores. Second, wholesale prices have been reduced, in some cases by 25 percent. Finally, manufacturers are searching for new promotional activities that may provide more value to consumers.[47] Overall, they hope that these changes will build customer loyalty for the long term—emphasizing a lifetime of purchases rather than a single transaction.

Self-Regulation

Unfortunately, over the years many consumers have been misled—or even deceived—by some promotions. Examples include sweepstakes in which the gifts were not awarded, rebate offers that were a terrible hassle, and advertisements whose promises were great, until the buyer read the small print.

Promotions targeted at special groups such as children and the elderly also raise ethical concerns. For example, providing free samples to children in elementary schools or linking product lines to TV programs and movies have led to questions about the need for restrictions on promotions.[48] Although the Federal Trade Commission does provide some guidelines to protect consumers and special groups from misleading promotions, some observers believe more government regulation is needed.

To rely on formal regulation by federal, state, and local governments of all promotional activities would be very expensive. As a result, there are increasing efforts by advertising agencies, trade associations, and marketing organizations at *self-regulation*.[49] By imposing standards that reflect the values of society on their promotional activities, marketers can (1) facilitate the development of new promotional methods, (2) minimize regulatory constraints and restrictions, and (3) help consumers gain confidence in the communication efforts used to influence their purchases. As organizations strive for effective self-regulation, marketing executives will need to make sound ethical judgments about the use of existing and new promotional practices.

CONCEPT CHECK

1. What is a news release?

2. What is the difference between government regulation and self-regulation?

SUMMARY

1. Communication is the process of conveying a message to others and requires a source, a message, a channel of communication, a receiver, and the processes of encoding and decoding.

2. For effective communication to occur, the sender and receiver must have a shared field of experience. Feedback from receiver to sender helps determine whether decoding has occurred or noise has distorted the message.

3. The promotional elements consist of advertising, personal selling, sales promotion, and public relations. These tools vary according to whether they are personal; can be identified with a sponsor; and can be controlled with regard to whom, when, where, and how often the message is sent.

4. In selecting the appropriate promotional mix, marketers must consider the target audience, the stage of the product's life cycle, characteristics of the product, decision stage of the buyer, and the channel of distribution.

5. The target for promotional programs can be the ultimate consumer, an intermediary, or both. Ultimate consumer programs rely more on advertising, whereas personal selling is more important in reaching industrial buyers and intermediaries.

6. The emphasis on the promotional tools varies with a product's life cycle. In introduction, awareness is important. During growth, creating brand preference is essential. Advertising is more important in the former stage and personal selling in the latter. Sales promotion helps maintain buyers in the maturity stage.

7. The appropriate promotional mix depends on the complexity of the product, the degree of risk associated with its purchase, and the need for ancillary services.

8. In the prepurchase stage of a customer's purchase decision advertising is emphasized; at the purchase stage personal selling is most important; and during the postpurchase stage advertising, personal selling, and sales promotion are used to reduce postpurchase anxiety.

9. When a push strategy is used, personal selling and sales promotions directed to intermediaries play major roles. In a pull strategy, advertising and sales promotions directed to ultimate consumers are important.

10. Integrated marketing communications programs coordinate all promotional activities to provide a consistent message across all audiences.

11. More money is spent on sales promotion than on advertising. Selecting sales promotions requires a good understanding of the advantages and disadvantages of each option.

12. There is a wide range of consumer-oriented sales promotions: coupons, deals, premiums, contests, sweepstakes, samples, continuity programs, point-of-purchase displays, rebates, and product placements.

13. Trade-oriented promotions consist of allowances and discounts, cooperative advertising, and training of distributors' salesforces. These are used at all levels of the channel.

14. The most frequently used public relations tool is publicity—a nonpersonal, indirectly paid presentation of an organization, good, or service conducted through news releases, news conferences, or public service announcements.

15. Efforts to improve the value of promotion include emphasizing long-term relationships and increasing self-regulation.

KEY TERMS AND CONCEPTS

communication p. 496
source p. 496
message p. 496
channel of communication p. 496
receivers p. 496
encoding p. 497
decoding p. 497
field of experience p. 497
feedback p. 498
noise p. 498
advertising p. 498
personal selling p. 500

public relations p. 500
publicity p. 500
sales promotion p. 501
promotional mix p. 501
push strategy p. 505
pull strategy p. 506
integrated marketing communications p. 506
consumer-oriented sales promotions p. 508
product placement p. 512
trade-oriented sales promotions p. 512
cooperative advertising p. 514
publicity tools p. 514

CHAPTER PROBLEMS AND APPLICATIONS

1. After listening to a recent sales presentation, Mary Smith signed up for membership at the local health club. On arriving at the facility, she learned there was an additional fee for racquetball court rentals. "I don't remember that in the sales talk; I thought they said all facilities were included with the membership fee," complained Mary. Describe the problem in terms of the communication process.

2. Develop a matrix to compare the four elements of the promotional mix on three criteria—to *whom* you deliver the message, *what* you say, and *when* you say it.

3. Explain how the promotional tools used by an airline would differ if the target audience were (a) consumers who travel for pleasure and (b) corporate travel departments that select the airlines to be used by company employees.

4. Suppose you introduced a new consumer food product and invested heavily both in national advertising (pull strategy) and in training and motivating your field salesforce to sell the product to food stores (push strategy). What kinds of feedback would you receive from both the advertising and your salesforce? How could you increase both the quality and quantity of each?

5. Fisher-Price Company, long known as a manufacturer of children's toys, has introduced a line of clothing for children. Outline a promotional plan to get this product introduced in the marketplace.

6. Many insurance companies sell health insurance plans to companies. In these companies the employees pick the plan, but the set of offered plans is determined by the company. Recently Blue Cross–Blue Shield, a health insurance company, ran a television ad stating, "If your employer doesn't offer you Blue Cross–Blue Shield coverage, ask why." Explain the promotional strategy behind the advertisement.

7. Identify the sales promotion tools that might be useful for (*a*) Tastee Yogurt—a new brand introduction, (*b*) 3M self-sticking Post-it notes, and (*c*) Wrigley's Spearmint Gum.

8. Design an integrated marketing communications program—using each of the four promotional elements—for Music Boulevard, the on-line music store.

9. When the Gannett Corporation introduced the daily newspaper *USA Today,* free copies were distributed at airports and check-in counters of car rental companies such as Hertz and Avis. (*a*) What was the rationale behind this promotional strategy? (*b*) Who was the original target audience?

10. Describe a self-regulation guideline you believe would improve the value of (*a*) an existing form of promotion and (*b*) a new promotional practice.

CASE 19–1   Sprint

Video

What do you think of when you think of Sprint? Regardless of the long distance company you may use, Sprint hopes you associate its name with two characteristics: the first all fiber optic long distance phone system in the country, and sound quality so fine that you can hear a pin drop.

competition among these three companies is not surprising given that each share point in the long distance market is worth about $320 million in revenue. Sprint has played an increasingly important role in the long distance market rivalry. While AT&T and MCI have dominated the industry for many years, Sprint has steadily attracted a base of customers and now captures close to 10% of the market for long distance communication.

THE COMPANY

US Sprint was formed from US Telecom, GTE Sprint and GTE Telenet in 1986. Probably best known for long distance service and its fiber optic communications network, Sprint offers outbound and 800 telephone services, data services for exchange of voice, data, video and image information, calling card services for exchange of voice, data, video and image information, calling card services such as the FONCARD (Fiber Optic Network Card), and multimedia and strategic services such as electronic data interchange (EDI) services for consumer and business markets.

THE COMPETITION

Sprint faces stiff competition in the communication industry and particularly in the long distance market from larger rivals AT&T and MCI. The intensity of

THE SERVICE

Sprint has used product innovation as a means of differentiating its services. For instance, Sprint has touted its 100% digital fiber optic network for its clarity—you can hear a pin drop as demonstrated in Sprint advertisements. Sprint's newest product, introduced in January of 1994, is a voice activated phone card called Voice FONCARD. Voice FONCARD is described by Sprint as the "first widely available voice-activated calling card". To use Voice FONCARD customers call an 800 number to gain access to the system and then direct the system to make calls. It allows you to store frequently called numbers and call them up with your voice—"Call Ed" or "call home". The system searches for Ed's number or your home number and places the call. The voice matching system is quite sophisticated allowing for some variation in the caller's voice due to fatigue or illness but secure enough to recognize only the subscriber.

THE VOICE FONCARD COMMUNICATION PROGRAM

J. Walter Thompson (JWT) developed the Voice FON-CARD integrated marketing communication program. The program was targeted at business travelers. Business travelers, it was believed, would likely have the greatest interest and need for the convenience of the FONCARD. Business travelers are often away from home and office, and are willing to adopt products and make expenditures that make their lives easier when they're on the road.

The program integrated a variety of promotional elements. First, a press release was designed to appeal to the media and stimulate publicity for the service. Second, print advertisements for Voice FONCARD were placed on airline ticket jackets and in in-flight magazines, and commercials were designed for placement before in-flight movies. National print and television advertising campaigns were also developed. Third, direct-mail materials were sent to business travelers. Finally, telemarketing was utilized to handle inquiries and provide support for the other communication elements. Many of the communication program elements utilized Sprint's now familiar spokesperson, Candice

Bergen, because she represented Sprint's image—smart, spunky, and hipper than AT&T.

The national campaign utilized what JWT describes as a 'game'. Photos of well know personalities—showing only part of their faces—were used for the print advertising. In the case of the television advertising, only the voices of the well known personalities were used. The readers and viewers were then asked whether they could identify the person. The primary point of the advertising was to illustrate the voice recognition capability of the card. Another more subtle message to the advertisements, however, was not only that this was a very special product but that it is a very special company that recognizes every single person by voice.

Research conducted by JWT found that Voice FONCARD customers received an emotional benefit from using the card because the card and the company recognized the customer uniquely. In addition, the Voice FONCARD enhances the image of Sprint as a whole. Results also indicated that while business customers were responding to the campaign, the Voice FONCARD was appealing to other market segments. One surprise to JWT and Sprint was the number of students calling the telemarketing center to learn more about acquiring the Voice FONCARD.

Questions

1. What were Sprint's promotional objectives when launching the Voice FONCARD? How did Sprint's integrated marketing communications program fit Sprint's objectives?

2. How did Sprint measure the effectiveness of their marketing communications program? Are these methods consistent with Sprint's objectives? What other methods do you feel would be beneficial for evaluating the effectiveness of the marketing communication program?

3. Now that Voice FONCARD has been on the market for a number of years, what changes should Sprint make in their promotional objectives and integrated marketing communications program?

ESPNET SPORTSZONE

A SERVICE OF STARWAVE AND ESPN ™

Baseball	NHL	NBA	College Basketball	Other Sports
SCORES	SCORES	SCORES	SCORES	

March 19, 1996, 2:32pm ET

Click here to play in the big leagues.

networkMCI that's HOW

Click here to find out how to get live scores.

◇ Subscribers Log in here

Explore Subscriber Benefits

Features

Gretzky still a hit in Hollywood

Reuters/Sam McC...

Wayne Gretzky got his wish Monday night: He played for a winning team in Los Angeles. Unfortunately for the Kings he was just passing through as a member of the St. Louis Blues. The Great One fed Hollywood's love for drama by scoring a goal and an assist as the Blues dumped the Kings 3-1. In the first game against his former team, Gretzky built on his all-time NHL scoring mark with his 2,600th career point. And L.A. saw up close that No. 99 plans many more points before he's through.

CHAPTER 20

Advertising

AFTER READING THIS CHAPTER YOU SHOULD BE ABLE TO:

• Explain the differences between product advertising and institutional advertising and the variations within each type.

• Understand the steps used to develop, execute, and evaluate an advertising program.

• Understand alternative ways to set an advertising budget.

• Explain the advantages and disadvantages of alternative advertising media.

WHO IS ADVERTISING IN CYBERSPACE? WHO ISN'T?

For thousands of businesses, the past year has been a race to advertise their products and services in cyberspace—the network of World Wide Web sites on the Internet. From virtually nothing only a few years ago, experts now predict that "on-line advertising" expenditures will exceed $5 billion by the year 2000.[1] Current advertisers include such companies as Levi Strauss, Pizza Hut, Visa International, Ford Motor Company, AT&T, and Microsoft.

How does it work? Generally, businesses start by creating a Web site, or page, that contains information in text, audio, and graphical form. At the Music Boulevard site (http://www.musicblvd.com), for example, users can search by artist, CD title, song, or label for a particular music selection. Consumers can then access 30-second sound samples, view album art or artist photos, read album reviews or musician bios, and make purchases by credit card through an 800 number or via fax. Today, more than 15,000 businesses have Web sites in operation.

Many firms with Web sites also advertise on other sites. ESPN's popular SportsZone (http://espnet.sportszone.com), for example, charges sponsors $37,500 per month for a banner and a "bridge" that serves as an interim page between the ESPN content and the advertiser's site. Microsoft paid $225,000 for six weeks as the title sponsor of the National Football League's Super Bowl Web site. Other Web sites that sell advertising space include HotWired, Vibe Online, Time Inc.'s Pathfinder, and Yahoo Web guide.

To direct consumers to a particular Web site, businesses are developing customized software packages called Web browsers. Guests at Hilton Hotels now find in their rooms a computer disk with software to install on their PCs that then links the guests directly to the Hilton Web site. Similarly, Volkswagen of America will soon place disks with customized software in the glove compartment of its new cars. MasterCard International recently distributed 22,000 browser packages to member institutions. In addition to facilitating purchases, encouraging use of a Web site provides direct contact with customers, creates an opportunity for relationship marketing, and improves customer service.[2]

What does the future hold? A recent survey shows that one third of all businesses are planning to advertise on the Internet, and even more will use it to sell directly to consumers. The number of people with access to the Internet is approaching 40 million, and the number of those people who regularly utilize the Internet already exceeds 20 million. In the words of one marketing expert, "To not be on the Internet in the 90s is going to be like not having a phone!"[3]

On-line advertising is one example of the many exciting changes taking place in the field of advertising today. Chapter 19 described **advertising** as any *paid* form of *nonpersonal* communication about an organization, good, service, or idea, by an identified sponsor. This chapter describes alternative types of advertisements, the advertising decision process, and other important changes in advertising.

TYPES OF ADVERTISEMENTS

As you look through any magazine, watch television, listen to the radio, or browse on the Web, the variety of advertisements you see or hear may give you the impression that they have few similarities. Advertisements are prepared for different purposes, but they basically consist of two types: product and institutional.

Product Advertisements

Focused on selling a good or service, **product advertisements** take three forms: (1) pioneering (or informational), (2) competitive (or persuasive), and (3) reminder. Look at the ads by AT&T, Corel, and Godiva, and determine the type and objective of each ad.

Advertisements serve varying purposes. Which ad would be considered (1) pioneering, which is (2) competitive, and which is used as a (3) reminder?

Used in the introductory stage of the life cycle, *pioneering* advertisements tell people what a product is, what it can do, and where it can be found. The key objective of a pioneering ad (such as that for the AT&T wireless wrist telephone) is to inform the target market. Informative ads have been found to be interesting, convincing, and effective.[4]

Dial soap uses reinforcement ads to encourage consumers to keep using the product.

Advertising that promotes a specific brand's features and benefits is *competitive.* The objective of these messages is to persuade the target market to select the firm's brand rather than that of a competitor. An increasingly common form of competitive advertising is *comparative* advertising, which shows one brand's strengths relative to those of competitors.[5] The Corel ad, for example, highlights the competitive advantage of CorelFlow 3 over its primary competitor, Visio 4. Firms such as P&G, which began using comparative ads for the first time in 1993, are attracted by studies showing that comparative ads attract more attention and increase the perceived quality of the advertiser's brand.[6] Firms that use comparative advertising need market research and test results to provide legal support for their claims.[7]

Reminder advertising is used to reinforce previous knowledge of a product. The Godiva ad shown reminds consumers about the association between its product and a special event—in this case, your birthday. Reminder advertising is good for products that have achieved a well-recognized position and are in the mature phase of their product life cycle. Another type of reminder ad, *reinforcement,* is used to assure current users they made the right choice. One example: "Aren't you glad you use Dial? Don't you wish everybody did?"

Institutional Advertisements

The objective of **institutional advertisements** is to build goodwill or an image for an organization, rather than promote a specific good or service. Institutional advertising has been used by companies such as GTE, Beatrice, and IBM to build confidence in the company name.[8] Often this form of advertising is used to support the public relations plan or counter adverse publicity. Four alternative forms of institutional advertisements are often used:

1. *Advocacy* advertisements state the position of a company on an issue. Miller places ads encouraging the responsible use of alcohol, as shown on the next page.

2. *Pioneering institutional* advertisements, like the pioneering ads for products discussed earlier, are used for announcement about what a company is, what it can do, or where it is located. Recent Bayer ads stating "We cure more headaches than you think" are intended to inform consumers that the company produces many products in addition to aspirin.

3. *Competitive institutional* advertisements promote the advantages of one product class over another and are used in markets where different product classes compete for the same buyers. The State of Florida, Department of Citrus developed the "Are You Drinking Enough" campaign to show the benefits of

An advocacy advertisement about the responsible use of alcohol by Miller and a competitive institutional advertisement about the benifits of orange juice by the state of Florida.

orange juice. The goal of these ads is to increase demand for orange juice as it competes against other beverages.

4. *Reminder institutional* advertisements, like the product form, simply bring the company's name to the attention of the target market again.

CONCEPT CHECK

1. What is the difference between pioneering and competitive ads?

2. What is the purpose of an institutional advertisement?

DEVELOPING THE ADVERTISING PROGRAM

Because media costs are high, advertising decisions must be made carefully, using a systematic approach. Paralleling the planning, implementation, and control steps described in the strategic marketing process (Chapter 2), the advertising decision process is divided into (1) developing, (2) executing, and (3) evaluating the advertising program (Figure 20–1). Development of the advertising program focuses on the four *W*s:

- *Who* is the target audience?
- *What* are (1) the advertising objectives, (2) the amounts of money that can be budgeted for the advertising program, and (3) the kinds of copy to use?
- *Where* should the advertisements be run?
- *When* should the advertisements be run?

Identifying the Target Audience

The first decision in developing the advertising program is identifying the *target audience,* the group of prospective buyers toward which an advertising program is

FIGURE 20-1

The advertising decision process

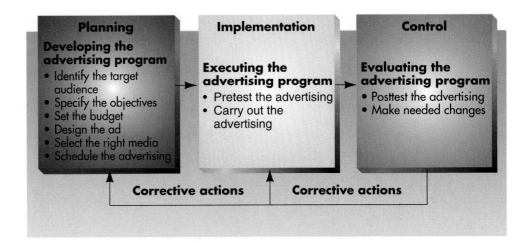

directed. To the extent that time and money permit, the target audience for the advertising program is the target market for the firm's product, which is identified from marketing research and market segmentation studies. The more a firm knows about its target audience's profile—including their lifestyle, attitudes, and values—the easier it is to develop an advertising program. If a firm wanted to reach you with its ads, it would need to know what TV shows you watch and what magazines you read.

Specifying Advertising Objectives

After the target audience is identified, a decision must be reached on what the advertising should accomplish. Consumers can be said to respond in terms of a **hierarchy of effects,** which is the sequence of stages a prospective buyer goes through from initial awareness of a product to eventual action (either trial or adoption of the product).[9]

- *Awareness.* The consumer's ability to recognize and remember the product or brand name.
- *Interest.* An increase in the consumer's desire to learn about some of the features of the product or brand.
- *Evaluation.* The consumer's appraisal of the product or brand on important attributes.
- *Trial.* The consumer's actual first purchase and use of the product or brand.
- *Adoption.* Through a favorable experience on the first trial, the consumer's repeated purchase and use of the product or brand.

For a totally new product the sequence applies to the entire product category, but for a new brand competing in an established product category it applies to the brand itself. These steps can serve as guidelines for developing advertising objectives.

Although sometimes an objective for an advertising program involves several steps in the hierarchy of effects, it often focuses on a single stage. Regardless of what the specific objective might be, from building awareness to increasing repeat purchases,[10] advertising objectives should possess three important qualities. They should (1) be designed for a well-defined target audience, (2) be measurable, and (3) cover a specified time period.

Setting the Advertising Budget

You might not remember who advertised during the 1980 Super Bowl, but it cost the companies $500,000 a minute. By 1996 the cost of one minute during Super Bowl

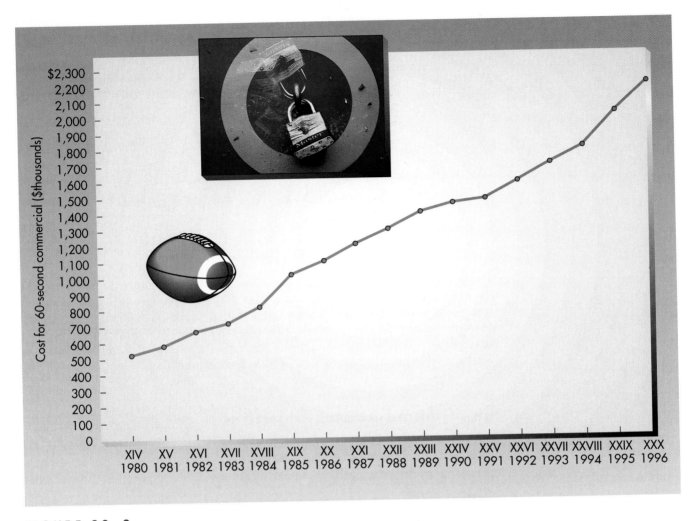

FIGURE 20-2

Rising media costs: Super
Bowl, super dollars

XXX was $2.2 million (Figure 20–2). The reason for the escalating cost is the growing numbers of viewers: an estimated 133 million people tune in, approximately 90 percent of them watch the entire game, and 66 percent report total day-after aided recall of the commercials. As a result some companies are regular Super Bowl advertisers. Master Lock, for example, has been on 21 Super Bowl's![11]

From Figure 20–3 it is clear that the advertising expenditures needed to reach U.S. and non-U.S. households are enormous. Note that 10 companies—P&G, Philip Morris, General Motors, Ford, Sears, AT&T, PepsiCo, Unilever, Nestlé, and Toyota—each spend a total of more than a billion dollars annually on advertising.

After setting the advertising objectives, a company must decide on how much to spend. Determining the ideal amount for the budget is difficult because there is no precise way to measure the exact results of spending advertising dollars. However, there are several methods used to set the advertising budget.[12]

Percentage of sales   In the **percentage of sales budgeting** approach, funds are allocated to advertising as a percentage of past or anticipated sales, in terms of either dollars or units sold. A common budgeting method,[13] this approach is often stated in terms such as, "Our ad budget for this year is 3 percent of last year's gross sales." The advantage of this approach is obvious: it's simple and provides a financial

FIGURE 20-3

Advertising expenditures by companies in 1994

| | U.S. ADVERTISERS | | NON-U.S. ADVERTISERS | |
RANK	COMPANY	ADVERTISING EXPENDITURES (MILLIONS)	COMPANY	ADVERTISING EXPENDITURES (MILLIONS)
1	Procter & Gamble	2689	Unilever	2208
2	Philip Morris	2413	Procter & Gamble	2199
3	General Motors	1929	Nestlé	1216
4	Ford Motor Co.	1186	Philip Morris	778
5	Sears	1134	PSA Peugot	773
6	AT&T	1102	Toyota	697
7	PepsiCo	1097	Volkswagen	696
8	Chrysler Corp	971	General Motors	650
9	Walt Disney Co.	934	Nissan	611
10	Johnson & Johnson	933	Mars	604
11	Nestlé	894	L'Oreal	563
12	Time-Warner	860	Ford	544
13	Warner-Lambert	831	Renault	533
14	Toyota	766	Fiat SpA	521
15	Grand Metropolitan	764	Kao Corp.	507

Sources: "100 Leading National Advertisers," *Advertising Age* (September 27, 1995), p. 3; and Todd Pruzen, "Top Global Marketers," *Advertising Age* (November 20, 1995), p. I–20.

safeguard by tying the advertising budget to sales. However, there is a major fallacy in this approach, which implies that sales cause advertising. Using this method, a company may reduce its advertising budget because of a downturn in past sales or an anticipated downturn in future sales—situations where it may need advertising the most.

Competitive parity   A second common approach, **competitive parity budgeting,** is matching the competitor's absolute level of spending or the proportion per point of market share. This approach has also been referred to as *matching competitors* or *share of market*. It is important to consider the competition in budgeting.[14] Consumer responses to ads are affected by competing ads, so if a competitor runs 30 radio ads each week, it may be difficult for a firm to get its message across with only five messages.[15] The competitor's budget level, however, should not be the only determinant in setting a company's budget. The competition might have very different advertising objectives, which require a different level of advertising expenditures.

All you can afford   Common to many small businesses is **all you can afford budgeting,** in which money is allocated to advertising only after all other budget items are covered. As one company executive said in reference to this budgeting process, "Why, it's simple. First, I go upstairs to the controller and ask how much they can afford to give us this year. He says a million and a half. Later, the boss comes to me and asks how much we should spend, and I say 'Oh, about a million and a half.' Then we have our advertising appropriation."[16]

Fiscally conservative, this approach has little else to offer. Using this budgeting philosophy, a company acts as though it doesn't know anything about an advertising–sales relationship or what its advertising objectives are.

Objective and task   The best approach to budgeting is **objective and task budgeting,** whereby the company (1) determines its advertising objectives, (2) outlines the tasks to accomplish these objectives, and (3) determines the advertising cost of performing these tasks.[17]

FIGURE 20-4

The objective and task approach

OBJECTIVE

To increase awareness among college students for a new CD player. Awareness at the end of one semester should be 20 percent of all students from the existing 0 percent today.

TASKS	COSTS
Advertisements once a week for a semester in 500 college papers	$280,000
Advertisements weekly for a semester on the nationally syndicated "Rockline" radio show	25,000
Three monthly, full-page ads in *Audio* magazine	9,000
Total Budget	$314,000

FIGURE 20-4

The objective and task approach

This method takes into account what the company wants to accomplish and requires that the objectives be specified.[18] Strengths of the other budgeting methods are integrated into this approach because each previous method's strength is tied to the objectives. For example, if the costs are beyond what the company can afford, objectives are reworked and the tasks revised. The difficulty with this method is the judgment required to determine the tasks needed to accomplish objectives. Would two or four insertions in *Time* magazine be needed to achieve a specific awareness level? Figure 20–4 shows a sample media plan with objectives, tasks, and budget outlined. The total amount to be budgeted is $314,000. If the company can only afford $200,000, the objectives must be reworked, tasks redefined, and the total budget recalculated.

Designing the Advertisement

The central element of an advertising program is the ad itself. Advertising messages consist of advertising copy and the artwork (including audio) that the target audience is intended to see (as in magazines, newspapers, and TV) or hear (as on radio and TV). The message usually focuses on the key benefits of the product that are important to a prospective buyer in making trial and adoption decisions.

Message content   Most advertising messages are made up of both informational and persuasional elements. These two elements, in fact, are so intertwined that it is sometimes difficult to tell them apart. For example, basic information contained in many ads such as the product name, benefits, features, and price are presented in a way that tries to attract attention and encourage purchase. On the other hand, even the most persuasive advertisements have to contain at least some basic information to be successful.

Information and persuasive content can be combined in the form of an appeal to provide a basic reason for the consumer to act. Although the marketer can use many different types of appeals, common advertising appeals include fear appeals, sex appeals, and humorous appeals.

Fear appeals suggest to the consumer that he or she can avoid some negative experience through the purchase and use of a product or through a change in behavior. Insurance companies often try to show the negative effects of premature death on the relatives of those who don't carry enough life or mortgage insurance. Food producers encourage the purchase of low-fat, high-fiber products as a means of reducing cholesterol levels and the possibility of a heart attack.[19] When using fear

MARKETING NEWSNET

Customer

$

Value

DESIGNING ADS THAT DEAL WITH NEGATIVE ISSUES

Have you ever developed anxiety over a message you've received from an advertisement? If your answer is yes, chances are that your reaction was the result of what advertisers call a *fear appeal*. Examples you may be familiar with include fire or smoke detector ads that depict a family home burning, political candidate endorsements that warn against the rise of other unpopular ideologies, or social cause ads warning of the serious consequences of drug use, alcoholism, or AIDS. This approach is based on three steps—the creation of a fearful situation by giving the audience information about the severity of the threat and the probability of its occurrence, describing the effectiveness of a solution or coping response, and suggesting how the solution can be implemented.

How individuals react to fear appeals, though, varies significantly with their prior knowledge and experience. Indeed, the varying levels of anxiety that result from the ads suggest several ethical concerns for the psychological well-being of consumers. Therefore, advertisers need to consider four guidelines when developing their ads:

1. Whenever possible, use low or moderate (rather than high) levels of fear.
2. Offer more than one alternative as a solution.
3. Avoid deceptive implications (e.g., that a product will completely eliminate a fearful condition).
4. Pretest each ad to ensure a balance between the message and the associated level of anxiety.

Some examples of fear appeal advertisements include the following:

SPONSOR	MEDIUM	THEME
American Express Travelers Checks	Television	A couple on a vacation was shown victimized by a robbery and left in a state of shock and desperation.
American Trauma Society	Television	The inside of a car with a broken windshield was shown with a voice stating, "The head that could make the decision to buckle up no longer can."
Radio Shack	Television and radio and newspaper	The TV advertising featured blue-tinged night scenes in a house, including a baby in a crib, and urged people to empower themselves to prevent crime.
Cease fire	Print	The ads show a gun with a tag describing an accidental shooting of a child. The copy reads: "A gun in the home is much more likely to kill a family member than to kill an intruder."
Prudential Insurance	Television	A man was shown dying on an operating table. The message focused on who will take care of his children.
Partnership for a Drug-Free America	Print and television	Photos of an unbroken egg, a hot pan, and the egg frying in the pan are shown. The copy reads: "This is your brain on drugs."

appeals, the advertiser must be sure that the appeal is strong enough to get the audience's attention and concern, but not so strong that it will lead them to "tune out" the message. The accompanying Marketing NewsNet suggests some guidelines for developing an ad with a fear appeal.[20]

In contrast, *sex appeals* suggest to the audience that the product will increase the attractiveness of the user. Sex appeals can be found in almost any product category, from automobiles to toothpaste. The Ethics and Social Responsibility Alert on page 530

ETHICS AND SOCIAL RESPONSIBILITY ALERT

DID CALVIN KLEIN GO TOO FAR?

Over the years Calvin Klein has built a reputation for controversial advertising— from the Brooke Shields "Nothing comes between me and my Calvins" campaign to ads with various degrees of nudity. His recent campaign, which used teen models in suggestive poses, however, drew a barrage of criticism. The campaign was also the focus of a Justice Department investigation to determine if the models were under 18 years old.

In the past, some publications have asked Calvin Klein to reshoot ads before they are published. While no magazines rejected the teen ads, Klein decided to stop running the ads in the United States, sparking a national debate about advertising to (and with) children. Janice Grossman, publisher of *Seventeen*, argued that the ads were "too blatant," while Ira Garey, publisher of *Sassy*, suggests that "kids look at things differently than adults do." Meanwhile, Calvin Klein has reserved the ads for use in the European market.

Why has this campaign been so controversial? What is your opinion?

discusses how Calvin Klein has used sex appeals in clothing ads.[21] Unfortunately, many commercials that use sex appeals are only successful at gaining the attention of the audience; they have little impact on how consumers think, feel, or act. Some advertising experts even argue that such appeals get in the way of successful communication by distracting the audience from the purpose of the ad.

Humorous appeals imply either directly or more subtly that the product is more fun or exciting than competitors' offerings. As with fear and sex appeals, the use of humor is widespread in advertising and can be found in many product categories. Unfortunately for the advertiser, humor tends to wear out quickly, thus boring the consumer. Eveready ads, featuring the Energizer battery bunny, frequently change to avoid this advertising "wearout." Another problem with humorous appeals is that their effectiveness may vary across cultures if used in a global campaign.[22]

Creating the actual message   The "creative people" in an advertising agency— copywriters and art directors—have the responsibility to turn appeals and features such as quality, style, dependability, economy, and service into attention-getting, believable advertisements.

Advertising agency DDB Needham Worldwide was recently designated as *Advertising Age* magazine's advertising Agency of the Year for infiltrating "the American vernacular with its ad copy." Robert Scarpelli, the agency's creative director, says, "We try to do advertising that gets into the language, is remembered, and talked about." An example of DDB Needham's approach is the television campaign for Frito-Lay's Rold Gold pretzels. In the commercials, "Seinfeld's" Jason Alexander fantasizes about all the feats he can accomplish while eating the fat-free pretzels. Not only has "Prove it, Pretzel Boy" become part of the American lexicon, the product's market share has increased from 11 percent to 25 percent! Other successful campaigns with memorable taglines include Lotto ads that proclaim, "Hey, you never know," and Bud Light ads, in which "everyman" falsifies his identity to get a Bud Light by claiming, "Yes, I am."[23]

DDB Needham's use of television actor Jason Alexander is an example of a very popular form of advertising today—the use of a celebrity spokesperson. In homes across the United States, sports heros, rock stars, and movie stars are talking directly

A creative advertisement with a catchy phrase ("Prove it, Pretzel Boy!") for Rold Gold Pretzels.

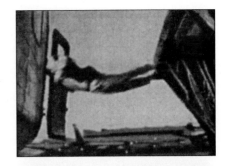

to consumers through ads in all of today's many media options. Advertisers who use a celebrity spokesperson believe that the ads are more likely to influence sales. The "Milk, what a surprise!" campaign features model Christie Brinkley, tennis player Gabriela Sabatini, singer Tony Bennett, and many other celebrities in an attempt to reverse the decline in per-capita milk consumption. Similarly, football player Jerry Rice and images of Alfred Hitchcock were part of the "Don't laugh, it works," campaign used to introduce Breath Right nasal strips. A campaign may also encourage consumers to associate a product with a celebrity. For example, when consumers see or hear Bill Cosby they may think of Jello or Kodak. Who is the top TV endorser as ranked by consumers? According to Video Storyboard Tests, a company that conducts an annual survey of 3,000 people, Candice Bergen tops the list![24]

Translating the copywriter's ideas into an actual advertisement is a complex process. Designing quality artwork, layout, and production for the advertisements is costly and time consuming. High-quality TV commercials typically cost about $268,000 to produce a 30-second ad, a task done by about 2,000 small commercial production companies across the United States. High-visibility commercials can be even more expensive: two 15-second Rolaids commercials involved $500,000 and 75 people over a six-month period. About 70 "takes" are necessary, and typical, to get things "right."[25]

CONCEPT CHECK

1. What are characteristics of good advertising objectives?

2. What is the weakness of the percentage of sales budgeting approach?

Selecting the Right Media

Every advertiser must decide where to place its advertisements. The alternatives are the *advertising media,* the means by which the message is communicated to the target audience. Newspapers, magazines, radio, and TV are examples of advertising media. This "media selection" decision is related to the target audience, type of product, nature of the message, campaign objectives, available budget, and the costs of the alternative media. Figure 20–5 shows the distribution of the $150 billion spent on advertising among the many media alternatives.

Choosing a medium and a vehicle within that medium In deciding where to place advertisements, a company has several media to choose from and a number of alternatives, or vehicles, within each medium. Often advertisers use a mix of media forms and vehicles to maximize the exposure of the message to the target audience

FIGURE 20–5

U.S. advertising expenditures, by category (data in billions of dollars)

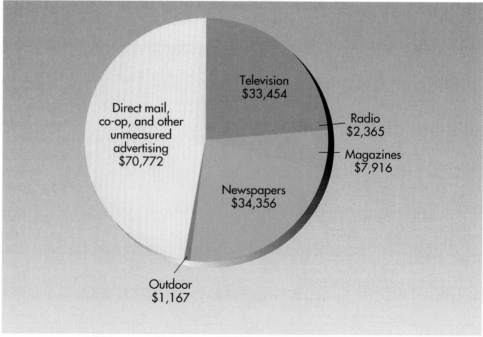

Source: "National Ad Spending by Media," *Advertising Age* (September 27, 1995), p. 62.

TERM	WHAT IT MEANS
Reach	The number of different people or households exposed to an advertisement.
Rating	The percentage of households in a market that are tuned to a particular TV show or radio station.
Frequency	The average number of times an individual is exposed to an advertisement.
Gross rating points (GRPs)	Reach (expressed as a percentage of the total market) multiplied by frequency.
Cost per thousand (CPM)	The cost of advertising divided by the number of thousands of individuals or households who are exposed.

while at the same time minimizing costs. These two conflicting goals of (1) maximizing exposure and (2) minimizing costs are of central importance to media planning.

Basic terms   Media buyers speak a language of their own, so every advertiser involved in selecting the right media for their campaigns must be familiar with some common terms used in the advertising industry. Figure 20–6 shows the most common terms used in media decisions.

Because advertisers try to maximize the number of individuals in the target market exposed to the message, they must be concerned with reach. **Reach** is the number of different people or households exposed to an advertisement. The exact definition of reach sometimes varies among alternative media. Newspapers often use reach to describe their total circulation or the number of different households that buy the paper. Television and radio stations, in contrast, describe their reach using the term **rating**— the percentage of households in a market that are tuned to a particular TV show or radio station. In general, advertisers try to maximize reach in their target market at the lowest cost.

Although reach is important, advertisers are also interested in exposing their target audience to a message more than once. This is because consumers often do not pay close attention to advertising messages, some of which contain large amounts of relatively complex information. When advertisers want to reach the same audience more than once, they are concerned with **frequency,** the average number of times a person in the target audience is exposed to a message or advertisement. Like reach, greater frequency is generally viewed as desirable.[26]

When reach (expressed as a percentage of the total market) is multiplied by frequency, an advertiser will obtain a commonly used reference number called **gross rating points** (GRPs). To obtain the appropriate number of GRPs to achieve an advertising campaign's objectives, the media planner must balance reach and frequency. The balance will also be influenced by cost. **Cost per thousand** (CPM) refers to the cost of reaching 1,000 individuals or households with the advertising message in a given medium (*M* is the Roman numeral for 1,000).

Different Media Alternatives

Figure 20–7 summarizes the advantages and disadvantages of the important advertising media, which are described in more detail below.

MEDIUM	ADVANTAGES	DISADVANTAGES
Television	Reaches extremely large audience; uses picture, print, sound, and motion for effect; can target specific audiences.	High cost to prepare and run ads; short exposure time and perishable message; difficult to convey complex information.
Radio	Low cost; can target specific audiences; ads can be placed quickly; can use sound, humor, and intimacy effectively.	No visual excitement; short exposure time and perishable message; difficult to convey complex information.
Magazines	Can target specific audiences; high-quality color; long life of ad; ads can be clipped and saved; can convey complex information.	Long time needed to place ad; limited control of ad position; relatively high cost; competes for attention with other magazine features.
Newspapers	Excellent coverage of local markets; ads can be placed and changed quickly; ads can be saved; quick consumer response; low cost.	Ads compete for attention with other newspaper features; can't control ad position on page; short life span; can't target specific audiences.
Direct mail	Best for targeting specific audiences; very flexible (3-D, pop-up ads); ad can be saved; measurable.	Relatively high cost; audience often sees it as "junk mail"; no competition with editorial matter.
Outdoor	Low cost; local market focus; high visibility; opportunity for repeat exposures.	Message must be short and simple; low selectivity of audience; criticized as a traffic hazard, eyesore.

Sources: William F. Arens, *Contemporary Advertising*, 6th ed. (Homewood, Ill.: Richard D. Irwin, 1996), p. 241; and William G. Nickels, James M. McHugh, and Susan M. McHugh, *Understanding Business*, 4th ed. (Homewood, Ill: Richard D. Irwin, 1996), p. 495.

Television   Television is a valuable medium because it communicates with sight, sound, and motion. Print advertisements alone could never give you the sense of a sports car cornering at high speed or communicate Ford's excitement about its new Probe. In addition, network television is the only medium that can reach 95 percent of the homes in the United States.[27] Recent studies have shown that *out-of-home TV* reaches another 20 million viewers in bars, hotels, offices, and college campuses each week.[28]

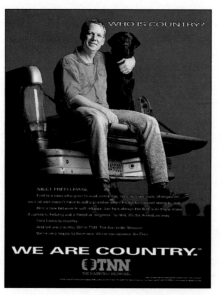

Television's major disadvantage is cost: the average price of a prime-time 30-second network spot is now $129,000.[29] Because of these high charges, many advertisers have reduced the length of their commercials from 30 seconds to 15 seconds. This practice, referred to as *splitting 30s*, reduces costs but severely restricts the amount of information and emotion that can be conveyed. Research indicates, however, that two different versions of a 15-second commercial, run back-to-back, will increase recall over long intervals.[30]

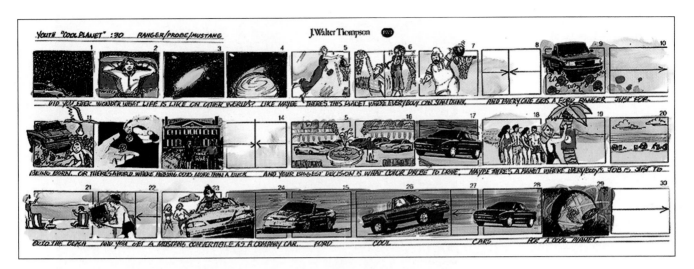

TV storyboards lead to commercials, which communicate with sight, sound, and motion.

Another problem with television is the likelihood of *wasted coverage*—having people outside the market for the product see the advertisement. In recent years the cost and wasted coverage problems of TV have been reduced through the introduction of cable TV. Advertising time is often less expensive on cable channels than on the major networks. In addition, there are currently about 150 cable channels—such as The Nashville Network, MTV, and the Golf Channel—that reach very narrowly defined audiences.[31]

A relatively new, and increasingly popular, form of television advertising is the infomercial. **Infomercials** are program-length (30-minute) advertisements that take an educational approach to communication with potential customers. Their use has increased since 1984 when the Federal Communications Commission lifted a restriction on the amount of commercial time television stations could air. Today more than 90 percent of all TV stations air infomercials, and more than 25 percent of all consumers have purchased a product as a result of seeing an infomercial. Volvo, Club Med, General Motors, Bank of America, Mattel, Revlon, Texaco, and many other companies are using infomercials as a means of providing information that is relevant, useful, and entertaining to prospective customers.[32]

Radio   There are seven times as many radio stations as television stations in the United States. The major advantage of radio is that it is a segmented medium. There are the Farm Radio Network, the Physicians' Network, all-talk shows, and hard rock stations, all listened to by different market segments. The average college student is a surprisingly heavy radio listener and spends more time during the day listening to radio than watching network television—2.2 hours versus 1.6 hours. Thus, advertisers with college students as their target market must consider radio.

The disadvantage of radio is that it has limited use for products that must be seen. Another problem is the ease with which consumers can tune out a commercial by switching stations. Radio is a medium that competes for people's attention as they do other activities such as driving, working, or relaxing. Peak radio listening time is during the drive times (6 to 10 A.M. and 4 to 7 P.M.).

Magazines   Magazines are becoming a very specialized medium, primarily because more than 400 new magazines are launched in the U.S. each year.[33] The marketing

Strong images increase an
ad's effectiveness.

Who is the target audience?
In what type of magazine
should it be run? What action
is it supposed to trigger? For
the answers, see the text.

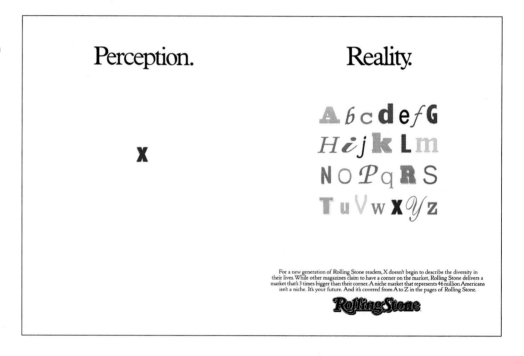

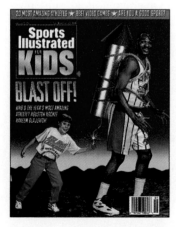

advantage of this medium is the great number of special-interest publications that appeal
to narrowly defined segments. Runners read *Runner's World,* sailors buy *Sail,* gardeners
subscribe to *Organic Gardening,* and children peruse *Sports Illustrated for Kids.* More
than 200 publications cater to the computer industry, and high-tech companies fill
about one fourth of the ad pages in *Fortune, Forbes, Business Week,* and *Dun's.*[34]
Each magazine's readers often represent a unique profile. Take the *Rolling Stone* reader,
who tends to travel, backpack, and ski more than most people—so a manufacturer of ski
equipment that places an ad in *Rolling Stone* knows it is reaching the desired target
audience. In addition to the distinct audience profiles of magazines, good color production is an advantage that allows magazines to create strong images.[35] The image
created by the Levi's ad used in Italy (shown above) helped it win the International
Advertising Festival print advertising award in Cannes.[36]

Rolling Stone has had a perception problem: many prospective advertisers in the magazine saw it as a magazine read only by 1960s-era hippies. To alter this misperception, it developed a series of "Perception–Reality" ads targeted at its prospective advertisers and ran them in magazines such as *Advertising Age,* which media buyers read. The advertising succeeded in describing the diversity of the magazine's readers and increased the number of pages of advertising sold in *Rolling Stone.*

The cost of advertising in national magazines is a disadvantage, but many national publications publish regional and even metro editions, which reduce the absolute cost and wasted coverage. *Time* publishes well over 100 different editions, ranging from a special edition for college students to a version for the area around Austin, Texas. In addition to cost, a limitation to magazines is their infrequency. At best, magazines are printed on a weekly basis, with many specialized publications appearing only monthly or less often.

Newspapers   Newspapers are an important local medium with excellent reach potential. Because of the daily publication of most papers, they allow advertisements to focus on specific current events, such as a "24-hour sale." Local retailers often use newspapers as their sole advertising medium.

Newspapers are rarely saved by the purchaser, so companies are generally limited to ads that call for an immediate customer response (although customers can clip and save ads they want). Companies also cannot depend on newspapers for color reproduction as good as that in most magazines.

National advertising campaigns rarely include this medium except in conjunction with local distributors of their products. In these instances both parties often share the advertising costs using a cooperative advertising program, which was described in Chapter 19. Another exception is the use of newspapers such as *The Wall Street Journal* and *USA Today,* which have national distribution.

Two trends are influencing newspapers today. The first is a dramatic increase in their cost of paper. In response, many newspapers have attempted to cut costs through hiring freezes, while others have raised prices. The Sunday *New York Times,* for example, recently raised its price by $0.50. The second trend is the rush to deliver on-line newspapers. More than 60 newspapers, including the *Chicago Tribune,* the *New York Times,* the *Dallas Morning News,* the *San Jose Mercury News,* and the *Washington Post,* are already on-line, and many others are expected soon.[37]

Direct mail   Direct mail allows the greatest degree of audience selectivity. Direct-mail companies can provide advertisers with a mailing list of their target market, such as students who live within two miles of the store, product managers in Texas, or people who own mobile homes. Direct mail has an advantage in providing complete product information, compared with that provided in 15-second, 30-second, or 60-second television or radio spots. Many advertisers now use direct mail in combination with other media to create *integrated marketing communications programs.* Mass media are used to create awareness, while direct mail builds a relationship and facilitates a purchase. In fact, 48 percent of all Americans have purchased something by mail in the past six months.[38]

One disadvantage of direct mail is that rising postal costs are making it more expensive. In fact, many direct-mail advertisers are beginning to use private delivery services, which charge less than the U.S. Postal Service, for catalogs and other "flats."[39] The major limitation is that people often view direct mail as junk, and the challenge is to get them to open a letter. Databases, which help marketers send their target market only mail that is relevant to them, are improving consumers' response to advertising they receive in the mail.

Outdoor   A very effective medium for reminding consumers about your product is outdoor advertising, such as the scoreboard at Chicago's Comiskey Park. The most common form of outdoor advertising, called *billboards,* often results in good reach

and frequency and has been shown to increase purchase rates.[40] The visibility of this medium is good supplemental reinforcement for well-known products, and it is a relatively low-cost, flexible alternative. A company can buy space just in the desired geographical market. A disadvantage to billboards, however, is that no opportunity exists for lengthy advertising copy. Also, a good billboard site depends on traffic patterns and sight lines. In many areas environmental laws have limited the use of this medium.

If you have ever lived in a metropolitan area, chances are you might have seen another form of outdoor advertising, transit advertising. This medium includes messages on the interior and exterior of buses, subway cars, and taxis. As use of mass transit grows, transit advertising may become increasingly important. Selectivity is available to advertisers, who can buy space by neighborhood or bus route. One disadvantage to this medium is that the heavy travel times, when the audiences are the largest, are not conducive to reading advertising copy. People are standing shoulder to shoulder on the subway, hoping not to miss their stop, and little attention is paid to the advertising.

Although outdoor advertising expenditures grew to more than $1.1 billion in 1994, the industry must address environmental concerns through self-regulation or be restricted by legislation. For example, four states have banned billboards, and New York City's Metropolitan Transportation Authority has banned tobacco advertising on buses and subways.[41]

Other media   As traditional media have become more expensive and cluttered, advertisers have been attracted to a variety of nontraditional advertising options, called *place-based media.* Messages are placed in locations that attract a specific target audience such as airports, doctors' offices, health clubs, or theaters (where ads are played on the screen before the movies are shown).[42]

Selection criteria   Choosing between these alternative media is difficult and depends on several factors. First, knowing the media habits of the target audience is essential to deciding among the alternatives. Second, occasionally product attributes necessitate that certain media be used. For example, if color is a major aspect of product appeal, radio is excluded. Newspapers allow advertising for quick actions to confront competitors, and magazines are more appropriate for complicated messages because the reader can spend more time reading the message. The final factor in selecting a medium is cost. When possible, alternative media are compared using a common denominator that reflects both reach and cost—a measure such as CPM.

Scheduling the Advertising

There is no correct schedule to advertise a product, but three factors must be considered. First is the issue of *buyer turnover,* which is how often new buyers enter the market to buy the product. The higher the buyer turnover, the greater is the amount of advertising required. A second issue in scheduling is the *purchase frequency;* the more frequently the product is purchased, the less repetition is required. Finally, companies must consider the *forgetting rate,* the speed with which buyers forget the brand if advertising is not seen.

Setting schedules requires an understanding of how the market behaves. Most companies tend to follow one of three basic approaches:

1. *Steady ("drip") schedule.* When seasonal factors are unimportant, advertising is run at a steady or regular schedule throughout the year.
2. *Flighting ("intermittent") schedule.* Periods of advertising are scheduled between periods of no advertising to reflect seasonal demand.
3. *Pulse ("burst") schedule.* A flighting schedule is combined with a steady schedule because of increases in demand, heavy periods of promotion, or introduction of a new product.

For example, products such as dry breakfast cereals have a stable demand throughout the year and would typically use a steady schedule of advertising. In contrast, products such as snow skis and suntan lotions have seasonal demands and receive flighting-schedule advertising during the seasonal demand period. Some products such as toys or automobiles require pulse-schedule advertising to facilitate sales throughout the year and during special periods of increased demand (such as holidays or new car introductions). Some evidence suggests that pulsing schedules are superior to other advertising strategies.[43]

CONCEPT CHECK

1. You see the same ad in *Time* and *Fortune* magazines and on billboards and TV. Is this an example of reach or frequency?

2. What is the most selective medium available?

3. What factors must be considered when choosing among alternative media?

EXECUTING THE ADVERTISING PROGRAM

As shown earlier in Figure 20–1, executing the advertising program involves pretesting the advertising copy and actually carrying out the advertising program. John Wanamaker, the founder of Wanamaker's Department Store in Philadelphia, remarked, "I know half my advertising is wasted, but I don't know what half." By evaluating advertising efforts marketers can try to ensure that their advertising expenditures are not wasted.[44] Evaluation is done usually at two separate times: before and after the advertisements are run in the actual campaign. Several methods used in the evaluation process at the stages of idea formulation and copy development are discussed below. Posttesting methods are reviewed in the section on evaluation.

Pretesting the Advertising

To determine whether the advertisement communicates the intended message or to select among alternative versions of the advertisement, **pretests** are conducted before the advertisements are placed in any medium.

Portfolio tests   Portfolio tests are used to test copy alternatives. The test ad is placed in a portfolio with several other ads and stories, and consumers are asked to read through the portfolio. Afterward subjects are asked for their impressions of the ads on several evaluative scales, such as from "very informative" to "not very informative."

FIGURE 20–8

Alternative structures of advertising agencies used to carry out the advertising program

TYPE OF AGENCY	SERVICES PROVIDED
Full-service agency	Does research, selects media, develops copy, and produces artwork
Limited-service agency	Specializes in one aspect of creative process; usually provides creative production work; buys previously unpurchased media space
In-house agency	Provides range of services, depending on company needs

Jury tests   Jury tests involve showing the ad copy to a panel of consumers and having them rate how they liked it, how much it drew their attention, and how attractive they thought it was. This approach is similar to the portfolio test in that consumer reactions are obtained. However, unlike the portfolio test, a test advertisement is not hidden within other ads.

Theater tests   Theater testing is the most sophisticated form of pretesting. Consumers are invited to view new television shows or movies in which test commercials are also shown. Viewers register their feelings about the advertisements either on hand-held electronic recording devices used during the viewing or on questionnaires afterward.

Carrying Out the Advertising Program

The responsibility for actually carrying out the advertising program can be handled in one of three ways, as shown in Figure 20–8. The **full-service agency** provides the most complete range of services, including market research, media selection, copy development, artwork, and production. Agencies that assist a client by both developing and placing advertisements have traditionally charged a commission of 15 percent of media costs. As corporations have reorganized and cut costs, however, new methods of paying agencies have been introduced. About 45 percent of advertisers now pay less than 15 percent, while other pay preset fees. A small but growing number of advertisers pay performance-based fees. Advertising agency Young and Rubicam, Inc., for example, actually earned more than 15 percent from Sears because its "Softer Side of Sears" campaign has been so successful.[45] **Limited-service agencies** specialize in one aspect of the advertising process such as providing creative services to develop the advertising copy or buying previously unpurchased media space. Limited-service agencies that deal in creative work are compensated by a contractual agreement for the services performed. Finally, **in-house agencies** made up of the company's own advertising staff may provide full services or a limited range of services.

EVALUATING THE ADVERTISING PROGRAM

The advertising decision process does not stop with executing the advertising program. The advertisements must be posttested to determine whether they are achieving their intended objectives, and results may indicate that changes must be made in the advertising program.

Posttesting the Advertising

An advertisement may go through **posttests** after it has been shown to the target audience to determine whether it accomplished its intended purpose. Five approaches common in posttesting are discussed here.[46]

Starch scores an
advertisement

Aided recall (recognition-readership)   After being shown an ad, respondents are asked whether their previous exposure to it was through reading, viewing, or listening. The Starch test shown in the accompanying photo uses aided recall to determine the percentage (1) who remember seeing a specific magazine ad *(noted)*, (2) who saw or read any part of the ad identifying the product or brand *(seen-associated)*, and (3) who read at least half of the ad *(read most)*. Elements of the ad are then tagged with the results, as shown in the picture.

Unaided recall   A question such as, "What ads do you remember seeing yesterday?" is asked of respondents without any prompting to determine whether they saw or heard advertising messages.

Attitude tests   Respondents are asked questions to measure changes in their attitudes after an advertising campaign, such as whether they have a more favorable attitude toward the product advertised.[47]

Inquiry tests   Additional product information, product samples, or premiums are offered to an ad's readers or viewers. Ads generating the most inquiries are presumed to be the most effective.

Sales tests   Sales tests involve studies such as controlled experiments (e.g., using radio ads in one market and newspaper ads in another and comparing the results) and consumer purchase tests (measuring retail sales that result from a given advertising campaign). The most sophisticated experimental methods today allow a manufacturer, a distributor, or an advertising agency to manipulate an advertising variable (such as schedule or copy) through cable systems and observe subsequent sales effects by monitoring data collected from checkout scanners in supermarkets.[48]

Making Needed Changes

Results of posttesting the advertising copy are used to reach decisions about changes in the advertising program. If the posttest results show that an advertisement is doing poorly in terms of awareness or cost efficiency, it may be dropped and other ads run in its place in the future. On the other hand, sometimes an advertisement may be so successful it is run repeatedly or used as the basis of a larger advertising program, as with Colgate's "White on White" laundry detergent commercials now used in 30 countries.

IMPORTANT CHANGES IN ADVERTISING AND SOCIETY

Several aspects of advertising are likely to change in the near future. First, in place of traditional mass media, new media such as CD-ROMs, the Internet, and interactive channels are evolving. Some experts suggest that the success of these media may reduce the number and effectiveness of mass media advertising opportunities. In response, some large marketers have begun to produce their own programs to guarantee an outlet for their ads. Procter & Gamble, for example, is working with Paramount Television Group to produce "Frazier" and "Wings." Similarly, Hallmark invested $365 million to purchase a company to produce its "Hall of Fame" programs.[49]

Second, new technologies may change how advertising is created. A small New Jersey company, Princeton Electronic Billboard, has developed a product that can place a corporate logo or message in a television transmission electronically. Fans watching a baseball game on television, for example, would see an ad on the wall behind the batter even though the wall is blank for fans at the game. One advantage of this form of advertising will be that viewers will only see ads that are relevant to them.[50]

Another change is the declining difference between advertising and editorial material. You may have noticed special advertising sections in newspapers and magazines with nonadvertising content, called *advertorials*. Like infomercials, the advertorials provide large amounts of relevant information in a form that readers may find entertaining. The growth of on-line advertising has created an electronic variation of the advertorial. At New Balance Athletic Shoe's Web site, for example, consumers can find tips on exercise, diet and running, content provided by *Runner's World*, *Men's Health*, and *Women's Sport and Fitness* and, of course, information on New Balance products and events.[51]

CONCEPT CHECK
1. Explain the difference between pretesting and posttesting advertising copy.

2. What is the difference between aided and unaided recall posttests?

SUMMARY

1. Advertising may be classified as either product or institutional. Product advertising can take three forms: pioneering, competitive, or reminder. Institutional ads are one of these three or advocacy.

2. The advertising decision process involves developing, executing, and evaluating the advertising program. Developing the advertising program focuses on determining who is the target audience, what to say, where the message should be said, and when to say it.

3. Setting advertising objectives is based on the hierarchy of effects. Objectives should be measurable, have a specified time period, and state the target audience.

4. Budgeting methods often used are percentage of sales, competitive parity, and the all you can afford approaches. The best budgeting approach is based on the objectives set and tasks required.

5. Copywriters and art directors have the responsibility of identifying the key benefits of a product and communicating them to the target audience with attention-getting advertising. Common appeals include fear, sex, and humor.

6. In selecting the right medium, there are distinct trade-offs among television, radio, magazines, newspapers, direct mail, outdoor, and other media. The decision is based on media habits of the target audience, product characteristics, message requirements, and media costs.

7. In determining advertising schedules, a balance must be made between reach and frequency. Scheduling must take into account buyer turnover, purchase frequency, and the rate at which consumers forget.

8. Advertising is evaluated before and after the ad is run. Pretesting can be done with portfolio, jury, or theater tests. Posttesting is done on the basis of aided recall, unaided recall, attitude tests, inquiry tests, and sales tests.

9. To execute an advertising program, companies can use several types of advertising agencies. These firms can provide a full range of services or specialize in creative or placement activities. Some firms use their own in-house agency.

10. Important future changes in advertising include the growth of new media, the development of new advertising technologies, and the use of advertorials.

KEY TERMS AND CONCEPTS

advertising p. 522
product advertisements p. 522
institutional advertisements p. 523
hierarchy of effects p. 525

percentage of sales budgeting p. 526
competitive parity budgeting p. 527
all you can afford budgeting p. 527
objective and task budgeting p. 527

CHAPTER PROBLEMS AND APPLICATIONS

1. How does competitive product advertising differ from competitive institutional advertising?

2. Suppose you are the advertising manager for a new line of children's fragrances. Which form of media would you use for this new product?

3. You have recently been promoted to be director of advertising for the Timkin Tool Company. In your first meeting with Mr. Timkin, he says, "Advertising is a waste! We've been advertising for six months now and sales haven't increased. Tell me why we should continue." Give your answer to Mr. Timkin.

4. A large life insurance company has decided to switch from using a strong fear appeal to a humorous approach. What are the strengths and weaknesses of such a change in message strategy?

5. Some national advertisers have found that they can have more impact with their advertising by running a large number of ads for a period and then running no ads at all for a period. Why might such a flighting schedule be more effective than a steady schedule?

6. Which medium has the lowest cost per thousand?

MEDIUM	COST	AUDIENCE
TV show	$5,000	25,000
Magazine	2,200	6,000
Newspaper	4,800	7,200
FM radio	420	1,600

7. Each year managers at Bausch and Lomb evaluate the many advertising media alternatives available to them as they develop their advertising program for contact lenses. What advantages and disadvantages of each alternative should they consider? Which media would you recommend to them?

8. Federated Banks has just developed two versions of an advertisement to encourage senior citizens to direct deposit their Social Security checks with the bank. Direct deposit means the government sends the funds directly to the bank, so that the consumer does not have to go and deposit the check. Suggest how the bank can evaluate the two ads.

9. The Toro Company has a broad product line. What timing approach would you recommend for the advertising of (*a*) the lawn mower line and (*b*) the new line of lawn and garden furniture?

10. What are two advantages and two disadvantages of the advertising posttests described in the chapter?

CASE 20–1   Fallon McElligott

Tucked away in Minneapolis, Minnesota, far from the traditional, perhaps conventional, headquarters of advertising's powerbrokers, is Fallon McElligott. Just 15 years old, it is considered one of the country's most respected creative advertising agencies. Fallon McElligott's stated philosophy about advertising has the same crispness as some of its most celebrated campaigns:

- Today's marketplace is burdened by unprecedented obstacles. Consumer lifestyles are in a state of rapid, almost daily flux. An ever-increasing proliferation of new brands is fragmenting the market more and more.

Consumer skepticism is making brand loyalty harder and harder to achieve.

- Amid all this, advertising clutter continues to expand. Increasing advertising spending is not the answer. In fact, in many cases, it's not even an option.

- Imagination is what will separate the companies that will thrive from those that will disappear.

"A number of companies have looked to us to help them outsmart rather than outspend the competition," explains Steve Sjoblad, Fallon McElligott's managing director. Clients today include *Rolling Stone* and *Time* magazines, Lee Jeans, Timex, Jim Beam brands, Ralston Purina, and Continental Bank, among others.

DEVELOPING AN ADVERTISING CAMPAIGN

Outsiders who see simply a newspaper or print advertisement rarely understand that hundreds of hours from dozens of people often contribute to a successful campaign. For Fallon McElligott, the sequence of activities generally includes the following three successive steps.

Planning and Research: Developing an Advertising Program

This involves the agency's account managers, account planners, and creative teams meeting with a client's marketing managers. "We must understand the client's marketing and communications goals, and the target audience and objectives for the advertising campaign," says account executive Maryanne O'Brien. "Frequently, additional research is required to understand consumer needs and wants and how to best position the client's product or service to consumers," she continues.

A Fallon McElligott creative team (copywriter and art director) translates this information into print or broadcast "concepts"—the words, pictures, and sounds the target audience sees and hears. Next, the agency's media planners and buyers select and schedule appropriate advertising media to carry the client's message to the target audience.

Implementation: Executing the Advertising Program

As with each of the other steps involved in a successful campaign, producing or executing the actual advertisements requires attention to hundreds of details. Fallon McElligott's production standards are very exacting. It is common to rework layouts and rewrite copy many times before a campaign is implemented.

Control: Evaluating the Advertising Program

The agency and its clients want to know if an advertising program is "working"—whether it is increasing awareness, inquiries, or sales. When this information becomes available through research, Fallon McElligott can fine-tune the direction and media selection of future creative work.

DEVELOPING IDEAS FOR TWO ADVERTISING PROGRAMS

The needs of two Fallon McElligott clients—*Rolling Stone* magazine and Lee Jeans— illustrate the kinds of problems that challenge an agency's creative efforts.

Rolling Stone Magazine

Rolling Stone brought to Fallon McElligott this positioning problem: too many advertisers and agencies perceived it as a magazine of the 60s, with political commentary and entertainment news reaching only a very young audience. "Many potential advertisers saw *Rolling Stone* as a hippie, counterculture magazine whose readers didn't have any spending power," says copywriter Bill Miller, who has worked on the *Rolling Stone* ads since the account came to Fallon McElligott. In fact, the opposite was true. The typical *Rolling Stone* reader is an upscale middle-class male.

Fallon McElligott's objectives were to change the outdated attitudes among major advertisers and key media influencers, convince them that *Rolling Stone* is the primary medium for the hard-to-reach young adult audience, and achieve deeper penetration of current advertiser categories and expand into new targeted areas.

Lee Jeans

Jeans are considered a "badge" product. More than any other item of clothing, they are often an emotional purchase tied to the brand displayed on the jean's back pocket. Lee Jeans, the nation's number one female brand and the number two brand in the category, had developed a "rational" franchise with consumers because of its unique product competence: the best fitting jeans. But research showed that it had failed to establish an emotional bond with consumers, which was considered critical if Lee was to establish a strong consumer preference for its jeans. This was the challenge facing Fallon McElligott. "We've met this challenge by combining the best-fitting-jeans idea with humor," comments copywriter Mike Lescarbeau.

Questions

1. (*a*) Give examples for each of the following statements/observations made in Fallon McElligott's agency philosophy provided at the beginning to the case:

- Consumer lifestyles are in a state of rapid flux.
- A proliferation of new brands is fragmenting the market.
- Consumer skepticism is making brand loyalty harder to achieve.
- Advertising clutter continues to expand.

(*b*) In what way do these affect the agency's creative work?

2. Think about the marketing problems described for *Rolling Stone* magazine as you scan a recent issue. (*a*) What kinds of advertisers do you find represented? (*b*) Can you recommend new groups of advertisers that the magazine might seek to attract? (*c*) What other images or messages could Fallon McElligott juxtapose in its Perception/Reality campaign (see page 536 in the chapter) to appeal to these new groups of advertisers? (*d*) What general and specific measures of success should *Rolling Stone* use to evaluate the effectiveness of Fallon McElligott's campaign?

3. Consider the current selling environment for Lee jeans. (*a*) What demographic changes and external forces affect the marketing and advertising of Lee jeans? (*b*) What is Lee's unique selling proposition (primary point of difference/competitive advantage)? (*c*) Consider Lee's three major target audiences: women, men, and teens. For each target group, list (1) the key communications messages and accompanying copy points and (2) a prioritized list of media that should be selected, with specific magazine titles, television programs, etc.

CHAPTER 21

Personal Selling and Sales Management

AFTER READING THIS CHAPTER YOU SHOULD BE ABLE TO:

- Recognize different types of personal selling.

- Describe the stages in the personal selling process.

- Specify the functions and tasks in the sales management process.

- Determine whether a firm should use manufacturer's representatives or a company salesforce and the number of people needed in a company's salesforce.

- Understand how firms recruit, select, train, motivate, compensate, and evaluate salespeople.

- Describe recent applications of salesforce automation.

MARY KAY COSMETICS: SELLING BEAUTY IN RUSSIA

What images come to mind when you hear the words "sales" and "sales management" mentioned as a career? Whatever they are, they would surely change after meeting Julie Rasmussen (shown on the opposite page).

Ms. Rasmussen exudes the entrepreneurial spirit sought in today's challenging global world of cosmetic and skin care marketing. After arriving in Moscow in 1992 with nothing more than a suitcase and an American Express Corporate Card, she employed a mixture of persistence and creativity to build the Russian subsidiary of Mary Kay Cosmetics from nothing to an all-female salesforce of independent representatives stretching across Russia, Ukraine, Kazakhstan, and the Baltics. Today she is president of the venture, which fills as many as 500 orders a day.

Drawing on her education as a Russian literature major at the University of Virginia and a master's degree in international relations from Columbia University, plus fluency in the Russian language, Ms. Rasmussen recruited, selected, and trained a salesforce that has since grown to 7,000. Ms. Rasmussen attributes the success of Mary Kay, in a region where people have been denied access to Western beauty products for almost 70 years, to an abundance of intelligent women who are "amazingly entrepreneurial." Mary Kay salespeople make an average of $350 a month, which is significantly more than Russia's $90 average monthly salary. Sales directors, who organize their own sales team, average as much as $6,000 a month, says Ms. Rasmussen.

Ms. Rasmussen acknowledges the challenges of sales and marketing in Russia, including inflation and political instability. But she adds, "In terms of fast-moving consumer goods, Russia is where it is happening."[1]

This chapter examines the scope and significance of personal selling and sales management in marketing.

547

It first highlights many forms of personal selling and outlines the selling process. The functions of sales management are then described, including recent advances in salesforce automation.

SCOPE AND SIGNIFICANCE OF PERSONAL SELLING AND SALES MANAGEMENT

Chapter 19 described personal selling and management of the sales effort as being part of the firm's promotional mix. Although it is important to recognize that personal selling is a useful vehicle for communicating with present and potential buyers, it is much more. Take a moment to answer the questions in the personal selling and sales management quiz in Figure 21–1. As you read on, compare your answers with those in the text.

Nature of Personal Selling and Sales Management

Personal selling involves the two-way flow of communication between a buyer and seller, often in a face-to-face encounter, designed to influence a person's or group's purchase decision. However, with advances in telecommunications, personal selling also takes place over the telephone, through video teleconferencing and interactive computer links between buyers and sellers. For example, customers of Haggar Apparel Company can enter purchase orders into their computer, have it contact Haggar's computer, and find out when the requested products can be shipped.[2]

Personal selling remains a highly human-intensive activity despite the use of technology. Accordingly, the people involved must be managed. **Sales management** involves planning the selling program and implementing and controlling the personal selling effort of the firm. Numerous tasks are involved in managing personal selling, including setting objectives; organizing the salesforce; recruiting, selecting, training, and compensating salespeople; and evaluating the performance of individual salespeople.

Pervasiveness of Selling

"Everyone lives by selling something," wrote author Robert Louis Stevenson a century ago. His observation still holds true today. The Bureau of Labor Statistics reports that almost 16 million people are employed in sales positions in the United

FIGURE 21–1

Personal selling and sales management quiz

> 1 What percentage of chief executive officers in the 1,000 largest U.S. corporations have significant sales and marketing experience in their work history? (check one)
>   10% _____   30% _____   50% _____
>   20% _____   40% _____   60% _____
>
> 2 About how much does it cost for a consumer product salesperson to make a single personal sales call? (check one)
> $100 _____ $150 _____ $200 _____
> $125 _____ $175 _____ $225 _____
>
> 3 "A salesperson's job is finished when a sale is made." True or false? (circle one)
>   True   False
>
> 4 On average, sales training programs devote about what percentage of time to sales techniques? (check one)
>   20% _____   40% _____   60% _____
>   30% _____   50% _____   70% _____

Victor Kiam, Chairman and CEO of Remington Products, Inc., is also Remington's "principal salesperson."

States, and this figure will grow to 18 million in 2000. Included in this number are manufacturing sales personnel, real estate brokers, stockbrokers, and salesclerks who work in retail stores. In reality, however, virtually every occupation that involves customer contact has an element of personal selling. For example, attorneys, accountants, bankers, and company personnel recruiters perform sales-related activities, whether or not they acknowledge it.

Many executives in major companies have held sales positions at some time in their careers. For example, Victor Kiam, the flamboyant chairman and chief executive officer of Remington Products, Inc., previously held a sales position at Lever Brothers. It might be said that today Kiam is Remington's most visible salesperson. It is no accident that these individuals rose from sales and marketing positions to top management. About 20 percent of the chief executive officers in the 1,000 largest U.S. corporations have significant sales and marketing experience in their work history.[3] (What percentage did you check for question 1 in Figure 21–1?) Thus, selling often serves as a stepping-stone to top management, as well as being a career path in itself.

Personal Selling in Marketing

Personal selling serves three major roles in a firm's overall marketing effort. First, salespeople are the critical link between the firm and its customers. This role requires that salespeople match company interests with customer needs to satisfy both parties in the exchange process. Second, salespeople *are* the company in a consumer's eyes. They represent what a company is or attempts to be and are often the only personal contact a customer has with the company. For example, the "look" projected by salespeople for Avon Products, Inc. is an important factor in communicating the benefits of the company's cosmetic line. Third, personal selling may play a dominant role in a firm's marketing program. This situation typically arises when a firm uses a push marketing strategy, described in Chapter 19. Avon, for example, pays almost 40 percent of its total sales dollars for selling expenses.[4] Pharmaceutical firms and office and educational equipment manufacturers also rely heavily on personal selling in the marketing of their products.

Creating Customer Value through Salespeople: Relationship Selling

As the critical link between the firm and its customers, salespeople can create customer value in many ways.[5] For instance, by being close to the customer, salespeople can identify creative solutions to customer problems. Salespeople at U.S. Surgical observe hospital surgical practices and devote hours to questioning surgeons on how surgeries can be improved. One result of this activity was the creation of a new product that makes gallbladder surgery safer, cheaper, and less painful. The product is now used in over 60 percent of gallbladder surgeries in the United States. Salespeople can create value by easing the customer buying process. This happened at AMP, Inc., a producer of electrical products. Salespeople and customers had a difficult time getting product specifications and performance data on AMP's 70,000 products quickly and accurately. The company now records all information on

U.S. surgical salespeople visit hospital operating rooms to find better ways to create customer value.

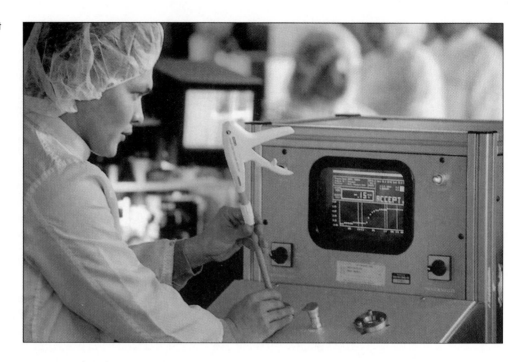

CD-ROM disks that can be scanned instantly by salespeople and customers. Customer value is also created by salespeople who follow through after the sale. At Jefferson Smurfit Corporation, a multibillion dollar supplier of packaging products, one of its salespeople juggled production from three of the company's plants to satisfy an unexpected demand for boxes from General Electric. This person's action led to the company being given GE's "Distinguished Supplier Award."

Customer value creation is made possible by **relationship selling,** the practice of building ties to customers based on a salesperson's attention and commitment to customer needs over time. Relationship selling involves mutual respect and trust among buyers and sellers. It focuses on creating long-term customers, not a one-time sale.[6] A recent survey of 300 senior sales executives revealed that 96 percent consider "building long-term relationships with customers" to be the most important activity affecting sales performance. Companies such as American Express, Electronic Data Systems, Motorola, and Owens-Corning have made relationship building a core focus of their sales effort.[7]

CONCEPT CHECK

1. What is personal selling?
2. What is involved in sales management?

THE MANY FORMS OF PERSONAL SELLING

Personal selling assumes many forms based on the amount of selling done and the amount of creativity required to perform the sales task. Broadly speaking, three types of personal selling exist: order taking, order getting, and sales support activities.[8] While some firms use only one of these types of personal selling, others use a combination of all three. Figure 21–2 compares order getters and order takers to illustrate some important differences between them.

FIGURE 21-2

Comparing order takers and order getters

BASIS OF COMPARISON	ORDER TAKERS	ORDER GETTERS
Objective	Handle routine product orders or reorders	Identify new customers and uncover customer needs
Purchase situation	Focus on straight rebuy or simple purchase situations	Focus on new buy and modified rebuy purchase situations
Activity	Perform order processing functions	Act as creative problem solvers
Training	Require significant clerical training	Require significant sales, product, and customer training

Order Taking

Typically, an **order taker** processes routine orders or reorders for products that were already sold by the company. The primary responsibility of order takers is to preserve an ongoing relationship with existing customers and maintain sales. Two types of order takers exist. *Outside order takers* visit customers and replenish inventory stocks of resellers, such as retailers or wholesalers. For example, Frito-Lay salespeople call on supermarkets, neighborhood grocery stores, and other establishments to ensure that the company's line of snack products (such as Doritos and Tostitos) is in adequate supply. In addition, outside order takers typically provide assistance in arranging displays. *Inside order takers*, also called *order* or *salesclerks*, typically answer simple questions, take orders, and complete transactions with customers. Many retail clerks are inside order takers. Inside order takers are often employed by companies that use *inbound telemarketing*, the use of toll-free telephone numbers that customers can call to obtain information about products or services and make purchases. In industrial settings, order taking arises in straight rebuy situations. Order takers, for the most part, do little selling in a conventional sense and engage in little problem solving with customers. They often represent simple products that have few options, such as confectionary items, magazine subscriptions, and highly standard-ized industrial products. Inbound telemarketing is also an essential selling activity for

Inbound telemarketing is an essential selling activity for companies such as National Flora in the long-distance floral delivery business.

A Xerox Corporation
advertisement featuring team
selling.

more "customer service" driven firms, such as National Flora in the long-distance
floral delivery business. At National Flora, for example, order takers undergo
extensive training so that they can better assist callers with their purchase decisions.

Order Getting

An **order getter** sells in a conventional sense and identifies prospective customers,
provides customers with information, persuades customers to buy, closes sales, and
follows up on customers' use of a product or service. Like order takers, order getters
can be inside (an automobile salesperson) or outside (an IBM salesperson). Order
getting involves a high degree of creativity and customer empathy and is typically
required for selling complex or technical products with many options, so considerable product knowledge and sales training are necessary. In modified rebuy or new
buy purchase situations in industrial selling, an order getter acts as a problem solver
who identifies how a particular product may satisfy a customer's need. Similarly, in
the purchase of a service, such as insurance, a Metropolitan Life insurance agent can
provide a mix of plans to satisfy a buyer's needs depending on income, stage of the
family's life cycle, and investment objectives.

Order getting is an expensive process.[9] It is estimated that the median direct cost
of a single sales call for an industrial product is $198.67; for a consumer product,
$210.43; and for a service, $193.58. (What amount did you check for question 2 in
Figure 21–1?) These costs illustrate why outbound telemarketing is so popular today.
Outbound telemarketing is the practice of using the telephone rather than personal
visits to contact customers. A significantly lower cost per sales call (in the range of
$20 to $25) and little or no field expense accounts for its widespread appeal. Inbound
and outbound telemarketing usage has grown about 25 percent per year.[10]

Sales Support Personnel

Sales support personnel augment the selling effort of order getters by performing a
variety of services. For example, **missionary salespeople** do not directly solicit

MARKETING NEWSNET

Cross

Functional

CREATING AND SUSTAINING CUSTOMER VALUE THROUGH CROSS-FUNCTIONAL TEAM SELLING

The day of the lone salesperson calling on a customer is rapidly becoming history. Many companies today are using cross-functional teams of professionals to work with customers to improve relationships, find better ways of doing things, and, of course, create and sustain value for their customers.

Xerox and IBM pioneered cross-functional team selling, but other firms were quick to follow as they spotted the potential to create and sustain value for their customers. Recognizing that corn growers needed a herbicide they could apply less often, a Du Pont team of chemists, sales and marketing executives, and regulatory specialists created just the right product that recorded sales of $57 million in its first year. Procter & Gamble uses teams of marketing, sales, advertising, computer systems, and distribution personnel to work with its major retailers, such as Wal-Mart, to identify ways to develop, promote, and deliver products. Pitney Bowes, Inc., which produces sophisticated computer systems that weigh, rate, and track packages for firms such as UPS and Federal Express, also uses sales teams to meet customer needs. These teams consist of sales personnel, "carrier management specialists," and engineering and administrative executives who continually find ways to improve the technology of shipping goods across town and around the world.

Efforts to create and sustain customer value through cross-functional team selling will become more popular as customers also seek greater value for their money. According to the vice president for procurement of a *Fortune 500* company, "Today, it's not just getting the best price put getting the best value—and there are a lot of pieces to value."

orders but rather concentrate on performing promotional activities and introducing new products. They are used extensively in the pharmaceutical industry, where they persuade physicians to prescribe a firm's product. Actual sales are made through wholesalers or directly to pharmacists who fill prescriptions. A **sales engineer** is a salesperson who specializes in identifying, analyzing, and solving customer problems and brings know-how and technical expertise to the selling situation but often does not actually sell products and services. Sales engineers are popular in selling industrial products such as chemicals and heavy equipment.

In many situations firms engage in cross-functional **team selling,** the practice of using an entire team of professionals in selling to and servicing major customers.[11] Team selling is used when specialized knowledge is needed to satisfy the different interests of individuals in a customer's buying center. For example, a selling team might consist of a salesperson, a sales engineer, a service representative, and a financial executive, each of whom would deal with a counterpart in the customer's firm. Team selling takes different forms. In **conference selling,** a salesperson and other company resource people meet with buyers to discuss problems and opportunities. In **seminar selling,** a company team conducts an educational program for a customer's technical staff, describing state-of-the-art developments. IBM and Xerox Corporation pioneered cross-functional team selling in working with prospective buyers. Other firms have embraced this practice and created and sustained value for their customers, as described in the accompanying Marketing NewsNet.[12]

CONCEPT CHECK

1. What is the principal difference between an order taker and an order getter?

2. What is team selling?

FIGURE 21-3

Stages and objectives of the
personal selling process

STAGE	OBJECTIVE	COMMENTS
Prospecting	Search for and qualify prospects	Start of the selling process; prospects produced through advertising, referrals, and cold canvassing.
Preapproach	Gather information and decide how to approach the prospect	Information sources include personal observation, other customers, and own salespeople.
Approach	Gain prospect's attention, stimulate interest, and make transition to the presentation	First impression is critical; gain attention and interest through reference to common acquaintances, a referral, or product demonstration.
Presentation	Begin converting a prospect into a customer by creating a desire for the product or service	Different presentation formats are possible; however, involving the customer in the product or service through attention to particular needs is critical; important to deal professionally and ethically with prospect skepticism, indifference, or objections.
Close	Obtain a purchase commitment from the prospect and create a customer	Salesperson asks for the purchase; different approaches include the trial close and assumptive close.
Follow-up	Ensure that the customer is satisfied with the product or service	Resolve any problems faced by the customer to ensure customer satisfaction and future sales possibilities.

THE PERSONAL SELLING PROCESS: BUILDING RELATIONSHIPS

Selling, and particularly order getting, is a complicated activity that involves building buyer–seller relationships. Although the salesperson–customer interaction is essential to personal selling, much of a salesperson's work occurs before this meeting and continues after the sale itself. The **personal selling process** consists of six stages: (1) prospecting, (2) preapproach, (3) approach, (4) presentation, (5) close, and (6) follow-up (Figure 21–3).

Prospecting

Personal selling begins with *prospecting*—the search for and qualification of potential customers.[13] For some products that are one-time purchases such as encyclopedias, continual prospecting is necessary to maintain sales. There are three types of prospects. A *lead* is the name of a person who may be a possible customer. A *prospect* is a customer who wants or needs the product. If an individual wants the product, can afford to buy it, and is the decision maker, this individual is a *qualified prospect*.

Leads and prospects are generated using several sources. For example, advertising may contain a coupon or a toll-free number to generate leads, as shown in the accompanying AT&T advertisement. Some companies use exhibits at trade fairs, professional meetings, and conferences to generate leads or prospects. Staffed by salespeople, these exhibits are used to attract the attention of prospective buyers and

An AT&T prospecting advertisement for its direct marketing service.

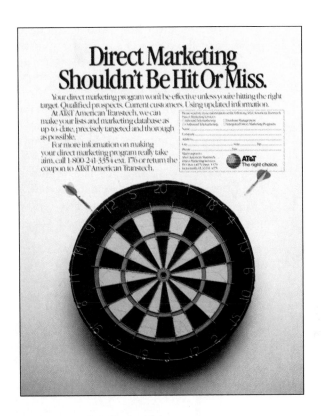

disseminate information. Another approach for generating leads is through *cold canvassing* in person or by telephone. This approach simply means that a salesperson may open a telephone directory, pick a name, and visit or call that individual. Although the refusal rate is high with cold canvassing, this approach can be successful. For example, 41 brokers at Lehman Brothers recently identified 18,004 prospects, qualified 1,208 of them, made 659 sales presentations, and opened 40 new accounts in four working days.[14] However, cold canvassing is frowned upon in most Asian and Latin American societies. Personal visits, based on referrals, are expected.[15]

Cold canvassing is often criticized by U.S. consumers and is now regulated. A recent survey reported that 75 percent of U.S. consumers consider this practice an intrusion on their privacy, and 72 percent find it distasteful.[16] The Telephone Consumer Protection Act of 1991 contains provisions to curb abuses such as early morning or late night calling. Additional federal regulations became effective January 1, 1996. They require more complete disclosure regarding solicitations, include provisions that allow consumers to avoid being called at any time, and impose fines up to $10,000 for violations.[17]

Preapproach

Once a salesperson has identified a qualified prospect, preparation for the sale begins with the preapproach. The *preapproach* stage involves obtaining further information on the prospect and deciding on the best method of approach. Knowing how the prospect prefers to be approached, and what the prospect is looking for in a product or service, is essential regardless of cultural setting. For example, a Merrill Lynch stockbroker will need information on a prospect's discretionary income, investment objectives, and preference for discussing brokerage services over the telephone or in person. For industrial products the preapproach involves identifying the buying role of a prospect (for example, influencer or decision maker), important buying criteria, and the prospect's receptivity to a formal or informal presentation. Identifying the best time to contact a prospect is also important. For example, Northwestern Mutual Life Insurance Company suggests the best times to call on people in different occupations: dentists before 9:30 A.M., lawyers between 11:00 A.M. and 2:00 P.M., and college professors between 7:00 and 8:00 P.M.[18]

This stage is very important in international selling where customs dictate appropriate protocol. In many South American countries, for example, buyers expect salespeople to be punctual for appointments. However, prospective buyers are routinely 30 minutes late. South Americans take negotiating seriously and prefer straightforward presentations, but a hard-sell approach will not work.[19]

Approach

The *approach* stage involves the initial meeting between the salesperson and prospect, where the objectives are to gain the prospect's attention, stimulate interest, and build the foundation for the sales presentation itself and the basis for a working relationship. The first impression is critical at this stage, and it is common for salespeople to begin the conversation with a reference to common acquaintances, a referral, or even the product or service itself. Which tactic is taken will depend on the information obtained in the prospecting and preapproach stages.

The approach stage is very important in international settings. In many societies outside the United States, considerable time is devoted to nonbusiness talk designed to establish a rapport between buyers and sellers. For instance, it is common that two or three meetings occur before business matters are discussed in the Middle East and Asia. Gestures are also very important. Business cards should be printed in English on one side and the language of the prospective customer on the other. Knowledgeable U.S. salespeople know that their business cards should be handed to Asian customers using both hands, with the name facing the receiver. In Asia, anything involving names demands respect.[20]

Presentation

The *presentation* is at the core of the order-getting selling process, and its objective is to convert a prospect into a customer by creating a desire for the product or service. Three major presentation formats exist: (1) stimulus-response format, (2) formula selling format, and (3) need-satisfaction format.

Stimulus-response format   The **stimulus-response presentation** format assumes that given the appropriate stimulus by a salesperson, the prospect will buy. With this format the salesperson tries one appeal after another, hoping to "hit the right button." A counter clerk at McDonald's is using this approach when he or she asks whether you'd like an order of french fries or a dessert with your meal. The counter clerk is engaging in what is called *suggestive selling.* Although useful in this setting, the stimulus-response format is not always appropriate, and for many products a more formalized format is necessary.

Formula selling format   A more formalized presentation, the **formula selling presentation** format, is based on the view that a presentation consists of information that must be provided in an accurate, thorough, and step-by-step manner to inform the prospect. A popular version of this format is the *canned sales presentation,* which is a memorized, standardized message conveyed to every prospect.[21] Used frequently by firms in telephone and door-to-door selling of consumer products (for example, Fuller Brush Company and Encyclopaedia Britannica), this approach treats every prospect the same, regardless of differences in needs or preference for certain kinds of information. Canned sales presentations can be advantageous when the differences between prospects are unknown or with novice salespeople who are less knowledgeable about the product and selling process than experienced salespeople. Although it guarantees a thorough presentation, it often lacks flexibility and spontaneity and, more important, does not provide for feedback from the prospective buyer—a critical component in the communication process and the start of a relationship.

Need-satisfaction format   The stimulus-response and formula selling formats share a common characteristic: the salesperson dominates the conversation. By comparison, the **need-satisfaction presentation** format emphasizes probing and listening by the salesperson to identify needs and interests of prospective buyers. Once these are identified, the salesperson tailors the presentation to the prospect and highlights product benefits that may be valued by the prospect. The need-satisfaction format, which emphasizes problem solving, is the most consistent with the marketing concept. Two selling styles are associated with this format. **Adaptive selling** involves adjusting the presentation to fit the selling situation, such as knowing when to offer solutions and when to ask for more information. **Consultative selling** focuses on problem identification, where the salesperson serves as an expert on problem recognition and resolution.[22] Both styles are used for industrial products such as computers and heavy equipment. Many consumer service firms such as brokerage and insurance firms and consumer product firms like AT&T and Gillette also subscribe to these selling styles.

Handling objections   A critical concern in the presentation stage is handling objections. *Objections* are excuses for not making a purchase commitment or decision. Some objections are valid and are based on the characteristics of the product or service or price. However, many objections reflect prospect skepticism or indifference. Whether valid or not, experienced salespeople know that objections do not put an end to the presentation. Rather, techniques can be used to deal with objections in a courteous, ethical, and professional manner. The following six techniques are the most common:[23]

1. *Acknowledge and convert the objection.* This technique involves using the objection as a reason for buying. For example, a prospect might say, "The price is too high." The reply: "Yes, the price is high because we use the finest materials. Let me show you. . . ."
2. *Postpone.* The postpone technique is used when the objection will be dealt with later in the presentation: "I'm going to address that point shortly. I think my answer would make better sense then."
3. *Agree and neutralize.* Here a salesperson agrees with the objection, then shows that it is unimportant. A salesperson would say, "That's true and others have

MARKETING NEWSNET

THE SUBTLETY OF SAYING YES IN EAST ASIA

By the year 2000, the economies of East Asia—spanning from Japan to Indonesia—will almost equal that of the United States and total about four fifths of the European Union. The marketing opportunities in East Asia are great, but effective selling in these countries will require a keen cultural ear. Seasoned global marketers know that in many Asian societies it is impolite to say *no*, and *yes* has multiple meanings.

Yes in Asian societies can have at least four meanings. It can mean that listeners are simply acknowledging that a speaker is talking to them even though they don't understand what is being said, or it can mean that a speaker's words are understood, but not that they are agreed with. A third meaning of *yes* conveys that a presentation is understood, but other people must be consulted before any commitment is possible. Finally, *yes* can also mean that a proposal is understood and accepted. However, experienced negotiators also note that this *yes* is subject to change if the situation is changed.

This one example illustrates why savvy salespeople are sensitive to cultural underpinnings when engaged in cross-cultural sales negotiations.

said the same. However, they concluded that issue was outweighed by the other benefits."

4. *Accept the objection.* Sometimes the objection is valid. Let the prospect express such views, probe for the reason behind it, and attempt to stimulate further discussion on the objection.

5. *Denial.* When a prospect's objection is based on misinformation and clearly untrue, it is wise to meet the objection head on with a firm denial.

6. *Ignore the objection.* This technique is used when it appears that the objection is a stalling mechanism or is clearly not important to the prospect.

Each of these techniques requires a calm, professional interaction with the prospect and is most effective when objections are anticipated in the preapproach stage. Handling objections is a skill requiring a sense of timing, appreciation for the prospect's state of mind, and adeptness in communication. Objections also should be handled ethically. Lying or misrepresenting product or service features are grossly unethical practices.

Close

The *closing* stage in the selling process involves obtaining a purchase commitment from the prospect. This stage is the most important and the most difficult because the salesperson must determine when the prospect is ready to buy. Telltale signals indicating a readiness to buy include body language (prospect reexamines the product or contract closely), statements ("This equipment should reduce our maintenance costs"), and questions ("When could we expect delivery?"). The close itself can take several forms. Three closing techniques are used when a salesperson believes a buyer is about ready to make a purchase: (1) trial close, (2) assumptive close, and (3) urgency close. A *trial close* involves asking the prospect to make a decision on some aspect of the purchase: "Would you prefer the blue or gray model?" An *assumptive close* entails asking the prospect to consider choices concerning delivery, warranty, or financing terms under the assumption that a sale has been finalized. An *urgency close* is used to commit the prospect quickly by making reference to the timeliness of the purchase: "The low interest financing ends next week," or, "That is the last model we have in stock." Of course, these statements should be used only if they accurately reflect the situation; otherwise, such claims would be unethical. When a prospect is clearly ready to buy, the final close is used, and a salesperson asks for the order.

Knowing when the prospect is ready to buy becomes even more difficult in cross-cultural buyer–seller negotiations where societal customs and language play a large role. Read the accompanying Marketing NewsNet to understand the multiple meanings of *yes* in Japan and other societies in East Asia.[24]

Follow-Up

The selling process does not end with the closing of a sale; rather, professional selling requires customer follow-up. One marketing authority equated the follow-up with courtship and marriage,[25] by observing, "... the sale merely consummates the courtship. Then the marriage begins. How good the marriage is depends on how well the relationship is managed." The *follow-up* stage includes making certain the customer's purchase has been properly delivered and installed and difficulties experienced with the use of the item are addressed. Attention to this stage of the selling process solidifies the buyer–seller relationship. Moreover, research shows that the cost and effort to obtain repeat sales from a satisfied customer is roughly half of that necessary to gain a sale from a new customer.[26] In short, today's satisfied customers become tomorrow's qualified prospects or referrals. (What was your answer to question 3 in the quiz?)

CONCEPT CHECK	**1.**	What are the six stages in the personal selling process?
	2.	What is the distinction between a lead and a qualified prospect?
	3.	Which presentation format is most consistent with the marketing concept? Why?

THE SALES MANAGEMENT PROCESS

Selling must be managed if it is going to contribute to a firm's overall objectives. Although firms differ in the specifics of how salespeople and the selling effort are managed, the sales management process is similar across firms. Sales management consists of three interrelated functions: (1) sales plan formulation, (2) sales plan implementation, and (3) evaluation and control of the salesforce (Figure 21–4).

Sales Plan Formulation

Formulating the sales plan is the most basic of the three sales management functions. According to the vice president of the Harris Corporation, a manufacturer of

FIGURE 21–4

The sales management process

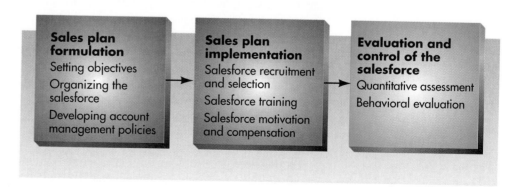

ETHICS AND SOCIAL RESPONSIBILITY ALERT

Ethics

THE ETHICS OF ASKING CUSTOMERS ABOUT COMPETITORS

Salespeople are a valuable source of information about what is happening in the marketplace. By working closely with customers and asking good questions, salespeople often have first-hand knowledge of customer problems and wants. They also are able to spot the activities of competitors. However, should salespeople explicitly ask customers about competitor strategies such as pricing practices, product development efforts, and trade and promotion programs?

Gaining knowledge about competitors by asking customers for information is a ticklish ethical issue. Research indicates that 25 percent of U.S. salespeople engaged in business-to-business selling consider this practice unethical, and their companies have explicit guidelines for this practice. It is also noteworthy that Japanese salespeople consider this practice to be more unethical than do U.S. salespeople.

Do you believe that asking customers about competitor practices is unethical? Why or why not?

---

electronics products, "If a company hopes to implement its marketing strategy, it really needs a detailed sales planning process."[27] The **sales plan** is a statement describing what is to be achieved and where and how the selling effort of salespeople is to be deployed. Formulating the sales plan involves three tasks: (1) setting objectives, (2) organizing the salesforce, and (3) developing account management policies.

Setting objectives   Setting objectives is central to sales management because this task specifies what is to be achieved. In practice, objectives are set for the total salesforce and for each salesperson. Selling objectives can be output related and focus on dollar or unit sales volume, number of new customers added, and profit. Alternatively, they can be input related and emphasize the number of sales calls and selling expenses. Output- and input-related objectives are used for the salesforce as a whole and for each salesperson. A third type of objective that is behaviorally related is typically specific for each salesperson and includes his or her product knowledge, customer service, and selling and communication skills. Increasingly, firms are also emphasizing knowledge of competition as an objective since salespeople are calling on customers and should see what competitors are doing.[28] But should salespeople explicitly ask their customers for information about competitors? Read the accompanying Ethics and Social Responsibility Alert to see how salespeople view this practice.

Whatever objectives are set, they should be precise and measurable and specify the time period over which they are to be achieved. Once established, these objectives serve as performance standards for the evaluation of the salesforce—the third function of sales management.

Organizing the salesforce   Establishing a selling organization is the second task in formulating the sales plan. Three questions are related to organization. First, should the company use its own salesforce, or should it use independent agents such as manufacturer's representatives? Second, if the decision is made to employ company salespeople, then should they be organized according to geography, customer type, or product or service? Third, how many company salespeople should be employed?

The decision to use company salespeople or independent agents is made infrequently. However, Apple Computer recently switched from using agents to its own

FIGURE 21-5

Break-even chart for comparing independent agents and a company salesforce

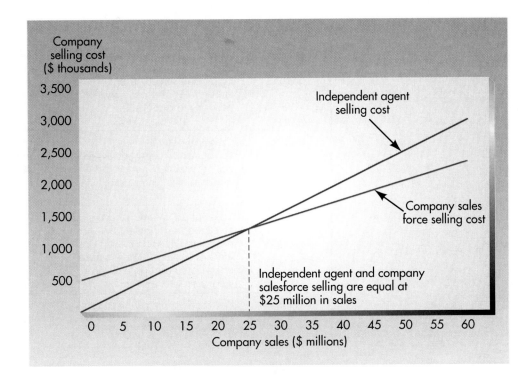

salesforce, and Coca-Cola's Food Division replaced its salesforce with independent agents (food brokers). The Optoelectronics Division of Honeywell, Inc. has switched back and forth between agents and its own salesforce over the last 25 years. The decision is based on an analysis of economic and behavioral factors. An economic analysis examines the costs of using both types of salespeople and is a form of break-even analysis.

Consider a situation in which independent agents would receive a 5 percent commission on sales, and company salespeople would receive a 3 percent commission, salaries, and benefits. In addition, with company salespeople, sales administration costs would be incurred for a total fixed cost of $500,000 per year. At what sales level would independent or company salespeople be less costly? This question can be answered by setting the costs of the two options equal to each other and solving for the sales level amount, as shown in the following equation:

$$\frac{\text{Total cost of company salespeople}}{0.03(X) + \$500,000} = \frac{\text{Total cost of independent agents}}{0.05(X)}$$

where X = sales volume. Solving for X, sales volume equals $25 million, indicating that below $25 million in sales independent agents would be cheaper, but above $25 million a company salesforce would be cheaper. This relationship is shown in Figure 21–5.

Economics alone does not answer this question, however. A behavioral analysis is also necessary and should focus on issues related to the control, flexibility, effort, and availability of independent and company salespeople.[29] Figure 21–6 shows the common behavioral arguments for independent agents versus a company salesforce. An individual firm must weigh the pros and cons of the economic and behavioral considerations before making this decision.

If a company elects to employ its own salespeople, then it must choose an organizational structure based on (1) geography, (2) customer, or (3) product (Figure 21–7). A geographical structure is the simplest organization, where the United States, or indeed the globe, is first divided into regions and each region is divided into districts or territories. Salespeople are assigned to each district with defined

CRITERIA	CASE FOR COMPANY SALESFORCE	CASE FOR INDEPENDENT AGENTS
Control	Company selects, trains, supervises, and can use multiple rewards to direct salespeople.	Agents are equally well selected, trained, and supervised by the representative organization.
Flexibility	Company can transfer salespeople, change customer selling practices, and otherwise direct its own salesforce.	Little fixed cost is present with agents; mostly there are variable costs; therefore, firm is not burdened with overhead.
Effort	Sales effort is enhanced because salespeople represent one firm, not several; firm loyalty is present; there is better customer service because salespeople receive salary as well as commission.	Agents might work harder than salespeople because compensation is based solely on commissions; customer service is good, since it builds repeat business.
Availability	Knowledgeable agents might not be available where and when needed.	Entrepreneurial spirit of agents will make them available where a marketing opportunity exists.

geographical boundaries and call on all customers and represent all products sold by the company. The principal advantage of this structure is that it can minimize travel time, expenses, and duplication of selling effort. However, if a firm's products or customers require specialized knowledge, then a geographical structure is not suitable.

When different types of buyers have different needs, a customer sales organizational structure is used. In practice this means that a different salesforce calls on each separate type of buyer or marketing channel. For example, Eastman Kodak recently switched from a geographical to a marketing channel structure with different sales teams serving specific retail channels: mass merchandisers, photo specialty outlets, and food and drug stores. The rationale for this approach is that more effective, specialized customer support and knowledge are provided to buyers. However, this structure often leads to higher administrative costs and some duplication of selling effort, since two separate salesforces are used to represent the same products.

A variation of the customer organizational structure is **major account management,** the practice of using team selling to focus on important customers so as to build mutually beneficial, long-term, cooperative relationships.[30] Major account management involves teams of sales, service, and often technical personnel who work with purchasing, manufacturing, engineering, logistics, and financial executives in customer organizations. This approach, which often assigns company personnel to a customer account, results in "customer specialists" who can provide exceptional service. Procter & Gamble uses this approach with Wal-Mart as does Black & Decker with Home Depot.

When specific knowledge is required to sell certain types of products, then a product sales organization is used. For example, Lone Star Steel has a salesforce that sells drilling pipe to oil companies and another that sells specialty steel products to manufacturers. The primary advantage of this structure is that salespeople can develop expertise with technical characteristics, applications, and selling methods associated with a particular product or family of products. However, this structure also produces high administrative costs and duplication of selling effort since two company salespeople may call on the same customer.

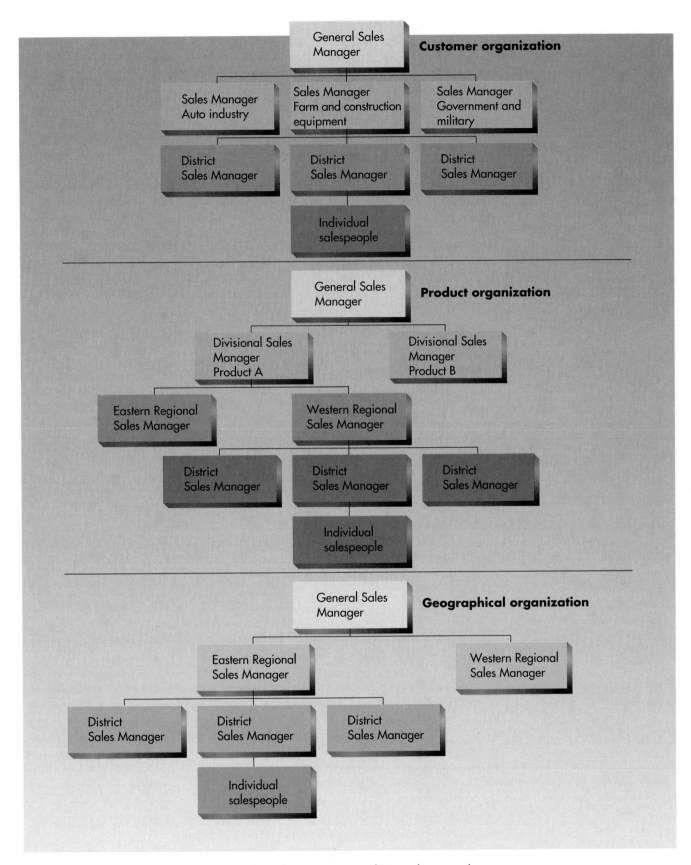

FIGURE 21–7   Organizing the salesforce by customer, product, and geography

In short, there is no one best sales organization for all companies in all situations. Rather, the organization of the salesforce should reflect the marketing strategy of the firm. Each year about 10 percent of U.S. firms change their sales organizations to implement new marketing strategies.

The third question related to salesforce organization involves determining the size of the salesforce. For example, why does Frito-Lay have about 13,500 salespeople who call on supermarkets, grocery stores, and other establishments to sell snack foods? The answer lies in the number of accounts (customers) served, the frequency of calls on accounts, the length of an average call, and the amount of time a salesperson can devote to selling.

A common approach for determining the size of a salesforce is the **workload method.** This formula-based method integrates the number of customers served, call frequency, call length, and available selling time to arrive at a figure for the salesforce size. For example, Frito-Lay needs about 13,500 salespeople according to the following workload method formula:

$$NS = \frac{NC \times CF \times CL}{AST}$$

where:

    NS = Number of salespeople

    NC = Number of customers

    CF = Call frequency necessary to service a customer each year

    CL = Length of an average call

    AST = Average amount of selling time available per year

Frito-Lay sells its products to 400,000 supermarkets, grocery stores, and other establishments. Salespeople should call on these accounts at least once a week, or 52 times a year. The average sales call lasts 55 minutes (0.91 hour). An average salesperson works 2,000 hours a year (50 weeks × 40 hours a week), but 12 hours a week are devoted to nonselling activities such as travel, leaving 1,400 hours a year. Using these guidelines, Frito-Lay would need

$$NS = \frac{400,000 \times 52 \times 0.91}{1,400} = 13,520 \text{ salespeople}$$

The value of this formula is apparent in its flexibility; a change in any one of the variables will affect the number of salespeople needed. Changes are determined, in part, by the firm's account management policies.

Developing account management policies   The third task in formulating a sales plan involves developing **account management policies** specifying whom salespeople should contact, what kinds of selling and customer service activities should be engaged in, and how these activities should be carried out. These policies might state which individuals in a buying organization should be contacted, the amount of sales and service effort that different customers should receive, and the kinds of information salespeople should collect before or during a sales call.

An example of an account management policy in Figure 21–8 shows how different accounts or customers can be grouped according to level of opportunity and the firm's competitive sales position. When specific account names are placed in each cell, salespeople clearly see which accounts should be contacted, with what level of selling and service activity, and how to deal with them. Accounts in cells 1 and 2 might have high frequencies of personal sales calls and increased time spent on a call. Cell 3 accounts will have lower call frequencies, and cell 4 accounts might be contacted through telemarketing or direct mail rather than in person. For example, Union Pacific Railroad recently put its 20,000 smallest accounts on a telemarketing

		COMPETITIVE POSITION OF SALES ORGANIZATION	
		HIGH	**LOW**
ACCOUNT OPPORTUNITY	**High**	1 *Attractiveness.* Accounts offer good opportunity, since they have high potential and sales organization has a strong position. *Account management policy.* Accounts should receive high level of sales calls and service to retain and possibly build accounts.	3 *Attractiveness.* Accounts may offer good opportunity if sales organization can overcome its weak position. *Account management policy.* Emphasize a heavy sales organization position or shift resources to other accounts if stronger sales organization position impossible.
	Low	2 *Attractiveness.* Accounts are somewhat attractive since sales organization has a strong position, but future opportunity is limited. *Account management policy.* Accounts should receive moderate level of sales and service to maintain current position of sales organization.	4 *Attractiveness.* Accounts offer little opportunity, and sales organization position is weak. *Account management policy.* Consider replacing personal calls with telephone sales or direct mail to service accounts. Consider dropping account.

FIGURE 21-8

Account management policy grid

program. A subsequent survey of these accounts indicated that 84 percent rated Union Pacific's sales effort "very effective" compared with 67 percent before the switch.[31]

Sales Plan Implementation

The sales plan is put into practice through the tasks associated with sales plan implementation. Whereas sales plan formulation focuses on "doing the right things," implementation emphasizes "doing things right." The three major tasks involved in implementing a sales plan are (1) salesforce recruitment and selection, (2) salesforce training, and (3) salesforce motivation and compensation.

Salesforce recruitment and selection   Effective recruitment and selection of salespeople is one of the most crucial tasks of sales management. It entails finding people who match the type of sales position required by a firm. Recruitment and selection practices would differ greatly between order-taking and order-getting sales positions, given the differences in the demands of these two jobs. Therefore, recruitment and selection begin with a carefully crafted job analysis and job description followed by a statement of job qualifications.[32]

A *job analysis* is a study of a particular sales position, including how the job is to be performed and the tasks that make up the job. Information from a job analysis is used to write a *job description,* a written document that describes job relationships and requirements that characterize each sales position. It explains (1) to whom a salesperson reports, (2) how a salesperson interacts with other company personnel, (3) the customers to be called on, (4) the specific activities to be carried out, (5) the physical and mental demands of the job, and (6) the types of products and services to be sold. The job description is then translated into a statement of job qualifications, including the aptitudes, knowledge, skills, and a variety of behavioral characteristics considered necessary to perform the job successfully. Qualifications for order-getting sales positions often mirror the expectations of buyers: (1) problem-solving ability, (2) honesty, (3) intimate product knowledge, and (4) attentiveness reflected in responsiveness to buyer needs and customer follow-up.[33] Firms use a variety of methods for evaluating prospective salespeople. Personal interviews, reference

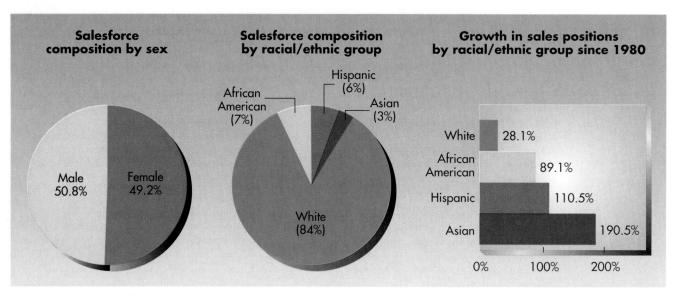

FIGURE 21–9

U.S. salesforce composition and change

checks, and background information provided on application forms are the most frequently used methods.[34]

The search for qualified salespeople has produced an increasingly diverse salesforce in the United States. Women now represent almost half of all professional salespeople, and minority representation is growing. The fastest growth rate is among salespeople of Asian and Hispanic descent (see Figure 21–9).[35]

Salesforce training   Whereas recruitment and selection of salespeople is a one-time event, salesforce training is an ongoing process that affects both new and seasoned salespeople. For example, Microsoft offers nearly 100 training courses annually for its experienced salespeople alone.[36] Sales training covers much more than selling practices. On average, training programs devote 35 percent of time to product information, 30 percent to sales techniques, 25 percent to market and company information, and 10 percent to other topics, including ethical practices.[37] (What was your answer to question 4 on the quiz?)

Training new salespeople is an expensive and time-consuming process.[38] The average cost of training a new industrial product salesperson (including salary during the training period) is $9,763 and takes four months. Training a new consumer product salesperson costs $4,995 and takes about three months, and training new salespeople in service industries costs $6,610 and takes almost four months. On-the-job training is the most popular type of training, followed by individual instruction taught by experienced salespeople. Formal classes and seminars taught by sales trainers are also popular.

Salesforce motivation and compensation   A sales plan cannot be successfully implemented without motivated salespeople. Research on salesperson motivation suggests that (1) a clear job description, (2) effective sales management practices, (3) a sense of achievement, and (4) proper compensation, incentives, or rewards will produce a motivated salesperson.[39]

The importance of compensation as a motivating factor means that close attention must be given to how salespeople are financially rewarded for their efforts. Salespeople are paid using one of three plans: (1) straight salary, (2) straight commission, or (3) a combination of salary and commission. Under a *straight salary compensation plan* a salesperson is paid a fixed fee per week, month, or year. With a *straight commission compensation plan* a salesperson's earnings are directly tied to the sales or profit generated. For example, an insurance agent might receive a 2 percent commission of $2,000 for selling a $100,000 life insurance policy. A *combination compensation plan* contains a specified salary plus a commission on sales or profit generated.

Each compensation plan has its advantages and disadvantages. A straight salary plan is easy to administer and gives management a large measure of control over how salespeople allocate their efforts. However, it provides little incentive to expand sales volume. This plan is used when salespeople engage in many nonselling activities, such as account servicing. A straight commission plan provides the maximum amount of selling incentive but can detract salespeople from providing customer service. This plan is common when nonselling activities are minimal. Combination plans are most preferred by salespeople and attempt to build on the advantages of salary and commission plans while reducing potential shortcomings of each. Today, 68 percent of companies use combination plans, 19 percent use straight salary, and 13 percent rely solely on commissions. The popularity of combination plans is evident in the recent decision by Digital Equipment Corporation to convert its 10,000 computer salespeople from straight salary to a salary plus commission plan.

Mary Kay Cosmetics recognizes a top salesperson at its annual sales meeting.

Nonmonetary rewards are also given to salespeople for meeting or exceeding objectives. These rewards include trips, honor societies, distinguished salesperson awards, and letters of commendation. Some unconventional rewards include the new pink Cadillacs, fur coats, and jewelry given by Mary Kay Cosmetics to outstanding salespeople.

Effective recruitment, selection, training, motivation, and compensation programs combine to create a productive salesforce. Ineffective practices often lead to costly salesforce turnover. U.S. and Canadian firms experience an annual 27 percent turnover rate, which means that about one of every four salespeople are replaced each year. The expense of replacing and training a new salesperson, including the cost of lost sales, can be as high as $75,000.[40] Moreover, new recruits are often less productive than established salespeople.

Salesforce Evaluation and Control

The final function in the sales management process involves evaluating and controlling the salesforce. It is at this point that salespeople are assessed as to whether sales objectives were met and account management policies were followed. Both quantitative and behavioral measures are used.

Quantitative assessments   Quantitative assessments, called quotas, are based on input- and output-related objectives set forth in the sales plan. Input-related measures focus on the actual activities performed by salespeople such as those involving sales calls, selling expenses, and account management policies. The number of sales calls made, selling expense related to sales made, and the number of reports submitted to superiors are frequently used input measures.

Output measures focus on the results obtained and include sales produced, accounts generated, profit achieved, and orders produced compared with calls made. Dollar sales volume, last year/current year sales ratio, the number of new accounts, and sales of specific products are frequently used measures when evaluating salesperson output.

Behavioral evaluation   Behavioral measures are also used to evaluate sales-people. These include assessments of a salesperson's attitude, attention to customers, product knowledge, selling and communication skills, appearance, and professional demeanor. Even though these assessments are sometimes subjective, they are frequently considered, and, in fact, inevitable, in salesperson evaluation. Moreover, these factors are often important determinants of quantitative outcomes.

Almost 30 percent of U.S. companies now include customer satisfaction as a behavioral measure of salesperson performance.[41] Indianapolis Power & Light, for example, asks major customers to grade its salespeople from A to F. IBM has been the most aggressive in using this behavioral measure. Forty percent of an IBM salesperson's evaluation is linked to customer satisfaction; the remaining 60 percent is linked to profits achieved. The relentless focus on customer satisfaction by Eastman Chemical Company salespeople contributed to the company being named a recipient of the prestigious Malcolm Baldrige National Quality Award, as described in the accompanying Marketing NewsNet.[42]

Salesforce Automation

Personal selling and sales management are undergoing a technological revolution in the form of salesforce automation. **Salesforce automation** (SFA) is the use of technology designed to make the sales function more effective and efficient. SFA applies to a wide range of activities including each stage in the personal selling

Toshiba America Medical System salespeople have found computer technology to be an effective sales tool and training device.

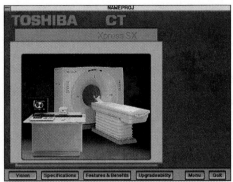

process and management of the salesforce itself. Computer and communication technologies have and will continue to play a central role in salesforce automation.[43]

Salesforce computerization   Computer technology has become an integral part of field selling through innovations such as laptop, notebook, palmtop, pad, and tablet computers. For example, salespeople for Godiva Chocolates use their laptop computers to process orders, plan time allocations, forecast sales, and communicate with Godiva personnel and customers. While in a department store candy buyer's office, such as Neiman Marcus, a salesperson can calculate the order cost (and discount), transmit the order, and obtain a delivery date within minutes using the buyer's telephone and the computer to communicate with Godiva's order processing department.[44]

Toshiba America Medical System salespeople now use laptop computers with built-in CD-ROM capabilities to provide interactive presentations for their computerized tomography (CT) and magnetic resonance imaging (MRI) scanners. In it the customer sees elaborate three-dimensional animations, high-resolution scans, and video clips of the company's products in operation as well as narrated testimonials from satisfied customers. Toshiba has found this application to be effective both for sales presentations and for training its salespeople.[45]

Salesforce communication   Technology also has changed the way salespeople communicate with customers, other salespeople and sales support personnel, and management. Facsimile, electronic mail, and voice mail are three common commu-

nication technologies used by salespeople today. Cellular (phone) technology, which now allows salespeople to exchange data as well as voice transmissions, is equally popular. Whether traveling or in a customer's office, these technologies provide information at the salesperson's fingertips to answer customer questions and solve problems.

Advances in communication and computer technologies have made possible the mobile sales office. Some salespeople now equip minivans with a fully functional desk, swivel chair, light, computer, printer, fax machine, cellular phone, and a satellite dish. Jeff Brown, an agent manager with U.S. Cellular, uses such a mobile office. He says, "If I arrive at a prospect's office and they can't see me right away, then I can go outside to work in my office until they're ready to see me."[46]

The mobile office for salespeople has grown in popularity with the advent of computer and communication technology.

Sales management in the age of automation Salesforce automation represents both an opportunity and a challenge for sales management. Examples of SFA applications include computer hardware and software for account analysis, time management, order processing and follow-up, sales presentations, proposal generation, and product and sales training. But, applications are not free. It is estimated that equipment, software, and training costs for automating a salesforce ranges from $2,500 to $5,000 or more per person. However, companies such as Tandem Computer report that savings from SFA by its 1,700 national and international field salespeople amount to $2 million annually.[47]

Some companies are using SFA to eliminate the need for field sales offices. Compaq Computer Corporation is a case in point. The company recently shifted its entire 224 person U.S. salesforce into home offices, closed three regional sales offices, and saved $10 million in staff salaries and office rent. A fully equipped home office for each salesperson costs the company about $8,000 and includes a notebook computer, fax/copier, cellular phone, two phone lines, and office furniture.[48]

Salesforce automation is clearly changing how selling is done and how salespeople are managed. Its numerous applications promise to boost selling productivity, improve customer service, and decrease selling cost. As applications increase, SFA has the potential to transform selling and sales management in the twenty-first century.

CONCEPT CHECK

1. What are the three types of selling objectives?

2. What three factors are used to structure sales organizations?

3. Sales training typically focuses on what two sales-related issues?

SUMMARY

1. Personal selling involves the two-way flow of communication between a buyer and a seller, often in a face-to-face encounter, designed to influence a person's or group's purchase decision. Sales management involves planning the sales program and implementing and controlling the personal selling effort of the firm.

2. Personal selling is pervasive since virtually every occupation that involves customer contact has an element of selling attached to it.

3. Personal selling plays a major role in a firm's marketing effort. Salespeople occupy a boundary position between buyers and sellers; they *are* the company to many buyers and account for a major cost of marketing in a variety of industries; and they can create value for customers.

4. Three types of personal selling exist: order-taking, order-getting, and sales support activities. Each type differs from the others in terms of actual selling done and the amount of creativity required to perform the job.

5. The personal selling process, particularly for order getters, is a complex activity involving six stages: (1) prospecting, (2) preapproach, (3) approach, (4) presentation, (5) close, and (6) follow-up.

6. The sales management process consists of three interrelated functions: (1) sales plan formulation, (2) sales plan implementation, and (3) evaluation of the salesforce.

7. A sales plan is a statement describing what is to be achieved and where and how the selling effort of salespeople is to be deployed. Sales planning involves setting objectives, organizing the salesforce, and developing account management policies.

8. Effective salesforce recruitment and selection efforts, sales training that emphasizes selling skills and product knowledge, and motivation and compensation practices are necessary to successfully implement a sales plan.

9. Salespeople are evaluated using quantitative and behavioral measures that are linked to selling objectives and account management policies.

10. Salesforce automation involves the use of technology designed to make the sales function more effective and efficient. It applies to a wide range of activities including each stage in the personal selling process and management of the salesforce itself.

KEY TERMS AND CONCEPTS

personal selling p. 548
sales management p. 548
relationship selling p. 550
order taker p. 551
order getter p. 552
missionary salespeople p. 552
sales engineer p. 553
team selling p. 553
conference selling p. 553
seminar selling p. 553
personal selling process p. 554

stimulus-response presentation p. 556
formula selling presentation p. 557
need-satisfaction presentation p. 557
adaptive selling p. 557
consultative selling p. 557
sales plan p. 560
major account management p. 562
workload method p. 564
account management policies p. 564
salesforce automation p. 568

CHAPTER PROBLEMS AND APPLICATIONS

1. Jane Dawson is a new sales representative for the Charles Schwab brokerage firm. In searching for clients, Jane purchased a mailing list of subscribers to *The Wall Street Journal* and called them all regarding their interest in discount brokerage services. She asked if they have any stocks and if they have a regular broker. Those people without a regular broker were asked their investment needs. Two days later Jane called back with investment advice and asked if they would like to open an account. Identify each of Jane Dawson's actions in terms of the steps of selling.

2. For the first 50 years of business the Johnson Carpet Company produced carpets for residential use. The salesforce was structured geographically. In the past five years a large percentage of carpet sales has been to industrial users, hospitals, schools, and architects. The company also has broadened its product line to include area rugs, Oriental carpets, and wall-to-wall carpeting. Is the present salesforce structure appropriate, or would you recommend an alternative?

3. Where would you place each of the following sales jobs on the order taker/order getter continuum shown below? (*a*) Burger King counter clerk, (*b*) automobile insurance salesperson, (*c*) IBM computer salesperson, (*d*) life insurance salesperson, and (*e*) shoe salesperson.

Order taker	**Order getter**

4. Listed here are three different firms. Which compensation plan would you recommend for each firm, and what reasons would you give for your recommendations? (*a*) A newly formed company that sells lawn care equipment on a door-to-door basis directly to consumers; (*b*) the Nabisco Company, which sells heavily advertised products in supermarkets by having the salesforce call on these stores and arrange shelves, set up displays, and make presentations to store buying committees; and (*c*) the Wang word-processing division, which makes word-processing system presentations to company buying committees consisting of purchasing agents and future users.

5. The TDK tape company services 1,000 audio stores throughout the United States. Each store is called on 12 times a year, and the average sales call lasts 30 minutes. Assuming a salesperson works 40 hours a week, 50 weeks a year, and devotes 75 percent of the time to actual selling, how many salespeople does TDK need?

6. A furniture manufacturer is currently using manufacturer's representatives to sell its line of living room furniture. These representatives receive an 8 percent commission. The company is considering hiring its own salespeople and has estimated that the fixed cost of managing and paying their salaries would be $1 million annually. The salespeople would also receive a 4 percent commission on sales. The company has sales of $25 million dollars, and sales are expected to grow by 15 percent next year. Would you recommend that the company switch to its own salesforce? Why or why not?

7. Suppose someone said to you, "The only real measure of a salesperson is the amount of sales produced." How might you respond?

Case 21-1   Contemporary Developments in Selling Today

Salespeople today often can no longer afford to behave like the pushy, stereotypical salesperson often portrayed in the media. More sophisticated customers, changes in technology, and a changing selling environment have meant that the 'old-fashioned' salesperson of the past is increasingly becoming obsolete.

Three contempory developments in selling are changing how the sales function is being performed. These developments include (1) changes in sales motivation and compensation programs, (2) the introduction of salesforce automation, and (3) higher expectations for ethics in selling.

Changes in Motivation and Compensation Programs

One of the areas where selling has changed has been in the way salespeople are motivated and compensated. Marshall Industries, a Southern California electronics firm, operated until 1988 with a sales compensation and motivation program that encouraged a competitive environment between members of the sales force. In such an environment, salespeople were not interested in helping one another and the company as a whole. Rather, salespeople were primarily concerned with *their* customers and *their* territory. Compensation and motivation programs that produce winners and losers tend to have this effect. Since 1988, however, a new compensation and motivation program has been in place that encourages and rewards salesperson cooperation by eliminating commissions and other individual bonuses. Marshall Industries' sales compensation program was redesigned to reward group performance. Salespeople focused more on serving the customer rather than on achieving quotas. The results have been dramatic. Sales have increased from $400 million to $700 million within a 5 year period, salesperson turnover was cut by 50%, and the company's stock price rose from $10 to $42 per share.

Introduction of Salesforce Automation

Improvements and innovations in salesforce automation have had a dramatic impact on the tools available to the salesforce as well as improving salesforce effectiveness. Navistar has turned to technology to gain an advantage in their markets by developing a selling tool that allows potential customers to compare its brand of International trucks against competitors on a component by component basis. For example, a potential customer can learn how the turn radius for an International truck compares to that of a competitive truck, or how gas consumption varies, or how engine efficiency differs. This approach helps identify specific customer needs and highlight the implications of the purchase decision; that is, how does the purchase of this truck impact operating and maintenance costs? It's an extremely powerful tool for helping the salesforce show the benefits of the International truck in a very quantitive and useful manner on the criteria of importance to a given buyer.

Selling Ethics

Salespeople cannot afford to take an "anything goes" approach to getting the sale. The potential for damage, not only to the individual's reputation but to the company as a whole, means that salesforce ethics are receiving increased attention.

Real estate agents can potentially be placed in a situation that can create a conflict of interest that can present an ethical problem. Dual agency occurs when a real estate agent or the company s/he represents is acting on behalf of both the seller and buyer in a transaction. For example, if the real estate agent helping you look for a new home also shows you a home listed by his/her company, the real estate agent's loyalties are divided. To prevent potential ethical dilemmas, a real estate agent should inform the client when such a situation is presented. This gives the client the option of deciding whether to continue under a dual agency, thereby assuming greater responsibility for their own interests than if a single agency situation occurred. In several states, laws govern or prevent dual agency situations from occurring to control for potential conflicts of interest.

Questions

1. What are the pros and cons of various salesforce compensation programs? What types of behaviors are encouraged under each?

2. Describe how salesforce automation can be used at different stages of the selling process to facilitate the sales person's efforts.

3. Dual agency is one type of ethical conflict that can arise in a real estate selling situation. However, there are many types of ethical conflicts that are faced by the salesforce due to the nature of the selling job—acting as an advocate for the customer within the organization and representing the company to the customer and the market. What steps can a salesperson and his/her company take to minimize the potential for ethical dilemas?

MANAGING THE MARKETING PROCESS

CHAPTER 22
The Strategic Marketing Process

Part Five discusses issues and techniques related to the planning, implementation, and control phases of the strategic marketing process. Chapter 22 explains how marketing executives search for a competitive advantage and allocate the firm's resources to maximize the effects of marketing efforts. Frameworks for improving marketing planning, guidelines for creating an effective marketing plan, and alternatives for organizing a marketing department are also discussed. In addition, General Mills's spin-off of a new company—Darden, Inc.—illustrates the planning activities of a successful marketing organization.

The Strategic Marketing Process

AFTER READING THIS CHAPTER YOU SHOULD BE ABLE TO:

• Explain how marketing managers allocate their limited resources, both in theory and in practice.

• Describe three marketing planning frameworks: Porter's generic strategies, profit enhancement options, and market-product synergies.

• Describe what makes an effective marketing plan and some problems that often exist with them.

• Describe the alternatives for organizing a marketing department and the role of a product manager.

• Schedule a series of tasks to meet a deadline using a Gantt chart.

• Understand how sales and profitability analyses and marketing audits are used to evaluate and control marketing programs.

MARKETING STRATEGY AT GENERAL MILLS: A RETURN TO ITS ROOTS

Marketing strategists at General Mills faced tough times in the mid-1990s. Its flagship Cheerios and Wheaties breakfast cereals and its Betty Crocker cake mixes were competing in a U.S. food industry growing at only 1 percent each year. Also, private brands were becoming tougher competitors, requiring General Mills to cut its prices, thereby hurting its margins and profits.[1] General Mills's restaurant chains—Red Lobster, Olive Garden, and China Coast—were growing fast but were constantly competing with its food lines for limited corporate resources.

In the end the corporate cultures—discussed in Chapter 2—in the General Mills food and restaurant sectors were far different, and real synergies between the two sectors didn't materialize. Therefore, corporate and marketing planners made a big decision: divide the original company into two new separate, focused companies:[2]

• General Mills, Inc.—a $5.5 billion consumer foods company that includes foods such as cereals, Betty Crocker cake mixes and desserts, Hamburger Helper, Yoplait yogurt, and Fruit by the Foot.
• Darden, Inc.—a $3.2 billion multiunit restaurant company that includes the Red Lobster, Olive Garden, and China Coast chains.

Marketing strategists planning the breakup hoped that the split would enable each new company to plan, implement, and control marketing efforts that would achieve higher growth in sales revenues and profits in their separated units than in the past. The breakup had at least one immediate result: the new product introduction of Frosted Cheerios—industry analysts have called it the most successful product launch of a ready-to-eat cereal in history.[3]

This chapter discusses issues and techniques related to the planning, implementation, and control phases of the strategic marketing process, the kind of topics marketing strategists at General Mills and Darden face in growing their businesses. The individual elements of the strategic marketing process were introduced in Chapter 2.

STRATEGIC MARKETING'S GOAL: EFFECTIVE RESOURCE ALLOCATION

As noted in Chapter 2, corporate and marketing executives search continuously to find a competitive advantage—a unique strength relative to competitors, often based on quality, time, cost, or innovation. Having identified this competitive advantage, they must allocate their firm's resources to exploit it.[4] The timing of product and market actions may also influence the magnitude and duration of a firm's competitive advantage.[5]

Allocating Marketing Resources Using Sales Response Functions

A **sales response function** relates the expense of marketing effort to the marketing results obtained.[6] For simplicity in the examples that follow, only the effects of annual marketing effort on annual sales revenue will be analyzed, but the concept applies to other measures of marketing success—such as profit, units sold, or level of awareness—as well.

Maximizing incremental revenue minus incremental cost   Economists give managers a specific guideline for optimal resource allocation: allocate the firm's marketing, production, and financial resources to the markets and products where the excess of incremental revenues over incremental costs is greatest. This parallels the marginal revenue–marginal cost analysis of Chapter 14.

Figure 22–1 illustrates this resource allocation principle. The firm's annual marketing effort, such as sales and advertising expenses, is plotted on the horizontal axis. As this annual marketing effort increases, so does the resulting annual sales revenue. The relationship is assumed to be S-shaped, showing that an additional $1 million of marketing effort results in far greater increases of sales revenue in the mid-range (such as $4 million) than at either end (such as $2 million or $7 million).

A numerical example of resource allocation   Suppose Figure 22–1 shows the situation for a recently introduced General Mills product such as Gushers. Also assume the sales revenue response function doesn't change through time. Point *A* shows the position of the firm in year 1, and point *B* shows it three years later in year 4. Marketing effort in the form of advertising and other promotions has increased from $3 million to $6 million a year, while sales revenue has increased from $30 million to $70 million a year.

Let's look at the major resource allocation question: what are the probable increases in sales revenue in years 1 and 4 for an extra $1 million of marketing effort? As Figure 22–1 reveals:

Year 1
 Increase in marketing effort from $3 million to $4 million = $1 million
 Increase in sales revenue from $30 million to $50 million = $20 million
 Ratio of incremental sales revenue to effort = $20,000,000:$1,000,000 = 20:1

Year 4
 Increase in marketing effort from $6 million to $7 million = $1 million
 Increase in sales revenue from $70 million to $73 million = $3 million
 Ratio of incremental sales revenue to effort = $3,000,000:$1,000,000 = 3:1

FIGURE 22-1

Sales response function showing the situation for two different years

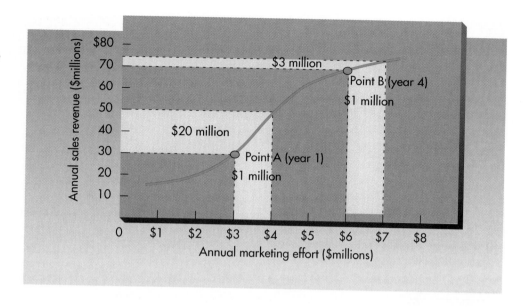

Thus, in year 1 a dollar of extra marketing effort returned $20 in sales revenue, whereas in year 4 it returned only $3. If no other expenses are incurred, it might make sense to spend $1 million in year 4 to gain $3 million in incremental sales revenue. However, it may be far wiser for General Mills to invest the money in products in one of its other business units, such as its new lighter texture Whipped Deluxe Frosting or its new Pop Secret Popcorn Bars. The essence of resource allocation is simple: put incremental resources where the incremental returns are greatest over the foreseeable future.

Allocating Marketing Resources in Practice

General Mills, like many firms in these businesses, does extensive analysis using **share points,** or percentage points of market share, as the common basis of comparison to allocate marketing resources effectively. This allows it to seek answers to the question "How much is it worth to us to try to increase our market share by another 1 (or 2, or 5, or 10) percentage point?"

This also enables higher-level managers to make resource allocation trade-offs among different kinds of business units owned by the company. To make these resource allocation decisions, marketing managers must estimate (1) the market share for the product, (2) the revenues associated with each point of market share (the present-day $82 million for a share point in breakfast cereals[7] may be five times what it is in cake mixes), and (3) the contribution to overhead and profit (or gross margin) of each share point.

The resource allocation process helps General Mills choose wisely from among the many opportunities that exist in its various products and markets.

Resource Allocation and the Strategic Marketing Process

Company resources are allocated effectively in the strategic marketing process by converting marketing information into marketing actions. Figure 22–2 summarizes the strategic marketing process introduced in Chapter 2, along with some details of the marketing actions and information that compose it. Figure 22–2 is really a simplification of the actual strategic marketing process: while the three phases of the strategic marketing process have distinct separations in the figure and the marketing actions are separated from the marketing information, in practice these blend together and interact.

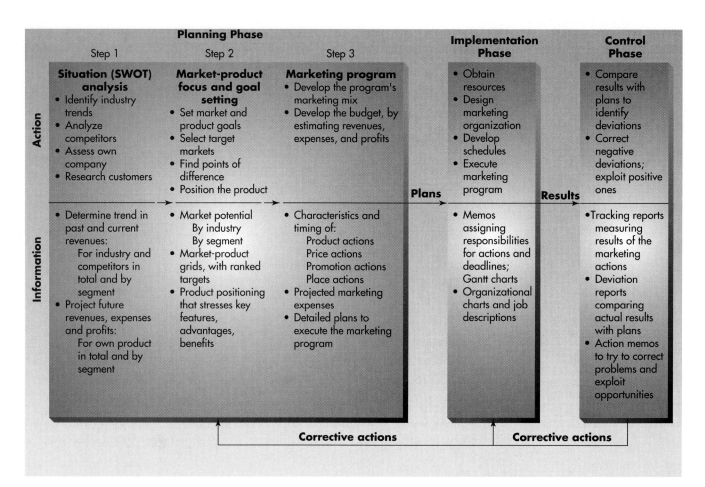

FIGURE 22–2

The strategic marketing process; actions and information

The upper half of each box in Figure 22–2 highlights the actions involved in that part of the strategic marketing process, and the lower half summarizes the information and reports used. Note that each phase has an output report:

PHASE	OUTPUT REPORT
Planning	Marketing plans (or programs) that define goals and the marketing mix strategies to achieve them
Implementation	Results (memos or computer outputs) that describe the outcomes of implementing the plans
Control	Corrective action memos, triggered by comparing results with plans, that (1) suggest solutions to problems and (2) take advantage of opportunities

The corrective action memos become "feedback loops" in Figure 22–2 that help improve decisions and actions in earlier phases of the strategic marketing process.

THE PLANNING PHASE OF THE STRATEGIC MARKETING PROCESS

Three aspects of the strategic marketing process deserve special mention: (1) the varieties of marketing plans, (2) marketing planning frameworks that have proven useful, and (3) some marketing planning and strategy lessons.

The Variety of Marketing Plans

The planning phase of the strategic marketing process usually results in a marketing plan that sets the direction for the marketing activities of an organization. As noted earlier in Appendix A, a marketing plan is the heart of a business plan. Like business plans, marketing plans aren't all from the same mold; they vary with the length of the planning period, the purpose, and the audience. Let's look briefly at three kinds: long-range, annual, and new-product marketing plans.

Long-range marketing plans   Typically, long-range marketing plans cover marketing activities from two to five years into the future. Except for firms in industries such as autos, steel, or forest products, marketing plans rarely go beyond five years into the future because the tremendous number of uncertainties present make the benefits of planning less than the effort expended. Such plans are often directed at top-level executives and the board of directors.

Annual marketing plans   Usually developed by a product manager (discussed later in the chapter) in a consumer products firm such as General Mills, annual marketing plans deal with marketing goals and strategies for a product, product line, or entire firm for a single year. Typical steps that firms such as Kellogg, Coca-Cola, and Johnson & Johnson take in developing their annual marketing plans for their existing products are shown in Figure 22–3.[8] This annual planning cycle typically starts with a detailed marketing research study of current users and ends after 48 weeks with the approval of the plan by the division general manager—10 weeks before the fiscal year starts. Between these points there are continuing efforts to uncover new ideas through brainstorming and key-issues sessions with specialists both inside and outside the firm. The plan is fine-tuned through a series of often excruciating reviews by several levels of management, which leaves few surprises and little to chance.

Marketing plans for new-product launches: Frosted Cheerios   Planning and implementing the introduction of Frosted Cheerios by a General Mills team shows the interactions of marketing strategy and tactics with the information, actions, and people needed for success. Central to all of this activity is a new-product marketing plan. As noted in Chapter 11, during 1993 and 1994 General Mills introduced a series of breakfast cereals that did poorly in the market. So when Mark Addicks was named director of marketing for new cereal products in March 1995, he knew the company needed a big winner. Figure 22–4 shows a time line of actions in the marketing plan that led to the shipment of Frosted Cheerios to stores in September 1995. The time from the new-product idea in March 1995 to first shipment in September took six months—half the normal new launch time for a new cereal product at General Mills.[9]

Figure 22–4 illustrates many key marketing concepts developed throughout this book:

- *Cross-functional teams.* The first thing Addicks did was recruit a team with a representative from every pertinent department: marketing, sales, research and development (R&D), marketing research, product development, and manufacturing.
- *Corporate goals.* Frosted Cheerios must contribute to General Mills's corporate targets of increasing earnings per share 12 percent annually and growth of unit volume 5 percent annually.
- *Marketing goals.* The new product must not cannibalize sales of the existing brands of Cheerios (plain Cheerios alone had 1995 sales of $289 million) or hurt their images. Also, 0.5 percent market share is considered a success.

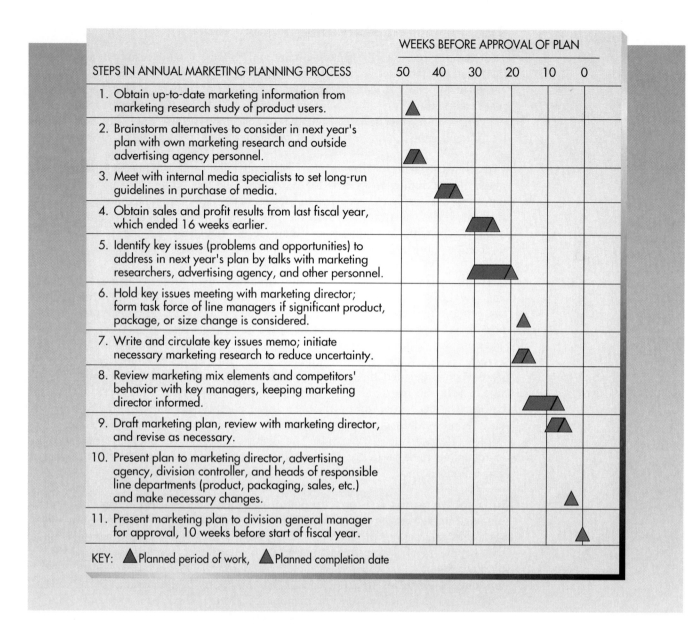

STEPS IN ANNUAL MARKETING PLANNING PROCESS	WEEKS BEFORE APPROVAL OF PLAN					
	50	40	30	20	10	0
1. Obtain up-to-date marketing information from marketing research study of product users.	▲					
2. Brainstorm alternatives to consider in next year's plan with own marketing research and outside advertising agency personnel.	◢◣					
3. Meet with internal media specialists to set long-run guidelines in purchase of media.		◢◣				
4. Obtain sales and profit results from last fiscal year, which ended 16 weeks earlier.			◢◣			
5. Identify key issues (problems and opportunities) to address in next year's plan by talks with marketing researchers, advertising agency, and other personnel.				◢◣		
6. Hold key issues meeting with marketing director; form task force of line managers if significant product, package, or size change is considered.				▲		
7. Write and circulate key issues memo; initiate necessary marketing research to reduce uncertainty.				◢◣		
8. Review marketing mix elements and competitors' behavior with key managers, keeping marketing director informed.					◢◣	
9. Draft marketing plan, review with marketing director, and revise as necessary.					◢◣	
10. Present plan to marketing director, advertising agency, division controller, and heads of responsible line departments (product, packaging, sales, etc.) and make necessary changes.					▲	
11. Present marketing plan to division general manager for approval, 10 weeks before start of fiscal year.						▲

KEY: ▲ Planned period of work, ▲ Planned completion date

FIGURE 22–3

Steps a large consumer package goods firm takes in developing its annual marketing plan

- *Marketing budget.* Top management allocated $40 million for the launch, the most of any product in its history.
- *Target market.* The target market is kids (60 percent) and baby-boomer adults (40 percent) who do not have the sugared cereals hangup that their parents do.
- *Benchmarking.* The team studied successful product launches of all kinds, including Disney movies and Nickelodeon TV programs, to learn lessons for its cereal launch.
- *Marketing research on consumers.* In April (see Figure 22–4) consumers were asked about the Frosted Cheerios concept; 88 percent of the kids saying they would eat them. In-home taste tests in May bore this out and identified the best from among three formulations.
- *Competitive advantages/points of difference.* A big concern was copycat imitations. So Addicks's team targeted these unique elements: complex enough to avoid copying, sweet enough to appeal to the target market, and grainy enough to maintain the Cheerios taste and image.

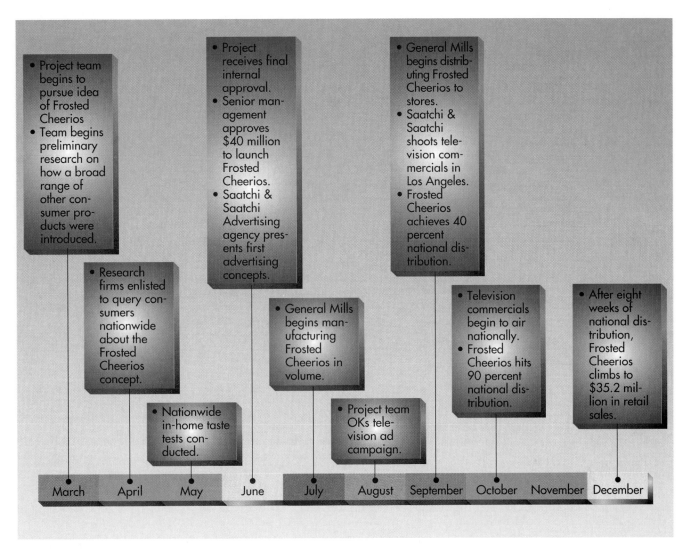

FIGURE 22–4

Frosted Cheerios: from idea to grocery shelf in six months

- *Product strategy.* Manufacturing Frosted Cheerios was a lot more complex than dipping regular Cheerios in sugar. R&D scientists found they had to blend corn flour in with the regular oat flour to give their new product the proper Cheerios "crunch." The final package, shown in Figure 22–5, was selected from seven competing designs. The figure shows the detailed planning needed to position the product favorably in the eyes and minds of consumers.
- *Pricing strategy.* The team set a price consistent with other Cheerios brands and competitive with other sugared cereals, like Kellogg's Frosted Flakes.
- *Promotion strategy.* Working with the team, its advertising agency shot the TV commercials in September (Figure 22–5), using contemporary and campy characters such as Underdog, rap artist Latifah, and loud-mouth comedian Gilbert Gottfried.[10]
- *Place strategy.* As shown in Figure 22–5, General Mills started shipping to stores in September and had 90 percent distribution the next month.

In terms of implementation, Frosted Cheerios was on retailer shelves when the TV ad campaigns started, always a huge concern with new grocery product introductions. After eight weeks, sales were $35.2 million, about 2.5 percent market share. At $82

FIGURE 22–5

The cross-functional team's thinking behind the Frosted Cheerios new package

million per share point, sales revenue projections for 1996 are more than $200 million. This market share is five times the minimum level needed to support the brand. Clearly Frosted Cheerios is a huge success by any standard—a success attributable to a cohesive cross-functional team's attention to detail and deadlines in its new-product marketing plan.

CONCEPT CHECK

1. What is the significance of the S-shape of the sales response function in Figure 22–1?

2. What are the main output reports from each phase of the strategic marketing process?

3. What are three kinds of marketing plans?

Frameworks to Improve Marketing Planning

Marketing planning for a firm with many products competing in many markets—a multiproduct, multimarket firm—is a complex process. Three techniques that are useful in helping corporate and marketing executives in such a firm make important resource allocation decisions are (1) Porter's generic business strategies, (2) profit enhancement options, and (3) market-product synergies. All of these techniques are based on elements introduced in earlier chapters.

Porter's generic business strategies   As shown in Figure 22–6, Michael E. Porter has developed a framework in which he identifies four basic, or "generic," strategies.[11] A **generic business strategy** is one that can be adopted by any firm, regardless of the product or industry involved, to achieve a competitive advantage.

FIGURE 22-6

Porter's four generic business strategies

		SOURCE OF COMPETITIVE ADVANTAGE	
		LOWER COST	**DIFFERENTIATION**
COMPETITIVE SCOPE	**BROAD TARGET**	1. Cost leadership	2. Differentiation
	NARROW TARGET	3. Cost focus	4. Differentiation focus

Some current research suggests that a firm needs several major competencies, not just one, to sustain its competitive advantage over longer periods;[12] other research suggests that the preferred strategy is to focus on a single discipline—such as operational excellence, product leadership, or customer intimacy.[13]

Although all of the techniques discussed here involve generic strategies, the phrase is most often associated with Porter's framework. In this framework the columns identify the two fundamental alternatives firms can use in seeking competitive advantage: (1) becoming the low-cost producer within the markets in which it competes or (2) differentiating itself from competitors through developing points of difference in its product offerings or marketing programs. In contrast, the rows identify the competitive scope: (1) a broad target by competing in many market segments or (2) a narrow target by competing in only a few segments or even a single segment. The columns and rows result in four business strategies, any one of which can provide a competitive advantage among similar business units in the same industry:

1. A **cost leadership strategy** (cell 1) requires a serious commitment to reducing expenses that, in turn, lowers the price or the items sold in a relatively broad array of market segments. Sometimes significant investments in capital equipment may be necessary to improve the production process to give these low unit costs. The cost leader still must have adequate quality levels. The original Model T Ford and today's South Korean shipbuilders are examples of

What benefit does Southwest Airlines give customers that underlies its "cost focus" generic strategy? This ad and the text provide the answer.

a cost leadership strategy. By mass producing only black Model T's, Henry Ford drove the price down to where the typical American family could buy a car. South Korean shipbuilders now dominate Asian competitors because of their cost efficiencies.

2. A **differentiation strategy** (cell 2) requires innovation and significant points of difference in product offerings, higher quality, advanced technology, or superior service in a relatively broad array of market segments. This allows a price premium. General Motors used this strategy against Ford in the 1920s when it developed an array of models with different colors and features in contrast to Ford's black Model T. It has taken Ford half a century to approach a similar level of differentiation through offering multiple product lines and, in some cases, higher quality.

3. A **cost focus strategy** (cell 3) involves controlling expenses and, in turn, lowering prices, in a narrow range of market segments. Retail chains targeting only a few market segments in a restricted group of products—such as Office Max in office supplies—have used a cost focus strategy successfully. Southwest Airlines has been very successful in offering low fares between very restricted pairs of cities.

4. Finally, a **differentiation focus strategy** (cell 4) utilizes significant points of difference to one or only a few market segments. Enterprise Rent-A-Car ("The Company that Picks You Up") has achieved spectacular success by offering to pick up or drop off their car renters at their homes or offices.

These strategies also form the foundation for Michael Porter's theory about what makes a nation's industries successful, as discussed in Chapter 5.

Profit enhancement options If a business wants to increase, or "enhance," its profits, it can (1) increase revenues, (2) decrease expenses, or (3) do both. Among these "profit enhancement options," let's look first at the strategy options of increasing revenues and then at those for decreasing expenses.

The strategy option of increasing revenues can only be achieved by using one or a combination of four ways to address present or new markets and products (Figure 22–7): (1) market penetration, (2) product development, (3) market development, and (4) diversification (which are described in Chapter 2).

Procter & Gamble has followed a successful strategy of market penetration (present markets, present products) by concentrating its effort on becoming the market leader in each of its 39 product categories. It is currently first in market share in more than half these product categories. Recent research, however, suggests that while market share may be directly related to profitability in some industries, this is not true for all. Corporate goals such as increasing customer satisfaction may be more successful than simply maximizing market share.[14]

In contrast, Johnson & Johnson has succeeded with a product development strategy—finding new products for its present markets—to complement popular brands such as Tylenol pain reliever and Accuvue contact lenses. To compete with Bristol-Meyers, American Home Products, and other companies, Johnson & Johnson developed Tylenol PM—a combination pain killer and sleeping pill—and Sure-vue—a long-lasting disposable contact lens.

Walt Disney Co. has pursued a market development strategy (new market, present product) since the success of the original Disneyland in Anaheim, California. The first market expansion, of course, was to Orlando, Florida, and more recently Disney has built theme parks in Tokyo and Paris.

Finally, Philip Morris, which depended on Marlboro cigarettes for 60 percent of its profits in 1988, has used a diversification strategy (new market, new product) to reduce its dependence on a single brand. In recent years Philip Morris has purchased Seven-Up, Miller Brewing, General Foods, and Kraft to create a portfolio of consumer products.

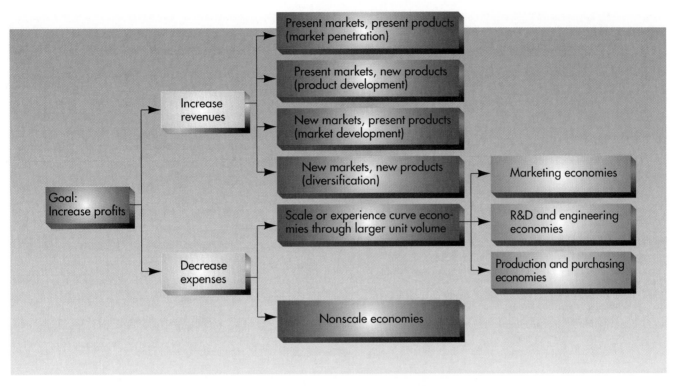

FIGURE 22–7   Generic marketing strategies for increasing a firm's profits

Strategy options for decreasing expenses fall into two broad categories (Figure 22–7). One is relying on scale economies or experience curve benefits from an increased volume of production to drive unit costs down and gross margins up, the best-known examples being electronic devices such as fax or voice-mail machines whose prices fell by half in a few years. Scale economies may occur in marketing, as well as in R&D, engineering, production, and purchasing.

The other strategy option to decrease expenses is simply finding other ways to reduce costs, such as cutting the number of managers, increasing the effectiveness of the salesforce through more training, or reducing the product rejects by inspectors. In an effort to decrease costs, IBM and AT&T have downsized through massive layoffs.

Market-product synergies   Let's use the market-product grid framework introduced in Chapter 9 to study two kinds of synergy that are critical in developing corporate and marketing strategies: (1) marketing synergy and (2) R&D–manufacturing synergy. While the following example involves external synergies through mergers and acquisitions, the concepts apply equally well to internal synergies sought in adding new products or seeking new markets.

A critical step in the external analysis is to assess how these merger and acquisition strategies provide the organization with **synergy**, the increased customer value achieved through performing organizational functions more efficiently. The "increased customer value" can take many forms: more products, improved quality on existing products, lower prices, improved distribution, and so on. But the ultimate criterion is that customers should be better off as a result of the increased synergy. The firm, in turn, should be better off by gaining more satisfied customers.

A market-product grid helps identify important trade-offs in the strategic marketing process. As noted in the Marketing NewsNet, assume you are vice president of marketing for Great States Corporation's line of nonpowered lawnmowers and

MARKETING NEWSNET

THE STRATEGY ISSUE OF THE 1990S: FINDING SYNERGIES

Chase Manhattan Bank and Chemical Banking merge "to get synergy." Time Warner buys Turner Broadcasting "to get synergy." Both Sun Microsystems and Sony considered buying Apple for the purpose of "getting synergy." With the current go-go days of giant mergers and acquisitions, the partners in these ventures are looking for synergies that have often proven elusive or impossible to achieve. For example, AT&T finally spun off its NCR computer group that it had bought only a few years earlier—to find synergies—after losing more than $1 billion dollars.

To try your hand in this multibillion dollar synergy game, let's assume you are vice president of marketing for Great States Corporation, whose product lines are nonpowered lawnmowers and powered walking mowers. A market-product grid for your business is shown below. You distribute your nonpowered mowers in the three market segments shown and your powered, walking mowers in suburban markets—but you don't yet sell your powered walking mowers in cities or rural areas.

Here are your strategy dilemmas:

1. Where are the marketing synergies (efficiencies)?
2. Where are the R&D and manufacturing synergies (efficiencies)?
3. What would a market-product grid look like for an ideal company for Great States to merge with?

For the answers to these questions, read the text and study Figures 22–8 and 22–9.

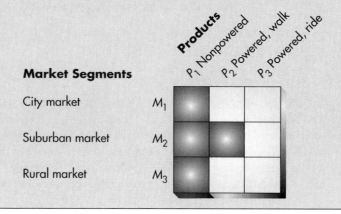

powered walking mowers sold to the consumer market. You are looking for new product and new market opportunities to increase your revenues and profits.

You conduct a market segmentation study and develop a market-product grid to analyze future opportunities. You identify three major segments in the consumer market based on geography: (1) city, (2) suburban, and (3) rural households. These market segments relate to the size of lawn a consumer must mow. The product clusters are (1) nonpowered, (2) powered walking, and (3) powered riding mowers. Five alternative marketing strategies are shown in the market-product grids in Figure 22–8.

As mentioned in Chapter 9, the important marketing efficiencies—or synergies—run horizontally across the rows in Figure 22–8. Conversely, the important R&D and production efficiencies—or synergies—run vertically down the columns. Let's look at the synergy effects for the five combinations in Figure 22–8:

A. *Market-product concentration.* The firm benefits from "focus" on a single product line and market segment, but it loses opportunities for significant synergies in both marketing and R&D–manufacturing.

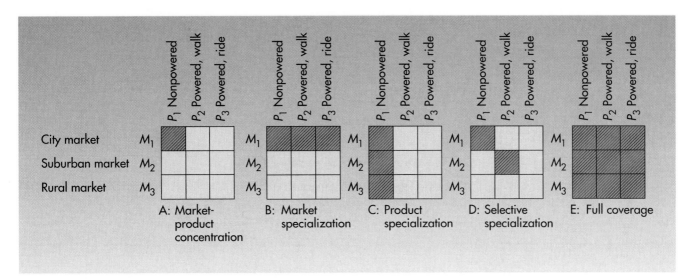

FIGURE 22-8

Market-product grid of
alternative strategies for a
lawnmower manufacturer

B. *Market specialization.* The firm gains marketing synergy through providing a complete product line, but R&D–manufacturing have the difficulty of developing and producing two new products.

C. *Product specialization.* The firm gains R&D–manufacturing synergy through production economies of scale, but gaining market distribution in the three different geographic areas will be costly.

D. *Selective specialization.* The firm doesn't get either marketing or R&D–manufacturing synergies because of the uniqueness of the market-product combinations.

E. *Full coverage.* The firm has the maximum potential synergies in both marketing and R&D–manufacturing. The question: Is it spread too thin?

The Marketing NewsNet posed the question of what the ideal partner would be, given the market-product combinations shown in the box. If, as vice president of marketing, you want to follow a full-coverage strategy, then the ideal merger partner is shown in Figure 22–9. This would give the maximum potential synergies—if you are not spreading your merged companies too thin. Marketing gains by having a

FIGURE 22-9

An ideal merger for Great
States to obtain full
market-product coverage

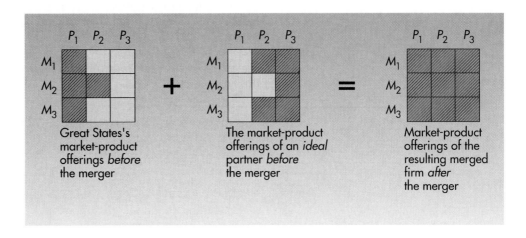

complete product line in all regions, and R&D–manufacturing gains by having access to new markets that can provide production economies of scale through producing larger volumes of its existing products.

CONCEPT CHECK

1. Describe Porter's four generic business strategies.

2. What are four alternative ways to increase a firm's profits when considering profit enhancement options strategies?

3. Where do (*a*) marketing synergies and (*b*) R&D–manufacturing synergies appear in a market-product grid framework?

Some Planning and Strategy Lessons

Applying these frameworks is not automatic but requires a great deal of managerial judgment. Commonsense requirements of an effective marketing plan are discussed next, followed by problems that can arise.

Guidelines for an effective marketing plan   President Dwight D. Eisenhower, when he commanded Allied armies in World War II, made his classic observation, "Plans are nothing; planning is everything." It is the process of careful planning that focuses an organization's efforts and leads to success. The plans themselves, which change with events, are often secondary. Effective planning and plans are inevitably characterized by identifiable objectives, specific strategies or courses of action, and the means to execute them. Here are some guidelines in developing effective marketing plans:

- *Set measurable, achievable goals.* Ideally, goals should be quantified and measurable in terms of what is to be accomplished and by when. So, "Increase market share from 18 percent to 22 percent by December 31, 1997" is preferable to "Maximize market share given our available resources." Also, to motivate people the goals must be achievable.
- *Use a base of facts and valid assumptions.* The more a marketing plan is based on facts and valid assumptions, rather than guesses, the less uncertainty and risk are associated with executing it. Good marketing research helps.
- *Utilize simple, but clear and specific, plans.* Effective execution of plans requires that people at all levels in the firm understand what, when, and how they are to accomplish their tasks.
- *Have complete and feasible plans.* Marketing plans must incorporate all the key marketing mix factors and be supported by adequate resources.
- *Make plans controllable and flexible.* Marketing plans must enable results to be compared with planned targets, which allows replanning—the flexibility to update the original plans.

Problems in marketing planning and strategy   From postmortems on company plans that did work and on those that did not work, a picture emerges of where problems occur in the planning phase of a firm's strategic marketing process. The following list explores these problems:

1. Plans may be based on very poor assumptions about environmental factors, especially changing economic conditions and competitors' actions. A Western

Domino's, a legend in effective implementation, stayed with its basic pizza-and-Coke menu into the 1990s. For the result, see the text.

Union plan failed because it didn't reflect the impact of deregulation and competitors' actions on business.

2. Planners and their plans may have lost sight of their customers' needs. Domino's Pizza is a legend for its implementation efficiency in home-delivered pizzas. But in the early 1990s it refused to recognize that its customers wanted a broader selection than its pizza-and-Coke menu, and its profits plummeted. The successful additions of buffalo wings and thin-crust pizza are helping it rebound.[15]

3. Too much time and effort may be spent on data collection and writing the plans. Westinghouse has cut its planning instructions for operating units "that looked like an auto repair manual" to five or six pages.

4. Line operating managers often feel no sense of ownership in implementing the plans. Andy Grove, CEO of Intel, observed, "We had the very ridiculous system . . . of delegating strategic planning to strategic planners. The strategies these [planners] prepared had no bearing on anything we actually did."[16] The solution is to assign more planning activities to line operating managers—the people who actually carry them out.

Balancing value and values in strategic marketing plans   Two important trends are likely to influence the strategic marketing process in the future. The first, value-based planning, combines marketing planning ideas and financial planning techniques to assess how much a division or strategic business unit (SBU) contributes to the price of a company's stock (or shareholder wealth). Value is created when the financial return of a strategic activity exceeds the cost of the resources allocated to the activity.

The second trend is the increasing interest in value-driven strategies, which incorporate concerns for ethics, integrity, employee health and safety, and environmental safeguards with more common corporate values such as growth, profitability, customer service, and quality. Some experts have observed that although many corporations cite broad corporate values in advertisements, press releases, and company newsletters, they have not yet changed their strategic plans to reflect the stated values. Because plans depend on goals, the next step will require that organizations learn to specify value-based objectives. See the accompanying Ethics and Social Responsibility Alert for guidelines that help add new values to the planning process.[17]

ETHICS AND SOCIAL RESPONSIBILITY ALERT

HOW TO ADD NEW VALUES TO STRATEGIC MARKETING PLANS

How can companies change their strategic marketing process to reflect the interests of the many stakeholders they serve—such as the community, customers, employees, shareholders, and suppliers? Although many approaches have had success, several actions are critical:

1. Identify, define, and prioritize critical values.
2. Measure employee perceptions of the values.
3. Assess customer perceptions of the degree to which company actions conform to these values.
4. Audit current management practices and modify them to reflect values.
5. Use a reward system that reinforces values.

Using these guidelines can help companies develop appropriate value-driven strategies. For example, Johnson & Johnson faced the cyanide crisis with its Tylenol brand by using its primary value—trust—that led to media cooperation and total recall of the product.

Ford Motor Company recently specified three values—people, products, and profits—to guide its attempts to become more competitive. Why are people first? "Because people are our most important asset. Everything that we are and can accomplish can only be done by people," says Ford chairman and CEO Donald Peterson. Ford's strategies now focus first on employees and their work environment.

What values would you specify for Ford? For your current employer?

THE IMPLEMENTATION PHASE OF THE STRATEGIC MARKETING PROCESS

The Monday morning diagnosis of a losing football coach often runs something like "We had an excellent game plan: we just didn't execute it."

Is Planning or Implementation the Problem?

The planning-versus-execution issue applies to the strategic marketing process as well: a difficulty when a marketing plan fails is determining whether the failure is due to a poor plan or poor implementation. Figure 22–10 shows the outcomes of (1) good and bad marketing planning and (2) good and bad marketing implementation.[18] Good planning and good implementation in cell 1 spell success, as with the Swiss firm that combined a strong product—its Swatch brand watches—with excellent advertising,

FIGURE 22–10

Results of good and bad marketing planning and implementation

MARKETING IMPLEMENTATION	MARKETING PLANNING AND STRATEGY	
	GOOD (APPROPRIATE)	**BAD (INAPPROPRIATE)**
GOOD (EFFECTIVE)	1 *Success:* Marketing program achieves its objectives.	2 *Trouble:* Solution lies in recognizing that only the strategy is at fault and correcting it.
BAD (INEFFECTIVE)	3 *Trouble:* Solution lies in recognizing that only implementation is at fault and correcting it.	4 *Failure:* Marketing program flounders and fails to achieve its objectives.

Swatch watches have benefited from having both good marketing planning and implementation.

distribution, and pricing. NeXT Computer, Inc. fell into the "bad-bad" cell 4 with its workstation that used a proprietary hardware strategy that discouraged many potential customers and a salesforce "just too small and strapped for cash to reach many prospects." NeXT has now closed its computer factory to focus on its software business.

Cells 2 and 3 indicate trouble because either the marketing planning *or* marketing implementation—not both—is bad. A firm or product does not stay permanently in cell 2 or 3. If the problem is solved, the result can be success (cell 1); if not, it is failure (cell 4).

Toyota used good implementation on a bad marketing strategy (cell 2) when it applied its superior automobile marketing skills to the introduction of its T100 pickup truck. Consumer response was well below forecasts because the truck was too big to compete with smaller "compact" pickups and too small and underpowered to compete with full-size options. Goodyear Tire and Rubber Co. found itself in cell 3 after it successfully developed all-season radial tires but created problems with the 640 dealer distribution network by raising wholesale prices. The poor implementation led to a two-point decline in market share—a drop of 3 million tires.

Increasing Emphasis on Marketing Implementation

In the 1990s, the implementation phase of the strategic marketing process has emerged as a key factor to success by moving many planning activities away from the duties of planners to those of line managers.

GE reorganized to reduce the size of its corporate strategic planning staff from 350 to approximately 20 and also reduced the number of layers of middle managers and pushed decision-making authority lower in the organization. Some experts argue that

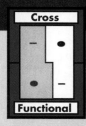

MARKETING NEWSNET

IMPLEMENTATION IN THE ORGANIZATION OF TOMORROW

In today's global marketplace, corporations struggle to reduce their response time to windows of opportunity. One of the reasons is that few companies have the complete expertise necessary to quickly launch new products in diverse and changing markets. To excel at implementation of marketing strategies, the organization of tomorrow will emphasize adaptability by taking advantage of information technology and acting, as Peter Drucker suggests, like a symphony orchestra.

Frank Ostroff and Doug Smith at the consulting firm McKinsey & Co. have suggestions for firms making the transition, including:

1. Organize around process, not task.
2. Flatten the hierarchy.
3. Give leaders responsibility for process performance.

4. Link performance to customer satisfaction.
5. Create teams that have managerial and non-managerial responsibilities.
6. Reward team performance.

In addition, companies will need to utilize networks of suppliers, customers, and even competitors to create *strategic alliances*.

These developments are described by many terms today, including the *boundaryless company*, the *virtual corporation*, and *capabilities-based competition*, but, regardless of the terminology, you can bet that the future will bring exciting changes in the way marketing plans are implemented. Organizations as diverse as GE, Hallmark Cards, Eastman Kodak, and even the Zoological Society of San Diego are already trying many of these ideas!

in the future "boundaryless organizations" in which technology, information, managers, and managerial practices are shared across traditional organizational structures will be necessary.[19] The Marketing NewsNet box describes how implementation activities may occur in tomorrow's organizations.[20]

Improving Implementation of Marketing Programs

No magic formula exists to guarantee effective implementation of marketing plans. In fact, the answer seems to be equal parts of good management skills and practices, from which have come some guidelines for improving program implementation.

Communicate goals and the means of achieving them   Those called on to implement plans need to understand both the goals sought and how they are to be accomplished. Everyone in Domino's Pizza—-from founder Tom Monaghan to telephone order takers, make-line people, and drivers—is clear on what the firm's goal is: to deliver tasty, hot pizzas quickly to homes of customers who order them by telephone. All Domino's personnel are trained in detail to perform their respective jobs to help achieve that goal.

Have a responsible program champion willing to act   Successful programs almost always have a **product or program champion** who is able and willing to cut red tape and move the program forward.[21] Such people often have the uncanny ability to move back and forth between big-picture strategy questions and specific details when the situation calls for it. Program champions are notoriously brash in overcoming organizational hurdles. The U.S. Navy's Admiral Grace Murray Hopper not only gave the world the COBOL computer language but also the word *bug*—meaning any glitch in a computer or computer program. This program champion's famous advice for moving decisions to actions by cutting through an organization's red tape: "Better to ask forgiveness than permission."

Reward successful program implementation   When an individual or a team is rewarded for achieving the organization's goal, they have maximum incentive to see a program implemented successfully because they have personal ownership and a stake in that success. At a General Electric surge protector plant, employees receive a bonus each quarter that the facility meets plantwide performance goals. Drivers delivering Domino's pizza take their job seriously—because it may lead directly to their owning a franchise in a few years.

Take action and avoid "paralysis by analysis"   Management experts warn against paralysis by analysis, the tendency to excessively analyze a problem instead of taking action. To overcome this pitfall, they call for a "bias for action" and recommend a "do it, fix it, try it" approach.[22] Conclusion: Perfectionists finish last, so getting 90 percent perfection and letting the marketplace help in the fine tuning makes good sense in implementation.

Lockheed Aircraft's Skunk Works got its name from the comic strip *L'il Abner* and its legendary reputation from achieving superhuman technical feats with a low budget and ridiculously short deadlines by stressing teamwork. Under the leadership of Kelly Johnson, in 35 years the Skunk Works turned out a series of world-class aircraft from the first American jet airplane (the P-80) to the nation's most untrackable aircraft (the F-117 Stealth fighter). Two of Kelly Johnson's basic tenets: (1) make decisions promptly and (2) avoid paralysis by analysis. In fact, one U.S. Air Force audit showed that Johnson's Skunk Works could carry out a program on schedule with 126 people, whereas a competitor in a comparable program was behind schedule with 3,750 people.[23]

For the unusual way GM developed its Saturn, see the text.

Foster open communication to surface the problems   Success often lies in fostering a work environment that is open enough so employees are willing to speak out when they see problems without fear of recrimination. The focus is placed on trying to solve the problem as a group rather than finding someone to blame. Solutions are solicited from anyone who has a creative idea to suggest—from the janitor to the president—without regard to status or rank in the organization.

Two more Kelly Johnson axioms from Lockheed's Skunk Works apply here: (1) when trouble develops, surface the problem immediately, and (2) get help; don't keep the problem to yourself. This latter point is important even if it means getting ideas from competitors.

Saturn is GM's attempt to create a new company where participatory management and improved communications lead to a successful product. For example, to encourage discussion of possible cost reductions, each employee receives 100 to 750 hours of training, including balance sheet analysis. To avoid the "NIH syndrome"—the reluctance to accept ideas "not invented here" or not originated inside one's own firm—Saturn engineers bought 70 import cars to study for product design ideas and selected options that would most appeal to their target market.

Schedule precise tasks, responsibilities, and deadlines   Successful implementation requires that people know the tasks for which they are responsible and the deadline for completing them. To implement the thousands of tasks on an orbiting satellite, GE's Aerospace Group typically holds weekly program meetings. The outcome of each of these meetings is an **action item list** that has three columns: (1) the task, (2) the name of the person responsible for accomplishing that task, and (3) the date by which the task is to be finished. Within hours of completing a program meeting, the action item list is circulated to those attending. This then serves as the starting agenda for the next meeting. Meeting minutes are viewed as secondary and backward looking. Action item lists are forward looking, clarify the targets, and put strong pressure on people to achieve their designated tasks by the deadline.

Related to the action item lists are formal *program schedules*, which show the relationships through time of the various program tasks. Scheduling an action program involves (1) identifying the main tasks, (2) determining the time required to

FIGURE 22–11

Tasks in completing a term project

Shown below are the tasks you might face as a member of a student team to complete a marketing research study using a mail questionnaire. Elapsed time to complete all the tasks is 15 weeks. How do you finish the project in an 11-week quarter? For an answer, see the text.

TASK	TIME (WEEKS)
1. Construct and test a rough-draft questionnaire for clarity (in person, not by mail) on friends.	2
2. Type and copy a final questionnaire.	2
3. Randomly select the names of 200 students from the school directory.	1
4. Address and stamp envelopes; mail questionnaires.	1
5. Collect returned questionnaires.	3
6. Tabulate and analyze data from returned questionnaires.	2
7. Write final report.	3
8. Type and submit final report.	1
Total time necessary to complete all activities	15

complete each, (3) arranging the activities to meet the deadline, and (4) assigning responsibilities to complete each task.

Suppose, for example, that you and two friends are asked to do a term project on the problem, "How can the college increase attendance at its performing arts concerts?"[24] And suppose further that the instructor limits the project in the following ways:

1. The project must involve a mail survey of the attitudes of a sample of students.
2. The term paper with the survey results must be submitted by the end of the 11-week quarter.

To begin the assignment, you need to identify all the project tasks and then estimate the time you can reasonably allocate to each one. As shown in Figure 22–11, it would take 15 weeks to complete the project if you did all the tasks sequentially; so to complete it in 11 weeks, your team must work on different parts at the same time, and some activities must be independent enough to overlap. This requires specialization and cooperation. Suppose that of the three of you (A, B, and C), only student C can type. Then you (student A) might assume the task of constructing the questionnaire and selecting samples, and student B might tabulate the data. This division of labor allows each student to concentrate on and become expert in one area, but you should also cooperate. Student C might help A and B in the beginning, and A and B might help C later on.

You must also figure out which activities can be done concurrently to save time. In Figure 22–11 you can see that task 2 must be completed before task 4. However, task 3 might easily be done before, at the same time as, or after task 2. Task 3 is independent of task 2.

Scheduling production and marketing activities—from a term project to a new product rollout to a space shuttle launch—can be done efficiently with Gantt charts. Figure 22–12 shows one variation of a Gantt chart used to schedule the class project, demonstrating how the concurrent work on several tasks enables the students to finish the project on time. Developed by Henry L. Gantt, this method is the basis for the scheduling techniques used today, including elaborate computerized methods. The key

FIGURE 22–12   Gantt chart for scheduling the term project

TASK DESCRIPTION	STUDENTS INVOLVED IN TASK	WEEK OF QUARTER 1 2 3 4 5 6 7 8 9 10 11
1. Construct and test a rough-draft questionnaire for clarity (in person, not by mail) on friends.	A	
2. Type and copy the final questionnaire.	C	
3. Randomly select the names of 200 students from the school directory.	A	
4. Address and stamp envelopes; mail questionnaires.	C	
5. Collect returned questionnaires.	B	
6. Tabulate and analyze data from returned questionnaires.	B	
7. Write final report.	A, B, C	
8. Type and submit final report.	C	

KEY: ▲ Planned completion date   ▢ Planned period of work   Current date
▲ Actual completion date   ▢ Actual period of work

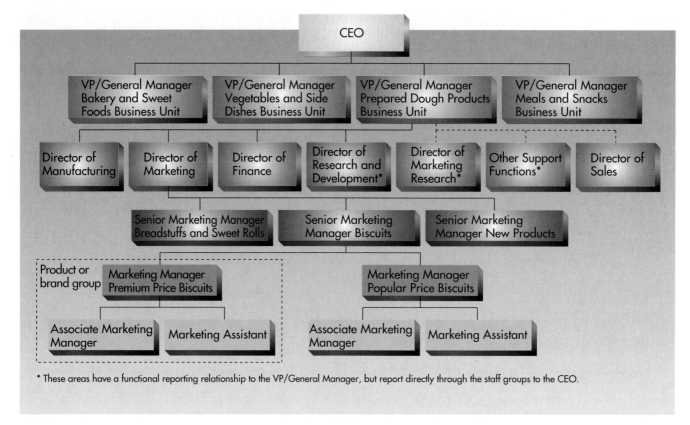

FIGURE 22-13

Organization of the Pillsbury Company

to all scheduling techniques is to distinguish tasks that *must* be done sequentially from those that *can* be done concurrently. As in the case of the term project, scheduling tasks concurrently often reduces the total time required for a project.

CONCEPT CHECK

1. Why is it important to include line operating managers in the planning process?
2. What is the meaning and importance of a program champion?
3. Explain the difference between sequential and concurrent tasks in a Gantt chart.

Organizing for Marketing

A marketing organization is needed to implement the firm's marketing plans. Basic issues in today's marketing organizations include understanding (1) how line versus staff positions and divisional groupings interrelate to form a cohesive marketing organization and (2) the role of the product manager.

Line versus staff and divisional groupings   Although simplified, Figure 22-13 shows the organization of Pillsbury's Prepared Dough Products Business Unit in detail and highlights the distinction between line and staff positions in marketing. People in **line positions,** such as group marketing managers, have the authority and responsibility to issue orders to the people who report to them, such as marketing managers. In this organizational chart, line positions are connected with solid lines. Those in **staff positions** (shown by dotted lines) have the authority and responsibility to advise people in line positions but cannot issue direct orders to them.

Products from Pillsbury's line of prepared dough products.

Most marketing organizations use divisional groupings—such as product line, functional, geographical, and market-based—to implement plans and achieve their organizational objectives. Three of these appear in some form in Pillsbury's organizational chart in Figure 22–13. At the top of its organization, Pillsbury organizes by **product line groupings,** in which a unit is responsible for specific product offerings. For example, Pillsbury has four main product lines: Bakery & Sweet Foods, Vegetables & Side Dishes, Prepared Dough Products, and Meals & Snacks.

The Prepared Dough Products Business Unit is organized by **functional groupings** such as manufacturing, marketing, and finance, which are the different business activities within a firm.

Pillsbury uses **geographical groupings** for its more than 500 field sales representatives throughout the United States. Each director of sales has several regional sales managers reporting to him or her, such as Western, Southern, and so on. These, in turn, have district managers reporting to them (although for simplicity these are not shown in the chart).

A fourth method of organizing a company is to use **market-based groupings,** which utilize specific customer segments, such as the banking, health care, or manufacturing segments. When this method of organizing is combined with product groupings, the result is a *matrix organization.*

A relatively new position in consumer products firms is the *category manager* (senior marketing manager in Figure 22–13). Category managers have profit-and-loss responsibility for an entire product line—all biscuit brands, for example. They attempt to reduce the possibility of one brand's actions hurting another brand in the same category. The popularity of category management among packaged goods manufacturers has increased rapidly as supermarket buyers have become responsible for purchasing, merchandising, and promoting entire categories.

Role of the product manager   The key person in the product or brand group shown in Figure 22–14 is the manager who heads it. As mentioned in Chapter 12, this person is often called the *product manager* or *brand manager,* but in Pillsbury he or she carries the title *marketing manager.* This person and the assistants in the product group are the basic building blocks in the marketing department of most consumer and industrial product firms. The function of a product manager is to plan, implement, and control the annual and long-range plans for the products for which he or she is responsible.

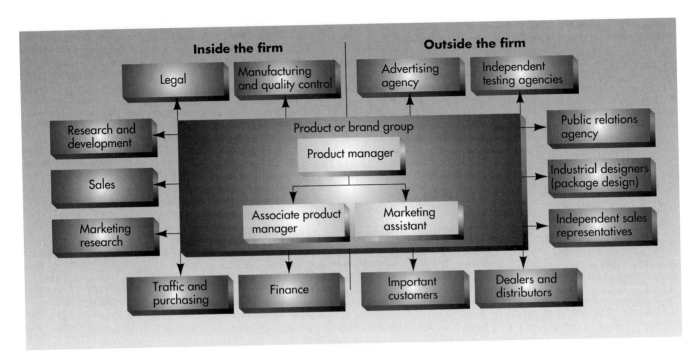

FIGURE 22-14

Units with which the product manager and product group work

There are both benefits and dangers to the product manager system. On the positive side, product managers become strong advocates for the assigned products, cut red tape to work with people in various functions both inside and outside the organization (Figure 22–14), and assume profit-and-loss responsibility for the performance of the product line. On the negative side, even though product managers have major responsibilities, they have relatively little direct authority, so most groups and functions shown in Figure 22–14 must be coordinated to meet the product's goals.[25] To coordinate the many units, product managers must use persuasion rather than orders.

THE CONTROL PHASE OF THE STRATEGIC MARKETING PROCESS

The essence of control, the final phase of the strategic marketing process, is comparing results with planned goals for the marketing program and taking necessary actions.

The Marketing Control Process

Ideally, quantified goals from the marketing plans developed in the planning phase have been accomplished by the marketing actions taken in the implementation phase (Figure 22–15) and measured as results in the control phase. A marketing manager then uses *management by exception,* which means identifying results that deviate from plans to diagnose their causes and take new actions. Often results fall short of plans, and a corrective action is needed. For example, after 50 years of profits Caterpillar accumulated losses of $1 billion. To correct the problem, Caterpillar focused its marketing efforts on core products and reduced its manufacturing costs. At other times the comparison shows that performance is far better than anticipated, in which case the marketing manager tries to identify the reason and move quickly to exploit the unexpected opportunity.

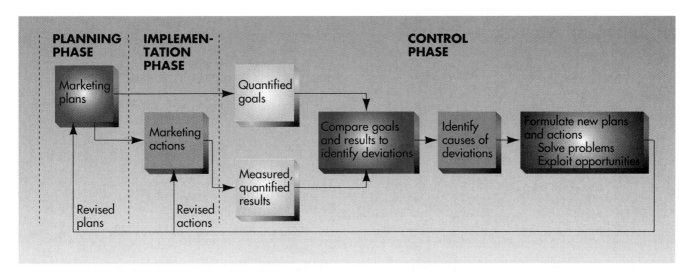

FIGURE 22-15

The control phase of the strategic marketing process

Measuring results   Without some quantitative goal, no benchmark exists with which to compare actual results. Manufacturers of both consumer and industrial products are increasingly trying to develop marketing programs that have not only specific action programs but also specific procedures for monitoring key measures of performance. Today marketing executives are measuring not only tangible financial targets such as sales revenues and profits, but also less tangible ones such as customer satisfaction, new-product development cycle time, and salesforce motivation.

Taking marketing actions   When results deviate significantly from plans, some kind of action is essential. Deviations can be the result of the process used to specify goals or can be due to changes in the marketplace. When MCI noticed its market share declining after an AT&T advertising blitz, it took decisive action. First, it consolidated some operations, and then it initiated the combined pricing and advertising campaign called "Friends and Family."

Sales Analysis

For controlling marketing programs, **sales analysis**—using the firm's sales records to compare actual results with sales goals and identify areas of strength and weakness—is critical. All the variables that might be used in market segmentation may be used in **sales component analysis** (also called *microsales analysis*), which traces sales revenues to their sources, such as specific products, sales territories, or customers. Common breakdowns include the following:

- Customer characteristics: demographics, Standard Industrial Classification, size, reason for purchase, and type of reseller (retailer or wholesaler).
- Product characteristics: model, package size, and color.
- Geographical region: sales territory, city, state, and region.
- Order size.
- Price or discount class.
- Commission to the sales representative.

Today's computers can easily produce these breakdowns, provided the input data contain these classifications. Therefore, it is critical that marketing managers specify the breakdowns they require from the accounting and information systems departments.

PRODUCTS/SERVICES: THE REASON FOR EXISTENCE

1. Is the product/service free from deadwood?
2. What is the life-cycle stage?
3. How will user demands or trends affect you?
4. Are you a leader in new-product innovation?
5. Are inexpensive methods used to estimate new product potentials before considerable amounts are spent on R&D and market introduction?
6. Do you have different quality levels for different markets?
7. Are packages/brochures effective salespeople for the products/services they present?
8. Do you present products/services in the most appealing colors (formats) for markets being served?
9. Are there features or benefits to exploit?
10. Is the level of customer service adequate?
11. How are quality and reliability viewed by customers?

CUSTOMER: USER PROFILES

1. Who is the current and potential customer?
2. Are there geographic aspects of use: regional, rural, urban?
3. Why do people buy the product/service; what motivates their preferences?
4. Who makes buying decisions; when; where?
5. What is the frequency and quantity of use?

MARKETS: WHERE PRODUCTS/SERVICES ARE SOLD

1. Have you identified and measured major segments?
2. Are small, potential market segments overlooked in trying to satisfy the majority?
3. Are the markets for the products/services expanding or declining?
4. Should different segments be developed; are there gaps in penetration?

COMPETITORS: THEIR INFLUENCE

1. Who are the principal competitors, how are they positioned, and where are they headed?
2. What are their market shares?
3. What features of competitors' products/services stand out?
4. Is the market easily entered or dominated?

PRICING: PROFITABILITY PLANNING

1. What are the objectives of current pricing policy: acquiring, defending, or expanding?
2. Are price policies set to produce volume or profit?
3. How does pricing compare with competition in similar levels of quality?
4. Does cost information show profitability of each item?
5. What is the history of price deals, discounts, and promotions?

FIGURE 22–16

Marketing audit questions

The danger is that marketing managers or chief executive officers get overwhelmed by the volume of computerized reports. To avoid this problem, each Tuesday, Ken Iverson carefully inputs into the computer numbers on the tons of steel each of Nucor's "minimills" produced the previous week. What makes the situation unique is that Iverson is chief executive officer of Nucor. Saving money is *not* the reason he does his own computer analysis. His explanation, "By keying in the numbers, you're forced to look at every figure for every week. That's the value."[26]

Profitability Analysis

To their surprise, marketing managers often discover the 80/20 principle the hard way, on the job. **Profitability analysis** enables the manager to measure the profitability of the firm's products, customer groups, sales territories, channels of distribution, and even order sizes. This leads to decisions to expand, maintain, reduce, or eliminate specific products, customer groups, or channels.

For example, following the 80/20 principle, a marketing manager will try to find the common characteristics among the 20 percent of the customers (or products, brands, sales districts, salespeople, or kinds of orders) that are generating 80 percent (or the bulk) of revenues and profits to find more like them to exploit competitive advantages. Conversely, the 80 percent of customers, products, brands, and so on that are generating few revenues and profits may need to be reduced or even dropped entirely unless a way is found to make them profitable.

The Marketing Audit

Often a broader marketing perspective is needed than is given by sales or profitability analyses, one that covers a longer time horizon and relates the marketing mix factors to environmental variables. This is the role of a **marketing audit,** which is a comprehensive, unbiased, periodic review of the strategic marketing process of a firm or SBU. The purpose of the marketing audit, which serves as both a planning and control technique, is to identify new problems and opportunities that warrant an action plan to improve performance.

Many firms undertaking a marketing audit use a checklist such as that shown in Figure 22–16 as a part of their situation analysis in their strategic marketing process. The checklist used covers factors ranging from the marketing mix factors and customer profiles to markets and competitors.

For a meaningful, comprehensive marketing audit, the individual or team conducting the audit must have a free rein to talk to managers, employees, salespeople, distributors, and customers, as well as have access to all pertinent internal and external reports and memoranda. They need to involve all levels of the organization in the process to ensure that resulting action recommendations have widespread support.

CONCEPT CHECK

1. What is the difference between a line and a staff position in a marketing organization?

2. What are four groupings used within a typical marketing organization?

3. What two components of the strategic marketing process are compared to control a marketing program?

SUMMARY

1. Marketing managers use the strategic marketing process to allocate their resources as effectively as possible. Sales response functions help them assess what the market's response to additional marketing effort will be.

2. The planning phase of the strategic marketing process usually results in a marketing plan that sets the direction for the marketing activities of an organization. Three kinds of marketing plans are long-range, annual, and new-product plans.

3. Three useful frameworks to improve marketing planning are (1) Porter's generic business strategies, (2) profit enhancement options, and (3) market-product synergies.

4. An effective marketing plan has measurable, achievable goals; uses facts and valid assumptions; is simple, clear, and specific; is complete and feasible; and is controllable and flexible.

5. The implementation phase of the strategic marketing process is concerned with executing the marketing program

developed in the planning phase and has achieved increased attention the past decade.

6. Essential to good scheduling is separating tasks that can be done concurrently from those that must be done sequentially. Gantt charts are a simple, effective means of scheduling.

7. Organizing marketing activities necessitates recognition of two different aspects of an organization: (a) line and staff positions and (b) product line, functional, geographical, and market-based groupings.

8. The product manager performs a vital marketing role in both consumer and industrial product firms, interacting with numerous people and groups both inside and outside the firm.

9. The control phase of the strategic marketing process involves measuring the results of the actions from the implementation phase and comparing them with goals set in the planning phase. Sales analyses, profitability analyses, and marketing audits are used to control marketing programs.

KEY TERMS AND CONCEPTS

sales response function p. 578
share points p. 579

generic business strategy p. 584
cost leadership (generic) strategy p. 585

CHAPTER PROBLEMS AND APPLICATIONS

1. Assume a firm faces an S-shaped sales response function. What happens to the ratio of incremental sales revenue to incremental marketing effort at the (*a*) bottom, (*b*) middle, and (*c*) top of this curve?

2. What happens to the ratio of incremental sales revenue to incremental marketing effort when the sales response function is an upward-sloping straight line?

3. In 1996 General Mills plans to invest millions of dollars in expanding its cereal and cake mix businesses. To allocate this money between these two businesses, what information would General Mills like to have?

4. Suppose your Great States mower company has the market-product concentration situation shown in Figure 22–8A. What are both the synergies and potential pitfalls of following expansion strategies of (*a*) market specialization and (*b*) product specialization?

5. Are value-driven strategies inconsistent with value-based planning? Give an example that supports your position.

6. The first Domino's Pizza restaurant was near a college campus. What implementation problems are (*a*) similar and (*b*) different for restaurants near a college campus versus a military base?

7. A common theme among managers who succeed repeatedly in program implementation is fostering open communication. Why is this so important?

8. Parts of tasks 6 and 7 in Figure 22–11 are done both concurrently and sequentially. How can this be? How does it help the students meet the term paper deadline?

9. In Pillsbury's organizational chart in Figure 22–13, where do product line, functional, and geographical groupings occur?

10. Why are quantified goals in the planning phase of the strategic marketing process important for the control phase?

CASE 22–1 Yoplait USA

Video

"A little bit of constructive restlessness is good," says Chap Colucci, "because you can become too satisfied with your own success, with the status quo. You take your foot off the gas and things begin to stall." Colucci is vice president of marketing and sales of Yoplait USA, a subsidiary of General Mills, Inc., whose experience is in more traditional grocery products like flour, breakfast cereals, and cake mixes.

THE ORIGINAL IDEA

Yoplait's sole product is yogurt, a business far removed from General Mills's regular product lines.

In the late 1970s top management at General Mills asked Steven M. Rothschild to head a team to investigate yogurt as a new business opportunity for the company. In the United States, yogurt had annual sales of $350 million with an annual growth rate of about 18 percent. Rothschild's team discovered that about 95 percent of the yogurt consumed in the United States was mixed with fruit or flavoring and about 5 percent was plain. About 95 percent was consumed in eight-ounce cups. The team also found the U.S. annual per capita consumption of yogurt was low (5 cups per person) compared with consumption in European countries (27 cups per person a year in France).

Further analysis showed there were four basic types of yogurt:

- Sundae style—fruit on the bottom of the cup.
- Swiss style—fruit blended throughout the cup to keep the fruit from settling on the bottom.
- Western style—fruit on the bottom and flavored syrup on the top.
- Frozen style—ice-cream or soft-custard form.

Other research showed that yogurt was available in 20 different flavors and a wide range of textures. When refrigerated, it had a shelf life of 21 to 60 days, depending on whether preservatives are added.

MEETING CORPORATE NEW PRODUCT GOALS

Rothschild and the team recommended that General Mills enter the yogurt market. In doing so, it committed the yogurt venture to achieve several brand goals set for new products at General Mills:

1. Fit with General Mills's strengths: "high value-added products distributed through supermarkets."
2. Achieve 20 percent share of the yogurt market in five years.
3. Achieve $100 million in sales in five years—double the minimum required by General Mills.
4. Meet internal financial goals of 25 percent ROI in five years.
5. Become a multiproduct business.

A yogurt product also met some other brand goals for a new product at General Mills: (1) a high-turnover branded item that allows a significant profit margin, (2) a product for which the firm's skills in positioning, advertising, packaging, and promotion will provide an advantage over competition, and (3) a business that will capitalize on trends resulting from long-term changes in consumer behavior.

THE COMPANY

Rothschild and his team decided General Mills should buy the rights to market Yoplait yogurt in the United States from Sodima, a large French cooperative. This enabled General Mills to gain Yoplait's technology of producing and distributing a refrigerated product and Yoplait to profit from sales of its product in the United States. It also saved General Mills three years of time in entering the yogurt business.

At that time Yoplait was the best-selling yogurt in France. Marketing research revealed what consumers perceived as Yoplait's key benefits: (1) 100 percent natural yogurt without artificial sweeteners or preservatives, (2) Swiss style, with real fruit mixed throughout, and (3) outstanding taste with a creamy texture. In terms of U.S. competition, there was no national brand of yogurt, but there was a two-tiered group of yogurt producers: (1) premium regional brands like Dannon and Kraft and (2) private-label brands produced by local dairies.

Yoplait USA moved quickly to gain acceptance for Yoplait as a national brand among American consumers. Yoplait USA positioned its yogurt as the "Yogurt of France" with creative TV commercials featuring personalities like Loretta Swit and Tommy Lasorda eating Yoplait and speaking French.

YOPLAIT TODAY

After its initial success, Yoplait underestimated the competition from national brands (such as Dannon and Kraft). Although number two nationally, Yoplait's market share and profit fell. Its first fruit-on-the-bottom line failed. Chap Colucci, the new vice president of marketing and sales at Yoplait USA, believed that the team had become too satisfied with its early success.

Now in the in the 1990s, Chap Colucci conducts a situation analysis in preparation for developing a new marketing strategy for Yoplait USA. His "constructive restlessness" turns up some serious concerns, including:

1. Retail prices. Yoplait's price for a 6-ounce cup is actually higher on some lines than competitors' 8-ounce cups. For example, the prices on Yoplait's 4 Pack are about 20 percent higher per cup than Dannon's and Kraft's 6 Pack.
2. Low gross margins. Margins have declined, at least partly because of high production and overhead costs.
3. Mix of spending weighted toward trade promotions. Most is directed at trade (retailers and wholesalers) and only a little at consumers.
4. Lack of "effective advertising with continuity." Yoplait has been living off the great Loretta Swit and Tommy Lasorda series of ads that launched the product without a similar creative, follow-up campaign.
5. Few coupons offered. In the late 1980s Yoplait cut way back on offering consumer coupons, while its competitors had heavy couponing.
6. Few new products. While Yoplait has developed its Lite product-line extension, the remaining new product pipeline is largely empty.
7. Geographic marketing organization. Yoplait is organized geographically with three regions—Eastern, Central, and Western. This organization has caused marketing managers to focus on geography, not basic marketing.

Yoplait's performance the previous two years isn't reaching the targets set for it by top management at General Mills. Chap Colucci concludes he must analyze these concerns and take marketing actions.

Questions

1. Without considering Chap Colucci's list of concerns:

a. Compare the situation both today and in 1980 (right after Yoplait appeared nationally in the United States) in terms of:

(1) Stage of the product life cycle for yogurt in the United States.

(2) Why Americans might eat yogurt.

b. Describe how these environmental factors might change today's Yoplait USA strategy from what it was in 1980.

2. Now look at Chap Colucci's list of concerns for Yoplait USA. Thinking in terms of the strategic marketing process:

a. Describe the implications for Yoplait USA of each concern.

b. Describe *planning* and *implementation* actions you believe Colucci and Yoplait USA should take to address the concerns.

c. Identify possible objectives that relate to each concern that could serve as a measure of *control* to determine if the new actions were achieving desired results.

Career Planning in Marketing

GETTING A JOB: THE PROCESS OF MARKETING YOURSELF

Getting a job is usually a lengthy process, and it is exactly that—a *process* that involves careful planning, implementation, and control. You may have everything going for you: a respectable grade point average (GPA), relevant work experience, several extracurricular activities, superior communication skills, and demonstrated leadership qualities. Despite these, you still need to market yourself systematically and aggressively; after all, even the best products lie dormant on the retailer's shelves unless marketed effectively.

The process of getting a job involves the same activities marketing managers use to develop and introduce products into the marketplace.[1] The only difference is that you are marketing yourself, not a product. You need to conduct marketing research by analyzing your personal qualities (performing a self-audit) and by identifying job opportunities. Based on your research results, select a target market—those job opportunities that are compatible with your interests, goals, skills, and abilities—and design a marketing mix around that target market. *You* are the "product"; you must decide how to "position" yourself in the job market. The price component of the marketing mix is the salary range and job benefits (such as health and life insurance, vacation time, and retirement benefits) that you hope to receive. Promotion involves communicating with prospective employers through written correspondence (advertising) and job interviews (personal selling). The place element focuses on how to reach prospective employers—at the campus placement center or job fairs, for example.

This appendix will assist you in career planning by (1) providing information about careers in marketing and (2) outlining a job search process.

CAREERS IN MARKETING

The diversity of marketing opportunities is reflected in the many types of marketing jobs, ranging from purchasing to marketing research to public relations to product management. The growing interest in marketing by service and nonprofit organizations—such as hospitals, financial institutions, the performing arts, and government—has added to the numerous opportunities offered by traditional employers such as manufacturers, retailers, consulting firms, and advertising agencies. Examples of companies that have opportunities for graduates with degrees in marketing include Ford, GTE, Hormel, Kellogg Co., JCPenney, Dell, Westinghouse, Kodak, Hewlett-Packard Co., and many others.[2] Most of these career opportunities offer the chance to work with interesting people on stimulating and rewarding problems. Comments one product manager, "I love marketing as a career because there are different challenges every day."[3]

Recent studies of career paths and salaries suggest that marketing careers can also provide an excellent opportunity for advancement and substantial pay. For example, a survey of chief executive officers (CEOs) of the nation's 1,000 most valuable publicly held companies revealed that marketing and finance were the most common career paths to their positions.[4] Similarly, reports of average starting salaries of college graduates indicate that salaries in marketing compare favorably with those in many other fields. The average annual starting salary of new marketing undergraduates in 1995 was $25,400, compared with $19,935 for journalism majors, and $22,494 for advertising majors.[5] The future is likely to be even better. The National Association of Colleges and Employers reports that the field of marketing, advertising, and public relations is one of the 20 fastest-growing occupations requiring a bachelor's degree. In addition, the Bureau of Labor Statistics suggests that "Increasingly intense domestic and foreign competition in products and services offered to consumers . . . should require greater marketing, sales, and public relations efforts through the decade."[6]

Figure C–1 describes marketing occupations in six major categories: product management and physical distribution, advertising, retailing, sales, marketing research, and nonprofit marketing. One of these may be right for you! (Additional sources of marketing career information are provided at the end of this appendix.)

Product Management and Physical Distribution

Many organizations assign one manager the responsibility for a particular product. For example, P&G has

PRODUCT MANAGEMENT AND PHYSICAL DISTRIBUTION

Product manager for consumer goods develops new products that can cost millions of dollars, with advice and consent of management—a job with great responsibility.

Administrative manager oversees the organization within a company that transports products to consumers and handles customer service.

Operations manager supervises warehousing and other physical distribution functions and often is directly involved in moving goods on the warehouse floor.

Traffic and transportation manager evaluates the costs and benefits of different types of transportation.

Inventory control manager forecasts demand for stockpiled goods, coordinates production with plant managers, and keeps track of current levels of shipments to keep customers supplied.

Administrative analyst performs cost analyses of physical distribution systems.

Customer service manager maintains good relations with customers by coordinating sales staffs, marketing management, and physical distribution management.

Physical distribution consultant is an expert in the transportation and distribution of goods.

SALES

Direct salesperson (door-to-door) calls on consumers in their homes to make sales.

Trade salesperson calls on retailers or wholesalers to sell products for manufacturers.

Industrial or semitechnical salesperson sells supplies and services to businesses.

Complex or professional salesperson sells complicated or custom-designed products to business. This requires understanding of the technology of a product.

NONPROFIT MARKETING

Marketing manager for nonprofit organizations develops and directs mail campaigns, fundraising, and public relations.

ADVERTISING

Account executive maintains contact with clients while coordinating the creative work among artists and copywriters. In full-service ad agencies, account executives are considered partners with the client in promoting the product and helping to develop marketing strategy.

Media buyer deals with media sales representatives in selecting advertising media and analyzes the value of media being purchased.

Copywriter works with art director in conceptualizing advertisements and writes the text of print or radio ads or the storyboards of television ads.

Art director handles the visual component of advertisements.

Sales promotion manager designs promotions for consumer products and works at an ad agency or a sales promotion agency.

Public relations manager develops written or filmed messages for the public and handles contacts with the press.

Specialty advertising manager develops advertising for the sales staff and customers or distributors.

RETAILING

Buyer selects products a store sells, surveys consumer trends, and evaluates the past performance of products and suppliers.

Store manager oversees the staff and services at a store.

MARKETING RESEARCH

Project manager for the supplier coordinates and oversees the market studies for a client.

Account executive for the supplier serves as a liaison between client and market research firm, like an advertising agency account executive.

In-house project director acts as project manager (see above) for the market studies conducted by the firm for which he or she works.

Marketing research specialist for an advertising agency performs or contracts for market studies for agency clients.

Source: David W. Rosenthal and Michael A. Powell, *Careers in Marketing*, © 1984, pp. 352–54. Adapted by permission of Prentice Hall, Englewood Cliffs, N.J.

FIGURE C–1

Twenty-six marketing occupations

separate managers for Tide, Cheer, Gain, and Bold. Product or brand managers are involved in all aspects of a product's marketing program, such as marketing research, sales, sales promotion, advertising, and pricing, as well as manufacturing. Managers of similar products typically report to a category manager and may be part of a *product management team.*[7]

College graduates with bachelor's and master's degrees—often in marketing and business—enter P&G as brand assistants, the only starting position in its product or brand group. Each year students from campuses throughout the United States accept

positions with P&G.[8] As brand assistants, their responsibilities consist primarily of selling and sales training.

After one to two years of good performance, the brand assistant is promoted to assistant brand manager and after about the same period to brand (product) manager. These promotions often involve several brand groups. For example, a new employee might start as brand assistant for P&G's soap products, be promoted to assistant brand manager for Crest toothpaste, and subsequently become brand manager for Folger's coffee, Charmin, or Pampers. The reason, as recruiter Henry de Montebello explains, is that "in the future everybody will have strategic alliances with everybody else, and the executives who thrive will be well-rounded."[9]

Several other jobs related to product management (Figure C–1) deal with physical distribution issues such as storing the manufactured product (inventory), moving the product from the firm to the customers (transportation), maintaining good relations with customers (customer service), and engaging in many other aspects of the manufacture and sale of goods. Prospects for these jobs are likely to increase as wholesalers increase their involvement with selling and distribution activities and begin to take advantage of overseas opportunities.[10]

Advertising

Although we may see hundreds of advertisements in a day, what we can't see easily is the fascinating and complex advertising profession. The entry-level advertising positions filled every year include jobs with a variety of firms. Advertising professionals often remark that they find their jobs appealing because the days are not routine and they involve creative activities with many interesting people.

Advertising positions are available in three kinds of organizations: advertisers, media companies, and agencies. Advertisers include manufacturers, retail stores, service firms, and many other types of companies. Often they have an advertising department responsible for preparing and placing their own ads. Advertising careers are also possible with the media: television, radio stations, magazines, and newspapers. Finally, advertising agencies offer job opportunities through their use of account management, research, media, and creative services.

Starting positions with advertisers and advertising agencies are often as assistants to employees with several years of experience. An assistant copywriter facilitates the development of the message, or copy, in an advertisement. An assistant art director participates in the design of visual components of advertisments. Entry-level media positions involve buying the media that will carry the ad or selling air time on radio or television or page space in print media. Advancement to supervisory positions requires planning skills, a broad vision, and an affinity for spotting an effective advertising idea. Students interested in advertising should develop good communication skills and try to gain advertising experience through summer employment opportunities or internships.[11]

Retailing

There are two separate career paths in retailing: merchandise management and store management (Figure C–2). The key position in merchandising is that of a buyer, who is responsible for selecting merchandise, guiding the promotion of the merchandise, setting prices, bargaining with wholesalers, training the salesforce, and monitoring the competitive environment. The buyer must also be able to organize and coordinate many critical activities under severe time constraints. In contrast, store management involves the supervision of personnel in all departments and the general management of all facilities, equipment, and merchandise displays. In addition, store managers are responsible for the financial performance of each department and for the store as a whole. Typical positions beyond the store manager level include district manager, regional manager, and divisional vice president.[12]

FIGURE C-2

Typical retailing career paths

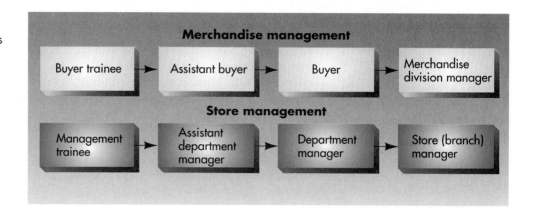

Most starting jobs in retailing are trainee positions. A trainee is usually placed in a management training program and then given a position as an assistant buyer or assistant department manager. Advancement and responsibility can be achieved quickly because there is a shortage of qualified personnel in retailing and because superior performance of an individual is quickly reflected in sales and profits—two visible measures of success.

Sales

College graduates from many disciplines are attracted to sales positions because of the increasingly professional nature of selling jobs and the many opportunities they

can provide. A selling career offers benefits that are hard to match in any other field: (1) the opportunity for rapid advancement (into management or to new territories and accounts); (2) the potential for extremely attractive compensation (the average salary of regional sales managers is $95,000)[13]; (3) the development of personal satisfaction, feelings of accomplishment, and increased self-confidence; and (4) independence—salespeople often have almost complete control over their time and activities. Many companies such as National Semiconductor now offer two sales career paths—one for people who want to go into management, and another for those who want to remain in sales for their entire career.[14]

Employment opportunities in sales occupations are found in a wide variety of organizations, including insurance agencies, retailers, and financial service firms (Figure C–3). Activities in sales jobs include *selling duties,* such as prospecting for customers, demonstrating the product, or quoting prices; *sales-support duties,* such as handling complaints and helping solve technical problems; and *nonselling duties,* such as preparing reports, attending sales meetings, and monitoring competitive activities. Salespeople who can deal with these varying activities are critical to a company's success. According to RJR Nabisco, their recruiting priority is "finding quality people who can analyze data from customers, see things from the consumer's eyes, use available sales tools like laptops and syndicated data, and interface with the marketing people at headquarters."[15]

OCCUPATION	1992 EMPLOYMENT	2005 EMPLOYMENT	PERCENTAGE CHANGE 1992–2005	AVERAGE ANNUAL GROWTH
Insurance agents and brokers	415,000	477,000	+15%	4,769
Retail sales workers	4,086,000	4,963,000	+21	67,461
Securities and financial services sales workers	200,000	265,000	+33	5,000
Real estate agents and brokers	397,000	460,000	+16	4,846
Travel agents	115,000	191,000	+66	5,846
Services sales representatives	488,000	673,000	+38	14,230

Source: "The 1992–2005 Job Outlook in Brief," *Occupational Outlook Quarterly* (Spring 1994), pp. 29–30.

FIGURE C–3

Employment opportunities in selected sales occupations (1992 to 2005)

One of the fastest areas of growth in sales positions is in the direct marketing industry. Interest in information technology, relationship marketing, and integrated marketing has increased the demand for contact with customers. Requests for "the most talented people" is "unprecedented," says Hal Crandall, president of New York recruiting firm Crandall Associates. For many firms this means new or additional telemarketing efforts; for other firms it means increasing the amount of time sales-people spend with clients. According to Mutual Life Insurance Company of New York, one of five companies selected by *Sales and Marketing Management* magazine for its Best Sales Force award, successful salespeople "focus on ways to get in front of the client more, by delegating tasks to staff and utilizing technology more effectively."[16]

Marketing Research

Marketing researchers play important roles in many organizations today. They are responsible for obtaining, analyzing, and interpreting data to facilitate making marketing decisions. This means marketing researchers are basically problem solvers. Success in the area requires not only an understanding of statistics and computers but also a broad base of marketing knowledge[17] and an ability to communicate with management. Individuals who are inquisitive, methodical, analytical, and solution oriented find the field particularly rewarding.

The responsibilities of the men and women currently working in the market research industry include defining the marketing problem, designing the question-naire, selecting the sample, collecting and analyzing the data, and, finally, reporting the results of the research. These jobs are available in three kinds of organizations. *Marketing research consulting firms* contract with large companies to provide research about their products or services.[18] *Advertising agencies* may provide research services to help clients with questions related to advertising and promotional problems. Finally, some companies have an *in-house research staff* to design and execute their research projects. Typical positions would include director, statistician, analyst, field work director, and interviewer.[19]

Although marketing researchers may start as assistants performing routine tasks, they quickly advance to broader responsibilities. Survey design, interviewing, report writing, and all aspects of the research process create a challenging career. In addition, research projects typically deal with such diverse problems as consumer motivation, pricing, forecasting, and competition. A recent survey of research organizations suggested that, to be successful in marketing research positions, students should develop skills in written, oral, and interpersonal communication; statistics and analysis; research design; and logic. The survey also suggested that practical work experience (e.g., internships) provides a useful supplement to class-room education.[20]

International Careers

Many of the careers just described can be found in international settings—in multinational U.S. corporations, small- to medium-size firms with export business, and franchises. The international public relations firm Burson-Marstellar, for example, has offices in New York, Sydney, Copenhagen, and Bangkok. Similarly, franchises such as Blockbuster Entertainment are expanding in many other markets outside of the United States. The dramatic changes in Europe and the need to rebuild the economies of the former Soviet republics may provide other opportunities. Variations of the permanent international career are also possible—for example, some companies may alternate periods of work at "headquarters" with "field" assignments in foreign countries.[21] Finally, a domestic international career—working for a foreign-owned company with an office in the United States—may be appealing.[22]

Applicants for international positions should first develop a skill that can be applied in an international setting. In addition, however, internationally competent employees will need language and cultural skills. A Conference Board description illustrates the point:

> The successful managers of the future will probably be those who speak both Japanese and English, who have a strong base in Brussels and contacts in the Pacific Rim, and who know the cafes and bars of Singapore.

Further, in many organizations, international experience has become a necessity for promotion and career advancement.[23]

THE JOB SEARCH PROCESS

Activities you should consider during your job search process include assessing yourself, identifying job opportunities, preparing your résumé and related correspondence, and going on job interviews.

Assessing Yourself

You must know your product—you—so that you can market yourself effectively to prospective employers. Consequently, a critical first step in your job search is conducting a self-analysis, which involves critically examining yourself on the following dimensions: interests, abilities, education, experience, personality, desired job environment, and personal goals.[24] The importance of performing this assessment was stressed by a management consultant:[25]

> Many graduates enter the world of work without even understanding the fact that they are specific somebodies, much less knowing the kinds of competencies and motivations with which they have been endowed. . . . The tragedy of not knowing is awesome. Ignorant of who they are, most graduates are doomed to spend too much of their lives in work for which they are poorly suited. . . . Self-knowledge is critical to effectively managing your career.

INTERESTS
How do I like to spend my time?
Do I enjoy being with people?
Do I like working with mechanical things?
Do I enjoy working with numbers?
Am I a member of many organizations?
Do I enjoy physical activities?
Do I like to read?

ABILITIES
Am I adept at working with numbers?
Am I adept at working with mechanical things?
Do I have good verbal and written communication skills?
What special talents do I have?
At which abilities do I wish I were more adept?

EDUCATION
How have my courses and extracurricular activities prepared me for a specific job?
Which were my best subjects? My worst? The most fun? The least?
Is my GPA an accurate picture of my academic ability? Why?
Do I aspire to a graduate degree? Before beginning my job?
Why did I choose my major?

EXPERIENCE
What previous jobs have I held? What were my responsibilities in each?
Were any of my jobs applicable to positions I may be seeking? How?
What did I like the most about my previous jobs? Like the least?
Why did I work in the jobs I did?
If I had it to do over again, would I work in these jobs? Why?

PERSONALITY
What are my good and bad traits?
Am I competitive?
Do I work well with others?
Am I outspoken?
Am I a leader or a follower?
Do I work well under pressure?
Do I work quickly, or am I methodical?
Do I get along well with others?
Am I ambitious?
Do I work well independently of others?

DESIRED JOB ENVIRONMENT
Am I willing to relocate? Why?
Do I have a geographical preference? Why?
Would I mind traveling in my job?
Do I have to work for a large, nationally known firm to be satisfied?
Must the job I assume offer rapid promotion opportunities?
If I could design my own job, what characteristics would it have?
How important is high initial salary to me?

PERSONAL GOALS
What are my short-term and long-term goals? Why?
Am I career oriented, or do I have broader interests?
What are my career goals?
What jobs are likely to help me achieve my goals?
What do I hope to be doing in 5 years? In 10 years?
What do I want out of life?

FIGURE C-4

Questions to ask in your self-analysis

Asking key questions   A self-analysis, in part, entails asking yourself some very important and difficult questions (Figure C–4). It is critical that you respond to the questions honestly, because your answers ultimately will be used as a guide in your job selection.[26] A less-than-candid appraisal of yourself might result in a job mismatch.

Identifying strengths and weaknesses   After you have addressed the questions posed in Figure C–4, you are ready to identify your strengths and weaknesses. To do so, draw a vertical line down the middle of a sheet of paper and label one side of the paper "strengths" and the other side "weaknesses." Based on your answers to the questions, record your strong and weak points in their respective column. Ideally this cataloging should be done over a few days to give you adequate time to reflect on your attributes. In addition, you might seek input from others who know you well (such as parents, close relatives, friends, professors, or employers) and can offer more objective views. They might even evaluate you on the questions in Figure C–4, and you can compare the results with your own evaluation. A hypothetical list of strengths and weaknesses is shown in Figure C–5.

FIGURE C–5

Hypothetical list of job candidate's strengths and weaknesses

STRENGTHS	WEAKNESSES
Enjoy being with people	Am not adept at working with
Am an avid reader	computers
Have good communication skills	Have minimal work experience
Am involved in many extracurricular activities	Have a mediocre GPA
Work well with others	Am sometimes impatient
Work well independently	Resent close supervision
Am honest and dependable	Work methodically (slowly)
Am willing to travel in the job	Will not relocate
Am a good problem solver	Anger easily sometimes
Have a god sense of humor	Lack of customer orientation
Am a self-starter, have drive	

Additional information about yourself can be obtained by developing a list of the five experiences or activities you most enjoy and analyzing what they have in common. Don't be surprised if the common characteristics are related to your strengths and weaknesses!

Taking job-related tests   Personality and vocational interest tests, provided by many colleges and universities, can give you other ideas about yourself. After tests have been administered and scored, test takers meet with testing service counselors to discuss the results. Test results generally suggest jobs for which students have an inclination. The most common tests at the college level are the Strong Interest Inventory and the Campbell Interest and Skill Survey. Some counseling centers also administer the Myers-Briggs Type Indicator—a personality measure that helps identify professions you may enjoy.[27] If you have not already done so, you may wish to see whether your school offers such testing services.

Identifying Your Job Opportunities

To identify and analyze the job market, you must conduct some marketing research to determine what industries *and* companies offer promising job opportunities that relate to the results of your self-analysis. Several sources that can help in your search are discussed below.

College placement office   Your college placement office is an excellent source of job information. Personnel in that office can (1) inform you about which companies will be recruiting on campus, (2) alert you to unexpected job openings, (3) advise you about short-term and long-term career prospects, (4) offer advice on résumé construction, (5) assess your interviewing strengths and weaknesses, and (6) help you evaluate a job offer. In addition, the office usually contains a variety of written materials focusing on different industries and companies and tips on job hunting. One major publication available in most campus placement offices is the National Association of Colleges and Employers publication *Job Choices,* which contains a list of employers, kinds of job openings for college graduates, and whom to contact about jobs in those firms.

On-line career and employment services   Many companies no longer make frequent on-campus visits. Instead, they may use the many on-line services available to advertise an employment opportunity or to search for candidate information. The National Association of Colleges and Employers, for example, maintains a site on the World Wide Web called JobWeb (http://www.jobweb.org). Similarly, the Online Career Center (http://www.occ.com) is a database of employment ads, candidate resumes, and other career-related information. Some of the information resources include career guidance, a cover letter library, occupational profiles, and resume templates.[28] Employers may contact students directly when the candidate's qualifications meet their specific job requirements. The advantage of this system for students is that regardless of the size or location of the campus they are attending, many companies have access to their résumé. Your school's career center may also have a "home page" that offers on-line job search information and links to other World Wide Web sites.

Library   The public or college library can provide you with reference material that, among other things, describes successful firms and their operations, defines the content of various jobs, and forecasts job opportunities. For example, *Fortune* publishes lists of the 1,000 largest U.S. and global companies and their respective sales and profits; Dun & Bradstreet publishes directories of all companies in the United States with a net worth of at least $500,000. *Careers in Marketing,* a publication of the American Marketing Association, presents career opportunities in marketing. The *Occupational Outlook Handbook* is an annual publication of the U.S. Department of Labor that provides projections for specific job prospects, as well as information pertaining to those jobs. A librarian can indicate reference materials that will be most pertinent to *your* job search.

Advertisements   Help-wanted advertisements provide an overview of what is happening in the job market. Local (particularly Sunday editions) and college newspapers, trade press (such as *Marketing News* or *Advertising Age*), and business magazines (such as *Sales and Marketing Management*) contain classified advertisement sections that generally have job opening announcements, often for entry-level positions. Reviewing the want ads can help you identify what kinds of positions are available and their requirements and job titles, which firms offer certain kinds of jobs, and levels of compensation.

Employment agencies   An employment agency can make you aware of several job opportunities very quickly because of its large number of job listings available through computer databases. Many agencies specialize in a particular field (such as sales and marketing). The advantages of using an agency include that it (1) reduces the cost of a job search by bringing applicants and employers together, (2) often has exclusive job listings available only by working through the agency, (3) performs much of the job search for you, and (4) tries to find a job that is compatible with your qualifications and interests.[29] Employment agencies are much maligned because some engage in questionable business practices, so check with the Better Business Bureau or your business contacts to determine the quality of the various agencies.

Personal contacts   An important source of job information that students often overlook is their personal contacts. People you know often may know of job opportunities, so you should advise them that you're looking for a job. Relatives and friends might aid your job search. Instructors you know well and business contacts can provide a wealth of information about potential jobs and even help arrange an interview with a prospective employer. They may also help arrange "informational interviews" with employers who do not have immediate openings. These interviews allow you to collect information about an industry or an employer and give you an advantage if a position does become available. It is a good idea to leave your résumé with all your personal contacts so they can pass it along to those who might be in need of your services. Student organizations (such as the student chapter of the American Marketing Association and Pi Sigma Epsilon, the professional sales fraternity) may be sources of job opportunities, particularly if they are involved with the business community. Local chapters of professional business organizations (such as the American Marketing Association and Sales and Marketing Executives International) also can provide job information; contacting their chapter president is a first step in seeking assistance from these organizations. In the past decade, small employers have provided the greatest growth in employment, and their most common source of new employees is through personal referrals.[30]

State employment office   State employment offices have listings of job opportunities in their state and counselors to help arrange a job interview for you. Although state employment offices perform functions similar to employment agencies, they differ in listing only job opportunities in their state and providing their services free.

Direct contact   Another means of obtaining job information is direct contact—personally communicating to prospective employers (either by mail or in person) that you would be interested in pursuing job opportunities with them. Often you may not even know whether jobs are available in these firms. If you correspond with the companies in writing, a letter of introduction and an attached résumé should serve as your initial form of communication. Your major goal in direct contact is ultimately to arrange a job interview.

Writing Your Résumé

A résumé is a document that communicates to prospective employers who you are. An employer reading a résumé focuses on two key questions: (1) What is the candidate like? and (2) What can the candidate do for me?[31] It is imperative that you design a résumé that addresses these two questions and presents you in a favorable light. Personnel in your campus placement office can provide assistance in designing résumés.

The résumé itself   A well-constructed résumé generally contains up to nine major sections: (1) identification (name, address, and telephone number), (2) job or career objective, (3) educational background, (4) extracurricular activities, (5) work experience or history, (6) skills or capabilities (that pertain to a particular kind of job for which you may be interviewing), (7) accomplishments or achievements, (8) personal interests, and (9) personal references.[32] There is no universally accepted format for a résumé, but three are more frequently used: chronological, functional, and targeted. A *chronological* format presents your work experience and education according to the time sequence in which they occurred (i.e., in chronological order). If you have had several jobs or attended several schools, this approach is useful to highlight what you have done. With a *functional* format, you group your experience into skill categories that emphasize your strengths. This option is particularly appropriate if you have no experience or only minimal experience related to your chosen field. A *targeted* format focuses on the capabilities you have for a specific job. This alternative is desirable if you know what job you want and are qualified for it.[33] In any of the formats, if possible, you should include quantitative information about your accomplishments and experience, such as "increased sales revenue by 20 percent" for the year you managed a retail clothing store. A résumé that illustrates the chronological format is shown in Figure C–6.[34]

Technology is creating a need for a new type of résumé—the electronic résumé. While traditional versions of résumés may be easily delivered through fax machines, today most career experts suggest that a second electronic version be available. The reason? Computers read differently than people. To fully utilize on-line opportunities, an electronic résumé with a popular font and relatively large font size—and without italic text, graphics, shading, underlining or verticle lines—must be available. In addition, because on-line recruiting starts with a key-word search, it is important to include key words and avoid abbreviations.[35]

FIGURE C-6

Chronological résumé

SALLY WINTER

Campus address (until 6/1/97):
Elm Street Apartments #2B
College Town, Ohio 44042
Phone: (614) 424-1648

Home address:
123 Front Street
Teaneck, NJ 07666
Phone:(201) 836-4995

Education
B.S. in Business Administration, Ohio State University, 1997, cum laude—3.3 overall GPA—3.6 GPA in major

Work Experience
Paid for 70 percent of my college expenses through the following part-time and summer jobs:
Legal Secretary, Smith, Lee & Jones, Attorneys at Law, New York, NY—summer 1995
• Took dictation and transcribed tapes of legal proceedings
• Typed contracts and other legal documents
• Reorganized client files for easier access
• Answered the phone and screened calls for the partners
Salesclerk, College Varsity Shop, College Town, Ohio—1994–1996 academic years
• Helped customers with buying decisions
• Arranged stock and helped with window displays
• Assisted in year-end inventories
• Took over responsibilities of store manager when she was on vacation or ill
Assistant Manager, Treasure Place Gift Shop, Teaneck, NJ—summers and Christmas vacations—1993–1996
• Supervised two salesclerks
• Helped select merchandise at trade shows
• Handled daily accounting
• Worked comfortably under pressure during busy seasons

Campus Activities
• Elected captain of the women's varsity tennis team for two years
• Worked as a reporter and night editor on campus newspaper for two years
• Elected historian for Mortar Board chapter, a senior women's honorary society

Personal Interests
• Collecting antique clocks, listening to jazz, swimming

References Available on Request

Letter accompanying a résumé   The letter accompanying a résumé, or cover letter, serves as the job candidate's introduction. As a result, it must gain the attention and interest of the reader or it will fail to give the incentive to examine the résumé carefully. In designing a letter to accompany your résumé, address the following issues:[36]

• Address the letter to a specific person.
• Identify the position for which you are applying and how you heard of it.
• Indicate why you are applying for the position.
• Summarize your most significant credentials and qualifications.
• Refer the reader to the enclosed résumé.
• Request a personal interview, and advise the reader when and where you can be reached.

A sample letter comprising these six factors is presented in Figure C–7. Some students have tried creative approaches to making their letter stand out—sending a gift with their letter or using creative packaging, for example. Although these tactics may gain a recruiter's attention, most hiring managers say that a frivolous approach makes for a frivolous employee. As a general rule, nothing works better than an impressive cover letter and good academic credentials.[37]

Interviewing for Your Job

The job interview is a conversation between a prospective employer and a job candidate that focuses on determining whether the employer's needs can be satisfied by the candidate's qualifications. The interview is a "make or break" situation: if the interview goes well, you have increased your chances of receiving a job offer; if it goes poorly, you probably will be eliminated from further consideration.

FIGURE C–7

Sample letter accompanying a résumé

Sally Winter
Elm Street Apartments #2B
College Town, Ohio 44042
January 31, 1997

Mr. J. B. Jones
Sales Manager
Hilltop Manufacturing Company
Minneapolis, MN 55406

Dear Mr. Jones:

Dr. William Johnson, Professor of Business Administration at the Ohio State University, recently suggested that I write to you concerning your opening and my interest in a sales position. With a B.S. degree in business administration and courses in personal selling and sales management, I am confident that I could make a positive contribution to your firm.

During the past four years I have been a salesclerk in a clothing store and an assistant manager in a gift shop. These two positions required my performing a variety of duties including selling, purchasing, stocking, and supervising. As a result, I have developed an appreciation for the viewpoints of the customer, salesperson, and management. Given my background and high energy level, I feel that I am particularly well qualified to assume a sales position in your company.

My enclosed résumé better highlights my education and experience. My extracurricular activities should strengthen and support my abilities to serve as a sales representative.

I am eager to talk with you because I feel I can demonstrate to you why I am a strong candidate for the position. I have friends in Minneapolis with whom I could stay on weekends, so Fridays or Mondays would be ideal for an appointment. I will call you in a week to see if we can arrange a mutually convenient time for a meeting. I am hopeful that your schedule will allow this.

Thank you for your kind consideration. If you would like some additional information, please feel free to contact me. I look forward to talking with you.

Sincerely,

Sally Winter

enclosure

Preparing for a job interview   To be successful in a job interview, you must prepare for it so you can exhibit professionalism and indicate to a prospective employer that you are serious about the job. When preparing for the interview, several critical activities need to be performed.

Before the interview, gather facts about the industry, the prospective employer, and the job. Relevant information might include the general description for the occupation; the firm's products or services; the firm's size, number of employees, and financial and competitive position; the requirements of the position; and the name and personality of the interviewer.[38] Obtaining this information will provide you with additional insight into the firm and help you formulate questions to ask the interviewer. This information might be gleaned, for example, from corporate annual reports, *The Wall Street Journal,* Moody's manuals, Standard & Poor's *Register of Corporations, Directors, and Executives, The Directory of Corporate Affiliations,* selected issues of *Business Week,* or trade publications. If information is not readily available, you could call the company and indicate that you wish to obtain some information about the firm before your interview.

Preparation for the job interview should also involve role playing, or pretending that you are in the "hot seat" being interviewed. Before role playing, anticipate questions interviewers may pose and how you might address them (Figure C–8). Do not memorize your answers, though, because you want to appear spontaneous, yet logical and intelligent. Nonetheless, it is helpful to practice how you might respond to the questions. You should also anticipate a substance abuse screening process—now common among a wide variety of organizations.[39] In addition, develop questions you might ask the interviewer that are important and of concern to you (Figure C–9).

When role playing, you and someone with whom you feel comfortable should engage in a mock interview. Afterward, ask the stand-in interviewer to candidly appraise your interview content and style. You may wish to videotape the mock interview; ask the personnel in your campus placement office where videotaping equipment can be obtained for this purpose.

Before the job interview you should attend to several details. Know the exact time and place of the interview; write them down—do not rely on your memory. Get the full company name straight. Find out what the interviewer's name is and how to pronounce it. Bring a notepad and pen along on the interview, in case you need to record anything. Make certain that your appearance is clean, neat, professional, and conservative. And be punctual; arriving tardy to a job interview gives you an appearance of being unreliable.

Succeeding in your job interview   You have done your homework, and at last the moment arrives and it is time for the interview. Although you may experience

FIGURE C-8

Questions frequently asked by
interviewers

INTERVIEWER QUESTIONS

1 What can you tell me about yourself?
2 What are your strengths? Weaknesses?
3 What do you consider to be your most significant accomplishment to date?
4 What do you see yourself doing in 5 years? In 10 years?
5 Are you a leader? Explain.
6 What do you really want out of life?
7 How would you describe yourself?
8 Why did you choose your college major?
9 In which extracurricular activities did you participate? Why?
10 What jobs have you enjoyed the most? The least? Why?
11 How has your previous work experience prepared you for a job?
12 Why do you want to work for our company?
13 What qualifications do you think a person needs to be successful in a company like ours?
14 What do you know about our company?
15 What criteria are you using to evaluate the company for which you hope to work?
16 In what kind of city would you prefer to live?
17 What can I tell you about our company?
18 Are you willing to relocate?
19 Are you willing to spend at least six months as a trainee? Why?
20 Why should we hire you?

some apprehension, view the interview as a conversation between the prospective employer and you. Both of you are in the interview to look over the other party, to see whether there might be a good match. You know your subject matter (you); furthermore, because you did not have a job with the firm when you walked into the interview, you really have nothing to lose if you don't get it—so relax.[40]

When you meet the interviewer, greet him or her by name, be cheerful, smile, and maintain good eye contact. Take you lead from the interviewer at the outset. Sit down

FIGURE C-9

Questions frequently asked by
interviewees

INTERVIEWEE QUESTIONS

1 Why would a job candidate want to work for your firm?
2 What makes your firm different from its competitors?
3 What is the company's promotion policy?
4 Describe the typical first-year assignment for this job.
5 How is an employee evaluated?
6 What are the opportunities for personal growth?
7 Do you have a training program?
8 What are the company's plans for future growth?
9 What is the retention rate of people in the position for which I am interviewing?
10 How can you use my skills?
11 Does the company have development programs?
12 What kind of image does the firm have in the community?
13 Why do you enjoy working for your firm?
14 How much responsibility would I have in this job?
15 What is the corporate culture in your firm?

after the interviewer has offered you a seat. Do not smoke. Sit up straight in your chair, and look alert and interested at all times. Appear relaxed, not tense. Be enthusiastic.

During the interview, be yourself. If you try to behave in a manner that is different from the "real" you, your attempt may be transparent to the interviewer or you may ultimately get the job but discover that you aren't suited for it. In addition to assessing how well your skills match those of the job, the interviewer will probably try to assess your long-term interest in the firm. William Kucker, a recruiter for General Electric, explains, "We're looking for people to make a commitment."[41]

As the interview comes to a close, leave it on a positive note. Thank the interviewer for his or her time and the opportunity to discuss employment opportunities. If you are still interested in the job, express this to the interviewer. The interviewer will normally tell you what the employer's next step is. Rarely will a job offer be made at the end of the initial interview. If it is and you want the job, accept the offer; if there is any doubt in your mind about the job, however, ask for time to consider the offer.

Following up on your job interview   After your interview, send a thank-you note to the interviewer and indicate whether you are still interested in the job. If you want to continue pursuing the job, "polite persistence" may help you get it. According to one expert, "Many job hunters make the mistake of thinking that their career fate is totally in the hands of the interviewer once the job interview is finished.[42] You *can* have an impact on the interviewer *after* the interview is over.

The thank-you note is a gesture of appreciation and a way of maintaining visibility with the interviewer. (Remember the adage, "Out of sight, out of mind.") Even if the interview did not go well, the thank-you note may impress the interviewer so much that his or her opinion of you changes. After you have sent your thank-you note, you may wish to call the prospective employer to determine the status of the hiring decision. If the interviewer told you when you would hear from the employer, make your telephone call *after* this date (assuming, of course, that you have not yet heard from the employer); if the interviewer did not tell you when you would be contacted, make your telephone call a week or so after you have sent your thank-you note.

As you conduct your follow-up, be persistent but polite. If you are too eager, one of two things could happen to prevent you from getting the job: the employer might feel that you are a nuisance and would exhibit such behavior on the job, or the employer may perceive that you are desperate for the job and thus are not a viable candidate.

Handling rejection   You have put your best efforts into your job search. You developed a well-designed résumé and prepared carefully for the job interview. Even the interview appears to have gone well. Nevertheless, a prospective employer may send you a rejection letter. ("We are sorry that our needs and your superb qualifications don't match.") Although you will probably be disappointed, not all interviews lead to a job offer because there normally are more candidates than there are positions available.

If you receive a rejection letter, you should think back through the interview. What appeared to go right? What went wrong? Perhaps personnel from your campus placement office can shed light on the problem, particularly if they are in the custom of having interviewers rate each interviewee. Try to learn lessons to apply in future interviews. Keep interviewing and gaining interview experience; your persistence will eventually pay off.

SELECTED SOURCES OF MARKETING CAREER INFORMATION

The following is a selected list of marketing information sources that you should find useful during your academic studies and professional career.

Business and Marketing Reference Publications

Peter D. Bennett, ed., *Dictionary of Marketing Terms,* 2nd ed. (Chicago: NTC Business Books, 1995). This dictionary contains definitions of more than 3,000 marketing terms.

Victor P. Buell, ed., *Handbook of Modern Marketing,* 2nd ed. (New York: McGraw-Hill, 1986). This handbook was designed to provide a single authoritative source of information on marketing and marketing-related subjects. Sections and chapters contain conceptual background material to aid the reader in overall understanding, followed by "how-to" information.

Business Periodicals Index (BPI) (New York: H. W. Wilson Company). This is a monthly (except July) index of almost 300 periodicals from all fields of business and management.

Chase Cochrane and Kenneth L. Barasch, *Marketing Problem Solver,* 3rd ed. (Radnor, Penn.: Chilton Book Company, 1989). A good reference for "how-to" problems, this handbook contains chapters on marketing research, marketing planning, product planning, pricing, advertising, trade shows, sales promotion, legal aspects of marketing, and other topics.

Jill Cousins and Lesley Robinson, eds., *The Online Manual,* 2nd ed. (Cambridge, Mass.: Blackwell Publishers, 1993). This manual is a practical tool to help both the experienced and inexperienced information user select from the thousands of databases now available online.

Lorna M. Daniells, *Business Information Sources,* 3rd ed. (Berkeley, Calif.: University of California Press, 1993). This comprehensive guide to selected business books and reference sources is useful for business students, as well as the practicing businessperson.

Jeffrey Heilbrunn, ed., *Marketing Encyclopedia* (Chicago: NTC Business Books, 1995). This book provides a collection of essays by professional and academic marketing experts on issues and trends shaping the future of marketing.

Jerry M. Rosenberg, *Dictionary of Business and Management,* 3rd ed. (New York: John Wiley & Sons, 1992). This dictionary contains more than 10,000 concise definitions of business and management terms.

Jean L. Sears and Marilyn K. Moody, *Using Government Publications,* rev. ed. (Phoenix: Oryx Press, 1993). An easy-to-use manual arranged by topics such as consumer expenditures, business and industry statistics, economic indicators, and projections. Each chapter contains a search strategy, a checklist of sources, and a narrative description of the sources. Volume 1: Searching by Subjects and Agencies; Volume 2: Finding Statistics and Using Special Techniques.

Career Planning Publications

Richard N. Bolles, *What Color Is Your Parachute? A Practical Manual for Job Hunters and Career Changers* (Berkeley, Calif.: Ten Speed Press, 1995).

Karmen Crowther, *Researching Your Way to a Good Job* (New York: John Wiley, 1993).

Ronald W. Fry, ed., *Advertising Career Directory* (Detroit, Mich.: Visible Ink Press, 1992).

Fred E. Jardt and Mary B. Nemnich, *Using the Internet in Your Job Search* (Indianapolis, Ind.: JIST Works, 1995).

Joyce Lain Kennedy and Thomas J. Morrow, *Electronic Job Search Revolution* (New York: John Wiley & Sons, 1994).

Bradley J. Morgan, ed., *Marketing and Sales Career Directory,* 4th ed. (Detroit, Mich.: Visible Ink Press, 1993).

Tom Jackson, *The Perfect Résumé* (New York: Doubleday, 1990).

Ronald L. Krannich and Caryl R. Krannich, *The Complete Guide to International Jobs and Careers,* 2nd ed. (Woodbridge, Va.: Impact Publications, 1992).

Dorothy Leeds, *Marketing Yourself* (New York: HarperCollins, 1991).

Adele Lewis, *How to Write Better Résumés,* 4th ed. (Hauppauge, N.Y.: Barron's Educational Services, 1993).

David W. Rosenthal and Michael A. Powell, *Careers in Marketing* (Englewood Cliffs, N.J.: Prentice Hall, 1984).

Selected Periodicals

Advertising Age, Crain Communications, Inc. (semiweekly). Write to 965 E. Jefferson Ave., Detroit, MI 48207-3185 (subscription rate: $99).

Business Horizons, Indiana University (bimonthly). Write to JAI Press, Inc., 55 Old Post Rd. No. 2, Greenwich, CT 06836 (subscription rate: $70).

Business Week, McGraw-Hill (weekly). Write to 1221 Avenue of the Americas, New York, NY 10020 (subscription rate: $46.95).

Fortune, Time, Inc. (biweekly). Write to P.O. Box 60001, Tampa, FL 33660-0001 (subscription rate: $57).

Harvard Business Review, Harvard University (bimonthly). Write to Harvard Business Review, Harvard University, Harvard Business School Publishing Corp., 60 Harvard Way, Boston, MA 02163 (subscription rate: $75).

Industrial Marketing Management, Elsevier Science Publishing Co., Inc. (quarterly). Write to 655 Avenue of the Americas, New York, NY 10010 (subscription rate: $350).

Journal of the Academy of Marketing Science, The Academy of Marketing Science (quarterly). Write to Sage Publications, Inc., 2455 Teller Rd., Thousand Oaks, CA 91320 (subscription rate: $67).

Journal of Advertising Research, Advertising Research Foundation (bimonthly). Write to Advertising Research Foundation, 641 Lexington Ave, 11th Fl., New York, NY 10022 (subscription rate: $100).

Journal of Business and Industrial Marketing, MCB University Press (quarterly). Write to 60/62 Toller Ln., Bradford, West Yorkshire, England, BD89BY (subscription rate: $279).

Journal of Consumer Marketing, MCB University Press (quarterly). Write to 60/62 Toller Ln., Bradford, West Yorkshire, England, BD89BY (subscription rate: $279).

Journal of Consumer Research, Journal of Consumer Research, Inc. (quarterly). Write to University of Chicago Press, Journals Division, 5720 S. Woodlawn Ave., Chicago, IL 60637 (subscription rate: $84, $20 for students).

Journal of Health Care Marketing, American Marketing Association (quarterly). Write to 250 S. Wacker Dr., Suite 200, Chicago, IL 60606 (subscription rate: $50 for nonmembers, $40 for members).

Journal of Marketing, American Marketing Association (quarterly). Write to 250 S. Wacker Dr., Suite 200, Chicago, IL 60606 (subscription rate: $70 for nonmembers, $35 for members).

Journal of Marketing Education, University of Colorado (three per year). Write to University of Colorado, Graduate School of Business Administration, Campus Box 420, Boulder, CO 80309 (subscription rate: $30).

Journal of Marketing Research, American Marketing Association (quarterly). Write to 250 S. Wacker Dr., Suite 200, Chicago, IL 60606 (subscription rate: $70 for nonmembers, $35 for members).

Journal of Personal Selling and Sales Management, Pi Sigma Epsilon (quarterly). Write to 6560 S. 27th St., Oak Creek, WI 53154 (subscription rate: $55).

Journal of Retailing, Institute of Retail Management (quarterly). Write to JAI Press, Inc., 55 Old Post Pd. No. 2, Greenwich, CT 06836 (subscription rate: $60).

Marketing News, American Marketing Association (biweekly). Write to 250 S. Wacker Dr., Suite 200, Chicago, IL 60606 (subscription rate: $50 for nonmembers, $30 for members).

Media Week, BPI Communications, Inc. (monthly). Write to 49 E. 21st St., New York, NY 10010 (subscription rate: $40).

Sales and Marketing Management, Bill Communications, Inc. (16 per year). Write to P.O. Box 10667, Riverton, NJ 08076 (subscription rate: $48).

Stores, National Retail Federation (monthly). Write to 325 7th St. NW, Suite 1000, Washington, DC 20004 (subscription rate: $49).

Marketing Education Review, CTC Press (three times a year). Write to CTC Press/MER, P.O. Box 1826, Clemson, SC 29633 (subscription rate: $28).

Professional and Trade Associations

American Advertising Federation
    1101 Vermont Avenue, NW, Suite 500
    Washington, DC 20036
    (202) 483-3399
    http://www.aaf.org/pub/aaf/

American Marketing Association
    250 S. Wacker Dr., Suite 200
    Chicago, IL 60606
    (312) 648-0536
    http://www.ama.org

American Society of Transportation and
    Logistics
    216 East Church Street
    Lockhaven, PA 17745
    (717) 148-8515
    http://www.cranfield.cc.uk/som/cclt/
        cclt.html
    http://www.its.leeds.ac.uk:8000/
        interesting-transport.html

Bank Marketing Association
1120 Connecticut Avenue, NW
Washington, DC 20036
(202) 663-5268

Business Professional Advertising
Association
21 Kilmer Road
Edison, NJ 08899-0001
(201) 985-4441

Direct Marketing Association
1120 Avenue of the Americas
New York, NY 10036-8096
(212) 768-7277

International Franchise Association
1350 New York Ave., NW, Suite 900
Washington, DC 20005
(202) 628-8000

Life Insurance Marketing and Research
Association International
Box 208
Hartford, CT 06141
(800) 235-4672

Marketing Research Association
2189 Silas Deane Hwy., Suite 5
Rocky Hill, CT 06067
(203) 257-4008

Marketing Science Institute
1000 Massachusetts Ave.
Cambridge, MA 02138
(617) 491-2060

National Association of Purchasing
Management
2055 E. Centennial Circle
P.O. Box 22160
Tempe, AZ 85285-2160
(602) 752-6276

National Association of Wholesaler-
Distributors
1725 K St. N.W.
Washington, DC 20006
(202) 872-0885

National Retail Federation
325 7th Street, NW
Suite 1000
Washington, DC 20004-2802
(202) 783-7971

Public Relations Society of America
33 Irving Place, 3rd Fl.
New York, NY 10003
(212) 995-2230
http://www.prsa.org/

Sales and Marketing Executives International
Statler Office Tower, #977
Cleveland, OH 44115
(216) 771-6650

Women in Advertising and Marketing
4200 Wisconsin Ave., N.W.
Suite 106-238
Washington, DC 20016
(301) 369-7400

Women in Sales Association
8 Madison Avenue
P.O. Box M
Valhalla, NY 10595
(914) 946-3802

Alternate Cases

It would be hard to have missed the introduction of Microsoft Corporation's Windows 95. Windows 95 is probably the biggest marketing story of the decade. Although Windows 95 was years in the making, the marketing war for personal computer (PC) operating systems was virtually over before Microsoft formally launched the product in August 1995.

THE PRODUCT

A computer's operating system controls exactly how the computer hardware interacts with other software and directs the basic functions of the computer. For years, the PC industry—defined here as IBM-compatible personal computers—was dominated by DOS (for Disk Operating System). However, the old DOS was user-unfriendly and required PC users often to learn and use cryptic codes to interact with the computer. Microsoft observed how successful Macintosh computers were in enabling computer users to interact easily with their computers using a graphical interface, and consequently, it developed MS (Microsoft) Windows, a user-friendly interface to DOS. MS Windows was the precursor, or first generation, which would ultimately be replaced by Windows 3.1, and then—two generations later—by Windows 95. Windows 95 acts as both an interface and an operating system, completely replacing DOS.

Even somewhat recently, computers were the exclusive domain of computer specialists, and complex, unfriendly operating systems abounded. The systems were also designed for early, relatively slow, computers. Declining prices, rapidly improving technology, and the widespread acceptance of computers among the general population were the driving forces behind the development of a new PC operating system. To contend with these factors, Microsoft was determined to provide an advanced, stable operating system that would be more "user oriented" than existing systems. Microsoft spent several years and millions of dollars testing its new Windows 95 operating system. This 32-bit operating system was designed to take advantage of the full power of today's 32-bit chips, look prettier on the screen than Windows 3.1, allow more than one application program to run simultaneously, and generally make life easier for PC owners.

THE INDUSTRY

The highly competitive PC operating system market is driven by two important factors. First, modern high-performance PCs have been criticized as being unable to perform to their full potential because the common DOS operating system was developed for much more primitive computers. New 32-bit operating systems (such as Windows 95) can unleash the full power of the 486 and Pentium processors to take advantage of demanding software. Second, there is little doubt that the company with the most widely adopted operating system will have a competitive advantage in terms of developing other system-compatible software. For example, consumers may perceive that other Microsoft software would run faster and more reliably on a Microsoft operating system. Operating system dominance is particularly important given the rapidly growing PC industry. Industry growth rates are around 30 percent annually.

There have also been rapid changes in consumer attitudes toward computers. The purchase of a computer for the home is no longer for an elite segment of the population. As acceptance of PCs expands, operating system dominance may lead to industry dominance.

THE COMPETITION

Microsoft's largest competitor in the PC operating system market was IBM's OS/2 Warp. OS/2 Warp had the advantage of being released earlier than Microsoft's highly touted Windows 95 system. In fact, Warp beat

Windows 95 to the market by almost a year. OS/2 Warp was released to the market with mixed reviews, however. While the *New York Times* and *PC Week* were unimpressed with the product, another trade journal, *InfoWorld*, claimed Warp was superior to a prerelease version of Windows 95.

IBM also took a big gamble by announcing that OS/2 Warp would not provide any way for users to run programs designed for Windows 95. This would force OS/2 to stand on its own in the market. If software developers were persuaded to create special OS/2 versions of their programs, it could give OS/2 a boost. If the move failed to encourage software manufacturers to develop OS/2 programs, it could kill OS/2 completely.

IBM also faced other obstacles. OS/2 had a hard time gaining an inroad to the market because most PC manufacturers were selling their PCs preloaded with the Windows 3.1 operating system simply because they had paid for it. Microsoft had a practice of charging computer makers a licensing fee on each machine sold, regardless of whether it contained MS-DOS or Windows. Microsoft got away with this because computer manufacturers lived "in fear of retribution from Microsoft," according to Lee Reiswig, IBM's personal software chief.

In July 1994, the Justice Department ordered Microsoft to end this practice of charging computer makers a licensing fee on each machine sold. The Justice Department settlement with Microsoft encouraged IBM's Reiswig, who felt more optimistic about OS/2 Warp's chances in the market.

THE ISSUES

Both OS/2 Warp and Windows 95 entered the U.S. market priced at about $90. Windows entered the market at this price despite the fact that millions of dollars had gone into extensively testing the software; further millions went into promoting the package. In fact, Microsoft practically gave away more than 500,000 copies of Windows 95 to test the system on a variety of PCs and in a variety of conditions, and worldwide promotional expenditures for the Windows 95 launch was estimated at $700 million. Microsoft wanted to ensure that its operating system would be priced within reach of the average PC owner.

To ensure widespread acceptance of its operating system, Microsoft depended on PC user input during the "beta-testing" phase. Beta testing is taking a new product to lead users for input and feedback prior to full-scale product introduction. At Microsoft headquarters, software developers carefully studied exactly how users interacted with the operating system and what confused them. They then made modifications to the product to try and make sure that computer users could focus on the tasks they wanted their computers to do and not on how to navigate a complicated operating system.

Microsoft also spared no expense in promoting the "product of the decade." Millions of dollars were spent on advertising and special promotions. Great pains were taken to ensure that sufficient quantities of Windows 95 were shipped to stores worldwide so that no store faced shortages of the product when the customers came for the product. Windows 95 was available at computer stores, electronic stores selling computers, and mass merchandisers. After the product was launched, Microsoft also made sure that there were adequate support staff personnel available at the end of a toll-free support line to answer any questions new users had or solve any early problems.

By early August 1995, industry speculation was that IBM had given up on the home PC market. OS/2 Warp was relatively strong in the corporate market but was facing strong competition from yet another Microsoft operating system—Windows NT. IBM's chairman claimed that the consumer and stand-alone desktop markets were always secondary to the company and that IBM intended to continue its long-standing focus for OS/2 on the corporate market. Despite having almost a year advantage on Microsoft in getting to the market, it appeared by early 1996 that Microsoft's Windows 95 would win the desktop operating system war.[1]

Questions

1. What are the various environmental factors influencing the potential success of Windows 95 and OS/2 in the marketplace?

2. If you were in charge of launching Windows 95 in late 1995, what would be your marketing mix decisions (4Ps) for the product, and why?

3. What role did customer needs play in Microsoft's Windows 95 development and launch? How did Microsoft's marketing mix add customer value?

Case D-2 Girl Scouts of America

BE PREPARED. The motto of the Girl Scouts of America (GSA) has been the same since Mrs. Juliette Gordon Low founded the organization in 1912 with money from an inheritance and a divorce settlement. However, Girl Scout membership has declined from an all-time high of 3.9 million in 1969 to 2.3 million in the early 1990s. Had the principles underlying GSA become obsolete, or were there other forces operating that could explain declining membership? Furthermore, would recent changes adopted by GSA lead to success?

When Low founded the GSA, she wanted young girls to be self-reliant and independent and to uphold the highest standards of citizenship and moral character. The many activities of the GSA focused on young girls developing into wives and mothers, and merit badges were awarded for accomplishments such as dressmaking, homemaking, and being a hostess. The GSA also had focused on traditional family life and increasingly found itself following population migration to the suburbs and away from the cities. This meant that the GSA recruited many scouts from white, middle-class families.

However, the environment has changed in recent years. Divorce has fractured the traditional family, opportunities for women to work outside the home have expanded, more married women are working, fewer children are being born, and the technology affecting everyday living has become more complex. The racial and ethnic composition in the United States also has changed, with a growing number of African-Americans, Hispanics, and Asian Americans.

In addition to fewer girls becoming scouts, the GSA observed that girls who had become Girl Scouts as youngsters did not continue as they grew older. Many girls who had progressed from Brownies (the youngest group of 6- to 8-year-olds) to Juniors (ages 9 to 11) had dropped out before attaining the rank of Cadette at age 12, and thus never achieved the highest rank of Senior (ages 14 to 17). It seemed that the scout troop organizational structure had contributed to the loss of scouts as they grew older. The troop format required frequent meetings and was believed to be too confining as teenagers became involved in a wider range of activities. Another disadvantage of the troop format was that it demanded considerable time from the adult troop leader.

To counteract the forces in the environment, the GSA has adopted different approaches for attracting and retaining young people. For example, the GSA has focused attention on recruiting young girls, particularly African-Americans and Hispanics, in cities as well as the suburbs. Emphasis has been placed on recruiting lower-income and delinquent girls as well. The GSA has reached out to pregnant teenagers with a program dealing with career opportunities. GSA activities also have changed, as evidenced by the new merit badges. Today they are awarded in categories such as "Aerospace," "Business-Wise," "Computer Fun," and "Ms. Fix-it," which recognizes skill in home repairs. An increasing emphasis on careers is also evident. The troop concept and requirement has been relaxed. Girls can now become scouts without joining a troop, provided they attend one official event per year. Once members, they are invited to participate in special-interest projects that include field trips, guest speakers, and conferences.

These efforts were detailed in a print, radio, and television public service campaign titled "Brainstorm," aimed at encouraging girls to become scouts and stay in the program even after they entered high school. The campaign included a 30-second TV message that covered sights and sounds related to ocean liners and travel, tap dancing, piano playing, airplanes, filmmaking, a space capsule taking off, and meeting young men.[2]

Questions

1. Did the business definition of GSA change?

2. How did the product-market grid for the GSA change, given environmental trends?

3. What is your prognosis for the GSA, given its response to the environment?

Case D-3   The Juice Club

What were you doing in 10th grade? Waiting to get your driver's license? Kirk Perron was thinking about his future and putting together a deal that would help launch the successful Juice Club chain. It sounds incredible, but Kirk Perron bought the real estate for the first Juice Club when he was in 10th grade. He borrowed money from a high school counselor, the librarian, and his school bus driver to put together the $12,000 down payment.

The Company

Kirk Perron opened up his first Juice Club in 1990. He hit on the idea for a convenient, delicious, healthful food store on a long weekend bike ride. An avid cyclist with a life-long interest in health and nutrition, he wanted to offer an alternative to typical fast-food fare. The idea was a hit and quickly spread. Today the Juice Club has more than 24 stores offering a wide variety of healthy drinks and snacks. Customers can choose from a variety of Juice Club specialties such as a Boysenberry Blitz or a Guava Gulp smoothie.

The Idea

Walk into a Juice Club and you are confronted with almost two dozen choices for smoothies, additional natural juice blend options, and healthy snacks. Read about the benefits of raw fruit and vegetable juices from Juice Club's selection of affordable, interesting books by health industry authors. Check out the in-store *Nutrient Analysis Book,* showing a complete nutritional breakdown for all the Juice Club menu products.

Smoothies are about 80 percent of the Juice Club's business. They are made with juice and fruit and often yogurt, sherbet, or ice milk. A typical smoothie gets most of its calories from carbohydrates and protein, providing a low- or no-fat, nutritious meal. Nutritional supplements from wheat germ to bee pollen are also available. The Juice Club offers customers up to two "Club Additions." Add more vitamins, calcium, or protein. How about adding some spirulina? A blue-green micro-algae, spirulina provides a good source of B vitamins, iron, and protein.

As you sit at the counter in a Juice Club, you can watch friendly, well-schooled Juice Club employees whip, beat, and blend your smoothie right before your eyes. Prices range from $0.95 for an 8-ounce glass of a natural juice blend to $3.75 for the Ironman/Woman, the healthiest nondairy smoothie containing orange, strawberry, and banana as well as about half of the Juice Club's "Club Additions."

These Juice Club outlets are busy! The outlet near Stanford University typically has 50 customers waiting in line outside on Saturday mornings and reportedly takes in about $1.7 million per year, or more than $2,000 per square foot annually.

The Competition

Juice bars are one of the hottest new trends. Several California, Arizona, and Louisiana juice bar chains have ambitious plans for hundreds of new locations in the coming months. Barriers to entry are fairly low. Single store outlets or small chains within a city or region are common.

The Market

Juice bars have been around for decades, often in health food stores and gyms. Associated with what used to be a small group of intensely health-conscious customers, that small demographic group has boomed in recent years, fueling the market for fat-free foods, fitness equipment, and apparel. Many wonder, however, whether juice bars will go too far. There are doubts about whether a significant number of men will substitute a healthful smoothie for a fat-laden fast-food lunch.

However, the Juice Club is optimistic about the opportunities for expanding the market. About two-thirds of Juice Club's customers are between the ages of 15 and 25—not exactly the same demographic group as the traditional health-conscious baby boomer. Age and education level are important selection criteria for opening new Juice Club outlets. Kirk Perron believes that the more highly educated potential customers are, the more likely they will be to stop in for a nutritious smoothie. In fact, many current and planned Juice Club outlets are in college towns.

The Issues

Purists insist that the best drinks come from completely fresh products. Fresh produce can be hard to work with to provide consistent tasting drinks. Also, the price of fresh produce can change drastically throughout the year. The Juice Club has developed its own frozen juice blends.

As a response to this problem Michael Owings developed the California Juice Oasis concept, which utilizes bag-in-the-box "mother juices," such as apple, cranberry, and nonpulp orange, and frozen fruit to create bases for the various mixed drinks. Bar guns dispense the mother juices in four different ounce-based measures for convenience and portion-size control.

With fairly limited menus, juice bars are considered great as an add-on rather than a stand-alone retail establishment since they are usually not strong enough to draw huge volumes on their own. Personnel are important to the success of a juice bar—described as "bartenders" they have to be able to put on a good show for the customer.[3]

Questions

1. Conduct an environmental scan for the Juice Club as it considers a new juice bar to open near your university. Identify factors that you feel have an impact on the juice bar market, and indicate whether these factors would tend to enhance opportunities or represent threats.

2. Given your environmental analysis, which environmental force do you feel is most critical for the Juice Club and why?

3. Examine the competitive environment for juice bars. Consider the likelihood of new entrants, barriers to entry, existing competitors, and substitutes. How would you summarize the current competitive environment?

4. Find a growth strategy for the Juice Club to expand its number of outlets and sales revenue by suggesting (*a*) market segments to target and (*b*) kinds of locations to select.

Case D–4   H. B. Fuller

In January 1996, H. B. Fuller was sued in U.S. District Court for allegedly causing the 1993 death of Joel Linares, a 16-year-old Guatemalan boy. The lawsuit claims that Fuller's toxic glue product, Resistol, caused severe physical and neurological injuries to the boy, who had inhaled it, which led to his death.

The Company and Product

H. B. Fuller is a long-time manufacturer of glues and inks, competing in many international markets. It has a tradition of social responsibility. Like only a handful of other American companies, it contributes 5 percent of its earnings to charitable causes. H. B. Fuller takes pride in its research center designed to be environmentally sensitive and energy efficient. *Fortune* magazine has named H. B. Fuller one of the best U.S. firms for which an employee can work.

Through its research H. B. Fuller developed Resistol, a glue used in shoe manufacture and repair, leather work, and carpentry. Its advantages over water-based glues include rapid setup time, better adhesion, and superior water resistance. In the early 1980s Resistol was sold in Central America in small packages affordable by firms that used the product for legitimate purposes. Many of the firms using Resistol were small businesses and could not afford to buy or store large containers of the product. Fuller's profits from selling Resistol in Central America are less than $500,000 annually. Resistol was sold in Central America by a wholly owned, but autonomous, subsidiary of H. B. Fuller. This subsidiary is one of the 500 largest firms in Latin America. This firm's management also stressed its ethical obligations.

The "Resistoleros"

In 1985, Fuller's product Resistol was publicized because of its use by Honduran street children seeking a cheap "high." Inhaling the product dulled their hunger pangs and sensitivity to the cold, but it caused addiction and irreversible brain damage. While children throughout Central and South America abuse a variety of chemical substances, the name "Resistoleros" became synonymous with Latin American street children, whether they used inhalants or not.

Central American countries are very poor, have high infant mortality rates, and have short life expectancies among their citizens. Primary exports are agricultural products such as bananas and coffee. Surplus rural workers migrate to overcrowded cities in search of work. In the cities, they find high rates of unemployment and low wages. Children work to help support their families. It is these city children that have been given the Resistoleros name.

In the 1980s H. B. Fuller's Latin American subsidiary responded to reports of abuse of Resistol by children by pointing out that Resistol was not the only product abused by street children; glue-sniffing was a social, not a corporate concern, and Resistolero should not be used as a term synonymous with drug addict. Social activists asked the subsidiary to add mustard oil to the glue. H. B. Fuller's researchers found that mustard oil is carcinogenic and causes short-term damage to the respiratory tract, eyes, and skin of any workers who come into contact with even minute quantities of this oil. It induces nausea in anyone who sniffs the glue. The oil has a shelf-life of only six months, greatly complicating distribution.

THE 1992 DECISIONS

In 1992 Fuller announced it would stop sales of Resistol in Central America "wherever it is being misused." As a result, Fuller said it was removing the product from retail sales in Central American countries such as Guatemala and Honduras. After extensive study the company also concluded the following:

1. It would fund social, educational, and drug treatment programs to try to help Central American street children.
2. It would not add mustard oil to its adhesives because adding another toxic ingredient would harm legitimate users such as shoemakers.
3. It would put labels warning against the product's misuse on large containers—unaffordable by street children—in which it shipped Resistol from its U.S. production site to Central America.
4. It would continue research to try to find a water-based, nontoxic replacement glue for toluene, the chemical that gives Resistol its glue-sniffing "high."

These decisions—particularly the first one—caused children's advocates to laud the company for its position that inhalant abuse should be attacked on a broader scale.

THE ISSUES TODAY

The 1996 lawsuit alleges that H. B. Fuller was negligent in that it knew that its glue was dangerous when inhaled but did not issue adequate warnings of this fact. The Texas attorney who filed the suit on behalf of the boy's family said that he will try to convert this lawsuit into a class action on behalf of all children in Central America

who have sniffed glue. H. B. Fuller replied that it put warning labels on the containers in which it shipped the glue to Central America, but that its subsidiary repackaged the product into smaller containers that did not have warning labels. It also observed that most of the street children who abuse the product are illiterate, so warning labels on small containers would have no effect. The lawsuit also claims that tighter controls on distribution would have prevented Fuller's products from "falling into the hands of children such as Joel Linares."

This U.S. District Court suit is a product-liability action. Product-liability law embodies the expectations held by some segments of American society about the high level of safety they expect to be built into consumer products. However, achieving safety is not free. Furthermore, it may be impossible to produce absolutely safe products or to foresee all situations or uses of the products that might cause harm to its users or to bystanders.

Questions

1. Do you see H. B. Fuller's position today as ethical but illegal, ethical and legal, unethical but legal, or unethical and illegal? Why?
2. (a) Who are the primary stakeholders affected by the decision about whether to continue producing and marketing Resistol, and (b) how is each affected positively or negatively?
3. Should H. B. Fuller be held liable for the physical effects on Central American children or their possible deaths? Explain.
4. What are the implications of your answer to Question 3 (a) for the employees of manufacturers producing products that might be misused? (b) for the distributors? (c) for consumers?
5. What should H. B. Fuller do now about its production and marketing of Resistol to Central American customers?

CASE D-5 Kingpin Snowboarding

What looks like a slalom water ski, feels like surfing, but takes place on snowy downhill ski slopes? The answer is snowboarding—one of the fastest growing sports.

THE COMPANY

In 1992 Doran Nurmi and Roger Walsberg started Kingpin Manufacturing with an initial investment of $2,400. In the first year, the partners sold 15 of the 30

snowboards produced. Production increased to 300 boards the second year, 1,500 boards the third year, and 2,900 in 1995. With firm orders already received for more than 6,500 boards, Kingpin estimates total sales of more than 9,500 boards in 1996. Initially, more than 70 percent of the snowboards produced by Kingpin were custom orders. Now, however, a majority of the snowboards manufactured by Kingpin are "private labels" manufactured for other companies. Also, as the popularity of their snowboards rapidly rose, Kingpin moved away from custom orders and now offers 10 different models as standard products.

Photo by Mike Cousino.

THE IDEA

Snowboarding is a wintertime sport that resembles surfing on a ski hill. The modern snowboard industry began around 20 years ago. Currently, snowboarding is considered the hottest sport around. With an annual growth rate of 20 percent and more than 2 million snowboarders in the United States, the National Sporting Goods Association estimates that the snowboard population will increase to more than 4 million riders by the year 2000. The number of snowboarders is expected to exceed the number of skiers by 2010.

There are about 20 manufacturers producing snowboards within the United States. Barriers to entry are relatively low, so new entrants can be expected. Industry giants such as Burton, Nitro, Sims, and Santa Cruz account for about 60 percent to 65 percent of the market and offer entire lines of boards that range in price from $300 to $800.

THE JAPANESE MARKET

Snowboarding is also achieving worldwide attention and acceptance. The International Olympic Committee and the International Ski Federation have accepted snowboarding as a medal sport in the 1998 Winter Olympics to be held in Nagano, Japan. In fact, the Japanese market is an important one for Kingpin. Kingpin has been selling boards in Japan since 1993. Nurmi finds some interesting differences between the U.S. and Japanese markets. The Japanese market is much more "fashion conscious" than the U.S. market. In the United States, snowboarding has been around long enough that it has become a fairly well established sport. It is still very much a fashion trend in Japan. Wants are strongly dictated by what is seen in snowboarding magazines, especially U.S. magazines. As a result, the number one attribute sought in snowboards by the Japanese consumer is the appearance of the board, followed by quality. Performance is probably at the bottom of the list. In contrast, Nurmi finds that performance is the number one buying criterion for consumers selecting snowboards in the U.S. market.

Snowboards in Japan are smaller in size than the boards sold in the United States and styled a little differently. The Japanese in general have a smaller average foot size than their U.S. counterparts. The size and style are also different because of differences in snowboarding style. The Japanese ride differently—freestyle snowboarding is much more common in Japan. Interestingly, this ties into the influence of U.S. snowboarding magazines. Despite the fact that more than half of the snowboarders in the United States are either "free riders" or "all-mountain riders," they get little publicity in the popular snowboarding magazines. Since freestyle gets a lot more space in magazines, Japanese desire snowboards styled for freestyle riding. Free riders or mountain riders tend to ride on steeper terrain, in deep powder, and at the better resorts. These riders tend to be more expert than freestyle riders, who use different maneuvers on easier runs. Accordingly, Kingpin manufactures four snowboard models designed exclusively for the Japanese market.

The ski industry environment is also different. Snowboarding is not as widely accepted on Japanese slopes as it is in the United States. (The number of U.S. ski resorts allowing snowboarding went from 7 percent in 1985 to 90 percent in 1990.) Apparently many Japanese ski slope managers still see snowboarding as a fad that will die soon and, consequently, provide only limited ski slope access to snowboarders.

Kingpin's business dealings with the Japanese market also differ. According to Nurmi, the biggest difference is that all communications are via fax because of the time zone difference and the language barrier. Nurmi finds it inconvenient doing business this way since he is more comfortable dealing one-on-one with customers, and he finds it difficult to judge 'tone' when reading faxes.

Kingpin sells to the Japanese market through a distributor. This eliminates extensive dealings with individual Japanese retailers. While Kingpin also utilizes an indirect channel of distribution in the United States, the channel is longer in Japan. Kingpin generally sells directly to U.S. retailers in order to reach the U.S. consumer. An additional intermediary is used for the Japanese market. According to Nurmi, this indirect exporting market entry strategy is more appropriate than any direct market entry strategy for two important reasons. First, the Japanese consumers do not want to buy Japanese-made boards. As mentioned earlier, the image associated with American snowboards is important to the Japanese consumers. Second, manufacturing snowboards in Japan would be difficult since the most important component of the snowboard is the wood core. Given Japan's limited natural resources, the wood would probably have to be imported into Japan anyway. It is easier to export the completed snowboard rather than components for assembly in Japan.

Wholesalers, such as Kingpin's Japanese distributor, are offered a special wholesale price. In addition, there are quantity discounts to encourage large orders.

THE ISSUES

What does the future hold? Doran Nurmi thinks that the inclusion of snowboarding in the 1998 Olympics will significantly influence future demand in Japan. He is certain that it will change the Japanese market. In addition to expanding the market in Japan, he feels it will change how the Japanese view snowboarding: not only will snowboarding be taken more seriously, but the

market will shift from a focus on appearance to performance.[5]

Questions

1. What are the pros and cons of a global versus a multidomestic approach to marketing snowboards in Japan? Which approach do you feel would have more merit, and why?

2. What are some of the significant environmental factors that could have a *major* impact on the marketing of snowboards internationally? Describe each factor and what the nature of the impact would be. For example, one of the social/cultural factors that could have an impact is whether there is a tradition, an interest level, critical mass of skiers and snowboarders, and an interest in snowboarding in a given country or area.

3. What marketing mix recommendations do you have for Kingpin as they look toward the 1998 Olympics in Japan and beyond?

4. Kingpin currently uses indirect exporting. What are the advantages and disadvantages of indirect exporting versus other methods of global marketing such as direct exporting, licensing, joint venture, or direct ownership?

CASE D-6   The Johnsons Buy a Food Processor

At 4:52 P.M. on Friday, January 19, 1994, Brock and Alisha Johnson bought a food processor. There was no doubt about it. Any observer would agree that the purchase took place at precisely that time. Or did it?

When questioned after the transaction, neither Brock nor Alisha could remember which of them at first noticed or suggested the idea of getting a food processor. They do recall that in the summer of 1992 they attended a dinner party given by a friend who specialized in French and Chinese cooking. The meal was delicious, and their friend Brad was very proud of the Cuisinart food processor he had used to make many of the dishes. The item was expensive, however—about $200.

The following summer, Alisha noticed a comparison study of food processors in *Better Homes and Gardens*. The performance of four different brands was compared. At about the same time, Brock noticed that *Consumer Reports* also compared a number of brands of food processors. In both instances, the Cuisinart brand came out on top.

Later that fall, new models of the Cuisinart were introduced, and the old standard model went on sale in department stores at $140. The Johnsons searched occasionally for Cuisinarts in discount houses or in wholesale showroom catalogs, hoping to find an even

lower price for the product. They were simply not offered there.

For Christmas 1993, the Johnsons traveled from Atlanta to the family home in Michigan. While there, the Johnsons received a gift of a Sunbeam Deluxe Mixer from a grandmother. While the mixer was beautiful, Alisha immediately thought how much more versatile a food processor would be. One private sentence to that effect brought immediate agreement from Brock. The box was (discreetly) not opened, although many thanks were expressed. The box remained unopened the entire time the Johnsons kept the item.

Back home in Atlanta in January, Alisha again saw the $140 Cuisinart advertised by Rich's, one of the two major full-service department stores in Atlanta. Brock and Alisha visited a branch location on a Saturday afternoon and saw the item. The salesperson, however, was not knowledgeable about its features and not very helpful in explaining its attributes. The Johnsons left, disappointed.

Two days later, Alisha called the downtown location, where she talked to Ms. Evans, a seemingly knowledgeable salesperson who claimed to own and love exactly the model the Johnsons had in mind. Furthermore, Ms. Evans said that they did carry Sunbeam mixers and would make an exchange of the mixer, which had been received as a gift and for which no receipt was available.

On the following Friday morning, Brock put the mixer in his car trunk when he left for work downtown. That afternoon, Alisha and 6-month-old Brock, Jr., rode the bus downtown to meet Brock and make the transaction. After meeting downtown, they drove through heavy rainy-day traffic to Rich's to meet Ms. Evans, whom they liked as much in person as they did on the telephone. After a brief, dry-run demonstration of the use and operation of the attachments for all of the models, the Johnsons confirmed their initial decision to take the $140 basic item. They then asked about exchanging the Sunbeam mixer that they had brought with them. "No problem," said Ms. Evans.

After making a quick phone call, Ms. Evans returned with bad news. Rich's had not carried that particular model of mixer. This model mixer (i.e., I-73) was a single-color model that is usually carried at discount houses, catalog sales houses, and jewelry stores. The one carried by the better department stores, such as Rich's, was a two-tone model. Ms. Evans was sorry she could not make the exchange, but suggested that other stores such as Davison's, Richway Discount, or American Jewelers might carry the item. She even offered to allow the Johnsons to use her phone to verify the availability of the item. The Johnsons did exactly that.

Alisha dialed several of the suggested stores, looking for a retailer who carried both the Cuisinart and the Sunbeam Model I-73, but she quickly learned that they were distributed through different types of retail stores. The young man who answered the phone at American Jewelers, however, seemed friendly and helpful, and Alisha was able to obtain his agreement to take the item as a return if she could get there that afternoon.

American Jewelers was about ½ mile away. Brock volunteered to babysit for Brock, Jr., at Rich's while Alisha returned the mixer. She took the downtown shoppers' bus to American Jewelers with the still unopened mixer box under her arm.

About an hour later, Alisha returned, cold and wet, with a $57 refund. Brock, having run out of ways to entertain a 6-month-old, was very happy to see her. Together they bought the Cuisinart at 4:52 P.M. and proudly took it home.[6]

Questions

1. Which of the Johnsons decided to buy a food processor? The Cuisinart?

2. When was the decision to buy made?

3. What were the important attributes in the evaluation of the Cuisinart brand?

4. Would you characterize the Johnsons' purchase decision process as routine problem solving, limited problem solving, or extended problem solving? Why?

CASE D-7   Honeywell, Inc.: Optoelectronics Division

After several years of developing fiber-optic technology for Department of Defense projects, executives in the Optoelectronics Division of Honeywell, Inc. decided to pursue commercial applications for their products and technology. The task would not be easy because fiber optics was a new technology that many firms would find unfamiliar. Fiber optics is the technology of transmitting light through long, thin, flexible fibers of glass, plastic, or other transparent materials. When it is used in a commercial application, a light source emits infrared light flashes corresponding to data. Millions of light flashes per second send streams through a transparent fiber. A light sensor at the other end of the fiber "reads" the data transmitted. It is estimated that sales of fiber-optic technology could exceed $3 billion in 1995. Almost half the dollar sales volume would come from telecommunications, about 25 percent from government or military purchases, and about 25 percent from commercial applications in computers, robotics, cable TV, and other products.

Interest in adapting fiber-optic technology and prod-ucts for commercial applications had prompted Honeywell executives to carefully review buying behavior associated with the adoption of a new technology. The buying process appeared to contain at least six phases: (1) need recognition, (2) identification of available products, (3) comparison with existing technology, (4) vendor or seller evaluation, (5) the decision itself, and (6) follow-up on technology performance. Moreover, there appeared to be several people within the buying organization who would play a role in the adoption of a new technology. For example, top management (such as the president and executive vice presidents) would certainly be involved. Engineering and operations management (e.g., vice presidents of engineering and manufacturing) and design engineers (e.g., persons who develop specifications for new products) would also play a major role. Purchasing personnel would have a say in such a decision and particularly in the vendor-evaluation process. The role played by each person in the buying organization was still unclear to Honeywell. It seemed that engineering management personnel could slow the adoption of fiber optics if they did not feel it was appropriate for the products made by the company. Design engineers, who would actually apply fiber optics in product design, might be favorably or unfavorably disposed to the technology depending on whether they knew how to use it. Top management personnel would participate in any final decisions to use fiber optics and could generate interest in the technology if stimulated to do so.

This review of buying behavior led to questions about how to penetrate a company's buying organization and have fiber optics used in the company's products. Although Honeywell was a large, well-known company with annual sales exceeding $5 billion, its fiber-optic technology capability was much less familiar. Therefore the executives thought it was necessary to establish Honeywell's credibility in fiber optics. This

was done, in part, through an advertising image campaign that featured Honeywell Optoelectronics as a leader in fiber optics.[7]

Questions

1. What type of buying situation is involved in the purchase of fiber optics, and what will be important buying criteria used by companies considering using fiber optics in their products?
2. Describe the purchase decision process for adopting fiber optics, and state how members in the buying center for this technology might play a part in this process.
3. What effect will perceived risk have on a company's decision of whether to use fiber optics in its products?
4. What role does the image advertising campaign play in Honeywell Optoelectronics' efforts to market fiber optics?

CASE D-8   Bookworms, Inc.

Late one August morning, Nancy Klein, co-owner of Bookworms, Inc., sat at her desk near the back wall of a cluttered office. With some irritation, she had just concluded that her nearby calculator could help no more. "What we still need," she thought to herself, "are estimates of demand and market share . . . but at least we have two weeks to get them."

Klein's office was located in the rear of Bookworms, Inc., an 1800-square-foot bookstore specializing in quality paperbacks. The store carries more than 10,000 titles and sold more than $520,000 worth of books in 1995. Titles were stocked in 18 categories, ranging from art, biography, and cooking to religion, sports, and travel.

Bookworms, Inc. was located in a small business district across the street from the boundary of Verdoon University (VU). VU currently enrolled about 12,000 undergraduate and graduate students majoring in the liberal arts, the sciences, and the professions. Despite national trends in enrollment, the VU admissions office had predicted that the number of entering students would grow at about 1 percent per year through the 1990s. The surrounding community, a city of about 350,000, was projected to grow at about twice that rate.

Bookworms, Inc. carried no texts, even though many of its customers were VU students. Both Klein and her partner, Susan Berman, felt that the VU bookstore had simply too firm a grip on the textbook market in terms of price, location, and reputation. Bookworms also carried no classical records, as of two months ago. Klein recalled with discomfort the $15,000 or so they had lost on the venture. "Another mistake like that and the bank will be running Bookworms," she thought. "And, despite what Susan thinks, the copy service could just be that final mistake."

The idea for a copy service had come from Susan Berman. She had seen the candy store next door to Bookworms (under the same roof) go out of business in July. She had immediately asked the building's owner, Ed Anderson, about the future of the 800-square-foot space. Upon learning it was available, she had met with Klein to discuss her idea for the copy service. She had spoken excitedly about the opportunity: "It can't help but make money. I could work there part-time and the rest of the time we could hire students. We could call it 'Copycats' and even use a sign with the same kind of letters as we do in 'Bookworms.' I'm sure we could get Ed to knock the wall out between the two stores, if you think it would be a good idea. Probably we could rent most of the copying equipment, so there's not much risk."

Klein was not so sure. A conversation yesterday with Anderson had disclosed his desire for a five-year lease (with an option to renew) at $1,000 per month. He had promised to hold the offer open for two weeks before attempting to lease the space to anyone else. Representatives from copying-equipment firms had estimated that charges would run between $200 and $2,000 per month, depending on equipment, service, and whether the equipment was bought or leased. The copy service would also have other fixed costs in terms of utility expenses, interest, insurance, and the inventory (and perhaps equipment). Klein concluded that the service would begin to make a profit at about 20,000 copies per month under the best-case assumptions, and at about 60,000 copies per month under the worst-case assumptions.

Further informal investigation had identified two major competitors. One was the copy center located in the Krismann Library on the west side of the campus, a mile away. The other was a private firm, Kinko's, located on the south side of the campus, also one mile away. Both offered service while you wait, on several machines. The library's price was about ½ cent per copy higher than Kinko's. Both offered collating, binding, color copying, and other services, all on a seven-days-a-week schedule.

Actually, investigation had discovered that a third major "competitor" consisted of the VU departmental machines scattered throughout the campus. Most faculty and administrative copying was done on these machines, but students were allowed the use of some, at cost. In addition, at least 20 self-service machines could be found in the library and in nearby drugstores, grocery stores, and banks.

Moving aside a stack of books on her desk, Nancy Klein picked up the telephone and dialed her partner. When Berman answered, Klein asked, "Susan, have you any idea how many copies a student might make in a semester? I mean, according to my figures, we would break even somewhere between 20,000 and 60,000 copies per month. I don't know if this is half the market or what."

"You know, I have no idea," Berman answered. "I suppose when I was going to school I probably made 10 copies a month—for articles, class notes, old tests, and so on."

"Same here," Klein said. "But some graduate students must have done that many each week. You know,

I think we ought to do some marketing research before we go much further on this. What do you think?"

"Sure. Only it can't take much time or money. What do you have in mind, Nancy?"

"Well, we could easily interview our customers as they leave the store and ask them how many copies they've made in the past week or so. Of course, we'd have to make sure they were students."

"What about a telephone survey?" Berman asked. "That way we can have a random sample. We would still ask about the number of copies, but now we would know for sure they would be students."

"Or what about interviewing students in the union cafeteria? There's always a good-sized line there around noon, as I remember, and this might be even quicker."

"Boy, I just don't know. Why don't I come in this afternoon and we can talk about it some more?"

"Good idea," Klein responded. "Between the two of us, we should be able to come up with something."[8]

Questions

1. What sources of information should Klein and Berman use?

2. How should Klein and Berman gather data?

3. What questions should they ask?

4. How should they sample?

CASE D-9   Heart Rate Inc.: The Versa-Climber

Ms. Kimberly Dubois, director of Advertising and Promotion for Heart Rate Incorporated (HRI), was assigned responsibility for preparing a marketing plan for the introduction of the 108H Versa-Climber, the home version of the institutional models sold by the company. Mr. Dick Charnitski, president and founder of HRI and inventor of the Versa-Climber, was enthusiastic about the new introduction. Institutional Versa-Climber models had been successful in the health club and physical therapy markets, and users persuaded Mr. Charnitski to develop a more economical model for home use shown in the photo. While institutional models were occasionally sold to individuals, the 108H Versa-Climber would be HRI's first targeted entry into the aerobic home-fitness market.

THE COMPANY

HRI designs, develops, and markets a variety of products for use in health clubs, hospitals, and rehabilitation

clinics. Company sales have grown from $9,433 when HRI was founded 9 years ago, to more than $3 million today. The Versa-Climber is a full-body, aerobic, and strength exercise machine that simulates the physical motion of climbing a ladder. It is HRI's principal product and accounts for the great majority of company sales.

The Versa-Climber utilizes one of the most intensive and rigorous activities to which the body can be subjected—continuous vertical climbing. All major muscles of the arms, shoulders, chest, back, hips, buttocks, and legs are engaged while climbing. This combined upper- and lower-body muscle contraction maximizes peripheral blood flow, resulting in higher energy expenditure and calorie consumption. The workout is effective and efficient because it takes less time and perceived effort to burn more calories and achieves better results than other exercise activities. The rhythmic and continuous nature of the climbing exercise provides the benefits of aerobic training as well.

The machine itself consists of a column that houses the mechanical operations, pedals and handles, and a digital display module. To exercise, the user stands on two stirrup-style foot pedals and holds on to the two hand grips. All of the movement is powered by the user. The climbing motion is achieved by alternately stepping and pulling down on the handles with the left and right arms and legs. The left pedal and handle move vertically downward while the right move upward, and then alternate cyclically. This action simulates the motions of climbing a ladder.

HRI sells the Versa-Climber primarily in California, through a network of manufacturer's representatives and dealers who sell to institutional buyers. HRI spends little money on advertising. However, the Versa-Climber is displayed at trade shows and conventions.

The institutional Versa-Climber sells in the price range of $1,995 to $3,450, depending on the model. The 108H Versa-Climber for home use would be priced at $1,295. The price level was set after interviews with prospective buyers and a design and manufacturing cost analysis, which indicated that certain features could be eliminated for home use. The variable production cost per machine was estimated to be $430.

THE HOME-FITNESS MARKET

The home-fitness market is composed of weight-lifting equipment, exercise bicycles, rowers, treadmills, and cross-country skiing simulators. While estimates vary, it is believed that present retail sales of these products exceed $1.4 billion. The average annual sales dollar growth is 16 percent.

Exercise bicycles are the most popular home-fitness product, with 3.1 million units sold annually. Weight-lifting equipment is the second-most popular product category, with 1.8 million units sold each year.

Home-fitness products are sold through sporting goods stores, catalogs, and direct marketing, including television, magazines, and direct mail. The home-fitness product buyer is typically between the ages of 30 and 50 and has an annual income of more than $60,000. The buyer usually owns two or more types of home-fitness equipment and engages in athletic activities outside the home. Industry research indicates that buyers prefer equipment that is easy and fun to use and provides the benefits promised when used properly. This research also indicated the exercise equipment purchased for home use was first used at a health club or similar facility and that buyers preferred to operate the equipment before making a purchase.

MARKETING OPTIONS FOR THE 108H VERSA-CLIMBER

HRI considered two broad options for marketing the 108H Versa-Climber: (1) direct marketing and (2) marketing through retail stores. Alternative approaches within each option were also possible. However, HRI was prepared to spend no more than $300,000 annually to market the 108H Versa-Climber for home use. The manufacturer's suggested retail price to the customer would be $1,295, regardless of the option considered.

Direct Marketing

Two direct-marketing approaches were identified: (1) direct-response media advertising with promotional literature to supplement inquiries, and (2) catalog houses, which assume nearly all direct-marketing functions and costs. Direct-response media advertising involved three main costs: media expenditures, brochure costs, and video costs. Because of the high cost of spot television advertising and the firm's limited resources, media expenditures would be limited to print advertising.

The direct-response strategy involved soliciting inquiries and orders through print media advertising. When inquiries were made, the company would follow up by mailing out a brochure and video and ideally making a subsequent phone call to solicit the sale. Costs associated with the direct-response channel strategy included advertising, video, brochure, telephone, and postage. The total expenditure on promotional materials sent to inquiries would be about $5.50. Shipping units individually through UPS would be $29 per unit.

Media placement costs would vary by magazine and the number of insertions. For example, a full-page color advertisement in *Men's Fitness*, a monthly magazine, would cost $4,350 for a single insertion, $22,968 for an ad run six times, and $40,428 if an ad ran in all 12 issues of a year. The advertising cost for a single full-page color insertion in *National Body & Fitness*, a monthly magazine, would be $1,700, $9,000, and $15,840 for 1, 6, and 12 insertions respectively.

Distribution through special-interest, enthusiasts', and unique product catalogs was a second approach. Some catalogs, such as *The Sharper Image*, also had showrooms where products were displayed and purchased. In placing the product in a catalog, HRI would have to design and produce the print ads, and, depending on the catalog, pay a placement fee to the catalog house per mailing or edition. These costs would be about $12,000. Catalog houses obtained a 100 percent price markup on the product and required large minimum starting inventory levels. Catalog companies stock inventory in their own warehouses, which would reduce shipping costs to bulk rates, or $15 per unit.

Retail Stores

The second option involved selling through sporting goods and fitness equipment retailers. Several approaches were possible. First, HRI could sell direct to retailers, who would be recruited at trade shows and conventions. HRI believed that the sales effort, including providing service to retailers, would require at least one dedicated company salesperson. This person would be paid $55,000 a year, including travel expenses and fringe benefits. In addition, point-of-purchase displays, brochures, and related promotional materials would cost about $12,000 per year. HRI also felt that a minimum of $50,000 should be budgeted for annual cooperative advertising allowances for retailers to promote the product in their local market. Retailers would expect a gross profit of 54 percent per unit sold. Therefore, HRI would sell the Versa-Climber to retailers at a price of $842. Shipping costs would still be $29 per unit.

A second approach involved using manufacturer's representatives rather than a company salesperson to recruit and call on retailers. Manufacturer's reps would receive a commission of 15 percent on the Versa-Climber selling price to retailers ($842) for performing the sales function. HRI would provide the same promotional support to retailers as the direct-to-retailer alternative and incur the same unit shipping expense.

A third approach considered was using athletic supply and sporting goods equipment wholesalers to stock and sell equipment to retailers. HRI would sell the Versa-Climber to these wholesalers who would then sell to retailers. Wholesalers would expect a 20 percent profit margin on each unit sold to retailers, or $168. It was believed that a half-time salesperson would be needed to work with the wholesalers and retailers. This person would also work half-time in the institutional market. The annual fixed cost of the person assigned to the home-fitness marketing program would be $27,000. The same promotional support would be provided to retailers as was planned with the two previous alternatives. In addition, sales literature for wholesalers would be prepared at an annual cost of $5,000. The shipping expense per unit would be $12, due to cost savings from bulk shipments.[9]

Questions

1. What market-product strategy is HRI considering with the introduction of the 108H Versa-Climber to the home-fitness market?

2. What are the pros and cons of each of the five marketing options under consideration?

3. What will be HRI's contribution per unit for each 108H Versa-Climber sold for each of the five marketing options?

4. Calculate the number of units HRI must sell for each of the five marketing options to break even.

5. Which marketing option would you select? Why?

CASE D-10   The Hummer

What in the world is a Hummer? The Hummer was originally designed for the U.S. Army as a jeep. This rugged vehicle is constructed of corrosionproof aircraft aluminum. The chassis is made of massive, hollow girders; hundreds of rivets cover the exterior and interior surface. At 6 feet 3 inches in height, 15 feet 4 inches long, with giant front tires, and twice the diameter of a passenger car, the Hummer can splash through water 30 feet deep. It can climb 45-degree inclines, hills, and mountains. It is virtually unstoppable. Not surprisingly, it gets a whopping 11.5 miles to the gallon.

THE COMPANY

The Hummer is produced by AM General of South Bend, Indiana. AM General and its predecessor companies have been a leader in the design and manufacture of light- and medium-duty trucks for the military for more than 50 years.

The company, which has become known as AM General, has been bought, sold, and renamed numerous times over its history. AM General's history is traced to the Standard Wheel Company, a bicycle manufacturer, in Terre Haute, Indiana. In 1903, Standard Wheel made the decision to diversify into automobile manufacture, introducing, as their first product, the Overland "Runabout" through the newly formed Overland Automotive Division. Acquisition of Overland created the Willys-Overland company in 1908, and the new company began producing the Willys-Knight series of vehicles. In 1953, the company was again purchased and renamed Willys Motors, Inc.—later changed to Kaiser-Jeep Corporation following the company's acquisition of a contract from the defunct Studebaker Corporation to manufacture military trucks. American Motors purchased the company in 1970, renaming it Jeep Corporation. Two divisions were created—the Commercial Products Division and the General Products Division. The General Products Division was spun off as a wholly owned subsidiary of American Motors in 1971 under its current name, AM General Corporation. In 1983 AM General was acquired by LTV Corporation, and most recently, it was purchased by its current owner, the Renco Group in 1992.

THE PRODUCT

The Hummer's history is much shorter than that of AM General. In 1979 AM General entered competition for the development of a High-Mobility Multi-Purpose Wheeled Vehicle (HMMWV) to meet the demanding standards of the U.S. Army.

The Army created a list of objectives for the vehicle. For instance, the Army wanted a vehicle that could climb a 60-degree grade without bogging down as well as traverse a 40-degree side slope with stability while carrying a two-ton payload. The Army's requirements were for a new kind of vehicle, one that would be versatile, reliable, and easy to maintain. AM General engineers were not told *how* to reach these objectives but rather what was desired in the vehicle. AM General engineers then found unique design solutions to solve the problems created by the performance objectives.

The prototype Hummer went to test in the Nevada desert in July 1980, less than one year after initial designs were drawn. After extensive testing, the Army awarded three contracts for test vehicles to General Dynamics, Teledyne, and AM General. Within 10 months, AM General delivered its Hummer prototypes to the Army. After five months of testing, the AM General Hummer was judged the superior product, and AM General was granted an initial production contract of 55,000 vehicles over a five-year period.

Since production began in 1983, AM General has sold 110,000 Humvees, or Hummers as it was affectionately nicknamed, to the military. The Hummer replaced several vehicles in the U.S. Army's fleet including the jeep. More than 20,000 Hummers were used in the 1991 Gulf War alone, where they were transformed into everything from ambulances to missile launchers.

The Hummer has many unique design features. Independent suspension for all four wheels avoids ground clearance limits of most conventional four-wheel drive vehicles. The truck's wide track and well-distributed weight keep the center of gravity low, preventing the truck from tipping over. Tire pressure can be adjusted on the go—from 15 pounds per square inch (psi) in soft sand to 30 psi on asphalt—to obtain the best traction and handling on changing terrain.

THE CONSUMER MARKET

The development of the Hummer illustrates collaboration between one type of customer, the military, and AM General. The development of a new market for the Hummer—the consumer market—was the result of close interaction with selected consumers or perhaps one key consumer.

Believe it or not, Arnold Schwarzenegger is reportedly responsible for AM General's entry to the consumer market. Shortly after the Gulf War began, AM General's president, James Armour, received a call from Arnold Schwarzenegger. Armour thought his secretary was joking when she said "Arnold is on the phone." Armour recounts the conversation this way: "This is Arnold. I want to see you." Armour told Schwarzenegger that he wouldn't sell Arnold the Hummer unless they were able to sell them to everyone. Arnold's response was, "What do I have to do to get you to sell them to the public?" From this, the development of the consumer version of the Hummer developed.

Arnold became the first civilian customer for the Hummer. But there have been many more. First sold in 1992, there are currently six different 1996 civilian models available at more than 52 Hummer dealerships around the country. Prices range from $43,000 for a two-passenger hard top to more than $61,000 for a four-passenger wagon. Standard equipment includes auxiliary fuel tank, halogen headlights, power door locks, power steering, high-back bucket seats, and more. Options include your choice of diesel, gas, or turbo diesel engine (diesel is standard); a 12,000-pound winch; power windows and power mirrors; and even a CD player. However, even the largest Hummer only has room for four passengers with narrow, airplane-style seats: two in front, two in back.

The typical Hummer consumer customer makes $200,000 to $300,000 per year. Most buyers have two or three other cars already. Reportedly, doctors buy Hummers but not attorneys. Hummers sell well on the East Coast and West Coast but not in mid-America. Entrepreneurs, not corporate conformists, tend to buy the Hummer. Let's face it. This is not a vehicle to own if you want to be inconspicuous. The Hummer is not a product for everyone, even if the product is now available to you, the U.S. Army, and Arnold Schwarzenegger.[10]

Questions

1. How might AM General utilize relationship marketing in reaching the consumer market?

2. What sort of database should AM General develop to successfully implement a relationship in the consumer market. Explain what types of information should be collected on an on-going basis.

3. How could AM General utilize relationship marketing to pursue new market opportunities, for example, selling the Hummer to logging and mining companies?

Case D–11   Upjohn Company: Rogaine

Rogaine, the brand name for a hair-growing drug called *minoxidil,* was expected to reap worldwide sales of $500 million per year when it was approved by the Food and Drug Administration (FDA) in August 1988. However, by the end of 1992, estimated sales for Rogaine were $121 million. What factors contributed to the shortfall in expected sales? Some industry analysts and marketing and advertising consultants have pointed toward the marketing plan and execution, while others have cited the consumer buying process as a stumbling block. Uncovering the reasons for Rogaine's sales performance to date might provide clues to its future performance.

DEVELOPMENT OF ROGAINE

The development of Rogaine can be traced to the mid-1960s, when researchers at Upjohn Company noticed that the drug minoxidil reduced the heart rate of laboratory animals. Further testing on humans for cardiac use uncovered an interesting side effect—hair growth on a person's forehead or upper chest. Then, in 1973, a bald patient using minoxidil developed new hair on his head. Subsequent testing of 2,356 men with a 2 percent minoxidil solution between 1977 and 1982 showed that hair growth was apparent for a sizable number. Upjohn claimed that 39 percent of patients achieved "moderate to dense" hair growth after a year's use—a claim approved by the FDA. Moreover, hair growth was most evident for men under 30. Some side effects existed, including itching, skin irritation, and possibly a rise in heartbeat.

The properties of minoxidil and its use as a topical ointment for hair growth meant that the solution had to be applied twice every day. When not applied daily, hair loss would result. In other words, minoxidil was a lifetime treatment if its effects of hair growth and retention were to be permanent.

Upjohn began selling its minoxidil solution in other countries in 1986, under the trade name Regaine. However, more stringent and time-consuming review procedures by the FDA slowed approval for use in the United States until late 1988. The name Regaine was replaced with Rogaine because an FDA official believed that the name Regaine suggested that the solution would result in complete hair growth. During this time, minoxidil had received considerable publicity in the media as a miracle cure for baldness.

MARKETING OF ROGAINE

Introductory marketing plans for Rogaine in the United States were developed concurrently with the FDA approval process. Since Rogaine had FDA approval as a prescription drug, Upjohn's initial attention was placed on educating its salesforce, which called on physicians. In October 1988, Rogaine was introduced to physicians by its salesforce and through advertisements in medical journals. According to an Upjohn spokesperson, "We couldn't begin marketing Rogaine to consumers until we felt the awareness level was adequate in the medical community."

The pricing of Rogaine was such that a user would spend between $700 and $900 per year for the solution and periodic visits to a physician to monitor progress. This cost would continue as long as a person used the solution.

Consumer advertising for Rogaine began in November 1988, two months ahead of the originally planned program. Slow prescription sales prompted this action. Television and print advertising emphasized a soft sell, which urged consumers to "see your doctor . . . if you're concerned about hair loss." The ads contained no mention of Rogaine since federal regulations prohibit the use of brand names in prescription-drug advertising to consumers. With a sales rate of $4 million per month for the first quarter of 1989, a decision was made to revamp the advertising campaign. The new campaign featured a bald man standing before his bathroom mirror. Like the earlier message, viewers were urged to see their doctor. While sales improved, they remained below expected levels. Accordingly, a third advertising campaign was developed and launched in February 1990. Print advertisements featured the Rogaine name for the first time, with FDA approval, and emphasized that Rogaine was the only FDA-approved product for hair growth with the headline: "The good news is there's only one product that's proven to grow hair . . . Rogaine." Companion television advertising, however, did not mention Rogaine.

Upjohn invested heavily in advertising for Rogaine. It is estimated that $50 million was spent for advertising in 1989, 1990, and 1991. The same amount would be spent in 1992.

A variety of sales promotion activities have been implemented to complement consumer advertising. For instance, Upjohn offered rebates to people who got a Rogaine prescription from their physician. The patient would either get a certificate worth $10 toward the purchase of the first bottle of Rogaine or $20 for sending in the box tops from the first four bottles used. Selected barbershops and salons were provided with information packets to be given to customers worried about hair loss.

New Initiatives and Developments

As early as 1987, Upjohn researchers began studying the effect of Rogaine on women. Positive results led the company to seek FDA approval for Rogaine's use by women, which it received in August 1991, even though some physicians had been already prescribing the solution for them. (Physicians can legally prescribe drugs for uses not approved by the FDA.) Company officials believe women represent an opportunity for future sales growth. For example, consumer research suggests that women might be more receptive to a hair growth product than men. This research indicates that 13.3 percent of surveyed women losing their hair have sought treatment, while 9.9 percent of men have done so. Furthermore, 38.6 percent of women say they would seek treatment if they were losing hair, compared with 30.4 percent of men who say they would seek treatment. While estimates vary, it is believed that about 30 million men and 7 million women are balding, of which an estimated 35 percent are under 30 years old.

In early 1989, Upjohn introduced Progaine Shampoo, a hair-thickener product, for use by men and women. This product does not promote hair growth but serves as a treatment for thinning hair. It is believed the shampoo will benefit from the sound-alike name and be considered a companion to Rogaine. In April 1990, Upjohn received approval to market Rogaine in Great Britain, which opened yet another market for the product. By late 1991, the product was sold in more than 50 countries.[11]

Questions

1. How might the buying process for a product like Rogaine be described?

2. Which psychological and sociocultural variables affect the buying process for Rogaine?

3. How would you assess the effectiveness of the overall marketing program for Rogaine to date?

4. What marketing program changes, if any, would you recommend for Rogaine?

Case D–12   Pepsico Foods International

Should Pepsico Foods International enter the Polish fast-food market? And since this international subsidiary of Pepsico, Inc. has not one, but three fast-food restaurants—Pizza Hut, Taco Bell, and Kentucky Fried Chicken—which one of these restaurants might "work" in Warsaw? One? Two? All three? This was the dilemma facing Pepsico Foods International in early 1993.

Pepsico and Pepsico Foods International

Most people recognize Pepsico as a global corporation whose Pepsi-Cola soft drink has been in many Latin American, Western European, and Asian markets for decades. What is less well known is the diversity of products in the Pepsico and Pepsico Foods International product line; besides soft drinks and the fast-food chains mentioned, Pepsico owns Frito-Lay and its global snack brands, including Fritos, Doritos, Tostitos, and Ruffles.

In fact, when the Berlin Wall fell, Pepsico Foods International moved quickly into Central and Eastern Europe. By 1990, it had opened the first Pizza Hut restaurant in Moscow. In 1991, Pepsico purchased 40 percent of E. Wedel S.A., a respected Polish chocolate

candy business that had been in operation more than 140 years. Despite its lack of experience in the chocolate industry, Pepsico has invested heavily in the improvement of Wedel's manufacturing facilities while utilizing Wedel's distributors in order to expand distribution and sales of its snack-food line in Poland. The snack foods are produced in a new plant in Grodzinsk, Poland, whose annual 600-million-bag capacity is able to supply 15 bags of snacks for every man, woman, and child in Poland. In August 1993, Pepsico announced it would invest $500 million in Poland in the coming five years.

Polish Consumers and Their Eating Habits

Eating habits of Americans and Poles differ. Americans are accustomed to an early afternoon break for lunch (12:00 NOON to 1:00 P.M.), often away from the workplace or at a company cafeteria. In Poland, white- and blue-collar workers alike work 8 hours per day without a formal lunch break. Polish workers take a short break whenever time permits to eat a meal brought from home. There is some evidence that this custom is

TABLE 1

A comparison between American and Polish consumers in the early 1990s

FACTOR	AMERICAN CONSUMER	POLISH CONSUMER
Average household income	$43,237	Not available
Fast-food restaurant patronage	83% of the U.S. adult population eat one or more meals at a fast-food restaurant in a 1-month period	Data not available; fast-food restaurants nonexistent prior to 1990
Typical daily eating pattern	Nine-to-five workday with a noon lunch break; major evening meal between 6:00 and 7:00 P.M.	Work through noontime, often with a sandwich on the job; begin work before 8:00 A.M.; major evening meal between 4:30 and 5:30 P.M., featuring meat, potatoes, vegetables, and soup
Consumer familiarity with Pizza	Very familiar	Familiar to Poles due to opening of on-site and take-out restaurants since 1990
Fried chicken	Very familiar	Little known to Poles
Tacos, burritos	Very familiar	Not familiar at all to Poles

changing as a result of the growing prominence of Western European and North American firms in Poland. Also, an increasing number of privately held Polish companies have adopted business practices of foreign firms, including the formal lunch break.

In addition to custom, economics plays a role in Polish eating habits. The average per-capita monthly salary of Polish workers is one-tenth that of U.S. workers. Per-capita income is related to eating away from home and the patronage of fast-food restaurants. For instance, 83 percent of U.S. adults consume at least one fast-food meal per month; 16 percent of the adults have two or more fast-food meals monthly. Fast-food patronage is not known in Poland because of the limited number of such restaurants. However, the growing number of small, privately owned pizzerias in Poland suggests that patronage is related to availability of outlets. Table 1 summarizes differences between American and Polish consumers. While this table describes "typical" or "average" consumers, Polish eating habits are changing rapidly.

McDonald's Experience in Poland

Lacking up-to-date information on Polish eating habits generally, and those of Warsaw residents specifically, Pepsico Foods International executives can look at McDonald's experience in Poland. While Poles have no tradition of eating American-style hamburgers, McDonald's experience with its Polish restaurant openings has been astounding. The 1992 opening of its Warsaw McDonald's had 31,000 transactions on its opening day, and the Gdansk McDonald's opening in September 1993 had 34,000 transactions its first day!

Somewhat surprisingly in this era of globalization—in which global corporations utilize the successful global strategy of the company but allow local in-country managers to modify the strategy to meet local conditions—the Warsaw McDonald's menu is no different from what a customer in New York or Chicago would see: Big Macs, French fries, and chocolate shakes, without the frills of new menu items or beer as would be seen in a McDonald's in Britain or France.

A comparison of 1993 McDonald's menu items and prices looks like this:

MCDONALD'S ITEM	U.S. MCDONALD'S PRICE (U.S. DOLLARS)	WARSAW MCDONALD'S PRICE (POLISH ZLOTYS)
Big Mac	$1.89	32,000
Hamburger	$0.59	14,000
French fries	$0.79	11,000
	$0.99	14,000
	$1.19	17,000
Large Coke	$1.14	15,000
Milk shake	$1.09	13,000
	$1.29	16,000
Apple pie	$0.74	13,000

These 1993 prices are based on an exchange rate of 20,000 zlotys = $1.00. In addition, McDonald's in Poland, like Pepsico Foods International, has to face an average inflation rate of 35 percent per year.[12]

Questions

1. Thinking about today's Polish consumers, what are the (*a*) favorable factors and (*b*) unfavorable factors in terms of their demographic characteristics and eating behavior in introducing one or more of the three proposed Pepsico restaurants?

2. Which, if any, of the three restaurants would you introduce into Warsaw, and why? What are the benefits and dangers to Pepsico of introducing (*a*) all three restaurants in Warsaw in a single location, (*b*) only one of the restaurants, or (*c*) no restaurants at all.

3. If you introduced one or more of these restaurants in Warsaw, (*a*) what points of difference would you stress to prospective customers, and (*b*) what flexibility would you give to the Polish managers to adapt the menu to Polish tastes?

CASE D–13 Memorial Hospital Medical Emergency Clinic

"We've been open for 11 months and have yet to break even in any one month," mulled Heather Waite as she scanned last month's revenue and expense summary for the Medical Emergency Clinic (MEC) operated by Memorial Hospital. As the administrator for MEC, Waite knows that something has to change. Even

though Memorial is a nonprofit hospital, the charter for MEC stipulates that it has to be self-supporting in its second year of operation.

MEC was established to serve the health care needs of people who work in the central business district. The specific services offered by MEC included (1) preventive health care (such as physical examinations), (2) minor emergencies, (3) specialized employer services (such as preemployment examinations and workers' compensation injuries), and (4) primary health care services (for personal illnesses). A breakdown of average monthly service usage and the average charge for each service is as follows:

SERVICE	PERCENTAGE OF VISITS	AVERAGE CHARGE
Personal illness	39%	$25
Physical examinations	14	25
Workers' compensation	25	39
Employment or insurance examinations	19	47
Emergency	3	67

The weighted average charge per visit is $33.94, and the weighted average variable cost per visit is $5.67. Fixed costs per month average $17,500. The average number of visits per month is 590.

Since its opening, MEC has surveyed patients to find out how it might better serve their needs. Patient concerns fell into two categories: service hours and waiting time. To date, MEC has been open from 8 A.M. to 5 P.M., Monday through Friday. However, patients have requested extended hours, with an opening time of 7 A.M. and a closing time at 7 P.M. A second concern is waiting time, particularly during lunch hours (11 A.M. to 2 P.M.). A check of MEC records indicate that 70 percent of patient visits occur during this period, and most of these visits are for personal illnesses and examinations for various reasons. Further checking revealed that people actually left MEC because of congestion and did not return at a later date. Waite believes these concerns could be dealt with if MEC increased its personnel. Her plan is to add another physician and support personnel to create two staffs. One staff could work from 7 A.M. to 3 P.M., and a second staff could work from 11 A.M. to 7 P.M. By using paramedical personnel and part-time medical assistants, she estimates that average monthly fixed costs will increase by only 25 percent, even with a raise in personnel salaries next year. The staff overlap at lunchtime will alleviate some of the congestion.

Still, Waite feels that something has to be done about the uneven demand for MEC's services during operating hours. She knows that personal physical examina-

tions and employment and insurance examinations can be handled by appointment. Moreover, these services might be provided before or after normal working hours (before 8 A.M. or after 5 P.M.). Her interviews with employers and insurance companies revealed that they will schedule employment and insurance examinations during this period. Based on her interviews, she estimates that MEC could significantly modify its visit mix and number of patients in an average month. Specifically, she believes MEC will have an average of 749 patient visits per month if the hours were expanded. Almost all the additional visits will be for employment and insurance examinations. In addition, Waite received approval to increase the prices of MEC's major services. The new prices, which will become effective at the beginning of the second year of operation, and the forecast mix of patient visits are as follows:

SERVICE	PERCENTAGE OF VISITS	AVERAGE CHARGE
Personal illness	31%	$27
Physical examinations	11	37
Workers' compensation	20	41
Employment or insurance examinations	36	50
Emergency	2	70

Waite believes that the average variable cost per patient visit will be $6 next year, regardless of the mix of patient visits.

As she prepared her recommendation to the Memorial Hospital administrator, she identified at least two options to enable MEC to break even. She could simply institute the price increase, or she could increase prices, expand hours, and incur higher fixed costs. Whatever she recommends, she knows has to support her argument from both a profit and service perspective.[13]

Questions

1. How many visits below the break-even point is MEC at the present time?

2. Can MEC break even when the price increases are put into effect, assuming fixed costs remain unchanged, the visit mix is the same, but variable costs become $6 per visit?

3. Can MEC expand its hours, thereby increasing fixed cost, and break even given a price increase, the increased variable cost per visit, and the new patient visit mix expected by Waite?

CASE D-14   Health Cruises, Inc.

Health Cruises, Inc. packages cruises to Caribbean islands such as Martinique and the Bahamas. Like conventional cruises, the packages are designed to be fun. But the cruise is structured to help participants become healthier by breaking old habits, such as smoking or overeating. The Miami-based firm was conceived by Susan Isom, 30, a self-styled innovator and entrepreneur. Prior to this venture, she had spent several years in North Carolina promoting a behavior-modification clinic.

Isom determined that many people were very concerned about developing good health habits, yet they seemed unable to break away from their old habits because of the pressures of day-to-day living. She reasoned that they might have a chance for much greater success in a pleasant and socially supportive environment, where good health habits were fostered. Accordingly, she established Health Cruises, Inc., hired 10 consulting psychologists and health specialists to develop a program, and chartered a ship. DeForrest Young, a Miami management consultant, became the chairperson of Health Cruises. Seven of Isom's business associates contributed an initial capital outlay totaling more than $250,000. Of this amount, $65,000 went for the initial advertising budget, $10,000 for other administrative expenses, and $220,000 for the ship rental and crew.

Mary Porter, an overweight Denver schoolteacher, has signed up to sail on a two-week cruise to Nassau, departing December 19. She and her shipmates will be paying an average of $1,500 for the voyage. The most desirable staterooms cost $2,200.

Mary learned of the cruise by reading the travel section of her Sunday newspaper on October 16. On that date, the Pittsford and LaRue Advertising Agency placed promotional notices for the cruise in several major metropolitan newspapers. Mary was fascinated by the idea of combining therapy sessions with swimming, movies, and an elegant atmosphere.

Pittsford and LaRue account executive Carolyn Sukhan originally estimated that 300 people would sign up for the cruise after reading the October 16 ads. But as of November 14, only 200 had done so. Isom and Health Cruises, Inc. faced an important decision.

"Here's the situation as I see it," explained a disturbed Ms. Isom at the Health Cruises board meeting. "We've already paid out more than a quarter of a million to get this cruise rolling. It's going to cost us roughly $200 per passenger for the two weeks, mostly for food. Pittsford and LaRue predicted that 300 people would respond to the advertising campaign, but we've only got 200.

"I see three basic options: (1) we cancel the cruise and take our losses; (2) we run the cruise with the 200

and a few more that will trickle in over the next month; or (3) we shell out some more money on advertising and hope that we can pull in more people.

"My recommendation to this board is that we try to recruit more passengers. There are simply too many empty rooms on that ship. Each one costs us a bundle."

At this point, Carolyn Sukhan addressed the board: "I've worked out two possible advertising campaigns for the November 20 papers. The first, the limited campaign, will cost $6,000. I estimate that it will bring in some 20 passengers. The more ambitious campaign, which I personally recommend, would cost $15,000. I believe this campaign will bring in a minimum of 40 passengers.

"I realize that our first attempt was somewhat disappointing. But we're dealing here with a new concept, and a follow-up ad might work with many newspaper readers who were curious and interested when they read our first notice.

"One thing is absolutely certain," Sukhan emphasized. "We must act immediately if there's any hope of getting more people on board. The deadline for the Sunday papers is in less than 48 hours. And if our ads don't appear by this weekend, you can forget it. No one signs up in early December for a December 18 sailing date."

Isom interrupted, shaking her head. "I just don't know what to say. I've looked over Carolyn's proposals, and they're excellent. Absolutely first-rate. But our problem, to be blunt, is money. Our funds are tight, and our investors are already nervous. I get more calls each day, asking me where the 300 passengers are. It won't be easy to squeeze another $6,000 out of these people. And to ask them for $15,000—well, I just don't know how we're going to be able to justify it."[14]

Questions

1.   What is the minimum number of passengers that Health Cruises must sign up by November 20 to break even with the cruises? (Show your calculations.)

2.   Should Health Cruises go ahead with the cruise, since 200 passengers had signed up as of November 14?

3.   Would it be worthwhile for Health Cruises to spend either $6,000 or $15,000 for advertising on November 20? If so, which figure would you recommend?

4.   How realistic are Carolyn Sukhan's estimates of 20 more passengers for the $6,000 advertising campaign and 40 more passengers for the $15,000 campaign?

5.   Should Health Cruises consider cutting its prices for this maiden voyage health cruise?

CASE D-15   The Easy Embers™ Charcoal Starter

"I know barbecuers are going to love Easy Embers™, as long as we price it right so they'll give it a try," said Julie Brighton to herself, as she pondered recent market data regarding consumer buying and behavioral trends in the barbecue industry. According to the Barbecue Industry Association, consumers spent $4.35 billion in 1995 on all barbecue-related items. This greatly excited Brighton because Alma Products, Inc., her new business venture, intended to enter the barbecue market with its newly created charcoal starter.

This latest demand information (see Exhibit 1) was an important consideration for Brighton before making a final pricing decision for her company's first product (see illustration). With this industry and census data, Brighton had as much information as she could get before determining the manufacturer's suggested retail price and the wholesale price retailers would pay for Easy Embers™.

EASY EMBERS™ PRODUCT BENEFITS

For the moment, Alma Products planned to market a single product, the Easy Embers™ Charcoal Starter. Easy Embers™, with its brightly colored label, was intended for sale through hardware stores, home centers, and discount department stores. The charcoal starter was a metal cylinder, approximately one foot high and tapered toward the top, with an attached wooden handle and a heat shield. Inside, a metal grate was located two inches from the bottom to support charcoal. Instructions for use were quite simple. Two sheets of newspaper were crumpled and stuffed underneath the grate; then the charcoal starter was set inside the barbecue. Charcoal was poured into the top, and the newspaper lit from holes along the bottom rim of the device. Once the coals were hot, they were ready to be dumped into the barbecue. The Easy Embers™ starter held up to 4½ pounds of charcoal briquettes, and Brighton's tests showed that it was twice as fast as using lighter fluid (10 to 12 minutes to start a typical four-pound batch of charcoal, compared with 20 to 25 minutes for lighter fluid), which was the most prevalent method of starting barbecue charcoal. The tapered design concentrated the rising heat around each briquette, allowing an even burn and a hotter fire.

Brighton designed the product after having seen some campers light charcoal using a crude device made of a three-pound coffee can with holes punched around the bottom and coat hanger wire. She thought she could

have some fun and make some money building a business around this simple but ingenious idea.

COSTS

Brighton negotiated an arrangement with a local sheet metal fabricator, Santa Fe Engineering, Inc., to manufacture the Easy Embers™ in lots of 1,000 units at a cost of $3.00 each to Alma Products, which included all packaging, labor, and materials. Santa Fe was also charging a one-time tooling cost of $10,000 to make the dies with which the metal parts would be stamped. Furthermore, since Alma did not own a warehouse facility, Santa Fe agreed to ship finished products directly to Alma's customers using shipping labels and packing lists provided by Alma. The product would be shipped in a display carton of 12. Brighton estimated that freight charges to ship the products to Alma's retailers would average $6.00 per case for small orders and about $3.00 per case when 10 or more cases were shipped.

EXHIBIT 1

Barbecue industry market data

UNIT SALES: BARBECUE GRILLS

YEAR	CHARCOAL	GAS	ELECTRIC	TOTAL
1993	8,661,621	4,002,279	190,809	12,854,709
1994	8,074,623	4,261,181	142,734	12,478,538
1995	7,946,738	4,283,387	155,895	12,386,020

CHARCOAL BRIQUETTE SALES

YEAR	TONS	% CHANGE FROM PRIOR YEAR
1993	747,055	0.23
1994	752,699	0.75
1995	789,667	4.91

SELECTED BARBECUE INDUSTRY DATA

	1985	1995
Households owning barbecue grills	79%	83%
Households owning charcoal grills	73	62
Households owning gas grills	15	54

1995 CENSUS DATA

Number of households—United States	94,312,000
Number of households—California	10,381,000

FREQUENCY OF BARBECUE OCCASIONS

FREQUENCY OF BARBECUING AMONG HOUSEHOLDS OWNING GRILLS	% OF HOUSEHOLDS
More than 16 times/year	20%
12-15 times/year	45
6-11 times/year	25
Less than 6 times/year	10

Note: Dates and names have been disguised.

Sources: Barbecue Industry Association, Statistical Abstract of the United States, Alma Products, Inc.

Another variable cost associated with the products included sales commissions to be paid to a manufacturer's representative agency retained a month ago. Davis & Davis Associates, whose other clients included well-known manufacturers of barbecue grills and other summer seasonal products, had agreed to a 10 percent commission on all sales made to retail stores and exclusive coverage of retail accounts in California. Brighton hired the agency, in part, because it was easily more affordable than hiring an internal salesforce. Alma would simply pay the commission to the agency, which, in turn, was responsible for providing the salary, benefit, travel, individual commission, and overhead expenses for each of its reps. Aside from being more cost effective, Davis & Davis also had well-established contacts with the retail buyers in the barbecue industry, contacts that could take years for Alma to form on its own.

Fixed costs associated with running Alma were expected to be minimal. Brighton, living off consulting income and savings from her career as a retailing executive, planned to forego any salary for the first year of business. Using Brighton's home as an office for the company would save monthly rent expense, and for now, only a part-time secretary would be needed to help handle orders. Therefore, total monthly office expenses, including the phone and the secretary's salary, were expected to be around $500.

TARGET MARKET

In its first year of business, Alma planned to target retail stores located in California. Home centers, hardware stores, and mass merchandisers sold most barbecue grills and seemed (to Brighton) to be the best retail distribution channels for her product. Brighton's knowledge of retailing and discussions with her manufacturer's representative indicated that these retail chains would require a 40 percent gross margin on their selling price on an item like Easy Embers™.

COMPETITION

In its home state of California, Alma found a few local retailers that sold a similar item, the Adamson Quick-Fire, for $9.95. However, this item was also new, and the manufacturer, Adamson, Inc., did not appear to have established distribution with any large retail chains. Brighton looked in the stores of large chain retailers and found the QuickFire in none of them. The only stores that carried the QuickFire seemed to be small, individually owned hardware stores. A clerk in one of the small stores told Brighton that the store bought the QuickFires from "some guy from Berkeley." Brighton was able to find no telephone listing for Adamson, Inc. in Berkeley or its surrounding area.

Broader competition included manufacturers of electric charcoal starters, which sold for about $5.95 in most stores, and companies marketing charcoal lighter fluid. Lighter fluid still dominated the market for starting barbecue charcoal. A quart can of lighter fluid sold for about $2.00 in most stores and contained enough fluid to start 8 to 12 barbecue fires.

BRIGHTON'S PRICING DECISION

Brighton knew that by Friday she needed to have suggested retail and wholesale prices determined. She was not yet sure whether a skimming or a penetration pricing strategy made more sense. She did know, however, that her decisions must include her intended prices to the consumer (even though she could not really control the retailers' pricing) as well as the prices she would charge the retailers. Brighton had no expectations of making much money her first year in business, but she did want to be certain to at least break even on a cash basis.[15]

Questions

1. Based on the data in Exhibit 1, how many charcoal starters do you estimate that the company will sell in California in its first year?

2. Does a skimming or penetration pricing strategy make more sense in this situation. Why?

3. What price should Brighton charge the retailers for Easy Embers™, and what should the suggested retail selling price be for the product?

4. How many Easy Embers™ units must be sold for Alma Products to break even on a cash basis in its first 12 months of operation?

CASE D-16   Starbucks Coffee Company

What'll you have? Non-fat latte, espresso? Americans are increasingly turning to Starbucks to quench a growing thirst for specialty coffee.

THE COMPANY

Starbucks Coffee has been hugely successful. Net sales have grown from $65,309,000 in 1991 to $465,213,000 in 1995. Starbucks got its start in 1971 as a gourmet coffee bean store in Seattle. In 1987, Starbucks' current chairman and CEO, Howard Schultz, opened the first Starbucks location with a coffee bar. The focus then and now has been on high-quality specialty coffees. Customers can buy fresh roasted beans from around the world, gift packs, Starbucks coffee cups and sweets, as well as freshly brewed coffees. All coffee beans are roasted in-house to maintain quality. The company prides itself on buying top-quality beans, vacuum packs the beans two hours after roasting, and donates to local charities any beans that go unsold seven days after opening the bag.

Starbucks employees (referred to as partners) are given more than 24 hours of coffee making training and lore. Starbucks maintains designers and architects in-house to develop, maintain, and update the hip, upscale image of the stores. All of this has led to the high-quality service that has built Starbucks brand loyalty.

Citing concern about maintaining quality, Starbucks has turned down lucrative franchising agreements. All stores are company owned. Starbucks plans to have more than 950 stores in place by the end of 1996 and expects to open new stores at a rate of 300 per year in markets across the United States. The company purposely opens stores near one another, even if it involves some cannibalization, to ensure quality customer service and convenience.

Upscale grocery store chains such as Star Markets in Boston have large Starbucks coffee bars on site. Customers can often enter such stores through the grocery store or from a separate outside entrance.

There are still concerns about the long-term trend in coffee consumption. While specialty brews have increased, Americans are now drinking an average of 1.87 cups a day, a decline from the early 1960s when the average per-capita consumption was more than 3 cups per day.

THE COMPETITION

Today, Starbucks faces competition from a number of national, regional, and even local coffee bars and houses. Starbucks is credited with helping to educate the public about specialty coffee, creating the opening for large and small competitors. For example, Seattle's Best Coffee plans to open more than 500 stores within the next five years. Even fast-food outlets such as Dunkin Donuts are improving their coffee offerings. Not all of these competitors attempt to follow Starbucks' lead as an elite coffee product. Competitors such as Ft. Lauderdale–based Brothers Gourmet Products describe Starbucks as "more of a cult." Brothers is aiming for a classic American look in their 80-store chain of coffee bars.

Supermarkets are a primary competitor in the specialty coffee arena. Supermarkets sell about 70 percent of all coffee and are increasingly going upscale, selling whole beans to be ground in the store. Starbucks has also turned down opportunities to distribute its coffee through supermarkets.

Another unique approach to distributing their product is developing special coffee blends for others. For example, Barnes and Noble bookstores have their own coffee bars in many locations, and these coffee bars exclusively sell the Starbucks "Barnes and Noble Coffee Blend." United Airlines is running advertising touting the fact that they now serve Starbucks coffee in every class on every flight worldwide.

Research also is a key part of Starbucks' success. A sophisticated point-of-sale systems allows the company to track store and regional buying trends. The Starbucks real estate division sifts through data on potential markets and market characteristics for at least nine months prior to opening in a new market.

THE ISSUES

A major issue for Starbucks is the price of coffee, which can fluctuate wildly. Frost in Brazil, the world's largest coffee producer, can damage coffee plants for years. New bushes can take five years to mature. As little as two years ago commodity coffee prices doubled, while specialty premium coffees briefly tripled in price.

With increasing domestic competition, plans have been announced to expand to Asia. It is not clear whether Starbucks's chic appeal will sell well in other markets.

There are even plans to develop a new bottled coffee drink in a deal with Pepsico. Pepsi's venture with Lipton Tea Company produced the number one product in the ready-made iced tea category. However, few Americans drink cold coffee, and a cold cappuccino drink from General Foods called Cappio was a market failure in the United States.

Some industry analysts also question whether Starbucks will be able to maintain their rapid growth and profitability and see a cooler future for the coffee market.[16]

THE COFFEE MARKET

The coffee market wasn't always perking along. As recently as 10 years ago, the National Coffee Association was concerned about declining coffee consumption among younger adults. However, the growth of specialty coffees has not only boosted coffee consumption (nationally, 47 percent of Americans consider themselves coffee drinkers today) but has repositioned a product category that had little differentiation. Coffee was coffee, almost a generic product.

Questions

1. What type of distribution strategy is Starbucks employing? How does this distribution strategy fit in with Starbucks' product and positioning?

2. What is Starbucks' competitive advantage? Discuss whether you feel this is a sustainable competitive advantage.

3. Starbucks' current distribution system can be described as corporate vertical marketing system (VMS). Starbucks has turned down lucrative franchising agreements, which would create a contractual VMS. What are the pros and cons of continuing the present distribution system versus a contractual (franchising) VMS as Starbucks' continues to grow and expand? What recommendations would you make to Starbucks concerning changes in their distribution strategy and their growth objectives?

Case D-17   UPS (B)

How can you guarantee delivery of a package to more than 4 billion people (double the number of people who can be reached by any telephone network) in more than 185 countries and territories around the world? UPS does it with more than 315,000 employees, 500 aircraft, 130,000 vehicles, and 2,400 facilities around the globe. Getting customer packages to the right place at the right time, of course, is the core of their business and this would not be possible without a superefficient physical distribution system.

The Company

In 1907, six years before the U.S. Postal Service began its parcel post system, a Seattle teenager borrowed $100 from a friend to establish the American Messenger Company. The teenager was James ("Jim") Casey, and the company he ran with his brother, George, and a handful of other teenagers would eventually grow into UPS—the world's largest package distribution company.

Logistics Management at UPS

When UPS was still a fledgling parcel delivery service in 1918, they pioneered the concept of consolidated delivery—combining packages addressed to a certain neighborhood onto one delivery vehicle—in order to use manpower and motorized equipment most efficiently. This focus on efficient physical distribution has made UPS a pioneer in logistics management.

In 1988, UPS received authorization from the Federal Aviation Administration to operate its own aircraft, thus officially becoming an airline. Not content to simply operate freight aircraft normally, UPS strove to integrate the airline into an optimized physical distribution process by aggressively adopting advanced information systems. UPS Airlines' COMPASS (Computerized Operations Monitoring, Planning, and Scheduling System) can be used to plan optimum flight schedules up to six years in advance! To streamline their delivery operations, UPS has built an impressive global electronic data communications network that includes 500,000 miles of communications lines, including a UPS satellite. In order to equip more than 50,000 UPS vehicles with wireless communications capability to provide real-time package tracking and real-time vehicle dispatch and rerouting, UPS succeeded in getting GTE, PacTel, McCaw, and Southwestern Bell to cooperate so that UPS could work with a single service arrangement in all 722 U.S. cellular markets.

UPS Worldwide Logistics

Perhaps lesser known than its package delivery business are UPS's subsidiaries that take advantage of their expertise in logistics and huge investments in physical distribution infrastructure. A wholly owned subsidiary is UPS Worldwide Logistics. UPS Worldwide Logistics is a comprehensive consulting service in which UPS combines services based on customer needs to provide cost-effective, service-intensive solutions for all distribution needs. The services include order processing, inventory control, fleet management, electronic data interchange, tracking, warehousing, freight payment, and customs clearance. In fact, UPS Worldwide Logistics has the ability to move goods from raw materials through the entire manufacturing and wholesale/retail distribution process to the final destination. To accommodate the growing base of customers who contract with UPS for just-in-time inventory management, UPS announced in 1995 that it will build a 116-acre warehousing and logistics center near its international hub in Louisville, Kentucky. Plans are to eventually build eight warehouses at the site with a combined 1.33 million square feet of space.

Under the umbrella of UPS Worldwide Logistics are four other UPS subsidiaries. Inventory Express is a contract logistics management service in which UPS actually physically stores the customer's merchandise in UPS-owned warehouses and then ships the merchandise as needed "just in time." In general, Inventory Express is responsible for critical parts, inventory, and warehousing management. RoadNet Technologies provides customers with access to services such as route scheduling and other communications systems. Another subsidiary, UPS Truck Leasing, offers private fleet management and dedicated contract carriage and vehicle leasing services. Finally, MarTrac offers services that include refrigerated truckload transport.

In January 1996, when UPS Worldwide Logistics opened its first warehouse and distribution center in Asia, computer giant IBM was its first user. The state-of-the-art facility located in Singapore features a warehouse management system that automatically identifies the location of stock keeping units (SKU), updates inventory, and supports documentation necessary for local or export distribution. On explaining why IBM decided to outsource logistics support in Asia, Ms. Gela Russell of IBM's Storage Systems Division said,

"Time-definite, door-to-door delivery systems will help our customers reduce both replenishment cycle times and inventory investment. This partnership is part of IBM's continued effort to serve our customers better." Now orders for components will be forwarded electronically from the IBM order desk to the new UPS Worldwide Logistics distribution center for immediate processing and direct dispatch to the customer.[17]

Questions

1. How did UPS's long-standing expertise in physical distribution help make it a pioneer in logistics management?

2. Why should a firm consider outsourcing its logistics management to UPS? Are there any drawbacks to a firm contracting with UPS Worldwide Logistics for their logistics management?

3. How does logistics management relate to the marketing concept?

CASE D–18   Nordstrom, Inc.

Company lore says that John Nordstrom founded the department store that bears his name today using his stake from the Alaska gold rush. Whether the story is fact or fiction, the philosophy behind the company has made its success one of the real gold nuggets in U.S. retailing.

THE COMPANY

Started in Seattle in 1901 as a shoe store by Swedish immigrant John Nordstrom and a partner, Carl F. Wallin, the business prospered. In 1928, John Nordstrom sold his stake in the company to his three sons: Everett, Elmer, and Lloyd. Wallin sold his stake the following year. By 1959, Nordstrom was the largest independently owned shoe store in the country. Nordstrom operated 27 stores by 1963 and also acquired Best's Apparel that same year, a decision that moved Nordstrom beyond shoes and launched it into women's fashions.

The third generation took over Nordstrom management in 1970. At this point Nordstrom not only offered shoes but apparel and accessories for the entire family. Although Nordstrom went public as Nordstrom, Inc. in 1971, the Nordstrom family still maintains controlling interest in the company.

Nordstrom has grown from a single shoe store to more than 36 fashion specialty stores with annual sales of more than $600 million. Expansion has moved it

from the West Coast and Seattle area where Nordstrom has had a major presence to strategic locations in the Midwest and East. Nordstrom has a number of stores in Washington, Oregon, Alaska, California, Utah, New Jersey, Maryland, and Illinois. In addition, Nordstrom has single stores in Minnesota (Mall of America), Virginia, Texas, and New York. Prospective sites for new stores are Indiana, Connecticut, Michigan, and Colorado. Nordstrom stores are generally located in major or regional malls and feature a wide selection of apparel and shoes for men, women, and children. Nordstrom stores may include a gift department and often a small restaurant. Nordstrom does not carry furniture, linens, housewares, or electronics—items often found in department stores.

THE IDEA

The hallmark of Nordstrom is service. The initial philosophy of the two founders, still guiding Nordstrom today, was to offer the *very best* service, selection, quality, and value to the customer. This commitment to exceptional customer service has been combined with an environment that encourages and supports entrepreneurial spirit among employees to react to customer needs.

Extraordinary tales are told of sales associates that went the extra mile to satisfy the customer. Reportedly a customer fell in love with a pair of Donna Karan slacks that had just gone on sale at the Nordstrom store in downtown Seattle. The salesperson, unable to track down the slacks at any of the other five Seattle area stores, secured some petty cash from her department manager, ran across the street to the Frederick and Nelson department store, where she bought the slacks at full price, and returned triumphantly to Nordstrom to sell them to the customer at the Nordstrom sale price.

Another fabled story is of a loyal Nordstrom customer who died with her Nordstrom account $1,000 in arrears. Nordstrom not only settled her account but also sent flowers to the funeral.

Nordstrom salespeople make the customer feel special. You won't find Nordstrom customers running to another part of the store to find a gift box (gift boxes are provided, complete with gift card and complimentary bow, in the department in which you make your purchase). One surprised father found that the Nordstrom's men's room had a changing table with complimentary diapers when he went inside to change his young son.

It is not unusual to receive a thank-you note from your Nordstrom salesperson or a phone call or note concerning new merchandise of particular interest to you. Salespeople keep customer books listing customer information such as likes and dislikes, sizes, and past purchases. This allows the salesperson to notify customers when merchandise comes in that could be of interest. One salesperson had the challenge of selling different "looks" to 40 different partners within the same 120-attorney office. It simply wouldn't do for the attorneys to show up in the office with the same suit!

Nordstrom is known not only for its salespeople but also for its unconditional money-back guarantee return policy and welcoming, comfortable, and hassle-free store designs. One pleased spouse of a devoted Nordstrom customer wrote: "Of all the stores, Nordstrom was best. They gave a husband a place to rest."

THE ISSUES

In an increasingly competitive environment, Nordstrom's emphasis on building customer loyalty and retaining customers provides an advantage. While Nordstrom provides customers with what they consider an unsurpassed commitment to quality and value, increasing price competition and price-conscious consumers may be a threat.

Primary competition for Nordstrom could come from popular specialty stores such as Talbots or Ann Taylor for women's clothing, Brooks Brothers for men's clothing, Joseph Banks, Abercrombie and Fitch, and J. Crew for both men and women, and Kids Talbot and Gymboree for children. Since apparel specialty stores focus on more narrow product lines, such as professional apparel, sportswear, or casualwear, or on type of customer, the competition can be quite diverse. In addition, traditional department stores such as Dayton's, Hudson's, Bloomingdale's, and Nieman Marcus are primary competitors. Department store competitors and specialty store competitors vary somewhat, depending on the particular market and geographic location, since many are regional rather than national in scope. It is worth noting that Nordstrom will experience competition not only from specialty stores for particular product lines (e.g., shoes) but also from stores offering broader lines, such as traditional department stores. Continued geographic expansion can provide Nordstrom with additional opportunities for growth but also exposes it to new competitors, which may attempt to imitate Nordstrom's famous service and quality.[18]

Questions

1. How would Nordstrom be classified as a retail outlet in terms of form of ownership, level of service, and merchandise line?

2. What type of retail position does Nordstrom own? Whom do you see as its primary competitors, given this position?

3. How do you reconcile Nordstrom's growth and success with the fact that department stores as a category are in the maturity stage of the retail life cycle? What implications are there for Nordstrom, given the maturity of the category as well as the wheel of retailing concept?

CASE D–19   Windows 95 (B)

It's been variously described as "marketing history," "a defining moment," and "a global sensation." Combined international marketing expenditures for Microsoft's personal computer (PC) operating system Windows 95 promotional campaign were estimated at $700 million.

Beyond just an intensive advertising campaign, Microsoft used every element of the promotional mix to ensure that only the remotest corners of the globe remained unaware of Microsoft's new product.

THE PRODUCT

Microsoft's Windows 95 is an operating system for IBM-compatible personal computers. A computer's operating system controls exactly how the computer hardware interacts with other software and directs the basic functions of the computer. The Windows 95 interface enables computer users to easily interact with their computers with a graphical interface, inspired by Apple Computer's icon-friendly interface and operating system. In addition to providing a more user-friendly operating system, Windows 95 was designed to take full advantage of the power of today's 32-bit chips.

THE PROMOTIONAL LAUNCH

In promoting Windows 95, Microsoft made effective use of integrated marketing communications to get the best return on its promotional investment. It was essential that all of Microsoft's promotional and marketing activities were integrated to promote a consistent image to consumers. In the case of the Windows 95 launch, Microsoft was communicating with its consumers with a variety of media. Each event added to the message that Windows 95 was not simply a slightly modified version of Windows 3.1 but rather a major replacement for Windows 3.1. Microsoft used the Windows 95 logo prominently in all its advertising and promotional efforts. The company provided retailers with point-of-purchase displays that were bathed in the logo and prominently displayed the "START" button to demonstrate the easy interface Windows 95 used to launch programs within Windows 95. Product packaging, advertising, and everything at the Windows 95 launch site—signs, cups, the polo shirt worn by Bill Gates—all carried the Windows 95 design elements: the "START" button and the blue-sky-and-clouds motif. To help reinforce this unified theme, Microsoft is rumored to have spent more than $10 million simply to gain the rights to use the Rolling Stones song "Start Me Up" in their promotional campaign. To communicate the dominance of Microsoft in the PC industry to consumers, Microsoft even required marketers demonstrating the software to use Microsoft brand keyboards and computer mice.

In New York City, the Empire State Building was bathed in the colors of the Windows 95 logo. In Toronto, a massive banner announcing the arrival of Windows 95 graced the CN Tower—the world's largest free-standing structure. In the United Kingdom, *The Times* was distributed free, courtesy of Microsoft. Of course, the free issue contained a prominent Windows 95 advertising supplement. To ensure that travelers in between two U.K. destinations didn't miss out on the event, entire fields were painted with the Windows 95

logo so that it was visible from the air. In the land down under, Australian residents on the country's eastern coast witnessed an unusual sight—a four-story-high Windows 95 box sailed into Sydney Harbor on a barge. At Microsoft headquarters in Redmond, Washington, a large event was planned that people around the globe could attend—virtually. Microsoft set up a World Wide Web (WWW) site that anyone could connect to if they wanted to participate "live" in the events on launch day.

Combined with these spectacular events, Microsoft benefited from a great deal of publicity spurred on by the grand scale of the launch. According to an analysis by MediaLink Public Relations Research, in the week preceding the launch, Windows 95 was the topic of 345 U.S. television news stories compared with 432 for the war in Bosnia during the same period. The publicity machine was also churned by Bill Gates's designation as the wealthiest human being in the solar system.

Microsoft spent years testing and, one could argue, even sampling the product. Windows 95 has been hailed as the most tested software program in history. Lead users could download beta versions of the program from the Internet for trial and testing at several stages of product development.

The Windows 95 launch was not simply Microsoft's show. Several manufacturers of computer hardware and software jumped on the bandwagon, eager to take advantage of this strategic window. Software manufacturers readied their Windows 95 products for shelves to try to take advantage of the enormous traffic the Windows 95 launch was expected to generate. PC hardware managers were optimistic—of the 200 million PCs now in use globally, only 39 percent have the horsepower necessary to run Windows 95.

Computer retailers planned their own events around the launch date. Some planned to stay open 95 minutes past midnight into August 24 so that consumers could get their hands on the software as soon as Windows 95 was available for sale. Since PC owners of a whole range of PCs were expected to feel the urge to buy into the Windows 95 hype, most also prominently displayed hardware upgrades in terms of larger disk drives, more memory, and faster video cards that consumers could snatch up along with their copies of Windows 95.

THE COMPETITION

Interestingly, IBM did virtually no promotion for their OS/2 Warp operating system, considered the primary direct competition for Windows 95, during the Windows 95 launch or subsequently. While it could be argued that doing any promotion during this launch period would have been counterproductive, IBM has been surprisingly quiet since the Windows 95 launch, seemingly conceding the battle for PC operating system dominance to Microsoft. Only Apple made a play for media attention during the Windows 95 hoopla, poking fun at Microsoft's attempt to mimic the user-friendly format of Apple computer systems. To remind consumers that Windows 95 developed from the IBM PC operating system was still more complex than Apple's operating system ever was, Apple took out a full page ad in *The Wall Street Journal* on the day of the launch which simply said, in bold letters "C:\ONGRTLNS.W95" followed by the Apple logo.[19]

Questions

1. What are the primary promotional objectives for Microsoft's launch of Windows 95?

2. How did Microsoft use integrated marketing communication to launch Windows 95? What are the strengths and weaknesses of each element of the promotional mix, and how do they correspond to Microsoft's promotional objectives for Windows 95?

3. The promotional tactics described in the case appear to be part of a pull promotional strategy. Discuss whether you feel a push strategy is necessary to support this pull promotional strategy. How could Microsoft utilize a push strategy (what types of tactics for the trade would be effective)?

CASE D–20   Timex

"Takes a licking and keeps on ticking." For years this is the image that has been associated with Timex watches—dependable, reliable, almost indestructible. Timex's advertising was closely associated with the Timex image. The advertising campaign featured different attempts to destroy Timex watches that failed to stop the Timex from ticking. One memorable ad showed a Timex watch strapped to the propeller of a motor boat before being driven across the lake. The dripping watch was proudly displayed as the second hand swept past the face of the watch.

THE COMPANY

Timex has been the industry leader since 1960. In fact, Timex's share of the of the U.S. watch market was 50 percent by the late 1960s, and as much as 20 percent worldwide. However, Timex missed several important environmental trends that changed the industry. For one thing, Timex stuck to analog technology, losing money and market share to competitors that adopted digital technology in the 1970s. By the time Timex caught on to the importance of the electronic watch, competitors had already developed and marketed far-superior products. Timex employees dubbed the first Timex electronic watches "quarter pounders" because of their clumsy, clunky appearance. In 1982, a Swiss company approached Timex and asked it to do the worldwide marketing for a new product. Timex turned down the offer, believing the garish plastic watches would be a flop. It was a major blunder for Timex. Swatches

became a fashion success around the globe. By 1983, U.S. market share for Timex had fallen to about 17 percent, with operating losses approaching $100 million.

THE MARKET

Times changed and so did consumer needs and wants for watches. C. Michael Jacobi, Timex president since 1992, says that Timex's biggest mistake was failing to keep up with the watch's evolution from a functional object to a fashion accessory. Your watch tells the world who you are or what you want to be. Coordinating watches with clothing, changing watch bands for different occasions, and wearing designer watches that convey status and prestige is increasingly important to consumers. According to the Jewelers of America, the average consumer today owns five watches compared with 1½ 30 years ago. Timex was left behind as the rest of the industry moved from watches as a functional tool to watches as fashion statements.

THE PRODUCT

Timex appears to have learned from its mistakes. Fashion consultants now visit twice a year from New York and Paris to provide insight to Timex on trends and interests that can translate into new watch styles. Jacobi and other executives travel to retailers and other trade shows to spot fashion trends.

Timex took advantage of consumer interest in sport watches to develop the Indiglo watch. Indiglo patented technology uses energy from the watch battery to excite electrons in the watch face. Unlike other watches that require exposure to the sun or lamp, the Timex Indiglo does not need to be "charged" to emit light.

Timex was also very successful advertising the Indiglo watches when the technology was introduced in 1992. Its introductory commercial effectively conveyed the simple message about the glowing watch face while hinting at the "takes a licking and keeps on ticking" theme. In the background, Sinatra sings "strangers in the night . . . " as a smitten firefly hovers over the glowing watch dial. Smack! A huge hand suddenly swats at the infatuated firefly but misses, hitting the watch. *Time* magazine called this campaign "the best television campaign of 1992." The 1992 Gallup Watch Brand Survey found that 98 percent of consumers knew the Timex brand, followed by Seiko (87 percent).

Recognizing that simply introducing a unique product with a patented technology is insufficient to gain market share, Timex boosted its 1993 ad budget by more than 50 percent. Timex also faced increasing competition from major competitors. Hearing that Seiko, Armitron, and Citizen planned to add watches to their lines with a lighting technology similar to Indiglo, Timex spent a record $10 million on advertising—just in the fourth quarter of 1993. Additionally, Timex made a major change in its advertising strategy. Watch companies traditionally focused their advertising campaigns in the spring and fall. In what industry executives called a first, Timex began advertising continuously throughout the year. As a result, in 1993 Timex unit sales rose about 30 percent, with more than half the increase attributed to Indiglo.

Given its success, it is not surprising that Timex continued to put almost its entire advertising budget into campaigns for Indiglo in 1994. And the Indiglo is *HOT.* Timex was fortunate enough to get some impressive testimonials from customers that rolled in along with sales. These stories provided some fascinating material for potential ad campaigns. Consider the following:

- A man led a group of people down 34 unlit flights of stairs in the bombed World Trade Center in New York City by the light of an Indiglo.
- A Los Angeles couple lit their way to safety after an earthquake with an Indiglo watch.
- Four people clung to a capsized fishing boat overnight, comforted by the reassuring blue beam of a Timex Indiglo.

The Indiglo technology is "making ho-hum Timex kind of hip." In fact, earlier attempts to upscale the product line and develop more fashionable products were hampered by perceptions that the products have "got a $12.95 name on them."

Currently Timex has 20 to 30 watch styles with the Indiglo technology, part of a product line that includes 1,500 styles, up from 300 in 1970. Indiglo models accounted for 40 percent to 50 percent of all Timex sales. And Timex has some dramatic stories to tell, rivaling those of the old "takes a licking and keeps on ticking" ads.

THE COMPETITION

Competitors are taking two positions with respect to the popularity of the Timex Indiglo. Some are attempting to imitate the technology. For example, Seiko's LumiBrite watch has dials coated with a nonradioactive compound that absorbs light during the day and re-emits it for up to five hours in the dark. Others suggest that the light-up dial is a novelty that will not appeal to the masses. Bulova's marketing vice president, Philip Shaw, does not feel that night-lighting technology will become a watch standard, unlike water resistance. Shaw states, "People buy our watches for style."

THE ISSUES

Industry observers expect the next big technological trend in watches to be two-way voice communication timepieces—Dick Tracy style. Prototypes have been too large, they don't easily fit on the wrist. However, early test models of the Indiglo were too large as well.

Timex also scored a critical hit with its high-tech Data-Link watch. Coupled with Microsoft personal computer (PC) software, the watch allowed users to download a variety of information from their PCs, such as phone numbers, appointments, and birthdays, to their Timex watches simply by pointing the face of their watches to a flashing PC screen.[20]

Questions

1. What advertising objectives should Timex have for the Indiglo? How do objectives for the Indiglo affect advertising objectives for other Timex products?

2. Discuss what sort of promotional message should be emphasized in Timex ads. (Emphasize the technology, the styling, competitive advantages.)

3. What type of advertisements, media, and scheduling would you recommend?

4. Should the Indiglo advertising program be part of a comprehensive advertising program for all Timex products?

CASE D-21   Field Furniture Enterprises

Edward Meadows, president of Field Furniture Enterprises, met with representatives of Kelly, Astor, & Peters Advertising (KAP) and Andrew Reed, Field's vice president of marketing and sales, to discuss the company's advertising program for 1997. The KAP representatives recommended that Field Furniture increase its advertising in shelter magazines (such as *Good Housekeeping* and *Better Homes and Gardens,* which feature home improvement ideas and new ideas in home decorating) by $250,000 and maintain the expenditures for other promotional efforts at a constant level during 1997. The rationale given for the increase in advertising was that Field Furniture had low name recognition among prospective buyers of furniture and it intended to introduce new styles of living and dining room furniture. Reed, however, had a different opinion as to how Field Furniture should spend the $250,000. He thought it was necessary to (1) hire additional salespeople to call on the 30 new retail stores to be added by the company in 1997, (2) increase the funds devoted to cooperative advertising, and (3) improve the selling aids given to retail stores and salespeople.

THE COMPANY

Field Furniture is a medium-sized manufacturer of medium- to high-priced living and dining room furniture. Sales in 1996 were $50 million. The company sells its furniture through 1,000 furniture specialty stores nationwide, but not all stores carry the company's entire line. This fact bothered Meadows because, in his words, "If they ain't got it, they can't sell it!" The company employs 10 full-time salespeople, who receive a $40,000 base salary annually and a small commission on sales. A company salesforce is atypical in the furniture industry since most furniture manufacturers use selling agents or manufacturer's representatives who carry a wide assortment of noncompeting furniture lines and receive a commission on sales. "Having our own sales group is a policy my father established 30 years ago," noted Meadows, "and we've been quite successful having people who are committed to our company. Our people don't just take furniture orders. They are expected to motivate retail salespeople to sell our line, assist in setting up displays in stores, coordinate cooperative advertising plans, and give advice on a variety of matters to our retailers and their salespeople."

In 1996, Field spent $2.45 million for total promotional expenditures, excluding the salary of the vice president of marketing and sales. Promotional expenditures were categorized into four groups: (1) sales expense and administration, (2) cooperative advertising programs with retailers, (3) trade promotions, and (4) consumer advertising. Cooperative advertising allowances are usually spent on newspaper advertising in a retailer's city and are matched by the retailer's funds on a dollar-for-dollar basis. Trade promotion is directed toward retailers and takes the form of catalogs, trade magazine advertisements, booklets for consumers, and point-of-purchase materials such as displays for use in retail stores. Also included in this category is the expense of trade shows. Field Furniture is represented at two trade shows a year. Consumer advertising is directed to potential consumers through shelter magazines. The typical format used in consumer advertising is to highlight new furniture and different living and dining room arrangements. Dollar allocation for each program in 1996 was as follows:

PROMOTIONAL PROGRAM	EXPENDITURE
Sales expense and administration	$ 612,500
Cooperative advertising	1,102,500
Trade advertising	306,250
Consumer advertising	428,750
TOTAL	$2,450,000

THE INDUSTRY

The household wooden furniture industry is composed of more than 5,000 firms. Industry sales at manufacturers' prices were $10 billion. California, North Carolina, Virginia, New York, Tennessee, Pennsylvania, Illinois, and Indiana are the major U.S. furniture-producing areas. Although Ethan Allen, Bassett, Henredon, and Kroehler are the major furniture manufacturers, no one firm captured more than 3 percent of the total household wooden furniture market.

The buying and selling of furniture to retail outlets centers around manufacturers' expositions at selected times and places around the country. At these marts, as they are called in the furniture industry, retail buyers view manufacturers' lines and often make buying commitments for their stores. However, Field's experience has shown that sales efforts in the retail store by company representatives account for as much as half the company's sales in a given year. The major manufacturer expositions are held in High Point, North Carolina, in October and April. Regional expositions are also scheduled in June through August in locations such as Dallas, Los Angeles, New York, and Boston.

Company research on consumer furniture-buying behavior indicated that people visit several stores when shopping for furniture, and the final decision is made jointly by a husband and wife in about 90 percent of furniture purchases. Other noteworthy findings are as follows:

- Eighty-four percent of buyers believe "the higher the price, the higher the quality" when buying home furnishings.
- Seventy-two percent of buyers browse or window shop in furniture stores even if they don't need furniture.
- Eighty-five percent read furniture ads before they actually need furniture.
- Ninety-nine percent agreed with the statement, "When shopping for furniture and home furnishings, I like the salesperson to show me what alternatives are available, answer my questions, and let me alone so I can think about it and maybe browse around."
- Ninety-five percent get redecorating ideas from shelter magazines.
- Forty-one percent have written off for a manufacturer's booklet.
- Sixty-three percent feel they need decorating advice for "putting it all together."

BUDGETARY ISSUES

After the KAP Advertising representatives made their presentation, Reed again emphasized that the incremental $250,000 should not be spent for consumer advertising. He noted that Field Furniture had set as an objective that each salesperson would make six calls per year at each store and spend at least four hours at each store on every call. "Given that our salespeople work a 40-hour week, 48 weeks per year, and devote only 80 percent of their time to selling due to travel time between stores, we already aren't doing the sales job," Reed added. Meadows agreed but reminded Reed that the $250,000 increment in the promotional budget was a maximum the company could spend, given other cost increases.[21]

Questions

1. How might you describe furniture buying using the purchase decision process described in Chapter 6?
2. How might each of the elements of the promotional program influence each stage in the purchase decision process?
3. What should Field's promotional objectives be?
4. How many salespeople does Field need to adequately service its accounts?
5. Should Field Furniture emphasize a push or pull promotional strategy? Why?

CASE D–22 Hasbro, Inc.

How does a toy company become a leader in an industry marked by fads? Just ask the executives at Hasbro, Inc., a market leader with worldwide sales exceeding $1.4 billion. Recognizing that toy companies must replace 60 percent of their toy volume each year with new products and that 80 percent of new toys introduced each year are failures, Hasbro executives know that the secret lies in deft product development and marketing.

HASBRO PRODUCT DEVELOPMENT AND MARKETING

Hasbro, Inc. looks for three qualities in new products: (1) lasting play value, (2) the ability to be shared with other children, and (3) the ability to stimulate a child's imagination. In addition, the company provides differ-ent toys for the various stages of a child's development. Beginning with items for infants and preschool children, it also has toys and games for pre-adolescents of both sexes, and some adults (e.g., the game Scruples).

For example, preschool toys include Glo Worm and Teach Me Reader, young boys' toys include action figures like Transformers and G.I. Joe, and young girls have items such as My Little Pony. In addition, Hasbro markets stuffed toys such as Yakity Yaks and Watchi-mals and games and puzzles including Candyland and Bed Bugs. An element of the company's marketing strategy includes reaching mothers at the time of the child's birth, for infant toys. As the child develops, toys such as G.I. Joe are promoted through Saturday morning cartoon shows where complementary toys (aircraft carriers) are advertised.

However, even Hasbro had found it difficult to compete against Mattel, Inc.'s Barbie doll for young girls. Two entries, Jem and Maxie, were both dropped after disappointing sales. Similarly, Hasbro's investment of $20 million in its Nemo videogame, designed to compete against Nintendo in the late 1980s proved to be a failure.

TOY INDUSTRY

The toy industry produces more than $16 billion in sales annually. This figure has remained largely unchanged in recent years. A percentage breakdown of volume by toy category, excluding videogames and children's books, is shown here:

CATEGORY	PERCENTAGE OF MARKET
Dolls and action figures	31.6
Games and puzzles	11.6
Preschool and infant toys	10.1
Activity toys	9.5
Toy vehicles	9.0
Riding toys	8.6
Stuffed toys	7.6
Arts and crafts	4.2
Other	7.8
	100.0

According to the editor of *Toy & Hobby World,* a trade publication, the toy industry is a "hit-driven business." Some hits include Cabbage Patch Kids by Coleco, which produced estimated sales of $600 million in 1985 but fell to an estimated $115 million in 1987. Teddy Ruxpin, made by Worlds of Wonder, Inc. was the hit of 1986 and 1987; but sales declined rapidly by 1990. Creating a hit in the children's toy industry also involves making large marketing expenditures. It is estimated that a full-scale introduction of a major toy requires $5 million to $10 million in advertising, plus $12 million to $15 million to produce a cartoon show featuring the toy or character.

In recent years, some toy companies have focused on specific children. For example, some firms have recently produced African-American, Hispanic, and Asian dolls and action figures to reach previously untapped buyers. More than 54 million (10 percent of the dolls' total volume) African-American Cabbage Patch Kids have been sold since 1983. Other firms have produced dolls for disabled children. Mattel, for example, markets the Hal's Pals line, which includes a girl with leg braces and a cane and a boy in a wheelchair. The company donates the proceeds from Hal's Pals sales to disabled-children groups.[22]

Questions

1. How do toy marketers, including Hasbro, apply concepts from consumer behavior in the marketing of toys?
2. What variables might be used to segment the toy market?
3. What might a product-market grid for Hasbro look like, and where are new product-market opportunities for the company?
4. What are your thoughts on the subject of marketing ethnic dolls, action figures, and dolls of disabled children?

GLOSSARY

80/20 rule The principle that 80 percent of sales (and costs) are generated by 20 percent of the items or customers, and vice versa, thus suggesting priorities.

above-, at-, or below-market pricing Pricing based on what the market price is.

accelerated development The second stage of the retail life cycle, characterized by rapid increases in market share and profitability.

account management policies Policies that specify whom sales people should contact, what kinds of selling and customer service activities should be engaged in, and how these activities should be carried out; in advertising agency, refers to policies used by an account executive in dealing with clients.

action item list An aid to implementing a market plan, consisting of three columns: (1) the task, (2) the name of the person responsible for completing the task, and (3) the date by which the task is to be finished.

adaptive selling A need-satisfaction sales presentation involving adjusting the presentation to fit the selling situation.

advertising Any paid form of nonpersonal communication about an organization, good, service, or idea by an identified sponsor.

advocacy advertisements Institutional advertisements that state the position of a company on an issue.

all you can afford budgeting Allocating funds to advertising only after all other budget items are covered.

alternatives The factors over which the decision maker has control.

anchor stores Well-known national or regional stores that are located in regional shopping centers.

approach stage In the personal selling process, the initial meeting between the salesperson and prospect where the objectives are to gain the prospect's attention, stimulate interest, and build the foundation for the sales presentation.

aseptic packaging Germfree packaging that allows products to be sealed in paper containers and stored for extended periods of time without refrigeration.

assumptions Conjectures about factors or situations that simplify the problem enough to allow it to be solved within the existing constraints.

atmosphere A store's ambiance or setting.

attitudes Learned predispositions to respond to an object or class of objects in a consistent manner.

average revenue The average amount of money received for selling one unit of a product.

baby boomlet The generation of children born in 1977 and later.

baby boomers The generation of children born between 1946 and 1965.

back translation The practice of retranslating a word or phrase into the original language by a different interpreter to catch errors.

bait-and-switch advertising An advertising practice in which a company shows a product that it has no intention of selling to lure the customer into the store and sell him a higher-priced item.

balance of trade The difference between the monetary value of a nation's exports and imports.

barriers to entry Business practices or conditions that make it difficult for a new firm to enter the market.

barter The practice of exchanging goods and services for other goods and services rather than for money.

basing-point pricing Selecting one or more geographic locations (basing point) from which the list price for products plus freight expenses are charged to buyers.

beliefs A consumer's subjective perception of how well a product or brand performs on different attributes; these are based on personal experience, advertising, and discussions with other people.

benchmarking Discovering how other organizations do something better than yours so your firm can imitate or leapfrog competition.

bidder's list A list of firms believed to be qualified to supply a given item.

blended family Two families from prior marriages merged into a single household as spouses remarry.

brand equity The added value a given brand name provides a product.

brand extension The practice of using a current brand name to enter a completely different product class.

brand loyalty A favorable attitude toward and consistent purchase of a single brand over time.

brand manager (see product manager)

brand name Any word or device (design, shape, sound, or color) that is used to distinguish one company's products from a competitor's.

branding Activity in which an organization uses a name, phrase, design, or symbol, or a combination of these, to identify its products and distinguish them from those of a competitor.

breadth of product line The variety of different items a store or wholesaler carries.

break-even analysis An analysis of the relationship between total revenue and total cost to determine profitability at various levels of output.

break-even chart A graphic presentation of a break-even analysis.

break-even point (BEP) Quantity at which total revenue and total cost are equal and beyond which profit occurs.

brokers Channel intermediaries that do not take title to merchandise and make their profits from commissions and fees by negotiating contracts or deals between buyers and sellers.

buildup forecast Summing the sales forecasts of each of the components to arrive at a total forecast.

bundle pricing The marketing of two or more products in a single "package" price.

business analysis Involves specifying the features of the product and the marketing strategy needed to commercialize it and making necessary financial projections.

business analysis stage Step 4 of the new-product process, which involves specifying the product features and marketing strategy and making necessary financial projections to commercialize a product.

business culture Comprises the effective rules of the game, the boundaries between competitive and unethical behavior, and the codes of conduct in business dealings.

business firm A privately owned organization that serves its customers in order to earn a profit.

business marketing The marketing of goods and services to commercial enterprises, governments, and other profit and not-for-profit organizations for use in the creation of goods and services that they then produce and market to other business customers as well as individuals and ultimate consumers.

business plan A roadmap for the entire organization for a specific future period of time, such as one year or five years.

business portfolio analysis Analysis of a firm's strategic business units (SBUs) as though they were a collection of separate investments.

business unit Element of a firm that markets a set of related products to a clearly defined group of customers.

business unit competencies Special capabilities resulting from the business unit's personnel, resources, or functional units.

business unit goal A performance target the business unit seeks to reach to achieve its mission.

business unit level Level at which business unit managers set directions for their products and markets.

business unit mission A statement specifying the markets and product lines in which a business unit will compete.

buy classes Groups of three specific buying situations organizations face: new buy, straight rebuy, and modified rebuy.

buyer turnover The frequency with which new buyers enter the market to buy a product.

buying center The group of persons within an organization who participate in the buying process and share common goals, risks, and knowledge important to that process.

buying criteria The factors buying organizations use when evaluating a potential supplier and what it wants to sell.

capacity management Managing the demand for a service so that it is available to consumers.

case allowance A trade-oriented sales promotion in which retailers receive a discount on each case ordered during a specific time period.

cash and carry wholesaler A limited-service merchant wholesaler that takes title to merchandise but sells only to buyers who call on it and pay cash for and transport their own merchandise.

category killers Specialty discount outlets that focus on one product category such as electronics or business supplies at very competitive prices

cause-related marketing Tying the charitable contributions of a firm directly to the customer revenues produced through the promotion of one of its products.

caveat emptor A Latin term that means "let the buyer beware."

cease and desist order An action by the Federal Trade Commission (FTC) ordering a company to stop practices it considers unfair.

cells Boxes in a table or cross tabulation.

central business district The oldest retail setting; the community's downtown area.

channel captain A marketing channel member that coordinates, directs, and supports other channel members; may be a manufacturer, wholesaler, or retailer.

channel of communication The means (e.g., a salesperson, advertising media, or public relations tools) of conveying a message to a receiver.

channel partnering Agreements and procedures among channel members for ordering and physically distributing a producer's product through the channel to the ultimate consumer.

Clayton Act (1914) A law that forbids certain actions that lessen competition, like tie-in sales, exclusive dealing arrangements, and acquisitions whose effect might be to lessen competition or help create a monopoly.

closed-end question (see fixed alternative question)

closing stage The stage in the personal selling process that involves getting a purchase commitment from a prospect.

co-branding The pairing of two brand names of two manufacturers on a single product.

code of ethics A formal statement of ethical principles and rules of conduct.

cognitive dissonance The feeling of postpurchase psychological tension or anxiety a consumer often experiences.

combination compensation plan A compensation plan whereby a salesperson is paid a specified salary plus a commission based on sales or profit.

commercialization The final phase of the new-product process in which the product is positioned and launched into full-scale production and sale.

communication The process of conveying a message to others. Six elements—a source, a message, a channel of communication, a receiver, and the processes of encoding and decoding—are required for communication to occur.

community shopping center A retail location that typically has one primary store (usually a department store branch) and 20 to 40 smaller outlets and serves a population base of about 100,000.

company forecast (see sales forecast)

comparative advertisements Advertisements that show one brand's strengths relative to those of competitors.

competition The set of alternative firms that could provide a product to satisfy a specific market's needs.

competitive advantage A unique strength relative to competitors, often based on quality, time, cost, or innovation.

competitive advertisements Advertisements that promote a specific brand's features and benefits.

competitive institutional advertisements Institutional advertisements that promote the advantages of one product class over another and are used in markets where different product classes compete for the same buyer.

competitive parity budgeting Matching the competitors' absolute level of spending or the proportion per point of market share.

computer-assisted retailing A retailing method whereby customers order products over computer linkups from their home after viewing items on the TV or on their computer monitor.

concept tests External evaluations of a product idea that consist of preliminary testing of the new product idea (rather than the actual product) with consumers.

conference selling A form of team selling where a salesperson and other company resource people meet with buyers to discuss problems and opportunities.

consolidated metropolitan statistical area (CMSA) The largest designation in terms of geographical area and market size, made up of several primary metropolitan statistical areas (PMSAs).

constraints The restrictions, such as time and money, placed on potential solutions by the nature and importance of the problem.

consultative selling A need-satisfaction sales presentation where the salesperson focuses on problem definition and serves as an expert on problem recognition.

consumer behavior Actions of a person to purchase and use products and services, including the mental and social processes that precede and follow these actions.

Consumer Bill of Rights The rights of consumers in the exchange process including the right to safety, to be informed, to choose, and to be heard.

consumer ethnocentrism The tendency to believe that it is inappropriate, indeed immoral, to purchase foreign-made products.

consumer goods Products purchased by the ultimate consumer.

Consumer Product Safety Act (1972) A law that established the Consumer Product Safety Commission to monitor product safety and establish uniform product safety standards.

consumer socialization The process by which people acquire the skills, knowledge, and attitudes necessary to function as consumers.

consumer-oriented sales promotion Sales tools used to support a company's advertising and personal selling efforts directed to ultimate consumers; examples include coupons, sweepstakes, and trading stamps.

consumerism A movement to increase the influence, power, and rights of consumers in dealing with institutions.

contest A sales promotion in which consumers apply their analytical or creative thinking to win a prize.

continuity programs Sales promotions used to encourage and reward repeat purchases by acknowledging each purchase made by a consumer and offering a premium as purchases accumulate.

continuous innovations New products that require no new learning to use.

contracting A strategy used during the decline stage of the product life cycle in which a company contracts the manufacturing or marketing of a product to another firm.

contractual vertical marketing system A channel arrangement whereby independent production and distribution firms integrate their efforts on a contractual basis to obtain greater economies and marketing impact.

control group A group not exposed to the experimental variable in an experiment.

controlled distribution minimarkets Test markets run in smaller test areas that electronically monitor product purchases at checkout counters for more careful testing at reduced costs.

convenience goods Items that the consumer purchases frequently and with a minimum of shopping effort.

cooperative advertising Advertising programs in which a manufacturer pays a percentage of the retailer's local advertising expense for advertising the manufacturer's products.

corporate chain A type of retail ownership in which a single firm owns multiple outlets.

corporate culture The shared values, beliefs, and purpose of employees that affect individuals and group behavior.

corporate culture A system of shared attitudes and behaviors held by the employees that distinguish an organization from others.

corporate goals Strategic performance targets that the entire organization must reach to pursue its vision.

corporate level Level at which top management directs overall strategy for the entire organization.

corporate philosophy The values and "rules of conduct" for running an organization.

corporate takeover The purchase of a firm by outsiders.

corporate vertical marketing system A channel arrangement whereby successive stages of production and distribution are combined under a single owner.

corporate vision A clear word picture of the organization's future, often with an inspirational theme.

corrective advertising FTC action requiring a company to spend money on advertising to correct prior misleading ads.

cost of goods sold Total value of the products sold during a specified time period.

cost focus strategy Involves controlling expenses and, in turn, lowering prices, in a narrow range of market segments.

cost leadership strategy Using a serious commitment to reducing expenses that, in turn, lowers the price of the items sold in a wide range of market segments.

cost per thousand (CPM) The cost of reaching 1,000 individuals or households with an advertising message in a given medium. (M is the Roman numeral for 1,000.)

cost plus fixed-fee pricing A pricing method where a supplier is reimbursed for all costs, regardless of what they may be, plus a fixed percentage of the production or construction costs.

cost plus percentage-of-cost pricing Setting the price of a product or service by adding a fixed percentage to the production or construction costs.

cost-plus pricing The practice of summing the total unit cost of providing a product or service and adding a specific amount to the cost to arrive at a price.

countertrade Using barter rather than money in making international sales.

coupons Sales promotions that usually offer a discounted price to consumers.

cross-cultural analysis The study of similarities and differences between consumers in two or more nations or societies.

cross-functional teams A small number of people from different departments in an organization who are mutually accountable to a common set of performance goals.

cross-tabulation Method of presenting and relating data on two or more variables to display summary data and discover relationships in the data.

cue A stimulus or symbol perceived by the consumer.

cultural ethnocentricity The belief that aspects of one's culture are superior to another's.

cultural symbols Things that represent ideas and concepts.

culture The sets of values, ideas, and attitudes of a homogeneous group of people that are transmitted from one generation to the next.

cumulative quantity discounts The discount given to a buyer based on the accumulation of purchases of a product over a given time period, typically a year.

customary pricing A method of pricing based on a product's tradition, standardized channel of distribution, or other competitive factors.

customer contact audit A flow chart of the points of interaction between a consumer and a service provider.

customer service The ability of a logistics system to satisfy users in terms of time, dependability, communications, and convenience.

customer value   The unique combination of benefits received by targeted buyers that includes quality, price, convenience, on-time delivery, and both before-sale and after-sale service.

customs   Norms and expectations about the way people do things in a specific country.

data   The facts and figures pertinent to the problem, composed of primary and secondary data.

database marketing   An organization's effort to collect demographic, media, and consumption profiles of customers in order to target them more effectively.

database marketing   An organization's effort to collect demographic, media, and consumption profiles of customers in order to target them more effectively.

deal   A sales promotion that offers a short-term price reduction.

deceptive pricing   A practice by which prices are artificially inflated and then marked down under the guise of a sale.

decision   A conscious choice from among two or more alternatives.

decision factors   The different sets of variables—the alternatives and uncertainties— that combine to give the outcome of a decision.

decision making   The act of consciously choosing from alternatives.

decision-making unit (DMU)   The people in a household or an organization's buying center who are involved in the decision to buy a product.

decline stage   The fourth and last stage of the product life cycle when sales and profitability decline.

decoding   The process of having the receiver take a set of symbols, the message, and transform them back to an abstract idea.

deletion   A strategy of dropping a product from the product line, usually in the decline stage of the product life cycle.

delivered pricing   A pricing method where the price the seller quotes includes all transportation costs.

Delphi forecast   Polling people knowledgeable about the forecast topic to obtain a sequence of anonymous estimates.

demand curve   The summation of points representing the maximum quantity of a product consumers will buy at different price levels.

demand factors   Factors that determine the strength of consumers' willingness and ability to pay for goods and services.

demand-backward pricing   Setting a price by estimating the price consumers would be willing to pay for goods and services.

demographics   A description of the population according to selected characteristics such as age, sex, ethnicity, income, and occupation.

dependent variables   The change in the behavior of what is studied.

depth of product line   The assortment of each item a store or wholesaler carries.

derived demand   Sales of a product (typically industrial) that result from the sales of another item (often consumer).

desk jobber   (see drop shipper)

development   Phase of the new product process in which the idea on paper is turned into a prototype; includes manufacturing and laboratory and consumer tests.

dichotomous question   A fixed alternative question that allows only a "yes" or "no" response.

differentiation focus strategy   Using significant points of difference in the firm's offerings to reach one or only a few market segments.

differentiation positioning   Positioning a product in a smaller market niche that is less competitive.

differentiation strategy   Using innovation and significant points of difference in product offerings, higher quality, advanced technology, or superior service in a wide range of market segments.

diffusion of innovation   The process by which people receive new information and accept new ideas and products.

direct channel   A marketing channel where a producer and ultimate consumer interact directly with each other.

direct exporting   A firm selling its domestically-produced goods in a foreign country without intermediaries.

direct forecast   An estimate of the value to be forecast without the use of intervening steps.

direct investment   In global marketing, a domestic firm actually investing in and owning a foreign subsidiary or division.

direct marketing   Selling products by having consumers interact with various advertising media without a face-to-face meeting with a salesperson.

direct ownership   In international trade, a domestic firm actually investing in and owning a foreign subsidiary or division.

discontinuous innovations   New products that require totally new consumption patterns.

discounts   Reductions from list price that a seller gives a buyer as a reward for some buyer activity favorable to the seller.

discretionary income   The money that remains after taxes and necessities have been paid for.

disposable income   The money a consumer has left after taxes to use for food, shelter, and clothing.

diversification   A strategy of developing new products and selling them in new markets.

downsizing   The practice of reducing the content of package without changing package size and maintaining or increasing the package price.

drive   A stimulus that moves an individual to action.

drop shipper   A merchant wholesaler that owns the merchandise it sells but does not physically handle, stock, or deliver; also called a desk jobber.

dual distribution   An arrangement by which a firm reaches buyers by employing two or more different types of channels for the same basic product.

dumping   When a firm sells a product in a foreign country below its domestic price.

durable good   An item that lasts over an extended number of uses.

dynamically continuous innovations   Products that disrupt the consumer's normal routine but do not require learning totally new behaviors.

early adopters   The 13.5 percent of the population who are leaders in their social setting and act as an information source on new products for other people.

early growth   The first stage of the retail life cycle, when a new outlet emerges as a sharp departure from competitive forms.

early majority   The 34 percent of the population who are deliberate and rely on personal sources for information on new products.

ecology   The relationship of physical resources in the environment.

economic infrastructure A country's communication, transportation, financial, and distribution systems.

economy The income, expenditures, and resources that affect the cost of running a business and household.

elastic demand A situation where a percentage decrease in price produces a larger percentage increase in quantity demanded, thereby actually increasing sales revenue.

electronic data interchange (EDI) Computers linked in two different firms to transmit documents such as purchase orders, bills of lading, and invoices.

elements of the marketing mix (see marketing mix)

encoding The process of having the sender transform an abstract idea into a set of symbols.

environmental factors The uncontrollable factors involving social, economic, technological, competitive, and regulatory forces.

environmental scanning Acquiring information on events occurring outside the company and interpreting potential trends.

ethics The moral principles and values that govern the actions and decisions of an individual or group.

euro-branding The strategy of using the same brand name for the same product across all countries in the European Community.

Eurostyle A no frills, monochrome, geometric look to product design.

evaluative criteria Both the objective and subjective attributes of a brand important to consumers when evaluating different brands or products.

everyday low pricing The practice of replacing promotional allowances given to retailers with lower manufacturer list prices.

evoked set The group of brands a consumer would consider acceptable out of the set of brands in the product class of which he or she is aware.

exchange The trade of things of value between buyer and seller so that each is better off after the trade.

exclusive dealing An arrangement a manufacturer makes with a reseller to handle only its products and not those of competitors.

exclusive distribution A distribution strategy whereby a producer sells its products or services in only one retail outlet in a specific geographical area.

exclusive territorial distributorship A manufacturer grants a reseller sole rights to sell a product in a specific geographic area.

experience curve pricing A method of pricing where price often falls following the reduction of costs associated with the firm's experience in producing or selling a product.

experiment Obtaining data by manipulating factors under tightly controlled conditions to test cause and effect.

experimental group A group exposed to the experimental variable in an experiment.

experimental independent variable The causal condition manipulated or controlled by the experimenter.

exporting Producing goods in one country and selling them in another country.

express warranties Written statements of a manufacturer's liabilities for product deficiencies.

external secondary data Published data from outside the firm or organization.

extraneous independent variable The causal condition that is the result of outside factors that the experimenter cannot control.

facilitators Intermediaries that assist in the physical distribution channel by moving, storing, financing, or insuring products.

fad A product whose life cycle has two stages consisting of rapid introduction and equally quick decline.

failure fees A penalty payment made to retailers by manufacturers if a new product does not reach predetermined sales levels.

Fair Packaging and Labeling Act (1966) A law that requires manufacturers to state on the package the ingredients, volume, and identity of the manufacturer.

family branding (see multiproduct branding)

family life cycle The concept that each family progresses through a number of distinct phases, each of which is associated with identifiable purchasing behaviors.

Farm Bill (1990) Legislation that sets the standards for organic foods and products that use the term "organic."

fashion product A product whose life-cycle curve may decline, then return through another life cycle.

feedback The communication flow from receiver back to sender; indicates whether the message was decoded and understood as intended.

field experiment A test of marketing variables in actual store or buying settings.

field of experience A person's understanding and knowledge; to communicate effectively, a sender and a receiver must have a mutually shared field of experience.

field warehouse A specialized public warehouse that takes possession of a firm's goods and issues a receipt that can be used as collateral for a loan.

finance allowance A trade-oriented sales promotion in which retailers are paid for financing costs or financial losses associated with consumer sales promotions.

fixed alternative question A question in which the respondent merely checks an answer from predetermined choices.

fixed cost An expense of the firm that is stable and does not change with the quantity of product that is produced and sold.

flexible-price policy Offering the same product and quantities to similar customers, but at different prices.

flighting schedule A scheduling approach in which periods of advertising are scheduled between periods of no advertising to reflect seasonal demand.

FOB (free on board) Refers to the point at which the seller stops paying transportation costs.

FOB origin pricing A method of pricing where the title of goods passes to the buyer at the point of loading.

FOB with freight-allowed pricing A method of pricing that allows the buyer to deduct freight expenses from the list price of the product sold; also called freight absorption pricing.

focus group An informal session of 6 to 10 current or potential users of a product in which a discussion leader seeks their opinions on the firm's or a competitor's products.

follow-up stage The phase of the personal selling process that entails making certain that the customer's purchase has been properly delivered and installed and that any difficulties in using the product are promptly and satisfactorily addressed.

Food, Drug, and Cosmetic Act (1938) A law that prevents the adulteration or misbranding of these three categories of products.

forced distribution markets (see selected controlled markets)

Foreign Corrupt Practices Act A law that makes it a crime for U.S. corporations to bribe an official of a foreign government or political party to obtain or retain business in a foreign country.

forgetting rate The speed with which buyers forget a brand if advertising is not seen.

form of ownership Who owns a retail outlet. Alternatives are independent, corporate chain, cooperative, or franchise.

form utility The value to consumers that comes from production or alteration of a good or service.

formula selling presentation The selling format that consists of providing information in an accurate, thorough, and step-by-step manner to persuade the prospect to buy.

forward buying A response to discounts offered by manufacturers in which supermarkets purchase more merchandise than they plan to sell during the promotion. The remaining stock is sold at regular price later, or diverted to another store.

four I's of service Four unique elements to services: intangibility, inconsistency, inseparability, and inventory.

four P's (see marketing mix)

franchising The contractual agreement between a parent company and an individual or firm that allows the franchisee to operate a certain type of business under an established name and according to specific rules.

freight consolidators (see freight forwarders)

freight forwarders Firms that accumulate small shipments into larger lots and then hire a carrier to move them, usually at reduced rates.

frequency The average number of times a person in the target audience is exposed to a message or advertisement.

FTC Act (1914) A law that established the Federal Trade Commission (FTC) to monitor deceptive or misleading advertising and unfair business practices.

full warranty A statement of liability by a manufacturer that has no limits of noncoverage.

full-service agency An advertising agency providing a complete range of services, including market research, media selection, copy development, artwork, and production.

full-service retailer A retailer that provides a complete list of services to cater to its customers.

functional groupings Organizational groupings in which a unit is subdivided according to the different business activities within a firm, such as manufacturing, marketing, and finance.

functional level Level at which groups of specialists create value for the organization.

gap analysis An evaluation tool that compares expectations about a particular service to the actual experience a consumer has with the service.

General Agreement on Tariffs and Trade (GATT) An international treaty intended to limit trade barriers and promote world trade through the reduction of tariffs.

general merchandise stores General merchandise stores carry a broad product line with limited depth.

general merchandise wholesaler A full-service merchant wholesaler that carries a broad assortment of merchandise and performs all channel functions.

Generation X The generation of children born between 1966 and 1976.

generic brand A branding strategy that lists no product name, only a description of contents.

generic business strategy Strategy that can be adapted by any firm, regardless of the product or industry involved, to achieve a competitive advantage.

geographic information systems (GIS) Technology that represents different layers of data on one map.

geographical groupings Organization groupings in which a unit is subdivided according to geographical location.

global competition A competitive situation that exists when firms originate, produce, and market their products and services worldwide.

global consumers Customer groups living in many countries or regions of the world who have similar needs or seek similar features and benefits from products and services.

global marketing strategy The practice of standardizing marketing activities when there are cultural similarities and adapting them when cultures differ.

goal A targeted level of performance set in advance of work.

government units The federal, state, and local agencies that buy goods and services for the constituents they serve.

gray market A situation in which products are sold through unauthorized channels of distribution; also called parallel importing.

green marketing Marketing efforts to produce, promote, and reclaim environmentally sensitive products.

gross domestic product The monetary value of all goods and services produced in a country during one year.

gross income The total amount of money earned in one year by a person, family, or household.

gross margin Net sales minus cost of goods sold.

gross rating points (GRPs) A reference number for advertisers, created by multiplying reach (expressed as a percentage) by frequency.

growth stage The second stage of the product life cycle characterized by rapid increases in sales and by the appearance of competitors.

harvesting A strategy used during the decline stage of the product life cycle in which a company continues to offer a product but reduces support costs.

head-to-head positioning Competing directly with competitors on similar product attributes in the same target market.

hierarchy of effects The sequence of stages a prospective buyer goes through from initial awareness of a product to eventual action (either trial or adoption of the product). The stages include awareness, interest, evaluation, trial, and adoption.

high learning product A product that has a long introductory phase to its life cycle because significant education is required for consumers to use the item or appreciate its benefits.

horizontal conflict Disagreements between intermediaries at the same level in a marketing channel.

horizontal price fixing The practice whereby two or more competitors explicitly or implicitly collaborate to set prices.

hypermarket A large store (over 200,000 square feet) offering a mix of food products and general merchandise.

hypothesis A conjecture or idea about the relationship of two or more factors or what might happen in the future.

hypothesis evaluation Research to test ideas discovered in the hypothesis generation stage to assist in making recommendations for marketing actions.

hypothesis generation A search for ideas that can be evaluated in later research.

idea generation   A phase of the new product process, in which a firm develops a pool of concepts as candidates for new products.

idle production capacity   A situation where a service provider is available but there is no demand.

implied warranties   Warranties assigning responsibility for product deficiencies to a manufacturer even though the item was sold by a retailer.

inbound telemarketing   The use of toll-free telephone numbers that customers can call to obtain information about products or services and make purchases.

inconsistency   A unique element of services; variation in service quality because services are delivered by people with varying capabilities.

independent retailer   A retail outlet for which there is an individual owner.

indirect channel   A marketing channel where intermediaries are situated between the producer and consumers.

indirect exporting   A firm selling its domestically produced goods in a foreign country through an intermediary.

individual interviews   A situation where a single researcher asks questions of one respondent.

industrial distributor   A specific type of intermediary between producers and consumers that generally sells, stocks, and delivers a full product assortment.

industrial espionage   The clandestine collection of trade secrets or proprietary information about a company's competitors.

industrial firm   An organizational buyer that in some way reprocesses a good or service it buys before selling it again.

industrial goods   Products used in the production of other items for ultimate consumers.

industry   A group of firms offering products that are close substitutes for each other.

industry potential   (see market potential)

inelastic demand   A situation where a small percentage decrease in price produces a smaller percentage increase in quantity demanded.

information technology   Involves designing and managing computer and communication systems to satisfy an organization's requirements for information processing and access.

infomercials   Program length advertisements, often 30 minutes long, that take an educational approach to communicating with potential customers.

in-house agency   A company's own advertising staff which may provide full services or a limited range of services.

innovators   The 2.5 percent of the population who are venturesome and highly educated, use multiple information sources, and are the first to adopt a new product.

inseparability   A unique element of services; the fact that a service cannot be separated from the deliverer of the service or the setting in which the service occurs.

institutional advertisement   Advertisements designed to build goodwill or an image for an organization, rather than promote a specific good or service.

intangibility   A unique element of services; the fact that services cannot be held, touched, or seen before the purchase decision.

integrated marketing communications   The concept of designing marketing communications programs that coordinate all promotional activities—advertising, personal selling, sales promotion, and public relations—to provide a consistent message across all audiences.

intensive distribution   A distribution strategy whereby a producer sells products or services in as many outlets as possible in a geographic area.

intermodel transportation   Combining different transportation modes in order to get the best features of each.

internal marketing   The notion that a service organization must focus on its employees, or internal market, before successful programs can be directed at customers.

internal secondary data   Data that have already been collected and exist inside a business firm or organization.

intertype competition   Competition between dissimilar types of retail outlets brought about by scrambled merchandising.

introductory phase   The first stage of the product life cycle in which sales grow slowly and profit is low.

inventory   (1) Physical material purchased from suppliers, which may or may not be reworked and is available for sale to customers. (2) A unique element of services; the need for and cost of having a service provider available.

involvement   The personal, social, and economic significance of the purchase to the consumer.

ISO 9000   International standards for registration and certification of a manufacturer's quality management and quality assurance system.

job analysis   A written description of what a salesperson is expected to do.

job description   Written document that describes job relationships and requirements that characterize each sales position.

joint venture   In international trade, an arrangement in which a foreign company and a local firm invest together to create a local business.

jury of executive opinion forecast   Asking knowledgeable executives inside the firm about likely sales during a coming period.

jury test   A pretest in which a panel of customers is shown an advertisement and asked to rate its attractiveness, how much they like it, and how much it draws their attention.

just-in-time (JIT) concept   An inventory supply system that operates with very low inventories and requires fast, on-time delivery.

laboratory experiment   A simulation of marketing-related activity in a highly controlled setting.

laggards   The 16 percent of the market who have fear of debt, use friends for information sources, and accept ideas and products only after they have been long established in the market.

Lanham Act (1946)   A law that allows a company to register a trademark (symbol or word) for its exclusive use.

late majority   The 34 percent of the population who are skeptical, below average in social status, and rely less on advertising and personal selling for information than do innovators or early adopters.

laws   Society's values and standards that are enforceable in the courts.

lead time   Lag from ordering an item until it is received and ready for use.

learning   Those behaviors that result from (1) repeated experience and (2) thinking.

level of service   The degree of service provided to the customer by the retailer: self, limited, or full.

licensing   A contractual agreement whereby a company allows another firm to use its brand name, patent, trade secret, or other property for a royalty or fee.

lifestyle   A mode of living that is identified by how people spend their time and resources (activities), what they consider important in their environment (interests), and what they think of themselves and the world around them (opinions).

Likert scale   A fixed alternative question in which the respondent indicates the extent to which he agrees or disagrees with a statement.

limited-coverage warranty   A manufacturer's statement indicating the bounds of coverage and noncoverage for any product deficiencies.

limited-line store   A retail outlet, such as a sporting goods store, that offers considerable assortment, or depth, of a related line of items.

limited-service agency   An agency that specializes in one aspect of the advertising process such as providing creative services to develop the advertising copy or buying previously unpurchased media space.

limited-service retailer   A retailer that provides selected services such as credit or merchandise return to customers.

line extension   The practice of using a current brand name to enter a new market segment in its product class.

line positions   People in line positions, such as group marketing managers, have the authority and responsibility to issue orders to the people who report to them, such as marketing managers.

local approach   (see customized approach)

logistics management   Organizing the cost-effective flow of raw materials, in-process inventory, finished goods, and related information from point of origin to point of consumption to satisfy customer requirements.

loss-leader pricing   Deliberately pricing a product below its customary price to attract attention to it.

lost-horse forecast   Starting with the last known value of the item being forecast, listing the factors that could affect the forecast, assessing whether they have a positive or negative impact, and making the final forecast.

low-learning product   A product that has an immediate gain in sales in the introductory phase because the benefits are easily observed by consumers and little education is required to use it.

macromarketing   The study of the aggregate flow of a nation's goods and services to benefit society.

Magnuson-Moss Warranty/FTC Improvement Act (1975)   An act that regulates the content of consumer warranties and also has strengthened consumer rights with regard to warranties through class action suits.

mail-order retailer   A retailing operation in which merchandise is offered to customers by mail.

maintained markup   The difference between the final selling price and retailer cost; also called gross margin.

major account management   The practice of using team selling to focus on important customers to build mutually beneficial long-term, cooperative relationships.

make-buy decision   An evaluation of whether a product or its parts will be purchased from outside suppliers or built by the firm.

management by exception   A tool used by a marketing manager that involves identifying results that deviate from plans, diagnosing their cause, making appropriate new plans, and taking new actions.

manufacturer branding   A branding strategy in which the brand name for a product is designated by the producer, using either a multiproduct or multibranding approach.

manufacturer's agents   Individuals or firms that work for several producers and carry noncompetitive, complementary merchandise in an exclusive territory; also called manufacturer's representatives.

manufacturer's branch office   A wholly owned extension of a producer that performs channel functions, including carrying inventory, generally performed by a full-service merchant wholesaler.

marginal analysis   Principle of allocating resources that balances incremental revenues of an action against incremental costs.

marginal cost   The change in total cost that results from producing and marketing one additional unit.

marginal revenue   The change in total revenue obtained by selling one additional unit.

markdown   Reduction in retail price usually expressed as a percentage equal to the amount reduced, divided by the original price and multiplied by 100.

market   People with the desire and ability to buy a specific product.

market-based groupings   Organizational groupings that assign responsibility for a specific type of customer to a unit.

market development   Selling existing products to new markets.

market growth rate   The annual rate of growth of the specific market or industry in which a firm or SBU is competing; often used as the vertical axis in business portfolio analysis.

market modification   Attempts to increase product usage by creating new-use situations or finding new customers.

market orientation   Focusing organizational efforts on (1) continuously collecting information about customers' needs and competitors' capabilities, (2) sharing this information across departments, and (3) using the information to create customer value.

market penetration   A strategy of increasing sales of present products in their existing markets.

market potential   Maximum total sales of a product by all firms to a segment under specified environmental conditions and marketing efforts of the firms (also called industry potential).

market segmentation   Aggregating prospective buyers into groups, or segments, that (1) have common needs and (2) will respond similarly to a marketing action.

market segments   The groups that result from the process of market segmentation; these groups ideally (1) have common needs and (2) will respond similarly to a marketing action.

market share   The ratio of sales revenue of the firm to the total sales revenue of all firms in the industry, including the firm itself.

market testing   A phase of the new product process, in which prospective consumers are exposed to actual products under realistic purchase conditions to see if they will buy.

market-product grid   Framework for relating market segments to products offered or potential marketing actions by a firm.

marketing   The process of planning and executing the conception, pricing, promotion, and distribution of ideas, goods, and services to create exchanges that satisfy individual and organizational objectives.

marketing audit   A comprehensive, unbiased, periodic review of the strategic marketing process of a firm or a strategic business unit (SBU).

marketing channel People and firms involved in the process of making a product or service available for use or consumption by consumers or industrial users.

marketing concept The idea that an organization should (1) strive to satisfy the needs of consumers (2) while also trying to achieve the organization's goals.

marketing decision support system (MDSS) A computerized method of providing timely, accurate information to improve marketing decisions.

marketing mix The marketing manager's controllable factors of product, price, promotion, and place he or she can take to solve a marketing problem.

marketing orientation When an organization focuses its efforts on (1) continuously collecting information about customers' needs and competitors' capabilities, (2) sharing this information across departments, and (3) using the information to create customer value.

marketing plan A written statement identifying the target market, specific marketing goals, the budget, and timing for the marketing program.

marketing plan A roadmap for the marketing activities of an organization for a specified future period of time, such as one year or five years.one year or five years.

marketing program A plan that integrates the marketing mix to provide a good, service, or idea to prospective consumers.

marketing research The process of defining a marketing problem and opportunity, systematically collecting and analyzing information, and recommending actions to improve an organization's marketing activities.

marketing strategy The means by which a marketing goal is to be achieved, characterized by (1) a specified target market and (2) a marketing program to reach it.

marketing tactics The detailed day-to-day operational decisions essential to the overall success of marketing strategies.

markup The amount added to the cost of goods sold to arrive at a selling price, expressed in dollar or percentage terms.

materials handling Moving goods over short distances into, within, and out of warehouses and manufacturing plants.

mature households Households headed by people over age 50.

maturity phase The third stage of the product or retail life cycle in which market share levels off and profitability declines.

measures of success Criteria or standards used in evaluating proposed solutions to the problem.

Meat Inspection Act (1906) An act that regulated that meat products be wholesome, unadulterated, and properly labeled.

mechanical observational data Data collected by electronic or other impersonal means, such as meters connected to television sets in viewers' homes.

merchandise allowance A trade-oriented sales promotion in which a retailer is reimbursed for extra in-store support or special featuring of the brand.

merchandise line The number of different types of products and the assortment a store carries.

message The information sent by a source to a receiver in the communication process.

methods The approaches that can be used to solve all or part of a problem.

metropolitan statistical area (MSA) An area within (1) a city having a population of at least 50,000 or (2) an urbanized area with a population in excess of 50,000 with a total population of at least 100,000.

micromarketing How an organization directs its marketing activities and allocates its resources to benefit its customers.

missionary salespeople Sales support personnel who do not directly solicit orders but rather concentrate on performing promotional activities and introducing new products.

mixed branding A branding strategy in which the company may market products under their own name and that of a reseller.

modified rebuy A buying situation in which the users, influencers, or deciders change the product specifications, price, delivery schedule, or supplier.

monopolistic competition A competitive setting in which a large number of sellers offer unique but substitutable products.

monopoly A competitive setting in which there is a single seller of a good or service.

moral idealism A personal moral philosophy that considers certain individual rights or duties as universal regardless of the outcome.

motivation Motivation is the energizing force that causes behavior that satisfies a need.

multibranding A manufacturer's branding strategy in which a distinct name is given to each of its products.

multidomestic marketing strategy A firm's worldwide marketing strategy that offers as many different product variations, brand names, and advertising programs as countries in which it does business.

multiple-zone pricing Pricing products the same when delivered within one of several specified zones or geographical areas, but with different prices for each zone depending on demand, competition, and distance: also called zone-delivered pricing.

multiproduct branding A branding strategy in which a company uses one name for all products; also called blanket or family branding.

national character A distinct set of personality characteristics common among people of a country or society.

need That which occurs when a person feels deprived of food, clothing, or shelter.

need-satisfaction presentation A selling format that emphasizes probing and listening by the salesperson to identify needs and interests of perspective buyers.

new buy The first-time purchase of a product or service, characterized by greater potential risk.

new-product concept A tentative description of a product or service a firm might offer for sale.

new-product process The sequence of activities a firm uses to identify business opportunities and convert them to a saleable good or service. There are seven steps: new-product strategy, idea generation, screening and evaluation, business analysis, development, testing, and commercialization.

new-product strategy development The phase of the new-product process in which a firm defines the role of new products in terms of overall corporate objectives.

news conference A publicity tool consisting of an informational meeting with representatives of the media who received advanced materials on the meeting content.

news release A publicity tool consisting of an announcement regarding changes in the company or product line.

noise Extraneous factors that work against effective communication by distorting a message or the feedback received.

noncumulative quantity discounts   Price reductions based on the size of an individual purchase order.

nondurable good   An item consumed in one or a few uses.

nonprobability sampling   Using arbitrary judgments to select the sample so that the chance of selecting a particular element may be unknown or zero.

nonprofit organization   A nongovernmental organization that serves its customers but does not have profit as an organizational goal.

nonrepetitive decisions   Those decisions unique to a particular time and situation.

North American Industry Classification System (NAICS)   A system for classifying organizations on the basis of major activity or the major good or service provided used by the three NAFTA countries—Canada, Mexico, and the United States.

objective and task budgeting   A budgeting approach whereby the company (1) determines its advertising objectives, (2) outlines the tasks to accomplish the objectives, and (3) determines the advertising cost of performing these tasks.

objectives   Specific, measurable performance targets and deadlines.

observational data   Facts and figures obtained by watching, either mechanically or in person, how people actually behave.

odd-even pricing   Setting prices a few dollars or cents under an even number, such as $19.95.

off-peak pricing   Charging different prices during different times of the day or days of the week to reflect variations in demand for the service.

off-price retailing   Selling brand name merchandise at lower than regular prices.

oligopoly   A competitive setting in which a few large companies control a large amount of an industry's sales.

one-price policy   Setting the same price for similar customers who buy the same product and quantities under the same conditions.

one-price stores   A form of off-price retailing in which all items in a store are sold at one low price.

open-end question   A question that a respondent can answer in his or her own words.

opinion leaders   Individuals who exert direct or indirect social influence over others.

order cycle time   (see lead time)

order getter   A salesperson who sells in a conventional sense and engages in identifying prospective customers, providing customers with information, persuading customers to buy, closing sales, and following on customer experience with product or service.

order taker   A salesperson who processes routine orders and reorders for products that have already been sold by the company.

organizational buyers   Units such as manufacturers, retailers, or government agencies that buy goods and services for their own use or for resale.

organizational buying behavior   The decision-making process that organizations use to establish the need for products and identify, evaluate, and choose among alternative brands and suppliers.

organizational buying criteria   The objective attributes of the supplier's products and services and the capabilities of the supplier itself.

organizational goals   Specific objectives a business or nonprofit unit seeks to achieve and by which it can measure its performance.

original markup   The difference between retailer cost and initial selling price.

outbound telemarketing   Use of the telephone rather than personal visits to contact customers.

outsourcing   Contracting work that formerly was done in-house by employees such as those in marketing research, advertising, and public relations departments to small, outside firms.

Pacific Rim   The area of the world consisting of countries in Asia and Australia.

packaging   The container in which a product is offered for sale and on which information is communicated.

panel   A sample of consumers or stores from which researchers take a series of measurements.

parallel development   An approach to new product development that involves the simultaneous development of the product and production process.

patent   Exclusive rights to the manufacture of a product or related technology granted to a company for 17 years.

penetration pricing   Pricing a product low in order to discourage competition from entering the market.

per se illegality   An action that by itself is illegal.

perceived risk   The anxieties felt because the consumer cannot anticipate the outcome but sees that there might be negative consequences.

percent of sales budgeting   Allocating funds to advertising as a percentage of past or anticipated sales, in terms of either dollars or units sold.

perception   The process by which an individual selects, organizes, and interprets information to create a meaningful picture of the world.

perceptual map   A graph displaying consumers' perceptions of product attributes across two or more dimensions.

personal selling   The two-way flow of communication between a buyer and seller, often in a face-to-face encounter, designed to influence a person's or group's purchase decision.

personal selling process   Sales activities occurring before and after the sale itself, consisting of six stages: (1) prospecting, (2) preapproach, (3) approach, (4) presentation, (5) close, and (6) follow-up.

personality   A person's consistent behaviors or responses to recurring situations.

physical distribution management   Organizing the movement and storage of finished product to the customer.

piggyback franchising   A variation of franchising in which stores operated by one chain sell the products or services of another franchised firm.

pioneering advertisements   Advertisements that tell what a product is, what it can do, and where it can be found.

pioneering institutional advertisements   Institutional advertisements about what a company is or can do or where it is located.

place-based media   Advertising media alternative that places messages in locations that attract a specific target audience such as airports, doctor's offices, and health clubs.

place utility   The value to consumers of having a good or service available where needed.

point-of-purchase displays   Displays located in high-traffic areas in retail stores, often next to checkout counters.

points of difference   Those characteristics of a product that make it superior to competitive substitutes.

population   The universe of all people, stores, or salespeople about which researchers wish to generalize.

portfolio test   A pretest in which a test ad is placed in a portfolio with other ads and consumers are questioned on their impressions of the ads.

possession utility   The value of making an item easy to purchase through the provision of credit cards or financial arrangements.

posttests   Tests conducted after an advertisement has been shown to the target audience to determine whether it has accomplished its intended purpose.

power center   Large strip malls with multiple anchor (or national stores), a convenient location, and a supermarket.

preapproach stage   The stage of the personal selling process that involves obtaining further information about a prospect and deciding on the best method of approach.

predatory pricing   Selling products at a low price to injure or eliminate a competitor.

premium   A sales promotion that consists of offering merchandise free or at significant savings over retail.

presentation stage   The core of the personal selling process in which the salesperson tries to convert the prospect into a customer by creating a desire for the product or service.

prestige pricing   Setting a high price so that status-conscious consumers will be attracted to the product.

pretests   Tests conducted before an advertisement is placed to determine whether it communicates the intended message or to select between alternative versions of an advertisement.

price   The money or other considerations exchanged for the purchase or use of the product, idea, or service.

price discrimination   The practice of charging different prices to difference buyers for goods of like trade and quality; the Clayton Act as amended by the Robinson-Patman Act prohibits this action.

price elasticity of demand   The percentage change in quantity demanded relative to a percentage change in price.

price fixing   A conspiracy among firms to set prices for a product.

price lining   Setting the price of a line of products at a number of different specific pricing points.

pricing constraints   Factors that limit a firm's latitude in the price it may set.

pricing objectives   Goals that specify the role of price in an organization's marketing and strategic plans.

primary data   Facts and figures that are newly collected for the project.

primary demand   Desire for a product class rather than for a specific brand.

primary metropolitan statistical area (PMSA)   An area that is part of a larger consolidated statistical metropolitan area with a total population of 1 million or more.

prime rate   The rate of interest banks charge their largest customers.

private branding   When a company manufactures products that are sold under the name of a wholesaler or retailer.

proactive strategies   New product strategies that involve an aggressive allocation of resources to identify opportunities for product development.

probability sampling   Using precise rules to select the sample such that each element of the population has a specific known chance of being selected.

product   A good, service, or idea consisting of a bundle of tangible and intangible attributes that satisfies consumers and is received in exchange for money or other unit of value.

product advertisements   Advertisements that focus on selling a good or service and take three forms: (1) pioneering (or informational), (2) competitive (or persuasive), and (3) reminder.

product (program) champion   A person who is able and willing to cut red tape and move a product or program forward.

product class   An entire product category or industry.

product counterfeiting   Low cost copies of a popular brand, not manufactured by the original producer.

product development   A strategy of selling a new product to existing markets.

product differentiation   A strategy having different but related meanings; it involves a firm's using different marketing mix activities, such as product featuring and advertising, to help consumers perceive the product as being different and better than other products.

product form   Variations of a product within a product class.

product item   A specific product noted by a unique brand, size, and price.

product life cycle   The life of a product over four stages: introduction, growth, maturity, and decline.

product line   A group of products closely related because they satisfy a class of needs, are used together, are sold to the same customer group, are distributed through the same outlets, or fall within a given price range.

product line groupings   Organizational groupings in which a unit is responsible for specific product offerings.

product line pricing   The setting of prices for all items in a product line.

product manager   A person who plans, implements, and controls the annual and long-range plans for the products for which he or she is responsible.

product mix   The number of product lines offered by a company.

product modifications   Strategies of altering a product characteristic, such as quality, performance, or appearance.

product placement   Advertising media alternative in which the manufacturer pays for the privilege of having a brand name product used in a movie.

product positioning   The place an offering occupies in a consumer's mind with regard to important attributes relative to competitive offerings.

product repositioning   Changing the place an offering occupies in a consumer's mind relative to competitive products.

production goods   Products used in the manufacturing of other items that become part of the final product.

profit   A business firm's reward for the risk it undertakes in offering a product for sale; the money left over after a firm's total expenses are subtracted from its total revenues.

profit equation   Profit = Total revenue − Total cost.

profit responsibility   The view that companies have a single obligation, which is to maximize profits for its owners or stockholders.

profitability analysis   A means of measuring the profitability of the firm's products, customer groups, sales territories, channels of distribution, and order sizes.

program schedule   A formal time-line chart showing the relationships through time of the various program tasks.

promotional allowance   The cash payment or extra amount of "free goods" awarded sellers in the channel of distribution for undertaking certain advertising or selling activities to promote a product.

promotional mix   The combination of one or more of the promotional elements a firm uses to communicate with consumers. The promotional elements include: advertising, personal selling, sales promotion, and publicity.

prospecting stage   In the personal selling process, the search for and qualification of potential customers.

protectionism The practice of shielding one or more sectors of a country's economy from foreign competition through the use of tariffs, or quotas.

protocol In the new product development process, an early statement that identifies a well-defined target market; specifies customers' needs, wants, and preferences; and states what the product will be and do.

psychographics Characteristics represented by personality and lifestyle traits (activities, interests, and opinions).

public relations A form of communication management that seeks to influence the feelings, opinions, or beliefs held by customers, stockholders, suppliers, employees, and other publics about a company and its products or services.

public service announcement (PSA) A publicity tool that uses free space or time donated by the media.

publicity A nonpersonal, indirectly paid presentation of an organization, good, or service.

publicity tools Methods of obtaining nonpersonal presentation of an organization, good, or service without direct cost. Examples include news releases, news conferences, and public service announcements.

pull strategy Directing the promotional mix at ultimate consumers to encourage them to ask the retailer for the product.

pulse schedule The combination of a steady schedule and a flighting schedule because of increases in demand, heavy periods of promotion, or introduction of a new product.

purchase decision process Steps or stages a buyer passes through in making choices about which products to buy.

purchase frequency The frequency of purchase of a specific product.

pure competition A competitive setting in which a large number of sellers compete with similar products.

push strategy Directing the promotional mix to channel members or intermediaries to gain their cooperation in ordering and stocking a product.

quality Those features and characteristics of a product that influence its ability to satisfy customer needs.

quantity discounts Reductions in unit costs for a larger order quantity.

questionnaire data Facts and figures obtained by asking people about their attitudes, awareness, intentions, and behaviors.

quota In international marketing, a restriction placed on the amount of a product allowed to enter or leave a country.

rack jobber A merchant wholesaler that furnishes racks or shelves to display merchandise in retail stores, performs all channel functions, and sells on consignment.

rating (TV or ratio) The percentage of households in a market that are tuned to a particular TV show or radio station.

reach The number of different people or households exposed to an advertisement.

reactive strategies New product strategies are defensive approaches in response to competitors' new items by developing new products.

rebate A sales promotion in which money is returned to the consumer based on proof of purchase.

receivers The consumers who read, hear, or see the message sent by a source in the communication process.

reciprocity An industrial buying practice in which two organizations agree to purchase products from each other.

reference group People to whom a person turns as a standard of self-appraisal or source of personal standards.

regional marketing A form of geographical segmentation that develops marketing plans to reflect specific area differences in taste preferences, perceived needs, or interests.

regional rollouts Introducing a new product sequentially into geographical areas to allow production levels and marketing activities to build up gradually.

regional shopping centers Suburban malls with up to 100 stores that typically draw customers from a 5- to 10-mile radius, usually containing one or two anchor stores.

regulation The laws placed on business with regard to the conduct of its activities.

reinforcement A reward that tends to strengthen a response.

relationship marketing An organization's effort to develop a long-term cost-effective link with individual customers for mutual benefit.

relationship selling The practice of building ties to customers based on a salesperson's attention and commitment to customer needs over time.

relative market share The sales of a firm or SBU divided by the sales of the largest firm in the industry; often used as a horizontal axis in business portfolio analysis.

reminder advertisements Advertisements used to reinforce previous knowledge of a product.

reminder institutional advertisements Institutional advertisements that bring a company's name to the attention of the target market.

repeat purchasers People who tried the product, were satisfied, and buy again.

repetitive decisions Decisions repeated at standard intervals during the work year.

replenishment time (see lead time)

requirements contract A contract that requires a buyer to meet all or part of its needs for a product from one seller for a period of time.

reseller A wholesaler or retailer that buys physical products and resells them again without any processing.

restructuring (reengineering or streamlining) Striving for more efficient corporations that can compete globally by reducing duplicate efforts in multiple company locations, closing or changing unprofitable plants and offices, and laying off employees.

retail life cycle A concept that describes a retail operation over four stages: early growth, accelerated development, maturity, and decline.

retailer-sponsored cooperative chain A contractual system involving independently owned stores that bind together to act like a chain.

retailing All the activities that are involved in selling, renting, and providing goods and services to ultimate consumers for personal, family, or household use.

retailing mix The strategic components that a retailer manages, including goods and services, physical distribution, and communication tactics.

retailing positioning matrix A framework for positioning retail outlets in terms of breadth of product line and value added.

return on investment (ROI) The ratio of after-tax net profit to the investment used to earn that profit.

returns Refunds or credit granted a customer for an item returned to the seller.

reverse marketing The effort by organizational buyers to build relationships that shape suppliers' products, services, and capabilities to fit a buyer's needs and those of its customers.

Robinson-Patman Act (1936) A regulation that makes it unlawful to discriminate in prices charged to different purchasers of the same product where the result is to substantially lessen competition or help create a monopoly.

sales analysis   A tool for controlling marketing programs where sales records are used to compare actual results with sales goals and to identify strengths and weaknesses.

sales component analysis   A tool for controlling marketing programs that traces sales revenues to their sources such as specific products, sales territories, or customers.

sales engineer   A salesperson who specializes in identifying, analyzing, and solving customer problems and who brings technological expertise to the selling situations, but does not actually sell goods and services.

salesforce automation   The use of technology designed to make the sales function more effective and efficient.

salesforce survey forecast   Asking the firm's salespeople to estimate sales during a coming period.

sales forecast   What one firm expects to sell under specified conditions for the uncontrollable and controllable factors that affect the forecast.

sales management   Planning, implementing, and controlling the personal selling effort of the firm.

sales plan   A statement describing what is to be achieved and where and how the selling effort of salespeople is to be deployed.

sales promotion   A short-term inducement of value offered to arouse interest in buying a good or service.

sales response function   The relationship between the expense of marketing effort and the marketing results obtained. Measures of marketing results include sales revenue, profit, units sold, and level of awareness.

samples   (1) Some elements taken from the population or universe, or (2) a sales promotion consisting of offering a product free or at a greatly reduced price.

sampling   (1) the process of selecting elements from a population, or (2) the process manufacturers use of giving away free samples to introduce a new product.

scrambled merchandising   Offering several unrelated product lines in a single retail store.

screening and evaluation   The phase of the new product process in which a firm uses internal and external evaluations to eliminate ideas that warrant no further development effort.

seasonal discounts   Price reductions granted buyers for purchasing products and stocking them at a time when they are not wanted by customers.

secondary data   Facts and figures that have already been recorded before the project at hand.

selected controlled markets   These sites also referred to as forced distribution markets are where a market test for a new product is conducted by an outside agency and retailers are paid to display the new product.

selective comprehension   Interpreting information to make it consistent with one's attitude and beliefs.

selective demand   Demand for a specific brand within a product class.

selective distribution   A distribution strategy whereby a producer sells its products in a few retail outlets in a specific geographical area.

selective exposure   The tendency to seek out and pay attention to messages consistent with one's attitudes and beliefs and to ignore messages inconsistent with them.

selective perception   The tendency for humans to filter or choose information from a complex environment so they can make sense of the world.

selective retention   The tendency to remember only part of all the information one sees, hears, or reads.

self-concept   The way people see themselves and the way they believe others see them.

self-liquidating premium   A sales promotion offering merchandise at a significant cost savings to the customer, its price covering the cost of the premium for the company.

self-regulation   An industry policing itself rather than relying on government controls.

selling agent   A person or firm that represents a single producer and is responsible for all marketing functions of that producer.

semantic differential scale   A seven-point scale in which the opposite ends have one- or two-word adjectives with opposite meanings.

seminar selling   A form of team selling where a company team conducts an educational program for a customer's technical staff describing state-of-the-art developments.

semiotics   The field of study that examines the correspondence between symbols and their role in the assignment of meaning for people.

sensitivity analysis   Asking "What if . . . " questions to determine how changes in a factor like pricing or advertising affect marketing results like sales revenues or profits.

service continuum   A range from the tangible to the intangible or good-dominant to service-dominant offerings available in the marketplace.

services   Intangible items such as airline trips, financial advice, or telephone calls that an organization provides to consumers in exchange for money or something else of value.

share points   Percentage points of market share; often used as the common basis of comparison to allocate marketing resources effectively.

shelf life   The time a product can be stored before it spoils.

Sherman Anti-Trust Act (1890)   A law that forbids (1) contracts, combinations, or conspiracies in restraint of trade and (2) actual monopolies or attempts to monopolize any part of trade or commerce.

shopping goods   Products for which the consumer will compare several alternatives on various criteria.

shrinkage   A term used by retailers to describe theft of merchandise by customers and employees.

single-line store   A store that offers tremendous depth in one primary line of merchandise; for example, a running shoe store.

single-source data   Information provided by a single firm on household demographics and lifestyle, purchases, TV viewing behavior, and responses to promotions like coupons and free samples.

single-zone pricing   Pricing policy in which all buyers pay the same delivered product price, regardless of their distance from the seller; also known as uniform delivered pricing or postage stamp pricing.

situation analysis   Taking stock of where the firm or product has been recently, where it is now, and where it is headed in terms of the organization's plans and the external factors and trends affecting it.

situational influences   A situation's effect on the nature and scope of the decision process. These include (1) the purchase task, (2) social surroundings, (3) physical surroundings, (4) temporal effects, and (5) antecedent states.

skimming pricing   A high initial price attached to a product to help a company recover the cost of development.

slotting fees   Payment by a manufacturer to place a new product on retailer's shelf.

social audit A systematic assessment of a firm's objectives, strategies, and performance in the domain of social responsibility.

social classes The relatively permanent and homogeneous divisions in a society of people or families sharing similar values, lifestyles, interests, and behavior.

social forces The characteristics of the population, its income, and its values in a particular environment.

social responsibility The idea that organizations are part of a larger society and are accountable to society for their actions.

societal marketing concept The view that an organization should discover and satisfy the needs of its customers in a way that also provides for society's well-being.

societal responsibility The view that firms have obligations to preserve the ecological environment and benefit the general public.

solution The best alternative that has been identified to solve the problem.

source A company or person who has information to convey.

special merchandise wholesaler A full-service merchant wholesaler that offers a relatively narrow range of products but has an extensive assortment within the products carried.

specialty outlet Retailers that offer large selections in a narrow range of products.

specialty goods Products that a consumer will make a special effort to search out and buy.

splitting 30s Reducing the length of a standard commercial from 30 seconds to 15 seconds.

staff positions People in staff positions have the authority and responsibility to advise people in the line positions but cannot issue direct orders to them.

stakeholder responsibility The view that an organization has an obligation only to those constituencies that can affect achievement of its objectives.

standard markets Sites where companies test market a product through normal distribution channels and monitor the results.

standard markup pricing Setting prices by adding a fixed percentage to the cost of all items in a specific product class.

Starch test A posttest that assesses the extent of consumers' recognition of an advertisement appearing in a magazine they have read.

statistical inference Drawing conclusions about a population from a sample taken from that population.

steady schedule A scheduling approach in which advertising is run at a steady schedule throughout the year; sometimes called "drip" scheduling.

stimulus discrimination The ability to perceive differences in stimuli.

stimulus generalization When a response elicited by one stimulus (cue) is generalized to another stimulus.

stimulus-response presentation A selling format that assumes the prospect will buy if given the appropriate stimulus by a salesperson.

stock keeping unit (SKU) A distinct ordering number to identify a product item.

store audits Measurements of the sales of the product in stores and the number of cases ordered by a store from the wholesaler.

straight commission compensation plan A compensation plan where the salesperson's earnings are directly tied to his sales or profit generated.

straight rebuy The reordering of an existing product or service from the list of acceptable suppliers, generally without checking with the various users or influencers.

straight salary compensation plan A compensation plan where the salesperson is paid a fixed amount per week, month, or year.

strategic alliances Agreements between two or more independent firms to cooperate for the purpose of achieving common goals.

strategic business unit (SBU) A decentralized profit center of a large firm that is treated as though it were a separate, independent business.

strategic business unit (SBU) (see business unit)

strategic channel alliances A practice whereby one firm's marketing channel is used to sell another firm's products.

strategic marketing process The activities whereby an organization allocates its marketing mix resources to reach its target markets.

strip location A cluster of stores that serves people who live within a 5- to 10-minute drive in a population base of under 30,000.

subcultures Subgroups within the larger or national culture with unique values, ideas, and attitudes.

subliminal perception Means that a person sees or hears messages without being aware of them.

supply partnerships A relationship between an organizational buyer and its supplier created to adopt mutually beneficial efforts to lower the cost and/or increase value delivered to the ultimate consumer.

support goods Items used to assist in the production of other goods.

survey of buyers' intentions forecast A method of forecasting sales that involves asking prospective customers whether they are likely to buy the product or service during some future time period.

survey of experts forecast Asking experts on a topic to make a judgment about some future event.

sustainable competitive advantage A strength, relative to competitors, in the markets served and the products offered.

sweepstakes Sales promotions consisting of a game of chance requiring no analytical or creative effort to win a prize.

SWOT analysis An acronym describing an organization's appraisal of its internal strengths and weaknesses and its external opportunities and threats.

synergy The increased customer value achieved through performing organizational functions more efficiently.

target market One or more specific groups of potential consumers toward which an organization directs its marketing program.

target profit pricing Setting a price based on an annual specific dollar target volume of profit.

target return-on-investment pricing Setting a price to achieve a return-on-investment target.

target return-on-sales pricing Setting a price to achieve a profit that is a specified percentage of the sales volume.

tariff In international marketing, a government tax on goods or services entering a country.

team selling Using a group of professionals in selling to and servicing major customers.

technological forecast Estimating when scientific breakthroughs will occur.

technology An environmental force that includes inventions or innovations from applied science or engineering research.

telemarketing Involves the use of the telephone to interact with and sell directly to consumers.

television home shopping   (see telemarketing)

test marketing   The process of offering a product for sale on a limited basis in a defined area to gain consumer reaction to the actual product and to examine its commercial viability and the marketing program.

theater test   A pretest in which consumers view test ads in new television shows or movies and report their feelings on electronic recording devices or questionnaires.

TIGER (Topologically Integrated Geographic Encoding and Reference)   A landmark project in demography by the U.S. Census Bureau that will provide a minutely detailed computerized map of the entire United States that can be combined with a company's own data.

time utility   The value to consumers of having a good or service available when needed.

timing   The issue of deciding when to discount the price of merchandise.

top-down forecast   Subdividing an aggregate forecast into its principal components.

total cost   The total expense a firm incurs in producing and marketing a product, which includes fixed cost and variable cost; in physical distribution decisions, the sum of all applicable costs for logistical activities.

total logistics cost   Expenses associated with transportation, materials handling and warehousing, inventory, stockouts, and order processing.

total revenue   The total amount of money received from the sale of a product.

trade (functional) discounts   Price reductions granted to wholesalers or retailers on the basis of future marketing functions they will perform for the manufacturer.

trade feedback effect   A country's imports affect its exports and exports affect imports.

trade name   The commercial name under which a company does business.

trade-oriented sales promotions   Sales tools used to support a company's advertising and personal selling efforts directed to wholesalers, distributors, or retailers. Three common approaches are allowances, cooperative advertising, and salesforce training.

trademark   Legal identification of a company's exclusive rights to use a brand name or trade name.

Trademark Law Revision Act (1988)   A legislative change to the Lanham Act by which a company can secure the rights to a name before actual use by declaring intent to use the name.

trading down   Reducing the number of features, quality, or price of a product.

trading up   Adding value to a product by including more features or higher quality materials.

trend extrapolation   Extending a pattern observed in past data into the future.

trial   The initial purchase of a product by the consumer.

truck jobber   Small merchant wholesalers that usually handle limited assortments of fast-moving or perishable items that are sold directly from trucks for cash.

tying arrangement   A seller's requirement that the purchaser of one product also buy another product in the line.

ultimate consumers   People who use the goods and services purchased for a household; sometimes also called ultimate users.

uncertainties   The uncontrollable factors that the decision maker cannot influence.

uncontrollable factors   (see environmental factors)

uniform delivered pricing   A geographical pricing practice where the price the seller quotes includes all transportation costs.

unit train   A train that is dedicated to one commodity, is loaded and unloaded with sophisticated equipment, and runs from origin to destination at high speed.

unit variable cost   Variable cost expressed on a per unit basis.

unitary demand elasticity   A situation where the percentage change in price is identical to the percentage change in quantity demanded.

universal product code (UPC)   A number assigned to identify each product, represented by a series of bars of varying widths for scanning by optical readers.

unsought goods   Products that the consumer does not know about or knows about and does not initially want.

usage rate   Refers to quantity consumed or patronage during a specific period, and varies significantly among different customer groups.

utilitarianism   A personal moral philosophy that focuses on the "greatest good for the greatest number" by assessing the costs and benefits of the consequences of ethical behavior.

utility   The benefits or customer value received by users of the product.

Valdez Principles   Guidelines that encourage firms to focus attention on environmental concerns and corporate responsibility.

value   Specifically, value can be defined as the ratio of perceived quality to price (Value = Perceived benefits/Price).

value added   In retail strategy decisions, a dimension of the retail positioning matrix that refers to the service level and method of operation of the retailer.

value analysis   A systematic appraisal of the design, quality, and performance requirements of a product to reduce purchasing costs.

value consciousness   Consumer concern for obtaining the best quality, features, and performance of a product or service for a given price.

value pricing   The practice of simultaneously increasing service and product benefits and decreasing price.

values   The beliefs of a person or culture; when applied to pricing, the ratio of perceived quality to price (Value = Perceived benefits/Price).

variable cost   An expense of the firm that varies directly with the quantity of product produced and sold.

vending machines   A retailing operation in which products are stored in and sold from machines.

venture teams   Multidisciplinary groups of marketing, manufacturing, and R&D personnel who stay with a new product from conception to production.

vertical conflict   Disagreement between different levels in a marketing channel.

vertical marketing systems   Professionally managed and centrally coordinated marketing channels designed to achieve channel economies and maximum marketing impact.

vertical price fixing   The practice whereby sellers are required to not sell products below a minimum retail price, sometimes called resale price maintenance.

want   A need that is shaped by a person's knowledge, culture, and individual characteristics.

warehouse A location, often decentralized, that a firm uses to store, consolidate, age, or mix stock; house product-recall programs; or ease tax burdens.

warehouse clubs Large retail stores (over 100,000 square feet) that require a yearly fee to shop at the store.

warranty A statement indicating the liability of the manufacturer for product deficiencies.

wasted coverage People outside a company's target audience who see, hear, or read the company's advertisement.

weighted-point system A method of establishing screening criteria, assigning them weights, and using them to evaluate new product ideas.

wheel of retailing A concept that describes how new retail outlets enter the market as low-status, low-margin stores and change gradually in terms of status and margin.

whistleblowers Employees who report unethical or illegal actions of their employers.

wholesaler-sponsored voluntary chain A contractual system involving independently owned wholesalers who band together to act like a chain.

word of mouth People influencing each other during their face-to-face conversations.

workload method A formula-based method for determining the size of a salesforce that integrates the number of customers served, call frequency, call length, and available time to arrive at a salesforce size.

World Trade Organization An institution that sets rules governing trade among its members through a panel of experts.

Chapter Notes

CHAPTER 1

1. Chad Rubel, "Advertisers Go to Extremes to Target Young Athletes," *Marketing News* (August 28, 1995), pp. 26, 29; and Lisa Feinberg Densmore, "Taking Extreme Mainstream," *Inline* (November 1995), pp. 30–37, 62.
2. Joshua Rosenbaum, "Wheeler Dealers," *Continental Profiles* (February 1991), pp. 22–42.
3. Mary Horwath, "Rollerblade: Creation of an American Original," a talk in Rome, Italy, November 1992.
4. Steven A. Meyerowitz, "Surviving Assaults on Trademarks," *Marketing Management* (1994, No. 1), pp. 44–46; and Carrie Goerne, "Rollerblade Reminds Everyone That Its Success Is Not Generic," *Marketing News* (March 2, 1992), pp. 1–2.
5. Peter D. Bennett, *Dictionary of Marketing Terms,* 2nd ed. (Lincolnwood, IL: NTC Publishing Group, 1995), p. 166.
6. Frederick E. Webster, Jr., "The Changing Role of Marketing in the Corporation," *Journal of Marketing* (October 1992), pp. 1–17; and Jagdish N. Sheth and Rajendra S. Sisodia, "Feeling the Heat," *Marketing Management* (Fall 1995), pp. 9–23.
7. Richard P. Bagozzi, "Marketing as Exchange," *Journal of Marketing* (October 1975), pp. 32–39; and Gregory T. Gundlach and Patrick E. Murphy, "Ethical and Legal Foundations of Relational Marketing Exchanges," *Journal of Marketing* (October 1993), pp. 35–46.
8. Patricia Sellers, "So You Fail. Now Bounce Back!" *Fortune* (May 1, 1995), pp. 48–66; and Christopher Power, Kathleen Kerwin, Ronald Grover, Keith Alexander, and Robert Hof, "Flops," *Business Week* (August 16, 1993), pp. 76–82.
9. E. Jerome McCarthy, *Basic Marketing: A Managerial Approach* (Homewood, Ill.: Richard D. Irwin, 1960); and Walter van Waterschoot and Christophe Van den Bulte, "The 4P Classification of the Marketing Mix Revisited," *Journal of Marketing* (October 1992), pp. 83–93.
10. Carl P. Zeithaml and Valarie A. Zeithaml, "Environmental Management: Revising the Marketing Perspective," *Journal of Marketing* (Spring 1984), pp. 46–53; and P. Rajan Varadarajan, Terry Clark, and William M. Pride, "Controlling the Uncontrollable: Managing Your Market Environment," *Sloan Management Review* (Winter 1992), pp. 39–47.
11. Michael Treacy and Fred D. Wiersema, *The Discipline of Market Leaders* (Reading, Mass.: Addison-Wesley, 1995); Michael Treacy and Fred Wiersema, "How Market Leaders Keep Their Edge," *Fortune* (February 6, 1995), pp. 88–98; and Michael Treacy, "You Need a Value Discipline—But Which One?" *Fortune* (April 17, 1995), p. 195.
12. Michael Hammer and James Champy, *Reengineering the Corporation: A Manifesto for Business Revolution,* (New York, NY: HarperCollins Publishers Inc., 1993); and Thomas O. Jones and W. Earl Sasser, Jr., "Why Satisfied Customers Defect," *Harvard Business Review* (November–December 1995), pp. 88–99.
13. Horwath.
14. Ibid.
15. Lee Schafer, "It's Not a Fad," *Corporate Report Minnesota* (April 1992), pp. 31–39.
16. "The Best of 1994," *Business Week* (January 9, 1995), p. 119.
17. Justin Martin, "Minor Diversions Draw Sports Fans," *Fortune* (September 18, 1995), p. 24; and Jeff Jensen, "NHL's Icebreaker," *Advertising Age* (April 17, 1995), p. 35.
18. For a contrary view, see Ronald A. Fullerton, "How Modern Is Modern Marketing? Marketing's Evolution and the Myth of the 'Production Era'," *Journal of Marketing* (January 1988), pp. 108–25.
19. Robert F. Keith, "The Marketing Revolution," *Journal of Marketing* (January 1960), pp. 35–38.
20. *1952 Annual Report* (New York: General Electric Company, 1952), p. 21.
21. Stanley F. Slater and John C. Narver, "Market Orientation and the Learning Organization," *Journal of Marketing* (July 1995), pp. 63–74; Stanley F. Slater and John C. Narver, "Market Orientation, Customer Value, and Superior Performance," *Business Horizons* (March–April 1994), pp. 22–28; George S. Day, "The Capabilities of Market-Driven Organizations," *Journal of Marketing* (October 1994), pp. 37–52; and Robert Monagham, "Customer Management Teams Are Here to Stay," *Marketing News* (November 6, 1995), p. 4.
22. N. Craig Smith, "Marketing Strategies for the Ethics Era," *Sloan Management Review* (Summer 1995), pp. 85–97; Oswald A. J. Mascarenhas, "Exonerating Unethical Marketing Executive Behaviors: A Diagnostic Framework," *Journal of Marketing* (April 1995), pp. 43–57; and Russell Mitchell and Michael Oneal, "Managing by Values," *Business Week* (August 1, 1994), pp. 46–52.
23. Donald P. Robin and R. Eric Reidenbach, "Social Responsibility, Ethics, and Marketing Strategy: Closing the Gap between Concept and Application," *Journal of Marketing* (Summer 1982), pp. 9–26.
24. Minette E. Drumwright, "Socially Responsible Organizational Buying: Environmental Concern as a Noneconomic Buying Criterion," *Journal of Marketing* (July 1994), pp. 1–19; Michael E. Porter and Claas van der Linde, "Green and Competitive: Ending the Stalemate," *Harvard Business Review* (September–October 1995), pp. 120–34; Jacquelyn Ottman, "Edison Winners Show Smart Environmental Marketing," *Marketing News* (July 17, 1995), pp. 16, 19; and Jacquelyn Ottman, "Mandate for the '90s: Green Corporate Image," *Marketing News* (September 11, 1995), p. 8.
25. Shelby D. Hunt and John J. Burnett, "The Macromarketing/Micromarketing Dichotomy: A Taxonomical Model," *Journal of Marketing* (Summer 1982), pp. 9–26.
26. Philip Kotler and Sidney J. Levy, "Broadening the Concept of Marketing," *Journal of Marketing* (January 1969), pp. 10–15.
27. Horwath.

Rollerblade, Inc.: This case was written by Linda Rochford of the University of Minnesota–Duluth and William Rudelius.

CHAPTER 2

1. Geoffrey Smith, "Life Won't Be Just a Bowl of Cherry Garcia," *Business Week* (July 18, 1994), p. 42.
2. Joseph Pereira and Joann S. Lublin, "A New CEO for Cherry Garcia's Creators," *The Wall Street Journal* (February 2, 1995), pp. B1, B11.
3. Blair S. Walker, "Good-Humored Activist Back to the Fray," *USA Today* (December 8, 1992), pp. 1B–2B.
4. Jim Castelli, "Finding the Right Fit: Are You Weird Enough?" *HR Magazine* (September 1990), pp. 38–39.
5. Franco Salvoza, "Ben & Jerry's New Boss," *USA Weekend* (December 22–24, 1995), p. 6; and Mark Lowery, "Sold on Ice Cream," *Black Enterprise* (April 1995), p. 60.
6. Roger A. Kerin, Vijay Mahajan, and P. Rajan Varadarajan, *Contemporary Perspectives on Strategic Marketing Planning* (Boston: Allyn & Bacon, 1990), Chapter 1; and Orville C. Walker, Jr., Harper W. Boyd, Jr., and Jean-Claude Larreche, *Marketing Strategy* (Homewood, Ill.: Richard D. Irwin, 1992), Chapters 1 and 2.
7. Gary Hamel and C. K. Prahalad, "Strategic Intent," *Harvard Business Review,* (May–June 1989), pp. 63–76.
8. "Coca-Cola Co. Restructures Itself into Units Covering Globe," *Star Tribune* (January 13, 1996), p. D2.
9. Theodore Levitt, "Marketing Myopia," *Harvard Business Review* (July–August 1960), pp. 45–56.
10. John M. Ivancevich, Peter Lorenzi, Steven J. Skinner, with Philip B. Crosby, *Management: Quality and Competitiveness* (Burr Ridge, Ill.: Richard D. Irwin), pp. 176, 621.

11. W. Edwards Deming, *Out of the Crisis* (Cambridge, Mass.: MIT Center for Advanced Engineering Study, 1986).

12. Jeffrey Abrahams, *The Mission Statement Book* (Berkeley, CA: Ten Speed Press, 1995), p. 41.

13. Susan Chandler, "Drill Bits, Paint Thinner, Eyeliner," *Business Week* (September 25, 1995), pp. 84–85; and Gregory A. Patterson and Christina Duff, "Sears Trims Operations, Ending an Era," *The Wall Street Journal* (January 26, 1993), pp. B1, B8.

14. Danny A. Zottoli, Jr. (Publisher), *Moody's Industrial Manual,* vol. 1 (New York: Moody's Investors Service, 1995), pp. 4168–73.

15. Robert Berner, "Sears' Softer Side Paid Off in Hard Cash This Christmas," *The Wall Street Journal* (December 29, 1995), p. B4.

16. Robert S. Kaplan and David P. Norton. "The Balanced Scoreboard Measures That Drive Performance," *Harvard Business Review,* (January–February 1992), pp. 71–79.

17. Adapted from "The Experience Curve Reviewed, IV. The Growth Share Matrix of the Product Portfolio" (Boston: The Boston Consulting Group, 1973).

18. Kerin, Mahajan, and Vardarajan, p. 52.

19. Strengths and weaknesses of the BCG technique are based largely on Derek F. Abell and John S. Hammond, *Strategic Market Planning: Problem and Analytic Approaches* (Englewood Cliffs, N.J.; Prentice Hall, 1979); and Yoram Wind, Vijay Mahajan, and Donald Swire, "An Empirical Comparison of Standardized Portfolio Models," *Journal of Marketing* (Spring 1983), pp. 89–99.

20. Rich Brown, "Making the Product Portfolio a Basis for Action," *Long Range Planning* (February 1991), pp. 102–10.

21. J. Scott Armstrong and Roderick J. Brodie, "Effects of Portfolio Planning Methods on Decision Making: Experimental Results," *International Journal of Research in Marketing* (Winter 1994), pp. 73–84.

22. George Stalk, Phillip Evans, and Lawrence E. Shulman, "Competing on Capabilities: The New Rules of Corporate Strategy," *Harvard Business Review* (March–April 1992), pp. 57–69.

23. Roger A. Kerin and Robert A. Peterson, *Strategic Marketing Problems: Cases and Comments,* 7th ed. (Englewood Cliffs, NJ: Prentice-Hall, 1995), pp. 2–3; and Derek F. Abell, *Defining the Business* (Englewood Cliffs, N.J.: Prentice Hall, 1980), p. 18.

24. Christopher Meyer, *East Cycle Time* (New York: Free Press, 1993); and Michael E. Porter, *Competitive Advantage* (New York: Free Press, 1985).

25. *1994 Hewlett-Packard Annual Report* (Palo Alto, Calif.: Hewlett-Packard, 1995).

26. Thomas C. Powell, "Total Quality Management as Competitive Advantage: A Review and Empirical Study," *Strategic Management Journal,* vol. 16 (1995), pp. 15–37.

27. Loyd Eskildson, "TQM's Role in Corporate Success: Analyzing the Evidence," *National Productivity Review* (Autumn 1995), pp. 25–38; and Keith Naughton, "This Taurus Sure Won't Blend into the Crowd," *Business Week* (October 30, 1995), pp. 168–70.

28. William M. Bulkeley and Joann S. Lublin, "Ben & Jerry's New CEO Will Face Shrinking Sales and Growing Fears of Fat," *The Wall Street Journal* (January 10, 1995), pp. B1, B4.

29. Peter Nulty, "Kodak Grabs for Growth Again," *Fortune* (May 16, 1994), p. 76–78.

30. Ibid.

31. Mark Maremont, "Kodak's New Focus," *Business Week* (January 30, 1995), p. 63–68.

32. Mark Maremont, "The Times of Your Life—As Many Times As You Want," *Business Week* (January 30, 1995), p. 68.

33. Wendy Bounds, "Kodak Under Fisher: Upheaval in Slow Motion," *The Wall Street Journal* (December 22, 1994), pp. B1, B4; and Wendy Bounds, "Fuji, Accused by Kodak of Hogging Markets, Spits Back: 'You Too' " *The Wall Street Journal* (July 31, 1995), pp. A1, A4.

34. Mark Maremont, "The New Flash at Kodak," *Business Week* (May 16, 1994), p. 32.

35. Stephen H. Wildstrom, "Not Yet Picture Perfect," *Business Week* (November 20, 1995), p. 30.

Specialized Bicycle Components, Inc.: This case was written by Giana Eckardt of the University of Minnesota.

CHAPTER 3

1. Karen Ritchie, "Marketing to Generation X," *American Demographics* (April 1995), pp. 34–39; Nicholas Zill and John Robinson, "The Generation X Difference," *American Demographics* (April 1995), pp. 24–33; Faye Rice, "Making Generational Marketing Come of Age," *Fortune* (June 26, 1995), pp. 110–14; Randall Lane, "Computers Are Our Friends," *Forbes* (May 8, 1995), pp. 102–108; and Kemba Johnson, "Generation X Finds a Voice for Advertising," *Advertising Age* (September 18, 1995), p. 12.

2. Shannon Dortch, "Coffee at Home," *American Demographics* (August 1995), pp. 4–6; and Marcia Mogelonsky, "Instant's Last Drop," *American Demographics* (August 1995), p. 10.

3. Peter Francese, "America at Mid-Decade," *American Demographics* (February 1995), pp. 23–29.

4. For an interesting description of age distribution, see Judith Waldrop, "Secrets of the Age Pyramids," *American Demographics* (August 1992), pp. 46ff.

5. Bruce Nussbaum, "What Works for One Works for All," *Business Week* (April 20, 1992), pp. 112–13; and Walecia Konrad and Gail DeGeorge, "U.S. Companies Go for the Gray," *Business Week* (April 3, 1989), pp. 64–67.

6. Patricia Braus, "The Baby Boom at Mid-Decade," *American Demographics* (April 1995), pp. 40–45; and Cheryl Russell, "On the Baby-Boom Bandwagon," *American Demographics* (May 1991), pp. 24–31.

7. Marcy Magiera and Pat Sloan, "Levis, Lee Loosen Up for Baby Boomers," *Advertising Age* (August 3, 1992), p. 9.

8. Diane Crispell, "Generations to 2025," *American Demographics* (January 1995), p. 4; and Scott Donaton, "The Media Wakes Up to Generation X," *Advertising Age* (February 1, 1993), pp. 16–17.

9. Susan Mitchell, "The Next Baby Boom," *American Demographics* (October 1995), pp. 22–31.

10. Rice; Geoffrey Meredith and Charles Schewe, "The Power of Cohorts," *American Demographics* (December 1994), pp. 22–31.

11. Francese.

12. Diane Crispell, "Dual-Earner Diversity," *American Demographics* (July 1995), pp. 32–37; and Jan Larson, "Understanding Stepfamilies," *American Demographics* (July 1992), pp. 36–40.

13. Francese.

14. This discussion is based on Francese; Maria Shad, Christopher Power and Laura Zinn, "Suddenly, Asian-Americans Are a Marketer's Dream," *Business Week* (June 17, 1991), pp. 54–55; and Joe Schwartz and Thomas Exter, "All Our Children," *American Demographics* (May 1989), pp. 34–37.

15. Zachary Schiller, "Stalking the New Consumer," *Business Week* (August 28, 1989), pp. 54–62.

16. Christine Dugas, Mark N. Vamos, and Jonathon B. Levine, "Marketing's New Look," *Business Week* (January 26, 1987), pp. 64–69; see also Shawn McKenna, *The Complete Guide to Regional Marketing* (Homewood, Ill.: Business One Irwin, 1992).

17. Jeffery D. Zbar, "In Diverse Hispanic World, Image Counts," *Advertising Age* (April 3, 1995), pp. 518–519.

18. Diane Crispell, "Workers in 2000," *American Demographics* (September 1992), pp. 27–28.

19. Nina Munk, "The Best Man for the Job Is Your Wife," *Forbes* (November 20, 1995), pp. 148–54; Michele Galen and Ann Theresa Palmer, "White, Male, and Worried," *Business Week* (January 31, 1994), pp. 50–55.

20. Julie Ralston, "Chevy Targets Women," *Advertising Age* (August 7, 1995), p. 24; Ruby Roy Dholakia, "Even PC Men Won't Shop by Computer," *American Demographics* (May 1994), p. 11; Tim Triplett, "Women and Cigars," *Marketing News* (December 4, 1995), pp. 1, 5; and Chad Rubel, "Parents Magazines Make Room for Daddy," *Marketing News* (February 27, 1995), pp. 1, 5, 14.

21. Jill Smolowe, "Do You Still Know Me?" *Time* (September 12, 1994), p. 60; and Judann Dagnoli, "Value Strategy to Battle Recession," *Advertising Age* (January 7, 1991), pp. 1, 44.

22. Kathleen Kerwin, Larry Armstrong, and Thane Peterson, "The Big Three Think They Smell Blood," *Business Week* (September 28, 1992), pp. 34–35.

23. Blayne Cutler, "The Feel-Good Index," *American Demographics* (September 1992), pp. 56–60.

24. Jon Hull, "The State of the Union," *Time* (January 30, 1995), pp. 53–75.

25. "The Future of Spending," *American Demographics* (January 1995), pp. 12–19.

26. Robert Lenzner, "The Reluctant Entrepreneur," *Forbes* (September 11, 1995), pp. 162–68; Joshua Quittner, "A Mighty Morphing," *Time* (January 16, 1995), p. 56; Amy Cortese, John Verity, Russell Mitchell, and Richard Brandt, "Cyberspace," *Business Week* (February 27, 1995), pp. 78–86; Rebecca Piirto, "Cable TV," *American Demographics* (June 1995), pp. 40–43; and David Woodruff, Larry Armstrong, and John Carey, "Electric Cars," *Business Week* (May 30, 1994), pp. 104–14.

27. Neil Gross, Peter Coy, and Otis Post, "The Technology Paradox," *Business Week* (March 6, 1995), pp. 76–84.

28. Leon Jaroff, "Smart's the Word in Detroit," *Time* (February 6, 1995), pp. 50–52.

29. Eugene Carlson, "Business Maps Plans for the Use of TIGER Geographic Files," *The Wall Street Journal* (June 8, 1990), p. B2; and Ruth Hamel "AAA Goes GIS," *American Demographics* (September 1992), p. 53.

30. Jacquelyn Ottman, "Mandate for the '90s: Green Corporate Image," *Marketing News,* (September 11, 1995), p. 8.

31. Jacquelyn Ottman, "A Little Creativity Could Lead to a Big Advantage," *Marketing News* (March 27, 1995), p. 11; and Stephanie Anderson, "There's Gold in Those Hills of Soda Bottles," *Business Week* (September 11, 1995), p. 48.

32. Maxine Wilkie, "Asking Americans to Use Less Stuff," *American Demographics* (December 1994), pp. 11–12.

33. Jacquelyn Ottman, "New and Improved Won't Do," *Marketing News* (January 30, 1995), p. 9: and Wilkie.

34. Timothy K. Smith, "Why Air Travel Doesn't Work," *Fortune* (April 3, 1995), pp. 43–56; Nikhil Hutheesing, "Who Needs the Middleman?" *Forbes* (August 28, 1995), pp. 110–11; and Christopher Farrell, "Media Control Is Narrowing. Should We Worry?" *Business Week* (August 14, 1995), p. 37.

35. Michael Porter, *Competitive Advantage* (New York: Free Press, 1985); and Michael Porter, *Competitive Strategy* (New York: Free Press, 1980).

36. James B. Treece, Kathleen Kerwin, and Heidi Dawley, "Ford," *Business Week* (April 3, 1995), pp. 94–104; Keith Hammonds, Kevin Kelly, and Karen Thurston, "The New World of Work," *Business Week* (October 17, 1994), pp. 76–87.

37. Michael Mandel, Christopher Farrell, and Catherine Yang, "Land of the Giants" *Business Week* (September 11, 1995), pp. 34–35; and Howard Chua-Eoan, "Too Big or Not Too Big?" *Time* (October 2, 1995), pp. 32–33.

38. Perri Capell, "Small Companies Dominate Growth," *American Demographics* (October 1995), pp. 17–18.

39. Kevin Goldman, "L'eggs Wins Injunction Against Leg Looks," *The Wall Street Journal* (December 31, 1992), p. B3.

40. "Washington Outlook," *Business Week* (July 5, 1993), p. 43; "Soft on 'Green' Crime?" *Business Week* (August 10, 1992), p. 40; "Execs Get Little Sympathy for Crimes against Nature," *The Wall Street Journal* (March 11, 1992), p. B1; and "Poll: Execs as Green as Public," *Advertising Age* (May 25, 1992), p. 18.

41. Dorothy Cohen, "Trademark Strategy Revisited," *Journal of Marketing* (July 1991), pp. 46–59.

42. Paul Barrett, "High Court Sees Color as Basis for Trademarks," *The Wall Street Journal* (March 29, 1995), p. A6; Paul Barrett, "Color in the Court," *The Wall Street Journal* (January 5, 1995), p. A1; and David Kelly, "Rainbow of Ideas to Trademark Color," *Advertising Age* (April 24, 1995), pp. 20, 22.

43. Dick Mercer, "Tempest in a Soup Can," *Advertising Age* (October 17, 1994), pp. 25–29.

44. Joanne Lipman, "Double Standards for Kids' TV Ads," *The Wall Street Journal* (June 10, 1988), p. 21.

45. Jeffrey Tannenbaum, "Listen, Anything That Eats Mice Isn't Going to Be That Choosey," *The Wall Street Journal* (June 22, 1990), p. B1.

Imagination Pilots Entertainment: This case was prepared by Steven W. Hartley.

CHAPTER 4

1. "Anheuser Resolution Concerns Marketing," *The New York Times* (April 25, 1995), p. D11; *Fighting Alcohol Abuse Through Awareness & Education* (St. Louis: Anheuser-Busch Companies, 1994); "Earth Crisis," *The National College Magazine* (Fall 1992), p. 11.

2. For a discussion of the definition of ethics, see Eugene R. Lazniak and Patrick E. Murphy, *Ethical Marketing Decisions: The Higher Road* (Boston: Allyn & Bacon, 1993), Chapter 1.

3. Verne E. Henderson, "The Ethical Side of Enterprise," *Sloan Management Review* (Spring 1982), pp. 37–47.

4. M. Bommer, C. Gratto, J. Grauander, and M. Tuttle, "A Behavioral Model of Ethical and Unethical Decision Making," *Journal of Business Ethics,* vol. 6 (1987), pp. 265–80.

5. "Just How Honest Are You?" *Inc.* (February 1992), p. 104.

6. Ray O. Werner, "Marketing and the Supreme Court in Transition, 1982–1984," *Journal of Marketing* (Summer 1985), pp. 97–105; Jane Bryant Quinn, "Computer Program Deceives Consumers," *Dallas Times Herald* (March 2, 1990), p. B3.

7. "The Bottom Line on Ethics," *U.S. News & World Report* (March 20, 1995), pp. 61–66; "Business Week/Harris Poll: Is an Antibusiness Business Backlash Building?" *Business Week* (July 20, 1987), p. 71; "Looking

to Its Roots," *Time* (May 27, 1987), pp. 26–29; and "Who's Trusted, Who's Not?" *American Demographics* (June 1995), p. 55.

8. "What Bosses Think about Corporate Ethics," *The Wall Street Journal* (April 6, 1988), p. 21. See also J. Badaracco, Jr., and A. Webb, "Business Ethics: A View from the Trenches," *California Management Review* (Winter 1995), pp. 8–28.

9. N. Craig Smith, "Marketing Strategies for the Ethics Era," *Sloan Management Review* (Summer 1995), pp. 85–97; Kenneth Labich, "The New Crisis in Business Ethics," *Fortune* (April 20, 1992), pp. 167ff.

10. Paula Mergenhagen, "Product Liability: Who Sues?" *American Demographics* (June 1995), pp. 48–54; "Primate Lab Thrives as Controversy Continues," *The Dallas Morning News* (September 3, 1995), pp. 47A–52A; and "Special Report: Animal Uproar," *Advertising Age* (February 25, 1990), pp. S1–S11.

11. For a comprehensive review on marketing ethics, see John Tsalikis and David J. Fritzche, "Business Ethics: A Literature Review with a Focus on Marketing Ethics," *Journal of Business Ethics,* vol. 8 (1989), pp. 695–743.

12. "Levi Only Comfortable Dealing with Countries that Fit Its Image," *The Dallas Morning News* (January 9, 1994), p. D2. See also William Beaver, "Levi's Is Leaving China," *Business Horizons* (March–April 1995), pp. 35–40.

13. "It's All in the Cards," *Time* (November 7, 1988), p. 101.

14. Russell Watson, "A Little Fight Music," *Newsweek* (February 13, 1995), pp. 38–39; and Damon Darlin, "Where Trademarks Are Up for Grabs," *The Wall Street Journal* (December 5, 1989), pp. B1, B4.

15. "Nabbing the Pirates of Cyberspace," *Time* (June 13, 1995), pp. 62–63; "A Little Fight Music," *Newsweek* (February 13, 1995), pp. 38–39; "What Information Costs," *Fortune* (July 10, 1995), pp. 119–21; see also Moshe Givon, Vijay Mahajan, and Eitan Muller, "Software Piracy: Estimation of Lost Sales and the Impact of Software Diffusion," *Journal of Marketing* (January 1995), pp. 29–37.

16. Vern Terpstra and Kenneth David, *The Cultural Environment of International Business,* 3rd ed. (Cincinnati: South-Western Publishing Co., 1991), p. 12.

17. For an extended treatment of ethics in the exchange process, see Gregory T. Gundlach and Patrick E. Murphy, "Ethical and Legal Foundations of Business Marketing Exchanges," *AMA Winter Marketing Educators' Conference* (Chicago: American Marketing Association, 1990).

18. Malcolm Gladwell, "Group Challenges Parts of Dalkon Shield Pact," *The Washington Post* (August 25, 1989), p. C2; "Some Dalkon Shield Claimants Attack Trust's Settlement Policies," *The Wall Street Journal* (March 12, 1992), p. B4.

19. "FTC Forces Car Rental Firms to Reveal All," *The Wall Street Journal* (August 14, 1992), p. B4.

20. Lois Therrion, "Want Shelf Space at Supermarkets? Ante Up," *Business Week* (August 7, 1989), pp. 60–61.

21. "In Crackdown on Fraud, FTC Moves to Regulate Telemarketing Practices," *The Wall Street Journal* (February 10, 1995), p. B12.

22. Robert Johnson and Edward T. Pound, "Hot on the Trail of Trade-Secret Thieves, Private Eyes Fight All Manner of Snakes," *The Wall Street Journal* (August 12, 1992), pp. B1, B4. See also "Companies on the Lookout for Spies," *USA Today* (February 24, 1995), p. 48.

23. "P&B Expected to Get about $120 Million in Settlement of Chewy-Cookie Lawsuit," *The Wall Street Journal* (September 11, 1989), p. B10.

24. "Former Honda Officials Sentenced for Kickbacks," *The Wall Street Journal* (August 22, 1995), p. B16.

25. Andy Pasztor, *When the Pentagon Was for Sale: Inside America's Biggest Defense Scandal* (New York: Scribner 1995).

26. Warren J. Keegan, *Global Marketing Management,* 5th ed. (Englewood Cliffs, N.J.: Prentice-Hall, 1995), p. 170.

27. "Hard Graft in Asia," *The Economist* (May 27, 1995), p. 61.

28. David J. Fritzche, "Ethical Issues in Multinational Marketing" in Gene R. Lazniak and Patrick E. Murphy, eds., *Marketing Ethics: Guidelines for Managers* (Lexington, Mass.: Lexington Books, 1985), pp. 85–96; and "Hard Graft in Asia," reference cited.

29. "Good Grief," *The Economist* (April 8, 1995), p. 57; and "Odds and Ends," *The Wall Street Journal* (February 25, 1992), p. B1.

30. "Good Grief," reference cited.

31. Ismael P. Akaah and Daulatram Lund, "The Influence of Personal Values and Organizational Values on Marketing Professionals' Ethical Behavior," *Journal of Business Ethics,* vol. 13 (1994), pp. 417–30.

32. "Doing the 'Right' Thing Has Its Repercussions," *The Wall Street Journal* (January 25, 1990), p. B1. See also "Business Ethics: A View from the Trenches," reference cited.

33. "The Uncommon Good," *The Economist* (August 19, 1995), pp. 55–56; "Workers Who Blow the Whistle on Bosses Often Pay a High Price," *The Wall Street Journal* (July 18, 1995), p. B1.

34. For an extensive discussion on these moral philosophies, see R. Eric Reidenbach and Donald P. Robin, *Ethics and Profits* (Englewood Cliffs, N.J.: Prentice-Hall, 1989); and Shelby D. Hunt and Scott Vitell, "A General Theory of Marketing Ethics," *Journal of Macromarketing* (Spring 1986), pp. 5–16.

35. "Bad Apple for Baby," *Financial World* (June 27, 1989), p. 48; and "What Led Beech-Nut Down the Road to Disgrace," *Business Week* (February 22, 1988), pp. 124–27.

36. James Q. Wilson, "Adam Smith on Business Ethics," *California Management Review* (Fall 1989), pp. 59–72; and Edward W. Coker, "Smith's Concept of the Social System," *Journal of Business Ethics,* vol. 9 (1990), pp. 139–42.

37. George M. Zinkhan, Michael Bisesi, and Mary Jane Saxton, "MBAs: Changing Attitudes toward Marketing Dilemmas," *Journal of Business Ethics,* vol. 8 (1989), pp. 963–74.

38. Alix M. Freedman, "Bad Reaction: Nestlé's Bid to Crash Baby-Formula Market in the U.S. Stirs a Row," *The Wall Street Journal* (February 16, 1989), pp. A1, A6; and Alix Freedman, "Nestlé to Drop Claim on Label of Its Formula," *The Wall Street Journal* (March 13, 1989), p. B5.

39. Milton Friedman, "A Friedman Doctrine: The Social Responsibility of Business Is to Increase Profits," *New York Times Magazine* (September 13, 1970), p. 126.

40. "Beating the Odds in Biotech," *Newsweek* (October 12, 1992), p. 63.

41. "Can Perrier Purify Its Reputation?" *Business Week* (February 26, 1990), p. 45; and "Perrier Expands North American Recall to Rest of Globe," *The Wall Street Journal* (February 15, 1990), pp. B1, B4.

42. The following examples are based on "Shell Pumps Cleaner Gas in 'Dirtiest' Cities in U.S.," *The Wall Street Journal* (April 12, 1990), pp. B1, B6; "Efforts to Save Dolphins Are Set by Tuna Canners," *The Wall Street Journal* (April 13, 1990), p. B5; "Downy Refill Makes a Splash on Shelves," *Advertising Age* (July 8, 1991), p. 16; and "Levi's Esprit Spin New Cotton Into Eco-friendly Clothes," *Marketing News* (April 24, 1992), p. 11.

43. For an extended discussion on this topic, see P. Rajan Varadarajan and Avil Menon, "Cause-Related Marketing: A Coalignment of Marketing Strategy and Corporate Philanthropy," *Journal of Marketing* (July 1988), pp. 58–74. The examples given are found in this article and "McD's Ties to World Cup," *Advertising Age* (April 13, 1992), p. 17; Scott M. Smith and David S. Alcorn, "Cause Marketing: A New Direction in the Marketing of Corporate Responsibility," *The Journal of Consumer Marketing* (Summer 1991), pp. 19–35; and "Are Good Causes Good Marketing?" *Business Week* (March 21, 1994), pp. 64–65.

44. These steps are adapted from J. J. Carson and G. A. Steiner, *Measuring Business Social Performance: The Corporate Social Audit* (New York: Committee for Economic Development, 1974). See also E. M. Epstein, "The Corporate Social Policy Process: Beyond Business Ethics, Corporate Social Responsibility, and Corporate Social Responsiveness," *California Management Review* (Spring 1987), pp. 99–114.

45. *Research Report: The Only Environment We Have: How Can We Save It?* (New York: Council on Economic Priorities, November 1989); and Rajib N. Sanyal and Joao S. Neves, "The Valdez Principles: Implications for Corporate Social Responsibility," *Journal of Business Ethics,* vol. 10 (1991), pp. 883–90.

46. "Soft on 'Green' Crime," *Business Week* (August 10, 1992), p. 40.

47. "The Drought Is Over at 3M," *Business Week* (November 7, 1994), pp. 140–41; and "How to Make Lots of Money, and Save the Planet Too," *The Economist* (June 3, 1995), pp. 57–58.

48. For a listing of unethical consumer practices, see Robert E. Wilkes, "Fraudulent Behavior by Consumers," *Journal of Marketing* (October 1978), pp. 67–75. See also Catherine A. Cole, "Research Note: Determinants and Consumer Fraud," *Journal of Retailing* (Spring 1989), pp. 107–20.

49. "Coupon Scams Are Clipping Companies," *Business Week* (June 15, 1992), pp. 110–11; Paul Bernstein, "Cheating: The New National Pastime?" *Business* (October–December 1985), pp. 24–33; "Video Vice: 1 in 10 Copy Videotapes Illegally," *USA Weekend* (February 9–11, 1990), p. 18; and "Trade Tripwires," *The Economist* (August 27, 1994), p. 61.

50. "Consumers Keen on Green But Marketers Don't Deliver," *Advertising Age* (June 29, 1992), pp. S-2, S-4.

51. "Green Campaigns Don't Always Pay Off, Survey Finds," *The Wall Street Journal* (April 11, 1994) p. 88; "Green Product Sales Seem to Be Wilting," *The Wall Street Journal* (May 18, 1992), p. B1.

52. "Keeping Hair in Place—Without Messing Up the Air," *Business Week* (January 25, 1990), p. 85.

53. "Rush to Endorse 'Environmental' Goods Sparks Worry about Shopper Confusion," *The Wall Street Journal* (April 16, 1990), pp. B1, B3; and JoAnn S. Lublin, "Environment Claims Are Sowing More Confusion, 2 Reports Say," *The Wall Street Journal* (November 8, 1990), p. B8.

54. Steven W. Colford, "FTC Green Guidelines May Spark Ad Efforts," *Advertising Age* (August 3, 1992), pp. 1, 29; see also Dorothy Cohen, *Legal Issues in Marketing* (Cincinnati, OH: South-Western, 1995), pp. 53–55.

Pricing in the Pharmaceutical Industry: This case was prepared by Roger A. Kerin. Sources: "How Many Times Must a Patient Pay?" *Business Week* (February 1, 1993), pp. 30–31; "What's Up Doc?" *U.S. News & World Report* (April 12, 1993), pp. 26–29; "Doctor Assails J&J Price Tag on Cancer Drug," *The Wall Street Journal* (May 14, 1990), pp. B1, B5; Richard A. Spinello, "Ethics, Pricing, and the Pharmaceutical Industry," *Journal of Business Ethics* (August 1992), pp. 617–26; "The Big Pill," *The Economist* (March 6, 1993), p. 67; Brian O'Reilly, "The Inside Story of the AIDS Drug," *Fortune* (November 5, 1990), pp. 112–29; Wellcome PLC 1989 *Annual Report,* p. 13; and Shawn Tully, "Why Drug Prices Will Go Lower," *Fortune* (May 3, 1993), pp. 56–66.

CHAPTER 5

1. "Selling in Russia: The March on Moscow," *The Economist* (March 18, 1995), pp. 65–66; "Buyers Want Better Value in E. Europe," *Advertising Age* (April 17, 1995), P. I-18; "The Rival Japan Respects," *Business Week* (December 19, 1989), pp. 69–76; "Guess Who's Selling Barbies in Japan Now?" *Business Week* (December 9, 1991), pp. 72–75; and "Revolution in Japanese Retailing," *Fortune* (February 7, 1994), pp. 143–46.

2. These estimates are based on statistics reported in *International Financial Statistics Yearbook* (New York: International Monetary Fund, 1995) and trend projections by the authors.

3. "Regionalism in World Trade: The End of an Era?" *The Economist* (March 25, 1995), p. 66.

4. Nathaniel Gilbert, "A Case for Countertrade," *Across the Board* (May 1992), pp. 43–45; and E. Amann and D. Marin, "Risk-Sharing in International Trade: An Analysis of Countertrade," *The Journal of Industrial Economics* (March 1993), pp. 63–77.

5. This discussion is based on Karl E. Case and Ray C. Fair, *Principles of Economics* (Englewood Cliffs, N.J.: Prentice-Hall, 1989), p. 930; "No Free Lunches Here," *Newsweek* (February 20, 1995), pp. 39–40; "U.S. Firms Take Chances in Korea," *The Wall Street Journal* (June 15, 1992), pp. B1, B5; "Kodak Zooms in on Pro Photographers," *The Wall Street Journal* (February 27, 1991), pp. B1, B5; "GM Finally Discovers Asia," *Business Week* (August 24, 1992), pp. 42–43; and "P&G Viewed China as a National Market and Is Conquering It," *The Wall Street Journal* (September 12, 1995), pp. A1, A6.

6. Michael R. Czinkota and Ilkka A. Ronkainen, "The Globalization of the U.S. Economy," *Journal of International Consumer Marketing,* vol. 3, no. 4 (1991), pp. 51–68.

7. "Balancing Act," *The Economist* (January 4, 1992), p. 30; and "Eyeball to Eyeball with China," *Business Week* (February 20, 1995), pp. 32–33.

8. Michael E. Porter, *The Competitive Advantage of Nations* (New York: The Free Press, 1990), pp. 577–615; and Michael E. Porter, "Why Nations Triumph," *Fortune* (March 12, 1990), pp. 94–108.

9. "Japan's Price of Protection," *Fortune* (March 6, 1995), p. 48; "New World Trade Chief Fears Economic Nationalism," *Dallas Morning News* (March 22, 1995), p. 11D; and Gary C. Hufbauer and Kimberly A. Elliott; *Measuring the Costs of Protection in the United States* (Washington, D.C.: Institute for International Economics, 1994).

10. "A Survey of Multinationals," *The Economist,* Special Report (June 24, 1995).

11. R. Jacob, "Export Barriers the U.S. Hates Most," *Fortune* (February 27, 1989), pp. 88–89.

12. Shawn Tully, "Europe 1992: More Unity than You Think," *Fortune* (August 24, 1992), pp. 136–38; and "10,000 New EC Roles," *Business Week* (September 7, 1992), pp. 48–49.

13. "It Ain't Just Peanuts," *Business Week* (December 18, 1995), p. 30.

14. For a concise overview of the WTO, see Philip R. Cateora, *International Marketing,* 9th ed. (Chicago: Richard D. Irwin, 1996), pp. 51–53.

15. "The EU Goes Cold on Enlargement," *The Economist* (October 28, 1995), pp. 57–58.

16. For a comprehensive report on strategy for the European Union, see Colin Egan and Peter McKiernan, *Inside Fortress Europe: Strategies for the Single Market* (Reading, Mass.: Addison-Wesley, 1994).

17. "Meanwhile, to the North, NAFTA Is a Smash," *Business World* (February 27, 1995), p. 86; and "What Has NAFTA Wrought? Plenty of Trade," *Business Week* (November 21, 1994), pp. 48–49.

18. "Asia, Par for the Course," *The Economist* (December 16, 1995), pp. 31–32.

19. "Kimberly-Clark and P&G Face Global Warfare," *The Wall Street Journal* (July 18, 1995), pp. B1, B6; and "Coca-Cola Still in India Despite Fight from Pepsi," *Advertising Age* (July 18, 1994), pp. I-1, I-4.

20. "A Hunger for Growth," *Chicago Tribune* (September 20, 1992), pp. 7–1, 7–11; and "Spoon-to-Spoon Combat Overseas," *The New York Times* (January 1, 1995), p. 17.

21. For an excellent overview of different types of global companies and marketing strategies, see Warren J. Keegan, *Global Marketing Management,* 5th ed. (Englewood Cliffs, N.J.: Prentice Hall, 1995), pp. 43–54.

22. "The Avon Lady of the Amazon," *Business Week* (October 24, 1994), pp. 93–94.

23. E. S. Browning, "In Pursuit of the Elusive Euroconsumer," *The Wall Street Journal* (April 23, 1992), pp. B1, B3; and "Global Campaigns Don't Work; Multinationals Do," *Advertising Age* (April 18, 1994), p. 23.

24. "Ford: Alex Trotman's Daring Global Strategy," *Business Week* (April 3, 1995), pp. 94–104.

25. For an extensive discussion on identifying global consumers, see Jean-Pierre Jeannet and H. David Hennessey, *Global Marketing Strategies,* 3rd ed. (Boston: Houghton Mifflin Company, 1995), pp. 236–39.

26. Chip Walker, "The Global Middle Class," *American Demographics* (September 1955), pp. 40–47; William Echikson, "Luxury Steals Back," *Fortune* (January 16, 1995), pp. 112–19; Ricardo Sookdeo, "The New Global Consumer," *Fortune* (Autumn-Winter 1993), pp. 68–72; Sala S. Hassan and Lea Prevel Katsanis, "Identification of Global Consumer Segments: A Behavioral Framework," *Journal of International Consumer Marketing,* vol. 3, no. 2 (1991), pp. 15–22; and "Capturing the Global Consumer," *Fortune* (December 13, 1993), p. 166.

27. Chip Walker, "Can TV Save the Planet?" *American Demographics* (May 1996), pp. 42–49; "Teens Seen as the First Truly Global Consumers," *Marketing News* (March 27, 1995), p. 9; John Greenwald, "No Passage to India," *Time* (September 18, 1995), pp. 91–92; "Rock Around the World," *Newsweek* (April 24, 1995), p. 65; "The Universal Teenagers," *Fortune* (April 4, 1994), p. 14; and Shawn Tully, "Teens: The Most Global Market of All," *Fortune* (May 16, 1994), pp. 90–97.

28. For an extended discussion on cross-cultural analysis, see Vern Terpstra and Kenneth David, *The Cultural Environment of International Business,* 3rd ed. (Cincinnati: South-Western Publishing, 1991).

29. These examples are adapted from Terpstra and David; "In India, Beef-Free Mickey D," *Business Week* (April 17, 1995), p. 52; and "After Early Stumbles, P&G Is Making Inroads Overseas," *The Wall Street Journal* (February 6, 1989), p. B1.

30. Louis Kraar, "Meet 25 People You Ought to Know," *Fortune,* Pacific Rim Special Issue (Fall 1989), p. 108; and Susan Feyder, "In 3M's Eyes, All the World's a Market," *Minneapolis Star Tribune* (April 16, 1990), pp. 1D, 7D.

31. See Terpstra and David; and "Valentine's Day in Japan: Ladies Don't Expect a Gift," *The Christian Science Monitor* (February 13, 1989), p. 6.

32. R. L. Tung, *Business Negotiations with the Japanese* (Lexington, Mass.: Lexington Books, 1983).

33. These examples are found in John C. Mowen, *Consumer Behavior,* 2nd ed. (New York: Macmillan Publishing, 1990), p. 604; and Richard Tansey, Michael R. Hyman, and George M. Zinkham, "Cultural Themes in Brazilian and U.S. Auto Ads: A Cross-Cultural Comparison," *Journal of Advertising,* vol. 19, no. 2 (1990), pp. 30–39.

34. "Greeks Protest Coke's Use of Parthenon," *Dallas Morning News* (August 17, 1992), p. D4.

35. "What Soviets Think: A Gallup Poll," *Advertising Age* (February 19, 1990), p. 46; and "The Japanese Talk about Themselves," *Fortune,* Pacific Rim Special Issue (Fall 1990), p. 17. For a comprehensive review of research on country-of-origin effects, see Saeed Samiee, "Customer Evaluation of Products in a Global Market," *Journal of International Business Studies,* third quarter, 1994, pp. 579–604.

36. These examples are adapted from Terpstra and David, p. 21; David A. Ricks, "Products that Crashed into the Language Barrier," *Business and Society Review* (Spring 1983), pp. 46–50.

37. "Global Thinking Paces Computer Biz," *Advertising Age* (March 6, 1995), p. 10.

38. "U.S. Firms Sometimes Lose It in the Translation," *Dallas Morning News* (August 17, 1992), pp. D1, D4.

39. Terrence A. Shimp and Subhash Sharma, "Consumer Ethnocentrism: Construction and Validation of the CETSCALE," *Journal of Marketing Research* (August 1987), pp. 280–89.

40. Nancy Giges, "Europeans Buy Outside Goods, But Like Local Ads," *Advertising Age* (April 27, 1992), pp. I-1, I-26.

41. Subhash Sharma, Terrence Shimp, and Jeongshin Shin, "Consumer Ethnocentrism: A Test of Antecedents and Moderators," *Journal of the Academy of Marketing Science* (Winter 1995), pp. 26–37; Joel Herche, "A Note on the Predictive Validity of the CETSCALE," *Journal of the Academy of Marketing Science* (Summer 1992), pp. 261–64; Richard G. Netemeyer, Srinivas Durvasula, and Donald R. Lichtenstein, "A Cross-National Assessment of the Reliability and Validity of the CETSCALE," *Journal of Marketing Research* (August 1991), pp. 320–27; Shimp and Sharma; and Giges.

42. This example is based on Shawn Tully, "Nestlé Shows How to Gobble Markets," *Fortune* (January 16, 1989), pp. 74–78; "Global Coffee Market Share Comparisons," *Advertising Age* (December 10, 1995), p. 47; and Carla Rapoport, "Nestlé's Brand Building Machine," *Fortune* (September 19, 1995), pp. 147–56.

43. "Finding the Next Japan," *Sales & Marketing Management* (August 19, 1995), p. 83.

44. "Selling in Russia: The March on Moscow."

45. Carole Howard, "*Reader's Digest* Meets Eastern Europe," *Express Magazine* (Summer 1992), pp. 28–31.

46. "Selling in Russia: The March on Moscow."

47. This discussion is based on "Multinationals in Vietnam," *The Economist* (December 9, 1995), pp. 63–64; Bill Saporito, "Where the Global Action Is," *Fortune* (Autumn/Winter 1993), pp. 63–65; and Walker.

48. "Whirlpool Makes a Splash in Global Market," *Dallas Morning News* (April 2, 1995), p. 5H.

49. "Not Grieving for the Greenback," *Business Week* (May 1, 1995), pp. 40–41.

50. Cateora, p. 560.

51. This discussion is based on "Why Japanese Deregulation Won't Much Help America," *Business Week* (April 3, 1995), p. 72; Ford S. Worthy, "A New Mass Market Emerges," *Fortune,* Pacific Rim Special Issue (Fall 1990), p. 57; "EC Vote May Threaten Ads Aimed at Kids," *Advertising Age* (December 11, 1995), p. 4; "Japan's Big Problem: Freeing Its Economy from Over-Regulation," *The Wall Street Journal* (April 25, 1995), pp. A1, A6; and "Euro Telemarketing in Trouble," *Advertising Age* (November 27, 1995), p. 4.

52. For an extensive discussion on ISO 9000, see H. Michael Hayes, "ISO 9000: The New Strategic Consideration," *Business Horizons* (May–June 1994), pp. 52–60.

53. For an extensive examination of these market entry options, see Cateora, pp. 340–345; Keegan, pp. 351–59; and Jeannet and Hennessey, pp. 296–316. See also Krishna M. Erramilli and C. P. Rao, "Service Firms' International Entry-Mode Choice: A Modified Transaction-Cost Analysis," *Journal of Marketing* (July 1993), pp. 19–38; and Franklin R. Root, *Entry Strategies for International Markets* (Lexington, Mass.: D. C. Heath, 1994).

54. Harley-Davidson, Inc., Form 10K (Milwaukee, Wis., 1994).

55. "Special Report: It's a Small (Business) World," *Business Week* (April 17, 1995), pp. 96–101.

56. Andrew E. Serwer, "McDonald's Conquers the World," *Fortune* (October 17, 1994), pp. 103–16.

57. Avraham Shama, "Entry Strategies of U.S. Firms to the Newly Independent States, Baltic States, and Eastern European Countries," *California Management Review* (Spring 1995), pp. 90–109.

58. S. Lanier, "Joint Ventures Are Not Just for Giants," *Trade & Culture* (September–October 1994), pp. 37–38.

59. Cateora, p. 480.

60. Shama.

61. "Potato Chips to Go Global—Or so Pepsi Bets," *The Wall Street Journal* (January 30, 1995), pp. B-1, B-10; "Pizza in Japan Is Adapted to Local Tastes," *The Wall Street Journal* (June 4, 1993), p. B-1; and "Campbell: Now Its M-M-Global," *Business Week* (March 15, 1994), pp. 52–54.

62. "From Cookies to Appliances, Pan-Euro Efforts Build," *Advertising Age* (June 22, 1992), pp. I-1, I-29. See also, "Can the Queen of Cosmetics Keep Her Crown?" *Business Week* (January 17, 1994), pp. 90–91.

63. This discussion is based on John Fahy and Fuyuki Taguchi, "Reassessing the Japanese Distribution System," *Sloan Management Review* (Winter 1995), pp. 49–61.

64. For an excellent treatment on global pricing, see S. Tamer Cavugil, "Unraveling the Mystique of Export Pricing," in Sidney J. Levy et al., eds., *Marketing Manager's Handbook,* 3rd ed. (New York: The Dartnell Corporation, 1994), pp. 1356–74.

65. A. A. Flynn, "New U.S. Recipe for China Relations: More Honey, Less Vinegar," *China Business Review* (November–December 1994), pp. 4–5; and "Eyeball to Eyeball with China."

66. Cateora, pp. 552–55.

The Coca-Cola Company: Japan: This case was prepared by Roger A. Kerin. Sources: The Coca-Cola Company 1994 *Annual Report,* p. 29; "We Got the Achtung Baby," *Brandweek* (January 18, 1993), pp. 23–26; and "Cola War Bubbles in Japan," *Advertising Age* (March 23, 1992), p. 4.

CHAPTER 6

1. "Automotive Marketing," *Advertising Age* (April 3, 1995), p. S2; "Auto Update," *Better Homes and Gardens* (May 1995), p. 230; "Automakers Recognizing Value of Women's Market," *Marketing News* (April 11, 1994), pp. 1, 2; "Vehicle for Growth," *Dallas Morning News* (May 28, 1995), pp. 1H, 3H; and "Nice Guys Finish First?" *Time* (July 25, 1994), pp. 48–49.

2. James F. Engel, Roger D. Blackwell, and Paul Miniard, *Consumer Behavior,* 8th ed. (Fort Worth, Tex.: Dryden Press, 1995), p. 176. See also Gordon C. Bruner III and Richard J. Pomazal, "Problem Recognition: The Crucial First Stage of the Consumer Decision Process," *Journal of Consumer Marketing* (Winter 1988), pp. 53–63.

3. For thorough descriptions of consumer experience and expertise, see Stephen J. Hoch and John Deighton, "Managing What Consumers Learn from Experience," *Journal of Marketing* (April 1989), pp. 1–20; and Joseph W. Alba and J. Wesley Hutchinson, "Dimensions of Consumer Expertise," *Journal of Consumer Research* (March 1987), pp. 411–54.

4. For in-depth studies on external information search patterns, see Joel E. Urbany, Peter R. Dickson, and William L. Wilkie, "Buyer Uncertainty and Information Search," *Journal of Consumer Research* (September 1989), pp. 208–15; Narasimhan Srinivasan and Brian T. Ratchford, "An Empirical Test of a Model of External Search for Automobiles," *Journal of Consumer Research* (September 1991), pp. 233–42; and Julie L. Ozanne, Merrie Brucks, and Druv Grewal, "A Study of Information Search Behavior during the Categorization of New Products," *Journal of Consumer Research* (March 1992), pp. 452–63.

5. Engel, Blackwell, and Miniard, p. 208.

6. John A. Howard, *Consumer Behavior in Marketing Strategy* (Englewood Cliffs, NJ: Prentice Hall, 1989), pp. 176–77, 361. For an extended discussion on consumer choice sets, see Allan D. Shocker, Moshe Ben-Akiva, Bruno Boccara, and Prakesh Nedungadi, "Consideration Set Influences on Consumer Decision-Making and Choice: Issues, Models, and Suggestions," *Marketing Letters* (August 1991), pp. 181–98.

7. For an extended discussion on why consumers postpone decisions, see Eric A. Greenleaf and Donald R. Lehman, "Reasons for Substantial Delay in Consumer Decision Making," *Journal of Consumer Research* (September 1995), pp. 186–99.

8. Ruth N. Bolton and James H. Drew, "A Multistage Model of Customers' Assessments of Service Quality and Value," *Journal of Consumer Research* (March 1991), pp. 376–84.

9. See Chip Walker, "Word of Mouth," *American Demographics* (July 1995), pp. 38–45; and Damon Darlin, "Although U.S. Cars Are Improved, Imports Still Win Quality Survey," *The Wall Street Journal* (December 12, 1985), p. 27.

10. Rahul Jacob, "The Struggle to Create an Organization for the 21st Century," *Fortune* (April 3, 1995), pp. 90–99; and "Putting a Price on Customer Loyalty," *Dallas Morning News* (June 26, 1994), p. 2H. See also "What's a Loyal Customer Worth?" *Fortune* (December 11, 1995), p. 182.

11. Steven E. Prokesch, "Competing on Customer Service: An Interview with British Airways' Sir Colin Marshall," *Harvard Business Review* (November–December 1995), pp. 100–18; "For Customers, More than Lip Service?" *The Wall Street Journal* (October 6, 1989), p. B1; Patricia Sellers, "How to Handle Customers' Gripes," *Fortune* (October 24, 1988), pp. 88–89ff; and "For Marketers, No Peeve Is Too Petty," *The Wall Street Journal* (November 14, 1990), pp. B1, B6.

12. "Customers, 800-Lines May Not Connect," *The Wall Street Journal* (November 20, 1990), p. B1.

13. Many different definitions and perspectives on involvement exist. See, for example, Judith Lynne Zaichkosky, "The Personal Involvement Inven-tory: Reduction, Revision, and Applications to Advertising," *Journal of Advertising Research* (December 1994), pp. 59–70; Richard L. Celsi and Jerry C. Olson, "The Role of Involvement in Attention and Comprehension Processes," *Journal of Consumer Research* (September 1988), pp. 210–24; and Deborah J. MacInnis and C. Whan Park, "The Differential Role of Characteristics of Music on High- and Low-Involvement Consumers' Processing of Ads," *Journal of Consumer Research* (September 1991), pp. 161–73.

14. J. Paul Peter and Jerry C. Olson, *Consumer Behavior: Marketing Strategy Perspectives,* 4th ed. (Homewood, Ill.: Richard D. Irwin, 1996), p. 101; Del Hawkins, Roger J. Best, and Kenneth J. Coney, *Consumer Behavior: Implications for Marketing Strategy,* 6th ed. (Homewood, Ill.: Richard D. Irwin, 1995), pp. 423–26; and Engel, Blackwell, and Miniard, pp. 164–66.

15. Russell Belk, "Situational Variables and Consumer Behavior," *Journal of Consumer Research* (December 1975), pp. 157–63. Representative studies on situational influences include Ronald Milliman, "The Influence of Background Music on the Behavior of Restaurant Patrons," *Journal of Consumer Research* (September 1986), pp. 286–89; Meryl Gardner, "Mood States and Consumer Behavior: A Critical Review," *Journal of Consumer Research* (December 1985), pp. 281–300; Robert Donovan and John Rossiter, "Store Atmosphere: An Environmental Psychology Approach," *Journal of Retailing* (Spring 1982), pp. 34–57; and Sevgin A. Eroglu and Karen A. Machleit, "An Empirical Study of Retail Crowding: Antecedents and Consequences," *Journal of Retailing* (Summer 1990), pp. 201–21.

16. K. H. Chung, *Motivational Theories and Practices* (Columbus, Ohio: Grid, 1977). See also A. H. Maslow, *Motivation and Personality* (New York: Harper & Row, 1970).

17. Arthur Koponen, "The Personality Characteristics of Purchases," *Journal of Advertising Research* (September 1960), pp. 89–92; Joel B. Cohen, "An Interpersonal Orientation to the Study of Consumer Behavior," *Journal of Marketing Research* (August 1967), pp. 270–78; and Rena Bartos, *Marketing to Women Around the World* (Cambridge, Mass.: Harvard Business School, 1989).

18. Terry Clark, "International Marketing and National Character: A Review and Proposal for an Integrative Theory," *Journal of Marketing* (October 1990), pp. 66–79.

19. J. Neher, "Toro Cutting a Wide Swath in Outdoor Appliances Marketing," *Advertising Age* (February 25, 1979), p. 21.

20. For further reading on subliminal perception, see Timothy E. Moore, "Subliminal Advertising: What You See Is What You Get," *Journal of Marketing* (Spring 1982), pp. 38–47; Joel Saegert, "Why Marketing Should Quit Giving Subliminal Advertising the Benefit of the Doubt," *Psychology & Marketing* (Summer 1987), pp. 107–20; Dennis L. Rosen and Surendra N. Singh, "An Investigation of Subliminal Embed Effect on Multiple Measures of Advertising Effectiveness," *Psychology & Marketing* (March/April 1992), pp. 157–73; and Kathryn T. Theus, "Subliminal Advertising and the Psychology of Processing Unconscious Stimuli: A Review of Research," *Psychology & Marketing* (May/June 1994), pp. 271–90.

21. "Dr. Feelgood Goes Subliminal," *Business Week* (November 6, 1995), p. 6; and Michael R. Soloman, *Consumer Behavior,* 3rd ed. (Englewood Cliffs, NJ: Prentice Hall, 1996), pp. 68–72.

22. "Ex-Soviet States Lead World in Ad Cynicism," *Advertising Age* (June 5, 1995), p. 3; "Europeans Buy Outside Goods, But Like Local Ads," *Advertising Age* (April 27, 1992), pp. I-1, I-26; Ronald Alsop, "Brand Loyalty Is Rarely Blind Loyalty," *The Wall Street Journal* (October 19, 1989), p. B1; and *Brand-Driven Marketers Are Beating Themselves in the War Against Price-Based and Private Label Competition* (New York: Bates USA, 1994).

23. Gordon Allport, "Attitudes," in Martin Fishbein, ed., *Readings in Attitude Theory and Measurement* (New York: John Wiley & Sons, 1968), p. 3.

24. Hawkins, Best, and Coney, pp. 364–65; See also Richard J. Lutz, "Changing Brand Attitudes through Modification of Cognitive Structure," *Journal of Consumer Research,* Vol. 2 (1975), pp. 49–59.

25. "Pepsi's Gamble Hits Freshness Dating Jackpot," *Advertising Age* (September 19, 1994), p. 50.

26. For an extended discussion of self-concept, see M. Joseph Sirgy, "Self-Concept in Consumer Behavior: A Critical Review," *Journal of Consumer Research* (December 1982), pp. 287–300. For a broader perspective, see Russell Belk, "Possessions and the Extended Self," *Journal of Consumer Research* (September 1988), pp. 139–68.

27. This description of the VALS Program is based on Judith Waldrop, "Markets with Attitude," *American Demographics* (July 1994), pp. 22–32; *The VALS 2 Segmentation System* (Menlo Park, CA: SRI International, 1989); Martha Richie, "Psychographics for the 1990s," *American Demographics* (July 1989), pp. 25–31, 53; and "SRI's New Psychographic Typology Reasserts Old Stereotypes of Aging," *Maturity Market Perspective* (September/October 1989), pp. 1, 6.

28. See, for example, Lawrence F. Feick and Linda Price, "The Market Maven: A Diffuser of Marketplace Information," *Journal of Marketing* 51 (January 1987), pp. 83–97; and Peter H. Block, "The Product Enthusiast: Implications for Marketing Strategy," *Journal of Consumer Marketing* 3 (Summer 1986), pp. 51–61.

29. "Survey: If You Must Know, Just Ask One of These Men," *Marketing News* (October 25, 1992), p. 13.

30. "Maximizing the Market with Influentials," *American Demographics* (July 1995), p. 42.

31. "Put People Behind the Wheel," *Advertising Age* (March 22, 1993), p. S-28.

32. "Importance of Image," *The Wall Street Journal* (August 12, 1985), p. 19; and "What Soviets Think: A Gallup Poll," *Advertising Age* (February 28, 1990), p. 46.

33. Representative work on positive and negative word of mouth can be found in Jacqueline Brown and Peter H. Reingen, "Social Ties and Word-of-Mouth Referral Behavior," *Journal of Consumer Research* (December 1987), pp. 350–62; Marc Weinberger and Jean B. Romeo, "The Impact of Negative Product News," *Business Horizons* (January–February 1989), pp. 44–50; Barry L. Bayers, "Word of Mouth: The Indirect Effects of Marketing Efforts," *Journal of Advertising Research* (June–July 1985), pp. 31–39; and Marsha L. Richins, "Negative Word of Mouth by Dissatisfied Consumers: A Pilot Study," *Journal of Marketing* (Winter 1983), pp. 68–78.

34. "Pork Rumors Vex Indonesia," *Advertising Age* (February 16, 1989), p. 36.

35. John C. Mowen, *Consumer Behavior*, 2nd ed. (New York: MacMillan, 1990), pp. 464–65.

36. William O. Beardon and Michael G. Etzel, "Reference Group Influence on Product and Brand Choice," *Journal of Consumer Research* (September 1982), pp. 183–94; and Terry L. Childers and Akshay R. Rao, "The Influence of Familial and Peer-based Reference Groups on Consumer Decisions," *Journal of Consumer Research* (September 1992), pp. 198–211.

37. "Honda Revs Up a Hip Cycle Campaign," *The Wall Street Journal* (July 31, 1989), p. B1.

38. For an extended discussion on consumer socialization, see George P. Moschis, *Consumer Socialization* (Lexington, Mass.: Lexington Books, 1987). See also Laura A. Peraccio, "How Do Young Children Learn to Be Consumers? A Script-Processing Approach," *Journal of Consumer Research* (March 1992), pp. 425–40.

39. "How Children Decide on Gifts They Want, and Plot to Get Them," *The Wall Street Journal* (December 23, 1993), pp. A1, A5.

40. This discussion is based on Robert E. Wilkes, "Household Life-Cycle Stages, Transitions, and Product Expenditures," *Journal of Consumer Research* (June 1995), pp. 27–42; *Lifestages: A Study of Dramatic Changes in the Consumer Market* (New York: J. Walter Thompson USA, 1989); Patrick E. Murphy and William A. Staples, "A Modernized Family Life Cycle," *Journal of Consumer Research* (June 1979), pp. 12–22; "Married in the 1990s," *American Demographics* (August 1992), p. 63; and "How Spending Changes During Middle Age," *The Wall Street Journal* (January 14, 1992), p. B1.

41. "What's Good for the Goose May Gag the Gander," *American Demographics* (May 1994), pp. 15–16; and Diane Crispell, "Dual-Earner Diversity," *American Demographics* (July 1995), pp. 32–36.

42. "Real Men Buy Paper Towels, Too," *Business Week* (November 9, 1992), pp. 75–76; "Women Help Van Heusen Collar Arrow," *The Wall Street Journal* (May 22, 1992), pp. B1, B5.

43. "Blow Dryers Leave Men's Hair Dry, But Their Image Slick," *The Wall Street Journal* (August 11, 1992), pp. A1, A6.

44. "Kids Market Keeps Growing Up," *Advertising Age* (May 15, 1995), pp. 3, 22.

45. For a recent description of social class structure in the United States, see Kenneth Labich, "Class in America," *Fortune* (February 7, 1994), pp. 114–26. For research on social classes in other countries, see "Gallup Offers New Take on Latin America," *Advertising Age* (November 13,

1995), p. 21; Sarah O'Brien and Rosemary Ford, "Can We at Last Say Goodbye to Social Class?" *Journal of the Market Research Society* (July 1988), pp. 289–331; and Donald W. Hendon, Emelda L. Williams, and Douglas E. Huffman, "Social Class System Revisited," *Journal of Business Research,* vol. 17 (1988), pp. 259–70.

46. For a review of this research, see Hawkins, Best, and Coney, pp. 98–102; Engel, Blackwell, and Miniard, pp. 647–57.

47. Mowen, p. 626.

48. This observation is based on a series of articles in H. P. McAdoo, ed., *Black Families* (Newbury Park, Calif.: Sage Publications, 1988).

49. "Special Report: Marketing to Hispanics," *Advertising Age* (January 23, 1995), pp. 29–37; Judith Waldrop and Thomas Exter, "What the 1990 Census Will Show," *American Demographics* (January 1990), pp. 20–30, 28–32; and Christopher Palmeri and Joshua Levine, "No Habla Espanol," *Forbes* (December 23, 1991), pp. 140–42.

50. "How Asian-Americans Make Purchasing Decisions," *Marketing News* (March 13, 1995), p. 9; "Asians in the Suburbs," *American Demographics* (May 1994), pp. 32–38; "Retail Trails Ethnic Changes," *Advertising Age* (May 1, 1995), pp. 1, 41; and "Suddenly, Asian-Americans are a Marketer's Dream," *Business Week* (June 17, 1991).

Ken Davis Products, Inc.: This case was prepared by William Rudelius.

CHAPTER 7

1. Interview courtesy of Bob Proscal, Honeywell, MICRO SWITCH Division.

2. Peter LaPlaca, "From the Editor," *Journal of Business and Industrial Marketing* (Summer 1992), p. 3.

3. Peter LaPlaca, "From the Editor," *Journal of Business and Industrial Marketing* (Winter 1988), p. 3.

4. "FAA Announces Contract for New Workstations," *Dallas Morning News* (April 30, 1995), p. 16H.

5. This discussion is based on *The Federal Register,* "Economic Classification Policy Committee: Standard Industrial Classification Replacement—The North American Industry Classification System Proposed Industry Classification Structure" (Washington, D.C.: Office of Management and Budget, July 26, 1995).

6. An argument that consumer buying and organizational buying do not have important differences is found in Edward F. Fern and James R. Brown, "The Industrial/Consumer Marketing Dichotomy: A Case of Insufficient Justification," *Journal of Marketing* (Spring 1984), pp. 68–77. However, most writers on the subject do draw distinctions between the two types of buying. See, for example, Michael D. Hutt and Thomas W. Speh, *Business Marketing Management,* 5th ed. (Ft. Worth, Tex.: The Dryden Press, 1995); and V. Kasturi Rangun, Benson P. Shapiro, and Rowland T. Moriarity, Jr., *Business Marketing Strategy* (Chicago: Richard D. Irwin, 1995).

7. This discussion is based on Robert E. Reeder, Edward G. Brierty, and Betty Reeder, *Industrial Marketing,* 2nd ed. (Englewood Cliffs, N.J.: Prentice-Hall, 1991); Robert W. Eckles, *Business Marketing Management* (Englewood Cliffs, N.J.: Prentice Hall, 1990); Frank G. Bingham, Jr., and Barney T. Raffield III, *Business to Business Marketing Management* (Homewood, Ill.: Richard D. Irwin, 1990); and Robert W. Haas, *Business Marketing Management* (Boston: PWS-Kent Publishing Company, 1992).

8. Based on "The I-Way Will Be Paved with Silicon," *Business Week* (January 9, 1995), p. 77; and *1995 U.S. Industrial Outlook* (Washington, D.C.: U.S. Department of Commerce, January 1995).

9. For a study of buying criteria used by industrial firms, see Daniel H. McQuiston and Rockney G. Walters, "The Evaluative Criteria of Industrial Buyers: Implications for Sales Training," *Journal of Business & Industrial Marketing* (Summer/Fall 1989), pp. 65–75. See also "What Buyers Look For," *Sales & Marketing Management* (August 1995), p. 31.

10. David L. Blenkhorn and Peter M. Banting, "How Reverse Marketing Changes Buyer-Seller Roles," *Industrial Marketing Management* (August 1991), pp. 185–90; and Michael R. Leenders and David L. Blenkhorn, *Reverse Marketing: The New Buyer-Supplier Relationship* (New York: The Free Press, 1988).

11. David Woodruff and Karen Lowry Miller, "Chrysler's Neon," *Business Week* (May 3, 1993), p. 119.

12. Richard N. Cardozo, Shannon H. Shipp, and Kenneth Roering, "Proactive Strategic Partnerships: A New Business Markets Strategy," *Journal of Business & Industrial Marketing* (Winter 1992), pp. 51–63.

13. For a discussion of JIT, see Gary L. Frazier, Robert E. Spekman, and Charles R. O'Neal, "Just-in-Time Exchange Relationships in Industrial Markets," *Journal of Marketing* (October 1988), pp. 52–67; Paul A.

Dion, Peter M. Banting, and Loretta M. Hasey, "The Impact of JIT on Industrial Marketers," *Industrial Marketing Management* (February 1990), pp. 41–46; and Steve McDaniel, Joseph G. Ormsby, and Alicia Gresham, "The Effect of JIT on Distributors," *Industrial Marketing Management* (May 1992), pp. 145–49.

14. Shirley Cayer, "Welcome to Caterpillar's Quality Institute," *Purchasing* (August 16, 1990), pp. 81–84.

15. Haas, *Business Marketing Management*, p. 3.

16. Mary C. LaForge and Louis H. Stone, "An Analysis of the Industrial Buying Process by Means of Buying Center Communications," *Journal of Business & Industrial Marketing* (Winter/Spring 1989), pp. 29–36.

17. "$35 Million Machine: Wires not Included," *Newsweek* (April 15, 1995), p. 25.

18. Bingham and Raffield III, p. 11.

19. This discussion is based on N. Craig Smith and John A. Quelch, *Ethics in Marketing* (Homewood, Ill.: Richard D. Irwin, 1993), p. 796; Nathaniel Gilbert, "The Case for Countertrade," *Across the Board* (May 1992), pp. 43–45; Alan J. Dubinsky, Marvin A. Jolson, Masaaki Kotobe, and Chae Un Lim," A Cross-National Investigation of Industrial Salespeople's Ethical Perceptions," *Journal of International Business Studies* (Fourth Quarter 1991), pp. 651–70; and Jacob Schlesinger, "Fenced Out," *The Wall Street Journal* (June 10, 1993), pp. A1, A9.

20. Pratibha A. Dabholkar, Wesley J. Johnston, and Amy S. Cathey, "The Dynamics of Long-Term Business-to-Business Exchange Relationships," *Journal of the Academy of Marketing Science*, vol. 22, (1994), pp. 130–45.

21. "Boeing Receives a Key Order for Airliners," *The Wall Street Journal* (March 15, 1995), pp. A3, A10.

22. This discussion is based on Robert D. Buzzell and Gwen Ortmeyer, "Channel Partnerships Streamline Distribution," *Sloan Management Review* (Spring 1995), pp. 85–96; James C. Anderson and James A. Narus, "Partnering as a Focused Market Strategy," in *Marketing Manager's Handbook,* 3rd ed. Sidney J. Levy, George R. Frerichs, and Howard L. Gordon, eds. (Chicago: The Dartnell Corporation, 1994); Paul A. Herbig and Bradley S. O'Hara, "The Future of Original Equipment Manufacturers," *Journal of Business and Industrial Marketing*, vol. 9, (1994), pp. 38–43; and Donald G. Norris, "Intel Inside," *Journal of Business & Industrial Marketing*, vol. 8, (1993), pp. 14–24.

23. Thomas V. Bonoma, "Major Sales: Who Really Does the Buying?" *Harvard Business Review* (May–June 1982), pp. 111–19. For recent work on buying groups, see Ajay Kohli, "Determinants of Influence in Organizational Buying: A Contingency Approach," *Journal of Marketing* (July 1989), pp. 50–65; and John R. Ronchetto, Jr., Michael D. Hutt, and Peter H. Reingen, "Embedded Influence Patterns in Organizational Buying Systems," *Journal of Marketing* (October 1989), pp. 51–62.

24. Carl R. Ruthstrom and Ken Matejka, "The Meaning of 'Yes' in the Far East," *Industrial Marketing Management*, vol. 19 (1990), pp. 191–92; John L. Graham and Yoshihiro Sano, "Across the Negotiating Table from the Japanese," *International Marketing Review* (Autumn 1986), pp. 58–71; and Peter Banting, Jozsef Beracs, and Andrew Gross, "The Industrial Buying Process in Capitalist and Socialist Countries," *Industrial Marketing Management* (May 1991), pp. 105–13.

25. Julia M. Bristor, "Influence Strategies in Organizational Buying: The Importance of Connections to the Right People in the Right Places," *Journal of Business-to-Business Marketing*, vol. 1 (1993), pp. 63–98; and Herbert E. Brown and Roger W. Brucker, "Charting the Industrial Buying Stream," *Industrial Marketing Management* (February 1990), pp. 55–61.

26. Based on an interview with Bob Procsal, Honeywell, MICRO SWITCH Division.

27. These definitions are adapted from Frederick E. Webster, Jr., and Yoram Wind, *Organizational Buying Behavior* (Englewood Cliffs, N.J.: Prentice-Hall, 1972), p. 6.

28. For an extensive description of 18 industrial purchases, see Arch G. Woodside and Nyren Vyas, *Industrial Purchasing Strategies: Recommendations for Purchasing and Marketing Managers* (Lexington, Mass.: Lexington Books, 1987); see also Joseph A. Bellizzi, "Business-to-Business Selling and the Organizational Buying Process," in *Marketing Manager's Handbook*, 3rd ed., Sidney J. Levy, George R. Frerichs, and Howard L. Gordon, eds. (Chicago: The Dartnell Corporation, 1994).

29. For insights into buying industrial services, see James R. Stock and Paul H. Zinszer, "The Industrial Purchase Decision for Professional Services," *Journal of Business Research* (February 1987), pp. 1–16; and Ralph W. Jackson, Lester A. Neidell, and Dale A. Lunsford, "An Empirical Investigation of Differences in Goods and Services as Perceived by Organizational Buyers," *Industrial Marketing Management*, vol. 24 (1995), pp. 99–108.

30. Patrick J. Robinson, Charles W. Faris, and Yoram Wind, *Industrial Buying and Creative Marketing* (Boston: Allyn & Bacon, 1967).

31. Recent studies on the buy-class framework that document its usefulness include Erin Anderson, Wujin Chu, and Barton Weitz, "Industrial Purchasing: An Empirical Exploration of the Buy-Class Framework," *Journal of Marketing* (July 1987), pp. 71–86; Morry Ghingold, "Testing the 'Buy-Grid' Buying Process Model," *Journal of Purchasing and Materials Management* (Winter 1986), pp. 30–36; P. Matthyssens and W. Faes, "OEM Buying Process for New Components: Purchasing and Marketing Implications," *Industrial Marketing Management* (August 1985), pp. 145–57; and Thomas W. Leigh and Arno J. Rethans, "A Script-Theoretic Analysis of Industrial Purchasing Behavior," *Journal of Marketing* (Fall 1984), pp. 22–32. Studies not supporting the buy-class framework include Joseph A. Bellizi and Philip McVey, "How Valid Is the Buy-Grid Model?" *Industrial Marketing Management* (February 1983), pp. 57–62; and Donald W. Jackson, Janet E. Keith, and Richard K. Burdick, "Purchasing Agents' Perceptions of Industrial Buying Center Influences: A Situational Approach," *Journal of Marketing* (Fall 1984), pp. 75–83.

32. See, for example, R. Venkatesh, Ajay Kohli, and Gerald Zaltman, "Influence Strategies in Buying Centers," *Journal of Marketing* (October 1995), pp. 61–72; Gary L. Lilien and Anthony Wong, "An Exploratory Investigation of the Structure of the Buying Center in the Metal Working Industry," *Journal of Marketing Research* (February 1984), pp. 1–11; and Wesley J. Johnston and Thomas V. Bonoma, "The Buying Center: Structure and Interaction Patterns," *Journal of Marketing* (Summer 1981), pp. 143–56. See also Christopher P. Puto, Wesley E. Patton III, and Ronald H. King, "Risk Handling Strategies in Industrial Vendor Selection Decisions," *Journal of Marketing* (Winter 1985), pp. 89–98.

33. Interview courtesy of Ward McClure, Industrial Automation Division, Texas Instruments.

34. Interview courtesy of David Dornbush, Alternative Pioneering System.

Energy Performance Systems, Inc.: This case was written by William Rudelius. Sources: Personal interviews with L. David Ostlie, Tom Kroll, and Paul Helgeson.

CHAPTER 8

1. Brent Schlender, "Steve Jobs' Amazing Movie Adventure," *Fortune* (September 18, 1995), pp. 155–72; and Ronald Grover, "This Movie Winds Up Old Favorites," *Time* (November 20, 1995), p. 8.

2. Ivor Davis, "Costner Braces for Opening of Notorious 'Waterworld'," *Star Tribune* (July 23, 1995), p. F3.

3. Thomas R. King, "How Big Will Disney's 'Pocahontas' Be?" *The Wall Street Journal* (May 15, 1995), pp. B1, B8.

4. Richard Turner and John R. Emshwiller, "Movie-Research Czar Is Said by Some to Sell Manipulated Findings," *The Wall Street Journal* (December 17, 1993), P. A1.

5. Helene Diamond, "Lights, Camera . . . Research!" *Marketing News* (September 11, 1989), pp. 10–11; and "Killer!" *Time* (November 16, 1987), pp. 72–79.

6. Thomas R. King, "Sad Endings: How Sure-Fire Films Flopped," *The Wall Street Journal* (February 15, 1995), pp. B1, B8.

7. "New Marketing Research Definition Approved," *Marketing News* (January 2, 1987), pp. 72–79.

8. Joseph Pereira, "Unknown Fruit Takes on Unfamiliar Markets," *The Wall Street Journal* (September 9, 1995), pp. B1, B5.

9. The bubble gum and hair dye examples are adapted from Roger Ricklefs, "Success Comes Hard in the Tricky Business of Creating Products," *The Wall Street Journal* (August 23, 1978), p. 1.

10. The definitions of marketing research suppliers are adapted from William G. Zikmund, *Exploring Marketing Research,* 5th ed. (Fort Worth, Tex.: Dryden Press, 1994).

11. Kenneth Wylie, "Special Report: Eager Marketers Driving New Globalism," *Advertising Age* (October 30, 1995), pp. 28–29.

12. Susan Feyder, "It Took Tinkering by Twin Cities Firms to Save Some Sure Bets," *Minneapolis Star Tribune* (June 9, 1982), p. 11A.

13. Cyndee Miller, "Kiddi Just Fine in the U.K., But Here It's Binky," *Marketing News* (August 28, 1995), p. 8.

14. Scott B. Dacko, "Data Collection Should not Be Manual Labor," *Marketing News* (August 28, 1995), p. 31.

15. Adapted from Donald S. Tull and Del I. Hawkins, *Marketing Research: Measurement and Method,* 5th ed. (New York: Macmillan Publishing Company, 1990), Chap. 23.

16. Personal communications with Dr. Scott Augustine, Augustine Medical, Inc.

17. Betsy D. Gelb and Gabriel M. Gelb, "New Coke's Fizzle—Lessons for the Rest of Us," *Sloan Management Review* (Fall, 1986), pp. 71–76.

Envirosell: This case was prepared by Linda Rochford of the University of Minnesota–Duluth.

CHAPTER 9

1. Kenneth Labich, "Nike vs. Reebok: A Battle for Hearts, Minds, and Feet," *Fortune* (September 18, 1995), p. 90–106.

2. Joseph Pereira, "Women Jump Ahead of Men in Purchases of Athletic Shoes," *The Wall Street Journal* (May 26, 1995), p. B1.

3. Labich, p. 106.

4. Labich, pp. 90–106; and Geoffrey Smith, "Sneakers That Jump into the Past," *Business Week* (March 13, 1995), p. 71.

5. "Shoe for Hoops Named after Sheryl Swoopes," *Star Tribune* (October 29, 1995), p. E4.

6. Issues in using market segmentation studies are described in William Rudelius, John R. Walton, and James C. Cross, "Improving the Managerial Relevance of Market Segmentation Studies," in Michael J. Houston, ed., *1987 Review of Marketing* (Chicago: American Marketing Association, 1987), pp. 385–404.

7. Clara Germani, "Chicken for Russia," *Star Tribune* (October 20, 1995), pp. D1, D6.

8. Laura Zinn, "Real Men Buy Paper Towels, Too," *Business Week* (November 9, 1992), pp. 75–76.

9. Jean C. Darian and Judy Cohen, "Segmenting by Consumer Time Shortage," *Journal of Consumer Marketing,* vol. 12 (1995), pp. 32–44; Bill Saporito, "What's for Dinner?" *Fortune* (May 15, 1995), pp. 50–64; and Susan Chandler, "The Grocery Cart in Your PC," *Business Week* (September 11, 1995), pp. 63–64.

10. Robert Metz, "Apple Now a Strong Investment," *Minneapolis Star Tribune* (October 1, 1987), p. 2M.

11. Jim Carlton, "Apple's Choice: Preserve Profits or Cut Prices," *The Wall Street Journal* (February 22, 1995), pp. B1, B4.

12. Kathy Rebello, "Apple's Assault," *Business Week* (June 12, 1995), pp. 98–99.

13. Peter Burows and Kathy Rebello, "Is Spindler a Survivor?" *Business Week* (October 2, 1995), p. 62; "Apple Lowers Prices on its Macintosh Computers," *Star Tribune* (October 17, 1995), p. D4; and Jim Carlton, "Apple Reduces Prices on Line of Power Macs," *The Wall Street Journal* (August 7, 1995), pp. B1, B3.

14. Jim Carlton, "What's Eating Apple? Computer Maker Hits Some Serious Snags," *The Wall Street Journal* (September 21, 1995), pp. A1, A8; Julie Pitta, "Apple Braces for Windows 95," *Star Tribune* (September 17, 1995), p. 5D; and Jim Carlton, "Apple's Net Fell 48% in 4th Quarter as Computer Shortages Hurt Results," *The Wall Street Journal* (October 19, 1995), p. B10.

15. Jim Carlton, "Apple Is Facing Widespread Shortages of Its Products," *The Wall Street Journal* (August 11, 1995), p. B8.

16. Pitta, p. 5D.

17. Rebello, p. 98.

18. Bart Ziegler, "PC Makers Big Push into the Home Market Comes at Risky Time," *The Wall Street Journal* (November 1, 1995), pp. A1, A13.

19. Advantages and disadvantages of cross tabulations are adapted from Roseann Maguire and Terry C. Wilson, "Banners or Cross Tabs? Before Deciding, Weigh Data-Format, Pros, Cons," *Marketing News* (May 13, 1983), pp. 10–11.

20. Andrew Purris, "Cheaper Can Be Better," *Time* (March 18, 1991), p. 70.

21. Alex Taylor III, "GM's $11,000,000,000 Turnaround," *Fortune* (October 17, 1994), pp. 54–74; David Woodruff and Mark Maremont, "GM Learns to Love an Outsider," *Business Week* (July 3, 1995), p. 32; Alex Taylor III, "GM: Some Gain, Much Pain," *Fortune* (May 29, 1995), pp. 78–84; Jesse Snyder, "4 GM Car Divisions Are Repositioned in an effort to Help Sales," *Automotive News* (September 15, 1986), pp. 1, 49; and Joseph B. White, "GM Puts Low Price on Saturn to Sell in Small-Car Field," *The Wall Street Journal* (October 5, 1990), pp. B1, B6.

22. Gabriella Stern, "As Old Cadillac Buyers Age, the GM Division Fights to Halt Slippage," *The Wall Street Journal* (August 24, 1995), pp. A1, A9.

Paisley Park Records: This case was prepared by Tom Davies from a personal interview with Alan Leeds.

CHAPTER 10

1. Raymond Serafin and Julie Ralston, "Jeep Sets Up Camp to Help Build Stronger Bonds with Owners," *Advertising Age* (June 26, 1995), p. 40; Don Peppers and Martha Rogers, "Ask the Marketing Doctors," *Inc.* (October 1995), pp. 68–70; Jonathan Berry, John Verity, Kathleen Kerwin, and Gail DeGeorge, "A Potent New Tool for Selling: Database Marketing," *Business Week* (September 5, 1994), pp. 56–62; Sally Apgar, "Fingerhut Wins with a Personal Touch," *Star Tribune* (November 25, 1991), pp. 1D, 4D; and Robert C. Blattberg and John Deighton, "Interactive Marketing: Exploiting the Age of Addressability," *Business Edge* (May 1992), pp. 12–17.

2. Adapted from David Shani and Sujana Chalasani, "Exploiting Niches Using Relationship Marketing," *Journal of Consumer Marketing* (Summer 1992), pp. 33–42.

3. Jeffrey F. Rayport and John J. Sviokla, "Exploiting the Virtual Value Chain," *Harvard Business Review* (November–December 1995), pp. 75–85; Robert Benjamin and Rolf Wigand, "Electronic Markets and Virtual Value Chains on the Information Superhighway," *Sloan Management Review* (Winter 1995), pp. 62–72; and Jeffrey F. Rayport and John J. Sviokla, "Managing in the Marketspace," *Harvard Business Review* (November–December 1994), pp. 141–50.

4. Bill Gates, *The Road Ahead* (New York: Viking, 1995); Gary McWilliams, "Small Fry Go Online," *Business Week* (November 20, 1995), pp. 158–64; and Rayport and Sviokla.

5. Antonio Kovacevic and Nicolas Majluf, "Six Stages of IT Strategic Management," *Sloan Management Review* (Summer 1993), pp. 77–87.

6. Michael J. McCarthy, "What Micromarketing Taught Our Reporter about His A&P," *The Wall Street Journal* (March 18, 1991), p. B1.

7. Julie Tilsner, "Lillian Vernon: Creating a Host of Spin-offs from Its Core Catalog," *Business Week* (December 19, 1994), p. 85; and Lisa Coleman, "I Went Out and Did It," *Forbes* (August 17, 1992), pp. 102–04.

8. Don Peppers and Martha Rogers, *The One to One Future: Building Relationships One Customer at a Time,* (New York: Doubleday, 1993).

9. Mark Gleason, "Time to Perform or Perish," *Advertising Age* (October 2, 1995), p. 32; and Bradley Johnson, "Behind All the Hype Lies a Hidden, Crucial Asset," *Advertising Age* (October 2, 1995), pp. 30, 32.

10. Shelby D. Hunt and Robert M. Morgan, "Relationship Marketing in the Era of Network Competition," *Marketing Management* no. 1 (1994), pp. 19–27.

11. Richard S. Teitelbaum, "Companies to Watch: Viking Office Products," *Fortune* (November 30, 1992), p. 87.

12. Max D. Hopper, "Rattling SABRE—New Ways to Compete on Information," *Harvard Business Review* (May–June 1990), pp. 118–25; and F. Warren McFarlan and James C. Wetherbe, "SABRE Rattling and the Future of the Chief Information Officer," *Harvard Business Review* (July–August 1990), pp. 176–77.

13. *American Airlines, Inc.: Revenue Management* (Boston, Mass.: HBS Case Services, Harvard Business School, 1989), pp. 3–7.

14. Wendy Zellner, "Putting a Keener Edge on SABRE," *Business Week* (October 23, 1995), p. 118.

15. Faye Rice, "How to Deal with Tougher Customers," *Fortune* (December 3, 1990), pp. 39–48.

16. Frank Rose, "Now Quality Means Service Too," *Fortune* (April 22, 1991), pp. 99–100; Patricia Sellers, "What Customers Really Want," *Fortune* (June 4, 1990), pp. 58–68; and Anne B. Fisher, "What Consumers Want in the 1990s," *Fortune* (January 29, 1990), pp. 108–12.

17. Rose, p. 102.

18. Gary Levin, "Media Ads Blasted for Loss of Impact," *Advertising Age* (November 2, 1992), p. 14.

19. Laura Loro, "Package Goods Expands Database," *Advertising Age* (August 14, 1995), p. 29; Berry, Verity, Kerwin, and DeGeorge.

20. Gary Levin, "Package-Goods Giants Embrace Databases," *Advertising Age* (November 2, 1992), p. 1, 37.

21. Levin, "Package-Goods Giants Embrace Databases," p. 37.

22. Frank V. Cespedes and H. Jeff Smith, "Database Marketing: New Rules for Policy and Practice," *Sloan Management Review* (Summer 1993), pp. 7–22.

23. Dom Del Prete, "Advances in Scanner Research Yield Better Data Quicker," *Marketing News* (January 7, 1991), p. 54.

24. Jeremy Main, "Computers of the World, Unite!" *Fortune* (September 24, 1990), pp. 115–22.

25. Laurence N. Gold, "High Technology Data Collection for Measurement and Testing," *Marketing Research* (March 1992), pp. 29–38.
26. Joe Schwartz, "Back to the Source," *American Demographics* (January 1989), pp. 22–26; and Felix Kessler, "High-Tech Shocks in Ad Research," *Fortune* (July 7, 1986), pp. 58–62.
27. Chad Rubel, "CD-ROM Takes a Back Seat to Other Tools," *Marketing News* (January 15, 1996), p. 10.
28. W. Steven Perkins and Ram C. Rao, "The Role of Experience in Information Use and Decision Making by Marketing Managers," *Journal of Marketing Research* (February 1990), pp. 1–10.
29. Regis McKenna, *Relationship Marketing* (Reading, Mass.: Addison-Wesley, 1991).
30. Richard S. Teitelbaum, "Reader's Digest: Are Times Tough? Here's an Answer," *Fortune* (December 2, 1991), pp. 101–02.
31. William Keenan, Jr., "Numbers Racket," *Sales and Marketing Management* (May 1995), pp. 64–76.
32. "Analyzing Promotions: The Free-Standing Insert Coupon," *Nielsen Researchers*, no. 4 (1982), pp. 16–20.
UPS (A): This case was prepared by Linda Rochford of the University of Minnesota–Duluth. Sources: Laurie M. Grossman, "Federal Express, UPS Face Off on Computers," *The Wall Street Journal* (September 17, 1993), pp. B1, B6; "UPS Awarded $1 Billion JC Penney Contract: Extends Partnership into Year 2000," UPS Home Page.

CHAPTER 11

1. John J. Oslund, "More than Meets the Eye," *Star Tribune* (May 8, 1995), pp. 1D, 4D.
2. Bob Kearney, "Joining Forces: 3M Puts Stock in Bonding," *3M Today* (January, 1995), pp. 2–5.
3. "Ribbon Sales All Tied Up with Home Shopping Network," *3M Stemwinder* (January 18, 1995), p. 3.
4. Definitions within this section are from Committee on Definitions, *Marketing Definitions: A Glossary of Marketing Terms* (Chicago: American Marketing Association, 1960).
5. Brenton R. Schlender, "How Sony Keeps the Magic Growing," *Fortune* (February 24, 1992), pp. 76–84.
6. R. G. Cooper and E. J. Kleinschmidt, "New Products—What Separates Winners from Losers?" *Journal of Product Innovation Management* (September 1987), pp. 169–84. Copyright © 1987 by Elsevier Science Publishing Co., Inc.; and Robert G. Cooper, *Winning at New Products*, 2nd ed. (Reading, Mass.: Addison-Wesley Publishing, 1993), pp. 49–66.
7. An example is the Stanford Innovation Project studies of the U.S. electronics industry, whose results are reported in B. J. Zirger and M. A. Maidique, "A Model of New Product Development: An Empirical Test," *Management Science* (July 1990), pp. 867–83.
8. Greg Burns, "Has General Mills Had Its Wheaties?" *Business Week* (May 8, 1995), pp. 68–69.
9. Fara Warner, "On-Line Services Try to Define Their Identities," *The Wall Street Journal* (July 12, 1995), p. B1.
10. John Gilbert, "To Sell Cars in Japan, U.S. Needs to Offer More Right-Drive Models," *Star Tribune* (May 27, 1995), p. M1.
11. John Helyar, "Licensed Sports Gear Takes a Hit from Alienated Fans," *The Wall Street Journal* (February 23, 1995), pp. B1, B10.
12. James Walsh, "New Products Elbow for Space on Grocery Shelf," *Star Tribune* (June 7, 1995), p. T1.
13. Larry Armstrong, "Channel-Surfing's Next Wave," *Business Week* (July 31, 1995), pp. 90–91.
14. "They're Still Talkin' about 'Team Talk'," *3M Stemwinder* (May 17, 1995), pp. 1, 4.
15. Thomas M. Burton, "Drug Company Looks to 'Witch Doctors' to Conjure Products," *The Wall Street Journal* (July 7, 1994), pp. A1, A4; and letter from Professor Goran Hellekant, University of Wisconsin-Madison dated January 9, 1995.
16. William M. Bulkeley, "Scientists Try to Make Broccoli 'Fun'," *The Wall Street Journal* (July 17, 1995), pp. B1, B3.
17. Steve Alexander, "New Product Machine," *Star Tribune* (June 5, 1995), pp. 1D, 4D.
18. Don Clark, "Amid Hype and Fear, Microsoft Windows 95 Gets Ready to Roll," *The Wall Street Journal* (July 14, 1995), pp. A1, A4.
19. Stephanie Simon, "Imposter Merchandise," *Star Tribune* (July 7, 1995), p. 1D; and Anne O'Connor, "Investigators Wrinkle Plans of Clothing Counterfeiters," *Star Tribune* (August 4, 1995), p. 3B.
20. William M. Carley, "Engine Troubles Put GE Behind in Race to Power New 777s," *The Wall Street Journal* (July 12, 1995), pp. A1, A6.
21. Gabriella Stern, "GM Puts off Launch of Some Models," *The Wall Street Journal* (August 4, 1995), pp. A4, A12.
American Harvest: This case was prepared by William Rudelius. Sources: Personal interviews with David Dornbush and Chad Erickson.

CHAPTER 12

1. "Can Coke and Pepsi Make Quaker Sweat?" *Fortune* (July 10, 1995), p. 20; "Gatorade Rivals Will Heat Up Summer," *Advertising Age* (May 1, 1995), p. 29; "Gatorade Is Starting to Pant," *Business Week* (April 18, 1994), p. 98; "The Sultan of Swamp," *Beverage World* (October 1994), pp. 88–92; and "Mega-brands of the 100 Leading National Advertisers," *Advertising Age* (September 27, 1995), p. 34.
2. For an extended discussion of the generalized product life-cycle curve, see David M. Gardner, "Product Life Cycle: A Critical Look at the Literature," in Michael Houston, ed., *1987 Review of Marketing* (Chicago: American Marketing Association, 1987), pp. 162–94.
3. "The SunChip Also Rises," *Advertising Age* (April 27, 1992), p. S2, S6; "Gillette to Launch Women's Sensor," *Advertising Age* (February 10, 1992), p. 36.
4. Orville C. Walker, Jr., Harper W. Boyd, Jr., and Jean-Claude Larréché, *Marketing Strategy,* 2nd ed. (Chicago: Richard D. Irwin, 1996), p. 215.
5. Portions of the discussion on the fax machine industry are based on "U.S. SemiCon Corporation: Facsimile Technology Program," in Roger A. Kerin and Robert A. Peterson, *Strategic Marketing Problems: Cases and Comments,* 7th ed. (New York: Prentice-Hall, Inc., 1995), pp. 454–67; "The Fax Gets a Face-Lift," *Business Week* (November 7, 1994), p. 15; and "Fax-on-Demand Grows," *ComputerWorld* (January 17, 1995), p. 59.
6. "Shocker at GM: People Like the Impact," *Business Week* (January 23, 1995), p. 47; Alex Taylor III, "Why Electric Cars Make No Sense," *Fortune* (July 26, 1993), pp. 126–27; "Saturn May Market GM's Electric Vehicles," *Automotive News* (March 13, 1995), p. 6; "French EVs Hinted for Calif.," *Automotive News* (March 14, 1994), pp. 1, 47; and "Ford Electric Truck Set for California," *The New York Times* (June 14, 1995), p. D19.
7. Lawrence P. Feldman and Albert L. Page, "Harvesting: The Misunderstood Market Exit Strategy," *Journal of Business Strategy* (Spring 1985), pp. 79–85.
8. "Car Bodies Can Sport Tatoos Too," *Advertising Age* (January 11, 1993), p. 12; "Making the Cut in a Retail Niche Driven by Fads," *The Wall Street Journal* (September 25, 1995), pp. B1, B2.
9. Based on "Sega Leaps Ahead by Shipping New Player Early," *The Wall Street Journal* (May 11, 1995), pp. B1, B4; "The Christmas Videogame Massacre," *The Economist* (November 19, 1994), p. 71; and "Sega!" *Business Week* (February 21, 1994), pp. 66–74.
10. Everett M. Rogers, *Diffusion of Innovations,* 3rd ed. (New York: The Free Press, 1983).
11. S. Ram and Jagdish N. Sheth, "Consumer Resistance to Innovation: The Marketing Problem and Its Solution," *Journal of Consumer Marketing* (Spring 1989), pp. 5–14.
12. "Everyone Is Bellying Up to This Bar," *Business Week* (January 27, 1992), p. 84.
13. For an historical perspective on the product/brand manager system, see George S. Low and Ronald A. Fullerton, "Brands, Brand Management, and the Brand Manager System: A Critical-Historical Evaluation," *Journal of Marketing Research* (May 1994), pp. 173–90.
14. "Haggar, Farah, Levi's Iron Out the Wrinkles," *Advertising Age* (March 6, 1995), p. 12; and "Modified Screwdrivers May Prevent Slips," *The Wall Street Journal* (March 1, 1990), p. B1.
15. "Brand Scorecard: Premium Products Lather Up Sales," *Advertising Age* (July 24, 1995), p. 24; and "Vitamin Shampoo Brings Shine to P&G Profits," *The Wall Street Journal* (October 21, 1993), pp. B1, B7.
16. "P&G Plans Big New Ivory Push," *Advertising Age* (November 23, 1992), p. 12; and "P&G's Soap Opera: New Ivory Bar Hits the Bottom of a Tub," *The Wall Street Journal* (October 23, 1992), p. B11.
17. Bob Geiger, "Liquid Yogurts Pour in the U.S.," *Advertising Age* (June 1, 1987), pp. 3, 62.
18. Cyndee Miller, "Food Producers Appeal to Fat-Free Crowd," *Marketing News* (August 14, 1995), p. 3.
19. "Et tu, Brut?" *Consumer Reports* (March 1992), p. 205.
20. "Marketers Try to Ease Sting of Price Increases," *Marketing News* (October 9, 1995), pp. 5–6; "It's the Pits," *Consumer Reports* (February

1992), p. 203; and John B. Hinge, "Critics Call Cuts in Package Size Deceptive Move," *The Wall Street Journal* (February 5, 1991), pp. B1, B8.

21. "Hello Mother Russia: Smirnoff Returns to Its Roots," *The New York Times* (May 5, 1995), p. D6; "Smirnoff Distributor Continues Battle for Name," *The Dallas Morning News* (September 22, 1995), p. 11D; and "Vodka Battle Continues for Smirnoff Name in Russia," *Advertising Age* (February 15, 1993), p. I-8.

22. For an extended treatment of brand equity, see David Aaker, *Managing Brand Equity* (New York: The Free Press, 1991); also see, Betsy Morris, "The Brand's the Thing," *Fortune* (March 4, 1996), pp. 72–86.

23. "Corporations Latch onto Licensing," *Advertising Age* (August 14, 1995), p. 28.

24. "Ruffles Makes Waves in Israel," *Advertising Age* (November 23, 1992), p. J-12.

25. Daniel L. Doden, "Selecting a Brand Name that Aids Marketing Objectives," *Advertising Age* (November 5, 1990), p. 34.

26. "Buying the Ranch on Brand Equity," *Brandweek* (October 26, 1992), p. 6; and "Kellogg Changes Name of Controversial Cereal," *Marketing News* (August 19, 1991), p. 22.

27. "A Survey of Multinationals," *The Economist* (June 24, 1995), p. 8.

28. For a review of brand extensions, see David A. Aaker and Kevin Lane Keller, "Consumer Evaluations of Brand Extension," *Journal of Marketing* (January 1990), pp. 27–41.

29. "Missteps Mar Church & Dwight's Plans," *The Wall Street Journal* (April 28, 1995), p. B5.

30. "Mixed Companies," *The Dallas Morning News* (June 8, 1995), pp. 1F, 4F. For an in-depth discussion on co-branding, see Akshay R. Rao and Robert W. Ruekert, "Brand Alliances as Signals of Product Quality," *Sloan Management Review* (Fall 1994), pp. 87–97.

31. "Brands Fight Back Against Private Labels," *Marketing News* (January 16, 1995), pp. 8–9.

32. "Kodak Pursues a Greater Market Share in Japan with New Private-Label Film," *The Wall Street Journal* (March 7, 1995), p. B11.

33. *These Prices Are Killing Us: What Brand-Driven Marketers Must Do to Combat Price-Based Competition* (New York: Bates Advertising USA, Inc., 1994).

34. "The National Peztime," *The Dallas Morning News* (October 9, 1995), pp. 1C, 2C; and David Welch, *Collecting Pez* (Murphysboro, IL: Bubba Scrubba Publications, 1995).

35. Fred W. Morgan, "Tampered Goods: Legal Developments and Marketing Guidelines," *Journal of Marketing* (April 1988), pp. 86–96.

36. "Coca-Cola Finds Success Trading New for the Old," *The Wall Street Journal* (March 24, 1995), p. B5.

37. Carl McDaniel and R. C. Baker, "Convenience Food Packaging and the Perception of Product Quality," *Journal of Marketing* (October 1977), pp. 57–58.

38. "Which Hue Is Best? Test Your Color I.Q.," *Advertising Age* (September 14, 1987), pp. 18, 20.

39. "Supreme Court to Rule on Colors as Trademarks," *Marketing News* (January 2, 1995), p. 28.

40. This discussion is based, in part, on Barry N. Rosen and George B. Sloane III, "Environmental Product Standards, Trade and European Consumer Goods Marketing," *Columbia Journal of World Business* (Spring 1995), pp. 74–86; "Life Ever After," *The Economist* (October 9, 1993), p. 77; and "How to Make Lots of Money, and Save the Planet Too," *The Economist* (June 3, 1995), pp. 57–58.

41. This example is based on John A. Quelch, "The Procter & Gamble Company: The Lenor Refill Package," Harvard Business School case N9-592-016; and "Procter and Gamble, Inc.: Downy Enviro-Pak," University of Western Ontario Case 9-90-A006.

42. Paula Mergenbagen, "Product Liability: Who Sues?" *American Demographics* (June 1995), pp. 48–54; "Bottled Up," *The Economist* (December 17, 1994), p. 69.

43. Sonia L. Nazario, "Microwave Packages that Add Crunch to Lunch May also Pose Chemical Risks," *The Wall Street Journal* (March 1, 1990), pp. B1, B6.

Golden Valley Microwave Foods, Inc.: This case was prepared by William Rudelius. Sources: Personal interviews with James Watkins and Sara Risch.

CHAPTER 13

1. Sandra Dallas and Gary McWilliams, "Going To Extremes—To Lure the Hot Dogs Back," *Business Week* (March 13, 1995), p. 100; Sandra Dallas, "How Purgatory Is Climbing Out of Hell," *Business Week* (November 27, 1995), p. 132; Roy Furchgott, "Downhill Biker: Cycling the Ski Slopes," *Business Week* (July 10, 1995), p. 134; and Sandra Atchinson, Evan Schwartz, and Gregory Sandler, "At These Prices Who Needs the Alps?" *Business Week* (February 10, 1992), p. 131.

2. *Survey of Current Business* (Washington, D.C.: U.S. Department of Commerce, January 1993); John Greenwald, "The New Service Class," *Time* (November 14, 1994), pp. 72–73; and Amy Borrus and Ronald Grover, "Suddenly, Services Aren't Such World Beaters," *Business Week* (September 18, 1995), p. 45.

3. Susan Greco, "The Road to One to One Marketing," *Inc.* (October 1995), pp. 56–66; Chad Rubel, "Banks Go Mobile to Serve Low-Income Areas," *Marketing News* (November 20, 1995), p. 12; Kelly Shermach, "Movie Reviews Go Interactive," *Marketing News* (June 19, 1995), p. 8; and Cyndee Miller, "An Oasis of Hip Consumers," *Marketing News* (February 19, 1990), p. 2.

4. Frederick F. Reichheld and W. Earl Sasser, Jr., "Zero Defections: Quality Comes to Services," *Harvard Business Review* (September–October 1990), pp. 105–11; "Standardized Services Run Gamut from Mufflers to Wills," *Marketing News* (April 10, 1987), pp. 17, 43; and Valarie A. Zeithaml, Leonard Berry, and A. Parasuraman, "Communication and Control in the Delivery of Service Quality," *Journal of Marketing* (April 1988), pp. 35–48.

5. Howard Schlossberg, "Electric Utilities Finally Discover Marketing," *Marketing News* (November 20, 1989), pp. 1, 2.

6. Paul Magnusson, "It's Open Season on Nonprofits," *Business Week* (July 3, 1995), p. 31.

7. Ani Hadjian, "Follow the Leader," *Fortune* (November 27, 1995), p. 96; John A. Byrne, "Profiting from the Nonprofits," *Business Week* (March 26, 1990), pp. 66–74; Kathleen Vyn, "Nonprofits Learn How-to's of Marketing," *Marketing News* (August 14, 1989), pp. 1–2; and Peter Drucker, "What Businesses Can Learn from Nonprofits," *Harvard Business Review* (July–August 1989), pp. 88–93.

8. Anne Faircloth, "The World Takes on the USPS," *Fortune* (July 24, 1995), p. 28; Christy Fisher, "Postal Service Looks to Stamp Out Woes," *Advertising Age* (September 12, 1994), p. 4; and Cyndee Miller, "U.S. Postal Service Discovers the Merits of Marketing," *Marketing News* (February 1, 1993), pp. 9, 18.

9. Keith B. Murray, "A Test of Services Marketing Theory: Consumer Information Acquisition Activities," *Journal of Marketing* (January 1991), pp. 10–25.

10. Dawn Iacobucci, "An Empirical Examination of Some Basic Tenets in Services: Goods-Services Continua," Teresa Swartz, David E. Bowen, and Stephen W. Brown, eds., in *Advances in Services Marketing and Management,* vol. 1 (Greenwich, Conn.: JAI Press), pp. 23–52; and Valarie A. Zeithaml, "How Consumer Evaluation Processes Differ Between Goods and Services," in James H. Donnelly and William R. George, eds., *Marketing of Services* (Chicago: American Marketing Association, 1981).

11. Murray.

12. John Ozment and Edward Morash, "The Augmented Service Offering for Perceived and Actual Service Quality," *Journal of the Academy of Marketing Science* (Fall 1994), pp. 352–63.

13. A. Parasuraman, Valarie A. Zeithaml, and Leonard L. Berry, "Reassessment of Expectations as a Comparison Standard in Measuring Service Quality: Implications for Further Research," *Journal of Marketing* (January 1994), pp. 111–24; and Leonard L. Berry, *On Great Service* (New York: Free Press, 1995).

14. Valerie A. Zeithaml, A. Parasuraman and Leonard L. Berry, *Delivering Quality Service* (New York: Free Press, 1990); and Stephen W. Brown and Teresa Swartz, "A Gap Analysis of Professional Service Quality," *Journal of Marketing* (April 1989), pp. 92–98.

15. Amy Ostrom and Dawn Iacobucci, "Consumer Trade-Offs and the Evaluation of Services," *Journal of Marketing* (January 1995), pp. 17–28; and J. Joseph Cronin, Jr., and Steven A. Taylor, "Measuring Service Quality: A Reexamination and Extension," *Journal of Marketing* (July 1992), pp. 55–68.

16. "Burger King Opens Customer Hot Line," *Marketing News* (May 28, 1990), p. 7.

17. Vicki Clift, "Everyone Needs Service Flow Charting," *Marketing News* (October 23, 1995), pp. 41, 43; Mary Jo Bitner, Bernard H. Booms, and Mary Stanfield Tetreault, "The Service Encounter: Diagnosing Favorable and Unfavorable Incidents," *Journal of Marketing* (January 1990), pp. 71–84; Eberhard Scheuing, "Conducting Customer Service Audits," *Journal of Consumer Marketing* (Summer 1989), pp. 35–41; and W. Earl

Sasser, R. Paul Olsen, and D. Daryl Wyckoff, *Management of Service Operations* (Boston: Allyn & Bacon, 1978).

18. "Services Marketers Must Balance Customer Satisfaction Against Their Operational Needs," *Marketing News* (October 10, 1986), pp. 1, 14.

19. Thomas S. Gruca, "Defending Service Markets," *Marketing Management* (1994 No. 1), pp. 31–38; and Leonard L. Berry, Jeffrey S. Conant, and A. Parasuraman, "A Framework for Conducting a Services Marketing Audit," *Journal of the Academy of Marketing Science* (Summer 1991), pp. 255–68.

20. Patriya Tansuhaj, Donna Randall, and Jim McCullough, "A Services Marketing Management Model: Integrating Internal and External Marketing Functions," *Journal of Services Marketing* (Winter 1988), pp. 31–38.

21. Christian Gronroos, "Internal Marketing Theory and Practice," in Tim Bloch, G. D. Upah, and V. A. Zeithaml, eds., *Services Marketing in a Changing Environment* (Chicago: American Marketing Association, 1984).

22. Ibid.

23. Scott W. Kelly, "Developing Customer Orientation among Service Employees," *Journal of the Academy of Marketing Science* (Winter 1992), pp. 27–36; Sybil F. Stershic, "Internal Marketing Campaign Reinforces Service Goals," *Marketing News* (July 31, 1989), p. 11; James L. Heskett, "Lessons in the Service Sector," *Harvard Business Review* (March–April 1987), pp. 118–26; Leonard Berry, "Big Ideas in Services Marketing," *Journal of Consumer Marketing* (Spring 1986), pp. 47–51; and Ray Lewis, "Whose Job Is Service Marketing?" *Advertising Age* (August 3, 1987), pp. 18, 20.

24. David E. Bowen and Edward E. Lawler III, "Empowering Service Employees," *Sloan Management Review* (Summer 1995), pp. 73–84; James Hirsch, "Now Hotel Clerks Provide More Than Keys," *The Wall Street Journal* (March 5, 1993), pp. B1, B2; Christopher W. L. Hart, Leonard A. Schlesinger, and Dan Maher, "Guarantees Come to Professional Service Firms," *Sloan Management Review* (Spring 1992), pp. 19–29; and Michael J. Showalter and Judith A. Mulholland, "Continuous Improvement Strategies for Service Organizations," *Business Horizons* (July–August 1992), pp. 82–87.

25. Dan R. E. Thomas, "Strategy Is Different in Service Businesses," *Harvard Business Review* (July–August 1978), pp. 158–65.

26. Haim Oren, "Branding Financial Services Helps Consumers Find Order in Chaos," *Marketing News* (March 29, 1993), p. 6; and Leonard L. Berry, Edwin F. Lefkowith, and Terry Clark, "In Services, What's in a Name?" *Harvard Business Review* (September–October 1988), pp. 28–30.

27. Frederick H. deB. Harris and Peter Peacock, "Hold My Place, Please," *Marketing Management* (Fall 1995), pp. 34–46.

28. Christopher Lovelock, *Services Marketing* (Englewood Cliffs, N.J.: Prentice Hall, 1991), pp. 122–27.

29. Kent B. Monroe, "Buyer's Subjective Perceptions of Price," *Journal of Marketing Research* (February 1973), pp. 70–80; and Jerry Olson, "Price as an Informational Cue: Effects on Product Evaluation," in A. G. Woodside, J. N. Sheth, and P. D. Bennett, eds., *Consumer and Industrial Buying Behavior* (New York: Elsevier North-Holland, 1977), pp. 267–86.

30. B. D. Colen, "Hospitals Turn to Advertising," *Washington Post* (June 25, 1979), pp. 1, 6A.

31. Robert E. Hite, Cynthia Fraser, and Joseph A. Bellizzi, "Professional Service Advertising: The Effects of Price Inclusion, Justification, and Level of Risk," *Journal of Advertising Research* 30 (August/September 1990), pp. 23–31; William R. George and Leonard L. Berry, "Guidelines for the Advertising of Services," *Business Horizons* (July–August 1981), pp. 52–56; and Eugene M. Johnson, Eberhard E. Scheuing, and Kathleen A. Gaida, *Profitable Service Marketing* (Homewood, Ill.; Dow Jones-Irwin, 1986).

32. Sak Onkvisit and John J. Shaw, "Service Marketing: Image, Branding, and Competition," *Business Horizons* (January–February 1989), pp. 13–18.

33. *Bates and O'Sheen* v. *State of Arizona,* 433 U.S. 350, 391–395 (1977); and "Supreme Court Opens Way for Lawyers to Advertise Prices for Routine Services," *The Wall Street Journal* (June 28, 1977), p. 4.

34. "Blond Ambition," *ABA Journal* (January 1996), p. 12.

35. Joe Adams, "Why Public Service Advertising Doesn't Work," *Ad Week* (November 17, 1980), p. 72.

36. Thomas A. Stewart, "A New 500 for the New Economy," *Fortune* (May 15, 1995), pp. 166–78; Philip Elmer-Dewitt, "Mine, All Mine," *Time* (June 5, 1995), pp. 46–54; and James Brian Quinn and Penny C. Paquette, "Technology in Services: Creating Organizational Revolutions," *Sloan Management Review* (Winter 1990), pp. 67–78.

37. Anne B. Fisher, "What Consumers Want in the 1990s," *Fortune* (January 29, 1990), pp. 108–12.

38. Mark L. Clifford, "A Vein of Gold in the Bush," *Business Week* (December 4, 1995), p. 28; Suzanne Oliver, "Ecoprofitable," *Forbes* (June 20, 1994), p. 110; Pamela Wight, "Ecotourism: Ethics or Eco-Sell?" *Journal of Travel Research* (Winter 1993), pp. 3–9; and Louis J. D'Amore, "A Code of Ethics and Guidelines for Socially and Environmentally Responsible Tourism," *Journal of Travel Research* (Winter 1993), pp. 64–66.

The Philadelphia Phillies, Inc.: This case was prepared by William Rudelius. Sources: *Phillies Yearbook* and personal interviews with Philadelphia Phillies executives: David Montgomery, executive vice president; Dennis Mannion, director of marketing; and Jo-Anne Lery, assistant director of marketing.

CHAPTER 14

1. *Boeing 1995 Annual Report* (Seattle: The Boeing Company, 1996); and *Boeing 1994 Annual Report* (Seattle: The Boeing Company, 1995).

2. Valerie Reitman and Jathon Sapsford, "To See Issues Vexing Japanese Business Now, Consider JAL Flight 176," *The Wall Street Journal* (August 9, 1994), pp. A1, A6.

3. Jeff Cole, "Boeing Is Offering Cuts in Prices of New Jets, Rattling the Industry," *The Wall Street Journal* (April 24, 1995), pp. A1, A8.

4. Alex Taylor III, "Boeing: Sleepy in Seattle," *Fortune* (August 7, 1995), pp. 92–98.

5. This box is based on Boeing 1995 Annual Report; Boeing 1994 Annual Report; Cole; Taylor; and Alison L. Sprout, "How to Sit Pretty in the Boeing 777," *Fortune* (August 7, 1995), p. 29.

6. Sprout.

7. Raymond Sarafin, "Even Lamborghini Must Think Marketing," *Advertising Age* (May 1, 1995), p. 32.

8. Adapted from Kent B. Monroe, *Pricing: Making Profitable Decisions,* 2nd ed. (New York: McGraw-Hill, 1990), chapter 4. See also David J. Curry, "Measuring Price and Quality Competition," *Journal of Marketing* (Spring 1985), pp. 106–17.

9. Numerous studies have examined the price-quality-value relationship. See, for example, Jacob Jacoby and Jerry C. Olsen, eds., *Perceived Quality* (Lexington, Mass.: Lexington Books, 1985); Kent B. Monroe and William B. Dodds, "A Research Program for Establishing the Validity of the Price-Quality Relationship," *Journal of the Academy of Marketing Science* (Spring 1988), pp. 151–68; Askay R. Rao and Kent B. Monroe, "The Effect of Price, Brand Name, and Store Name on Buyers' Perceptions of Product Quality: An Integrative Review," *Journal of Marketing Research* (August 1989), pp. 351–57; William B. Dodds, Kent B. Monroe, and Dhruv Grewal, "Effects of Price, Brand, and Store Information on Buyers' Product Evaluations," *Journal of Marketing Research* (August 1991), pp. 307–19; and Roger A. Kerin, Ambuj Jain, and Daniel J. Howard, "Store Shopping Experience and Consumer Price-Quality-Value Perceptions," *Journal of Retailing* (Winter 1992), pp. 235–45. For a thorough review of the price-quality-value relationship, see Valarie A. Ziethaml, "Consumer Perceptions of Price, Quality, and Value," *Journal of Marketing* (July 1988), pp. 2–22. Also see Jerry Wind, "Getting a Read on Market-Defined 'Value,'" *Journal of Pricing Management* (Winter 1990), pp. 5–14.

10. These examples are from Roger A. Kerin and Robert A. Peterson, "Morgantown Furniture, Inc. (A)," *Strategic Marketing Problems: Cases and Comments,* 7th ed. (Englewood Cliffs, NJ: Prentice-Hall, 1995), pp. 282–291; and "Software Economics 101," *Forbes* (January 28, 1985), p. 88.

11. Julie Chao, "Is Kona Coffee Good to the Last Drop? That's All You Get," *The Wall Street Journal* (August 24, 1995), pp. A1, A6.

12. David Wessel, "The Price Is Wrong, and Economists Are in an Uproar," *The Wall Street Journal* (January 2, 1991), pp. B1, B6.

13. Patricia Sellers, "Busch Fights to Have It All," *Fortune* (January 15, 1990), pp. 81ff.

14. "Price War Is Raging in Europe," *Business Week* (July 6, 1992), pp. 44–45.

15. Michael Garry, "Dollar Strength: Publishers Confront the New Economic Realities," *Folio: The Magazine for Magazine Management* (February 1989), pp. 88–93; Cara S. Trager, "Right Price Reflects a Magazine's Health Goals," *Advertising Age* (March 9, 1987), pp. 5–8ff; and Frank Bruni, "Price of Newsweek? It Depends," *Dallas Times Herald* (August 14, 1986), pp. S1, S20.

16. For an overview of price elasticity studies, see Ruth N. Bolton, "The Robustness of Retail-Level Elasticity Estimates," *Journal of Retailing*

(Summer 1989), pp. 193–219; and Gerald J. Tellis, "The Price Elasticity of Selective Demand: A Meta-Analysis of Econometric Models of Sales," *Journal of Marketing Research* (November 1988), pp. 331–41.

17. See, for example, Susan L. Holak and Srinivas K. Reddy, "Effects of a Television and Radio Advertising Ban: A Study of the Cigarette Industry," *Journal of Marketing* (October 1986), pp. 219–27; and Rick Andrews and George R. Franke, "Time-Varying Elasticities of U.S. Cigarette Demand, 1933–1987," *AMA Educators' Conference Proceedings* (Chicago: American Marketing Association, 1990), p. 393.

18. This box is based on references X, Y, and Z.

19. Andrew E. Serwer, "Head to Head with Giants—and Winning," *Fortune* (June 13, 1994), p. 154.

20. Kent B. Monroe, *Pricing: Making Profitable Decisions,* 2nd ed. (New York: McGraw-Hill, 1990), pp. 24–26.

21. W. Nylen, *Marketing Decision-Making Handbook* (Englewood Cliffs, N.J.: Prentice Hall, 1990), pp. G237–G239.

Washburn International, Inc.: This case was prepared by William Rudelius.

CHAPTER 15

1. "Picture-Phone Marketers Target the Home PC," *The Wall Street Journal* (February 27, 1996), p. B1, B6; "The Difficult Art of Videophone Conversation," *New Scientist* (January 14, 1995), p. 20; "Voyeurs vs. Exhibitionists," *Forbes* (May 23, 1994), p. 210; and "An Eye on Phones," *U.S. News and World Report* (June 22, 1992), pp. 78–82.

2. "U.S. Invents, Japan Profits (Again)," *Fortune* (March 12, 1990), pp. 14–15.

3. "Fight to the Finish," *Newsweek* (December 12, 1994), pp. 56–57; and "Sonic Boom," *The Economist* (January 25, 1992), p. 69.

4. "Sony Prices Its Advanced Game Player at $299, Near Low End of Expectations," *The Wall Street Journal* (May 12, 1995), p. B4; and Jeffrey A. Trachtenberg, "Sony Sells 100,000 Video-Game Units on First Weekend," *The Wall Street Journal* (September 12, 1995), p. A12.

5. For the classic treatment of skimming and penetration pricing, see Joel Dean, "Pricing Policies for New Products," *Harvard Business Review* (November–December 1976), pp. 141–53. See also Thomas T. Nagle and Reed K. Holden, *The Strategy and Tactics of Pricing,* 2nd ed. (Englewood Cliffs, NJ: Prentice-Hall, 1995).

6. "PC Prices Cut in Japan," *The Wall Street Journal* (October 21, 1992), p. B7.

7. Jeffrey H. Birnbaum, "Pricing of Products Is Still an Art, Often Having Little Link to Costs," *The Wall Street Journal* (November 25, 1981), p. 25.

8. "Luxury Steals Back," *Fortune* (January 16, 1995), pp. 112–19.

9. See, for example, V. Kumar and Robert P. Leone, "Measuring the Effect of Retail Store Promotions on Brand and Store Substitution," *Journal of Marketing Research* (May 1988), pp. 178–85.

10. Robert C. Blattberg and Scott A. Neslin, *Sales Promotion Concepts, Methods and Strategies* (Englewood Cliffs, NJ: Prentice-Hall, 1990); and Kent B. Monroe, *Pricing: Making Profitable Decisions,* 2nd ed. (New York: McGraw-Hill, 1990).

11. "PCs: The Battle for the Home Front," *Business Week* (September 25, 1995), pp. 110–14; and David Kirkpatrick, "The Revolution at Compaq Computer," *Fortune* (December 14, 1992), pp. 80–82ff.

12. Nagle and Holden.

13. "It's Not as Easy as 1-2-3 Anymore," *Business Week* (October 14, 1991), pp. 112–14.

14. "Lawyers Start to Stop the Clock," *Business Week* (August 17, 1992), p. 108.

15. George E. Belch and Michael A. Belch, *Introduction to Advertising and Promotion,* 2nd ed. (Homewood, IL: Richard D. Irwin, 1993).

16. For a comprehensive discussion on the experience curve, see Roger A. Kerin, Vijay Mahajan, and P. Rajan Varadarajan, *Contemporary Perspectives on Strategic Market Planning* (Boston: Allyn and Bacon, 1990).

17. Based on information provided by Amber, Bergen and Drecker Associates; "Digital Daze," *The Economist* (October 3, 1992), p. 65; and Andrew Kupfer, "Phones that Will Work Anywhere," *Fortune* (August 24, 1992), pp. 100–12.

18. William Taylor, "Message and Muscle: An Interview with Swatch Titan Nicolas Hayek," *Harvard Business Review* (March–April 1993), pp. 98–110.

19. Jim Carlton, "Hewlett-Packard Cuts Office-PC Prices in Wake of Moves by Compaq and IBM," *The Wall Street Journal* (August 22, 1995), p. B11.

20. Susan Carey "Pechin's Mart Breaks Many Rules, But Not the One on Pricing," *The Wall Street Journal* (March 5, 1984), p. A1.

21. "Retailers Using Cut-Rate Videos as Lures," *The Dallas Morning News* (October 4, 1992), p. 5H.

22. "Single-Price Stores' Formula for Success: Cheap Merchandise and a Lot of Clutter," *The Wall Street Journal* (June 30, 1992), pp. B1, B6.

23. Ian Ayres and Peter Siegelman, "Race and Gender Discrimination in Bargaining for a New Car," *The American Economic Review* (June 1995), pp. 304–21; "Saturn's Uniform Pricing Extended to Used Cars," *The Dallas Morning News* (August 14, 1995), p. 4D; and "Automotive Marketing," *Advertising Age* (April 3, 1995), pp. S1–S32.

24. Trachtenberg.

25. Monroe.

26. "Store-Brand Pricing Has to Be Just Right," *The Wall Street Journal* (February 14, 1992), p. B1.

27. Timothy Smith, "Why Air Travel Doesn't Work," *Fortune* (April 3, 1995), pp. 42–56.

28. "Bob Allen Is Turning AT&T into a Live Wire," *Business Week* (November 6, 1989), pp. 140–41ff.

29. For a review of quantity discounts, see George S. Day and Adrian B. Ryans, "Using Price Discounts for a Competitive Advantage," *Industrial Marketing Management* (February 1988), pp. 1–14; and James B. Wilcox, Roy D. Howell, Paul Kuzdrall, and Robert Britney, "Price Quantity Discounts: Some Implications for Buyers and Sellers," *Journal of Marketing* (July 1987), pp. 60–70.

30. "Burger King, in Big Blow to Pepsi, Is Switching to Coke," *The Wall Street Journal* (May 2, 1990), pp. B1, B6.

31. "Everyday Low Profits," *Harvard Business Review* (March–April 1994), p. 13; Stephen J. Hoch, Xavier Dreze, and Mary E. Purk, "EDLP, Hi-Lo, and Margin Arithmetic," *Journal of Marketing* (October 1994), pp. 16–27; and Tibbett Speer, "Do Low Prices Bore Shoppers?" *American Demographics* (January 1994), pp. 11–13. See also Philip Zerrillo and Dawn Iacobucci, "Trade Promotions: A Call for a More Rational Approach," *Business Horizons* (July–August 1995), pp. 69–76.

32. Dorothy Cohen, *Legal Issues in Marketing Decision Making* (Cincinnati, OH: South-Western, 1995).

33. "More Airlines to Settle Suit on Price Fixing," *The Wall Street Journal* (June 23, 1992), p. A3.

34. "Reebok and FTC Settle Price-Fixing Charges," *The Wall Street Journal* (May 5, 1995), pp. B1, B8.

My Own Meals: This case was prepared by William Rudelius. Sources: Personal interview with Mary Anne Jackson; Mike Duff, "New Children's Meals: Not Just Kids Stuff," *Supermarket Business* (May 1990), p. 93; Heidi Parsons, "MOM, Incorporated," *Poultry Processing* (August/September 1989); Lisa R. Van Wagner, "Kids Meals: The Market Grows Up," *Food Business* (May 20, 1991); Mary Ellen Kuhn, "Women to Watch in the 90's," *Food Business* (September 10, 1990); Arlene Vigoda, "Small Fry Microwave Meals Become Big Business," *USA Today* (June 4, 1990).

CHAPTER 16

1. Christie Brown, "Pooper-scooper dooper," *Forbes* (February 13, 1995), pp. 78–79; "Reigning Cats and Dogs," *American Demographics* (April 1995), p. 10; "Deluxe Brands, Pet Supers Wag the Market," *Advertising Age* (September 27, 1995), p. 22; "Why True Love Is Like Puppy Chow," *American Demographics* (January 1996), pp. 14–15; and "Sick Pets: A Healthy Pharmaceutical Market," *The Wall Street Journal* (January 3, 1996), pp. B1, B6.

2. See Peter D. Bennett, ed., *Dictionary of Marketing Terms,* 2nd ed. (Chicago: American Marketing Association, 1995).

3. Based on Frederick E. Webster, Jr., *Industrial Marketing Strategy,* 2nd ed. (New York: John Wiley & Sons, 1988).

4. "Pepsi, Concerned about Market Share in France, Will Break with Local Bottler," *The Wall Street Journal* (November 7, 1989), p. A12.

5. This discussion is based on John A. Quelch, "Why Not Exploit Dual Marketing?" *Business Horizons* (January–February 1987), pp. 52–60; *PepsiCo, Inc. 1994 Annual Report;* "GM Says Sales Arm Plans to Distribute Saab Cars in Canada," *The Wall Street Journal* (May 10, 1990), p. B2; and Rustan Kosenko and Don Rathz, "The Japanese Channels of Distribution: Difficult but Not Insurmountable," *AMA Educator's Proceedings* (Chicago: American Marketing Association, 1988), pp. 233–36.

6. For a recent discussion on strategic channel alliances, see P. Rajan Varadarajan and Margaret H. Cunningham, "Strategic Alliances: A Synthesis of Conceptual Foundations," *Journal of the Academy of Marketing Science* (Fall 1995), pp. 282–96; and Johny K. Johansson, "International Alliances: Why Now?" *Journal of the Academy of Marketing Science* (Fall 1995), pp. 301–04.

7. "Spoon-to-Spoon Combat Overseas," *New York Times* (January 1, 1995), p. 17; "Cafe au Lait, a Croissant and Trix," *Business Week* (August 24, 1992), pp. 50–51; and "Cereal Partners Gains in European Market," *Advertising Age* (May 17, 1993), p. I-10.

8. For an extended treatment of direct marketing, see Mary Lou Roberts and Paul D. Berger, *Direct Marketing Management* (Englewood Cliffs, N.J.: Prentice Hall, 1989); and Herbert Katzenstein and William S. Sachs, *Direct Marketing* (Columbus, Ohio: Merrill, 1986).

9. "Telemarketing Cited as Chief Form of Direct Marketing," *Advertising Age* (January 1, 1996), p. 9.

10. Adapted from Louis W. Stern, Adel I. El-Ansary, and James R. Brown, *Management in Marketing Channels* (Englewood Cliffs, N.J.: Prentice Hall, 1989), pp. 99–108; Kenneth G. Hardy and Allan J. McGrath, *Marketing Channel Management* (Glenview, Ill.: Scott, Foresman, 1988), pp. 3–5, 310–34; and Bert Rosenbloom, *Marketing Channels* 3rd ed. (Hinsdale, Ill.: Dryden Press, 1987), pp. 44–47.

11. *Health o meter Products, Inc. 1994 Annual Report;* and Interview with Mr. James Yurak, executive vice president, Mr. Coffee, June 1, 1990.

12. Louis W. Stern and Adel I. El-ansary, *Marketing Channels,* 4th ed. (Englewood Cliffs, N.J.: Prentice Hall, 1991).

13. Statistics provided by the International Franchise Association.

14. For a review of channel partnering, see Robert D. Buzzell and Gwen Ortmeyer, "Channel Partnerships Streamline Distribution," *Sloan Management Review* (Spring 1995), pp. 85–96.

15. Edwin R. Rigsbee, *The Art of Partnering* (Dubuque, Iowa: Kendall/Hunt Publishing, 1994), pp. 82–83.

16. *Kroger 1994 Annual Report.*

17. "Distributors: No Endangered Species," *Industry Week* (January 24, 1983), pp. 47–52.

18. This exhibit is based on "PCs: The Battle for the Home Front," *Business Week* (September 15, 1995), pp. 110–14; "The Computer Is in the Mail (Really)," *Business Week* (January 23, 1995), pp. 76–77; "Mass Market Transforms PC Retailing," *The Wall Street Journal* (December 18, 1990), p. B1; "More Computer Marketers Taking the Direct Approach," *Marketing News* (October 26, 1992), p. 6; and "A Surprise Lift for Computer Retailers," *Business Week* (October 4, 1992), pp. 63–64.

19. "Revolution in Japanese Retailing," *Fortune* (February 7, 1994), pp. 143–46.

20. "Japanese Retailing: The Emporia Strike Back," *The Economist* (October 29, 1994), pp. 83–84.

21. "Gillette Tries to Nick Schick in Japan," *The Wall Street Journal* (February 4, 1991), pp. B3, B4.

22. This discussion is based on John Fahy and Fuyuki Taguchi, "Reassessing the Japanese Distribution System," *Sloan Management Review* (Winter 1995), pp. 49–61; and Michael R. Czinkota and Jon Woronoff, *Unlocking Japanese Markets* (Chicago: Probus Publishing, 1991), pp. 92–97.

23. Based on an interview with Pamela Viglielmo, Director of International Marketing, Fran Wilson Cosmetics, November 10, 1992; and "U.S. Firm Gives Lip (Coloring) Service to Japan," *Marketing News* (March 16, 1992), p. 6; and "At Last, a Product that Makes Japan's Subways Safe for Men," *Advertising Age* (January 16, 1995), p. I-24.

24. "Distributors' Links to Producers Grow More Fragile," *The Wall Street Journal* (October 28, 1992), p. B2; and "Wal-Mart Draws Fire," *Advertising Age* (January 13, 1992), p. 3.

25. "Bloody, Bowed, Back Together," *Business Week* (March 19, 1990), pp. 42–43.

26. "Heinz Struggles to Stay at the Top of the Stack," *Business Week* (March 11, 1985), p. 49.

27. "Black Pearls Recast for Spring," *Advertising Age* (November 13, 1995), p. 49.

28. Studies that explore the dimensions and use of power and influence in marketing channels include the following: Gul Butaney and Lawrence H. Wortzel, "Distributor Power versus Manufacturer Power: The Customer Role," *Journal of Marketing* (January 1988), pp. 52–63; Kenneth A. Hunt, John T. Mentzer, and Jeffrey E. Danes, "The Effect of Power Sources on Compliance in a Channel of Distribution: A Causal Model," *Journal of Business Research* (October 1987), pp. 377–98; John F. Gaski, "Interrelations among a Channel Entity's Power Sources: Impact of the Exercise of Reward and Coercion on Expert, Referent, and Legitimate Power Sources," *Journal of Marketing Research* (February 1986), pp. 62–67; Gary Frazier and John O. Summers, "Interfirm Influence Strategies and Their Application within Distribution Channels," *Journal of Marketing* (Summer 1984), pp. 43–55; Sudhir Kale, "Dealer Perceptions of Manufacturer Power and Influence Strategies in a Developing Country," *Journal of Marketing Research* (November 1986), pp. 387–93; George H. Lucas and Larry G. Gresham, "Power, Conflict, Control, and the Application of Contingency Theory in Channels of Distribution," *Journal of the Academy of Marketing Science* (Summer 1985), pp. 27–37; and F. Robert Dwyer and Jule Gassenheimer, "Relational Roles and Triangle Dramas: Effects on Power Play and Sentiments in Industrial Channels," *Marketing Letters,* vol. 3 (1992), pp. 187–200.

29. Based on Gene R. Laznick and Patrick E. Murphy, *Ethical Marketing Decisions: The Higher Road* (Boston: Allyn & Bacon, 1993), pp. 117–18; and N. Craig Smith and John A. Quelch, *Ethics in Marketing* (Chicago: Richard D. Irwin, 1993), pp. 478–79.

30. For a comprehensive treatment of legal issues pertaining to marketing channels, see Dorothy Cohen, *Legal Issues in Marketing* (Cincinnati, Ohio: South-Western, 1995).

31. "Kodak Takes a Shot in the Mug," *Business Week* (June 22, 1992), p. 40.

Creston Vineyards: This case was prepared by Steven W. Hartley.

CHAPTER 17

1. Ronald Henkoff, "Delivering the Goods," *Fortune* (November 28, 1994), p. 64.

2. Henkoff, pp. 64–78.

3. Definition provided by the Council of Logistics Management, Chicago, 1986. Emphasis added.

4. Elizabeth Edwardson, "Workers at L.L. Bean Busy as Santa's Elves Filling Christmas Orders," *Minneapolis Star Tribune* (December 23, 1992), p. 5D.

5. Bernard Wysocki, Jr., "Improved Distribution, Not Better Production, Is Key Goal in Mergers," *The Wall Street Journal* (August 29, 1995), pp. A1, A2; Laura Landro, "Giants Talk Synergy but Few Make It Work," *The Wall Street Journal* (September 25, 1995), pp. B1, B2; and Henkoff, pp. 64–78.

6. Henkoff, p. 64.

7. John Holusha, "P&G Downy Bottles Use Recycled Plastic," *The New York Times* (January 14, 1993), p. C5; and Bruce VanVoorst, "The Recycling Bottleneck," *Time* (September 14, 1992), p. 52.

8. Lee Smith, "The Customer with Clout," *Fortune* (October 2, 1995), p. 100.

9. Jon Bigness, "In Today's Economy, There Is Big Money to Be Made in Logistics," *The Wall Street Journal* (September 6, 1995), pp. A1, A9.

10. Joseph Pereira, "In Reebok-Nike War, Big Woolworth Chain Is a Major Battlefield," *The Wall Street Journal* (September 22, 1995), pp. A1, A5; and Kenneth Labich, "Nike vs. Reebok: A Battle for Hearts, Minds and Feet," *Fortune* (September 18, 1995), pp. 90–116.

11. Michael Saul, "Penney-UPS Deal Valued at $1 Billion," *The Dallas Morning News* (July 11, 1995), p. 4D; and Scott McCartney, "Dell to Outsource All its Shipping to Roadway Unit," *The Wall Street Journal* (February 15, 1995), p. B8.

12. Bigness, p. A9.

13. Henkoff, pp. 66–74; and Philip Evers and F. J. Beier, "The Portfolio Effect and Multiple Consolidation Points: A Critical Assessment of the Square Root Law," *Journal of Business Logistics* (Fall 1993), pp. 117–126.

14. "Europeans Think Alike when It Comes to Customer Service," *International Ambassador* (August 1990), p. 25; and "The European Customer Service Survey: Results," *Europa* (September 1990), p. 1.

15. John J. Coyle, Edward J. Bardi, and C. John Langley, Jr., *The Management of Business Logistics,* 5th ed. (St. Paul, Minn.: West Publishing, 1992), pp. 85–90.

16. Bigness, p. A1.

17. *Railroad Facts* (Washington, D.C.: Association of American Railroads, 1992), p. 29.

18. David Greising, "Watch Out for Flying Packages," *Business Week* (November 14, 1995), p. 40; and Roy Rowan, "Business Triumphs of the Seventies," *Fortune* (December 1979), p. 34.

19. Christina Duff and Bob Ortega, "How Wal-Mart Outdid a Once-Touted Kmart in Discount-Store Race," *The Wall Street Journal* (March 24, 1995), pp. A1, A4; and Thomas J. Winninger, "Price Wars," *Minnesota Ventures* (September/October 1994), pp. 31–34.

20. Henkoff, pp. 64–78.

Navistar International (B): This case was prepared by Steven W. Hartley.

CHAPTER 18

1. Stratford Sherman, "Will the Information Superhighway Be the Death of Retailing?" *Fortune* (April 18, 1994), pp. 98–110; and Allyson L.

Stewart, "Future of Shopping: Shop as You Flop," *Marketing News* (November 21, 1994), p. 15.

2. Suzanne Oliver, "Virtual Retailers," *Forbes* (April 24, 1995), pp. 126–27; and Susan Chandler, "The Grocery Cart in Your PC," *Business Week* (September 11, 1995), pp. 63–64.

3. Robert Lenzner and Philippe Mao, "Banking Pops Up in the Strangest Places," *Forbes* (April 10, 1995), pp. 72–76; Faye Rice, "One Writer's Hunt for the Perfect Jeans," *Fortune* (April 17, 1995), p. 30; and Cyndee Miller, "Gaze into the Crystal Ball for '95 and Beyond," *Marketing News* (January 30, 1995), pp. 1, 10.

4. "The Fortune Global 500," *Fortune* (August 7, 1995), pp. F1–F42; and "Fortune 500," *Fortune* (May 15, 1995), pp. F1–F65.

5. *Statistical Abstract of the United States,* 115th ed. (Washington, D.C.: U.S. Department of Commerce, Bureau of Census, September 1995), p. 782.

6. Carla Rapoport and Justin Martin, "Retailers Go Global," *Fortune* (February 20, 1995), pp. 102–8; William Symonds, "Invasion of the Retail Snatchers," *Business Week* (May 9, 1994), pp. 72–73; and Eugene Fram and Riad Ajami, "Globalization of Markets and Shopping Stress: Cross-Country Comparisons," *Business Horizons* (January–February 1994), pp. 17–23.

7. Gene Koretz, "Those Plucky Corner Stores," *Business Week* (December 5, 1994), p. 26.

8. Alison L. Sprout, "Packard Bell Sells More PCs in the US than Anyone," *Fortune* (June 12, 1995), pp. 82–88; Marcia Berss, "We Will Not Be in a National Chain," *Forbes* (March 27, 1995), p. 50; and Steve Kichen, "Pick a Channel," *Forbes* (March 2, 1992), pp. 108, 110.

9. Christopher Palmeri, "Who's Afraid of Wal-Mart?" *Forbes* (July 31, 1995), p. 81.

10. Richard C. Hoffman and John F. Preble, "Franchising into the Twenty-First Century," *Business Horizons* (November–December 1993), pp. 35–43.

11. Allen Whitehead, "Trouble in Franchise Nation," *Fortune* (March 6, 1995), pp. 115–29; and Jennifer S. Stack and Joseph E. McKendrick, "Franchise Market Expands as Rest of Economy Slumps," *Marketing News* (July 6, 1992), p. 11.

12. Robert E. Bond and Christopher E. Bond, *The Source Book of Franchising Opportunities* (Homewood, Ill.: Dow Jones-Irwin, 1991).

13. Marc Rice, "Competition Fierce in Complex Business of Delivering Packages," *Marketing News* (May 22, 1995), p. 5; Tim Triplett, "Scanning Wand Makes Checkout Lines Disappear," *Marketing News* (July 4, 1994), p. 6; and Tara Parker-Pope, "New Devices Add Up Bill, Measure Shoppers' Honesty," *The Wall Street Journal* (June 6, 1995), pp. B1, 13.

14. Cyndee Miller, "Nordstrom Is Tops in Survey," *Marketing News* (February 15, 1993), p. 12; "Daytons Is Top Retailer in Customer Satisfaction Survey," *Marketing News* (June 6, 1994), p. 8; and Richard Stevenson, "Watch Out, Macy's, Here Comes Nordstrom," *New York Times Magazine* (August 27, 1989), p. 40.

15. Joseph Pereira, "Toys 'R Us Grows Up," *The Wall Street Journal* (March 20, 1995), p. B4.

16. Zina Moukheiber, "Retailing," *Forbes* (January 2, 1995), pp. 190–92.

17. Laurie M. Grossman, "Hypermarkets: A Sure-Fire Hit Bombs," *The Wall Street Journal* (June 25, 1992), p. B1.

18. Peter D. Bennett, ed., *Dictionary of Marketing Terms* (American Marketing Association, 1995).

19. Edward Nash, "The Roots of Direct Marketing," *Direct Marketing* (February 1995), pp. 38–40; and Edith Hill Updike and Mary Kurtz, "Japan Is Dialing 1 800 BUYAMERICA," *Business Week* (June 12, 1995), pp. 61–64.

20. Susan Chandler and Therese Palmer, "Can Spiegel Pull Out of the Spiral?" *Business Week* (August 28, 1995), p. 80; Gary McWilliams, Susan Chandler, and Julie Tilsner, "Strategies for the New Mail Order," *Business Week* (December 19, 1994), pp. 82–85; and Annetta Miller, "Up to the Chin in Catalogs," *Newsweek* (November 20, 1989), pp. 27–58.

21. Lenzner with Mao; Dyan Machan, "Sharing Victoria's Secrets," *Forbes* (June 5, 1995), pp. 132–33; and Charles Waltner, "Interactive Catalogs a Tough Sell," *Advertising Age* (March 6, 1995), p. 19.

22. Donna Bursey, "Targeting Small Businesses for Telemarketing and Mail Order Sales," *Direct Marketing* (September 1995), pp. 18–20; "Inbound, Outbound Telemarketing Keeps Ryder Sales in Fast Lane," *Direct Marketing* (July 1995), pp. 34–36; "Despite Hangups, Telemarketing a Success," *Marketing News* (March 27, 1995), p. 19; Kelly Shermach, "Outsourcing Seen as a Way to Cut Costs, Retain Service," *Marketing News* (June 19, 1995), pp. 5, 8; and Greg Gattuso, "Marketing Vision," *Direct Marketing,* (February 1994), pp. 24–26.

23. Laura Loro, "Downside for Public Is Privacy Issue," *Advertising Age* (October 2, 1995), p. 32; Cyndee Miller, "Concern Raised over Privacy on Infohighway," *Marketing News* (January 2, 1995), pp. 1, 7; "Telemarketing Rules OK'd," *Marketing News* (September 11, 1995), p. 1; Judith Waldrop, "The Business of Privacy," *American Demographics* (October 1994), pp. 46–55; and Mag Gottlieb, "Telemarketing and the Law," *Direct Marketing* (February 1994), pp. 22–23.

24. Gail DeGeorge and Lori Bongiorno, "Polishing Up the Cubic Zirconia," *Business Week* (July 31, 1995), pp. 83–84; Chad Rubel, "Home Shopping Network Targets Young Audience," *Marketing News* (July 17, 1995), pp. 13, 26; and Kathy Haley, "Keys Are Interactive TV and Channel Expansion," *Advertising Age* (February 22, 1993), p. C16.

25. David Fryxell, "How to Succeed in Executive Shopping," *Link-Up* (March/April 1992), pp. 8–10; and Gary Robins, "On-Line Service Update," *Stores* (February 1990), pp. 24–29.

26. Hanna Liebman, "The Microchip Is the Message," *Mediaweek* (November 2, 1992), pp. 22–29; and "How Long Will Prodigy Be a Problem Child?" *Business Week* (September 10, 1990), p. 75.

27. Robert Benjamin and Rolf Wigand, "Electronic Markets and Virtual Value Chains on the Information Superhighway," *Sloan Management Review* (Winter 1995), pp. 62–72; "Malling the Net," *Adweek* (September 25, 1995), pp. 32–37; Paul Judge, "Mr. Smith Goes to Cyberspace," *Business Week* (October 30, 1995), pp. 72–73; Scott Danaton and Dagmar Musey "Online's Next Battlefront: Europe," *Advertising Age* (March 6, 1995), p. 18; and Philip Elmer-Dewitt, "Battle for the Internet," *Time* (July 25, 1995), pp. 50–56.

28. Mathew Schifrin, "Okay, Big Mouth," *Forbes* (October 9, 1995), pp. 47–48; Veronica Byrd and Wendy Zellner, "The Avon Lady of the Amazon," *Business Week* (October 24, 1994), pp. 93–96; and Ann Marsh "Avon Is Calling on Eastern Europe," *Advertising Age* (June 20, 1994), p. I16.

29. "Vending Machine Software," *Marketing News* (May 8, 1995), p. 1; and "Coke Machine Modems Send Distress Signals," *Marketing News* (October 9, 1995), p. 2.

30. The following discussion is adapted from William T. Gregor and Eileen M. Friars, *Money Merchandising: Retail Revolution in Consumer Financial Services* (Cambridge, Mass.: Management Analysis Center, Inc., 1982).

31. Gail Tom, Michelle Dragics, and Christi Holdregger, "Using Visual Presentation to Assess Store Positioning: A Case Study of J. C. Penney," *Marketing Research* (September 1991), pp. 48–52.

32. William Lazer and Eugene J. Kelley, "The Retailing Mix: Planning and Management," *Journal of Retailing* (Spring 1961), pp. 34–41.

33. Francis J. Mulhern and Robert P. Leon, "Implicit Price Bundling of Retail Products: A Multiproduct Approach to Maximizing Store Profitability," *Journal of Marketing* (October 1991), pp. 63–76.

34. Gwen Ortmeyer, John A. Quelch, and Walter Salmon, "Restoring Credibility to Retail Pricing," *Sloan Management Review* (Fall 1991), pp. 55–66.

35. William B. Dodds, "In Search of Value: How Price and Store Name Information Influence Buyers' Product Perceptions," *Journal of Consumer Marketing* (Spring 1991), pp. 15–24.

36. "Annual Report on Discount Retailing," *Discount Store News,* (July 3, 1995), p. 23; "Combined Annual and Revised Monthly Trade," *Current Business Reports* (April 1995). Faye Rice, "What Intelligent Consumers Want," *Fortune* (December 28, 1992), pp. 56–60.

37. Rita Koselka, "The Schottenstein Factor," *Forbes* (September 28, 1992), pp. 104, 106.

38. Rice; and Gary Strauss, "Warehouse Clubs Heat Up Retail Climate," *USA Today* (September 7, 1990), pp. 1B, 2B.

39. James M. Degen, "Warehouse Clubs Move from Revolution to Evolution," *Marketing News* (August 3, 1992), p. 8; Dori Jones Yang, "Bargains by the Forklift," *Business Week* (July 15, 1991), p. 152; and "Fewer Rings on the Cash Register," *Business Week* (January 14, 1991), p. 85.

40. Stephanie Anderson Forest, "I Can Get It for You Retail," *Business Week* (September 18, 1995), pp. 84–88; and Adrienne Ward, "New Breed of Mall Knows: Everybody Loves a Bargain," *Advertising Age* (January 27, 1992), p. 55.

41. Barry Brown, "Edmonton Makes Size Pay Off in Down Market," *Advertising Age* (January 27, 1992), pp. 4–5.

42. Kenneth Labich, "What It Will Take to Keep People Hanging Out at the Mall," *Fortune* (May 29, 1995), pp. 102–6; Cyndee Miller, "Retailers Do What They Must to Ring Up Sales," *Marketing News* (May 22, 1995), pp. 1, 10–11; and Laura Zinn, "Steady Traffic at the Mall," *Business Week* (January 9, 1995), p. 86.

43. Eric Peterson, "Power Centers! Now!" *Stores* (March 1989), pp. 61–66; and "Power Centers Flex Their Muscle," *Chain Store Age Executive* (February 1989), pp. 3A, 4A.

44. Pierre Martineau, "The Personality of the Retail Store," *Harvard Business Review* (January–February 1958), p. 47.

45. Julie Baker, Dhruv Grewal, and A. Parasuraman, "The Influence of Store Environment on Quality Inferences and Store Image," *Journal of the Academy of Marketing Science* (Fall 1994), pp. 328–39; Howard Barich and Philip Kotler, "A Framework for Marketing Image Management," *Sloan Management Review* (Winter 1991), pp. 94–104; Susan M. Keaveney and Kenneth A. Hunt, "Conceptualization and Operationalization of Retail Store Image: A Case of Rival Middle-Level Theories," *Journal of the Academy of Marketing Science* (Spring 1992), pp. 165–75; and James C. Ward, Mary Jo Bitner, and John Barnes, "Measuring the Prototypicality and Meaning of Retail Environments," *Journal of Retailing* (Summer 1992), p. 194. For a review of the store image literature, see Mary R. Zimmer and Linda L. Golden, "Impressions of Retail Stores: A Content Analysis of Consumer Images," *Journal of Retailing* (Fall 1988), pp. 265–93.

46. Mary Jo Bitner, "Servicescapes: The Impact of Physical Surroundings on Customers and Employees," *Journal of Marketing* (April 1992), pp. 57–71.

47. Jans-Benedict Steenkamp and Michel Wedel, "Segmenting Retail Markets on Store Image Using a Consumer-Based Methodology," *Journal of Retailing* (Fall 1991), p. 300; and Philip Kotler, "Atmospherics as a Marketing Tool," *Journal of Retailing,* vol. 49 (Winter 1973–74), p. 61.

48. Susan Chandler, "Drill Bits, Paint Thinner, Eyeliner," *Business Week* (September 25, 1995), pp. 83–84.

49. The wheel of retailing theory was originally proposed by Malcolm P. McNair, "Significant Trends and Development in the Postwar Period," in A. B. Smith, ed., *Competitive Distribution in a Free, High-Level Economy and Its Implications for the University* (Pittsburgh: University of Pittsburgh Press, 1958), pp. 1–25; see also Stephen Brown, "The Wheel of Retailing—Past and Future," *Journal of Retailing* (Summer 1990), pp. 143–49; and Malcolm P. McNair and Eleanor May, "The Next Revolution of the Retailing Wheel," *Harvard Business Review* (September–October 1978), pp. 81–91.

50. Andrew E. Serwer, "McDonald's Conquers the World," *Fortune* (October 17, 1995), pp. 103–16; and Lois Therrien, "McRisky," *Business Week* (October 21, 1991), pp. 114–22; Gail DeGeorge, "Someone Woke the Elephants," *Business Week* (April 4, 1994), p. 52.

51. Bill Saporito, "What's for Dinner?" *Fortune* (May 15, 1995), pp. 51–64.

52. William R. Davidson, Albert D. Bates, and Stephen J. Bass, "Retail Life Cycle," *Harvard Business Review* (November–December 1976), pp. 89–96.

53. Gretchen Morgenson, "Here Come the Cross-Shoppers," *Forbes* (December 7, 1992), pp. 90–101.

54. Russell Mitchell, "The Smart Money Is on Smart Cards," *Business Week* (August 14, 1995), p. 68; Thomas McCarroll, "No Checks. No Cash. No Fuss," *Time* (May 9, 1994), pp. 60–62; and Robert Shaw, "How the Smart Card Is Changing Retailing," *Long Range Planning* (February 1991), pp. 111–14.

55. Mary Kuntz, Lori Bongiorno, Keith Naughton, Gail DeGeorge, and Stephanie Anderson Forest, "Reinventing the Store," *Business Week* (November 27, 1995), pp. 84–96; David Fischer, "The New Meal Deals," *U.S. News & World Report* (October 30, 1995), p. 66.

56. Mary Kuntz, "These Ads Have Windows and Walls," *Business Week* (February 27, 1995), p. 74; Richard Corliss, "What's Hot, Doc? Retail! *Time* (May 9, 1994), pp. 64–66.

Mall of America: This case was prepared by Steven W. Hartley.

CHAPTER 19

1. Blair R. Fischer, "Making Your Product the Star Attraction," *Promo* (January 1996), pp. 42–47, 88; Damon Darlin, "Junior Mints, I'm Going to Make You a Star," *Forbes* (November 6, 1995), pp. 90–94; Lisa Bannon, "Will Natty 007 Charm the Grunge Generation?" *The Wall Street Journal* (November 7, 1995), pp. B1, B11; and Fara Warner, "Why It's Getting Harder to Tell the Shows from the Ads," *The Wall Street Journal* (June 15, 1995), pp. B1, B10.

2. Wilbur Schramm, "How Communication Works," in Wilbur Schramm, ed., *The Process and Effects of Mass Communication* (Urbana, Ill.: University of Illinois Press, 1955), pp. 3–26.

3. E. Cooper and M. Jahoda, "The Evasion of Propaganda," *Journal of Psychology,* vol. 22 (1947), pp. 15–25; H. Hyman and P. Sheatsley,

"Some Reasons Why Information Campaigns Fail," *Public Opinion Quarterly,* vol. 11 (1947), pp. 412–23; and J. T. Klapper, *The Effects of Mass Communication* (New York: Free Press, 1960), chapter VII.

4. David A. Ricks, Jeffrey S. Arpan, and Marilyn Y. Fu, "Pitfalls in Advertising Overseas," *Journal of Advertising Research,* vol. 14 (December 1974), pp. 47–51.

5. Adapted from *Dictionary of Marketing Terms,* 2nd ed., Peter D. Bennett, ed. (Chicago: American Marketing Association, 1995), p. 231.

6. B. C. Cotton and Emerson M. Babb, "Consumer Response to Promotional Deals," *Journal of Marketing,* vol. 42 (July 1978), pp. 109–13.

7. Robert George Brown, "Sales Response to Promotions and Advertising," *Journal of Advertising Research,* vol. 14 (August 1974), pp. 33–40.

8. Siva K. Balasubramanian and V. Kumar, "Analyzing Variations in Advertising and Promotional Expenditures: Key Correlates in Consumer, Industrial, and Service Markets," *Journal of Marketing* (April 1990), pp. 57–68.

9. Dunn Sunnoo and Lynn Y. S. Lin, "Sales Effects of Promotion and Advertising," *Journal of Advertising Research,* vol. 18 (October 1978), pp. 37–42.

10. J. Ronald Carey, Stephen A. Clique, Barbara A. Leighton, and Frank Milton, "A Test of Positive Reinforcement of Customers," *Journal of Marketing,* vol. 40 (October 1976), pp. 98–100.

11. James M. Olver and Paul W. Farris, "Push and Pull: A One-Two Punch for Packages Products," *Sloan Management Review* (Fall 1989), pp. 53–61.

12. Julia Flynn and Michael Oneal, "A Tall Order for the Prince of Beers," *Business Week* (March 23, 1992), pp. 66–68; and Patricia Sellers, "How Busch Wins in a Doggy Market," *Fortune,* (June 22, 1987), pp. 99–111.

13. Joseph Weber, "Drug Ads: A Prescription for Controversy," *Business Week* (January 18, 1993), pp. 58–60.

14. Fischer, p. 88.

15. Tom Duncan, "Is Your Marketing Communications Integrated?" *Advertising Age* (January 24, 1994), p. 26.

16. Kim Cleland, "Few Wed Marketing, Communications," *Advertising Age* (February 27, 1995), pp. 10.

17. Don Schultz, "Objectives Drive Tactics in IMC Approach," *Marketing News* (May 9, 1994), pp. 14, 18; and Neil Brown, "Redefine Integrated Marketing Communications," *Marketing News* (March 29, 1993), pp. 4–5.

18. Kate Fitzgerald, "Sega 'Screams' Its Way to the Top," *Advertising Age* (March 20, 1995), pp. S2, S9; and Kerry Smith, "Sega Creates a $20 million 'Sonic' Boom," *Promo* (February 1994), pp. 1, 6.

19. "The 1995 Annual Report on the Promotion Industry," *Promo* (July 1995), p. 33; and "Promotion Expenditures Shift," *Promo* (August 1995), pp. 1, 9.

20. Magid M. Abraham and Leonard M. Lodish, "Getting the Most Out of Advertising and Promotion," *Harvard Business Review* (May–June 1990), pp. 50–60; Steven W. Hartley and James Cross, "How Sales Promotion Can Work for and against You," *Journal of Consumer Marketing* (Summer 1988), pp. 35–42; Robert D. Buzzell, John A. Quelch, and Walter J. Salmon, "The Costly Bargain of Trade Promotion," *Harvard Business Review* (March–April 1990), pp. 141–49; and Mary L. Nicastro, "Break-Even Analysis Determines Success of Sales Promotions," *Marketing News* (March 5, 1990), p. 11.

21. "The 1995 Annual Report on the Promotion Industry," *Promo* (July 1995), pp. 38–39.

22. Kapil Bawa and Robert W. Shoemaker, "Analyzing Incremental Sales from a Direct-Mail Coupon Promotion," *Journal of Marketing* (July 1989), pp. 66–78.

23. Roger A. Strang, "Sales Promotion—Fast Growth, Faulty Management," *Harvard Business Review,* vol. 54 (July–August 1976), pp. 115–24; Ronald W. Ward and James E. Davis, "Coupon Redemption," *Journal of Advertising Research,* vol. 18 (August 1978), pp. 51–58; similar results on favorable mail-distributed coupons were reported by Alvin Schwartz, "The Influence of Media Characteristics on Coupon Redemption," *Journal of Marketing,* vol. 30 (January 1966), pp. 41–46.

24. Larry Armstrong, "Coupon Clippers, Save Your Scissors," *Business Week* (June 20, 1994), pp. 164–66.

25. "Nine Steps to a Fraud-Proof Rebate Form," *Promo* (December 1994), p. 16; Kerry Smith, "The Promotion Gravy Train," *Promo* (August 1995), pp. 50–52; Christopher Power, "Coupon Scams Are Clipping Companies," *Business Week* (June 15, 1992), pp. 110–11; and Kerry J. Smith, "Coupon Scam Uncovered in Detroit," *Promo* (December 1992), pp. 1, 45.

26. Blair Fischer, "The Top 10 Premium Promotions of the Past Ten Years," *Promo* (May 1995), pp. P17–P21.

27. Jack Kenny, "The Prize Is Right," *Promo* (August 1995), pp. 78–85.

28. Fred C. Allvine, Richard D. Teach, and John Connelly, Jr., "The Demise of Promotional Games," *Journal of Advertising Research,* vol. 16 (October 1976), pp. 79–84.

29. Kerry Smith, "Free Lunch: Product Sampling Earns Respect as a Strategic Marketing Tool," *Promo* (September 1995), pp. 93–105; and "The Bell Tolls for Free," *Promo* (June 1995), p. 8.

30. Kerry Smith, "Building a Winning Frequency Program—The Hard Way," *Promo* (December 1995), pp. 36–38.

31. Gary McWilliams and Mark Maremont, "Forget the Green Stamps—Give Me a Ticket to Miami," *Business Week* (February 24, 1992), pp. 70–71; Glenn Heitsmith, "Credit Cards Form Hub of Loyalty Programs," *Promo* (October 1992), pp. 30, 56; and Howard Schlossberg, "Frequency Programs Work Best when Data Are Leveraged Properly," *Marketing News* (November 9, 1992), pp. 3, 5.

32. "New Handy Snack Display Is Dandy," *Marketing News* (October 9, 1987), p. 15.

33. Cyndee Miller, "P-O-P Gains Followers as 'Era of Retailing' Dawns," *Marketing News* (May 14, 1990), p. 2.

34. Kathleen Deveny, "Displays Pay Off for Grocery Marketers," *The Wall Street Journal* (October 15, 1992), pp. B1, B5; "VideOcart Is Rolling Again," *Promo* (August 1991), pp. 1, 36; and Bradley Johnson, "Retailers Check Out In-Store," *Advertising Age* (December 16, 1991), p. 23.

35. "Marketers Trumpet 'Swan Princess,' " *Promo* (June 1995), p. 1.

36. Marvin A. Jolson, Joshua L. Wiener, and Richard B. Rosecky, "Correlates of Rebate Proneness," *Journal of Advertising Research* (February–March 1987), pp. 33–43.

37. Alison Fahey, "Rebate Program Rings Wright Bell," *Advertising Age* (May 21, 1990), p. 44.

38. Darlin, pp. 90–94.

39. This discussion is drawn particularly from John A. Quelch, *Trade Promotions by Grocery Manufacturers: A Management Perspective* (Cambridge, Mass.: Marketing Science Institute, August 1982).

40. Michael Chevalier and Ronald C. Curhan, "Retail Promotions as a Function of Trade Promotions: A Descriptive Analysis," *Sloan Management Review,* vol. 18 (Fall 1976), pp. 19–32.

41. G. A. Marken, "Firms Can Maintain Control over Creative Co-op Programs," *Marketing News* (September 28, 1992), pp. 7, 9.

42. Leon Reinstein, "Intel's Pentium: A Study in Flawed Public Relations," *Business Week* (January 23, 1995), p. 13; and David Kirkpatrick, "Intel's Tainted Tylenol?" *Fortune* (December 26, 1994), pp. 23–24.

43. Scott Hue, "Free 'Plugs' Supply Ad Power," *Advertising Age* (January 29, 1990), p. 6.

44. Marc Weinberger, Jean Romeo, and Azhar Piracha, "Negative Product Safety News: Coverage, Responses, and Effects," *Business Horizons* (May–June 1991), pp. 23–31.

45. Irving Rein, Philip Kotler, and Martin Stoller, *High Visibility* (New York: Dodd, Mead & Co., 1987); and Steven Colford, "Ross Perot: A Winner after All," *Advertising Age* (December 21, 1992), pp. 4, 18.

46. Michael Treacy and Fred Wiersema, "Customer Intimacy and Other Value Disciplines," *Harvard Business Review* (January–February 1993), pp. 84–93.

47. Scott Hume and Ricardo Davis, "Successful Promos Stress Value-Added," *Advertising Age* (September 21, 1992), p. 35; Zachary Schiller, "Not Everyone Loves a Supermarket Deal," *Business Week* (February 17, 1992), pp. 64–68; and Patricia Sellers, "The Dumbest Marketing Ploy," *Fortune* (October 5, 1992), pp. 88–94.

48. "Kid Stuff," *Promo,* vol. 4 (January 1991), pp. 25, 42; Steven W. Colford, "Fine-Tuning Kids' TV," *Advertising Age* (February 11, 1991), p. 35; and Kate Fitzgerald, "Toys Star-Struck for Movie Tie-Ins," *Advertising Age* (February 18, 1991), pp. 3, 45.

49. Herbert J. Rotfeld, Avery M. Abernathy, and Patrick R. Parsons, "Self-Regulation and Television Advertising," *Journal of Advertising,* 19, no. 4 (1990), pp. 18–26.

Sprint: This case was prepared by Linda Rochford of the University of Minnesota–Duluth. Sources: Jaclyn Fierman, "When Genteel Rivals Become Mortal Enemies," *Fortune* (May 15, 1995), pp. 90–91.

CHAPTER 20

1. Debra Aho Williamson, "Marketers Link Up to the Tune of $54.7 Mil," *Advertising Age* (January 22, 1996), p. 28.

2. Cyndee Miller, "Music Marketers Hoping to See a Net Gain," *Marketing News* (January 15, 1996), p. 2; Arsenio Oloroso, Jr., "So, You're on the Internet. Okay, Now What?" *Crain's Chicago Business* (July 10, 1995), pp. 3, 36; Debra Aho Williamson, "Score One for ESPN, Starwave," *Advertising Age* (October 2, 1995), p. 34; Debra Aho Williamson, "Microsoft Pays Record for Super Bowl Web Ad," *Advertising Age* (December 18, 1995), p. 2; Wendy Marx, "Marketers' Home Page Advantage," *Advertising Age* (August 21, 1995), p. 19; and "Ad Age's Cybermarketing Leaders," *Advertising Age* (September 18, 1995), p. 15.

3. Paul Eng, "Big Business on the Net? Not Yet," *Business Week* (June 26, 1995), pp. 100–1; Cyndee Miller, "Marketers Find It's Hip to Be on the Internet," *Marketing News* (February 27, 1995), p. 2; and Julian Dibbell, "Nielsen Rates the Net," *Time* (November 13, 1995), p. 121.

4. David A. Aaker and Donald Norris, "Characteristics of TV Commercials Perceived as Informative," *Journal of Advertising Research,* vol. 22, no. 2 (April–May 1982), pp. 61–70.

5. William Wilkie and Paul W. Farris, "Comparison Advertising: Problems and Potentials," *Journal of Marketing,* vol. 39, no. 4 (October 1975), pp. 7–15.

6. Jennifer Lawrence "P&G Ads Get Competitive," *Advertising Age* (February 1, 1993), p. 14; Jerry Gotlieb and Dan Sorel, "The Influence of Type of Advertisement, Price, and Source Credibility on Perceived Quality," *Journal of the Academy of Marketing Science* (Summer 1992), pp. 253–60; and Cornelia Pechman and David Stewart, "The Effects of Comparative Advertising on Attention, Memory, and Purchase Intentions," *Journal of Consumer Research* (September 1990), pp. 180–92.

7. Bruce Buchanan and Doron Goldman, "Us vs. Them: The Minefield of Comparative Ads," *Harvard Business Review* (May–June 1989), pp. 38–50; Dorothy Cohen, "The FTC's Advertising Substantiation Program," *Journal of Marketing* (Winter 1980), pp. 26–35; and Michael Etger and Stephen A. Goodwin, "Planning for Comparative Advertising Requires Special Attention," *Journal of Advertising,* vol. 8, no. 1 (Winter 1979), pp. 26–32.

8. Lewis C. Winters, "Does It Pay to Advertise to Hostile Audiences with Corporate Advertising?" *Journal of Advertising Research* (June/July 1988), pp. 11–18; and Robert Selwitz, "The Selling of an Image," *Madison Avenue* (February 1985), pp. 61–69.

9. Robert J. Lavidge and Gary A. Steiner, "A Model for Predictive Measurement of Advertising Effectiveness," *Journal of Marketing* (October 1961), p. 61.

10. Brian Wansink and Michael Ray, "Advertising Strategies to Increase Usage Frequency," *Journal of Marketing* (January 1996), pp. 31–46.

11. Jeff Jensen, "Oscar Mayer Scores Super Bowl Halftime," *Advertising Age* (January 8, 1996), pp. 1, 32; Bob Garfield, "Wieners and Losers," *Advertising Age* (January 29, 1996), pp. 1, 37; and Elizabeth Jensen, "NBC Super Bowl Coverage Attracts Record 133.4 Million TV Viewers," *The Wall Street Journal* (February 3, 1993), p. B8.

12. J. Enrique Bigne, "Advertising Budgeting Practices: A Review," *Journal of Current Issues and Research in Advertising* (Fall 1995), pp. 17–31.

13. John Philip Jones, "Ad Spending: Maintaining Market Share," *Harvard Business Review* (January–February 1990), pp. 38–42; and Charles H. Patti and Vincent Blanko, "Budgeting Practices of Big Advertisers," *Journal of Advertising Research,* vol. 21 (December 1981), pp. 23–30.

14. James A. Schroer, "Ad Spending: Growing Market Share," *Harvard Business Review* (January–February 1990), pp. 44–48.

15. Jeffrey A. Lowenhar and John L. Stanton, "Forecasting Competitive Advertising Expenditures," *Journal of Advertising Research,* vol. 16, no. 2 (April 1976), pp. 37–44.

16. Daniel Seligman, "How Much for Advertising?" *Fortune* (December 1956), p. 123.

17. James E. Lynch and Graham J. Hooley, "Increasing Sophistication in Advertising Budget Setting," *Journal of Advertising Research,* 30 (February/March 1990), pp. 67–75.

18. Jimmy D. Barnes, Brenda J. Muscove, and Javad Rassouli, "An Objective and Task Media Selection Decision Model and Advertising Cost Formula to Determine International Advertising Budgets," *Journal of Advertising,* vol. 11, no. 4 (1982), pp. 68–75.

19. Bob Garfield, "Allstate Ads Bring Home Point about Mortgage Insurance," *Advertising Age* (September 11, 1989), p. 120; and Judann Dagnoli, " 'Buy or Die' Mentality Toned Down in Ads," *Advertising Age* (May 7, 1990), p. S-12.

20. Jeffery D. Zbar, "Fear!" *Advertising Age* (November 14, 1994), pp. 18–19; John F. Tanner, Jr., James B. Hunt, and David R. Eppright, "The Protection Motivation Model: A Normative Model of Fear Appeals," *Journal of Marketing* (July 1991), pp. 36–45; Michael S. LaTour and

Shaker A Zahra, "Fear Appeals as Advertising Strategy: Should They Be Used?" *The Journal of Consumer Marketing* (Spring 1989), pp. 61–70; and Joshua Levine, "Don't Fry Your Brain," *Forbes* (February 4, 1991), pp. 116–17.

21. "Calvin Klein Gets Clip Job," *Marketing News* (January 15, 1996), p. 1; "Dumbest Moves of 1995," *Business Week* (January 8, 1996), p. 6; Kirk Davidson, "Calvin Klein Ads: Bad Ethics, Bad Business," *Marketing News* (November 6, 1995), p. 11; "Ad Follies," *Advertising Age* (December 18, 1995), p. 20; Kevin Goldman, "Calvin Klein Ad Rekindles Debate as It Runs in Youths' Magazine," *The Wall Street Journal* (July 10, 1995), p. B7; and "Racier Ads to Be Reserved for Europe, Klein Says," *The Wall Street Journal* (December 19, 1995), p. B2. For a review of research on advertising ethics, see Michael Hyman, Richard Tansey, and James Clark, "Research on Advertising Ethics: Past, Present, and Future," *Journal of Advertising* (September 1994), pp. 5–15.

22. Dana L. Alden, Wayne D. Hoyer, and Chol Lee, "Identifying Global and Culture-Specific Dimensions of Humor in Advertising: A Multinational Analysis," *Journal of Marketing* (April 1993), pp. 64–75; and Johny K. Johansson, "The Sense of 'Nonsense': Japanese TV Advertising," *Journal of Advertising* (March 1994), pp. 17–26.

23. Iris Cohen Selinger, "DDB Needham Turns a Clever Phrase," *Advertising Age* (April 10, 1995), pp. S-4, 34.

24. Alan R. Miciak and William L. Shanklin, "Choosing Celebrity Endorsers," *Marketing Management,* vol. 3, no. 3, pp. 51–59; and Kevin Goldman, "Candice Bergen Leads the List of Top Celebrity Endorsers," *The Wall Street Journal* (September 17, 1993), pp. B1, 10.

25. Kim Cleland, "More Advertisers Put Informercials into Their Plans," *Advertising Age* (September 18, 1995), p. 50; and John Pfeiffer, "Six Months and a Half a Million Dollars, All for 15 Seconds," *Smithsonian* (October 1987), pp. 134–35.

26. Giles D'Souza and Ram C. Rao, "Can Repeating an Advertisement More Frequently than the Competition Affect Brand Preference in a Mature Market?" *Journal of Marketing* (April 1995), pp. 32–42.

27. Katherine Barrett, "Taking a Closer Look," *Madison Avenue* (August 1984), pp. 106–9.

28. Joe Mandese, "Out-of-Home TV: Does It Count?" *Advertising Age* (January 18, 1993), p. 53.

29. "How Much a 30-Second Spot Costs in Fall's Prime-Time Schedule," *Advertising Age* (September 7, 1992), p. 36.

30. Surendra N. Singh, Denise Linville, and Ajay Sukhdial, "Enhancing the Efficacy of Split Thirty-Second Television Commercials: An Encoding Variability Application," *Journal of Advertising* (Fall 1995), pp. 13–23; Scott Ward, Terence A. Oliva, and David J. Reibstein, "Effectiveness of Brand-Related 15-Second Commercials," *Journal of Consumer Marketing,* no. 2 (1994), pp. 38–44; and Surendra N. Singh and Catherine Cole, "The Effects of Length, Content, and Repetition on Television Commercial Effectiveness," *Journal of Marketing Research* (February 1993), pp. 91–104.

31. Joe Mandese, "In New Growth Phase, Cable Feeding on Itself," *Advertising Age* (March 27, 1995), pp. S-1, 2, 10.

32. Jacqueline M. Graves, "The Fortune 500 Opt for Infomercials," *Fortune* (March 6, 1995), p. 20; and William McCall, "Infomercial Pioneer Becomes Industry Leader," *Marketing News* (June 19, 1995), p. 14.

33. George R. Milne, "A Magazine Taxonomy Based on Customer Overlap," *Journal of the Academy of Marketing Science* (Spring 1994), pp. 170–79.

34. "Clutter Bucks," *Fortune* (October 29, 1984), pp. 78–79.

35. Julia Collins, "Image and Advertising," *Harvard Business Review* (January–February 1989), pp. 93–97.

36. Joshua Levine, "Advertising's Summer Games," *Forbes* (August 3, 1992), pp. 70–71.

37. Kim Cleland, "Online Soon to Snare 100-plus Newspapers," *Advertising Age* (April 24, 1995), p. S-6.

38. Carrie Goerne, "Direct Mail Spending Rises, but Success May Be Overblown," *Marketing News* (March 2, 1992), p. 6; and Don Schultz, "Integrated Marketing Communications: Maybe Definition Is in the Point of View," *Marketing News* (January 18, 1993), p. 17.

39. Stephen Barlas, "Cataloguers Seek Cheaper Alternative to Mail," *Marketing News* (February 18, 1991), pp. 1, 19.

40. Arch G. Woodside, "Outdoor Advertising as Experiments," *Journal of the Academy of Marketing Science,* 18 (Summer 1990), pp. 229–37.

41. Charles R. Taylor and Weih Chang, "The History of Outdoor Advertising Regulation in the United States," *Journal of Macromarketing* (Spring 1995), pp. 47–59; Cyndee Miller, "Outdoor Advertising Weathers Repeated Attempts to Kill It," *Marketing News* (March 16, 1992), pp. 1, 9; Ricardo

Davis, "Outdoor Ad Giants Trim Pay to Agencies," *Advertising Age* (January 18, 1993), p. 54; and Patricia Winters, "Outdoor Builds New Areas to Replace Tobacco and Liquor," *Advertising Age* (October 12, 1992), pp. 5–24.

42. John Cortex, "Growing Pains Can't Stop the New Kid on the Ad Block," *Advertising Age* (October 12, 1992), pp. 5–28; Allen Banks, "How to Assess New Place-Based Media," *Advertising Age* (November 30, 1992) p. 36; and John Cortex, "Media Pioneers Try to Corral On-the-Go Consumers," *Advertising Age* (August 17, 1992), p. 25.

43. Sehoon Park and Minhi Hahn, "Pulsing in a Discrete Model of Advertising Competition," *Journal of Marketing Research* (November 1991), pp. 397–405.

44. Rob Norton, "How Uninformative Advertising Tells Consumers Quite a Bit," *Fortune* (December 26, 1994), p. 37; and "Professor Claims Corporations Waste Billions on Advertising," *Marketing News* (July 6, 1992), p. 5.

45. Mary Kuntz, "Now Mad Ave Really has to Sing for Its Supper," *Business Week* (December 18, 1995), p. 43.

46. The discussion of posttesting is based on William F. Arens, *Contemporary Advertising,* 6th ed. (Burr Ridge, Ill.: Richard D. Irwin, 1996), pp. 181–182.

47. David A. Aaker and Douglas M. Stayman, "Measuring Audience Perceptions of Commercials and Relating Them to Ad Impact," *Journal of Advertising Research,* 30 (August/September 1990), pp. 7–17; and Ernest Dichter, "A Psychological View of Advertising Effectiveness," *Marketing Management,* vol. 1, no. 3 (1992), pp. 60–62.

48. Dave Kruegel, "Television Advertising Effectiveness and Research Innovation," *Journal of Consumer Marketing* (Summer 1988), pp. 43–51; and Laurence N. Gold, "The Evolution of Television Advertising-Sales Measurement: Past, Present, and Future," *Journal of Advertising Research* (June/July 1988), pp. 19–24.

49. Roland T. Rust and Richard W. Oliver, "The Death of Advertising," *Journal of Advertising* (December 1994), pp. 71–77; Richard J. Fox and Gary L. Geissler, "Crisis in Advertising?" *Journal of Advertising* (December 1994), pp. 79–84; and Zachary Schiller and Ron Grover, "And Now, a Show from Your Sponsor," *Business Week* (May 22, 1995), pp. 100–2.

50. Ronald B. Lieber, "Here Comes the TV Commercial No Remote Control Can Zap," *Fortune* (October 16, 1995), p. 31.

51. Jeffery D. Zbar, "Blurring the Ad-Editorial Line," *Advertising Age* (November 13, 1995), p. 14; Keith J. Kelly, " 'Time,' 'Newsweek' Say Hi to Tech Titles," *Advertising Age* (July 31, 1995), p. 7.

Fallon McElligott: This case was prepared by Mary Weber of Fallon McElligott and Gwen Achenreiner of Bradley University.

CHAPTER 21

1. Peter Serenyi, "The Pink Revolution," *The Dallas Morning News* (September 25, 1995), pp. 1C, 11C.

2. "Tying the Knot," *The Economist* (May 14, 1994), p. 3.

3. "A Portrait of the Boss," *Business Week* (November 25, 1991), p. 180.

4. Paul S. Busch and Michael J. Houston, *Marketing: Strategic Foundations* (Homewood, Ill.: Richard D. Irwin, 1985), p. 706.

5. Jaclyn Fierman, "The Death and Rebirth of the Salesman," *Fortune* (July 25, 1994), pp. 80–91; "Teaming Up," *Sales & Marketing Management* (October 1993), pp. 98–104; "Getting Hot Ideas from Customers," *Business Week* (May 18, 1992), pp. 86–87; and Brian Tracy, "Stop Talking and Start Asking Questions," *Sales & Marketing Management* (February 1995), pp. 79–87.

6. For different perspectives on relationship selling, see Catherine Romano, "Death of a Salesman," *Management Review* (September 1994), pp. 10–15; Robert F. Dwyer, Paul H. Schuer, and Sejo Oh, "Developing Buyer–Seller Relationships," *Journal of Marketing* (April 1987), pp. 11–27; Lawrence A. Crosby, Kenneth R. Evans, and Deborah Cowles, "Relationship Quality in Services Selling: An Interpersonal Influence Perspective," *Journal of Marketing* (July 1990), pp. 68–81; Barry J. Farber and Joyce Wycoff, "Relationships: Six Steps to Success," *Sales & Marketing Management* (April 1992), pp. 50–56; and Gerrard Macintosh, Kenneth A. Anglin, David M. Szymanski, and James W. Gentry, "Relationship Development in Selling: A Cognitive Analysis," *Journal of Personal Selling and Sales Management* (Fall 1992), pp. 23–34.

7. David W. Cravens, "The Changing Role of the Sales Force," *Marketing Management* (Fall 1995), pp. 49–57.

8. For a perspective on types of selling, see Thomas R. Wotruba, "The Evolution of Personal Selling," *Journal of Personal Selling & Sales Management* (Summer 1991), pp. 1–12.

9. For up-to-date information on selling costs, see *Sales & Marketing Management* magazine's yearly June issue.

10. "Despite Hangups, Telemarketing a Success," *Marketing News* (March 27, 1995), p. 19.

11. For recent research on team selling, see Dawn R. Deeter-Schmelz and Rosemary Ramsey, "A Conceptualization of the Functions and Roles of Formalized Selling and Buying Teams," *Journal of Personal Selling & Sales Management* (Spring 1995), pp. 47–60.

12. "The Selling Game," *The Wall Street Journal* (March 29, 1994), p. A1; "Smart Selling," *Business Week* (August 3, 1992), pp. 46–50; and Susan Caminti, "Finding New Ways to Sell More," *Fortune* (July 27, 1992), pp. 100–103.

13. For further reading, see Marvin A. Jolson and Thomas R. Wotruba, "Prospecting: A New Look at This Old Challenge," *Journal of Personal Selling & Sales Management* (Fall 1992), pp. 59–66. See also Bob Donath et al., "When Your Prospect Calls," *Marketing Management,* vol. 3, nb. 2 (1994), pp. 26–37.

14. Carol J. Loomis, "Have You Been Cold-Called?" *Fortune* (December 16, 1991), pp. 109–15.

15. "Corporate Cultures: Clearing Customs," *SKY Magazine* (July 1995), pp. 35–40.

16. These results are reported in Irma Zandl and Richard Leonard, *Targeting the Trendsetting Consumer* (Homewood, Ill.: Business One Irwin, 1992), p. 141.

17. "Tele-Sale Rules Zoom in on Abuse," *Advertising Age* (August 21, 1995), p. 6; and "Paying to Avoid Pitches," *Marketing News* (November 8, 1995), p. 1.

18. Ronald B. Marks, *Personal Selling: An Integrative Approach* 3rd ed. (Boston: Allyn & Bacon, 1988), p. 239.

19. "Doing Business in Chili," *American Way Magazine* (July 15, 1995), p. 40.

20. "Corporate Cultures: Clearing Customs."

21. For a variation on the "canned presentation," see Marvin A. Jolson, "Canned Adaptiveness: A New Direction for Modern Salesmanship," *Business Horizons* (January–February 1989), pp. 7–12.

22. Research on these formats can be found in Barton A. Weitz, Harish Sujan, and Mita Sujan, "Knowledge, Motivation, and Adaptive Behavior: A Framework for Improving Selling Effectiveness," *Journal of Marketing* (October 1986), pp. 174–91; Thomas W. Leigh and Patrick F. McGraw, "Mapping the Procedural Knowledge of Industrial Sales Personnel: A Script-Theoretic Investigation," *Journal of Marketing* (January 1989), pp. 16–34; David M. Symanski, "Determinants of Selling Effectiveness: The Importance of Declarative Knowledge to the Personal Selling Concept," *Journal of Marketing* (January 1988), pp. 64–67; Rosann L. Spiro and Barton A. Weitz, "Adaptive Selling: Conceptualization, Measurement, and Normological Validity," *Journal of Marketing Research* (February 1990), pp. 61–69; and Thomas Blackshear and Richard E. Plank, "The Impact of Adaptive Selling on Sales Effectiveness within the Pharmaceutical Industry," *Journal of Marketing Theory and Practice* (Summer 1994), pp. 106–25.

23. Based on David Mercer, *High-Level Selling* (Houston, TX: Golf Publishing, 1990), pp. 130–31; and Ronald D. Balsley and E. Patricia Birsner, *Selling: Marketing Personified* (Hinsdale, Ill.: Dryden Press, 1987), pp. 261–63.

24. Philip R. Cateora, *International Marketing,* 9th ed. (Chicago: Richard D. Irwin, 1996), pp. 126–27; Carl R. Ruthstrom and Ken Matejka, "The Meanings of 'Yes' in the Far East," *Industrial Marketing Management,* 19 (1990), pp. 191–92. See also Terri Morrison, Wayne A. Conaway, and George A. Borden, *Kiss, Bow, or Shake Hands* (Newton Square, Pa.: Adam Media Group, 1994).

25. Theodore Levitt, *The Marketing Imagination* (New York: Free Press, 1983), p. 111.

26. "Leading Edge," *Sales and Marketing Management* (July 1995), p. 13.

27. *Management Briefing: Marketing* (New York: The Conference Board, October 1986), pp. 3–4.

28. Based on Barton A. Weitz, Stephen B. Castleberry, and John F. Tanner, Jr., *Selling: Building Partnerships* (Homewood, Ill.: Richard D. Irwin, 1992), pp. 7–8; Alan J. Dubinsky, Marvin A. Jolson, Ronald E. Michaels, Masaaki Kotobe, and Chae Un Lim, "Ethical Perceptions of Field Sales Personnel: An Empirical Assessment," *Journal of Personal Selling & Sales Management* (Fall 1992), pp. 9–21; and Alan J. Dubinsky, Marvin A. Jolson, Masaaki Kotobe, and Chae Un Lim, "A Cross-National Investigation of Industrial Salespeople's Ethical Perceptions," *Journal of International Business Studies* (Fourth Quarter 1991), pp. 651–70.

29. Benson Shapiro, *Sales Program Management: Formulation and Implementation* (New York: McGraw-Hill, 1977), pp. 250–55.

30. Several variations of the account management policy grid exist. See, for example, Gilbert A. Churchill, Jr., Neil M. Ford, and Orville C. Walker, Jr., *Sales Force Management: Planning, Implementation, and Control,* 5th ed. (Chicago, Ill.: Richard D. Irwin, 1997), p. 249; and David W. Cravens, Thomas N. Ingram, and Raymond W. LaForge, "Evaluating Multiple Channel Strategies," *The Journal of Business & Industrial Marketing* (Fall 1991), pp. 37–48.

31. Patricia Sellers, "How to Remake Your Sales Force," *Fortune* (May 4, 1992), p. 103.

32. This discussion is based on Douglas J. Dalrymple and William L. Cron, *Sales Management,* 5th ed. (New York: John Wiley & Sons, Inc., 1995), pp. 421–24.

33. "What Buyers Look For," *Sales & Marketing Management* (August 1995), p. 31.

34. Neil M. Ford, Orville C. Walker, Jr., Gilbert A. Churchill, Jr., and Steven W. Hartley, "Selecting Successful Salespeople: A Meta-Analysis of Biographical and Psychological Selection Criteria," in Michael J. Houston, ed., *Review of Marketing 1987* (Chicago: American Marketing Association, 1988), pp. 90–131.

35. "What's Selling? Sales Jobs," *Sales & Marketing Management* (September 1993), p. 11; and *Occupation Outlook Quarterly* (Washington D.C.: U.S. Department of Labor, Fall 1995).

36. "Is There a Payoff?" *Sales & Marketing Management* (June 1995), pp. 64–71.

37. Earl D. Honeycutt, Jr., Clyde E. Harris, Jr., and Stephen B. Castleberry, "Sales Training: A Status Report," *Training and Development Journal* (May 1987), pp. 42–47.

38. Dalrymple and Cron.

39. See, for example, William L. Cron, Alan J. Dubinsky, and Ronald E. Michaels, "The Influence of Career Stages on Components of Salesperson Motivation," *Journal of Marketing* (January 1988), pp. 78–92; Pradeep K. Tyagi, "Relative Importance of Key Job Dimensions and Leadership Behaviors in Motivating Salesperson Work Performance," *Journal of Marketing* (Summer 1985), pp. 76–86; Richard C. Beckerer, Fred Morgan, and Lawrence Richard, "The Job Characteristics of Industrial Salespersons: Relationship to Motivation and Satisfaction," *Journal of Marketing* (Fall 1982), pp. 125–35; and Walter Kiechel III, "How to Manage Salespeople," *Fortune* (March 14, 1988), pp. 179–80.

40. For statistics and research on salesperson turnover, see "Turnover Rates by Industry Group," *Sales & Marketing Management* (June 22, 1992); George H. Lucas, Jr., A. Parasuraman, Robert A. Davis, and Ben Enis, "An Empirical Study of Salesforce Turnover," *Journal of Marketing* (July 1987), pp. 34–59; and René Y. Darmon, "Identifying Sources of Turnover Costs: A Segmental Approach," *Journal of Marketing* (April 1990), pp. 46–56. See also Edward F. Fern, Ramon A. Avila, and Dhruv Grewal, "Salesforce Turnover: Those Who Left and Those Who Stayed," *Industrial Marketing Management,* vol. 18 (1989), pp. 1–9; and Thomas R. Wotruba and Pradeep K. Tyagi, "Met Expectations and Turnover in Direct Selling," *Journal of Marketing* (July 1991), pp. 24–35.

41. "More Companies Link Sales Pay to Customer Satisfaction," *The Wall Street Journal* (March 29, 1994), p. A1; and "IBM Leans on Its Sales Force," *Business Week* (February 7, 1994), p. 110. For a recent study on this topic, see Arun Sharma and Dan Sanel, "The Impact of Customer Satisfaction Based Incentive Systems on Salespeople's Customer Service Response," *Journal of Personal Selling & Sales Management* (Summer 1995), pp. 17–29.

42. Melissa Campanelli, "Eastman Chemical: A Formula for Quality," *Sales & Marketing Management* (October 1994), p. 88; William Keenan, Jr., "What's Sales Got to Do With It?" *Sales & Marketing Management* (March 1994), pp. 66–70; and Cravens.

43. George W. Colombo, *Sales Force Automation* (New York: McGraw-Hill, 1994).

44. Cravens.

45. Robert L. Lindstrom, "Training Hits the Road," *Sales & Marketing Management,* part 2 (June 1995), pp. 10–14.

46. "Going Mobile, Part 2," *Sales & Marketing Management* (June 1994), p. 5.

47. Cravens.

48. "The Office That Never Closes," *Forbes* (May 23, 1994), pp. 212–13.

Contemporary Developments in Selling Today: This case was prepared by Linda Rochford of the University of Minnesota–Duluth.

CHAPTER 22

1. Greg Burns, "A Fruit Loop by Any Other Name . . . " *Business Week* (June 26, 1995), pp. 72–76.

2. *General Mills 1995 Midyear Report* (Minneapolis, MN: General Mills, Inc., 1995); and Richard Gibson, "General Mills to Spin Off Restaurants in Effort to Focus on Its Core Business," *The Wall Street Journal* (December 15, 1994), pp. A3, A9.

3. Kevin Goldman, "General Mills to Launch Frosted Cheerios," *The Wall Street Journal* (July 25, 1995), p. B3; Terry Fledler, "Soul of a New Cheerios," *Star Tribune* (January 28, 1996), pp. D1, D4; and Tony Kennedy, "New Cheerios about to Sweeten Cereal Market," *Star Tribune* (July 25, 1995), pp. 1D, /2/d.

4. Pankaj Ghemawat, "Sustainable Advantage," *Harvard Business Review* (September–October 1986), pp. 53–58.

5. Roger A. Kerin, P. Rajan Varadarajan, and Robert A. Peterson, "First-Mover Advantage: A Synthesis, Conceptual Framework, and Research Propositions," *Journal of Marketing* (October 1992), pp. 33–52.

6. Murali K. Mantrala, Prabhakant Sirha, and Andris A. Zoltners, "Impact of Resource Allocation Rules on Marketing Investment-Level Decisions and Profitability," *Journal of Marketing Research* (May 1992), pp. 162–75.

7. Leah Rickard, "General Mills Gathers Rewards of Change," *Advertising Age* (July 10, 1995), p. 4.

8. This discussion and Figure 22–3 are adapted from Stanley F. Stasch and Patricia Longtree, "Can Your Marketing Planning Procedures Be Improved?" *Journal of Marketing* (Summer 1980), p. 82; by permission of the American Marketing Association.

9. Fledler.

10. *Ibid.*

11. Adapted with permission of The Free Press, a Division of Macmillan, Inc., from *Competitive Advantage: Creating and Sustaining Superior Performance* by Michael E. Porter. Copyright 1985 by Michael E. Porter.

12. William B. Wertner, Jr. and Jeffrey L. Kerr, "The Shifting Sands of Competitive Advantage," *Business Horizons* (May–June, 1995), pp. 11–17.

13. Michael Treacy and Fred Wiersma, "How Market Leaders Keep Their Edge," *Fortune* (February 6, 1995), pp. 88–89.

14. J. Martin Fraering and Michael S. Minor, "The Industry-Specific Basis of the Market Share-Profitability Relationship," *Journal of Consumer Marketing,* vol 11, no. 1 (1994), pp. 27–37.

15. Michael Oneal, " 'God, Family, and Domino's—That's It,' " *Business Week* (January 30, 1995), pp. 57–60.

16. Stratford Sherman, "How Intel Makes Spending Pay Off," *Fortune* (February 22, 1993), pp. 57–61.

17. Lee Ginsburg and Neil Miller, "Value-Driven Management," *Business Horizons* (May–June 1992), pp. 23–27; Richard L. Osborn, "Core Value Statements: The Corporate Compass," *Business Horizons* (September–October 1991), pp. 28–34; and Charles E. Watson, "Managing with Integrity: Social Responsibilities of Business as Seen by America's CEOs," *Business Horizons* (July–August 1991), pp. 99–109.

18. Reprinted by permission of the *Harvard Business Review.* An exhibit from "Making Your Marketing Strategy Work" by Thomas V. Bonoma (March/April 1984). Copyright © 1984 by the President and Fellows of Harvard College; all rights reserved.

19. Larry Hirschhorn and Thomas Gilmore, "The New Boundaries of the 'Boundaryless' Company," *Harvard Business Review* (May–June 1992), pp. 104–15.

20. John Byrne, Richard Brandt, and Otis Port, "The Virtual Corporation," *Business Week* (February 8, 1993), pp. 98–103; Hans Hinterhuber and Wolfgang Popp, "Are You a Strategist or Just a Manager?" *Harvard Business Review* (January–February 1992), pp. 105–13; Thomas Steward, "The Search for the Organization of Tomorrow," *Fortune* (May 18, 1992), pp. 92–98; George Stalf, Philip Evans, and Lawrence Shulman, "Competing on Capabilities: The New Rules of Corporate Strategy," *Harvard Business Review* (March–April 1992), pp. 57–69; and Jon Katzenbach and Douglas Smith, *The Wisdom of Teams* (Boston: Harvard Business School Press, 1992).

21. Don Frey, "Learning the Ropes: My Life as a Product Champion," *Harvard Business Review* (September–October 1991), pp. 46–56.

22. Thomas J. Peters and Robert H. Waterman, Jr., *In Search of Excellence: Lessons from America's Best-Run Companies* (New York: Harper & Row, 1982).

23. Ralph Vartabedian, "Built for the Future," *Minneapolis Star Tribune* (April 7, 1992), pp. 1D, 70; Roy J. Harris, Jr., "The Skunk Works: Hush-Hush Projects Often Emerge There," *The Wall Street Journal* (October 13, 1980), p. 1; and Tom Peters, "Winners Do Hundreds of Percent over Norm," *Minneapolis Star Tribune* (January 8, 1985), p. 5B.

24. The scheduling example is adapted from William Rudelius and W. Bruce Erickson, *An Introduction to Contemporary Business,* 4th ed. (New York: Harcourt Brace Jovanovich, 1985), pp. 94–95.

25. Robert W. Ruekert and Orville W. Walker, Jr., "Marketing's Interaction with Other Functional Units: A Conceptual Framework and Empirical Evidence," *Journal of Consumer Marketing* (Spring 1987), pp. 1–19; and Steven Lysonski, Alan Singer, and David Wilemone, "Coping with Environmental Uncertainty and Boundary Spanning in the Product Manager's Role," *Journal of Consumer Marketing* (Spring 1989), pp. 33–43.

26. John Grossman, "Ken Iverson: Simply the Best," *American Way* (August 1, 1987), pp. 23–25; Thomas Moore, "Goodbye, Corporate Staff," *Fortune* (December 21, 1987), pp. 65–76; and Michael Schroeder and Walecia Konrad, "Nucor: Rolling Right into Steel's Big Time," *Business Week* (November 19, 1990), pp. 76–81.

Yoplait USA: This case was prepared by William Rudelius. Sources: Personal interviews with Chap Colucci and Steven M. Rothschild.

APPENDIX C

1. Denny E. McCorkle, Joe F. Alexander, and Memo F. Diriker, "Developing Self-Marketing Skills for Student Career Success," *Journal of Marketing Education* (Spring 1992), pp. 57–67.

2. *Job Choices in Business: 1996,* 39th ed., (Bethlehem, Pa.: National Association of Colleges and Employers, 1995).

3. Nicholas Basta, "The Wide World of Marketing," *Business Week's Guide to Careers* (February–March 1984), pp. 70–72.

4. "The Corporate Elite," *Business Week* (October 12, 1992), pp. 119–46.

5. *Salary Survey,* (Bethlehem, Pa.: National Association of Colleges and Employers, September 1995), p. 2.

6. "Occupations to Watch," *Job Choices in Business: 1996,* p. 7; and David Gumpert, "Reaching for the Best Opportunity: 10 High-Flying Businesses to Join in the 90s," *Managing Your Career,* (Spring 1992), pp. 4–6.

7. Linda M. Gorchels, "Traditional Product Management Evolves," *Marketing News* (January 30, 1995), p. 4; "Focus on Five Stages of Category Management," *Marketing News* (September 28, 1992), pp. 17, 19; and Sandy Gillis, "On the Job: Product Manager," *Business Week's Guide to Careers* (April–May 1988), pp. 63–66.

8. Phil Moss, "What It's Like to Work for Procter & Gamble," *Business Week's Guide to Careers* (March–April 1987), pp. 18–20.

9. David Kirkpatrick, "Is Your Career on Track?" *Fortune* (July 2, 1990), pp. 38–48.

10. Robin T. Peterson, "Wholesaling: A Neglected Job Opportunity for Marketing Majors," *Marketing News* (January 15, 1996), p. 4.

11. "Advertising," *Career Guide to America's Top Industries* (Indianapolis, Ind.: JIST Works, 1994), pp. 142–45.

12. "The Climb to the Top," *Careers in Retailing* (January 1995), p. 18.

13. Justin Martin, "How Does Your Pay Really Stack Up?" *Fortune* (June 26, 1995), pp. 79–86.

14. Milan Moravec, Marshall Collins, and Clinton Tripoli, "Don't Want to Manage? Here's Another Path," *Sales and Marketing Management* (June 1990), pp. 62–72.

15. William Keenan, Jr., "America's Best Sales Forces: Six at the Summit," *Sales and Marketing Management* (June 1990), pp. 62–72.

16. Perri Capell, "Direct-Marketing Pros Enjoy Surging Demand," *National Business Employment Weekly* (January 1–January 7, 1995), pp. 23–24; and "1995 Best Sales Force Awards," *Sales and Marketing Management* (October 1995), pp. 52–63.

17. Michael R. Wukitsch, "Should Researchers Know More about Marketing?" *Marketing Research* (Winter 1993), p. 50.

18. "Market Research Analyst," in Les Krantz, ed., *Jobs Rated Almanac,* 3rd ed., (New York: John Wiley & Sons, 1995).

19. Cyndee Miller, "Marketing Research Salaries Up a Bit, But Layoffs Take Toll," *Marketing News* (June 19, 1995), pp. 1, 3.

20. Joby John and Mark Needel, "Entry-Level Marketing Research Recruits: What Do Recruiters Need?" *Journal of Marketing Education* (Spring 1989), pp. 68–73.

21. Susan B. Larsen, "International Careers: Reality, Not Fantasy," *CPC Annual: A Guide to Employment Opportunities for College Graduates,*

36th ed. (Bethlehem, Pa.: College Placement Council, Inc., 1992), pp. 78–85.

22. John W. Buckner, "Working Abroad at Home," *Managing Your Career* (Spring 1992), pp. 16–17.

23. Kathryn Petras and Ross Petras, *Jobs 95* (New York: Fireside, 1994), pp. 100–18.

24. "Your Job Search Starts with You," *Job Choices: 1996,* 39th ed. (Bethlehem, Pa.: National Association of Colleges and Employers, 1995), pp. 6–9; Hugh E. Kramer, "Applying Marketing Strategy and Personal Value Analysis to Career Planning: An Experiential Approach," *Journal of Marketing Education* (Fall 1988), pp. 69–73; Alan Deutschman, "What 25-Year-Olds Want," *Fortune* (August 27, 1990), pp. 42–50; and Dawn Richerson, "Personality and Your Career," *Career Woman* (Winter 1993), pp. 46–47.

25. Arthur F. Miller, "Discover Your Design," in *CPC Annual,* vol. 1 (Bethlehem, Pa.: College Placement Council, Inc., 1984), p. 2.

26. Robin T. Peterson and J. Stuart Devlin, "Perspectives on Entry-Level Positions by Graduating Marketing Seniors," *Marketing Education Review* (Summer 1994), pp. 2–5.

27. Diane Goldner, "Fill in the Blank," *The Wall Street Journal* (February 27, 1995), pp. R5, R11.

28. James C. Gonyea, *The Online Job Search Companion* (New York: McGraw-Hill, 1995).

29. Ronald B. Marks, *Personal Selling* (Boston: Allyn & Bacon, 1985), pp. 451–62.

30. Constance J. Pritchard, "Small Employers—How, When & Who They Hire," *Job Choices: 1996,* 39th ed., (Bethlehem, Pa.: National Association of Colleges and Employers, 1995), pp. 66–69.

31. John L. Munschauer, "How to Find a Customer for Your Capabilities," in *1984–1985 CPC Annual,* vol. 1 (Bethlehem, Pa.: College Placement Council, Inc., 1984), p. 24.

32. C. Randall Powell, "Secrets of Selling a Résumé," in Peggy Schmidt, ed., *The Honda How to Get a Job Guide* (New York: McGraw-Hill, 1984), pp. 4–9.

33. Powell, p. 4.

34. Adapted from C. Randall Powell, "Secrets of Selling a Résumé," in Peggy Schmidt, ed., *The Honda How to Get a Job Guide* (New York: McGraw-Hill, 1985), pp. 4–9.

35. Joyce Lain Kennedy and Thomas J. Morrow, *Electronic Resume Revolution* (New York: John Wiley & Sons, 1994).

36. Arthur G. Sharp, "The Art of the Cover Letter," *Career Futures,* vol. 4, no. 1 (1992), pp. 50–51.

37. Perri Capell, "Unconventional Job Search Tactics," *Managing Your Career* (Spring 1991), pp. 31, 35.

38. Julie Griffin Levitt, *Your Career: How to Make It Happen* (Cincinnati: South-Western Publishing Co., 1985).

39. Deborah Vendy, "Drug Screening and Your Career," *CPC Annual* (Bethlehem, Pa.: College Placement Council, 1992), pp. 61–62.

40. Marks, p. 469.

41. Terence P. Pare, "The Uncommitted Class of 1989," *Fortune* (June 5, 1989), pp. 199–210.

42. Bob Weinstein, "What Employers Look For," in Peggy Schmidt, ed., *The Honda How to Get a Job Guide* (New York: McGraw-Hill, 1985), p. 10.

APPENDIX D

1. This case was prepared by Professors Rajiv Vaidyanathan and Linda Rochford, University of Minnesota–Duluth, from the following sources: Amy Cortese, "Windows of Opportunity for Big Blue?" *Business Week* (October 17, 1994), p. 184; Laurie Flynn, "IBM Software Chief Sees an Opening for OS/2," *New York Times* (July 24, 1994), p. 7; Craig Stedman, "What's Ahead for OS/2?" *Computerworld,* vol. 29 (August 7, 1995), p. 4; Bart Ziegler, "Glitch Halts IBM Software Production," *The Wall Street Journal* (October 27, 1994), p. B8; Bart Ziegler, "IBM Won't Provide Way for Programs for Windows 95 to Run on OS/2 System," *The Wall Street Journal* (June 20, 1995), p. B6; and Laurence Zuckerman, "IBM Chief Concedes OS/2 Has Lost Desktop War," *New York Times* (August 1, 1995), p. D4.

2. This case was prepared by Professor Roger A. Kerin, Southern Methodist University, from the following sources: "Girl Scout Campaign Active Image," *Advertising Age* (September 4, 1989), p. 28; "Profiting from the Nonprofits," *Business Week* (March 26, 1990), pp. 66ff; and Maria Shao, "The Girl Scouts Make Many Changes to Stay Viable in the 1980's," *The Wall Street Journal* (June 15, 1982), pp. 1, 22.

3. This case was prepared by Professor Linda Rochford, University of Minnesota–Duluth, from the following sources: Nancy Rivera Brooks, "How to Get a Business Loan," *Los Angeles Times* (May 16, 1993); David Eddy, "Juice Club: Smoothin' Its Way to Success," *San Luis Obispo County Telegram–Tribune* (April 23, 1993); Kinney Littlefield, "Slurp to Heart's Content at Juice Club," *The Orange County Register* (April 23, 1993); and Beth Lorenzini, "Turn Up the Juice," *Restaurants and Institutions,* vol. 105, no. 3 (February 1, 1995), p. 113.

4. This case was adapted by Mark Weber from a case originally written by Norman Bowie and Stefanie Ann Lenway and from additional sources, including Paul McEnroe and Susan E. Peterson, "H.B. Fuller Sued in Teen's Death," *Minneapolis Star Tribune* (January 4, 1996), pp. D1, D2.

5. This case was prepared by Professors Linda Rochford and Rajiv Vaidyanathan, University of Minnesota–Duluth, from the following sources: Interview with Doran Normi, Kingpin Manufacturing; and the National Sporting Goods Association, "1993 Sports Participation Study."

6. This case was prepared by Roy D. Adler, Professor of Marketing, Pepperdine University–Malibu, as a basis for class discussion. Copyright © by Roy D. Adler. Reproduced with permission.

7. This case was prepared by Professor Roger A. Kerin, Southern Methodist University.

8. This case was prepared by Professor James E. Nelson, University of Colorado at Boulder. Used with permission.

9. The cooperation of Heart Rate Incorporated in the preparation of this case is gratefully acknowledged. This case was prepared by Steve O'Brien and Kris Sirchio, graduate students at Southern Methodist University. Some information is disguised, while other information is illustrative and not useful for research purposes. Used with permission.

10. This case was prepared by Professor Linda Rochford, University of Minnesota–Duluth, from the following sources: Stuart F. Brown, "Quest for the Boojum," *Popular Science* (July 1995), pp. 77–81; Brian O'Reilly, "What's a Hummer? Aah! Thought You'd Never Ask," *Fortune* (October 2, 1995), p. 146; "His Summer in a Hummer," *Fortune* (October 2, 1995), pp. 154–55; and AM General press package 1996.

11. This case was prepared by Professor Roger A. Kerin, Southern Methodist University, from the following sources: "For Rogaine, No Miracle Cure—Yet," *Business Week* (June 4, 1990), p. 100; "Britain Approves Upjohn Hair Drug," *New York Times* (April 6, 1990), p. D4; Stephen W. Quickel, "Bald Spot," *Business Month* (November 1989), pp. 36–37ff; "Hair Today: Rogaine's Growing Pains," *New York Times* (October 30, 1990), p. 20; "Upjohn Turns to Women to Increase Rogaine Sales," *Advertising Age* (January 2, 1992), p. 4; "Blondes, Brunettes, Redheads, and Rogaine," *American Druggist* (June 1992), pp. 39–40; and "Rogaine: Promises, Promises, Promises," *Advertising Age* (October 3, 1993), p. S14.

12. This case was prepared by Krzysztof Przybyowski, Warsaw School of Economics, Susan Rosen, graduate student, and William Rudelius, University of Minnesota, from the following sources: Jane Perlez, "Poles a Quick Study with Fast Food," *New York Times* (October 6, 1993), p. C3; "Global Hustle," *Forbes* (September 13, 1993), p. 222; and site visits to U.S. and Polish restaurants.

13. This case was prepared by Professor Roger A. Kerin, Southern Methodist University.

14. This case was prepared by Professors Maurice Mandell and Larry J. Rosenberg. Reprinted by permission of Prentice-Hall, Inc.

15. This case was prepared by Professor John W. Mullins and Christina L. Grippi, University of Denver. Copyright © by the *Case Research Journal.*

16. This case was prepared by Professor Linda Rochford, University of Minnesota–Duluth, from the following sources: John Welbes, "Coffee Connoisseurs," *Duluth News Tribune* (September 25, 1995), pp. 1B, 3B, 5B; Dori Jones Yang, "The Starbucks Enterprise Shifts into Warp Speed," *Business Week* (October 24, 1994), pp. 76–77; and Rhonda Brammer, "Grounds for Caution," *Barrons* (August 15, 1994), p. 20.

17. This case was prepared by Professor Rajiv Vaidyanathan, University of Minnesota–Duluth, from the following sources: Curt Harler, "Logistics on the Cutting Edge of Wireless," *Transportation and Distribution,* 36 (March 1995), pp. 30–35; "The UPS Story," Information at UPS WWW site (http://www.ups.com/news/); "UPS Facts," Information at UPS WWW site (http://www.ups.com/news/); "UPS Strengthens Worldwide Logistics Unit," May 10, 1995 Press Release at UPS WWW site (http://www.ups.com/news/); "UPS Worldwide Logistics Opens Regional Distribution Center in Singapore," January 15, 1996 Press Release at UPS WWW site (http://

www.ups.com.news/); and "UPS Worldwide Logistics to Develop Warehouse Complex Near UPS International Air Hub in Louisville," March 22, 1995 Press Release at UPS WWW site (http://www.ups.com/news/).

18. This case was prepared by Professor Linda Rochford, University of Minnesota–Duluth, from the following sources: Brian Silverman, "Shopping for Loyal Customers," *Sales and Marketing Management* (March 1995), pp. 96–97; Nordstrom Employment Opportunities, Publication P3003, Rev. 5/94; Robert Spector and Patrick D. McCarthy, *The Nordstrom Way: The Inside Story of America's #1 Customer Service Company* (New York: John Wiley and Sons, 1994).

19. This case was prepared by Professor Rajiv Vaidyanathan and Linda Rochford, University of Minnesota–Duluth, from the following sources: "Heights and Depths of Hype," *Advertising Age* (August 28, 1995), pp. 1, 33; Matt Carmichael, "Web Sites Showcase Win 95," *Advertising Age* (August 28, 1995), p. 33; Alice Z. Cuneo, "Apple Gets Gnarly Over Introduction," *Advertising Age* (August 28, 1995); Michael Himowitz "Windows 95: Do You Need the Most Overhyped Product of the Decade?" *Fortune* (September 18, 1995), pp. 191–96; Bradley Johnson "D-Day Countdown for Win 95, Microsoft Net," *Advertising Age* (August 7, 1995), p. 3; and Bradley Johnson, "Windows 95 Opens with Omnimedia Blast," *Advertising Age* (August 28, 1995), pp. 1, 32.

20. This case was prepared by Professors Linda Rochford and Rajiv Vaidyanathan, University of Minnesota–Duluth, from the following sources: "Image-conscious Consumers Wear Social Ambitions on Wrist," *Duluth News Tribune* (August 2, 1995), p. 6; "Timex Plans $10M Push in 4th Quarter," *Advertising Age* (September 6, 1993), p. 23; "Timex, Swatch Campaigns Set for Battle," *The Wall Street Journal* (May 31, 1995), p. B9; "The Best Advertising of 1992," *Time* (January 4, 1993), p. 70; Riccardo A. Davis, "More Ads to Watch," *Advertising Age* (February 7, 1994), p. 50; Elaine Underwood, "Indiglo Watch Lights Up, Better Times for Timex," *Brandweek* (April 25, 1994), pp. 30–32; Neal McGrath, "Timex, After a Licking, They're Back Ticking," *Asian Business* (December 1994), pp. 18–20; and Chris Roush, "At Timex, They're Positively Glowing," *Business Week* (July 12, 1993), p. 141.

21. This case was prepared by Professor Roger A. Kerin, Southern Methodist University.

22. This case was prepared by Professor Roger A. Kerin, Southern Methodist University, from the following sources: "Hasbro's Hopes for Maxie Model Come to an End," *The Wall Street Journal* (February 12, 1990), p. B4; "For Video Games, Now It's a Battle of Bits," *The Wall Street Journal* (January 9, 1990), pp. B1, B4; "Barbie Is on the Front Line for Marketing Ethnic Dolls," *Dallas Times Herald* (August 30, 1990), pp. D1, D4; "It's Kid Brother's Turn to Keep Hasbro Hot," *Business Week* (June 26, 1989), pp. 152–53; "Toyland Turnaround," *Forbes* (January 9, 1989), pp. 168–69; Andrea Stone, "Toy Fair No Picnic for Toy Industry," *USA Today* (February 8, 1988), pp. B1–B2; and "Mattel Takes Page from Hasbro Playbook," *The Wall Street Journal* (January 30, 1996), p. B7.

Name Index

A

Aaker, David A., 684 n, 690 n, 691 n
Abell, Derek, 675 n
Abernathy, Avery M., 690 n
Abraham, Magid M., 689 n
Abrahams, Jeffrey, 675 n
Abrahms, Rhonda M., 58
Abramson, Tom, 507
Achenreiner, Gewn, 691 n
Adams, Joe, 685 n
Adams, Scott, 242
Addicks, Mark, 581–582
Adkins, Derrick, 233
Adler, Roy D., 694 n
Aerosmith, 387
Ajami, Riad, 688 n
Akaah, Ismael P., 676 n
Alba, Joseph W., 679 n
Alcorn, David S., 677 n
Alden, Dana L., 691 n
Alexander, Jason, 530
Alexander, Joe F., 693 n
Alexander, Keith, 674 n
Alexander, Steve, 683 n
Allman, Greg, 386
Allport, Gordon, 679 n
Allvine, Fred C., 690 n
Alsop, Ronald, 679 n
Amann, E., 677 n
Amelio, Gilbert F., 250, 252
Anderson, Erin, 681 n
Anderson, James C., 681 n
Anderson, Stephanie, 676 n
Andrews, Rick, 686 n
Anglin, Kenneth A., 691 n
Apgar, Sally, 682 n
Arens, William F., 534, 691 n
Armour, James, 638-639
Armstrong, J. Scott, 675 n
Armstrong, Larry, 675 n, 683 n, 689 n
Arpan, Jeffrey S., 689 n
Atchison, Sandra, 684 n
Augustine, Scott, 226–227, 682 n
Avila, Ramon A., 692 n
Ayres, Ian, 686 n

B

Babb, Emerson M., 689 n
Badarocco, J., Jr., 676 n
Bagozzi, Richard P., 64 n
Baker, Julie, 689 n
Baker, R. C., 684 n

Bakken, Earl, 304
Baksha, Joe, 387
Balasubramanlan, Siva K., 689 n
Balsley, Ronald D., 692 n
Banks, Allen, 691 n
Bannon, Lisa, 689 n
Banting, Peter M., 680 n, 681 n
Barasch, Kenneth L., 622
Bardi, Edward J., 687 n
Barich, Howard, 689 n
Barlas, Stephen, 691 n
Barnes, Jimmy D., 690 n
Barnes, John, 689 n
Barnum, P. T., 492
Barrett, Katherine, 691 n
Barrett, Paul, 676 n
Bartos, Rena, 679 n
Bass, Stephen J., 689 n
Basta, Nicholas, 693 n
Bates, Albert D., 689 n
Bawa, Kapil, 689 n
Bayers, Barry L., 680 n
Beardon, William O., 680 n
Beckerer, Richard C., 692 n
Beier, F. J., 687 n
Belch, George E., 686 n
Belch, Michael A., 686 n
Belk, Russell, 679 n
Bellizzi, Joseph A., 681 n, 685 n
Ben-Akiva, Moshe, 679 n
Benjamin, Robert, 682 n, 688 n
Bennett, Peter D., 622, 674 n, 685 n, 686 n, 688 n, 689 n
Bennett, Tony, 531
Beracs, Joszef, 681 n
Bergen, Candice, 519, 531, 691 n
Berger, Paul D., 687 n
Berner, Robert, 675 n
Bernstein, Paul, 677 n
Berry, Jonathan, 682 n
Berry, Leonard L., 684 n, 685 n
Berss, Marcia, 688 n
Best, Roger J., 679 n, 680 n
Bettencourt, Nuno, 387
Bigne, J. Enrique, 690 n
Bigness, Jon, 687 n
Bingham, Frank G., Jr., 680 n, 681 n
Birnbaum, Jeffrey H., 686 n
Birsner, E. Patricia, 692 n
Bisei, Michael, 677 n
Bitner, Mary Jo, 684 n, 689 n
Blackshear, Thomas, 692 n
Blackwell, Roger D., 679 n, 680 n

Blair, Bonnie, 27
Blanko, Vincent, 690 n
Blattberg, Robert C., 682 n, 686 n
Blenkhorn, David L., 680 n
Bloch, Tim, 685 n
Block, Peter H., 680 n
Boccara, Bruno, 679 n
Bolles, Richard N., 622
Bolton, Ruth N., 679 n, 685 n
Bommer, M., 676 n
Bond, Christopher E., 688 n
Bond, Robert E., 688 n
Bongiorno, Lori, 688 n, 689 n
Bonoma, Thomas V., 681 n, 693 n
Booms, Bernard H., 684 n
Borden, George A., 692 n
Boring, Christopher, 484
Borrus, Amy, 684 n
Bounds, Wendy, 675 n
Bowen, David E., 684 n, 685 n
Bowie, Norman, 694 n
Boyd, Harper W., Jr., 674 n, 683 n
Brammer, Rhonda, 694 n
Brandt, Richard, 675 n, 693 n
Braus, Patricia, 675 n
Breen, Brady, 386
Brierty, Edward G., 680 n
Brighton, Julie, 645-647
Brinkley, Christie, 531
Bristor, Julia M., 681 n
Britney, Robert, 686 n
Brockwell, Ed, 284
Brodie, Roderick J., 675 n
Brooks, Nancy Rivera, 694 n
Brown, Barry, 688 n
Brown, Christie, 686 n
Brown, Herbert E., 681 n
Brown, Jacqueline, 680 n
Brown, James, 259
Brown, James Paul, 445
Brown, James R., 680 n, 687 n
Brown, Jeff, 569
Brown, Neil, 689 n
Brown, Rich, 675 n
Brown, Robert George, 689 n
Brown, Stephen, 689 n
Brown, Stephen W., 684 n
Brown, Stuart F., 694 n
Browning, E. S., 678 n
Brownson, Carol, 345
Brucker, Roger W., 681 n
Brucks, Merrie, 679 n
Bruner, Gordon C., III, 679 n

COMPANY INDEX

INDEX

CREDITS

CHAPTER 1

p. 4, Photograph by Douglas Mason/Woodfin Camp & Associates; p. 8, Courtesy of Rollerblade, Inc.; p. 11, New Product Showcase and Learning Center Inc./Photograph by Robert Haller; p. 13, Courtesy of American Library Association; p. 14, Courtesy of Dell Computer Corporation; p. 14, Courtesy of NIKE, Inc.; p. 14, Courtesy of Lands' End; p. 17, Courtesy of Rollerblade, Inc.; p. 18, Courtesy of Rollerblade, Inc.; p. 19, Courtesy of *Inline* Magazine/Photograph by Tony Donaldson; p. 23, Courtesy of ProChile; p. 23 © American Museum of Natural History, New York; p. 26, Photograph by Larry Marcus.

CHAPTER 2

p. 28, Photograph ©1996 E. Lee White; p. 32, Courtesy of Norfolk Southern Corporation; p. 36, Courtesy of Sears Roebuck & Co., model: Megan Griffith/Wilhelmina Models, photographer: Gilles Bensemon; p. 37, *Moody's Industrial Manual*; p. 39, Courtesy of Black & Decker; p. 39, Courtesy of Intel Corporation; p. 40, Courtesy of Hewlett-Packard; p. 44, Courtesy of Ben & Jerry's Homemade, Inc.; p. 47, ©1996 Paradise Kitchens, Inc. Reprinted with permission; p. 50, Reprinted with permission from Eastman Kodak Company; p. 52, Reprinted with permission from Eastman Kodak Company; p. 54, Specialized Bicycle Components, Inc.; p. 55, Courtesy of Specialized Bicycles; p. 56, DILBERT reprinted by permission of United Features Syndicate, Inc. **Appendix A:** pp. 59, 61, 65, 67, 69, 70 ©1996 Paradise Kitchens Inc. All photos and ads reprinted with permission.

CHAPTER 3

p. 74, Photograph © 1996 Amy Guip; p. 78, Percent of U.S. population by age, 1900–90, and projections to 2050, p. 52, *American Demographics* Magazine, © 1995, reprinted with permission; p. 79, Courtesy of Club Med Sales, Inc.; p. 83, Courtesy of Saturn Corporation; p. 84,

"The Feel-Good Index," pp. 56-60, *American Demographics* Magazine, © 1992, reprinted with permission; p. 86, Courtesy of Westin Hotels & Resorts, agency: Cole & Weber/Seattle, photographers: Kathleen Norris Cook and Tim Bieber/Image Bank Northwest and Tony Stone Images; p. 87, Courtesy of Ford Motor Company; p. 87, Courtesy of USSB; p. 88, Graphic image supplied courtesy of Environmental Systems Research Institute, Inc. (ESRI); p. 89, Courtesy of Young & Rubicam/Frankfurt; p. 89, Courtesy of Lever Brothers Company; p. 90, Courtesy of Irwin Professional Publishing; p. 95, Photograph © Sharon Hoogstraten; p. 98, Imagination Pilots Entertainment.

CHAPTER 4

p. 100, © 1995 Anheuser-Busch, Inc. Budweiser® Beer, St. Louis; p. 105, REX USA LTD.; p. 106, © Mark Fisher/SIS; p. 109, Photograph by Sharon Hoogstraten; p. 111, Photograph by Sharon Hoogstraten, p. 112, Photograph by Sharon Hoogstraten; p. 113, Courtesy of McDonald's Corporation; p. 114, Courtesy of 3M.

CHAPTER 5

p. 120, Courtesy of Toys "R" Us; p. 126, Courtesy of Mackay Photopak; p. 130, Courtesy of Avon Products, Inc.; p. 131, Courtesy of Ford Motor Company; p. 132, Courtesy of DMB&B/Frankfurt; p. 134, Travelpix/FPG International; p. 134, Photograph by Leo Cullum; p. 136, Photography © Sharon Hoogstraten; p. 137, Reprinted with permission of *Reader's Digest*/photograph by Richard Hong; p. 138, "Percent Distribution of Households by Annual Purchasing Power Level," from "World Bank and Global Business Opportunities, p. 44, *American Demographics* Magazine, © 1995, reprinted with permission; p. 139, Courtesy of Saskatchewan Tourism Authority; p. 142, "Special Report: It's a Small (Business) World, pp. 96-101, reprinted from *Business Week*, April 17, 1995 by special permission, copyright ©

1995 by The McGraw-Hill Companies; p. 143, Courtesy of McDonald's Corporation; p. 144, Global Marketing Management 5/e, pp. 489-494, from *Global Marketing Management* 5/e by Keegan, © 1995, adapted by permission of Prentice-Hall, Inc., Upper Saddle River, NJ; p. 145, Courtesy of Campbell Soup Company.

CHAPTER 6

p. 150, Courtesy of *American Woman Motorscene*; p. 153, "CD Players," Copyright 1995 by Consumers Union of U.S., Inc., Yonkers, NY 10703-1057. Adapted with permission from *Consumer Reports,* March 1995, Although this material originally appeared in *Consumer Reports,* the selective adaptation and resulting conclusions presented are those of the authors and are not sanctioned or endorsed in any way by Consumers Union, the publisher of *Consumer Reports;* p. 159, Used with permission of Michelin North America, Inc. All rights reserved; p. 160, Courtesy inscape for Time Warner Interactive; p. 161, Photograph by Lee Salem/Shooting Star; p. 161, Courtesy of The Procter & Gamble Company; p. 161, Photograph by Greg Wolff; p. 163, Reproduced with permission of PepsiCo, Inc., 1996, Purchase, New York; p. 165, VALS 2, SRI International Menlo Park, CA; p. 167, Courtesy of adidas America; photo by Walter Iooss, Jr.; p. 167, Courtesy of Revlon Consumer Products Corporation; p. 168, Courtesy of Sony Consumer Electronics Inc.; p. 171, "KENYA" doll and trademark property of Tyco Industries, Inc. Used with permission; p. 172, Courtesy of Goya Foods, Inc.; p. 173, Courtesy of Pacific Bell; pp. 175, 176, Courtesy of Ken Davis Products, Inc.

CHAPTER 7

p. 178, Photograph by Mark Romine/SUPERSTOCK; p. 181, Courtesy of Marvol USA, New York, NY; p. 185, Courtesy of SGS-Thomson Microelectronics; p. 186, Courtesy of Sylvania/GTE Products Corp.; p. 187,

Courtesy of Chrysler Corporation; p. 189, Courtesy of Intel; p. 190, Courtesy of Honeywell MICRO SWITCH Division; p. 194, Courtesy of Allen-Bradley Company, Inc.; p. 196, Courtesy of American Harvest, Inc.

CHAPTER 8

p. 204, Photograph by Archive/Fotos International; p. 207, Courtesy of Ocean Spray; p. 209, Courtesy of Fisher-Price, Inc.; p. 210, Courtesy of Fisher-Price, Inc.; p. 212, Courtesy of Clean Duds Inc., for Duds 'n Suds; p. 214, Courtesy of Lexus and Team One Advertising/Photograph by Vic Huber; p. 217, Courtesy of Intersearch Corporation, Horsham, Pennsylvania; p. 217, Courtesy of Meridia Interactive Information Services; p. 218, Top 10 National Television Programs: 1996 Ratings; p. 218, Photograph by Viacom/Shooting Star; p. 218, Courtesy of Nielsen Media Research; p. 219, Courtesy of Campbell Soup Company; p. 220, Courtesy of Binky-Griptight, Inc.; p. 223, Courtesy of Wendy's International; p. 226, *Marketing Research: Measurement and Method,* 5/e by Tull & Hawkins © 1984, adapted by permission of Prentice-Hall, Inc., Upper Saddle River, NJ; p. 227, Courtesy of Augustine Medical, Inc.

CHAPTER 9

p. 232, Photograph by AP/Wide World Photos; p. 235, "U.S. Market Share, 1994" and "Global Market Share, 1993" from "Nike vs. Reebok: A Battle for the Hearts, Minds, and Feet, pp. 90-106, Reprinted with permission of Kenneth Lebiche, "Nike vs. Reebok: A Battle for the Hearts, Minds, and Feet, FORTUNE, September 18, 1995, © 1995 Time, Inc. All rights reserved; p. 237, Courtesy of *Street & Smith's*; p. 238, Courtesy of 3M; p. 242, DILBERT reprinted by permission of United Features Syndicate, Inc.; p. 242, Courtesy of MicroFridge, Inc.; p. 243, *Simmons 1993 Study of Media and Markets: Restaurants, Stores, and Grocery Shopping,* P-10 (New York: Simmons Market Research Bureau, Inc., 1993), pp. 0001 and 0026 in Summary Appendix; p. 243, Photograph by John Abbott; p. 244, *Simmons 1993 Study of Media and Markets: Restaurants, Stores, and Grocery Shopping,* P-10 (New York, Simmons Market Research Bureau, Inc., 1993), p. 0003 in Summary Appendix; p. 245, Courtesy of Panasonic; p. 248, Courtesy of Wendy's International; p. 250, Courtesy of Apple Computer, Inc.; p. 254, "Cheaper Can Be Better," p. 70, © 1991 Time, Inc. Reprinted with permission; p. 255, Courtesy of Buick; p. 255, Courtesy of Pontiac.

CHAPTER 10

p. 262, Courtesy of Jeep, agency: Bozell Worldwide, Inc.; p. 264, Map Courtesy of Strategic Mapping, Inc.; p. 266, Courtesy of Acer America Corporation; p. 267, Courtesy of Fingerhut; p. 267, Courtesy of Marshall Field's; p. 268, SABRE Courtesy of American Airlines; p. 270, Courtesy of Advance Promotion Technologies; p. 272, Photograph © by David Wahlberg; p. 272, Courtesy of Kirin USA, Inc.; p. 274, © Time Inc. New Media, Reprinted with permission; p. 275, Courtesy of The Reader's Digest Association, Inc., 1996; p. 278, S&MM, "1995 Survey of Buying Power"; p. 284, UPS and UPs shield design are registered trademarks of United Parcel Service of America, Inc., Used by permission.

CHAPTER 11

p. 288, Photograph Courtesy of 3M; p. 291, Courtesy of NIKE, Inc.; p. 292, © Tiffany & Co.; p. 295, Courtesy of Sony Electronics Inc.; p. 295, Breathe Right nasal strips are manufactured by CNS, Inc., Minneapolis, MN/Advertising agency: Seitsema, Engel and Partners, Minneapolis, MN; p. 297, Courtesy of American Harvest, Inc.; p. 297, New Product Showcase and Learning Center, Inc./Photograph by Robert Haller; p. 297, Courtesy of The Original Pet Drink Co., Inc.; p. 300, "Many Predictions from the Past Missed Mark Badly," p. 2D, Reprinted from Bob Schwabach's column ON COMPUTERS, January 12, 1995, © 1995 Universal Press Syndicate, reprinted by permission; p. 300, Photograph by Sharon Hoogstraten, p. 303, Photograph by Caroline Parsons; p. 305, Courtesy of Frito-Lay, Inc.; p. 306, Photograph by AP/Wide World Photos; p. 307, "Imposter Merchandise," 7/7/95, p. 1D, "Investigators Wrinkle Plans of Clothing Counterfeiters," 8/4/95, p. 3B; p. 307, Photograph by Jose Azel/AURORA; p. 308, Photograph by John Madere/The Stock Market; p. 309, S&MM "The Nation's Most Popular Test Markets," pp. 65-69; p. 310, Courtesy of Campbell Soup Company; p. 311, Photo courtesy of Hewlett-Packard Company.

CHAPTER 12

p. 316, Courtesy of The Quaker Oats Company; p. 327, Courtesy of Mars, Incorporated; p. 328, Courtesy of Oscar Mayer Foods. Oscar Mayer, Lunchables, the Oscar Mayer rhomboid, Will Snore No More are trademarks of Oscar Mayer Foods, Madison, Wisconsin; p. 331, Photograph by Chuck Nacke/Woodfin Camp & Associates; p. 332, Courtesy of

Elite Foods Inc.; p. 334, Courtesy of Black & Decker (U.S.), Inc.; p. 334, Courtesy of DeWalt Industrial Tool Company; p. 335, Courtesy of Eastman Kodak Company; p. 336, Courtesy of Pez Candy, Inc.; p. 337, Photograph by Sharon Hoogstraten; p. 338, Courtesy of The Coca-Cola Company; p. 339, Courtesy of Owens-Corning; p. 340, Courtesy of McDonald's Corporation.

CHAPTER 13

p. 344, Photograph by Lori Adamski Peek/Tony Stone Images; p. 347, Courtesy of American Express Co.; p. 347, Courtesy of Continental Airlines; p. 348, Courtesy of Hyatt Hotels Corporation; p. 350, HBR, "Strategy Is Different in Service Businesses," reprinted by permission of *Harvard Business Review,* an exhibit from "Strategy Is Different in Service Businesses" by Dan R. E. Thomas, July-August 1978, © 1978 by the President and Fellows of Harvard College, all rights reserved; p. 351, Reprinted with permission of the United States Postal Service, agency: Young & Rubicam/New York; p. 352, Elvis and Elvis Presley are Registered Trademarks of Elvis Presley Enterprises, Inc., Reprinted with permission of the United States Postal Service; p. 353, "On Great Service," p. 79, Reprinted with the permission of The Free Press, a division of Simon & Schuster from ON GREAT SERVICE: A Framework for Action by Leonard L. Berry; p. 356, UPS and UPS shield design are registered trademarks of United Parcel Service of America, Inc., Used by permission; p. 357, Logos Courtesy of McDonald's Corporation, Courtesy of Sprint, and Courtesy of American Red Cross; p. 358, Courtesy of Hartej S. Sood, DDS; p. 359, Courtesy of Deloitte & Touche; p. 359, Courtesy of Singapore Airlines; p. 360, "Ecotourism: Ethics of Eco-Sell," by Pamela Wright, pp. 3-9, and "A Code of Ethics and Guidelines for Socially and Environmentally Responsible Tourism, by Louis J. D'Amore, pp. 64-66, Reprinted by permission of the publisher; p. 361, Courtesy of Charles Schwab & Co., Inc.; p. 361, Courtesy of United Airlines, agency: Leo Burnett; p. 363, Photograph by Focus on Sports.

CHAPTER 14

p. 364, Photograph by Kevin Horan/Tony Stone Images; p. 366, © Kohler Company; p. 368, Photograph by Robbie McClaran; p. 370, Courtesy of Sony Electronics Inc.; p. 371, "Is Kona Coffee Good to the Last Drop? That's All You Get," Reprinted by permission of The Wall Street Journal,

© 1995 Dow Jones & Company, Inc., All Rights Reserved Worldwide; p. 372, Photograph by Sharon Hoogstraten; p. 373, Courtesy of H.J. Heinz Company; p. 374, Courtesy of Fiat USA Inc.; p. 375, Photograph by Sharon Hoogstraten; p. 379, Courtesy of Luigino's Inc.

CHAPTER 15

p. 388, Photograph by Pascale de Laubier; p. 392, "Sony Prices Its Advanced Game Player at $299, Near Low End of Expectations," 5/12/95, p. B4 and "Sony Sells 100,000 Video-Game Units on First Weekend," 9/12/95, p. A12, Reprinted by permission of The Wall Street Journal, © 1995 Dow Jones & Company, Inc., All Rights Reserved Worldwide; p. 392, Courtesy of Sony Entertainment of America; p. 394, Courtesy of Compaq Computer Corporation; p. 396, Courtesy of Rock & Roll Hall of Fame and Museum; p. 401, Photograph by Sharon Hoogstraten; p. 402, Photograph by Sharon Hoogstraten; p. 405, Courtesy of The Toro Company; p. 408, Photograph by Monci Jo Williams, FORTUNE, © 1983 Time Inc. All rights reserved.

CHAPTER 16

p. 422, Photograph © Amy Etra; p. 424, "Dictionary of Marketing Terms," Reprinted by permission of the publisher from *Dictionary of Marketing Terms*, Peter D. Bennett, Editor, © 1996 by The American Marketing Association; p. 429, Courtesy of L.L. Bean, Inc.; p. 430, Courtesy of General Mills, Inc.; p. 433, Photograph by Voyles; p. 436, Courtesy of the Kroger Company; p. 438, Courtesy of Q Lube Inc.; p. 439, Courtesy of Dai-Ichi Kikaku Co., Ltd. and Warner Lambert; p. 440, Courtesy of Sanyu Boh Co., Ltd.

CHAPTER 17

p. 446, Photograph by Robert Ziebell; p. 451, Courtesy of United Parcel Service; p. 451, Photograph by Sharon Hoogstraten; p. 456, Courtesy of Southern Pacific; p. 459, Courtesy of Maersk, Inc.; p. 460, Courtesy of United Airlines; p. 462, Courtesy of Federal Express Corporation; p. 463, Courtesy of Supervalu Inc.; p. 464, Courtesy of Rapistan Demag Corp.; p. 465, Photograph by Fritz Hoffmann/JB PICTURES.

CHAPTER 18

p. 468, Courtesy of eShop, Inc.; pp. 470-471, Courtesy of Levi Strauss & Co.; p. 472, Photograph by The Bettmann Archive; p. 474, Courtesy of Midas

International Corporation; p. 476, "Hypermarkets: A Sure-Fire Hit Bombs," p. B1, Reprinted by permission of The Wall Street Journal, © 1992, Dow Jones & Company, Inc., All Rights Reserved Worldwide; p. 477, Courtesy of Lillian Vernon Corporation; p. 477, Courtesy of L.L. Bean, Inc.; p. 478, Courtesy of BayBank; p. 478, Courtesy of Interactive Catalog Corporation, Seattle, Washington; p. 478, Courtesy of CompuServe® Incorporated; p. 478, Courtesy of Cybersmith, Cambridge, MA; p. 480, Photograph by Paul Chesley/Tony Stone Images; p. 486, Courtesy of The Forum Shops at Caesar's—a joint venture of Simon Property Group, Inc. & The Gordon Company; p. 488, Courtesy of Taco Bell; p. 491, Courtesy of NIKE, Inc.; p. 493, Courtesy of Mall of America.

CHAPTER 19

p. 494, James Bond and car courtesy of MGM/UA; p. 497, Courtesy of Lexus, agency: Team One Advertising, photographers: © Rick Rusing and © 1996 Kathleen Norris Cook; p. 499, Courtesy of Eastpak; p. 500, Photograph by Voyles; p. 501, Courtesy of Fence Magazine; p. 502, Photograph by Gregg Wolff; p. 503, Courtesy of IBM, agency: Ogilvy & Mather/New York; p. 506, Courtesy of Marion Merrell Dow, Inc.; p. 507, Courtesy of Sega of America; p. 509, Courtesy of Friday's; p. 509, © 1996 Hertz System, Inc. Hertz is a registered service mark and trademark of Hertz System, Inc.; p. 511, Courtesy of GM Credit Card Operations; p. 512, Photograph by Ray Marklin; p. 513, Courtesy of ACTMEDIA, Inc.; p. 515, Photo courtesy of National Broadcasting Company, Inc.; p. 519, Courtesy of Sprint.

CHAPTER 20

p. 520, Photos Courtesy of ESPN and Starwave Corporation and Courtesy of Telebase System Co.; p. 522, Courtesy of AT&T, agency: NW Ayer & Partners, photographer: ©Hunter Freeman Studio; p. 522, Courtesy of Corel Corporation; p. 522, Courtesy of Godiva Chocolatier; p. 523, Courtesy of DDB Needham Worldwide and The Dial Corporation; p. 524, Courtesy of Miller Brewing Company; p. 524, Courtesy of the State of Florida Department of Citrus; p. 526, Courtesy of Master Lock Company; p. 527, "100 Leading National Advertisers," 9/27/95, p. 7 and "Top Global Marketers," 11/20/95, pp. i-20, Reprinted with permission from *Advertising Age*, November 20, 1995, copyright Crain Communications, Inc. All

rights reserved; p. 531, Gabriela Sabatini © 1995 National Milk Processor Promotion Board, agency: Bozell Worldwide, Inc., photographer: Annie Leibovitz; p. 531, Courtesy of Frito-Lay, Inc., agency: DDB Needham, Chicago; p. 532, "National Ad Spending by Media," p. 62, Reprinted with permission from *Advertising Age*, September 27, 1995, Copyright Crain Communications, Inc. All rights reserved; p. 535, Courtesy of Ford Motor Company; p. 534, Courtesy of Group W Satellite Communications; p. 536, Courtesy of Sports Illustrated for Kids; p. 536, Courtesy of McCann-Erickson Italiana S.P.A. and Levi Strauss International; p. 536, Courtesy of Straight Arrow Publishing; p. 538, Courtesy of Chicago White Sox; p. 541, Courtesy of Roper Starch Worldwide Inc.; p. 544, Courtesy of Lee Apparel Co.

CHAPTER 21

p. 546, Photograph by Peter Serenyi, Special to *The Dallas Morning News*; p. 549, Courtesy of Remington Products Company; p. 550, Photograph by John Madere; p. 551, Courtesy of National Flora; p. 552, Courtesy of Xerox Corporation; p. 555, Courtesy of AT&T; p. 556, Photograph by C/B Productions/The Stock Market; p. 567, Courtesy of Mary Kay, Inc.; p. 569, Courtesy of Toshiba America Medical Systems and Interactive Media; p. 569, Photograph by SUPERSTOCK; p. 570, Courtesy of MO-V.

CHAPTER 22

p. 576, Photograph by Michael Hruby; p. 578, Photograph by Sharon Hoogstraten; p. 585, "Competitive Advantage: Creating and Sustaining Superior Performance," Reprinted with permission of The Free Press, a division of Simon & Schuster from COMPETITIVE ADVANTAGE: Creating and Sustaining Superior Performance by Michael E. Porter, copyright © 1985 by Michael E. Porter; p. 585, Courtesy of Southwest Airlines; p. 591, Courtesy of Domino's Pizza International; p. 592, "Making Your Marketing Strategy Work," Reprinted by permission of *Harvard Business Review*, an exhibit from "Making Your Marketing Strategy Work," by Thomas V. Bonoma, March-April 1984, copyright © 1984 by the President and Fellows of Harvard College, all rights reserved; p. 593, © 1996 Swatch/A division of SMH (U.S.) Inc.; p. 594, Courtesy of Domino's Pizza International; p. 595, Courtesy of Lockheed Advanced Development Company; p. 595, © 1995

APPENDIX C

APPENDIX D